DATE DUE

MR 25 '88		

AMERICAN FICTIONS

Also by Frederick R. Karl

A Reader's Guide to Joseph Conrad *(1960; revised edition, 1969)*

The Quest, *a novel (1961)*

The Contemporary English Novel *(1962; revised edition, 1972)*

C. P. Snow: The Politics of Conscience *(1963)*

An Age of Fiction: The Nineteenth Century British Novel *(1964; revised edition, 1972; paperback edition:* A Reader's Guide to the Nineteenth Century British Novel)

The Adversary Literature: The English Novel in the Eighteenth Century. A Study in Genre *(1974; paperback edition:* A Reader's Guide to the Eighteenth Century English Novel)

Joseph Conrad: The Three Lives *(1979)*

EDITED:

Joseph Conrad: A Collection of Criticism *(1975)*

The Mayor of Casterbridge *by Thomas Hardy (1966)*

The Portable Conrad *(Morton Dauwen Zabel's edition, revised, 1969)*

COEDITED:

The Existential Imagination *(1963)*

Short Fiction of the Masters *(1963, 1973)*

The Shape of Fiction *(1967, 1978)*

The Radical Vision *(1970)*

The Naked i: Fictions for the Seventies *(1971)*

The Existential Mind: Documents and Fictions *(1974)*

The Fourth World: The Imprisoned, the Poor, the Sick, the Elderly and Underaged in America *(1976)*

Frederick R. Karl

AMERICAN FICTIONS

1940 / 1980

A Comprehensive History and Critical Evaluation

1817

HARPER & ROW, PUBLISHERS, *New York*

Cambridge, Philadelphia, San Francisco,
London, Mexico City, São Paulo, Sydney

Grateful acknowledgment is made for permission to reprint:

Lines from "North Labrador" from *The Complete Poems and Selected Letters and Prose of Hart Crane,* edited by Brom Weber, copyright 1933, © 1958, 1966 by Liveright Publishing Corporation. Reprinted by permission of Liveright Publishing Corporation.

Lines from "The Fifth Elegy" and "The Ninth Elegy" from *Duino Elegies* by Rainer Maria Rilke, translated by J. B. Leishman and Stephen Spender, copyright 1939 by W. W. Norton & Company, Inc., copyright renewed 1967 by Stephen Spender and J. B. Leishman. Reprinted by permission of W. W. Norton & Company, Inc.

Lines from "The Panther" from *Translations from the Poetry of Rainer Maria Rilke,* translated by M. D. Herter Norton, copyright 1938 by W. W. Norton & Company, Inc., copyright renewed 1966 by M. D. Herter Norton. Reprinted by permission of W. W. Norton & Company, Inc.

Lines from "The Most of It" from *The Poetry of Robert Frost,* edited by Edward Connery Lathem, copyright 1942 by Robert Frost, copyright © 1969 by Holt, Rinehart and Winston, copyright © 1970 by Lesley Frost Ballantine. Reprinted by permission of Holt, Rinehart and Winston.

Excerpts from "The Quaker Graveyard in Nantucket" from *Lord Weary's Castle* by Robert Lowell, reprinted by permission of Harcourt Brace Jovanovich, Inc. and Faber and Faber Ltd., London.

Lines from "The Kingfisher" from *The Kingfisher and Other Poems* by Charles Olson, copyright © 1960 by Charles Olson, reprinted by permission of the Estate of Charles Olson.

Lines from "The Snow Man" from *The Collected Poems of Wallace Stevens* by Wallace Stevens, copyright 1923 by Wallace Stevens, renewed 1951 by Wallace Stevens. Reprinted by permission of Alfred A. Knopf, Inc.

First HARPER COLOPHON edition published 1985.

Library of Congress Cataloging in Publication Data

Karl, Frederick Robert, 1927–
    American fictions, 1940–1980.

    Includes bibliographical references and index.
    1. American fiction—20th century—History and criticism.   I. Title.
PS379.K24   813′.54′09   81–47659
ISBN 0–06–014939–6
ISBN 0–06–091150–6 (pbk.) 85 86 87 88 89 10 9 8 7 6 5 4 3 2 1

For Dolores, no American fiction she

CONTENTS

FOREWORD

The Alps neglect their Curtain
And we look farther on!

EMILY DICKINSON,
"Our Lives are Swiss"

The American novel since the Second World War is, obviously, that fiction which came after 1945; but it is also more than a body of work in chronological sequence. In attitudes, recognitions, ideologies, disturbances, and techniques, it is a fiction that molded itself to post-atomic ideas and responses and reached out to become something new. We have an era, really sustained for the first time, of what we may broadly call "American modernism,"* the rough equivalent in fiction of abstract expressionism or action painting, of the *nouvelle vague* in cinema, of the post-Pound-Williams era in poetry, of serial and electronic music, of increasing forms of abstraction which have characterized all the arts. On the stage, where our cultural

---

*Postmodernism, fabulation, Gothicism, the antinovel, the post-antinovel novel, the self-reflective (or self-conscious) novel, Nabokovian discontinuities, Borgean fantasies, as we shall observe, are all derivatives of modernism, either developments, expansions, or reductions of the original impulse. Because modernism came relatively late to American fiction, critics have been eager to relabel what are impulses from a movement that never dissipated its original energies. In the prewar novel, only Faulkner and Dos Passos, among major novelists, assimilated European ideas of modernism and even there in limited quantities, and certainly without establishing any equivalent American movement.

ideals are visualized more directly, the bare, abstract, symbolic look is part of this general movement. Theater manifested the perfect expression of the era in Beckett's *Waiting for Godot*—in language, characters, themes, staging, even clothes. In all its diversity, the postwar novel has striven for precisely this achievement: to defamiliarize the familiar, to make the reader reinvent the world, and while moving human experience to the margins, to move the margins toward the center.

Several studies of this period have attempted to categorize its fiction. Each characterization is an effort to convey coherence to a massive body of very individualized work. It has been called a "city of words" (by Tony Tanner), a "waste land beyond" (Raymond Olderman), a literature "after alienation" (Marcus Klein), a period of "radical innocence" (Ihab Hassan), in part a "world elsewhere" (Richard Poirier), a literature of "disruption" (Jerome Klinkowitz), the inheritor of an eroticism based on "love and death" (Leslie Fiedler). Most of these diagnoses are ingenious, and some are quite useful as critical tools. They all fall short, however, of being sufficiently inclusive, and nearly all neglect both patterns and details of the larger culture.

Although *American Fictions* is primarily an interpretation of key American fiction in the four decades since the 1940s, it is, also, a reading of the culture from which the novels and writers derived. By "culture," I mean not only literature or the arts, but the social, political, and economic institutions that help define a society. If we seek coherence in the fiction, we must discover a profile for the era.

I play two roles: first, locating and identifying several paradoxes that reflect a complex, even profound cultural experience; second, redefining the nature of our taste in fiction by distinguishing between novels (even very adroit ones) and literature. My two points interpenetrate. The great vitality and inventiveness of the postwar American novel derive from its confrontation with what, ultimately, will help to frustrate it. It is doubtful whether in any other period in history the serious writer has had to respond to so many unyielding, rapidly altering, and irreconcilable conflicts. Yet the American writer boldly pursues the paradoxes of the American experience, trying to reconcile the irresolvable, unwilling to be defeated by the presence of so much diversity. The resonance of a baffled Melville and an embattled Whitman can be heard.

Unlike his English contemporaries, who seem comfortable within reductive and unresolved elements, the American writer continues to chip away at uncertainties, perhaps hoping that in this somewhat stale Eden he or she against all odds to the contrary can gain a foothold. Every grappling point, however, is slippery and hostile. What is remarkable about America is that even while it appears to assimilate, indeed to devour, the new, it is resistant to nearly everything important. The serious writer bangs his head against this particular irony.

We must nevertheless emphasize that many of our experiences that seem so startlingly innovative are anchored deep in our past. Postwar discontinuity, of course, exists, but it frequently prospers within the context of continuous lines. Although Emerson and Thoreau, not to speak of Jefferson and, further back, the Puritans, may have receded from our *active* imagination, their presence *is* clear in the themes, obsessions, conflicts, and even techniques of our contemporary novelists.

My second point is directed at a cultural phenomenon of considerable importance, which is that our tastes in serious fiction are increasingly being guided by the mass media: that is, reduced to television or film. The distinctions between novels and literature have become so fuzzy that even our more responsible critics look to "big names" as our cultural luminaries

and "big books" as cultural events. The star system has so confused our cultural values that much which passes for literature is simply fiction. Novels, rather than literature, are part of the "now" and are, for that reason, more appealing and accessible to the media.* It is not that bad drives out good—although that may occur—but that mediocrity is hailed. Novels are pumped up to seem like literature, when they are simply—novels. *The Catcher in the Rye* and *Lie Down in Darkness* were early examples, *One Flew Over the Cuckoo's Nest* another, *Herzog* a fourth. Sometimes a writer produces several novels that are greeted extravagantly as significant literature—the work of William Styron, exemplifies that,† or John Updike—and yet retrospection suggests a different order of being.

To discover where literature does exist, we must seek beyond media favorites and those who gain publicity on nonliterary grounds. Readability and accessibility, while *never* to be discounted as essential to entertainment, cannot preempt other values. Yet many of those whom I cite as makers of literature are, admittedly, difficult in their point of view and execution. I have in mind John Hawkes, William Gaddis, John Barth, Flannery O'Connor, Thomas Pynchon, Joseph McElroy, William Burroughs, Donald Barthelme, with more traditional fiction by Saul Bellow,

*The negative response to John Barth's *Letters* (1979) is instructive and should be juxtaposed to the acclamation afforded John Irving's *The World According to Garp*. While very difficult to read and in many aspects a display of authorial self-indulgence, *Letters* is a significant cultural event. For it does what literature is supposed to do, which is to probe new modes of perception, however tedious the process. *Letters* must be given time to find its level.

†Jerome Klinkowitz, an academic critic, views Vonnegut as an important "post-contemporary," the senior member of a group that is remaking the novel through "radical disruption" of novelistic conventions. "Vonnegut's rise to eminence [Klinkowitz writes] coincides precisely with the shift in taste which brought a whole new reading public—and eventually critical appreciation—to the works of Richard Brautigan, Donald Barthelme, Jerzy Kosinski, and others. Ten years and several books their elder, Vonnegut by his long exile underground was well prepared to be the senior member of the new disruptive group, and the first of its number to be seriously considered for the Nobel Prize." Academic criticism here becomes indistinguishable from media hype; this could have come from *Time, Newsweek, People* magazine, or a CBS television commentator. The opposite of such hyperbole comes from *Commentary* mercenaries who, as the result of conservative political allegiances and/or toadying to the editor, feel obliged to denigrate what are often solid literary impulses.

, Walker Percy, Philip Roth, Joyce
, Bernard Malamud, providing and con-
provide literary events. Literature in the
postmodern period is often inaccessible or
greeable—as were Joyce's *Ulysses* and
aste Land" in 1922—but it has a shaping
goes well beyond the novel of the "now."
nce more make that leap, as though it had
made before. We must never forget that
found Proust unintelligible, a poor writer of
French; that early readers of *Ulysses* reeled without
guidelines; that "The Waste Land" remained impenetrable for years.

Most (not all) major work of this forty-year span
in American fiction derives from its reliance on the
modern movement, the willingness of our authors to
experiment, to have sensational failures (such as
Barth's *Giles Goat-Boy*) as well as inaccessible triumphs (Gaddis's *JR*). We find European ideas of
fiction entering as early as the 1940s, in John Hawkes
(especially *The Cannibal*) and Saul Bellow *(Dangling
Man),* then in the 1950s in William Gaddis and John
Barth, with some intimations from Norman Mailer;
followed by an avalanche of work in the modern
mode—more Barth, more Gaddis, Coover, Pynchon,
Gass, Barthelme, McElroy, Sukenick, Kosinski, the
English novels of Nabokov. Even less experimental
novelists—Roth, Bellow, Ellison, Heller, Baldwin,
for example—were not immune. An early draft of
Catch-22, for one, was an almost unintelligible version of a Joycean stream. The models were not always
the same, but they included Joyce (apparent in
Faulkner and Dos Passos, in an earlier generation),*
Kafka, Céline, Borges, French existentialist novelists
and philosophers (handled very derivatively), Robbe-
Grillet and Nathalie Sarraute, Heidegger and
phenomenology, Freud, Jung, and their epigones,
plus aspects of Proust, Beckett, Gide, Woolf, Conrad,
Mann, Hesse.

The era gains its coherence from the interpenetration of foreign ideas and techniques with typically
American ones. European sense of time had to work
through with American stress on space; European
dread with American escape; European historical dimensions with American presentness; European
sense of decline and last-ditch philosophy with
American bustle, growth, its own forms of entropy,
frustration, and dejection. American pastoral had to
accommodate European "counterfeit"; American
openness, European disguise and invisibility. Even
American underground—as in Ellison or Wright—
had to adjust to European subterranean modes,
whether Dostoyevskian or Kafkan.

Through a decade-by-decade arrangement, this
book can locate the larger culture as it lies in the
individual writer and focus on how he or she is both
continuous and discontinuous with European and
American themes. Discussion by decade rather than
chapter readings of a particular novelist's work can
help us account for such apparently divergent materials as the combat and war novels of the late forties
and the fifties, a large body of fiction by black Americans, an equally large outpouring by ethnic novelists
(mainly Jewish), the appearance of an ever increasing
body of work by female writers, the presence, in fact,
of writers as culturally different as Hawkes, Oates,
Ellison, Flannery O'Connor, Barthelme, Mailer,
Roth, Gaddis, Baldwin, Bellow, Burroughs, and
Barth. What can they possibly have in common: a
writer like Bellow, who, after *Dangling Man,* used his
intelligence to resist European models, and one like
Pynchon, who has subscribed to everything the Europeans can offer? At first look they would appear not
even to share the same map of the United States, or
else to share the America of Jasper Johns, distorted
on canvas almost beyond recognition. (The decade
arrangement has some few exceptions: when a particular career—such as Burroughs's—is as a whole
more illuminating culturally than if parceled out; and
when certain themes—for example, those pertaining
to politics, growing up, minimalism, the female experience, and the nonfiction novel—cut significantly
across the decade pattern.)

In this period, American fiction is no longer simply American; just as America itself is no longer
purely American. The Atlantic, once divisive, has
receded in favor of overseas linguistic modes, experiments with structure, a willful difficulty. As our culture has turned, so has our fiction. We cannot read
postwar fiction—and this is a factor common to all of
it—without reference to European novels, philosophy, cultural modes. And yet the American novel is

---

*The earlier generation—Dos Passos, Faulkner, and Hem-
ingway, of course, Wright Morris, John O'Hara, John Steinbeck, Katherine Anne Porter—was at the time of World War
II alive and writing; but its most significant work either belonged to an earlier period, the twenties or thirties, or else did
not respond to the vast changes that the war brought. The most
ambitious book from that group in the postwar era was
Faulkner's *A Fable* (1954). For this, Faulkner selected an episode in the First World War, creating a religious mythology
which, while very powerful, would have little meaning in the
larger culture after the later war. For all its energy and reach,
the book is a holding action, not an exploration.

still American. The point is that "American" has a different sense and feel to it, a different weight, both a tentativeness and a resolution that are its own and not quite its own. In brief, postwar fiction spins out in reflected images what the culture is becoming. Rather than dying or becoming extraneous or a false guide, the novel at no time in history has illuminated more a country, a people, a direction.

We should think of the postwar novelist in America as fitting into that description Jung made of the "Trickster Figure." His subject was the coyote, both a natural and a magical creature. At one time, the coyote had become, for the American Indian, a figure capable of changing from a physical to a spiritual state, and back again—in a series of transformations that suggested a huge, mysterious center. But with the coming of the white man, the coyote lost its magical presence, and its transformation from one role to another was observed no longer as spiritual or shamanistic, but as mean cunning, something in the world of the trickster, not the magician. It became part of that definition in which the cowboy or Westerner refers to a low-spirited person as a "coyote."

Yet the coyote continues, working its changes, altering its personality, and it survives. In a sense, without being mean-spirited as individuals, our novelists must become tricksters; for they have lost their aura as magicians and spiritualists. That power has passed elsewhere, to the culture in which the novel counts little: to the world of sound and sensation;* to the world of psychology and psychoanalysis; or to the social sciences, which have preempted the flashier elements of the novelist's material. The novelist survives, of course, but like the coyote, he must work

---

*William Burroughs is our novelist of that "aural culture," where sounds can be used as forms of power and control. For Burroughs, the tape recorder is more potent than a nuclear bomb. Warhol's *a,* which poses as the new, is derivative Burroughs.

along the contours of different frontie[...] proach borders differently, and he mus[...] to accept his lesser role in a white ma[...] The magic has gone out, not only from h[...] from the world; and it has passed elsewh[...] extinguished. What the novelist needs, [...] only a vision but strategies for holding on[...] still embodies the crises, conflicts, and tensi[...] we associate with a culture—although preci[...] the culture embodies has become part of Ameri[...] fictions.

Jung speaks of a savior: "Only out of disaster can the longing for the savior arise—in other words, the recognition and unavoidable integration of the shadow create such a harrowing situation that nobody but a savior can undo the tangled web of fate." But Pynchon, in *Gravity's Rainbow,* gives us less pretentious perspectives: "Ghosts used to be either likenesses of the dead or wraiths of the living. But here in the Zone categories have been blurred badly. The status of the name you miss, love, and search for has grown ambiguous and remote, but this is even more than the bureaucracy of mass absence—some still live, some have died, but many, many have forgotten which they are. Their likenesses will not serve. Down here are only wrappings left in the light, in the dark images of the Uncertainty." To negotiate as ghosts in the shadow—not as saviors—is the function of the novelist, the one-time shaman now turned trickster. Behind those shadows, the novelist, like the coyote, survives by redefining himself and his culture.

Those who lament that the postwar American novel has not produced its Proust, Mann, or Joyce should recall that the earlier generation of American novelists—Fitzgerald, Hemingway, Dos Passos, Wolfe, Dreiser, the source now of so much nostalgia—lacked a Proust and Mann also. We must return to the last century for that, when Melville was our Joyce, Hawthorne our Proust, Emerson our Mann, Poe our Gide. For giants, except for Faulkner, look backward.

AMERICAN
FICTIONS

*Notes appear at the end of the book and are iden-
tified by a page number and a lead-in phrase.*

A POLEMICAL INTRODUCTION: WHO WE ARE

We are double-edged blades, and every time we whet our virtue the return stroke straps our vice. Where is the skilful swordsman who can give clean wounds, and not rip up his work with the other edge?

THOREAU,
A Week on the Concord and Merrimack Rivers

. . . it is unlawful to do what one will spoil by doing.

Ibid.

Many writers, during their lifetime, occupy the very center of novel-making. This is a large, rather disorganized center, and they fill it at different levels and removes from each other. Such novelists are of widely different kinds, but I am speaking of Saul Bellow, Norman Mailer, Kurt Vonnegut, Jr., William Styron, Irwin Shaw, Truman Capote, James Baldwin, among many others. Because some have been able to dramatize their lives (through public appearances and political appeals), or gain an inordinate amount of media attention (by appearances at Elaine's or literary parties), in ball games in the Hamptons, or through drinking brawls, multiple marriages, talk shows), they appear as central cultural figures. And some of them are, some of the time.

For several of these writers, however, their significance is guaranteed only by their physical presence; remove *them* and their work recedes rapidly. Mailer's last unqualified novel (a considerable achievement) was in 1967. Often, the attention paid to them is disproportionate to their body of work, although in some of their books they indicate serious intentions. Saul Bellow, for one, has for thirty-five years sailed close to the real centers of fictional achievement, but his critical sense has lagged behind his novelistic gifts, and he early on connected himself to a self-defeating conservative aesthetic. As a consequence, he did not permit his talent to take him where it could, and moderation itself—except in *Henderson the Rain King* (1959)—appears to have hobbled his imagination. He is, in this respect, almost the obverse of Norman Mailer, who has absorbed the "new" without being able to reflect it fictionally. Yet an adulatory press still hails them as literary heroes, cultural lions.

My quarrel is not with these writers—let them seek their fame where they may—but with the neglect literarily and aesthetically of possibly more important writers and their books. Some of these, such as Barth and Pynchon, are suitably praised; but they are not considered touchstones of literary effort, either in the press or other media, or in much of the academy. Many of these writers—besides Barth and Pynchon, I have in mind William Gaddis, John Hawkes, Donald Barthelme—are physically removed from the scenes where fame accrues. And their work certainly does not lend itself to certain kinds of staff reviewing or popular reception.

We encounter a curious phenomenon, in its complexities almost uniquely applicable to postwar fiction. That is the entrance of the serious novel into the world of entertainment (more varied and competitive than ever before), with the novelist himself as entertainer.* Sports figures have become a more vulgarized version of the same process. In an earlier generation, Ernest Hemingway was perhaps the leading practitioner of this kind of substitute for literary effort. As his work declined in significance, he increasingly offered himself: fishing, hunting, eating and drinking, divorcing, remarrying, following the bulls, romancing the media. His activities have spawned an entire generation, and in some ironic way, if we seek Hemingway's influence on postwar fiction we find it more in his public personality than in his work.

Running parallel to the above is something equally invidious, and paradoxically, this phenomenon is connected to our strengths as well as weaknesses. We are all familiar with the fact that the more extreme and outlandish the event, vision, or people, the more readily it or they are accommodated to our sense of things. One of our postwar shibboleths is that everything reflects us; we are everywhere—a spinoff of Emerson's dictum that man is the source of all. In quick order, the culture embraces and assimilates the vision, and then through imitations reduces the original, until, finally, the latter is replaced by the substitute, which comes to stand for the whole. When a literary vision is involved, such as Pynchon's *Gravity's Rainbow,* only the substitute enters the marketplace of ideas.

The man with the vision gives way to the man who has a vision to sell—a commentator, reviewer, columnist, media personality, that middle ground of literacy and competency. The seductiveness of the marketplace for ideas is indeed one of our glories, the result of egalitarianism in all aspects of our culture. None of this involves "selling out" to capitalism, as the left once labeled it; it is part of our ideology as Americans.

Yet the marketplace establishes its own paradoxes. For even as it expresses our uniqueness as a people and a culture, it must reduce everything it touches. An extended example: The American novel of the last two decades has been like a beehive, equaled only by the aggregate of Latin American fiction—full of invention and energy, innovative techniques, daring use of language. Nevertheless, the impact of the novel as an art form has been slight becuase of its very accessibility, and chiefly because of the ease with which every aspect of experience can be expressed and published. Dilution begins with publication and ends with media reductionism. In the Soviet Union, any idea expressed in an art form or as a criticism of official policy must push its way against incredible odds—to get written, to be published (publicly or underground), to be distributed, finally to be read. An idea that rubs the culture wrong becomes a spearlike thrust.

In a tolerant society such as ours, an idea loses its power long before it has the opportunity to simmer in the marketplace. All this is greatly to be preferred, of course, to the suppression of art and the terrorizing of the artist. Yet it is in just such a flexible atmosphere and in just such a society that art dissipates its values. The artist becomes part of the society, no matter how severe his vision, how extreme his criticism. Heller's vision of America as nightmare, in *Something Happened,* goes on to become a best-seller, a bourgeois artifact. Burroughs's revolutionary stances made him a sought-after speaker. It is not only a question of money, or of the salability of a product, not only a question of hyperbolic overkill—it is the very nature of a tolerant society to absorb whatever seems dangerous and turn it into mass communication. Good art can survive, however, only if its ideas are given their run.

The very term "novelist" has become suspect in the postwar era, and many novelists prefer to call themselves "writers," which can be packaged better. Part of this confusion of realms is a by-product of the 1960s–70s concern with the "new journalism," where borders were, in the view of some, blurred; so that one could speak of the nonfiction novel, or novelistic journalism. "Writing," rather than journalism or novelmaking, was the acceptable phrase for those who moved along the contours. Much of this nomenclature was nonsense, for novels and nonfiction or journalism, new or otherwise, are very different things. This new form could be stressed only because of a general disdain for the novel.

The "death of the novel" controversy (d.o.n.c.) is connected to the assimilationist tendencies of the marketplace and to the role of the novel as entertainment, the novelist as entertainer. D.o.n. talk had begun as early as the 1950s, but in the 1960s, passions flared. In the earlier decade, Lionel Trilling had denied the phenomenon in an essay called "The Novel Alive or Dead" (February 1955), although he granted

---

*John Aldridge picked up this development in the 1950s and wrote, in the 1960s, that it may be better for a young writer not to continue writing and "far more strategic for him just to lean back and enjoy the advantages that come simply from being well known." Celebrity, he adds, becomes self-perpetuating, dependent less on work produced than on skillful public relations.

the temptation to add his signature "to the certificate of the novel's death." Leslie Fiedler later spoke of "The End of the Novel," part of the apocalypse, indeed Armageddon, he saw in American culture as a whole. In "The Ivory Tower and the Dust Bowl," Albert Guérard, in 1953, had tried to lay a different groundwork, so that the novel could be perceived as alive, based no longer on history but on language, withdrawal, new stances to fit new circumstances. And in 1969, John Barth's "The Literature of Exhaustion," which was misread as part of the d.o.n.c., was really about revivals.

Of course, revivals and resurrections can lead to excesses. James Tuttleton cautioned that "when the idea gains currency that a whole genre is exhausted in the achievement of its first great example, writers whose genius may best find expression in traditional forms are driven toward the extremes of a futile dead-end experimentalism—simply to be 'inventive,' to escape the charge of 'imitation.' " Nevertheless, the drive to bury the novel went on, with Louis Rubin's book called *The Curious Death of the Novel: Essays in American Literature* (1967). Rubin felt that the novel is now in the stage of "rearrangement and replenishment of literary energies," an interval. We are marking time "while a group of very talented writers—Styron, Bellow, Malamud, Barth, others—explore the already mostly discovered ground to see whether anything important has been overlooked."

To press his point, he says that we have no Faulkners, Joyces, Hemingways, Fitzgeralds, Prousts, Manns, and the like in the postwar era. Yet by citing Joyce, Proust, and Mann, Rubin overloads his circuits, since only Faulkner can compete there, and to compare American contemporaries with them is both critically and culturally unsound. Even in Rubin's own terms, Hemingway and Fitzgerald are not at the level of Proust, or Joyce, or Kafka.

Ronald Sukenick offered a witty reply to d.o.n. critics in his novella "The Death of the Novel" (1969). Sukenick provides his own version of what has died in the novel—not the genre but its materials—and then writes a novella as a film sequence to demonstrate the vitality of fictional forms. To clear the ground, Sukenick lists what no longer exists, like James's dismissal of American culture in his biography of Hawthorne: "Reality doesn't exist, time doesn't exist, personality doesn't exist. God was an omniscient author, but he died; now no one knows the plot, and since our reality lacks the sanction of a creator, there's no guarantee of the authenticity of the received version." Chance rules, and all reality is indi-

vidual experience—German phenomenology transferred to fiction. So, Sukenick agrees, the novel *has* died, and one must seek ways to resurrect it. While we should hail Sukenick's defense of the novel, we should be wary of his dismissals. What has kept the novel from dying has not been an awareness of the loss of time, destiny, reality, personality, et al., but a perception that these older ideas exist in a dialectic with their denial; that the old is very much with us, but only as one element of a "reality." What is needed is not a further dismissal of the old—Sukenick leans on Robbe-Grillet as if the latter had already transformed fiction—but modes in which the dialectic can dissolve, reform, and defamiliarize. As this occurs, the novel survives the marketplace, assimilation, and its critics.

In many instances, novelists who are considered marginal—while perhaps treated respectfully—are experimenters: inventors on their own or ingenious borrowers of European forms. There is an apparent division which fits in perfectly with American social leveling. The novelists who offer themselves in the marketplace as "writers" are traditionalists who eschew experiment or adventurousness. The writers who either reject the limelight outright, or shun it because celebrity insists on assimilation, are frequently the experimenters. It is a premise of this book that in the latter group we are more likely to find literature; in the former, novels. The latter are, admittedly, difficult, and often when their books go wrong, as Barth's *Giles Goat-Boy* does, they are unreadable. Yet even when accessible, their books can present such a challenge even to the experienced reader that they become coterie writers—consider Gaddis and especially his *JR*, or some of Barthelme (*The Dead Father*, for example), or Pynchon of *The Crying of Lot 49* and *Gravity's Rainbow*. Even so, difficult works are not always permanently difficult. The later fiction of these writers often opens up the earlier, so that in the light of *JR, The Recognitions* becomes more accessible, or with *Chimera* in mind, even *Giles Goat-Boy* becomes approachable.

In point of fact, many readers (and reviewers) are still fighting battles about modernism, which had already altered our consciousness by 1930, no less 1960 or 1980. We can, for ironic purposes, return to over a century ago, when Herman Melville, beginning with *Moby-Dick*, decided to be new, and lost the readership gained from his earlier romances of the South Seas. Melville's pronouncement that he wanted to be different, that he deemed (surface) inconsistency a virtue to be achieved, is echoed in John Hawkes's youthful statement that his work will eliminate plot and character in their traditional roles. Such an overstatement, which Hawkes later retracted in part, is well within an established American tradition. Emerson's stress upon intuition, his proposition that every "natural fact is a symbol of some spiritual fact," his assertion that he has taught one doctrine, "namely, the infinitude of the private man"—all support disarrangement, inconsistency, the shadowy and the vague as against the bright and the clearly delineated. If man shares in the "divine superabundance" and if the sole integrity in life is the integrity of one's own mind, under such conditions the author immerses himself, like all men, in the universal mind; what is consequent is a synesthesia and disarrangement that we ordinarily associate with the nineteenth-century *poètes maudits.* American experimentalism has a long lineage, not only from its European sources but from its own American tradition.

Hawkes's very early novella "The Owl" begins: " *'Him?/Think not of him for your daughter, Signore, nor for her sister either. There will be none for him. Not him. He has taken his gallows, the noose and knot, to marry.' "* There is no discernible speaker. An unknown voice comes out of what might be a recording hidden in a tree. Even the prepared reader is disconcerted. The place mentioned in the next line is Sasso Fetore ("stinking rock" or "tomb," in Italian), no known geographical location; and the "I" of the story, but not the narrator of the first words, is Il Gufo (the goof), the owl of the title. We already feel exhausted, as if some terrible weight were being laid upon us.

Words pour out, as though the writer has forgotten us or assumes we know where he is heading, where he came from. There is none of the traditional information or linkage, as in Bellow, Mailer, or Malamud. The very rationale here is missing, and Hawkes has himself seemed to vanish. Coherence, if it does exist, resides inside the form, and that comfortable reader settled in his chair must work out what the Owl means, what Sasso Fetore is, locate it (or not) in time and space, and pursue intelligibility.

Experimentation is not, of course, the only thing; but it does suggest that fiction is responding to the culture, reflecting it with vitality.* Our postwar era

has been called, variously, the age of narcissism, the "me too" age, the age of anxiety, of liberation, of depression, of melancholy, the post-atomic age. Fiction is hard-pressed to respond, in subject matter as in treatment. An unorthodox "novel" such as Nabokov's *Pale Fire* (1962) is, because of the circularity of its form, a greater reflection of American narcissism than (say) Bellow's *Herzog* (1964), which seems more directly self-indulgent.

By way of disconnections and disruptions, the novelist—and the reader by implication—is doing no more than experiencing Emerson's dictum: "the *all in each* of human nature," the universal residing in each individual, by way of intuition. The novelist must move along the lines of that intuition, even when it leads toward disaster. Emerson repeated: "nothing is at last sacred but the integrity of your own mind." This may have proved pernicious, a prod to solipsism, or else the ultimate in democratic egalitarianism. The paradox here, in Emerson, nourishes the novel, and nowhere more than in the postwar era. What may be destructive in the larger culture can frequently provide the right mix of drama, paradox, and irony for fiction.

I suggested that an experimental fiction like *Pale Fire* might be more expressive of the culture's subjectivism than a more traditional work such as *Herzog,* or *Goodbye, Columbus;* although all three expertly characterize the sixties, with elements of the Roth collection preternaturally prophetic. Yet still another example, Hawkes's *Second Skin*—an intensely American work in the Emerson, Thoreau, Whitman, Edenic tradition—suggests even more fully how experimentation can jar us into a sense of the culture, or how the culture can be filtered through a work of fiction.

By the time of *Second Skin* (1964), Hawkes had worked through to more traditional forms than in *The Cannibal* or *The Owl,* while retaining his disturbing method of limning characters and events as if his eyes were pieces of glass refracting even as they observed. The prose has some greater flexibility, but it is stilted and oblique, not the language of discourse but a self-conscious literary mode. He begins:

> I will tell you in a few words who I am: lover of the humming-bird that darts to the flower beyond the rotted sill where my feet are propped; lover of bright needlepoint and the bright stitching fingers of humorless old ladies bent to the sweet and infamous designs;

---

*Saul Bellow disagrees not only about experimentation but about vitality. Writing in *Modern Occasions* (Winter 1971), he begins: "I'm not sure that what we have *is* a literary situation; it seems rather to be a sociological, a political, a psychological situation in which there are literary elements. Literature itself has been swallowed up."

lover of parasols made from the same puffy stuff as a young girl's underdrawers; still lover of that small naval boat which somehow survived the distressing years of my life between her decks or in her pilot-house; and also lover of poor dear black Sonny, my mess boy, fellow victim and confidant, and of my wife and child. But most of all, lover of my harmless and sanguine self.

The materials so far presented center the fiction within the consciousness of an individual "I," but without any identification and without sign of development or direction. The novel is motionless; the key image is stasis. Yet our bewilderment about roles is precisely what Hawkes has attempted to evoke: self against self, our wonder against his strategies. Bewilderment raises consciousness, as does frustration. The process of defamiliarization has begun, from the first lines, and our grappling for fixed points relates as much back to us as to the desire for location.

As the section called "Naming Names" moves along, we discover little help. Hawkes turns to mythical forms, to Clytemnestra, Iphigenia, Antigone, then into a mixture of Hamlet, Gertrude, and Cassandra. He has begun, apparently, with a very compressed reprise of the past, such as we find in the Shakespearean Prologue, spoken rapidly while everyone is still being seated. Words provide, not guidance, but a whiff of chaos, a sense of anarchy. Language divides us from meaning and from reality.

Once carried along, we note that Hawkes works through tensions created by adversary lines of development. Whatever he gives in one instance, he withdraws in another. His central intelligence, Skipper or the Captain, is the writer of his tale, and we are located in the familiar territory of "remembrance of things past," a fable of self unfolding to create its own text. This narrative method establishes a complicated time sequencing and, as well, turns outward space into space denied, into space as having already been experienced even as we the reader observe it shaping up. Setting his present view of himself against what occurred in the past, Skipper has developed a second skin and can deny the reality of the first. While he appears to be a picaro of sorts (and encourages this manly aspect), there is always the "other" dimension, alien to the picaresque, of the inner self having already unfolded before the story is related.

For Hawkes, this double bind, with its inner core of negative energy, is particularly necessary, since his vision at its best withholds as much as it releases. What creates the dimension of "otherness" is the reader's consciousness seeking order, while the writer is reluctant to reveal his pattern. He pays out information in bits, and even names—the profusion of Gertrudes, Cassandras, Pixies, Mirandas, Catalina Kates—disallow an easy narrative until the reader has sorted out their almost interchangeable roles as mother, daughter, granddaughter, one island woman, second island woman, and so on. Hawkes slants in as part of his strategy to upset traditional narrative styles, routine plot structure, customary notions of character and setting. His world is composed of half-moons, where the other side remains a mystery; darks and lights, as if in some Manichee vision, dominate landscape and background.

As a twilight writer, a kind of Munch in words—Fiedler misleadingly places him among the Gothicists—Hawkes burrows into paradoxes and adversary possibilities by way of distortion of perspective, convoluted time, inverted sequences, antirealist devices. His fiction is an adversary force, still within the terms of the traditional novel, but extending its countering potentialities to the inner reaches of time and space. His scenes are themselves nonsequential, noncausal; often they appear to have no association with each other, for they move laterally as well as horizontally and vertically. Whether judged successful or not, his methods aim at a transformation of our fictional consciousness, an attempt to reflect, in terms of perspective, the larger culture as we would find it in the 1960s. Although some of Hawkes's materials look back to European modernism, he had adapted himself to his own time and place. Read *Second Skin* and observe the sixties unfold.

If the postwar era in America is characterized by tentativeness, lack of completion and fulfillment, a sense of shivering disappointment, frustration amid plenty, the fear that everything is temporary (ready either to collapse or to disappear), the recognition that while all matters, little counts—if this is the mood which swings up and down, then fiction is sorely tested; or else left behind by the more popular media, which can shift attitudes overnight. If the postwar American is a difficult target to focus upon, then the postwar American novelist seems to arrive and depart like Merlin. Crèvecoeur called our country "this great American asylum," but the noun has taken on quite a different connotation. Can we even define what an American novelist is in this "great American asylum"? De Tocqueville spoke of "three races" in the United States, but when we look at our fiction writers, we find closer to thirty, or more.

The postwar era has become noted for the proliferation of designations. Among black writers alone, we have black Americans, Afro-Americans, Negroes, then subdivisions for each sex; among Jews, we find Jewish-Americans, Jewish novelists, subdivisions into male and female, occasionally further subdivisions into the particular Jewish orientation—German, Eastern European, Sephardic, and eventually we can expect South American Jews, North African Jews, Israelis, and so on. Among other ethnic authors, we have Irish and Italian, but few females. Then we have Southern novelists, a subdivision that began in an earlier generation, but still is used, catching as wide a group as Walker Percy (a Catholic and, like J. F. Powers, often referred to as a "Catholic novelist"), Flannery O'Connor (also Catholic, but referred to as a "lady Southern novelist"), Eudora Welty (not noted for any religious affiliation), William Styron, a transplanted Southerner, and so on. Then among the so-called WASP writers, we have divisions that cut across numerous categories, from William Burroughs to John Cheever, John Updike, Joyce Carol Oates, James Purdy, Donald Barthelme, John Barth, John Hawkes, Thomas Pynchon, William Gaddis. This is a group of such variety—except for the preponderance of John and William as Christian names—that we have no justification for labeling it a group or category. We can expect still further subdivisions, for even now male and female homosexual writers are distinguishing themselves from heterosexual authors, so that we will have the lesbian Jewish-American novelist or the gay black-American writer.

This diversification, which is generally healthy for a democracy but is a nightmare for the classifier of materials, whether literary critic or taxonomist, is an inevitable reflection of American culture. If de Tocqueville could speak of Indian, Negro, and white, we must speak of such variousness that only language holds our fictional literature together. One of the tenets of this study is that no matter what the sex, the race, the ethnic or religious affiliation of the writer, he or she is first and foremost an American writer because of the use of American English.* The commitment to writing in American English, for the black, Jew, Italian, Irish Catholic, WASP, male or female, gay or straight, is a commitment to American values,

no matter what the stresses, attitudes, antagonisms, degrees of separation, and hostilities of the writer. John Cheever and James Baldwin may appear widely separated (although after *Falconer* one cannot be certain of anything), but commonality of language makes them foster brothers. This is not to say that their language, or their literary usage, is the same. After commonality comes diversification.

An excellent example of cultural bifurcation comes in the work of Vladimir Nabokov, who grew up bilingual in English and Russian. Although his career divides into the Russian half and the English half, when Nabokov turned to "American" as his novelistic language, he carried over such a burden of Russian culture and language that his English works are truly "Russian-American."† *Pale Fire* exemplifies this bifurcation: for within the confines of the English Commentary by Charles Kinbote, the preponderance of Zemblan (a mock Russian) overlays the American English and creates a cultural divide which we do not find in Jewish-American, black-American, or Italian-American novelists. *Their* thinking is clued in to American themes, reflected in their language; whereas Nabokov, no matter how Americanized his terminology, was thinking as a highly sophisticated European with particular reference to Russian culture. We have no equivalent of Nabokov in this respect. No serious American novelist, home bred, can carry such a weight of another culture, and, therefore, his or her language—idiom, usage, vocabulary—is critical in demonstrating cultural roots. The use of a language reflects a culture so profoundly that it orders virtually every aspect of human perception. Jerzy Kosinski by writing in English and not Polish —even when his grasp of the learned language was uncertain—placed himself in a vastly different literary culture which would affect everything he could envisage or relate.

What we say here pertains particularly to black and Jewish novelists. Writers who identify strongly with the black experience, such as Morrison, Baraka, Williams, Reed, Brown, Killens, could, if they wished, cast their novels in what they consider to be black English. Reed, in fact, has moved toward a kind of "middle language" so as to convey a different kind of experience from that of (say) Ellison or Baldwin. Such a use of English, which would be heavily dependent upon a specialized idiom, vocabulary, and tonality, would come closer to conveying the sense of a distinctive black experience than does the "alien" lan-

---

*For this reason, I have omitted Isaac Bashevis Singer. Jewish or black novelists—Cynthia Ozick and John Williams, for example—who pepper their English with Yiddish or black idiom are nevertheless connected by a shared language and its traditions.

†Especially his final masterwork, *Ada*.

guage of standard American English, even when the latter is peppered with images and idioms from black culture.

Yet black writers have rejected this form of expression. It would, of course, seal them off from most of their readership; but more importantly, I think, in terms of their own creative development, it would deny a large part of their experience as Americans. As a result of schooling they grew up, as did many of us, in a two-language culture: one, the home language, the other the standard language of public school. Since writers are usually early and serious readers, the language they read in their formative years was a standard English, which carried with it a cultural freight they could not easily shuffle off. Further, when they read foreign literatures, the language was the standard English of translations, of Dostoyevsky and Tolstoy, Kafka, Sartre, and Camus. When LeRoi Jones (not yet Baraka) wrote his powerful play *Dutchman,* he drew on the universal myth of the Flying Dutchman, adapting *it* to the black experience; that is, wedding his reading to his own experience, as he would later do with Dante's *Inferno.*

Similarly, novelists with certain ideas about life and people and culture that we consider "Jewish" are American writers, not Jewish writers, not members of a Jewish club, affiliated to each other not as Jews but as Americans. They are not part of a Yiddish or Hebrew tradition, but of an American historical background. The distinctions among them are far greater than the similarities, and to speak of them as "Jewish-American" is to homogenize what should be particularized. Even when Yiddish seems close to the surface of their English usage, how intensely American they are in their response to the culture! Malamud's *The Assistant,* for example, is ostensibly about a "Jewish experience," flavored with Yiddish expressions, its English inverted as if a translation from Yiddish; and yet it is full of 1950s upward mobility —for the Italian Frank Alpine, being Jewish means a higher economic status. His name is his destiny. In *A New Life,* S. Levin, a New York Jew, seeks rebirth in an American Eden, and in so doing flirts with every motif in American culture since the Puritans. Despite some Yiddish tonalities, Malamud's English is solidly American, full of hip idiom, mocking the clichés, aware of nuances, using a contemporary modish language as the means of shaping character and event.

None of this denies the specifics of the Jewish and black experiences; each is clearly very different from that of the American WASP or the Italian Catholic —but different in its secondary characteristics. Primary characteristics are part of shared values. Growing up in the 1920s and 1930s was, for most of our authors in question, a problem of relating to American forms of reality, American schizophrenia in regard to race, ethnicity, sex, sense of gain and loss, the good and the bad life. The main considerations were, for the older writers, the Depression, the agonizingly slow recovery, the Second World War, the raising of hopes in its aftermath, the cold war, the political malaise and counterfeit of the fifties, the manic mood swings of the sixties, the vague drift of the seventies. And these cultural pressures were all associated with language, which itself expanded radically to meet the changes, including terms from black and Jewish literature, from music (swing, jazz, rock 'n' roll), science and technology, films and television: all common terminology.

John Williams's *The Man Who Cried I Am* (1967), a novel which has never received its due, is an ambitious effort to view the black experience on a world scale. Cast mainly in Amsterdam, the novel mixes the adventures of transplanted American blacks (thinly disguised Richard Wright, James Baldwin, Martin Luther King, Williams himself) with African themes and a plot to exterminate blacks altogether. Its swelling form cuts across everything that concerned blacks in the 1960s—breadth of reach, in fact, vitiates some of the impact—and yet it is intensely American in its values. Its language is not a form of black or Africanized English, but the standard American of the white literary establishment. Since blacks and whites speak the same language, and mix socially and sexually, Williams's insistence on distinctions, while real, must be based on secondary considerations.

If language creates continuity both laterally and historically, then ideologically and philosophically the postwar American novel is continuous with American themes, even when the influence of European ideas and modes of thought is insistent. Kafka's presence may seem extraordinarily pervasive, but his influence does not snap the thread of continuity in American fiction. One of the most persistent motifs is that of the regaining of paradise by means of spatial movement; that is, to stop the clock or move back in time by way of space. This awareness of the loss of Eden, or the wasting of it, and the compulsive need to regain even the sense of it lead to terrible conflicts in American thinking and particular narrative forms. Not for nothing did the son of Kurt Vonnegut, Jr., call his book on self-destructiveness and American culture *Eden Express* (three of the four chapters express "traveling," "arriving," "going"); or Emma

Rothschild title her book on the fate of the automobile (emblematic of America itself) *Paradise Lost.* Kafka and Camus link up with Emerson, Thoreau, and Melville.

The full force of the modernist movement did not strike American writers until the years after the Second World War; and with the influence of Virginia Woolf, not until the 1960s and 1970s. Although modernism in its major phases had almost run its course in Europe by the early 1930s, its impact then on American fiction was minimal. Unlike the poets, only Dos Passos, Faulkner, and Hemingway among major American novelists can be related to this movement, but the more we scrutinize Hemingway's work the more we can perceive its American forebears rather than European models. The spareness, the lulls and silences, the unspoken words, are sui generis, patterns of Midwestern speech and outgrowths of journalistic usage, owing little to Joyce or others. As for Dos Passos, modernism had to struggle against native naturalism, and the latter won.

When European models flooded American shores beginning in the 1940s, it was mainly Kafka's presence, reinforced, somewhat incongruously, by French existentialism, the general ideas rather than precisely the fiction of Sartre, de Beauvoir, or Camus. Camus's most popular novel, *The Stranger,* offered little new to the American sensibility; marginality, bizarre patterns of behavior, and anomie had long been staples of the American imagination. European existentialism, whose various strands are not simple, was reduced and modified for American taste; but however diluted, it did have its impact on nearly every major talent here, as that of Robbe-Grillet would a decade later. Each import, we should stress once again, whether existentialist or not, became assimilated to American needs. The purely French "novel of ideas" rarely caught on.* Existential angst (that of Sartre,

_____
*An excellent exception to this is Albert Guerard's *The Bystander* (1958), which in its controlled prose, tones, and narrative strategies uncannily foreshadows the novels of Robbe-Grillet. Guerard's frame of reference is a play of ideas, his protagonist a voyeur who chooses freedom, and options that include cheap happiness and exalted suffering. The novel functions well at both its abstract and its realistic levels. Earl Rovit's *The Player King* (1965) fits roughly into the same genre, owing more to the postwar French novel than to the American. Reminiscent of Gide in *The Counterfeiters,* Rovit offers polyphonic voices. His three levels are a first-person narrator, who provides continuity; a man who is starting out to write a novel; and a novelist who keeps a journal. The three voices are carefully

Kierkegaard, later Heidegger) became hostage to American need for escape; European modes of depression, despair, enclosure became secondary to American dependence on spatiality and denial of temporal modes.

The marked antirationality of modernism, even when couched in a heavy intellectual frame of reference, was also attractive to the American novelist, giving him (her) some philosophical foundation for his pursuit of sensory experience. Nearly every major novelist in this country has indulged in marked anti-intellectuality, something that goes well beyond attacks on the academy, where so many of the writers have found support. We are speaking of authors as diverse and distinct as Barth, Bellow, Pynchon, Heller, Vonnegut, Mailer, Malamud, and Barthelme. Possibly, the very anti-intellectual aspects of modernism—its stress upon consciousness and vitality as against mentality, its reliance on "inner states," its attacks upon officialdom, experts, and administrators as automatons, its emphasis upon memory and unmeasurable data, its disruptiveness and discontinuities—account for its appeal.

It is not money or immediate reward that makes American novelists repeat themselves, but an inability to grow because of a persistent anti-intellectuality, which, in turn, I associate with the masculine tradition. Even Bellow, whose work is frequently cited for its "braininess," is least satisfactory when discussing ideas. His manner is hit and run (as is Mailer's), the offering up of tidbits, sometimes spuriously, as though learning had to convince us of something unconnected to intellect. Herzog as an intellectual is the least convincing part of him, Herzog as a parasite compelling. We should add that female writers describing the "female experience" seem little different in their marked anti-intellectuality, as if the masculine-anticulture stance were a gigantic trap for all.

We are, of course, in the middle of one of our cultural paradoxes. The anti-intellectual tradition is one of our glories, the mainstay of our great literary flowering in the mid-nineteenth century. And the masculine tradition—in Cooper, Melville, later Twain—is intricately associated with it. *Moby-Dick* is, in one of its aspects, the working out of the dialectics of this tradition, the interplay between "masculine" (Ahab) and "feminine" (Ishmael), all against a

_____
orchestrated to suggest an "inscape," which is, in fact, the title of the first section. "Outscape" ends it. Between are alternations among the questing narrator, his efforts to write, and the Journal, three voices that ultimately blend.

background of mind and intellect struggling with other levels of experience. Further, because of the masculine tradition, Americans write so well about war. Some recent books about the Vietnam conflict, *A Rumor of War, Dispatches,* and *Going After Cacciato,* indicate that the American talent for the war/combat book has not subsided, with the latter itself strongly suggestive of *Catch-22, The Gallery,* and *The Naked and the Dead.*

The very mobility that is at the core of an egalitarian society militates against a strong intellectual tradition in the arts, since mobility has its own dictates and the slow development of a talent or mind cannot be encouraged. Clearly, the last forty years in America celebrated a kind of frenzy that is not conducive to stable intellectual traditions. Even the proliferation of educational opportunities under the G.I. Bill did not provide the basis for such a tradition; although many of our novelists have been splendidly trained. Stress on the academy in postwar years led, in fact, to parody of learning rather than to learning within the framework of a large body of fiction.

For the postwar writer, there is only now; the past ended in 1945. That lack of historical sense, and in many instances an active rejection of history, means that our major writers did their best work when the full force of the postwar era was upon them—in anger, rebellion, withdrawal, adversary action. Freshness, wit, and stylistic adventurousness characterized the earlier work of Bellow, Mailer, Roth, Heller, Percy, and several others, qualities often not to be found in their later work. Their perception of our society, or their adaptation of these perceptions to fictional use, did not lead them into new modes of seeing, but often into repetition.

That ahistorical, anti-intellectual masculine pressure on the individual talent (female as well as male) can only intensify in the present arena of publishing. The free-for-all policies that have taken hold of all but a small number of publishing houses cannot help but exacerbate that celebration of the Now. Only our most heroic novelists—Pynchon and McElroy, perhaps—can allow their talent to mature before they display it. More frequently, we find writers (like Joan Didion, Paul Theroux, John Gardner) entering the galaxy of "major novelists" before they have produced even one book ambitious enough to gain entrée. It is not just the marketplace, where rewards can be very high indeed, but the larger society of publishing, entertainment, competition with films, television, and nonfiction that must be accounted for. The novel, as we have observed, finds itself in a terrible struggle to exist as a serious form of entertainment and moral instruction. There are no villains, only a process.

Much of this is familiar, but bears repeating. The changes in the nature of publishing, and, in turn, of bookstores, must influence the novel in a myriad of ways. Such changes involve the acquisition of publishers by conglomerates for whom books are commodities; an increase in the level of hyperbole from publishers, reviewers, and all those involved in the book industry; the celebration of authors in general and novelists in particular, whereby they vie with sports figures and film and television stars; the celebration of editors, agents, and publishers themselves. All such events are good for the ego, but what happens to the book?

It is not, as I have suggested, that good novels fail to be published; there are enough small houses so that nearly anything of merit will appear. Also, bad novels do not necessarily drive out good—not if we look to the long run. Gaddis's *JR* did get published and won the National Book Award, although it remains unread and undiscussed. What does occur in the present razzle-dazzle situation is that potentially fine novelists are not permitted to develop; that those who have produced a solid first work are preempted too rapidly; that the thinking that goes into a serious novel is diluted at the source; that books will appear at intervals from large talents simply to provide a holding action; and that critical theories develop to protect certain favorites which have little relationship to what they are actually producing. Such criticism has supported Styron, Updike, Vonnegut, Mailer, many others, despite terrible unevenness.

All changes in the publishing industry, as all changes in society, involve, ultimately, matters not only of economics but of taste, aesthetics, the entire structure of a literary culture and how it is shaped. Mergers between publishing houses, purchases of already large houses by conglomerates, external pressures on houses to multiply profits as apart from quality, tie-ins (a continuing process begun in the 1950s) between hardcover and paperback houses, the publishing of original, "catchy" paperbacks, or paperbacks tied in not to hardcover books but to films or television, the radical increase in books by celebrities —movie and ballet stars, athletes, media people, criminals, rock stars—all these are related to "bookmaking," but marginal to literature. What they involve, unlike developments in the past, is not the increase in the book-reading population (that is, of real books) but a way of reaching those for whom a book is little different from a film or a television program.

The argument in an egalitarian country is that any product which makes people read is a positive act. It is an argument that in decency we should support. But by reinforcing the type of reading in which the nonbook printed and bound is coequal to the real book, we put additional pressure on writers. Perhaps we do not touch those who can remain enclosed within their own talents, those who consider themselves, still, priests of literature—Pynchon, Gaddis, Gass, Barth—but a literature requires a strong supporting cast. American postwar fiction sees that supporting cast dropping away, one good-sized talent after another dissipating its skills on frivolity, or repeating what once was an original spark. Mailer is an obvious example; Bellow less obvious—but did any of the reviewers notice how repetitive of his own work *Humboldt's Gift* is, a step backward into already stale Bellow, not a development?

We move in three-to-five-year cycles, and a writer who would normally space out his life in far longer units of development must react to the culture—catch it, as it were, as it passes by—before his imagination has had the opportunity to adjust and digest. A fine exception to this formulation is Bernard Malamud, who waited until he had assimilated the import of the sixties and seventies before publishing *Dubin's Lives,* which has the pace and feel of a well-conceived, well-developed fiction. Malamud aside, Mailer is our archetype here, the novelist turned writer who picks and drops pieces of the larger culture in two- or three-year intervals: anti-Vietnam demonstrations and marches, moon shots and big shots like Ali, Monroe, and Miller, Gilmore and the death penalty.

Yet not only must the serious novelist negotiate his or her way through the above developments, he must catch the reader once attracted to fiction and now engaged by nonfiction, not to speak of the "new journalism." We observe an outpouring of pseudo-historical works, pop sociological and psychological studies, as well as casual biography and autobiography alongside excellent books like Robert Caro's life of Robert Moses, David McCullough on the Johnstown flood, the Brooklyn Bridge, or the Panama Canal, Gay Talese on *The New York Times.* Not entirely history, not novel, these personalized books are excellent of their kind. Barbara Tuchman's studies, for example, are not original history, but they are expertly done, well researched, written with verve and awareness of the reader, and they, like others of this type, cut into a novel-reading audience. They

make real events so compelling that the novel, in comparison, may seem tepid. Have we recognized, though, that however expertly these books are crafted they are really responses to the needs of a more broadly based media audience? They compete not with "acts of the imagination" but with the demands of film, television, and magazines.

The nature of the American experience swamps all generalities. Philip Roth spoke of the multiplicity of the American cultural experience, which boggles the novelist's mind; Barth cited the "exhaustion" of traditional modes of plot and narration; many writers stress entropy (Henry Adams's concept now become fashionable), the winding down of our energies; others warn of the apocalypse, in which black and white will together find their doom. Donald Barthelme mocks all those who formulate these warnings. Others continue their faith in renewal, dreams, fantasy, escape into space, the redemptive power of the land, nature as salvation. All are American experiences, many of them contradictory, and yet, often, crisscrossing in the same author. They lie well beyond verbal constructs, for the language in which they are expressed often involves the terrible silences of the American experience: that silence which strikes nearly every novelist who pauses to listen to the vast spaces and what they might say to him.

When Joseph Conrad in another era said (in his preface to *The Nigger of the "Narcissus"*) that his aim was to make the reader *see:* "by the power of the written word to make you hear, to make you feel— it is, before all, to make you *see"*—he was not only defining his own form of impressionism; he was asserting a literary truth, whether derived from Homeric mimesis or Old Testament elevation. If the writer insists on making you "see," he or she is attempting to prevent an art form from expiring. Such a novelist takes tremendous chances. Language, point of view, spatial and temporal arrangements, tonal and textural varieties, conceptions of plot and narrative, even silence, must be defamiliarized and then reassociated. We can expect large-scale mistakes, misjudgments, unusual demands, in some instances failure alongside ambitious effort. In this light, "entertainment" takes on different qualities.

Yet within these wrenchings of the familiar into the unfamiliar, often a test of reader tolerance and endurance, we still have our units of reference: sexual relationships, marriage, associations with friends and enemies, parental roles, clashes between individual and social unit or systems, antagonism between individual and technology, hierarchies of time and space. The new arrangements, however, are the structural equivalents of Conrad's injunction to make you see. Linguistically, also, we must enter fresh territory, in the stylized speech of Nabokov's American novels, in the technical demands of Barth and Pynchon, the obscenities of Mailer, the colloquialisms of Gaddis, the flattened-out phrasing of Gass, the crowded imagery and crabbed quality of Hawkes, the apocalyptic prose-poetry of Burroughs. These, too, are literary languages, stylizations that return us to writers as disparate as Rabelais, Sterne, and Dickens, or, more recently, to Woolf, Joyce, Beckett, Kafka, Faulkner, and Hemingway.

Yet the paradoxical importance of the modernist impulse in contemporary fiction is that it keeps the novel as an unsettling force. Whatever else it may have been at different times, the novel has served as an adversary element, reflecting the larger culture and yet undermining it. If we think of Dickens, for one, as typically Victorian, we may forget how radical he was within Victorian terms, cutting and slashing at every form of organization and rule, apotheosizing the individual, offering sensory experience as a form of salvation to a society which counseled rationality and logic. The novel has traditionally forced its way into the seams of disorder and anarchy, seeking out those working connections between people and institutions where a given society is at its weakest. At the same time, the novel poses questions, in fresh terms, of order and sanity. It is a unique medium for working out balances between surface and subsurface, between the observed and the unseen.

The postwar novel fits that function, giving the lie to those who try to reduce it to popular entertainment or seek to castigate it for lacking weight. In America of the last forty years, no print medium has acted more responsibly as a moral force, as a means of making us see ourselves. Yet a great danger to the novel, admittedly, lies in the inability of the American novelist to grow or develop at the rate necessary for himself. There appears to be no solution here, since exciting times are also perilous. Whenever an art form is threatened, in fact, it becomes more intensely exciting and more ruthless toward the individual talent. In the eighteenth century, the fledgling novel was treated with contempt by the literary establishment; critics demeaned it as suitable only for female readers. Almost alone, Fielding attempted to salvage the novel as a form against onslaughts which could have destroyed it at its source. He did so by identifying everything in the novel ("prose fiction") as aspects of realism, although what constitutes it for any particular era makes the concept slippery and undefinable. For our own era, since the Second World War, realism in fiction must embrace as many "realities" as we discover in our culture. The quest is as perilous as it was in Fielding's time, when Sterne worked as hard to undermine the novel, by way of the novel, as Richardson and Fielding did to define it, by way of the novel.

Chapter One

||||||||||||||||||||||||||||||||||||||||||||||||

THEMES AND COUNTERTHEMES

Solitude is naught and society is naught. Alternate them and the good of each is seen.

EMERSON, *Journals*

America as shit, America as a shit-producer, America as beshitten, America as a gigantic asshole out of which energy and waste pour, Texans as the biggest assholes of them all—such are the ways of explaining why we were in Vietnam. If Mailer was correct, we still are what we were. What is remarkable about his 1967 novel *Why Are We in Vietnam?* is how continuous it is with the American past, more immediately with Faulkner and the Southern Agrarians, back through them to Teddy Roosevelt and Manifest Destiny, tunneling into Emerson, Thoreau, and the woods of Cooper.

In a passage as if written by William Burroughs in a drug-induced hallucinatory state, Mailer binds old and new America in his final "Terminal Intro Beep" —a cosmic flash: "A ring of vengeance like a pitch of the Saracen's sword on the quiver (what a movie was that, madame!) rings out of the air as if all the woe and shit and parsimony and genuine greed of all those fucking English, Irish, Scotch and European weeds, transplanted to North America, that sad deep sweet beauteous mystery land of purple forests, and pink rock, and blue water, Indian haunts from Maine to the shore of California, all gutted, shit on, used and blasted, man, cause a weed thrives on a cesspool, piss is its nectar, shit all ambrosia, and those messages at night—oh, God, let me hump the boss' daughter." The passage is an incantation, in which Thoreau's America meets Lyndon Johnson's, from pond hole to asshole.

What is further remarkable about Mailer's achievement is that he broke away from self-serving fantasies so inadequately dramatized in *The Deer Park* and *An American Dream* and found a sustaining vision in America. In *Dream,* he internalized American spatiality and turned it into masturbatory fantasies, power and sex intermixed indiscriminately. In *Why Are We,* he was able to exploit the spatial metaphor without losing its dimensions. Moreover, the intensely political Mailer found his exact center, where sex, power, dread, spatiality, exploration, adventure, and even guilt crisscrossed. If Mailer is apt to pose as the "American guide," Cooper's Hawkeye updated, then Vietnam was his perfect subject, provided he could explore it indirectly; as he showed, also, in *The Armies of the Night.* The political discussions that were so earnest in *The Naked and the Dead,* so sophomoric in *Barbary Shore* and *The Deer Park,* give way to images and symbols of a politicized America.

Defoliation of a hostile landscape is the American dream—we worship the land, we destroy it to make others feel our power, we replenish it out of charity, and then we fill it with factories. Mailer has found here, in the region where "Hell Sucks," a central metaphor for American life and its key paradox, what Thoreau suggested when he said "it is unlawful to do what one will spoil by doing." Machine and garden are the duelists. "Fyodor Kierkegaard," as Mailer calls him, is the intellectual and spiritual guide.*

Mailer's "newest American" is D.J., also known as Ranald, son of Rusty and, at eighteen, disc jockey to the world. D.J. is all talk, as befits a disc jockey, and looks back to Melville's confidence man and forward to Gaddis's JR, another "Rusty, Junior" caught in verbal coils. D.J.'s father is a "Dallas ass" bigwig, Rutherford David Jethroe Jellicoe Jethroe, or Rusty, who is L.B.J. to D.J.'s 1960s American youth. Father and son: the father leads the son into a bear hunt which tempts death; if the son refuses, he denies his masculinity (his "Texas Dallas assness"). D.J., who favors talk, must act, the confidence man and artist turned hunter and soldier.

The two work out in space America's violent destiny. The novel moves from Texas to Alaska, from the former biggest state to the present one. In Alaska, America's newest state of mind, animals are brought within range of hunters with helicopters; once frightened, excited, driven nearly crazy, big game becomes easy targets for men whose guns could destroy elephants or whales or dinosaurs. The Alaskan safari guarantees a shot at a grizzly, or money back. Rusty, however, insists on more than a shot; he demands a head count. He and D.J. leave the main body of the safari hunters to get their own catch. If in Texas Rusty is L.B.J., in Alaska he is Westmoreland. Their breakaway is the first of the two quests that structure the novel.

For Rusty, to "search and destroy" a bear—something in nature that exceeds him—is a compulsion. Mailer, however, poses his hunt on grounds apposite to Faulkner's in "The Bear." With that novella in mind, he turns the killing of the bear into Rusty's need to destroy whatever interferes with his sense of power and control. In the Faulkner story, the hunt is itself the thing; it is a purification rite, a vestigial gesture, and the monstrous beast of nature represents only partially something to be conquered, more some-thing to be experienced. Ultimately, "The Bear" is about the introduction of the corrupt self into a transcendent world. In Rusty's case, one must kill or be killed. Death is the latest toy from Neiman-Marcus.

The mechanical principle is always present in Rusty's figuring: his large-scaled firearms, powerful enough to stop a tank; the helicopter overhead—"Cop Turd," Mailer calls it—which now he wants to avoid. The copter is searching for them, to carry them out, but he wants only a body count; like the "Lurps" described by Michael Herr in *Dispatches.* Before they sight the bear they will wound and then pursue to the kill, D.J. recognizes that his father is the death principle. His urge is to kill *him:* "cause D.J. for the first time in his life is hip to the hole of his center which is slippery desire to turn his gun and blast a shot into Rusty's fat fuck face thump in the skull, whawng! and whoong!" Playing through the boy's mind is an episode when Rusty almost killed him, as a child of five. With brilliant images of rot and corruption, Burroughs-like descriptions made Mailer's own, the conflict is observed not in Freudian but in classical Greek terms. The House of Atreus is reborn in the house of Jethroe, Texas as the new Athens, Alaska its Sparta.

Then the grizzly comes on—like a tank, Hemingway's bull, all one's nightmares accumulated into nine hundred pounds of fury and rush. Mailer takes us inside panic and fear. The grizzly is severely wounded, but becomes even more dangerous when it vanishes into the brush. The "search and destroy" mission is on. When Rusty and D.J. sight the hulk, sitting in a vast puddle of its own blood, D.J. moves ever closer, looking deep into dying and death, the bullfighter honoring his victim. For D.J., the grizzly represents the peace and cool of every dying thing in nature; he wishes to respect it by being present at its moment of passing. Here is an aspect of "The Bear" working itself out as a ritual of life and death. At that moment, when elements are about to connect, Rusty shoots, and the bear rises into death, "all forgiveness gone." Rusty can now claim the kill. The war in Vietnam is on.

This episode ends a phase of the novel, and one brief period in D.J.'s life as a sixteen-year-old. There will be one more "hunt" and then the final phase, the party in Dallas two years later, which celebrates his induction into the army. Dallas is the midpoint between Alaska and Vietnam. Dread now passes to shit, Kierkegaard to Texas bragging. The party leads D.J. to reminisce, back to the bear hunt in Alaska when he and his friend Tex had broken away on their own —to escape from machines, and guns, and Rusty

---

*The literary and psychological models are numerous and diverse: Dostoyevsky, Kierkegaard, and Faulkner, as already suggested, plus Joyce, Burroughs, Thoreau, Henry Miller, Freud, even Kafka, among others, a rich blend of American and European sources.

types. This is the second of the two quests: for themselves. Tex is himself the son of a braggart, a man who tries to screw everything that walks. He is always dragging out his dick, a little one for such a big man, but one so full of vitality that Gutsy Hyde is a living terror to man, woman, and beast. D.J. and Tex want moments of self away from big-dick fathers, and they abandon guns and knives to try the wilderness on its own terms.

They hope for challenge, but fear it. On the edge, they come alive. "Lying there in the wilderness, for all they know no other man for fifteen or twenty miles, the moon was on the pond, little sounds coming from that pond, fish of the North breaking surface time to time could that be, and on the ground the restlessness of lemmings and voles, and foxes no doubt and the wolf, nothing sleeping easy in this bowl around this pond." Only their fire protects the pair, lying weaponless and naked, not touching, two Thoreaus or Bumppo and Chingachgook out of time and space, their phase having long since passed.

D.J., compulsive talker—Mailer's freaked-out "easy rider" of the airwaves—has sought and found, now deep in memory, that moment of absolute silence. "Cop Turd" has given up; there can be no shots. The moment cannot last, for Alaska is now America, no longer a wilderness but a state, a part *of* instead of divided *from.* The two boys eventually return to the camp, where the "older men's voices were filled with the same specific mix of mixed old shit which they had heard before in the telepathic vaults of their Brooks Range electrified mind." The past is over, the present has arrived, and D.J. will be inducted the day after the reminiscence. One ritual gives way to another. He had been destined for Vietnam all along, even when he lay in the open Alaskan night, weaponless. "Cop Turd" was simply waiting for daylight.

Why Are We in Vietnam? is Mailer's last novel in fifteen years. (His attempt at the final moment to make *The Executioner's Song,* 1979, appear as a novel cannot disguise its documentary nature.) Apart from its place in his canon—it is, I think, his finest work of fiction—it is remarkable for its expression of both a continuous and a discontinuous America. Mailer's compulsion to talk and to seek anarchic social forms has found a focus, even a dramatic center.* His inter-

est in Reich's theories of vitality and sexuality, his sense of political and personal power, his admiration for Henry Miller and William Burroughs as prose writers, his absorption of America as idea and as dream/nightmare all coalesce in time and place. A prophetic work of fiction reverberates throughout the culture, and we should not be surprised that the Mailer novel is a form of palimpsest or pentimento. Beneath the text of *Why Are We* we find images and metaphors of every aspect of American culture, past and present. Mailer is not usually associated with Southern Agrarians, Henry Adams, Emerson and Thoreau, Cooper, or Puritan fascination with the Indian, but with jazzier, more modish, figures; yet his novel serves as a magnet for all those divergent views that establish American paradox, irony, and conflict.

The antecedents of *Why Are We,* a prototypical postwar fiction, lie ever deeper in the American past. In his *Journal,* Thoreau speaks of America as a receptacle, a she-wolf prepared to nurse the disaffected children of foreign lands; America as a gigantic mother awaiting her Romulus and Remus. The battles over space, seeking, the loss of pastoral, the ways in which America will be used are fought out on these grounds, on how to relate to the mother: as rapist, perhaps, or as dutiful son-daughter.

Although the Agrarian Statement or Manifesto of 1930, "I'll Take My Stand," is anathema politically and racially to nearly all postwar American novelists, it represents a part of the culture that has engaged them compellingly. The statement by twelve Southern Agrarians† has a cultural potential that overrides its political and racial implications, which were and are poisonous; from its points we can observe how American culture, even when so reactionary, profoundly touches upon careers in conscious recoil from what the 1930s statement implies. Slighting as the manifesto is to blacks—by implication, they do not exist—we find that many of the cultural forms suggested by the twelve signatories find their way into contemporary black writing.

The statement is such a significant document in American cultural history that some of its familiar points are worth repeating. Even its placement, in

---

*A comparable talkathon in recent American fiction is Stanley Elkin's Dick Gibson, also a disc jockey, but the brilliance of Elkin's formulation is exhausted long before the novel runs its course (*The Dick Gibson Show,* 1970). More to the point

is William Gaddis's intricately sustained and extremely difficult *JR.*

†It was signed by, among others, John Crowe Ransom, Allen Tate, Robert Penn Warren (who later disclaimed much of what he had signed), Donald Davidson, Andrew Lytle, John Gould Fletcher, and Stark Young; many of them having been Ransom's students.

1930, when American industrial capitalism seemed to be collapsing after the stock market crash, was critical; for the very elements the manifesto attacked had, ostensibly, failed. The statement was prophetic even before its issuance.* If the Crash was the American equivalent of the Russian Revolution, then the statement by the twelve (apostles) would be the Southern version of the Bolshevik manifestos.

The Southern statement asserted that the South as a coherent region has something valuable to offer in human terms, but that if Southerners succumb to temptation—heavy industry, loss of regionality— then the South will not differ from the rest of the nation. A sense of exclusion is palpable. What affords the South its distinctiveness is its moral, social, and religious superiority. The devil has offered the nation as a whole dubious economic benefits based on "applied science." The latter means the introduction of machines into every form of life, and that concentration of machinery will result in a form of life which will, satanically, destroy Southern values. God lives in the land. Although the kind of religion is not stipulated, one can assume the Agrarians had in mind a "Christian state," based on a medieval or early Renaissance model, such as Eliot posited in his *The Idea of a Christian Society* ten years later.

Just what is an agrarian society? Historically, as a result of the Crash, farms would be foreclosed all over the nation, and one of the great migrations of modern times would occur, rural people heading for towns and cities and, they hoped, work.† Steinbeck's *The Grapes of Wrath* would catch one aspect of this phenomenon, which would be irreversible even when the economy revived and farmland was cheap. With our hindsight, we can see that the statement outlined not only a cultural style but a historical position; for it offered the South as an adversary to virtually everything the rest of the nation would be embracing. The signatories asserted they did not desire to return to pre–Civil War days, but their vagueness on economic issues—machines, for example, would be permitted only when they satisfied a "basic need"—suggests that their entire cultural position rested on nostalgia for a cotton-producing South, which, from the van-

tage point of a white man in the 1930s, seemed like prelapsarian Eden itself.

Most important, the signatories saw themselves as rebels, and therefore as romantic fools, part of the hopelessness of the American dream. Theirs would be a "city of God" instead of a secular state; a Calvinist submission to the inscrutable. Their political sympathies, we shall observe, would surface throughout the twentieth century in "paranoid" groups, whether informers of the late forties and fifties, the religious and political right wing (Birchers, Moon-worshipers, Jesus freaks) of the sixties, or anti-ERA, fundamentalist, and anti-abortion movements of the seventies. Such people, as Richard Hofstadter defined them, feel that America "has been taken away from them and their kind, though they are determined to try to repossess it and to prevent the final destructive act of subversion." Theirs is a pastoral dream, in which the "old American virtues have already been eaten away by cosmopolitans and intellectuals; the old competitive capitalism has been gradually undermined by socialist and communist schemers." Their dream or fantasy is continuous with Jeffersonian agrarianism, but without Jefferson's great doubts, his play of ideas and sense of the individual's worth—that is, Jeffersonian without Jefferson's idea of democracy.‡ It appealed, also, to many of the Populist feelings of the late nineteenth and early twentieth centuries, but eschewed the egalitarian assumptions of the movement.

How can such a manifesto, almost incoherent as a model for a contemporary American society, have touched so many hearts and minds? It has reached them, apparently, because it and others like it express a strain of such magnitude in American society that almost no one can escape: Gaddis, in *The Recognitions* and particularly *JR;* Malamud, *The Natural, A New Life,* and, twenty years later, *Dubin's Lives;* Bellow, *The Adventures of Augie March, Henderson the Rain King,* and *Herzog;* Heller, *Catch-22* and, a decade later *Something Happened;* Walker Percy, *Love Among the Ruins, Lancelot,* and *The Second Coming;* Vonnegut, *Player Piano, Cat's Cradle,* and several later novels; Roth, the novella *Goodbye, Columbus* and *The Ghost Writer;* Barth, *Giles Goat-Boy;* Clancy Sigal, *Going Away;* Whittaker Chambers, *Witness* (a

---

*Prophetic, also, for national land policy, for in 1935 the government would end all private purchase of public land, closing out an era that began with the Homestead Act of 1862.

†Quite different from what Hamlin Garland described in his *A Son of the Middle Border,* wherein his family migrated not to cities but to different farmlands, Maine to Ohio to Wisconsin to Iowa to the Dakota Territory.

‡He held that farmers with interests that are entirely agricultural are the real representatives of great American interests, and they alone are to be relied on for expressing correct American sentiments. And if God had a chosen people, it is those "who labour in the earth," small landholders as the most precious part of a state.

nonfiction novel); Ellison, *Invisible Man;* Updike, *Rabbit, Run;* Matthiessen, *At Play in the Fields of the Lord;* Flannery O'Connor, *Wise Blood* and, especially, several "peacock" stories. What is remarkable is that the political liberalism of most novelists does not vitiate their attraction to agrarian ideals, which are reactionary, even paranoid, certainly anti-intellectual (in the urban sense), and anti–twentieth century.

Much of the anarchy and discontinuity that underlie fiction (and life styles) in America derive from such paradoxes. The statement in its extreme resistance to change and modernism is far more radical than anything coming from comparable contemporary groups, like the Wobblies or the American Communist Party.* For it suggests nothing less than a rollback of what America had come to mean: egalitarianism and leveling. The agrarian ideal was not diminished by this social, political, and racial jumbling; for it also offered a Golden Age America, as Arcadian and unique. The Puritan injunction to the American to live out his life as something favored and distinct, as based on the "minority right to live its own kind of life," is restated.

In effect, the restatement of the ideal split off the bucolic aspect of America (the dream and fantasy life) from what America had actually become: heavily dependent on science and technology (already a "car culture"); industrialized and urbanized; capitalistic and centralized; migratory, from rural areas to ever larger urban centers; egalitarian and increasingly leveling (except for blacks). All these movements were becoming clear by 1930. The statement, then, divides the American experience up the middle, and its paradoxes, ironies, misconceptions, irresolvable conflicts become the stock-in-trade of the postwar novelists.

If, briefly, we update that manifesto, we note its appropriateness in the 1940s, as another literary era was emerging. In 1940, the Committee to Defend America First ("America Firsters") was formed; and its touchstones were rejection of England (foreign, aristocratic, tainted by centuries of corruption), support of rural and small-town values, isolation of a "purified" America from European entanglements.

_____
*My reading of McCarthyism in the 1950s is that it expressed a profound radicalism, that McCarthy and Cohn and many of their supporters were anarchistic and nihilistic; populists only as a façade, true successors to Camus's Meursault and typical men out of modernist literature. That their base was an agrarian America only points up the terrible discontinuities of our political and, by extension, our literary styles.

The battleground was the Garden of Eden, replayed as politics and ideology; America as prelapsarian, Europe as post-. Some of the early supporters were Joseph P. Kennedy (who insisted that England was fighting not for democracy but for self-preservation), John Foster Dulles (who denied that Germany, Japan, or Italy planned war upon America), Charles Lindbergh (the embodiment of small-town culture), Henry Ford, Robert A. Wood (board chairman of Sears, Roebuck, entrepreneur of agrarian economics), and several representatives and senators, including Taft, Vandenberg, and Burton K. Wheeler.

When James Burnham, in 1940, wrote of a "managerial revolution," he was perpetuating ideological battle lines that had been defined in "I'll Take My Stand." For when the managers take over—men related to production, not to ownership—the American way as we have known it disappears. America becomes diluted; the devil of socialism enters. Burnham's turn to the right (he had been a *Partisan Review* Trotskyite in the 1930s) was less a response to Communist threats than to the un-American threat of the managerial revolution. For in that phenomenon, as he defined it, we have the end of small-town America.

From Mailer to the Southern Agrarians and the attractions of their reactionary "pure" America, back to Emerson, assisted by Thoreau, the passage is conditioned by the bizarre nature of the American experience itself. Yet connections are there, Emerson speaking to American postwar novelists with an insistence and intensity that would surprise sons of immigrants, Afro-Americans, women. The historical route is as full of paradoxes and ironies as the novel which reflects it and them. As in some vast Hegelian dialectic, every American theme plays against its counter.

In "Nature," that radical expression of oneness, Emerson referred to himself, in his now well-worn phrase, as a "transparent eyeball." The phrase, and what it describes, is far more ambiguous, far richer as a metaphor, than is usually granted. We can, to start, note the words as describing a man who is receptive to all varieties of experience. Emerson adds: "I am nothing; I see all." We can, also, observe him as the passive recipient of whatever passes through him— "all mean egoism vanishes," Emerson says. If so, the "transparent eyeball" serves no more function than does a microscopic lens, a piece of glass that while functioning as a conduit for observation is itself neutral, an object. We can, still further, view the comment as being part of that voracious American appetite for experience, analogous to Whitman's "I am of old and young, of the foolish as much as the wise

well as paternal, a child as well as a [...] To me the converging objects of the [...] ually flow."

[...] ate Emerson's phrase in only these [...] merican self subsumes all experience [...] self or ego becomes primary. We must [...] ever, that the eyeball does not become pure [...] does it mean that all ego disappears. A [...] rent eyeball," like the microscopic lens, [...] istortion, however slight; and that distortion [...] equivalent in a sense of the way the artistic [...] ocess distorts in order to make more real. By stressing the transparency of the eyeball, Emerson emphasized that the seer brought a sensibility to the experience that changed, or distorted, both it and the seeing eye. The latter process, however it occurs and whatever its exact dimensions, is the creative act itself. "Every natural fact [Emerson continues] is a symbol of some spiritual fact. Every appearance in nature corresponds to some state of the mind, and that state of the mind can only be described by presenting that natural appearance as its picture." The "correspondence" here provides that circuitry we associate with all art and creativity, with the projection and reception that occur in alternating waves to produce something.

As soon as we approach Emerson's words in this way, as not simply those of an egoist or a self-serving guzzler of the world, we see him and other American writers as providing a very thick kind of experience. If we simplify him, we note the raw egoism; if we resist simplification, we note how his words express the desire to create and recreate: how the individual is involved in a very complicated kind of experience. Instead of simply turning the universal into the one, the world into the individual, Emerson was attempting to discover how transformation could occur. Optimistically, he felt that such remaking of change itself was indeed possible; that the American experience called for just this transformation. If we resist reductionism, we note the American archetype, the very fount of the American paradox: the ego that wishes to subsume all is also the ego that, in this new Zion, makes all change possible. In postwar terms, renewal, not stagnation, is necessary, even when self-destructive.

In Thoreau's reflections on his walk across Cape Cod, he comes close to Emerson's sense of the "transparent eyeball." Cape Cod is a "wild rank place," where shipwrecks and dead bodies dot the shore, an antiparadise with Edenic potentialities. It was a hos-

tile place until the walker "could perceive, at last, how its beauty was enhanced by wrecks like this, and it acquired thus a rarer and sublimer beauty still." We are taken from death of human bodies and ships' hulks, who have no friends but worms and fishes, to a "newer world than ever Columbus dreamed of." The "transparent eyeball" catches glimpses of mortality which peculiarly enhance our sense of life. The shipwrecks suggest to us the distant shore of death which is man's fate; but also, they create another perspective, a closer one, which is the tangibility of life, intensified by its juxtaposition to final things. This expression of what is an intense experience by way of contrast or denial—a kind of litotic or oxymoronic negation—engages us in its immediacy. It is part of our own ideal of the "now," as well as a definition of life for Emerson and Thoreau, and it reaches back profoundly to the Puritan ethic.

Back of Emerson and Thoreau, located deep in our mythical existence amidst Puritans and Indians, the idea of resurrection runs like a leitmotif; not only in the more obvious sense of a novel land, an earthly Eden, the new Zion, but in the deeper sense of an insistent desire to return to fundamentals, to experience purification. Cleansing oneself was an act of faith. The radical movements of the 1960s were quasi-religious, continuous with ideas set forth in the earliest days of American cultural life. The American Communists of the 1930s and the anti-Communists of the 1950s, similarly, saw their experience as being reborn or purified, either in a new belief or in opposing it. Basics, rebirth, and purification met at the intermingling of religion and ideology. Whereas European radicals based themselves on Marx, American radicals were nourished by pastoral fantasies.

The English Puritans who came to America for religious and political reasons were, also, radicals, in the original sense of the word: to get at causes or roots. Theirs was an agricultural ideal—to work the land, earn a living, and worship the God who was immanent in every aspect of their life. Their goal was to strike away all trappings: to return to the New Testament, which was the word of God spoken by Jesus, without interference from bishops or kings.

To preserve original Christian values, live off the land, return to basic premises and fundamental styles: how familiar these ideas sound from the 1960s, and yet they were the precise notions of the Puritans. The latter particularly took to heart Augustine's citation, in his *Confessions,* of Paul's Epistle to the Romans: "And this, knowing the season, that already it is time for you to awake out of sleep: for now is salvation nearer to us than when we *first* believed." If we cast off darkness and seek the "armor of light," we have placed ourselves in a closer relationship to fundamental ideas than if faith had first come upon us. Full consciousness precedes transformation. Implicit is the Puritan desire for rebirth and renewal, so that faith acquired in this manner is more forceful and meaningful than faith acquired effortlessly.

The Great Awakening of the early eighteenth century, fostered by the sermons of Jonathan Edwards, led to revivalist religion and to intense belief in rebirth and renewal, a "second skin" for the spirit. Although it took on many excesses—of ecstatic rolling on the ground, shrieking, mass hysteria, the soul running amok—it nevertheless promoted that return to fundamentals so characteristic of the American experience, that desire indeed to return to the Garden.* Further, it placed religious ecstasy within the individual, not as part of any established ceremony; and although the individual was considered secondary to the experience, nonetheless that experience proved self-centered to the extent that the individual was the mirror by which Jesus was reflected. When belief in God waned, narcissism, the ideal of the Garden, insistence on purification and renewal remained. In the early nineteenth century, Cooper and the Indian became our guides here: Cooper as the recorder of old dreams; the Indian as the "other," that primitive life at war with encroaching civilization.

In that struggle of pastoral against civilization, with renewal at stake, our "representative man" is Thomas Jefferson. His public life in the Enlightenment falls almost midway between the present and the early Puritan settlements in New England. He is, in almost every way, pivotal, probably more influential in our cultural life than any other public figure in our history. Washington is a "father," Lincoln a healer, Roosevelt a savior (or devil!); but Jefferson is connected to a world of ideas in a way unequaled by any other President or politician. He is, also, our ideological link to continental thought, to Locke and Montesquieu, among others.

In his running argument with Hamilton, Jefferson was possibly "wrong" on nearly every stand he took, but his position embodied American ideals far more than did Hamilton's. Yet Hamilton, the city slicker,

was the genius and the prophet, far astute, foreseeing an America bas rather than loose republican princi sense of individuality, with intimati revolution, and narcissism intermixed philosophically pure, but was unworka mental terms. Jefferson looked in every took on every paradoxical belief and con embodied the irreconcilables of the Americ ence. The man who yearned after pastoral p a gourmet, a lover of fine wines, a devotee of F culture. Jeffersonianism stands for the ideals of individual, while Jefferson was a slave owner. Hami ton, with all his aristocratic notions, eschewed slavery, as did John Adams, who leaned toward monarchistic ideas for the fledgling democracy.

After his presidency, Jefferson returned to Monticello, to rejoin his family (now diminished by death) and to continue the development of his beloved retreat. His mulatto mistress was there, Sally Hemings, and very probably several of his children by her, none of whom could be recognized. His son-in-law, Thomas Mann Randolph, went mad and threatened to kill his wife, Martha. Two of Jefferson's nephews murdered a slave for breaking a valuable teacup (a crime dramatized in Robert Penn Warren's *Brother to Dragons*). Nature itself became a threat, with a flood sweeping away a needed dam on the river. Jefferson's debts mounted, forcing him to sell his library to gain funds for routine expenses. Monticello was so full of children and visitors that Jefferson had to leave to gain quiet. Thus, the pastoral ideal is intermixed with the stuff of America: madness, murder, miscegenation, unrecognized children, near-bankruptcy. The idea of a retreat was already an illusion, and yet the Jeffersonian Arcadia remains basic to our history.

Paradoxes in Jeffersonian ideals are intrinsic to the American experience. Cooper and the Indian may have been our ideological guides in the early nineteenth century, but Jefferson straddled the two, the old pastoral dream found in the novelist and the primitive spiritual fervor of the Indian. The very astute purchase of the Louisiana Territory in 1803, for example, would extend America's western frontiers, and by so doing bring civilization to an "earthly paradise." Jefferson took away with one hand what he gave with the other.

We need, in fact, look no further than the Puritans and the Indians for that basic contradictoriness which has characterized every stage of our culture. The Puritans stood for organization and repression of self;

---

*In the 1960s, many demonstrations (and of course, rock concerts like Woodstock) had the look and feel of revival meetings, wild expressions of "belief," reliance on something special happening, or about to occur. The first coming may have been sexual, but the second was connected to spirit.

...ans for the flow with nature and the wilderness: the two eternally at war in fact and ideology. Yet through it all, we know the Puritans coveted what the Indian felt and knew, and wanted to ingest the Indian experience into themselves; since what the Indian knew suggested areas of knowledge closed out to the Puritan. There is far more here than mere trafficking with forbidden knowledge or fascination with the exotic. It would be repeated in the white American's obsession with the Negro, his way of life, his sexuality, his "African nature."* And it would recur when native Americans had to deal with millions of bizarre foreigners, those overseas Indians.

What we find occurring in each phase is a peculiar American process, of initial curiosity, then inexorable assimilation or wholesale effacement. There is little middle ground—either assimilate or be effaced. Part of the reason our postwar (and earlier) novelists have such a difficult time relating to what is American is that the country offers so little of the middle, where novels traditionally flourished. When we speak of the classic novel, which is usually located in the previous century (Eliot, Dickens, Tolstoy, Dostoyevsky, Flaubert), we refer to fictions and cultures that had a definable middle. Even Dostoyevsky maneuvered from extremes back toward the center: faith, Mother Russia, love of a good woman. American writers have few such common anchors.

For the Puritans, the Indian was part of what had to be assimilated and effaced; and so the Indian represented to the white American settler what was attractive (primitive, mythical, exotic) and forbidden (the devil incarnate). The Indian suggested a dualism: a source of strength and yet a threat to civilization. The very qualities that gave the Indian his mystical power were elements that had to be erased, in the Indian himself and in the Puritan. With his "Red Brother," the Puritan could flirt with every aspect of what later became standard American themes: rebirth, pastoral values, the primitive versus civilization, tribal life versus more sophisticated social forms, the lure of romantic ideas as against practical considerations.

In that ambivalent Puritan relationship to the Indian, we have, in fact, the very first collision between elements of a technological society (Puritan control, order, logic, reason) and the romanticism of the primitive mind (Arcadia, pastoral, Garden); a clash that

---

*Mailer's "The White Negro" is in many ways an updating of Puritans and Indians; as are, in different terms, Bellow's *Henderson the Rain King* and Matthiessen's *At Play in the Fields of the Lord.*

would dominate our literature in the nineteenth century and remain unabated in the twentieth. For Emerson, Thoreau, Whitman, Melville, Hawthorne, Henry Adams, our classical writers, this conflict of ideas was a primary ideological consideration. American culture is defined less by its literary or artistic content than by ideological struggles which, worked out over the centuries in Europe, were telescoped into a few decades here. The overriding concern in the later nineteenth century, best characterized by Henry Adams's attacks on technology, had its base two hundred years earlier and is updated in the postwar novel.

The first generation of twentieth-century novelists recognized that Adams's technology—car, railroad, highway—would never again allow the pastoral dream. Hemingway, nevertheless, still believed such frontiers could exist, if not in America then elsewhere. Part of the malaise which claimed him was surely personal and psychological, but part was also the ending of his intensely felt universe: both *it* and his power to control it. Long ago, the Puritans had ingested the Indian, and the primitive was not only in final retreat, it no longer represented anything. The larger question is how the next generation of writers, our concern here, could deal with this altered sense of reality: the final disappearance of what had started to diminish three hundred years ago.

Broadly, the old belief in the pastoral ideal, with its connection to renewal and rebirth, has been transformed into an obsession with changing relationships: movement, escape, spatiality (being spaced out), divorce, reformation of family structures, remarriage, proliferating affairs. Each new attachment is perceived, optimistically, by the author as the "freeing process" we associate with immersion in the new Eden, *even when Eden is itself an illusion.*

Sex, under such conditions, loses guilt, confinement, inhibition; one can experiment (oral, anal), seek group experience, dabble in homosexuality. Mailer's "The Man Who Studied Yoga," a mid-fifties fiction, is prophetic; not drugs, but a pornographic home film, is the turn-on, a glimpse of the beyond that is traditionally assigned to pastoral. Postwar writers have found in shifting attachments and relationships (to one's self as well as to others) that expression of feeling which Emerson associated with energies that lead to development and maturity.

Even as Emerson wrote, the machine was settling in, at least the railroad. The railroad was for the American the quintessential machine, the one that commanded romantic dreams of space and escape, as its proliferating lines brought boundaries. While offering spatiality, it frightened cows, sent clouds of soot over crops and farmhouses, allowed for huge speculation in goods, transforming food to commodities, and it brought settlements to areas that might have remained wilderness or desert. Nourishing as it destroyed, it was the archetypal machine of the nineteenth and early twentieth centuries, as the car has become the equivalent in midcentury.*

While Emerson misjudged, Hawthorne and Melville detected that the intrusion of the machine was more than the interruption of a pastoral idyll. They foresaw that the machine, the slums of Europe, the inroads of new experiences would permanently transform American life: that Eden, no longer attainable, would shape itself into utopian dreams, become the stuff of romance and nostalgia, and mislead us repeatedly about the nature of reality.

The Blithedale Romance (1851), Hawthorne's version of a utopian venture in communal living, Brook Farm or otherwise, stands, also, as a corrective to an easy pastoral life. The fire burning so brightly at the beginning of the novel creates an illusion, and everyone observing the fire becomes like the denizens watching the flames in Plato's parable of the cave: misled by the nature of reality, unable to distinguish real from unreal. Even Coverdale, our man of reason, succumbs to the flames, to the transformation, even purification, they create. In their light and heat, all earthly creatures take on a beauty they do not intrinsically possess; and the utopian experiment itself suggests a metamorphic state, returning them to a paradise regained. But the flames mislead. Once Coverdale falls ill and awakens distant from the fire, he recognizes how it has falsified. Flame, heat, warmth, glow itself are illusory; paradoxically, their enhancement of life makes them deceptive. The fire is emblematic of the entire experiment, and only Silas Foster, a worker, remains outside the deception; for he is connected to the farm as a working area, land, animals, crafts, not to its utopian potentiality. Hawthorne's tale is cautionary. He warns of utopia, nostalgia, the falsifications of pastoral ideals.

---

*That, too, is passing; *Paradise Lost* is Emma Rothschild's ironic title for our own form of nostalgia. We observe nostalgia also in the proliferation of "baseball novels," an effort to regain a lost paradise. See Chapter Three for discussions of Philip Roth's *The Great American Novel,* Robert Coover's *The Universal Baseball Association: J. Henry Waugh, Prop.,* and Mark Harris's Henry Wiggen trilogy; one could add Wallace Stegner's *Big Rock Candy Mountain* and others.

One century later, in Malamud's *The Natural* (1952), we can find the contemporary version of Hawthorne's tale. Baseball is Malamud's utopia, a magical rite instead of a magical place. Roy Hobbs, the protagonist, through his fantastic bat called Wonderboy, is able to become a superstar. Hobbs's career is symbolic of America: country boy makes good, a young man deeply attached to pastoral life (the bat is made of a strange wood, as Siegfried's sword is made of special metal), a Huck Finn type, yet stalked by disaster. Reality is Memo, a witch girl who shoots athletes in their prime—Hobbs is only nineteen. The shooting, recalling that of Eddie Waitkus, of the Philadelphia Phillies, sends Hobbs into a fifteen-year oblivion. He returns from the shadow of defeat at thirty-four and is almost "saved" by Iris, a lovely flower of a woman, a grandmother in her thirties. But Hobbs is hobbled by disaster—the shooting, an attack of appendicitis, a stroke, the acceptance of a bribe in a playoff game so he can marry Memo. What is of interest, however, is not the sequence of defeats, but how Malamud identifies the natural with pastoral values. Everything good about Hobbs is natural, prelapsarian; everything weak or corrupt is urban, sophisticated, materialistic. The bribe (recalling the Chicago White Sox of 1919) is capitalism at its crudest. Despite Malamud's recognition of Hawthorne's warning, we have, here, an Emersonian dialectic of American experience.

Our writers since the Second World War have, in the main, leapfrogged over Melville and Hawthorne to embrace a vision that was by 1860 already moldy. This has, obviously, created a relationship to historical patterns that affects every aspect of American fiction. It means that the American attitude toward its past is based on evasions, distortions, nostalgia, sentimentality, false hopes, and an illusory sense of historical process. Nabokov's *Pale Fire* fits curiously into this pattern—very possibly a truer view of American disruption and dislocation than *Lolita,* which seems more obvious.

In an effort to overcome these evasions, the writer has sought the only possible areas where he or she can go—self-serving impulses, spatiality, escape from time, constant movement, ever shifting new relationships. These are the source of both strength and weakness. The self holds it all together; or else everything fragments, and the self is indulged. *Nearly every technical innovation in postwar American fiction is designed not to disguise or veil the self, but to display its greater glory,* like the peacock with its tail. Gaddis in *JR* evades the expected associations of scene and character not to bleach out his main character but to give him greater presence. Unlike Kafka, the American writer cannot posit an entire universe on withdrawal. Kafka never makes failure a form of success, whereas the American writer indulges in failure as a formula for eventual success.

For the European writer, the life or force against which he reacts has always been clear: historical, traditional, customary. His weapons may be wit, irony, and parody, but whatever is out there firmly remains itself, even during periods of tremendous change. His difficulty is to give his characters individuality, to find an identity for them outside so much settled "beyond." Kafka's solution was to bury his characters, giving them space away from it all. K. gains a separate identity by forsaking all identity. The negation of self is self. Stendhal's Julien Sorel is eager to establish his own romantic self, but cannot discover exactly what it is that exists beyond him. He struggles to free himself, not to achieve personal freedom.

European search for self amidst a rooted "other" leads to phenomenology, the interior space where history is less of a burden. American search for the "other" as a place to attach the self opens up all experience, where the outer reaches are chaotic or disastrous. Melville's Pierre wonders if beneath the bricks and shaven faces—the finite of our everyday world—there may be something subtle, exotic, and infinite. Yet coexistent with this speculation is the fear that there may be nothing more than what he sees. Kafka had no doubts: the forefront *was* the beyond, and the equation was reversible.

The very assets of the "new American"—that is, his or her ability to start cleanly, without the weight of history—become here the burden. Everything must be filled in, or the empty (black?) holes are sources of doom. We recall Crèvecoeur's paean to American life, in which the *absence* of burdensome elements becomes the basis for his praise. These absent elements, which Crèvecoeur celebrates, were, incidentally, almost precisely what Henry James, in his comments on Hawthorne, found so debilitating about American life. Crèvecoeur wrote: "Here are no aristocratical families, no courts, no kings, no bishops, no ecclesiastical dominion, no invisible power giving to a few a very visible one; no great manufacturers employing thousands, no great refinements of luxury. . . . We are a people of cultivators, scattered over an immense territory, communicating with each other by means of good roads and navigable rivers. . . . We are all animated with the spirit of any industry which is unfettered and unrestrained, because each person works for himself."

Crèvecoeur's image is one of unlimited space into which the American can fit himself in any way he wishes. For Melville's Pierre, who is doomed by space, that empty terrain is a fearful vacuum. He desires solidity and obtains liquidity, or atmosphere. Since he romanticizes all experience, he can create illusions, even when there is nothing to imagine. The vision of emptiness can be turned into a densely populated city, as his imagination works upon it, or it can remain exactly what it is: a vision of emptiness. The choice for Pierre, whether to accept that Isabel may be only "two-score words" or to imagine in her enigma a fully fleshed-out history, is too much for him. Revitalized by the need to fill in, he is enervated by that need to find what must be filled in. Rather than his occupying space, space occupies him. Transformed into the vacuum which he imagines as being out there, he becomes, in his crazy, skew way, the prototype of the American hero. He, not Hester Prynne, fills out our landscape, that mixture of innocence, nostalgia, sentimentality, illusory hopes and dreams, that desire for spatiality and pastoral idylls, that compulsion to fill up spatiality so as to define oneself.

"History is now," Emerson warned, and these words, if we accept them as a true definition of the American experience, make it difficult for the novelist to function with intellectual completeness. Emerson counseled: "We, as we read, must become Greeks, Romans, Turks, priest and king, martyr and executioner; must fasten these images to some reality in our secret experience, or we shall learn nothing rightly." In this formulation, all history becomes autobiographical materials, personalized images.

The writer faces terrible problems of assimilation and resolution. William Gaddis's Wyatt Gwyon, with his family association to the American past, can only establish recognitions or realities for himself by way of forgery. For him, the counterfeit is a greater reality, a greater awareness, than is the real thing, which has died in history. The counterfeit or forgery is *now,* lending itself to the historical present even while encapsulating the past. The writer through an act of will, ego, or subjective projection must recreate an America that is more myth than reality. It is not so much, as Philip Roth has asserted, that American reality is too bizarre for the writer, who cannot "out-invent" reality; rather, it is that America rarely coheres or achieves a reality. An analogy would be the deepest or blackest parts of the cosmos, which shift constantly as new constellations are created, disintegrate, reform; so that the pattern can only be measured by mathematics, not by the eye pressed to the looking glass. That deliquescent reality slips through the writer's imagination, setting up infinite potentialities for an art form that seems to possess finite tools.

If the novelist is a first- or second-generation American or someone who traces his lineage to another culture, or not even an American (Nabokov, Kosinski), then he or she must doubly recreate an America whose traditions and history he has learned, not absorbed through family and tradition. He must first expunge his own past (African, Eastern European, Catholic, Judaic), then adopt another past, with all *its* contradictions, and finally reject whatever has resulted, itself disorderly and discontinuous. In his autobiography, *Speak, Memory,* and in his American fiction, Nabokov grappled directly with these irreconcilable factors. Like Nabokov, the American writer is isolated: no culture is precisely his, although he seems to have access to several cultures. In point of fact, he is not even a peninsula, but an island.

These ideas play back and forth in the American experience in the second half of the twentieth century, like ghosts haunting an attractive but mysterious house. We carry ourselves as perpetually new—and our writers often voice old truths as revelation—but our novelty is old newness. Behind it all is the myth of the Garden, that myth played out by the Puritans with the Indians and then duplicated, in part, in the nineteenth century: the Puritans themselves, with their repression of self so as to achieve a stronger self; Emerson, with his ideas of renewal, his call to novelty; Thoreau, with his pond and reflected face, that combination of salvation and narcissism; Melville, with his Ahab seeking to overcome original sin and yet seemingly excluded from it; Hawthorne, with his awareness of the illusory nature of flame, passion, heat, the Garden itself. Now, after our emergence from a winning war, victor in a depleted world, how could the American novelist avoid believing he was someone unique who, although baptized by the Old World experience, had emerged, nevertheless, to re-enact the myth of Adam and the Garden?

The war ended, and after the jungle rot, bombings, and holocaustic horrors, the American felt pristine. Little of the disaster really penetrated the American psyche; and even the writers who saw action continued to perceive it through American eyes. We must insist on this: that the American novelist Americanized the war or the wartime situation, as if it were a local action.* We have an outpouring of sophisticated provincialism. Irwin Shaw's romanticization in *The Young Lions* needs no further gloss. Cozzens's *Guard of Honor* turns the war into a legal squabble. James Jones's prewar Prewitt resists the Treatment because he insists on being Adam; he carries with him a purity, an untouchability. Heller's Yossarian observes horrors all around, but assumes he can be saved, and at the end rows toward Sweden, an earthly paradise (although, in part, a Nazi sympathizer). Mailer was almost alone in questioning this view, but he, too, came to embrace it; and in his fiction shortly after *The Naked and the Dead,* he was nothing if not the avatar of the new, Adam reborn.

Although the war experience could not be romanticized as it was in Hemingway, nor seen as a testing ground for heroes and villains, nor even viewed, in the mode of Dos Passos, as the basis for attacks upon exploitative capitalism, it could also not be observed in the disastrous terms of the European. When "nothingness" and nihilism entered our postwar fiction, they were borrowings, not from Hemingway and his Lost Generation, nor from any other American tradition, but from Europeans—Camus, Sartre, Céline. This is an important distinction, because nothingness such as we find mouthed by Bourjaily's Skinner Galt is unearned. It is neither the *nada* of Hemingway, which it resembles, nor the deeper nothingness we find in the French and Germans. It is a distinctly postwar American nothingness, an elected melancholy, boredom, depression, which was loosely translated into a quasi-melancholy nihilism. Real nihilism, nothingness, negativism are countered by American spatiality, booze, or, later, drugs.

When the war ended and those men who had fought in it returned to become writers—Mailer, Jones, Bourjaily, Heller, Mandel—they reassumed roles as Americans, with horizons and opportunities (G.I. Bill, credit plans, cheap mortgages), despite what they had experienced in Europe or the South Pacific. The country, undisturbed by the war (with casualties far fewer than those of any large European country), its optimism untouched, was experiencing a great industrial surge. Part of the sourness of fiction in the 1950s resulted not from conditions but from hopes dashed; as Americans, writers had believed in their illusions.

---

*When we come, later, to the Vietnam conflict, the complete Americanization of the war is to be expected. Korean War fiction is not a factor in this study.

Another very significant fact remained: that we had won; the enemy had been identified and conquered, and there was no question there had been an enemy. The idea of the "perfect war" was as reassuring as the idea of the Garden. We could do anything we wanted with impunity—relocate the Japanese from the West Coast, firebomb Dresden, atomic bomb Japanese cities, acquiesce to Soviet plans for Eastern Europe. Had the Vietnamese My Lai incident occurred twenty years earlier, Calley and his superiors would have received commendations. In the name of a "good war," anything can be perpetrated.

Despite the horrors that sneaked back, this feeling served in part as continuity with the era of Emerson and Thoreau. It brought us over the bad years of the Depression, when the Garden turned to the dust bowl and unemployment lines. How quaint seemed the march on Washington in 1932 of the Bonus Expeditionary Force to seek relief from unemployment, and the fact that the marchers were routed, with several deaths, by our new heroes of the 1940s: Patton, MacArthur, and Eisenhower!

Further, if people wished to communicate, the new tower was not Babel, but English, the language of trade, diplomacy, and literature. American novelists established norms for fiction: horizons, energy, a nihilism predicated on abundance, a nothingness amidst plenty. British fiction obliged by withdrawing, becoming increasingly insular. The language of the world was American, and this suddenly made our postwar novel—more than its poetry or drama—a language that spoke almost universally. It also opened up the past in fiction and gave new weight to our nineteenth-century writers. The beginning of the Fulbright awards, by which American professors and students went throughout the world to teach or spread American literature and culture, was a recognition of American literary influence. The important element here is not only that the contemporary American novel was spread abroad, but that the earlier culture was examined; so that continuity with contemporary fictions could be established. In turn, large American studies programs were established by foreign countries, and the Puritans, American romantic poetry, the Transcendentalists, Cooper, Melville, Poe (our previous "export"), Hawthorne, Emerson, and Thoreau became objects of intense study. We had our literary Peace Corps.

Intermixed with complex attitudes toward the past were elementary questions of language. For one of the hurdles the postwar novelist had to clear, far more than any other group in our history, was lin-

guistic. The major prewar novelists, with few exceptions, were old Americans, on at least one side of their family—Hemingway, O'Hara, Fitzgerald, Steinbeck, Wolfe, Anderson, Miller, Porter, Dos Passos (one side). The language they turned to, no matter how they modulated it in their work, was a received English. For the postwar novelists, the situation was different. For now besides the historically American writers—Cheever, Purdy, Styron, O'Connor, Oates, Updike—we have those whose ears as children had been filled with Yiddish or an Eastern European language, or with a black version of English or English particularized in the ghettos of large cities, or with Italian; or those who had grown up with an accented English, with inflections and tones that derived from another language.

Additionally, there was the influence of modernism, bringing with it yet another kind of English— Joyce's in particular, the poetry of Yeats and Eliot (whose rhythms and cadences would prove almost as influential as Joyce's). Besides British English, translations of the major modernists would throw in a vast new experience, the "English" of Proust, Mann, Kafka, Céline, Gide, Malraux, Camus, Sartre, de Beauvoir, Sarraute, Robbe-Grillet, later Borges, Grass, García Márquez. This English filtering in by way of reading formed a three-part linguistic unit: the foreign language from one's childhood already in one's ear, reading in the English of modernists, especially Joyce and Eliot, and readings in translation from highly influential Europeans.

In his excellent book on the role the Negro intellectual must play in forging black nationalism in the sixties and thereafter, Harold Cruse, unfortunately, omits language. Yet the language a black novelist or poet chooses for himself will shape his vision; and if he writes in a standard English he has entered in some part a "white culture," no matter the other emphases in his work. Similarly, in "Envy; or, Yiddish in America," a satire on a Yiddish novelist who is translated into English as well as on those who are called "Jewish-American" novelists, Cynthia Ozick is aware of how language alters the entire vision. Her protagonist, Edelshtein, writes in Yiddish, so that the uniqueness of the Jewish experience should not be lost. In translation, the Yiddish writer becomes Americanized, and, comparably, those American writers who sprinkle their work with Yiddish expressions are little more than whores, selling out their language in the marketplace. Edelshtein is a fanatic, a dreamer, and not a little crazy; but the premise holds, that the novelist writing in postwar America finds himself in a unique relationship to language.

In a parallel (but vastly different) point, Mailer tries to locate an American style as derivative from Henry Miller, who has perhaps "influenced the style of half the good American poets and writers alive today: it is fair to ask if books as different as *Naked Lunch, Portnoy's Complaint, Fear of Flying,* and *Why Are We in Vietnam?* would have been as well received (or as free in style) without the irrigation Henry Miller gave to American prose. Even a writer as removed in purpose from Miller as Saul Bellow shows a debt in *Augie March.*" Mailer observes, further, that young writers thirty years ago "learned to write by reading him along with Hemingway and Faulkner, Wolfe and Fitzgerald."

The impact on style which Mailer pinpoints in Miller is more a general freeing process, in language, sexual notation, rhythms, swinging outward and around, than a distinctively Miller phenomenon. Miller was himself part of a general liberating tendency in prose, not the initiator. It is a freedom that extends as much to poetry—from Whitman, to Williams, on to Lowell and Ginsberg—as it does to prose. In prose, in fact, we can locate this freedom in Thomas Wolfe, whose work was obtainable at a time when Miller's was banned in this country. Even Wolfe's influence is only a small part of a much larger force, for liberating elements in prose are as much generally cultural as they are specifically literary. D. H. Lawrence, for example, was alert to the culture as a whole and carries the freeing process back to the time of the first war, well before Miller began writing *Tropic of Cancer* (in 1931) and fully twenty years before that book was published in France.*

Every writer who decides upon American English not only identifies with a history that may not be his, but inherits a spatial tradition that is distinctly American; he as well succeeds to a secular heritage at odds with his own religious practices. Every attempt

---

*More than purely linguistically, Miller's total presence as a narcissist in both language and sex places him solidly in an American tradition. Part of the attraction he provides for Mailer—and for Roth, Jong, Burroughs—is his fearlessness in reveling in mechanical sex: sex without passion and surely without love. His narcissism gave him a single-mindedness in the sexual act that isolated it from the people performing it. That proximity to pornography—observing it or participating in it, as Mailer caught so well in "The Man Who Studied Yoga"—defines much of the sexual combat in the postwar novel, and not simply because legal restrictions on candid descriptions have been lifted.

on the part of the novelist to become ahistorical, to move himself and his characters beyond a particular national destiny, is connected to a countertension that binds him to America; and since the postwar novelist's desire for individuality, for anarchic indulgence, for display of self is more intense than ever, the tensions are more acute, the play between past and present more violent. Paradoxically, the more furious is the tug toward freedom from history on the part of the postwar novelist, the greater is the attraction of past writers and themes.

The American does not believe so much in the world or in America, which he judges harshly, as he assumes the individual can escape that world, deny its validity for him, run from history or doom, establish his own values, and live as though spatial escape were always possible. Mailer's halfhearted "American dream" is Rojack's belief he is Proteus combined with Odysseus and a Texas cowboy: the man who can alter his shape, the great wanderer, and the marginal drifter who recognizes only the stars overhead. America is a world without fences. Odysseus, in reality, was attempting to get home.

Part of the significance of the modernist influence on the postwar American was its reinforcement of his sense of removal from history, by immersing him in ideas and techniques that transcended this time or that place. Pure modernism can be read as art for art's sake, but the American novelist rarely embraced the new with that kind of aesthetic fervor. What we find is not a Yeatsian removal to Byzantium or a Kafkan castling, but a different relationship to the historical process. The very shapelessness of American life and language offered freedom, so that novelty could be turned against itself, in a dialectic of release from self and search for self. Emerson denied there was evil, only the absence of good; Melville, aware of history, scoffed at him: twins of past and present.

While the postwar writer swipes at several heritages, how does he or she discover a center? A theme of this study is that the American novelist of the postwar era is constantly working out a process of adjustment: fully conscious of other cultures and yet himself in pursuit of something essentially American. A parallel motif is that with this period of fiction, because of the influence of European modernism, something distinctly American is almost impossible to achieve. Located among those who have tried are Gaddis, Pynchon, McElroy, Gass, Barth (to a lesser extent), Barthelme, Bellow (in two works), Roth (in one work).

In several ways, Walker Percy's *Lancelot* (1977)

underscores this terrible dilemma, in which the novelist is divided, even torn, rejecting history and yet yearning after it. A Catholic convert, a Southerner, a medical doctor by training, an outsider to the New York partying and literary scene, a man of considerable wit and a consumer of paradoxes, Percy is particularly equipped for the tightrope act of American fiction. Yet with *Lancelot,* he apparently gave up trying to find delicate holes in the fabric through which he can score; and he moved to apocalyptic endings. For his protagonist, Lancelot, wants to stop the world: "The point is, I will not tolerate this age." He insists on his uniqueness, on the singularity of the individual experience, on clear-cut sexual definitions and social roles. He wants to identify with a historical process, to return to an era when he felt this was possible, an Eden that never existed. It is (shades of "I'll Take My Stand") a Southern version of a Greek ideal, when a ruling class had slaves to live for it.

Yet whether the point is well taken or not does not really matter, because in context it derives from a man already a lunatic. We meet Lancelot, not in a tournament, but in a madhouse, prepared to settle down with the young woman in the next cell, a psychotic who has been gang-raped. Thus, the driving need to regain sanity, balance, social structuring, individual worth is given by Percy to a crazed criminal. R. D. Laing is reflected: the mad are saner; the crazy may be holy.

Like the Lancelot of Arthurian legend, Percy's protagonist has been victimized by a woman, his wife, and in his rage he plans revenge, which leads to her death and the death of the two other men in her life. One dies by the knife, two by fire, and Lancelot goes mad, if not already crazed when he systematically plots their deaths. This man, then, becomes the repository of moral wisdom about the modern world, the man seeking a pattern. The ironies cannot disguise that Percy is building upon shifting ground, his view of the sixties and early seventies: that insanity is really sanity if the rest of the world is insane. This is another way of posing the confrontation between a historical process and an anarchic behavior which rejects all history. The dilemma passes into ironies, and ironies into paradoxes that cannot work literarily unless the author is Dostoyevsky writing about holy fools.

All social and personal signals have shifted. To be sane is to be ahistorical, adrift; to be insane is to discover a set of moral values. Hemingway still believed, in *A Farewell to Arms,* that one could retreat from the retreat at Caporetto. Although death would eventuate, Henry's escape is worth the effort, his retreat with one woman worth the experience. Such a probe at stability, however evanescent, is not possible for the post–World War II novelist. Hemingway's Henry is updated and transformed into Yossarian and Rabbit, who because they cannot conceivably seek wholeness—what is it? where is it?—must run; not only to escape a war or marriage that will kill them, but to evade feelings that cannot be resolved. They have entered history and now want to escape it. Jones's Prewitt chooses to buck the system, to cultivate anarchy within discipline, but he does not achieve wholeness; for he dissolves in alcohol and lost hopes, lying dead on a golf course. Examples multiply. Bellow's young and older men, from Joseph and Augie through Herzog and Sammler, run or else lie around, cut off from whatever resources would make it possible for them to resolve themselves. Only Henderson seems capable of wholeness, and that in a narrative that becomes mythical and fantastic, an aberration for Bellow. Barth's Horner seeks salvation in a witch doctor, Gaddis's Gwyon in counterfeit paintings, McElroy's Hind in reconstructing a kidnapping that may never have occurred.

Paradoxically, the strength of the postwar novel lies here: in that intense, fervid quest for wholeness which will undermine, and perhaps destroy, freedom. The desire to link oneself to a historical tradition is equaled only by the impossibility of it. Flannery O'Connor's "perverted heroes" are men who know all routes are blocked. When the Misfit in "A Good Man Is Hard to Find" says that " 'Jesus was the only One that ever raised the dead . . . and He shouldn't have done it,' " in his perverse way he is straddling the American dilemma. For if He actually did raise the dead, then one must seek wholeness by seeking Him; there is no other course. But if He didn't raise the dead, then one is free to kill, enjoy, burn, destroy. *The point is that one never knows.* As the Misfit says, he wasn't there and so he can't say.

The wars fought in American fiction are ego wars. The nineteenth century gave them impetus; the postwar era, definition. It was Emerson who suggested that "life was a matter of having good days," by which he *did* mean self-indulgence. He feared that the shivering of men into fragments was destructive of the whole and subversive of those "good days" which gave life meaning, which *were* life. This was, also, Thoreau's romantic, agrarian side, his espousal of a circuitry of self (at Walden, Cape Cod, on the Concord and Merrimac), the individual whose culture was his labor, his labor his culture. Almost from its beginnings and intensifying in the postwar years,

American fiction has shown a disequilibrium between the individual with his isolated ego and that same individual within marriage, group, family, or society. The individual functions only at the extremes, in a hole or cubby or within an institutional atmosphere that the novelist feels obligated to parody (army, college, office) as a mechanical system. In our earlier fiction, imagery was oceanic, of vastitudes, white whales and infinite Pacifics, or sweeps of time that carried us back to the Puritans. Now it is holes and cubbies and small rooms or labyrinths as equally seductive. Once one went out to meet frontiers, which kept receding; now one searches downward, within, which also keeps receding. Kafka wars with the horizon.

The consequence of this, as of other incongruities, is a bifurcation of reality, creating several realities which reshape themselves at every turn. The reliance on tactile, sensory experience in the novel of recent years is an attempt to reach beyond these unresolvable complexities, to achieve some contact with a vital process; and therefore the self is probed narcissistically—*Invisible Man* is prototypical—as the sole source of life, *even when* the given novel has a larger conceptual frame of reference. The fiction that results is "phenomenological narcissism," the self and its projects as the single reality. Gaddis's *JR* is a great triumph of an oral tradition that vaunts the self as its subject.

Attempts at resolution, meaningful as they are in the abstract, can only carry forward as dream, reverie, fantasy—what we find in Barth, Barthelme, Pynchon, Coover, and Burroughs. We may still honor the holy fool, in Salinger, for example, but his time has passed. In his quest for deeper meaning, the postwar novelist, far more than the generation lost after the first war, is almost completely separated from the past; and even a Southern novelist like Styron has, in *Sophie's Choice,* forsaken his heritage for a Northern and European experience.

Does the American novelist need any sense of the past at all? Possibly, we have become so protean that the search for earlier shapes is chimerical. Numerous novels since 1965 about the female experience do away with the past altogether. All that matters is "a life," "one's life," "my life" or "our life together," or the escape from "my present life" and the gaining of "my new life." Although intensely male, *An American Dream* is prototypical of such novels, and the appearance now of female writers in this area means women are entering a previous male preserve, not initiating something new.

This mode is based on infinite renewability, a kind of Hegelian dialectic, but adapted to American tastes and predilections. Since such developments have little historical past and few cultural traditions, the result can be either a brittleness of language or a reliance on language alone, the great strength *and* weakness of the American postwar writer. Yet despite ingenious attempts, few writers have forged a distinctly American prose, what we find in the Hemingway stories, in Fitzgerald's *Gatsby* and shorter pieces, in early Dos Passos. Gaddis in *JR,* Pynchon in *V.,* Heller in *Catch-22,* Bellow in *Augie March,* Roth in *Portnoy's Complaint,* Reed in *The Free-Lance Pallbearers,* Ellison in *Invisible Man* have attempted a prose "voice," but such efforts are rarely sustained. They are, by and large, one-shot efforts, without that continuity which allows something distinctive to take hold. Barthelme in his early stories and then in *The Dead Father* has been most consistent, but the danger is repetition. Similarly, Didion's nervous minimalist prose seems significant, but may be lost if she cannot move from self-pity to larger themes.

In *JR,* Gaddis has moved beyond all the other novelists into a world dominated completely by torrents of language: a novel of over 350,000 words almost all in dialogue. Gaddis marks dialogue by dashes, but it would have been more of an assault on the reader if he had forgone the dashes and made dialogue indistinguishable from the rare narrative passages. Nevertheless, the barrage of words, as conversation, publicity and advertisements, as echoes and reechoes, radio and television talk—words to the right and left of us—serves as a large cultural commentary; words become the American universe. Gaddis, like Pynchon in *Gravity's Rainbow,* has found not in language but in words the way we think and live. Thoreau thought we lived best in silences, but Gaddis, an urbanist, shows us that we survive by way of verbal barrages: words that rarely shape sentences or need end punctuation, that are aspects of gesture, that telegraph themselves by way of syllables or fragments. Words form outlines of a fabulous land, like the metaphors of Borges, but then fall back as just words.

An alternative to linguistic experimentation is to preserve amenities by means of an outdated figure, one out of phase with his time, such as Bellow's Sammler and even his Herzog; or, in some respects, Jones's Prewitt and Malamud's Dubin. Yet this method, no matter how well used, creates unbridgeable schisms, for the very reason that the contemporary novelist is also so scornful of the present. While the past may evoke a nostalgia derived from a fantasy life, the present is almost always a foul place—not just people and events, but the very texture of life.

For Roth, unpleasantness is associated with assimilated Jews and their values; for Bellow, it is modern youth, always horny, high on drugs, or else blacks, with their big cocks, their alien culture; for Mailer, it is modern life as a whole, which is weak and unchallenging, debilitating, unsexed. For Pynchon, it is more cosmic, a falling off, heading toward disintegration; for Barth, a general exhaustion in everything from people to literary ideas; for Baldwin, unresolved elements of color, sex, one's emotional life. For Heller, it is the failure of life to provide sustained happiness, so that one must search memory for fantasies by which the present can be supported. For Joyce Carol Oates, life is so devoid of satisfaction that her protagonists seek meaning in supermarkets and drive-ins, in murky streets and byways, where the present is narrow and restrictive, already self-defeating.

The most ingenious, perhaps, of them all has been a brilliant stringer together of words and scenes; and yet Bellow, despite his insight into the paradoxes and incongruities of American life, has an impulse toward stability and resolution, toward social values, that much of his material legitimately denies. Reason pulls against intuition, consciousness against imagination. Bellow uses words to show us disintegration, decline, fragmentation—what we routinely expect from Pynchon and Barth—but then switches; so that words deny themselves and become flimsy bridges over values and systems Bellow generates from himself.

Traditionally, humor, wit, satire, even burlesque and mockery, were verbal efforts to resolve life elements by way of style. All forms of humor have had a commonsensical base to them, supporting a system in which laughter was a means of comprehension, of pressing elements toward a center. Our contemporary humorists, however—whether sardonically as in Barth, Pynchon, Barthelme, more openly as in Vonnegut and Heller, or less intellectually as in Friedman or Brautigan—deploy comedy as a way of splitting off those who are cool and authentic (a distinct minority) from those who are square and of bad faith (ones connected to society or a system). Since the terms of the split have little basis in historical detail or philosophical belief, the humor can be fleeting. We may revel in the mockery, but the novel in question falters or flattens, as comic episodes are strung out without supporting substance—thus, not only Friedman, but Vonnegut.

Our novelists slug away at the realities they scorn, but lacking philosophical bases and holding to patterns of anti-intellectuality, they frequently sink when their sensations (good for a novel or two) are exhausted. Depletion of resources results from their inability to take intellect seriously. Even Walker Percy, a novelist of ideas—philosophical, scientific, religious, a far deeper thinker than most—ran from all of them to write his novel of rage, *Lancelot*. Ideas turn into diatribes. Rational discourse vanishes. For another, Saul Bellow is often spoken of as a novelist of ideas; but it is here, in sustained thought, that he is weakest. He, in fact, writes best not at the level of ideas, where his protagonists express puerile views, but at the level of parody, mockery, sarcasm, wit, where panache replaces intellect.

Translated into cultural values, wit and mockery by themselves have little lasting value. Even in the best of such fiction, *Gravity's Rainbow,* one is made aware of attenuated skits stitched on to previous segments, rather than baked in by a defined point of view. In the European/Borges sense of the comic, wit is a form of historical process. Baudelaire, for instance, spoke of the comic impulse as based on laughter caused by the grotesque; that, in turn, expresses the superiority, not of man over man, "but of man over nature." For the American, man's superiority over nature splits him away as someone separate and distinct: that special Adamic sense implicit in so much American comedy, in which the protagonist becomes the "first man," pristine and innocent despite personal devilry.

As a consequence of his conception of Adamic man, the American novelist removes his protagonist from the very social and political context which nourishes the comic.* The distinction is crucial here, since, as we shall see, the American form of comic impulse stresses the individuality of the protagonist, who stands outside comedy, except perhaps as a temporary victim; and in so doing, he weakens the very impulses that make the comic dimension possible. By means of such separation of the individual from his context, the American writer denies realities that have created more traditional comic situations, substituting a dualism where none can exist. For these realities, whether social, political, situational, or institutional, cannot be nullified, except ideally as aspects of mind and will. In Europe, these external pressures

---

*Robert Coover's *The Public Burning*—the Rosenbergs and Nixon—must strain at every seam to achieve its comic effects, and yet Coover to his credit is virtually alone in trying to write a witty political novel.

exist historically and traditionally. The process of existence is not denial or exclusion or escape, but a dialectic which is inescapable. Inevitably, European existentialism would be reduced when it became adapted to American needs.

Modernism for the American writer means he must first assimilate and then repeat his dilemmas. The more he seeks individuality and responds to that liberating aspect of the modernist tradition, the more he must deny the past and weaken his protagonist's frame of reference. Elements which have characterized our culture since the Second World War have all been openings up, some of them cataclysmic in terms of what a society can absorb. The war was itself a radical opening up; but not in the obvious sense of young men and women going abroad and becoming cosmopolitan: rather, in the way that literary modernism invaded this country as authors and techniques. Every serious novelist who wrote after the war, whether he attended college or not, was caught up by the intensities of literary modernism and new critical methods of reading it. Even the most solidly based traditionalists, such as Jones, Cheever, Updike, and Cozzens, were moved by new freedom in language, situation, narrative possibilities, although repelled by stresses on tones, textures, moods, antiheroes, scene and plot discontinuities, narrative convolutions.

After the first postwar years, decisions and events took on the shape of an avalanche. The Hiss-Chambers confrontation had little permanent effect on our literary culture, but it, like the McCarthy years, poisoned the atmosphere and entered into many of our writers: Heller, Mailer, Malamud, Trilling, Coover later, Doctorow.* Far more important than these for the culture at large was the Supreme Court decision in *Brown* v. *Education,* which struck down a previous court ruling sanctioning segregated school facilities. This decision was, in many ways, the opening up of black life in this country, and it certainly was instrumental in the outpouring of fiction by blacks in the later 1950s and throughout the next two decades. For many of the younger writers, the decision coincided with their own childhood or adolescence—L. Jones, Morrison, Reed, et al. And although desegregation did not effectively change the way schools were run, it did offer a step toward another opening up, the civil rights movement five years later.

Of almost equal importance, measured in terms of a life style adopted by the larger culture, was the very loose federation of types called Beats. The adversary movement for the 1950s, when intense political commitment broke down, was directed almost completely inward, toward forging a life style rather than a political statement. The movement that replaced Marxism, Trotskyism, Stalinism, Communism, the United Front, the Popular Front, Marxist Socialism was "inner politics": the old spatiality, but shaped inward. The frontiers were now defined by Zen or some other form of worship, with drugs the catalyst for inner visions. "Give me space" was born here, and it was quite different from Turner's application to the American frontier.

What gave the Beats holding power was the emergence of genuine literary talent: in the poetry of Allen Ginsberg and Gary Snyder, the visionary fictions of William Burroughs, some parts of Kerouac's and Holmes's work. The Beats differed enormously among themselves and should not be confused with the Lost Generation of the 1920s, whose values were far more product-oriented. Those we associate with the generation labeled by Gertrude Stein—Hemingway, Dos Passos, Cowley, Harry Crosby, Fitzgerald, Cummings—were obsessed by work. They went to Europe or rode the rails or drank themselves into oblivion while practicing their craft. Theirs was not only a life style, but an approach to the work they sensed within themselves. Often their self-destructiveness was a means of tapping their literary resources. Although some Beats were indeed poets and novelists, their ideology involved an entire mode of life, not simply the clearing away of bourgeois elements so that words could flow. Their ideal was the remaking of themselves into something different and new: renewal through the utilization of inner space.†

Their life style became coherent to the extent that they became committed to alternative forms of experience, wherever such forms could be found. Frenzied travel (by car), for some, became the "high" that Ginsberg found in William Blake's visionary poetry. Kerouac's Dharma expressed a religious dimension to the style, the open road having now turned inward,

---

*In "The Political Novel," Chapter Seven, I demonstrate how the more traditional values of political fiction are transformed to fit the American experience.

†Just as Beats differed from the Lost Generation, so hippies differed from Beats. The hippies, more action- and politically oriented, developed in the 1960s as part of the rebellion against social/political values; they became more a reaction than a movement, more protesters than doers. In Chapter Three, I discuss Beats in pastoral terms, and then more fully in Chapter Five, on the 1950s.

to a spatiality defined by Buddhism. Castaneda's "weeds," Kesey's Merry Pranksters, and Muktananda worship are, by extension, Beat modes of gaining transcendence. At the highs and lows, one found the authentic human potential. The charms of Neal Cassady in the Beat movement are incomprehensible unless we observe him as a young man daring the lows in order to achieve the highs; the *poète maudit* without the poetry. Beat personal audacity—a mixture of melancholia and frenzied energy—was American existentialism in action.

Running parallel to this cultural opening up in the "under world" of American society were more direct developments in the over world. Supreme Court decisions on obscenity, which granted new freedom in print, films, and even television, brought laws into mainstream culture. What had seemed to be counterthemes in American life now surfaced as themes, that characteristic discontinuity assimilated rapidly into continuity. The novelist was under the gun, especially since these cultural shifts had given rise to competition in the form of the nonfiction novel, the new journalism, the personalizing of history. Could fiction keep pace?

In John Cheever's *Falconer* (1977), his "now" book, Farragut (a solid American name, an admiral in the Civil War) is a college professor who tries to keep pace with the new. As a creature of the 1960s, he becomes separated from the ordinary run of academics by virtue of fratricide and drug addiction. To achieve the oddity of his creation, Cheever had to cut Farragut off from everything that nourished him; he moves in the prison atmosphere as though "dewilled" and disembodied, exempt from history.

Cheever's dilemma is that of the postwar novelist; driven ever deeper into paradoxes, unable to see any way out, he would like to nullify complexity by means of running, sensation, sensory perception. He or she would like to recreate childlike fantasies and observations into the lines and rhythms of his own needs. According to this, all old myths are outdated; nothing holds, because there is no center. Not only is the ceremony of innocence lost, all ceremony is empty. Only "I" remains. Everything becomes fodder for sensation; nothing can be believed, for all has turned to deception and loss. We hear and see a replay of Lost Generation themes, only now with a disbelief in everything except booze or exploitative sex. Booze works, but kidneys and arteries give way. Styron built a reputation on exploiting, in *Lie Down in Darkness* and *Set This House on Fire,* the myths of alcohol: Lost Generation poses, lost Southerners and other gentlemen.

New myths are harder to come by, and yet the novelist must struggle to discover them. They, too, involve words, more booze, more running, a hope for some earthly paradise, more inventive sex. Pynchon has found such a myth in the rocket; Gaddis in counterfeiting and sheer talk; Hawkes in words, brilliant images which approximate the best in modern poetry; Barth in mockeries of the past and of fiction itself.

We are not, however, as Emerson thought and hoped, tragic comedians, but comic tragedians, a different phrase and a different world. Our man of the world wears not the garb of Emerson's scholar—his costume for the emancipated self—but a space suit and lifeline to protect him against the atmosphere. The salient images of the 1960s are demonstrations; or an astronaut dangling by his lifeline outside a spaceship, then striding out on the moon. Comparably, our literary heroes in the sixties and seventies are those who left the world behind, a notable distance from the nineteenth-century creature for whom Emerson said "Life only avails." *His* man, as Hawthorne's and Thoreau's, was of the world; ours, rejecting earth as overpopulated, sealed off, its problems unresolvable, is already stretching out toward heaven. We straddle planets. We escape through space. The search for space objects, frontiers, worlds of adventure has left us snared between past myths—never actively rejected, often embraced as still viable—and future hopes, rarely rooted in more than sensation. The novelist plays out his role as trickster.

Chapter Two

|||||||||||||||||||||||||||||||||||||||||||||||||

AMERICAN SPACE AND SPATIALITY

Every man is an impossibility until he is born; every thing impossible until we see a success.

EMERSON, *"Experience"*

There is no country as extensive as a thought.

EMERSON, *Journals*

Implicit in the American pastoral ideal—whether it derives from Jew, black, or white Protestant—is the notion of space, vertical as well as the more obvious horizontal. In Walker Percy's *Love in the Ruins* (1971), the apocalypse has arrived, and America lies in ruins; the novel a montage of Percy's view of the 1960s. What remains after a secular Armageddon is a small group of people, their so-called leader a sympathetic doctor, all holed up in an abandoned Howard Johnson's.

What could be a more telling metaphor than America's favorite rest stop! Ruins lie around, after a "15-year Ecuadorian war," but salvation rests in those emblems of bourgeois America on the road. More, the protagonist, digs in with food, drink, and three women. This particular Howard Johnson's, deserted and overgrown as it is, has extraordinary facilities, all weighted toward the male point of view, our basic and traditional allegory. The women need a doctor, or More, but he requires three different women: Mormon love in an orange villa.

The significant element is the spacing: More is spaced in, spaced out, distanced from the rest of the world. With the closing of the frontier, only Howard, not Lyndon, Johnson remains, and "he" becomes

"it," our new pastoral. Since we need space, then pastoral settings (wherever), skyscrapers, and even those roadhouses which dot the landscape at intervals like the forts of an earlier age are our new notion of distancing.

The survival of the picaro in the American novel can help to explain that compulsive need for space—outward (on the road) or upward (to the moon). With the building up of cities, the closing out of space, one alternative form of spatial arrangement is the Howard Johnson's of reality and fantasy (white building, bright orange roof, almost unlimited flavors of ice cream, free rest rooms, et al.), the new Tower of Babel. Instead of dispensing languages, it dispenses flavors, new taste sensations, and minimum comforts.

In a novel set in the forties, enclosed by fifties attitudes, but published in the sixties, Heller's Yossarian heads for Sweden, believing that Scandinavia is the new Eden, having replaced America as the avatar of the new. Since it is distant and somewhat mythical, the Sweden of blondes, travel posters, the mystical north, not the Sweden that sold high-grade steel to the Nazis as a benign collaborator, it has the sense of Huck Finn's escape to Montana territory. Both runs are to the north, which means they are wrapped up in spatial mysteries and partake of northern—purifying—myths. Yossarian's run, the archetypal American escape, rings true at one level of the novel, false at another, as do most spatial metaphors for the American novelist. In an updating of *Catch-22*, Tim O'Brien's *Going After Cacciato* replaces Sweden with Paris. Since the latter is halfway around the world from Vietnam, the point of departure, O'Brien was able to inject the war itself into the spatial metaphor. In still more ambitious terms, Pynchon has done this with technology.

Space—wherever—was of course an obsession long before Frederick Jackson Turner's theory of the frontier was articulated as an explanation of the American experience, and it remained an obsession long after he said (as of 1890) spatial frontiers were closed. Space in early settler communities was connected to the openness of Eden: the equation between an Edenic pastoral and the sense of endless space was apparent, as though America were viewed by a new Moses from Mount Pisgah, the Promised Land stretching to infinity. The paradox was already there, since Eden in our minds is enclosed like a middle-sized ranch, fenced in against intruders; yet it is also infinity, where the first couple could roam without restrictions.

The first American was indeed Columbus, who felt the pull of space, finding the boundaries of Europe confining and needing that release that comes with exploring the horizon. With a crew of mixed sorts, he was the first to use water as escape; clearly the ocean and the river are both aspects of the frontier myth. Later, the Great Plains would be spoken of as an ocean, of wheat and grains, endless and treeless space, an Eden without contrasts or lushness. The early settlers, similarly, were space men and women, using America then as many Americans now hope to use the moon and stars: to free themselves of bondage, of earthly restrictions. The moon in the 1960s and early 1970s was that uncontaminated "new place"; not merely was it novel, it was untainted because uninhabited.

Americans abhor a vacuum and have, accordingly, structured a literature in which they can pursue the limitless. In space their aspirations lie, and in space they find either fulfillment or, more often, despair. Everything will be sacrificed to the inner need to move on. Success in America, in fact, is often measured in terms of mobility, not in the fruits. In this respect, *Moby-Dick* for its insight into an American obsession is our archetypal expression of space

and spatiality, perhaps equaled in ambition only by *Gravity's Rainbow* in our century.*

One of the dilemmas of the American postwar novelist has been, in fact, the need to resolve the influence of Kafka with native American spatiality. Much of my argument in later pages will be directed at trying to discover the cultural implications of a Kafkan drift in American fiction paralleled by the compulsion for motion, energy, vitality, space. This is a phenomenon that underlies our postwar culture, exacerbated by many liberal critics (Schlesinger, Galbraith, etc.) who have identified with space, energy, opening up, while ignoring the adversary movement. On that other side, in the undertow, the tension lies.

Those who are optimistic about America—those who, having gone "beyond the melting pot," find the country affluent, the position of blacks improved or improving, intellectuals becoming more accommodating to social need—stress the spatial variety of America, rather than the cubbyhole, enclosed, subterranean view that we can trace to Kafka. Bellow, in 1953, limns a Kafkaesque family in the Einhorns, but then has Augie March explore a different America, a spacious country that spreads into Mexico. Bellow identifies with the expansionists. Ralph Ellison, on the other hand, places his protagonist in an underground room, where the "sun" is not the light over the Great Plains but that provided by hundreds of light bulbs.

Augie seeking an America of space, Ellison's protagonist plumbing the depths of a subterranean existence: here we have the dilemma of the American novel. One form turns outward, one inward. Although Bellow appears to be in the tradition of Kafka, he is really quite a different kind of writer, exploring inward experience in his early fiction—*Dangling Man, The Victim,* and *Seize the Day*—but coming to deny its realities even by *Herzog,* in 1964. In his later work, Bellow toys with Kafka, especially in *Sammler,* but needs a different America.

Kafka's ability to turn a structured universe into a surreal nightmare tested several elements of the American experience, or else highlighted existing disruptions. Kafka's world is so highly ordered and organized that it operates like a machine, an infernal

---

*Our need to conquer continental space by the railroad and national highway systems was ambiguous: to pursue a dream while encased in a warm box; to escape from a lost paradise by speeding, enclosed, toward a still emerging Eden.

machine. While compelling and even realistic for Middle and Eastern Europe, this vision of people and their lives is difficult for the American to absorb. He is drawn to it literarily, and yet harmony in his own frame of reference is connected to space, eluding pursuers, seeking still another good life. Malamud's S. Levin *(A New Life)* straddles the spatiality of America (he teaches at Cascadia College in the Northwest) and the enclosed, stuffy world of Kafka. Reminiscent of K. and Joseph K., the name "S. Levin" (in the Russian style of an initial and a family name) begins the novel. The epigraph is from *Ulysses,* and it speaks of space, of heading westward: "Lo, levin leaping lightens / in eyeblink Ireland's westward walkin!" All the familiar tensions are here: the Kafkan mode of burrowing, along with an American desire for movement and escape, encapsulated in a character who is Jewish, of Russian origin, city oriented. The novel, although not fully developed, is a literary archetype of the American dilemma in the postwar years.

Nearly every American novelist has touched upon Kafka and Kafkan themes, perhaps more significantly in novels by Jews, but not exclusively: Bellow, Roth, Heller, Malamud, Salinger, but also Ellison, Wright, Williams, Oates, Percy, Styron, Barth, Nabokov. Barthelme's *The Dead Father* is an American transformation of Kafka's "Letter to His Father." Yet there is virtually no sustained way in which the Kafkan stress on reductiveness or his ordered nightmare can be incorporated into an American vision. One literary reason, possibly, that Salinger entered his long period of silence was the fact that his burrowing in the Kafkan mode led him up against an Americanism rooted in space and escape, and he could not resolve conflicting elements.

The American novelist, at a loss when faced by Kafkan irony and countertensions, cannot assimilate it, and yet remains fascinated: takes from Kafka and rejects him.* The result is an uneasy hybrid, such as we see in Roth's *The Breast* (1972), part memory, part mammary, part mummery. In *The Professor of Desire,* Roth explores the earlier life of David Kepesh, the man who will ultimately turn into a breast, and explores some peripheral Kafka material, such as an episode with the invented "Kafka's whore," who could be the writer's vision that eludes the American writer.

*Malamud in *The Fixer* (1966) does not speak of Kafka, but *The Trial* lies heavily over the novel, even though Malamud's Jew goes beyond the doglike obedience of Joseph K.

It is rare to have one novelist working so consciously within the vein of another that his chief character speaks of that other's influence on his life. It is even rarer to have, at the same time, an essay by the creator of this character. We have Roth's essay "Looking at Kafka: A Biographical Study," published at approximately the same time as *The Breast,* his Kafkan story of metamorphosis. Thus we have dual documents in Roth's Kafkan quest: the essay published in May 1973 and the novella issued in 1972.

In the first half of the essay, Roth writes very sensitively about Kafka's sense of entrapment, the "Kafka whose fictions refute every easy, touching, humanish daydream of salvation and justice and fulfillment with densely imagined counter-dreams that mock all solutions and escapes." How does this Kafka, Roth wonders, finally escape from his own circuitry of torture? How does this trapped animal achieve the transformation so that he *"awoke one morning from uneasy dreams . . .* [and] *found himself transformed in his bed into a father* [of the twenty-year-old Dora], *a writer, and a Jew"?*

The question Roth grapples with is not how the writer creates a character who is transformed into something grotesque, but how the writer—the creator of creatures who are transformed—is himself changed into a new shape. At its best, this is a subject Proust addressed himself to, for it is really a dimension beyond anything in Kafka. It is, in fact, a final dimension, the stage at which the author rises out of entrapment and through the powers of his own imagination or art becomes one with his fictional creation. It demands self-renewal of the kind only the greatest masters experience. By directing his sense of Kafka to this, Roth is attempting to bring him around to ideas of expansion and spatiality.

This assumption of new shapes is paradigmatic of *The Breast.* Instead of turning into a vermin, Roth's protagonist, David Alan Kepesh, a literature professor at the State University at Stony Brook, changes into a gigantic breast that is almost indistinguishable from a gigantic roach, with a long penis-like antenna at its top. As an instructor in Gogol, Kafka, and other writers of transformation (one may add Landolfi's "Gogol's Wife" and, surely, Rabelais), Kepesh has become the subject matter of the fiction he teaches, somewhat along the lines of Kafka's Gregor, who has assumed the shape of the insect he feels he has become in the eyes of his family.

The quotation at the conclusion of the novella of Rilke's poem "Archaic Torso of Apollo," with its final line, "You must change your life," indicates

d
he
en
of
he
or
ates
un-
eas are
, spatial-

ption of the
be observed
1944). Bellow
orlds of his Jo-
aspect of the Kaf-
eterminacy and passiv-
ly new in American fiction.
ing induction into the army,
European protagonist, lost his
being; he is caught between types
ything about him dangles, even his
espite his flirtation with Kafkan modes
n, here and elsewhere, Bellow really fits
traditions. His Joseph does not accept his
g nature, no more than does Melville's Ish-
n... Nearly one hundred years separate the two works, and yet a thematic presence is continuous: the hope is to break free, to float away. The beyond beckons. Bellow may have thought he was working in the Kafkan mode, but he was transforming Kafka to fit the American novel.

The serious American prison novel—as apart from prison literature and the popular detective story—is rare, since enclosed, Kafkan aspects of prison life negate one of the traditional weapons of the novelist, his use of spatiality.† In Cheever's novel, "Falconer" prison (based on Sing-Sing) turns spatiality into cells, lanes, cubbyholes. Kafka hovers at every turn. Yet

---

*The obverse of this process occurred in the "easy rider" mentality of the 1960s. The salient idea was to open oneself up, and yet the result was to fill oneself with another kind of authority: drugs, hallucinations, fantasies, et al. Parallel to this is the "consciousness-raising" phenomenon of the 1970s, the desire to liberate oneself, which takes the form of seeking new authority, whether est or otherwise. One's "inner hole" waits expectantly to be filled. Much that passed for anarchy in the last two decades was a search for such new forms of control.

†Coover's *The Public Burning* and Doctorow's *The Book of Daniel* contain significant prison scenes—Sing-Sing and the Rosenbergs—but they are not prison novels.

Cheever is concerned with forms of energy that can be discharged even within an arena that calls for enervation, passivity, and anomie. By attempting to merge aspects of space with situations that deny space, Cheever Americanized Kafka when, I feel, he had attempted to write a Kafkan tale. However ambitious the effort, the result is a curious hybrid of Kafkan and American themes: loss of Eden, the fear one might not be among the elect, the need for and hatred of isolation, the presence of great energy seeking outlets in an enclosed situation.

If we move back more than a decade, we observe Bellow's *Herzog,* in the prison of his own failures and the prison of a series of enclosed spaces. Herzog's torpor characterizes a 1950s attitude carried forward into the early 1960s, where it becomes the other side of that decade's anarchy and energy. Bellow stresses passivity, ennui, Kafkaesque conditions adapted to American notions of space, escape, and development. Moses Herzog, the archetypal Eastern Jew, Joyce's Bloom, is Bellow's Gregor Samsa, his K. and Joseph K. From the spaciousness of *Augie March* and *Henderson,* Bellow has moved within, where tensions occur in tunnels, labyrinths, subterranean passages.

Bellow, of course, cannot maintain the Kafkaesque vision. The very problems inherent in the novel derive from this: his deference to a kind of existential Kafka while he attends to other matters. The surface bubbles with wit and charming irony, all of which moves us toward openness. The surface is American "escape," whereas subsurface movement is European, the underground man attempting to find a niche where he can live unnoticed. Once the novelist has chosen this mode, the difficulty comes in blending disparate elements. Further, the matter above— witty, ironic, comic—is often tonal or attitudinal; whereas the material beneath is physical, good old American pastoral fantasy: a good lay with a deep-thighed shepherdess, a satisfying meal, some room to breathe in (a hut of one's own), perhaps an escape route—all with little continuity to the witty superstructure. Comedy, which is socially based, wars against individual expression.

It is a measure of Bellow's ambition that, in *Herzog,* he tried to confront the terrible dilemma of the American writer, where ideology struggles against the terms of the American experience. Bellow apparently went into the teeth of the problem, attempting a balance between a solipsistic Kafkan "self" and a more complete person moving outward in space. Had he angled his vision somewhat differently, his 1964 novel would have picked up what was to occur later in the decade; but even without that prophetic element, he cast the book well within the key tensions that American culture demands.

Perhaps more intently than any other contemporary American novelist except Barth, Bellow has tried to reconcile what he feels are extremes. In *Encounter* in 1962, the time of the writing of *Herzog,* he warned of the romantic "over-valuation of the self" and yet, at the same time, recoiled from the American novelists' depreciation of the self. He was, apparently, responding to still ambiguous signals in the 1960s, when selfness came to dominate and ran parallel to a literature in Barth, Pynchon, and Roth that degraded the self. The novel of the 1960s, with *Herzog* almost paradigmatic, became the battleground for cultural confrontations that seemed all fragments of self, society, and space, whether civil rights marches, antiwar demonstrations, social and economic upheavals, assassinations, or the moon shot. Bellow's argument bears reproducing, since it led so directly into *Herzog* and could have become a basic text for the decade. He wrote:

> We are dealing with modern attitudes toward the ancient idea of the individual and the many, the single self in the midst of the mass of species. In modern times the idea of the unique self has become associated with the name of Rousseau. Nietzsche identified the self with the God of Apollo, the god of light, harmony, music, reason and proportion, and the many, the tribe, the species, the instincts and passions, with Dionysus. Between these two principles, the individual and the generic, men and civilisations supposedly work out their destinies. It is to Nietzsche, too, that we owe the concept of the "last man." His "last man" is an obituary on the unitary and sufficient self produced by a proud bourgeois and industrial civilisation. Dostoievsky's Underground man is an analogous figure.

The description is of the self, given its free rein as the result of a romantic assessment of man's powers, developing into a monster, a king or god gone mad. Against this apotheosis of the self is the American conception of the individual as a "colonist who has been sent to a remote place, some Alaska of the soul. What he has to bring under cultivation, however, is a barren emptiness within himself." Between these antipodes—self and space—Bellow finds the excesses that deny man his mystery, indeed his humanity; a concept he struggled with at the comic level of his novel and then surrendered to intellectually in the

him
as it
connec
conflict
strung-out
American
(Barth's *Sot-*
sire for shape,
from European
periment with na
emptiness," for Bellow,
ism, optimism, opening up a
ening mindlessness and irresp
and solipsism negate mature
major reason American novelis
out, picaresque narrative is that a
tions come on the run. Bellow had been
kind of narrative himself in the second
March. Attempting to blunt openness and
narrative, he tried a semi-parodic mode in
but lost out to solipsism. The novel collapses from its
own self-indulgence—as we have observed, one of the inherent dangers in all efforts to adapt the Kafkan mode to American spatiality.

This tension between the openness of life and the need to impose form or restrictions has a long history, going back to Puritan psychology, in its contrast between individualism and personal responsibility. The Puritans believed in the welfare of the individual self (its need to expand) and, at the same time, in a fervent hatred of the self. Self meant expression, openness, to which they contrasted soul, which starts with a "holy despair" of the self.* The soul leads to Another and is, therefore, a restriction on self, which is narcissistic: the antiself or soul serves as a trap for spatiality and expansion. Puritan ideology, accordingly, encouraged individual spatiality by reinforcing every manifestation of self-consciousness; yet, in the same breath, the Puritans cautioned against that same spatiality found in self-examination. Each growth of consciousness or awareness was accompanied by con-

*We could argue that the Puritans' insistence on the covenant between themselves and God was an effort to enclose space: that is, to bring the infinite down to manageable levels.

strictions of self; each advancement of self indicated the need for the self to be conquered by a counterself, or soul or spirit. Every movement out of the self had its counterstep in an act of submission to a transcendental Being.

Of all American novelists in the nineteenth and early twentieth centuries, only Melville fully engaged the ambiguities connected to a self reaching out into space, an oceanic self, which is opposed to constrictions placed upon it by a counterself or society. Melville posited that man must be the reflection of immensity: that vastness becomes conscious of itself through man. For the contemporary American, that consciousness of immensity is transformed into the consciousness of emptiness, so that escape into vastness—whether of self or of geographic space—does not fill, but empties one out. One must move to avoid being static, sterile, a failure. The new always beckons; and failure, to a large extent, is marked by remaining.

Hawthorne, too, was cautionary. Hollingsworth is Ahab to Coverdale's Starbuck. Hollingsworth desires to go well beyond a communal utopian existence, into the very soul of man. His sense of spatiality is exploration of self and soul, to the end of collecting out of "a thousand human hearts" their great sense of sin and then "transmuting it into virtue." Hollingsworth's dream, based on an expansive self, is nothing less than the transformation of the unredeemed. To gain this, he needs power, control, the organization of others' lives. Threatened by a strong woman, Zenobia, he says of women: "I would call upon my own sex to use its physical force, that unmistakable evidence of sovereignty, to scourge them back within their proper bounds!" Hollingsworth's is a male vision, an egomania based not only on physical but on social and political power. His kind of spatiality seems the shadow substance which we associate with many of our contemporary novelists: Mailer, Bellow, Kesey, Pynchon. Mailer's Deer Park is Blithedale updated in some ways, as is Coover's West Condon in *The Origin of the Brunists.* Examples multiply. Even Gaddis's *JR,* that sardonic paean to American success and expansionism, becomes carried away by spatiality: the country as a vast treasure trove that even a sixth grader can tap for its wealth.

By judging man potentially perfectible, Emerson placed tremendous pressure on the individual to expand; standing still was contemptible. It would be a failure of everything we are, not only of self but of America, a cultural ideal. This is, of course, a carryover from the Enlightenment, nourished by belief in

rational man in a rational society. For Emerson, the America that could reach perfection was still the Eden of the myth, the garden before the machine took over. Here was all potential, and space awaited man to fill it. As Martha Banta describes it, in her *Failure and Success in America:* "Failure is thereby the betrayal of the total space we inhabit, whether it is defined as God's universe joined with the innermost regions of the soul, or as the American continent interlaid with the multiple layers of the self."

If success is connected to space and expansion of self, difficult complications are created for the American novelist, especially in the postwar era when affluence and opening up marked the culture. What can be counted as stable? Where is the home in serious American fiction? *It becomes a place that exists in order to be left behind or to disappear.* The wife? love? —there is little enough time. Lust is preferable because faster, and it can be rationalized as a "happy orgasm." Spending, an ambiguous sexual and economic term, is more important than holding back, saving. The child in the family—unless he or she rebels and moves out—hardly counts. Oates is one of the few to write seriously about children, family life, the houses and neighborhoods people live in—but almost always as disintegrating or violence-ridden elements, places from which younger family members must escape. A man's profession is usually a step toward something else, or work to which he is not committed; women professionals are not yet perceived. Relaxation is an interlude, not a period for growth. If how we spend our leisure time is a mark of maturity, then the novel shows us as perpetual adolescents. The road, whether train, river, ocean, or air, consumes all energy; the quest to escape self to discover ego becomes a national mystique. Rabbit must run, in Updike's apt image.

American idealism, rarely more buoyant than at the end of the Second World War, ran up against a national purpose which involved military action in two unpopular wars that helped keep our economy strong. Development, expansion, and mobility became possible for the individual, at the expense of depletion, compromise, cultural and moral shame. Every height had the potential of depth, every gain the potential of tremendous loss. Each maneuver by the individual involved a trap or entrapment. Unless the novelist turned to mockery, satire, or fantasy, he could not capture the sense of the fifties or sixties.

We can observe the difficulties even as early as 1948, in *The Naked and the Dead.* The men Mailer focuses upon view the army and the war as a form of escape from drifting, failed lives. The flashbacks, awkwardly labeled "the time machine," are really a space mechanism, a path backward into the individual's history to demonstrate how he arrived at his desire for escape. Yet their history turns out to be a snare; the men were as trapped in their past, as if in some fiercely naturalistic novel, as they are in the present, which they consider to be a form of escape. Although presented as "time" capsules, their past demonstrates that spatial considerations are pitfalls for the individual.

One area in which the postwar American novel uniquely differs from its European counterpart, despite several external similarities, is in its denial of the Faustian pact. Because of this denial, the American novelist must work in comedy rather than tragedy; philosophical formulations give way to variety, textures, tones, and imaginative flights, in some instances to linguistic experimentation and strains of fantasy and fabulation. The Faust legend works out in time, not space, and grows in a culture where events move slowly. Change is gradual, if at all apparent; growth occurs over centuries, not in the individual's lifetime.

The paradox of the American rejection of the Faust legend nevertheless remains. The American, picaro or not, from Wyatt Gwyon, S. Levin, Sergius O'Shaugnessy, and Yossarian to Herzog, Portnoy, Rabbit, Benny Profane, and Isadora Wing, desires many of the objects attainable only through a pact with the devil. He (she) traffics with the forbidden as a way of displaying the colors of his self, and he exposes himself to all kinds of physical and moral dangers in his attempt at self-expression. The American must flirt with the extremes of behavior so as to test Faustian potentialities; and yet when the time comes to balance accounts, he believes he can avoid accounting by running. In theory, the devil—who tires easily, this American hopes—will not follow; or else the devil will pursue the weak and enervated, not those who remain strong and defiant. New territory is too arduous for the devil to assay, and the picaro can try to escape damnation in the prairie, mountains, desert; or in recesses, holes, and underground refuges offered by large cities.

Alternatives to running mean digging in. This is the Kafkan route—Ellison's nameless protagonist, Bellow's Herzog, Gaddis's Wyatt, Malamud's tenant, Heller's Slocum, McElroy's Cartwright and Hind, Barthelme's counter people: burrowing in, clawing out a space, then holding on. Energy is internalized, transmuted into memory and/or fantasy. Yet we must admit that part of the moral slipperiness we experience in contemporary American fiction, where often so much more is promised than delivered, is the result of inadequate accounting. Ellison's protagonist earns his hole, but Herzog, for one, does not. First he wallows in self-pity and then he depends on life-support systems from a host of others. Even for such a moral accountant as Bellow, escape is still possible.

The rogue, American style, may work through many girls while he is on the road, but finally he sinks his head into the belly of a motherly woman. He may prefer to play with girls, but he wants to marry a woman, for girls demand attention, whereas women give it. Comforted, patted, assuaged, cosseted, stroked, he is ready to run as soon as her disenchantment begins or his own returns. One reason male-female relationships in American novels are so tentative or juvenile is that spatial considerations can always intrude. Few cementing temporal elements obtain: family, church, work. All three are traps, not permanent sources of strength; to survive, one must evade them.

Dubin in Malamud's novel strengthens his long-term marriage by pursuing a young lady named Fanny; she gains wisdom, while he grows young. His relationship to her, whatever the mutual benefit, is based on spatial considerations: running from age, wife, years of boredom. We can chart somewhat similar marriages in Updike *(Rabbit, Run; Couples)*, Cheever *(Bullet Park)*, Heller *(Something Happened)*, Donleavy *(The Ginger Man)*: either ridicule of or release from wife. Understanding rarely derives from within the individual. There is too much self-indulgence for that, and with the frontier of choice open, the protagonist need only gallop away. In the later 1960s and the 1970s, female writers (Gould, French, Jong, Rossner, Oates) confronted the same dilemma. Seeking themes that were more quintessentially female than male, or bringing female perceptions to bear upon familiar problems, they could not evade the spatial trap.

One returns to Melville as a novelist who sensed this dilemma. He observed that the American, the reborn Ahab-Adam, denies not only the past but all limitations. Defying time and using space for purposes of self-aggrandizement, this American commits crimes against the order of things by taking space as a commodity he can manipulate. Melville saw, further, that Faust had nothing to offer this new creature, who believed he could himself manufacture whatever Faust had obtained by bartering away his soul. This denial of limitations, this condescension toward the devil, Melville viewed as the source of one's strength and one's destruction.

Since Melville was writing about a Hebrew king, an Old Testament outcast in Ishmael, a lost tribe of the Indians in the *Pequod,* an indestructible force of nature in the white whale, his vision had the quality of Armageddon. The contemporary novelist has chosen a different scale, for the most part, and his "Armageddon" involves acts of freedom: desertion of home, adultery, homosexual love, rebellion against authority, defiance of social rules, departure from regulations, flouting of sexual mores, or military desertion. In the postwar period, only a few novelists catch the violence and sense of an ending: Burroughs, of course; Coover, in *The Origin of the Brunists;* Pynchon, in *Gravity's Rainbow;* Mailer, in *Why Are We in Vietnam?;* Gaddis, in *The Recognitions;* some of Barth and Barthelme, perhaps Ellison in *Invisible Man* and Williams in *The Man Who Cried I Am,* O'Connor in her "peacock" stories. Even as Kafkan enclosure seems so seductive, most of our novelists slide away into space.

Can Faulkner's mythical woods, once realities, still regenerate, or have they become a remote idea, like the Golden Age? Where does a Mississippian go now? The courts, as Faulkner feared, have replaced the woods; and if bears were tracked for the first fifty years of the century, legal loopholes remain to be sought for the next fifty. Where can the American run? D. H. Lawrence felt that man denies his freedom as long as he moves away. He argued for a temporal community, a denial of the spatial-pastoral experience. "Men are free," he wrote, "when they belong to a living, organic, *believing* community active in fulfilling some unfulfilled, perhaps unrealized purpose. Not when they are escaping to some wild west. The most unfree souls go west, and shout of freedom. . . . The shout is a rattling of chains, always was."

Lawrence offered struggle, not escape. Yet while we have imported European ideas and ideologies, especially in the 1950s, the American experience is resistant. Reconsider Faulkner's "I am a farmer," a pose he held in the years before he received the Nobel Prize, for literature, not agriculture, in the same decade as the very unagrarian Hermann Hesse, André Gide, and T. S. Eliot. Faulkner, whose work is saturated with history, fled the idea of history.

American fiction flirted despairingly and longingly with time, and for a while in the 1920s its expatriate literary men and women found meaning only in temporally oriented cultures. Having sought the burden of history, the weight of the past, the wise answers to a thousand riddles, they returned baffled to embrace largeness, openness, the supreme individual. Yet trying to be the emperor of ice cream comes at a terrible personal and professional price. The American writer burns out; space rarely lasts for an entire career. "There is no breath of friends and no more shore," Hart Crane wrote, "Where gold has not been sold and conscience tinned."

Many readers and critics have failed to assimilate difficult novelists such as Gaddis and Pynchon not only for their technical density, but for their denial of resolutions, their attempt to explore the paradoxes American culture makes the writer face. In both *V.* and *Gravity's Rainbow,* Pynchon has tried to find physical and psychological equivalents for the chaos and aimlessness that the American experience enforces. The extraordinary spatial arrangements of the latter novel can only be explained as a conflict between infinite room and the pull of gravity: i.e., our soaring spirits (the rainbow) and the physical forces (gravity) that pull us back. Translated into human behavior and action, this means that the voyage out is made at great personal expense, even while the individual fights to preserve what remains close—his sexuality, identity, personal history, responses, appetites. By solving the technological difficulties of rocketry, the American has pushed forward his freedom from gravity, from a cosmic universal force (war in other guises); yet that very rocketry, which promises limitless liberation, is not only order and scientific beauty, but anarchy. In its order lies a terrible disorder.

The American may float free in space, beyond gravitational pull, but then he has lost the very elements he might connect to. The wonder of Pynchon's metaphor is that it promises so much and delivers on so little. It is our novel of the 1960s (when it was mainly written) in its manifestations of solipsism which, when turned outward, ultimately leads to encapsulation in space.

If only we could be existential! Mailer tried "existential errands" as a means of transforming himself into something more than a consuming self; and Bellow, Roth, Percy, and Barth flirt with existential situations to balance their protagonists' self-indulgent impulses. Inevitably, we must inquire if our "frontier" fictional American (cowboy, gangster, city dweller) is a disguised new-world model of the existential hero. Put another way: is the new-world mode of experience existential, and therefore universal, or peculiarly American, and cut off even from *that* tradition? Superficially, it would appear that our postwar fiction with its isolated antihero, denied power and romance, caught between desire and failure, buffeted by fate, victimized by unknown forces, is broadly existential.

Yet the American experience rarely fits easily into this mode, and when it does, only marginally. Spatiality precludes the claustrophobia implicit in time-oriented societies. Existentialism is meaningful literarily only where death (time, mortality, inescapability) is an ever-present reality, not in a society where it can be disguised with all the resources of wealth and ingenuity. Joan Didion's spare antiheroines take existential poses, consider themselves victims, and conspire in creating parapet-like lives for themselves. But at their most anxious, they play with despair in snappy Corvettes and luxurious homes.

Because other societies have faced annihilation and been forced to contemplate its meaning, their philosophy subsumes an inescapability. Having confronted death, the European must construct a philosophy of life that includes death and shapes itself on the edge of an abyss. This is a norm, not an anomaly. As we have seen, Philip Roth has attempted, in recent fiction and essays, to move in and out of an existential Franz Kafka, very movingly in " 'I Always Wanted You to Admire My Fasting'; or Looking at Kafka." But even the title suggests he must showboat with Kafka, role-play at it. How can he find that witty Kafkan sense of frustration akin to annihilation, which is so basic to existentialism, in his own American experience? Here, frustration is connected to one's loss of momentum in self-love, to a blockage of happiness, or to a shutdown of erotic impulses or social successes.

In the end, the American believes he can conquer death, just as in coming to the new world as settler, pioneer, or immigrant he placated the devil. The Puritanical quest for religious freedom was always cast in terrible paradoxes; for even while the Puritans theorized about damnation and lived in the shadow of Satan, they sought out areas of life that bespoke renewal and resurrection of self. The very sermons of the clergy were couched in spatial terms, in the phraseology of cosmic space, which provided either salvation or damnation.

In his "personal Narrative," Jonathan Edwards writes of rising and falling, of huge spaces becoming familiar to him, of God's voice and thunder coming to him from great "outer space"; holiness itself could not have existed without the spatial metaphor. And "Sinner in the Hands of an Angry God," Edwards's most famous sermon, delivered during the period of the Great Awakening, is nothing if not a spatial message: everything yawning and gaping and surging, spatial even more than sexual. Man's soul and God's redemption must approach each other from across great distance. God holds the soul of the individual over the pit of hell, His wrath like great waters ready to burst over man, a vast flood that will engulf all space.

The Puritan ministers of course viewed the individual as emblematic of a universal design, not simply as a performing secular self. In this respect, we have gutted the Puritan sense of the individual in order to extract his importance and deny his divine connection. Yet implicit in Puritan rhetoric is our secularization of man in space, our representative man capable of perfection, democratic values interconnected with technological progress. In our most sensational wedding of man and machine, the moon shot and walk, we have brought together men who acted like machines and machines with virtually the will of man. Everything was there except the Puritan injunction to the divine principle.

When Malamud's S. Levin heads for Cascadia College, he assumes he can achieve Thoreau's intensity and wholeness in the Edenic West, where he can efface the alcoholism of his past. Drunk on spatial hopes, the European East Coast having proved a false friend, he opts for Western freshness and novelty. Of course, when he arrives in this virgin paradise, the chairman of Levin's department tells him his function is to satisfy the needs of the professional school. While Levin seeks renewal, he is informed that the area's needs are based on a land economy: "We need foresters, farmers, engineers, agronomists, fish-and-game people, and every sort of extension agent." English majors are unnecessary; there is no poetry in the forest, only lumber. Levin's job will be to turn timber into poetry.

Such ironies are at the heart of postwar fiction—in Didion as much as Salinger, Gass as much as Morrison, Williams as much as Updike. This need for space is not simply personal but political and, over all, cultural; for I believe that, literarily, obsessive spatiality and the politics of the cold war were interconnected in a very complex way. The cold war created obvious confrontation, between two types of government, two specific systems of thought; and it froze choices. One was for us, or against us, and subtleties of position, the mediating ideas that inform a culture and make it a functioning civilization, were jeopardized or repressed.* For the serious novelist, the situation was precarious, although for the popular writer —Wouk in *The Caine Mutiny,* Shaw in *The Young Lions*—the cold war fed directly into his fiction. Such choices polarized the writer in a deleterious way, since they could rigidify his imagination, or discourage large-scale confrontation with ideas and make visionary spatiality even more attractive. Fantasy and fabulation were born here, and Barth and Burroughs are representative.

Malamud set *A New Life* in 1950, right on the edge of the cold war era: the Korean War, beginnings of McCarthyism and Nixonism, red baiting, polarization between Ivy League East and the rest of the country, disenchantment with Communists and the Soviet Union, loss of wartime mutuality, start of the alliances that would forge the politics of the next three decades. How does Malamud translate these forms of data into novelistic terms? S. Levin has hardly arrived when he recognizes that he—a Jew, a reformed drunkard, a representative of European culture—is misplaced; for his choices have narrowed to cold war positions. Give up ideas of literature and accept notions of grammatical drill, or else move on. Yet if this is the frontier, then where to? He is already at the edge, and America has told him to choose. Even sex is affected. When he goes off with a waitress for a tumble in the hay, he feels a wondrous moment: sexual intercourse amidst elements that made the country and the West great. Yet the sexual act is interrupted, by a jealous Syrian student—international complications!—and Levin and the young woman make their way back to town without their clothes. Paradise has been reversed, with pain the consequence.

How Levin yearns to be the first man! For Levin, a nonsporting type, his newly grown beard is his whale-hunting, leatherstocking experiences, floating on a Mississippi raft, hunting big game. He is bearding lions, and recalls us to the bullring. Yet every aspect of his practical situation will negate every cultural assumption he has, whether social, political, or pedagogical. Levin may be badly off, Malamud suggests, but the culture is worse. We have, in this prescient novel, nearly all the strands of the American experience in the immediate postwar years.

The American poet of spatiality is, of course, Whitman—not by chance, resurrected in the 1950s, his confessional, open style suddenly prophetic. To some extent, Levin and those ideologically similar would choose to follow the injunctions of Whitman. But which Whitman? The Whitman who asserted that "a man only is interested in anything when he identifies with it"? Or the Whitman who insisted that we are redeemed by "the sexual fibre of things"? Or his open-chested manliness, the Hemingway pose which disguised a sick soul or an unhappy emotional life—when his lack of manliness was precisely what disturbed his contemporaries and kept Emerson equivocating? Or is it the Whitman of space who embraced all experience ("I was there," "America is me"), representative of the huge expanse of the Edenic experience? Yet spatiality is, for the novelist, the very trap that snares him.

The alienation or estrangement of the space-oriented hero or antihero is quite unlike that of existential man, if Dostoyevsky's narrator in *Notes from Underground* is our representative figure. Dostoyevsky's narrator, in a prototypical gesture, makes a final rejection, accepting its anguished suffering, while refusing a compromised happiness. Only James Purdy's protagonists, on a considerably reduced scale, offer a comparable view. Far too many current American protagonists, after struggling with their consciences, seem to accept a cheapened form of happiness as their birthright, even if in a cosmic hell. As a consequence, experience becomes delusional. Memory plays such a vital role in contemporary American fiction because it becomes a spatial concept, a point in motionless time that can be moved around, coughed up in analysis, played off against the present, viewed nostalgically. For the American writer, memory is rarely static, as in Proust, but motionlessness given momentum. Space as such creates perspectives. Because it promises that the reverse is as true as the forward movement, it upsets all preconditions. When contemporary Latin American writers work with delusional materials, they do so in the knowledge that delusion is a universal condition. The American novelist, however, senses the potentiality of escape from delusion.

A further dilemma arises in the fact that space is male, or connected to men. In American fiction, it is, overwhelmingly, men who make use of space: who escape, run, look ahead to renewal. Only in more recent fiction does the woman begin to think in these

*Mailer's career is instructive in this respect. *Barbary Shore* (1951) and *The Deer Park* (1955), clearly wrong directions for his fictional talents, attempted to sort out cold war ideas and ideologies in a confrontational simplistic way. Until his fine essay "The White Negro," Mailer's 1950s were self-defeating.

terms, in Erica Jong's *Fear of Flying,* Judith Rossner's *Looking for Mr. Goodbar* and *Attachments,* or Lois Gould's *A Sea Change.* But spatiality is not, as yet, fully fashioned into the fiction. Female novelists, chiefly, have presented the idea as part of women's freedom to separate, lead their own lives, pursue careers, without space becoming an ideological concept.

When Huck Finn lights out for Montana territory, he does something his sister could not do, no more than Shakespeare's sister could have headed for London to pursue a dramatic career. When Ahab destroys life and seeks self-destruction, as his Biblical namesake does, he chooses a spatial quest of the most cosmic kind—Melville's prefiguration of the moon shot or rocketry. However, when a woman is the focus, as Hester Prynne, she is placed in historical perspective, that is, turned into a temporal figure, with her movement severely restricted. Early in *The Scarlet Letter,* Hawthorne asks why such a woman as Hester remains where she is; why, in fact, she does not seek relief in space.

Hawthorne presents the classic female condition, and does so sympathetically. The male would head into the forest to seek another state of being, and thus use space as a mode of renewal. But Hester eschews this structuring of a new exterior, in order, apparently, to remain not only where she is, but what she is. This prefiguration of the role women will play, contrasting Hester's temporality with Huck's and Ahab's spatial orientation, reminds us that the American literary frame of reference was already set in the nineteenth century.

The war or combat novel, by necessity a male prerogative, is such a popular American form because it offers the ultimate in escape, renewal, spatial potentialities, even while it presents the final word in time: death itself. When Jones's Prewitt is shot down on a golf course in Hawaii, he encapsulates nearly every dimension of the American spatial metaphor. He is a young man manifest as Gawain, in quest of a personal grail. He has ingested faith, turning from an external God to the personal God he senses within. His quest has kept him on the run, from violence-ridden Harlan County to the army; and then, once in the army, from a series of careers, as boxer and bugler, which he rejects. Prewitt is a man moving, a spatial being, and not unusually, he is killed when AWOL, on the run.

There is, as we have observed, delusion at the heart of the spatial metaphor. When Huck in all innocence yearns after a land without fences or boundaries, he hardly expects to find savagery, discomfort, uncivil-ized whites and reds. He expects to find a finer way of life, at least one more attuned to a person of good faith. He believes in this fully. If he maintains the delusion, he can seek anywhere and find what he is looking for. By running, he can assume there will always be a future for him, when, in point of fact, the future has already foreclosed on him as he runs.

To what degree, we must ask, is the American novelist aware of the contradictions in this double bind? Does he acknowledge not only that he is caught in an irresolvable situation, but that American culture works on discrete lines of development which do not cohere and certainly cannot through a spatial metaphor? In *JR,* William Gaddis attempted to deal with these elements by giving us only voices which flow with American capitalism, which advance finance as a grand impersonal force. By depersonalizing his characters—that is, by making them voices which vibrate on the telephone—Gaddis tried to create a confluence of people and things, characters and objects "out there." The novel works at so many levels of invention because Gaddis foresaw that spatiality and temporality were potential traps, and so he turned expression into voices coming out of phones and radios or as advertisement and publicity gimmicks. If the entire country is a financial sideshow, then everything coheres as words and voices. Essentially, Pynchon achieves the same synthesis through rocketry, his scientific wizardry, as we have suggested, the counterpart of JR's financial wizardry.

To escape from space is for the American novelist as important as escaping into space. In *The Poetics of Space,* Gaston Bachelard hovers above our theme. He writes about the "hut dream," an archetypal pastoral and spatial ideal, "which is well-known to everyone who cherishes the legendary images of primitive houses. But in most hut dreams we hope to live elsewhere, far from the overcrowded house, far from city cares. We flee in search of a real refuge." The contradictions of the hut dream are analogous to the contradictions of the American spatial metaphor. The hut dream involves both an enclosed space which will be a refuge and a space that is far from all other refuges, from all other huts. The focus of the dream is an isolated place which is protected, part of a house dream we all carry within us. One thinks of the ranch, the farmhouse, the suburban "fortress," the rural homestead, the archetypal Thoreau cottage at Walden Pond. This is also, in general, the idea behind the small town in America, what politicians point to as the heart and soul of American life. This "small town," like Bachelard's hut dream, is a spatial idea which gets caught up in time. It is order beyond chaos, and its quality is frequently measured not by its life—which may be mad, alcoholic, full of inbred disorders—but by its distance from real turmoil, the city. Space is evasion.

In another section, Bachelard speaks of the house as an "inhabited space" which "transcends geometrical space." Once again, in this complex image, we have enclosed space as refuge itself caught in immensity, and yet our view of that inhabited place transcends the immensity of geometrical space. We have several levels of experience here. The phenomenology of the imagination works to reshape the smallness of the space so that it becomes limitless, and it reshapes the limitless space so that it is subsumed under the small space. This opening out and closing down of space, this use of space as something which can be large even when small, and diminished even when vast, has its counterpart in the American novelist's use of spatial concepts. And it is, as we have stressed, self-defeating.

In the novel an unresolved attitude toward space —whether as refuge, escape, entrapment, or cage—is divisive, since spatiality is intrinsically part of novelistic development. From the very beginning of the genre, as we have seen, the basic premise has been space. The early picaresque, even when modified as in *Tom Jones,* used space for forms of escape, an idea that lent itself readily to the American experience. This is connected not only to frontiers but to the phenomenology of space: that idea of the Garden, in the American mind, as equivalent to Bachelard's "hut dream" or "dream hut."

The Garden is suspended in limitless space, with vast distance between it and anything else, and yet it is enclosed, a pocket of earthly paradise. When we think of it, we see it as a refuge, a pleasant houselike structure with extensive cultivation, *a garden within the Garden:* smallness and vastness brought together as part of our "reverie" of it. Since this becomes the key spatial metaphor for the novel, the problem becomes apparent. That search for the Garden in space is self-defeating because it places on a spatial metaphor, which has its truth in fantasy and imagination, a burden that is social and psychological. In the latter, the only space that matters is real space, countable and accountable spatiality. In the space of reverie, there is immeasurability, and this is conducive to poetry, where immensity within finds its counterpart in immensity without. In the novel, that vastitude or oceanic sense which may exist within ourselves cannot find its counterpart outside, where measurement comes in miles or kilometers.

Chapter Three

▌▌

THE PERSISTENCE OF PASTORAL

Spontaneous me, Nature   WHITMAN, *"Children of Adam"*

The decisive moment in human evolution is perpetual. That is why the revolutionary spiritual movements that declare all former things worthless are in the right, for nothing has yet happened."

KAFKA,
"Wedding Preparations in the Country"

So persistent is the theme, indeed the obsession, that it would be possible to arrange this entire study around the idea of pastoral. American writers have never lost sight of a combined Edenic and pastoral background, not even those whose immigrant origins had little enough of nature, the natural, or Arcadia. Yet the memory of a mythical America as the new Eden, as a haven for those seeking perfect freedom, as a land in which such freedom is associated with a pastoral or purely natural dream, illuminates large numbers of our novelists and their novels: even when particular works seem to point in other directions. That "vision of innocence" is the key ingredient in American tragedy, and of course in our comedy. If the idea seems blurred, that is because too many of our novelists who believe in the "fortunate fall" forget there *was* a Fall. But that neglect of the Fall is also part of the American experience, perhaps what makes it unique. To seek the paradoxes of pastoral-worship is to explore the American experience.*

We can cite, among numerous examples, novels as diverse as Cheever's two Wapshot chronicles, much of his shorter fiction, and *Bullet Park,* itself a hymn to a dispossessed Garden; Updike's *Rabbit, Run* and its sequels; very obviously Salinger's *The Catcher in the Rye;* Mailer's *An American Dream, The Deer Park,* as well as the famous essay "The White Negro"; Wright Morris's *The Field of Vision* and *Ceremony in Lone Tree;* William Gass's *Omensetter's Luck* and stories in *In the Heart of the Heart of the Country;* Malamud's *A New Life;* Richard Brautigan's *Trout Fishing in America* and other books; a group of novels arranged around baseball themes by Coover, Roth, Malamud, and Harris; both shorter and longer works of Purdy, Bellow, Wright, and Styron. We could, in fact, read *The Confessions of Nat Turner* from an alternate angle of vision, from the point of view of a vanishing America implicit in the Turner rebellion, a first step toward a realignment of the South, which in turn was the end

---

*Near the end of *The Great Gatsby* Fitzgerald says that perhaps all along his story had been one of the West, that the characters were Westerners, and "perhaps we possessed some deficiency in common which made us subtly unadaptable to Eastern life." The West, then, represents unblighted nature, the East blight itself; the key is pastoral purity, those moments when natural perfection creates personal identity—that is, experience of the Garden.

of one kind of pastoral dream.*

In his profound study *The Sacred and the Profane*, Mircea Eliade explains how even in the profane or secular world there remain vestiges of that sacred world which lives in us as memory and archetype. Although our postwar novelists have probably never (or rarely) lived in the "little house on the prairie" or in a tent or hut, or even in the heart of the country, their dream is of such a magical existence. Whatever the practical problems of living in such splendid isolation, we perceive the experience as having been transformed by a spiritual presence—what we sense in Thoreau's otherwise very practical cottage at Walden. Awareness of that spiritual force carries the novelist back to a sacred existence, to what Eliade has defined as the house located in an *imago mundi.*

The house, as such, is an "image of the world," a symbol of the sacred life implicit in every structure; and around it extends the magical land which contains the supporting elements for the house. A secular state is transformed, momentarily at least, into a transcendental experience.† And when that is lost, all is apparently lost: innocence, spirit, even physical strength. The loss of that sacred feeling, or the sense that it cannot be assimilated into our lives, creates in the postwar writers a terrible debilitation. The widespread use of the idea of entropy—the matter of the world becoming irreplaceable—is connected to this loss of archetypical magic. And the pervasive spatial dimension in postwar American fiction is associated with the willful desire to discover that magic, to seek a mythical locale in the next town, road, outpost. That obsessive seeking of a new spatial dimension which recurs in our fiction is part of what Eliade calls a "creative ritual": life cannot be repaired, "it can only be recreated through symbolic repetition of the cosmogony."

Running away also has reference to the need to find a door. Such images abound in our novelists: the doors of perception, to the outside, to freedom from

*What Louis Simpson labeled the "dispossessed Garden." In this conception, once driven from the Garden, man makes every effort to reachieve its organic unity, even when imperfect conditions—slavery itself—seem antithetical to Garden perfection.

†That is, a pastoral image or metaphor becomes Edenic; Arcadia is transformed into Paradise; a bucolic setting becomes that "first place." Eden in this respect is neither a farm nor a wilderness, but an ever-changing mixture of reality and fantasy. By turning nature into pastoral or a rural Eden, Americans have established a midpoint between primitive and civilized, between Indian savagery and European models.

marriage, to liberation from restraints, to illegal acts, to acts of defiance and rebellion, all expressed in portal metaphors. Burroughs in his discussion of drugs as leading to a kind of dispossessed Eden—to perpetual exile into the unknown—speaks repeatedly of doors which open up and out, and to. That image of an opening is, as it were, a means of communicating with sacred and magical elements: "Communication with the gods [writes Eliade] is made possible: hence, there must be a door to the world above, by which the gods can descend to earth and man can symbolically ascend to heaven." The morbidity and ennui we sense in the American novelist derive from his awareness that such doors may no longer open, that we cannot ascend and the gods cannot descend.

To go from house to apartment is to move from sacred to profane. The house is in the country, or by a lake, or near some spiritual retreat, Bachelard's "hut dream"; whereas the apartment is an "enclosed hole" in an urban setting, already given over to secular and corruptive life. At the turn of the industrial revolution, movement toward cities was always portrayed in devilish or hell-like images. However, Jane Jacobs's influential 1961 study, *The Death and Life of American Cities,* demonstrates that even cities have a paradisiacal component. Jacobs shows they have elements of transfiguration: that is, they develop their own forms of magic, and people in them are not demeaned or debased if the city functions along the lines of what it is. The city then becomes a refuge from a heartless world; becomes, indeed, the opposite of that heartless world, which lies somewhere outside city boundaries. In an urban setting, she discovers a version of pastoral.

It is clear that certain ideas about pastoral life became focused in the 1960s, after the great industrial surge of the previous decade. Such ideas appeared in the most unlikely areas, even in the black power movement, which was urban oriented. The radical wing of that movement, the one more concerned with ideology than with immediate economic improvement of blacks, divorced itself from a technologically based white America and saw itself as established on a pastoral, primitive, agricultural model. In an ironic reworking of the "I'll Take My Stand" statement, the ideologues of black power stated that gains by blacks must be achieved within an alternative pastoral model.

For this group, civilization was a white trap, first because it was white, but more significantly because it was unconnected to any primitive sources of energy. In such a civilization, blacks, successful or not, will live as second-class citizens; accepted perhaps as workers, but not as blacks. The inference is that such a civilization is anathema to the black perspective and imagination. A black who accepts a technological civilization, the argument goes, will prostitute himself, not as a worker but as a person.*

This argument was formed and expounded in various ways by Ron Karenga, LeRoi Jones (Baraka), Stokely Carmichael, Bobby Seale, Huey Newton, and others, though not always in the same terms. Remarkably, such a stand was already strong, even strident, in many of our novelists—white and black— who hardly considered themselves radical or revolutionary. In other words, the left wing of the black power movement was using an argument for separatism that was already a cliché of literary culture, in which reversion to pastoral becomes a battle cry for rebels.

The pastoral split we find, perhaps unexpectedly, in black separatism can be discovered in every seam of our existence. To a recent study of the automotive industry, Emma Rothschild attached the title *Paradise Lost.* It is a title of considerable irony, for the paradise that is lost is borrowed from our pastoral metaphor and transformed into the "good old days" when there was a car in everybody's future, and the potential was unlimited. Here, technological magic became transformed into our sense of America as a magical place where anything was possible. If America was a paradise on earth, then its technology would support and define its Edenic elements, not blunt them. Although in the previous century our sages had warned of technology as a fatal intrusion on our Arcadian potentialities, in 1842 a book called *The Paradise Within the Reach of All Men . . . By Powers of Nature and Machinery* argued otherwise.

As continuity, an October 1939 issue of *Life* magazine panegyrized the automotive industry as a giant suited to the country. *Life* described Ford's River Rouge plant as a miracle of technology, with its quarter-mile-long motor assembly plant, its near hundred miles of railroad, a mass-production unit with a greater capacity than that of many countries. *Life,*

like *Time,* which had picked up the theme, saw the automotive industry not as a sign of American reliance on a chimera, but as our transformation of what was already a paradise into Paradise.

If we swing widely, another movement, this one associated with the 1950s, focuses upon transportation by automobile; its ideology having been derived from jazz and the practice of Zen, its goal is to live out pastoral fantasies. The "high" the Beats pursued was not at all unlike the transcendence Emerson spoke of a century earlier in his Journals. Emerson: "God hides the stars in a deluge of light," both a religious and a personal transcendence, a moment of illumination. Implicit is association between outer nature or pastoral epiphanies and inner exploration. It is an image that allows for successive moments of great intensity; in the words of Charles Olson: "When the attentions change / the jungle leaps in, even the tones are split." What Gary Snyder, poet laureate of the Beats, called "Hatching a new myth" and Lawrence Ferlinghetti, borrowing from Henry Miller, labeled "A Coney Island of the Mind" were areas where jazz, Zen, and drug-induced hallucinations move us toward Eden.

In this scene, jazz and Zen join, one outer, one inner, both associated with drugs by way of "highs." Jazz had the element of danger; played by blacks, performed often in seedy bars, connected to reefers and even more dangerous drugs, allied to booze and open sexuality, it went further than music, into areas of open rebellion against an organized, technologically oriented society. Jazz was a total environment, a value system. Its lack of verbal content was essential to its impact as a purely aural form of experience; within it, one could trace one's own mountains and valleys.

Not unusually, the Beat experience was generated from a California city, San Francisco. While high art in the 1950s was identified with the Eastern Seaboard, life styles were the prerogative of the West Coast. California faced neither toward Europe nor toward the rest of America; it was a territory responsible to no one, where the Edenic dream could be played out in idyllic settings. Pastoral fantasies could be recovered in forms of nakedness or loose clothing; in diverse sexual styles (Neal Cassady as the model, Burroughs not a distant second); classlessness, the result of an influx of "immigrants" from the rest of the country; a rough democratization that forced Anglos to make peace with Hispanics; and a cultivated

---

*From our perspective of the 1980s, we can observe that this seemingly aberrant position was deeply involved in more central 1960s ideology, and after being blunted would become transformed into aspects of the conservationist movement, basically white.

roughness, the Barbary Coast feel of Frisco itself. In the 1950s, people came to be renewed in an alternative country, to discover themselves.

Zen allowed "travel" to another country, where one could, as the Gautama Buddha said, get out of the house of the self, which is on fire. This, too, was a trip, an on-the-road experience, although to a new place that receded even as one tried to approach it. Its inaccessibility, its sense of an unattainable Eden, was its strength. One could travel eternally and never reach the end; the journey was all.

Allen Ginsberg in poetry and Burroughs in his novels tried to achieve this sense of merging the one with the all that we find in Zen. Everything becomes process. The Zen Buddhist experience worked particularly well with the confessional mode in poetry, what we associate with Ginsberg as well as Lowell, Plath, and Sexton. Since confessional poetry is self-oriented and eliminates the interposing of another voice or persona, it fits well into religious beliefs where the self is unmasked, defamiliarized, and reshaped either in or out of existence. Confessional poetry allowed real life and fantasy to be combined, as products of experience emanating from the self. Such an emanation was also necessary in Zen, one of the first stages before self could be effaced.

In quite another visitation to the pastoral mode, we have the example of Vladimir Nabokov transforming himself from a Russian novelist to an American writer (however odd that sounds) by way of memory. He began his entry into Emerson's "pleached garden" through a chapter in French of what would become *Speak, Memory;* the rest of that book flowed when he settled in America. Once here, he returned to his past—*Pale Fire*'s Zembla—as a "lost Eden," turning himself inside out, as it were, going from Russian memories into an English version, which he then later put into Russian.

In his Edenic past, two elements are emblematic: his focus on butterflies and chess. For each presupposes a perfect world, something going even deeper than Emerson's "ideal world," so deep into what has been lost that it can only be an archetypal paradise. Butterflies represent visual and structural beauty; chess, the clear lines of definition which open up to the potentialities of an infinite place. Chess becomes in its insistence on balance something close to Emerson's organic community: an element singular, unified, yet creative, all of which supposes an Edenic memory. In the butterfly, Nabokov viewed an "art"

unchanged by time, the universe that once was, emblematic of a childhood idyll.

The point for us is that Nabokov felt impelled to move back toward that pastoral past in the thrall of Mnemosyne (he wanted to call his memoir "Speak, Mnemosyne"), the goddess of memory itself. The Russian Revolution having turned the past into disharmonies, he was, like Adam, displaced from a Garden, thrust into an indifferent world. The protection of a benevolent God having been removed, he was obliged, like our mythical parents, to mature; but memory remained, no matter what else intervened. Part of the problem with Nabokov's book, in fact, is that his memories of a "perfect world" are based on privileges afforded him, when in fact that world was quite imperfect. The ahistorical nature of the book may fit the scheme of a lost Eden, but placed in a more human context, the book lacks a tragic dimension, despite the presence of much tragedy. Nabokov's personalization of events does not help: "that trite *deus ex machina,* the Russian Revolution, came, causing my removal from the unforgettable scenery."

Nabokov becomes curiously like Emerson as he moves from his worlds of Russian, German, and French to American pastoral at Ithaca. Seeking perfection, he fits himself into aspects of Emerson's unities, realms, organic community—all, we must stress, at the expense of what is modern. That paradisiacal memory is associated with hatred of modernism, as it was for Emerson, and emphasis on pastoral for both became a way of controlling the spread of modern ideas. We perceive how interrelated pastoral and modernity are, not only here, not only in the statement of the Southern Agrarians, but in the rhetoric of the black power movement. It is worth repeating that set deep within American progress, a vein tapped by the very European Nabokov, is a reactionary lode with pastoral as its ideology. Thoreau, in many ways politically progressive, saw his sojourn at Walden Pond as serving two functions, enabling him both to contemplate his soul in isolation, and parallel to that, to oppose society's efforts at modernization. Louis Simpson has called him "a figure of the apostate gardener in the New England garden of the literary covenant."

Like Thoreau, so Jefferson before him. Part of Jefferson's dilemma over slavery was connected to his anxiety about the role of the new in the old. Jefferson's "pastoral ideal," as we shall examine it, ran athwart the slavery issue, but in a very complicated way. For while slavery was immoral and traduced human rights, it seemed a way of containing that very modernity which threatened the pastoral model. Slavery, then, had to be condemned even while it appeared as a bulwark against modernization, industry, urbanization.

For those unlike Jefferson, who defended slavery or who became part of the Agrarian movement of the 1920s, slavery established its own cultural lines: antimodern, agrarian, Edenic, with the master-slave relationship reminiscent of the noblesse oblige between God the guardian and his wards in the Garden. The Garden is severely compromised by its association with slavery, but the need to defeat change preempted all other considerations.

This battle between supporters of slavery (embodied in the work of William Gilmore Simms) and those who saw it as a "garden of chattel" (Harriet Beecher Stowe) was not an isolated one. Stowe observed that behind the pastoral façade there lurked, in Simon Legree's methods, an economic exploitation, a leaching out of the pastoral ideal. Such ideas of a waste land, where Eden was a kind of palimpsest, would engage generations of Southern novelists, feeding into writers as similar as Faulkner and Styron, as dissimilar as Flannery O'Connor, Eudora Welty, and James Purdy. In all of them, the compromise of the Garden in terms of Southern history has left some version of pastoral, although it, too, is receding.

While this action and reaction occurred before the advent of our postwar generation, many of them grew up within sight of such ferment. The immediate previous generation of Faulkner, Warren, Tate, Caroline Gordon, among others, recognized that memory and history were being degraded in the opposition to modernity, and they tried to understand the past truthfully, to perceive the redemptive meaning of the Southern past as an influence on the present. Eudora Welty's work fits here; as does a book so different from any of hers, Styron's *Nat Turner*.

The shift from that earlier order of Southern writer, of whom Faulkner is obviously the greatest and most inclusive, to the present generation is instructive. The constant is a pastoral ideology. Faulkner's sense of a Christian-humanist civilization that is connected to the recovery of memory and history—*even when* they are doomed—gives way to Styron's emphasis on the disorderly, unbalanced self, skew to those very values of memory and history. None of this should suggest Styron is alone. Virtually all major Southern writers must deal with pastoral values, the sense of transcendence amidst a profane life. Their resemblance to Faulkner in many instances exists only because they all overlap in their obsessions. *Sophie's Choice,* which may seem to be light-years from the South, dredges up ideological conflicts that are reprises of Southern tensions: i.e., the concentration camps as forms of master-slave relationships, a prebellum South.

Forewarned and armed, we can now move back to Jefferson, our quintessential American, who hated the machine as an infernal device, yet nevertheless saw it, paradoxically, as a means by which the American could be freed from drudgery. For Jefferson, the key to an enriched American life was the pastoral experience, and the machine (an alien, external threat) was Satan personified. From pastoral, he extrapolated peace, balance, stability, sanity. It was a very personal, very human view of American life, and it was connected in its major aspects to the terrible religious trauma experienced at the loss of Eden. During the War of 1812, Jefferson associated the expulsion of "our first parents" from Eden with our transformation from a peaceful to a military nation. And in parallel political terms, he distinguished for John Adams between the "natural aristocracy" and the "artifical aristocracy," the implication being that the first derived from a pastoral existence, the latter from everything associated with privilege, an antipastoral.

As the technological ability of America intensified, science became a mixed blessing, a source of strength and an impersonal giant to be attacked and vilified, even personified as demonic. The ideal remained a rural society regenerated by its proximity to that original nature which sustained "our first parents."

If this is a fair summary of the Jeffersonian ideal, and by extension of the "American dream" long after it had proved unworkable, we can see nearly every aspect of the postwar novel infused by that ideal. The war was itself viewed as a cleansing agent. Americans came out victors, the new Romans, with their legions winding through every village and hamlet of Europe: the conqueror dispensing chocolate to children and cigarettes and nylons to adults. The cold war, in many of its ideological aspects, was a "natural" response to that ideal. Here the threat was something alien, impersonal, foreign, subversive of real values—all those assessments once connected to the mechanization of society. Repeatedly, we find images of mechanical elements, of drill, precision, facelessness—everything associated with the machine—applied to the Soviet Union and its sympathizers. The few Communist followers in America were almost always identified with gears in a system, whereas loyal Americans were associated with the pastoral ideal.*

The ideal is attractive and human, but like so much else in American ideology, it is rooted in a view that neglects consequences. The unresolved elements have caught the American novelist in impossible dilemmas.* The "virtue and talent" which Jefferson described to John Adams as part of a "natural aristocracy," as opposed to an artificial or pseudo aristocracy founded on birth and wealth, can only take hold in an expansionist society. That society, based on spatial maneuvers, must constantly renew itself. It cannot remain fixed in the Edenic past, which is a still point outside time and space. The pastoral idea remained, however, so located, even when the influx of the machine and mechanical principles said otherwise. Jefferson, and those who followed him 150 years later, hoped that somehow *there would be no change even while change occurred.* Pastoral, Eden, the good life, the simple life, and "virtue and talent" become intermixed and, inevitably, sentimentalized. There would, the hope went, be continuity within discontinuity. How these opposing values were to be resolved was left to chance, goodwill, providence.

The literary tradition that grew and developed with two competing systems, with rural life as the ideal while cities became the center of "civilized" values, had to reflect the sense of continuity within the discontinuities of the model. All this becomes far more complicated after the Second World War, when the war was itself viewed, in some transformation of values and ideals, as the very cleansing agent which would return us, as individuals and nation, to that

*In 1932, when America could still perceive herself as a pastoral or agrarian society, the Communist Party here, already an agent of Soviet Communism, enlisted the support of the following writers for its candidate for President: Hemingway, Dos Passos, Dreiser, Wright, Hughes (Langston), Farrell, Porter (Katherine Anne), Wilson (Edmund), Cowley, Steffens, West (Nathanael), Caldwell (Erskine). Twenty years later, Communism and the Party enlisted the support of no major writers, few minor writers, and its ideology was viewed as death to the pastoral ideal, indeed as a juggernaut crushing its supporters.

*Emerson's City of the West, "that fusion of the frontier and the cosmopolitan," is ultimately—despite the magnificence of the conception—a fantasy, like Yeats's Byzantium. Hawthorne and Melville, on the other hand, foresaw that every "ideal realm" was contaminated by poison, whether in Rappaccini's Garden or Pierre's New York.

Edenic myth. Europe may have been an old whore—the very image in a dozen war novels—but we saved it by way of our pastoral ideal. Such a view abetted a fantasy life that would prove fateful to many writers and their work.

Novelists were caught in impossible dilemmas. Part of the pastoral ideal meant that conquest in bed and on the battlefield (sex and war) was still a manly pursuit. One expressed oneself thus, and the social ideal sustained the effort. But the impersonality of the machine undermined the Edenic myth; the "happy orgasm" was a contradiction in a mechanical universe. One expended positive energy on what, one knew, was wasteful effort. As a consequence, every writer working on a large scale became split.

Whether represented realistically, sentimentally, or fantastically, pastoral has the quality of "ideal realms" implicit in it. Emerson's sense of "angelic use," in which large spaces could join with inner possibilities and poetic imagination, finds its meaning in the pastoral experience. The City of Man and the City of God had to be merged with each other for Emerson, and in that juncture we have the meeting ground of an ever-running American theme, where pastoral allows for the immanence of both, interconnected. Emerson's warning that the individual can destroy himself outside a context meant he foresaw the dangers of ego-worship and self-indulgence. Yet excesses are the price we pay for the individual's right of freedom from the limitations of the past. Recognizing this, Emerson also tried to bring the individual back to a sense of history, to a balance between social past and present self.

Pastoral works toward this end, although it is never really successful as an ideological mode in American thought. It works better as a fictional idea, as an image, as a fantasy interlarded with real people and events. At its worst, it becomes an "easy rider" vision, a perversion of its real qualities in which self-indulgence can be justified by space and countryside. Those who express pastoral there are infantile, while those who close out the dream altogether are contemptible.

The farm may have been a "holy emblem" to Emerson, but farms now are desolate places; land is too expensive to be tilled and given over to food. People have replaced the "holy emblem" of growth and development. In William Whyte's description of the organization man in Lake Forest, Illinois, we observe how pastoral purity has given way to belief in the group and faith in technology as the means to achieve a sense of belonging. With this, the nineteenth-century dialectic between pastoral and machine is finished; pastoral lost. De Tocqueville warned that conformity would undermine the unique American genius; that a social ethic would be destructive, even fatal. The perfect machine rather than a pastoral memory would become our emblem of Eden, and with that a social consensus achieved. "Paradise Lost" ironically becomes the breakdown of the automotive age, not the decline of a human value system.

Kenneth Keniston speaks of "unprogrammatic alienation"—a condition he finds unique, for it involves "dissent without a fully articulated foundation," or rebellion without a cause. He was writing in 1965, before civil rights and the Vietnam War provided the causes; but his point does cover a general malaise that began to reveal itself in the 1950s. Our fiction, in its stress on frenetic space, on the counterfeit and factitious, on futile attempts to recall Eden and pastoral moments, seems to reflect qualities associated with alienation: "distrust, pessimism, resentment, anxiety, egocentricity, the sense of being an outsider, the rejection of conventional values, rejection of happiness as a goal, and a feeling of distance from others."

While malaise was generally a worldwide response, we must stress that such feelings were speeded up in America, were more massive, if our fiction is a valid reflection of underlying national attitudes. Behind the malaise is that broken association of self and nature, of individual and community; that loss the individual suffers when he recalls a once Edenic existence, the hostility he senses toward ideas that remain only fantasies. A good part of the problem is our paradoxical need for Edenic memories even as we recognize they are mythical—i.e., no longer visible, even if irresistible.

Keniston found that among his alienated students there was a constant: they cultivated sentience and solitude, and they associated those qualities which sustained them with a pastoral past, a whiff of Eden, the myth of the "hut dream"; so that Thoreau at Walden or communes based on Brook Farm remained as generating ideas and images. In this respect, our students are not alienated, but mainstream: they have, despite their passivity and disdain for an active or adventurous life, found agreement with the larger America, the America we find in our fiction. Its reflection of pastoral paradoxes is not marginal, "crazy," or exaggerated, but loyally American.

Those images of broken lives, dislocated individuals, fragmented existences are not simply examples of decline; they are images of how a life must be structured when it lives with paradoxes and fantasies. We need only contrast what we made of the West in an earlier generation and how we view California now, in terms of what Edwin Fussell has called "a condition of the soul [rather] than . . . a physiographical region." The West has become a mythical place, especially since its depiction in novels and stories came from Easterners, who could "invent" its qualities unobserved. Like Eden, the West remained out of sight for those who wrote about it; and its physical aspects could become part of mythology.

When Turner drew his line at the "frontier" and indicated it had vanished, he was saying, in effect, that American civilization has overtaken Eden, that the line between civilization and undeveloped nature no longer existed. He was not clarifying the myth, but exploiting it; so that our writers became even more frenzied about an Edenic past, as it seemed to have receded. Thoreau foreshadowed this "frenzy" and in "Walking" perceived the West as "the wild" (the essay's original title), as a place of absolute freedom, a contrast with civilization.

None of this transformation of realities into myth and then our living with the myth rather than the reality is a break with our history; it is, rather, a continuation of some of our earliest attitudes, embedded deep in the Puritan past. As we have observed elsewhere, the Indian was for the Puritans a very complex phenomenon they had to master ideologically as well as physically. The Indian represented nature, which the Puritans associated with an adversary relationship to civilization; therefore, the Puritans had to discover ways in which the Indian became significant for what civilized man should *not* be or become. Yet the Puritan could not forsake nature, which included Indians, as part of the God-patterned universe. It was necessary for the Puritans first and then their successors to formulate a theory that established a new order which excluded the Indian. Part of this was accomplished by identifying the Indian with Satan, so that the struggle with the Indian became not an example of colonialism, but "a sign of earthly struggle and sin," a "religious enterprise." To grab Indian land, to kill Indians, to exclude them by way of reservations and other deprivations were ways of containing Satanism and carrying out God's divine plan.

With this thread running through our history and

implicit in our history books (as Frances FitzGerald shows),* the Indian, the West, development, colonialism, et al. come together as myth; and this myth is associated with an Edenic past, a pastoral rite, a sense of ever-receding time and space. A young country's life is extended back to the beginning of time, to the cosmogony itself. We must become aware of how our youthful country is transformed by our sense of space and time, so that we extend back to the Garden, which is where our frontier really ends (or begins).

Not surprisingly, in the 1960s, when so much of our past and so many of our myths were being reexamined, the Indian reemerged. Several nonfiction studies of Indians include Vine Deloria, Jr.'s *Custer Died for Our Sins,* Alice Marriott and Carol K. Rachin's *The American Epic: The Story of the American Indian,* and Leslie Fiedler's *The Vanishing American;* fiction, Kesey's Chief Bromden in *One Flew Over the Cuckoo's Nest,* Heller's Chief White Halfoat in *Catch-22,* Berger's *Little Big Man,* Matthiessen's Meriwether Lewis Moon in *At Play in the Fields of the Lord,* and numerous others.

For these books, in one way or another, circle around to Indian forms of existence as ways of responding to the very qualities that civilization is proud of quieting. After the display of civilized values represented by the 1950s, that mixture of imitation, counterfeit, economic advances, personal aggrandizement, that confusing display of American might and pusillanimity, we needed something simpler or purer or less contrived. Indian life and values seemed worth recalling, and that memory, we have observed, was never too distant from our sense of an Edenic past.

_____

*The textbook description of white-Indian relationships can be even more explicit, as Vine Deloria, Jr., shows: "It was," he quotes from one such book, "perhaps fortunate for the future of America that the Indians of the North rejected civilization. Had they accepted it the whites and Indians might have intermarried to some extent as they did in Mexico. That would have given us a population made up in a measure of shiftless half-breeds." Deloria tells an interesting counterstory. Whites who tell him they have Indian blood have, with one exception, claimed it on their grandmother's side; so that they have as their ancestor an Indian princess. They do not wish to have a male ancestor, for that "has too much of the savage warrior, the unknown primitive, the instinctive animal." The idea of the princess gives the white imagination a chance to enter the exotic pastoral of Indian life and still have a measure of stability, since princesses can be subdued to the "hut dream," whereas warriors turn an Edenic memory into a battleground.

The "savage Indian" now becomes the purest form of civilization. The myth remains.

Every American writer attempting to enter the mainstream of fiction must arrive at what Empson called some "versions of pastoral." Most of our major writers began their careers with such incursions, although in their later fiction they may move on to other matters. Yet some careers have been so closely identified with pastoral modes they cannot be perceived otherwise. It is, as we have observed, the "matter of America."

John Cheever's two Wapshot novels—and many of his short stories by implication—are shadowy existences of Hawthorne's sense of the flawed pastoral. In *The Scarlet Letter* and elsewhere, Hawthorne observed man as living in a "dispossessed garden," that is, in a garden of potential perfection upset by man's own imperfections. Hawthorne's sense of the mode is almost as archetypically American as is Emerson's "ideal realm," the latter leading to fantasies, the former to waste lands. For Hawthorne, the "perfect place" can never be free of evil or sin; the ideal must always be balanced by the dysfunctioning human, beset by some demonic force which he or she cannot resolve. Cheever's adaptation of this removes much of the fierce intensity, the fire of madness we perceive in Hawthorne's vision, and turns the material into a comically dispossessed pastoral: life remains appetizing although profoundly disturbed. He is concerned as much with "American dreams" as nightmares.*

Cheever's dispossessed pastoral is St. Botolphs, an inland port in the great days of the Massachusetts sailing fleets; now it has been reduced to a small factory town. Yet even so, St. Botolphs has within it pastoral dimensions, so that proximity to nature in an unthreatening environment still obtains. There the Wapshot family lives in a pastoral balance: Leander, captain of the riverboat *Topaze*, Mrs. Sarah Wapshot, and their two sons, Coverly and Moses. The boys' names suggest the pastoral dimension, as well as the Hawthorne tradition.

When Moses and Coverly leave St. Botolphs for New York and Washington, respectively, their point of reference is not just home, represented by St. Botolphs, but a locale signifying for them a prior existence associated with Edenic, not just idyllic, life. Their memories include alternating trips with Leander into the wilderness, where they fish for trout and

_____

*The obverse of *Wapshot*'s St. Botolphs is Bullet Park.

live in squalor. For the sake of the Edenic setting, they accommodate themselves to desperate camp conditions. Yet the period has its magical dimension: they are reliving, within distance of St. Botolphs, a wilderness life that contains no threat, no women, no social life—simply Leander and one son cooking hamburgers on a pot lid and trolling for trout, separate from the world, in a Garden of their own making, untouchable from the outside. That camp is like being present at the creation.

Yet even there, everything is decaying, a reminder that Eden is ephemeral. "Everything was dead; dead leaves, and branches, dead ferns, dead grass, all the obscenity of the woods death, stinking and moldy, was laid thickly on the trail. A little white light escaped from the clouds and passed fleetly over the woods, long enough for Moses to see his shadow, and then this was gone." Against this sense of dying and sere nature, still there is the wonder of the present.

The boys strike out to make their fortunes, but their inner life is turned back toward St. Botolphs by a kind of magnetic force. Although St. Botolphs is seriously flawed—Leander is a wastrel, Mrs. Wapshot caught in a marriage that has long since gone sour, old Honora lost in a disconnected time zone—even so, it is "some reminder of paradise—some happy authentication of the beauty of the summer countryside. . . . It was all real and they were flesh and blood."

Personal dimensions broaden into sociopolitical ones when Cheever contrasts Coverly's background with the places he is sent as a taper. As a man involved in computers, he is himself systematized, sent by way of a preselected program to locations he knows nothing about, then further programmed into government villages, also standardized. This institutionalization of life finds its lateral movement in the destruction of the *Topaze* on the rocks—Leander's quest for Byronic experience dashed on the shoals—and in the flawed quality of Clear Haven, the castle-like home where Moses pursues his fair Melissa. Thus, all three locations are faulted, with St. Botolphs the most resistant to the ravages of civilized change.

Clear Haven, despite recalling that "first place," is a prison of sorts, where Justina, Melissa's old aunt, rules as dictator, keeps all the inmates in thrall to her, and tries to prevent Melissa from functioning as an individual. Before Moses has insight into the castle, he sees it as a perfect place for the early months of his marriage. Since his conception of love and a relationship is intensely associated with sexual fulfillment, his dreams of paradise are filled with lovely women. Fair Haven is such a refuge: "even the benches in the garden were supported by women with enormous marble breasts and in the fall his eye fell repeatedly on naked and comely men and women in the pursuit of the glow of love."

But like everything else beyond the domain of St. Botolphs, life is infected by ego, self-indulgence, power games. Justina boasts of her own power: "I could be all these things [wicked, rude, boorish] and worse and there would still be plenty of people to lick my boots." As she smiles sweetly on Moses, he "saw for once how truly powerful this old dancing mistress had been in her heyday and how she was like an old Rhine princess, an exile from the abandoned duchies of upper Fifth Avenue and the dusty kingdoms of Riverside Drive." Moses perceives more than Eve; he sees, as if for the first time, evil.

The novel is of an ideological piece with Cheever's stories. For unlike Updike, with whom he can be superficially compared, Cheever is very conscious of the darkening sky that lies just beyond every endeavor to live and/or expand. The suburban railroad which runs through the center of so many of his stories is a monster of civilization, a freak which becomes indispensable, and a deceptive element in the life of every commuter. For while it is a lifeline, it is also a passage into anonymity. The railroad connects two forms of life: St. Botolphs, based on illusions, and its morbid replacements—Clear Haven and government villages. Near the end of the novel, a new cycle is about to begin, with the death of Leander by drowning and the birth of sons for Coverly and Moses. Leander's death clears the way for another round of illusions based on pastoral dreams. For the new generation, St. Botolphs will prove a magnet for their dreams; and they will repeat that alternation of refuge and escape which gives them vitality.

When Cheever returned to the Wapshot chronicle in *The Wapshot Scandal,* published six years later, in 1963, he sharpened the divisions. Here everything that disconnects the individual from St. Botolphs has within it forms of death, usually by way of machinery and technology. The Garden and the machine are in deadly conflict, and illusions gain in significance. In a key episode, Coverly has become attached to the team of Cameron, a man whose scientific achievements have made him an arbiter over life and death for much of the world. Yet Cameron is himself woefully incomplete, lacking a dimension, the archetype for Cheever of those who have made no progress "in solving the clash between night and day, between the head and the groin."

Coverly's dilemma is how to behave in a society which increasingly retreats from any values he can recognize or assimilate as forms of behavior. Old cousin Honora, also, no longer recognizes the familiar and must flee St. Botolphs in disgrace. Cheever is neither intense nor tragic about such conflicts between individual behavior and a world in which values no longer matter. But in his laid-back, suburban manner, he is reaching toward broad themes, what we find more comprehensively in books as different as *Giles Goat-Boy* (only a few years removed from the second *Wapshot*) and *Gravity's Rainbow*. Barth and Pynchon are more panoramic novelists, but they limn similar experiences. And if we dip back into Barth's earlier career, before *Giles,* we see in his *The Floating Opera* and *The End of the Road* the same kind of world that Cheever has illuminated. The end is a rounding off, with Christmas Eve in St. Botolphs; in the end is the beginning. The brothers welcome a busload of blind people into Coverly's house, and the seeing and the blind sit down to dinner together. With that, the omniscient narrator indicates that it is time to pull out. He leaves on an incantatory note, to the effect that all will fade, St. Botolphs and whatever it stands for—like Eden itself: "I will never come back, and if I do there will be nothing left, there will be nothing left but the headstones to record what has happened; there will really be nothing at all." Leander's final message, that man's soul is able to "endure every sort of good and every sort of evil," will become an idle fancy. Once the illusions pass, the machine has triumphed.

From Cheever, it is less than a full step back to Wright Morris, that almost forgotten American writer of dispossessed gardens, epiphanies of doom, ceremonies of a pastoral existence on the edge of extinction or diminution. From an earlier half-generation, Morris looks ahead to Gass as well as Cheever, although he lacks Gass's finely honed lyricism. Both, however, move us by boring us; that is, they slow down our perceptions, so that we sink into tedium, and at the same time marvel at how differently things look from that diminished pace. Morris achieves his sense of pastoral by way of threats to it, not by sentimentalizing it. Unlike Hemingway, with whom he shares an interest in bullfighting, Morris in *The Field of Vision* (1956) does not view the corrida as masculine or an aspect of bravado. Instead, he tried to blend two main strands in American fiction: the masculine tradition associated with "ordeals," of which the bullfight is one test; and the pastoral tradition, in which man wrestles not a finite foe but the forces of destiny. Morris's pattern is to bring together a seemingly disparate group of people at a Mexico City corrida,* and his plan within the pattern is to observe his characters as the bullfights continue within their "field of vision."

The most interesting of the characters is Boyd, a failed actor and failed person. Boyd has tried to reach beyond his background in Nebraska, given up the land and what it means, and made himself into a gypsy. He is as dedicated to failure as McKee, his counterbalance, is to success on the land. "A dedicated no-man, one who had turned to failure as a field that offered real opportunity for success, Boyd had come to Lehmann [his analyst] when it was clear that he had failed to fail. That he had failed to touch the floating bottom within himself. Having run the full gamut of success-clichés—including the quick rise and fall from favor—he had found Failure a nut that refused to crack."

McKee has remained a Nebraska man, deeply devoted to Mrs. McKee, but lacking the sensitivity to her and to himself that would give him a full field of vision. He is like the tortoise that wins through perseverance, rather than the rabbit that flashes wit and style. Pastoral values have blinded him, especially to the fact that Mrs. McKee and Boyd had an affair in the deep past. McKee is the pivotal force in the book: made strong by his close feeling for the land of his birth, but hobbled in imagination by his concentration on one thing.

Scanlon is Mrs. McKee's father, now blind, but full of memories of a pioneering past. He sits at the bullring seeing nothing, but picking up associations. A plainsman, he has made the plains into a sea, a world, which he travels endlessly in his mind. He lives backward, the man who has made the western part of the country possible; the very opposite of the image the others carry of Boyd, a hopeless individual living out failure in the emptiness of a shell-like New York loft filled with nothing. As Boyd perceives the field of loneliness in himself, the blind Scanlon has visions of what can be. In Lone Tree, he stares at the fields:

---

*The structure may recall Thornton Wilder's *The Bridge at San Luis Rey,* but the point of Wilder's short novel is that the victims of the bridge are connected only by way of the accident. Wright's group have known each other for a long time, two are married, one has had an affair with another; and the tangled strands of their relationships return them deep into their pasts. Wright's method is, accordingly, less naturalistic than Wilder's, where the hand of fate has fallen; in Wright, the hand of fate is in balance with man's asserted will.

"The faded sky was like the sky at sea, the everlasting wind like the wind at sea, and the plain rolled and swelled quite a bit like the sea itself. Like the sea it was lonely, and there was no place to hide. Scanlon had never been to sea, of course, but that was beside the point."

Despite the extreme range of the group and its diversity of focus (or field of vision), the activity in the bullring brings each to a privileged moment, an existential crisis of sorts. Each must discover the self that he (or she) clings to, and each must redefine himself in the light of the bullring's field of vision. Morris meets Hemingway's sense of the corrida in that he makes it the measure of the individual: in Morris's case, for the spectator, not the performer. We go from the 1920s and 1930s to the 1950s, when introspection and counterfeit have replaced acts of (foolish) heroism. Morris's very point is that while acts of great daring may occur in the bullring, the spectators are forced into an examination of themselves, into, mainly, perceptions of failure, evasion, withdrawal from life. The matador's immersion in life before them is not a measure but a contradiction of them. They are defined by the negative of their field of vision, or, put another way, by another kind of field of vision.

Morris is able to handle all this by way of interior monologue, meanderings into the past, either generally as with the McKees or more specifically with Scanlon, to a time when his survival depended on his wits. For Boyd's analyst, the bullring is an even greater test, for his carefully structured irony, cynicism, impersonality begin to show seams. "Each man," Morris writes, "his own bullfighter, with his own center, a circle overlapped by countless other circles, like the pattern of expanding rings rain made on the surface of a pond. How many had been traced on the sand of the bullring that afternoon?"

At the center of disorder, a dispossessed Garden, is Boyd, who will, along with some of the others, appear also in Ceremony in Lone Tree. Boyd serves part of the function we find in Virginia Woolf's Percival, in The Waves: a man, not so remarkable in himself, who becomes remarkable under the gaze of others. It is not what he is, but how he is perceived, part of a field. Somehow Boyd was considered, once, the best in themselves, as now, in his seediness, he is considered to have failed them. Boyd's prowess made him and them feel he could walk on water, and although he almost drowned, the attempt remains in memory as an Edenic moment. Yet juxtaposed to this memory, as of Jesus himself, is one of equal intensity:

when the crowd from Nebraska come in on Boyd in his New York cold-water flat and see a man reaching for the bottom. Boyd lives at these extremes, and since the Nebraska group shelters itself at the center, he is their beacon: his early successes and now his later failures illuminate them. He is a figure in both the Garden and the dispossessed Garden.

Near the end of the book, Boyd helps the McKees' grandson into the bullring to give him the same moment of excitement that he, Boyd, once felt when he attempted to walk on water. Although the bull is dead, there are suggestions of danger—the darkening arena, blood everywhere, groups of local children racing around, young Gordon wild and untamable, and Boyd urging him on to his "privileged moment," the young boy under the coonskin cap sharing for the moment the matador's excitement. The scene is all bogus pastoral. The book ends with McKee herding everyone back to his car, but young Gordon, who had wanted everything he saw, is yelling for something he will not be able to buy. The spatiality of pastoral has been shrunk to the size of the bullring; then expanded to include an alternative life style, with its possibilities of expansion and escape.

Ceremony in Lone Tree, with many of the chief characters from The Field of Vision, focuses on the breakup of a pastoral existence by way of two small Nebraska towns: Polk, where the McKees live, and Lone Tree, Scanlon's place. Local crimes and the blank eyes of the young people (future Manson-worshipers!) indicate that a major transformation is taking place, with someone like McKee being phased out. Boyd can survive in this atmosphere because he has already ingested many of the destructive elements implicit in the new mode of living and thinking. In this novel, on the eve of the 1960s (published in 1960), Morris foresees the generational struggle; but even more, some of the cultural nihilism implicit in the revolt of the young. When McKee is displaced, little is left of old pastoral values; rural areas have gone the way of towns and cities.*

The pastoral dream in Lone Tree is embodied in the half-mad and blind Scanlon and some of the people gathered there for his ninetieth birthday. McKee

---

*The emergence of the new at the expense of the old is also the subject of Fire Sermon, Morris's 1971 novella. A hippie couple picks up an old man and a young boy, and the struggle in the boy between the old man, representing the rural and pastoral past, and the hippie couple, who represent the new, becomes the central conflict. Their destination in the car is a point in the plains where the past no longer has meaning.

himself attempts to continue as if nothing has changed, even when his relative, Lee Roy Momeyer, has gone mad, using his hot rod to crush two bullies in the schoolyard. Morris, however, does not romanticize McKee as the holder of the torch, for he lives in a kind of fantasy, in which he fails to recognize that his way of life is fraught with self-deception. Boyd, however, tries to be a voice of truth, even while he is cynical about himself and human life in general.*

The "ceremony" in Lone Tree celebrates death coequally with life; and the sense of life there is more fantasy than reality. The central image is of a ghost town and a man who should have died in Death Valley. Only memories can sustain him and Lone Tree. Morris's Nebraska is receding into a place of the imagination; reality is in the blank eyes of the young, or the careless way of Boyd, who sees it all and recoils into his own ceremonies. In a witty denial of McKee's pastoral Nebraska, Boyd offers his own, a state of mind:

> It's lovely country. Know it well. Game, wild fowl and snotweed abound. Traveling from east to west, one gets the impression of a verdant grassland, congenial to man, along with bones of the woolly mammoth and the dinosaur. Spaghetti made in Omaha very popular in Italy. . . . The people of Nebraska being conservative by nature, living close to the soil and the round of the seasons are not swept by the tides of shifting opinion and still refer to most Negroes as coons. A predictable percentage of the women go mad, books are sold in most of the drugstores, and Mr. Charles Munger, celebrated gunman, is a native son.

In *Plains Song,* Morris's American Book Award winner for 1980, we have a version of pastoral in the form of "As I Lay Dying." The dying person is Cora Atkins, whose comatose figure begins the novel and who dies thirty pages from the end. The novel is, in a sense, a flowing out of experience from the dying Cora into the family which she begins with the nightmare of her first sexual experience with Emerson, a farmer. This is a pastoral of women; not shepherdesses, but female children who radiate out from Cora, either into suburban life or into the distant life of cities. In the four generations Morris covers, America is settled in her outreaches and then begins to fill up. Cora's driving sense of function, in which work is essential for her survival, ends up in the suburban life of her children and their children, in the 1970s, for whom machines function.

Cora's sense of purpose is counterweighted, most of all, by her niece, Sharon Rose, daughter of Emerson's brother, Orion, and the wild Ozark girl he marries, Belle. Product of Orion and Belle, Sharon is different, very possibly lesbian, a musician and teacher, a woman who lives near cities. She fears the family, for its strange demands on her, and yet recognizes that her life "led back to where it had started," that her eyes had "fastened on the darkness where . . . [she] hoped to see a glimpse of familiar light." Unable to accept the mindless, boring, uncommunicative routines of the family when she returns to Lincoln for Cora's funeral, Sharon nevertheless recognizes the immense sadness that lies at her center. She ascribes it to the world's sorrow, but it is her own, and it is the self she has lost in finding her role, what she gave up of the plains, of the Cora and Belle in her, in order to seek out life near cities, in modern life as a modern woman. Her role as a 1970s woman is inescapable—she *is* different from Madge, Fayrene, the others—but there, not diminution, simply loss. Morris has become our poet laureate or bard of such losses, sadness, sense of hollowness.

Although his subject matter associates him with Morris and Cheever in some respects, William Gass is very much a writer of the 1960s. Gass is an avatar of the new, a minimalist, whose aim is to create the sense of a journey as occurring *between* words, sentences, paragraphs. White space or visual void (Mallarmé's "absence") counts as much as words, which, for Gass, are "opaque as objects." Words, in fact, are objects of a kind, since they tell us as much about an object as the object does. Thus, for Gass, the words creating a pastoral image are *that:* the thing itself. It is in these pastoral associations, the heart of the heart, that he rubs up against many of his seemingly dissimilar contemporaries.

Full of Gertrude Stein's repetitions,* caught up by the "angel of death" which resides in all rural life, engaged by the "ontology of the sentence" or "a

---

*The drift of Boyd's argument recalls Anderson's Winesburg stories, which are the archetypal literary expression of small-town life. Our romantic sense may be Wilder's "Our Town," but the reality is closer to Anderson's view, which is also what we find in *Wisconsin Death Trip,* that chronicle of madness, alcoholism, and murder which accompany the lovely scenery and intimate life of small-town America.

*And her mapping of "body space." Gass's brilliant essay on "Gertrude Stein and the Geography of the Sentence" is full of words (Stein's "tender buttons"), visions, and voices, all the elements of his own work.

world of words," Gass rejects an art based on windows, or peering through. As a trained philosopher, he perceives fiction as itself an existential act: contingent, which is to say open to chance; the author as a nonchalant god, omnipotent and capable of anything; the fact that "nothing necessarily follows, and anything plausibly may." Like Barth in his occasional essays, Gass is unusual in trying to formulate an idea of fiction, as the European writers have traditionally done. Very much aware of contemporary French theory—Robbe-Grillet, Nathalie Sarraute, Roland Barthes—Gass posits a pastoral whose actuality differs from its more conventional forms; and yet once we cut through theory and even his arrangements, we discover familiar American cultural patterns: lost Edens, fallen men, dispossessed Gardens, bitter contrasts between what God has made and man has wrought.

Gass's characters shape themselves along the line of the action, as if separable from the words that identify them. Since images of life are "faded sensations," and themselves falsifications, we must deal with a reality that always slides away from the language which particularizes an author's vision of his material. We recall a kindred spirit in Walker Percy, whose Will Barrett focuses his telescope on a distant scene and is able to move, through stages of space, from a world of "pure possibility" to one of more defined shape. On similar ground, Gass rejects simply focused perceptions and prefers "blueness," or that which is capable of a more ambiguous clarity. "On Being Blue" is another way of keeping all options available.

"Words in daily life are signposts, handles, keys," Gass writes in "The Concept of Character in Fiction," by which he suggests they serve, request, command. But they are not themselves ways of seeing; they are only themselves. This does not necessarily mean they lose their suggestivity, their "imaged" quality. On the contrary, even if opaque, even if the thing itself, they recall and evoke. Gass titled his second collection of essays *The World Within the Word,* by which he suggests—as presented in his essay on "Proust at 100"—that the author lives in his book, not outside it; that all life, as the structuralists would have it, must be found within the forms of words. Proust's world or Valéry's Monsieur Teste fits Gass's internal areas, where all life pushes out between the words, into white spaces.

"In the Heart of the Heart of the Country" contains headings of a conventional nature: "A Place," "Weather," "My House," "Politics," etc., many of them repeated. The categories suggest an idyll or pastoral of some balance and refinement; but "the heart of the heart of the country" is a place of waste and madness, like Winesburg, Ohio, or, with modifications, Sinclair Lewis's small towns and Hamlin Garland's villages. Billy Holsclaw, who is the heart of this heart, is "as vacant and barren and loveless as the rest of us are—here in the heart of the country." And his residences fit: "These houses are now dying like the bereaved who inhabit them; they are slowly losing their senses—deafness, blindness, forgetfulness, mumbling, an insecure gait, an uncontrollable trembling has overcome them." The houses themselves will soon be occupied by "some kind of Northern Snopses. . . . These Snopses will undertake makeshift repairs with materials other people have thrown away; paint halfway round their house, then quit; almost certainly maintain an ugly loud cantankerous dog."

In "Education," the children will "be taught to read and warned against Communism" by a teacher with a face like a "mail-order ax," her voice hoarse from screaming abuse. The narrator muses that he would rather "it was the weather that was to blame for what I am and what my friends and neighbors are —we who live here in the heart of the country." For the weather drives the people in upon themselves, even though it is better to live in the country than in the city, which is "swollen and poisonous with people." At least, that's what one wants to believe: that the country is better. But the country has changed, and the "modern husbandman uses chemicals from cylinders and sacks, spike-ball and claw machines, metal sheds, and cost accounting. Nature in the old sense does not matter. It does not exist." So he can say, "My window is a grave, and all that lies within it's dead." Beyond his window lie the three passions of the poorly educated: sports, politics, and religion. The church is the basketball gymnasium, and business is represented by endless Christmas carols. "Joy to the World" rings out, ironically.

In the collection of stories that make up *In the Heart of the Heart of the Country,* Gass has entered Twain territory, that division between poisonous shore and idyllic waterway, between deadly city and living river. The bucolic idyll, if discovered, lies under layers of man-made deception and lies. In "The Pedersen Kid," the other considerable fiction in the collection, the themes are deep hatred, revenge, the harboring of the deepest rages: patricide, burying the family, killing off the children. The snow does the job of death that lies in everyone's heart, especially in the young. The pastoral idyll lies there in the snow; but impacted beneath, in the heart of the people as in the heart of the country, are worlds we can define as "death trips."

The term is borrowed from a book that conveys the fear and trembling of small-town America, *Wisconsin Death Trip* (1973) by Michael Lesy. It is a work of brilliant juxtapositions. Photographs of graduations, infants, young men and women, nursing mothers, old people, men of the town are set next to news items from the state and local papers: tales of horror, mayhem, acts of violence, suicides, madness, brutal killings. Although the book seems indebted to *Now Let Us Praise Famous Men,* madness, not poverty, is the motif, small-town life and insane rage as constant companions. "James McDonald and his wife were arrested in Eau Claire on the charge of having killed their own team of horses which were found in McDonald's barn with their throats cut about 2 weeks ago." Horses give way to people: "Mrs. John Larson, wife of a farmer living in the town of Troy, drowned her 3 children in Lake St. Croix during a fit of insanity." She asserted that devils pursued her. Not only do we find here a dispossessed Garden, but the very witches of Salem.

Such a book, like Gass's work, is in part a response to the Vietnam War and issues raised by it. Gass's fiction, while minimalist in structure and language, is deeply concerned with political and social issues; but in the mode of modernist fiction, it is indirect and oblique. "The Pedersen Kid" seems leagues away from any social or political content, but in the year of its book publication (1968), it fits quite well into a life-and-death generational struggle: a war empowered by the old which consumes the young. Like Roth's urban stories, Gass's lean on generational conflicts. But while Roth's end in masturbation, nasty words, defiance of mother, Gass, closer to the heart of the country, senses the violence that lies in American conflict, that readiness to kill off the oppressor and be done with it. Release through masturbation may be suitable for the Jewish writer, who sentimentalizes America; but not for the Christian—there, awareness of a more savage America is very real: murder, not masturbation.

Gass's only full-length novel (*Omensetter's Luck,* 1966) centers on Brackett Omensetter's "luck," and that quality in turn on his ability to move along the contours of nature. Omensetter is an oafish sort, his center far from that of others; yet because he marches to a different drummer, he is deeply focused on something that lies outside others' perception. Gass writes:

"Omensetter lived by *not* observing—by joining himself to what he knew." He adds: "Necessity flew birds as easily as the wind drove these leaves, and they never felt the curvature which drew the arc of their pursuit." Omensetter, whose name could as easily have been a sign of doom, moves along the curvature of necessity, working through it or manifesting it, by "joining" it. Rather than trying to discover what makes gravity's rainbow, he forsakes exploration for fitting himself along its perimeters.

The novel, then, is a celebration of life in Gilean, Ohio, Gass's mythical past America. The book begins with an auction,* then moves back into the early years of the town, all held together not only by Omensetter's aloof form of salvation but by the Pimbers. It is Missus Pimber's goods which are being auctioned at the beginning, and it is Henry Pimber whose life threads through Omensetter's, all framed in the past. When Omensetter saves Pimber's life by use of a poultice soaked in beet juice, he enfolds himself in the life of Gilean by way of natural means: what makes him tick becomes *the* mystery for Henry Pimber and the entire town, but especially for the preacher, Jethro Furber.

The main parts of the book give way to Jethro Furber's meditation on Omensetter: Furber cannot understand someone like him, and, therefore, the meditation—at once religious, sexual, blasphemous, personalized—is hostile and antagonistic. Furber is a tortured man, and what enrages him is Omensetter's apparent imperviousness to disaster, his "stony mindlessness," which makes Furber think of Eden. That Omensetter "does without desire in the ordinary sense, with a kind of abandon," makes Furber blaspheme his own beliefs. He sees sin as simply exile, a life in which God has withdrawn, and he tries to identify Omensetter's exile from ordinary life as sin itself; everything "seems fine beyond the fence," as Furber puts it. This recognition makes his own position doubly difficult. For he perceives evil, and Omensetter simply does not. If this is so, Furber decides, then it means Omensetter is the worst of all—although a more charitable perception would be that he is the best, beyond evil, but not good. Furber becomes enraptured by his own hostility, by his own toiling in the garden of desires; he must observe Omensetter

---

*Suitably an auction, which is not language, but words. "In the Medium of Fiction," Gass modulated the roles of words: "A dedicated storyteller, though—a true lie-minded man—will serve his history best . . . by following as closely as he can our simplest, most direct and unaffected forms of daily talk."

from the point of view of the man who struggles daily to achieve his faith, while the former seems to fall into his effortlessly.

Omensetter's "luck," which so galls Furber, is that he appears outside normal desires, something Furber cannot deal with; for he is himself a man of intense passions, like Hawthorne's Dimmesdale, outwardly pious, but inwardly roiled by conflict. In response to his own turbulence, he must destroy Omensetter; and the sole way to do that in a small town like Gilean is by way of his reputation. Furber starts out to undermine Omensetter's position, his passiveness, his family life—and he will do this by way of the pulpit, through the word of God.

The story within the story—the major part of the narrative is long flashback that tails off from the auction of Missus Pimber's household goods—is one of passion versus passivity, sexuality and fire versus ease. For Furber, the man of barely controlled passion, sees Omensetter as a devil whose "luck" leaves in its wake a series of victims: Pimber (himself a spectacular suicide) and Watson (the man who gave Omensetter his first job). Yet all this derives from Furber's imagination, for Omensetter, while strange, is not icy, is passionate in his own way. Yet because he is different, does not fit in, Furber musters the town against his foe, making Omensetter into the leader of the army of devils bringing ill luck, bad omens, upon Gilean.

"Omensetter cast an interest like a shade," Gass writes, and as a consequence his every action has, for the townspeople and Furber, a dual meaning. Omensetter's "simple harmony and ease" must be condemned by those accustomed to living with misfortune; and it is believed that if his activity is monitored, somehow the sum total of his routine acts will lead to a perception of his secret. The townspeople put him in glass. Space becomes multiple. His planting, his trapping of a fox, his ability to survive on low land near the river, the cowlike qualities of his wife, the strangeness of his daughters are all scrutinized for signs of his secret, as if the innards of a recently slain goat.

Yet Omensetter's luck is not connected to any secret self, any witchlike shadow. He is a man among men, hearing—like Thoreau, perhaps—distinct sounds which only he can define and embody. He is, in fact, a man of little interest except for this ability to move in harmony with, not against, nature. This ability extends to his family, for when his infant son, Amos, falls ill with diphtheria and is considered lost, the boy hangs on and survives. Omensetter's own

survival becomes a legend, although, in fact, it is unremarkable. Furber, however, cannot remain content in the face of his foe's stable life. He must insist that paradise has been lost, not retained.

In his sermons he whips up the town, so that when Henry Pimber is found hanging from a tree limb, the townspeople are ready to lynch Omensetter. In a dark scene in Omensetter's house, while his wife is frantic over the dying Amos, the townspeople close in on him, only to be dissuaded by Furber and, chiefly, Dr. Orcutt. Omensetter's "luck" holds, and he is permitted to leave town. Furber goes mad, and the story is ready to wind back to its beginning, to the auction of the Pimber goods, including Amos's cradle. The auctioneer, Israbestis Tott, was present at the near-lynching, witness to the loss of paradise. "It's a long story, Israbestis was saying, a long story. This is Brackett Omensetter's cradle. It's not a name that means anything to you, I imagine, but there are a few of us left, like old leaves, I guess."

Gass's triumph is in bringing together the ordinary and trivial, and giving them the aura of the extraordinary; in packing his story with routine matters and by way of an intense and dense prose creating an American legend, a truly dispossessed Garden. Omensetter (the name, of course!) arrives mysteriously, lives in a damp, dark house on low land near the river, takes a job working with leather, raises a family outside the life of the town, has an antagonistic relationship with Henry Pimber, his landlord, is accused of murdering him, and finally leaves town, as quietly as he arrived. But his story is never *his* story: through most of the narrative, it is viewed from the outside, by Furber. Gass is careful not to write directly of Omensetter, whose life would not be dramatic if related from within; it gains drama from secrets, mystery, conspiracies, all generated by the town preacher, who fights with his God as he struggles with his conflicts over Omensetter. The battle is in Furber, while life continues for his foe; and this external post of observation allows Gass to perceive characters, town, land as if they exist beyond words.

"Literature is language," Gass says at the beginning of his essay "The Medium of Fiction," and he apologizes for the simplicity of his remark: "It seems a country-headed thing to say." He continues, more phenomenologically: "The purpose of a literary work is the capture of consciousness, and the consequent creation, in you, of an imagined sensibility, so that while you read you are that patient pool or cataract of concepts which the author has constructed; and though at first it might seem as if the richness of life had been replaced by something less so—senseless noises, abstract meanings, mere shadows of worldly employment—yet the new self with which fine fiction and good poetry should provide you is as wide as the mind is, and musicked deep with feeling." The author attempts to achieve a "consciousness electrified by beauty," and so the function of fiction is to create a new area of stillness for the reader, Eliot's still center, Joyce's epiphany, Yeats's Byzantium. *Omensetter,* on a smaller scale, is set within that frame of reference.

Analogously to Gass, the work of Peter Matthiessen exemplifies the pursuit of Eden(s) and dispossessed Gardens—whether in the Caymans, the Himalayas, where the legendary snow leopard resides, or the Amazon jungles of Brazil, in *At Play in the Fields of the Lord.* In *Far Tortuga* (1975), Matthiessen writes of the *Lillias Eden,* a schooner which goes down on an ill-fated voyage. The *Eden* moves in the waters of the Caribbean around the Caymans. These are legendary islands, once known as Columbus's islands, also called Tortugas—Far Tortugas. Their background in the mists of Columbus's islands, as part of that "new Eden" which was America, gives the ship and its novel its pastoral dimension. The sail out is into a pastoral paradise; what eventuates is a disaster, a doomed voyage on a doomed ship—we recall the *Pequod,* a ship named after an extinct Indian tribe. America goes down, in the form of a "flowered Eden."

At Play in the Fields of the Lord (1965) is a far more complicated vision of Eden, a potential paradise transformed into a nightmare and hell reminiscent of Conrad's Congo. The attempt to weave a way through this "paradise lost" occurs in Meriwether Lewis Moon, part Indian, college educated: a man on the edge of civilization and savagery. Moon can go in either direction, equipped as he is for the white man's world as well as for that of the Brazilian natives. The world of the savages is a battlefield, fought over by missionaries on one hand and government forces on the other. The missionaries (a priest and several Protestants) wish to win the souls of the Indians, whereas the government wants the land. The latter operation is directed by the Comandante, Guzmán, who uses Moon and his sidekick, Wolfie, to bomb and exterminate the Indians.

While Wolfie, a Jew, is as cynical about events as Father Xantes, the lone Catholic, Moon has not given up on finding himself. He is not at ease in the white man's world, although he can function there; but as a sign of his unease, he had at the final moment

thrown over his degree. Having hit bottom, he is like innumerable other American questors, drifting from one low job to another; trapped by Guzmán, who controls his documents; unable to find some seam in the system where he can live.

The "fields of the Lord," then, are peopled by few who can comprehend what the Lord means. The missionaries see the Indians and the land as something to be tamed; in that respect, they are Puritans/Pilgrims bringing their faith and sense of martyrdom to a place completely hostile. The jungle, Matthiessen stresses, is a trial for them at every turn, especially for Hazel Quarrier, whose faith is strong, but whose mental condition cannot support the isolation, insects, threats from hostile Indians. When her son, Billy, dies of backwater fever, she begins to lose her mental control, her faith insufficient.

The Hubens also become a divided couple: he fervent, unbending, humorless; she, Andy, beginning to understand that the Indians have their own culture and faith, their own forms of worship, their own gods. Similarly, Quarrier—a man as torn as any Graham Greene priest, something of a burnt-out case himself—starts to unfold; something of the human being behind the missionary goal begins to emerge. He tries to perceive the Indians and the situation in terms outside his mission, and this of course puts him on a collision course with himself, Les Huben, the very mission. Also, his own sexual life forbidding, he lusts after Andy Huben. At best, Hazel is not accessible, and Quarrier, withal, is racked by physical desires he can barely control.

These ingredients, so far, provide Matthiessen with somewhat stereotypical elements: missionaries befuddled by the people they are attempting to convert; squabbles between Catholic and Protestant, the Reformation refought, in which numbers saved preempt quality of salvation; tension within a main character between his service to God and demands of the flesh; conflicts in a marriage threatened by a hostile environment, a strange people, the death of a child; presence of a tyrannical force—Guzmán as a typical South American military man, right out of Conrad's *Nostromo;* and surrounding them all a form of life at the station—and then at the mission site—which is completely different from anything they had prepared for back in North Dakota. Home seems like a distant, inaccessible paradise. Added to the familiar elements is a heavy dosage of Greene and Conrad. *Heart of Darkness* hovers over the entire enterprise: impenetrable jungle, the mission itself as the "inner station," savages barely seen, hostility at every stage of the jungle journey, presence of the warrior Aeore as a kind of avenging Kurtz.

In this scene, Wolfie and Moon are catalysts. Guzmán expects them to kill the Indians because the latter have become unnecessary for the development of the Amazon region. But legal justification must be found. Faced by killing those who are as innocent as the Cheyennes of his own background, Lewis Moon defects with a plane and flies off to join the Niaruna, a savage tribe, with its own hierarchies and forms. Like Lévi-Strauss in *Tristes Tropiques* (1955; 1961 in English), Matthiessen observes the Niarunas as not at all anarchic savages; they have evolved—their beliefs, daily life, ideas about life and death—into a highly structured culture. It is into this that Moon must fit, aided only by the fact of his Indian heritage.

Parachuting in, he takes on the guise of one of their gods, but does not completely deceive the warrior Aeore, whose bravery he had once observed when Aeore aimed an arrow at his and Wolfie's plane. Aeore's spirit cannot be broken, and his presence is a constant threat to Moon, who is otherwise accepted. Life with the Niarunas is not Edenesque, although Moon's apprenticeship to their ways is a kind of crash course in Indian lore. Here Matthiessen breaks away from what was at first cliché-ridden, and has moved into Cooper territory, without Cooper's sentimentality. For if the Niarunas teach Moon anything, it is to not be sentimental about Indians: they simply are.

In Moon's break from the world of Guzmán and the missionaries, he has discovered a different way of colonizing the jungle savage: by blending in with him. It is as if the Pilgrims had come to New England to join the Indians, rather than to colonize the land and establish a parallel camp. Moon journeys into the primitive, not as some sentimental quest for simplicity, but as a course essential for life. Matthiessen makes us believe this, and that is the triumph of the novel. Moon must choose between darkness, which brings enlightenment of a sort, and light, which carries with it its burden of darkness, unremitting darkness. He is caught in paradoxes, halfway between two worlds: deadened by the repetitions of the savage world and disheartened by the missionaries'. He plays with disclosure: "More and more Moon was drawn toward the mission, to test his disguises again and again, just for the fun of it. Boronai [a chief] watched him. Yet he knew that to visit the mission was to dissipate a mystery, to break a spell, before he had penetrated to the heart of it and made it part of him."

Moon becomes caught in the middle, unsuitable since birth for any particular world. Here, for the first time, he observes an opening, and yet it is not easy: he remains a stranger in each culture, unless he can accept the Indians for what they are and adapt to them. Moon's survival depends on the Indians, and their survival in turn depends on him, since he can help them against Guzmán's plans for extermination. Moon enters into the profoundly complicated structure of daily life, tribal politics, religious worship, which make up the Niaruna world. He must deal not only with physical facts—his soft feet, unsure hand, inability to live off the land—but with elements of worship which they do not reveal to him. While he presents himself as one god, as Kisu, the Niarunas believe in another with greater finality, Witu'mai. Moon has fallen between their beliefs in the same way as have the missionaries, who, because of an interpreter's error, have confused themselves about the Indian gods.

To become an Indian, Moon comes to learn, means leaving everything behind. He must drift out, literally, into their world and *be.* There is no process, only existence; and whenever Moon wavers, he stares into the eyes of the savage and all he sees is *there,* nothing beyond it but the savagery of the savage. Matthiessen is superb at conveying this sense of cultural difference. At the end of the novel, Moon has floated free of his past, and brought down by malarial hallucinations, he is finally transformed into a man of the river and jungle. "He was neither white nor Indian, man nor animal, but some mute, naked strand of protoplasm. He groaned with the ache of his own transience under this sky, as if, breathing too deeply, he might rise on the wind as lightly as a seed, without control or intimation of his fate." He wonders if he is the first or last man on earth; there is no certainty, only life. "Laid naked to the sun and sky, he felt himself open like a flower. Soon he slept. At dark he built an enormous fire, in celebration of the only man beneath the eye of Heaven."

There is something of the Lawrentian world here, but Lawrence never shows actual transformation, even in *The Plumed Serpent,* which this novel vaguely recalls. Lawrence was interested in the power of primitive symbols as counters to civilized weakness; but Matthiessen demonstrates, without Lawrentian dramatization, the "nothingness" that lies behind primitive celebration. Once one achieves that identification with Indian existence, one is terribly alone; not first or last man: only man.

Written in the early 1960s, *At Play* is a finely

wrought novel but also a significant cultural document. Not simply prophetic of the decade that will emerge, it is definitive of an acute American dilemma. In its tortured workings, it is a "Walden" of the postwar era. Only now Walden Pond is not part of nature's benevolence. In the transformation that has occurred in Eden, a truly dispossessed arena, nature is either malevolent or totally threatening. Moon survives, but barely, and only because he is part of it: a moon, a Meriwether or explorer, part Cheyenne, and educated in a white man's world. Half bred to everything, he has the lore and instincts to come through the seams of what is already a fantasy life for others. What is for the missionaries a living hell, for Guzmán an area to exploit, for the surviving Indian tribes a losing battle to avoid extinction, becomes for Moon a search for Eden. Here is pastoral shifted to the Amazon jungles, but close to the bone of the American experience. Given the alternatives, redefinition is the sole way to survival. The only comparable novel to deal with such crucial issues is Bellow's *Henderson the Rain King,* also a marvel of language and cultural insights.

It can be instructive to play off the maturity of the Matthiessen novel against the puerilities of Ken Kesey's *One Flew Over the Cuckoo's Nest* (1962). Although ideas of pastoral are fundamental to both, Kesey establishes categories which are reductive and self-defeating. For he posits that whatever is antisystem belongs to pastoral and whatever is system is antipastoral. The categories, as worked out, are limited, ideologically infantile. Not for nothing did *One Flew* become a cult novel.

Kesey's novel is a response to the 1950s world of Skinner's utopian *Walden Two,* where systems control everyone and aim at infinite potential for happiness. In Kesey's reworking of a cuckoo utopia, everyone's potential for happiness is stunted. The system blights, and the individual exists to the degree he can undermine or evade the system. Counterfeiting is all.

Kesey's narrator is Chief Bromden or Broom, half Indian—and therefore someone whose instinctive life is being destroyed by the systems of Nurse Ratched's cuckoo's nest. He has assumed a condition of deafness and muteness, so that he functions as a drugstore Indian, silent, observing, unresponsive. Accustomed, as an Indian, to being treated as "not there," he has, as a consequence, taken on that persona. Since he is the registering intelligence of the novel, real changes

that can occur in an individual are suggested by changes that occur within him. Unlike Matthiessen's Moon, however, Bromden is not to be redefined; he must simply revert.

The asylum in Oregon, the cuckoo's nest, is under the operation of Nurse Ratched,* who has devised the systems which govern the institution. These systems are likened, by Kesey, and more directly by Chief Broom, to programs: the inside of the asylum is like the guts of a computer, all elements wired and interconnected. (Barth's university in *Giles Goat-Boy!*) Ratched is the programmer, the inmates the programmed, the entire system the computer.

In order to ensure that her organization runs smoothly, Ratched plans every move like a military maneuver. She is the epitome of Whyte's "organization man," her organization a cuckoo's nest, not a business or university. The system does not fit the men; the men fit the system.

"Practice has steadied and strengthened her until now she wields a sure power that extends in all directions on hair-like wires too small for anybody's eye but mine; I see her sit in the center of this web of wires like a watchful robot, tend her network with mechanical insect skill, know every second which wire runs where and just what current to send up to get the results she wants. What she dreams of there in the center of those wires is a world of precision efficiency and readiness like a pocket watch with a glass back, a place where the schedule is unbreakable and all the patients who aren't Outside, obedient under her beam, are wheelchair Chronics with catheter tubes run direct from every pantleg to the sewer under the floor." Her section of Acutes, Chronics, and Disturbed is akin to a totalitarian state, overseen by a dictator, its inmates marked for a kind of death as social misfits.

What can upset this is a rebel, a radical, a Panurge —the force or element designed to disrupt systems. This Panurge comes in the shape of an ex-con, ex-farm worker, current brawler, gambler, funster— Randle Patrick McMurphy, Donleavy's Ginger Man. Since we are dealing with a cult novel of the 1960s, it may prove interesting to examine what occurs behind the brawling scenes of the novel, for *One Flew* in its reception became far more than the sum total of its parts. So caught up did Kesey become in his

---

*"Wretched," or "ratchet," a toothed bar or wheel that is engaged by a pawl so as to make sure movement occurs in one direction only. The image is only too clear.

own cult that, later, as leader of the Merry Prank-sters, he tried out McMurphy's very role. If *The Catcher in the Rye* was the cult novel of the fifties, *Cuckoo's Nest,* along with *Catch-22,* expressed enough of the sixties to become "in" novels of that decade.

What is remarkable is how Kesey played off traditional elements: we are immersed here in an updated pastoral. The asylum epitomizes urban values—programmed, organized, systemized. The sole way to counter urban order is by way of the pastoral, whether actual pastoral or with values usually assigned to the idea: release, escape, ease of movement, lack of control, individual decision-making, ordering of one's life. The novel ends, in fact, with a note reminiscent of Huck Finn, as Chief Broom escapes from the asylum and comments, "I been away a long time."

If the asylum is the city, and the world outside is represented by Broom's past and McMurphy's rebellion, then Nurse Ratched designates all that stands between freedom and imprisonment. The ideology is, of course, very familiar; for behind all the difficulty is not the men's individual insanity but a woman who forces men into the condition of children. With her benign manner, her huge frontal development, her "big nurse" quality, Nurse Ratched is, of course, the "great mother," the great bitch goddess, woman as monster. She is the embodiment of what women do to men: she slices off their manhood and turns them into incompetents, fearful, helpless charges. One thinks of Thurber's cartoon in which the man arrives home, to see his wife's form rising out of the very roof, a dominant goddess waiting to engulf him in her power.

What gives her mechanical possession of the section is the control panel, a piece of metal weighing perhaps a quarter of a ton, anchored to the floor by any number of connections. To upend the control panel is, in a way, to strike directly at Nurse Ratched, equivalent in the terms of the novel to raping her. First McMurphy tries to rip the panel out, but he is unable to do it. So his next strategy is to build up Chief Broom, a much larger man, until he is capable of doing it—the novel, after all, belongs to him. As for McMurphy, his rebellion must be lobotomized; to become a vegetable is his destiny in the order of things.

Overall, hatred of women fuels the novel, far less subtly than it does in so many fictions of our postwar novelists. A career woman is a monster, and the "good women" are the whores McMurphy brings in.

Kesey's formulation does not even fit into Leslie Fied-ler's division of female stereotypes into Rose (bitch, whore, temptation, seducer) and Lily (maiden, passive, pious) whose influence rarely extended beyond sexual matters: the Rose offered good sex, but danger; the Lily offered weak sex, but security. The Rose was "built," the Lily slender, willowy, very white. The Rose could be, on occasion, part Indian, part black, or wholly so, possibly Jewish or Italian; whereas the Lily was American.

The central episode, and one that is very well handled, contains the fishing expedition. It is solidly within the pastoral tradition, the embodiment of the antisystem which counters programming. The men who choose to go have put themselves on the line: for they have exchanged the "fog" of Big Nurse's machinery for the clarification of fishing. The fishing expedition—openness, sex with women who give it away, freedom for the day—embodies McMurphy's sense of life: but given the circumstances, it is fraught with dangers. This the inmates recognize, and thus their fear in joining him and the expedition. Their manhood is on the line.

McMurphy represents "tall tale" America: braggart, physicality, audacity, adventurousness. Such a man roams forests and rivers. His predecessors include those rogues who appeared on the frontier or on the Mississippi, Simon Suggs coming to mind; and it is perhaps not coincidental that in *Huckleberry Finn*—Kesey's inspiration—Twain presents a meeting between the King and the Duke which seems very close to Johnson Jones Hooper's description of Suggs in "Camp-Meeting." The tradition is a long one in American frontier humor, from Paul Bunyan on.* McMurphy's relationship to this tradition, dipping also into Rabelais's Panurge, of course makes him anathema to any system. Systems exist for him to sunder.

The fishing expedition, then, expresses everything McMurphy is capable of. When he lacks authorization to take the men out, he steals the boat. When the captain intervenes and insists on order, McMurphy

---

*McMurphy has many of the qualities we associate with the "Yankee," the man who fulfilled the myth of the archetypal American: crude, vulgar, humorous, strong, swaggering. Connected to him is the backwoodsman, a Mike Fink or a Davy Crockett. Cooper's Natty Bumppo is a distant relative: the rifle that never misses, the legends and feats attached to his prowess, his inability to fit suitably into civilized life, and yet his superiority to all systems. McMurphy combines these qualities, and, not untypically, women do not fit in this world, except as whores, and even there infrequently.

deceives him and then wins him over; he finds chinks in the system everywhere. By showing the men that their fears are conditioned, not innate, he undermines order. He brings them back into normal time, not the temporal distortions Ratched has enforced on them. Although deeply troubled, the men have become organization men; the need is to reorganize their problems by creating self-reliance. McMurphy's romanticism is clear, as is Kesey's: disorder is sanity, order the real insanity.

Implicit in such pastoral fiction is awareness that the immediate asylum situation emblemizes the "nation-wide Combine," the big force in which Nurse Ratched is "a high-ranking official." To strike a blow against Big Nurse is to rebel against the entire Combine, which represents a colonialism embodying death, like the Tristero System in Pynchon's *The Crying of Lot 49.* McMurphy's organization of Acutes and Chronics is an attempt to pull off a minority rebellion: revolutionary America against England, minorities against their colonial oppressors.

Inevitably, Kesey touches all the bases of what will be 1960s ideology, but he founders on one shoal after another. Despite brilliant episodes and some inventiveness of scene, the book lacks center because ideologically it is so soft, and in the case of its women, insidious and infantile. Not only are its themes in the American romantic tradition, its sexual divisions stereotypical—Cooper, Twain, Hemingway, Mailer —but its view of life is not far removed from Holden Caulfield's. The fact that *One Flew* became a more "adult" cult novel than its counterpart in the 1950s, *Catcher,* is not coincidental. Both strike at that "Animal House" mentality which underlies the making of a cult book. The 1960s were, in fact, far more sophisticated and significant than Kesey's view of the decade would make it appear. Yet, necessarily, any fantasy view of pastoral or the "new Eden" must include the kind of simplification and elementalism which underpin *Cuckoo.* *

We return to Chief Bromden as the central intelligence of the novel. Kesey has, of course rightfully, always insisted on Bromden as his pivotal figure. When the very fine film was made of the novel, he protested that the screenwriter and the director had refocused the novel so as to make McMurphy central. This was perhaps inevitable given the actor who

---

*Did *One Flew* perhaps become a cult novel, not despite, but because its best women are whores, its blacks slaveys and morons, its ideology the Laingian equation of the insane as wise, the sane as truly destructive?

played McMurphy, Jack Nicholson. The film did shift the value system around, from the one who survives (the vanishing Indian) to the one who succumbs (the lobotomized McMurphy). A great deal in Kesey's novel functions only if we perceive that the Chief's values, observations, and final act—smothering the lobotomized McMurphy—are crucial.

Kesey's relegation of Bromden to a central intelligence, as both the observer and the recipient of the action, is connected to his "soft" ideology. For Bromden represents what will perhaps save us from the Nurse and the Combine she represents. He, the deaf-mute Indian, is "witness" to what is happening, to his people and to all the oppressed (the cuckoos). And the quality that makes him a survivor is his Indian half, his association with that part of America which has remained pure and true. Because Bromden is uncorrupted, he feels a kinship with McMurphy, his primitive half. It is to McMurphy that Bromden first reveals he can speak, and that revelation is linked to his brotherhood with him, their awareness of a pure, green America. The puerilities that went into Charles Reich's "greening" of America can also be found in Bromden's sense of it.

Unfortunately, once Bromden makes his escape, he has nowhere to go except dreamland. He plans to make a journey into his past, stopping along the Columbia River for some former haunts. He will look back into the time the government intruded and tried to "buy their right to be Indians." In their associations, Indians have somehow held on to some revelation that the white man is not privy to, and Bromden, by making contact with that, will be revived.

Not unusually, we pick up Kesey later in the decade in the hallucinatory trips that Tom Wolfe wrote about so brilliantly in *The Electric Kool-Aid Acid Test.* The psychedelic bus and its spaced-out travelers replace the vision of the Indian. The "new purity" is that of visions, hallucinations, fantasies reinforced by drugs, all held together by Kesey's charismatic figure. He has, in a sense, come to live out what Bromden cannot possibly fathom; the Chief's sense of things must fail, or else trail off into the drug culture. The sole purity left is not Bromden's defiance of a dispossessed Garden, but a spaced-out individual: his sense of spatiality now given over to a transformation of inner space. The movement out to discover America and destroy the machine becomes an ego trip.

Walden Two has in the main won. There is no reason to rejoice that Kesey's vision failed, that Bromden will be assimilated into the mainstream of the Combine. When Bromden escapes at the end of the novel, he disappears into what will swallow him. We need not applaud that order has returned, or the seventies brought systems back into favor. We are only indulging the counterfeit which poses as stability. Whatever the excesses and deficiencies of Kesey's visions, they were deeply rooted in America, but by the end of the sixties, *that* America could no longer function. In fact, it never did.

John Gardner's work falls roughly into the pastoral mode, as many of his titles and characters suggest romantic forms of Eden, either lost, rediscovered, or decaying. His own name suggests his destiny, but more Candide than Adam. *The Resurrection, The Sunlight Dialogues, Nickel Mountain,* and *October Light* are all titles having to do with the rediscovery of something lost, or something transfigured by a new sensibility, or something in decline that can be recovered by a magical presence. Gardner's world offers a struggling Edenic vision which civilization and whatever else is embedded in it violates: to regain the presence behind the vision is the task of his literary endeavors. But the rigidity of Gardner's mind, a failure to allow openness and flexibility, his refusal to let adversary ideas violate his moral sense, turns him into a scold. Without major ideas, he strives to be a major writer.

Gardner could have made a real point: which would have explained why our novelistic vision seems negative, even life-denying. He would have, first, had to establish that such is the case, and it is by no means self-evident. Once established, that position would then need a thick cultural argument to sustain it. Instead, he takes his polemic from thinly argued texts such as Tolstoy's *What Is Art?* and George Steiner's *The Death of Tragedy,* shrill, ill-begotten works in the minor mode, and dismisses the very points that need to be argued. Gardner neglects to mention that the great novelist, in order to sustain his dubious argument, must dismiss Shakespeare; or that Steiner strings together a number of platitudes about tragedy and tragic man, all derivative and stereotypical.

To reestablish a different kind of fiction, his own brand of "moral fiction," Gardner mounts an obligatory attack upon modernism, Freud, and Sartre, and misreads Wittgenstein altogether. He lowers himself to the level of popular reviewers by distorting and/or simplifying every argument. He makes Dante his literary hero, and then comments: "Freud, at least as he is popularly read [the qualification means Gardner is excused to read him at a debased level], would have sought to persuade Dante that he did not really love

Beatrice, nor she him. He saw in her an image of his mother, or, of food: he transferred the physical gratification of suckling at his mother's breast, and his mother's sexual gratification and burden-relief, to the useful misconstruction 'mutual love.' "

Taking up Sartre, Gardner substitutes the names of Dante and Beatrice for the French philosopher's more generalized pronouns in *Being and Nothingness.* Gardner admits that such substitutions are not "scrupulously fair," but goes ahead, moving one context into another, then standing by his analysis. As for Wittgenstein, who is admittedly difficult, Gardner says that he has shown that "language is very tricky."

Gardner then scoops up a generation of writers and links them: "Mobs of contemporary writers—writers very different in other respects—follow Gass [for whom he has some affection] in focusing their attention on language, gathering nouns and verbs the way a crow collects paper clips, sending off their characters to take a long nap." The writers Gardner groups are so varied the list may as well contain Joyce, Beckett, and Proust, all of whom were concerned with the primacy of words. The real villain, obviously, is modernism itself.

Gardner also has his enemies list: Gaddis ("pure meanness"), Pynchon ("intellectual blight," "academic narrowness"), Barth (his later fiction characterized as "puerilely obscene," setting up the possibility of his early fiction as "adultly obscene"), Updike (an example of bourgeois pornography), Heller ("imitates the Satanist's leer" and dodges all moral issues), Bellow (self-indulgent). Through all these blurblike characterizations, Gardner evades his responsibility as a critic, while revealing his own shallowness as a writer. His point should concern the role of moral issues in modern fiction, and the ancillary questions of how language has perhaps usurped such issues, how dislocation has made morality expendable, how inconclusiveness works at cross purposes with any sustained moral vision. These are issues that obviously concern Gardner, and his own work is an attempt to reach through modernism—so as to find soft spots in social, political, and personal terms. That he fails in all his enterprises is not because he needs grander themes, but because he perceives problems in insufficient terms. These critical failures carry over into the fiction, which apotheosizes pastoral as against modernism and its disruptive, disintegrative modes.

Nickel Mountain, begun in 1952, when Gardner was nineteen, spans his early and middle career. When it was published in 1973, Gardner was the author of several other novels—*The Resurrection* (1966), *Grendel* (1971), *The Sunlight Dialogues* (1972)—and therefore it is representative; or else *October Light* (1976) is. Henry Soames, in 1954, is a loser in every way. He runs a diner, but it is a borderline business. He has suffered from heart trouble, is terribly overweight, and is close to a nervous breakdown. He is drifting toward inexorable decline which will lead to both spiritual and physical death. He has nothing to live for, and the area around Batavia, New York, does not provide much moral support, for winners or losers. His chief images, in his diner, are of trucks heading up the local highway, and of Nickel Mountain, whose purity and solitary splendor set off everything below.

The novel explores the "salvation" of Henry; not his spiritual rejuvenation, but the salvation of his wasting life. He is brought back by the appearance in his diner of Caillie Wells, a very young girl who offers to work. Henry takes her in, and a symbiotic attachment forms—he needs her presence as a source of life, she needs him as a surrogate father. When she becomes pregnant with another man's child, Henry insists on marrying her and rearing the child as his own.

As narrative, this sounds familiar. Gardner's aim is to take an ordinary situation and invest it with mysterious events and sensations. Nickel Mountain lies just beyond. Its relationship to the community below is like spirit to physical; like the river in Huck Finn or deer hunting in the film *The Deer Hunter*. Nickel Mountain, however, is only one such "beyond." Gardner introduces Simon Bale, a man of such intense religious vision that he lives outside the pale, more than half maddened. There is also a Goat Lady, who is so closely associated with the goats she travels with that she is indistinguishable from them. Her presence suggests an animal world, a harlequin figure, Hardy's furmity woman, who has passed over to another world. Her cart is drawn by goats, like some classical chariot: "The Goat Lady sat up in front like a midget stage-coach driver or a burlesque of the fiery charioteer, her legs splayed out like an elderly madam's, her skirt hiked up over her dust-specked, yellow-gray thighs, on her head a dusty black bonnet like an Amish woman's."

Gardner works hard—and the prose is a little forced—at conveying sensations to justify the fullness of life. Death must not be given its dominion. Sartre and his ilk must be fought at every turn. George Loomis, despite the crippling of a foot in the Korean War and the loss of an arm in a corn binder, remains

life oriented, a pressure on Henry not to succumb to bad heart, overeating, depression. Henry must reenter his own life, forage around in its wastes, and derive elements of vitality. "So it was that Henry Soames had discovered the holiness of things (his father's phrase), the idea of magical change." "Magical change" means going beyond the all-devouring self; or else extending the self beyond itself to other phenomena.

The main problem with the novel lies in the inadequacy of the connections between the ordinary qualities associated with the characters and the magical elements. Parts are more substantial than the whole. The contraries, once established, are supposed to suffice. Gardner has accepted the fantasies of pastoral as real and has been trapped. For the novelist who offers up pastoral as a resolution, or even an alternative, is cheating us, deceiving himself and us about the nature of Nature. Small-town America, except perhaps in religious communities (Amish, Mormon), is not an outpost against anything, but a frontier town in the middle of a cultural war. It cannot be offered, literarily, as Edenic.*

In *October Light*, the main narrative "experiment" comes in the intertwining of Sally Page's reading in a trashy novel and the line of development associated with her own life, as prisoner of her tyrannical brother, James. She is imprisoned in her room, the result of his attack on all senseless forms of modern life, which she has embraced. These siblings in their dotage become the contrasting elements of modern and past, intermixed with the kind of trashy fiction which represents, for Gardner, the modern cultural response.

The point at issue in Sally's imprisonment, which lasts the entire novel, is her attachment to television and James's hatred of it. He blasts a hole in the set with his shotgun, and then puts his sister in an upstairs room until she repents. James is a fundamentalist in his ideas, although not formally religious. In his Bennington, Vermont, working farm, he peers out at

---

*In a *Bookviews* interview with Ralph Tyler, Gardner tried to dissipate that simplistic sense of rural and pastoral. After praising his parents, he admitted that the country produces as many troubled people as the city. Yet this recognition is not built into his novels, nor is it part of the structure of his moral view. On the contrary, he divides existence into "life" and "death," sides with life, and equates the latter to rural living, pastoral, bucolic self-sufficiency. If Gardner had been able to roughen up this view, create greater counterpoint, he could have offered a more complex vision to accompany much fine prose.

what is a godless, materialistic world. "He'd taken the twelve gauge shotgun to it, three weeks ago now, for its endless, simpering advertising and, worse yet, its monstrously obscene games of greed, the filth of hell made visible in the world: screaming women, ravenous for refrigerators, automobiles, mink coats, ostrich-feather hats; leering glittering-toothed monsters of ceremonies . . . those panderers to lust, and their programs were blasphemy and high treason."

About one-quarter of the book is given over to the novel Sally reads in her upstairs prison. It is about two sets of smugglers, of grass, who meet and join up. Captain Fist (Faust in German) and a black named Luther Santisillia, the leaders of each group, both speak exceptionally well, quote from learned sources, and cite philosophical evidence for their various acts. The novel is a spoof of all kinds of fiction, but mainly of ideas that can be adapted to support terrible crimes. We recall Gardner's remarks on Freud, Sartre, and others in his *On Moral Fiction.* Sally reads the book in spurts, in between her eating of apples (her sole food) and her use of a chamber pot (her sole outlet), which she empties out of her window. First the smugglers try to kill each other, and then almost all of them are killed by an earthquake and a hail of police bullets, in that order. The man who emerges as their guide is Arthur (seeker of the Grail?), who had once tried suicide, only to be saved; and the man who attempts to investigate their activities is in a wheelchair. Intermixed in all this is a young woman who offers herself to either one or to all. Gardner touches all bases.

In the outside world, "October light," like Nickel Mountain before, is transformational. Transformation is essential, for Gardner believes in simple things: a farmer farms, a worker works; life in its essentials counts far more than whatever lies beyond it. Tolstoy's message is repeated: morality lies in working, joining, bringing forth the fruits of the earth. In "October light," the "stones and grass of the pasture turned spiritual in this light, radiating power, as if charged with some old, mystic energy unnamed except in ancient Sumerian or Indian."

The world of James and "October light" somehow saves, whereas the world of Fist dooms. Gardner has made his equation. But its contrasts cannot disguise its simplicities. Through Fist and Luther, Gardner can condemn modern excesses which trammel human freedom; and through James, he can cite basics which we need. But James is as unattractive as Fist, and Gardner's equation leads him into the simple formulas of *On Moral Fiction,* where he argues in literary terms what he poses here in human terms. Despite witty scenes—the gathering in James's house of relatives and friends to draw Sally from her room is very fine—Gardner is caught in a dualism which sucks out meaning, rather than infusing it. In arguing for a transformation through "October light," he reduces, not extends; limits, not expands; binds, not frees.

A very fine addition to American pastoral has been a group of novels about baseball: the game as such, the game as a metaphor for life, the game as a tribute to a passing America—like Brautigan's *Trout Fishing in America,* which adapts fishing to that vanishing America. At least three of these baseball novels have not received their due: Robert Coover's *The Universal Baseball Association,* the finest of the lot; Philip Roth's *The Great American Novel,* which was unjustly dismissed; and Bernard Malamud's *The Natural* (discussed in Chapter One), his auspicious debut as a novelist. To these we add Mark Harris's Henry Wiggen trilogy, *The Southpaw, Bang the Drum Slowly,* and *A Ticket for a Seamstitch,* of which the first is the most substantial.* With these novelistic treatments of a pastoral tradition, we should consider a nonfiction account of the game, the very moving *The Boys of Summer* by Roger Kahn, who showed that the "new journalism" can reflect a sense of America as intensely as fiction.

What all these books have in common is the sense of a lost paradise. Baseball becomes as much an act of memory as the game played out in the present. In no other sport are statistics so essential. At the front of our minds, we recall home run totals, batting averages, rankings in league play, World Series winners, et al., in a way unduplicated in football or basketball. Certain baseball statistics have entered American legend, sunk deep in our archetypal past as part of an Edenic existence. When Roger Maris hit his historic sixty-one home runs in 1961, breaking Babe Ruth's record of sixty in 1927, an asterisk was attached to the figure in the record book. The asterisk indicated that Maris needed 162 games, whereas Ruth accomplished his feat in 154.

Yet the asterisk suggests a world. Ruth's record existed to be broken, of course, but infamy awaited the man who broke it. Ruth's sixty was a magical number, because 1927 was a magical year—it was the moment in the 1920s when America seemed in per-

---

*Still another entry is Jerome Charyn's *The Seventh Babe,* 1979.

fect balance, in sports, finance, political stability. It was the year Lindbergh flew the Atlantic, an event like Ruth's sixty. In our collective memories, 1927 was part of an Eden regained, and Ruth was a key symbol. Even the imperfections of the man helped to support the legend; for Ruth—beer guzzler, womanizer, foul-mouthed, inarticulate—was an unlikely hero, and yet an archetypal American: heir to the loudmouths and braggarts of the tall tale, Mike Fink reincarnate. Maris could not compete here, and except for a spurt here or there, he was quite an average player, finishing with a career average of .260. In 1961, he hit only .269; Ruth in the year of his sixty homers hit .356 and had a career average of .342.

The asterisk pointed to an altered America, in which 162 games made up a different kind of season, somehow less meaningful than the earlier 154. No one, of course, pointed out that to compensate for those eight additional games, Maris had to hit against night lights, had to travel more, faced more long doubleheaders—all of which were heavy penalties for a hitter to pay. Yet those disadvantages were not so significant as the fact that a legendary and Edenic memory had been shattered, and the asterisk was there to remind us that the legend not only remained untouched, but was, in fact, besmirched by the man who broke the record.

Baseball, basically a spring and summer game, is associated with the revival of life—our one sustained summer activity. It is played, in the main, only in good weather; and that dimension, together with spatiality, is part of its Edenic presence. "Spring training" is itself a time of renewal, when stiff muscles and bones are revived for the long season. Inevitably, the game is a nostalgia trip, but also a more serious journey into a vernal memory. Our baseball novels all exploit and explore these possibilities, although all four novels turn the "real game" into forms of legend and magic. Baseball becomes totemic. Wonderboy, the magical bat of Malamud's Roy Hobbs, so deeply rooted in the natural, is the game itself.

Robert Coover's *The Universal Baseball Association: J. Henry Waugh, Prop.* (1968) is related generically and thematically to the war and combat novel, even though the term of reference is baseball. But just as war becomes a metaphor for an even larger sense of life in Mailer, Burns, Heller, and Jones, so baseball for Coover carries us deeply into American dream and reality, Eden and doom, choice and destiny. The brilliance of Coover's formulation lies in the fact that his baseball association is not the real one of our national pastime, but the product of Henry Waugh's

imagination. He has imagined, or reimagined, the game in his room; and its intensity is, for him, far greater than the real game. Coover was, in a sense, writing a political novel of the 1960s; and we can read the book not only as a gloss on America in general but on America in the sixties in particular.

The central metaphor of the novel is the playing off of Henry Waugh's game versus the real one, which assumes a shadowy existence. He comments on this, saying that his time at the ball park was unhappy, whereas his time at home on his own records was fulfilling. "I found out the scorecards were enough. I didn't need the game."* The "games" Henry does need are those he manufactures out of three dice, which, when rolled, relate to various charts that take into consideration every possibility that baseball can provide—from stealing home to being killed by a pitched ball, from winning a batting championship to killing the pitcher with a batted ball. His baseball lies outside the real world, yet touches it at every point. The tragic moment—and it is quite touching—comes when Henry recognizes that his roll of the dice, triple 1's, will lead to the beaning death of Damon Rutherford, whose career was destined for greatness; the young man beaned, in fact, on the very day his father, Brock, was being honored.

The "sacrifice" of Damon—and Henry is tempted to tamper with the dice to prevent the tragedy—is a political statement, apparently about Kennedy, Johnson, Vietnam, the country. The sacrifice of the "best and brightest," those condemned to death by a cast of the dice, leads, eventually, to a cult of Damonites,

---

*In a magical paragraph, Roger Angell deifies the box score: "The box score, being modestly arcane, is a matter of intense indifference, if not irritation, to the non-fan. To the baseball-bitten, it is not only informative, pictorial, and gossipy but lovely in aesthetic structure. It represents happenstance and physical flight exactly translated into figures and history. Its totals—batters' credit vs. pitchers' debit—balance as exactly as those in an accountant's ledger. And a box score is more than a capsule archive. It is a precisely etched miniature of the sport itself, for baseball, in spite of its grassy spaciousness and apparent unpredictability, is the most intensely and satisfyingly mathematical of all our outdoor sports. Every player in every game is subjected to a cold and ceaseless accounting; no ball is thrown and no base is gained without an instant responding judgment—ball or strike, hit or error, yea or nay—and an ensuing statistic. This encompassing neatness permits the baseball fan, aided by experience and memory, to extract from a box score the same joy, the same hallucinatory reality, that prickles the scalp of a musician when he glances at a page of his score of *Don Giovanni* and actually hears bassos and sopranos, woodwinds and violins."

a mythology which is itself far removed from reality. Coover is moving, sometimes heavily, into deeper American themes. The game fits the larger American sense of doom and chance, destiny and play, death and opportunity. Implicit in every choice for recognition and gain is the throw of the dice—Mallarmé's "a throw of the dice will never abolish chance"; but added to that, the American's dictum that a throw of the dice is part of chance.

Henry's game has as its locale a diamond, but greater than the baseball diamond, since it is the legendary diamond of the imagination, Yeats's "great-rooted blossomer." When Henry tries to introduce his friend Lou to the Association, the game loses all its flavor; that diamond only sparkles when Henry can imagine it, apart from other people. Every play, player, record, score, hit, win, error, loss, season standing—each depends on his "move" with the dice. His cast, once translated into his charts, becomes the history of the game, from year 1 past its centennial. Since Henry plays out a season in six weeks or so, in a given year he can work through eight or more seasons. Godlike, he regulates seasons. That diamond in his head is truly Edenesque in its perfection—although fraught with tragedy as well as triumph—and yet too frail to sustain external intrusion.

By working with "diamonds," Henry has tried to achieve the perfect phenomenological experience: to ingest all data into his mind, and there to reform it according to his own rules. Coover has, in fact, taken the national pastime and turned it into an art form, a reflection of Henry's imagination. Although the model for his game is the existing game, nevertheless by throwing the dice he has intruded himself into pure chance. Coover's plan is diabolically clever. For Henry has at once added to and taken away from the real game in the process, transforming *it* into *his*.

Eventually, the game possesses him. The coolness and objectivity of earlier years give way to passions Henry cannot control. The death of Damon from Casey's beanball never leaves his mind, and he desires revenge. By turning over one die to a 6 (the other two are already 6's), he can have Casey killed by a batted ball, from Royce Ingram, Damon's former battery mate. Balance in the world means a death for a death; possibly Johnson for a generation of youths, America for Vietnam. The gods will be avenged, Henry appeased.

With that act of manipulation, things go awry— Henry's relationship to the Association, the standings, all the noise and excitement. The game settles down to silence. Eventually, in future time, the parti-sans of the game divide into parties, Damonites versus Universalists, later called Caseyites; a Universal Baseball Association chancellor is assassinated; there is a full revolt. The Association, honored in history, begins to come apart, like the country. Some "are saying that Damonism is a perversion and a tyranny, while others say the original Damonites had the truth, but have been betrayed by opportunity; others . . . hold that power itself is proof they are still in the right." The game has become apocalyptic in its implications, because it and life cannot be separated, as Henry Waugh thought they could be. What he played out in his imagination is now a mythology with its own rules and stresses. A religion has sprung up around what was once a throw of the dice which established chance. Damon is, as it were, reborn, to remind us that there is still the game, that it is preferable to life, that it must go on. "Play ball."

Coover's novel is so American in its idea and development that one hesitates to look for a non-American source; but Hermann Hesse's *Magister Ludi* is an obvious model. In the Hesse novel (also called *The Bead Game*), the "play" (the *spiel* in the German title, *Das Glasperlenspiel*) involves a bead game whose philosophical complexities touch upon every aspect of life; become, in fact, a parallel of existence. Coover's novel is too brief to be this ambitious an undertaking; but the idea is comparable. Role-playing, the Edenic locale on which the game is played (that perfect diamond), its triumphs and tragedies, its openness to chance and destiny, its proximity to human feelings and yet its distance, its self-consciousness and self-indulgence—all of these parallel life in the 1960s. Once more reflecting the decade, Coover constructed an America of the pastoral imagination, an Arcadian potential, preferable to the real thing. But it is only temporary, a stopgap. Pastoral dreams cannot take hold. The game, like all else, begins to decline. Henry's sheets are stained by beer and pizza, he stops keeping accurate records, and his efforts pass into mythology, which end an era even as they portend another. That "imaginary" America of the sixties is the dream of the Garden, a timeless past made possible by a throw of the dice, a frontier miracle based on chance. In a related dimension, Coover has cut Henry Waugh off from history; when he plays his game alone in his room, he organizes space/time. The sole space is the diamond before him, men moving around, charts on the wall. The only time is Henry's manipulation of the seasons, without reference to real time, in which games and seasons pass. This, too, is Arcadian, that stepping outside time, even while one is responsible to destiny. Lou's intrusion is like Eve's into Adam's world: the latter's desire for company leading to resentment that perfection has been destroyed. Lou spills over into the real world, and Henry wants him out. The game is the thing! The 1960s flatten out before us.

In Philip Roth's *The Great American Novel* (1973), one question we ask immediately to understand his strategy is: How is this novel connected to the early 1970s, or the late 1960s? What cultural context does this strange fiction fit into or try to accommodate itself to?

Roth's conception of the "great American novel" is baseball. An alternative organization to the two major leagues is the Patriot League, composed of teams like the Ruppert Mundys (the focus of the novel) and the Tri-City Tycoons; cities like Kakoola, Aceldama, and Asylum. The great star of baseball was not Ruth, Cobb, or Gehrig, but Luke Gofannon, who played for the Ruppert Mundys in his prime. And the singer of the Ruppert Mundys' epic is Word Smith, an octogenarian, self-appointed historian of America's past, who begins his tale with a prologue comparable, he feels, to Hawthorne's Custom House section of *The Scarlet Letter*.

This is "a glorious epic of failure," for the Ruppert Mundys are a dismal team as Word Smith limns their fortunes during the war years. Roth mixes his mythical team with real names; and in many ways, if we project, the Mundys of the 1940s are comparable to the Mets of the early 1960s. They finish in last place by fifty games, lose by lopsided scores, their play in the field is as dismal as at bat. Their one undeniably great player, Roland Agni, wants to be traded, for his career with the Mundys is in limbo.

How, then, does any of this fit its cultural context? Much of the novel is, in fact, a throwback to the 1940s —for the mise-en-scène, but also for the beginning of domestic Communist purges. Yet the feel of the book has that dualism of energy and exhaustion which characterized the early 1970s, when expenditure and depletion seemed to crest simultaneously. Word Smith's attempt to call up the greatness of baseball— "Call me Smitty," he begins—by pegging his story to America's great pastoral epics of whales, Mississippi rafts, and Puritan witch hunts, is defeated by conventional forces. His appeals for recognition to Mr. Bowie Kuhn, Commissioner of Baseball, and to other officials are all ignored; he is humored, and dismissed. Thus, his great tale of an alternative life, another league of cities, teams, stars, and yearnings, is forgotten except by him, and Luke Gofannon, the greatest of them all, will never make it into the Cooperstown Hall of Fame.

By way of this greatly expanded tall tale, the distinctive genre of the novel, Roth was attempting to capture that sense of waste the early 1970s suggested. What had been great in the country, the conflicts and vitality of the 1960s, the vain attempts to regain Arcadia, was dissipated, dismissed, lost forever. The Patriot League eventually becomes an ideological battleground, between those who see it infiltrated by Communist agents and those who want to manipulate it in other ways. Whatever the interests of the participants, the great American game became an extension of Washington's paranoia. The legendary pitcher Gil Gamesh—banished from the league a decade ago for having thrown a baseball at an umpire's windpipe and cutting off his voice—has emerged as the manager of the Ruppert Mundys. Gamesh, whose claim to Babylonian heritage is as suspect as Yossarian's to Assyrian, is not, however, what he seems, but a highly placed Soviet agent.

He is only one element infiltrating the team. Several of the Mundys players, none of whom could even locate the Soviet Union on a map, are accused of foreign collaboration, spying, acts of espionage; and their failures in the field are attributed to their undermining of the American system. "On instruction from Moscow Astarte [a French Canadian, not the goddess of fertility] dropped the pop fly in the last of the ninth of the last game of the '42 season, the error that cost the Mundys a tie for seventh and set the stage for the expulsion from Port Ruppert"—the Mundys must play an entire season on the road.

The game is contaminated. The game is, also, a shadow game, a mirror of the culture at large, baseball as America. A one-armed player recalls Pete Gray; Frank Mazuma stages spectacles during pregame ceremonies that recall the antics of Bill Veeck; a fourteen-year-old player, the size of a jockey, reminds us of Joe Nuxhall, the fifteen-year-old pitcher for the Cincinnati Reds; and two midgets, one who never swings his bat, the other who pitches so low nobody can hit him, recall Veeck's stunt in putting a midget at bat. But behind the players are other elements which go behind baseball, to ideology, social struggles, racial matters. For potential in the 1940s is the introduction of a black player; also, the presence of a Jewish owner.

Roth's use of the Jewish owner of the Tri-City Greenbacks is very witty, and part of the wittiness is that he plays on every anti-Semitic stereotype. The owner is tight, he lives in the scoreboard to save money, his wife babies the players with warm clothes and hot tea, he is anti-black—as much as everyone else in the league is anti-Semitic—and he speaks with a comic's Yiddish accent. His son, Isaac Ellis, a scientific genius, wants to become manager of the team so that he can apply his own theories of percentage baseball to the game. Toward that end, he has "Jewish Wheaties" secretly put in the food of the Mundys, and it proves a magic elixir. Truly possessed, they perform prodigious feats and win by enormous scores. Jewish science applied to the American pastime could transform it!

The novel is brilliantly clever, but parts are like comic set pieces in a Yiddish vaudeville show, connected only by threads. Word Smith's presentation is mind boggling in the early pages—a barrage of words like a Shakespearean prologue in a foreign language. Roth's epigraph is from Frank Norris, that "the Great American Novel is not extinct like the Dodo, but mythical like the Hippogriff." Roth works mightily to convey that mythical quality, and his beginning with a near-mythical Word Smith is an attempt to reach back deep into the American past so as to haul out what is still the great novel, the great game, the great play, Emerson's sense of the country. No one, however, wants to listen, and rightfully so, for Smith's story can knock you out with his prologue, his display of verbal ingenuity that almost deadens all. Most reviewers went little further, and missed out on a fine fictional experience. The Great American Novel, the game of baseball, is passing on, as Word Smith and his relationship to the past, to Melville, Twain, Hawthorne, is also vanishing. Baseball, in the early 1940s, is a shadow of the culture of the 1970s, already turning counterfeit.

For all our writers, baseball *when played*—not the individual players, not the time spent between games, not the life behind the player—is the reenactment of a regained paradise. In Mark Harris's *The Southpaw* (1953), Henry Wiggen writes: "Give me a baseball in my hand and I know where I am at. Give me a piece of machinery and I may be more or less in the dark. Give me a book and I am lost. Give me a map and I cannot make heads or tails, nor I could no more learn another language than pitch with my nose."

The baseball field becomes something special, where Henry Wiggen and his kind have magical powers. Like Malamud's "Natural" with his Wonderboy, Henry has his magic arm. Within the realm of the field and within the restrictions of the game, Henry

extends toward infinity, toward that world of command possessed by the true artist. Off field, he falters, as he explains in a "pastoral language" that imitates Twain's in his Sawyer and Finn novels. We can, in fact, see Harris's Wiggen trilogy—*The Southpaw, Bang the Drum Slowly* (1956), and *A Ticket for a Seamstitch* (1956)—as related to the family of novels suggested by *Sawyer* and *Finn.*

The game of baseball permits all forms of nostalgia; for it approximates, for the youngster growing up, a world apart or elsewhere. With its fairly easy play, its lobbing of the ball, its fungo hitting and workouts, spring training is part of a Garden existence. Henry feels his body singing in training: "I could of shouted and sung, for I felt so good. Did you ever feel that way? Did you ever look down yourself, and you was all brown wherever your skin was out in the sun, and you was all loose in every bone and every joint of your body, and there was not a muscle that ached, and you felt like if there was a mountain that needed moving you could up and move it, or you could of swam an ocean or held your breath an hour if you liked, or you could run 2 miles and finish in a sprint?"

If one's talent is sure, as Henry's is, then one becomes indeed God's favorite. Powers emanate out, from the infinite to the individual; and these powers can be demonstrated for the delight and wonderment of crowds. Epics and myths are created on the green field, comparable to great battles in history. All eyes focus on Henry's arm. A southpaw is a rarity to begin with, since baseball is mainly for right-handed players. Many positions are out of the question for a left-hander; pitching is one of the few remaining. But even here, a team needs more right-handed than left-handed pitching. "Southpaw" in itself denotes someone off center, marching to a different drummer, unique.

The paradise, however, is not perfect. It can be a dispossessed Garden.* Henry beans a player early in his major league career, and the player's face is badly smashed; he will eventually be sent down to the minors, where he will do badly, whereas Henry will sail on. It is a minor imperfection, but a harbinger of what life is really like. During his first season, which is sensationally successful, Henry develops a back problem; so that he must work on the mound against constant pain, and even attempt to alter his delivery.

Bang the Drum Slowly, with its tale of a dying ballplayer, at times a dying god, has all the elements of a spoiled Garden, a corrupted Eden.

Even while he scales the heights toward the Hall of Fame, he is made conscious of his mortality.

Other elements begin to taint Henry. He is reprimanded by Holly, his girl friend and then wife, for moving slowly into corruption; in his indecent desire to win at all costs, he loses his innocence. Leo Durocher's "Nice guys finish last" is the supreme ideology. He throws a spitter, gets away with it, but knows that its dipsy-doodle flight can deceive the batter and seriously injure him. His use of the spitter is connected to his enthrallment by Miss Moors, who runs the ball club and uses her seductive wiles to get her way.

Miss Moors—the wealthy owner of the Mammoths (a composite of the Giants and the Yankees) —recalls the witch Memo, who does in Roy Hobbs in *The Natural;* whereas Holly recalls Iris, who tries to save him. The paradisiacal dimension is recreated, with Miss Moors the serpent of temptation, Holly a steady Eve. Holly's Arcadian name, like Iris's, suggests she will remain true; and she not only tries to keep Henry honest, she also attempts to educate him, to make him a person. Holly here, Iris in Malamud: women sacrifice themselves for their men, in order to counterbalance women who are witches with men. Simple equations almost collapse the respective novels. Yet stereotypes aside, baseball remains in the world of wonder. The realm of the unique southpaw prevails on the diamond.

In *The Boys of Summer* (1973), Roger Kahn takes his theme and title from Dylan Thomas's lovely lines: "I see the boys of summer in their ruin / Lay the gold tithings barren, / Setting no store by harvest, freeze the souls." These lines, in turn, recall to us A. E. Housman's memorial lines to various Shropshire lads; and the juxtaposition, inevitably, of baseball wars and war, which leaches out youth, is not inappropriate. For Kahn's theme is no less than a form of paradise gained, then lost, in equal proportions.

The few years those Brooklyn Dodgers, the boys of summer, spend in baseball exhaust their youth; once that youth is depleted by the baseball wars, they sink back into obscurity. Nothing is sadder than how, for most, their second lives—the longer part by far— are so removed from the first. They are fallen heroes, lying in the dust, barely names to the public after those great moments in Ebbets Field as pitchers, fielders, hitters.

Like the four novelists, Kahn is writing seriously about America, and of the four—possibly because he has the advantage of a real team in a real time and place—he comes closest to human tragedy, American style. Only Coover approaches him in this respect. For American tragedy must always be measured in how one's youth is spent, how that youth measures up against certain ideals, and then how it further measures up against oneself once youth is expended. Tragedy in America, unlike that in European writing, is not only about a fall in personal terms; it concerns a fall from certain ideals of achievement or success. Kahn's book gains its grandeur from that consciousness of possibility which he brings to the subject; so that he is not ashamed to observe baseball as associated with the Edenic past that exists so vividly in American thought. For while terrible things are occurring outside of Ebbets Field—the cold war, the rise of Joseph McCarthy, Dulles's brinkmanship ploys, the surrender of Eisenhower to right-wing ideologues—the game itself takes us out of ourselves into a finer existence. There, war has all the grander aspects of War.

Kahn traveled with the Dodgers in 1952 and 1953 and wrote for the New York *Herald Tribune.* Like Tom Wicker, in his superb *A Time to Die,* Kahn makes his own changing consciousness part of the unfolding drama. He comes to the Dodgers as a very young man, green in almost every way—a rookie trying out his skills. Furthermore, when he writes this book twenty years later, the Dodgers are no longer a Brooklyn team, the *Herald Tribune* has gone under, Kahn's own personal life has undergone radical changes, and the Dodgers he wrote of, those "boys of summer," have dispersed into the wintry corners of Indiana, Ohio, and Arkansas. The lean, whiplash figure of Preacher Roe, who had a three-year won-lost record of 44 and 8, has ballooned to 223 pounds.

The greatest of all the boys of summer is Jackie Robinson. Here is, for Kahn, but not for many of Robinson's teammates, a true hero for our times. For when Branch Rickey brought Robinson up for the 1947 season and introduced a black into major league baseball, the full tragic potentialities of America became apparent.* The introduction of Robinson recreated in 1947 a Civil War situation; for as the roll call of the team goes on, we recognize that, like the army, baseball was populated by Southerners. It was meat and potatoes for poor boys from poverty regions, and the arrival of blacks meant that competition for each position would become bitterly based on color lines.

---

*For many players, baseball became a dispossessed Garden, a Garden traduced by the imperfections of a black player.

Some Dodgers could adapt—Peewee Reese, at shortstop, was a leader in this respect, a quiet hero of sorts. Preacher Roe, while not a leader, treated Robinson like a man. Dixie Walker, the bravo of so many late Dodger rallies, said he would not play alongside a black and was traded a year later. Entire teams in the league threatened to secede. The St. Louis Cardinals were warned by the league president that if they struck, they would all be suspended.

At the center of this was Robinson, Kahn's Clyde Griffiths, the man striving to get it all for himself and in doing so becoming a legend. We could argue that the 1954 Supreme Court decision in *Brown* v. *Education,* striking down school segregation, as well as a host of other pro-black decisions, received its impulse from Robinson's breakthrough in the late 1940s. What gives Robinson tragic status, however, is not only being first, but his magnificence under pressure, his greatness under taunts, threats, beanballs, spikings; then following that intense career, his subsequent life when black youths accused him of Tomism.

In both 1952 and 1953, the Dodgers won the pennant but lost to the Yankees in the World Series. While the Yankees went on winning, the Dodgers missed out, as they missed the pennant in 1951, when Bobby Thomson hit his historic playoff home run in the ninth. The Dodgers did not fall into the lap of paradise, as the Yankees seemed to do. They had to claw their way in. And while the Yankees would not have a black player until 1954, the Dodgers dared themselves, the league, the game itself by moving toward a half-black team, with Robinson, Campanella, Joe Black, Gilliam, Newcombe, and others.

Kahn is always conscious of this movement; it is an essential element of the paradise motif. For even as baseball dawdled on moral issues, a great moment had arrived: Robinson was a god of sorts (Kahn calls him "The Lion at Dusk"). A black in baseball meant more than integration of the sport; it involved integrated trains, hotels, restaurants. Its message spread out into every aspect of society, including desegregation of crowds at all games—so that large parts of the population were affected.

Here is Kahn's great theme. And he places himself right in the ideological middle. Jewish, middle class, entering a new career as a baseball writer, he discovers a moment when life holds together and the Dodgers reenter paradise. The inevitable fall was implicit in the moment: boys pass, summer passes. Pastoral fantasies, dreams not only of glory but of our mythical paradisiacal existence, heroic moments of youth— all will give way to Robinson and his heart attacks,

Hodges also a heart victim, Campanella a paraplegic from an automobile crash, Furillo in hard-hat obscurity, Cox tending bar in racist territory, Erskine watching carefully over his Mongoloid son, Robinson and Hodges dead as the book ends. Only Joe Black, the great reliever, seems to have found balance. Joe Black kept his wits, used his intelligence, worked his way through the myths, did not live entirely off the past, and maintained stability. But except for him, the glory was moments, before the expulsion. The rest was the Fall.

Beyond baseball, pastoral can readily lend itself to other forms of fantasy—as in Peter S. Beagle's *The Last Unicorn* (1968), Richard Brautigan's *Trout Fishing in America* (1967), and Truman Capote's *The Grass Harp* (1951). Or it can accommodate Eudora Welty, a celebrant of rural life, a tester of the individual against rural exigencies. In her work, pastoral finds its most traditional expression, as in the classical Greek poets who first explored the genre of "nature writing."

In Beagle's *The Last Unicorn,* the legendary animal is the final version of perfection, a remnant of paradise and our earlier existence. Symbolic of purity, the companion of virgins, the unicorn recalls prelapsarian man; it suggests not only the perfect creature but the perfect place. That it is "the last unicorn" suggests the recurring American theme of Eden approaching its demise. The last unicorn cannot mate, since no mate exists, and yet she is immortal—here is the paradox of an American fate. She recalls a work of art, a beauty that is immortal, yet a finality. Beagle writes: "Unicorns are immortal. It is their nature to live alone in one place: usually a forest [thus, it becomes part of our "hut dream"] where there is a pool clear enough for them to see themselves [Narcissus]—for they are a little vain, knowing themselves to be the most beautiful creatures in all the world, and magic besides. They mate very rarely, and no place is more enchanted than the one where a unicorn has been born."

Beagle's story of this final act of nature becomes an allegory of America in the 1960s, a working out of our traditions, attitudes, and identity as part of a pastoral fantasy, extinction facing us. Brautigan's *Trout Fishing in America* picks up a similar idea, but rather than agree to the "final" or "last" image, fantasizes an America in which every activity takes us close to trout fishing, which is its own kind of perfection. What throws Brautigan's story off balance as an American fantasy is that it is completely male, and his companion is "his woman"—"my woman" is her name—their child "his child." The male possessiveness blunts the visionary quality, since the vision seems to belong to only half of the population: the other half is owned.

Trout Fishing is, nevertheless, both ingenious and evocative. The book comprises a series of brief episodes, a minimalist journey: essentially a dialogue between the narrator and a character named Trout Fishing in America. The latter is not only an activity but an embodiment, a direction, a way of American life. It is the pastoral side of the narrator's experience, first as a child, then as an adult.

Early on, Brautigan tells of when he first heard of Trout Fishing in America, from a drunk, in 1942, when the narrator was a child. The drunk described trout as if they were a precious metal; silver at first comes to mind, although it is not quite right. "I'd like to get it right. Maybe trout steel. Steel made from trout. The clean snow-filled river acting as foundry and heat. Imagine Pittsburgh. A steel that comes from trout, used to make buildings, trains and tunnels. The Andrew Carnegie of Trout!"

The basic image for the book is there; trout and trout fishing as the emblem of the America that lies behind achievement, ambition, and possession (except of "my woman"). It is the Huck Finn in all of us, but especially in the child growing into adulthood in the sixties. Trout Fishing is not only the alter ego or double of the narrator, it is the double, actual and potential, of all life in America. As trout fishing becomes increasingly difficult—encroachments are everywhere—the narrator describes, late in the book, the sale of trout stream footage. "Used Trout Stream for Sale. Must be Seen to Be Appreciated," reads a big sign at a Family Gift Center. One can buy the stream by the foot, along with associated items like waterfalls, trees, birds, flowers, grass, ferns, and animals. Insects are given away free. Stream is $6.50/foot, for the first 100 feet, thereafter $5/foot; birds are, of course, additional. Animals are now rare, but flowers are still abundant and there are a few trout left in the stream. One takes one's chances. Eden is not readily recoverable.

One of the most evocative episodes occurs in a school, where the sixth graders become "trout fishing in America terrorists." The sixth graders use white chalk to mark "Trout Fishing in America" on the backs of the first graders, missing only one, who spent the period in the lavatory. Yet the sixth graders cannot escape the system so easily: trout fishing has its other side: authority, order, discipline. Their principal is a man who arranges order benevolently, not dictatorially. He calls in the perpetrators and goes "into his famous $E=MC^2$ sixth-grade gimmick, the thing he always used in dealing with us." He argues how order is maintained, and how each level of society depends on the good sense of the one beneath it. Would they like it, he asks, if the teachers had "Trout Fishing in America" on their backs, if he had it on his? That won't do, they all agree, and gradually it is washed from the clothing.

The narrator takes his small son everywhere, getting him acquainted with Trout Fishing in America, but by the time he grows up, perhaps only footage, not entire streams, will remain. Trout Fishing, however, is not only trout and fishing; it is food, ingredients, isolation, marginal life. What passes with Trout Fishing is the end of the era, the end of the Edenic myth. The sixties witnessed an attempt to recall those times, to seek out contemporary "doubles" of those times. Trout Fishing is just that.

Because her work settles so solidly within a reasonable version of pastoral, Eudora Welty hardly fits into a scheme of postwar novelists. She recalls earlier lives and earlier worlds, the organic community Emerson foresaw as a duplication of that "first place," to become the model for all life in America. Without becoming philosophical about nature, Welty has attempted to demonstrate that such forms of pastoral have timeless values which touch every life coexistent with it.

In *Losing Battles* (1970), a family clan gathers for the ninetieth birthday of Granny Vaughn. Her children, grandchildren, and great-grandchildren, as well as friends and townspeople, come to celebrate; and it is as if the entire country were coming together, since Granny's life spans several eras. Once gathered, they tell and retell tales, stories of their own and others' losing battles, an aural orgy. But lost or not, the battles indicate life met on its own terms, as part of an organic community. Voices drone on and on, regional accents piled on regional accents, stories blending, family members somewhat indistinguishable, a cast of characters that recalls *War and Peace* in length and diversity; yet behind it all is insistence on a timeless life, a pastoral existence which, whatever loss it may have entailed, allowed for a community of interests.

Welty's entire distinguished career can be perceived as having been organized around this idea. She breaks out of regionalism by virtue of her sharply observed, rarely sentimentalized sense of how pastoral values shape and reshape individual or family lives. Like so many of her contemporaries among Southern writers, she must counter modernism, not stridently but with a balancing set of values: scars.

The Optimist's Daughter (1972) is almost a paradigm of this Welty dialectic. Laurel McKelva, a designer in Chicago, returns to New Orleans, where her father is to undergo a routine eye operation. Even as the eye improves, however, Judge McKelva dies, from unforeseen complications. The Judge's second wife, Fay, a woman of about forty (Laurel is forty-one), is silly, self-centered, without regard for the past or the finer points of the present. She lives self-indulgently, full of affectations, deceptive (about background, relatives), directionless.

Laurel has the Judge's body returned to the ancestral home, a small, self-enclosed town in Mississippi, Mount Salus. Laurel, herself a widow, having been married to an apparently fine man who went down on a ship during the war, is brought back to her beginnings, enabled to recover what she was and manifestly still is, under the big-city veneer.

Welty's purpose, like Faulkner's in many respects, is the recovery of the Old South through memory and history. This comes about by way of one who has "escaped," who must return for some reason, and in that return confront herself and all those who did not escape. The drama is archetypal, closely associated with the expulsion from the Garden. Laurel McKelva —her name suggests her quest for Arcadia—must undergo some wrench or loss, or else become anonymous. The death of the Judge cannot be a wasted event, unconnected to the world in which she grew up. By way of memory, she relives private history: ontogeny recapitulates phylogeny.

Welty will not let the history of the South, her South, die. However provincial, even claustrophobic, it is immanent even in those who leave it. That rediscovery of the Old South through memory, that recapitulation of its history as a form of vital existence, is necessary for Welty so as to counterbalance directionless, dislocated urban life. Someone like Fay, who tries to straddle both worlds, has in fact left behind the small town without being able to deal emotionally and intellectually with life beyond. As such, she is ineffective, willful, infantile in her demands.*

---

*In *The Ponder Heart,* Fay has a precursor in Bonnie Dee Peacock, a toylike girl who moves outside any real culture. Her existence is emblematic of what occurs when modern elements enter the Garden experience.

Laurel has successfully bridged the two worlds, but Welty does not accept the urban hold upon Laurel; she insists, rather, on Laurel's recognition of Mount Salus (the ancient Roman goddess of prosperity, also identified with the goddess Hygeia) as the connecting point, the door leading to well-being and stability. In Mount Salus, even Fay is treated decently, and the return of the Judge's body is celebrated as a true homecoming. Instead of weeping, there is a ritualization of the human spirit. Mount Salus is home, a Mount Olympus for the lesser gods.

Once the burial has taken place, Laurel spends a long weekend in the family home. The "optimist's daughter" seeks the source of her father's spirit, communes with the spirit of her mother, Becky, with her own dead Phil, and searches for that optimism which circulated in the air of a modest house in Mount Salus. She rummages through desks and her father's books, discovers his letters to her mother, even her grandmother's letters. This *is* history, and her communion with the past is complete. With the aid of the old servant Missouri, she brings the house back to life, temporarily, by way of artifacts of the past. "There was nothing she was leaving in the whole shining and quiet house now to show for her mother's life and her mother's happiness and suffering, and nothing to show for Fay's harm; her father's turning between them, holding onto them both, then letting them go, was without any sign."

But the fragile balance of the house is not to be. For the showdown must come between Laurel and Fay, who distrust and despise each other. The issue is a breadboard, Becky's old breadboard (made by Laurel's husband), which she used for baking and kept immaculate. It is now scored, battered, streaked, the result of Fay's hammer blows and cigarette burns. It becomes the issue: how life is to be lived, how one uses objects, how balance is struck between human needs and the uses made of objects. Reverence is called for in certain areas; and desecration can be accomplished as much in the home as in the church.

Fay's life has simply not "taught her how to feel." Fay is part of the Snopes complex, people who struggle with life and foul their nests wherever they are. "For Fay was Becky's own dread. What Becky had felt, and had been afraid of, might have existed right here in the house all the time, for her. Past and future might have changed places, in some convulsion of the mind, but that could do nothing to impugn the truth of the heart. Fay could have walked in early as well as late, she could have come at any time at all. She was coming."

But even if Fay is Becky's fate, ten years after her death, then the breadboard, that fine piece of carpentry, made true, fitted, is Laurel's fate. For with the breadboard, she can hold together memory and history in some balance with her present life back in Chicago. It is "the whole story. . . . the whole solid past." Laurel half-heartedly starts to strike Fay with it, puts it down, and then recovers herself; the board is sacred, not a weapon. Since the past is frozen in time, "and can never be awakened," it is "memory that is the somnambulist. It will come back in its wounds from across the world. . . . It will never be impervious." With that recognition of memory as joining material, Laurel can give up even the breadboard. "Memory lived not in initial possession but in the freed hands, pardoned and freed, and in the heart that can empty but fill again, in the patterns restored by dreams."

Actualization of memory, dreams, and personal history gives Laurel the strength to leave; she is not evading or escaping, but taking with her what is essential. Chicago will be different. She will continue to design her way into a successful career, but intermixed with that will be something more essential, that touch and memory of the breadboard. An object has been transformed from an artifact into human life. With Laurel's departure from Mount Salus, waved out by the goodbyes of first graders, she has come full cycle. Her life in Chicago is not a rebirth, for her true rebirth occurred in her visit home. Death has energized her, given her optimism, and she can return to the modern world ready to confront it. Unlike Orpheus, who is destroyed by looking back, she has made the journey back as a form of discovery.

The first paragraph of Welty's *Delta Wedding* (1945) suggests how the life of this region, the Mississippi Delta, is integrated. Despite the presence of the railroad, life remains traditional and patterned, with little intrusion from the modern spirit. The railroad, in fact, is accommodated, its local nickname serving to take the edge off its functional name. The paragraph is a masterpiece of coherent life:

> The nickname of the train was the Yellow Dog. Its real name was the Yazoo-Delta. It was a mixed train. The day was the 10th of September, 1923—afternoon. Laura McRaven [an avatar of Laurel McKelva in *The Optimist's Daughter*], who was nine years old, was on her first journey alone. She was going up from Jackson to visit her mother's people, the Fairchilds, at their plantation near Shellmound, at Fairchilds,

Mississippi. When she got there, "Poor Laura, little motherless girl," they would all run out and say, for her mother had died in the winter and they had not seen Laura since the funeral. Her father had come as far as Yazoo City with her and put her on the Dog. Her cousin Dabney Fairchild, who was seventeen, was going to be married, but Laura could not be in the wedding for the reason that her mother was dead. Of these facts the one most persistent in Laura's mind was the most intimate one: that her age was nine.

The novel takes a familiar pattern: a small child watches all manner of behavior in the adult world, which does not quite register because she is too young. She is, then, like James's Maisie or Elizabeth Bowen's Portia, although what she sees is basically comic, with tragic elements intermixed. She perceives not only adult perfidy, but the whole fabric of Southern society, the focus being the marriage of the Fairchild girl, the prettiest of the clan. It is a clan affair, a tribal custom being performed, and it is made up of insiders. Such a celebration could never occur in the city, for it requires not only a halcyon time, 1923, but a rooted place. Everything external is excluded; so that Laura's very presence is foreign. That marriage is a moment fixed in time and space, an Edenic moment indeed. Although several members of the extended Fairchild family have "fallen," all is forgiven in the celebration, a kind of secular mass.

What Welty has forged in this brief novel is a panoramic view of the Old South, an integrated society which has exchanged black slaves for black servants; the old plantation for the new landed property; Civil War disruption and chaos for an ordered, Edenic existence. Insofar as modern ideas have not penetrated, this part of the Delta has returned to prebellum South. Welty has revived the old pastoral Eden, without the stain of slave chattel—a benevolent, carefully wrought society in which the "good Negro" still does his work, but without the contamination of a slave culture. The novel balances for only the briefest time; for its moment passes into the next one, when we begin to think. Then we recognize that the Delta, no less than the earthly paradise, is, in the main, fantasy.

In *The Ponder Heart* (1954), Welty demonstrates that the Southern pastoral ideal *is* fading. Snopses are everywhere, and the town of Clay is slowly being turned to concrete. The highway has altered life—the intrusion of the modern element—turning a sleepy place into a municipality where people roar in and out at ninety miles an hour. Such people want a room that minute, or ask what there is for dinner; and they are not a class of people "you'd care to spend the rest of your life with at all."

This class of people is never defined—neither Jews nor blacks nor foreigners in particular—but it is composed of all those who do not belong, who see in the landmark Beulah Hotel not a focus of traditions but a conglomerate of beds. They are traditionless people, responding to the automobile and the highway, to objects rather than to sensibilities.

The propensity of Uncle Daniel, he of the "ponder heart," to give away his goods and money is a response to change which he cannot accept, no less assimilate. His choice of a disaffected girl-bride, the vulgar Lolita-like Bonnie Dee Peacock, is his way of seeking a kind of Dickensian arrangement, where brother-sister relationships blissfully contrast with husband-wife arrangements, power struggles that the man always loses. By choosing a daughter, Daniel tries to bypass what marriage means. For a woman his equal would introduce into his life the full force of modernity, and this he cannot accept. Welty's rather casual method, then, suggests more than casualness; it adumbrates very distinct social elements working their way threateningly into Southern life, the nuances and subtleties of ever-changing patterns. Like Jane Austen in this respect, she perceived how tiny rents enter the social fabric, and she set herself a grand goal: to prevent those rents from becoming gigantic, unfillable holes. Nothing less was at stake than pastoral ideals themselves.

Chapter Four

‖‖‖‖‖‖‖‖‖‖‖‖‖‖‖‖‖‖‖‖‖‖‖‖‖‖‖‖‖‖‖‖‖‖‖‖‖‖

THE WAR AND THE NOVEL— BEFORE AND AFTER

It is the desperate moment when we discover that this empire, which had seemed to us the sum of all wonders, is an endless, formless ruin, that corruption's gangrene has spread too far to be healed by our scepter, that the triumph over enemy sovereigns has made us the heirs of their long undoing."

Calvino, *Invisible Cities*

Before and During

The 1940s were a unique literary period. The demise of an earlier generation of major writers, the end of the great literary (and political) wars of the 1930s, the war itself as a watershed,* the appeal of foreign ideas and modernist literary techniques, the influence in particular of French and German existentialism (much watered down), the literary presence of Joyce and Kafka and, to a lesser extent, Gide, Yeats, Eliot, Proust, and Mann, the tremendous impact of film— all of these occurred at one end or the other of the 1940s. By the latter part of the decade, it is fair to say we were immersed in a new literary endeavor, tied as it was to the larger cultural shifts.

These changes, which will be detailed as we move along, put considerable pressure on writers, older ones as well as those younger, but especially on the newer generation, many of whom had served in the war. It is a continuing theme of this study that the 1940s and what they meant literarily and culturally made it incumbent upon a serious novelist to rethink

purely traditional forms and ideas. The novelist moving on a large scale, even if sympathetic to Hemingway and Faulkner, as writers like Styron, Flannery O'Connor, and Mailer were, had to respond to new themes, new tensions, new attitudes and ways of expressing them, new linguistic modalities and textures; or else he could not be taken seriously. The 1930s were over, *even if* the war and foreign influences had not also become so important in creating a literary watershed.

The point seems obvious, but it has been blurred because of the presence of the earlier generation of major writers well after the war's end. Hemingway was alive and writing (although not well); Faulkner's *A Fable,* an ambitious work and by no means an example of sheer decline, was about to be written; Richard Wright, Steinbeck, O'Hara, Wright Morris, were working prolifically, and in O'Hara's case, with some of his more highly recognized longer fiction. Fitzgerald was only recently dead (1940), leaving work which spilled over into the decade.† The very presence of these older talented writers, whose major work lay in a previous generation, acted as a sluggish

---

*Walter Rideout puts it well: "One of the effects of modern war is to alienate us from the recent past. . . . In our consciousness war drops like a trauma between 'after' and 'before,' until it is sometimes hard to believe that 'before' was part of us at all."

†*The Last Tycoon* was published in 1941, Edmund Wilson's edition of *The Crackup* in 1945.

influence on the novel; or else disguised the fact that different cultural circumstances dictated new beginnings. What James Baldwin was later to say of his relationship to Wright, that the sons had to kill the fathers to free themselves, was fundamentally true of an entire generation. Beloved as Hemingway, Fitzgerald, and Faulkner were to those growing up on American fiction, they had to be put behind.

Not unnaturally, a similar situation was developing in poetry. Two examples can demonstrate the parallelism between the literary genres. In 1946, Robert Lowell published a volume of poetry called *Lord Weary's Castle,* an ambitious collection of forty-one brief poems. Although not Lowell's first volume of published poetry—*The Land of Unlikeness* came before—*Lord Weary's Castle* is generally considered as his first mature work, the first authentic Lowell. In the sole longer poem in the collection, "The Quaker Graveyard in Nantucket," Lowell works in and out of Captain Ahab and the *Pequod:* whaleboats, corpses, forms of doom. By way of the poem, Lowell was responding to history and the historical process, elucidating American traditions and yet pointing up discontinuity within those traditions. In language, rhythms, image clusters, Lowell was desperately new, which is not to say that he did not incorporate other elements. His language and rhythms owe a great deal to Hopkins, Pound, Eliot, and Auden; but the coherence of his line owes itself to Lowell and his uses of history.

What is further remarkable about the poem is how close it comes to what John Hawkes was doing in fiction at approximately the same time, especially in *The Cannibal* (1949), extending even to voices, images, clustering of phrases, the crackle and forward thrusting of discontinuous narrative lines. For both, the theme was very somber. Lowell's poem is on its surface an elegy for his lost cousin, but below that an elegy on America as a continuing graveyard for its young, a theme Lowell would continue during the Vietnam War. America as a graveyard is curiously part of Hawkes's frame of reference. His Nantucket Quaker Graveyard, however, is Germany, defeated after one war, rebounding, defeated after a second, and still planning to spring back. Hawkes's Germany is all death and destruction, fumes replacing foam. Both energize the jaggedness of defeat, and the American presence is as doomed as the *Pequod.*

Lowell in poetry, Hawkes in fiction, were part of the new, with a vengeance. By becoming "new," they were forcing upon us a redefinition of what our cultural traditions would become, of what use we could make of them. They were suggesting new identities; and the challenge for the artist, whether writer, painter, or composer, was immense. What occurs culturally is nothing less than a different expectation. Something momentous occurs in our thinking about literature and the other arts, and we suddenly recognize that the work even of writers we revered has become, not less good, but no longer definitive of what and who we are. If we are different, we must be defined differently.

"Ask for no Orphean lute / To pluck life back," Lowell writes near the end of the harried and rushed first part of his poem. Poetry is not sufficient for salvation, but, then, neither is prayer. "The Lord survives the rainbow of His Will," but it is questionable whether man's fate depends on that Will. "The world shall come to Walsingham," but for the unrepentant, there is no salvation there. Like Hawkes, who is far more secular, Lowell throws man into a maelstrom, where muscle, bone, and blood are helpless elements in what doomed even obsessive Ahab. The waters off Nantucket are all "sucking," "spouting," "thrashing," whirlpools of murderous intent. Here we have Lowell's location of self and will: *not in defeating these elements, as we would find in Hemingway or Faulkner, but in being defeated so as to be elegized.*

Even elegy, however, is a luxury. Orpheus, who could not save Eurydice, is superfluous for contemporary man. Only God survives, but whether or not he makes contact with man is dubious.

To arrive at Lowell's poetry and Hawkes's fiction of the 1940s, we must travel great distances from the 1930s. What is amazing in recent American history is how dissimilar decades are, as though the demarking of ten-year periods dictated actual differences. The thirties were themselves vastly distinct from the twenties, and we usually ascribe the Great Crash of 1929 as the watershed for that distinction in economic conditions, personal lives, the fortunes of the country. Yet upon examination, we find that relatively few people out of the 120 million in the nation were involved in the market crash, perhaps one percent in all—those marginally trading and speculating.* Nevertheless, the Crash became a central cultural fact; people lost their confidence and reexam-

---

*Since five percent of the population owned one-third of capital and income, most people had little to lose in money or property.

ined the idea of a nation, what would also occur in the sixties. The thirties, then, were not only a period of economic deprivation, unemployment, loss of market values, creation of millions of marginal people and families; but also a time when trust in the country and its institutions was severely tested. The myth of an Edenic America was shaken.

The 1930s were, in a Biblical sense, the years of drought—literally in the dust bowls of the Midwest, symbolically in the lives of the people. This is the sense of the decade that we carry away, although for most people the 1920s were not that much better. The twenties, however, had a better feel to them; and our nostalgia and fantasies focus there. The year 1925, for example, was a golden age for fiction, with major novels by Dreiser, Lewis, Fitzgerald, Dos Passos, and Hemingway.* The Depression, however, whether as fact or idea, did not translate into a considerable fiction, if we except Dos Passos's trilogy *U.S.A.* and Steinbeck's *The Grapes of Wrath.* Farrell's *Studs Lonigan,* which is currently undergoing more critical praise than the trilogy really warrants, is not a Depression novel. Deprivation is not economic—the Lonigan family is not poor—but emotional and cultural. *Call It Sleep*—one of the most elegant fictions of the 1930s—is not a Depression work either, but a proletarian novel of immigrant life in the city. It is only tangentially connected to the larger society and, in fact, it was attacked by leftist critics, for its lack of a social ethic.

Dos Passos's *The 42nd Parallel, 1919,* and *The Big Money,* published respectively in 1930, 1932, 1936, were books that carried well past the Depression years into the postwar era, traveling as well as Hemingway's early stories and novels and Faulkner's major work, somewhat better than much of Fitzgerald or Wolfe. The Dos Passos novels, furthermore, could not be slighted for lack of technical daring; like Faulkner, Dos Passos incorporated modernist experiments into his work. Along with *The Sound and the Fury, Absalom, Absalom!* and "The Bear," the trilogy was a bona fide American experimental fiction. And because the novels were technically daring, their political message penetrated. As immediately after the war as Jones's *From Here to Eternity* and Mailer's

first two novels, *The Naked and the Dead* † and *Barbary Shore,* political aspects of *U.S.A.* are apparent. We can see the reach of the trilogy, also, in Richard Wright, John Horne Burns, Alfred Hayes, even in later writers like Pynchon, Doctorow, and Gaddis.

Faulkner's influence, on the other hand, has been mainly on Southern writers—his intense themes dissipated even as his popularity grew. Although primarily a 1930s writer, he will appear in many sections of this book. Hemingway's influence, while apparent in Mailer and other members of the redskin school, was curiously diffuse. The prose style was absorbed into American stylistics, but the typical Hemingway world passed into nostalgia or was incorporated into pastoral and spatial traditions. Although all three, Dos Passos, Faulkner, and Hemingway, continued to publish in the postwar years, Dos Passos's break with his earlier work was so radical that his reputation paradoxically remained intact. Faulkner and Hemingway, however, kept doing the same thing, only less well, and their reputations suffered. The thinness of the latter's postwar fiction—*Across the River and into the Trees, The Old Man and the Sea,* the posthumous *Islands in the Stream*—gave him an old-fashioned look. The media were cruel to Hemingway when he faltered, what we can expect also for those who have taken on his poses. Only Dos Passos survived as a strong influence, perhaps the case of the lesser artist being more accessible.

Rereading *U.S.A.* now is an unusual experience, for the impact of the work is not from the set-in narratives of Mac and Morehouse and Mary French, but from the other three elements: the Biographies in particular, as well as the Newsreels and the Camera Eyes. What is remarkable about Dos Passos's achievement is how he assimilated European modernism to American traditions. Those three elements or voices, if connected to each other throughout the three volumes, would be a powerful American fiction in themselves.

U.S.A. is the quintessential political novel-document for those who are children or grandchildren of immigrants; made significant by the fact that its presentation is innovative and experimental. It was continuous with American protest literature and Dreiserian naturalism, yet not unaware of the novel as a developing genre. What Dos Passos achieved were many voices, moving polyphonically, printed

---

*In 1979–80, we had a comparable outpouring: major fiction from Roth, Styron, Baldwin, Malamud, Hawkes, Kosinski, Barth, Mailer, Oates, and others. Nothing, however, quite equaled *An American Tragedy, Arrowsmith, Gatsby, Manhattan Transfer,* etc.

---

†In *The Naked and the Dead,* the biographical time capsules are borrowed directly from *U.S.A.*

out by necessity sequentially, as type dictates, not simultaneously, as music permits. The aim is to assault us aurally.* The Newsreels, with their insistence on events, things, happenings, propel us forward with tremendous thrust toward unforeseen occurrences, whether apocryphal or not, a first and last judgment. The propulsion is like Pynchon's rocketry, that great thrusting forward toward an apocalyptic happening. The Camera Eye gives an "I" in stream of consciousness, a lyrical movement of the self attempting choice amidst a welter of experiences. It fits that persistent American theme of the individual struggling against the gears of the machine, which either crush him or propel him into success. The brief Biographies present a sweep of history, a large spatial dimension of America; men of vision, energy, destructive power—Veblen, Ford, Morgan, Edison.

The order is asymmetrical (sometimes a Camera Eye with a Newsreel, or a Biography with a Newsreel), determined not by any one element, but by all. The rhythms derive from an interplay of parts, even when individual segments are predictable or lacking in sufficient invention. To meet Dos Passos on common ground, as Pynchon and Gaddis have attempted to do, is to master the logistics of huge masses of material which contain several voices and several varieties of experience, all in an achieved rather than a received prose style. Dos Passos had to create a language for the trilogy, since the romantic prose of the aesthetes as well as the clipped quality of Hemingway were inadequate. Dos Passos contrived an "Americanese," made up of slang, gutter phrases, sardonic, lyric, choppy prose, an idiom with its own rhythms and tones. It is a voice that prefigured much in American literature, from novelistic language to Beat poetry.

Dos Passos has a narrator, a surrogate like Conrad's Marlow, who keeps his eye to the camera to record what he sees; then he has that narrator, the Camera Eye, record not only data but impressions. Although we may not be completely aware of the workings of the device as we read, we do sense the polyphonic play, the several voices, the different levels of experience which cohere in our minds. *U.S.A.* is experimentally modernist because it forces the reader to bring together disparate materials, to locate himself in the observing process, and to create the

novel out of his experience of the reading. The expected is turned into the unexpected, order into disorder; and even the mechanical, naturalistic doom involved in virtually every individual life—what will characterize Mailer, Jones, Burns in their war novels—takes on new colors and hues from the multiplicity of devices.

Joe Williams shuttling back and forth on freighters—the yo-yoing Pynchon uses in *V.*—may seem purely mechanical, like the production line in an assembly plant; but the mechanical nature is both enlarged and diminished by other technical elements working in and around it. The fact that Dos Passos leaves one narrative to jump to another, picks up the first, then drops it for a third, having characters finally meet or cross each other in *1919* and *The Big Money,* helps break up the expected or mechanical sense of the stories.

Dos Passos repeatedly tried to overcome the fate of naturalism for the American writer; and perhaps more successfully than any other author except Faulkner in the first half of the century, he brought American fiction right up against what gave it its strength. Dos Passos's ideology, his commitment to radical change in America, did not usurp the novelistic experience, but abetted it. Those vicious, mordant, lyrical Biographies of America's "enemies" as well as its great individuals, are not purely political, but part of the energy of the country. Dos Passos broke completely with the lostness of Hemingway's *nada,* that generation's search for a personal style amidst the ruins. The business of life in America is life.

But well beyond individual traits, or even aspects of experimentation, the trilogy marked something more meaningful for future writers: Dos Passos's intense hatred of authority, whether other individuals or institutions. His radicalism really consisted of anti-authoritarian stances, far more than prescriptions for change. This radical stance permeates postwar American fiction, even when the writer is not political or ideologically left. That hatred of authority, which we have traced to Emerson and Thoreau, intensified after the war, abetted by the military experience. It became translated into the generation wars that began, really, in the forties (not the sixties), that characterized the Beat movement of the fifties, the demonstrations of the sixties and seventies.

The Dos Passos novels were part of the literary wars of the 1930s, which ended when the real war

---

*As Gaddis's *JR* does, especially the buried radio which beams out commercials from beneath mountains of goods, sound vibrating not into ears but into space.

began. The call to arms was Michael Gold's boisterous "Towards Proletarian Art," by which he meant radical art, in which the writer identifies with the worker and reflects him in his art. Although this appeared in 1921, it became in its various guises the basis for much of the literary infighting of the later twenties and thirties. I am interested here in how these literary wars, which died formally, threaded their way as influential concepts into 1940s fiction. Gold's ideas of "huge-hewn poets, those striding, outdoor philosophers and horny-handed creators" may smack of Soviet literary realism; but they play upon certain anti-intellectual themes which dominate in postwar American fiction. The proletariat may have lost out in our more recent fiction—except perhaps for Oates, Morrison, Jones—but the idea of a classless society, a rough democratic hatred of education and learning, a radical rejection of authority all remain active, viable, compelling.

At the other end of this fifteen-year struggle for the hearts and minds of poets and novelists was James Farrell, a Marxist himself. In 1936, he published *A Note on Literary Criticism,* a critique from within the house of American realism. As Walter Rideout comments, Farrell's attack was twofold: first, to prick Gold's "revolutionary sentimentalism," then to puncture Granville Hicks's more "mechanical Marxism," which stressed a direct connection between economics and literature. In his *The Great Tradition,* which prefigured Leavis's title but not his substance, Hicks based literary evaluation on how the writer discussed the common man. Class consciousness was the touchstone of literary value, and using this measure, Hicks found Faulkner to be the Sax Rohmer for the sophisticated. Farrell himself was praised for moving to the left in *Judgment Day,* and this novel to that extent would be preferable to *Studs Lonigan,* then being written.

Farrell's own reputation and career were on the line and in danger, in 1936, of being smothered. In his response, Farrell asked for judgment, not measurement, qualitative evaluation, not quantitative. Terms of attack like "bourgeois" and proletarian" were not measuring rods but descriptions. Literature is not propaganda for the class struggle, nor is it frivolous, Farrell is quick to add. Literature may advance the class struggle more efficiently by being indirect, suggestive, embedded in life, not in generalities. Farrell makes it clear he is not arguing for the "art novel" or for "art for art's sake." James was definitely out. In a sense, he was defending his own kind of realism, and

through that the artist's conscience about his material. Farrell was, of course, in turn attacked and defended in *The New Masses* and *The American Spectator;* but literary confrontation was itself beginning to wind down.

Literary struggles were assimilated into the war and combat novel of the later 1940s and thereafter. Ideologies, while subsumed within the war itself, were manifest in terms of class, caste, and race. Officer and enlisted man confrontations were the wartime equivalent of the class/caste struggle of the 1930s. Thus, the inheritors of the thirties clashes were writers as disparate as John Horne Burns, Mailer, Irwin Shaw, Cozzens, Wouk, James Jones. Literary wars themselves— that is, the development of arguments outside the body of fiction, in essays, articles, books, forums, conferences—declined in importance and volume until the later 1960s. The most important organ of criticism, *Partisan Review,* lost its class consciousness and moved, at its best, to aesthetics and elitism, and at its worst, to a celebration of American affluence.

In the 1960s, the literary wars became, on one hand, racial in nature: white (arty) versus black (1930s realism, class, caste); and shortly after that, sexist: feminism versus more traditional male/female attitudes. Feminist aesthetics, ably abetted by Kate Millett's *Sexual Politics,* is still in the process of developing; whereas black aesthetics, despite Harold Cruse's influential book *The Crisis of the Negro Intellectual,* seems to have run its course. At least as of 1980, it is silent, part of the "benign neglect" that has taken over the nation in most racial matters. The period of discussion, which included the heated response to Styron's *Nat Turner,* lasted about five years, and its brevity can be attributed not to the lack of things to say, but to the vehemence (often justifiable) of black rhetoric. White critics refused to respond, and one hand clapping shortly ceases to be heard.

For us, the black-white disagreement about ends and means in the later sixties and early seventies recalls those brutal arguments of the thirties. Race, caste, attitudes, separation, exclusionary tactics dominated the later polemics as much as class struggle did the earlier. And class struggle was not itself alien to sixties rhetoric, since many black writers and critics assumed blacks were a different race economically as well as ideologically. Eventually, blacks came to speak only to each other; and even here only selected blacks. "Negroes" like Ellison and Baldwin were sellouts; blacks like Wright, Jones, and Williams more acceptable. This has the ring of the thirties, when exclusionary tactics aimed at purification of literature and, indirectly, of writers. For blacks, the desire for separation has indeed been gratified; the races have ceased to speak to each other on literary or larger cultural matters. There is now a certain groundswell for this among women, an exclusionary sexist policy among poets led by Adrienne Rich which has not, however, flowed over into fiction.

If we move back to the 1930s, there was no lack of rejoinders. During the height of the acrimonious debate, nearly every major novelist, poet, and critic was drawn into combat. The scene was like an octagon at war with itself. There were the theoretical Marxists (Farrell), the Stalinists (Gold, Hicks), the vague Communist sympathizers (Hemingway, Dos Passos, Dreiser), the John Reed Clubbers (who split off, forming *Partisan Review*), the Trotskyites, the humanists (More, Babbitt), the aesthetes (Eliot, Wilder, Burke), the independent leftists (Wilson, Porter, Farrell doubling), the Southern Agrarians (Warren, Tate, Ransom). Once the Communists relented and tried to broaden their appeal, they became an umbrella for nearly all these groups except for the Southern Agrarians (who yearned after an antebellum South), the humanists (whose appeal was for a highly structured past), and the more recalcitrant of the aesthetes (who embraced modernism in literature, which was often reactionary politically). The aim was to gain a united front of literary talents against capitalism.

Since this activity did occur in the 1930s, when the Depression seemed like a Biblical accounting for the failures of industrial capitalism, the energies that went into such debate were not completely frivolous. Also, the height of the acrimony occurred before the Moscow trials and purges (1936–38) and, of course, before the Soviet-Nazi Nonaggression Pact in August 1939. From the viewpoint of the socially committed, capitalism had failed, whereas the Soviet Union, observed from a great distance and before the purges, seemed like an avatar of the future. The gullibility of many writers is apparent to us, but partly because we have removed their protest from its context and we have ourselves forsaken formal ideologies. Our ideology is now in five-year cycles, one "chic" after another. There is no way to revive the 1930s battles. For capitalism survived, strengthened and reinforced by the war, and Soviet ruthlessness, anti-Semitism, and indifference to social justice have irremediably changed the terms of the dialogue.

What the 1940s lacked, in fact, was some comparable dialectic or polemic. For writers such as Mailer, Wright, and even Bellow, there was almost a void, into which they plunged without external support. There was no corrective dialogue, or else Mailer's *Barbary Shore* would not have taken its present form; Richard Wright's work would have received more support in America; and Faulkner's epigones, especially Styron, might not have been so extravagantly hailed. These are all "if"'s, but of extreme intellectual concern. Hoping to create discussion, *Partisan Review* held several serious forums, but its efforts, as Mailer's own remarks indicate, were out of touch with fictional ideas; and the magazine's symposia fell into a vacuum.*

There was little in the 1940s, or 1950s, to equal Kenneth Burke's early attempts to straddle complex and seemingly intractable issues. Gold's unyielding argument was that the laboring masses could not be left to rot in an indifferent capitalist society, and if no one else cared, then at least writers should pay attention. Burke offered an "aesthetic solution" at the First Writers' Congress in New York, in 1935, his topic being "Revolutionary Symbolism in America." The title must have made the audience suspect a gigantic hoax. Burke, however, was apparently serious, for he attempted to define a position that we would see repeated in the 1960s: the desire to accommodate a social and political ideology, but not at the expense of art.

Burke offered a kind of "Oblomovism," in that the artist would be an adversary, taking a negative attitude on everything that capitalism deemed important. For the latter's stress on efficiency, the artist would embody inefficiency and negativism; for initiative, he would substitute dissolution; for the machine, he would offer the impractical. Thus, the artist would insist on his (or her, but there were few women here) own kind of reality while still supporting a sociopolitical position. Political action in Burke's terms

---

*Mailer perceived, almost alone, that the symposium on "Our Country and Our Culture" (in 1952) was really a hygienic tour, not a way of connecting fiction, culture, and nation. "A symposium of this sort I find shocking. . . . Everywhere the American writer is being dunned to become healthy, to grow up, to accept the American reality, to integrate himself, to eschew disease, to re-value institutions. Is there nothing to remind us that the writer does not need to be integrated into his society, and often works best in opposition to it? I would propose that the artist feels most alienated when he loses the sharp sense of what he is alienated from."

was to be fought out not in action but in words that gave the artist, not the Party, ultimate control over his thoughts.

Although Burke came to modify this attitude—which *was* somewhere between burlesque and hoax—his refusal to toe the line was symptomatic of the drifting away, later, of nearly all the major writers. The Party had afforded a temporary "common front" to writers as disparate as Hicks, Hemingway (an especial favorite after *For Whom the Bell Tolls*), Farrell, Dos Passos (who refused to follow Party dictates), Cowley, and others. Since creative writers were following inner dictates that influenced their art more than external pressures could, in an open society where government kept its hands off, such alliances had to prove temporary. For our purposes, the literary battles, the attempts to define lines of argument, the twisting and turning of individual talents, the desire to find socially redeemable dimensions for every kind of art, the effort to retain an aesthetic based on an upper-middle-class culture, even Southern Agrarianism with its reactionary and implicitly racist ideology—all suggested an exciting ferment.

In the 1940s and 1950s, such reverberations were missing. That exploration of self which, later, would be characterized as "me-tooism" was already in existence two decades earlier. Also, the influx of modernist ideas and techniques stressed extreme subjectivism; social commitment was for lesser fiction. French existentialism, no matter how reductive it appeared in its American guises, was intensely subjective, concerned with self and ego as a given. If, later, we would speak of "me too," earlier we spoke of "how about me?" or "why me?" The simultaneous loss of external ideological pressure and the literary wars attendant upon that, along with the positive influence of modernism and existentialism, led the writer ever deeper into his own psyche.

The intellectual scene in the 1930s with *The New Masses, The New Republic, The Nation, The New Leader,* three of them stressing novelty, along with the "new" *Partisan Review,* could never be duplicated. We cannot argue that literature was better —it apparently was not—but the individual writer before the war had, virtually for the first time, something close to what Eliot called a tradition. It was not Eliot's "common tradition" by any means; but it was an American tradition of a broad kind. Despite strong influence from the Soviet Union, the loose amalgamation of writers who fell under the wing of the Party was far more American in its makeup than foreign.

There was no Party line, as became apparent when Dreiser did not relent on his anti-Semitic remarks, to the embarrassment of his left-wing affiliates, Gold himself, and rank-and-file members of the Party, a large number of them Jewish.*

A postwar fiction that uncannily recalls a thirties sense of life is Harvey Swados' *On the Line* (1957). Based on Swados's own experience in the Mahwah, New Jersey, Ford plant, *On the Line* is a series of interconnected stories of men on an automobile assembly line. The tradition is working class, modeled on the proletarian novel of the 1930s, almost prototypical of Michael Gold's call for a committed fiction. To be "on the line" is indeed to be involved in a kind of war, social, political, military. Instead of the squad, there are the teams involved in working together. Instead of drill sergeants and squad leaders, there are inspectors and, observing them, the officers or white-collar workers—engineers, efficiency experts, men from the office. Beyond it all are staff officers, the company directors, who remain out of sight. Replacing shells and enemy soldiers are the hulks of automobile frames, oncoming as in a banzai attack, relentless, part of a production plan the men cannot question. They are, literally, sent into the line. Quotas are set, comparable to the amount of ground a company must capture or, later, to body counts in the Vietnam War.

On the Line recycles so much of the American character from the 1930s through the 1950s that it transcends its literary limitations. The experience on the assembly line is a war against an omnipresent and omniscient enemy. It is the ultimate secular place; unless the quota is God, part of a covenant the men assume. One survives, as in war, by finding the correct rhythms—something Walter, the young man who hopes to save enough for college, never discovers. He seeks perfection when the goal is volume. " 'Make it look good, and confusing. Be a camouflage artist and the bosses'll very seldom bother you.' " This is the inspector's advice, for in a real war, Walter would not survive. Only in a counterfeit war, the assembly line, can Walter get by.

---

*Dreiser spoke of New York, the very heart of the Party's work with writers, as a "Kyke's dream of a ghetto." As Daniel Aaron shows, his sentiments fell easily among Mencken, Cabell, O'Neill, George Jean Nathan, Vachel Lindsay, Edgar Lee Masters; to whom we could add Hemingway, Cummings, and others.

Yet the line offers its rewards. Each man, like the members of the multiracial army squad, has his sense of America. Mailer's and Jones's army is updated, brought home. Outside, beyond the line, is the dispossessed paradise of an industrial America, the prizes offered by the fifties, the fantasies of the unemployed in the thirties. We recognize that all the literary wars of the 1930s came down to employment, wages, a market economy that functioned. America seduces. Each man makes his own Nazi-Soviet pact; he may think his work is temporary, that he can run, but once he buys into the goodies, he is caught. The line may damn, but it is also salvation. It is like war to peacetime soldiers; the directionless become guided.

All the men—who have only first names—live by illusions, the sole exception being "Joe, the Vanishing American." The single black, LeRoy, wants to be a singer at the Metropolitan Opera; Walter intends to be a civil engineer; Orrin hopes to become a "hero" of the assembly line; Pop saves to buy his son a new car; Harold is trying to overcome alcoholism; Kevin, an Irishman, finds America too frustrating, although full of promise; the foreman, Buster, seeks responsibilities he cannot handle; Frank needs the work to balance repeated failure outside. The true test for all is that oncoming, swinging automobile body: dangerous, heavy, yet graceful, shining, expensive, the American dream hung on heavy chains. The car is ultimate freedom, not only on the road but as a sense of personal achievement.

The car joins our sense of the thirties with our sense of the forties and fifties. To have a car in the thirties was to beat the Depression; yet in the following decades, the car, now attainable for most, became part of everything counterfeit about America. The automobile is emblematic of the country: under the shine, as the men know, the rot has already begun. Camouflage and deceive.

Only Joe, the vanishing American, understands this so fully that he refuses to acquiesce. Joe spreads himself between the thirties and fifties, the proletariat-artist hero who connects with Clancy Sigal's "on the road" protagonist and with Kesey's Chief Bromden. Like all those who perceive the counterfeit, he flees his version of it, the line. This section, published separately in *The Hudson Review,* deserves to be better known. Although Joe has an American eagle tattooed on his arm, not to celebrate pastoral values but to scream forth class and caste rage, he himself really stands for nothing. He is "passing through," existing as subjective matter that refuses to be reified. By rejecting his permanent place in the assembly, he avoids

being a movable part in the control of the bosses. He rejects the covenant.

Swados's book is rarely novelistic, nor does it owe anything to modernism. With a few changes, it could be a nonfiction study, a companion to Paul Goodman's *Growing Up Absurd* or David Riesman's *The Lonely Crowd,* both of which it complements. Yet if the prose had been pegged higher (it is mainly neutral), it could have been a prose poem, for Swados provides many lovely images: the line itself, the thin red line of the military; the hulking cars which become graceful objects; planets hoving into view; the sheen and finish which disguise incipient decay, like the human skin; the hopes and dreams of the men themselves, quickened by the American ideal and yet redeemed by the actuality of the line. The ultimate dream is the ultimate trap. And we have the final image of Joe, the vanishing American, with his own car, in which he and the machine become like a mirage. Joe argues: " 'things came up that were more important than the making of automobiles.' "

A novel with few literary pretensions and far outside our coordinates for modernism, *On the Line* nevertheless touches the culture at numerous points, without sentimentalizing or staining what it reaches, as many more ambitious novels do. Swados catches the American dream, its underside, the frustration and waste involved in that dream. Joe's insistence on personal and human values may be an avatar of the sixties, but we must recall that much of the protest of that decade came from youths whose parents had worked on the line or its equivalent. Money came from mindless, "absurd" work.

If *On the Line,* a fifties fiction, recreates for us the class and caste struggles of the thirties, we can see, by contrasting two novels that appeared within four years of each other, how those thirties themselves passed into the forties. Richard Wright's *Native Son,* in 1940, and Saul Bellow's *Dangling Man,* in 1944, seem to belong to different worlds, not to be books published in the same language at almost the same time.* In its attitudes and, as well, in its approach to

---

*If we had to cite one nonfiction book that signaled the shifting of decades, it would be James Burnham's *The Managerial Revolution* (1941). Written in 1940, Burnham's argument is a simple one, yet it thrusts itself into nearly everything America was and was to become. In its several aspects, it touches on *Native Son* as much as on *Dangling Man,* and it throws the thirties as much as the fifties and sixties into perspective. Citing the "managerial revolution" as nothing less than a radical shift from the capitalist-owner of a small business to the

fiction as naturalistic, social, concerned with questions of class, caste, and race, *Native Son* is clearly a product of the 1930s. *Dangling Man* is an early entrance into 1940s modernism, concerned with vague, undefined philosophical issues, an existential dangling, sexual innuendo, a world turned inward. The two novels, located against each other, would appear to provide that division between prewar and postwar, which in cultural terms meant, on one hand, a direct and frontal attack, on the other, indirection, impersonality, ambiguity.

I plan to show how Bellow—along with Hawkes—was moving us out into new areas for American fiction even as Wright was keeping the past well before us. But I want to do this without rejecting Wright's achievement, since I consider it very high, and also because this kind of novel remained quite active, threading itself through early Mailer and remaining constant in Jones and many other war/combat novelists. A book like *Native Son,* to focus on that, has many lives. It has its 1930s life as a novel about class, caste, and race; it has its reverberations in war novels of the late 1940s, so that we can look back at *Native Son* as Wright's version of a combat novel; it has its life in the 1950s and 1960s as a book that says critical things about black-white relationships and the victimization of poor blacks; it has its parallel cultural life in the attacks made on Wright by blacks themselves—Baldwin, among others.

------

technocrat-manager of a large corporation, Burnham demonstrates the growing alienation not of the worker from his work but of the owner from his business. The warning reinforces those who hold to a pastoral-rural tradition as the backbone of America, as against those who see vitality deriving from the city.

Taking his cue from Marx's analysis of capitalism, Burnham traces four stages of managerial assumption of power: from those who are in charge of operations, to those concerned with selling the product, then to directors, finally to those who own the company because they own the stock. The ruling class is now the managers, who become the cornerstone of a state bureaucracy. The New Deal, in Burnham's paranoiac interpretation, was the evil genius behind all this, Roosevelt hoping to end capitalism and "begin a new type of social organization, the same forces which at later stages and under different local circumstances produced the revolutions in Russia and Germany."

From Burnham's analysis, we can see how 1930s concerns —in terms of power, holding it or gaining it—will pass over into a different conception, what we associate with postwar philosophies. The "old world," Edenic, was manageable by an owner on the scene; the new world dangles from the hands of men removed from whatever they control.

Curiously enough, critics who have rejected the novel for being part of the "Wright School" (Robert Bone's depreciatory phrase)—meaning that it is a naturalistic protest novel now outdated—have failed to perceive how mainstream it is. Using modernism as a club, critics could beat Wright to death. Yet this is his "war novel," in which the consciousness of one man, rather than a squad or platoon, becomes central. By focusing on a single figure, Wright worked certain symbolic lines, as Mailer's single squad or Jones's "thin red line" becomes emblematic of a more universal condition. And while Wright uses naturalistic settings, much as James T. Farrell—dismal rooms, empty apartment houses, desolate rooftops, garbage-strewn streets, a furnace that devours—despite these familiar presences, Wright moves beyond the matrix of determinism to establish individual identity.

Wright differed, also, from his contemporary John O'Hara, in his ability to separate individual character from the fate that besets all. O'Hara's use of "ironic determinism" to resolve what should be left to the writer is what helps to undermine his fiction. The audacity of Wright's conception still grips us: to move an individual out from the sea of blackness (and therefore invisibility) into which he has been born. In Ellison's *Invisible Man*, which owes so much to Wright, the protagonist remains faceless, even nameless; Wright, however, makes us "see." His daring is to make Bigger's two murders his means of gaining an identity. The black man's potential for murder, since all other avenues were closed, gave him recognition and leverage. Mailer's "White Negro" picks up from Wright's conception. "The knowledge that he had killed a white girl they loved and regarded as their symbol of beauty [Wright explains] made him feel the equal of them, like a man who had been somehow cheated, but had now evened the score."

A strong 1930s element comes in the support the Communists give Bigger Thomas. The Communists were, of course, interested in blacks for their own reasons, to discredit capitalism, a point Ellison makes. What he blurs and what Wright stresses is that many individual Communists believed fervently in black equality and fought off both the terror tactics of society and manipulative tactics from within. Jan and Mary Dalton, who seem soft-headed, were nevertheless such individuals. Wright's prophetic power is amazing. The headlines that follow Mary Dalton's disappearance—she has already been fed into the Dalton furnace—read: "Seek Hyde Park Heiress Missing from Home Since Saturday, Girl Believed Hiding Out with Communists." The Patty Hearst case, allowing for significant differences, rests here: that alliance in the public mind between radical politics and heinous crimes. By connecting race and political ideology, and that in an individual life creating the terms of his own consciousness, Wright was able to move beyond race and ideology into the larger culture, precisely as the war/combat novel could do.

What has put off the postwar critics? Tony Tanner omits him altogether, although Wright published extensively in the 1950s. Other critics have pushed him back to the era of Hemingway and Fitzgerald, in a kind of no-man's-land. In his revised edition of *The Negro Novel in America,* Robert Bone does not devote space to later Wright. Some have designated him a "black writer," found him wanting either artistically or ideologically, and managed to dismiss him. Baldwin suggested he had to be figuratively killed, and other blacks have dealt with his work sociopolitically, dismissing his aesthetic base as insufficiently "black." He has been strangely located in American fiction, berated as too naturalistic, denied "modern" status, found wanting ideologically. Compared with Ellison, it is true, Wright lacks elegance and stylistic felicities; but there is no reason to compare him with another black writer. Compared with James Jones, for example, he has equivalent power and intensity. Some recognition of this is beginning to return.

The thematic novel now seems excessively old-fashioned. One characteristic of prewar fiction is thematic insistence; whereas postwar fiction suggests vague coordinates, discontinuous lines. The balance hangs in ambiguity, both character and plot dimmed. Wright drives for certainties. Yet *Native Son* still has something of a modern feel, chiefly in its presentation of an emerging consciousness. Let us attempt what seems a wild comparison: bring in Jerzy Kosinski's *The Painted Bird* (1965) as an analogy, with the hunted Jewish boy in Eastern Europe as a counterpart of the hunted black in Wright's South Side of Chicago.

Images of incredible brutality characterize both experiences; and each writer revels in the violence done to and by his protagonist. Strikingly, *The Painted Bird* is always discussed as a novel immersed in a postwar sensibility. I assume that the emergence of a human consciousness from surrounding detritus is what is meant here, along with a certain spareness and impersonality of presentation. While Wright is more passionate, certainly, than Kosinski, his Bigger Thomas in Chicago is not that different from Kosinski's hunted protagonist. The former is brutalized, before he kills, for the fact of being black; and Kosin-

ski's young boy is brutalized for his "blackness" or darkness, which associates him with Jews or Gypsies, marginal elements. His coloring also allies him, in Polish eyes, with the devil; protection from damnation must be sought through exorcism. Chicago's whites see blacks such as Bigger, allied with Communists and labor unions, as no less demonic; and they must drive him from society before he corrupts it.

Within that frame of reference, Bigger must, somehow, emerge, and he does so as an ambiguous figure of vengeance, by killing brutally. His crimes are not only the price of his previous repression, but also the mark of his emergence. Expressing himself through murder serves a twofold purpose: it will lead to his end, but also to a sense of life. Kosinski's boy has tried to live by hiding, but gradually he, too, recognizes that he must redeploy his energies and act as an angel of vengeance on those who have persecuted and tortured him. Both Bigger and the Kosinski protagonist serve as particular forms of a 1950s and 1960s experience, that of the emerging consciousness in a society that has lost all sense of the sacred, celebrated even when such consciousness passes beyond narcissism into destruction and self-destruction.

When we turn to Bellow's *Dangling Man,* we overlap with Wright's Bigger, but also enter different ground. Not only is the social sense different; the self-consciousness of the protagonist extends to a self-conscious mode of narration, in which everything reflects aspects of itself. The title lacks "the" and therefore mirrors the general human condition as well as Bellow's protagonist, Joseph—Kafka's Joseph, the Biblical Joseph, a persona for mankind.* Joseph worships his own imagination, the tender configurations of his mind. The journal that he keeps is part of his self-love, but also part of a new direction in twentieth-century American fiction. For Joseph's rage is, like Joseph's coat, many-colored. He respects his uniqueness, and yet rages against his holelike enclosure; and he forthrightly eschews the external world, leaving it to those who "fly planes or fight bulls or catch tar-

---

*The persona as a schlemiel—the fool or passive individual whose very resistance and fixedness become a threat to the status quo. Singer's "Gimpel the Fool" (translated by Bellow), Isaac Rosenfeld's "The Hand That Fed Me" (Bellow introduced Rosenfeld's work), Malamud's Fixer and Levin, Friedman's Stern, Bellow's own Asa Leventhal ("the victim"), Tommy Wilhelm, Herzog, and others, all fit into the schlemiel tradition. The original Peter Schlemiel, in the Chamisso story, sells his shadow for wealth and becomes an outcast. His sole alternative is to turn his marginality into strength.

pon." He floats, as it were, in indeterminate space, a spatial, dangling man without definition.

The entire first paragraph of *Dangling Man* puts distance between the Hemingway generation and the "new" as represented by the inward-turning Joseph. The method is a journal, the attitude nervous disorder, and the characterization by way of a persona: Joseph as analogous to Conrad's Marlow, with Bellow circling just beyond. "Do you have an inner life? It is nobody's business but your own. Do you have emotions? Strangle them. To a degree, everyone obeys this code. And it does admit of a limited kind of candor, a closemouthed straightforwardness. But on the truest candor, it has an inhibitory effect. Most serious writers are closed to the hard-boiled. They are unpracticed in introspection, and therefore badly equipped to deal with opponents whom they cannot shoot like big game or outdo in daring." Instead of energy, there will be "dangling": a physical condition that bottles enervation, a dubious sexuality in which the male hangs rather than erects, a territory between the vigorous and the dead. Except for *Henderson the Rain King*, this, with variations, will be Bellow's territory.

This is also the country of the new; novel, that is, for the American writer, who was still assimilating the European avant-garde well after it had passed into other phases. Bellow absorbed the sensibility in temporal and spatial dislocations, ahistorical patterns, and a flexible linguistic medium. He was alive to the literary vibrations that would make Sartre and Camus key figures in the 1940s and 1950s, as indebted to Sartre, whose Roquentin (in *Nausea*) he recalls, as he is to Kafka.

Nausea is an intermediate illness between health and real sickness, not unlike dangling between life and death. Sartre's protagonist is a historian whose interest lies in dead societies, feelings that have passed, and whose account of himself is caught in a diary, like Joseph's journal later. The diary entries are cold weather notations, with Roquentin's beginning in January, Joseph's in December and running through the winter. Both agree with Dostoyevsky's underground man that "One can't be a man of action"; action corrupts, whereas enervation and dangling bring the individual sufficiently close to sickness unto death, where he has distance on life the better to observe it and himself. Both, further, are struggling to deny the unconscious, which would make its own unique demands on choice, determine direction, and make the protagonist accept dangling as a permanent condition. Roquentin and Joseph, in their differing ways, insist on the contingency of phenomena, not causality or necessity, but chance or uncertainty, so they can impose their own patterns.

It is remarkable that Bellow, in a novel he wrote in his mid-twenties, had already developed a mature metaphysics: that need to turn all life into contingency and chance so as to give his protagonists the opportunity to pattern it, if and when they can. The idea of dangling—after several delays and errors, Joseph waits for the army to induct him—afforded Bellow a limbo-like state for his protagonist. The view can be either from life toward death, or from death (at the end of a rope) toward rebirth, or even intermediate gradations. What is further remarkable is how novelistic Bellow was from the beginning, using his materials as ways of modulating reality and yet reflecting it. The book ripples with fictional effects, of time and space displaced or distorted, narrative distancing, retrospection, events observed through both ends of the telescope.

Because the dangling gives Joseph a unique angle of perspective, everything outside him becomes clarified. Had he been a participant—that is, working, accumulating, settling in—his powers of observation would have been dulled. He is an eye, an "I," an observer not only of man's follies—like his brother's family and its desire to accumulate goods—but of the futility of man's strivings. When he contemplates whether he will kill or not kill in the war, he reasons he will, and that, in turn, he will be killed, which is the way things are. Dangling lets him penetrate all illusions and counterfeit feelings.

One of the props Bellow does not deny Joseph is cosseting by sympathetic females: a wife who becomes motherly, girl friends solicitous for his welfare, women feeding him in bed when he has a cold. This is a constant in Bellow's work, that ministering to male needs by sympathetic females. Bellow's men may like to think they are saved by intellect and choice, but often it is the right female at the right time. Since this drama is a motif in Bellow's fiction (not only in Joseph but in Herzog, Leventhal, Tommy Wilhelm, even Henderson), one cannot ignore the apparent superficiality of what constitutes salvation. His protagonists may be sick unto death, but what they need is beef broth and a tempting nipple, not Kierkegaardian faith. Joseph's wife may be named Iva (Eva), but she does not tempt him into destruction. On the contrary, she works for him, feeds him when he is ill, puts up with his temper fits, blithely ignores his two-month affair with another woman, and generally supports "her man" as though a working-class wife. Although women are essential to Bellow's view of his men, his sense of his female characters turns them either into patsies or bitches, nurses or emasculators.

The dimension Bellow exploits as the result of his character's metaphorical and actual dangling is a disarrangement of temporal and spatial perspectives. Joseph speaks of the "leveling of occasions" that has resulted from his condition, and by that he means that days have flowed into each other so fluidly that the usual distinctions we make in twenty-four-hour units have been erased. From this derangement of the usual, Joseph can sense how close he is to death; or else, how distant he is from normal life, which is measured in working and leisure hours. All Joseph's waking hours are the same, just as all meals are essentially similar—he gets hungry around the clock, since duties do not regulate his meals. Undifferentiated time transforms ordinary procedures into contingency.

In temporal terms, Bellow has returned Joseph to a kind of prehistorical accounting, when food, shelter, and sleep were the sole essentials. He becomes a Crusoe without work. As he says: "There were formerly baking days, washing days, days that began events and days that ended them." When every day is a holiday, there are no holidays; "it is [he comments] difficult to tell Tuesday from Saturday." Deranged temporality is in conflict with ordinary time. One day is all days, even while he recognizes that sanity and stability depend on unit measurement.

As Kafka insisted, if temporal arrangements are upset, then spatial dimensions cannot remain untouched. Perspectives are altered, especially since Joseph sticks so closely to his rented room, "this six-sided box." The room, a cage and a trap, also becomes a refuge. But even as he perceives he is trapped—out of choice, since his forays are always discouraging or frustrating—he realizes that "goodness is achieved" in the company of other people, "attended by love." His sense of things is that while others are mingling in love, his perspectives "end in the walls."

Like Roquentin, he lives only in the past, while the future either is unknown or passes him by. One room holds him, though other men "cross whole Siberias" to pursue their opportunities. Much of this sense of entrapment is, of course, self-pity, self-indulgence, but it informs Bellow's work in exquisite modulations; culminating in that most entrapped of creatures, Herzog, a Kafkaesque character who is, finally, saved only by the ministrations of the deep-thighed Ramona. One of the problems in dealing with the

serious side of Bellow's work is the paltriness of his solutions (which he insists upon), the superficiality of the way he pulls his characters out, the optimistic nature of his endings when the material seems to disallow resolution.

The hanging, dangling Joseph is all mind, all observation, all contemplation, like Kafka's mole. Hanging on to life precariously, he recognizes how indifferent a phenomenon is death, a theme that surfaces insistently in the 1940s novel of war and combat, intensified by European themes of absence, emptiness, and finality. The foreground is Sartre, Camus; the background Kierkegaard. The guru is Dostoyevsky, with his hatred of the works of modern man, his detestation of science and technology, his rejection of materiality. Joseph is such a man updated, but without faith; a modern man facing all the trials of Job, but desacralized. As Joseph comments, once we float free of history, as modern man does, we lose all perspectives, and only self matters. Joseph must fight pride to maintain his priorities, which are that reason wins out weakly, that man must not surrender to any contrivance which promises salvation, and finally, that "from the antidote itself another disease would spring." Such is the fate, as Dostoyevsky insisted, of every man who is secularized. Nevertheless, the recognition that every solution establishes a dialectic of problems, and that, therefore, there can be no solution but man's feeble attempt at reason, informs Bellow's universe. He know it is insufficient, also that we have no other.

The novel's metaphysics is established in those two sections in which Joseph argues with the "Spirit of Alternatives," something like Faust with Mephistopheles. This turning of the self into two parts, also reminiscent of Diderot's *Rameau's Nephew,* allows Bellow his ideological grounding. The "Alternative," or *"Tu As Raison Aussi,"* attempts to undermine Joseph's sense of choice, reason, his rejection of the shoddy and meretricious. Joseph recognizes, in his dangling state, that the "world comes after you . . . singles you out for this part or that." The world waits to make a whore of you, if you are compliant. One can only meet these matters with ideal constructions that are well made and thought out, even when one recognizes that such constructions—whether God, money, art—are insufficient to meet the world with. Joseph's final position is not unlike that of Conrad's Marlow, to immerse oneself in the destructive element and swim until pulled down.

In the second of the dialogues, Joseph insists on life, not antilife; he stresses man's humanity, choice, survival with reason. These are all 1940s considerations, intensified by the war years, ideological concerns that had to do with questions of individual versus social survival. *These* questions are the real world, Joseph insists. The conditions posed by the war will pass, and the war will not in itself be of essential or lasting value. What is crucial is what occurs to the individual destiny, the singular spirit, the ethical modes by which we guide our lives as separate beings. Here is Bellow's permanent territory. Joseph insists on this, as he dangles, although when domestic matters sour, he rushes to surrender his freedom to the army and welcomes regimentation. "Long live regimentation," he shouts at the end of the novel, a realization, ironically put, of how fragile personal ideologies can be when confronted with reality, whether domestic or real war.

The final lines, in which Joseph embraces standardization, turn the novel into an ironic statement, in which Bellow establishes the attractions of "alternative spirits" to his own point of view. The moral struggle is on: to preserve oneself against all the traps and snares, whether overindulgence in self or the regimentation of what lies beyond. Bellow has established his guidelines: Kierkegaardian woe, Sartrean nausea, Camus's rebellion of the self, American spatiality and temporality, Emerson's organic community, Kafkaesque enclosure. It's a strange mix, as much a trap as a jumping-off ground, and only *Henderson the Rain King* and parts of *Augie March* break out. Just past his mid-twenties, Bellow had defined, more or less, his sense of the modern.

Another kind of modern novel emerged with John Hawkes's *The Cannibal* (1949), a remarkable achievement for a young man barely past his Harvard undergraduate years. *The Cannibal* is a war novel, part of that outpouring of fiction just after the end of the conflict. Unlike Mailer or Jones, however, Hawkes was not interested in a blockbuster or a realistic presentation of what the army looked and felt like. A contemporary designer, a maker of mosaics, a Mondrian, he wanted conceptualization, the phenomenology of war, so to speak. Pouring into Hawkes's "war novel" is the whole modernist tradition: use of a split-screen reality and montage of events, play with history and time, utilization of special perspectives and spatiality, jagged prose to approximate jaggedness of defeat, blurring of point of view and line of narration, reliance on incomplete characters or characters completed only in the reader's mind, stress on extraordinary images, lack of talk or words, sense of silence, replacement of point of view by fragmentation, the result of cutting. Film-making suggests itself as a considerable pressure on both conception and execution.

Hawkes is uninterested in any particular campaign of the war against Germany, nor is he interested in the military itself. He is unresponsive to winners and losers, even ideology. He is, however, overwhelmingly concerned with creating a sense of Germany right after the war, in 1945, a conquered and devastated country.* So he gives us a Germany of the mind, fleshed out with a few physical elements. Hawkes's radical break with naturalism and realism —details of particular campaigns, the drive to win, efforts of the men, losses, et al.—creates a dimension we rarely find in Mailer's novel, in which the lack vitiates the intellectual drive he tried to convey.

While Mailer is all words—foreshadowing the barrage of rhetoric he lays down in his later work— Hawkes downplays words themselves by way of shifting the focus, telescoping people and events, even entire wars (the first as well as the second), changing perspectives, shortening and foreshortening, hitting obliquely at angles, working along obscure situations. He avoids all centrality. *The Cannibal* is a refracted picture of a marginal Germany, the sense of the country deep in defeat, already planning to renew itself with American aid—the surreal, nightmarish sense of the conqueror's abetting the defeated's rise.

Nothing is more marginal than Hawkes's conception of the conqueror, a brilliant image which the careless reader may minimize, a single motorcyclist who controls one-third of the conquered territory. The motorcyclist is named Leevey, a variation on a Jewish name, and his "patrolling" of the countryside puts him near Spitzen-on-the-Dein, where Zizendorf, the new German Führer, has risen from the ashes of defeat to lead the German people. Zizendorf's plan is to unseat the motorcyclist, through a log placed across his path, and then steal the machine. A movement begins with one machine. This, along with broadsides printed clandestinely and spread to the population, will be the basis of the new movement: all against scenes of appalling desolation, destruction, and deprivation.

The motion in the novel is twofold: the motorcyclist rushing toward his doom in Spitzen-on-the-Dein, and Zizendorf, the narrator, attempting to recreate a Germany now left in ashes and defeat. With

---

*Walter Abish's *How German Is It* (1980) is a fine complement to the Hawkes novel.

these two as his frame of reference—and never clearly delineated—Hawkes moves the reader back and forth in time, with the major time shift occurring between the period of 1914, the first war, and 1945, the end of the second. The telescoping of the two eras is often remarkable for its brevity, and for its difficulty. For even within the telescoping of the eras, there is further intense condensation. In the final section of the novel, when 1914 has returned to 1945, Hawkes titles a chapter "Leader." He roves back and forth between the onrushing Leevey and the narrator, Zizendorf, with all the characters brought together, finally, *Götterdämmerung* revisited. At one point, as the local madhouse prepares to riot, and Madame Snow, a woman whose fortunes stretch between the two wars, is about to wrench off the head of a stolen chicken, an image appears at the window: "The soft broken claws [of the chicken] kicked at her wrist. For a moment the Kaiser's face, thin, depressed, stared in at the cell window, and then was gone, feeling his way over a land that was now strange to his touch. The old woman watched the fowl twisting its head, blinking the pink-lidded eyes."

The image may seem purely surrealistic, but it is quite functional, given the telescoping of the two wars into one, the two defeats into one, the resurgence of Germany under Hitler and now Zizendorf's attempt at renewal. The Kaiser's face becomes a linkage of considerable significance, although it is fleeting, like everything else in the novel. We recall Lowell's poem on the Quaker graveyard in Nantucket, with its brief, telescoped glimpses of *Moby-Dick,* the *Pequod,* Ahab, whaleboats. In the next chapter of *The Cannibal,* in the same section, a further telescoping occurs in the 1945 period: first forty years of Kaiser updated, then one year's events compressed. The Mayor of the town had acquiesced to the execution by the American occupation forces of a Nazi named Miller—the Mayor had been forced to drop the handkerchief that signaled the firing squad. The American colonel had put a live bullet into only one rifle, Zizendorf's, and then, savagely, congratulated him on being a good marksman. Zizendorf plots his revenge, waits out the occupation, and then burns down the building with the Mayor in it. The passage suggests how all have become cannibals:

> "Here, Miller," he [the Mayor] said, "let's sit down to the soup together. That woman's an excellent cook and the bird's from my own flock. I have hundreds, you know. Miller, let me give you this broth." Tears were in the old man's eyes, he reached

for the soup. But Miller wouldn't drink. The Mayor's nose and mouth were bound in the red bandanna [belonging to the Pastor, who had told the Mayor *he* would die], it choked about his throat, and at the last minute, Miller knocked over the tureen.

> "I think we can go," I [Zizendorf] said. The fire was filling the street with a hot, small amount of ash.

> The Mayor did not cry out, but died, I was very glad, without recompense or absolution.

The remarkable thing, besides the intense condensation of events, is the use of prose in the manner of compact poetry. Lowell's contemporary work has already been cited. One recalls the knotted quality of Yeats's later poetry, or some of the closely wrought phrases in Shakespeare's tragedies, in which a line or two, even a phrase, carries the weight of entire explanations. Hawkes's economy here, carried over into his novellas and novels of the next ten years, requires the closest of reading and an adaptation to a tightness of phrasing that will recur, not in the popular novelists, but in Gaddis, Barth, Barthelme, and Pynchon. Hawkes, in the 1940s, was grappling with what would be for the American novelist new literary ideas and new forms of craftsmanship, all outside the pleasing of a particular readership, on a much smaller scale what Joyce had attempted in the previous generation.

Mailer's and Jones's barrage of words does not describe the army or war, but makes them part of everything familiar. Hawkes defamiliarizes war. It is his obliqueness that makes us "see" the many dimensions of occupation: hatred of the Germans toward their conquerors, desolation of their spirit, madness of their endeavors to recover, equal madness of the Americans to help them recover. Some of the final images of the novel are concerned with a riot at the local madhouse, with inmates pouring out and only women at hand to control them with staves or household weapons. Just as Zizendorf announces that Germany has been liberated and the new era begun, the madhouse is put in order and opened once again: "and before the day had begun the Nation was restored, its great operations and institutions were once more in order, the sun was frozen and clear." Everything comes together and another mad cycle is ready to start, Yeats's rough beast slouching toward Bonn.

Despite economy of word, scene, and character, despite obliqueness of approach, there is vastness here. Space implied can be more compelling than space defined. In Mailer's novel, despite the vastness of the arguments between Cummings and Hearn, and even the near-infinitude of the terrain, there is the sense of limitation, of history denied. By use of constant reshapings and refocusing, as well as telescoping and oblique commentary, Hawkes evaded the verbal traps awaiting his more popular contemporaries. With landscapes drawn from authors as disparate as Hardy, Eliot, and Kafka, Hawkes combined spatial dimensions with silence, motionlessness, isolation: energy underpinned by enervation. In a novel about one-quarter the length of *The Naked and the Dead, The Cannibal* presents a far more sophisticated political view of war, of America and Europe, than Mailer could do in his extended dialogues. Furthermore, Hawkes had not forsaken a historical context; by refracting the two wars (like Grass, in *The Tin Drum,* later), he allowed both frame and range. Potentiality is all. This is not, incidentally, minimalist art, since the issues are huge, the outlines on a grand scale, the execution moving toward the large gesture. A motorcyclist racing across one-third of a conquered nation, while a third-rate Führer plots comeback, a country that itself exists only to prepare for war—these are not only modernist images, but historical counters of great moment.

The War as Literary and Cultural Barrier Reef

In many salient ways, Flannery O'Connor, who, as a retiring Southern lady afflicted with a crippling disease, was as distant from war as a novelist could possibly be, assimilated the sense of the war in her stories (less so in her novels). The presentation of elements dissolving and breaking apart (an "artificial nigger," the first step toward "seeing" the black), the breakdown of all restrictions (criminality on a par with Christian ethics), the intense awareness of clash among final things all characterize her fiction and reflect the values of the postwar period, in a way that Hemingway does not or could not.

Even Faulkner's "war novel," *The Fable,* fails as an ambitious attempt to frame war values because it ennobles the (first) war, turns it into fable, at the very time postwar novelists defabulized the war, demythicized it, saw it as different from what war had seemed before. In his novel, Faulkner attempted to bring war together with an admittedly outmoded morality, to make coherent for us elements that were already flying apart for his contemporaries. For him, with all other avenues of heroism closed out, war had become the way in which the heroic life, even in defeat, could still be lived. It was just this point his younger contemporaries were questioning or mocking.

What these "new" generational novelists had in common was a desire to get beyond what the United States was becoming in the late 1940s and the 1950s. Unlike the previous generation, they did not have to fight against poverty; they had to struggle against acceptance, compromise, assimilation. The war stimulated the economy in ways that Roosevelt's prewar measures could not, leading to many accusations that Roosevelt had created the war to end the Depression. Motivation aside, it did. Once the war began, the economy leaped ahead with such momentum that every aspect of the system benefited. *One could create oneself in those postwar years.*

We observe, on one hand, an America that finally fulfilled all its promises as the result of a *felix culpa,* the war itself; yet, on the other, the need to oppose marketplace affluence to allow serious culture to develop and flourish. The war was a literary barrier reef or watershed because it made America seem so easy; when, for cultural purposes, it had to be viewed as impossible, intractable, with irresolvable tensions and conflicts.

That surface of life so beloved by the popular press and by *Time* and *Life* magazines drove an ever deeper wedge between the serious novelist (who appeared subversive, unpatriotic) and the more popular panderers to a confectionery culture. Serious writers faced a terrible uphill struggle. For everything—except them—was up: wages, employment, population growth (a one-third increase over the 1930s), and of course, the industrial boom, which continued, in the main, unbroken through the Korean War and the cold war into the early years of the Vietnam War. As long as the pump was primed, no one minded. Yet our novelists peered out at a counterfeit, deceptive, artificial society that bolstered a bogus culture.

On that surface, America's relationship to the rest of the world, depleted by the war, was Roman. Nuclear power was ours alone, and even when the Soviet Union joined the club, our technology seemed invincible. The war had indeed made us rich. The tremendous growth of the economic plant and the superiority of American industry over the rest of the world combined postponed the divisive elements—political, social, cultural—that would surface in the 1960s; although many novelists by the mid-1950s perceived that such divisions existed and remained unresolved. The dissolution, the counterfeiting, the entropic sense that seemed central to novelists was marginal at most to corporate America and its spokesmen in the popular press.

America was, literally, growing fat. How fat? Food surpluses, not deficiencies, were the problem. Storing the huge grain crops of the 1950s became an increasing difficulty. The average American ate enough each day for two Europeans or three Orientals. In many sectors, such as oil, steel, electricity, industrial equipment, manufactured goods, chemicals, the United States produced more than half of the world's total. Its railroads ran, its airlines were modernized. Almost five out of every six cars were American manufactured. The buying power of the average American exceeded that of the rest of the world's citizens by 1500 percent. Poverty areas here, as Michael Harrington later demonstrated, existed abundantly, but they were silent, hidden, unaccounted for. The average poverty-level poor white or Southern black was in any case better off than almost all the rest of the foreign population. Miserable by American standards, Harrington's hidden one-third fared far better than the average European, although they were mired in a poverty cycle that would remain unaltered. Some integration of blacks into the economy, however slow and torturous, was made possible by way of labor unions (especially in auto assembly plants), integration of the armed forces (with much resistance), and educational benefits under the G.I. Bill.

Of equal importance is that the civilian population of the United States and its cities and towns had suffered no war damage. There was no coming back from rubble, or from the moral problems of defeat and occupation. Everything in America was incremental; we could add, not replace. (Of course, this would come to haunt us in the 1970s, when the physical plant was worn down and too expensive to replace.) Educational establishments, from first-rate universities to fourth-rate colleges, dance schools, vocational centers, began their spectacular growth, aided by the G.I. Bill. Funds existed for everything, from Harvard to cosmetology.

Yet the felt sense of that period was of a very different kind of reality; of a drift in which valuable years and great opportunities were being wasted by men of little vision, supported by a general populace indifferent to larger issues. The surge of support intellectuals and academics gave Adlai Stevenson's candidacy in 1952, and again in 1956, was a sign of desperation; for the Stevenson whom they supported so generously was a conservative man, a man who had vacillated on civil rights, whose position on minorities was not at all defined, and whose foreign policies, although phrased brilliantly, were indistinguishable from Truman's and Eisenhower's. While his great rhetorical ability was exhilarating, especially when contrasted with Truman's homespun* and Eisenhower's non sequiturs, the rhetoric was more style than substance; more the forays of an agile intellect and a mannered man than the result of deeply held convictions or a philosophical mind.

A good deal of this was apparent to novelists, for many of the books published in the early 1960s—such as Percy's *The Moviegoer,* Heller's *Catch-22,* Pynchon's *V.,* Roth's *Letting Go,* Bellow's *Herzog,* Malamud's *A New Life*—were begun in the 1950s and reflect the decade's attitudes and cultural concepts. Some are direct responses. Since these books—and my listing is partial—are so antagonistic to the 1950s we have observed in the economic sphere, their adversariness must have some basis. Or else we are dealing with an art form gone mad.

How do we account for the rejection, indifference, and nausea we discover in the fiction of the 1950s themselves and in those novels which derived from that decade but were published in the 1960s? Foreign influences, as we have noted, abounded; but could those foreign themes and techniques have gripped the American novelists' imagination unless certain domestic elements had prepared the way? We are speaking of those novelists preparing themselves as well as those already achieving; yet both groups, the en-

---

*The nostalgia for Truman that ran through the mid-1970s is truly inexplicable in rational terms; as is the case with most nostalgia, the fuel that keeps it running is made up of two parts forgetfulness to one part ignorance. It can only be explained as a pastoral fantasy, those postwar Truman years having been relatively Edenic.

trenched writers as well as the novices, agreed that to understand America one had to deny it. While the visions of the writers remained individualized and varied, there was some basic consensus that the novel and the general culture were two halves of a schizoid existence.

Are the following answers sufficient response to why the novel became such an adversary force? (1) The war and its immediate aftermath had raised so many expectations that the only place to look was down; as avatars of the future, novelists were concerned with "down" factors before the general public (or media) recognized how its hopes would be dashed. Yet since this reason has application to many eras, its specific application to the late 1940s and early 1950s is unchanged. (2) Much of the fiction of this early postwar period was written by minority novelists, chiefly Jews and blacks; and therefore their ideology was already outside the mainstream, pointing toward a European or generally foreign orientation. Yet many non-Jewish writers (Hawkes, Gaddis, Barth, Burroughs, for example) were writing a wilder, far more adversary kind of novel than their ethnic contemporaries.

Or: (3) Themes based on alcoholism, homosexuality, dissidence, or on being "beat" were ways of calling attention to oneself. Thus, novelists were forsaking social commitment to seek personal publicity, pursuing outlandish themes as a means of locating themselves outside a bourgeois frame of reference. This was the crux of the *Life* article in 1955 castigating novelists for not showing America as it really was. Accordingly, the adversary quality of the novelist was connected to his narcissism; so that he or she was eager to display a self rather than to understand the nature of things. (4) Adversariness was based on the self-hatred of the writer. The writer, in this view, has had such a dismal childhood or unhappy adolescence that he will make the country (his parents *in extenso*) pay for his miseries. This argument, incidentally, although vague, has interesting psychological aspects and cannot simply be dismissed. The problem is that it applies in every era—would a happier, less ill Kafka have written *(a)* happier novels; *(b)* the same novels; or *(c)* no novels at all? Would he have been Kafka? (5) The American has always been a rebel, so that matching his imperial self against the country is his heritage, and behind the rebellion is a real love-hate relationship to the country. Ultimately, the writer tries to understand America by way of his rebellion against her.

Nearly all these arguments, however generalized, contain a partial truth, a partial answer. Certainly, the problems they point to do exist: that the novelist, with an almost desperate and obsessive intensity, fails to accept America as others see it; that his or her America is doom filled, populated with marginal creatures who are maddened, enraged. Implicit in postwar fiction are Lee Harvey Oswald, Jack Ruby, Sirhan Sirhan, James Earl Ray, Arthur Bremer, the Manson clan, the Symbionese Liberation Army— they were in the fiction well before they appeared in public life; as were the public figures they targeted, or the issues such public figures disguised, lied about, or simply distorted. Joseph McCarthy was a fictional presence before he appeared in person. What all these arguments except the final one fail to accept, however, is that the postwar novel is not unique as a subversive force.

We can see the American 1850s, when Hawthorne wrote his adversary fictions, as a decade of tremendous excitement, the years preceding the Civil War as full of political maneuvering, polemics, economic expansion, growth of railroads, considerable migration. And yet Hawthorne moved outside this, to marginal discontinuous areas. Poe, for his part, sought his vision of America in aspects of English Gothic, in tales of horror and nightmare, an unrecognizable America for those interested in contemporary values. Melville moved his protagonists to sea, to remove them from an America that apparently was only a source of confusion to him. There, on the sea, they make their decisions, freed of any close attachment to the country, pure decisions of salvation and/or doom. Emerson preached a new man, discontinuous with the past, a man reborn to his own devices, self-indulgent to some degree, egotistical, a worthy individual. Thoreau sought himself in nature, and then in everything he perceived in nature he saw himself. The rest of the world, as he pictures us, remains outside the self.

Captain Vere, in *Billy Budd,* has come to stand for many things: support of existing value systems, one who defends capitalistic exploitation of the innocent, the father figure who condemns the son, the Jewish God who recondemns the Jesus figure, Billy; but it has been insufficiently stressed how dangerous his ideas are before he agrees to hang Billy. We recall that he speaks in a time of war, a period when even our contemporary writers were hesitant to condemn America, and yet his recognition of Billy's act contains sympathetic responses to rebellion and even subversion. Before Vere decides on his course of action, he does not capitulate to simplistic notions of Billy's danger to the body politic; but argues that while Billy may be innocent, his action will be seen by others as subversive. Vere himself views Billy as beyond evil, and in these thoughts he flirts, in wartime, with ideas subversive of the common good.

Such examples suggest that the American writer has always moved quite explicitly outside any official version of American life and culture, in this respect very different from English writers of either the nineteenth or the twentieth century. The English novelist has worked from within, cherishing the very institutions he or she mocks, neither subversive nor adversary in the larger sense. The American writer, whether in romantic or realistic fiction, diverges, moving along outside of institutions and history, always discontinuous with normalizing cultural patterns, taking a countering role as a matter of course, Adam reborn.

The postwar novel differs only in its intensity of antagonism, its enlargement of ways in which fiction can oppose the direction of the country. One of the by-products of the war and the influx of modernism was the release of sexual energies: the earlier legalization of *Ulysses,* later the decision over *Lady Chatterley's Lover,* more importantly Supreme Court decisions about the written word, decisions made quite clearly within the modernist influence. Sexual rebellion—as hetero- or homosexual activity, masturbatory play, voyeurism, soft and later hard pornography, whatever—played no small part in the novel's insurgency. A chapter of *Portnoy's Complaint* was called "Whacking Off." A few years earlier, whacking off would have remained a private matter; by 1967, it gained head listing on the cover of *Partisan Review,* the Trotskyite journal of the thirties.

But we should not overstress sexual rebellion at the expense of other elements. The war generated an opening out that was more than sexual; it was, surely, more than physical experience. A world conflict is a state of mind, and even a winning conflict kills a good deal of the old while generating an increased sense of the new. What we find in our postwar novelists is that American desire to be reborn; the war and its aftermath were the means. It does not matter that much of the new was already old; when American novelists imported modernism, it was no longer modern, but post-, meta-, or para-.

Even though the new was old—Melville would have appreciated the irony—for the American it signaled that periodic need for renewal. And rebirth with modernism as one's support meant subversion, adversariness, separation, as much as one can generate in a culture which absorbs everything as rapidly as it appears. Any writer who failed to be "after" was observing the world through the wrong end of the telescope; or else charting his course on a map with the wrong projection.* Before the war, the map was, more or less, straight lines; after, it was the curves of great circles, where all that seemed distortion was really only a different angle of perspective, another particle in the field of force.

---

*Gore Vidal's *Williwaw* (1946), as one of the first war novels, was a fine performance for a nineteen-year-old author; similarly, *The City and the Pillar* (1948), as one of the first American novels to touch directly on homosexual themes, was a fine performance for an only slightly older author. I have, however, omitted Vidal from this study. By assiduously separating himself from modernism and the modern novel, he has produced a large body of work that rejects the new. He apparently hears a different drummer and would surely be embarrassed to be considered alongside novelists many of whom he has repeatedly disparaged for running with the academic pack: i.e., writing modern novels, cultivating fashion, trying to be new. "Eventually the novel [he told *Paris Review*'s Gerald Clarke in 1974] will simply be an academic exercise, written by academics to be used in classrooms in order to test the ingenuity of students. A combination of Rorschach test and anagram. Hence, the popularity of John Barth, a perfect U[niversity]-novelist, whose books are written to be taught, not to be read." The same lines could have described Joyce's *Ulysses* when it appeared in 1922. Like Louis Auchincloss, Vidal has made literary choices that—despite trendy themes—look back, not forward.

The War and Combat Novel

In the years immediately after the war, an entire subgenre of the novel developed, the war and combat novel, which then appeared regularly thereafter in the 1950s and 1960s, mainly connected to the Second World War, skipping the Korean War, and then trying to come to terms with the Vietnam War. Except for Tim O'Brien's *Going After Cacciato,* the major achievements in the subgenre have been associated with the 1940s conflict.* The war/combat novel becomes for the American novelist a sociopolitical fiction; for at their most incisive, such novels reflect the culture. Even more, they demonstrate continuity with traditional American themes, mirroring not only contemporary culture but the American past. We can see this most immediately in a spare fiction written during the war about the Italian campaign, *A Walk in the Sun* (1944) by Harry Brown. Although brief, this novel has within it many or most of the dimensions of war/combat fiction associated with Mailer, Jones, et al.

Small scale is the dimension here: one platoon, one section, one goal. The question is of leadership, for the group of men heading toward a farmhouse along a bombed-out coast has no leader. Leaders die, and the men must become a coherent group because of some element from within. The farmhouse is only a spot on a map, and since they are not certain where it is, it takes on mythical properties. It will save them (as a refuge), but it also exposes them to terrible danger on their journey toward it. That farmhouse "at the end of the road" is either pastoral salvation or violent death.

The achievement of the goal itself is a great lyrical moment. The men, after severe losses from strafing, storm the farmhouse, their objective, the sole reason for their society, after a walk in the sun. "Tyne [now in charge of the platoon] knew that he was running gracefully toward the farmhouse, the mysterious farmhouse, the farmhouse that was waiting to gather him in and hide him from the world. Its windows were eyes, and they were looking at him, studying his every move and the movements of the men with him. The farmhouse loomed up, and it was waiting."

Brown has evoked the elemental nature of war, in which it is associated with the pastoral tradition: the earth, which the men hug as though their mothers; the farm and farmhouse as mythical salvation; the silent planes, like birds, which loom up and bring instant death, only to disappear rapidly; the road in the sun, the bright light of Italy, its heat and also its death. Leading away from the farmhouse is a bridge, which must be blown; so that the platoon and the Germans are cut off, in the farmhouse in the middle of nowhere: Thoreau's cottage transformed into a death house.

A Walk in the Sun owes a good deal to Crane's *The Red Badge of Courage,* which has become the archetypal American war novel. Crane caught the ineffectuality of the American as a soldier, his basic distrust of military life, his inability to follow authority, his confusion when faced with disruption of his pastoral dream, his desire to escape anything that makes him joyless. Brown's men also wander in and out of death, refusing to accept it as a badge of war. They are not really soldiers, but civilians playing at war; yet caught in a mission that will save or kill them.

That immersion in pastorality is clear; as is the intensity with which space is evoked. The sun is played off against the earth: one withering, the other offering protection. A "walk" becomes the means by which the men expose themselves, as if on a picnic or family outing; and yet they men are picked off, dying not in combat but in idle, marginal acts of strafing by silent birdlike planes. Space is both the friend and the enemy; friend, because the farther the men walk, the farther they move from the main area of combat; enemy, because the closer they come to their objective, the closer they are to a conclusion of whatever their mission entails. They are chess pieces in a game whose rules are made, not by man, but by sun, earth, farmhouse, space and time. "Earth is a marvellous thing," Brown writes, because it is a motherly space; hugged by earth, or hugging it, one is safe.

A Walk in the Sun, a compelling fiction in itself, is also exemplary of that entire subgenre of war and

---

*The Vietnam War saw some superb nonfiction: Michael Herr's *Dispatches* and Philip Caputo's *A Rumor of War* (both 1977). Of note as fiction are James Webb's *Fields of Fire* (1978) and O'Brien's earlier *If I Die in a Combat Zone* (1973). Robert Stone's *Dog Soldiers* (1974) uses Vietnam as a backdrop, drugs as the civilian equivalent of war; ideologically, the novel works through themes derived from *Heart of Darkness.* Midway between fiction and nonfiction is John Sack's *M* (1966), which, however, lacks the verbal distinction of Herr or the imaginative power of O'Brien.

combat novels. But then the question arises of whether we can even speak of war and combat novels together. How do we distinguish, for example, between *Guard of Honor* and *The Naked and the Dead,* both of them written about the Second World War and published within a short time of each other? Or *The Gallery* and *From Here to Eternity,* also "war novels" published only a few years apart. Or *Catch-22* and *The Thin Red Line?* There does appear to be a distinction between the novel about the war and the novel about combat in the war. The former—I have in mind besides *Guard of Honor, From Here to Eternity,* and *Catch-22, The Caine Mutiny, The Young Lions, Going After Cacciato,* and Bourjaily's *The End of My Life*—may have scenes of combat, but it is essentially more about the society that generated the war, or about a societal equivalent found in the military, than it is about combat.

The sensibility underlying the war novel has within it the strands of the social writer. A masculine world, it is not so exclusively masculine as in the novel of combat. The essential element is that war novels use the military as social commentary. *From Here to Eternity,* arguably the best of any of these novels, in its prewar scenes is the "war novel" equivalent of *The Grapes of Wrath,* the army base in Hawaii substituting for the dust bowl of the Steinbeck novel. The Jones book is, of course, more than that; but it is as much an atomization of the society—class, caste, upward mobility, political infighting, matters of power, controlled capitalistic systems—as of the military. Although there is no war in most of the novel, it points toward the attack on Pearl Harbor, and when the attack comes, Jones has suggested for us a military society that reflects the larger society.

The war novel, then, is not solely a subgenre of the novel, but is, in this respect, as much a part of fictional representation as the novel of manners in James, Fitzgerald, or Wharton, the novel of social disaster in Steinbeck or Dos Passos, the novel of class and caste in Dreiser, the novel of individual dislocation in Wolfe, Norris, or even Hemingway. What the war provided was a huge arena for all the social and political energies of the novelist. Politics were not at all ignored in the 1940s and 1950s, but were frequently incorporated into the war (not combat) novel.*

---

*The two most effective American novels about the First World War were war rather than combat novels. E. E. Cummings's *The Enormous Room* (1922) reverberates with images, motifs, situations, that are updated in Heller's sense of World

The combat novel—*The Thin Red Line* and *Whistle, The Naked and the Dead, A Walk in the Sun*—is more exclusive, and it is far more masculine. While it would be possible for a woman to write a war novel —*Guard of Honor* is within a woman's range of experience—it is unlikely that a woman could write a novel of combat, unless as purely an act of imagination, perhaps the way Crane and Stendhal invented battle scenes. Even so, theirs are perspectives on battle, rather than purely battle. This stress is important, for the novel of combat has within it the same kind of masculine preoccupations that we find in western and gangster novels; combat legitimizes the killing, yet many rules of conduct still hold true.

The novel of combat is essentially a subgenre of the war novel, not the main thing. The war novel sweeps, the combat novel focuses. Only indirectly does it mirror the culture; for its violence is legalized, and its special conditions create a special kind of man and response. It carries over very little; it *is.* Despite its focus on a battle situation, the combat novel becomes an intensely individual thing; for behind the war focus is the testing out of the individual: not the winning of the battle or the war, but the individual's victory over himself. Because of that focus on self, Americans are particularly fine combat novelists.

War II in *Catch-22.* The war for Cummings is viewed through a prison system. Connected, like so many other writers during World War I, to the Norton-Harjes Ambulance Corps, Cummings refused to repudiate a charge that he did not hate the Germans. As a result, he begins a journey of rooms and imprisonment until he reaches the "enormous room" in the gendarmerie in Marseilles. His refusal and fate are the "catch-22" of the First War. The enormous room is like the Tower of Babel, an image of Europe, not the war. Here he has established a vast symbol, a Bosch-like world, a milling and heaving collection of languages, customs, types, and frauds. With the room as focus, Cummings has an instrument for observing a completely dislocated, discontinuous society.

Similarly, in *Three Soldiers* (1921), Dos Passos, in more conventional terms, distances himself in the military from the world, only to reflect it. His three soldiers are three levels of society: upper, as represented by John Andrews, a composer, an artist seeking expression; lower, as represented by Fuselli, uneducated, a loser; the indeterminate middle, as represented by Chrisfield, a farm boy from Indiana with violent tendencies. Since the army reflects a naturalistic, fated society, military life is repressive, doom-filled. Freedom for Andrews is to be free of the army so his art can flow. Like John Brown, whom Dos Passos compares him to, Andrews must become the embodiment of liberation. Through the army, Dos Passos has created a military society that represses and constricts; overthrow it or break out, and one helps to remake that society and oneself.

From Mailer's ability to handle combat scenes, which are the most effective parts of *The Naked and the Dead,* we can foresee the entire career: the need to define a world that belongs to men. Mailer's world is limited to the male's response to challenge, and this response—since bullfighting and big-game hunting are not ordinarily accessible to a Jewish writer—must come through combat. Physical courage in the face of fear becomes the way in which a man can measure not only himself but the quality of life. By way of bravery, the individual can break through historical restrictions.

Writers of combat fiction are happiest when they can bring the placid, rather stodgy American soldier up against a situation in which he becomes a killer, rapist, brutal wielder of power. The idea in Mailer, Jones, and others is to find that means by which the American soldier can be "awakened" to the primitive elements lying beneath, to what the Indian once meant to the Puritan and then to the pioneer. The experience in combat also has reference to a religious awakening, being touched; it has elements, in our fiction, of revivalism, the sense of doom in the sermons of ministers of the Great Awakening, of religious apocalypse. Combat, which may confer swift death, also means a kind of quickened life. We are not in the presence of the Greek tragic sense of violence and death, which leads, ultimately, to a reckoning with the gods. For the American, there is no reckoning; violence establishes a purity with its own rules, its own field of force. When an American soldier reaches beneath his unfocused history toward the elemental or primitive force, he is reaching toward the vitality which identifies him as American.

The novel of combat connects the American experience in war to that in detective* and western fiction. It brings back the sole frontier remaining to us and

---

*Running parallel to many combat/war novels was the gangster/detective fiction of Mickey Spillane. His Mike Hammer is the ultimate, in popular culture, of the masculine military type. Hateful of Communists, patriotic, associated with the right, a male chauvinist, a defender of a reductive form of democracy, Hammer represents a kind of caricatured military. As in the novel of combat, Spillane's work simplified and reduced to violent endings all social, political, and ideological conflicts—hammered them down, as if in a gigantic air raid. Spillane surely had his success because of how well he conformed with McCarthyism in the fifties—his Hammer and McCarthy were no strangers to each other—but even more, Spillane and Hammer were working out combat situations in peacetime. In both fiction forms there are resolutions of elements which peacetime leaves as loose ends.

provides an alternative to a bourgeois society, which deals death to the instinctual life. Of equal importance is the fact that the novel of combat removed the writer from ideological concerns, placing him outside a political stance in an elemental area that both transcends and falls beneath politics. This was, and is, obviously important for the American novelist, who is traditionally uncomfortable with ideological materials. We have only to observe the passage of Norman Mailer from the superb combat scenes of *The Naked and the Dead* to a static ideological dialectic in *Barbary Shore,* his next novel. Mailer had, in a sense, to leap over political problems and return to the visceral aspects of his first novel before his imagination was freed: in his "combative nonfiction," the essay on "The White Negro," and the personal journalism at the end of the fifties.

Just as musical comedy, not opera, became a distinctive American musical tradition, so the novel of combat became a distinctive American form, rather than the socially oriented fiction associated with the Continent. The American in combat, in a sense, was returned to that era in which the American was created in the wilderness Zion of the Puritans, or even more, in the Adamic wilderness of earliest man. This is the time before Eve; or else Eve was not wife, but mistress or whore. There are no children, no responsibilities except to other men, and there is the camaraderie of fellow souls, untouched by the feminizing world, which, seemingly desirable, is so feared. This is the vision James Jones has, and he captures it in parts of *The Thin Red Line,* but misses it altogether in his final novel, *Whistle,* which was intended to bring together all these aspects of the American mentality.

Even spatially, the combat novel is a sympathetic form. For space in combat is measured in the proximity to enemy fire, which is death, and the distance between it and oneself, which is salvation.† Distant space has to do with life; nearness of space with imminent death. When the soldier closes with the enemy —caught in that transcendent experience that results from company spirit—he exposes his body in order to salvage his soul. If he can remain distant from the enemy, space represents rewards existing in a limitless world beyond. In that "beyond," there lies his spatial fantasy of insatiable women, a bottomless well of booze, uncomplicated pleasures.

---

†Somewhere in between is a third distancing, connected to the "good wound," one that does not disable but leads to a rest cure, R & R, even being sent home.

In temporal terms, the obverse of the spatial universe, the novel of combat establishes short bursts of action, with periods of exhaustion and rest intervening. The rapidity of battle is in contradistinction to the long-drawn-out sequences necessary for the social novel. There, scenes must occur over years; in combat, minutes—at the most, on patrol, hours. The purpose of combat, which is pure American in this respect, is expenditure of a lifetime of energy in a short burst, which determines whether one lives or dies. In the social novel, preparation for action is longer, and there may be several opportunities or choices, unless the deck is marked. But even when the individual's fate is determined, the downfall, if it comes, is not precipitous, but serpentine. For the postwar novelist, the war had created a different sense of speeded-up time.

We need only to compare James Jones with Dreiser, both of them on the surface apparently loyal to naturalistic determinism. Jones, like Dreiser, rarely permits his characters to slip out of a mechanical universe, however much they fancy their own freedom. Prewitt attempts to liberate himself, but it is Warden, who never leaves the system, who prevails —that is, stays alive. Yet while Dreiser plays out his narrative over a lifetime, Jones telescopes his into days, months, or a limited run of years. The nature of their difference, despite superficial similarities, is that between the social mentality and the combat mentality, the consequence of postwar fiction-making.

SOME SPECIMENS

When Mailer conceived of *The Naked and the Dead,* he did so in traditionally naturalistic terms, those of Hemingway, Dreiser, Crane, Dos Passos, Norris, possibly Conrad and Melville. The focus was man versus machine, or fate; man at the mercy of a neutral nature—Hardy's neutral-malevolent nature —or subverted by forces he cannot understand, or conquer; man as the butt of whatever lies in store for him, or ruled by ideologies he cannot comprehend. Victory, if it comes, is the result of blunders, chance, even misadventure, Tolstoyan in this respect. All this Mailer encapsulates on the island of Anopopei, and it takes heroism out of the war, placing it in the traditional narrative of the individual sunk into a group. Yet the American drive for the single self must assert itself regardless of group fate; so Mailer drives frantically toward the individual. The problems begin.

It is true that war establishes its own universe of relationship and sensations, different from those in civilian life. Men are transformed into mechanical objects by fear and desire for survival. Nothing surpasses Jones's portrait of men in the line in *The Thin Red Line,* and they cannot escape, except perhaps into fantasy or their own history. Superior officers and general command have otherwise placed a wall around individual need and desire; only their minds and sensations can still respond, and these severely circumscribed. Within this frame of reference, *all* war experiences, as Crane and Stendhal recognized, are essentially the same, all wars comparable.

This much we can understand. The homogeneity of war and of war experiences, once differences of place and time are located, means that basic activity preempts the novel's attention: matter, not manner, count. Yet manner styles the individual, matter the generalized area. A war novel obviously need not be cast in terms of *Ulysses* or *Finnegans Wake,* or become a dream sequence like Proust's novel. A large fiction, however, which hopes to capture the particulars of a war situation, needs more than conventional tools, or tools once used to write about the First War. What gives *The Cannibal* its strength—that is, its innovativeness—is the very element lacking in *The Naked and the Dead.* An alternative to technical innovation would have been intellectual distinction.

Part of the problem lay in Mailer's plan. As he stated in *Advertisements for Myself,* he wanted to write a war novel. And yet he avoided the theater of war where issues were thickly textured, in Europe, for the one in the Far East, which was relatively straightforward. I am suggesting that the ideological discussions in the novel between Hearn and Cummings, which provide the intellectual underpinning, are misplaced in the Far Eastern war. Simply their location, apart from content, dissipates their significance, since the issues at hand are uncomplicated: to take an island, then another, then still another. What they discuss becomes words—modeled possibly on Naphta and Settembrini in *The Magic Mountain*—but talk unconnected to anything outside it except pure violence.

To stand back for a moment. The country at large was split in its own relationship to the war. Those favoring a Pacific war as the higher priority were quite different from those who felt Germany had to be beaten first. Behind that division were questions of patriotism, ideological and political complexity, and racial attitudes. These divisions incidentally did not die with the war, but remained well into the 1960s.

Since Japan had attacked us, and Germany did not, the pro-Pacific argument focused on matters of national survival, revenge, honor. Supporters of the Pacific war tended to be from less urban states, from smaller towns and cities, more conservative elements in the country, for whom MacArthur was a hero. Anti-Roosevelt forces saw his German priority as simply another sellout. Anti-Japanese feeling on racial grounds ran high, also. While the German soldier received begrudging admiration, as did the German war machine, the Japanese was ridiculed personally as bucktoothed, squat, bandy-legged, little more than a savage. Jones's combat scenes in *The Thin Red Line* reflect this sense of the enemy.

The German war was of another kind, supported heavily by urbanites, professionals, those politically committed, and those who tended to find liberal solutions more satisfactory than conservative ones. These are traditional divisions in American life and thought, and it is not unusual to find them reflected in wartime attitudes. For those who would support the Japanese war, we need look no further than characters in novels by John O'Hara, John Marquand, and James Gould Cozzens.

Given the lack of coherence between larger elements—the discussions and the narrative line—all efforts at cohesion prove awkward. The flashbacks and choruses which occur periodically, for example, are attempts to give the ideological conflicts, as well as racial and social tensions, some historical reference, as Dos Passos did in *U.S.A.* Yet even as Mailer evidently needed these biographical capsules to fill out his characters' perspectives, they are, given their brevity, clumsy and platitudinous. Since they function naturalistically, well within cause and effect, deterministically, they do not differentiate; one Jew is like another, one Pole similar to all Poles. Despite Mailer's skill, we rarely see them clearly in the flashback material, but only in their actions; so that narrative forward and history backward clash technically.

The long dialogues between Hearn and Cummings in the first half of the novel are similarly misplaced, clogging rather than clarifying the narrative. Necessary as they are to Mailer's plan, which is to pit varying ideologies against each other—Cummings's reactionary view, typical of Pacific war advocates, Hearn's liberalism, more suited to the European war, and Croft's stress on survival, the ultimate in lower-class ethics—except for the latter they are antithetical to the war elements. The novel may read well, but it is intellectually flaccid; the tensions which form its skeleton are too often undermined by naive presentation.

The kind of novel Mailer chose to write reflected postwar culture at its most obvious. It was to be a narrative of a small group caught in a larger conflict —we think of Crane and Conrad as the prototypes— a frame based on microcosm and macrocosm. Melville and Dreiser are other obvious practitioners. Crane and Conrad, however, gained their intensity by means of obliqueness of reference, compression, imagistic condensation. Mailer constructed his novel on principles of expansion—word, scene, flashback, ideological conflict.

His construction is like two pyramids, the first, as is customary, lying on its broad base and pointing toward the heavens; the second inverted so that its tip touches the base of the first and its base lies across the horizon. Mailer starts with the broad base of the first, moves with the patrol toward the tip, then keeps moving beyond that to the other pyramid by means of the dialogues and the "time machine" device that moves us into the Depression, ethnic issues, varying levels of the poor and oppressed.

Although Mailer handles the patrol itself expertly —the Hardyesque sense of the individual dwarfed by immensity of landscape, by a universal fate—the conventionality of his approach to a scene partially vitiates it beyond the physical fact. A related problem is his uncompelling characters: their lives, their mode of speech, the level of their ideas. Mailer's need to present a cross section of soldiers meant each had to be typical, and each indeed speaks and thinks typically. A more elaborate technique might have enabled Mailer to get at his characters obliquely and thus disguised their ordinariness; but as they stand, it is impossible, even after close readings, to remember what anyone said or stood for. Only the Hearn-Cummings dialogues have any residue; yet not because of their quality, but rather as periodic breaks from the narrative.

Only Croft has individuality, and he is Mailer's provisional triumph. As Mailer himself developed, it became clear that Croft represented to him what counted: a massive ego, only partially disguised as devotion to the army; a vast struggle between self and antiself, that is, between strength and weakness; a desire to turn everyone and everything to his own will; reserves of sadism, cruelty, as well as endurance, fitting qualities for a man who survives while others go under. Croft, nevertheless, understands fear, and at the moment the Japanese cross the river, he believes in recurring nightmares.

He is pure Being, as against Nothingness, which he brushes. A Heideggerian sense of Being exists, in that Croft attempts to transcend human "being" to achieve pure Being, and yet runs up against the fact that "being" in its temporality restrains "Being," which lies outside time. That play of the impossible straining against ordinary restraints was to preoccupy Mailer; so that while he has matured, we can say he has grown within the dictates of what he manifested in his mid-twenties. Not surprisingly, Croft is free of ideology. He moves physically and emotionally, aspects of himself he can control; ideology is for him meaningless. By way of naturalism, Mailer was attempting to reach pure Being.

It is quite incorrect to see Croft as part of the reactionary claptrap General Cummings spouts to Hearn. Croft is the ideal, however unsettling such an ideal may be to the liberal-humanistic mind, of what the army demands. To be a man, a soldier, a functioning member of a squad or patrol, one must emulate Croft. Mailer revels in this, those restraints and disciplines necessary to be a man. Even Hearn, when he moves out with the patrol behind Japanese lines, must confront the "Croft" within as well as the real Croft. Hearn's death, in fact, comes from his inability to comprehend fully how someone like Croft functions.

Croft is not Nietzschean, no overman. Driven by his need to be himself, he has visions of fear, weakness, and capitulation to the unknown. He is a miniature of organizations that function on the individual's fear. Croft is such a perfect embodiment of the army because the men fear him more than they fear death, which is the way an organization can function best. Although lacking ideology, Croft is in a sense Mailer's representative of a political idea, for he demonstrates the way an organization—army, business, industry—functions. Similarly, in *From Here to Eternity,* Jones, who was almost totally apolitical, nevertheless offered a highly structured political community by way of the peacetime army, officers and men in their tiered responses playing out the balletic movements of a political state.

Croft admires and embraces violence. He enjoys killing Japanese the way a hunter enjoys a turkey shoot. By killing, he can smother his own fear of the situation the Japanese have created; but even more, he can display his response to fear. He has a product —a body count—that denies the very fear he knows to exist. Although essentially irrational, he applies thought when personally threatened. He pits himself against nature, for he knows he can withstand the threats of men, and only nature holds any challenge

for him. Croft is a Hemingway-like embodiment of responses, but without charm, sensitivity, or fineness. He is not decent, he is not courageous in any conventional way; in a corrida, he would go after the bull with an automatic weapon or a grenade. He is pure existence: for Mailer, the purest form of survival.

It is important to emphasize that Mailer's attitudes revolve around Croft, not Hearn or Cummings, so we recognize that intellectual discussion, ideological dialogues, political debate are not the center of Mailer's universe. Survival *on any terms* is. The ironies are all there: from the start, we observe how few serious intellectual ideas will permeate Mailer's fiction, this in a supremely intelligent writer, well read, percipient, brimful of intellectual notions in his nonfiction. Given this as a premise, then, we can say that Mailer's development as a novelist had to be restricted; growth is really embroidery of a very few visceral ideas. The Croftness of Croft will remain, in Rojack, in the White Negro, in Mikey Lovett, in D.J. and his friend, in Sergius O'Shaugnessy, in various personae in the nonfiction.

Rojack's parapet walk in *An American Dream* is analogous to Croft's assertion of his essential being. Mailer's own descriptions of himself in his various political roles, whether arrested on the Pentagon steps or daring arrest in Chicago, are all variations of the Croft syndrome, expanded, made far more sophisticated, given rational explanations, but essentially embodying that nub of being (Being?) which exists outside rationality and ideology. A good part of Mailer's difficulty in achieving a satisfactory novel since *The Naked and the Dead* is that he is trapped in the Croft syndrome; and his temporary ability to break out in *Why Are We in Vietnam?* was connected to that novel's subject matter, the war as reflected on the home front, but with Croftness intact.

Mailer's every opportunity to emulate the masculinity of Croft is a dare, and yet, as a New York intellectual, he must embroider ideas; thus his fiction dangles between worlds that remain incoherent. *An American Dream* exemplifies a novel undermined by the author's intellectual ambivalence, his inability to recognize what belongs to him as the writer and what pertains to his material once it is created independently of him. The solipsism of present-day writers— Mailer, of course, but also Bellow, Barth, Vonnegut, Heller, Roth—makes it difficult for any particular writer to remain outside his work; and recent interest in what has been called the nonfiction novel or new journalism has not helped, for that literary subgenre has further fudged lines between objective and subjective, a confusion of realms reciprocated in fiction.

That line of demarcation, however subtle, however smoothed out, between subjective and objective—and it is a line profoundly affected by modernism—involves taste, discretion, literary intelligence. It was once called aesthetic distance, a term used not so much as a demarcation but as a way of defining artistic objectivity. As we see the full influence of modernism, we recognize that objectivity is not so significant; yet lines drawn between objective and subjective are. Since Mailer blurred such lines almost from the start, we can understand why he has been more comfortable with personal journalism than with fiction. We perceive that his nonfiction and journalism are all forms of autobiography; their strengths and weaknesses lie there. Even the moon shot is observed by Mailer as a Jewish astronaut. His preoccupations with White Negroes, drug traffickers, prizefighters, crime rings, conspiracies are all ways, subtle and not so subtle, by which he can measure himself against them, as Croft measures himself against each member of the squad and his superiors.

Whenever the fiction has failed to come—for thirteen years, as I write this in 1982—Mailer offers himself as the greater presence, as the truer fiction; measuring himself against Marilyn Monroe, Henry Miller, Muhammad Ali, Gary Gilmore, or women as a whole. In some super-romantic sense, he becomes, first, his work, then greater than the subject of his work. We find the counterpart to Mailer in nonfiction in Tom Wolfe, whose brilliant perceptions are almost always overridden by Wolfe's dramatization of himself, lest we forget who is the ultimate performer. Similarly, Mailer teases us that he is more important than the Vietnam War; his role in the march on the Pentagon is crucial to the antiwar movement. There is an amusing, witty side to this, for each of us who has demonstrated against something has felt superiority to the issue simply because *we* are there. Yet for the fiction writer, such loss of distinctions is fatal, since all good fiction inevitably goes beyond the author's ego, even the most reflexive fiction, in which subject circles subject.

When we return to our original point, that the war brought with it recognition that old forms must change, we find Mailer inhibited from the beginning by his immersion in the old guard, the giants of the 1920s and 1930s. That pull from naturalism caught him early, and even his later career has been a struggle not to achieve new forms but to break away from old ones, each step forward inhibited by a step backward. When literature was being formed around

Joyce, Yeats, Eliot, Proust, and Lawrence, Mailer was working within Hemingway and Dos Passos. Their way of seeing was valid and, at its best, a permanent part of our culture; but what they saw was no longer there.

Unlike *The Naked and the Dead,* a fully fleshed war novel that attempted to enter into modernist modes was John Horne Burns's *The Gallery* (1947). With varying degrees of success, Burns tried to find techniques equivalent to war; and his effort *there* locates the intellectual content of the novel, not, as in Mailer, in political and ideological discussions.

This novel about a fierce war in Europe and North Africa has only one combat scene, the war being in fact reflected in men trying to relieve themselves from the fatigue, anxiety, and fear of combat. There is almost no war except that which can be mirrored in their destructive means of relaxation—drink, gay and straight bars, staring, forms of madness which allow withdrawal. Burns's method reflects Nietzsche's paradoxical formulation that letting go is unnatural, antithetical to our temperament, even when it apparently relaxes us. In our leisure we demonstrate our true insanity.

The means for Burns's formulation is the vast Galleria Umberto Primo in Naples, a temple of glass which is a fitting symbol of the reflected pleasure that soldiers seek. In Mailer, the long sections on the patrol working behind Japanese lines preempt the shape of the novel, giving it a snakelike, episodic quality with its own tensions and dialectic. The trouble lies there, for those sections, the best in the book, have no structural reference to the earlier political episodes. In Burns, the dominant symbolic shape of the crystal gallery, whose glass has been shattered by Allied bombers, gives him a literal container for the novel: a pleasure dome, a sacred place where black masses occur; yet also a church that offers salvation and life but is, like the war itself, a magnet for destruction, doom, and death.

With this reverse image of the war as his symbolic form, Burns had an integrative shape, something lacking in most other war novels of the forties and fifties. Within it he located two kinds of material; first, the nine Portraits, which enfold the novel, beginning it and ending it. Intermixed with these are eight Promenades, five of which do not take place in the Galleria or even in Naples, but assume a kind of North African equivalent. They are first-person narratives which are expected to bring together the Portraits of war with the recording consciousness of the novelist-narrator. The aim, one assumes, was to integrate the external aspects, the Portraits, with the internal aspects, the Promenades; further, there was the need to achieve geographical integration, Italy and North Africa. In the final three Promenades, the recording consciousness moves from Algiers to Naples, so that external and internal intertwine.

Our judgment of the novel's success, or whether it is really even a novel, depends on how we view Burns's attempts at integration. That is, he took great chances in what he tried to do, and if he failed, as some critics suggested, then his novel becomes a series of discrete, well-written episodes or portraits. On the other hand, if he succeeded, even in part, then he had found some technical means for expressing the war.

Burns employed what was essentially the idea of the Greek chorus, a commentary on the main action. But the commentary, since it is modernist, is oblique to the Portraits, where the war lies. The effect of the Promenades, or commentaries by an I-narrator, is cumulative, not at all a direct relationship to the Portraits before or after them. The commentaries tend to be affirmative of human values, but then even the Portraits contain some affirmation, although they may end in death or frustration. But the key image is the Galleria, which is life and death, affirmation and negation, heaven for some, nightmare for others. If the Galleria reflects the war and, ultimately, all life, then it is everything we are, can be, hope to be. As "glass" and reflector, it sends back no more and no less than what we are; as Moby-Dick's whiteness mirrors those who challenge him. The Promenades all finally point toward the Galleria, and the Portraits are all somehow contained by it, through meetings, deals, values.

Probably the rising arch of the book comes with the episode called "Giulia," the seventh Portrait. Just before it is the first Promenade, called "Naples," and right after it is another "Naples." Giulia is a young Neapolitan lady who insists on being herself despite what the war has done to the city, her brother and father, her friends, and her total society. She will be a "gift" to any man who finally obtains her, but before that she will retain her virginity, and her identity, no matter what persuasion is brought to bear upon her. She insists on respect, love, decency. A man whom she trusts asks her to give herself to him on his last night, yet she refuses, even though he may never return from the front, or if he returns, may never claim her as his bride. She stands fast, although she "knew he'd be coming back to her." The Promenades sur-

rounding this Portrait are both positive elements, in that the narrator tries to find a meaningful existence in Naples despite the general whoredom of the city. And he concludes: "I drowned in mass ideologies, but was fished out by separate thinking and will. I remember watching the mad hordes in the streets of Naples and wondering what it all meant. But there was a certain unity in the bay, in the August moon over Vesuvius. Then humanity fell away from me like the rind of an orange, and I was something much more and much less than myself."

At this stage of the novel, less than one hundred pages from the end, the unity of Portraits and Promenades is accomplished—more by tone, of course, than by content or ideology. There is no equation between one element and the other, but the attempt by the narrator to discover individual meaning beneath the values of a war society informs all the commentaries in the Promenades, and that attempt—halting, sometimes sentimentalized, sometimes misjudged—nevertheless serves as a cohesive force. To understand that life is more than the war, more than the society brought to Naples by the American occupation, more than the Fascistic undertow in the Italian—to understand this is to move into novelistic areas Mailer rejected.

Further, Burns tried to discover where real feeling begins in a wartime situation, where sexual relief amidst fear and danger is often the sole outlet, itself a form of power. Mailer pushes everything into a call for power—whether Cummings at the top, Hearn in the middle, or Croft at the bottom—a dialectic of inexorable power he will repeat in sexual variations later. Burns also recognizes that power obtains, obtains absolutely, when one element is the conqueror and the other the defeated. Yet he is concerned with finding a mode of existence that, while it exists within the urgency of power, is also something else, varietal, as some plants are intermediary between deciduous and evergreen. Still further, he tried to move outside that destructive naturalism which appears to grip every war novel. Since war, its terrain, its power, were all external forces which become fate for the individual, it would appear that all life is sucked toward some black hole one can never understand.

By means of his gigantic metaphor for life, the reflecting power of the Galleria glass, Burns restores some individual will to living, and is much truer to the sense of the late 1940s than is Mailer in his novel. What came out of the 1940s for the American who understood the war was the sense of the individual's terrible fragility when confronted by the "enormous room" of the war, whether as part of the civilian or the military effort. The dialectic of individual and social/political forces had altered; proportions changed, but never so much that the individual lost his belief in himself or his ability to control his destiny. The 1950s bear this out. A period of deadening ennui in national politics, a waste land of ideas and actions at the ideological level, a good deal of deception at the actively political level, a period of tremendous conflicts and ideological struggles, it nevertheless became the matrix of development for many who tried to effect radical changes in the decade following. Apparently, the individual will had not been stupefied by the Eisenhower regime, McCarthy, intellectual complacency and compromise, the newly fat cats of foundations, finance, and academia, these forms of political entropy and intellectual sellout having failed to homogenize everyone.

Burns has a passage near the end of the third Portrait, "Hal," in which his hollow, emptied-out young man, educated, psychoanalyzed, full of New York sophistication, meets a parachute captain who says he is "buried near Taormina on the island of Sicily." All he wants is a few flowers on his grave. He enters Hal's psyche, and he offers the philosophy— Nietzsche's "gay science"?—that nails Hal to his doom: he becomes a nut who believes he is Jesus Christ. The parachute captain, dead at twenty-two, offers a view of mankind that helps counter life as an unrelieved power struggle: "In wartime the greatest heroes are the sensitive and shy and gentle. They're great because they have to live in a world which is dedicated in wartime to an annihilation of everything they stand for. They're the unsung. No one will ever sing to them. Except us, the dead." The others, the crude ones, come out of their ordeal "more brutal and crass and cocky" than when they went in. "That's the way civilizations die, gradually. A premium is put on physical courage in wartime which kills off the gentle, because they're too noble to admit of cowardice."

This is not always true of Burns's view of war. Even the dead parachute captain was mixed in his gentleness, since he chose the parachute corps, volunteers, and rose to captain, only to be shot in the face when he landed in Sicily. The point is that Burns has provided modulations of human experience within the war, the way Conrad showed that an ordeal creates many different kinds of reactions in men, not simply a homogeneous response. Marlow understands Kurtz's temptations, yet resists becoming Kurtz. Not all men respond to power in the same way, nor do all men indulge themselves by the same

means or for the same goals. Bellow modulated this view in *The Victim* and then repeated it, in greatly different shape, in *The Adventures of Augie March;* both novels, despite vast differences, concerned with the uses of power and the men who have it to dispense. This is, as Burns recognized, a novelistic insight, not simply a political one, especially when it can be gathered into meaning by a technical device that makes it cohere with other conflicts, insights, and tensions generated by the material.

One of the major problems with the postwar novel, particularly with the novel focused on war and/or combat, is the need to provide modulation—of character type, scene, tone, attitude; which is to say, the novel had to move outside deterministic patterns. Even with the considerable influence of existentialism and other aspects of modernism in the 1950s and 1960s, the postwar American novel remained indebted to a patterned, deterministic, or cyclical shape. And this patterning of thought translated into forms.

The novelist is caught in a bind, no one more than the novelist of war. If he stresses the overall power of the war and its commanders, then we lose interest in individuals; or else we have no ultimate reason for caring. If, on the other hand, he stresses individuals, then he is being unfaithful to what war is and what its values are. In a sense, this problem is endemic to the American novel as a whole; it is the "catch" of our fiction, the perpetual trap, theme, dance of death. Heller's frenetic comedy in *Catch-22* was an effort to break from this; turning the war into metaphor was one means of evading either/or. If the writer makes his characters dance, they are less liable to be doomed by technology. Pynchon works similar ploys in novels that are reflections of war fictions.

The writer who carried naturalism as far as it would go in the postwar period was James Jones, and his use of this mode is both his glory and the source of some of his weaknesses. In *From Here to Eternity* (1951), he decided to meet the problems raised by naturalism head-on. Using the peacetime army not as a metaphor for society but as society itself—life does not extend for Jones beyond army life on Hawaii before the Japanese attack on Pearl Harbor—he attempted to fight through the old Dreiser, Farrell, Dos Passos, Hemingway battle. This is a quintessentially American novel, full of the difficulties the American writer must face squarely. Aside from the achievement of the work, whether one finds for or against, the reader must marvel at Jones's courage in taking up such old forms and giving them vitality. For ideologically, the confrontation between doom and the individual is a trap; there is no fictional escape. Jones does not try to parry the blow, by making Prewitt's problems inherent. That is, rather than succumbing to the "fate versus individual" format of traditional tragedy, he has shifted his ground and made Prewitt the architect of his own demise, more Elizabethan than classically conceived. Consciousness and self join with coercive forces.

It is a trap, nevertheless. For all Jones's ingenuity and Prewitt's dogged refusal to succumb, the peacetime army circumvents maneuverability. Jones attempts a large-scale presentation by catching Prewitt between Art (the bugle), which he gives up, and War (boxing), which he withdraws from formally while remaining a fighter. The conception here is ambiguous, although we can see it, through Jones's eyes, as an effort to thrust Prewitt into the larger world which his lowly role in the army negates. He is, in this larger sense, a young man moving between Art and War, Apollo and Mars, a small man who defies the army after he has moved in regions unknown to those who imprison and punish him. He has had his moments of greatness, as bugler and as boxer, and now he comes to us as a legend. Jones's aim was to make him life-size, but to provide an immortal past, from Kentucky coal fields to the worlds of Art and War.

But even that attempt runs into ideological problems. For Prewitt's forsaking of Art and War in order to carry on his own kind of war has diminished him. His past may be glorious, but his present is small-scaled. And Jones is never clear how Prewitt's struggle to remain an individual can make sense when he has volunteered for an organization that punishes individuality. Prewitt is in the army by free choice—it is peacetime—because it is somehow preferable to coal mining or other demeaning work; and yet once within that organization, he insists on antithetical forms of behavior. The terms of the army are clear: forgo individuality, except when drunk, submit to discipline dictated by the organization, show mechanical obedience to superiors. Prewitt has accepted this insofar as he thinks of himself as a "thirty-year soldier." He has limited his area of maneuverability by virtue of his choices, and yet he insists on his choices, even when he has divested himself of those skills which would have enlarged his ability to move.

The three sides, Prewitt, the army, and skills, do not add up to a triangle. They are, in fact, three sides seeking a structure they can form. Jones's admirable desire to search out Prewitt's individuality in an organization that stifles it cannot ideologically sustain the novel. Only Maggio has found a means, by seeking a Section 8 discharge, as a crazy; but then he leaves the army and enters civilian life a marked man, decisions Prewitt rejects.

With the ideological underpinning so shaky, even untenable, the novel succumbs to naturalistic traps, just as Mailer's book yielded to the framework of ideas represented by Cummings and Hearn. And precisely as Mailer found his métier not in ideology but in the felt sense of Croft, so Jones finds his measure in individuals: Prewitt to some extent, Karen Holmes, and Warden (the Sergeant appears to be a type American writers are most at home with).

Jones's lower-class soldiers—here, in *The Thin Red Line,* and in *Whistle*—are of a class only occasionally seen in the postwar novel; outside of "war fiction," it appears mainly in female writers: O'Connor, Oates, Morrison, some other blacks.* It is Jones's point that whatever good feeling or honesty derives from army life, derives from the lower-class soldier, and more so from the dog soldier. Like his American Indian namesake, an outcast of sorts who became a kamikaze in action, the dog soldier moves along the margins of the army, but is useful during combat or other crucial situations. He is, to some degree, sacrificial, a scapegoat, allowed his eccentricities and marginality as long as he does his combat job.

There is, of course, a good deal of Wobblyism and romanticism here, such as we find in Dos Passos's biographical insets in *U.S.A.* Jones brings to the army this sense of the outsider socially, economically, and politically who, somehow, expresses something valuable. Unlike Mailer, who was clinical in his treatment of these men, Jones is sympathetic and yet honest in the face of their terrible flaws and self-destructiveness. Among the "other" class, the officers, only Karen Holmes—the wife of a captain—is presented sympathetically, a strange turnabout which has not drawn much attention, and since Karen Holmes is

---

*One way to explain this phenomenon, and it is a compelling one, is to view the male writer as concerned with the upwardly mobile, whereas the female writer sticks to those who have not made it—their own class, women. No explanation, however, is satisfactory. We could use an in-depth study of the subjects of women writers since World War II and especially in the 1960s and 1970s as compared with those of their male counterparts.

such a remarkable portrait of a woman for a male novelist in the 1940s, both sexist and class aspects deserve attention.

Warden faces Holmes with the terrible fact that his wife had had an affair with Stark, now the mess sergeant, in the earlier days of her marriage. She then goes into her then famous discourse on hysterectomy, but the clinical details—and Jones's awkwardness in handling them—are subsumed in her passion for expressing her rights. What is most important, novelistically, is that Jones can cross class lines, so that the woman who expresses and defines herself is of a class Jones and Warden detest and is, further, married to a man who embodies a caste structure that is also anathema. Thus, in the depiction of Karen Holmes, we have a threefold fictional experience which is almost unique: the wife of an officer, a woman herself not lower class, and a woman who insists on her priorities, understands her victimization, and resents what she is expected to accept.

When Captain Holmes gives gonorrhea, like a gift, to his young wife, he imposes upon her not only a social disease but a multilevel experience: she is to accept, she is the receiver of whatever the male offers, she must assume inferiority (he is, after all, the captain), and she must make believe nothing is wrong. All this she rebels against, first with Stark and then with Warden, in the sole way she has of breaking even, by cuckolding her husband with men in his company. The wife who cuckolds is ordinarily in war novels a woman of the lowest sensibility, where here she is not only understandable but sympathetic. The modulations of class and sex in Karen are, in a sense, freakish in a war novel, only possible because most of *From Here to Eternity* occurs during peacetime. Once the war novel involves combat, then all sexual contact will be on the run or on the road, part of the American novelists' submission to spatiality.

In any event, Karen has not only to present her case, which Jones justifies, but to win over Warden to her point of view, a task made all the more difficult because of their class and rank differences. This is not a situation Jones stumbled into—he is far too conscious of every nuance—and we can only say he has described in detail the kind of male-female relationship that we do not associate with a male American novelist. And when female novelists of the 1960s and 1970s began to present a woman like Karen Holmes, they tended to declass her and make her experiences sexual; freedom starts there, or in her finances. Jones has Karen use her sex—it is, after all, her sole weapon

—but ultimately it is marginal to her need to define herself and what has happened to her. Although Warden may not completely accept this, he does understand it; and if it does not change all his attitudes about women, it changes his attitude toward one woman and toward himself in relationship to her. At the end, when Karen heads for the States, he seeks spatiality in drunkenness and whores; but as long as she is available, he lives with her situation and connects to something quite alien to him and his own ideas.

Warden is the sole character in the novel capable of change. One of the problems with the war novel is that characters remain static, part of that naturalistic noose the war situation tightens around the novelist's skills. Peculiarly, the peacetime army is more amenable to character change. For while Warden has significant doubts about himself before Pearl Harbor, once the attack occurs, he reverts, not unusually, to form: a brawling, drunken tough guy. Yet whatever the immediate situation, Warden represents a center of sorts, a bellwether. The form of the novel, as with nearly all novels of the military, depends on an ideological center; with the exception of *The Gallery,* such novels are rarely experimental with point of view, narrative positioning, tone, or elements of discontinuity. But if innovative form is not the key, then focus is. Mailer's dilemma was that he wanted to argue ideas, the Cummings-Hearn dialogues; but his sympathies were with Croft, who believed only in himself. Jones made no such error. He centered on Warden, in the sense that Warden is dead center, a warden or keeper of what is, the very middle of the army. To his left (with no direct political identification) stand Prewitt, and Jack Malloy—men who while identifying with the army want the kind of movement a military organization denies. To the right stand the officers, or Fatso, and those like them, men who can carry on because Warden holds the center together. The structure of the novel lies here, not in narrative but in ideological terms.

And ideology depends on class. For every major decision made in the novel is based on class differentiation. Prewitt kills Fatso because the latter is an enlisted man and, therefore, "a traitor against his kind." Warden refuses the commission that would have kept him together with Karen Holmes, because he would then become bourgeois, and it is the middle class that lives by brown-nosing. "And now I'm supposed to go on and become an officer, the very symbol of every goddamn thing I've always stood up against, and not feel anything about it." To be honest, he must reject the commission; to be dishonest means he can claim Karen.

Warden has mastered the amount of give the army allows without ceasing to be a mechanical organization.* Having tested out the potentialities of every situation, he knows that the army runs on its first sergeants, not on its officers or enlisted men. Those on either side dare the risk of self-destruction. By exploiting the center, Warden controls the vitals of the organization, while he can drink, make love to an officer's wife, and even keep the AWOL Prewitt on the company roster. If, with Warden, Jones has found his structural premise, then Prewitt is, of course, condemned; for he passes outside that central structural concept where continuity is possible. By moving beyond the center, he flirts with discontinuity, as would Warden if he had accepted the commission. Prewitt tries not to be himself: he should box and play the bugle, he should not read books; he should keep his eye on the main goal, to be a thirty-year man, his own decision. Anything that deviates from that, and he deviates in all, will prove destructive in terms of the ideological centering of the novel.

It is very easy to mock Jones's achievement, especially if we measure it against the sophisticated works that appeared in the 1950s and 1960s. The later period, with the sleeker, worldly novels of Bellow and Roth, as well as Gaddis and then Pynchon, make Jones appear in comparison as a primitive. Further, one can always point to the infelicities of phrasing. They abound. The novel will never become a primer of how the craft of fiction is carried out. But such criticism, like Leavis's of Conrad's adjectival excesses in *Heart of Darkness,* ultimately gives way to other, more significant matters. For when we think of a service culture, Jones's novel is our archetype; just as Conrad's novella becomes our archetypal vision of Africa.

Perhaps it is inevitable that the novels of the 1940s, *The Naked and the Dead, From Here to Eternity,* and *The Gallery,* generated all other war or military fiction and nonfiction of later decades, including Korean War and Vietnam War works. Even Jones's own *The Thin Red Line* is a throwback in which he "redoes" Mailer's turf, the invasion of a

Pacific island, here Guadalcanal. Very possibly, we can see Mailer's own Vietnam War, recounted in *The Armies of the Night,* as a replay of his earlier war novel.†

Jones carried his social beliefs deeply into the makeup of the peacetime army, finding there an exact mirror of the world outside. That world outside need not be a Depression era, although it is always a Depression era for the enlisted man. In this respect, we find Dos Passos's *U.S.A.* writ large in Jones's sensibility, especially those tales which chronicle men like Joe Williams and Mac. What gives Jones's Depression-era enlisted men such reality is their vitality in situations they must exploit very carefully or else they fail. Bloom, for example, the Jew who wants acceptance and who boxes to gain it, moves around the edges. Jones's handling of him (from the author's point of view) is vibrant but noxious; Bloom has almost no redeeming features, and we are always reminded that his personality derives from his Jewishness. Like Hemingway with Robert Cohn, Jones loads on Bloom sufficient noisomeness to carry on the tradition of anti-Semitism characteristic of American fiction. Although Prewitt says his struggle with Bloom has no Jewish overtones, Jones's treatment indicates it does. When the voice is Prewitt's, we are warned against a racial motive; but when the voice is Jones's, racial overtones are present.

Bloom has no business in the army; it is no place for Jews, even poor ones. Maggio, on the other hand, is presented sympathetically: the feisty, lower-class Italian who defies authority. Maggio's successful achievement in gaining a Section 8 discharge brings about a significant reordering of Prewitt's priorities. Maggio has made his mark on the company, on the army, on life. He has demonstrated that a skinny outsider can conspire to outwit the army, and succeed where others have failed. Those who share Warden's center are Stark, the mess sergeant, and Chief Choate, a romanticized Indian, a type we see later in Kesey's *One Flew Over the Cuckoo's Nest.* Chief Choate has modeled himself on Jim Thorpe, the extraordinary Indian athlete, but drinks himself into a stupor every night because he knows what people really think of

---

*If we compare the army to the "managerial revolution" in the larger culture, we can parallel Warden and Heller's Slocum. In *Something Happened,* Heller's view of a company is comparably structured; the managers run it, and Slocum is a civilian Warden, central to the organization but lacking ultimate power.

†The one author who sidestepped these novels is Heller in *Catch-22,* and that is really because its coordinates are a different kind of society; its literary influences not American writers, but Céline, Kafka, Joyce. Its sensibility is closer to *Death on the Installment Plan* than to novels of war/combat, and its philosophy is based not on the class/caste of officers and enlisted men, but on a denial of ideology in favor of the individual ego.

Indians, Thorpe having been stripped of all his medals. The Chief stands as the kind of character who succeeds in the army by doing its business; like Prewitt, he has given up boxing, but he compensates in other ways.

When Prewitt moves outside the center, he, strangely enough, shares territory with the really despicable characters, men like Ike Galovitch, a Yugoslav, and Fatso, who has no meaning except as a sadist. Probably based on men whom Jones detested beyond control, or else emblematic of the peacetime army, they are lost as characters; even Bloom is redeemed by his suicide. Similarly, Jack Malloy, the Stockade philosopher, has a purity that aligns him, as a character, with those of pure evil: no give, no life. His philosophy of passive resistance in the individual's life has, finally, no more meaning for Prewitt than does passive resistance for Americans once Pearl Harbor was attacked.

The structure of the novel, then, carries down into every character whose departure from the center marks his doom. Thus, Jones has, in this intensely American work of fiction, exploited the trap or inescapable paradoxes awaiting the writer: seeking holes in the fabric, looking for ways to escape doom, then dooming any character who attempts an assertion of individuality; finally, demonstrating that the center locates salvation, whereas the margins, however interesting, romantic, nostalgic, or exploratory, prove destructive. Romance comes up against the real world: Prewitt, our man of Art and War, against Warden, our man, finally, of order growing out of personal disorder. Prewitt is our Orpheus, torn to pieces; Warden our Apollo, fun-loving but aware of the godlike powers invested in him, the man who makes things work. It is the old American paradox. Melville saw it clearly, with his Ahab our Prewitt, his Ishmael our Warden, the *Pequod* our peacetime army.

While we tend to think of *From Here to Eternity* as a "war novel," the war is incidental; it is part of the working out, not of the forward drive. When the attack on Pearl Harbor does occur, the shape of the novel has presented itself; we are only one hundred pages from the end. The war, of course, dooms Prewitt. What was possible in the peacetime army is no longer feasible in war. This, too, is part of the trap—we recall it from *A Farewell to Arms.* But heavy as the influence of that novel is, in presence, tone, even prose style, Jones has tried to keep his distance, being more brutal and honest than Hemingway in his own portrait of the "doomed" lovers," Karen and Warden.

Hemingway's Catherine, brave, courageous, a woman of good faith, is nevertheless a receptacle for Henry's needs. Karen Holmes insists on her needs, and Warden does not mince words about his desire for regular sex. Jones is more tuned in to how fleeting a romantic attachment is even when it is profound and honest, how it moves in waves of sexual passion and then fades, the lovers moving out of each other's lives. For a novel that several critics have labeled immature, poorly written, and beneath literary notice, *From Here to Eternity* has maturities that few other novels have duplicated.

Jones tried to infuse some lyricism into *From Here to Eternity:* that is, to give it a turn away from purely military matters toward something culturally larger, as in Prewitt's bugling. Through "The Re-enlistment Blues," toward the latter part of the novel, Prewitt recognizes that in his doom-filled relationship to the army his own life is encapsulated. "So you short-times, let me tell you / Don't get yourself throwed in the can / You might as well be dead / Or a Thirty-Year Man / Recruitin crews give me the blues, / Old Re-enlistment Blues." This is the final tribute to the dog soldier, as Prewitt thinks of himself, one of those crazy, marginal soldiers whose daring marks them for early death.

Such lyricism is missing from Jones's next novel, *The Thin Red Line,* a combat novel, a different order of being from war fiction. Here Jones has accepted naturalism and decided to exploit it head-on. He defies, among others, Philip Rahv's depreciatory characterization of naturalism: "I would classify as naturalistic that type of realism in which the individual is portrayed not merely as subordinate to his background but as wholly determined by it—that type of realism, in other words, in which the environment displaces its inhabitants in the role of the hero." Dreiser, not a favorite of *Partisan Review* editors and contributors, is Rahv's chief example of that salient feature of the mode. As we continue with his description, which is by no means unjust, we see how it cannot explain the very power of Dreiser, or the combat novel, which must be deterministic. What makes *The Thin Red Line* such a telling piece of fiction is that Jones found the perfect medium for his sense of America, not only in the army, but in the army in combat.

Although the format is combat—enclosed space and time, restricted cast of characters, equally limited area of maneuver, no meaningful ideology, stark tensions and conflicts, mainly fear—Jones's plan was ambitious. The novel was published in 1962, but it was written in the 1950s, and its subject matter is from the 1940s. The time span of the action is brief, but the time span of Jones's pattern is two decades of American society. Also, as noted, the book was an effort to take on Mailer on his own grounds, in a combat novel about a South Pacific island, Jones's a real campaign, Mailer's an invented one. Even the title has several resonances: the line formed by British soldiers when faced by large numbers of attackers, the traditional "thin red line"—Jones picked this up from a Kipling quotation; his own sense, from an "Old Midwestern Saying," that "There's only a thin red line between the sane and the mad"—a conception of considerable significance in combat. There is also a potential third meaning, the thin red line of blood that trails from the dying and dead. The blood is as substantial as the men, which means it is expendable in combat, a lifeblood meaningful only to those who lose it, not to the army. Within all three meanings, Jones has written our archetypal novel of combat.

The governing idea of this intense, brutal book is that an army is made up of infinitely replaceable parts, soldiers and equipment alike. An army is like Zola's mine in *Germinal,* La Voreux, the gigantic maw or stomach, something that will consume all who enter and replace them with identical pieces, until they in turn are consumed. Chunks of the Jones book are given over to the relocating of men as they assume different titles within the company: men become temporary this or that, then permanent this or that as the temporary ahead of them is wounded or killed; executive officers are moved around, and even higher-ups gain promotions as a campaign goes well. Men as links, as objects—as against their feelings—is Jones's subject matter.

The army in wartime combat is the perfect vehicle for what Jones only suggested in *From Here to Eternity.* It fits into his sense of America, a carry-over of the Dos Passos of *Three Soldiers* and many parts of *U.S.A.* It presents the point of view, completely, of the marginal or "out" man whom the army subdues and then usually kills. Jones's quintessential marginal man in *The Thin Red Line* is Welsh, a successor to his own Warden, but even more, to Mailer's Croft. Welsh is not so fully done as Croft, since he disappears for large parts of combat. But he is a figure directly associated with the Depression and Dos Passos's lower-class misfits, a man whose sole hope for survival lies in the values of the army.

Like an old Wobbly, Welsh sees all war, all combat, all struggle as the rich man's way of protecting his property. He is contemptuous of human life, although afraid; but he does not weaken as Croft does during the Japanese night attack. As the first sergeant of C Company, Welsh does not feel protective toward his men, since he knows they are pawns. A live soldier one moment is dead the next, or the next. He sees even himself as a piece of property, and gloats over the fact that if he dies "the government wouldn't have anybody to send a Regrets card to for him." At enlistment, he had given a false first name and middle initial, cutting himself off from any recognizable kin, so that if he was wounded or disabled, the government would be responsible for him.

More than anyone else in the novel, Welsh sees it all happening, although as in most naturalistic fiction, to observe it he has to forsake some of himself. Welsh barely lives as a person, so small is the margin he permits himself. This becomes a problem with the novel, in fact, as soon as we step back from the combat. That, intensely and brutally narrated, becomes everything, the entire narrative, plot, theme, characterization, as well as tone, texture, point of view—all the elements we associate with fiction. But as soon as combat ends, when the Dancing Elephant series of hills and ridges is taken, then the novel has nowhere to develop; the second episode, on the Giant Boiled Shrimp, is supernumerary.

Fictionally, Jones's novel has devoured itself, so well has he achieved his thematic purpose. The cycle recurs until the army's gigantic stomach has consumed all the participants. Meanwhile, a new batch is preparing to step in. "Those who did not die [Jones writes] would be entered upon the elaborate shuttling movement back out from this furthermost point of advance, as only a short time back they had been entered upon the shuttle forward into it." There is fictionally no way out here, for once Jones enters this kind of novel, he accepts the traps. He can work only within areas of intensity: making the reader "see" the war, the fate of the soldier, doom itself.

War, here, Jones suggests, is the way we can be carried outside ourselves, the way drugs carry us beyond the corporeal, beyond memory and self. For the drugs of the fifties and sixties Jones offers combat, the numbing, the rage, the anxiety, all of which become dimensions in themselves. Pursuing this point, we can see combat as having the intensity we usually identify with creativity or the formation of an artwork: the effacement of or carrying oneself beyond self, that participation in an "objective" enterprise associated with the making of art.

This is a considerable achievement, of course, but

because it is illusory, it does not hold. It is true that the soldier, like the artist, loses himself in something beyond, the subject reshaping and becoming object. But the artist loses himself in what ultimately includes him, only larger, more dimensional, reshaped or reformed; the artwork as the artist in a different guise. For the soldier, while the squad, company, patrol become his "artwork," these groups have nothing of himself in them; his presence is illusory, *because they succeed to the extent he becomes faceless and bodiless.* For the soldier, loss of himself in larger units means he is interchangeable, expendable, selfless.

Nevertheless, some part of the idea remains. Jones's soldiers "create themselves" in the only way they can, by offering themselves, their bodies, their fears and anxieties as the sole artwork they, in their limited way, are capable of becoming. Bakunin, the anarchist, said that the urge to destroy "is also a creative urge," and while he meant this remark as a description of those who destroy for some creative purpose—a better or more equitable society—nevertheless the remark carries weight for all those, psychopaths as well as soldiers, who have only themselves to offer. When the soldier's living spirit or individual life is all there is, then, Jones recognizes, he is giving, in his way, as much as the artist gives in his.

This recognition allows Jones to find human worth everywhere, even when numbness sets in and individuals become agents of other-dimensional forces. We can find examples throughout, but Jones's handling of Fife, the file clerk, is suggestive. For Fife is, normally, the man never noticed, a fearful nonentity, who either survives or is killed almost anonymously: surely not a figure who imposes himself on other men or the author. Yet Jones observes Fife carefully and sympathetically, until we perceive that the file clerk, who is never interesting or compelling, has demanded of us a kind of attention we ordinarily give to someone of greater presence. Jones describes Fife as depressed, and we realize that depression is not a commodity many war novelists trade in; fear, anxiety, a rumbling bowel, a tight ass—these are the stock-in-trade. But Fife is depressed:

> Fife was suffering from a deep depression of an intensity he had never known before. Even his eyelids seemed immobilized by this slumping awareness of his total inability to cope. All the little dirts of life were attacking him en masse, threatening to destroy him, and they terrified him because there was nothing he could do. He could not even keep his files clean.

He was wet and filthy dirty. His toes squished in his wet socks in his shoes, and he had not heart or energy to go and change them. Tomorrow he would probably be sick. Mosquitoes swarmed around him in the dark and bit his face and neck and the backs of his hands. He did not even attempt to dislodge them. He simply sat. Temporarily he had ceased to function. He stagnated in the close darkness, consciously rotting toward some indefinite future death, and the most painful thought of all was knowing that eventually he would have to move again. He continued to touch the mud-gritty tips of his fingers against the tabletop.

His depression is connected to his intense desire to survive, to gain immortality. Nearly every line of Jones's description can be applied to the unconscious center of the artist, of that giving in to whatever will seize him, and then that moving along its contours. Fife floats, dimensionless for the time being, toward what will claim him in that cyclical movement which brings him his turn. And yet he resists, using his depression now, then his head wound, and finally all of himself to insist on his primary self.

In this frame of reference, sex is equivalent to love, and sex is further connected to ideas of war. The sexual feeling for another soldier among men who will be heterosexual when they return to civilian life is associated with their desire to survive. Images of need, which in civilian life can be sorted out, become interconnected in a combat situation, even in the peacetime army. Thus, the army establishes its own frame of reference, so that elements we think of as only distantly connected suddenly become randomly linked to each other. Seemingly patternless, sex, love, war, life, death are thrown together; and in this sense, we have the metaphor of chance and cycle which enter into the artwork. Of course, Jones is not concerned with drawing out this metaphor, nor could he do so. But its mere presence with such insistence in Jones's novel suggests why he portrays combat so effectively; each soldier counts, and even within the naturalistic trap of large force operating on individual units, the unit is sharply limned and refuses to succumb easily.

In a curious sense, *Whistle* (1978) is less the final volume in a projected trilogy than it is the negative of Cozzens's *Guard of Honor.* The Florida air base of the latter becomes Jones's Southern hospital base (Luxor or Memphis). In Cozzens's novel, we have a "war" situation in which virtually no one suffers; whereas in Jones's book, all is disability, illness, operations, suffering, although the war is distant, as nightmare and flashback. Everything Cozzens has erased from the war, Jones has sketched, as though redrawing the map of experience. Even Jones's prose, more uncontrolled than ever, appears like a negative of Cozzens's imitative Jamesian constructions.

Cozzens's world is one of high-ranking officers, administrative problems, decision-making; Jones's world is of sergeants, those who, having lower-echelon power, are themselves puppets controlled by the upper world. Cozzens is balletic and delicate, eager not to get his hands dirtied; Jones revels in muck, blood, wounds, sexual odors and juices.

Jones's plan was an excellent one: the war and the world as a gigantic hospital, to which Pacific campaign veterans have returned to be rehabilitated, so as to be readied for further campaigns. The three major images that control this very long and unfinished novel are the hospital itself—wounds, suppurations, cripples, unworkable limbs; the men's nightmares—of combat, of a hospital ship with a big red cross, of fear and horror; and finally, women's vaginas—something akin to the suppurating wounds in the hospital, but invested with mythical and magical qualities, a totem of civilian life. Much of the sex of the novel is, in fact, focused on men either enjoying cunnilingus or hesitating before its terrors, fearful that the practice is perverted. Most of the women, for their part, say that only cunnilingus can bring on orgasms; vaginal sex was minor-league stuff by comparison.

This three-part equation in the novel cannot hold, for one part—that given over to the sexual world—is at a twelve-year-old level. Jones had been hearing about new dominions of sex that feminists claimed were necessary for orgasm, and he introduced them into his 1940s novel. Instead of having men in wartime simply satisfy themselves with a quick screw, now they aim to please their women. The plan is commendable, but the execution, which replaces any serious relationship between the sexes, becomes ludicrous.

As the final segment of a planned trilogy—Jones said he conceived of it in 1946, began it in 1947, when he wrote about it to Maxwell Perkins at Scribner's—*Whistle* contains characters of *From Here to Eternity* and *The Thin Red Line* reborn and reshaped as necessary: Prewitt and Witt become Prell; Warden and Welsh are Winch; and Stark and Storm become Strange. The men represent different kinds of experiences and war wounds. All are sexually viable, even when casts, crutches, and water-filled lungs would appear to interfere with performance. Nevertheless,

their combat experiences have so changed them that they cannot see reality in the way of those who have missed combat. The world of Jones is divided, those who have seen it, those who have not, and they remain two different kinds of people in two different kinds of world.

Whistle, despite touches, descends precipitously from the two novels preceding it. The prose, which had wobbled in the early novels and in places gone out of control, is here barely functional, so crude and uneven has it become. Sex is described: "She was blowing him well, he was teaching her. And he was blowing her well. Apparently. And the fucking they had going was of a superior quality." It would work as parody—of Hemingway in the final sentence, of Mailer and Roth in the rest— except that Jones sees the passage as the basis for a relationship.

The men reveal themselves at such a low level of performance as civilians that it is difficult to take them seriously in combat. In the previous novels of the trilogy, the men, enclosed—on base, in combat—generated their own culture, which Jones understood and could describe with great power. Here the men have too great a freedom for Jones to handle, and his abilities as novelist waned, not only conceptually but in the prose, in maturity, in everything that sustains a long narrative.

Although James Gould Cozzens's *Guard of Honor* (1948) is about World War II, it is barely a war novel, and of course not a novel about combat. But for more compelling reasons than this, it does not belong with Mailer, Burns, Jones, or later, Heller and O'Brien. It is a novel that looks backward, in language, character, situation, but also in tone and attitude. It very consciously eschews the new. Cozzens wants not novelty, not surprise or excitement, but solidity. What damages the novel, further, is that it does not suit the 1940s, or the 1930s; it is, rather, a paean to an America that has never suffered. The one area in which suffering is suggested—the company of blacks who attempt to integrate the facilities of a white airfield—eventually becomes part of a larger issue: the war effort, the stability of a Florida airfield, the needs of the country at large.

Suffering, although spelled out in a few paragraphs, is glossed over. Cozzens accepts the words of his Judge Ross, now attached to the airfield staff, that blacks owe it to their country to accept conditions which may seem demeaning; that in fact, the country can measure their patriotism and qualities of leadership by the way they handle a situation, segregation of facilities, that is debasing to them. The tortured logic, all intended to keep Southern servicemen on the base contented, indicates Cozzens's manipulation of human feeling and attitudes to gain his ground.

His quest for small victories in the novel—matters of tone, nuance, modulation—while admirable in itself is unsuitable for a novel of such length. The working front is so minute that Cozzens has exchanged filigree work for any chance of expansion. Possibly his master was James, but James's filigree work was always within an ever-enlarging context of meaning. Cozzens's method is the opposite: by siphoning his novel through a small-town judge now attached to the general staff, he has taken a large issue—the question of Southern segregation in the face of Washington's order to the contrary—and reduced it to small details.

Cozzens has himself written, in *By Love Possessed,* that "whatever happens, happens because a lot of other things have happened already." Cozzens's point of attack is not on what results, but on that sequence of events; and not even on the larger elements, but on details which work their way into the sequence. Judge Ross, now Colonel Ross, is a decent man ready to make the compromises that Cozzens sees as necessary for the existence of the majority. Ross expresses all the right feelings about blacks—their suffering, the inequality of their opportunity, the frustration of those who desire justice. "It was fair to form the conclusion that they [the commissioned officers] were an unusually sensitive, intelligent, and courageous lot." Yet Ross must turn these sentiments into action: "They [the Negro officers] feel they are unjustly treated. I think in many ways they are; but there are insurmountable difficulties in doing them justice."*

---

*We can observe the other side of the color line in John Oliver Killens's *And Then We Heard the Thunder* (1964). Solomon Saunders, an educated young black, a kind of Candide, enters the army, of course in an all-black unit. There, a sequence of episodes based on discrimination and injustice turns him from an American patriot into a black nationalist, from hopes of assimilation to identification with blackness as his sole mode of survival. What Cozzens omits is how practices that placate a mainly white Southern officer corps erode black men's faith in themselves and in the country; how injustice destroys the very nature of what the army and the war are all about. William Jay Smith touched on similar points in his novel of postwar occupation of Germany, *Last of the Conquerors* (1948), in which a young black sees German destruction of Jews as little different from American repression of blacks. Although he exaggerates, since there is a distinction between extermination and discriminatory repression, his point raises profound ethical issues. Both Killens and Smith question what the black is

The question I raise here is not the views Cozzens expresses; nearly any view if presented with intensity and sufficient causation is fictionally valid. The question is methodological: the reductionism inevitably occurring in every judgment, and Cozzens's support for that reductiveness. Cozzens has often complained that readers and critics have missed his sly wit. But none of that underlies Ross. The Colonel is a sobersides, a conscientious family man, a worrier about propriety; he represents the exact center: decency, tempered by the ability to compromise one's beliefs, the Cozzens trademark. There is no passion, no commitment, no expression of self. Ross is a judge in every waking hour.

The aim is to bring disorder down to order, not to show the potentiality of disorder, or the impossibility of order. Here is Cozzens's conservatism, not so much social or political doctrine as one of attitude. He proceeds as if Galsworthy's London clubs were still the measure of human experience. A war based on a gentleman's view of the rules and the means of conduct is bound to be a war that exists only as a pastoral idyll once existed in the mind of the romancer. Only near the end of the novel, when the death of seven parachutists intrudes upon the orderly manner of the base operation, do we have any insight into the nature of a war. Granted that Cozzens has not intended a war novel in any traditional sense, nevertheless his choice of point of view, that of colonels and generals, rarely anyone lower than captain, suggests the kind of stratified society which revels in authority.

By the end of the 1940s, our sensibility had altered; it had, in fact, fifty years earlier, to the extent that stratification must be a source of irony or parody. Cozzens defends his reordering of our responses by claiming an "adult intelligence," a term he uses in a review of Oliver La Farge's *The Eagle in the Egg.* He goes on: "not many [war books] have addressed themselves and their material to readers reasonably well acquainted with human beings and human experience, not born yesterday, and not insensible to statements merely self-serving or to sentimental nonsense and bonehead contradictions in terms or facts."

Although this is directed at La Farge's history of

---

fighting for when his life is jeopardized or sacrificed for values from which he is excluded. The issue is a live one as the volunteer peacetime army becomes increasingly black in its composition: those for whom the social system has failed to function find themselves in an organization that asks them, possibly, to die for what has rejected them as expendable.

the Air Transport Command, Cozzens suggests that it extends to fiction as well as fact. And yet the very elements he describes derisively are ingredients that make fiction possible, and apparently the more contradictory, the more intense. His sense of human beings is far more limited than that of the Edwardian novelists he emulates. Even his much-vaunted prose is an affectation when put into the service of a mandarin point of view. Cozzens aims at an Alexandrian entanglement: "He [Colonel Ross] did not pretend to that special knowledge of Negroes that Southerners always, and not, after all, implausibly, insisted was to them reserved." The postpositioning of the verb gives the sentence a Germanic flavor, almost that of a poor translation. Further, the qualification of adverbs just before the end—"and not, after all, implausibly"—is not only awkward in its placement, it is deceitful. It shifts our sympathies by way of something that is not inherent in either the Colonel or in anything we have been shown. It is something we must accept on faith as being true in the mind of Judge Colonel Ross; and yet it is doubly deceitful for turning the Colonel's mind toward what he will eventually do, which is to compromise his own sense of justice toward the black commissioned officers.

Cozzens's prose, then, is not a weapon, but in several areas a source of disguise. It hedges on itself, not as a way of conveying complexity, as James's later mandarin style, but as a way of reducing. Cozzens's supporters (De Voto, for example) have cited his prose style as perfection itself, leaving nothing to chance and nothing to the critic. The opposite is true. The style builds up complexities of grammar—oddly placed modifiers, postpositioned verbs, vague references, muddy progressions—but not to thicken meaning; rather, to reduce it to "common sense" or

"adult intelligence," whatever these phrases mean in fiction. Cozzens seeks out certainty—*Guard of Honor* is neatly encapsulated in a three-day sequence—whereas the play of surface as well as what is beneath should be all uncertainty, or at least the novelistic presentation of it.

The cross in the novel is borne by General Beal, a hotshot two-star officer, the youngest two-star man in the air force, whose life is disrupted by the "mutiny" of the black commissioned officers. But the disruption is always seen through the eyes of Ross, not Beal, who remains relatively untouchable. As a consequence, we have no direct access to the man whose career is being challenged. Even the incident with Benny Carricker, a tempestuous fighter pilot who exceeds military propriety, is a sport, something we see Beal handling easily, almost casually. The dramatic components of command, challenge, threat, radical or violent movement are all missing. Beal glides along, helped by Ross, who is himself untroubled by little except the incursions of age and intimations of mortality.

The tremendous amount of care paid to the establishment of situations or scenes, the characters in them, their agonizing over the course of events is so bloodless, so qualified by unqualified acceptance of compromise, that the pieces simply do not cohere. We become terribly aware of how the novel is held together merely by words, a recognition that destroys the reader's relationship to the material. In many ways, Cozzens is a more careful craftsman than Mailer or Jones, but their energies are directed toward discovering, whereas his is directed toward concealing, withholding, modulating everything to flatness and bloodlessness.

The War Novel as Imitation

The following books, several of them expertly crafted, run on secondhand ideas, on conflicting or opposing elements which cancel each other or value slickness over subject matter. In the final analysis, they offer little we did not already know, and I include them because (1) they provide a good look at the culture as it moved into the 1950s, and (2) they are often treated seriously by reviewers and critics. It is a commonplace of criticism to note that the lesser work is often the more culturally revealing, if not the more culturally lasting; and we discover that *The Caine Mutiny* tells us more about the national mood in 1951 than do some of its more considerable contemporaries. The division between cultural relevance and aesthetic distancing was never more clear: what can be culturally revealing can also be aesthetically of little value.

The Caine Mutiny (1951) is an expertly narrated novel that has no dimensions beyond itself; it is precisely what Wouk tells us it is. This aspect of novel-making, which we also find in O'Hara and Cozzens in the 1940s, is something very different from the novel as meaning. The making of such fiction is based on the old verities: good story told with a clear plot line and several varieties of character. Wouk does not play the ethnic game, but the class one—Willie Keith is "upper," May is "lower," as is Maryk, the *Caine*'s executive officer. Most of the others are middle, since we see this war from the officers' point of view. The class structure is part of the novel's meaning; for Willie Keith, a self-serving young man, must mature sufficiently so that he returns from the war intent upon marrying May, despite her Italian background and slightly vulgar manner.

What makes Willie mature are the episodes on the *Caine* involving Captain Queeg. Wouk's overt plan is to demonstrate that Queeg is an incompetent skipper, not to speak of one suffering borderline madness, as demonstrated in arbitrary and cruel punishments and an inability to respond to crucial situations. His behavior drives Maryk, the executive, and Keith and Keefer, a novel-writing officer, to believe he is incapable of command. Seduced by the amateur psychologizing of Keefer, Maryk is persuaded Queeg must be replaced as skipper when the *Caine* moves into the eye of a typhoon and almost capsizes. Citing three articles of navy regulations, Maryk, along with Keith and Keefer, takes over the ship and brings it safely back to port.

This much is straightforward, and given the nature of the type of novel Wouk chose to write, expertly done. The meanings of the novel are, of course, evident, and not a single paragraph holds out promise for a dimension beyond the line itself. But narrative is adroitly handled, and the characters have been well established. Had Wouk left it at that, he would have had a traditional novel about a young man growing up in the vicissitudes of war, an honest work done well at a certain level. But Wouk's purpose was hardly fulfilled by this; he was after a much larger ideological point, which involved the nature of responsibility, the limits of individuality, the question

of command, and the role of the military in the life of the individual. Behind the *Caine,* the captain, the mutiny is the analogy of the state and its leader, and the responsibility the individual has to that state and its leader. And in this area, Wouk shows not only weak thinking, but an insidiousness that is strangely prophetic; for in the poisonous creation of Greenwald, Wouk has evoked the deceptive motives and intentions that would help characterize the 1950s as a counterfeit decade.

Greenwald is Wouk's super-Jew, a lawyer in civilian life, and a pilot in the military; he must be a Jew for Wouk's purpose to have the correct political resonance. As a Jew, Greenwald has a "true" intellectuality; but he is no armchair liberal intellectual—he is the Jew as activist, the man who puts his neck on the line. We savor the creation of the state of Israel as a shadowy presence behind Greenwald. At the trial of Maryk, who is held responsible for the mutiny, Greenwald argues brilliantly that Queeg was indeed mad at the moment he had to decide the fate of the *Caine,* although he may be considered sane when beyond periods of stress. Greenwald demonstrates this in the face of testimony by two (Gentile) psychiatrists. Of course, Greenwald never "proves" his case, but by sagacious courtroom tactics, he throws doubt on the prosecutor's case. Maryk is acquitted. At the party celebrating Maryk's acquittal and the acceptance of Keefer's novel, *Multitudes, Multitudes,* Greenwald describes himself as a Jew and then attacks Keefer as the guilty one. For Keefer misused his intellect to mislead Maryk, a relatively ignorant man, into mutinying; and it is Keefer, that shallow, nonresponsible, dilettante of an intellectual, who should have been on trial. "I defended Steve [Maryk] because I found out the wrong guy was on trial. . . . Queeg deserved better at my hands. I owed him a favor, don't you see? He stopped Hermann Goering from washing his fat behind with my mother."

Here is the equation: Queeg, despite his limitations as a skipper, fought for his country, represented its values; and he was done in by the viper on board his ship, the intellectual, novel-writing Keefer, who knew nothing of the nature of the individual's responsibility or of obedience to a higher authority. And Keefer, by virtue of his glibness and shallow sense of human rights, was able to foment a mutiny, all based on duplicitous issues, and then withdraw when the going became difficult. The real enemy is Keefer, and behind him the Nazis. The reasoning is tortuous, of course, but also somewhat prophetic; for even before the main onslaughts in the 1950s against intellectuals, many of whom whined and cringed in return, Wouk was establishing his defenses: the loyal Jew, the active defender of his country, the man who knows the limitations of the individual when leadership is involved, the lawyer who understands the chain of command in a wartime navy, the line of authority in the state.

Unlike his contemporaries, Irwin Shaw conceived of the war in *The Young Lions* (1948) as taking place at two levels, the level of individual lives and that of the larger culture. He tried to place three men in their own backgrounds without losing sight of the war itself, as a large theater of operations. Unlike Mailer and Jones, he does not preoccupy himself with a company, although C Company dominates the individual action. Nevertheless, his stress is upon the interrelationship between C Company, as it shapes and reshapes itself, and the larger movements that characterize the European theater of operations. War becomes the catalyst for individual lives.

In this larger conception, the Nazi (Christian Diestl) and the Jew (Noah Ackerman) "kill" each other, and the victor is Michael Whitacre, a playboy turned man by his knowledge of the war. Diestl directly kills Noah, and the latter's death leads to Michael's killing of Diestl. The symmetrical arrangements of the deaths and the survival of Whitacre are characteristic of the entire novel, in which expert narrative skills are put at the service of a mind that conceives of ideas and history as stereotypes. The Nazi is strong from the start; the Jew achieves strength through adversity; and the WASP, Michael, attains maturity as the result of challenge.

Each life, denied the urgency of its own stresses, falls into those stereotypical patterns of Nazi, Jew, WASP. Not a single stray act can interfere with Noah's determination to make the company respect him. The unlikely event of a puny boy, Noah, challenging and fighting the ten largest members of the company is actualized, so that Israel fights its larger neighbors to gain their respect, and finally beats the last one. Michael, in his way, fits every stereotype of the Hollywood writer: expensive lunches, countless affairs, broken marriage, easy charm, access to wealth and influence, sense of drift and worthlessness despite external signs of success.

Potentially, the Nazi seems the most promising. Diestl is caught within a good deal of local color, his activities have the strangeness of another culture, and he seems to have a streak of decency. But Shaw forsakes all complexity when he attempts to demonstrate ruthlessness, loss of decency; then we have a stock Nazi, concerned only with the survival of the Fatherland, a machine for killing.

The narrative skills remain. In some ways, despite the platitudes, this novel has a more honest thrust to it than a failed attempt at grand art, such as we find in *Lie Down in Darkness*. The two novels, in fact, create the classic confrontation along the edges of real art: that collision between the traditional storyteller and the writer who consciously redeals the deck so as to strain after artistic effects. Neither worker in these fields can achieve art, even temporarily; a brief novel like Hawkes's *The Cannibal* says more about war than *The Young Lions* and a good deal more about twisted human motives than *Lie Down*, although *The Cannibal* is difficult, baffling, and frustrating.

A tributary of the war/combat novel is the novel of occupation, with Italy the more favored country, very possibly because an Italian mistress seems more toothsome than a German. The problem with all such novels is a technical one, in that the novelist needs devices to modulate his material, more than in the war/combat novel. So many levels of experience are presented, from the battle-scarred soldier, to the remnants of a decadent culture, to the young woman who is bought, that stylistic modes must reflect shifts in content. This is precisely where the novelist runs into difficulty and becomes imitative.

In *All Thy Conquests* (1946), Alfred Hayes uses the alternations of Hemingway's *In Our Time;* only he has, like Burns in *The Gallery,* expanded it. He includes, also, as in *U.S.A.,* a Chorus (Dos Passos's Newsreel or perhaps Camera Eye), which stands for all Rome, where the narrator is located. He links many elements: the trial of a man implicated in the Nazi murder of 350 Cave victims; the city itself—the perspective of a liberated Rome; several characters: Giorgio, a former barman; Harry, a soldier, on the lookout for the virginal Francesca, among the Roman whores; the Marchese, a *dolce vita* type who spends the occupation in Italy as a representative of aristocratic and decadent Rome; Carla, a romantic young lady who becomes pregnant by a married American soldier.

This is Part I. Part II repeats the characters and methods. "Trial" becomes "Prosecution"; "Liberated City" I becomes II; and the order is shifted somewhat among the characters. Part III becomes "The Defense," in which Italy is viewed as complicitous. The novel ends with "The Sentence," in which the crowd takes justice into its own hands and lynches the man who led to the death of the 350.

Stylistically, the novel belongs to the Hemingway

school—hard-bitten English, *tristesse,* use of Italian as Hemingway uses Spanish, lost people in a lost city. Only one character, the Professore, offers hope of recovery, of decency. Romantic love goes down the drain against a background, not of war, but of a war ended. The set-in pieces themselves, unfortunately, are insufficient. Hemingway props with Dos Passos contrivances, they have little of the driving energy of Dos Passos; nor do they have the subdued lyricism of Hemingway. The stories are lacking in any great interest; the prose, in fact, often picks up the enervation of the subjects without the author's providing any distance. Their exhaustion is his. Hayes's attempt is to capture something he knew would be ephemeral: the liberation of a great city, the joy having turned to survival alone, the beauty of Rome now become the urgency of food, shelter, even light. The Professore speaks of what it will be like when the *luce* goes on; Rome will, once again, be a city of light. Yet the very significance of the idea, to capture that passing moment of triumph, defeat, liberation, and joylessness amidst joy, is defeated by the means. Those chopped-up episodes are advisable for a picture of America, or even of a city, as in *Manhattan Transfer;* but are historically and culturally unsuitable for revelations about Rome.

Robert Lowry's *The Wolf That Fed Us* (1949), a collection of eight interrelated stories, continues the theme of American soldiers in Italy as the occupying force, the conquerors. Lowry's point is to use the leave of one Joe Hammond, a gentle, kind soldier, and his friend so as to intermix them with various Italian whores. The main objective is Joe's desire to have everything, "every girl . . . I was looking for several lifetimes squeezed into a few days." Rome is a reflection of this desire, with everything messed up, the bottom having fallen out, and all saving themselves in the only way they know. The title is, of course, from the statue of Romulus and Remus feeding from the she-wolf that gave Rome its life—a life now perverted by the occupation. The style, however, modified Hemingway, allows for few modulations. Unlike Burns in *The Gallery,* Lowry cannot find the right expression.

Despite great energy and considerable craft, this group of novels is imitative and reductive, using styles and techniques remaindered from a previous generation. In Hemingway's own *Across the River and into the Trees* (1950), we see him imitating himself; and what he could not avoid, a whole stable of novelists also fell into. The postwar genre we have called the war/combat novel produced, in fact, three distinctive books: *From Here to Eternity,* in a traditional naturalistic mode; *The Gallery,* an attempt to break loose and establish new grounds for such fiction; *The Cannibal,* which looks ahead and is itself the new. Cutting across several categories is *The Naked and the Dead,* its force partially vitiated by weak technical devices and a general intellectual flaccidity.

When we turn to two novels of the Vietnam conflict, we find a distinct revival of the genre. Robert Stone's *Dog Soldiers* and Tim O'Brien's *Going After Cacciato* have assimilated their models and yet moved into new areas for war/combat fiction.

Vietnam as a Metaphor for Life

In *Dog Soldiers* (1974), Stone needed a metaphor for the Vietnam War, some emblem or central image which would carry over into civilian life what American soldiers experienced in Vietnam. In that sense, this is a war novel; not a frontal assault on war, as in Mailer, but war carried into our larger imagination.

Stone's key metaphor is the struggle over a three-kilo package of scag, or heroin. His three main characters are John Converse, a journalist; Brenda, his wife, the daughter of a newspaper owner and left-winger; and their courier, Hicks, whose sensibility assumes the center of the novel. Since no character calls for sympathy or empathy from the reader, Stone has had to locate his novel not in characters but in their mission: the transporting of the heroin from Vietnam to Brenda, who will then dispose of it, enriching everyone along the way. While the transfer of the heroin is an actual event, its chief import is symbolic. We must comprehend the characters at the level of what the war has done to them, as evidenced by the effect the heroin has on them.

In one way or another, they are all "users." Converse needs the excitement of the transaction to give his life some meaning—he is close to being a zombie; Brenda starts to pick up a habit, after experimenting with pills; and Hicks has a taste for the stuff—he also needs the experience to provide some thrills. Hicks reads Nietzsche, who "had overwhelmed him"—the Nietzsche of nihilism, not renewal. Hicks keeps repeating his own formula, which he has derived chiefly from the German: "Form is not different from nothingness. Nothingness is not different from form. They are the same." Hicks has imagined a triangle in his future, and he uses the idea of the triangle—a form for enclosing vast space, a means of journeying into various sides of experience—as his way of bringing space under control. His head is a vast arena of antisystems—the heroin transaction becomes for him a way of moving among them—but he still needs the triangle as a form to hold back the nothingness.

One key element involved in the transaction is the establishment of loyalties. Loyalties centering on heroin are the equivalent of bonds formed by men in Vietnam. Once again, Stone's problem, novelistically, was to find in civilian life or some marginal transaction the way the men had banded together during the war; how they survived what was a descent into nothingness. The epigraph for the novel comes, appropriately, from *Heart of Darkness,* to the effect that Marlow saw the "devil of violence and the devil of greed and the devil of hot desire," but even more, would "become acquainted with a flabby, pretending weak-eyed devil of a rapacious and pitiless folly."

Nevertheless, loyalties, however significant, are not all. What is also needed is the activization of a marginal group doomed by their position and definition. These are the dog soldiers. In American Indian tribes, there were male braves who were marginal to the general practices of the tribe; such males might be homosexual and live as married couples, or be deviant in other ways. They were permitted their deviance because they were dog soldiers: braves who were ready to sacrifice themselves in the most daring exploits. They were, in the eyes of the tribe, men who were already dead, therefore especially useful in war. They led the charge.

In Stone's terms, people unfitted for leadership in normal terms have qualities that can be called upon under special circumstances. They are not pleasant, Converse, nor Brenda, nor Hicks. But if the right transaction or common experience can be found, they have qualities that float to the surface: their ability to work along the boundaries of nothingness, greed, descent. To experience fear and to survive it is part of their mental equipment, although they approach it in different ways. Brenda fears for her small daughter, who is moved along from one person to another during the reign of terror perpetrated by the corrupt narcs; Converse is tortured and threatened by the same group, who move him from one place to another; and Hicks gradually takes the heat as he tries to hold on to the heroin.

In one sense, heroin does to the characters, those who have it as well as those who want it, what ivory in *Heart of Darkness* does to the agents and, most of all, to Kurtz. As Stone's version of Kurtz, Hicks has memories mainly of horrors, nightmares, "apocalypse now." He thinks of punitive patrols when his squad is wiped out, or of acts that pass beyond even Nietzschean formulations of human degradation. He has touched bottom, as has Kurtz, and so the heroin for him is simply another journey into blackness: Kurtz's final mission, which will bring together nothingness and form.

Badly wounded by narcs, pursued by the relentless Antheil and a Mexican agent, Hicks allows Converse and Brenda to escape, and tries to wind his way back so that they can pick him up. But his blood ebbs out, his attempt foredoomed to failure. He slows up, makes the rendezvous, but dies before Converse arrives. The latter, having the opportunity to escape with the heroin, chooses to leave it, to attempt something that will make Brenda and him other than dog soldiers. Antheil and the Mexican agent come upon Hicks, and decide to keep the heroin for themselves, precisely what they had intended all along. The fight for the totem goes on, now white snow, as ivory was white gold; purity perverted.

Like ivory in the Conrad novella, smack has its own qualities of purity: the greater the purity, the more it can be diluted on the streets; the greater the purity, the more intense its effects. When Hicks is driven to near-madness, he injects a deadly load into a man's thigh, a man who wanted to go along on a heroin joyride for the experience so as to write about it. Hicks will not permit scag to be trivialized. All the black deceit and corruption that lie around the acquisition of heroin are at odds with its pure appearance, its simplicity. Whiteness mocks the intentions of those who attempt to grapple with it.

What remains is the cycle of corruption. Once Hicks is dead and the Converses have fled, Antheil and the Mexican hold the ground. Converse has attempted to work out the contradictions of his name, which imply, on one hand, connection, intercourse; on the other, an adversary role, a contrary presence. His name suggests still another possibility: Converse may be converted, may exchange one state or condition for another. This, too, is possible; as the dog soldier may reenter his tribe after several brushes with death. Converse will not be a solid citizen, nor will Brenda, but in their abandonment of heroin they have indicated something of a conversion. The field is left to the corrupt, the narcs who will profit from a resale of the smack. The cycle will not end. The war will, simply, continue on new grounds; in other terms, a Nietzschean-Spenglerian cycle of doom.

Like the image of Adam's fingers reaching out to touch those of the Creator in Michelangelo's painting of the Creation, *Going After Cacciato* reaches out to touch several other war novels. Eventually, it becomes its own book, but the sources help define it. Cacciato—in Italian, "hunted one"—derives in idea from Heller's Yossarian. Cacciato's plan parallels Yossarian's escape to Sweden; he will escape the Vietnam War by going to Paris. One day, he packs his gear in an AWOL bag and leaves camp, walking away, destination Paris, the city of magic, life, a form of salvation. For those in Vietnam, Paris is comparable to Eden for those in America. A squad, with Paul Berlin, Tech 4, and an old lieutenant regular, takes off after Cacciato, whom they corner in a mountain, on a small greasy hill. They surround the spot and send up flares in the dawn, certain they have trapped their prey. They expect his surrender and encounter his escape. That is the last known fact. The rest is fantasy, the fantasy of Cacciato's run for Paris, across Asia and Europe until he is home safe, in the "capital of the world."

O'Brien's ingenious and convincing book concerns the fantastic journey of the squad chasing Cacciato until it, too, reaches Paris. At each stage in their journey, they catch glimpses of the "hunted one," who even seems to help them, certainly when the Shah's SAVAK is about to execute them. The squad comes alive as Paris becomes a realizable dream; fantasy takes on shape. Along the way, they pick up a Chinese girl named Sarkin Aung Wen, whose two old aunts die and leave her as an adoptee of the squad and of Paul, in particular. Sarkin represents "reality" within the fantasy, for she hopes to create a real life

out of the escape, to break from the army. She pulls ever harder at Paul to desert, in a sense suggesting that if the fantasy is to become real, Paul must indeed seek Paris. When he refuses, she runs off with the lieutenant, who is rejuvenated.

The main thrust of the novel is that fantasy journey to the fount of vitality and magic, Paris. Crossing the journey at several points, ten in all, are holding actions, comprising the "observation post." These brief sections, pages rather than chapters, recall the Promenades in John Horne Burns's *The Gallery*. Facing toward journey aspects, yet static, they hold the action back in the real world of Paul's first day in combat. The "observation post" is a four-hour watch Paul stands, which stretches to six, and it provides commentary on his dreams and sense of things. The segments are spaced in an irregular pattern, which allows basic rhythms to emerge, with closeness giving way in the middle pages to distant spacing, then returning to smaller intervals, the end as at the beginning. The idea is ingenious, in that its static element —the post never moves, of course—works with and against the fantasy journey, giving it grounding and still affording it dimensions.

Playing against the "post" and the journey is a third element, the description of Paul's first day in combat. Thus, the interplay of these elements gives us a three-part frame: the present of the journey; the present of the observation post; and the present of the combat experience, from which he had run only in his imagination. Little is future or past; all is now.

Vietnam War novels and nonfiction (*A Rumor of War* and *Dispatches*, for example) are, in a sense, removed from history, roving outside time and space. The writers who turn to the war—O'Brien here, Robert Stone, Michael Herr, Philip Caputo—have converted it into an ahistorical aberration by thrusting it almost entirely into a present disconnected from past or future. By handling it in this way, they make the war more nightmarish: that is, so removed from anything familiar in time or space that it hangs there, itself a fantasy life of sorts. What distinguishes fiction about the Vietnam War from that about World War II is its disembodied quality; it is unassociated with anything occurring back home or even back on the base. The men enter a surreal area when they fight a battle—jungle, sky, mud, whirling copters, a phantasmal enemy, loss of distinction between friend and foe.

The lack of differentiation, the sense that the world has receded, the recognition that individual sacrifice is worth nothing, all make the men hang together in the presentness of Now. What remains is escape, to Paris, to Mandalay (another magical name), even to Teheran. Cacciato, the hunted, is the sole one to make sense: desertion and escape into space, that old replay of American forms of salvation.

A third influence on O'Brien's novel is *The Naked and the Dead,* the narrative structuring based on a squad heading out into enemy territory, like a posse or band of cowboys (or bandits) on their own in the vastness of enemy territory. Those pioneers out to conquer all space are a traditional American phenomenon, part of the Puritan, frontier, and nineteenth-century experience; connected, of course, to pastoral images, to Eden as salvation, and to spatiality as a form of renewal. The squad in *Going After Cacciato* achieves a coherence and unity denied to the larger body of men, who are at the mercy of whatever the enemy throws their way. On the other hand, the squad, while it also may be exposed to great danger, has forsaken a passive for an active role. It goes out, explores, takes chances; it has a mission, and even though Paul Berlin's expedition here seems to have an official authorization, it is missionary in its zeal and dedication to purpose: to overtake Cacciato, return him as a deserter, and deny him his right to Paris while the rest fight.

A fourth force playing through *Cacciato* is Paul Theroux's *The Great Railway Bazaar,* with its rail lines extending across the vastnesses of Asia, connecting Mandalay to Paris. The idea of a linking railroad creates a curious imagery: the two lines of track working their way through every difficulty of terrain have their counterpart in the squad moving through one troublesome area after another. Further, the idea of taming the wilderness by means of a mechanical monster is a deeply rooted American image, railroad as savior and destroyer, as the nineteenth century saw it. Where once cows grazed, there is noise, smoke, and soot; but coherence is obtained at the same time, distances conquered, markets brought closer, urban culture transported to the prairie.

Verbally, *Cacciato* establishes its own style, a mixture of realism and fantasy at the level of language. But it owes a great deal, once more, to *Catch-22;* for example, in that juxtaposition of disparate elements which helps account for patterns of craziness in the Heller novel: "They were drunk. Their singing bounced off the buildings [in Teheran]. Clams, Stink Harris kept saying. He wanted clams for supper, so they went in search of clams. Instead they were arrested"—by SAVAK, when they ask a cop about clams. Tonally, the presence of Heller is there, as is Hemingway "flatness." "The sand smelled of sour milk. The air, so clean near the water, smelled of mildew. He was scared, yes, and confused and lost, and he had no sense of what was expected of him or of what to expect of himself. He was aware of his body." When Paul reminisces, he thinks of his father taking him to a Wisconsin camp, to hunt and to see Indians; experiences we recall from Hemingway stories, from Nick Adams, whom Paul resembles.

The literary influences are all there. War novels generate their own characteristics in common. But part of the triumph of *Going After Cacciato* is that it establishes a dimension to the war novel only hinted at before: the fantasy of removal juxtaposed to combat itself, with an intervening "observation post" of interfacial matter which mediates, judges, serves as choral effect. The result is an opening up of dimensions of the present, an absorption of rather sophisticated modernist time sequencing into a genre not known for its experimental nature.

In *A Flag for Sunrise* (1981), Stone returned to Vietnam by way of Tecan. The route is circuitous, but the shadow of "Nam" is everywhere, in memory and image, in ideological alignments, in individual ambivalence to the political process. No matter the geography, Vietnam is a metaphor for life.

To get back to Nam, Stone masses various groups and individuals in and around a mythical Central American republic called Tecan, which is propped up by American aid. It is a country reminiscent of Nicaragua, under Somoza, the prototypical oligarchy which America favors. Stone's elements are familiar: Father Egan, a burnt-out priest; Sister Justin, a nearly burnt-out nun who refuses to forgo her idealism; Holliwell, an American professor who wanders in and becomes a focus for the police; Pablo Tabor, a ne'er-do-well, drifter, drinker, pill popper, savage killer; the Callahans, rich Americans whose fortune is based on smuggling; Zecca, part of the American government presence in Tecan; the insurgents, made up of several groups, including those who have defected and are American spies; the Guardia, represented by Lieutenant Campos, a devout Catholic who kills freely for his tyrant; the Tecan government itself, which never appears. The two large elements are the Guardia, protecting the tyrannical government and American interests, and the insurgents, whose presence, at first shadowy and threatening, is finally embodied in the final apocalypse.

Since Tecan does not exist except in Stone's imagination, he must create it for the reader as an artwork is created. This is, in a sense, the most ambitious undertaking of his three novels; for the first time, he has a location that is not a place. And for that very reason, he runs into problems which he tries to solve with pastiche: of Conrad and Greene, but also of *The New York Times* and other news media. For what he provides, in theme and individual, is what we already know. He finds himself, in each instance, dealing with known quantities, whether the church figures or the repressive forces, the intellectual opposition or the dipso professor, Holliwell, or the drifter, Pablo. Each is predictable in the course of the novel because each has been noted before in fiction or the media. There are no literary surprises, nor can there be any. Stone freshens the scene with edgy, jagged language, but he cannot break through the familiarity of his material. Tecan is Conrad's Sulaco, or Greene's Haiti, Southeast Asia, Africa, and Mexico, or the *Times*'s Nicaragua, or some other repressive Central or South American republic.

What is original, though Stone does not quite connect it thematically to the various elements, is the ever present shadow of Vietnam. That conflict hovers over the main characters and over the American presence in Tecan; for Vietnam made hollow men of Holliwell and others, and it has cramped the American style thereafter. America can be neither a military nor a moral force. The opposition knows America will not interfere with troops; and it also knows America is bankrupt morally.

An apt metaphor for Tecan is that shadowy Nam and its mix of cultures: "Beside the beach at Danang he [Holliwell] had seen a leper with a 'Kiss Me' tee shirt. There was nothing to get angry about; some stern wit had made a statement and the leper had got a shirt." The convergence of elements in Tecan is little different. The innocent Holliwell gets caught in a revolutionary/counterrevolutionary movement to keep Tecan safe for rich tourists. Behind the move to keep Tecan "safe" in the hands of a friendly dictator (who never appears and who flees when the insurgents make their move) are the "corporations that own land here." So it is explained to Holliwell by Heath, an agent for Investors Security International, whose aim is to guarantee a "favorable environment" for business ventures. This is, of course, a familiar explanation, and while "true," it is, for fiction, a restrictive truth.

For the explanation was too simple when Greene made it in *The Quiet American* twenty-five years ago. In Greene, as in Stone, the "quiet American" looks toward a better society, meddles, and is killed, after causing many others to die. Stone's "quiet American"

is not Holliwell, who is really passive—one of the novel's errors, in fact—but Sister Justin, May Feeney. She is the sole appealing character in the novel, the only one who tries to break out of the "banality of evil" which underlies the theme. May has worked in the Tecan region for six years and has concluded that her devotion as nun and nurse has been wasted. An extremely attractive young woman, an idealist, she insists on being reborn—that is, on becoming "May" instead of Sister Justin. But rebirth in Tecan is preparation for trouble. She nurses Holliwell when he is stabbed by sea urchins, at the same time acting as an agent for the insurgents, thus compromising herself with Campos, a murderous member of the Guardia. Her release from Sister Justin is activated when she sleeps with Holliwell, but this radical act does not liberate her in the way she had thought it would. " 'A Wife—at Daybreak I shall be,' " she quotes. " 'Sunrise—Hast thou a flag for me?' " She says this ruefully, to indicate that the reality, the sexual act here, was less than what she had expected; that she will have to will herself into liberation—it does not come naturally. Here we have the quintessential Stone theme, the connection with his two previous novels. It is a lovely passage, a lovely moment in the novel, when May, seeking rebirth, beds down with Frank, whose name is somewhat of a mockery for such a passive man.

May is doomed. The insurgents cannot help her when Campos picks her up and proceeds to beat her to death. Her final words to him are: " 'Behold the handmaid of the Lord.' " With this, he knows he is doomed; that he has been caught out by God, and that his desire for power through brutality has been compromised by those simple words. She gains *her* power not by being a free woman but by re-becoming a nun.

The various narrative threads of the novel converge when Holliwell and Pablo Tabor are thrown together on a small boat and must try to slip away from Tecan. Pablo is a desperate killer, Holliwell now a man exposed to Tecan in all its varieties, as slippery as Nam. When they move out into the sea, the two recall very vividly the great scene in *Nostromo* when Decoud and Nostromo remove the silver from Sulaco and head out into the night of the Gulf on a lighter, each suspicious of the other, Decoud knowing that Nostromo will kill if necessary. Stone's Pablo plays the Nostromo role, Holliwell Decoud; but here the resemblance ends. In Conrad, the two men have been developed as opposites who overlap at many points; Nostromo has his charms, Decoud his. In Stone—

whether he modeled his final scene on Conrad or not —Pablo has no charms, no attractions, no presence except that of inexplicable evil (shades of Mailer's Gary Gilmore!); and Holliwell has not come to stand for anything except a drifting, dipso anthropologist, with little sense of introspection. His so-called love for May never penetrates into him; it is connected to his desire to allay loneliness, and is little different from hitting the bottle for the same purpose.

Despite the lively, fresh prose, Stone has kept feeling, motivation, and behavior on the surface. For a novel which attempts to explain so much—which is, in fact, a meeting of personal and political, of North and South, of capitalism and insurgent socialism/ Marxism/communism/Catholicism—there is little depth. The priest with whom the novel begins, Father Egan, burnt-out, alcoholic, sick, becomes increasingly madder; he comes, eventually, to mean little, although we have been led to expect much. Holliwell, with his memories of Vietnam, comes to the fore; but he rarely achieves presence. The various elements floating through and around him, the good as well as the evil, are embodiments of motives and emotions we do not comprehend, nor are we, I feel, expected to. Stone has chosen surfaces, and thus, measured against Conrad and even Greene, he has disappointed us. The fault lies not in the ambition but in the execution, and the novel does not seem an advance over the first two but a standing still, a measuring of skills: superbly fresh prose seeking the level to maintain it; which is another way of saying Stone is caught in a familiar American literary trap.

The Other Forties

Fiction of the 1940s was "inferno" oriented, inferno intensified. Beyond war/combat novels, the most representative fiction came from Bellow *(The Victim),* Capote (short pieces and *Other Voices, Other Rooms),** Willard Motley *(Knock on Any Door,* a continuation of the Wright tradition),† Carson McCullers (her major work preceding our lines of interest), Faulkner (whose *Fable* was begun in December 1944), Lionel Trilling *(The Middle of the Journey),* * Chester Himes *(If He Hollers Let Him Go,* also in the Wright tradition),‡ plus work by Hemingway, O'Hara, Farrell, and Dos Passos, whose careers we associate with the previous era. In most instances, their fiction of the forties and fifties was inferior to their best, although O'Hara and Farrell hung on even while the novelistic world they represented was slipping away in the work of younger and more culturally attuned writers.

The most ambitious work of these younger writers derived from Bellow and Faulkner, even though *A Fable,* despite the large ethical and moral issues exposed, is curiously a period piece. *The Victim* is surely the most significant fiction of this nonwar group, however overrated it has been by his admirers. It is still journeyman work, Bellow on his way toward discovering a distinctive voice; although, not to underrate it, it *is* a voice on the way to that discovery. Its intense Jewishness should not disguise the fact that its ethical considerations are not restrictive but generally postwar: Bellow's equivalent of the war novel brought into the postwar period.

The Victim (1947) is continuous with *Dangling Man* in its ethical modalities, both novels part of Bellow's 1940s "Inferno." His work is generally characterized by passage of his protagonists from Infernolike situations and attitudes toward Purgatorio, or Limbo, where an individual awaits movement into Purgatorio: the Dantesque positioning a good indicator of postwar America, poised for Heaven but resting on a line that stretches from Inferno to Limbo or Purgatorio. Rarely does Bellow's individual achieve Paradiso, and if so, only momentarily, in sexual bliss or with a finely prepared dish. Bellow's Christian, who is almost always a Jew, moves between the lower and intermediary levels of existence; for in the author's canon, to achieve Purgatorio signifies not the

---

*In "Growing Up in America."
†In "The American Political Novel."
‡In "Growing Up in America."

road to happiness but the attainment of an ethical mode of behavior.

Dangling Man was ambiguous because Joseph had his power of freedom removed, first, by war, and second, by his draft board. Caught in a maze of changing rules, none of which makes sense to him, he finds his self draining away. Thus his increasing acts of temper, his bursts of rage, his physical as well as psychical need to break out into forms of expression and individuality. The end of the novel is paradigmatic, Bellow's paradox: that Joseph has achieved his greatest freedom at the moment he embraces regimentation. All movement is ironic maneuvering.

The Victim picks up from there. Asa Leventhal, far more Jewish than Joseph, gains a sense of himself only when he is hounded by guilt feelings embodied in the person of Kirby Allbee. The latter, a sponger, drinker, loser, the traditional Gentile from a Jewish point of view, feels wronged by Leventhal. And yet he retains a hold over Leventhal by virtue of the fact of their common humanity, so Bellow claims. Although the nature of the hold remains vague, and we feel Leventhal is a born sufferer, rather than a man of choice, there is no question his life gains significance to the degree Allbee violates it. Here Bellow joins with Dostoyevsky, in this, one of his most Russian novels.

Allbee is, apparently, all men who are or have being; if he is All-be or All-being, he is, in this narrow sense, an ever-present, demanding God. If Allbee is there as a persistent gadfly, then what he makes of Leventhal is Job: molested by this man from his past, by his sister-in-law, by all those unable to make adjustments to modern life, who heap their ills and maladjustments on Leventhal. As a Leventhal—a man from the Levant or East—he takes on Biblical characteristics: not only Job, but a suffering godlike creature, embodied in a weary, enervated man. Leventhal simply yearns to be, to be left alone to live out his days, without either great pleasure or great pain. He desires a middle course of existence, which Bellow will not permit, since it denies sensitive feeling. Leventhal's reaction must be sharpened—as later happens to Augie March, Herzog, Tommy Wilhelm, Sammler, Citrine—or else he remains in Limbo, even if unknown to him.

We glimpse Leventhal's intensification or deepening as early as the fifth chapter, about one-sixth into the novel. As he heads for Staten Island, in response to an SOS from his sister-in-law, he sees his new life, one assaulted by others. He observes the New York skyline. "The notion brushed Leventhal's mind that the light over them [towers on shore] and over the water was akin to the yellow revealed in the slit of the eye of a wild animal, say a lion, something inhuman that didn't care about anything human and yet was implanted in every human being too, one speck of it, and formed a part of him that responded to the heat and the glare." We recall images in *Death in Venice,* when a complacent, ordered Aschenbach has dreams of savage, primitive experiences, orgiastic in nature, a view of the inhuman, as it were.

Having lived without full awareness, Leventhal is set for redemption through suffering; not only that, but redemption by way of becoming responsible for every one of his acts. In that arena of trivial and minor events Bellow casts his novel. Here, in fact, he establishes the ethical mode that will govern his fiction, proving the strength of his vision and the weakness of his novelistic sense. For in his pursuit of ethical modes, Bellow often allows his fiction to deteriorate into didacticism, or, worse, into shrill rejection of alternative modes of being or countering forms of behavior, or even into incomprehension of such adversary modes. As a consequence, Bellow found the 1960s a challenge to man's very humanity, seeing in the frenzy of the decade a return to savagery, the worst in man. Bellow had to resolve the 1960s by way of rejection or through parodic forms; so that, in a real sense, his intellectual development *as a novelist* ceased after the 1950s. Since formal matters were rarely of primary importance to him, he located himself essentially by the time he was forty.

The Victim is Bellow's attempt to find an equivalent of what Mailer, Jones, Burns, and others were doing with the army and with combat.* Paradigmatic is the Biblical book of Job. The key polemical ideas are suffering, at one end, and one's belief in a transcendent power (by no means God) at the other. Man lies stretched on a rack in between, and he may gravitate in either direction, toward suffering, with or

---

*In *Ship of Fools* (written 1941–61, published 1962), Katherine Anne Porter reproduced a form of combat on board a ship out of Vera Cruz heading for Bremerhaven. Based loosely on Sebastian Brant's late-medieval *Das Narrenschiff,* which headed for a "fool's paradise," Porter's ship makes for Germany in 1931. Her scheme, like that of the war novelist, is an anatomy of the culture, a mirroring in a given cast of characters (voyagers, like a squad or platoon) of the workings of a society. Porter reflects prewar society as rent by irreparable conflicts: Jew-Gentile, male/female, generational, social/political, matters of class and caste. Her ship is the typical cross section, here a "ship of fools," in the army or war novel an arena of impostors.

without understanding, or toward escape, by assuming he is beyond any fixed reference. Near the end, Leventhal asserts it "came into his head that he was like a man in a mine who could smell smoke and feel heat but never see the flame." The image is Platonic, about those who confuse the flame on the wall with reality, while missing what is real altogether. In Bellow's inversion of the image, Leventhal must strive to see the flame, for he has attempted to go through life satisfied with smoke and heat, even less.

The average sensual man must be brought to understanding, and this only by an accrual of disasters. Leventhal's wife is away (in the South), his nephew dies, he meets an alienated brother for the first time in years, he is accused by Kirby Allbee of having destroyed his life, even of having caused Allbee's wife's death, he serves in a job whose other employees make anti-Semitic remarks, he incurs the hatred of his brother's wife and mother-in-law. Bellow has transformed the large-scaled disasters of Job's predicament into the trivialities of contemporary life, which are, however, no less essential to the growth of awareness.

Allbee, who victimizes Leventhal, and is, to some extent, victimized, is also a Job of sorts. He is a man who preys on others because of flaws in himself. Bellow never really focuses him, and while we can see that some of that vagueness is designed, we are also bothered by Bellow's inability to pin him down uniquely. As much as Leventhal is the paradigmatic Jewish sufferer, Allbee is the classic Gentile, so true to the so-called type that he remains unclear as an individual. He drinks heavily, is disorderly, flouts family life, is as unsteady at work as he is at play. If the Jew represents the principle of order, the Gentile is filthy, chaotic, inconsiderate, racially intemperate. He represents qualities inherent in those who assume the world belongs to them; whereas the Jew is orderly so that he can live undisturbed, invisibly.

Bellow's narrative strategy is to keep the reader immersed in trivia. Events are so ordinary as to pass beneath notice, except that Bellow charges each with significance. Once suffering begins, then every aspect of being becomes intensified, as in pain a patient invests details with meaning they otherwise lack. Even conversations, which later, in Bellow, would become witty and parodic, here are ordinary, without resonance. So much in the novel, in fact, expresses clearly what it means that the reader wonders how Bellow expected to gain significance from so little. Yet as we know from repetition of a word, it gains exotic dimensions from rehearing. By way of the ordinary repeated

in various guises, Bellow makes the ordinary fresh. Things that exist about Leventhal serve to estrange him, as Meursault's characteristics make him a stranger.

The reader recognizes that Bellow has attempted a mode of American existentialism, at the very time it was spreading over the French literary scene. Character is the snaillike movement that results from the accumulation of trivial details; a funeral, a monotonous job, a careless love affair. The ordinary magnified can be the stuff of a life experienced on the edge of a precipice. Bellow could have picked up much of this from home-grown American naturalism, except that naturalism had aspects of determinism, violence, and sloth alien to his type of world. The French variety of precipitous living is closer to Bellow's conception of life, although he has removed real violence (only some shoving and fistfighting, Jewish violence) and replaced it with suffering. Bellow has, in a sense, created a bourgeois existentialism, its precipices often connected to marriage and jobs.

The culmination of Leventhal's relationship with Allbee comes when the former stays out one night and the latter takes over the apartment, locking the door while he enjoys a female pickup in Leventhal's own bed. The sexual triangle is, somehow, completed. If this novel had been written in the 1950s, we could have seen a Chambers-Hiss examplar in the Leventhal-Allbee duo. For when Allbee accommodates himself to Leventhal's bed, he is in a sense sharing it with Leventhal by way of a woman. The sharing of the bed with Allbee disgusts Leventhal so much he throws him from the apartment. There is, further, the suggestion that when Allbee chains the door, he has taken over Leventhal's life, not only the apartment; and with that taken over Leventhal's wife, even though she is away. They share the wife when they share the bed. Part of the brilliant undersurface of the novel derives from just such intimations. Leventhal must be redeemed from entanglements he never dreamed existed.

In a direct war novel setting that parallels many aspects of *The Victim,* Faulkner in *A Fable* (1954) mixes Job, Jesus, suffering, martyrdom, repentance—the elements of Dante's experience. Faulkner worked on the novel formally from late 1944 to late 1953; so that it spanned the war decade, encompassing the postwar reaction. Faulkner sought, like Bellow in *The Victim,* some way of comprehending what man was like in situations of extreme stress, Faulkner near the end of his career, in a summation; Bellow at the beginning of his, a foreshadowing. Both writers were reacting to American war victories by stressing victims, victimizing, the cold war already implicit.

A Fable was Faulkner's attempt to write a visionary novel that brought together past and present, myth and actuality, as he had attempted more sparely in "The Bear." The myth of war, rather than its purely active elements, was the focus of the vision—what we saw, minimally conceived, in Hawkes's *The Cannibal.* At the end of the Second World War, both Hawkes and Faulkner concentrated on the First (although Hawkes slides from one to the other). By returning to the earlier war, they have written philosophical novels, transforming the war/combat novel into sociohistorical fiction, or into complex political statement.

Faulkner has interwoven complex themes: a generational struggle that is also a political struggle (worked through in class and caste terms) that is also a religious struggle (between Jesus and God); and all that played out in the conflict between Allied and German armies on the western front, where the ultimate is life and death. Here, a corporal who organizes the mutiny of a regiment of three thousand men on the French front is a Christ-like figure in struggle against generals (his father the supreme commander) and politicians, who demand that the war continue.

Faulkner's effort at a vast war and peace links him to many contemporary war novels, but, more aptly, provides a thread of continuity with a fiction like *Gravity's Rainbow* in the 1970s. What connects Faulkner and Pynchon, apart from their common attempt to collect the things of the world into one book, is a rhetorical manner, which in its way is as inclusive as what the words mean. Faulkner needed a language for the novel, and what he attempted was a variation on his own rhetoric in *Absalom, Absalom;* just as later Pynchon was to try out a linguistic exploration of ways in which visions could be verbalized. Unfortunately, the visionary quality of Faulkner's novel is undermined by ill-chosen language: excessive and indulgent, it rarely moves, and frequently serves to confuse.

Linguistically, then, the book is an indulgence, as the following passages suggest:* ". . . couldn't forget you because you were why we were where we were." "That you were chosen by destiny out of the paradox

---

*Yet Malcolm Cowley quotes Faulkner: " 'I am writing and rewriting, weighing every word which I never did before. I used to hang it on like an apprentice paper hanger and never look back.' "

of your background, to be a paradox to your past in order to be free of human past to be the one out of all earth to be free of the compulsions of fear and weakness and doubt which render the rest of us incapable of what you were competent for." Language strains for Biblical significance, but it does not find a level and it misses one's ear. Faulkner writes of "not even the crashing ejaculation of salute this time." Sometimes the same rhetoric clicks into place: "the vast cumbrous machinery of war grinding to its clumsy halt in order to reverse itself to grind and rumble in a new direction—the proprietorless wave of victory exhausted by its own ebb and returned by its own concomitant flux, spent not by its own faded momentum but as though bogged down in the refuse of its own success." Prose is on the edge, almost a parody of itself, and then redeemed in that final image, where language and vision of war encounter each other.

At the structural level, Faulkner has worked daringly, unfolding his tale of mutiny through flashback and parallelism of event, revealing small segments at a time; so that anyone who hopes to grapple with events must reread, not read. Faulkner has worked on disguises, dribbling out information of the regiment's mutiny, the corporal, the general in charge (Gragnon), and the supreme commander who arranges the façade. Since the mutiny must be disguised, so that the soldiers do not end the war themselves, Faulkner can come at his material as if from the narrow end of a funnel. As he burrows toward divulgation, we begin to perceive the political-religious-social patterns.

The mutiny is arranged by a corporal who seems ubiquitous, who, at thirty-three, is destined for martyrdom, and who refuses the role of dutiful son when the general offers him escape. The corporal may be France's unknown soldier after his death, as well as its savior; when he dies, he gains a crown of thorns of barbed wire, war and religion touching. War is all wars, past and future as well as present. The German general who flies in to agree to the arrangement by which the mutiny can be disguised from the rest of the army speaks of the next war and tells the British that they will not even prepare for it. "You will wait until an enemy is actually beating at your front gate. Then you will turn out to repel him exactly like a village being turned out cursing and swearing on a winter night to salvage a burning hayrick—gather up your guttersweepings, the scum of your slums and stables and paddocks; they will not even be dressed to look like soldiers, but in the garments of ploughmen and ditchers and carters; your officers look like a country-house party going out to the cutts for a pheasant drive."

The German foresees that the future belongs to those who can mobilize force, not moral persuasion; and by means of his presence and speech, Faulkner has extended his "fable" forward, just as by means of the Christ-like corporal he has extended it backward. At the heart of the struggle, on all levels of the novel, is the split between man's endurance as measured by his power and man's endurance by virtue of his spirit. Archetypally, the supreme general is indicative of political power and intrigue, whereas his son is a sacrifice to the elements marshaled by spiritual, moral, and ethical considerations. This ideological division defines the structure of the novel, much as the political discussions between Cummings and Hearn define the ideological setting of *The Naked and the Dead,* the difference being that Hearn is a weak idealist, whereas the corporal is a strong one.

Faulkner's Nobel Prize speech in 1950 is echoed in the novel, in that man endures "not because he is immortal but [is] immortal because he endures." He may endure from several points of view, even rapacity; but ultimately, man cannot fail man, or else he ceases. Every life experienced intensely and with comprehension of all the stakes is a form of endurance, and by extension a form of immortality.

There is an ethical imperative in the Faulkner novel that is considerably at odds with many other novels of the 1950s, where the drive was to achieve liberation from moral positions, exemplified by parts of *Augie March, Henderson the Rain King,* Barth's early fiction, Gaddis's *The Recognitions.* Faulkner's own concern is retold by Malcolm Cowley, in *The Faulkner-Cowley File:* "Then he told me [October 25, 1948] about his new novel, of which he has written 500 pages. It is about Christ in the French army, a corporal with a squad of 12 men—and a general who is Antichrist and takes him upon a hill and offers him the world. Symbolic and unreal, except for 300 wild pages about a three-legged racehorse in Tennessee. Mary Magdalene and the other two Marys." Faulkner clearly saw it as within a Biblical frame of reference, for as early as 1943, he wrote to Harold Ober, his agent: "It continues on, through the Three Temptations, the Crucifixion, the Resurrection," this being at a time when he had half or less of an earlier draft. We observe the ethical dimension in a follow-up letter to Robert Haas (January 15, 1944), in which he comments that when Christ reappeared he was recrucified: i.e., "we are in the midst of war again." Christ will be crucified each time he appears.

Faulkner wanted to grasp it all, more so than most of his younger contemporaries in the 1940s and early 1950s, except perhaps for Gaddis and, to some extent, Mailer. Even Bellow in *The Adventures of Augie March,* his most far-reaching novel, attempted less. Faulkner's narrative is more sermon than novel, for character, scene, plot elements give way to rhetorical streams intrinsic to the method. That Faulkner could not sufficiently control his rhetoric at this point in his career does not dissipate the largeness of the vision. We recognize as we read his ambitious contemporaries how they derive from Faulkner, not Hemingway; as Faulkner may have perceived when he wrote (June 28, 1947): "Hemingway did not have the courage to get out on a limb as the others [Wolfe, Dos Passos] did, to risk bad taste, overwriting, dullness, etc." Later, he apologized to Hemingway for these words.

The key observation is that "courage to . . . risk bad taste, overwriting, dullness." Although Faulkner's linguistic ability had slackened and he often miscalculated his verbal pyrotechnics, he had not lost that willingness to upset his readers. *A Fable,* we recall, appeared at the same time as *Across the River and into the Trees* (1950) and *The Old Man and the Sea* (1952), which, whatever their virtues, lacked what Faulkner called "risk." They were fictions for the Hemingway club. This was, indeed, the great danger for fiction in the 1950s: that with the rush of events so unwieldy, so fierce and anarchical, the reaction to it in novelistic terms would be to seek order, stability, surface organization. Faulkner knew better: that disorder and anarchy must be confronted head-on in equally fierce fictions, where order lies deep below the surface, while surface reflects turbulence. Man does not endure at a bar or in catching a fish or seeking his pleasures, but in vast works of myth, history, and ethical considerations.

Fictional guidelines were being set by Bellow, Jones, Hawkes, Mailer, and others, who would soon by joined by Gaddis, Barth, and Styron in the next decade. The remaining novelists seemed caught in older forms. I have in mind Carson McCullers and Nelson Algren, mining, respectively, Southern or American Gothic; John O'Hara and Robert Penn Warren in aspects of naturalism, which also carries over into William Carlos Williams's Stecher trilogy. But however expert these novels were—and Robert Penn Warren's *All the King's Men* reads as well in post-Watergate days as it did in the 1940s—they were set into forms that no longer expressed who and what we were. Even McCullers's grotesques looked back rather than forward, and Algren's drug-induced hallucinatory world is more in the naturalistic mode of Farrell and Dreiser than it is associated with the Beats, whom it appears to forerun.

In *The Heart Is a Lonely Hunter* (1940), McCullers's deaf-mute, John Singer, is akin to Dostoyevsky's Myshkin. He is the eye of the storm, a man deeply in love with the fat Greek, Spiros Antonapoulos, also a deaf-mute, with whom he communicates in sign language. Spiros goes mad and is put away, and from then on, Singer becomes the "ear" for that world circling around him: Mick Kelly, Biff Bannon, Jake Blount (the "Red"), and Dr. Copeland, a Negro medical doctor. Such a vision of life would be a remarkable achievement for a mature novelist, but it is extraordinary for one so young (McCullers was twenty-two); for her vision was no less than a way of seeking human conciliation. As she stated, her theme was "man's revolt against his own inner isolation and his urge to express himself as fully as possible. . . . Each man must express himself in his own way—but this is often denied to him by a wasteful, short-sighted society."

Yet she does not indulge runaway egos or pure narcissism; she also seeks "place," fit, order. Black life, with Dr. Copeland as the center of a large family, is superbly wrought. Burning with a rage for Negro justice, Copeland has children who are indifferent, who get into trouble, who work as maids or fight in bars. He dreams of making his children arms of retribution for injustice, but they turn out to be obedient Negroes with all the problems of their class. McCullers's description of Copeland's attempts to deal with his rage is the finest thing in the novel: his desire for advancement, his recognition that his race is doomed by failure (including that of his own children).

McCullers persists that the individual, suspended between love and terror, must find ways to emerge. This is Biff's vision at the end, alone in the café: "For in a swift radiance of illumination he saw a glimpse of human struggle and of valor. Of the endless fluid passage of humanity through endless time. And of those who labor and of those who—one word—love. His soul expanded. But for a moment only. For in him he felt a warning, a shaft of terror. Between the two worlds he was suspended." All are thwarted. Singer represents love, but is surrounded by terror; Spiros has his madness, his fat, his desire for food, for comforting, his inability to give; Biff, his hopeless feeling for Mick, a thirteen-year-old, which passes; Copeland, his frustrated plans; Jake Blount, his rage

for political justice; Mick, her entrapment as an employee for the five-and-ten.

All these incomplete or submerged people talk to Singer, who reads lips and makes them feel complete. Just speaking out calms them, and they crowd his room in the Kelly home, a boardinghouse. But when Spiros dies in the hospital, Singer, who has seemed to know all, shoots himself in the chest. One of the final scenes is the gathering at his graveside. His is a silent voice, a Jew who understands. Even Dr. Copeland, who hates whites, recognizes the specialty of Singer; a mute Singer, a bard, a maker of tones and textures, but without words, testimony to some internal experience he communicates to those around him. He calms white rage—Blount; and black rage—Copeland. He is the great conciliator.

This is a middle-ground fiction, technically straightforward. But the new tones of the novel are set by the unusual nature of the characters, the intensity of their internal experiences, the silences and pauses which fill the novel, the static quality of its life, and the fact that nothing much occurs except for self-destruction. Kafka is implicit here, as is Dostoyevsky; Faulkner, of course; but the writing is fresh, novel, textured.

In McCullers's second novel, *Reflections in a Golden Eye* (1941), the "reflections" are as much Lawrentian and from Poe or "Southern Gothic" as from herself; but her effort is still compelling. Although many of the literary devices were derivative— the use of Leonora's horse as metaphysical energy, the sun itself as a "golden eye," Private Williams's display of nudity—cumulatively they suggest a voice trying to break free. McCullers has moved in and out of Faulkner, toward a kind of grotesquerie we would find later in Truman Capote, Paul Bowles, James Purdy, Flannery O'Connor, parts of Hawkes, even Salinger. Of these, O'Connor and Hawkes proved the best able to assimilate various styles and forge something distinctively their own.

None of this is intended to discredit McCullers's achievement, except that we have tired of the mannerisms of this group of writers: the excessive drinking, the suggested or actual homosexuality, the helpless artistic sensibility (in the Filipino houseboy, Anacleto, a Tennessee Williams type), the visible adultery, and so on. But to all this—and it was relatively new when McCullers turned to it—she added qualities of stasis, silence, withdrawal, which are unique. She became successful here, and later, in depicting levels of retreat: Private Williams moves silently in forest and houses, he hovers over Leonora's bed like a statue, and he blends in with sun and moon, like a specter. His values are idiosyncratic, incapable of examination. His life is so withdrawn—he has spells that energize his actions—that it can only be expressed, not analyzed. His expression is intense voyeurism, but not distanced; he brings himself right up to the flesh, where sight becomes tactile.

Little of this aberration is weakness. Private Williams is strength itself—identified with nature's power, horses, sun, forests. Like a Lawrentian heroine, he gains strength from natural forces, whereas Leonora's husband, a weakling, locates his life in late studying, unresolved sexual feelings, inadequacy in bed, playing the cuckolded husband on an army base. Lawrence's short story "Sun" is a prototype.

What derives from this ballet—and the novel is a dance of fading forces—is a rhythm which indicates McCullers is moving out toward new forms of expression. Not always stylistically fresh, she is rhythmically innovative, introducing broad elements of movement and silence, intense frenzy combined with withdrawal. Except for the horses, *Reflections* is, like its title, almost completely lacking in sound. Reflections from the sun create another order of being, one of stealth, voyeurism, watchfulness. In this brief novel, written when McCullers was barely past twenty, we find a sensibility that has absorbed its novelistic lessons and is using form to express something distinct. This, too, is an army novel, about an army in peacetime, with war distant; and yet the sense of some kind of war is never beyond us.

Nelson Algren's *The Man with the Golden Arm* (1949; winner of the first National Book Award, in 1950) is a forerunner of the so-called Beat literature which would come in the 1950s. But the Algren novel harks back also to quite a different tradition, the naturalism that helped to fuel Farrell in his Studs Lonigan books, Crane in *Maggie,* some of Dreiser. The Beats explored an adversary life style which was achieved out of consciousness, a willed style that involved drugs, drink, poverty-level accommodations; whereas Algren's people take to this style out of necessity. They are not slumming; they are the slums.

Algren strains mightily to achieve their seemingly effortless accommodation to disaster. Eager to avoid the doom-filled prose of the naturalists, who are at his elbow, Algren yearns after a poverty-cycle lyricism; an analogy might be Styron, in *Lie Down in Darkness.* Caught within a web of Faulkner, Algren strains after language that will remove him from the Faulknerian grasp: "Till darkness brought her sleep on a weary handcar, switching her into a nowhere train that curved and descended, softly and endlessly, out upon the vast roundhouse of old El dreams." The lyricism is not achieved easily, since it involves romanticizing the El, which is noise, dirt, and grime.

Also, it is mechanical, part of a cycle of existence which is unending, like man's fate or destiny. To turn this into a lyrical artifact is to turn naturalism on its head, so to speak. For mechanical objects, ordinarily, are part of the doom-filled world; they drag down, not up. Algren moves in two directions, then, citing the mechanical El as man's fate; and yet attempting to transform it into an object that caresses the spirit. The entire world of Division Street is so "transformed," its inability to function in the outside world a sign of a certain nostalgia for purity of purpose, for a life that exists outside of demeaning work. Frankie Machine is a "dealer," a card dealer who also has a monkey on his back, a morphine need. Cardsharps, thieves, petty criminals of every stripe defy the world of the El, which carries working people to their form of doom overhead, whereas those on the ground pursue an adversary life.

Like the naturalistic novelists before him, Algren attempts to create an ethic from the lives of his characters. But this ethic, as suggested above, must not be work-oriented; it must hover between work and disaster, or even poke into art. Frankie is a man with a "golden arm," the reference being to his ability as a card dealer, THE DEALER, as he is called. The golden arm, however, suggests another dimension to Frankie: besides an arm filled with dope, one reaching halfway toward art, in transforming a deck of cards into a thing of beauty. Similarly, his best friend, Sparrow, is a sneak and a thief, but his name suggests flight, lightness, a certain style. This is a thieves' opera, the world of John Gay and of Brecht, a three-penny opera, where words attempt to become music.

The other side of this is its romanticization of pain and suffering. Inevitably, perhaps, Algren offers this not only as an adversary existence but a preferred one, closer to reality than the lives of those who record, document, work, stabilize. The indulgent life is superior to the puritanical; Poles, Algren's subjects, are preferable to Anglos, achievers and aspirers. Yet Algren's lyrical view puts his characters into a "high" that their lives and senses cannot support. Unlike Farrell, who wrote of frustration and dissatisfaction in flat, neutral prose, Algren makes his misery soar, zoom. The novel soars on the wings of a morphine high, Frankie's monkey; but without that sense of waste and frustration indigenous to the genre. It's as though a painter had tried to imitate Rembrandt and left black off his palette. Algren's characters lack definition, caught as they are between two types of thing: a naturalism that fixes them and a lyricism that suggests we should accept their despairing lives without knowing much about them.

Narrow lives can be of great literary interest; lives of despair are the stuff of twentieth-century fiction. Self-destruction is one of the major themes of our times, and characters whose only talent is to flaunt their self-hatred fill contemporary literature. But we are about to enter an entire sub-body of fiction, with Algren, the Beats, the narcissists of the 1960s and 1970s, with the so-called nonfiction novel, these and many other developments, in which narrowness of range and authorial misjudgment of tactics create fictions with ambitious overreach. Adroit language is there, as we can observe in Algren, but matters of tactics—tones, taste, attitudes, intellectual resources—militate against full use of linguistic abilities.

By the 1940s, John O'Hara's best work was behind him, in the 1930s, with *Appointment in Samarra* (1934) and *Butterfield 8* (1935), although these novels have been overrated. Even at his best, O'Hara skimmed surfaces. In *Butterfield 8,* Gloria Wandrous is more swirl than probe, and Weston Liggett is a stereotypical New York upper-middle-class young and middle-aged man. O'Hara was already accumulating external detail as a way of avoiding deeper analysis; and was hobbled, this early, by his literary ideas, which involved resisting everything that was new or trendy. More positively, he was remarkably prescient in his presentation of his female characters, who are rarely passive in the face of male aggression. Gloria makes men "pay," with money, but also with more than they had been willing to give.

In the later 1940s, at the time of *A Rage to Live,* O'Hara began to represent Matthew Arnold's definition of the "old master," who heard the plaudits of the world even as he recognized the slippage of his craft. While the regional novel dissipated rapidly after World War II and, in fact, became a sign of a prewar sensibility, O'Hara struggled heroically with regionalism. The sophistication he brought to the regional novel gave him a satirical weapon which, unfortunately, he used only lightly. He differs from more typical regional writers in that he brings New York (and *New Yorker*) attitudes to his region of Pennsylvania Dutch territory, instead of sharing the ingrown world of these people.

Naming is an important element in *A Rage to Live* (1949), and the use of family names is a mark of a prewar sensibility, particularly of the regional novel. Once the war intervened and the novel became urban, national, and international, family names became meaningless, as did the sense of idea of family. Early in the novel, after Sidney Tate and Grace Caldwell marry, O'Hara says that "at an intermediate point in their lives Sidney and Grace became the Tates." While the designation as Tates establishes the marriage, it does a great deal more culturally. It establishes the individual as part of the scene, the scene as part of the society; and it suggests interrelationships between elements that are distinctly regional. To be Sidney or Grace, apart from family name, has the mark of independence which is both the burden and the glory of postwar fictional characters. Or even to have no memorable name, neither given nor family—that, too, is a mark of the postwar character.

Further, the use of names, as well as other social devices, designates O'Hara as a chronicle writer. Near the conclusion of *A Rage to Live,* Grace Tate meets the twenty-year-old Julian English, who, we recall, committed suicide in *Appointment in Samarra,* a novel published in 1934. They meet in 1920, and by 1930 English is a suicide. The connection, the brief flirtation—Julian says something rather compromising and reveals the wildness under the socially acceptable exterior—all suggest connections to the chronicle and regional novel. Further, Sidney Tate's appearance as an outsider to the closed world of Fort Penn indicates not only a closing down of experience, but that whatever does occur must be out of sight. O'Hara's world is a voyeur's delight; whereas in the big city, a voyeur is defeated. The lens is too broad. When Walker Percy's Will Barrett trains his telescope on people, it is aimed at Central Park. O'Hara trains narrowly and then leaves out shadows, motives, even mind.

Ten North Frederick (1955) has comparable problems: an old-fashioned narrowness that dissipates what O'Hara did well. The courtship of Joe and Edith, for example, is the kind of thing the newer writers could not handle; also, O'Hara can convey intense physical awareness without sex. But once marriage settles in, he is predictable. Joe and Edith have no interest except for their snobbishness, concerned as they are with petty details. O'Hara generates no heat in this area. By now, his energy went into the writing, not the conception.

William Carlos Williams is a figure from a different era, associated more with Hemingway and Dos

Passos than with the postwar novel. His two prose works of the 1920s, *The Great American Novel* (1923) and *In the American Grain* (1925), were in the experimental mode. The first, which appeared in a limited edition of three hundred copies published in Paris, was among the earliest antinovels. Without plot, marginal to the traditions of the novel, seemingly incoherent in matters of time and place, it proceeds by way of associations, like the early pages of Joyce's *Portrait,* linked by the consciousness of the "I." *In the American Grain,* a prose poem of sorts, attempted to define the American character in the genre of Lawrence's *Studies in Classic American Literature:* a very personal history—an early version of the new journalism. By trying to make the reader "see," Williams evoked a living history of the American personality and character.

These prose works feed into Williams's Stecher trilogy. In *White Mule* (1937), Joe Stecher and his wife, Gurlie, come to New York at the turn of the century. Successive volumes, *In the Money* (1940) and *The Build-Up* (1946), chart their fortunes as paradigmatic of the American experience: their struggle to define themselves in the new world, their two babies, their fight to become part of American success, their achievements and move to a New Jersey suburb, their role as social leaders in their community. Although Williams's method is poetic, his debt is to naturalism. The rise (not fall) of the Stecher family emblemizes the rise of America at the turn of the century and thereafter. It is parallel to Gertrude Stein's *The Making of Americans,* but not so self-conscious as that work. By 1946, when the final volume was published, Williams had completed what he had begun, but the venture seems curiously outdated, despite his skill in evoking by way of detail a symbolic presence.

Robert Penn Warren's finest fictional achievement, *All the King's Men* (1946), worked along a similar vein: regional, naturalistic, yet symbolic of America in its details and its close attention to the "counterfeit" career of Willie Stark. What gives Warren's novel its old-fashioned quality is his insistence on turning all narrative elements into plot functions. Eventually, plot turns stifle us. *All the King's Men* is, in fact, a superb example of the kind of novel the postwar writer felt obligated to alter; for with all its excellent qualities, it represented an earlier form of fiction. Its moral flavor and cast of characters direct us toward George Eliot's *Middlemarch.* For a Southern novel by a Southerner, it owes surprisingly little to Faulkner, and in most ways jumps over the 1920s and 1930s in order to point toward the nineteenth-century triple-decker.

In its look backward, the novel catches some of the late twenties and certainly the sense of the thirties, as a political maverick, Willie Stark, rises from obscurity to governor of what appears to be Louisiana, a reenactment of many aspects of Huey Long's career. Yet the moral pivot of the novel is not Stark, but the narrator, Jack Burden. Part of Warren's strategy is to perceive Stark's unfolding through Burden's eyes. Burden is a historian by training, having gone through all the work on his Ph.D. except the final stages of the dissertation, a study of a pre–Civil War figure, Cass Mastern. In a life that straddled small events, all of them involving moral decisions and moral courage, Mastern struggled to be decent in an amoral world, and ended up a sacrifice to a Union bullet. His is a "small life," but from Burden's point of view, it proves instructive; for it parallels his own life as it drifts increasingly from moral to atavistic concerns.

From his position as aide-de-camp to Stark, Burden observes the unfolding of a drama in which Stark believes that good can derive from bad, though he no longer distinguishes good from bad or himself from power. As Stark's career develops, he identifies himself increasingly with the power that will enable him to do good; so that the good is compromised at every turn by the means bringing it about. Megalomania permits him to enter into so many shady deals that the people he injures increase severalfold. The disgruntled surround him, even as his circle of loyal supporters grows smaller.

Warren very shrewdly works class/caste lines. Stark, who is dirt poor at the start, is egalitarian, in that he wishes to bring everyone down to his level rather than to rise. He brings in Jack Burden, of Burden's Landing, a young man with a long family history of landed property. He wins over Doc Adam Stanton as director of his hospital—the son of the former governor; and he gains Anne Stanton, Adam's frosty sister, as his mistress. He sets Burden into researching Judge Irwin, who opposes Stark's political career, and brings Irwin down when Burden strikes dirt. Stark levels everyone, turning them from their good sense of themselves into people who must confront their compromises and defaults. The most compromised is, of course, Burden, and he pays by discovering, after Judge Irwin commits suicide rather than face the revelations of his past, that Irwin is his father.

Further, within the lower- and upper-class confrontation, Stark's women represent several classes and types: his wife, Lucy, the typical "lily" figure, loyal, honest, a woman of integrity, who leaves Willie when she cannot bear the dishonesty of his means; Sadie Burke, a dirt-poor, acne-pocked woman of great intensity, whose love for Willie permits her to enter into any deal, commit any act, go through any hell, as long as she can remain near his side; and finally, Anne Stanton, the aristocrat among Stark's respectable women. The governor's daughter agrees to become Willie's mistress so as to control Burden's discoveries about her father, to bring about some of her own projects, and because Stark touches in her forces she cannot resist.

Warren brilliantly demonstrates how such diversity, like the country itself, must lead to a violent resolution. Adam is "Adam," pure, frosty, a man of integrity who finds himself compromised at every turn, the final straw coming for him when he learns Anne is Stark's mistress. The crooked politicians around Stark, chiefly Tiny Duffy, create their own careers out of the former's enterprises, and will desert him as soon as they see him weaken. Burden is him-self intensely loyal, but he reserves a part for himself; and the death of Irwin begins the widening of the gap between himself and his father figure, Stark. Even Sadie Burke finds that Stark's philandering is more than she can accept, especially his power-hungry grab for a woman like Anne Stanton.

Power indeed corrupts. But the heavy plotting creates situations that dissipate political insights. Burden's sense of history, that all truth will out, is a search for stability. When he digs into Irwin's past, he is certain something will be there; for even the disorderly and deceptive past reveals an order. That quest for order thrusts Warren back into a previous era, thwarting the modern theme by presenting it in narrative terms of another society and world. A gloss on Nixon's Watergate caper would reach no conclusions, find no order; it would simply reveal that behind the depths of disorder lies ever greater disorder. The neatness of Warren's formulation in this excellent novel provided the very hurdle that the postwar novelists had to overcome. A highly plotted, neatly organized, historically based, morally ordered novel proved not only an achievement but an obstacle.

Toward the Fifties

Vance Bourjaily's *The End of My Life,* published just after the end of the war, in 1947, becomes an excellent expression of how new drives out old: not viciously or with celebration, but with regret and nostalgia. For Bourjaily, the war meant the end of things, and there was no going back. His Skinner Galt gains a "second skin"; but being skinned and reskinned will not lead to happiness or to an idyllic existence. Rather, it suggests the end, not the beginning, of innocence. The novel is that rarest of elements, a transitional fiction.

The End of My Life reeks of Hemingway and Hemingwayese, style and content. It is also full of Eliotic despair, the Eliot of "The Hollow Men" and early sections of "The Waste Land." Its ennui returns us to a period associated with the *nada* of 1920s fiction and poetry, with the (romantic) need to burn oneself out because tomorrow, if it came, would be as boring as today. "Then, returning to the possibility of separation, he [Skinner Galt] realized that what they faced was what all men face, over and over throughout their lives. That when they reach the ends of the miscellaneous little time compartments into which their lives are divided, they sum up the pleasures of the compartment they are leaving, making, each time, a last, futile effort to perpetuate them, forgetting that there were times when they considered the existence pattern of this particular compartment wearisome and unsupportable, and seeing the next compartment with unconfidence and fear."

A "Hemingway meal," says Skinner; "Good Hemingway country," says another; "Everything tasted fine, and they washed the dishes, and felt very domestic," says Bourjaily. From Skinner's point of view, once two and two are multiplied to make four, you have solved only the first part of the problem, the second being to divide by infinity; and that brings it all—effort, hope, desire, achievement—back to zero. There is always that second part, that division by infinity, which is something that most people forget. If they build their lives on two times two, without dividing, then they have isolated themselves from reality. Here are weltschmerz, the romanticism of ambulance driving, the enterprises of Dos Passos's *U.S.A.,* the war experiences of the lost generation, and the expatriation even of those who returned.

Skinner loves Cindy, whom he meets at college at a frat party, but he is a member of the lost generation; not those who came out of World War I, but those destined to end up in the Second War, children of war. " 'We were warborn. . . . Listen, the war made us. Let the bad joke of the past die decently, along with the clowns who tried to make it funny.' " This is Skinner's final comment, but it is the basis of all his action: he was a doomed child of the war even before the war. Before he sails for the Middle East, he tells Cindy, " 'We are the play,' " both a comedy and a tragedy, which proves nothing. " 'Nothing. No principles, no truths, no ethics, no standards.' "

When Cindy asks if there is anything, Skinner gives the Hemingway response of immediate sensation: " 'Just people you like, and people you don't like; people you love and people you hate.' " And when she questions further, he says this is not the philosophy of Skinner Galt, but "his lack of it." Such a philosophy allows him sex (with much sadness), plenty of liquor (with oblivion as the goal), and an awareness of decent acts (the basis of the philosophy or lack of it). Not unusually, the artistic equivalent of such feelings is music on New York's Fifty-second Street, Bessie Smith, Billie Holiday, and the sadness of black blues.

Bourjaily's Skinner can sustain his vision only by running. "Maybe I run for the sake of running," he thinks. He fears that while escapism may be a personal philosophy, it might also make him a romantic. And that is to be avoided as too positive. Once Skinner finds himself attached to an ambulance unit in the Middle East and then in Italy—the war is almost always at a distance—he defines his drift into nothingness. He holds himself together with a group of pals, whiskey, and whores, but their grip on him is incomplete. He comes to like a frisky nurse named Johnny, takes her in the ambulance near the front, where a stray bullet kills her. His attitude, which should have killed him, kills her; once more fate is fickle. But even before that, he attempts suicide on a sentry's bayonet, for he has realized he no longer has any love for Cindy, "or his friends or for himself, or for anything he had ever done or anything he ever would do." As he tells Cindy, who plays Catherine Barkham to his Frederic Henry, when she turns up in Italy: " 'Death and birth are not the spectator sports that you Twentieth Century humanitarians have tried to make of them. Dying is a private affair.' " But here even Hemingway is insufficient, too affirmative.

The novel ends with Skinner held responsible for Johnny's death, although she had insisted on a tour of the front, and imprisoned for a year. He has divested himself of the past, Cindy, his friends, his role in the war as an ambulance driver. Prison will purge him of any further aspects of himself. The cell seems, after all, very inviting, because it offers nothing. It is the world analogous to Skinner's self, an empty cell which he fills. This is, of course, distant from Hemingway's *nada,* which was founded on a positive denial. Skinner's is the negative denial that would characterize most important war fiction of the later 1940s and early 1950s; it accepted the war without believing it would solve anything.

Bourjaily has touched all bases of the 1940s, of young men who had been born in the 1920s, like many of our current novelists, who grew up aware in the Depression years, and who came of age in the war years. This was the initiation; birth in the years of false prosperity, childhood with poverty and hopelessness, young manhood with the war as both doom and salvation. Death in war: this becomes the initiation for every healthy young man in the 1940s, a Hemingway dream come true. Except that when it came true, it no longer meant anything, as Skinner comes to realize.

Skinner, we assume, will arrive fully armed into the counterfeit 1950s, ready for the political sport that characterized the individual's relationship to a government first under Truman and then dominated by Eisenhower. Skinner will be fully armed in the sense that his lostness will have prepared him for every aspect of the charade, for all the counterfeit feelings, policies, and ideologies that the fifties would bring. If he could paint, he would be Gaddis's Wyatt Gwyon; but since he cannot paint, he will become part of the Beat movement—where Skinner's running and escaping suggest a kind of ideology. Long before jogging became a national pastime, Skinner and the Beats after him found running was a characteristic American sport.

Chapter Five

GROWING UP IN AMERICA: THE 1940s AND THEREAFTER

A land of leaning ice / Hugged by plaster-grey arches of sky, /
Flings itself silently / Into eternity.

Hart Crane, *"North Labrador"*

The fictions about growing up in America, whether by Melville, Hawthorne, Hemingway, Dos Passos, or Fitzgerald, have always been extraordinary. In the postwar era, entire careers have focused on this aspect of American culture—Salinger's, for example—whereas others have written some of their best work in the area, Purdy, Baldwin, Roth coming to mind. Also, it was the "other Roth," not Philip but Henry, who wrote what is perhaps our archetypal twentieth-century novel of growing up, *Call It Sleep* (1934). It appears in relationship to the later manifestations of the genre what *Huckleberry Finn* meant to an earlier. *Call It Sleep,* in fact, is an urban *Huck Finn,* a reversal of every pattern, to such an extent that while Twain's novel is a siren call to the near-death of pastoral, Roth's is a hymn to what has replaced it, a truly dispossessed pastoral, where trolley tracks succeed country paths.

The range of growing up is enormous, from the children of Roth's Jewish immigrants to the young Maxine Hong Kingston and her Chinese mother, with her fantasies of a warrior existence in the old country; from the obsessive journey through death of Kosinski's unnamed boy in *The Painted Bird* back to Wright's Bigger Thomas in Chicago, whose life could also be fitted into terms we usually associate with war

fiction. Finally, we have the "Americanized" Nabokov in *Ada,* filtering through his American experiences his sense of growing up in Europe, an old world juxtaposed to a new. By way of Nabokov, we have a method of observing the American experience; by means of the American experience, we have a way of measuring Nabokov.

Every age has to grow up, but each age passes through the rite differently. Huck Finn's passage by way of the river remains fascinating for the American writer, and he continues to utilize the river-shore antagonism. But Twain's sense of things was for a shifting frontier society, where territories still existed; and his vision of youth allied to freedom is no longer applicable in the symbols he used. Now youth grows up in different ways, as much part of Keniston's "uncommitted" or Riesman's "lonely crowd" or Goodman's "absurd" or Lifton's "protean man," as committed to the search for willed freedom. Huck is not lost, but he is subsumed. He returns, even more broadly, in unlikely places, in Beats—in fiction of Kerouac and Holmes, poetry of Ginsberg. For Salinger, who pivots between 1940s and 1950s, there is no Montana territory, no river, no raft; simply a desire for innocence tantamount to forms of freedom.

Passage through childhood in such postwar fiction

has as its literary sources Huck in the nineteenth century, or in the twentieth, Clyde Griffiths, Studs Lonigan, and Bigger Thomas and Black Boy. The two extremes are "freedom," however qualified, and the loss of it: the meeting between the nineteenth and twentieth centuries creating an agon, a self against a system. If the goal is full freedom, it comes in the shape of Kerouac's Sal, who sets out by way of the car for territories as yet undiscovered, using roads instead of paths and trails. His freedom is defined by the degree of distance he can put between the last place and the next, not by any quality he discovers in himself. One reason, in fact, that fiction derived from the Beats is ultimately not satisfying is that while the problem is located in Huck's terms, resolution is defined by twentieth-century necessity: undifferentiated quantities of space, *as if it still existed.*

The goal is always to break out: from family, class, neighborhood, demons. We note, incidentally, how growing up fiction of the fifties and sixties is linked with novels about the feminine experience, since for females "growing up" was essentially to go from subservient girl to mature woman. In his revelatory essay on the American action painters, Harold Rosenberg speaks of how many painters had a double career, a full life as a regular painter, then five or seven years as an action painter. So, too, in the fiction of the female experience: the young lady grows up, and later enters a "new career," as a woman defined by a revived sense of self.

This procedure is, of course, archetypically American; also traditional is the fact that the quest is almost always foredoomed. Dreiser's Clyde Griffiths is emblematic here, or else Billy Budd, Pierre, or Hester Prynne. If the protagonist is not doomed, then he is baffled, or made to recognize that whatever his means, America contains him.

Paul Goodman called the quest *Growing Up Absurd,* in a book that gained its reputation in the sixties, but was actually a study mainly of fifties youth. Goodman's stress, unfortunately, was only on young men; but in the fifties, the assumption of most writers was that problems were male problems. We shall try to expand his terms. Goodman encouraged a different kind of existence from that offered by the dominant culture, which was either to live safely or to drop out: the two sides of much 1950s fiction. He counseled living dangerously, against the culture, each act a challenge. For those unable to fit in, organized society (systems, hierarchies, stabilities) offered only the Beat alternative. Goodman finds that acceptance of systems (what Pynchon in *V.* would call "stenciliza-

tion") dissipates one's unique qualities; whereas dropping out means forgoing potentialities.

This is, in effect, the absurdity of growing up in the 1950s. Each of the alternatives, Goodman finds, is part of role-playing, whereas to test the environment, not adjust to it or withdraw from it, is meaningful. Meaningful work helps the adjustment, although most jobs for young people lack significance, as does much of their leisure activity. Leisure, Goodman perceived, was often as organized as work, and would become even more systematized when television took hold. One must avoid role-playing, or what he labeled "canned self-exposure." The goal is to move toward some kind of existential reality; we note how his conditions link up with Mailer's in his "The White Negro." These out-of-phase elements involved "achieving a simpler fraternity, animality, and sexuality than we have had, at least in America, in a long, long time." Such self-expression would break out from Marcuse's sense of "one-dimensional life." What Goodman could not foresee was how some of this breakout would be achieved through drugs, which defeated his sense of self-achievement. He wanted sexual daring, probably more movement toward homosexuality or bisexuality, less stress on purely professional goals, development of mind as well as career.

Growing Up Absurd became something of a cult book in the later sixties, but, I think, for the wrong reasons. Those eager to break out read Goodman's analysis of one-dimensional American life correctly, but they did not comprehend his longer-range views. Goodman meant more than a tactile, sensual achievement. He was aiming for a Platonic conjunction of mind and body: a body ready to try out the unknown (new sexual connections) and a mind eager to test itself against antagonisms, counters, alternatives. He favored not only adversary relationships to community and society, but in-depth achievement up to the ability of the individual.

What Goodman was advocating, moving from roles to identity, involved becoming a "protean man," a man in the process of becoming. Influenced by Erik Erikson's conception of fluid selves, of change from one level of identity to another, Robert Jay Lifton used "protean man" to define an entire life style. The concept stresses self-process, whereby the self constantly struggles to emerge as what it is. The process is not final, nor is there any stable self that results. "The protean style of self-process, then, is characterized by an interminable series of experiments and explorations—some shallow, some profound—each of which may be readily abandoned in favor of still new psychological quests."

Each stage suggests an "identity crisis," in Erikson's sense, and each stage is the ground for a new phase. The crisis passes into change. Although Lifton formally defined the idea in 1968, he had gained his insights earlier, in his research on survivors of the atomic bombing of Hiroshima. "Protean man" is a postwar phenomenon, applicable directly to Japanese youth, but increasingly an American (and world) phenomenon. Eventually, American youth would become the model for world youth.

Protean man is noted for improvisation; in fiction, we see him in the literature of the Beats and before that in Henry Miller's novels. Since fixity is alien to his nature, mockery, satire, burlesque fit his scheme; and in the world of art, jazz, happenings, and television will replace books. Most social and community projects appear valueless, part of a systematized world in which protean man has no place. Boundaries exist for others, not for him. Part of him, at least, is an outlaw. Thus the role of drugs in the 1950s, as in Burroughs, who had assimilated the most destructive —but inevitable—quality of protean man's life. Growing up or maturing in the fifties brought home the nature of limitations; the key words were national security and anticommunism, the key figures Eisenhower, Nixon.

So much of major fiction in the 1950s is internalized, and therefore seemingly at odds with an extroverted country, because intensity of experience had already become the sole way one could remain valid, authentic, self-defined. Experience becomes in itself a goal, not something that can lead to some tangible success. Inevitably, the mode of expression becomes self-directed, narcissistic, oriented intensely inward. Goodman had hoped for greater mind/body balance; but protean man affirmed self, responses, self-consciousness, more than reason, which seemed part of systems rather than individuals. Drugs, Beats, counterfeiting, intensity of the artificial—all these became an arena for action, like the canvas on which the action painters massed their own troops. Such negations of national security, and by implication everything that it socially and politically stood for, was not necessarily nihilistic. For as we shall see, negation has its own momentum, narcissism its own energies, nihilism its own terms of challenge and response.*

*One of the deficiencies of David Riesman's otherwise very important *The Lonely Crowd* (1950) as a profile of the late 1940s was his neglect of those elements of withdrawal, what

Not only did fear of the counterfeit leak into every life growing up, but also an allied fear: fear the nation had become paranoiac and any divergence labeled one a fugitive. Postwar growing up is full of fugitive young people, foreshadowed by Henry Roth's early presentation of David Shearl and Richard Wright's of Bigger Thomas. Holden Caulfield, the Glass family, Capote's Joel, Demby's Johnny, Baldwin's John Grimes, Delmore Schwartz's personae are all fugitives in the actual sense, on the run, or else in their conception of their relationship to family, community, and society.

Although the atomic bomb does not enter directly into the experience of our protagonists growing up, a sense of the apocalypse is never distant from them. The paranoiac view of American life, Hofstadter shows,† is never far from an apocalyptic one. Ar-

would come to be called the counterculture. Riesman tied his character types to population changes, and it would have been instructive to see how he could have located large numbers of young people as they moved outside his inner-, other-, and tradition-directed group without fitting into his autonomous group. This element which withdrew, and which would grow sizably in the 1960s, called for a grouping of its own; for not only would it dominate the popular culture, with new modes of music, acting, and dancing, but it would become in one form or another the subject matter of our fiction. Riesman does, of course, observe certain breakups, in that small blocs of what he calls "veto-groups" were forming, replacing the larger groups of the past. Such dispersion was a key to what was happening out of sight in the 1950s, indicative of where the novelists saw movement. Further, each veto-group in pursuing its own sense of things was rejecting authority, from state toward that simplification of experience which we have associated with pastoral fantasies: the 1960s were already in the making.

†In *The Paranoid Style in American Politics* (1965), Richard Hofstadter defines his term as a mental disorder characterized by feelings of systematized delusions of persecution and of one's own greatness. Often, those who perceive such an experience—those deluded ones who, in turn, vaunt themselves as an alternative force—are "dispossessed," people who sense no connection to the main body or system. They fall into the "uncommitted," and their political type (Nixon, MacArthur, McCarthy) carries over into literary types, where politics are transformed into narcissism or delusions of power, as Mailer's Rojack and others like him. The sense of national paranoia, while subversive of political security, is a boon for fiction, not only feeding into the growing up subgenre but nourishing those large interpretive books that characterized the 1950s and 1960s: *Catch-22, The Sot-Weed Factor, V., Giles Goat-Boy, The Recognitions,* and, later, *JR, Gravity's Rainbow,* and *Letters.* The main issues here are conspiracy and subversion, political issues delivered over into fictional ideas. These are the big themes Melville spoke of as necessary for big books. The sense of entrapment characteris-

mageddon is close, the fatal day, week, month. Armageddon, that final struggle, will be between America and the Soviet Union, not for national security but for civilization itself: Jonathan Edwards's sermons on final things become translated into arguments about the development of the hydrogen bomb, which Truman finally approved. The Jim Jones cult and its mass suicides in the 1970s were a bizarre phenomenon, but not so strange if we connect them to early 1950s apocalypse, world struggle, Armageddon. Some set 1973 as the year the Communists would take over the world if not stopped.

The novel of growing up has assimilated this sense of America: its divided, groping self, its reliance on systems that deaden, its rootlessness, its search for status, which provides little solace, its bifurcated aims, its heterogeneity, which is both its glory and its problem. The paranoid style saw America as caught in a Manichaean struggle between the forces of good and evil, the Puritan view updated, the Civil War resurrected in different terms. But that paranoid style also saw America as Edenic, tainted by European corruption (whatever Chambers had assimilated from Europe he then had to exorcise) and demonry. Witchcraft had reentered the American soul and had to be driven out by way of martyrs; if not staked, then expelled.

It was a difficult time to grow up, but an excellently manured garden for fiction to develop in. One of the characteristics of the paranoiac personality is its dependence on respect and authority; authority replaced by self-indulgence signals things falling apart. Thus, family, school, work place, government, and state are all systemic forms of order, without which life is drained of meaning. Within such terms, the novelist as adversary has everything to mock. Hofstadter quotes from Barry Goldwater in the early sixties, and we wonder if we are in politics or absurdist fiction. Goldwater: " 'My aim is not to pass laws, but to repeal them.' " Or: " 'I fear Washington and centralized government more than I do Moscow.' " Out of this the counterfeit and artificial can grow like weeds in a garden, and those dispossessed from it have a richness that derives from their rebellion. Po-

tic of the paranoid condition creates for the novelist a marvelous adversary struggle, in which circumstance, history, tradition, conspiracy are all at odds with the emerging or stifled self. Anything *is* possible: the paranoid condition opens up an entire America. Emerson and Whitman meet at the crossroads with Dreiser and Dos Passos, freedom and determinism locked together, like Oedipus and Laius.

etry (Lowell, Plath, and Ginsberg, for example) and drama (Williams, in particular) as well as fiction can thrive here.

When our postwar novelists make their attack on state, governmental process, systems—everything ostensibly dear to the paranoiac vision in the guise of nation—they do so not from the left, which is inchoate, but from the point of view of the outsider in the land of pastoral fantasies. Our novelists of growing up have assimilated American systems as corruptive, as traducings of the original Edenic pact the settlers had made with the land. Politics or systems (racism is implicit here) destroy not only innocence and spirit but the American soul. What is remarkable is how American novelists of every kind, sons and daughters of immigrants as well as those with American roots, black and white, agree that the political process corrupts. However traditional and creaky its mechanisms, Robert Penn Warren's *All the King's Men* adumbrates the postwar novel of growing up.

TWO EARLY VERSIONS

It is strange to begin with a novel which does not fall within our frame of reference and which is, at the same time, possibly the finest example of the subgenre we are describing. But Henry Roth's *Call It Sleep* (1934) looks ahead, in subject matter, narrative detail, stress on individual development amidst social instability. In ways, it connects to novels as seemingly different as *The Adventures of Augie March, The Painted Bird, Portnoy's Complaint,* and some of Salinger, whether any of their authors knew the book or not.

Call It Sleep is almost a perfect book of its kind, lacking only that quality, which we find in Dickens's *Great Expectations,* of associating the individual with his larger society; or reflecting by way of the individual the social values that will intrude upon his consciousness. This is not to say Roth has no social pressure, but it is of David Shearl's own milieu, that tightly knit Jewish immigrant world which is, like its Italian and Irish counterparts, ready to break apart. What holds it together are the traditions of the old country and, usually, the understanding, compassionate mother rather than the tyrannical, anxiety-ridden father. The father seems unable to support the tremendous burdens of family, precarious finances (Albert Shearl is a milkman), and language difficulties.

While these are indeed social and familial pressures acting upon David, they still do not carry the weight of the larger society or culture. Part of the reason for this lack is connected to Roth's strategy. Like Joyce with Stephen Dedalus, an author and a character whose presence is everywhere in *Call It Sleep,* Roth creates a fluidity and fluency by filtering everything through David's eyes. He is the central and registering consciousness, the observer of note. Family background, Genya's relationship to a Gentile back in Poland, her association with the boarder, Luter, the reasons why she married Albert so hastily —these and other matters come to us as they come to David. Anything beyond that is beyond him. Of course, David's involvement in this information—it is *his* life at six, seven, eight that he is becoming conscious of—creates its own particular kind of web.

Even lacking those outside social matters which would have intertwined with David's life, Roth was able to bring to the novel something missing in most other growing up fictions except *Ada:* this by giving himself over to modern strategies. Most American versions of the genre were influenced more by traditional naturalism than by Joycean methods; the result a curiously attenuated development, a thinning out of texture such as we find in *Studs Lonigan* and extending right up through Italian, Jewish, and black equivalents. In Roth, Henry James and James Joyce come together on the Lower East Side.

The mise-en-scène is the home, sometimes the street. David rarely moves outside his apartment and street, except to go for Hebrew instruction, or earlier when he was lost, and later when he seeks out the trolley tracks (to play Isaiah). Like the culture, everything is enclosed; everything flows back upon itself. The family must stand strong, or else the world encroaches and destroys. David's mother is the "heroine," in that she mediates the terrible anger his father feels toward David. She softens, cares for, feeds; the son becomes her sole reason for living. Her own life, by now, is over, married as she is to a man so deeply embedded in his misery he is purely narcissistic. All activity in the family, even when well meant, wounds or enrages him. Genya, however, moves silently. She smothers David, in one sense protecting him against his day and night terrors, on the other emotionally crippling him by providing such a powerful shield. Whether he will escape that smothering is not part of this novel.

Except for Luter, the boarder, and Aunt Bertha, Genya's sister, who stays for six months, virtually no one breaks the atmosphere of the Shearl apartment. There are no friends, no neighborly visits. The apartment is like a temple, not to be profaned by the outside world. That enclosed existence, that type of claustrophobia—so different from the swirling, rhythmic Italian home, or the violent Irish and black one—is part of the culture. The apartment is a fortress where the deeper emotions are kept under check. Only Albert's rage intrudes. Everything is internalized, or saved for performance in school or in Hebrew lessons.

All Jewish family novels inevitably lead to Kafka, just as all apples lead to Milton. The enemy in the household is the father—not revered, not respected, simply feared. David's perception of his father is of a man with a hammer: "So that was how his father quit a place! He held a hammer in hand, he would have killed somebody. David could almost see him, the hammer raised over his head, his face contorted in terrific wrath, the rest cringing away." The right hand of the father becomes a potentially terrible weapon, the hammer of Thor, the hammer of vengeance, all punishing crimes David did not commit. Punishment without crime, this the Jewish heritage from the Kafkan vision of family relationships; so different from the black, where God may be vengeance, or the Italian, where outside conditions are the enemy, or the Irish, where whiskey creates breakdown. Each type of family novel has its own kind of retribution. "Nothing existed any longer except his father's right hand. *The hammer in that hand when he stood! The hammer!"*

But even with that right hand of vengeance, whether whip or hammer, Albert Shearl does have reasons for anger. Some may be inherent—his mother had warned Genya against marrying him—but some are also nurtured in America. Even by the time Genya and the infant David arrive at Ellis Island, Albert has sensed his victimization. He is a man full of his own powers who finds himself located nowhere. Even as he seeks definition, everything is alien, especially urban life, that loss of the pastoral tradition of the homeland in Austria. Albert dreams of vast spaces, farms, bulls and cows; and he ends up first as a printer and then, mockingly, as the driver of a milk wagon. He sits behind a horse's tail. His pride has nothing to focus upon, and his internal needs erupt in rages against David in particular, against family life as a whole. His past, upon which he has placed such value, is gone, and his present offers no ballast; he is a man floating free, toward a nihilism he senses but cannot control. His language is elegant Yiddish (if we can believe its English equivalent), but his attempts at English are demotic and humiliating. Unable to pass as an American, he is no longer a European.

With a righteous, angry father and a persecuted

son, the novel's Biblical dimensions are rarely distant. In Hebrew school, David comes alive in a passage relating Isaiah to his holy mission, the passage in which an angel touches Isaiah's lips with a live coal so that without sin or iniquity he can approach God and speak. For David, this is an incandescent moment: " 'He [Isaiah] said—he said he saw God and it —and it was light!' " This passage excites David immeasurably because it seems to resolve something he is striving to understand; it is part of self-definition, and the light, which he attempts to achieve near the end of the book, is that inner light of illumination. Since the novel moves from dark toward light, these passages in scripture about Isaiah are, in a sense, emblematic of the book's entire progress. David seeks illumination, and it can come only when he moves out from under the righteous arm of his father.

This he attempts when, in that final visionary scene, he strikes a milk dipper (symbolic of his father's job) into the third rail of the trolley tracks and almost electrocutes himself. His foot is burned— shades of the devil—but he is only deeply shocked. Yet the act, a sign of desperation as well as renewal, relocates him in the life of the family. The father relents. Although David has not repeated Isaiah's miracle, he does reestablish some son-father relationship. When the novel ends, we sense that Albert must listen, that David can speak, that the so-called fiery coal placed by the angel in his hand has achieved its end.

The final parts of the novel, labeled "The Rail," are notable also for Roth's adaptation of Joycean stream. "The Rail" is related, like a chapter of *Ulysses,* from the depths of the characters who run the trolleys and who will come upon David lying on the tracks. The method is interior monologue, free association, approximation to a stream of consciousness. The latter is not quite achieved since Roth does not bend language; it remains a fixed, denotative voice, although arranged for poetic dimensions. David lies half conscious on the tracks: "(W-e-e-e-e-e-p! Weep! Overhead the / brandished hammer whirred and whistled. / The doors of a hallway slowly opened. / Buoyed up by the dark, a coffin drifted / out, floated down the stoop, and while / confetti rained upon it, bulged and / billowed—)"

Many of David's preoccupations come together here in this delirious vision: hammer, death, and resurrection. The startling experimentation with language and levels of consciousness in the final sections does not come without preparation. For Roth has created a "poetic atmosphere" throughout, using the kind of language, often very close to the structure of Yiddish and yet elegantly Englished, that eschews the commonplace. Only on the streets do we find a barbaric English that marks the children of the immigrants as much as the immigrants themselves. Mainly, however, Roth uses the meeting of Yiddish, Hebrew, Polish, and English as a way of raising the level of discourse from the gutter toward a Biblical elegance. "Trinkets held in the mortar of desire, the fancy a trowel, the whim the builder. A wall, a tower, stout, secure, incredible, immuring the spirit from a flight of arrows, the mind, experience, shearing the flow of time as a rock shears water."

What is remarkable is how Roth in this his only novel has integrated the modern and new into a traditional fiction, the growth and development of a young boy toward illumination. He has entered into the horror of Kafka, the language of Joyce, as well as his positioning, the Jamesian use of a registering consciousness, and combined that with the sense of modern poetry, poetry oblique and evocative rather than descriptive and direct. Yet, withal, he has not relinquished the Biblical imperative, its language and moral message, its terrible stories and solace, its presentation of resurrection and transformation. Living with an Old Testament God who has not achieved a prophetic level, David must play out the roles of sons —David, Joseph, Jacob, et al. He will be the eternal son until he can provide his own illumination: not the fiery coal of the angel with Isaiah, but a milk dipper forced into the third rail. A light, a poof, a flash, a weakening of the current—and it all passes through David's foot, burning shoe and foot, leaving the body untouched.

"He might as well call it sleep," Roth writes. Only in sleep can dark be pierced by glinting images on things as commonplace as a tilted board, roller skates, gray stone stoops, the "tapering glitter of rails," night-smooth rivers, and son. Only in sleep can the ears reassemble the sounds of the street, the "roar of crowds and all sounds that lay fermenting in the vats of silence and the past." Only in sleep can one feel the cobblestones and all the feet and shoes that have rubbed over them. "One might as well call it sleep"; there one feels "not pain, not terror, but strangest triumph, strangest acquiescence." Only Joyce's *A Portrait* in this century has captured that level of existence, Dublin and New York City meeting in sleep, which leads to illumination. Roth has not integrated that larger world outside into his, but he has imbued the immigrants' world with such intensity that it becomes, indeed, the world.

Because of its Jamesian pacing and tones, its Whartonian rhythms, Jean Stafford's work seems more at home in a prewar context. But her three novels are very much part of the mid-forties to early fifties, and *The Mountain Lion* (1947; reissued in 1972) is quite a remarkable book about growing up. I include Stafford here not only because of the fine quality of her work, but because she is in danger of being omitted from studies of the novel. She appeared in a marginal time, neither prewar nor modern, and for that reason may be neglected. She deserves better.*

In *The Mountain Lion,* Jean Stafford has structured a family, the Fawcetts, that, because of parental death and remarriage, has extended itself into several kinds of associations. In the forefront are two children, Ralph and Molly, who belong to one grandfather's tradition, while their siblings belong to another. One tradition is Eastern, cultivated, cosmopolitan; the other Western, natural, outdoors, rough. The clash between the values of the two family halves recalls the conflicts in an Ivy Compton-Burnett novel, although Stafford does not have the Englishwoman's rapierlike wit and destructiveness. Nevertheless, Stafford's novel has its own kind of doom and destructiveness, the very subtly developed theme of the mountain lion.

The focus is on Ralph and Molly, first on the boy, then on the girl. He is two years older, a brother-father-husband figure for Molly. But the most remarkable feature of the novel besides their relationship and their association with their mother and

*The other two novels are *Boston Adventure* (1944) and *The Catherine Wheel* (1951, 1952), besides dozens of stories, collected in a single volume. *Boston Adventure* should be compared with Oates's *them* for their common exploration of lower-class life for a young woman. While Oates has more power and intensity, is more memorable, Stafford is more elegant, more shaped, more purely literary. Her Sonia Marburg and Oates's Maureen Wendall, nevertheless, meet in strange areas of choice, security, and near-destruction. *The Catherine Wheel* has as some of its loveliest moments Stafford's awareness of a young boy, Andrew Shipley, left alone, isolated, drifting from room to room in a deserted house, always on the margin of discovering secrets from diaries and letters. Although he is treated decently, no one cares for him; intrigue surrounds him, and we find ourselves back in an Elizabeth Bowen novel or in James's *What Maisie Knew.* Smothered by events just beyond his comprehension, blocked by secrets which he almost discovers, unable to break through to some truth that floats off in the distance, he becomes a demon in his own farce. His scene of rage when others return to the house and interrupt him is an epiphany of a boy's life, rare indeed in the fiction of our time.

family is Stafford's ability to chart Molly's development. For here better than anywhere else in postwar American fiction we have a child groping and developing toward becoming a writer. In the eyes of her family and even in Ralph's, Molly becomes "crazier and crazier." But her craziness is an acquisition of an angle of vision as well as a ruthless honesty which clears away veils. She maintains a list of those who fail to meet her standard, an ever-enlarging list, and it finally includes her. This is tantamount to a suicide pact. She sees herself as a "long wooden box with a mind inside," an image that fits rather well the way others see her. Her last anchor in the external world had been Ralph; but he has undergone his own transformation.

In a tunnel on their way to Uncle Claude's ranch, Ralph grows into self-knowledge and knowledge about the world. He admits to terrible things within himself and, by extension, in those outside him. "His mouth tasted foully of sulphur," from the tunnel air. This was a part of the journey he and Molly had always looked forward to, but now it takes on the nature of an ordeal, a nightmarish journey toward a hell he cannot fathom. Stafford is uncanny about finding natural images and symbols for modes of passage in the children's development. She recognizes that children observe details and that these details become for them the entire fabric of the universe. Yet she does not sentimentalize, having none of the cute mannerisms that make *A Catcher in the Rye* a young person's rather than an adult's book.

In that tunnel, Ralph sees into blackness, sulphur, coal smoke, and sees particularly a vile female passenger with children but no wedding ring; and what he observes is an urge to plunge downward. ". . . it would be so easy to lose his footing, relax his fingerholds, and plunge downward to wedge his bones in a socket of rocks." Surrounded by vileness, he looks to Molly as his sole shield against corruption. The tunnel experience becomes the apotheosis of his own sense of corruption, his passing feelings of incest toward an older sister, Leah, his passion for Winifred, who lives in his uncle's house, his pleasure at the degradation of the woman without a ring. Molly is his anchor in a pure world, but he cannot let her be. In a moment of uncontrollable weakness, he turns to her and says, " 'Molly, tell me all the dirty words you know.' " It is just a moment, during which the train emerges into the light, but the words, thoughts, intent move both children from childhood; they have acquired knowledge.

Once Molly crosses Ralph off her list, her course

is set. She is, somehow, connected to the mountain lion observed in the hills above Uncle Claude's ranch. The mountain lion is part of the terrain, the most "natural" object in a world of nature, in a sense superior to what is around it. It is always observed in an imperious pose, on top of a rock or loping away out of sight, like a golden god. For Ralph it becomes what he must overcome in order to attain that next phase of development; an initiation that is a more deadly version of Faulkner's bear hunt. "His passion for Goldilocks [their name for the lion] went over him like an ocean wave," and he is determined to kill her "out of his love for her golden hide." She is his Golden Fleece, his passage into adulthood. And as soon as he determines to kill the lion before Claude arrives, Molly, by extension, is doomed. For to kill the lion is for Ralph to put final distance between himself and Molly, to deny her completely, just as she has turned against him. The games of childhood, as Ivy Compton-Burnett also demonstrated, are deadly; not fun, not play.

Ralph shoots at the lion just as Claude appears and also shoots. But from the placement of the one wound, it is clear Claude's shot struck the lion and Ralph's struck Molly, the wound "like a burst of fruit in her forehead." It is, of course, the kind of accident that has within it intent and motive. Molly in her role as outsider and commentator becomes the scapegoat by whom Ralph can move, through tragedy, into self-awareness. Molly is supersensitive, a poet, a writer, an unattractive marginal adolescent, a female—elements which, like the lion, can be sacrificed to male experience and knowledge. Only in death does the mountain lion signify to the killers what they might know; and this knowledge is too late, for the lion is gone, and by extension so is what Molly represented.

Stafford's development of the children's lives with Mrs. Fawcett and then with Claude is full of sudden insights, most of them developed seamlessly. They are part of natural phenomena, whether a sick bull, or a skittish horse, or the black tunnel already cited. There is also a closely controlled wit, in the nosebleeds the children suffer together as though timed, in their extreme gawkiness and ugliness, their ruthless observation of the counterfeit. But wit never undermines the vision, for people and events are allowed to exist for themselves; and the children are not so witty that they become special in order to create a scene or event. Stafford works quite differently from Salinger, in that she does not caricature others in order to establish Ralph's and Molly's singularity. The outside simply reinforces what they already know and are.

Although there is movement—especially in the travel back and forth to the ranch, then on the ranch itself—motion is encapsulated, spatially removed or lessened. Stafford's method licks at the margins of enervation, but does not turn into ennui. Spirit is there, although contained. She seeks the unnatural in the natural, or reverses it and tries to discover the natural in the unnatural, in the process working toward the center of things. The man the children love, and their mother cannot tolerate, is grandfather Kenyon, a rough-hewn outdoorsman who has made millions from ranching. He dresses queerly, drinks at odd times, lacks cultivated conversation; and yet he travels widely and brings back sophisticated gifts. He never descends into oddity, but remains what he is, a foil for Mrs. Fawcett's gentility. Similarly, his son Claude is no oddball, nor is he a country bumpkin. He is intense about his life, with animals more important to him than people; his decency is in the way he holds himself together, in remaining what he is.

The natural world reveals its secrets as the rituals and lore of children and of adults who still have some child within them. What gives the rituals of childhood and adolescence their particular power is their connection to matters of class: not wide swings but subtle modulations. Normally, questions of class in the postwar novel come in naturalistic settings, in the gap between officers and men in the service, or in distinctions established by educational opportunities or fortunes of birth. But Stafford has created a class system based on taste, manners, speech, choice of dress, living styles, assumptions about family life, children, education. These are Jamesian rather than Dickensian factors, for Stafford sees them as miniature instead of huge, minor elements rather than major transfigurations. And yet they add up to class distinctions of the most vibrant and vital sort, placing grandfather Kenyon, consciously or not, in opposition to everything Mrs. Fawcett stands for.

TOWARD THE MAIN TRADITION

The placement of *The Catcher in the Rye* in our literary imagination is a compelling question. For since its publication in 1951, its holding power has been enormous. After segments appeared in *Collier's,* in 1943, and *The New Yorker,* in 1946, the hardcover book enjoyed twenty-six printings by 1968, and then had several other editions, before the paperback publication in 1964, which has itself gone through thirty-seven printings at this writing. Any claims that the novel was simply a postwar phenomenon which fitted itself into a more halcyon period runs up against this extraordinary staying power. It has charms, apparently, whether in 1951 or thirty years later. The question is: Are the charms those of a children's book or an adult's?

The time of publication unquestionably had a good deal to do with the book's initial success. The appearance of long war novels had conditioned the public for heavy reading that made it face up to the horrors of combat and the unresolved issues left by the victorious war. The domestic scene was a shambles, because of McCarthy, of course, but even more because it was becoming clear the American reaction to the world would be based on negative responses, despite Marshall Plan aid. The Korean War had begun, and it seemed inexplicable that American forces were fighting on the Asian mainland. Behind the American action was a desire by the right and center to seize something in Asia now that China was "lost." Hot and cold wars dominated the news, made all the more disquieting by the fact that the Soviet Union had acquired the atomic bomb, with or without the help of ubiquitous spies.

The Catcher in the Rye was our pastoral. Despite Holden Caulfield's series of disasters, he remains a figure of innocence, whose quest is to erase all the "Fuck You" signs in places where children like his sister Phoebe might see them. Even his inability to stick to any school never signals deeper problems, but returns us to Huck Finn's quest for open territory where a young man might grow, especially one who has grown tall so rapidly. School is an enclosure, a limited frontier, a restricted space full of miniature people with miniature mentalities. Outside school is experience, a potential pastoral of our Edenic preexistence. Holden is seventeen, and he demands for himself not learning, not training or discipline, but good faith. At every turn, he feels betrayed: by the values of his schoolteachers, by people like Antolini, who befriend and then importune him, by young ladies whose good looks belie the shriveled imagination lying beneath.

Experience is all, even when disastrous. Holden is the embodiment of an ego that wants to grow into a self; and he is, as well, a remnant of American innocence in the late 1940s and early 1950s. We could make a political reading of this novel: Holden is our archetypal decent American, the man who lives, like Thoreau, with a clean sense of himself. The result is that he must retreat, play Huck Finn in a world of deception and counterfeit. Politically, he must remain beyond ideology, for every kind is tainted and corrup-

tive. At seventeen, he is not old enough to vote, nor to care. The world spins off people of bad faith, bad intentions, unexamined lives. No one is really evil, unless it is the seemingly benevolent Mr. Antolini. Most people are simply being themselves.

Holden, then, insists on his own type of isolation, since people fail him. Only Phoebe, herself ten, sustains him, both his memories of her and her presence. She is still innocent; it is for her that he wants to rub out "Fuck You" from the universe, although very possibly she knows all about it. She is, for Holden, our first self, the purity of the Garden, their alliance a mirroring of the Edenic mating. When she puts away in a drawer the pieces of a childhood record, now shattered into fifty pieces, she treasures for herself what Holden treasures in her. It is this thread of innocence that the American must grip, or else madness will claim him.

Holden, of course, does not succeed, and his story, we note, is narrated from an institution, where he is recovering, with the help of a psychoanalyst, from being "pretty run-down." He needed help, and there is the possibility that he will be well enough to reenter the system "next September." Recovery, if it occurs, will be not into himself but into life; and the moment will have passed. The "gray flannel suit"—that counterfeit image of the 1950s—may await Holden; or else he may have his final fling in the 1960s, when the pastoral image reemerges, energized.

In the 1970s, William Gaddis published his own version of Huck Finn and Holden Caulfield in *JR*. A junior sixth grader whose genius is his ability to parlay penny-ante stuff into vast companies, corporations, and conglomerates, JR is the sensibility of the seventies, a Huck Finn whose innocence leads not to freedom but to the restrictions of great capitalistic responsibilities. His is a society gone mad, but unaware that it has; as though Huck Finn had gone to the Montana territory to buy up vast tracts of land to develop into an expensive housing development. The pastoral, the land, the natural wonder would all be huge selling points. Holden is the link between Twain's protagonist and Gaddis's.

In *The Catcher,* the pastorality of the title implies Holden's innocence, for he will catch young children as they play in the rye so as to prevent their falling over a cliff. The one thing he wants to do places him with children, and it is noble. But it forces us to locate the novel in a middle area of our imagination: between the book we read when much younger and the book we read now. Every novel that we consider adult must regain our imagination by presenting images we recognize, or symbolic presences that are still realities. The charms of *The Catcher* are the charms of a period piece; they cause not adult interest but nostalgia.

Its prose, which is a triumph of vernacular and colloquial, is self-limiting. One can go only so far with this kind of protest; it expands to allow for a young person's protest, but it does not engage, through either word or image, the larger world. People are either kind or mean; experiences are either fulfilling or hollow. There is not opportunity for complexity of experience, or for penetration of character. All elements in the novel, even Holden, depend on personality. Sex is incomplete, the groping in the back seat of a car or on a dark sofa; but it is the incompleteness of inexperience, not of knowledge compounded by frustration or lack of release. Each experience is limited by the nature of the challenge and response. This is not to deny Holden's attractiveness, nor Salinger's sympathetic portrayal of a youth trying to grapple with himself and his peers. Yet whenever we move beyond the world of Holden—for example, to compare him with Pip in *Great Expectations*—we see how restricted his social-personal-sexual experience is.

Once this is said, and it must be noted, the novel serves as a counter to its time, the counterfeit decade. Salinger saw that young manhood, as well as Phoebe's childhood, could be used to oppose the factitious and the fake; and he observed, further, that the pastoral tradition, in the yearning of his young protagonist, was still the American dream world of hope and expansion. Unfortunately, he did not sufficiently structure that experience so Holden could himself see the futility of the pastoral. It occurs to us, not to him, although he has intimations the frontier has receded. But despite his undeveloped realizations of self, Salinger forces us to accept his world, having had no other choice once he settled on a first-person narrative.

In Twain, meaningful experience lies in mythical places, the river, the northwest territory, even in Black Jim. In Gaddis, meaningful experience is part of a warped world where nature is rejected and only business-finance matters. In Salinger, we have the idyll, but only as the result of an incomplete vision, on the assumption an adult reader can and will accept the recognitions of a seventeen-year-old. The first time around that may have been possible, but after, our expectations, like our experiences, have shifted.

Half Jewish, half Irish, the Glass children reflect not only these two cultures, but several more. They are intensely part of the New York scene, and beyond that, the American; for as children, all seven Glass siblings appeared on a quiz show modeled on *The Quiz Kids* of the 1930s and 1940s. Their program is "It's a Wise Child"; and from Seymour, the oldest, and a suicide, to the youngest two, Franny and Zooey,* their lives have been marked by the attention, competition, and need to shine that the program afforded them. It is, also, a family doomed, with that quality now embodied in Franny and Zooey; Seymour, a suicide, and Walter, a twin, killed in the army of occupation in Japan. The other twin, Waker, has become a Roman Catholic priest; Buddy, the second eldest, is a writer in residence at a small female junior college, his life characterized by his desire for isolation. One other sister, Boo Boo, remains offstage, a wife and a mother of three.

The element connecting the two stories, as well as the two youngest Glass siblings, is Franny's "religious" conversion, although it seems a mixture of many elements: anorexia, psychological instability, a schizophrenic response to her life, a desire to wade through phoniness and hypocrisy in her college courses, an attempt to express her own ego intensely, a need to gain attention and at the same time efface herself in prayer, an effort, as the youngest, to establish her position in the family.

On the day of a big football game, Franny meets her boyfriend, and while he is full of the day's excitement and himself, she is seeking margins, where *her* day lies. She has been moved by the expression of faith of a Russian peasant in the books *The Way of a Pilgrim* and its sequel, *Pilgrim Continues His Way,* borrowed from Seymour. The peasant has read in the Bible about "unceasing prayer," and he goes on his pilgrimage to discover such a prayer, finally finding an old monk who tells him it is "Lord Jesus Christ, have mercy on me." The prayer repeated incessantly will come to take on a life of its own, shaping itself on the lips independently of the individual. As Zooey explains it: " 'The idea, really, is that sooner or later, completely on its own, the prayer moves from the lips and the head down to a center in the heart and becomes an automatic function in the person, right along with the heartbeat.' " Once the prayer becomes automatic, the person is released into the order of things. This is Franny's quest, and it leads to complete collapse.

Zooey begins a few days after her physical collapse

---

*Franny and Zooey, 1961 ("Franny," *The New Yorker,* 1955; "Zooey," *The New Yorker,* 1957).

on the day of the football game. She is all inner life now, refusing not only solace but chicken soup served by her Irish mother. Part of her rejection of outer life is her revulsion at the hypocrisy and phoniness of her professors, in this respect Holden updated. Also, she is in some ways attempting to move beyond the intense secularity of the Glasses. Zooey has himself embraced it, in acting, movies, role-playing, while mocking it and himself. His conversation is all defensive, full of wryness and ironies and forced witticisms. He is as intense about his secularity as she is about her religious conversion.

Yet Zooey is the only one to understand Franny. For he recognizes that in her quest for self-discovery she is pulling in two directions, alternately displaying ego and trying to efface it. In her desire to remove herself, from family, society, academic life, secularity, she condemns everything, a blanketing which disturbs her brother. He sees her motives as mixed, considers her no different in her religious fervor from the person who is greedy for material things. "Treasure's treasure," all a form of acquisitiveness. Zooey struggles with his own materialism by way of irony, he fights against what the 1950s have become, what their lives have become; but he wants to honor the self and the ego residing in all activity.

Zooey offers an alternative to Franny's ego-asserting religiosity. He speaks of religious life as meaning detachment, desirelessness, which he senses Franny is incapable of. As for himself, he says that one can, as a counter to detachment and false religiosity, aim at perfection, even when one is performing for morons. Audiences, reviewers, announcers, all the media flunkies, may be morons, but the performer shines his shoes and hones his talent for the "Fat Lady" out there. The "Fat Lady" is the ideal audience, one's own standard of excellence. A performer has no right to let her down, even though she is undefined, and may not even be there. No matter what, " 'There isn't anyone out there who isn't Seymour's Fat Lady.' " Then Zooey clinches his argument for Franny, asserting that the Fat Lady is " 'Christ Himself. Christ Himself, buddy.' " The kingdom of God is within her.*

The Glass family—beginning with the story "A Perfect Day for Bananafish" and ending with "Seymour—An Introduction"—forms the boundaries of Salinger's published work. Even while Holden is not

a Glass, he is in some respects a spin-off from the sequential series of stories and novellas. The sequence begins with Seymour's suicide in Florida on his honeymoon and then mythicizes him until his return in "An Introduction." The entire family hangs on Seymour, and so, apparently, does Salinger's writing career. What Seymour reflects, the Glass family reflects: great secular success, sickness unto death at that success, fear, trembling, angst, and all the other modern sicknesses, divisiveness in their heritage and their aims—a family that fragments despite the fondness of individual members for each other.

Through the family, Salinger achieves a cultural event more than a literary one. Starting in the 1940s and continuing into the late 1950s, when he vanished, Salinger would come back to the family, using various members to locate the cultural emblems of that postwar decade. The conception is a brilliant one, a kind of movable feast: to establish a large family, the parents and, originally, seven siblings, then to shift around from one to the other in order to establish a community of changing ideas, values, and attitudes.

Seymour is the apparent guru, the single force that both divides and joins the family. In "Raise High the Roof Beam, Carpenters," Salinger began to focus on the elusive Seymour, first from the outside, with Buddy as narrator, and then, in "Seymour—An Introduction," from the inside, but still with Buddy as narrator. In the latter, we learn that Buddy has also been the narrator or "maker" of the story "A Perfect Day for Bananafish"; or else Salinger has so entered into Buddy as his persona that the two, by the time of "Seymour," have become indistinguishable. Buddy is, as we learned in *Franny and Zooey,* a teacher of writing in an upstate New York junior college, a man who, seeing no one except students and colleagues, lives in a Thoreauvian cottage with few amenities. He is a self-conscious narrator who feels free to comment within his larger context, somewhat reminiscent, allowing for changes in values and attitudes, of Conrad's Marlow. The way in is Buddy, but the labyrinth is Seymour.

In "Raise High," Buddy retells the events of Seymour's wedding day in 1942. The title has a joyous reference, as against what actually occurs: the bridegroom, like Ares, walks so tall he needs a high roof beam. The reality is that Seymour fails to appear for the ceremony, then enters only when the guests have left the reception, elopes with Muriel, and commits suicide on their honeymoon in Florida. "Raise High," through Buddy's narrative, examines how the guests feel about Seymour. He is considered everything from

---

*We know, from "Seymour—An Introduction," that within five years Franny has recovered and is "a budding young actress."

a latent homosexual, who fears marriage, to a schizophrenic, whose behavior is completely unpredictable.

Buddy barely hints at Seymour's actual motives; but we can sense his distant manner by way of one of his avatars, a tiny deaf-mute, who is the bride's great-uncle. In *his* miniature, forbearing, accepting presence, we sense that Seymour is there; not tortured, not despairing, but Seymour of the moments of peace, Dostoyevsky's holy fool, settled into a peace that passes understanding. This tale from the outside is preparation for the tale from the inside, "An Introduction," the story that is the apex of Salinger's five about the Glass family. What Seymour reflects there will be not only his heritage but Salinger's; for both will disappear, fittingly enough, into the flow of things, no longer feeling the need to comment upon an alien culture.

To move beyond the Glass family successes and failures, we must get to matters of conscience. If Seymour is genuine, then he is a seer or an artist whose "creation" is religious. "I say that the true artist-seer, the heavenly fool who can and does produce beauty, is mainly dazzled to death by his own scruples, the blinding shapes and colors of his own sacred human conscience." Although this is highly unusual for fiction of the fifties, the dimensions lie in the sacred world of belief, conscience, guilt, redemption, the still center that is peace itself.

Toward the apotheosis of the oldest Glass child, Salinger wrote the crowning piece, "Seymour—An Introduction," the narrator, as indicated, Buddy. This is an introduction not only to Seymour's (184) poems, to his looks and habits, but to the making of a legend. With almost no intrusions, the narrative is a modified stream. Buddy hopes to sweep us up into the worship of Seymour, or to make us sense his uniqueness. Salinger's conception is grand: to get behind the reflections of the Glasses, to internality. In a sense, this is a fitting capstone to Salinger's work, continuous with *Catcher* and the earlier stories, a quest for integrity in an artificial America. Behind the phoniness, although well disguised, there is something worth preserving; and it rests in the man Seymour, the hero of an epic who has halted corruption by killing himself. Because he chose death at thirty-one, Seymour will not rot. Buddy describes his face, general appearance, games-playing abilities, as well as the poems based on Chinese and Japanese models. Is Seymour the last honest man, the man who refuses to be Nietzsche's degraded survivor? Is he our primeval American who exists beyond the confidence men of the fifties? Did Seymour fear that if he lived, he would, like everyone else, be sold?

What vitiates the grand scheme of Salinger's plan is the thinness of the realization. Several elements, unfortunately, appear wrong, unfocused. Narrating it all from Buddy's point of view dilutes the quality of Seymour; Buddy is himself unproven, and his sense of his older brother carries no resonance. Then, too, the voice is windy, self-indulgent, self-serving, too pregnant in its pauses and hesitations. "It's just got through to me [Buddy], that apart from my many other—and, I hope to God, less ignoble—motives, I'm stuck with the usual survivor's conceit that he's the only soul alive who knew the deceased intimately. *O let them come*—the callow and the enthusiastic, the academic, the curious, the long and the short and the all-knowing!"

Also misleading is Buddy's mockery of the academy, when he is himself a teacher of composition at a small college. He has earned little of that pretension to superiority; he is part of it, and his account of Seymour, accordingly, is not quite what he thinks it is. Seymour remains shadowy, rather leaden, without the swiftness Buddy tries to convey. Strategically, the long story remains an exercise in "Glass's disease." It is itself flatulent, Buddy at cross-purposes with himself, full of words without focus, swollen with desire to express something about Seymour, who remains out of range. Clotted and flushed, "Seymour—An Introduction" must have filled Salinger's imagination so fully—becoming his Zen, his Old and New Testament, his Jesus Christ, his Buddhism—that even that extraordinary Glass family ceased to reflect anything. The rest *was* silence.

Sylvia Plath's *The Bell Jar* appears to slide off Salinger in several ways; but not solely because, as some critics have suggested, her Esther Greenwood seems like a female Holden Caulfield. More, she is linked to Salinger by virtue of their ability to juxtapose highs and lows in rapid succession, their insight into how close one's sense of achievement is to one's end. Life in both is often a disguise for a very sudden death, which has already taken place without the individual knowing it.

The Bell Jar (published in England in 1963 under the pseudonym Victoria Lucas, in America in 1971) reaches for significance Plath is unable to deliver on. She is the tragedian of short bursts—intermixing death with lyric poetry—not of the longer haul. She opens the novel, which is mainly retrospective, with the "queer, sultry summer, the summer they electrocuted the Rosenbergs." She says she is stupid about electrocutions, but she is not stupid about forms of death, suicidal death. For the latter sections of the novel are bathed in suicides, sequences of them, either thought about (as wrist slashing or jumping from a speeding car) or else actual attempts, as in the one that almost succeeded. In that, she swallowed fifty pills and hid, fetuslike, in a breezeway in her mother's basement. Her mother, doing the laundry, heard groans and was able to get help in time. As for electrocutions, Esther Greenwood experiences something similar; she undergoes shock treatment on two separate occasions, and on the first, unprepared for it, she almost parallels what the Rosenbergs must have felt.

The latter sections, with the suicides, the shock treatments, the institutionalizations, are considerably at variance with the earlier segments. We understand that Esther has been driving herself, that she has felt little personal satisfaction, that there were unexamined areas of herself which were potentially explosive, that she was too passive. Also, we understand she was out of touch with whatever she was, that her feminine side was crushed in her attempts to make her way in a man's world; that all her efforts were judged by her role as a woman in that world. Nevertheless, her leap into suicide efforts is insufficiently prepared for. Their context is *suicide itself,* not the young woman attempting it. This is an important distinction, because if it is valid, efforts to claim more for the book are weakened. Then the book falls back into imitation Salinger, a weak link in that growing up subgenre.

Plath strives to intensify the narrative, to lay the groundwork for self-destruction and destruction. The importance of the title is there, the bell jar as container of Esther's ambience, the bell jar as lid, as a sense of the death awaiting her, her coffin. The jar with the embryo babies is introduced when Buddy Willard shows her around his hospital. Those embryos are forms, entombed in glass, which didn't make it, although the last one in the sequence looks as if it developed to a fetus. Esther perceives herself mirrored in those shapes, analogous to the role she chose to play in her mother's basement breezeway. As a multiple symbol, the bell jar is apt; but even here, Plath does not extend it. Implied in her character is a larger familial and social failure than Plath can develop. If she could have, that shift into tragedy from the earlier parts of the novel would have been sequential, not a leap.

We are left, then, with a suicidal Holden. We seem poised to understand Esther, but broader contexts are missing. Instead, Plath goes for laughs. Puking is a source of fun, or male genitals. We never comprehend the madness that will define her efforts to understand the world around her. Madness is at one level her exploration of what is still left for her to do, in a world that has defined her boundaries. Madness is revolt, in the Laingian sense of a personal reaction to social lunacy. What we miss in the novel are those coordinates which would have allowed Plath to make that huge leap from a "mad world" to true personal madness. The unevenness results from a crucial division between elements: those associated with the Holden-Salinger syndrome and those connected to the tragic element that lies in marginality, passivity, even innocence.

THE MAIN TRADITION

Salinger's novel and stories are characteristic forties and early fifties fiction, carrying us into pastoral, spatiality, the counterfeiting of emotional life, the flattening out of systems, and similar themes that define the decade. The five works that follow are, I believe, the major sources of postwar growing up fiction. Two derive from the 1950s, three from the 1960s; but except for the Nabokov, they seem continuous with each other.

Ada may appear unusually placed here—*Lolita,* perhaps, would be a more apt example of growing up in the fifties—but I include it as a kind of mirror image of the *Bildungsroman,* or "growing up novel," that American-born writers were publishing. By the time of *Ada,* in 1969, Nabokov had become so deeply an international writer, so much a combination of old world and new, that he provides in himself a gloss on our native writers—a European version of *Portnoy* and *Augie March,* a Russian counter to the Polish *Painted Bird,* all in all an amalgam of types and a grand work of American camp.

The Adventures of Augie March established Bellow as a major novelist at the beginning of the fifties, a position he consolidated with *Henderson the Rain King* at the end, the two novels forming his most considerable work: one devoted to growing up, the other to exploration and revival. Parts of *Augie March* appeared in the immediate years before its publication in 1953, so that both the writing and the partial publication belonged to the latter part of the 1940s rather than only to the early 1950s. The book and its protagonist, the quasi-picaresque Augie, are responses to the counterfeiting of ideas and feelings that developed in the decade after the war. But since this is a complicated, morally textured book, it is far more than a response to counterfeiting; for it demonstrates how imitational life can be assimilated even as one struggles against it. Bellow's point throughout, and a critical one for our postwar novelists, is that the individual will can become hostage to the very energies feeding it. Bellow places Augie in the Depression years in Chicago, but the twenty-year period to the present is telescoped from what we were to what we are. Bellow is nothing if not a social observer and a moral conscience. Growing up is as difficult, and complicated, as coming to terms with the nation.

In one of the many marvelous scenes early in the novel, Einhorn, the spunky, proud cripple, castigates Augie for having become involved in a cheap robbery of handbags. He comments: " 'All of a sudden I catch on to something about you. You've got *opposition* in you. You don't slide through everything. You just make it look so.' " The "opposition" Einhorn observes is Augie's dualism, that alternation of will and ennui, even anomie, which impels the novel. It moves along on two tracks, the driving energy of the I-narrator, Augie, and the enervation of the senses which acts as a countering force of equal strength. On one hand, Augie has the energy of Ulysses and something of his wily ability to survive; but on the other, he acts like Orpheus, although lacking artistic talent. Remarkable in Bellow's achievement is how convincing he makes Augie's potentiality; we always expect him to explode. Here, in contemporary terms, is a meeting of the forties and the fifties: energy confronting enervation and ennui.

Ambiguity is revealed from the first: "I am an American, Chicago-born [Call me Ishmael]—Chicago, that somber city—and go at things as I have taught myself, free-style, and will make the record in my own way: first to knock, first admitted." Yet this assertion of will is countered by the next statement, Heraclitus's warning that "man's character is his fate." Augie is not Augustus or august, but *Augie,* a name for a man of the people; he must march. Bellow's conception is grand, not simply based on but drawing on opposition between drives of the will and lack of it, will-lessness. Lionel Trilling ended his highly favorable review of the novel with a demurrer, that he resisted the book's propaganda, "holding an opinion the direct opposite of Mr. Bellow's, that without function it is very difficult to be a person and have a fate."

Augie slides away from any decision in which he must engage himself fully. He may glide into a situation with a strong display of will, but he insists, in his bouncy way, on his own sense of nature and men. Women appeal to him greatly, as do the things of the world, but he refuses the way of his brother Simon. The March family consists of three brothers (Karamazovs, Chicago and Jewish): George, who is simple-minded; Simon, hard as nails, always ready to strike for the main chance; and Augie, in between, a sexy Alyosha, more interested in "good" than in assertions of self.

Bellow, throughout, is delicately trying to get the feel of a period difficult to capture in literary terms, since one could not escape the contradictions of political and social life. Idealism is foolish, as Simon recognizes, seizing his opportunities. Augie is not so sure. He resists adoption, he cannot be bought, he acts in ways so that Lucy Magnus cannot be his, he rejects the hard, practical advice of Simon. No course of action seems appropriate. This makes him appear directionless, but he is, like a modern version of Henry James's Marcher, waiting for exactly the right moment: in one sense, an artist awaiting the combination for his kind of art.

If we examine character and symbol, we can see Augie as located between two large figures, each given an extended series of episodes. One extreme is Einhorn, a superbly drawn character. Crippled, ultimately dependent, Einhorn lives by his wits and achieves considerable fortune before the Crash. But even during the Depression years he does not surrender; pure will, all function, he claws his way and keeps himself from drowning.

The other part of the equation involves the adventure in Mexico, where Augie and Thea Fenschel travel to train the American bald eagle to capture gigantic iguanas. Earlier, Einhorn had been a kind of eagle, who would never release his talons once he obtained a grip. Augie could not identify with that, and here the giant bird, the principle of nature, suggests that same feral instinct for survival. Yet the bird proves cowardly. Bitten by a small iguana, it pulls back; attacked by a large one, it retreats altogether; it has been trained to sponge. Augie is delighted when Caligula, *el águila,* "preferred meat to prey." Augie applauds the eagle's cowardice, identifying it with love; whereas Thea is furious at the eagle's withdrawal, for she believes that love is only a stage toward action. Love being insufficient, Augie will fail her in action as Caligula has. The drift between the two occurs in their relationship to the eagle, which, in turn, is connected to the ambiguous relationship of man to nature. Not yet sure where the moral center is, Bellow refused to jump; later, no longer devoted to negative capability, more stern and judgmental, he jumped, and his fiction suffered.

Bellow is clearly using Einhorn and Caligula as comments on Augie's attempts to locate himself. Although the Mexican scenes convey some of his confusion—the circuslike atmosphere, the drift toward disaster, the kaleidoscope of disconnected images (fiestas, bands, Cossack chorus, Indian circus, card-playing, drinking)—they do not have sufficient rootedness. Even the brief glimpses of Trotsky are forced. The presence of Trotsky has a certain grandness, the legend himself, and Augie for a time thinks he may be employed as a disguise for Trotsky's entrance into the United States. But the idea does not cohere. Augie's drift is permitted to become the drift of the novel. Bellow so moves him around that we do not find sufficient braiding or textural variety. Augie is so defined by Chicago that, like Antaeus with the earth, he loses his strength when he departs.

Bellow had the problem of form. Picaresque calls for episodic development; but the social rootedness of modern-day picaresque requires greater texture than the old form demanded. Like Bellow's with form, Augie's dilemma is that he must leave himself open to experience. As a consequence, he prolongs that period we associate with adolescence well into his twenties. He takes different shapes, chameleonlike— a holding pattern while he tries to discover what is real. Ultimately, the narrative becomes so attenuated that its links cannot hold; as readers we are put in a holding pattern, which is quite a different aesthetic experience from observing the protagonist in such a pattern.

This insistence on life as against theories, ideologies, legends, and myths moves Bellow closer to storyteller than to novelist. If anything, the novel of our time has been one of ideas, often exploded in failure; or ideologies, which provide their own traps. In his *Paris Review* interview, Bellow stated his preference for nineteenth-century realism, of which Dreiser is a major American proponent. Favoring this kind of novel, which includes the Russians, has preempted Bellow's development in the postwar years. Not only has he not bent to new technical styles; he has refused, after *Henderson,* to move along the contours of new ideas. *Augie March* contains all these conflicting elements, Bellow struggling to let the new out even as he seeks to contain it.

He has himself divided novelists into those who are optimistic (the "cleans") and those who are rebellious and negative (the "dirties"), rather unfortunate designations given the complexity of the ideas involved. Claiming for himself the middle ground, he asserts that public figures hold modern literature (and writers and poets) in contempt because they sense no grappling with any "significant question." Most radical writers, he suggests, are like that, "for the sake of their dignity," and have little or no content. He stresses that a real radicalism is needed, but not a "radicalism of posture [which] is easy and banal."

The confusion here is immense, perhaps willfully so, because Bellow is too intelligent to bungle ideas unless strong personal feeling has interposed. Yet although the *Paris Review* interview (spring–fall 1965) came more than ten years after *Augie March,* the confusion of realms and ideas applies well to the novel —such a rich and rewarding experience novelistically that one can find in it sufficient material for several books as well as several ideas that pull both with it and against it. In his attack on "radical writers"— Mailer? Gaddis? Heller? Roth?—he suggests that the real novelist (neither "clean" nor "dirty") hugs the center, saying neither yea nor nay. Yet the center hugged so tightly in *Augie March* dissipates the tremendous energy Bellow obtains at the extremes— Einhorn is surely an extreme, and so is Simon, or Thea. Radicalism is surely not political, but a way of observing; so that we can say the great novelists of the twentieth century have all been radicals. Saying no is not simply negativism.

In the interview, Bellow was very possibly still defending *Herzog,* where passivity is celebrated. Augie is quite different from that, and yet he, too, is entrapped by Bellow's restrictive sense of the novel, especially a contemporary novel. We pick this up not only in the *Paris Review* interview but in several other journals and symposia where Bellow has stated his views. He says in the interview that when he began *Augie March,* he removed many of the restraints of his earlier two novels. "I think I took off too many, and went too far, but I was feeling the excitement of discovery." He fears he abused that freedom. The freedom Bellow sensed was not only of thought but of form, an open narrative as against the Flaubertian standard in *The Victim;* and yet an openness that connects to a character who admits passivity, willingness to be redirected by others.

The issue is of great moment literarily, because Bellow achieved the highest points of his art in sections of *Augie March,* and then dissipated them in the 1960s, in *Herzog* and *Sammler,* which are seriously flawed. In the interview, Bellow stresses that as the son of Russian Jews, he did not feel comfortable with the Anglo-Saxon traditions, even with English words. His center remained elsewhere, not in the English tradition.

In his first two novels, Bellow flirted with Dostoyevskian and Kafkan approaches, an ironic surface beneath which life drops off into endless tunnels of torment and anguish. Those tunnels of pain, in Asa Leventhal as well as in Joseph, are areas of grotesqueness which we recognize as modern equivalents—that is, psychological melodramas—of Gothic subterranean passages and underground dungeons. The strategy for novelists who attempt to utilize Kafka's insights is to bind together what seem disparate elements: fragments of wit and irony with portions of tragic awareness. The result must be tension between surface and elements lying beneath, what for an American writer would appear to function more effectively in short works, especially poetry. Bellow discovered as much with *Seize the Day* (1956), where he moved back to the European form after the expansionism of *Augie* and before the exuberance of *Henderson*. That novella, *Seize the Day,* is Bellow's only true attempt at a tragic posture within the closed form, his combined "Metamorphosis" and *Notes from Underground.*

The conflicts for the American novelist attempting a Kafkan or Dostoyevskian type of fiction are immense, the effort creating problems not only in content—those levels of philosophical extremism—but in technique. The surface of wit and irony moves toward openness, toward possibility. There is always the chance of disorder, even chaos; thus Bellow's assertion that he backed off from the implications of *Augie March.* The archetype here is the Rabelaisian epic of anarchy, elements of which do seem suited to Bellow's talent.

By *Augie March,* accordingly, Bellow was juggling novelistic traditions. An urban novelist attracted by nature, by a type of harmonious association between the individual and God's creation, he also knew man was solipsistic, impelled by needs he could neither disguise from himself nor fully comprehend. This, too, was a form of terrible knowledge: despite nature, man could easily become enclosed in his own circuitry, failing to grasp the experience that lay around, or growing up stunted. This other counter was the world itself, beyond simply "nature," and encompassing ideas, knowledge and self-knowledge, the life of the good man, the Socratic ideal. The problem was, still further, that to yearn for that world was to reach for anarchy; for the world out there, where everything lay ready to be picked or plucked, was entirely unpredictable. Thus the juggling act: Dostoyevskian chaos, Kafkan solipsism, American reliance on nature, with its concomitant escape, running, openness of forms and experience.

These were Bellow's problems by the end of *Augie March.* That long novel had really solved nothing; it had, by its writing, suggested where the problems would lie in Bellow's future career. He was now moving toward his late thirties, a crucial time for the novelist who wishes to succeed at the highest levels.

Bellow's specialty was in the writing of paragraphs. His paragraphs often have a small world in them, whereas most postwar novelists are sentence writers. One of the great qualities of nineteenth-century writers was their realization that the paragraph was far more than several sentences put back to back. Bellow tries to achieve that rhythm, beyond word, phrase, and individual sentence. Such writing requires information, thought, and a synthesizing ability.

Speaking of the hotel where Simon gets married, Augie comments:

> . . . But in this modern power of luxury, with its battalions of service workers and engineers, it's the things themselves, the products that are distinguished, and the individual man isn't nearly equal to their great sum. Finally, they are what becomes great —the multitude of baths with never-failing hot water. . . . No opposing greatness is allowed, and the disturbing person is the one who won't serve by using or denies by not wishing to enjoy.
>
> I didn't yet know what view I had of all this. It still wasn't clear to me whether I would be for or against it. But then how does anybody form a decision to be against and persist against? When does he choose and when is he chosen instead?

Bellow's paragraphs serve a corollary function. Although they may be tied to an individual, or a place, they suggest elements of the all. Each paragraph tends to move along on several fronts, glacierlike, giving him his thoughtful quality, far more than does any purely intellectual content of his material. Bellow quotes extensively from other writers, historians, philosophers; but these are usually tags and pieces, well-known to anyone familiar with the history of ideas and often lacking resonance. While they impress reviewers, they pretend to far more than they deliver.

What Bellow evidently feared from his work on *Augie March* was that excess of individuality, that threat of narcissism and reliance on personality, which he felt were disproportionate to what was significant in American life. As a reaction, he cultivated a literarily conservative aesthetic. He suspected that existence itself would be lost sight of, in that pursuit of whatever self-serving circuitry the individual pursued. He says he wanted to show (in *Herzog*) "that existence quite apart from any of our judgments, has value, that existence is worth-ful." He went from openness toward tunneling, closing down rather than expanding—*Henderson the Rain King* is the sole exception here. Just as much of *Augie March* seems to come from streets and open areas—from something as big as Chicago itself, or from the vast mountains and plains of Mexico, from the air surrounding the American bald eagle—so in the later novels experience derives from caves and grottoes, tombs, isolated houses, stuffy rooms, even beds.

Bellow was distressed that the American overevaluation of self derived from Rousseau, when it would better have come from Nietzsche. The latter saw the self as being associated with Apollo, god of light, god of harmony, music, reason; whereas the group or tribe was associated with Dionysus. In Nietzsche's formulation, Bellow stresses, the self served a real function, as part of the mediating process between "the individual and the generic." It was not an all-consuming commodity which demanded to be fed, as it was in Rousseau, villain of modern versions of selfdom. In these excesses of self, the American moves to antipodes of experience, from nihilistic denial of his own mysteries to the feeding of the self and the exclusion of the world. Bellow finds that man, caught in a "shameful and impotent privacy," needs to be freed from the intellectual privilege of his bondage.

The whole modern trend—in opposition Bellow becomes increasingly shrill in his sixties and seventies fiction—means that private and public have become unbalanced. In the onslaught of the public against the individual in twentieth-century technology, the individual has fought back by assuming superiority by way of sickness, retreat, enervation, exhaustion, displays of self without engagement of self. Self denies when it cannot engage; it becomes nihilistic when it debases existence in favor of the "sick soul." Bellow's formulations, which are tonic in many ways, become strangely limiting, since after a time they justify only his own kind of novel, not the wider range of human existence which he claims as his goal.

In a broad sense, all of James Baldwin's work—novels, stories, and key essays—can be perceived as part of growing up. It is, for him, the salient issue, and it carries over into his mature literary work. *Go Tell It on the Mountain* (1953), his first novel, and best, is so compelling because he had located himself precisely where his talent lay. So much of Baldwin's career has been based on the need to kill the father, resurrect him, and perhaps rekill him—not only his own father, of course, but Richard Wright and others—that he is in the constant condition of being a son.*

---

*Baldwin has generated a considerable round robin of critical reaction to his views, in a sense each article or essay by and about him a form of growing up for the writer. The developments are worth pursuing, but there is no clear chronology. At the center of the storm are Wright and Baldwin, although several offshoots appear. Originally, there was only Wright's *Native Son,* undeniably the most influential of all novels by black writers—in its content, ideology, even title, a beginning. In 1951, with his *Partisan Review* essay, "Many Thousands Gone," Baldwin began to peck away at the Wright image. Well before Harold Bloom's "anxiety of influence" spoke of fathers and sons, Baldwin tried to move out from under the man who had helped him but who, he felt, would smother him; thus his repudiation of Wright and his novel (far more subtly argued than his critics have granted him).

Baldwin was now poised to become a father, but still felt himself a son, a point he stressed in his 1955 "Notes of a Native Son," in *Harper's* magazine. In an essay saturated with father and son situations, Baldwin examined "fathers": his own father dying, the birth of his last child, Baldwin as the oldest of nine children now expected to become a father, whites as paternal figures, blacks as children, the Harlem riots in the background as a rebellion by sons. What Baldwin had to sort out was the extent to which the Negro must be perceived literarily as solely a social victim—the very point he had attacked in Wright—or whether the Negro could relocate as a distinct personality, as Baldwin would attempt to do after he disposed of fathers and their restrictive guideliness. Behind fathers lay growing up; behind growing up, color; behind color, sex; behind sex, the need for self-expression; and behind all that still lay several ambiguous regions in Baldwin which his fiction does not satisfactorily locate.

When Wright, in turn, became a sacred object, Baldwin was reviled. Brought in also to take some of the heat was Ralph Ellison, one of the many tributaries in this running argument, seemingly literary, but more apparently racial and social. In *his* "Notes on a Native Son," Eldridge Cleaver attacked Baldwin for his hatred of blackness. "The racial death-wish is manifested as the driving force in James Baldwin." Cleaver moved directly to Baldwin's attack on Wright, in which Baldwin argued that Bigger Thomas cannot be a symbol for for the American Negro, for he plays into American stereotypes of what the Negro is like. Cleaver turns nasty and, after accusing Baldwin of hating the blackness in himself, says he further despised Wright for his masculinity. "He cannot confront the stud in others—except that he must either submit to it or destroy it. And he was

Baldwin's fiction is all centered on "m·-ism," but the "me" recalls a recalcitrant son, whether of his own father, of his mentor, Wright, or of a religious and racial dimension. Spiritual and religious dimensions are so significant in Baldwin's work because these

elements informed his prose and helped counter the extreme narcissism of his interests. Baldwin's need to slay the father and assert himself as a son is so melodramatic a theme, so potentially uncontrollable for his art, that religious imagery and symbolism helped him to contain it literarily, giving his prose its rich burnish and yet distancing it just outside the self.

Chester Himes asserts, in an interview with John Williams, that the major mistake in Richard Wright's life was "to become a world writer on world events. . . . he should have stuck to the black scene in America. . . . he had the memory, so he was still there," even when in exile in Paris. The remark can be carried over to Baldwin; for within three years of *Go Tell It,* he moved to a French locale for *Giovanni's Room* (1956) and took on a persona that contained no resonance, depth, or even capacity for the suffering we are told the protagonist feels. Baldwin's lack of literary center here is portended by the pretentious epigraph from Whitman: "I am the man, I suffered, I was there." Far preferably, literarily, was John Grimes's plaint, in *Go Tell It,* that he *was rooted in silent fury.*

Baldwin's first novel has broad kinship with several books, by both whites and blacks, before and after it. In its general outlines and ambitions, it fits in with *Call It Sleep, Studs Lonigan, Black Boy,* Delmore Schwartz's *In Dreams Begin Responsibilities,* even *The Catcher in the Rye;* later, Mario Puzo's *The Fortunate Pilgrim,* then *Goodbye, Columbus* and *Portnoy's Complaint.* To these could be added Alfred Kazin's *A Walker in the City* and Leonard Kriegel's *The Long Walk Home* and *Notes for the Two-Dollar Window.* The basic frame is of a young man thrust into an atmosphere in which ethnicity or raciality is a conflict to be worked out in addition to the usual ones of boyhood and adolescence. We can see how the American version of the *Bildungsroman* has shifted the terms. Some of the original form is retained, such as the hostile, opposing father, the flight of the young person so as to gain freedom of expression. But in the original idea of the *Bildungsroman,* the youth comes through after he hurdles several obstacles, whereas in the American adaptation, race, religion, ethnicity, paternal authority are forms of doom, not to be overcome through simple initiation into life. Life never becomes a triumph, but remains a process; the individual life always hovers near destruction or abulia.

Baldwin's John Grimes is growing up in the intensely religious, and dangerous, atmosphere of New York's Harlem, expected to be a preacher like the stepfather, Gabriel, whom he detests, with a half brother (Royal) headed toward destruction at an

---

not about to bow to a *black man."*

Cleaver cites Mailer's long essay "The White Negro" approvingly, the Mailer piece having entered the fray somewhat tangentially. Mailer was concerned, as ever, with masculinity, and this fitted Cleaver's present argument, that Baldwin was useless in the coming revolutionary struggle because of his weak masculinity. Wright thus reenters the late 1950s and the 1960s not as a literary force but as a powerful heterosexual leader. It is, incidentally, this very quality which is examined perceptively by John Williams in *The Man Who Cried I Am* (1967), with characters including, besides Wright, Baldwin, King, Malcolm X, sons and fathers intermixed.

Forces are aligned now in the late 1960s: Baldwin, isolated, having attacked Mailer's "The White Negro" most recently and Wright in the previous decade; Cleaver, standing for the new "revolutionary" forces of Jones, Gayle, Killens, Hoyt, other black writers eager to resurrect Wright and dump Baldwin and Ellison; Mailer, standing alone, a white critic arguing for the black stud, for his existential experience as a black male aligned with danger. There is, however, more.

Ralph Ellison enters on several fronts, in the decade after *Invisible Man:* in the attacks made upon him by several black critics who found he was not black enough; in various defenses by white critics, who found him aesthetically more satisfactory than Wright; and most eloquently in his own defense, in an essay called "The World and the Jug." Ellison was responding to an article by Irving Howe called "Black Boys and Native Sons," which later appeared in his *A World More Attractive* (1963). Howe's closely argued point was located in a sympathetic view of the Negro's plight, to the extent that Howe views all black life as reflected in Wright's world of unredeemed violence: "violence is a central fact in the life of the American Negro, defining and crippling him with a harshness few other Americans need suffer." In a sense, Howe plays off Baldwin against Wright, perceiving that while the former has attacked the latter for presenting the Negro as a social victim, he has then done the same himself. Howe's point is that the Negro is caught in a social trap and that even the ending of *Invisible Man,* with its sense of ironic self-liberation, is something willed, not achieved, because it is incomprehensible culturally. Ellison responded in "The World and the Jug," reprinted in *Shadow and Act,* that black life is not all violence, that a cohesive culture exists and one can be free within it, that the individual can make choices, and that being black is not equivalent to being jailed, because one always has a thinking, conceiving, exploring mind.

Who has prevailed? Everyone except Cleaver seems to have come through. Baldwin still publishes, having become as black as Cleaver could have wished, Ellison and Wright are revered, and black revolutionary critics are cultivating their own gardens. The time is 1980, and few care.

early age, and a mother and an aunt who try to prevent the family's internal hatreds from destroying it. The family continues to exist, but only by a small margin. It is held together, however tentatively, by a religious faith, its Seventh-Day Adventism, practiced in a storefront church in Harlem.

By way of John Grimes, who is in the forefront mainly at the beginning and end, the novel finds focus; but Baldwin's maturity as a novelist—while still in his mid-twenties—allowed him to slide off John to other Grimeses: Gabriel, Aunt Florence, and the mother, Elizabeth. Placing the family and its religious tenets between himself and the fourteen-year-old John enabled Baldwin to avoid the inevitable narcissism that characterizes such fiction. It would be almost the last time in his fiction that he would eschew the expressly personal in favor of a more modulated, broadly based novel. His strength lies in family scenes, in tensions generated by terrible pressures exerted on the family as a whole, as well as on its individual members.

Flashbacks from the beginning of John's experience in the storefront church take up the entire middle of the novel. Although the structure seems simple —first, John on the threshold of his vocation as a preacher, then the Grimes family appearing seriatim, finally the return to the church and John's calling on the "threshing-floor"—Baldwin's accomplishment as a young novelist is remarkable. The background material even allows us to see Gabriel with some sympathy, although he is not sympathetic, a man who speaks of God and lies with the Devil. Unlike his Biblical namesake, a divine messenger, Baldwin's Gabriel strives to purify himself by punishing those around him. His is a deeply sensual nature at war with his religious needs. Only his spiritual calling keeps him from a life as a ne'er-do-well, a trifler and womanizer.

As a young man, Gabriel had got a young woman of dubious reputation pregnant, refused to recognize the child, let the woman (Esther) die without his help to save her; and then, as repentance, married a barren, very black, older woman, who as a young girl had been violated by white rapists. Gabriel can function only between intense sensuality and denial. When the older woman dies, he marries Elizabeth, who has a son, John, his father a young man who slashed his wrists after subjection to brutality and indignities in a police station. Gabriel's son by Esther, Royal, is murdered in a card game, all the while unrecognized; and Gabriel "acquires" John as a way of redeeming that sacrifice, also. He and Elizabeth have Roy and

Sarah, and that youth seems headed toward Royal's end, on the Harlem streets.

The middle of the novel is very busy, full of names and lives, too many for the brevity of the book. The pacing is off, although individual scenes and the language are eloquent. Baldwin's awareness of diverse voices, so heavily dependent on the language of the Bible and the oral tradition of black preachers, vibrates with passion and commitment even when scenes are relatively subdued. This play of language, with rhythms from the Old Testament, Harlem sounds, grammatical constructions of uneducated black people, has a quality we associate with early Roth and Malamud, some of Bellow; less so with Wright's *Black Boy,* which is already the more neutral language of a literary man. Baldwin is able to disguise his own "literary" qualities—as he could not do later—so that sounds and voices are authentic.

Esther pinpoints what kind of man he is. He speaks of being made to fall because of a wicked woman, and she responds: " 'You be careful . . . how you talk to me. I ain't the first girl's been ruined by a holy man, neither.' " She knows his talk of sinning is merely a façade to excuse his own weakness; and Baldwin uses her understanding of Gabriel as a wedge into a major conflict of the book. The drive for respectability sought by the black man against the debilitation and degradation foisted upon him by the white man's world is more than he can contain, with destruction or undermining of the individual as the consequence. While Gabriel cannot be excused for individual actions, his furious endeavors to become a man have almost destroyed him. With that conditioning, he will, in turn, crush John. Baldwin knew his fathers and sons.

At the end of the novel, John Grimes, to whom Baldwin finally returns, has his "moment of truth" on the church floor and thrashes around in the passionate embrace of the Lord. Unlike his half brother Royal, he will follow his stepfather into the church. But it is an ambiguous vocation, for he has also matured in these moments of passion and agony, and he announces to his unsmiling father that " 'I'm on my way.' " He has turned fourteen, and that is old enough for him to kill the father. The March wind strikes through his damp clothes, blowing away the dampness, the old, the musty; from the cocoon emerges a new self. It is doubtful if, except in individual essays, Baldwin ever surpassed the eloquence and intensity of this brief novel. His novelistic roots appear here, not in the wider areas of urban life that he attempted to portray. The broader he became in his interests, the more diluted became his powers, his vision, indeed his language.

Like Baldwin's *Go Tell It on the Mountain,* Philip Roth's novella "Goodbye, Columbus" locates growing up within generational struggles, but not solely Oedipal. For in Roth's work in 1959, we can find the foreshadowing of much of the generational conflict endemic to the 1960s. Family wars would become civil rights and Vietnam wars; but essentially Neil Klugman here—and Alexander Portnoy later—were working through large cultural shifts in which authority was itself the culprit. Whatever was anti-authoritarian was, somehow, good for the self, an idea still somewhat inchoate in the earlier fiction. What were systems for Holden Caulfield and orders of being for Augie March now become more directly family tensions; but, as for Baldwin, family tensions include entire worlds. Authority is a kind of prison for the young, and to break out, even in masturbation, as Portnoy demonstrates, is an act of life. Defiance has its own rationale. This, incidentally, will be the very theme of the novels focusing on the female experience later in the 1960s; and we observe how it is a central American theme, connecting not only black and Jewish men, but women.

As Roth became a more complicated writer, liberation was insufficient as an expression of life. Yet breaking out was itself richly paradoxical: a source of guilt, a loss of some part of the self, a step into chaos which even the strongest will could not control. In such ways, "Goodbye, Columbus" points toward both 1950s and 1960s, like a mirror in a Vermeer painting reflecting itself. *Portnoy's Complaint* (1969), however, pointed straight ahead, its self-indulgence a mark of Roth's deep exploitation of his material.

Alexander (not the Great, not the son of Philip) Portnoy must somehow escape his House Beautiful scene to become his own person. This is the primal theme of growing up fiction. In his document, which is narrated to his analyst, Dr. Spielvogel, Portnoy stresses his sexual disturbances, especially his fears of castration, which accompany shame and dread of retribution. He locates himself near Kierkegaard's Abraham and Isaac. He must, in order to discover himself, destroy the father (and mother) in himself; which is to say, he must erase his Jewishness. His Jewishness, however, goes well beyond fathers, to traditions which demand a Jewish wife, children, upward mobility, orderly life. It represents the bourgeois principle at its most civilized. Yet while it appears to vaunt self, Judaism actually devours it.

By stressing Roth as an exclusively Jewish writer, critics have lessened his cultural impact, which involves considerably more than "Jewishness," however it is defined. For by striving to become an American (however *that* is defined), by attempting to discover or rediscover America, Roth is setting himself against not only parents but the idea of America as chiefly a land of immigrants, refugees, foreign-born settlers. "What I'm saying, Doctor, is that I don't seem to stick my dick up these girls, as much as I stick it up their backgrounds—as though through fucking I will discover America. *Conquer America*—maybe that's more like it. Columbus, Captain Smith, Governor Winthrop, General Washington—now Portnoy."

This is a constant in Roth's fiction, the generational conflict which derives from younger people's desire to become American, American as exemplified by WASPs. "Goodbye Columbus," like *Goodbye, Columbus,* is an ambiguous title, but of course more than Columbus, Ohio, is indicated; for Columbus is also the first part of America, as it were. To say farewell to Columbus is to sail out oneself, away from where one element of America lies, to where another is situated. The opposite of this is the elder Portnoy's song-and-dance act, as well as Spielvogel, the German Jew, whose voice at the end suggests everything Alexander must escape, not embrace: " 'So. Now vee may perhaps to begin. Yes?' " To grow up is to explore, and in a curious way Alex recalls Huck, whose own father embodied a certain kind of repression.

The ironies of *Portnoy* derive from the form of the story: the anguished plaint from Alexander, at thirty-three, to his German analyst, who views the entire narrative not as explanation but as the beginning of the process. Because of the rich amusements of the narrative, it is easy to miss the brilliance of the formulation: along with content, which could indeed prove disturbing to conservative Jews, the chronology, winding back as if endings were beginnings and forcing the grown Portnoy to grow up again in his analysis.

What is clearly an act of narcissism—Portnoy's complaint as related by Portnoy to a man who is being paid to listen to Portnoy and then, we assume, help him—is mitigated by the placement of beginning and end comments. For Portnoy, whose pleasures derive from hand, mouth, asshole, vagina, is a figure Spielvogel can mock. Whatever is momentarily pleasurable for the analysand—"acts of exhibitionism, voyeurism, fetishism, auto-eroticism and oral coitus" —is a clinical matter for his analyst, and judged by Spielvogel on very different grounds. Given the format, Portnoy cannot break free, cannot grow up sequentially. Self-mockery makes the audacious display of self bearable.

In another sense, by retelling the story to his analyst, Portnoy is reexperiencing its pleasures: a form of auto-eroticism, a jerking off of the mind, so to speak; what we also find in Heller's tale of Slocum in *Something Happened,* a novel very much in the *Portnoy* tradition. In these terms, the Jewishness of the subject matter is less significant than the delineation of a kind of general life in America which Jews experience, between endpapers of Spielvogel, the still present European conscience.

When Portnoy makes his now famous comment about putting the "Id" back in "Yid" (and later the "oi" back in Goy), he is speaking metaphorically about life in America. Ronald Nimkin, who hangs himself while his mother enjoys mah-jongg, plays according to the rules: his life in order, his chores done meticulously. But he dies foolishly, as much a sacrifice to his mother's mah-jongg as to his ignorance of an alternative life. Roth cites "Civilization and Its Discontents," Freud's cynical assessment of human capability as it runs afoul of its own ordering sense; for the young Alexander, "civilization" is centered on getting laid, being blown, having a girl on her knees before him. So much for Freud—but not permanently; for side by side with the dismissal of "civilization" is an awareness of Freud's "degradation in erotic life," the condition in which sensuality is unaccompanied by tenderness, in which sex is distinct from love. Experiences are, thus, separated in Portnoy, who suffers from every divorce of elements Freud defined. Can Alexander survive so divided, so unbalanced, so demanding of erotic release and yet so miserable when gaining it? As his namesake discovered, all conquest leads to the morbid realization that the remaining territory has been diminished. Or else, as Italo Calvino puts it: "The traveler recognizes the little that is his, discovering the much he has not had and will never have."

The question, then, is not Jewishness, but survival as a discontent in a civilization: that is, as a guilt-ridden individual in a restrictive society. The Portnoy family represents that America which restricts; the string of Gentile girls and women represent that release. Between dangles Portnoy, one hand on Alexander, the other raised at the horror, the horror. Like Kurtz, whose consciousness of horror derives from a very different experience, Portnoy has glimpsed his own version of darkness; and it is the distinctly Emersonian theme lying deep within his psyche of how to

be, what to be, how to reach it, where to seek it. "It" lies outside "Id."

The relationship Roth describes between Portnoy, the guilt-stricken New York mama's boy, and The Monkey, the Gentile sexual acrobat from a border state, comes close to defining the cultural basis of the book. For if Portnoy can approach an understanding of this troubled, destructive, yet perceptive woman who cannot spell even the simplest words, then he has glimpsed some aspect of his own nature. A rapid reading of the book will stress those aspects of the relationship that are explicitly sexual, Portnoy's romance with the pornographic fantasy of his "whacking off" dreams.

But a good part of the relationship concerns other matters, implicitly how Portnoy fails this woman, how he cannot begin to accommodate her, even when she is not hostile and self-destructive. Her sexuality is for him a source of delight, awe, astonishment; but he only dimly glimpses that sex is for her a form of death as well as release, the sole way in which she is sure of expressing herself and making herself desirable. For Portnoy, she is, most of the time, the amazing Goy, the shiksa he has always been warned against, and therefore the very mysterious core of womanhood, to be probed at one hole or another. But for The Monkey, Portnoy is salvation: that Jewish man who treats her without violence or undue contempt, her first view of another world of relationships. When they come together, then, they release entire cultural entities, aspects of our civilization that focus on sex while really being located elsewhere.

Portnoy, torn between his awe at "such abandon in a woman" and "something close to contempt," does glimpse these aspects. He perceives she needs him to stay afloat, and yet her incredibly infantile spelling—"what am I doing having an affair with a woman nearly thirty years of age who thinks you spell 'dear' with three letters!"—and her immersion in an intellectual waste land make him despondent, in fact corroborate everything his mother had warned him against. In a very touching sequence, Portnoy recites from memory Yeats's magnificent sonnet "Leda and the Swan." The poem is quite appropriate, for Portnoy senses The Monkey will grasp the sexual aspect and yet miss larger meanings; thus, all at the same time, he can display New York brains, belittle her, and gain proof of her intellectual sterility. The recital, then, has a broad application: a male ploy, really, for he knows the language of the poem will baffle her, as it is intended to. It will be a literary equivalent of his other forms of degradation of her.

Her reaction to the poem is unpredictable. She comprehends, perhaps only slightly, that the poem is about a woman victimized, Leda being penetrated against her will—or perhaps not against her will—by a primitive force that does not recognize her rights. The Monkey's perception is only dim, but she does call Portnoy a "Jewish swan" and does grab his nose, "the indifferent beak"; and with that perception of the poem on her part, Portnoy on his recognizes she is a "marvellous girl." She is, he senses, a "quick and clever little girl. Not stupid at all"—that is, not stupid for a Gentile picked up on the streets.

To identify her, or to glimpse her in this way, is for Portnoy a revelation, a form of identity, but he cannot, of course, hold to it. Culturally, they must tear each other to pieces, and he must abandon her in Greece when he goes on to Israel, his true quest, for in Israel he can couple with Jewish women, the antidote to The Monkey and her self-destructive aimlessness. He needs Jewish purpose, commitment, dedication; and his response to such qualities is, predictably, impotence on his part or rejection on the women's. His problems, from their point of view, are irrelevant to the building of a state, to a definition of healthiness, to an identification of self with purpose. He is a self-indulgent, infantile, pleasure-seeking young man who is, to them, as self-destructive as The Monkey is to him; as he abandoned her, so they abandon him. He is their "Goy"; they are "his unapproachable Jews."

The novel lies here, in these cultural involvements, where paradox lurks at every turning. Portnoy in sexual terms is a figure of fun, but in his role-playing he manifests a self of considerable complexity. Put another way, the sexual component is the shield, behind which Portnoy disguises what is truly bothering him: thus Spielvogel's contemptuous words at the end, whose portent Roth is fully aware of and which undercut all Portnoy's narcissism. The level at which Portnoy must respond is not, of course, sexual, but cultural; and the role he plays at is one involving assimilation, acculturation, or else singular identity. It is no wonder Roth returned to Kafka in full force after this novel; for once he perceived that sensuality was a shield for deeper cultural elements, he found himself on Kafka's ground, where the "I" was not the letter in Id or Yid, but in a far deeper relationship between self and society.

Polish-born Jerzy Kosinski wrote *The Painted Bird* (1965) in English; it is a remarkable and original piece of work. On a different scale, Russian-born Vladimir Nabokov wrote *Ada or Ardor: A Family Chronicle* (1969) in English; it is, also, a remarkable and original piece of work, joining with *Lolita* and *Pale Fire* as his finest work in his adopted language.[*] The Kosinski and Nabokov novels pair off from their American counterparts in the growing up subgenre because they bring a historical dimension to their protagonists. No matter that Kosinski's "boy" is uprooted and on the move, that Nabokov's Van and Ada seem fixed; Kosinski's young protagonist is mired in Polish history, a victim of it, as much the heir of the European past as Nabokov's incestuous lovers. The textured quality of life each novelist evokes results from the depths of community and society which the protagonists touch upon: the boy in fleeing, Van and Ada in their search for havens.

The "painted bird" of the title appears one-quarter through the book, in Chapter 5. The unnamed boy has wandered from one village to another, ending up with Lekh, for whom he is to set snares. Lekh sells birds for money or for staples. Because of his craftiness, he is by village standards a rich man; and he is, by way of his contact with flying objects and natural wonders, transformed by this "pagan, primitive kingdom of birds and forests where everything was infinitely abundant, wild, blooming, and royal in its perpetual decay, death, and rebirth; illicit and clashing with the human world." Lekh's overpowering love for Ludmilla is connected to this world, although the villagers call her Stupid. For Lekh, she is indistinguishable from that natural world, and we find that in their gross coupling we have Adam and Eve in Eden, a small boy observing, birds snared; the rest of Poland and war forgotten.

This episode is, also, one of the few in which the boy is not mistreated or tortured. Lekh, however, is not without his moods, and when Ludmilla does not appear, he rages at the birds. He chooses the strongest, mixes his paints, and colors the bird until "it became more dappled and vivid than a bouquet of wildflowers." A work of art, the bird is conceived as something to deceive birds in nature. Lekh and the boy take the painted bird into the forest; the boy squeezes it until it twitters and chirps so that a flock of the same species appears overhead. Then Lekh

*Although Nabokov has spoken of learning English alongside Russian, even of learning English first, it is still an adopted language, one he used for his longer fiction only after he had come to this country and established himself in the new language, at first befriended by Edmund Wilson, then on his own as a Cornell University professor.

releases the bird. It soars free and happy and plunges into the center of the flock, seeking protection of the group. But the others are not convinced the painted bird belongs, and it flies to and fro seeking recognition.

It does not come, of course. The painted bird is a pariah, marked by its difference, doomed by its own flock. One bird after another "would peel off in a fierce attack," and the painted bird drops to the ground. Lekh's interference with the natural world is part of that warped experience the boy undergoes: whatever is natural is observed as unnatural, the converse also being true. The painted bird does not gain greater beauty through coloration but reaches toward doom; beautiful forms are really a veil for a greater degree of horror. What Lekh in his rage has done to the bird parallels the boy's treatment at the hands of the peasants. His "difference" is not paint but dark looks, swarthy complexion, similarity to a Gypsy or Jew, although he is never specifically identified as Jewish.

In the episode of the painted bird, Kosinski found an image or object in the natural world which correlates to the boy's condition; and the approximation of natural object to human presence is so appropriate that the novel becomes magical at that moment. Since so much of *The Painted Bird* depends on peasant superstitions and pagan beliefs, it is fitting that the controlling image should derive from Hieronymous Bosch,* and that nature itself should be not benign but essential to man's cruelty. Bosch had discovered the visual means by which man and nature could be combined to present an image of death and apocalypse, the sense of holocaust brought about by connivance of God and man. Kosinski's vision of the Holocaust is so effective because it focuses on a single life, and that life in the context of what made the Holocaust successful: people at the edge of the event who cheered it on. Kosinski saw the end of European Jewry not in camps but as routine, in the peasants who hated the outsider, who yearned for the death of Jews and Gypsies, and whose own lives were so filled with brutality and violence they could not react to human suffering outside their own.

But the young boy (twelve by the end of the book) is not simply a "painted bird." In a sense, he sets the pattern for all Kosinski's future books by choosing (in Chapter 12) to become an agent, not an object. He recognizes dimly that chance still rules, but he also realizes that he need not be a victim of it. Each person in his cruelty is involved in a vast, cosmic cruelty, the Bosch presence, and a specific act of cruelty can be countered only by a greater one, the Spinozan equation of a more intense passion negating a weaker one. Since the boy is already considered to be in league with the devil, he decides to take on the role. With this alliance, Kosinski has discovered his métier. The boy reasons: "Peasants also accused one another of accepting help from various demons . . . If the Powers of Evil were so readily available to peasants, they probably lurked near every person, ready to pounce on any sign of encouragement, any weakness." The devil gives one a chance against Chance: "the more harm, misery, injury, and bitterness a man could inflict on those around him, the more help he could expect." The man who succumbs to "emotions of love, friendship, and compassion" immediately becomes weaker.

Here, then, is the Kosinski novelistic pattern. A protagonist wanders like Cain, internally marked, unable to throw off his bitterness and cynicism. A Byronic "wound" is apparent; and sexual variety, love, encounter sessions, great wealth, daring adventures, revenge, ingenious gadgets, none can offer relief. Each act, each sexual experience in all its variety can only postpone that awareness of pain. The Kosinski protagonist, like the young boy, must be aware of how chance will destroy him; and since he experiences in himself the artifice of chance, he can never lie easily with himself or his situation.

Kosinski has no family scenes of consequence, little settled sense of a society. Acknowledging the weight of universal history, he shrugs off personal history as part of the chance world which will and ingenuity must oppose. His episodes are almost always "steps," because he conceives of life in terms of its brevity. His protagonists are more than "driven"; they are marginal—ill, unbalanced, objects of survival, unfeeling, always on trial. The Kafka of the trial is never distant: the sense that "They are coming for me, and I must be ready," although Kosinski's protagonists refuse the willing role of Joseph K., who

*The front jacket of the book is more than half filled by "Monster with a Basket," from Bosch's *The Last Judgment*. "Monster with a Basket" is a man with a bird's face, the huge beak dominating the entire figure and giving to the crippled creature a predatory, death-filled look. The Bosch reinforces Kosinski's own view of the book as "a *vision*, not an examination, or a revisitation of childhood. . . . This vision, this search for something lost, can only be conducted in the metaphor through which the unconscious most easily manifests itself, and toward which the unconscious most naturally navigates. The locale and the setting are likewise metaphorical, for the whole journey could actually have taken place in the mind."

connives in his own destruction. Jerzy Kosinski—a name like Joseph K.—has the young boy understand the nature of German power as the result of their common decision to sell out to the devil, then impose their methods on others. "Success was a vicious circle," and the more harm they inflict, the more power they acquire for future harm.

The boy, now mute, faces the future; the period of passivity is over, and he will become an agent of destruction. His last act of giving had been his love for Ewka, who preferred a stinking goat to the boy's tender caresses. "People who had contact with me would likewise become infected with evil. They would carry on the task of destruction, and every one of their successes would earn new powers for me." This picaresque, episodic novel—an apprenticeship to life of the most desperate kind—is transformed, now, into a Nietzschean drama of good and evil. With the young boy's decision, Kosinski now moves on to metaphysical levels, into modes of ethics and morality.

His theme of chance, or history itself, is multilayered, since chance may destroy if the individual cannot find a shape for himself; and at the same time, chance is the element one must bend with, for attempts to will a "life plot" may also prove destructive. A Kosinski character must always move along chance's contours and then oppose it with an assertion of self, yet be careful not to impose on chance too much of a human pattern, else chance will revenge itself.

That cautious movement comes in *Blind Date,* whose title suggests its manifold aspects. There, Levanter is a friend of Jacques Monod, the French Nobel Prize winner and author of *Chance and Necessity.* Monod cautions Levanter that each man must admit that "blind chance and nothing else is responsible for each random event of his life," but that this is no reason for despair, for a man can still savor "each unique instance of his own existence." Distortion comes when one attempts to ignore chance by substituting man-made order, those "life plots" which inevitably prove false gods.

Kosinski moves into this area when he makes the young boy in *The Painted Bird* assert his self. The boy is not creating "life plots," nor is he trying to dictate order. He hopes to identify chance with passivity, and the boy with near-extinction. Once he wills his own life, he becomes a force close to nature. In a remarkable image, Kosinski catches him as he moves along the ice, his "comet," or torchlight, burning, a sail over his head, skates on his boots; he whirls over the ice,

the "invisible hand of the wind" beginning to push him. "The howling wind drove me along, and dark gray clouds with light edges raced along with me on my journey." Now connected to nature, the boy is indistinguishable from it. Wind, ice, cold are all woven into his balancing act of sail, skates, and comet. He has discovered fire and movement to counteract cold and wind. He becomes part of the wintry scene, not a painted bird but like a "starling soaring in the air, tossed by every flurry, following a stream, unconscious of its speed, drawn into an abandoned dance." Whereas for the local people, deep in superstition, wind means "plague, paralysis, and death," it is now his friend. They attribute wind to the work of the devil, and that, too, is compelling to the boy. For as the wind moans, he hears the devil's own voice and he knows the latter is interested in him, a young dark boy working his way across Polish villages while war rages all around. All he knows, now, is that wind will not kill him, while everything else is conspiring to do so.

This use of primitive nature is linked to nearly every episode. Fire is particularly significant, as an element that lies at the border of life and death. The "comet" was a can with holes, filled with burning matter, which one kept alight by swinging it into the wind. The comet was essential to life, and to lose it or have it stolen was catastrophic, especially since cans were very scarce. Fire is associated with witches "hanging from trees," the "Shudders of wandering souls," and "plaintive voices and strange movements of mysterious ghosts and ghouls." When the boy decides to gain a comet, he aligns himself with elements that can reinforce or destroy him: the comet is part of a chancy world.

But earth is also part of that world. Early in the book, the boy is the property of Olga, a healer, midwife, and general practitioner in the use of primitive methods of cure. When the boy has a burning fever, she buries him to his head in a field, on the theory that the earth will draw out his heat and cool him. "Thus planted in the cold earth, my body cooled completely in a few moments, like the root of a wilting weed. I lost all awareness. Like an abandoned head of cabbage, I became part of the great field." The boy becomes a plant straining toward the sun; his head, solely exposed, begins to pick up a life of its own "until it finally struck the disk of the sun which had graciously warmed it during the day." But Olga had not figured on ravens, which pick at the boy's head, while he screams helplessly; unless rescued, he will be picked to death. When Olga comes, his scalp is lacerated, but his fever is gone. Earth is life, barely.

The great success of *The Painted Bird* derives from this fusion of elements and people. The peasants are never distant from the world of spirits, from those primitive beliefs which are a flowing part of their daily experience. The boy cannot be superior to what the peasants do, nor can he attempt to transcend them with knowledge of some other existence. He can deal with them only by experiencing their world. That wedding of will, chance, superstition, pagan belief gives the book a cohesion which makes it work at every level Kosinski attempts: as witness to the Holocaust, as witness to a young boy's initiation into an almost unbearable journey, as analyst of a particular people in a time and place, as witness to terrible events which take on a rhythm and life of their own, and finally, as witness to an apocalyptic vision.

Rats, scooped-out eyes, a dying horse, injured Jews on railroad tracks—all these are fused. Kosinski serves as witness so effectively because he animates the very objects that turn people into things. He does not need Germans for his Holocaust; nor does he need camps. The peasants on one side, trains with doomed passengers rushing to their deaths on the other, the boy in the exact center of it all—these three elements serve as his version of the Holocaust. When the boy reaches out to achieve some balance, by joining himself to evil, he is not only surviving; he is wedding himself to the way the world works when subject and object are fused.

The sole way the young boy can feel alive is by approaching ever closer to death. Late in the novel, when he is in the center for lost children, he links up with a boy called the Silent One, who can speak although no one has heard his voice. The narrator is himself mute, his statement not words but a form of flirtation with death, lying flat out on the railway bed while a long train passes over his face and body. He says that as the carriages roared over him, "nothing mattered except the simple fact of being alive." This experience of aliveness and freedom from injury gave him sufficient energy to deal with all other terrors; in contrast, *they* seemed pitiful. But he decides to use the feeling for more than that, as a stored-up memory he can bring out whenever he feels threatened. By daring death, he can face life; the pattern is set. This young boy is not only speaking for himself; he is speaking for all Kosinski protagonists. To live, they must live at the edge.

It is to Kosinski's credit that even when his work began to repeat itself after *Steps,* he did not fall into simplistic existential patterns, recognizing that that form of fiction had run its course. His marginal figures do not despair or sink for any length of time. The author denies them nothing—as if he had a bottomless bag of tricks or drugs—and melancholy, even temporary, is not for him a viable mode either in life or in fiction. Kosinski works with infinite care to prepare modes which will ward off depression before it gathers strength. These modes may be sexual, or objects of beauty, or, simply, activities—skiing, riding (as in *Passion Play*), traveling, luxuriating in sumptuous quarters.

By supporting his protagonists with life's gadgetry, Kosinski prevents them from thinking. There is, in actuality, very little thought, although his novels have an intellectual cast. Ideas are subsumed to action and narrative drive. The pattern established by the young boy in *The Painted Bird* remains in force: a wandering protagonist, armored against attack, always on the defense, ready to strike back, marginal to all, lacking in compassion or pity except under extraordinary circumstances, sadistic and cruel as needed, never unprepared. The covenant with himself made by the young boy was one Kosinski held to: passivity is a surrender to chance, whereas "life plots" are too extreme or positive to accommodate chance. One must fall into the seams.

The novel is an unfolding of a sensibility, rather than a shaped narrative. Kosinski's point, repeatedly, is that all elements, persecuted and persecutor (Germans, Polish), are involved together in some wasting drama of kill and be killed. At the midpoint, Chapter 9, the boy sees his first "different train," this one carrying living people to their death in the extermination camps. By now, the peasants were aware that Jews and Gypsies inside were doomed; that at the camp they would be stripped of their hair and gold teeth and sent to the ovens. The peasants feel it is all just punishment for the Jews' having crucified Christ; that God was using the Germans as an agent of punishment. The German camps are a windfall for the peasants, who pick along the embankment for belongings, sometimes finding a dying Jew, but almost always calendars, family albums, personal documents, old passports, diaries. Since the peasants could not read, photographs were the most desirable. The peasants use the photos as wall displays: "In some houses there was a picture of Our Lady on the wall, of Christ on another, a crucifix on the third, and pictures of numerous Jews on the fourth." They would trade the photos as cards, or use pictures of pretty girls in masturbatory fantasies.

What is so compelling about this chapter is that

Kosinski has blended life and death inextricably. The life after death afforded the Jews is their image in the hands of the peasants; ironically, everything that was dear to them in life and family is reified and blasphemed. They become the possession of the peasants, and even in death they cannot rest in peace. The use of one's most personal items after death destroys their sanctity, but such usage, in this curious dance of death, also ensures that one is not forgotten, no matter how abysmal the perpetuation. The peasants are, incongruously, receivers of the Jewish legacy; the Germans, agents of the gift.

Among the items that drop along the railroad embankment is a young Jewish girl, only bruised and with a sprained shoulder, age undetermined. She is found by a man named Rainbow, who claims her as his. When he rapes her that night, the two become locked together, Rainbow unable to extricate himself, the girl unable to expel him. It is a condition not unusual with animals, and Kosinski uses it here as a natural event, as well as for its symbolic significance. They are literally locked in, the man's penis consumed by her body, while she perpetuates his outrage to her virginal condition. If the Polish peasant is the rapist, the Jewish girl gains her revenge: both will be destroyed. Rainbow begins to beat the girl, but to no avail. The lock continues, until an old woman comes and cuts the girl away from around Rainbow, freeing him and killing her. Afterward, Rainbow speaks of having been "sucked in" by the Jewess. The "locking" simply reinforces everything the peasants believed about Jews, their desire to destroy the Gentile and the Christ in him even at the expense of their own life.

From this episode, which makes the young boy feel the "icy hand" of death reaching toward him, Kosinski moves to his protagonist's first sight of the German conqueror, a magnificently costumed SS officer. The boy is astonished by the striking uniform, the glittering cap, with its death's head and crossbones, the red badge with the swastika at the sleeve. This is surely the conqueror, a figure from beyond the boy's imagination. This is the man who will judge whether the boy lives or dies, a magnificent image of the god judging the nondescript, puny, emaciated boy. The latter worships the power implicit here: "I placed infinite confidence in the decision of the man facing me. I knew that he possessed powers unattainable for ordinary people." We enter into the drama between master and slave; that the boy is permitted to live is happenstance. The real drama is in the boy's turning himself into an object so that he can be judged; he so loses all sense of himself that he exists only in the other's eyes.

Kosinski locates here the most terrible crime of all, one that transcends beating, torture, even death. It is the ultimate in passivity, involving the boy's negation of himself because he has ceased to function as a subject, in-himself. He becomes of-himself, justifiable only when another judges him, chance having dissolved will. The young boy, transfixed by the splendor of the SS officer, has not yet learned how to fashion the moment, so that he is precariously poised between chance and "life plots."

Some of the novel's great driving force is dissipated when the boy's parents finally reclaim him; but then he foresees this: "rejoining my parents meant the end of all my dreams of becoming a great inventor of fuses for changing people's color, of working in the land of Gavrila and Mitka [Soviet army officers who save him]." The boy had become completely attuned to the world of the wild, to existence lived so close to extinction that it is sparked with the embers of the train passing over his head as he lies on the tracks. Being reclaimed means he will be domesticated, forced to live like other men. He identifies with Huck Finn: "The world was becoming cramped like the attic of a peasant's shed. At all times a man risked falling into the snares of those who hated and wanted to persecute him, or into the arms of those who loved and wished to protect him." The boy thinks of being a "painted bird, which some unknown force was pulling toward his kind." He also thinks of a captured hare which, offered its freedom after a long struggle to escape, retreats from the wild to the security of the cage. "He now carried the cage in himself; it bound his brain and heart and paralyzed his muscles." While once freedom had seemed all, now it is supererogatory, like the "fragrance evaporating from crushed, dried clover."

The winding down of the novel's energies, then, is accompanied by the winding down of the boy's expectations. He is twelve, and ready for a "normal" adolescence. *His* growing up is over, and what he can now expect is dull respectability, routine patterns. He is sent away into the mountains, and once reassociated with the wilds, the swirls of snow, the peaks and ridges, he almost dies in the cold, a recurring situation in Kosinski's fiction. Saved, he regains his voice while in the hospital; words are his. His brush with death in natural surroundings has enabled him to regain something once lost under somewhat similar conditions. He is now whole, ready for that combination James Bond–Don Quixote quest which will characterize the young boy grown up into Tarden, Levanter, Whelan, Fabian.

> Ada, spurning decorum, was hurrying toward him [Van, after several years]. Her solitary and precipitate advance consumed in reverse all the years of their separation as she changed from a dark-glittering stranger with the high hair-do in fashion to the pale-armed girl in black who had always belonged to him.

Ada is as much a memory as an experience, as much an artifact of the past as a sensation. She comes forward, from history, their history, as both the woman she has grown into and the girl she was: Van first possessed her when she was twelve and he fourteen. That passage, of the foreshortening of past and present (Nabokov dismisses the future as a lost cause), is only one of the several dualisms that comprise the novel. For dualism is the thing, as Nabokov himself sensed; in the end, there are really only two.

That past and present interplay is a temporal dimension, but it is, as Nabokov explains in the final chapters, a struggle against spatiality. Nabokov chose to tread Proustian ground while fighting Proust; to limn the European experience at the expense of the American; to bring back his Lolita in the form of an unshaped Ada, combine her Russian background with the American sensationalism of Lolita; to discover in Ivan Deen (Van Deen, son of Demon Deen, divine and demonic) that last remnant of a final family. *Ada* (1969) is a chronicle of growing up in a historical period, beginning with the Franco-Prussian War, continuing in the halcyon years prior to the First War, ending with the aging of individual and world in the postwar years. Everything changes, everyone ages. It is a novel of profound nostalgia, and one reason the prose is so affected is that Nabokov scorned sentimentality. Only by turning it into mandarin prose could he write such a nostalgic work.

Ada is his *Tempest,* Nabokov and Ariel with their wands, their pronouncements, their prose styles. Ada is his Miranda, Ivan his representative of the "brave new world"; together they are a family growing up, brother and sister, lover and mistress, man and wife. The hermetic quality of the chronicle is clear: a self-enclosed, incestuous Europe is impervious to change, while Europe beyond, in history, exhausts itself in destruction.

The novel is part of a diary or memoir kept by Van, commented on by Ada in marginal notes, and authorized, finally, by some presence beyond Van called the Editor (Ronald Oranger). This hovering consciousness, a Jamesian presence of sorts, speaks of returning us to the "novelistic structure"; or else moving us beyond the internal drama with commentary: "Therefore we find ourselves more comfortably sitting within Van while his Ada sits within Lucetta [Ada's younger half sister], and both sit within Van (and all three in me, adds Ada)." The novel's self-consciousness here meets with the novel's structure, as it were asymptotically, while Ada herself hovers ready with comments and asides. "Adds Ada," says Nabokov about a character who seems indifferent to her book.*

Language entwines Ada. Numerous references to and images of snakes, flowers, flora, and fauna suggest a pastoral setting in which Ada (something of a "natural scientist") is enclosed. She is almost always positioned in backgrounds or near foregrounds, either too far for us to see her or too close for us to focus upon her. A mirrored image, she is part of the past, rarely the present: the first part of the alphabet, which dims as we move along the letters. We meet her when she is twelve, a Lolita† in her seductive attractions to Van, at fourteen. Nabokov comments upon their love in language of such artificiality that, like the stream of Joyce or the interior monologue of Woolf, it establishes its own terms, the Nabokovian manner, and clearly a response to colloquial American languages of the 1960s.

> In this our dry report on Van Veen's early, too early love, for Ada Veen, there is neither reason, nor room for metaphysical digression. Yet, let it be observed (just while the lucifers fly and throb, and an owl hoots—also most rhythmically—in the nearby park) that Van, who at the time had still not really tasted the Terror of Terra—vaguely attributing it, when analyzing his dear unforgettable Aqua's torments, to pernicious fads and popular fantasies—even then, at fourteen, recognized that the old myths, which willed into helpful being a whirl of worlds (no matter how silly and mystical) and situated them within the gray matter of the star-suffused heavens, contained, perhaps, a glowworm of strange truth.

---

*Hovering over all is, of course, *Tristram Shandy,* that self-conscious mockery of eighteenth-century rationalism.

†As part of the nostalgia, Nabokov mentions a "lolita," "dubbed after the little Andalusian gipsy of that name in Osberg's novel," and referring to a long and ample black skirt. Osberg is Borges, his *La Gitanilla* modeled on *Lolita. Pale Fire,* John Shade, and references to Nabokov's other works run through the text, as if *Ada* in its roll calls and repetitions were an epic or saga of growing up.

The "Terror of Terra" adds to the doubling, punning voice; for Terra is the unmentionable, Russia, itself played off against the United States: the cold war embodied in Nabokov's prose war between Americanese and his own artificial invention, that mix of Russian and French which intermingles with English words, themselves given Latinized form.

The mixing of languages, as well as the exotic English, points toward parody of a family history; but it also adds a dimension to parody, for Nabokov creates an alternative family chronicle, the way Sterne did in *Tristram Shandy*. Nabokov's method is to turn the chronicle into a veritable hothouse: thus, the innumerable vegetative references, the use of green myths and legends, the "ardor" of *Ada*. This is the hidden or disguised part of the chronicle, the incestuous playoff that occurs between "cousins" really siblings. We suspect parody because of the outrageousness of the sexual activity: Van and Ada already understand they are siblings, even while Demon frantically tries to inform them. As incestuous siblings, they enclose each other as Egyptian princes and princesses did, the Isis and Osiris of nineteenth-century family life.

The chief quality of *Ada,* unlike many of its American counterparts, is its seamlessness, achieved through language working self-consciously and the novel as a memoir of growing up shaped by several hands. Since the subject is a family, an outmoded form, we have a delving into the past, which gives Nabokov the opportunity to explore Proustian memory and durational time, a subject he takes up theoretically near the end of the novel. *Ada* comes closer to autobiography than the much "protected" *Speak, Memory,* for it catches the felt quality of memory and past in images that are more liberating than those of the purported autobiography. Nabokov was less armored in the novel, which was a fiction, than in his own memoir, where he feared openness.

The long section on time, an unusual piece of theorizing in Nabokov, suggests how at the end of his career he tried to position himself beside Mann and Proust. With time, he insisted on Europe, not America. For Nabokov, less philosophical than Mann, less able to work in time aesthetically than Proust, the concept of time, which forms Part IV of the novel, is Van's valedictory to the past. Growth of a sort has been achieved. Van makes clear time is for him a sensual delight, whereas space, while still lovely, has something of the vulgar in it. "I wish to caress Time. . . . one can be an amateur of Time, an epicure of duration. . . . I delight sensually in Time, in its stuff

and spread, in the fall of its folds, in the very impalpability of its grayish gauze, in the coolness of its continuum." Time has an existence beyond space, and the latter is, for Van, merely a means by which he can better measure the former.

To understand the concept of time, Van tries to free it of content, so that he gains access to it as pure, perceptual, tangible; time that is contextless: "this is *my* time and theme. All the rest is numerical symbol or some aspect of Space." As an impostor, space is anathema to Nabokov because of its centrality in relativist literature: that hated concept of space/time, almost as detestable as "Sig" 's nonsense in Vienna. In relativist theory, space is a parasite, artificial; Van even sees it as a waste product of time, or its corpse. "Space . . . itself is incomputable." Time, on the contrary, affords "the utmost purity of consciousness to be properly apprehended"; it is "the most rational element of life, and my reason feels insulted by those flights of Technology Fiction."

Van-Nabokov is doing more than justifying a family chronicle. At stake is the entire European tradition, with those heavy literary references to Tolstoy *(Ada* can be read as a parodic gloss on *Anna Karenina),* Chateaubriand, Flaubert, Byron (the incest theme), Baudelaire, and numerous others. By concentrating on time, Nabokov has surrendered the spatial theme to American fiction; by denying space, he has returned to the European tradition, negating in particular the American sixties, with their spatial turbulence, their stress on change, the future. Everything about *Ada* responds to the 1960s; although Nabokov was living outside America (in Montreux, an "exile" like Mann and Hesse), his entire set of mind now turned against the American experience, American growing up.*

Discriminating measurement is necessary since present is always slipping off into past. Time *is* time passing, present as becoming past, present as intervals which slip by before we experience them. Everything swings in and out of focus in past even as we consider it present. Present is specious, Now a falsification even as we grasp at it.

---

*Toward the end of the 1970s, at least three American novelists, perhaps impelled by the example of *Ada,* or by Nabokov and Borges more generally, have attempted to move beyond space into some sense of Nabokovian time, all in fictions relating to growing up. I have in mind Styron, in *Sophie's Choice,* Roth, in *The Ghost Writer,* and Barth, in *Letters.* All three have made *their* past an essential element in the present, and have used their own careers, knowledge of which is important for the reader, as ways of supporting present literary activities.

This nowness is the only reality we know; it follows the colored nothingness of the no-longer and precedes the absolute nothingness of the future. Thus, in a quite literal sense, we may say that conscious human life lasts always only one moment, for at any moment of deliberate attention to our own flow of consciousness we cannot know if that moment will be followed by another.

This almost desperate attempt to grasp a tradition, a life, a sequence of moments—a campaign to deny American realities—forms itself in Nabokov's mind as a merging of past and present. "Our modest Present is, then, the time span that one is directly and actually aware of, with the lingering freshness of the Past still perceived as part of the nowness." That *true* Present" is outside enjoyment; it is an instant of "zero duration," represented "by a rich smudge." Nabokov's retreat from American optimism forms itself as "continuous becoming," as against American "being."

In his contemptuous dismissal of the future, Nabokov is at his most sardonic toward the America he had reflected in *Lolita,* an America which in the next decade became even more open, freer, less dependent on the past. "The future [not capitalized like Past and Present] is but a quack at the court of Chronos. Thinkers, social thinkers, feel the Present as pointing beyond itself toward a not yet realized 'future'—but that is topical utopia, progressive politics." The "veily substance" of time must be separated from "Siamese Space" and the "false future," both of which are inventions, Van implies, of a new world philosophy which denies the very "texture of time." At ninety-seven, Van has almost completed the century that began to change so rapidly in the year of his birth, 1870; that Nabokovian figure or persona has become a perpetual *puer,* denied the ravages of time by way of his treatise on Time. The reach toward Proust is obvious; and Nabokov's attempt demonstrates not a lesser effort but the greatness of the greater.

Nabokov would have entered the thickets of time and space only if he had felt the novel was reaching exhaustion; if, like Barth, Borges, and others, he had sensed that illusions about time were joining deceptions about reality to create a context alien for the novel. *Ada* is part of that ultimate parodic form which the novel was becoming in order to survive its purported demise. *Ada,* then, is an authorial swan song not only to an age, a time, even a place, but to something broader—the very form, language, and structure by which we have captured those elements of the past. A positive fiction in its felt sense, *Ada* is also a sense of an ending, the apocalypse suggested by Ada's resemblance to Anna Karenina, both novels caught by passions embodying both life and death.

The disquisition on time and space cannot be separated from another motif crucial to the novel's ideological framework: that temporal and spatial struggle implied by Antiterra and Terra, mythical kingdoms with vague resemblances, respectively, to America and the Soviet Union. Nabokov's division of the world into two forces recalls Barth's use of competing East and West Campus computers in *Giles,* with *their* broad relationship to cold warriors. Yet Antiterra and Terra should not be narrowed down to an ideological struggle, for Nabokov's purpose is considerably broader: a spatial and a temporal metaphor; for just as each place denotes a different spatial mode, so each maintains a different time scheme.

Use of mythical places is not new with Nabokov: Zembla in *Pale Fire,* Padukrad in *Bend Sinister,* America in *Lolita,* several others. Antiterra (antiterror) is the vague America where the action is located; it is also known as Demonia, a play on Demon Veen's nickname, counteracting any suggestions of divinity. Antiterra, although not Russia, is not divine, it is demonic; while Terra (Russia) hardly exists, or if so, only as a mental model of what Terra or terror can be. Early in his career as writer and philosopher, in 1891, Van writes *Letters from Terra,* but it is so neglected that when it is made into a film in 1940, only six copies remain. As a film, *Letters* indicates a fifty-year difference between Terra time (later) and Antiterra time (past). The film chronicles a kind of history which moves in and out of the history we know, using some dates, events, personages, distorting others, turning Hitler into Athauf Hundler, also known as Mittler, from "to mittle, 'mutilate.' "

What is significant is the value Nabokov places on such a work within the context of opposing elements in the larger novel. For *Letters from Terra,* the film of which Ada and Van see eleven times in seven different languages, points up near Van's death the problematical nature of that mythical land, with its own time and history; its contiguous hold on Antiterra, where Van and Ada live. The presence of Terra is so significant for Nabokov here and, however disguised, elsewhere because it gives him a fictional world he can oppose to the real one. That fictional world will exist regardless of what occurs in Antiterra. It is not simply the expatriate's or exile's movable feast; it is the nature of creativity itself, an ever shifting metaphor for the imagination and for the development of an artwork. Nabokov has invented a land, given it properties, reified it with historical events, and then cast it adrift, a kind of "painted bird," all as a means of measurement of or balance with the "other world," in which he must live.

Terra, then, exists as an act of imagination, a mental journey. It is not associated with those vague lands from utopian or science fiction materials, although it does partake of them. Far more than they, it influences "our land," Antiterra; that is, Terra's existence is important not only for itself but for what it means to Antiterra. Nabokov always works on reversals, dualisms. Van's favorite exercise, walking on his hands, becomes that physical reversal which characterizes the entire novel. Here we discover the mode: an unnatural effort to maintain narrative pace and speed, with reversal as its locus of interest.

Antiterra is composed of a vast province of Americans and Russians, comprising most of present-day America from the Arctic Circle to the Mexican border. The area is "Amerussia," with parts heavily Russian, others French, Bavarian, etc., all governed by Abraham Milton—the combined Jewish and Christian president, the Great Father of "Paradise Lost," "Zion Regained." The Terra gloss on this is the land mass split between Americans and Russians, the traditional division between the great powers. Antiterra enjoys a relaxed political atmosphere, except for the threat of Tartary, described as an "independent inferno" spread from "Kurland to the Kuriles," or from the Baltic to the Pacific. Tartary lies dormant, like the dragon of medieval tales, and it is duplicated to some extent in the names of our characters: Demon Deen; Ada, which suggests inferno in Russian; Aqua and Marina, twin sisters, one mad, one sane; in Van himself, with his reversal of walking, so that all forms of reality are twisted.

Reversal within opposing elements provides a reality which can be expanded infinitely within those terms. Nabokov has his metaphor for art, and *Ada* can be read as his Byzantium, Yeats's "place" of opposing elements, so transformed that its artifacts signify as acts of imagination. Nabokov has, in effect, created that reality and reflection as the sole place worthy of his inhabitancy. The French, Russian, and American cultural strains stretch over the world and even into imaginary worlds; so that Terra and Tartary as well as Antiterra contain elements that shaped the author. The solipsism of the 1960s, while mocked by Nabokov as culturally thin, even parched, is apotheosized in his vision of worlds within worlds, all of

them Nabokovian: like Barth in *Giles,* pleading for independent assessments while reflecting himself in all worlds—computer, campus, lenses. Rather than disappearing within the folds of historical eras, or into literary works mocked and exposed, or into spatial worlds stretching from sea to ocean, Nabokov has turned them all to his shape. The sixties could not have had a better representative.

Some critics have felt Nabokov mocked previous fiction—even writers like Flaubert and Chateaubriand, whom he admired—so that he could carry it forward in new means of expression. More probably, all fiction, as all ideas, is the source of parody so that Nabokov can suggest his own superiority. His well-advertised antagonism to Dostoyevsky is not literary, or even political, so much as personal; like Conrad, he felt the presence of a writer whose power he could not argue away and so he ridiculed him as bestial, as reflecting the worst of Russia. Only Chekhov can be praised, and even here Nabokov turns a Chekhovian scene or two into parody, such as using a motorcar for escape from a typical late-nineteenth-century duel in the Russian fashion.

Yet behind the inventiveness, the glossy surfaces, the reverberating wit and witticisms, the brilliant combinations of language and languages, the introduction of Russian and French as supplemental voices, the rarefied sensibility working on every page, the parodic sense seeping into crevices and seams, the seamlessness itself of the various levels of narrative, of Terra and Antiterra, of character permutations—behind all this, we are conscious of exhaustion and enervation. The book is a retrospective, Nabokov and Van turning back for memories—more tellingly than in *Speak, Memory*—as the sole parts of existence. Implicit in this, and in Van's comments in *Texture of Time,* is the sense that the genre has no more to yield. "I wish to caress Time," Van writes; and the time he caresses is "what was." What Nabokov lacks is a literary consciousness of the present which would lead all his devices to comprehension, not recapitulation. Too much is earned by rejection. His "summing up" does not add, but encapsulates himself: circuitry of self is overwhelming.

We are in the presence of such an overpowering presence that all of life, including time (his memories) and space (which he personally subsumes under time), exists only as Nabokovian, the self in perpetual incestuous romance with itself: a self that, despite its sophistication, has not grown up. The range of *Ada* lies here, but also the excesses. Nabokov needed to make time stand still, so that, ageless, he could constantly recreate himself. "I shall now proceed to consider the Past as an accumulation of sensa, not as the dissolution of Time implied by immemorial metaphors picturing transition," Van writes. Those "sensa" are all self, manifestations of personal needs and acquisitions, with little regard for any beyond. The incest motif fits perfectly,* of course, closing out the self in love with self: brother and sister together, children of a man committing adultery with his brother's wife, while he is married to her sister. Permutations and combinations are endless. There is a surfeit of self, of ego, of distortions of all knowledge (physical as well as literary) to support the individual's perception of himself. Nabokov provides few resonances beyond. The parodic element is not so much other-directed as reinforcement for his own perceptions. The excesses of the 1960s are mocked, but Nabokov fails to include himself. He fits.

The plasticity of growing up fiction is illustrated in the following selections. That the subgenre serves so many different kinds—and levels—of talent helps to illuminate its power. Realism, fabulism, apocalyptic visions, fantasies, ethnic earnestness—all can fit themselves into the mode. What better place to begin than with Delmore Schwartz's short story "In Dreams Begin Responsibilities," from 1935, a work which still sings and which foreshadows an entire genre, that of self-conscious fiction: fiction about the

---

*We can locate the contemporary chic of incest with *Lolita* in the mid-fifties: Humbert Humbert's relationship with Lolita being of an extended family type, stepfather and stepdaughter. In *Giles Goat-Boy,* Giles tries to mount his mother; and the inner scenario is parody of Oedipus. Further, sexual play among the goats is between siblings. The celebration of incest in *Ada,* however, is unique. Although her name suggests hell (Russian *ad* is hell, and *ada* in various combinations means torment), incest is pleasurable, guiltless, a fine replacement for masturbation. As Demon Veen gets older, he toys with Spanish girls "who were getting more and more youthful every year until by the end of the century, when he was sixty, with hair dyed a midnight blue, his flame had become a difficult nymphet of ten." The relationships are disguised father-daughter incest. We find further examples of incest in *The Sot-Weed Factor,* with the two Cookes, and *Lie Down in Darkness,* with father-daughter, among many others of this type.

The increased interest in the theme seems superficially connected to greater openness of sexual experience, to a testing of taboos; but I think incest motifs are more closely connected to our sense that personal needs can preempt everything. Then incest is not attached so much to sex as to power, self, individual authority.

self creating a fiction. With few exceptions, growing up novels and stories demonstrate a self in the process of being created, then dissolved as it rubs against a society or community, then redesigned to exhibit its flexibility or else withdrawn into areas of madness and/or death. The journey of the self in such fictions is no less than the journey of the American, writ here as elsewhere: that lonely self perched on some frontier of experience, venturing out into unknowns, caught by space, enticed to escape, restrained by mortal limitations, and yet ever straining to accomplish something beyond. It is, like the country it reflects, a quest both grand and futile.

If life is a film played backward, then the chief conceit is one of screening, the chief movement one of reeling. That narrator, young Delmore, is reeling from the marriage of his parents, one that, as the reel plays backward, he wants to stop. But he can only prevent it, or try to, in the film playing in his own mind—the film, the reel, the past, all acts of imagination. As Schwartz writes: "I feel as if I were in a motion picture theatre, the long arm of light crossing the darkness and spinning my eyes fixed on the screen." The film is, of course, a silent one, for the year Schwartz reels back to is 1909, when his father-to-be courted his mother-to-be, and their collective doom was almost upon them.

Beyond the conceit of the movie is the metaphor of life as a theater. The narrator, seated in the dark, an old lady next to him, is warned by the usher to be silent, etc. His life is staged, and his role, as he reels it back, is yet to be played. The brilliance of the formulation comes here: in the presence of a physical being, caught in the nightmare of his own forthcoming life, trying to comprehend a role that has not yet been played out. Not unusually, Nabokov selected "In Dreams" as one of the half-dozen American stories that impressed him.

By turning all into theater and role-playing on a reel reflected on a screen, Schwartz has made the story itself a commentary on the story. He has turned the actual events of his mother's courtship by his father, whatever those details really were, into a reflection caught on film so that it can be played back. The actual events, as those in some Borges fiction, may or may not have occurred; but their factuality is secondary to their reproduction. The reproduction is what gives them life.

In that prelife, opposites characterize his parents. His father is strong, his mother frail; his father seeks rougher entertainment, his mother a finer sort; his mother rides a white horse on the merry-go-round, his father a black one; his mother gains two rings, his father ten; they even disagree about a fortuneteller, and his father walks away, while his mother stays. And the boy in the audience of his fantasy film shouts that they do not know what they are doing, until his screams bring the usher and he is taken away.

Controlling all, in the film of the preparental walk along the boardwalk at Coney Island, is the image of the ocean, the waves "tugging strength from far back." Then: "The moment before they somersault, the moment when they arch their backs so beautifully, showing green and white veins amid the black, that moment is intolerable. They finally crack, dashing fiercely upon the sand, actually driving, full force downward, against the sand, bouncing upward and forward." The waves are the driving force that hurries all things toward some final end: that crashing and smashing power, that rush of water caught between "terrible sun" and "fatal, merciless, passionate ocean."

Although Schwartz's story is not simplistically Jewish, it does have within it a sense of Kafkan doom or fate: life unreeled in a movie theater. That fated quality reappears in several types of growing up fiction which are distinctly ethnic in nature; and in fact, the presence of these books suggests that forms of realism and naturalism, although in themselves no longer a major force in postwar fiction, still have vitality when connected to ethnic or racial themes.

Richard Wright's *Black Boy* (1937–45), which hovers on the margins between fiction and nonfiction, contains a typically naturalistic motif, that of food, hunger, emptiness. As in *The Grapes of Wrath,* it is a motif that fits the Depression more than the postwar era, but Wright gives it dimensionality. Hunger for food becomes, in the 1950s and 1960s, hunger for freedom and liberation: a naturalistic motif becomes a general cry of pain. Further, Wright relies on a typically American theme, that of the Edenic fantasy. The industrial North, for the hungry Southern black, becomes Eden, in that reversal of patterns that resulted from a slave culture. "I dreamed of going north and writing books, novels. The North symbolized to me all that I had not felt and seen; it had no relation whatever to what actually existed. Yet, by imagining a place where everything was possible, I kept hope alive in me." The North is Edenic in its offering of freedom; the South, with its rural beauty, is a dispossessed Garden, ultimately a trap. This theme plays throughout the book and becomes an archetypal experience for generations of black novelists after Wright.

SOME VERSIONS OF WRIGHT

In *If He Hollers Let Him Go* (1945), Chester Himes's young man, Robert Jones, has some of the anger associated with Bigger Thomas. Yet inspired though he was by the Wright novel, Himes tried to keep his subject and protagonist within a black mainstream. Despite murderous impulses, Jones resists acts that led Bigger to self-destruction. First, as a wartime worker in a shipyard with a draft deferment, Jones moves in a middle-class life style. Second, he has visions of growing into another life, of upward mobility, which he can achieve if he turns the other cheek when called "nigger" or suffers comparable indignities. Third, he has learned to control his anger at small insults, flaring only when the provocation accumulates.

Himes suggests that the "Bigger Thomas syndrome" exists in every black man despite his desire for stability and upward mobility. Jones functions as a supervisor, as an intermediary between blacks and whites in a potentially inflammatory situation, when he spots a flashy, whory-looking white Texas girl, Madge Perkins, who refuses to work with "niggers." His hatred of her hooks him, and he pursues her even as he is moving closer to marriage with Alice, a young black social worker, the daughter of a physician. The pursuit of Perkins, whom he wishes to humiliate at the same time he wishes to bed her, is the undoing of Jones. They become closed into a room at the shipyard, and she screams "rape." Herein lies the difficulty of the novel.

Writing in the 1940s, during wartime, Himes turns job, social status, promotional opportunities—all those aspects of black growing up—into sexual terms. The white man on the job humiliates the black because he fears his sexuality; and the white woman plays the tease with the black, desiring him and then retreating, to shrieks of rape, when he responds. While the general situation is true, documented innumerable times, fictionally the triangle of white man, black man, and white woman leads always to the same outcome. The black is victimized—Jones loses his deferment and is forced to enter the army—and the black woman is left holding the shreds. She, in particular, is victimized, since she lives outside the struggle proper and must stand and wait. If she is not loyal, she is a whore; if loyal, she becomes a cipher,

her individuality wiped out. Himes appears unaware of this dimension, although Wright was not.

A more conscious writer could have confronted these social contradictions as the very core of black existence. Jones is a battleground between self—he does not want blackness to define his total life—and a society that insists blackness is all, that no individual black can exist in a white society. This is a powerful theme, but after touching upon it, Himes slides away. Jones becomes defined by stereotypical circumstances, whereas he has insisted on self, will. In that potential, in that irresolvable conflict between needs of self and complex social pressures to fit a black stereotype, the focus of the novel lies.

William Demby's *Beetlecreek* (1950; reissued in 1967) works the "Bigger Thomas syndrome" with real originality. It is a novel that deserves more recognition. As its name implies, Beetlecreek is a Kafkaesque setting, a mined-out West Virginia town; enervated, a backwater, forgotten, where blacks and whites live uneasily, together in their doom but otherwise segregated. The novel has a triangular shape: Bill Trapp, a white recluse who decides to emerge from his shell; Johnny Johnson, an outsider from Pittsburgh, a young black boy who drifts psychologically until Trapp befriends him; and David Diggs, with whom Johnny lives, a black man who once wanted to be an artist and an intellectual, but found himself trapped by early marriage.

Under peer pressure of a gang of black youths, Johnny is forced to abjure Trapp, and in fact, to fire his place and, presumably, kill him. Diggs is so caught up in his misery that he decides to leave town with Edith, a former girl friend; and Diggs's wife is involved in a church festival, whose chief aim is to raise money. Every value is traduced: Johnny betrays Trapp's trust in him; Diggs flees town hoping for a brief glimpse of Eden; and Trapp's attempts to come closer to the black townspeople are mocked. The church is a force for money-making, and the town is itself described as a coffin, a mined-out, exhausted vein. Everyone's life is characterized by emptiness and boredom. In the townspeople's focus on Trapp, we recall Faulkner's "Dry September," when weather, dust, tedium combine to create a mob spirit and a Negro lynching.

Here, it is blacks who create the atmosphere in which the mob, a group of boys called "Nightriders," initiates Johnny by making him put the torch to Trapp's place. In what was apparently an earlier version of this novel, a story written for the *Fisk Herald* and called "Saint Joey," a white gang led by a religious fanatic murders an old hermit who has, in their eyes, violated the customs of the town. In his revision, Demby created a far more compelling situation, in which he, a black writer, makes his victim white, violated by a black gang who wear sheets and ride at night, a black Ku Klux Klan. Yet part of Demby's achievement is that his sympathies move along everyone's problems—Trapp's, Diggs's, Johnny's. They are all fighting forms of death. Trapp, Demby's Bigger, must be victimized, entrapped, because he seeks to break from the coffin to test out the air.

Problems accrue when Demby attempts to raise the motif of death into a pervasive one of evil. A dead pigeon, birds as victims, junk materials, mirrors, a swaying bridge: these are his images, and they are too slack and familiar as literary devices for the needed intensity. Yet racial feeling is presented in quite an original way. For Demby does not present the usual white anomosity toward blacks, but an uneasy truce between the races which a white man exacerbates when he tries to bridge the gap. By expressing antagonism toward the white man, Trapp, the town blacks reveal their own victimization, for they cannot perceive Trapp is different, does mean well, and is trying to create a situation based on love and trust. They miss this and, in fact, attribute his efforts to the devil's work; by so doing, they entrap themselves in racial conflict, which means further forms of dying.

Willard Motley's *Knock on Any Door,* published in 1947, is a novel that looks back. It is realistic, naturalistic, poetic, hard-boiled, but soft as mush in the inside, where it counts. It is in the Farrell, Algren, Chicago tradition, but pays strong debts to *Native Son,* published seven years earlier. Motley, a black writer, has repeated the environmental argument of Bigger Thomas's lawyer, to defend not a black man but an Italian, Nick Romano. But whereas Wright generated tremendous passion through his identification with Bigger and his crimes, Motley sees Nick completely from the outside, without those animating details of Italian life which would enable us to forget the schoolboy sociology. Not that the novel lacks power altogether; it has moments of poignancy, not the least in Nick's oft-repeated epitaph: "Live fast, die young and have a good-looking corpse."

One danger of such genre studies of growing up, which Wright avoided, is that the individual is not merely subordinated to his environment but swallowed up by it. When that occurs, as in Farrell's novels, then detail work is everything: that environment must be established without faltering. This Motley cannot accomplish. His Italians are mainly comic book figures: eaters, tomato-worshipers, devout Catholics, tyrannical fathers. There is little sense of genuine family life, and little sense of language, cadences, tones. It is highly praiseworthy that Motley tried to cross racial barriers, but the specificity of Italian immigrants required a different treatment. It is not all tomatoes and brawling. It is also fear, ritual, responsiveness.

Growing up Italian in Mario Puzo's *The Fortunate Pilgrim* (1964) is quite different from growing up Italian in Motley's *Knock on Any Door* or Edward Lewis Wallant's *Children at the Gate* (published posthumously in 1964). Puzo's Italians are always seeking to consolidate, whereas Wallant's Italian (from a Jewish perspective) looks beyond, to some source of life that can change him. Motley turned Nick Romano black, Wallant turns Angelo deMarco Jewish; Puzo writes about Italians.

The immigrant Italians in *The Fortunate Pilgrim* have staked out a piece of America that will be theirs forever. The Angeluzzi-Corbo family, doubly tiered, has made a part of west Manhattan a "little Italy." Here they play out the ways of the Old World as certainly as if they had never left the south of Italy; only here the dangers are intensified, for the young are continually tempted to break away. In Italy, the constant was no work, no chance of finding any; in the new country, the danger is of too many opportunities, leading to family rifts. In this respect, Lucia Santa plays a role comparable to Gabriel Grimes's in Baldwin's *Go Tell It on the Mountain*.

In both novels, the families are two-tiered. Like the Grimes family, the Italian one is made up of siblings, half brothers and sisters, stepchildren, stepfather, full father; the sole one to whom everyone belongs is Lucia Santa (or Holy Light), the connecting link and cementing force. Characteristic of all family novels are pressures that work from within (personal tensions, allegiances) and from without (opportunity, promise, freedom). Both types of pressure can dissipate individual strength and familial cohesiveness or, equally, reinforce them. As Puzo shows, the family, like the larger society, achieves a very delicate balance.

Although not working strictly within the dictates of naturalism, Puzo begins with a very powerful and lyrical naturalistic image: Larry Angeluzzi, at seventeen, rides a horse into his neighborhood with the freight train behind him. As the "eyes," he warns everyone the train is coming, to be put to bed in its terminal. Although Larry is a "dummy boy," he carries himself like the last of the cowboys, a mixture of horsemanship, bravura, and urban dress—sneakers, a peaked cap studded with union buttons, dungarees fastened at the ankles with bicycle clips. To the children of the neighborhood he is a hero, a combination policeman and cowboy, on a large horse. His slow progression uptown, where tracks and neighborhood intersect, is a meeting of worlds; and Larry is a glorious figure combining old and new. The image suggests immediately he will be magnificent and troublesome, an uncontrollable force; the horse makes him Valentino, but the freight behind indicates a presence he cannot control. This image of Larry will, in a sense, underlie every aspect of the novel.

The book thrusts not toward the fortunes of anyone of the family, but toward its survival as a whole. Foreshadowing his books on Mafia families, Puzo here manifests his best work in ensemble details: foods, which are vivid; rejection of the mentally ill stepfather, husband, and father; small acts of cruelty balanced by small acts of generosity; changes in the family's expectations, and the playing off of one child against another. These are the living moments of the book.

All life is a trade-off, and the family does survive as time passes. But as Lucia Santa recognizes, nothing works out exactly as one wanted. The dream of America is compromised by what one must do in America to survive: " 'I wanted all this without suffering. I wanted all this without weeping for two lost husbands [the second, mad, dies] and a beloved child. I wanted all this without the hatred of the son conceived in true love [Gino, who leaves for the army]. I wanted all this without guilt, without sorrow, without fear of death and the terror of a judgment day. In innocence.' " She had wanted, in effect, an untainted Garden, blending the fantasy of an Italy that never was, an America that could not be.

Angelo DeMarco is one of Wallant's "silent men" who must be brought out of themselves by pain and suffering, having come through so far by repressing all feeling, except what he senses for his idiot sister, Theresa. Angelo has cut himself off from the rest of his family, and from God and church. He works for his cousin Frank, in a pharmacy, and he spends much of his time taking orders at a local Catholic hospital, especially among the children. The "children at the gate" are the hospitalized cases, at the gate of death as much as at the gate of heaven; but Angelo, too, is not far removed from being a child at the gate of death.

In *Children at the Gate,* the familiar Wallant elements are there: deadness of spirit, a condition close to anomie, the desire to be left alone, lack of meaningful communication, a functioning body in a dormant head and heart, a glimmer, usually in development, of some other form of life. The protagonist then undergoes a series of experiences, or meets a particular person, and discovers alternatives which open him up. For Angelo, the medium is Sammy, a Jewish orderly at the hospital. Sammy is perpetually high—he both uses drugs and administers them secretly to the patients to make them feel better—and he preaches an ideology of life, not death. Sammy is the risen Jesus to the enervated Angelo, and to the half-dead nuns who run the hospital. Manic, criminal (in his use of drugs), virtually insane in his monologues, lies, tales of the past, he is, nevertheless, a small-scale Dostoyevskian figure. He is the marginal, suffering, hopeful, saintlike individual, anathema to those he cannot reach, beloved by those he can.

Through Sammy's preachments, Angelo finds himself changing. He begins to gain consciousness, and his differences with others seem to count for less. He does not structure himself so much on standing apart as on developing himself. He comes alive, slowly, at the edges, then toward the center. When Sammy, on the eve of being caught for drug usage, commits suicide—he jumps from a window and is impaled on an iron fence—Angelo is transfigured; especially since it was his anonymous note that alerted the hospital administrators. Judas benefits by his betrayal.

Angelo, the fallen Catholic, who tells Sister Louise he cannot believe and will no longer try, has moved through life like Camus's Meursault, although less willfully neutral. For him, all life is an accident. As he tells his mother when she bemoans her life: " 'Things happen for no reason—we're unlucky people, that's all. . . . So everything's an accident, so what? That don't seem too hard to take; it leaves things up to me. Just so long as I can see things clear, just so I don't have to take all that gas about Jesus Christ and Love and all the rest of them ghost stories.' " Here is, for a time, a true heir of Studs and Bigger. If everything *is* an accident, then Angelo is free to indulge himself as anomic, under no responsibility to himself or to others. Thus he can slide away from the feelings he fears to indulge, and he can drift. It is so written.

Sammy's preachments disallow this. Sammy speaks of human frailty, he asks forgiveness for a crazy orderly who has tried to rape a sick young girl, and he asserts man's eternal mortality. He offers, in his manic, insane way, a form of existence that confers both danger and salvation, without the protective covering Angelo demands. Sammy's way is to be exposed; only a naked man receives God's inspiration. The clothed man is beyond reach. Life demands exposure to everything, as Angelo begins to recognize. In its curious way, *Children at the Gate* embodies the sixties sense of opening up, living at the edge; adding, however, that self-indulgence must serve a social as well as an individual function.

OUTSIDE NATURALISM

In *Other Voices, Other Rooms* (1949), Truman Capote's Joel Harrison Knox is an internalized version of Huck Finn. As much as Huck travels outward into land and river, Joel travels inward, toward surrealistic images, literary descriptions—Miss Havisham, Rochester's Bertha, Faulkner's laboring blacks and domestics, all transformed into hallucinatory experiences. But unlike Twain's book, which starts as a boy's experience and becomes an adult's, Capote's remains a book primarily for precocious children—though many contemporary readers (such as Lewis Gannett and Diana Trilling) made that leap from childhood experience to adult assimilation.

They were, I sense, carried away by verbal virtuosity. There are lovely, lyrical passages, full of gently modulated melodies, especially toward the end, when Capote is bringing Joel through childhood toward adolescence and greater maturity. Such passages leave an impression of considerable control on the author's part. It could be quite easy to confuse the precocious young Capote (at twenty-three) with the maturity of some of the prose, and from that extrapolate meanings in the novel that appear adult. A more accurate reading perceives the novel as a cotton candy confection, in which the author indulges himself with terrors, nightmares, Gothic and surrealistic images. The book is composed of readings brought together in a hyped-up prose, with passages of considerable loveliness. The level of observation remains that of a nervous child in a child's world.

Everything is calculated for sensation. In the passage leading up to Joel's vision of the nightmarish lady at the window, he passes through several thoughts: the sun as a "white hot sphere," a sky of "pure blue fire," playing Blackmail, the time when he saw "two grown men standing in an ugly little room kissing each other," to the "diamond glitter" of the afternoon which hurt his eyes, to the bell which returns him to slave days, and then, finally, at the chapter break, to the vision or hallucination of the "queer lady." The lady has a "hazy substance" for a face, "suffused marshmallow features," and "white hair . . . like the wig of a character from history." The scene is played for its descriptive tricks, and yet what does it mean? Although the lady recurs in his imagination and in his revelations to his cousin Randolph, she really has little to do with Joel. Unlike Miss Havisham, whose presence is central to Pip's view of life, this queer lady is merely a sensation, a childish nightmare. And most tellingly, the passages of description, effective as some are separately, do not cohere.

Similarly, Randolph is presented as shaped by his campiness, his exhausted, played-out gayness. We understand he is part of that dream world of Joel's which lies between childhood and growing maturity; in that world lies a kind of swamp, nightmare, hallucinatory experience. To get through the muck, the underbrush, the terrorizing images, is to grow and develop. That we can accept. We can even accept that a child's world demands that all observations, like all experiences, must be drawn to him and expressed in terms of their meaning to him. Still, we must take Randolph on faith, and even if we do, what does he signify in the novel? Is he simply one of Joel's hallucinations? If so, then the narrative is not a form, but merely an episodic arrangement of highly wrought passages.

Contrast the Capote novel with one it superficially resembles, Carson McCullers's *The Heart Is a Lonely Hunter,* * also heavily indebted to Faulkner and to Southern fiction in general, written by an author in her early twenties, full of nightmarish characters and events. There is, even, an observer in Mick Kelly, a thirteen-year-old passing from childhood into maturity. But McCullers did not make the mistake of filtering everything through her; Mick is an observer, but within McCullers's direct control and modulation. Capote provides no such distance, so that when Joel sees something, that is not only his world but ours.

What keeps *Other Voices, Other Rooms* at the level of childhood is that the author blends himself with his chief observer, demanding equal love and attention.

*Or with *The Member of the Wedding* (1946). Frankie Adams observes, but McCullers always positions herself outside her observer. The result is not a reflection of reality but a refraction, a far richer experience.

This lack of authorial distance keeps us, as readers, focused only on what the chief consciousness experiences, and if he is very young, then his vision is young. Salinger does something similar with Holden Caulfield, fixing us, however effectively, at Holden's level. No matter how precociously talented, a young author who fails to differentiate in narrative terms between himself and his chief consciousness must reduce, not expand, experience. For Capote, the consequence is that we read paragraphs of immediate sensuousness which are like passages in an exercise book.

The neglect of James Purdy by both general readers and critics cannot be explained easily. Some writers are ignored because their timing is wrong, or they remain out of the limelight, or else they stick to a few given ideas and refuse to shift as tastes shift. Others, like Joseph McElroy, are simply too difficult to pick up a larger audience, although they have an underground critical response. Purdy, however, has missed at every level, even though his narratives do not in themselves present difficulties. There is no question that the homosexuality underlying his novels has led to some critical coolness, since his view of homosexual behavior does not easily lend itself to a wider application, whether sensually, ethically, or morally. But it would be a mistake to label Purdy a "homosexual writer," for he is dealing with very difficult fictional problems; and his wit, which has gone unrecognized, adds dimensions to his obsessive observations. His hatred of women would be another valid reason for some neglect, although such hatred has not kept readers from more famous contemporaries, perhaps because theirs is more attractively packaged.

I think the reason for his neglect lies in his lack of give, his failure to cheer on, his bottom-line reality, his refusal to provide guidelines for behavior, his painful, often masochistic, obsessions; finally, his lack of familiar people, scenes, and episodes. Purdy is an acquired taste, no question of that; but he deserves wider critical response. For if nothing else, he has fitted himself perfectly into a kind of washed-out America. Purdy does represent that anomie or abulia which accompanies extreme self-indulgence: those wide swings from enervation to manic needs, those rhythmic patterns of "growing up" into an indifference to moral values that is tantamount to infantilism. For that, Purdy is our representative man. He shows us at our worst, and we, in turn, have revenged ourselves by neglect.

Although not precisely about growing up, "63: Dream Palace" (in *Color of Darkness,* 1957) locates

Fenton Riddleway as far more youthful than his nineteen years suggest. His tastes, desires, utterances, in fact, are all young adolescent, even infantile, yet he is attractive to adults in the guise of a youth. Around Fenton gravitate homosexuals, quasi-homosexuals, or those with dubious sexuality; for in his presence they can flirt with pederasty; and even the greatwoman Grainger, whose sexuality is unclear, finds him beautiful. Names suggest the ambiguity: Grainger for the greatwoman, Claire for Fenton's brother, Parkhearst for the writer who picks up Fenton as part of his research for a book. The names are either masculine/feminine or else in some neutral area where sexual identification is lacking.

The "growing up" comes when Fenton is picked up by Parkhearst, meets the greatwoman, and discovers that his salvation lies in marrying this ruined hulk of a woman. He reminds her of her late husband, Russell, and he literally fits into the latter's clothing. In appearance at least, Fenton is then transformed from a street waif into a man of substance. But he is not the only "child" in the novella; there is also Parkhearst Cratty, whose wife, Bella, cannot oppose him without fear of his disintegrating "slowly, vanish[ing] before her eyes. He was a child who must not be crossed in the full possession of his freedom, one who must be left to follow his own whims and visions."

The location of the novella in a child's world comes in the profusion of fantasy images. The "dream palace" is itself a rooming house on "Sixty-three Street," more hell than place of dreams; for there Claire lies dying, full of bedbug bites, more child than young man. But "Sixty-three" is only one of the fantasy places; the movie house is another: Fenton languishes in all-night films, losing himself in the immensity of the "dark palace," which is full of riffraff. He has no interest in the film itself, only in the experience. The theater is a place for sleeping and dreaming: "The seats did not act as though they were required to hold you off the floor. Faces twisted around to look at you, or somebody's hand sometimes came out of the dark and touched you as though to determine whether you were flesh or not."

Purdy provides large spaces into which the individual pours whatever he or she is. Working with these spatial fantasies is a prose style so flattened that it becomes a form of negative adornment. An enormous number of sentences are subject-verb in construction (Fenton went there, Parkhearst came here), creating a grammatical repetition; ordinary words achieve distinctive rhythms. People speak of their intimate needs, expressing what is usually inhibited.

Since they seem to confess all, their presence seems guileless, childlike. Yet what they are thinking and doing has within it terrible countervailing potential. That conflict between what appears to be complete honesty and demonic guile provides Purdy with his agon. The conflict is always located out of sight, in the inner turmoil where language ends and human motivation lies undefined.

Fenton can only free himself from Claire by killing him, which he does, and disposing of the body, which he does. The place of rest is a chest in a vacant attic, a chest which turns out to be a dirty box filled with a "gauzy kind of veil," another "dream" sequence. The attic becomes like Miss Havisham's Satis House, of fantasies and lost dreams; and into this Fenton will introduce Claire's insect-ridden body. " 'Up we go then, motherfucker,' " is his final salute, the send-off into burial. It is Purdy's farewell address in a volume of stories based on hate that goes beyond hate, feelings that go beyond feelings; from a "dream palace" of images and words which are not the Eden of our fantasies, but the hell where Purdy's characters locate themselves.

As a beautiful boy, Malcolm (*Malcolm*, 1959) is an object of desire for everyone. Men and women want to possess him, either to screw him or simply to have him around as an art object. He is the lovely statue willed into being by every Pygmalion he meets. Surrounding Malcolm is a collection of stunted creatures whom we recognize from Carson McCullers, Flannery O'Connor, Tennessee Williams, who helped form Purdy's literary tradition. This tradition has been associated with Southern fiction, but it is not only regional but small-town, anywhere. Essential to it is its isolation from mainstream thought, which allows eccentricities, perversions, and self-indulgence to develop unrestrainedly. There is, also, madness from intermarriage, the presence of incest, the closet homosexual, secret drinking, suicides, of course, even homicides. Murderous impulses work like electric currents.

Malcolm is a catalyst and precipitate, as well as something of a sacrifice. As a beautiful object, he wilts. His hair turns white overnight, and he fades, never losing his beauty even as he approaches extinction. Once he is dead, the lives of those involved with him can proceed. In a sense, Malcolm has stopped them from living, even as his presence has made them live. It is a typical Purdy paradox, and perhaps helps to explain his continued lack of recognition: that the individual lives only in the depths of his pain, that pleasure can only be comprehended by way of its counterpart in torture, and that the normal relationships we make in life—marriage, family, children, at work—are meaningless when contrasted with associations that evince pain.

Bereft of his father, either dead or vanished, Malcolm is a typical Purdy waif, a young man waiting to be ravished, Edenic innocence sacrificed. Mr. Cox, "the most famous astrologer of his period," sees Malcolm and offers him his list. Cox (Cocks) is fundamentally a pimp, since the list will bring Malcolm to various individuals: to Estel Blanc, a mortician, number one on the list; then to Kermit (a midget) and Laureen Raphaelson; on to number three, Madame Girard and Girard Girard, a billionaire, both of whom want Malcolm for their own; finally to number four, the imposing Eloisa Brace, a painter. All these people pursue Malcolm, who remains, at fifteen, essentially will-less, a beautiful object with little or no sense of himself. As he tells Girard, " 'You see my difficulty is I can hardly place any estimate on myself. I hardly feel I exist.' " Malcolm's lack of affect, his role as an art object, makes him perfect for the surrounding cast, more zombies than living creatures.

Purdy's style is to steamroller everything. His dialogue, like his descriptive sentences, is reductive, so that it seems like words coming from a hollow chamber. His peculiar success, his unique quality, in fact, is to negate response, to wind things down. Although his literary tradition includes the American writers mentioned above, many of his mannerisms and stylistics derive from a French tradition, the kind of novel suggested by Robbe-Grillet, for whom, as well as for Butor and Sarraute, the world exists as a place in which "Things are things, and man is only man": that is, things remain unpenetrated, "hardy dry objects" foreign to us. For Purdy, *people* are impenetrable. They are as flat as the words he uses to describe them, their emotional lives so far out of sight that they are packed away as if in cold storage.

One area Purdy finds worthy of exploring more passionately than others is the excesses of women. When we first meet Madame Girard, she is dressed in a riding outfit, with her riding whip at her feet; several bottles, some partially empty, others empty, lie around. Her face is badly scratched, her makeup smeared so that she looks like a clown. She is a typical Purdy female, whipping her men into shape, demanding full attention, the better to demean them. Purdy's men, though not Girard Girard, revel in masochism, and seek out women who will humiliate them. Marriage is a farce; relationships bring only pain. Women are sadists, whores, demanding wives, sexually insatiable, like Melba, the singer who marries Malcolm.

Into this maelstrom the innocent Malcolm is drawn, a lamb fed to lions. As he enters the great world, he fills the need that people have of him, for he never becomes anything in himself. As a consequence, Purdy's world seems hallucinatory, for he reverses the ordinary order of things, in which a protagonist develops from his associations. The old picaresque form is used—the innocent who gains experience in the great world—but reversed; Malcolm is an experience for *them,* while they filter through his life ultimately to diminish him even as they try to bring him alive. As a Greek statuary beauty, the naked young man on a pedestal representing artistic form, Malcolm can only deteriorate from this attention, even as life is breathed into him. He starts out as a waif on a bench, deserted by his father, living alone in a great hotel, is brought alive by random contacts, but at the same time is diminished and reduced until he dies, used up.

The wit of a Purdy fiction derives from several factors, the chief of which is the bland presentation of a world of bleakness and even horror. Terrible things are said and done in a flat prose that superficially seems undistinguished. The opening sentence resonates with this flatness raised a notch by associations: "In front of one of the most palatial hotels in the world, a very young man was accustomed to sit on a bench which, when the light fell in a certain way, shone like gold." This recalls the beginning of "63: Dream Palace": " 'Do you ever think about Fenton Riddleway?' Parkhearst Cratty asked the greatwoman one afternoon when they were sitting in the summer garden of her 'mansion.' " The larger line of thought is undistinguished, but Purdy introduces an element of remorselessness which acts as contrast. The forlorn Malcolm is juxtaposed to a palatial hotel; the simple bench is struck by light that shines like gold; or else the exotic names and "greatwoman" work against the flatness. Tensions develop from small matters.

In *Malcolm,* as in most of his work, there is no "beyond." Not only are society, a political state or politics, a government, even a community, a neighborhood missing; to speak of them is beside the point. Purdy creates a vacuum within the larger world, in this respect recalling Kafka, and then excavates, as if it were a buried culture like Pompeii. The excavation is of buried types, buried even deeper by Purdy's prose. The wit lies here, in that pitiless, objective laser beam he directs upon creatures who seem to have no yield left.

The nephew of *The Nephew* (1960)—Cliff Mason, killed in the Korean War—is an extension of Malcolm of *Malcolm*. We never meet Cliff, and the novel is, in a sense, a recreation of the world in which he moved as a shadow creature before he went off to Korea to be blown to pieces. Not enough of him remains for it to be gathered together, a symbolic fragmentation, since that is all we ever know of him. His letters tell his aunt and uncle, Alma and Boyd Mason, almost nothing; and the sole evidence we have of his "presence" is a series of large photographs on the wall of Vernon Miller's room. To discover who Cliff was becomes the mysterious thread of the novel.

The Masons live in Rainbow Center, a name which indicates that while the novel proceeds realistically, it is a special kind of realism. Purdy is, in effect, interested in the counterfeit: appearances, deceptions, shadow lives, unlived lives, lack of fulfillment. Rainbow Center is, like Winesburg, Ohio, a town where dreams go unfulfilled, lives are depressed, feelings have few outlets. The scale of Purdy's novel is quite small, and yet by way of that peculiar extension through what we may call the "language of potentiality," Purdy implies a good deal.

The Purdy vision is not simply of simple people. When Alma Mason undertakes to write a book about her nephew, still believed to be missing in action, not dead, she will discover more about herself than about Cliff. He remains a mystery, the inner life preempting whatever one may learn of him. Yet Alma, that decent, snappish, but innocent elderly schoolteacher, learns for the first time what arrangements people make for themselves. She learns that Cliff's friends, Willard Baker and Vernon Miller, are homosexuals, that Vernon had given Cliff four thousand dollars under strange circumstances; she discovers that Professor Mannheim at the local college may have been sleeping with his coeds, that Mrs. Barrington, the local wealthy aristocrat, has had dealings with or knowledge of everything she, Alma, is ignorant of. Like sewage, knowledge seeps to the surface. *The Nephew* works on the assumption that reality is desperately incomplete, that the more we try to bridge the gaps of what we know, the less we can discover. The closet life is the only true life, because hidden. It only develops and expands concealed, so that the façade always counterfeits who we are. The Cliff of memory, those unrevealing letters, the reconstruction in Alma's mind are finally a more suitable and comprehensible Cliff than the one who begins to appear from historical fact.

Purdy is one of our most secretive of novelists.

Everything occurs out of sight: love, attachments, affection, real feeling. One reason he is so antagonistic toward women, besides whatever personal animus exists, is that they insist on bringing their emotional lives to the surface as voracious appetites. For him, repression is all. Cliff, like Malcolm, is the perfect Purdy protagonist—dead on arrival, an object to all who view him.

An even more appropriate image comes in those photographs revealed in Vernon Miller's room the night of the fire. The photos reflect a Cliff unknown to Alma and her brother, Boyd; and yet while they are real-life images, they only create greater mystery. For the presence of those photos, the reason for their existence in such a place, only suggests how little of Cliff they know. Professor Mannheim has scraps of Cliff's work in his files, but those scraps open up a record that recedes in veracity as more is known. The photos are part of that secret process, masturbatory fantasies in Vernon's past, or present; objects, not subjects, of attention and even worship. These photos are suggestive of the female bodies that are the object of rape in *Cabot Wright Begins*, Purdy's next novel. Wright does not care about the age or condition of the women he rapes; he cares only about relieving himself, although he is gentle, never brutal, never insistent.

Further, the antagonism to women, pitched so high in Purdy, but also characteristic of sixties fiction—Mailer, Updike, Pynchon, Roth, Barthelme, Heller—was part of the male defensive buildup to what was already in the air as female liberation in its early phases, foreshadowing Betty Friedan's *The Feminine Mystique,* which in turn reactivated Simone de Beauvoir's great study, *The Second Sex*. We have on the part of male novelists an attempt to build a wall that would protect them against a feminine sensibility, which was still formative; to build a base of male strength to withstand the inroads of female analysis. In some respects, *The Nephew* is anomalous in Purdy's canon, and yet in its repressive, secretive mode not such a departure.

Purdy's use of language works against language. It is the rhetoric of antirhetoric, almost a language in itself in its denial of suggestivity. Like Barthelme's prose, it works within the platitudes in which people express themselves; the platitudes and clichés become themselves sources of wit. "Mrs. B. cried in the manner of one clutching at a straw." " 'That's from the horse's mouth, I guess,' Vernon retorted." " 'It's so much fuss and feathers, Mrs. B.!' " The repetition, here and elsewhere, of that type of old-fashioned language used consciously goes beyond quaintness. It reveals a dimension of human intercourse in which all feeling has been deadened, words themselves no longer expressing or divulging, becoming merely sound. No one has to listen to such talk.

Platitudes bombard the ear, ketchup the nose, familiar sights the eye—all to deflate reality, and to make the secret life the only life worth investigating; except that it, in turn, will reveal nothing. Purdy moves ever deeper into mysteries which he knows have no bottom, not even a middle. The secretive life becomes its own justification. In an unloving, unfeeling world, all may as well be object, a prophetic statement for much fiction that would follow, in Barthelme, Barth, Pynchon. "Growing up" in Purdy is learning how to vanish in uncertainties, how to express oneself out of sight, how to counterfeit all feeling. This, too, is a social vision, albeit an unpalatable one.

The five remaining growing up fictions are characterized by a common attempt to utilize the mode as a way of expressing something well beyond their immediate subject. Kurt Vonnegut, Jr.'s science fiction *Cat's Cradle,* John Updike's myth-ridden *The Centaur,* Mary McCarthy's hymn to America, *Birds of America,* Tom Robbins's cowboy myth *Even Cowgirls Get the Blues,* John Irving's *The World According to Garp* all move well outside their youthful protagonists into larger, more universal areas, often with mixed results. They share a remarkable commonality, in their tribute to an America that was either passing or already past. Their dream is of Eden, their fantasies pastoral ones, their sense of life based mainly on space, flight, withdrawal. A great variety of talent feeds into a common stream: to grow up in America is still, in all, a struggle against systems, against authority, against those limitations waiting to tie down the "free American." Not only are the pioneer and Jefferson resurrected, but the pirate, the outlaw, the loner, and Emerson come together in this vision.

A good deal of Vonnegut's appeal comes from his ability to perceive trends; and his dialectic of elements in *Cat's Cradle* (1963) is representative of this talent. Growing up is surviving not technology and systems alone, but science itself, the pivotal form of destruction. The dualism is apparent in the uses of science, as manifest in the career of Dr. Felix Hoenikker, Nobel Prize winner and developer of the bomb dropped on Hiroshima; and the uses of humanism, as manifest in the career of Bokonon, a black man born Lionel Boyd Johnson. So apparent is the dualism, however, that the intellectual dialectic becomes as diagrammatic as that in any naturalistic or doggedly realistic novel. Yet Vonnegut is working along the lines of fantasy, with some reference to science fiction.

The science fiction referent is an apocalyptic vision of the world, first in the destructiveness of the Hiroshima bomb, but now even more implicitly in *ice-nine,* Dr. Hoenikker's bequest to the world via his children: small pieces of *ice-nine* being able to transform watery areas into solidity—that is, change the very nature of Nature. It is Vonnegut's perception that not huge political events but the small things of science, our inheritance from a wizard, will transform society. Politics will follow science and technology, unless humanistic concerns prevail, in the form of Bokonon's philosophy of kinship. Bokonon has developed a vocabulary for kinship, chiefly the *karass,* which jumps boundaries and allows the individual to identify with anyone else of comparable sympathies and typologies.* One may never discover the limits of one's own *karass,* for it can be as extensive as it is bound.

The modulating element in *Cat's Cradle* is a narrator named John: "Call me Jonah"—Jonah not because of his unlucky presence but because of his need "to be at certain places at certain times without fail." He is writing a book to be called *The Day the World Ended,* an account of what important Americans were doing on August 6, 1945, when the atomic bomb was dropped on Hiroshima. Because of that book, he researches the three children of the scientist Hoenikker: Newton, a midget; Franklin, who has disappeared; and Angela. John-Jonah (no surname) is now a Bokononist, and his pursuit of "endings" has moved from atomic bombing to *ice-nine.*

The locale for *ice-nine* is an island in the Caribbean, the Republic of San Lorenzo. John is drawn to the island on an assignment and, as well, to take his research from Ilium to the Hoenikkers. He also is attracted to the island to meet Mona, the adopted daughter of the local dictator, "Papa"; John had seen Mona on a tourist publicity notice, and after two failed marriages, considers her the most perfect woman in the world. Many of the elements are familiar from previous fiction, Vonnegut's and others: the locale of San Lorenzo, which owes much to Haiti and leans generally on Greene; the use of a made-up language, reminiscent of *Brave New World* and *1984;* a scientific patina from science fiction, which suggests

---

*Some other terms: *wampeter*—the pivot of a *karass,* anything that serves as a hub; *granfalloon*—a false *karass; foma*—evil; *duprass*—a *karass* for two persons.

the apocalyptic theme; and a tension between humanism and technology, which goes back to Vonnegut's own *Player Piano,* with Ilium the mythical center of a destructive force.

The addition is Bokonon (the island pronunciation of Johnson). Bokononism, a dressed-up basic Christianity, exists as an outlawed religious force, although nearly everyone, it turns out, is a Bokononian. Once we get past some of the charming words Vonnegut has conceived, Bokononism is a sentimentalized belief full of the author's sweetness and moral generosity. The outlaw Johnson-Bokonon (John-Jonah is a possible "son of John" himself, a Johnson, and therefore Bokonon in his new guise) has wandered the earth, is shipwrecked on San Lorenzo, and there develops his cult. But the irony of Bokononism is that even the evil elements—"Papa" himself, who puts all transgressors on the hook to die—are members of the cult; and its presence, like Christianity, does not always mitigate avarice and the abuses of power.

The cat's cradle is the symbol of connection, its name taken from the children's game of making a series of X-figures out of string held between the hands. It can be played with two hands, or four, so that one has the making of a *duprass.* Emblematically, the X-figures formed by the looped string make connections, joining fingers and hands, completing a loop, as it were, with the person. Such, apparently, is Vonnegut's use of this fanciful game, with its symbolic tying—together and/or up. The one character who identifies most strongly with the cat's cradle is Newt Hoenikker, whose brief fling with a Soviet ballet dancer–spy has probably given the Russians access to *ice-nine.*

The sole way apocalypse can be neutralized is through Bokononism. When *ice-nine* begins to take over San Lorenzo, Vonnegut's miniaturized world, only religion remains as a humanizing influence; and in fact, the novel ends with an old, frail black man, Bokonon, having the final gesture, thumbing his nose at whoever governs. What the religion stands for more than anything else is integrity: "Each one of us has to be what he or she is. And, down in the oubliette [used as a refuge, as *ice-nine* covers the world], that was mainly what I thought—with the help of *The Books of Bokonon.*" Behind the trappings are forms of old-fashioned American integrity and self-determination. Personal weakness translates directly into scientific destructiveness.

The construction of *Cat's Cradle,* 127 very brief chapters, reinforces its parable atmosphere. Apocalypse comes in short, readable sections, not in massive clots of prose. Vonnegut is nothing if not accessible, and it is his accessibility, transparency, and reductiveness that become part of the problem. One reason he was so popular in the sixties—by the seventies his reputation was undergoing revision—was that he caught a type of higher culture in the accents of pop culture. His provenance, with some exceptions, belongs not with serious practitioners of fiction but with the Beatles, McLuhan, and those who have probed into popular culture as ways of directly interpreting us. So much sweetness dissipates the chances of more light.

Even those charming Bokonon terms represent nothing more than concepts that can be expressed without any special language. The language, in fact, intensifies the sentimentality of the conception and exposes the simplistic equations that keep the novel moving forward. A special language is functional when it carries with it its own dimension, or when it illuminates elements that would otherwise remain vague. The Bokonon terms, on the contrary, highlight no other dimension; they state a basic humanism which has no fictional resonance. Once more, Vonnegut's charm for the 1960s, as apart from his literary value, was his entrance into a cultural netherland, in which old truths could be gussied up and presented as if fresh.

Once this is said, however, there remains a residue of elements which bear discussion. The cat's cradle is such an element, its emblematic quality potentially illuminative, especially in terms of growing up. Another is the mass suicide of San Lorenzans, poisoned with *ice-nine,* at the request of Bokonon, who has told them God was finished with them and they might as well die. The potential here is overwhelming, in the light of our hindsight of the Reverend Jones incident in Guyana in 1978; and we perceive Bokononism as an evil force as well, an aspect Vonnegut fails to develop sufficiently. A third example lies in the way Vonnegut has brought several seemingly disparate elements together: old pastoral themes, development of a cult following, the sense of apocalypse, growing up at the edge of doom, the world ready to topple—the sixties encapsulated.

John Updike's view of America—based implicitly on pastoral and Edenic visions updated by modern sex and contemporary openness—lacks the irony, distrust, and authorial suspicion that transform the ordinary into the extraordinary. Updike's fiction is founded on a vision of a compromised, tentative, teetering American, living in suburban New England or in rural Pennsylvania; an American who has broken with his more disciplined forebears and drifted free, seeking self-fulfillment, but uncertain what it is and how to obtain it. Updike may use epigraphs from Karl Barth, Sartre, and other chic authors, but his outlook is distinctly, almost provincially, native.

The Poorhouse Fair (1959), shaped around old people, is often cited as an unusual book for a young writer to have cut his teeth on. In retrospect, however, we can see that in fact, having discarded an autobiographical first novel, Updike moved to a topic that pure writing, alone, could dominate. For his feelings, while sympathetic to the old (John Hook, Updike says, is reminiscent of his grandfather), could not really be engaged when the difference between author and subject was from fifty to seventy years. The novel becomes an exercise in skill, an "act of writing" brought to bear upon something rather remote.

Updike from the beginning would have difficulty finding subjects for his great writing gift, which appears to run on under its own momentum. Fluency would prove an impediment. One of his major themes would be decay—how fitting, then, to begin with octogenarians—and yet what keeps back decay is not running, or disguise, or change, but walls of words. He uses words as a way of preventing his characters from dissolving or disintegrating, not, however, for probing them. The reason a novel such as The Centaur (1963) is incoherent is not Updike's ambitious reach, which is admirable, but that he had no way of integrating mythological references to daily characters. Words betrayed him. He had to make the characters artificial in their daily lives and speech so as to permit transitions to their mythological selves. Realistic foreground and mythical background struggle against each other, a monistic mind trying to be dualistic.

There is more than a clash of styles here. There is the need to replace with words what should have been integrated into structure. A high school teacher as Chiron, his car mechanic as Vulcan, the latter's wife as Venus (Vera), and so on are not really possible; ordinariness of character and setting pulls against the grandness of their other selves.

There is a problem endemic to postwar fiction, and it touches on everything Updike writes. On one hand, the novelist is impelled to reach out toward large themes, important statements: that is, to justify his or her entrance into the new. In The Centaur, for example, the epigraph is from Karl Barth's Dogmatics in Outline. Inside is quoted the sad tale of Chiron, the Centaur whose wound, like that of Philoctetes, will not heal until the gods hear his prayer and remove both his pain and his immortality. In Couples, one of the epigraphs is from Paul Tillich's The Future of Religions. Rabbit, Run features Pascal, Pensée 507, brief but very complex, and risible for Harry Angstrom. Of the Farm, a slight book, has an epigraph from Sartre, in which he speaks of existence, essence, and freedom. The seriousness of the epigraphs is commendable, but there is little functional connection between them and the characters and situations Updike creates.

Another side of the problem is the fear, also endemic to postwar novelists, that the American tradition has been exhausted, that a new start is necessary. It has not been thoroughly mined, as several writers have discovered, but with the war itself, the full onset of modernism in this country, the importation of French and European existentialism, the desire to seek renewal (a new era, new political alignments, a new potential for America, a new self)—with all these, the search for heavy meaning and novelty becomes frantic.

There is a third aspect to the problem, which several writers have commented upon. Not only must a novelist compete with excellent nonfiction books that draw on fictional materials, but they must compete against a phantasmagoria of American life. Fictional invention can barely keep pace with actuality. Whether on the larger national front or in the smaller, more intimate, family scene, events create such extremes that in comparison fiction seems a laggard. Updike writes earnestly about marriage, movingly about separation, divorce, personal entanglements, but his treatment is already a reprise of newspaper and magazine stories.

These three problems—the need to achieve largeness, the uncertainty about one's own traditions with the full onset of European modernism, and the fantastic rapidity and instability of American life—cause the novelist to lose his fictional bearings and in many cases, lose the sense of his own career. Updike's desire to enrich The Centaur was an effort to maneuver on this difficult ground. A talent for creating scenes of growing up in the rural area outside Alton, Pennsylvania, becomes engorged when it reaches for largeness. In the novel, Peter, son of the centaur George Caldwell, hopes to be a painter after his school years, and he particularly loves Vermeer, although he has seen only reproductions. The intimacy and detailing of Vermeer are a clue, also, to what Updike does best; a novel written along the lines of Vermeer and not centaurs, Prometheus, or Zeus would strike that middle distance between the miniature and the universal.

Vermeer is that middle ground for Peter, between the outlandish world of his schoolteacher father (a mixture of personal defeat as a schoolteacher and mythicized grandeur) and the grubby experience of Alton. "In all of Alton County only my mother and I seemed to know about Vermeer. . . . My white walls accepted a soft breeze scented with chalk and whole cloves. In the doorway a woman stood, shadow-mirrored by the polished tiles, and watched me; her lower lip was slightly heavy and slack, like the lower lip of the girl in the blue turban in The Hague." Complementing the Vermeer images are sounds from his radio, and the two sensations, aural and visual, make Peter the center of everything. In the Vermeer, Updike has a splendid image of small-town yearning, small-town futility, the frustration of growing up with a failure whom one loves while one's own mind is filled by the immaculate Dutch painter.

The images of waste land, impotence (Fisher King references), failure, wounding, pain, could have been generated by the interior story, without pretentious psychological dimensions. The old Buick, formerly an undertaker's car, which is always near collapse and finally does break down, is also an apt symbol. Updike is particularly good in working in and around the car, the only way George can get back and forth to school. When the car ceases to function, he must readjust his entire life, as must Peter, also dependent on it for transportation to school. Yet its vagaries— poor battery, broken drive shaft, cold engine—are perfectly centered metaphors for George. Like the car, he has wounds that are internal, and yet he keeps running, along the edge of breakdown.

A scene that works well within the solidity of a pastoral American tradition, and yet pulls us beyond into forms of death, comes after a basketball game, during a snowstorm. The snow, to Peter, is like a gigantic flock of birds ("an entire broadening wing of infinitesimal feathers"), endless spatiality ("broadening into the realization that this wing is all about them") which covers the horizon and vibrates. But as the snow falls, it becomes ghostly with shadows and light and darks of the parking lot: in a way, a Vermeer miniature, but somehow of the great, sweeping outside. Spaces play off against each other: that sense of a miniature working against the lateral, vertical, parabolic geometry of an endless universe. Into this comes that agent of death, and life, the undertaker's Buick; it takes on nature in the form of snow and hills, and ceases to function. Car and nature remain antithetical.

These antitheses generate the novel's qualities and meanings. Because of severe psoriasis, Peter refuses to undress so he can swim, this when George is the high school swimming coach. The psoriasis, however, is not simply painful for Peter; it is also magical, serving as a coat or shield. It has its dreamy quality, a covering that makes him unique. Only two other persons in Alton have it, his mother and the doctor who takes care of them. Yet even as the psoriasis provides a cover, its unsightliness makes Peter shy of displaying himself. An image of growing up shielded and disguised has found a perfect form.

Into these scenes of nature and antinature George carries the whiff of death. Identification with the Buick, belief he is dying of cancer, heedlessness in his conduct of his life, a dead tooth, a decaying digestive tract, a job at the school he is in jeopardy of losing, a career that has been a kind of ending, the ever-presence of pain—all these make him the dying centaur of Alton. The book begins with his taking an arrow in his leg, and that pain never leaves him, even when the arrow is removed and the wound heals.

Yet despite Updike's prompting, George never achieves that glorious transcendental pain which forces Chiron to beg the gods for respite. It is Updike who maneuvers George ever closer to death. Chiron is forced upon us, as are numerous changes in style, including an obituary notice in Chapter 5; some purely mythical inserts; lyrical passages in Peter's voice; overheard conversations, with no witness; other entries in George's and Peter's voice. Updike's plan was, apparently, to disarrange narrative lines so as to create that density of disorganization and fragmentation which would make more plausible the transformation of mortals into gods, of mortal scenes into godlike episodes.

Yet such transformation is possible only when the focus is singular, as in Kafka's presentation of Gregor or Mann's of Aschenbach. Here are tales of transformation at various levels: one downward, from person to insect; the other expansionist, from repressed, controlled author to Dionysiac destroyer of self. The voices are singular, the line of attack relentless; transformation becomes part of the ordinary, the extraordinary accomplished. Updike's attempt to disorganize us with stylistic shifts and changing verbal tonalities leaves the novel bifurcated: that meaningful realistic level at odds with the pretentious, uncompelling mythical. Even the index (compiled, Updike says, on his wife's advice) is a falsification, an attempt to win us over with the implication of it all, not the thing itself. In *Bech: A Book,* Bech's bibliography is a different matter altogether.

A NOTE: *Of the Farm* (1965) is the other side of *The Centaur:* the story updated and then retold, after George Caldwell's death, from the point of view of his widow and their son, now called Joey. "Of" the farm, rather than "On" the farm, is significant, since the farm, as once the Buick and the school, is now dominant. Joey returns to see his mother, accompanied by his new wife, Peggy, and her son, Richard. The dramatic pivot concerns how the farm (earth, pastoral, mother, enduring values) threatens everything that is impermanent (desire for joy, sex, wife, connection to city).

Of the Farm is the novel *The Centaur* would have been without the mythological paraphernalia, exactly what Updike does best, miniature work with filigree touches, sensitivity to ordinary things, frail existences, the give-and-take of relationships. The sole problem here is the relative placidity of Joey, the narrator, who assumes that during the visit he will have to modulate between his mother (used to living alone and communing with domestic animals) and his wife. At stake is the farm: the treasure lying equidistant between mother and wife, earth and sensuality, nature and wide-hipped mistress-wife. Given Updike's stress on Peggy's fleshy lower half, the stake is as much the treasure between her legs as that out there, the land. Not without irony, during their entire stay at the farm, Peggy menstruates; with her body in limbo for these days, he is offered up to his mother.

The farm, that neutral piece of eighty-odd acres, is the dividing space between old and new, the nineteenth and twentieth centuries. Joey's job in the city is the most modern of positions, "corporate image presentation." Joey had once yearned to be a poet, in the Wordsworthian tradition. Now he is an arranger, a fixer of images, a conniver. These are familiar themes, of course, in many ways archetypical American themes. But Updike handles them freshly, although even here there are incongruities. Updike presents a love that is really sensual slavery, a deception that justifies the mother's implication that Joey is moving along fleshy terrain without regard for values; and yet we are aligned against the mother's accusation of this, forced to take Joey and Peggy's part in what we cannot believe. Even in miniature, Updike breaks style, insufficiently defines the distinction between love and sensuality, and makes women into earth mothers.

The sixties gave birth to *Birds of America* (1971): old and new as the battleground in sensibility, culture, survival itself. Will the "birds of America," Audubon's America, survive the sanctuaries, neglect, ways in which "rare birds" are misplaced in the contemporary imagination? Mary McCarthy sets her protagonist, a modern-day Candide, Peter Levi, in his Garden setting: Rocky Port in Massachusetts, where he and his mother, Rosamund, go to live. A performer on the clavichord and harpsichord, Rosamund has just broken up with her second husband, Peter's stepfather. As a result of her two marriages, Peter is not only a child of divorce, he is the child of differing cultures, his father an Italian Jew, his mother an early American, and his stepfather a refugee German scientist (also Jewish).

From this diversity of backgrounds, the meeting of Europe and America, Jew and Gentile, old and new ways, Peter must forge some modern ethic. He is essentially an innocent, not victimized, but a youth out of phase with his time. The time is the sixties, the war is the Vietnamese conflict, and the issues are momentous, although much of the novel is caught from a perspective in Paris, where Peter spends his college junior year. Observations from this distance, unfortunately, give everything not only a stilted quality but an unreal substance; and yet Peter must react to real matters. For him, the war, the bombing of Hanoi, racial problems (he is very involved intellectually with the civil rights movement), one's relationship to historical values are not marginal but essential; integral to the good man and the good life.

Near the end of the novel, Peter and a friend visit the Paris zoo. In a deserted place, they see a black swan and decide to feed it. Peter, comfortable in his sense of wild things, assuming a rapport with the swan, tries to feed it a brioche and is, to his surprise, repeatedly struck by the beak, "wounded." The "bird of France" has failed to recognize a "bird of America": nature is, as it were, dead for Peter. That world of amazement and wonder with his mother back in Massachusetts is unregainable; every Garden is now tainted.

Peter has tried to live by the Kantian imperatives of duty, obligation, and moral intensity. On the final pages, when he lies in the hospital recovering from infection, Kant visits him, a considerable concession since the philosopher has never before left Königsberg. Peter's world, with the black swan's attack, the bombing of North Vietnam, and other events, has vanished, and Kant has reappeared to introduce him to a world where such things are commonplace. God is dead, Kant says, beating Nietzsche to the punch; then he says that "Nature is dead, *mein Kind,*" which is the real meaning of "God is dead." Audubon's America no longer exists. And indeed, it may have existed only in Peter's fervent imagination: that of an innocent young man growing up with a mother who plays the clavichord and harpsichord in Rocky Port, Massachusetts.

There is poetry here which the large middle of the novel lacks. When McCarthy moves beyond the liberal 1950s and 1960s message implicit in Peter's comments, the novel comes alive; when Peter expresses his (her) views, the novel turns leaden. This is unfortunate, but it is an inevitable concomitant of McCarthy's failure to dramatize or structure Peter's remarks. As commentary, it is a *Partisan Review* letter from Paris, or a message to middle America, simply the commonplaces of a sensitive young man. Peter's attachment, however, to a Thoreauvian America, which is also a landscape of the imagination, is a different order of business.

A cult novel, Tom Robbins's *Even Cowgirls Get the Blues* (1976) is a catchall of pastoral, Eden, spatiality, growing up, marginality, resourcefulness. It probes legends, and it recapitulates Thoreau, Kerouac, and early frontier life. Its protagonist, Sissy Hankshaw, has magic wands—abnormally large thumbs, more like baseball bats than fingers. With Sissy's abnormal thumbs, her hitchhiking ability, we have a parody of the American obsession with the road and, at the same time, an exploration of the legend.

The book has several segments about growing up, many of which, ultimately, fail to hold together. First: Sissy Hankshaw, with the big thumbs, which are legendary and which enable her to wield them as baseball bats when necessary. Sissy is the proverbial oddball who adapts to her affliction and turns it to her advantage. After having met and "gone with" Kerouac, she marries a Mohawk Indian, Julian, who becomes part of the establishment, whereas she struggles to remain herself. Second: the Rubber Rose Ranch, out in the Dakotas, a reducing farm now run by cowgirls. Many episodes are given over to the girls' life on the ranch: Delores del Ruby, with her whip; Bonanza Jellybean, with her bursting jeans; others. The ranch and its affairs feed directly into the feminist movement, which ideologically underlies the novel.

Third: off in the mountains the Chink—actually a Japanese named the Chink by the Clock People. Everything connected to the Chink (and beyond him, the Clock People) partakes of the *Whole Earth Catalog* view of life: he lives off yams, speaks of yin and yang, Zen principles, also of American individuality, and although ancient, screws like a rabbit. The Chink is guru, shaman, wizard. He learns from the Clock People about their sense of time, the two thirteen-hour segments that make up their history and that also, through water, keep them tuned in on the San Andreas Fault.

Because of this disdain for the disorderly, poetry and magic have vanished. "At every level. If civilization is ever going to be anything but a grandiose pratfall, anything more than a can of deodorizer in the shithouse of existence, then statesmen are going to have to concern themselves with magic and poetry." This message from the Chink recalls others, from Norman O. Brown or Castaneda's Don Juan: "the smoke is not for those who seek power. It is only for those who crave to see. I learned to become a crow because these birds are the most effective of all." The question is not one of survival, but the manner in which one survives.

Fourth: the workings of nature. After taking Sissy anally, the Chink argues: "Technology shapes psyches as well as environments, and maybe the peoples of the West are too sophisticated, too permanently alienated from Nature to make extensive use of their pagan heritage. However, links can be established. Links *must* be established. To make contact with your past, to re-establish the broken continuity of your spiritual development, is not the same as a romantic, sentimental retreat into simpler, rustic lifestyles."

Fifth: the whooping crane as natural model. The cowgirls at the Rubber Rose Ranch provide a sanctuary for the cranes, jeopardized by civilization—first "stoning" them slightly, and then feeding and taking care of them. It is this act that leads to invasion by enemies of nature, the police and FBI. The whooping crane is an apt model in that its courtship dance indicates an association with joy, and its life patterns suggest it has discovered that mode in nature the Chink espouses—neither a termite existence of survival (Nietzsche's "last man"), nor complete anarchy of self: instead, a balance of elements.

The reasons for the cult success of the novel are evident. It offers a critique of the larger society and technology in Jeffersonian and Emersonian terms without demanding a new society, simply a new person. Remake yourself, not the society: a comforting message for the 1970s, in a way an outgrowth and a repudiation of the previous decade. Foreign, combining sexual potency and balance, the Chink is a familiar figure in recent fiction—Kesey's Bromden, Berger's old Chief, and those other Indian wise men. Sissy is herself a very appealing character, with her deformity, her ability to make her way, her legendary hitchhiking powers. Then the Rubber Rose Ranch provides a feminist society, presented without condescension, with all the right arguments and activities.

Yet Robbins has written several kinds of novel. By far the most attractive sections concern Sissy growing up in South Richmond, Virginia, with those outsized baseball-bat thumbs. Everything connected with the thumbs makes the novel come alive, as part of her destiny, her growth into an extremely attractive woman who demonstrates feminine hygiene apparatuses. All such parts are worked through. Other elements are not integrated fictionally; they become set or insert pieces, especially the Chink, his teachings, the Clock People. The rest is a novel that seems part fiction, part sermon; and the wit, which is real, is often dissipated in the message. A novel turns into *Zen and the Art of Motorcycle Maintenance,* which is, after all, not a bad fate.

Quite understandably, newspaper and magazine staff reviewers found *The World According to Garp* (1978) "brilliant," "overwhelming," "extraordinary," "joyous," "superb," "enthralling," "original," "touching," "rich," and so on through Roget. Unlike many modern novels, for which publishers should hand out comic strip versions to aid reviewers, *Garp* presents few problems; but most of all, it conveys good feeling. Although it is in many ways a growing up novel, it bears few of the terrors that genre brings forth. Garp's mother, Jenny Fields, is an original and an eccentric, but she is a good mother; a nurse, she "nurses" her son carefully and correctly. His childhood has a few isolated incidents of terror, but the latter are only a small part of the story.

Curiously, Garp generates such good feeling because, except with his own children, he does not feel very deeply. In areas of emotion and response, he is passive; and part of his appeal in the novel is to a 1970s sense of "enough is enough." It is a long book, with a relatively untortured protagonist, surrounded as he is by eccentrics rather than cruel persons, a mother who does a strangely good job, a schooling that leaves few scars, an attractive appearance which encourages girls and women, and a stable personality that holds him together.

These ingredients, mixed, along with Irving's witty, irreverent manner, add up to a good read.

There is, also, just enough tampering with form, in temporal areas, to placate those who want a writer to be at least conscious he is in the second half of the twentieth century. In brief, something for all. In the early parts of the novel, which are much the best, Irving refers ahead: to Jenny Fields's autobiography, *A Sexual Suspect,* and to Garp's own later fiction. Added to that, he fills in on what occurs in later years to certain characters. Like Vonnegut, he settles matters long before they occur, so that the way is cleared for more important events. There are, then, three records: Irving's own commentary, with the jumping ahead; Jenny Fields's commentary on her yet to be written autobiography; Garp's own work at a later time. When Garp does begin to write, Irving includes his early effort: "The Pension Grillparzer," the attenuated story of episodes in an Austrian C-rated pension, visited by the narrator's father as a spy for the tourist bureau.

These elements, however, seem to exhaust themselves one-third through the novel. Despite some apparent borrowings—the hospital scenes with Garp's bandaged and crippled father recall the first chapter of *Catch-22*— the early parts are a crazy quilt of an extraordinary young woman (Jenny Fields), a witty outlook, and a school situation (Steering) that feels right. Once Garp and Jenny leave for Vienna, where she writes her famous autobiography, and Garp works on the "Grillparzer," the novel sputters. Garp is like a character in a picaresque novel whose activities can be endless, until the novelist wearies of the chase. A novel without intellectual underpinning needs imaginative thrust, or else self-indulgence controls the narrative. Less than halfway through, Irving has settled for what he knows he can do well: moving eccentric characters around on a board, permitting them relationships outside established ties (wife swapping, socking it to the baby-sitter), realigning these ties once they are strained, and then setting out on another round.

In both the full story and the internal stories by Garp, the common theme is Jenny's contention that lust destroys. Surely, it almost destroys the Garp family. While Garp's wife, Helen, is busy sucking off her student friend Michael, lying on the front seat of his huge station wagon, Garp returns early from the movies with the two boys. As he is accustomed to doing, he switches off his ignition and lights and moves silently into his parking place, now occupied by the wagon. In the ensuing crash, Helen bites off three-quarters of Michael's penis; the older boy, Duncan, loses an eye on the manual clutch, which lacks the protective knob; the younger son is thrown and killed; Garp breaks his jaw and must be wired; and Helen suffers numerous injuries, besides a funny taste in her mouth. The episode places them back in the hands of the nurse Jenny.

The gruesome sequence is related in witty fashion, and it is associated with another aspect of the "lust" theme, and incidentally the "growing up" theme: the overwhelming presence of rape episodes. Once Jenny becomes famous, she is surrounded by feminist groups, one of them being the Ellen James Society, named after an eleven-year-old girl who was raped and whose tongue was severed so she couldn't identify her assailants. Members of the society cut off their own tongues as a protest against what happened to Ellen James. They go around with pads and pencils. Whenever Garp meets a young woman who does not speak immediately, he thinks she is an Ellen Jamesian; and he is, himself, placed in their situation when his jaw is wired. Through this mockery of the rape situation, it becomes a theme, repeated in great detail in a Garp story of assault and murder called "The World According to Bensenhaver," which is to be the first section of his third novel.

Garp's writings depend on great rages, brutalization, violence, physical confrontation. He is, after all, a former contender in wrestling, where sudden bursts of violence determine a match. His own life seems passive, but beneath is a sadism and cruelty, which emerge in his story. Irving's lack of psychological probe, either explicitly or implicitly, leaves Garp's frame of reference uncertain. Irving has turned all behavior into narrative, which is possibly why the novel met such a popular reception.

Readable and clever as it is, *The World According to Garp* reaches for a profundity Irving cannot deliver. He ends with "we are all terminal cases," and his epilogue, after Garp's death at the hands of a fanatical feminist, has mythical qualities Garp has not earned. This failure to achieve the levels of distinction Irving is striving for derives from a playing with ideas, rather than ideas themselves. Even truly comic scenes have an unresolved quality. One of the best is Garp's appearance at a feminist funeral, the services for Jenny, which is restricted to women only. Garp must appear in drag, conceived of by Roberta Muldoon. When his disguise is penetrated—by Pooh Percy, who later shoots him—he is almost lynched by the irate women. One kicks him in the groin, and even Roberta, the ex–tight end running interference, does not help. Only an elderly nurse, reminiscent of his mother, gets him out alive. What is disturbing about this and other scenes is Irving's mocking exploitation of causes Garp seems sympathetic to. Garp's fascination with rape is part of this sensationalized use of extreme materials, capitalizing on what he purports to attack. Many people around him recognize this ambiguity, his hostility to the women's point of view even while he seems empathetic, and yet Irving does not integrate this ambiguity into Garp's imagination, nor does he seem to be aware of what is omitted. At this level alone, the novel reaches for more than that steely and witty narrative can fulfill.

The World According to Garp has been touted as the "big novel" of the second part of the 1970s; perhaps the humanistic counterpart of Pynchon's "unreadable" early 1970s exploration of science and technology. A modest novel, with modest underpinning, is done a disservice. Irving's talent, which is real, works most effectively in details, least compellingly when ideas must cohere. *Garp*'s great gift is its sustained narrative line; but we should not confuse ourselves that narrative is necessarily the place where literature is located.

Chapter Six

▪▪▪▪▪▪▪▪▪▪▪▪▪▪▪▪▪▪▪▪▪▪▪▪▪▪▪▪▪▪▪▪▪▪

THE COUNTERFEIT DECADE

By my faith, I am afraid he would prove the better counterfeit.

FALSTAFF, *Henry IV,* Part 1

. . . how could I be inside, there isn't any inside!

GADDIS, *JR*

Rules of the Game

Growing up, while retaining visions of innocence and pastoral glory, is an apt image for the 1950s. But while "development" may be a suggestive image for the decade, counterfeiting and invisibility are its most pungent metaphors. I take the first from William Gaddis's *The Recognitions,* the second from Ralph Ellison's *Invisible Man.* A third metaphor, which links the above two as well as growing up, is that spatial emblem, "on the road." And a fourth, which rearranges counterfeit feelings, visions of a lost Eden, and aspects of invisibility, is William Burroughs's hallucinatory, drug-induced universe.

While the country went one way—toward prosperity, cold war obsessions, national security and world power, industrial growth, egalitarian participation, school integration—fiction seemed to go another: toward rejection, withdrawal, aggressive hostility to systems, imitation as a mode of life, disintegration of acceptable modes of behavior. Implicit in the literature of the 1950s is a foreshadowing of nearly every aspect of social and political behavior of the 1960s; in literary terms, the two decades are seamless, Gaddis leading into Pynchon, Heller, Roth, and McElroy, Ellison and Burroughs into Barth,* Oates, Barthelme, and others.

American fiction of the 1950s took on the challenge of demonstrating that we were a "schizoid country," to use Adorno's characterization in *The Authoritarian Personality;* or the practitioners of a "paranoid style," to use Hofstadter's. For while our leaders spoke of prosperity and freedom, our fiction, and poetry, spoke of alternative existences based on rejection of *that* freedom, embracing of another kind. Yet the antagonistic modes are not, perhaps, so different. We found such dualism before in the American personality, in Hawthorne and, particularly, in Melville. His *Bartleby* and *Billy Budd* subsume heights and depths, as does his *Pierre.* Behind the schizoid appearance in American life, there is a coherent experience founded on paradox and irony, discontinuity and ahistorical development. Such elements fall just short of tragedy, just this side of comedy, an intermediate region characterized by counterfeiting and invisibility. Heller's phrase "Catch-22," paradigmatic

*I have omitted John Barth from "1950s and After" and used only *Giles Goat-Boy* in "The 1960s," preferring to group his work in "The 1970s," under *Letters.* Barth exemplifies an author who has worked toward a *summa,* and *Letters* provides just that, for both author and reader.

of the buried life, entered the language in the later sixties, but it derives from a book deeply embedded in the fifties, when it was written.

T. W. Adorno and his associates, preparing *The Authoritarian Personality,* conducted hundreds of interviews, which, first, isolated an especially clear type of psychological personality and, second, explored a psychological and political syndrome related to that personality type. Since the two parts did not cohere, Adorno felt he had discovered a schizoid personality among Americans, split between what they were and what they felt they were. Yet if he had examined our literature, he would have found that the schizoid factor lies deep within us, with its own form of coherence. It works in strange ways, and an example from popular culture will show how Americans, as a matter of course, divided themselves into warring, hateful elements.

Elvis Presley, whom many Americans in the 1950s epitomized as dissolute, crummy, and shabby, saw himself as clean-cut, patriotic, indeed supernationalistic. The same Presley who did so much to introduce the fifties and sixties to a counterculture in popular music was himself extremely disturbed by the Beatles, whom he considered to be "filthy and unkempt," their music "suggestive." He was also disturbed by the Smothers Brothers, Jane Fonda, and other entertainers who he felt were poisoning the minds of the young politically and culturally. With this in mind, he addressed a memo to J. Edgar Hoover, whom Presley considered to be "the greatest living American," and offered to be an informer.

Presley felt that because of his many associations in the entertainment industry he was in a particularly good position to report on those who did not have the best interests of the country in mind. (We see how Presley reaches back to Whittaker Chambers, early in the 1950s, and works the line of counterfeit and invisibility.) Hoover, advised by an assistant that the singer was himself suspect, what with hair down to his shoulders and exotic costumes, thanked Presley for his offer and said he'd keep him in mind for some future assignment.

We have in this amusing anecdote more than a "schizoid personality." We have a meeting of elements *typically,* not pathologically, American, in which real-life situations become personae of literary ones, until lines are blurred. In other guises and with other adversaries, Presley is a character in many fictions: Presley and Hoover, antisystem and system, counterfeit and invisible, raised to a definition of our culture. Novelists have complained bitterly that events outpace fiction. Personality swings, they allege, are so abrupt, so lacking in causal connections, so missing in plausible motivations that one must attribute character to rapid change alone. The sole stable element is change, which creates not one America, but several, and which assumes a whole history of types within a brief span.

These are, I feel, givens, not aberrations; points continuous with our entire cultural and literary history. If we seek political examples, we can find some equivalent of Burroughs's hallucinatory universe in Joseph McCarthy's sense of America. We recall that while McCarthy voted with the liberals in domestic policy, in foreign policy he created an imaginary world of names and lists, induced not by drugs but by alcohol and a shrewd perception of how power can be achieved. Or in Nixon's speeches and principles (he advocated the use of nuclear devices in France's effort to retain Southeast Asia), we have political life providing Gaddis with his image of counterfeit. The real chaos of the 1950s, we could argue, was in real life, not fiction. MacArthur's rebellion against Truman, his pose as Coriolanus, went deep into the culture; and admiration people felt for him was based as much on his defiance of a weak President as on the vague principles he stood for.

The 1950s, then, were a time not of restoring but of tearing apart; not of connecting but of separating. Our leaders spoke of bringing Americans together—even McCarthy used that theme—but their actions moved along the lines of anarchy, nihilism, outlawry. In effect, they were not distant from where our fiction would take us, into areas of counterfeit and invisibility, into hallucinations, into fantasies of spatial withdrawal and escape. Daniel Bell would see in this the "end of ideology"; it was, in fact, just the beginning of so many ideologies that a sociologist would need the precision of a nosologist to categorize them.

Everywhere we turn in the decade, we find paradox. In the larger sphere, our stress on national security and American power did not lead to greater feelings of confidence, but to an "enlargement of the range of perceived threats that must urgently be confronted." The paradox of our national survival becomes transformed into literary terms of counterfeiting as the more "natural" process, of invisibility as creating greater intensity than visibility, of hallucinations as having greater reality than real life. What occurred in the fifties was a reversal of values so that those who were perceived as "saving" us—

McCarthy, Nixon, MacArthur, a cabinet of car dealers, even Eisenhower—led us into a frame of mind in which they were necessary in order to save us from themselves. The idea of national security, simply one among many, encapsulated so many paradoxes that literary reflection could offer only equal paradoxes.

John Marquand called his 1949 novel *Point of No Return,* and while the book is diluted at every turn, the term, a military one, had its application to the fifties. Marquand saw the phrase in personal terms; once his Charles Gray had entered into a particular personal and professional arrangement, there was no turning back. So it seemed in each year of the 1950s: every turn of the social and political wheel changed the game, offered a new set of rules and standards. The Soviets moved along one notch, America matched them and upped the ante; in domestic life, one move toward affluence was followed by its successor at a faster pace than we were accustomed to. The opening up of a consumer society through broad television advertising, a 1950s phenomenon, turned consumption from a walk into a gallop, and then a sprint. We are not faced with something radically fresh, as we are with something so speeded up, like a camera reel, that it seems new.*

Television had massive importance in creating the counterfeit. For television must be reductive, artificial, must play with our sense of space even more than films ever did. Further, while raising our consumer expectations, television lowered our cultural standards, not only reducing images, events, even wars, but making us feel the distortion is the more real. By turning everything into a box, television could homogenize war, game and quiz shows, situation comedies, political commentary; the name of the sport was to erase distortions, which is essentially what the counterfeit aims for.

In the 1950s, the American novel began that divorce from history which would characterize its later development. Like action painting, in which the canvas becomes the historical ground, the novel—with its counterfeiting, invisible protagonist, its hallucinatory, self-destructive Burroughs prototype, its man fleeing from cities and from himself—attempted to be its own history. The text *is* the country. Moments replace the broader sweep, although a writer like Gaddis tried to provide Wyatt Gwyon with a long New England background. But background there, as elsewhere, is less for its historical validity than for its presence as something the protagonist can break from.

Speaking of the action painter, Harold Rosenberg remarked: "With the American, heir of the pioneer and the immigrant, the foundering of Art and Society was not experienced as a loss. On the contrary, the end of Art [in its traditional forms] marked the beginning of an optimism regarding himself as an artist." Of course, this dissociation of self from history was part of the larger modernist movement; but it had special significance for the American postwar novelist, who needed in the art object something that gained its glory from him (or her), not from its connection to an entailed world. In that frame of personal reference, all is possibility, associations are lacking,

*Two large *Partisan Review* symposia in the early 1950s, one on "Religion and the Intellectuals," the other on "Our Country and Our Culture," attempted to find common ground for American culture, beliefs, philosophy, as we shifted from postwar optimism to cold war national security. In the first, *Partisan* editors were interested in whether religious values could "now be maintained without a widespread belief in the supernatural." They also wondered if the "religious tradition of any civilization [will] have to be essentially pluralistic" and if a return to religion might be necessary "to counter the new means of social discipline that we all fear: totalitarianism." In the later symposium, the editors were concerned with nothing less than the writers' and intellectuals' relationship to American culture. Specifically, they asked if intellectuals (i.e., *Partisan Review* contributors) had made their peace with America, and if they had, they wondered further what their relationship to mass culture would be; if they had not, then where could they find "the basis of strength, renewal, and recognition" now that Europe no longer supplied ideas, examples, and vitality? Quite amusing is that several contributors, who entered freely into the symposia, seemed bewildered by the sweeping questions; having nothing to say, they filled several pages with opinions that sidestepped the issues.

Each symposium assumed American culture was becoming more conservative (more reliant on traditional beliefs, religious ones among them) and more narrowly American. The contributors (Burnham, Fiedler, Niebuhr, Trilling, Riesman, Schorer,

Rahv, Arvin, Agee, Arendt, Auden, Dewey, Richards, Marianne Moore, Clement Greenberg) all tried to deal with such sweeping matters in varying degrees of agreement or disagreement, some applauding, some defying, many dancing into the wings. I am not concerned with responses, but with the nature of the symposia themselves. For the assumption behind them is not too different from the assumptions behind *Life, Time,* and *Fortune* editorials: which is that Americans should come together and reflect a common heritage, especially in the face of a Soviet threat. The symposia imply that Americans should strive for coherence, that American values are worth defending, and that traditional beliefs, once so maligned, may be the source of considerable strength. To his credit, Norman Mailer refused.

and the artist confronts what Kierkegaard called the "anguish of the aesthetic," in which one kind of faith rubs up against another.

Those critics who make that loss of history into a point of attack underestimate our uniqueness. America may or may not have been betrayed by Communists and their sympathizers in the fifties; the larger cultural issue was that reality became hidden under layers, like an onion's core. The move toward world power which America made in the postwar decade established "history now." In a power vacuum created by the war, America stood to the rest of the world as Rome had once to its world. *History began with America in the 1950s.* Around that pose and fantasy, America became infinite. Thus, spatiality involves not only an investigation of what is "out there," but a demonic quest to see what filled it in. There was no discoverable core, no center, no stable locus, because there was no way to disentangle fantasies, political power plays, national security stands.

There was, finally, that rush to fill a centerless void, an effort made to achieve power by those who would normally have remained as critics of social and political events. The issue of communism gave academics and political critics the opportunity to blend: liberals such as Hook, Lasky, Koestler, Kristol, Bell, Fiedler, Schlesinger consorted with the right and reactionary, with Burnham, Dos Passos, John Chamberlain, etc. The American Committee for Cultural Freedom was founded by Schlesinger (a liberal of the "vital center"), Burnham (extreme right), Hook (diminishing into a neoconservative scold), and James Farrell (the 1930s Marxist). Intellectuals of every stripe had become part of the governmental process, what *Partisan Review* in the fifties and, later, *Commentary* would applaud.

Not only novelists and action painters celebrated "history now," but those who spoke of a "new America" and rejoiced in a fresh spirit of reality or actuality. Philip Rahv, ex-Trotskyite, wrote glowingly of the loss of "Utopian illusions and heady expectations." Intellectuals offered up a poisoned cultural and political atmosphere as a given, a semiliterate folk hero as President, the inevitable loss of expectations after a major crisis, the popular press and television media lauding American consumer fantasies; in this context, the novelists desperately needed some purchase. The sole movement could be to extremes, to mockery and/or withdrawal, into countering fantasies in which America would be barely recognizable.

The Tribunes, Gaddis and Ellison

In *The Recognitions* (1955), perhaps *the* novel of the fifties, William Gaddis makes counterfeiting his motif: for his characters, their activities, their emotional lives, and ultimately, for the entire surrounding culture. But counterfeiting, as we shall see, is not necessarily a purely negative form of expression; not always artificial or a form of plagiarism.* In some of its manifestations, it can lead to recognitions, especially in an era when "real things" are beyond attainment or themselves falsifications. Recognitions are related to Wordsworth's "spots in time," Joyce's

epiphanies, religious revelations (the protagonist, Wyatt Gwyon, was once a seminarian), Proust's "privileged moments." They are moments of personal truth or consciousness. When a person achieves a recognition, he has attained some connection between the universe and himself. Not to achieve a recognition is to remain unrealized or part of dead matter, unrecognized and unrecognizing—as, later, those impersonal creatures in Gaddis's *JR,* mutants attached only to "dummy corporations."

Halfway through this immense novel—half a million words—a character named Otto says what serves as a motif for the novel and for the period after the war when it was written. It serves, also, as a theme for *JR.* Otto is a failed playwright, a young man striving for the truth within a context of plagiarism

---

*When Pynchon picks up the theme in *V.,* counterfeiting becomes "stencilized," Herbert Stencil's programmed existence. But *V.* is a novel of the 1960s, when anything not natural was deemed unnatural.

or counterfeiting. He is unable to achieve recognition and searches reflections of himself for the "real person," which would be an act of recognition. If he could attain that reality, then he would be able to write a valid play, instead of one full of borrowed feelings and language. He has glimpses of his plight:

Like a story I heard once . . . a story about a forged painting. It was a forged Titian that somebody had painted over another old painting, when they scraped the forged Titian away they found some worthless old painting underneath it, the forger had used it because it was an old canvas. But then there was something under that worthless painting, and they scraped it off and underneath that they found a Titian, a real Titian that had been there all the time. It was as though when the forger was working, and he didn't know the original was underneath, I mean he didn't know he knew it, but it knew, I mean something knew. I mean, do you see what I mean? That underneath that the original is there, that the real . . . thing is there, and on the surface you . . . if you can only . . . see what I mean?

How traditionally American—Emersonian, in fact!—and yet how applicable it is to the decade in which it appeared. Layers of untruth piled on; beneath it, somewhere, the real, while all the time we demand the forgery. We recall how in the 1950s tags were used as forms of discourse—cold war, pinkos, left-winger, Red China, McCarthyism, Hiss, Rosenbergs, liberal intellectual, egghead—as though labels were a kind of totem. To repeat them was to reach for truth with a magic wand. We demeaned every experience and every response by means of a reductive vocabulary which transmitted only the artificial and factitious.

If this is granted, then *The Recognitions* becomes our archetypal experience for the fifties, a model or scenario for the way in which we saw and will continue to see ourselves. Rhetoric acts like a palimpsest, layer after layer disguising the real or actual. Exaggeration, hyperbole, rhetorical trivia all pile paint upon the old master. The ambitious reach of the Gaddis novel, sweeping up vertically the American past and horizontally present-day America and Europe, permits us to see inclusively. It is the opposite of the slice-of-life fiction that characterized the 1950s: Styron's *Lie Down in Darkness,* Bellow's *Augie March,* or Malamud's *The Assistant* and *A New Life.* The literary background of Gaddis recalls and goes well beyond Hawthorne, well beyond Joyce or the Joycean novel. His vast work is a kind of literary conglomer-

ate: the entire American literary past, Hawthorne, of course, but also Emerson and Thoreau, the Melville of *The Confidence Man,* Poe, and more Poe, Faulkner, Eliot; the Europeans—Dostoyevsky, Kafka, as well as Joyce and Céline. But these are only beginnings. Gaddis draws on extensive reading in and knowledge of religious literature, church fathers and historians, Latin works, theologians, all sufficiently assimilated so that they can be regurgitated for parodic purposes. The point throughout is that every belief once sincerely held is now a subject of mockery, unless one has achieved a recognition.

Wyatt Gwyon, heir to a New England past, realizes that recognition, of reality, actuality, truth itself, involves a commitment of self little short of obsessive. He is a man misplaced in his time, in a phase antithetical to his own nature. He is surrounded by people who live at the level of forgery, who must relate every feeling to advertisements, publicity, exaggeration of self, narcissism, and who, as a consequence, have removed themselves from "recognitions." Like Stephen Dedalus—the parallels are numerous and clearly pointed—he is moving on different levels of intensity and observation. And like Stephen, he will prove his difference from the mob by bringing forth with great personal suffering an art that distinguishes him from those who worship false idols. With this art, Wyatt will define his sense of "recognitions." He is the most appropriate deliverer of the vision, for, like Stephen, he is as much divinity student as creator. Wyatt has forsaken his religious studies in order to pursue new shapes and forms, the churchly past giving way to the artistic present.

Yet Gaddis is pursuing a course different from Joyce's, although not less significant. Wyatt's own work, as a definition of himself, lacks meaning, until he finds he can express himself only through a relationship with the past and, in particular, with the Flemish masters of the fifteenth and sixteenth centuries: Memling, the Van Eyck brothers, Roger Van der Weyden, Hugo van der Goes, Thierry Bouts, Patinir; and including the Venetian painter Titian. The Flemish masters, besides their religious themes, impressed Wyatt with their obsessive dedication to detail, their absolute devotion to fidelity of line and color. Each curve and shaping involved the sense of a world and universe; nothing was left to chance or coincidence. And their devotion seemed complete—no doubt, no removal of self, no narcissism. Instead of losing the subject in themselves, as in the narcissistic work of present-day creative artists, they lost themselves in their subject. If the 1950s were double-talk and double-think, labels that defaulted on thought, the Flemish masters were anchors in reality, in "recognitions."

So Wyatt, who must transform the religious passions of his father into forms in which he can believe, removes himself to the Flemish past. He finds his creative urge focused and shaped through his connection to a distinctive, identifiable art. Here, Gaddis expresses the originality of his motif, not only through technical experimentation with forms but through insight into how art can reflect the real, whereas contemporary discourse only falsifies it. Wyatt is not a conventional forger of great art. He paints pictures that his masters could have painted, Flemish "originals." By bringing together the styles, colors, and shapes of a particular master, he creates canvases that might have been done—pictures, often, that the masters were thought to have painted, but that have failed to turn up. He reconstitutes art history by "discovering" the work they did (but which has disappeared) and making them live in new shapes. As Valentine, a typically commercially-oriented art critic, says, "his work is so good it has almost been taken for forgery."

Valentine, then, caustically justifies Wyatt's kind of art, not for the sake of the art, but for the market value it retains despite changes of taste and style:

> Most forgeries last only a few generations, because they're so carefully done in the taste of the period, a forged Rembrandt, for instance, confirms everything that that period sees in Rembrandt. Taste and style change, and the forgery is painfully obvious, dated, because the new period has discovered him to be quite different. That is the curse that any genuine article must endure.

For Valentine, whenever one of Wyatt's "authentic forgeries" is questioned, it has nothing to do with art; it is simply because the dealers hope to discredit them and bring down the price. Every time the dealer guesses wrong, the market becomes that much better for the forgeries, since dealers become reluctant to question them. Wyatt's forgeries, accordingly, enter a market in which the authentic article is really no different from the forgery. The dealer and purchaser connive with the seller and art critic, since all have everything to gain from putting across a forgery and little to lose form the discovery of one.

The complicity of market, purchaser, seller, and art critic closes Gaddis's trap around Wyatt. We are now about one-fifth through the novel, and the terms are set. Like a fish struggling in a net, Wyatt must find a way through or be pulled in. As readers, we are in the position of complicity, like the figures in Plato who seek reality in appearances. If we assent to forgery frequently enough, we lose the definition of what is real, what is forged.

All this, however, is too simplistic for Gaddis, too heuristic. For while Wyatt may be a forger, he is a man of a distinct and original vision, for which he will lie, even kill. The ferocious demon is internal, and one recalls Faulkner's Sutpen, who created his "works" in order to define that demon. At the time of this conversation between Valentine and Recktall ("rectal") Brown, an art dealer, Wyatt is a fateful, Christ-like thirty-three, and we never lose sight of the religious dimension. With *his* forgeries, or "miracles," Wyatt will deliver us from the defilement of art, and the defilement of life beyond it.

The epigraph to the section (VII) compares Jesus Christ, who took upon Himself human nature in order to redeem mankind, to the artist, who must redeem us from those who defile creation. But Gaddis, once again, is not making the old, by now hackneyed plea for the superiority of the artist over life; he invokes the fixity of vision that rejects complicity, that marketplace notion of the real and actual. At stake, finally, is not solely art, but the quality of life, even when that life is itself based on counterfeiting. As in the religious parables, when the sinner achieves salvation, the less real here is more real, especially when those who market both do not care which is which.

Wyatt fulminates against reproductions because there is only *one* painting with its distinct aura, and the reproduction is a fake which cheapens the original, making the viewer think he is seeing something real, while the actual remains inaccessible to him. Reproduction, Wyatt indicates, is marketplace prostitution, in which the artist's vision is diluted by way of intervening methods.* His fanaticism brings from

---

*We find a parallel argument in Walter Benjamin's "The Work of Art in the Age of Mechanical Reproduction," which Gaddis may have been familiar with. Benjamin quotes Valéry to the effect that new techniques in reproduction of art will alter our entire perception of the beautiful, affecting artistic invention itself, changing how we view matter, time, and space. Benjamin's argument is that a work of art depends on its *aura* — that is, "its presence in time and space, its unique existence at the place where it happens to be." Changes in its physical condition, movement among owners, increase or decrease in its sales price, all have no effect on the essential work. It is that very control over the work that Wyatt wishes, one reason why he rejects original work in the present era, where reproduction and other mechanical forms have preempted the *aura* of a master.

Valentine the rejoinder that "Every piece you do is calumny on the artist you forge." We are now at the crossroads for the American and the American artist: at that choice between mechanical reproduction (marketplace) and purity of the original (art), between the pristine order (the Garden of Eden) and worldly rewards (the earthly paradise). Wyatt's defense of what he does is a defense of "recognitions" themselves; a defense of his journey into the past for a reality that is singular and intense, undiluted by the mechanical detection tools of the modern critic:

> Do you think I do these the way all other forging has been done? Pulling the fragments of ten paintings together and making one, or taking a . . . a Dürer and reversing the composition so that the man looks to the right instead of left, putting a beard on him from another portrait, and a hat, a different hat from another, so that they look at it and recognize Dürer there? No, it's . . . the recognitions go much deeper, much further back, and I . . . this . . . the X-ray tests and ultra-violet and infra-red, the experts with their photomicrography and . . . macrophotography, do you think that's all there is to it? Some of them aren't fools, they don't just look for a hat or a beard, or a style they can recognize, they look with memories that . . . go beyond themselves, that go back to . . . where mine goes.

Wyatt has repositioned himself: "I'm a master painter in the Guild, in Flanders, do you see? . . . because I've taken the Guild oath, not for the critics, the experts . . . to use pure materials, to work in the sight of God."

Wyatt is more than a crazy fool, for his is more than a vision of what could be. He makes the vision happen, and his fidelity to the masters is so great he becomes a master, whereas his contemporaries remain forgers of taste, panderers to the market. A modern-day visionary, a Christ of aesthetics, he insists that the purity of his materials—the gold he uses, his pigments, his exquisite colors—suggests the nature of his art. Valentine say that while Wyatt paints, "it's your own work," but what happens, he asks, when he attaches the signature? Wyatt admits he loses everything when that occurs; he is, at that moment alone, a forger. Valentine consoles him by saying that the sole thing he can be prosecuted for is the

---

At the time Gaddis wrote *The Recognitions,* controversy over originals, reproductions, and availability was created by André Malraux's contention that art now belonged to everyone, that museums no longer had walls. In this view, reproduction is the ultimate egalitarianism, to be not despised but applauded.

signature, *that* forgery. The paintings are authentic: "The law doesn't care a damn for the painting. God isn't watching them." Wyatt's greatest feat, he admits, would be to do a painting in the style of Hubert van Eyck, whose very existence as Jan van Eyck's older brother is in question. To paint a Hubert van Eyck, to document the painting, and prove not only that Hubert existed but that the painting is real—all this will fall on fertile ground, and the sole illegality would be the signature, not the painting.

Wyatt must live with this knowledge, that the moment he signs the painting and makes it valuable, at that moment he destroys the foundation of his art. The Faustian quality of his conflict is clear, and he follows it through by destroying everything, burning it, turning it into ashes, and then himself assuming the name Stephen Asche. He is the first Christian martyr born out of the ashes of his own work. The paradoxes and ironies are those of the very nature of the American experience, the Fall implicit in the beauties and purities of the Garden.

Themes of forgery and counterfeiting underlie every aspect of the novel, including Gaddis's method of novel-making. For a book of such great length, the author needed more than a conventional narrative; and the characteristic American picaresque, although appropriate to *Augie March* or *A New Life,* would have become untenable for a thousand pages—unless the entire book was parodic, as Barth's *Sot-Weed Factor.* Gaddis devised two, really three, kinds of scene development. The first involves the introduction of a character, unknown to the reader and, apparently, unconnected to the narrative, who then links up with someone we know from before. In section VII, for example, we read: "That afternoon Fuller sat on a bench, his back turned to Central Park in December." Since the novel is already so dense, we may feel we have missed Fuller's name in a previous passage, so confidently does Gaddis make the introduction. We remain unfocused until we catch Fuller's connection to Recktall Brown, who has been mentioned, at length, only once before. That, too, is part of the plan: when an association is made, it hangs by a single reference.

Brown brings us eventually to Wyatt Gwyon, and to the forgeries he is masterminding. But even when we meet Brown, along with Basil Valentine, the talk centers on a "he," who we assume is Wyatt. Once details flow in, we know it is "he," but not at first. The method, so far, creates immediate annoyance, especially since the tones and textures are also so ironic and paradoxical. A second method that Gaddis employs, possibly as a carry-over from Joyce and Faulkner, is to describe an entire episode without indicating the name or names of the characters; so that the reader must derive from the context who is involved. In a scene in which the Reverend Gwyon is never named, we find Wyatt returning to the New England town of his forebears, where Gwyon has gone mad, has been moved to a private institution, and now is dying. Gwyon is reduced to ashes—which, incidentally, turn up later in Spain, in loaves which the son eats—while the new minister, curled up with copies of *Reader's Digest,* prepares his sermon for the following Sunday. No names, and the Reverend Gwyon passes through his agony and madness without coming to us as an identified person, only as substance, ashes at that.

The final part (III) of the novel, one-quarter of its length, incorporates both methods: unnamed characters and characters who seem to have little connection to what came before. In addition, scenes are themselves so placed that they appear unassociated with people we have met. We have, then, actually three unknowns, so that reading becomes a kind of testing. Modernism with a vengeance! Because we may try out several alternative possibilities before we hit upon the "right one," we reconstruct many kinds of sequences. And in places, even the most careful reader cannot be certain of each character, event, scene.

Some of this Gaddis gained from Joyce, or from Eliot's modulations in "The Waste Land," but he differs from Joyce—I have in mind chiefly *Ulysses*—in some essential ways. The narrative line of *Ulysses* is frequently secondary to what occurs along the way; discourse and digression are at least as important as anything that happens. Part of the modernity of *Ulysses* was just this seeming indifference to narrative thrust. But *The Recognitions* has a strong narrative drive; it is not a secondary item, nor can it be ignored while we pursue method. A good deal does happen, including all kinds of forgery and counterfeiting, some conspiratorial work (Basil Valentine is a secret agent of sorts), even murder, and the exile of the main character, himself a murderer. What Gaddis has done is to locate his narrative under layers of disguise and deception, by doing so finding the equivalent in plot line of counterfeiting; like that Titian itself, which lies under layers of paint, Gaddis's narrative awaits someone willing to peel away coats which falsify and corrupt.

Are the difficulties presented to us as first-time readers of the novel worth the attention we must pay? Could not a more conventional method have worked as well? Since, except for Hawkes, so little of contemporary American fiction up to the mid-1950s was experimental, we are not conditioned to these labors, and part of the reading experience is to question the obstacles placed in our way. Yet the theme of the book is forgery, the motif recognitions. Gaddis's aim is clearly to defamiliarize the familiar so as to force us to experience it freshly. Thus, every kind of scene —some as familiar as cocktail party scenarios—gains fresh tonal varieties from the method of presentation. In this respect, Gaddis forces upon us that type of careful reading demanded by the early moderns, in both fiction and poetry.

For example: a man named Sinisterra ("sinister land") makes standard forgeries; he is a counterfeiter of existing forms, the American twenty-dollar bill, for instance. He runs through the lower criminal world as Wyatt does through the higher criminal world of art, artists, art dealers, and the wealthy. In both worlds, the aim is, literally, to make money. Sinisterra's first appearance in the novel occurs on page 5, in a fleeting reference amidst a good deal of frenetic authorial maneuvering. It becomes a typical Gaddis ploy.

His early importance is this: Wyatt's parents sail for Spain on the *Purdue Victory.* His mother develops acute appendicitis, and is operated upon by a so-called ship's surgeon, Sinisterra. She dies under the knife, and as it turns out, Sinisterra is not a doctor but a counterfeiter traveling under (his own) forged papers. In his defense, he offers evidence that he had once aided a vivisectionist in Tampa. He now leaves the scene, to reappear almost five hundred pages later, in Part II, the Purgatorio of our *Commedia.* * When we meet him, he appears in the standard Gaddis manner, apparently a new character who will, somehow, be connected to the others. Unless we have read with great care, his name recalls nothing, and we have no way of knowing he has already played a large role in Wyatt's life.

The epigraph for this section is Abraham Lincoln's request to the director of the mint to declare the "trust of our people in God" on our national coins. The mint was ordered to prepare a device with

---

*Dante placed counterfeiters in Bolgia Ten of Circle Eight of Malebolge. The falsifier of money is a "sinner of the third class," whose body is loathsome and racked by thirst. All he is capable of is abuse. The archetypal counterfeiter for Dante was Adamo di Bescia, who falsified the Florentine florin by making it of twenty-one rather than twenty-four carat gold, thus precipitating a currency crisis. Sinisterra aims lower.

a "motto expressing in the fewest and tersest words, this national recognition." The word "recognition," the presence of a counterfeiter, the large role of Sinisterra (the "killer" of Wyatt's mother) all point up Gaddis's ironies. The world as conspiracy, while not born here, is given sustenance and shape. This is not only high comedy, but high politics.

Sinisterra's chief reading is the *National Counterfeit Detector*, a publication devoted to describing the latest gaffes in counterfeiting. Since he values his art as much as Wyatt, he becomes more disturbed by poor evaluations of his work than by the prison sentences he serves. While Wyatt strives to achieve a perfect "Jesus figure," Sinisterra aims at a perfect Jackson portrait on the twenty-dollar bill. As we follow Sinisterra's intense career, we focus on the "real Jackson" much more attentively than we would without the counterfeit President; forgery energizes what the real deadens. By way of Sinisterra, Gaddis enters American history and finds forgery as establishing its own culture, including bank issues of money made on fictitious banks, banks that backed fictitious or worthless notes. That world based on forgery fills Sinisterra with extreme pride:

> Behind him lay the Protocols of the Elders of Zion; and the magnanimous grant of Constantine, though that emperor was some five centuries dead when the spirit of his generosity prevailed through forgers in Rome, to bequeath all of western Europe to the Papacy. Behind him lay decrees, land grants, and wills, whose art of composition became a regular branch of the monastic industry, busy as those monks in the Middle Ages were keeping a-kindle the light of knowledge which they had helped to extinguish everywhere else. Behind lay Polycrates, who minted gold-coated lead coins in his own kingdom of Samos; and Solon, who decreed death for such originality in his. Canute severed guilty hands; and England . . . removed not only hands but eyes.

Sinisterra's ideology parallels that of the other characters: Otto, the failed playwright, who plagiarizes; Esme, Wyatt's model, whose poems move in and out of plagiarism; the art dealers and critics, as well as buyers and sellers, already mentioned. His counterfeiting extends even to his parental role, for Sinisterra plays the false father to Otto and then later, as Mr. Yák, a Rumanian, takes a paternal role with Wyatt.

In a further extension of the forgery: while playing the false father to Otto (who hasn't seen his father since childhood), Sinisterra gives him a large bundle of beautifully printed twenty-dollar bills. The inno-cent Otto spreads them, even to his real father (a Mr. Pivner), and of course to his circle of artificial, partying friends. When the print on the bills runs, Otto and Pivner are identified with the forgery and caught. The bills pass through society, by way of people with counterfeit feelings, an entire society a vast marketplace.

About halfway through, Gaddis increasingly comes to favor a modified stream of consciousness narrative without authorial intrusion. While avoiding the breakup of language the true method calls for, Gaddis nevertheless slips narrative into individual consciousness, to the extent that consciousness is nearly all. There is no intervening narrator until near the end, when he provides some exposition of events. By the third chapter of Part III, with identification of characters left entirely to the reader—characters are merely voices—the end has circled around to the beginning. At the start of the novel, Reverend Gwyon and his wife made their ill-fated voyage to Spain and met Sinisterra as the bogus ship's doctor; now Wyatt, having burned his paintings and rejected his forgeries, has fled to Spain, a murderer. There, he meets Sinisterra, now Mr. Yák, whose aim is to prepare and sell a corpse done up as an ancient Egyptian mummy. The section is aptly titled "The Last Turn of the Screw."

Like Stephen and Bloom in *Ulysses,* the two meet oddly. By this time, Wyatt is ready to become Stephen, the name originally destined for him; and Sinisterra adds Asche on Stephen's false papers. As Stephen Asche, Wyatt attempts rebirth, the forger and murderer who once sought recognitions in counterfeit paintings. Obsessed with failure, pursued by demons, compulsively seeking some form of truth, Wyatt-Stephen has returned to Spain to seek his mother's grave, unaware, of course, that the man offering him aid is the man who butchered her. Further, because of a mixup with his father's ashes, Stephen does not know that the loaves he eats contain mixed in with the flour those very ashes, an act of true communion. Not only is he eating the wafer, he is consuming the actual body, indeed recognition of the real.

All these efforts at the real and actual on Wyatt-Stephen's part, however, occur under a mantle of deception, disguise, and forgery. Yák circles around like the Great Mother because he needs Wyatt's skill in preparing the mummy, which he hopes will be his consummate swindle. Sinisterra thinks he can win over Stephen by insisting he, too, is a craftsman and an artist; he insists he has fallen because "they" were jealous of his work. Wyatt is now so strung out it is questionable if he even hears Sinisterra. Having put all his energies into creating great Flemish "originals," an effort to transcend his contemporaries' inconsequence and technical deficiencies, he drifts: a battered Orpheus, or perhaps an avatar of 1950s "Beats."

The structural tension in the novel lies in that play between great energy and great passivity; between a surface of growth and development and the sense of nihilistic weariness, enervation, exhaustion, what could in fact be considered twin aspects of the American fifties. This tension can be spatially expressed. We note the great stress on traveling, Wyatt's frenzied movement from New England to New York, then to Europe, accompanied by the frenzied movements of the other characters. Even those who go nowhere move to and fro like Michelangelo, consuming space at cocktail parties. As against this, however, is the almost overwhelming desire to rest or drop out. In 1950s fiction, we have such a conflicting range of titles —"Lie Down" or "Flee the," become an "Invisible" or "Underground" man, or go "On the Road," or else have "Adventures of" and gain a "New Life." In swings of movement and passivity, we locate the contradictions of people who must get there so they can rest or disappear, or who become passive in the hope of gaining energy for a new foray.

In this respect, Gaddis's novel is archetypal. We can see how Pynchon, with his idea of the yo-yoing effect, is indebted to him: that expenditure of circular energy. We can, in turn, perceive how Gaddis sought in Hawthorne and Poe those intense inner energies which war with passivity; for this tension connects to larger American themes and paradoxes. Sweeps of limitless space and time run up against degeneration, entropy, paralysis, and withdrawal. As Gaddis will show here, and later in *JR*, American affirmation is "against," a value system erected on negativism and nihilism. The reason is that American attitudes are predicated on the Edenic myth and the Fall, and Gaddis plays diminution for faith gained and lost, like a yo-yo.

That desire to hide oneself, so evident in Wyatt, is the result of complications which work at the extremes: either easy acceptance and celebrity, which means a form of death, or desperate, often hopeless, opposition, which leads to a different kind of personal ruin. Every form of success—and Wyatt is an outstanding success as a forger, as an "original" counterfeiter—must be a form of death. This is a profoundly political idea, the American equivalent of European ideologies. The attack on the contemporary Ameri-

can novel *Life* magazine made in September 1955— the year of *The Recognitions*—went further than a misunderstanding of the fictional process; it was based on political outrage that the novelist had rejected those easy resolutions which, *Life* assumed, made up the good life and which the novelist saw as forms of death. The "good life" for Wyatt, as for art critics and dealers, would have been a continued exploitation of his talent for original counterfeits and his silence in the face of external demands made upon him. Success, in *Life*'s terms, was assured: the counterfeit was the real. Gaddis, however, insisted on a more layered sense of the counterfeit: that while it could falsify on one hand and still seek truth on the other, a more intense truth lay within, beyond the reach of all aspects of counterfeiting. The working out is extremely complex and requires the close reasoning of intricate scenes and dense structuring, not a flat statement of direction.

We are at that point when the novel as a genre had to respond or else succumb to its own success. There began, in the 1950s, the growing awareness that even the novel—a traditionally stable, solid presence—was insufficient as a reflection of reality; that, as Tony Tanner comments, "American writers seem . . . to have felt how tenuous, arbitrary, and even illusory are the verbal constructs which men call descriptions of reality." There began that need to seek more radical forms, so as to keep pace with or mirror the phantasmagoria called up by science and technology—what we find in Gaddis and Barth now, Pynchon and Barthelme later, Hawkes earlier.

Counterfeiting and invisibility work well with nearly any of these fictional developments. Tuned in as the American novelist has been to energy and linear development of character, counterfeiting and invisibility present a tension: counterfeiting, the use of imitative form and derivative life; invisibility, a negation of spatiality and vitality, a substitution of darkness for light, innerness for movement. The twin themes allow for that curious disaffection we discover in our novelists of the 1950s and 1960s. That is, they may seem dark or black or Gothic, but all too frequently they slip away from the ultimate nature of their observations, to resolve or slide off to areas of life which offer more dynamics than counterfeiting or invisibility allows. Such novelists flirt with the disintegration implicit in their themes, while fascinated by energy and movement. The point, except for a few, seems to be: *counterfeiting and invisibility accommodate their personal attitudes, but movement and energy preempt their ideology.* Even those who recognize the trap, such as Roth and Malamud, possibly Mailer, blur the full adversariness of their experience and fudge on the paralytic implications of their material.

Perhaps the novel of the 1950s except for *The Recognitions* which blurs least is *Invisible Man.* Counterfeiting and invisibility control Ellison's vision, just as narcissism, circuitry, and memories define his main character. We see how Ellison combines paralysis and enervation with typical American themes, building his tensions between traditional ideas of space and energy and the particularities of his narrator's experiences, which suggest exhaustion and stasis, self-examination and narcissism. He has blended the American sense of things, in Emerson, Whitman, Melville, Twain, and Wright, even Hawthorne, with the European—Dostoyevsky and Kafka, among others—to give us a sense of the period; in the same way Gaddis was working along a blend of Hawthorne and Kafka to produce a "counterfeit decade."

Once these things are said, Ellison and Gaddis part ways; for the former, however ironically, is more concerned with growth and development, characteristics firmly in the *Bildungsroman* tradition. Gaddis moves into the more doomed part of the American tradition, parts we associate with Melville's Ahab, Hawthorne's fated figures, Poe's nightmarish characters and scenes. Ellison foresaw enervation, but also the potentiality of growth. Gaddis identifies with the doom that lies beneath enervation. The images in the final sections of *The Recognitions* are of an incoherent Wyatt, a pilgrimage of doomed figures to Rome, a lunatic Otto, and Sinisterra with his counterfeit Egyptian mummy. Widely dispersed geographically, they are all circumscribed by the final scene of the novel. Stanley, an imitational composer, enters a church in Fenestrula, sees a gigantic organ, and indicates to a priest who understands no English that he intends to play it. When Stanley pulls out two particular stops, the priest puts them back, with the warning, in an Italian which Stanley cannot comprehend, that the church is so old the bass vibrations could be dangerous.

Like the poor reader with no Italian, Stanley understands nothing of the warning, and rolls out the deepest possible sound of the bass pipes. "Everything moved, and even falling, soared in atonement. He was the only person caught in the collapse, and afterward most of his work was recovered too, and it is still spoken of, when it is noted, with high regard, though seldom played." The apocalypse has arrived, with an explanation in Italian; and this experience of Stanley,

personally doomed, while his counterfeit work soars in atonement, is a perfect expression of Henry Adams's virgin and dynamo: the machine crushes, the Virgin saves.

Gaddis's vision, both hilarious and doom-filled, goes much farther than Ellison's toward a reading of the 1950s, even the entire postwar era. Since serious critics of the American novel—except for Tony Tanner, an Englishman—have ignored Gaddis's work, we have been spared their howls of outrage at his "nihilism" or his lack of "historical relevance." Yet whatever our individual response, we must view Gaddis's sense of the fifties as a guideline, and measure other novelistic experiences against it.

When Gaddis returned to fiction in the 1970s, with the monumentally conceived *JR* (1975), his world was a thriving, writhing, buzzing nightmare, a continuation of 1950s counterfeit. The key part here is the method: interrupted conversation, incomplete lines of thought, a shorthand language; language that no longer serves its traditional functions. Gaddis has tried to put gesture and expression into the written word. But it is, also, the language we feed into computers, set phrases programmed for rapidity, where our interest lies only in the printout.

The walls that come tumbling down at the finale of *The Recognitions,* Gaddis's Götterdämmerung, lead, fittingly enough, into an early part of *JR,* which presents a school production of *Das Rheingold,* with JR himself as the dwarfish Alberich. But Gaddis's Wagnerian model does not lead to the death of the gods or to human love, but to another kind of god, which is business, high finance. *Das Rheingold* accommodates the prologue of this immensely long novel, since gold, *Geld,* capitalism are forms of paradise or nightmare for all who enter.

We recall Alberich's key speech to Wotan and Loge in *Das Rheingold,* and we need only substitute JR, the school performer who becomes Alberich, Wagner's dwarf: "I will capture all you godly folk!/ As I have renounced love, / so all things living / shall renounce it; / lured by gold / you shall ever lust for gold alone. / On blissful heights / in happy meditation / you lull yourselves; / you immortal dwellers in luxury / despise the black goblins! / Beware, beware! / For once you people serve / my might / your pretty women, / who spurn my wooing, / the dwarf shall force to his pleasure, / though love smiles not on him. . . . Beware! / Beware of the dark legion / when the Nibelung treasure shall rise / out of the silent depths into the light of day!"

The content, once extracted, is familiar: the business of America is business; but Gaddis has found a form, a language as well as a focus for his view of postwar America. Many devices from *The Recognitions* remain. The withholding of vital information is crucial; for the retention of material creates a pressure on the reader. We are caught, in a guessing game, a suspense drama, a purely dramatic action. Postponement, as in drama, is the key; we push against unknowns.

That device in isolation does not convey Gaddis's method. Along with Hawkes, Barth, Pynchon, and Barthelme, Gaddis tried to parallel or even improve upon the major moderns in creating "voices." The withholding of information recalls Faulkner, in particular *Absalom, Absalom!,* perhaps *The Sound and the Fury.* The Faulknerian presence (and behind that, the Joycean) is, in fact, everywhere—in phrasing, in interrupted speech which suggests great unspoken depths, and in broad verbal wit. Intermixed with the incomplete or withheld information is an analogous device, also familiar from Faulkner: the unidentified speaker. The beginning of *JR* is one of the most deliberately confusing in literature:

—Money. . . ? in a voice that rustled.
—Paper, yes.
—And we'd never seen it. Paper money.
—We never saw paper money till we came east.
—It looked so strange the first time we saw it. Lifeless.

This continues for pages, with names slipped in that mean nothing, the speakers unidentified. The reader struggles not only for identification of the speakers, or for the information, but for some thread of argument which connects these discrete pieces of material. Long before recognition is forthcoming, the scene, we discover suddenly, has shifted to a school, where the main part of the plot eventually settles. Without warning, different speakers appear. Words and voices, however, seem disembodied. Location, direction, content are unclear. Compared with *JR,* *The Recognitions* is almost traditional.

The scene becomes fixed on a musical performance, *Das Rheingold,* with a shadowy schoolboy as the dwarfish Alberich, our JR. But the JR or Junior of the title rarely comes clearly into focus. He is a sixth grader, and a full-faced portrait, Gaddis realized, would be of little interest. Moving in shadows, however, he can be a giant, the mastermind of a vast corporate enterprise, something it takes us hundreds of pages to identify. In those early school scenes, we

know him only as Alberich, in an opera concerned with the Gold of the Rhine. Since the opening lines were fixed on paper money—that is, stocks and shares—we begin to perceive a theme, although unassociated with any particular characters. The theme, then, rather than characters, will dominate the novel. Just as in *Das Rheingold* the Gold of the Rhine will dominate the opera and the entire Ring, so money will open and close the cycles of *JR.*

This is still only a crude description of methods which could create initial difficulties. Paramount is the use of interrupted speech, in what approximates a contemporary lingo. About 75,000 words into the novel, we have our first clear indication of what is going to be significant. The unidentified JR says to Mr. Bast, the music coach:

. . . you know what I was thinking on the train hey? he came on righting his load, hurrying alongside —like I have this thing which what it is is it's this selling outfit where what you do is you send in and they send you all these different shoes which you get to wear them around so people can see them, you know? See that's how to sell them, see? I mean not the ones you're wearing right off your feet but like you take their order and then you make this commission, you know? Like it says you can make a hundred dollars a week in your spare time and you get to wear these shoes around too, you want me to find it?

This is one of JR's few long speeches, and it is interspersed with interrupted sentences, a printout or shorthand method. The long sequences are fluid and of a conversational ordinariness which is remarkable. Gaddis's execution is merciless; more than satirical, the style strikes at the heart of every type of communication. Later, a radio plays because the turn-off knob cannot be reached. It catches our attention in small bursts, then fades. Our speech patterns are similar: people listen, then stop, then are caught up in their own speech, interrupt, are interrupted, and the cycle renews itself on human self-indulgence. We hear, ultimately, only our own thought patterns, which we attempt to relocate in a language that is strangled before it reaches fulfillment. Counterfeit thoughts become part of an oral tradition.

Incomplete speech is the language of money-making. The director of the school operation, Whiteback, also heads a bank; and all school business is interrupted by his telephone, which signals bank business. The educational plant, and the language interred in it, is intermixed at every level with the world of the bank. A financial scheme advanced, in fact, is to advertise in textbooks, suitable to the needs of the reader; for example, in advanced algebra or French III, deodorant tampons. Within this frame of reference, the sixth grader JR is carrying out a function, with words he can barely pronounce, no less understand: to do the work of the banks and make money. We bank while we learn.

Obstacles are overwhelming: Gaddis is so unbending, and, one must add, obsessive, that the reader is forgotten.* If he makes the effort, however, there are scenes that are among the most hilarious in American fiction, despite this being be a doom-filled vision. We can cite the Marx Brothers scenario for the Ninety-sixth Street apartment that is the financial hub, with mail pouring in, Bast trying to write music for a "zoo movie," the hippie Rhoda protesting that the scene is too far out even for her, water cascading from a broken sink and then a broken tub faucet, a radio playing something beneath the books, the books themselves identified only by "III GRIN–LOC," the floor covered with cartons of "24–One Pint Mazola New Improved 36 Boxes 200 2-Ply" and "Wise Potato Chips Hoppin' with Flavor," volumes of *Textile World, Forest Industries, Supervisory Management* strewn everywhere—all this as part of the financial empire JR has been building by way of telephone and mails. This is incomparable comedy, although for the reader to reach it, he must come through a verbal and narrative obstacle course.

Gaddis is, in a sense, carrying on an extended, obsessively detailed dialogue with himself; he is the programmer and he receives the printout. All voices echo, a true universe of words, a parallel phenomenon to *Gravity's Rainbow.* The chief conduits for all information are telephones and mails. In no novel has there been so much fed into the telephone. Essentially, these are tools of obsession: placing calls, needing phone booths, making change for the call, and then gathering information without appearing. JR is a small, impersonal figure, in fact only a voice (often disguised) or a signature on a printed form requesting free goods.

The idea behind the novel is remarkable: that with the telephone and mails, money can be made by any marginal operator, by a sixth grader, through a self-perpetuating system. The basis of JR's fortune is a shipment of about one million surplus navy forks. The goods of the world are simply recycled: the forks, originally ordered by the navy, were produced for the navy, and then dumped by the navy as detritus, only to be picked by JR through the mails, started through the system once again, becoming the basis for further deals, all of which involve recycled materials, paper deals, penny stocks, goods which, having become unfashionable or dysfunctional, are then returned into fashion. JR is the new generation of entrepreneurs, and his fortune will result from his intuition that goods shuffling through the system become themselves the touchstones of wealth; movement, not production, is necessary. Without money or visible goods, JR is worth millions.

Gaddis stresses the depersonalization of money-making as part of the waste land in which people operate and thrive.* The structural equivalent of this is hundreds of thousands of words of dialogue, Gaddis's demonic way with conversational gambits: interrupted speech, run-together names and statements, broken-off phrases and barely uttered words, an oral shorthand. As in *The Recognitions,* we must pick up speakers from the situation and their words; but here the torrent of language pouring over us makes identification more difficult. In terms of language, Gaddis has tried to do for the oral American idiom what Joyce did for the written English—rediscover it as a literary voice, defamiliarize it so it seems fresh. His is the poetry, flow, and rhythm of routine speech, as much code as communication.

> . . . Oh J R I . . .
> —Oh hi Mrs. Joubert [a financial expert] . . . as quickly gone behind the glass panels clattering closed on the first ring. —Hello . . . ? pencil stub, paper scraps surfacing—this is him speaking yes, I'll accept it . . . portfolio jammed up against a knee—hello? Yes hi, boy it's a good thing you called hey I . . . where just now at the hotel? Did you . . . no but wait a second . . . No but see Bast that's what I was just . . . no what kind of full uniform, you mean with a gun and all . . . ? No but . . . no but sure I know we got this here hotel suite so you could partly use it to play the . . .

---

*I understand that his manuscript originally made no distinction between the spoken word and narration, and only when his publisher insisted on it did he insert dashes to indicate dialogue. Without dashes, the novel would have approximated the jigsaw puzzle of Little Red Riding Hood's hood.

*Although the sources for a book like *JR* are America itself, nevertheless one perceives parallels to the Brecht-Weill opera *The Rise and Fall of the City of Mahagonny.* The capital crime in Mahagonny is poverty; whereas wealth, acquired in whatever manner, rules. In a sense, this is the other side of Puritanism, a parodic view of earthly wealth as symbolic of the heavenly riches yet to come; a view Gaddis in both novels could accommodate.

For scenic development, Gaddis works with a very complicated montage: not simply shifting within a scene, or shifting from brief scene to brief scene, but moving from one long segment to another without any shading in or sense of direction. This fits his sense of modern communication, as aborted phraseology, undigested bits of information, false data purveyed as fact. It conveys, as well, his detestation of contemporary drift, lack of commitment, whether work, art, or even self. It is a true response to the vapidity one felt in the postwar years, when high finance *was* good for America and the life of the mind was considered counterfeit.

Since the goal is seamlessness and flow, there is considerable and conscious overlap of data. Gaddis's game is a form of suspense, based on incompletion and interruption, sudden shiftings of locale from school to bank to investment office to apartment, in a verbiage that permits no clear definition. This is a suspenseful story without crime or traditional criminals, and the reader must play along for clues. Since so much is a compulsion *not* to give, the reader desperately scrambles for what is given, like the tension we experience in crime stories. Our role is to be shaped by data.

In the deepest sense, Gaddis is concerned with crime: the crime of the decade, century, American history itself. For him, the deepest crime, whether in the counterfeiting process of the earlier novel or the financial recycling of the latter, is individual loss of recognition, actuality, perception of the real, if that can ever be determined. It may be impossible to achieve recognition, but to forgo the possibility is to collapse and subvert the individual.

A good example of a young man trying to attain perception and definition is Edwerd [sic] Bast, a composer. A serious composer in the contemporary mode, he is first seen directing and conducting a school performance of *Das Rheingold.* Yet despite his aspirations, Bast, whose name can be "enough" or "bastard," finds himself drawn into JR's financial schemes. He also becomes drawn into composing "animal music" for a zoo movie, a scheme intermixed with financial shenanigans by a man named Crawley. Like Whiteback, who blends education with banking, Crawley moves back and forth effortlessly between financial deals and his "zoo movie." Bast is caught between, drawn toward finance, which he cannot comprehend, and yet intent on music, which he tries to compose amidst the clutter of the Ninety-sixth Street apartment. Music, his kind, would help define him, whereas JR's schemes and Crawley's offer suck

him in. Unable to resist, he begins to float toward his own kind of doom, loss of recognition of himself and of what is outside.

One peculiarity of the novel is that the titular figure is really not a character in the book. As we suggested above, JR hovers, but is not a presence: somewhat like the Holy Ghost floating over Wyatt in *The Recognitions.* He is the catalyst for the financial empire that develops around the mail drop at Ninety-sixth Street, but the novel functions almost entirely without his appearance. We note the Joycean conceit: a Ulysses of the title who is absent from the book, and whose presence must be extrapolated from his opposite, Bloom. JR becomes, on his smaller scale, a mythical figure—only "Hey Mister" signals he is there.

One of his very few solid presences comes late in the novel, about two-thirds through, and characteristically, JR is on the telephone. He is speaking to Bast, but not as a sixth grader or an eleven-year-old. Here he is completely the corporate manager, the financial plunger, the man who has studied the market, futures, pork bellies, and margins. He has all the lingo of finance, although parts of it confuse him. He turns to his sixth-grade teacher, Mrs. Joubert, for further instruction: ". . . like now we already learned about the stock market and all with this here our share of America? See so now if we bought some of these futures like if we got in these here bellies and learned the . . ." He asks, further, about "hedged commodities," and wonders if it is possible to "hedge in these futures"—all questions she, as the "expert" in finance, cannot answer. JR sees millionaires wherever he looks; he is obsessed with the ideology of money and money-making, pointing to water-fountain millionaires, light-bulb millionaires, even locker millionaires, while Mrs. Joubert tries to make him *see* the evening, the sky, the wind, the moon.

Implied in this parodying of finance is the parody of technology and science, such as we see contemporaneously in Pynchon's *Gravity's Rainbow.* Gaddis works at several levels, describing devices such as an electric letter opener that is a devastating weapon, a "Steakwatcher," which computes the time necessary for cooking steaks and chops. Science parodies itself, as it tries to develop a "Frigicom:

> Dateline New York, Frigicom comma a process now being developed to solve the noise pollution problem comma may one day take the place of records comma books comma even personal letters in our daily lives comma according to a report released jointly today by the Department of Defense and Ray

Hyphen X Corporation comma a member of the caps J R Family of Companies period new paragraph. The still secret Frigicom process is attracting the attention of our major cities as the latest scientific breakthrough promising noise elimination by the placement of absorbent screens at what are called quote shard intervals unquote in noise polluted areas period operating at faster hyphen than hyphen sound speeds comma a complex process employing liquid nitrogen will be used to convert the noise shards comma as they are known comma at temperatures so low they may be handled with comparative ease by trained personnel immediately upon emission before the noise element is released into the atmosphere period.

The translation: Sounds can be frozen into a solid state.

Since all is flow, whether sound, water, conversation, a radio playing, publicity and advertising, or characters and scenes themselves, there is no order. Once caught in JR's international money schemes, the characters have no lives except what the flow determines. As a novelist who carries the 1950s into the 1970s, Gaddis is linked with Pynchon and Barthelme, writers who have constructed their universe almost entirely of words and whose basic theme is counterfeiting. To these we can add Nabokov, in *Ada,* as well as in the earlier *Pale Fire.* Behind them is Borges and parallel is Barth. For all, their verbal constructs are not solely connected to a more experimental phase in the arts—although that may be present—but to a distinct reaction to political and social themes. That stress on verbal constructs is not withdrawal from statement, but statement itself. Fiction has become an intensification of a verbal universe. Gaddis and Pynchon, in particular, do not use language to enter an interior world where all is self, narcissism, or indulgence; but as a way of exploring the outer reaches of language where it blurs into disorder. Their verbal construct is not a hiding behind words as a shield, but the forcing of words outward, where language and things merge into each other.

This distinction is quite important, for it separates Gaddis and Pynchon as wordsmen from Barthelme and Nabokov. The latter two are following in the Joycean tradition of internalizing experience, shunning the external, and locating activity by way of voices that point inward. Barthelme does this and, at the same time, disbelieves in it; whereas Nabokov pursues it for the sheer exuberance of his own versatility, especially in the fruitcake-like *Ada,* all performance.

Gaddis and Pynchon are social and political novelists, quite concerned with externals worlds, whether America as itself a corporate empire, in *JR,* or as part of a multinational cartel, as in *Gravity's Rainbow.* Their barrages of words, like Pynchon's rockets, are centrifugal, not centripetal, forces. The impersonality of *JR* results from Gaddis's construction of a huge "outer world" with an existence of its own; in that world, which spans two decades, we find an entire value system, not a retreat from it. Similarly, in *Gravity's Rainbow,* we discover that language works to thrust us into energy and movement, toward a confrontation not with enervation but with infinitude.

For both Gaddis and Pynchon, the corporate empire embodies tremendous energy. Once created, it takes on a vitality and vibrancy that is cataclysmic. The key image is Pynchon's: *thrust* and *thrusting,* sexual as well as financial, athletic as well as martial; the method based on movement. Both may parody finance, capitalism, the corporation, but they see in that a form of existence which gives real meaning to individual lives. While it may, in its multiplicity and energies, bury the individual, it also engages him. Edwerd Bast may reject the financial dealings of JR, but he comes alive in that chaotic, nightmarish Ninety-sixth Street apartment. And JR, that schoolboy, grows into an energetic, resourceful giant once he attaches himself to high finance.

Barthelme and Nabokov, to whom we could add Barth, are exuberant wordmen of exhaustion and enervation; they play not only with the death of the novel but with the death of feeling itself by constructing verbal analogies to the state of dying. Nabokov's work is almost always the end of something; and Barthelme has worked a similar vein: the death of the fairy tale in *Snow White,* the death of the father and an age of paternalism, the death of communication at social functions, the death of writing and painting, the death of verbal communication itself.

Gaddis and Pynchon, however, limn the contours of energy, even when their goals are satire and parody. *The Recognitions,* a more formal work than *JR,* is roughly equivalent in Gaddis's career to *V.* in Pynchon's, published eight years later. In both novels, the expression of the 1950s and early 1960s created a certain amount of exhaustion—the feeling of "the end of." Their novels of the 1970s are a different matter, however, a recovery from the malaise, an exuberance which may be a partial extension of the previous decade, and a direction for the American novel so outside the realist-naturalist tradition that the critic can point to a revitalized fiction.

We have, fortunately, I believe, entered another

modernist phase. This phase did not begin in the 1960s, but in long novels which, in Gaddis's case, reach back to the late 1940s, continue into the 1950s for their ideological base and textures, pick up again in the 1960s, with the gestation of *JR,* and continue into the early 1970s, when the novel was completed. For almost a thirty-year period, Gaddis had been developing two works displaying an American form of modernism. *JR,* in particular, has affinities to the other major developments in the arts. The electronic sounds of new music, for example, lead directly into the telephonic nature of the novel. The reliance there on sounds alone, in new sequences, or in seemingly random patterns, finds its parallel in the nature of media communication, a polyphony of voices that explodes into different and contrasting levels of meaning. The loss of melodic line in modern serial music finds still another parallel in the interrupted speech patterns of *JR.* In art, in particular, the laid-on paint we associate with Jackson Pollock, or the stress on linear arrangement and field of vision of the action painters, can be found in both *The Recognitions* and *JR,* although more recognizably in the latter. Pop art, whose development paralleled the gestation and writing of *JR* (itself a pop title), informs the novel at every turn, with the apartment on Ninety-sixth Street a repository of the junk objects that inform pop culture.

The first line, "I am an invisible man," establishes a tension in Ralph Ellison's novel (begun in 1945, published in 1952) which calls into question everything observed; for if the observer is himself invisible, it is questionable if what he says can be verified. Thus, we are involved in a vast counterfeit world: counterfeit observations, observer, "beyond." This is not to assert that Ellison's invisible man is himself counterfeit, but to suggest he undermines whatever he says or does by his insistence on invisibility. We are overwhelmed by images of veils, curtains, dreamlike states, fantasy lives, all of them part of that borderline between counterfeit and real, between invisible observer and observation.

Counterfeiting and invisibility control Ellison's vision, as self-examination and memory define his protagonist. Like Dostoyevsky's unnamed narrator in *Notes from Underground,* Ellison's begins with invisibility (skipping the Russian's sickliness and spitefulness) and concludes: "But live you must, and you can either make passive love to your sickness or burn it out and go on to the next conflicting phase." That is, one can remain in an underground hole as an alterna-tive to life above, or one can gain strength in the hole for further excursions outside. The latter alternative is often neglected, and black activists who attack Ellison forget: "Please, a definition: A hibernation is a covert preparation for a more overt action." Yet even if his protagonist forgoes action, he can choose antilife, antiparticipation, and still live richly. "I have stayed in my hole, because up above there's an increasing passion to make men conform to a pattern." The hole brings intensity; outside, enervation.

How neatly Ellison's novel hugs the experience of the decade, even though it comes only in 1952 and was written mainly in the 1940s! Although the invisible narrator, not only unnamed but physically nondescript, decides to shake "off the old skin" and leave it there in the hole, he has nevertheless recognized passivity and inertness as viable alternatives. The experience in the hole, he comes to realize, may be a more valuable, life-sustaining experience than any beyond it. The awareness of invisibility, which is a subterranean sensation and a reflector of narcissism, is surely more precious than anything experienced visibly. In his hole, he enters a redefined space-time continuum. Spatiality is, of course, restricted to his walls; but time has been radically altered. Sitting in his underground room, under the influence of a reefer, he gets beyond recognizable sounds and hears unheard melodies, of Louis Armstrong. "I not only entered the music but descended, like Dante, into its depths." Ordinary temporality gives way, until time is suspended.

Ellison's narrator later comes to write about his memories, but at one point in his hole experience he burns all his papers—as Gaddis's Wyatt his paintings—so that hole and blackness (relieved by 1,369 lights) become the entirety of his existence. In his *Paris Review* interview, Ellison spoke of the need to burn out the past: "Before he could have some voice in his own destiny he had to discard these old identities and illusions; his enlightenment couldn't come until then." He also described the progression of his narrator's movement: "from . . . purpose to passion to perception [Kenneth Burke's terms]." Perception, here, is an insight not only into himself and his need to define himself—Wyatt's "recognitions"—but into the potentialities of a world divided into light and black, enervation and vitality, paralysis and movement. He challenges everything. Like Dostoyevsky's underground man or Goncharov's Oblomov, he has insight into an alternative culture, with its own rules of time, space, movement, or lack of them. Since he deals with voids, he must create curtains, veils, and stages; Ellison is always working out theatrical poses for his narrator.

Ellison connects the paralysis and enervation of the 1950s with typical American themes, playing off stasis against spatiality and energy. Those tensions occur right at the beginning of the novel, in the words of the narrator's grandfather. Calling himself a "spy in the enemy's country," the dying old man says, "underline 'em with grins, agree 'em to death and destruction." This is followed shortly afterward by the "battle royal," the humiliation of black youths for the enjoyment of white men at a smoker. The narrator is blindfolded and then sent out to fight other blindfolded blacks. The image is a key one for the novel, that mixture of veil and struggle, of furious energies expended on a frustrating, degrading cause.

Yet *Invisible Man* is more than this. Like *The Recognitions,* it is several novels, although more compactly organized than Gaddis's sprawling work, even more ironically conceived, and capable of confronting irreconcilable elements more pointedly. Despite Ellison's stress on an enclosed, subterranean existence, he is also concerned, as his Prologue demonstrates, with growth. His line of development is a 1950s reflection of the *Bildungsroman* tradition, in this instance of the simpleton or fool who grows up into a realization of what the world really is, and then, as the result of setbacks, becomes capable of acting on his own condition. Since the narrator is black, his journey becomes a black man's journey, but his experience is not solely a black one. Salinger's Holden in a miniature way parallels Ellison's narrator; the upper-middle-class private-school white boy playing the fool, trying to be wise, attempting to grow up in a world of counterfeiters, offering honesty to their imitations.

Ellison's narrator is not born wise and cagey. He is idealistic, truthful, and optimistic about men and events, and he does not perceive the twists and turns of the labyrinth until he is prepared to go underground, when he recognizes he has been used. Because he is trusting, he is a fool; because he has not assimilated his grandfather's words and their implications, he must be deceived. Ellison stated that in the Prologue "the hero discovers what he had not discovered throughout the book: you have to make your own decisions; you have to think for yourself. The hero comes up from the underground because the act of writing and thinking necessitated it. He could not stay down there." Ellison's novel falls into several subgenres, not the least that of Melville's *Confidence Man,* a world composed of tricksters and power brokers. The premise is initiation and survival.

Although Ellison achieves many of his successes with set formulas—stress on folk idiom and humor, satirical wryness, rhetorical figures such as hyperbole, very carefully contained fantasy, staged shifts of focus—despite these very consciously conceived devices, the thrust is toward openness. The novel rests between end pieces: a Prologue and Epilogue, Dostoyevskian at one end, Kafkaesque at the other; with the main body of the narrative spiked by spatial and temporal openness, intensely American in these respects.* The form is basically linear, the experienced life of the novel progressive. A second skin here means a new life, not a cycle of existence.

The novel plays off American linear modes against European subterraneanism, American spatiality against Heideggerian notions of Being. The counterpoint or fugal movement derives, in large part, from "color strategies." Ellison hangs the novel on a string attached between black and white, in which permutations of extreme color schemes—Optic White, blackness, invisibility, visibility, black man on white Upper East Side, white man in Harlem—create a spectroscopic vision. Ellison's use of color is phenomenological. Since it extends into every aspect of his narrator's existence, color and its variations form a dimension that has little to do with action, progress, even direct relationships between the races. Color becomes, like Melville's use of shadows in "Benito Cereno"—upon which Ellison draws for an epigraph—a metaphysical state, a labyrinthine existence of "privileged moments," which exist outside time and space.

I am claiming for the novel something akin to the disordering effects of synesthesia. The color frame of reference carries beyond realism and empirical data, beyond any realistic-naturalistic narrative; into those dimensions of experience which critics who want protest fiction can never quite get right. "The end is in the beginning," Ellison following Eliot states at the beginning and end,† and he is suggesting that when

*Very early in the novel, the narrator drives the white benefactor, Mr. Norton, around the Negro college he attends, and the philanthropist asks if he has studied Emerson; Ralph Waldo Emerson, he says, when the narrator does not understand. Ralph Waldo Ellison poses the question, by way of the white benefactor, for his black narrator, who professes ignorance. " 'Not yet, sir. We haven't come to him yet.' " Emerson hangs like a parodic form over the entire novel; the narrator would like to reach Emersonian wisdom about America, but cannot because, black, he is curtained off from it.

†"In 1935 I discovered Eliot's *The Waste Land* which moved and intrigued me but defied my powers of analysis—such as they were—and I wondered why I had never read

one deals with color, holes, and appearances, then ends and beginnings are indistinguishable. At the beginning of the novel, we have the end: the narrator, now invisible, in his "hole in the ground," although a "warm hole." He says we should call him "Jack-the-Bear," albeit formless and outside normal spatial-temporal considerations. Invisibility enforces the suspension of routine expectations, just as visibility above ground once created *its* own kind of expectation.

All hangs on color, shades, and gradations, intermediate strains of existence. This is the "color equivalent" of paralysis and enervation, and it is as much Ellison's subject as is his stated need for that second skin. So compellingly has Ellison evoked those intermediate strains of existence that full-blooded activity —Ras, Rinehart, the Harlem and West Side Communists—all seems, by contrast, lacking in tension, reduced or simplified. If Ellison's real subject is subterranean life, intermixed with colors and shades, then that inevitably will clash with open forms which develop the novel's political and social themes.

As a cultural phenomenon, we have a curious confrontation of historical ideas. For Ellison's novel does prepare us for the activism of the 1960s: his underground protagonist will emerge as one of the angry young persons of that decade. If we can believe the Prologue, Ellison's protagonist—echoing James's Strether: "live you must"—will rise like the phoenix, as prototypical invisible men do. The enervation, which is Ellison's strongest element, will become connected to American "rising" and movement.

The dualism is implicit in every aspect of the novel's structure and color imagery. The narrative is itself a progression of three unfoldings, what Ellison characterized in the narrator as moving from "purpose to passion to perception." I would prefer to see the narrator as passing through various sets of unfoldings in which counterfeit ideas and events give him a slowly increasing perception of himself; so that, finally, as he comes to understand how men and systems work, he is armed. Ellison speaks of the innocence of his narrator, but nearly *everyone* in the novel, early and late, is blind to what he is doing; no one reveals his true role. Bledsoe may be in charge of the Southern black college that the narrator attends, and he may even tell the narrator about the nature of power. But Bledsoe, who thinks that the power given to him is really his, has bled so to achieve this power

anything of equal intensity and sensibility by an American Negro writer."

that he is hollowed, innocent of true comprehension, simply another husk. Similarly, Homer A. Barbee, the spellbinding preacher who pulls out all the rhetorical stops in his chapel address, is, literally, blind. But his blindness confers not wisdom, as it had on the poet Homer, but a condition in which things are invisible, so that he approaches a state not unlike the narrator's.

Even the letters Bledsoe gives the narrator— "Keep this nigger boy running"—are elements of blindness. For they are sealed, handed over as top secrets to secretaries; they penetrate into offices set deep within other offices, are perused behind barred doors of power. They are, in their deception, in their counterfeit sentiments, most of all in their physical imagery, the way the country works. As long as the narrator is under their influence—as long as he expects help from external sources—he cannot emerge. Those labyrinthine offices into which the letters disappear are the inner workings of a system based on naturalistic principles: the race is to the strong; the fittest and least innocent survive. They are areas that the narrator, with his strong work ethic, his sense of himself as a dedicated worker, thought he could enter. But he has no power; in fact, he represents negative power. As far as the white world is concerned, as far as Bledsoe is concerned, he represents entropy. He is worn out and down before he begins.*

The brilliance of Ellison's unfolding is that as his protagonist moves toward enervation, exhaustion, paralysis, he shows great energy; and he moves in a world that pits its energy against his, revving up as he begins to run down. Ellison argued, when the *Paris Review* interviewers questioned the shifting of styles in these two set pieces, that the Prologue and Epilogue to the novel were essential. His defense does not really go to the heart of the structure. It was necessary, first, to start with near-paralysis. Ellison says he wrote the Prologue afterward; but it does come at the beginning. It *stops* everything, before things begin to speed up. It establishes counterpoint. The Epilogue was necessary for different reasons. It brings the narrator back into action; it justifies mind now that body is in stasis, and it informs us that he must write about his experience, the narrative itself. In a way, the Epi-

*Only Emerson may save. It is the young Mr. Emerson who attempts to help the narrator by revealing to him the contents of the letter directed to the senior Mr. Emerson. Young Emerson's intentions are not completely pure—he is in a bad state himself, he is making what is perhaps a homosexual pass at the narrator—but, nevertheless, Emerson helps.

logue corrects the attitudes of the Prologue. It creates a dialectic of paralysis-activity, both intensifying invisibility and preparing for a greater shining forth.

Ellison needed a counterthrusting of elements, and he achieved this tension by way of three ongoing segments: Prologue, main body of the novel, Epilogue. Each has not only a different time sequencing, but a distinctive modulation of feeling, pacing, progress. The three parts seem interwoven elements of a large-scale symphony or concerto; and this observation would return us to Ellison's first love, for before he wrote in the language of words, he wrote in that of music. Orchestration, fugal counterpoint, tensions, harmonies are never distant from what I characterize as "unfolding," of paralysis set against energy; all edged by counterfeit, deception, flummery. For a novel in which whites fail to see blacks, make them invisible, and in which blacks cannot make whites see them, and thus cannot achieve visibility, musical elements are perfect vehicles of expression.

Readers caught up in the racial aspects of the novel, or in its protest qualities, or its allegiances to or deviations from "black causes," often fail to see how its energies depended on a time and place. Ellison's novel has of course survived 1952, a dismal year in American culture, but some of its survival qualities are connected to that original impact. Ellison explained to John Hersey why Russian novelists of the nineteenth century had such access to primary feelings. Their power derived from their involvement in emotional disruptions that in turn had come from social and political disruption, from disturbances in the normal hierarchical arrangements which give a society its stability. Although society under the Czar seemed controllable, in actuality it was moving inexorably toward chaos, a condition sensed by the great novelists.

On a somewhat smaller scale, we have a comparable situation in the immediate postwar years, when *Invisible Man* was written and published. The chaotic sense of social and political power that characterized the era was already set into motion by the ending of the war and movement toward peacetime conditions. Elements of control were superficial. Eisenhower's easy victories in the elections of 1952 and 1956 allowed a papering over of everything that would explode later. He was, like the Czar, our "Little Father," and for a vast majority almost as sacred. This idea of stability at the top could not, however, disguise that all was imitation and counterfeit. America was an imitation of America, and here Ellison's perceptions began to work on his material.

The entrapment of an innocent young man in the needs and desires of others is enhanced by a society that seems basically stable; that is, its systems, however counterfeit, appear to work. Only in Harlem, in Ellison's novel, is there terrible disharmony, systematic breakdown; and it is fitting that here the narrator begins to assert himself. His first step toward acceptance by the Brotherhood comes with his interference in an act of eviction, an episode in disharmonious living. When he sees a white marshal and two aides carrying out the meager belongings of an old black couple, he wonders what that couple had to show for all their years of life. Their paltry possessions, themselves dispossessed, become the theme of his harangue to the crowd, which turns it toward violence. The narrator's speech contrasts with his earlier behavior in a somewhat parallel episode, when he drove the benefactor, Mr. Norton, into a black slum. There he and Norton hear the story of incest from a sharecropper, and at the Golden Day, a disreputable bar, they see "crazies" act out roles they might have had if not black. In those scenes, the narrator is quiet, completely under the command of Norton's needs. He is a driver, but, in all senses, he is being driven.

In the Harlem dispossession scene, he is still going to be used, but he becomes a voice in a situation, before he is grabbed up by the Brotherhood for his race. After the fiasco of the Optic White episode, in which everything humiliating and manipulative that can occur does occur, he has moved to a new stage of consciousness. Part of the unfolding of Ellison's novel comes in that expert use of contrast: each stage of consciousness on the narrator's part accompanied by a new stage of manipulation by others. Yet in the process, whose working out is the novel, the narrator gains a greater sense of himself. He escapes from the eviction scene by walking along rooftops, a momentary freedom, a dizziness that derives from accomplishment. But the rooftop walk is followed quickly by a plunge downward, into a subway, where he drops "through the roar, giddy and vacuum-minded, sucked under and out into late afternoon Harlem." These spatial conflicts, between heights and depths, are the equivalent throughout of black and white, darkness and whiteness: structural concepts as states of mind.

Once the Brotherhood makes contact, the black-white tension is enhanced, even while the narrator is being used for his blackness (not black enough, one woman comments). Those who have found the Brotherhood (i.e., Communist) scenes too facile, too lacking in realistic detail to justify the narrator's allegiance, forget that the novel is not completely realistic. Every scene is slightly off key, surrealistic, as if the visual and verbal equivalent of a jazz rumination. Those early scenes at the college are deep pastoral marred by terrible divisiveness: pastoral on the surface, where systems function, dispossession beneath. Scenes that follow have an unreal texture, reinforced by folk idioms and songs, rhythms from slave life, broad comedy: eating of yams, offers of help on the street, bizarre characters met. Like the narrator, the reader is kept off balance, as Ellison manipulates a potentially realistic scene to create something eccentric; like scenes in "Benito Cereno," which seem normal on the surface, but seethe beneath with alternative experiences.

The paint company is superbly illustrative of this. It is, before all else, an actual place, with employment. It works. Paint is produced. The narrator heads there because of words spoken by young Emerson; it is a company where many young well-educated blacks are hired because they will work for nonunion wages. Optic White has as its slogan "If it's Optic White, it's the Right White," which the narrator perceives as a rerun of the old saying "If you're white, you're right." The world of Optic White carries the narrator into an allegorical, synesthesiac journey. The paint is the whitest that was, but its manufacture is overseen by a black, Lucius Brockway. For a paint that covers everything—that will coat coal—production is deep in the company's subterranean bowels, the controls like those of a nuclear plant. Every dial and switch and valve is fraught with danger. And controlling it all is a form of black Hades, an invisible man deep in the underworld existence of a vastly successful paint empire. Color schemes throw the episode out of kilter, toward surrealism on one hand, social comedy on the other.

In this area of Optic White, produced by Liberty Paints, its motto "Keep America Pure," its key man a black who recalls Loki, our narrator hopes to regain his destiny. Since leaving school, he has known only frustrated efforts, and he has come no closer to self-sufficiency or illumination than when he started out —except what is revealed by young Emerson, that he must break free of his past. Liberty Paints will be his means; Optic White his achievement.

The paint is, of course, a veneer, all imitation, a deception, like the palimpsest in *The Recognitions*. As he descends into the bowels of the company, where all the mechanical works reside, the narrator embraces the dynamo, hoping to make it work for him. His illusions about himself are cresting; he still lives, except for his knowledge of the letters' content (revealed by someone else), in a counterfeit world. And nowhere is there greater imitation than in Lucius Brockway's empire: those valves and pipes, knowledge of which constitute his grip upon the company. Lucius is half-crazed, isolated completely, an older man who fights all attempts by the union to penetrate his sanctuary, a man without his own teeth who bites the narrator and loses his dentures. Here is the "artificial nigger" whom Flannery O'Connor wrote about in a different context; but, also, a touching one, pursuing a craziness so that he, as a black in a white company, can survive.

There is, however, another side to Lucius. Even while he praises his paint and claims Optic White as his, he is, like a minor-league Samson, able to plan the destruction of his empire. For when he senses threat from the union, the narrator, his own loss of control, he tells the latter to turn a particular valve and then runs for his life. The explosion that follows, while destroying Optic White, thrusts the narrator ever deeper into the grip of the company. Lying helpless, but conscious, he hears himself discussed in terms of cures; one involves a "little gadget" that will solve everything, the other, surgery. When the gadget is tried, we enter a world that was to become the stock-in-trade of 1960s fiction, *One Flew Over the Cuckoo's Nest* being the most prominent of the type. The gadget alters personality: " 'The machine [this voice explains] will produce the results of a prefrontal lobotomy without the negative effects of the knife.' " Pressure on nerves—"our concept is Gestalt"—will result in a change of personality so radical it will recall villains turned into amiable fellows by way of surgery. Rather than cutting away, the machine controls; lost is the individual's psychology—" 'Absolutely of no importance!' "

The factory hospital turns out a new man. Compensated for his accident, the narrator is sent forth, his first stage of development completed. He senses his personality is different: "I had been talking beyond myself, had used words and expressed attitudes not my own," but he was no longer afraid: "Not of important men, not of trustees and such." He no longer fears them because he expects nothing from them. Circuitously and ironically, Liberty Paints has liberated him; he is on the edge of consciousness. Ellison's narrator now enters into his second skin, which leads toward new forms of consciousness, followed by choices.

The novel has been structured so that after eleven chapters, or about two-fifths along, the narrator can go forth; chastened by what has occurred, he still awaits final knowledge. Each choice involves a different kind of life, a distinct kind of consciousness. He can choose the Brotherhood, which is the way of least personal expression, a mode of discipline and sacrifice; or he can follow Ras, the separatist who challenges all efforts at white-black integration; or he can become Rinehart, that symbolic figure of the Harlem hipster who cuts into rackets, numbers, and related enterprises; or he can make a truly existential decision and carve out something for himself. As Ellison presents the choices, the most revolutionary act is not the Brotherhood (or Communist infiltration), not Ras (or African separatism), not Rinehart (the way of crime), but pursuit of self.

The latter is so radical because it does not involve imitation or counterfeiting. To escape illusions is a revolutionary act. Ellison is attempting, at the cultural level, to work his way through late 1940s fogs and veils; that burden of screening which made everyone and everything appear unreal. The real is in oneself; not in open pastoral or the urban jungle, but in the invisibility of oneself, in the dark. There, one can efface the past, as Richard Wright's protagonist had attempted in "The Man Who Lived Underground," or Cross Damon in *The Outsider*. Both men achieve a change of identification by way of a subterranean experience; and we see that Wright has as much of a hold upon Ellison as do Dostoyevsky and Kafka.

Adversary to the narrator is Tod Clifton, whose name, Tod, indicates his doom. Although in life graceful and athletic, he will be a figure of death. Clifton is loyal to the Brotherhood at first, fights Ras the Exhorter and, later, the Destroyer, with all his strength; and then drops away. He is, for the narrator, a man who has fallen outside history. When the former sights Tod on the street, he is selling Sambo dolls, becoming a street black, at the mercy of the market and the police. Since the narrator observes him from the outside, we do not understand what has occurred to him, but he must have broken with the Brotherhood ideologically, been tempted by Ras's exhortations for racial separatism, and found himself without an anchor, adrift socially, politically, personally. He foreruns Malcolm X. Clifton, then, is a true black tragic figure: fallen from grace in the Brotherhood and unable to find a position, a man sacrificed to ideology, race, and political expedience.

The narrator meditates upon history, which he begins to see as contingency. His fear is that history may pass him by unless he is attached to some movement. But what if history "was a gambler, instead of a force in a laboratory experiment, and the boys his ace in the hole?" History could be a madman, and young men like himself agents of a lunatic's direction. And what about the young men the narrator sees on the subway, in their zoot suits and casual indifference: what role do they play in history? Are they agents of something as yet unforeseen or are "they dodging the forces of history instead of making a dominating stand?"

Ellison has adapted French existential ideas of freedom, historical necessity, and individual positioning to accommodate the Harlem scene. These are, also, jazz components: group improvisation, individual performance, standing outside while inside. That the narrator still has no answers is connected to his invisibility. To evade invisibility he must both lose his blackness and become blacker.

His choice now is to hibernate and to write it all down. This desire to pass on his experience turns the typical quest novel into an art novel. End and beginning follow, touch, and the result is past effaced in favor of presentness of the mind. Out of chaos will come consciousness, and that insists he come forth. Louis Armstrong is the guide here: that half says, " 'Open the window and let the foul air out,' " whereas the other half comments, " 'It was good green corn before the harvest.' " Coming out is like some religious ritual; old skin moulting, second skin forming, personality restructured, insistent upon itself. Invisibility as a physical element has not been changed; but the man is visible to himself.

FINAL WORDS ON ELLISON

Almost thirty years after *Invisible Man,* Ellison's difficulties with his second novel have entered myth. Speculation whether Ellison can write more is really beside the point. *Invisible Man* as an achievement needs no second act; it established its author, entered into mainstream American fiction, and remains a touchstone of the 1950s. Condescension toward Ellison for his inability to produce another novel runs up against an essential fact: he wrote one. Many American novelists would have done well to stick by their first book and go no further. Ellison published several short fictions which derive from his work in progress, and these excerpts suggest some of the reasons for the difficulty.* In an interview with John Hersey, he

---

*"A Coupla Scalped Indians" (*New World Writing* 9, 1956); "It Always Breaks Out" (*Partisan Review,* Spring 1963); and "cadillac flambé" (*American Review,* February 1973).

spoke of his new novel as fitting into an "underground" experience, with images of coffins, of being buried, of attempts to transcend, all associated with black life. The key image is of resurrection: "In my mind all of this is tied up in some way with the significance of being a Negro in America and at the same time with the problem of our democratic faith as a whole." He perceives his vision as a big sponge, or "a waterbed, with a lot of needles sticking in it." Ellison says his difficulty has been in trying to "tie those threads together," without letting "whatever lies in the center leak out."

The most substantial of the stories is "cadillac flambé," which concerns a black man's burning of his Cadillac on the lawn of a senator who has made racist remarks. The black man, Minifees, creates a "cookout" of his own, comparable to that of the senator on his lawn. Yet the story lends itself more to an oral tradition than to print; it is part tall tale, part corn barrel chitchat. "Take the TAIL FINS and the WHITEWALLS. Help yourself to the poor raped RADIO. ENJOY the automatic dimmer and the power brakes. ROLL, Mister Senator, with that fluid DRIVE. Breathe that air-conditioned AIR." In a related story, Ellison produces a dialogue between newspapermen right after the burning. He pits an "I," a white liberal, against a Southern white, all this occurring in a club served by a silent but observant black waiter.

The third story, "A Coupla Scalped Indians," digs into the Tom Sawyer–Huck Finn repertory, two young boys setting out on a Boy Scout endurance test. As pure writing, it is effective. But the three pieces taken together suggest a clash of styles, whatever Ellison's other difficulties were with the larger plan. The language shifts, as if uncertainty of conception has extended into the prose. Further, what made Ellison's work in *Invisible Man* so corrosive was irony, itself a vision or patterning. Little or none of that is apparent in the stories. It is as if Ellison had turned his back on the sophistication of his novel in order to return to earlier, more simplistic modes; as if he had been touched so deeply by the attacks made on him by black critics for not being black enough that he was responding with more direct folksy material. And, as he must recognize, it is reductive.

In his reply to Irving Howe's essay on Richard Wright and protest literature, Ellison asserted that one may be loyal to the aspirations of black people without being Richard Wright; loyalty is measured, instead, in the steadiness and intensity of one's private vision. Yet despite Ellison's disclaimer, certain modes of thought seem continuous with Wright, and that is the kind of experience caught in Wright's "The Man Who Lived Underground" (1941, 1944) and elsewhere in his work. For Wright had, as early as *Native Son,* touched upon a traditional American theme of the outcast, with special reference to the black outcast: the man on the run from the police who eventually, because of some passive strain in his nature, embraces the police for his own destruction. Ellison's physical "refuge" in *Invisible Man* probably owes more to Wright's underground than to Dostoyevsky's. And just as Ellison's narrator lines his walls with bulbs, so Wright's Daniels lines his with bills. That papered wall, full of money he has no desire to spend, is his form of "light"; exactly as Ellison's lights are forms of spending, of enjoying something unearned, a black man's revenge.

The Man Who Lived Underground is the mythical Wright. That is, he was working a vein in which whatever he said was always more important than what his art could provide as the vehicle. He had discovered certain truths about human existence, outlaws, blacks on the run, the workings of a society, and they were not generated solely by economic causes. In the underground refuge, the treasure trove, where the black man builds his fortress against white incursions, Wright was moving toward some larger mythical insight, toward some myth of the races. The novella is insufficiently developed for the kind of statement he wanted and which his own anger reduced: police as devils, Daniels as pure victim, situations without dimensions; except underground, where the touch is sure. There, even his language changes, becoming more lyrical, more flexible. Withal, the idea of the novella preempts its workings. Wright thought in mythical modes which his practice did not allow him to exploit fully; in effect, the underground novel he suggests would become, not his, but Ellison's *Invisible Man.* *

---

*A minor spinoff from Wright's underground is LeRoi Jones's (Baraka's) *The System of Dante's Hell* (1963), where deep holes and invisibility are characteristic of the black experience. In rhapsodic and often moving prose, Jones speaks of the black as being "the unseen object, and the constantly observed object," of hell being in the head as an actuality. Jones uses Dante's systems of hell as metaphors and symbols of black life: first in Newark, then in a small Southern town, and finally in New York. One of the ironies of this brief book is that the black cannot afford the luxuries of Dante's hell; for his very existence above ground is that hell made palpable. Dante's hell is heaven for the black; when real hell is present, not as symbol but as actuality, then imagining hell becomes an artifact, not a fact.

Beats and Burroughs

If Gaddis is our new Hawthorne, Ellison our Emerson, then those who prefer to be "on the road" are our modern-day Thoreaus, and Burroughs our updated Whitman. The Beats of the 1950s and Burroughs were not only involved in opening up new or alternative experiences, they also pioneered in developing a new terminology. Much of the language we associate with succeeding decades derived from those early Beat novels, especially from George Mandel's *Flee the Angry Strangers.* This was Greenwich Village argot, terminology of a flourishing drug culture, and 1950s withdrawal from bourgeois language into its own forms.

Various code words for marijuana and heroin began to gain wider usage here—tea, grass, pot or pod, weed, gauge, horse. Also, our sexual terminology took on different dimensions. As Lawrence Lipton observes, "joint" has a dual meaning, as penis and as stick of marijuana. On the other hand, "joint" in common slang means a place—bar, restaurant, or even work site. Work itself has a sexual connotation, and place of work is a gig. This is not referred to very frequently, as work is itself anathema.

Other forms included to ball, cat, deal and dealer, dig, flip out, head, hip, making it (sexually not success oriented), push and pusher, split, turning on, getting or being stoned. The distinctive terminology suggests that a culture existed, since a language implies a community or society. John Clellon Holmes's *Go* (written 1949–51, published 1952) preceded Kerouac's *On the Road* and becomes our guide to what is clearly a counterculture, well before America knew the term or would have recognized the phenomenon.

Everyone recognizes that *Go* is a significant document in the development of the so-called Beat movement. What appears less apparent is that the book looks backward as much as forward, backward to the type of fiction we associate with Nelson Algren, and only a little removed from naturalistic fiction. Holmes's Beats are versions of Steinbeck's dropouts, urbanized Okies. And we find a similar phenomenon

---

A major spinoff from Wright's metaphor and locale is John Williams's *The Man Who Cried I Am,* which I discuss in "The 1960s." Williams works traditional American themes of liberation and space and relates them directly to black experiences, some of it personal history, some derived from his reading in Wright and Ellison.

in a lateral movement, in *Flee the Angry Strangers,* where the counterculture lives in Greenwich Village. Characteristic of all is the pursuit of leisure time, which may be filled in with drugs, booze, sex, talk, search for a transcendental being, self-destruction, frenetic movement, rearrangement of personal connections, reshuffling of lovers or mistresses, reliance on cars and spatial fantasies. Leisure is perceived as a form of liberation.

Go is representative in that Holmes was one of the first to prophesy the "counterfeit decade" in print. Searching for leisure is perhaps the most powerful way to indict a society hell-bent on acquisition and property. One of the paradoxes of the Beat phenomenon, however, is that while materialism is eschewed, each individual has a favorite kind of property. For some, it is drugs, whose acquisition depends on money; or books, some of which can be stolen from the university bookstore; or a private pad, which requires payment of rent, however minimal; or a car, which may be stolen. In *Go,* even Stofsky (Allen Ginsberg), Holmes's most ascetic figure, requires refueling by way of books and his own place: possessions, albeit reduced.

Holmes's Paul Hobbes, like Kerouac's Sal Paradise, like Kerouac himself, is a somewhat unwilling Beat, caught between desire for freedom and the need to have stable relationships, a pleasant apartment, a dependable home life. Hobbes's name, that of the author of *Leviathan,* indicates a man who cannot depend on dreams, who is rooted in actuality. He must will himself into freedom, since his attitudes tend toward order. He has been married for six years to Kathryn, an Italian, who wants a stable life, but who dabbles in the counterculture because of Paul. One of the catalysts here is Gene Pasternak (Kerouac); an even stronger catalyst is Hart Kennedy, a toned-down version of Neal Cassady, Kerouac's Dean Moriarty, the legendary centaur, half man, half car. *Go* and *On the Road* serve as palimpsests of each other. What one stresses, the other places in the distance, with characters moving in and out of each other's books. Holmes's recreation of Kerouac, Ginsberg, Cannastra, and others, however, is closer to fact. Many episodes are direct representations of what occurred: Cannastra's death, Ginsberg's brush with the law, Kerouac's experiences with his first novel.

But the chief contribution of *Go* is Holmes's attempt to define a movement that was still inchoate, really only a small number of urbanized countercultural individuals. "They made none of the moral or political judgments that he [Hobbes] thought essential; they did not seem compelled to fit everything into the pigeon holes of a system. . . . They never read the papers, they did not follow with diligent and self conscious attention the happenings in the political and cultural arena; they seemed to have an almost calculated contempt for logical argument. They operated on feelings, sudden reactions, expanding these far out of perspective to see in them profundities which Hobbes was certain they could not define if put to it." Their habitats were "a world of dingy backstairs 'pads,' Times Square cafeterias, bebop joints, night-long wanderings, meetings on street corners, hitchhiking, a myriad of 'hip' bars all over the city, and the streets themselves." Their activity is characterized by yo-yoing, "rushing around to 'make contact,' " suddenly disappearing into jail or on the road, only to turn up again to search one another out. Their medium of entertainment, except for booze, drugs, and sex, was jazz, a black mode. We see how this movement would feed into Mailer's essay on the White Negro.

The question for Hobbes is how much of this he can absorb, for he is a man torn by many different sensibilities. Besides his desire for stability and escape, there is still another side, which he expresses in letters to Liza, a sickly, hysterical young woman he has met at Columbia. For Hobbes, the correspondence is a form of mental masturbation; he sees himself as Dostoyevsky's underground man ("how brittle and will-less I have become," he begins), while she, namesake of the prostitute in the second part of the Russian's novella, is "a fascinating and sickly plant that thrived on the stifling atmosphere of argument over coffee."

The letters to Liza, many of them not sent or answered, provide Hobbes with what Kathryn cannot give him. In his letters, he speaks of suicidal impulses, of antilife. "Life is a perpetual defeat for us. . . . We have no eagerness, no ecstasy, only the likeness of this sense of defeat." This transformation of European existentialism into American angst and defeat is, of course, part of the Beat adaptation of ideas; but it serves as well as the other side of 1950s productivity, expansion, economic optimism. With all its weltschmerz, it is an effort to penetrate counterfeit feelings and derivative thought.

Doomed lovers, whether straight, homosexual, or bi, characterize Beat associations. The young women who attach themselves to the figure of Agatson (modeled on Cannastra) identify with his doom, his destructiveness, his nihilism, which does not have even the force of strong denial. It represents simply a blind force of nothing, which is less than nothingness. In predominantly male-authored Beat fiction, there is little in the way of male-female give-and-take. Women become pawns, preyed upon rather than satisfied, and they attach themselves out of some blind belief in the man. For novels that insist on choice, women curiously give up all choice and let men treat them like dirt. Often, the women do have a voice—Kathryn here, Diane in Mandel's novel—but this does not prevent them from being subservient to male domination.

More cerebral than Kerouac, Holmes was more likely to reveal Beat paradoxes, chiefly that ideas outstrip literary performance. The Beats attempted to confront the counterfeit decade head-on, and to offer a counterculture which would be anathema to every aspect of that troubled period. For the sense of achievement, it would offer failure; for organization and order, it would suggest chaos; for the man in the gray flannel suit, it offered sandals, Salvation Army rejects, beards, and long hair; for antisepsis, it paraded dirty bodies and matted hair; for marriage and family, it stressed promiscuous relationships, unmarried pregnancies; for discreet drinking in bars and home, it offered orgies of drugs, cheap wine, rotgut; for political commitment, it eschewed the cold war, the Rosenbergs, Hiss-Chambers-Nixon; for suburban living, it substituted communal living, people draped over couches and chairs; for progressive sanitary arrangements, it substituted filthy johns situated in hallways, toilets that did not flush, water that did not run. Even more, for the imitative happiness the decade offered, the Beats sought out pain; their attempts at joy compulsive, doomed to failure. They moved toward Dostoyevsky's sense of exalted suffering, while others, out there, settled for cheap happiness, counterfeit feelings.

Holmes perceived that the ideas would need far greater literary powers than the Beats could provide. While the latter indeed moved to extremes of behavior, toward compulsive Dostoyevskian themes, the novels themselves could hardly structure such themes into literary achievement. Recognizing the inadequacy of any single work, Kerouac from 1951 to 1956–57 tried to compensate with volume. But a problem common to all Beat novels is lack of moral differentiation. Since a recurring point is that each person has a distinct and worthy voice, then all experience becomes equally viable, or acceptable. Stofsky, for example, has no criminal intentions and is terribly frightened, but he does not try to prevent the use of his apartment to store stolen goods. If the author justifies all personal judgments equally, no moral, ethical, or even legal tensions are possible.

Corollary problems develop as well, particularly in Holmes's handling of Agatson. Bill Cannastra, who served loosely as the model for Agatson, had interesting qualities which countered his sense of doom. Among other achievements, he had a law degree from Harvard and worked responsibly for Random House, on an encyclopedia. Agatson has only Cannastra's destructive energy, his compulsive drinking habits, his need to destroy all relationships and humiliate women. The problem here is inherent in nearly all Beat literature: associations and relationships based on characters who wobble between fact and fiction.

The commitment to ideas in Holmes and Kerouac suffers. Hobbes strains for some dimension to give his life meaning. Holmes creates the brief fling between Pasternak and Kathryn, what he calls in the Introduction the "only completely invented incident in the book." The affair creates inevitable tension and gives Holmes the chance to plumb guilt, redemption, forgiveness. But this three-way relationship is so lacking in dimensionality that Hobbes treats Pasternak as if he had stolen his marbles, not his wife. Among good friends, some sharing of the little woman will not upset male bonding. The very lack of possessiveness feeds into flattened dramatic content; and the author's efforts to create tension are invalidated by his very premises. If everyone shares, then nothing is of value.

What remains is energy itself. "Go" is a great title, far superior to the original "The Daybreak Boys," named after a river gang on the New York waterfront in the 1840s; or the English title, "The Beat Boys." *Go* became an underground book long after it went out of print, long after it was cut and pirated. The title, I am certain, had a good deal to do with it. The word derives from Hart Kennedy's (Cassady's) cry of " 'go!' to everything, everything!" It is pure energy, unthinking. Also, it fits into a jazz scene, the Go Hole, where a tenor sax solo, stomping feet, and shouts of "Go" would crowd the air. The rush of energy in this would make everyone totally "gone." The past participle of "go" fits the jazz and drug scene. It has, as verbal cachet, as much significance as a later word, "wasted," derived from the Vietnam War, a term that signals the loss of energy, purpose, the shrinking back of human forms into phantoms, into waste matter or excrement. Energy in the 1950s was "go": all systems go, as the astronauts put it; "go" in its energy was the philosophy of both the culture and the counterculture. With entropy, in the 1960s and 1970s, the word became "waste"—human waste, material waste, the wasting of the environment, the sheer waste of human life. The Beats held to a different beat.

If we perceive the decade as an enclosed period, we think of conservative and reactionary elements dominant. But if we isolate particular years in the decade, we are astonished at the proliferation of countering forces, in social life, literature, even politics. As Eisenhower was nominated and elected in 1952, Kerouac in fiction was plotting to bring forth the "Beats," Ginsberg was moving along the lines of a new, more open form of poetry, and Burroughs was acting out the elements of his life that would describe a "drug culture." Robert Lowell was working fully in a type of confessional poetry that broadcast madness, instability, exhaustion. The abstract expressionist and action painters were turning life as lived into forms, geometric shapes, or masses, using spatial elements to indicate where "subjects" had been before. In these and other ways, the 1950s were either stretching tradition or moving toward adversary forms.

On the Road, written by 1951 but not published until 1957, expresses the new, although during his entire frantic writing career Kerouac never discovered a distinctive style. He tried to write his way into a style, but could not find a unique voice.* Kerouac

---

*The publication dates of Kerouac's novels give little indication of where they fitted in his life. *On the Road* is exemplary here: written from 1948 to 1951, then partially rewritten from 1951 to 1956, and published in 1957. In the decade before its publication, Kerouac started and completed *The Town and the City* (begun 1942, published 1950); then *Doctor Sax, Maggie Cassady, The Subterraneans, Tristessa, Visions of Cody* (also called *Visions of Neal*), *Visions of Gerard,* and other works. This incredible activity indicates Kerouac was searching frenetically for a style; for within these several books we have a variety of prose voices.

What is particularly interesting about Kerouac's work in this half decade is that he was moving stylistically on several fronts, always toward that discovery of language and forms which seemed to elude him. In *Visions of Cody,* he attempted to "open up" his form, but the work is more diary than novel. *The Town and the City* returns Kerouac to Thomas Wolfe, another man of insatiable appetites. The key element, as in Wolfe, is the individual's effort to find out something about life which he can apply to himself. *Doctor Sax,* an attempt to capture his sense of being with Burroughs in Mexico, in 1952, combines dream, nightmare, hallucination—the worlds of Bur-

intuited the subterranean world of the 1950s, but unlike (say) John Hawkes, he could not find either the prose or the right forms for his ideas. The first version of *On the Road* was presented to Kerouac's editor, Robert Giroux, on a 250-foot roll of Japanese paper which ran continuously, one long paragraph, only slightly indented for margins, and punctuated according to energy rather than grammatical breaks. The desire to achieve spontaneity or to confess was not so much experimental or "a dare," as it was an obsessional need to find print forms for the continuous racing of the mind, a drug-induced vision, with wild swings of manic and depressive feelings.

The first paragraph of *On the Road,* reorganized and presented traditionally when the book was published by Viking in 1957, still suggests the need for spontaneity and rush.

> I first met Dean not long after my wife and I split up. I had just gotten over a serious illness that I won't bother to talk about, except that it had something to do with the miserable weary split-up and my feeling that everything was dead. With the coming of Dean Moriarty began the part of my life you could call my life on the road. . . . Dean is the perfect guy for the road because he actually was born on the road, when his parents were passing through Salt Lake City in 1926, in a jalopy, on their way to Los Angeles.

The narrator is confessional and, too often, self-indulgent and self-serving. The split-up between narrator and wife prefigures splits that would characterize all male-female relationships in the fiction and poetry to come. The birth of Dean Moriarty (Neal Cassady) suggests the mythical hero, the figure shrouded in mist, the emergence of a Western type: mysterious birth, already on the road, in a car—the centaur standing in for modern, transitory man.* Dean will

___

roughs. Its key metaphor is the flooding of Lowell, Massachusetts; but the flood (the Flood) characterizes all those adversary elements which flow through Kerouac, the novel being subtitled "Faust Part Three." The most compelling part of the book is the author's effort to understand his companion's imaginative processes by way of water, flood, apocalyptic visions.

Maggie Cassady, written in two months in 1953, is part of the mosaic harking back to *The Town and the City.* This straightforward work is only a short time removed from the hallucinatory *The Subterraneans,* written at the end of 1953. Kerouac was moving, then, on so many fronts, between experimental and traditional, between opening up and restrictive naturalism, that we sense he had no stabilizing ego.

*Later, Neal Cassady drove the bus for Ken Kesey's Merry Pranksters. Even as he destroyed himself, the road meant life for him.

be Kerouac's Proteus and Prometheus, a man whose life, not his work, is the expression of how an era, otherwise constricted, can express itself.

Most significantly, the novel is an attempt to seek out another way of life, such as we find in the archetypal breakout novel, *Huckleberry Finn.* Twain's young hero serves many functions, not the least of which is his use of the river as a means of regaining an Edenic existence. Kerouac's narrator is named, suitably, Sal Paradise; and part of his quest for Eden is a lingering fantasy that it is achievable. One cannot fault young writers for their rebellion against fifties stodge and political deception; one can fault them for thinking that in running, jazz, drugs, dharma, or sexual combinations, they would find what Sal hopes to find. Similarly, Dean's desire for elements that a stable life cannot provide is the need of every "maker" or "creator" for elements lacking in his society. That much is clear, and acceptable. But Dean's antics become increasingly tiresome when we recognize he confuses process with results. In turn, Kerouac's narrative seems incompletely thought out, the material for the book, not the book.

Jazz, grass, visions, and, occasionally, sex may provide the high that suggests paradise does exist. In this respect, Kerouac's characters validly reach for a life beyond a respectable middle. The 1950s would appear to enclose us in what Dostoyevsky considered as the doom of "cheap happiness," what Nietzsche characterized as the fated life of the "last man." In their place, Kerouac, like Gaddis, Bellow, and Mailer in differing ways, offers the life of "exalted suffering," which can best be experienced in jazz. Jazz is particularly prophetic of "exalted suffering" since its origins are with Southern blacks, and its performance, mainly by blacks and marginal men, places it as an art form relatively untouched by bourgeois hands. George Shearing, the blind pianist, becomes the epitome of the man "who knows," "who sees"; the modern prophet hits the keys or blows a horn, and salvation is to be found there.

But if "exalted suffering" is the aim, the harrowing of hell, Paradise recognizes, is also a factor. He speaks of wrapping himself, drunk, around a toilet and going to sleep. "During the night at least a hundred seamen and assorted civilians came in and cast their sentient debouchments on me till I was unrecognizably caked." The use of a French vocabulary to describe being bathed in stinking shit cannot disguise that the obverse of this desire to reach highs is a terrible inability to throw off inferiority, to bathe oneself periodically in slime and filth as ways of expressing not only what man is but what one is. It is this deeper meaning, of degradation as well as exaltation, that Kerouac slights, and yet it is an essential part of his vision, as the real visionaries always realized.

Dean Moriarty as an avenging angel, as Prometheus, as the embodiment of vitality which can never express itself fully or sufficiently, is a brilliant idea, but, like the language, does not reach satisfactory form. That identification with cars is the sole area in which Dean (*the* Dean, the Christ, as it were) is supreme. Instead of a chariot, as in the myths, he drives jalopies and Cadillacs: "I saw his old jalopy chariot with thousands of sparking flames shooting out from it." He is superb with cars, so that machine and road afford him the opportunity to demonstrate a genius that has no other outlet in American society. He would be Ahab, but is, instead, a hired driver of someone else's Cadillac. If he owns a car, it is a jalopy, beat up and breaking apart. Traveling at eighty or more miles per hour, threading his way through traffic at high speeds, chancing death at routine moments, he should be a medieval knight, a samurai, a defender of the faith. Instead, he is a seedy-looking, always hungry, half-educated, word-spouting young man without anything to his name except ex-wives and children strewn across the country. The idea is so interesting, such a prophetic view of so many young men, that the reader only wishes Kerouac had matured sooner, so as to catch the sense of Dean and his world more completely.

The form he uses, but without sufficient connotative value, is the journey. The road becomes not only the means of escape but the locus of life. Once one arrives, the place proves disappointing or unfulfilling, a form of marriage. But with people packing the car, Dean at the wheel, Sal Paradise next to him, "life stories" as the form of entertainment, there *is* life. Riding through the desert or the plains is the trip to the moon, without the moon.

Life in the cities is a series of juvenile encounters, of adolescent expectations of women, who are required to wait and serve, or drink and drugs, and male companionship—an extended fraternity party, or a shore binge by sailors. Whereas life on the road has a lyrical energy. If the world is dualistic, life on the road is the irrational, energetic principle, while life in cities is enforced by reason; and one can break from reason only by way of excess.

In *The Town and the City,* town stood for nature's response to man, and city meant indifference or even hostility. Kerouac has shifted the equation, not the meaning: the road allows man's response, whereas the city, as ever, snares. One of the problems with the novel, as with the ideology behind it, is that it reduces; and a related problem is that it binds the writer to an equation that involves, on several levels, juvenile responses to life.

What is particularly unsettling is Sal Paradise's acceptance of Dean even when the latter goes beyond boys' tricks to real acts of deception and treachery, as in his treatment of his wives and women, his disregard of his children, present or coming, his ripping off of small store owners for cigarettes, his theft of cars and siphoning of gasoline.

Dean may be Gargantua, for whom "preparations had to be made to widen the gutters of Denver and foreshorten certain laws to fit his suffering bulk and bursting ecstasies." But he is also an antilife force for those who become the butts of his acts of aggression. Women are, for him, pure being, not becoming; and they are "being" because that state is static. Whatever pleasures they derive from Dean's presence, they are objects, reified for male pleasure.

Sex is not the thing; male bonding is. In the distant background on various encounters is Carlo Marx (Allen Ginsberg), with his voice of doom, his intellectual arguments, his warnings and cautions, his Jewish, Marxist, Marx Brothers-ish sense of self and life. But while he may have provided a corrective here, or a tension, he does not count; he exists only as the figure behind the name, not as a character in the book. Only Dean comes alive. Kerouac's point may have been that everyone except Dean is enervated, that only he brings magic and vitality; but the writer cannot bore in order to demonstrate boredom.

When Gaddis's Wyatt Gwyon goes on his forgery trips, he recognizes what he is doing; and the joy he derives from creating great paintings in the style of the old masters is qualified by the fact that he must sign another's name to his work. That signature subtracts as much as the act of painting an old master has brought. Gaddis realizes an act of joy is always balanced out by one of despair; to know this is part of "recognitions." But Kerouac either ignores this side of the experience or dilutes its impact. He is interested, mainly, in the highs that can bring the individual out of a deadly respectability and cheapening of happiness. This is a noble effort, one to be applauded as part of creativity itself. But the nature of a novelist's material is to gather in more. Mailer's *An American Dream* is a similar kind of novel, a Beat fiction given respectability.

Kerouac's career was so uneven, despite his phenomenal application to his writing career, because he could not find the right *literary* resolution of basic divisions within him, between a desire for a bourgeois life and an equal desire to break from it into some independent force or being. Though not necessary that he resolve these elements in his life, in his work it was essential. That five–six-year stretch of furious concentration in the early part of the fifties, as we have seen, caught Kerouac up in a million contradictory words of traditional writing and experiment, straight narrative and stream, formed characters and characters as process; the writer as Catholic, fallen-away Catholic, and devotee of Buddhism and Gnosticism. Even sexual identification was ambiguous. In his inability to stick with any belief or idea, he was typically American, driven and obsessed. For those who feel Kerouac provided a corrective to the 1950s, an alternative life style, he has succeeded; but for those who insist that such alternatives must be aesthetically satisfying, success is less apparent, if at all. Personal catharsis still needs a form. Open space may work for painting, but words are different from colors and phrases are not lines or strokes.

The Dharma Bums (1958) is a direct response by Kerouac and his publisher to the success of *On the Road*. Dean Moriarty is transformed into Jaffe Ryder (based on the poet Gary Snyder) and Sal Paradise becomes Raymond Smith. Whereas *On the Road* has a quality of innocence and freshness, *The Dharma Bums* has the consistency of a retread. Jaffe Ryder expresses to Kerouac or to his surrogate a triumph of the spirit over American bourgeois dullness and intellectual deception. Although Dean stood for protest in his energetic refusal to say yes to anything in American life, Ryder has discovered an alternative in the values of Buddhism. He is striving to reach another level of consciousness, which will, in effect, make him self-sufficient. Once able to throw over the American burden of materialism and dependency, he will have reached back beyond the fifties to a Whitmanesque expression of independence. The "open road," for him, is the effacement of self made possible by Buddhist discipline, brought about by communion with basic materials such as rock, air, and water, and by keeping a balance between intellectual and physical pursuits.

The Dharma bums of the title are those young men who turn the wheel of fortune to seek the true meaning as revealed by the various texts of Buddhism. Dharma has a mixed Hindu-Buddhist background. In Hindu belief, the progeny of Dharma are personifications of virtues and religious rites, while in a Buddhist sense, Dharma is worshiped by the lower castes in India, thus the application to California bums. In his way, Ryder is a Buddhist priest whose responsibility is to interpret the dharma, a universal code of conduct. As a monk, he is to have a moral function of the highest quality. Ryder's ability to break free of human restraints is connected, apparently, to his acceptance of Buddhist concepts of time as a continuum; in such a formulation, man and his life span are mere flickers of light. Implicit in such belief is the need to remove desire, whether yearning after material things or striving for recognition.

In this respect, Ryder has found some way to channel his energy, something that Dean Moriarty lacked. When Ryder speaks of materials and objects, he means those basics which are the making of the universe, "timeless objects." He seeks to align himself with Bodhisattva, himself a future Buddha who helps others less fortunate to seek the way of enlightenment.

But Kerouac's bums here are not really monks seriously seeking something within themselves, but surfers on Buddhist waves. They use religious beliefs as a way of breaking outside bourgeois life. Raymond Smith, Kerouac's narrator, loves his whiskey, but he is trying to discover some alternative to his mindless wanderings, which he seems to find in Ryder. What is remarkable in nearly all of Kerouac's fiction is how his protagonists must attach themselves to someone they admire (a male figure) and imitate their behavior and beliefs.

George Mandel's *Flee the Angry Strangers* (1952) is immersed in the life style of the Greenwich Village counterculture. Mandel's people differ somewhat from the Beats, in that they do not will themselves into an adversary position to the main culture: they are there by temperament, upbringing, inheritance. They are, like children in a ghetto, part of a scene not by choice but by having known nothing else. For many of them, there are no alternatives, although for Diane Lattimer, Mandel's protagonist, there are elements of choice. Chiefly, the dramatic movement of the novel depends on Diane, a young woman, barely eighteen, who senses doom, hooked on sex, "tea," and "horse"; her sister, Edna, who lies dying in a hospital, another doomed young woman; and Edna's husband, also beloved by Diane, Carter Webb. Webb represents choice for Diane, for he holds a regular job, as a film processer, and offers stability, though not his bed.

Around these, Mandel creates a large number of peripheral characters, each one representing further reaches of the Village jungle, or potential salvation.

Intermixed with this is a fierce parent-child conflict, focused mainly on Diane and her mother, Vivienne, who tries to bring up two rebellious daughters by religious and bourgeois doctrines. She fails to observe her dismal failure, has Diane put away, and is only slowly changed by circumstances and Webb's persistence.

Mandel holds down movement, so that the novel takes place almost entirely in bars, cafeterias, and run-down pads. The point is an important one, for as opposed to more spatial Beat fiction, this one is almost static. The Village is indeed like a village, a small enclosed place, with the central labyrinth defined by Bleecker, MacDougal, Eighth streets, the very heart of the heart. These sharply designated areas become like levels of Dante's Inferno, with danger lurking in each alley. The novel opens ominously with Robert Stoney observing a "new girl" on the street and accosting her; she is Diane, who knows him and his reputation, and is able to fend him off. But Stoney represents the least of the threats, which come from psychopaths like the dealer Buster or various addicts who represent stages of dying and death.

Diane is defined by her desire for ultimate forms of freedom: freedom from her mother's pressure, freedom from the internal demands consuming her, freedom to reclaim her baby, who has been put out for adoption, freedom to do whatever she chooses even if it destroys her. Mandel's idea of freedom for Diane is absolute: although what she chooses may well prove destructive, even so, at eighteen, she has the right to make such choices. We have, in this area, a linkage of European existentialism and Beat life style, together with plain American defiance of authority. Nevertheless, the motif of freedom which threads through the novel—especially freedom of child from parent—is a harbinger of a great deal to come, a distinct forerunner of much 1960s life and fiction, and a direct expression of postwar breakup.

Diane is a child of the new, even when the new means a doomed existence. Family is evil, since it depends on certain prerogatives of the parent not available to the child; bourgeois life, by extension, is as evil, since it allows the employer to suck the freedom of the employee; the political state, by further extension, is evil, since its order and organization, even stability, depend on obstructing the individual citizen's freedom.

Mandel's novel, historically, is very much part of the "counterfeit decade," in that it seeks out those elements which deflect the individual's drive toward fulfillment, although he defines fulfillment not as achievement but as choice alone. Further, we have the novelist's countering of the cold war, which is, in this respect, the ultimate in manipulation: parental figures on the largest scale possible, a face-down between two Big Brothers.

Mandel's novel comes at a crossroads in postwar fiction, since it points in so many directions. It is not quintessential Beat, although it brings together many Beat aspects of life style. It is not proletariat, although it sympathizes with the proles and rails against the bourgeoisie. It is not existentialist in any formal sense, but it does carry over one aspect of existentialism that lent itself readily to American life: the absolute belief in freedom. It is not Kafkaesque, but it does provide Kafka's sense of an enclosure, a small space which proves both refuge and potential source of destruction, the Village. It is not purely naturalistic, although it does revel in naturalistic detail, in pain and suffering, in areas of doom that seem beyond choice. It is not formally indebted to Joyce, but it does attempt a stream of sorts, and a tough lyricism that undertakes new forms of expression, such as we see in Algren and Kerouac.

The following passage describes the exquisite experience of shooting up: "In and out a couple of times while Horse burned gently in her [Diane's] arm. She was scarcely out with the needle when the charge set in. Not Nothingly like a skin pop, not scattered like a snort. It was a quick, sleek, golden Horse, a steed of gold, and gold all about, molten gold oozing into every last organ, erasing lead, enriching mush to cool gold forever. Forever was a long way from shadows." The Four Horses of the Apocalypse are encapsulated in that cap and needle, and they enter the bloodstream, to sow a kind of lyrical destruction. The patterns are set. What Mandel has caught is the five-year period after the war when the country headed in several directions, and its literature followed. Gaddis would come to define it more fully as the counterfeit decade; Bellow was to probe in *Augie March* many of the same patterns; Burroughs would turn the drug culture into a form of life itself; Heller was working out his own view of war as destroyer of human freedom; and Philip Roth at the end of the decade was to explore on several levels parent-child divisiveness.

Like many of the Beat novelists, Mandel assumes that any adversary move is in itself valuable. The individual must always break out. Liberation is a self-fulfilling process, even when the break cannot be handled, as in Diane's case. We find the novel, therefore, at still another juncture, where narcissism establishes its own terms. These terms are premised on individual experience and satisfaction, the supreme example of which is the golden horse riding through one's veins to bring every organ ecstasy. Those moments of ecstasy, destructive as they may be, are worth the aftermath; but whatever the individual chooses, this is the ultimate in the narcissistic experience. All else is pressure from without. Yet while Mandel sees that limitations must be placed, they must derive from within. There is no background, only foreground, the individual as sole product of civilization.

WILLIAM BURROUGHS AND THE SENSE OF THE FIFTIES

Well before he met the artist Brion Gysin, whose ideas of collages and cut-ups directly influenced the preparation of *The Exterminator* (written 1966–73, published 1974), William Burroughs had conceived of fiction as a plastic art. Burroughs is perhaps our best example of the writer borrowing from other art forms, the amalgamator of the arts by way of their infusion into the word. Like the action painters of the 1950s, Burroughs conceived of the field (canvas, page) as a series of clashes and conflicts; like the innovators in electronic music or John Cage, he found sounds more significant than traditional communication; like those shaping modern dance, he saw that movement existed for its own sake as much as for its continuity with other movements. Burroughs tried to discover a "montage language." What he found, however we respond to the particulars of his vision, has permanently entered our literature, not only as a reflection of our culture but as an avatar of what we are becoming. Burroughs has positioned himself as no less than an American prophet, a doom-filled Emerson, a no less lyrical Whitman.

Although *Naked Lunch* (published in Paris in 1959, in the United States in 1966) appears avant-garde, even postmodernist, as some critics would have it, the title has a traditional ring to it, recalling works from Dante's *Convivio* to Carlyle's *Sartor Resartus*. Common to each is a metaphor which strives to achieve the real. Despite obvious differences, Burroughs and Carlyle share common characteristics of anger, intensity, and desire to get beneath the "outer garment." Burroughs says that the title was suggested by Kerouac, and that it was unclear to him until his recent recovery from addiction. It means: "NAKED Lunch—a frozen moment when everyone sees what is on the end of every fork."

The metaphor of food recalls not only Dante's banquet but Swift's "Modest Proposal" for the disposition of Irish babies. For Burroughs, a "modest proposal" would be the elimination of all restraints. If we are to comprehend what we are, where we have gone, we must eat a "naked lunch." Since people, he says, favor capital punishment, then let them really rub their noses in "what they actually eat and drink. Let them see what is on the end of that long newspaper spoon." Burroughs's revilement of human practices, all heightened to cross both pleasure and pain, is aimed at liberation of the self, a Sadean measurement of self against others.

In such a probe, degradation is never distant from revelation. The overriding consideration is the self martyring itself in order to approach a form of joy otherwise unattainable. Everything must be experienced on the edge. To gain the junkie's paradise, one must sink to the junkie's hell; they are indistinguishable.* Burroughs's work in the 1950s is significant for its adversariness—it was banned in this country and became an underground book—and for its foreshadowing of that explosion of self which characterized the 1960s and 1970s. Through his fictions, we can observe the decades in change; the more the change, the closer the continuity to his racing imagination.

---

*Although the combination seems unlikely, *Junky* (originally published as *Junkie* by "William Lee") fits into the counterfeit decade, in 1953, in some of the ways that *Augie March* does, also in 1953. Two books that superficially seem so dissimilar are linked if we play them off not against each other but in counterpoint to the decade. The events of the Burroughs novel occur just near the end of the war, although the narration of them is somewhat later.

The motif that connects the two books and their association, in turn, to the decade is their accommodation to will-lessness. Burroughs's pursuit of heroin is almost passive. He comes to it casually, he is broken of the habit, and then he returns to it casually, because someone has it or offers it. He is willing to move along the lines of addiction in order to pursue a different dimension of reality, this in response to what he felt was the counterfeit quality of his times. Earlier, he had rejected Harvard for its "fake English setup" and its closed corporation quality. Ordinary life offered a comparable deadness, whereas junk and addiction threw his new self (or William Lee, as he called himself to get rid of the corporate name) into something more real, because dangerous, close to death, associated with criminals and confidence men. Like Augie, his straighter contemporary, he wishes to live without walls. Several varieties of drugs, homosexual experiences, toting a pistol (or more powerful weapons), rolling drunks offered alternatives to the grimness of routine, to imitative feelings.

Burroughs moves rapidly into that consummate expression of self, the junkie's self-indulgent paradise, a circuitry of pleasure which drugs can convey and which nothing else—neither sex, nor police, nor personal danger—can enter. Burroughs cites the ultimate trip as not that furious activity posited by Kerouac and Cassady, but the passivity of the junkie's inner journey. The junkie is never bored, he says, because he can focus on his shoe for eight hours; only the effectiveness of the drug alters his perception. That absorption in self was the line of liberation for Burroughs. What he is presenting is something very dangerous, and we can see that while he was banned here for his views on drugs and his sexual explicitness, he is really far more threatening in other areas.

Burroughs is Raskolnikov without restraints. For him, the supreme experience is the moment when life and death meet, as in hanging. For then, as is well known, the male ejaculates as the tension of spine and penis are broken. The bursting, explosive, flowing semen is for Burroughs a life force, stilled only by the drug trip. But just as the drug trip brings the individual down to the line between life and death, so does hanging. Burroughs must constantly seek encounters in which life and death meet on the edge. His role is demonic.

The method is to achieve the "ultimate moment" in the ultimate verbal montage, what he strove for more defiantly after he met Brion Gysin. That verbal montage is the linguistic equivalent of the drug-induced fantasies that make up most of his fictions. Almost arbitrarily divided into segments called novels or narratives, the fictions are really one. They are marked by a potentially endless sequence of fantasies, any number of which can be snipped off and combined into a book, called *Naked Lunch, The Soft Machine, The Ticket That Exploded, The Wild Boys,* or *Exterminator!* The center of this exploding universe of montage-ordered images is always William Burroughs or William Lee. Every narrative is also a journey, that journey into fantasy worlds where Burroughs seeks the real, the actual.* Interconnected

with this journey is the making of art, for the drug-induced fantasies are associated with those experiments with drugs, sex, and synesthetic experiences which characterized much nineteenth-century French poetry. Burroughs is our modern Rimbaud, only wilder, less artistically disciplined.

To gain balance, Burroughs plays off the fantasies in *Naked Lunch* against areas of fact: the Appendix (concerned with addiction), the Introduction (Burroughs's autobiographical "Deposition"), and excerpts from the book's obscenity trial in Massachusetts. Structurally, his so-called novel is also a montage of fact/fiction, long sections of fictional narrative interspersed with large bodies of factual material. In the latter, Burroughs is analytical, even clinical; whereas in the fictional parts, he develops what will be his characteristic style of verbal shorthand.

In the course of that trial, incidentally, in which *Naked Lunch* was found not obscene, Allen Ginsberg testified and read, from *Reality Sandwiches,* his poem "On Burroughs' Work." The final lines: "A naked lunch is natural to us, / we eat reality sandwiches. / Allegories are so much lettuce. / Don't hide the madness." Ginsberg's poem points up how Burroughs's presence was beginning to show itself in other works, not simply in individual lives around him. Ginsberg, Pynchon in *V.,* possibly Mailer in *Why Are We in Vietnam?,* Sontag in her shorter criticism, Gaddis in *JR* were influenced by aspects of Burroughs's work, especially his prose line.

The key to Burroughs's prose is condensation, a foreshortened voice, as it were. He drops off articles, both definite and indefinite; he leaves off the *s* in the third person singular verb—to achieve a mix of illiterate and literate; he often cuts out subjects for his verbs, or verbs for his subjects—to gain a notational effect. He treads a line between conventional narrative and free association; and although he does not dissolve words, as Joyce did in *Finnegans Wake,* he does dissolve passages by way of rapid movement, montage (long before the "cut-up" method of Gysin),

---

*Although a more traditional writer, Paul Bowles, in *The Sheltering Sky* (1949) and *Let It Come Down* (1952), like Burroughs, uses the journey as a form of discovery even when it leads to self-destruction. Only the "ultimate" expression of self can jar the self from exhaustion. In this respect, however differently literarily, both are recreating a war situation, using drugs, sexual experimentation, forms of sadism and masochism, to convey a form of combat.

In *The Sheltering Sky,* Port and Kit Moresby must make

the journey to North Africa, or else watch their lives waste away in inconsequential acts. They are driven not by social or political needs, but by inner pressures. The journey is their final effort to stay alive. Once it is started, Port's illness gives Kit her freedom, and then the desert provides opportunity for further choice—and as it turns out, what she desires most, bondage. Her deepest needs are met by an Arab on a caravan, who by degrees turns her into his slave, finally adding her to his harem. Kit feels most intensely at her greatest moments of servitude; this is the "female condition," presented as a form of liberation for her.

and spinoffs, reeling in his line and then suddenly letting it out. The overall sense is one of great nervousness, great movement and vitality. Burroughs's legacy for the future, I think, will not be his narratives as such, nor his sexual vision of rectums and hard cocks; but his fluid prose style, which conveys vitality in ways Kerouac never achieved despite years of intense experimentation.

Burroughs's description of the "buyer"—the man who sets up a seller for the police but is not himself a user—does not include the full run of his prose strategies, but it does support his sense of irony and negative force: energy expended on doing one thing, while the opposite is shaping up. "Well the buyer comes to look more and more a junky. He can't drink. He can't get it up. His teeth fall out. (Like pregnant women lose their teeth feeding the stranger, junkies lose their yellow fangs feeding the monkey.) He is all the time sucking on a candy bar. Baby Ruths he digs special. 'It really disgusts you to see the Buyer sucking on them candy bars so nasty,' a cop says."

The ultimate mechanical man, the buyer is the one for whom the "soft machine" was designed, the man who refuses to see the "naked lunch" at the end of his fork. He joins with Dr. Benway and all those other counterfeit creatures who make restrictive institutions possible, for he achieves his success by negating others' experiences. Burroughs here is moving along the line of pure anarchy, supporting the self that has the right to indulge itself and destroy itself as it sees fit, mounting an assault on all those elements—buyer, Benway, others—who place obstacles in their way. Burroughs's sense of individual freedom recapitulates de Sade's argument, that one achieves such freedom at the expense of others, regardless of consequences, with ruthlessness, cruelty, etc. Burroughs's narratives, then, are meaningful only as drug-induced fantasies, or as pure idea. For in the world outside fantasy or dream, they would be fascistic impulses, or impulses which literature (fiction or otherwise) cannot explain.*

_____

*Mailer's presentation of Gary Gilmore suggests a parallel figure, whose impulses for the satisfaction of the self, in two meaningless murders, cannot be contained in any literary form. Whenever Mailer tries to approach the aspect of Gilmore that led to the random crimes, he must retreat and describe Gilmore's stare or gaze, or back off onto neutral ground. The very area where Mailer's novelistic gifts might have functioned is left blank, and part of it may be that the novelist has no way of entering that ultimate sense of individual freedom, where the self goes wild and liberates itself with murder. The hangings in Burroughs's fiction would be equivalent crimes and tests.

As a writer of fantasies, with drugs as the catalyst, Burroughs can enjoy the same broad swings as the allegorist or parodist. He can be as outrageous as Swift in "A Modest Proposal" or the Laputa section of _Gulliver's Travels,_ or de Sade in _120 Days of Sodom and Gomorrah._ His hallucinatory version of "on the road" can infuse energy into areas Kerouac retreated from as too wild. The United States, as can be expected, is itself hallucinatory: "You can't see it, you don't know where it comes from. Take one of those cocktail lounges at the end of a subdivision street—every block of houses has its own bar and drugstore and market and liquorstores. You walk in and it hits you. But where does it come from?" This could be the America of _Lolita._

The literary advantage of Burroughs's world of hanging boys, endless sex (mainly anal), crumbling cities, continuous movement is that it highlights an America that lacks coherence, a real place which in its confusions equals the fantasy world. Dr. Benway, called in "as advisor to the Freedland Republic," is the organizing genius behind Kafka-land. Benway is an expert in "T.D.," Total Demoralization. In Annexia, he had abolished concentration camps and mass arrests, except under special circumstances, and substituted for brutality what he calls "prolonged mistreatment." The latter, when applied skillfully, gives rise to "anxiety and a feeling of special guilt." The subject does not, of course, recognize he is being mistreated; he must be "made to feel that he deserves _any_ treatment he receives because there is something (never specified) horribly wrong with him. The naked need of the control addicts must be decently covered by an arbitrary and intricate bureaucracy so that the subject cannot contact his enemy direct." In Freedland, confusing documents, missing park benches, ringing bells, police interference are all part of a disarray that allows the individual no opportunity to define himself, subject and object hopelessly jumbled. Burroughs describes a dystopia, pastoral not only gone sour but turned into hell.

Here, Burroughs can place his characters: the Vigilante, the Rube, Lee [Burroughs], the Agent, A.J., Clem and Jody, the Ergot Twins, Hassan O'Leary the After Birth Tycoon, the Sailor, the Exterminator, Andrew Keif, "Fats" Terminal, Doc Benway, "Fingers" Schafer—no longer literary or novelistic characters, but men (never women) who people a middle region of the imagination. Pynchon would pick up this ragtag bunch for his "Whole Sick Crew" in _V._ In common, they are figures of disorder, a crowd that breaks down rather than builds. Energy here is destructive, which is for Burroughs good energy, since it defuses the distorted satisfactions of the real world. Self-induced distortions are preferable to those imposed upon us.

Naked Lunch, then, is a blueprint, a how-to manual: "How-To extend levels of experience by opening the door at the end of a long hall. . . . Doors that only open in *Silence.*" We enter Bluebeard's castle. *Naked Lunch* demands silence from the reader; that is, he must approach it as holy text, its contents as sacred experience. Everything outside it is secular, waste matter. It is the Word. For Burroughs, the Word or Word horde "will leap on you with leopard man iron claws, it will cut off fingers and toes like an opportunist land crab, it will hang you and catch your jissom like a scrutable dog, it will coil round your thighs like a bushmaster and inject a shot glass of rancid ectoplasm." The point about the Word is that it is a prime mover. A little earlier, Burroughs had spoken of himself only as a "recording instrument," by which he meant that he was an automatic writer who did not impose story, plot, or continuity. He says in some instances he succeeds "in *Direct* recording of certain areas of psychic process," although he disclaims being an entertainer.

All is a definition of self. In each hanging, he relives his own final moment; in each act of sadism, he offers up his own life; in each moment of masochism, he shares pleasure/pain with all those who have ever been tortured; in each drug fantasy, he moves to the extremes of behavior where life exists; and in each cure or downer, he moves toward that hell which is everyman's lot. Burroughs has journeyed well beyond Genet's homosexual geography, well beyond criminal as saint, or homosexual as explorer of a holy world. He moves into a different order of experience, excluding women altogether, except as occasional substitutes for the male (a mouth, never a rectum); and uses male experience as the whole of life. But even here, he extracts a particular male experience: the male who is peddling his ass, or passively letting it be used. Yet arbitrary, even hateful as such a world may seem, as it does to Burroughs, he pursues its varieties with an integrity of purpose which is what we mean when we say a writer creates his own terms, wherever those terms may lead.

Burroughs is so continuous with himself that his work of the 1950s leads directly into the experiments of the next two decades. Once he discovered a prose style and a method of collage/montage, he cut himself adrift from contemporary sources, conceiving of himself as Lazarus returned from the dead to tell us what he has seen. The succeeding fictions become wilder and more intense efforts at liberation, and Burroughs's own embracing of Hubbard's Scientology movement is his way of negating the "Reactive Mind," which includes the practical world as well as history, Freud's unconscious and Jung's archetypes. Burroughs is moving toward Nietzsche's superman, but without Nietzsche's ironic morality.

Like Blake, he has a vast vision, each segment of which has personal significance for him. He must only find suitable words, words being his vehicle and also his curse. He says he wrote *Naked Lunch* under the influence of cannabis, but now that he has discontinued using it, he can achieve "the same results by non-chemical means: flicker and music through headphones, cut-ups and fold-ins of my texts, and especially by training myself to think in association blocks instead of in words." To be tied in to orthodox forms of language is to be part of the "switchboard" in *Naked Lunch,* a device for conditioning people. The switchboard updated will become the giant computer in Barth's *Giles Goat-Boy.*

Consistent throughout is the need to escape from words by finding an alternative aural culture, thus achieving the defamiliarization of the ordinary. Gaddis in *JR* was confronted by the same problems: how to use words, yet escape words, how to plug into an aural culture, oral as well. Words are for Burroughs a virus, part of the conditioning associated with the Reactive Mind. Words transformed by splicing, cut-outs, fold-ins, taping, are less manipulative, are in fact evocative. Once again we note how Burroughs was moving toward the literary equivalent of Cage in music, Pollock in painting, free or expressive form in dance.

Part of the advantage of the cut-in system is that words are wiped out on the tape at the point of the cut-in; then in splicing, juxtapositions appear random. But Burroughs insists randomness is not meaninglessness; for the splicings often suggest something, frequently refer to some future event. "I have seen enough examples to convince me that the cut-ups are a basic key to the nature and function of words." Burroughs sees breakdown in communication here as a form of radicalism; to rebel against the word is to take a step toward liberation of the self. We perceive how attuned he was to the nonverbal culture of the sixties, in which aurality, gesture, movement create their own voices outside formal languages. Far more than sex, nonverbal means of communication in Burroughs define him and shape his revolution.*

The Soft Machine (1961) is a series of montage images in which the machine is gutted. The ultimate enemy is Trak: "The Trak Reservation so-called includes almost all areas in and about the United Republics of Freelandt and, since the Trak Police process all matters occurring in Trak Reservation and no one knows what is and is not Reservation cases, civil and criminal are summarily removed from civilian courts with the single word TRAK to unknown sanctions." Dr. Benway, from *Naked Lunch,* is deeply involved in Trak activities. Trak serves here as cartels the way I. G. Farben does in Pynchon's *Gravity's Rainbow,* the cartel or organization (the soft machine) as an "invisible city" which controls all aspects of our experience, draining free will even as we try to exert it.

By use of the "soft machine" as his central metaphor for the way of the (American) world, Burroughs has a common image for the "sell-out": something accessible and yet mechanical. The softness of the machine† suggests its accommodation, which is another way of stressing its seductive powers and, thus, its increased destructiveness. In the section called "Gongs of Violence," the succession of images indicates Burroughs's prose as well as his vision. The context is a planet war brought on by the struggle between the sexes.

> Spectators scream through the track—The electronic brain shivers in blue and pink and chlorophyll orgasms spitting out money printed on rolls of toilet paper, condoms full of ice cream, Kotex hamburgers —Police files of the world spurt out in a blast of bone meal, garden tools and barbecue sets whistle through the air, skewer the spectators—crumpled cloth bodies through dead nitrous streets of an old film set— grey luminous flakes falling softly on Ewyork, Onolulu, Aris, Ome, Oston—From siren towers the twanging tones of fear—Pan God of Panic piping blue notes through empty streets as the berserk time machine twisted a tornado of years and centuries.

---

*Cf. Norman O. Brown's extraordinary Phi Beta Kappa address to the Columbia University chapter in 1960: "There is a hex on us, the specters in books, the authority of the past; and to exorcise these ghosts is the great work of magical self-liberation."

†Attuned to his Burroughs business machine background, Burroughs borrows computer terms: "soft-ware" is really "soft hardware" or "soft machine."

The listing is the obverse of Rabelaisian, not life force but death energy. The question arises whether or not we can cite "energy," even "prose style," for something so pathologically nihilistic. The omission of the first letter from cities suggests they lack a vital part, Burroughs dehumanizing them as they have their citizens. But what is left if death is the obsession? If all imagery and energy are consecrated to nihilism (well beyond anarchism), what role can Burroughs play in our literary imagination?

The question is a profound one that strikes at much in (post)modernist fiction. It arose fifty years ago with Kafka (especially) and Eliot, and is not distant from the contemporary sensibility. It became even more immediately apparent in the work of Céline, where death orientation, nihilism, and fascistic ideology combined to make him a pariah from the Western humanistic tradition. Yet if we reject Céline as a realist, view him as a prophet, or fantasist, read his books as "bibles" or holy texts, we can understand if not accept him.

The pairing of Céline with Burroughs, even more than Kafka, is not an idle one. Once we move past obvious differences—Burroughs's stress on homosexual sex, acts of sexual martyrdom, sadistic and masochistic impulses in all social activity—we can perceive common characteristics. Burroughs's intense sexual manipulation is part of his view of sex as power, and power is for him, as it is for Céline, the motivating element. Both bring great bursts of energy, a vibrating prose, a language that leaps from the page to nihilistic and anarchistic views. Both move close to the apocalypse; *The Soft Machine,* in fact, ends with an apocalyptic scene, as observed from a penny arcade. Burroughs's drug-induced fantasies are such visions, of nuclear devices dropped into the imagination, which then reacts with vistas of destruction, doom, final things. Céline is, along with Kafka, our prophet of Western doom, our incarnation of Nazi nihilism and the destruction of the Second World War. In his way, more fantasist than historian, Burroughs is our guide to the new apocalypse, the new wars of the world.

In a section called "Case of the Celluloid Kali," one Clem Snide (who calls himself "a Private Ass Hole," someone looking for a slavey's job) is confronted by a person suspiciously like Burroughs: "A thin grey man in a long coat that flickered like old film." Snide insists he was born in a nova, a star that begins to increase brilliantly and then gradually becomes fainter. The emphasis on the nova in Burroughs is apparent: a metaphor for earth itself, the way things have gone. The grey man explains that the "ticket has exploded," the apocalypse is here, and there is an evacuation plan, which he describes:

> The hanging gimmick—death in orgasm—gills—No bones and elementary nervous systems—evacuation to the Drenched Lands—a bad deal on the level and it's not on the level with Sammy sitting in—small timers trying to cross me up—Me, Bradly-Martin, who invented the double-cross—Step right up—Now you see me now you don't—a few scores to settle before I travel—a few things to tidy up and that's where you come in—I want you to contact the Venus Mob, the Vegetable People and spill the whole fucking compost heap through Times Square and Piccadilly—I'm not taking any rap for that green bitch —I'm going to rat on everybody and split this dead whistle stop planet wide open—I'm clean for once with the nova heat—like clean fall out——

The rhythms of this passage, and many others, are brilliantly conceived. But the referents come so rapidly and with such abandon, the play of thought is so far removed from our universe and yet solidly rooted in Burroughs's imagination, that the passage leaps away from us even as we grapple with its rhythmic energies. The matter of referents is crucial. All of Burroughs's preoccupations are present: the "hanging gimmick"; the apocalyptic sense of now; the conspiracies suggested, with scores to settle; the "Venus Mob," a group or groups from outer space; the transformation of man into some other creature, here into gilled bodies that can survive death by water.

In the final chapter, called "Cross the Wounded Galaxies," a penny arcade peep show provides "a long process in different forms." These forms recall Eliot's "Waste Land" before becoming Burroughs's own. "In the pass [he writes] the muttering sickness leaped into our throats, coughing and spitting in the silver morning. frost on our bones. Most of the ape forms died there on the treeless slopes. dumb animal eyes on 'me' brought the sickness from white time caves frozen in my throat to hatch in the warm steamlands spitting song of scarlet bursts in egg flesh, beyond the pass, limestone slopes down into a high green savanna and the grass-wind on our genitals. came to a swamp fed by hot springs and mountain ice. and fell in flesh heaps. sick apes spitting blood laugh."

Coming back to the point of Burroughs's significance—or marginality, for some—I think we must locate him as a "lyricist of nihilism." If one writer has brought himself down near death, flirted with it, examined it, tried to find the flimsy boundary between life and death, between personal death and death of a world, then Burroughs is that writer, and we must view him in those terms. His imagination is the film strip of our postwar world, an endless reel of images, scenes, characters, all of which are playbacks of himself. This goes beyond narcissism, however, since it involves indecent exposure. Burroughs has placed himself in a nuclear plant's core, so that radioactive waste can bathe him. He takes on all cancers, all illnesses, all spin-offs from the "soft machine," and if he survives, it is to return from the near-dead to tell us what he, Lazarus, has observed. The heir to the hard machinery of computers and other business hardware observes that not only toughness but "soft machines" destroy. Whatever accommodates us ends us.

Burroughs's remaining fiction of the last two decades becomes even wilder, more dire and threatening. His release from drugs, his association with Brion Gysin have intensified, not lessened, the horror. Often, as in *Nova Express,* he borrows heavily from science fiction to achieve another level of fantasy or nightmare. Communities and societies give way to universal struggles; the planet's survival rests in the balance. Burroughs, more demonic than ever, orchestrates our demise, each work a foray into *Götterdämmerung.*

Early in *The Ticket That Exploded* (1962, 1967), Burroughs indicates that his narrator is reading "a science fiction book called *The Ticket That Exploded.* The story is close enough to what is going on here so now and again I make myself believe this ward room is just a scene in an old book far away and long ago might as well be that for all the support I'm getting from Base Headquarters." The narrative is presented as a film strip, with film and journey image merging with each other. And the ticket that explodes is a multiple one—the ticket of admission to the film, but also the ticket that enables us to go on the "long trip." An exploding ticket has a personal reference, too, in that our ticket is up, canceled, or postponed for some future journey.

The exploding ticket also makes way for multiple roles; in an exploding universe, there is no room for a single personality. The narrator plays Burroughs, plays Burroughs's pseudonym William Lee, plays multiple roles as an agent of a group of assassins called the "White Hunters." The "White Hunters" are themselves uncertain about their goals. They may be white supremacists or an antiwhite organization, the extreme right or radical left; the CIA, the FBI, or any dehumanizing organization. When he joins, the recruit does not know what he will do; he gives himself up to uncertainty and will kill for it. Burroughs has an apt metaphor for an exploding ticket and, indeed, for violence.

As ever, the significant element for Burroughs amidst controls of every kind is liberation of the self. Each section of the book, arranged like a free-floating chapter, overlaps with the next so that all form a mosaic of alternating control and freedom. Drug fantasies of the war set free vaudeville acts of the imagination, which in turn becomes like a "second life" that each participant in the drama can put on, a sexual skin, as it were. An actual skin is described. "The guide slipped off his own skin like a garment, peeled penis pulsing red right, clouds drifting through his remote blue eyes—Hula hoops of color formed around the guide's body and enclosed Bradly weak and torn with pain cool hands on his naked flesh as he sank in blood and bones and intestines of the other suffocation panic of spermatozoa sucked through pearly genital passages and spurted out in a scratching shower of sperm—sunlight through bodies without cover—soft luminous spurts drifting in the cool blue wind——"

The passage is vintage Burroughs. However masochistic the act, release is gained even as one is almost suffocated. The presence of opposites is the catalyst, conflict in the individual heralding larger conflicts. In the section called "the nova police," Burroughs explains the "basic nova technique," which he says is very simple: "Always create as many insoluble conflicts as possible and always aggravate existing conflicts—This is done by dumping on the same planet life forms with incompatible conditions of existence. . . . Their conditions of life are basically incompatible in present time form and it is precisely the work of the nova mob to see that they remain in present time form, to create and aggravate the conflicts that lead to the explosion of a planet, that is to nova." The male hanging, Burroughs's favorite configuration, leads to the "basic nova technique": that final spurt of semen, the explosion of a planet, a nova in the making. The parabola of the semen is the star bursting into light and shape, brilliant for a brief time, then fading into the universe's overall structure.

The latter parts of *The Ticket That Exploded* are given over to explorations of the spliced tape principle, which Burroughs sees in terms of a universe of sound. This is, he says, an aural generation. Only sound (not sight) moves us, and we can manipulate sound so as to unbalance the universe. The tape principle, which involves recording and prerecording,

is Burroughs's form of synesthesia, but not solely for the individual's experience. He sees it as an ironic and parodic form of sensation, the natural outgrowth of a "soft machine" society. He cites Wittgenstein in support of his view: "No proposition can contain itself as an argument," which Burroughs interprets to mean: "The only thing *not* prerecorded in a prerecorded universe is the prerecording itself which is to say *any* recording that contains a random factor."

Burroughs uses Wittgenstein to locate chance in a recorded universe. For Burroughs, unlike the philosopher (who had other possibilities in mind), the goal is to seek out what is still sensation and yet to parody what sensation has become. With that double game, he finds dozens of uses for the spliced tape principle, everything from job applications to quiz program answers. The beauty of his formulation, like many of Swift's in Laputa, is that it lies along real lines: the assault on our ears, the massing of sound, the location of sound in areas we normally associate with quiet.

In the final section of *The Ticket,* called "the invisible generation," Burroughs repeats in essay form that "what we see is determined to a large extent by what we hear." The goal of the person who plays with a tape recorder is power. Aural power is not of course new. One need only recall that Mussolini wired every small village and hamlet in Italy for sound, placed a sound truck in the main square, and blared out speeches and propaganda unstoppable except at its source. Thus, all Italy became interconnected by way of particular sounds. Burroughs's scheme, which is parodic of soft-machine capability, would use sound to upset order, to create a form of aural anarchy. Think, he says, of bands of "irresponsible youths with tape recorders playing back traffic sounds that confuse motorists . . . put a thousand young recorders with riot recordings into the street." The potentialities are as infinite as the splicing itself, and any number can play. A current urban phenomenon is the sound from large portable stereos, often turned up as loud as they can go, which saturate the street with ferocious rhythms. Mass a thousand of these . . .

The Ticket is a sequence of such schemes, a montage of exploding images in seemingly random series. Besides tape splicing, Burroughs examines an orgone accumulator of creative energy; a writing machine that shifts from text to text in juxtaposition to each other, Shakespeare and Rimbaud, for example; various military units composed of compatible scholars, for instance, a Shakespeare Squadron; the sex skin. Some are considered seriously (as the orgone accumulator), some parodically, as the tape machine.

The goal for all is "to isolate and cut association lines of the control machine . . . the more you run the tapes through and cut them up the less power they will have cut the prerecordings into air into thin air." Only in that way can the exploding ticket be moved back toward recombination. It may, however, be too late. The book ends with a whimper, not a bang.

Nova Express (1964) presents a war between two elements for the survival of the universe. It is, like the medieval morality plays, a conflict between the forces of good and evil; and the outcome depends on moral force. There has been a strain of morality in Burroughs, a Puritan ethic of sorts, which is not usually cited: the desire to find the right way, despite the horrors piled on horrors. Like Kurtz, he hovers between nightmare and moral fervor.

The first words of the book, in fact, are a Jonathan Edwards sermon about the horrors of hell: "Listen to my last words anywhere. Listen to my last words any world. Listen all you boards syndicates and governments of the earth. And you powers behind what filthy deals consummated in what lavoratory to take what is not yours. To sell the ground from unborn feet forever——" Nova criminals have poisoned the world. Burroughs see his role as something of a filmmaker, to present before our eyes the fact that the "Garden of Delights is a terminal sewer." The pastoral vision has been turned into an urban nightmare; but more, our expectations of happiness have been transformed into sequences of destruction. The Nova criminals plan "Orgasm Death" and "Nova Ovens," which Burroughs warned about in *Naked Lunch* and *The Soft Machine.* He sees his writing of those books as martyrdom, to demonstrate to us what will happen if we do not arrest the Nova criminals.

"Howl" came from the same impulse, the poet taking upon himself the pain the individual must expose himself to so as to save the rest of us. It is a long tradition. What is unusual is that those who formed that loose group known as the Beats should have viewed their own self-destruction not as the pursuit of happiness but as forms of martyrdom to some cultural ideal.

In this struggle, we must fight back to survive. "Street gangs, Uranian born of nova conditions,* get

out and fight for your streets. Call in the Chinese and any random factors. Cut all tape. Shift cut tangle magpie voice lines of the earth." The criminals have a "Board Green deal" in which they plan to leave their "human dogs" under the "white hot skies of Venus," while they escape in "the first life boat in drag." The confusion of images is apt, as is disregard of ordinary punctuation; for Burroughs is intent on chaos: that mixture of sight, sound, smell (usually, rectal odors) which overpowers the senses. He calls for "Operation Total Exposure" as a way of fighting "Operation Total Disposal."

Of particular destructive power are words. "Verbal units" are inherent dangers, and we must discover ways of deactivating them. In Burroughs's crusade to have apomorphine used to cure drug addiction,† he speaks of it combating "parasite invasion by stimulating the regulatory centers to normalize metabolism— A powerful variation of this drug could deactivate all verbal units and blanket the earth in silence, disconnecting the entire heat syndrome." The struggle between silence and word, however, is not an easy one. Agent K9 is able to "Release Silence Virus" and a "Silence Sickness" flashes around the earth at the speed of light. But people are unprepared for the "Silence Sickness" and they go insane, since they are "composed entirely of word." For Burroughs, words have become so intolerable, and yet so essential, that any tampering with language causes madness.

Writing in the 1960s—for him a decade continuous with the 1950s—Burroughs saw the basic disorder of our time as forms of control by the "nova mechanism." "Always create as many insoluble conflicts as possible and always aggravate existing conflicts—This is done by dumping life forms with incompatible conditions of existence on the same planet." The "Nova Mob" exists to make certain the conflicts continue, to lead "to the explosion of a planet that is to nova." Like Pynchon with the Tristero System, he visualizes the "Nova Mob" as part of a continuous conspiracy: ". . . recording devices fix the nature of absolute need and dictate the use of total weapons." In the aural attack, feedback of recorded sounds, thrust into every situation, will create chaos, a playback of "nuclear war and nova." A character called the "Subliminal Kid" moves in and takes over "bars, cafés and juke boxes of the world cities and

---

*Burroughs's use of Uranus is of interest, since Uranus is a "Big Father" myth: son and husband of the Earth, he was father of the Titans and the Cyclops, was dethroned by Cronus. Uranus is the very emblem of that first world order overthrown by the first "Nova criminal," Cronus, who mutilated his father when he overthrew him.

---

†Nova police are compared to apomorphine, Nova criminals to morphine. Like apomorphine, which can be dispensed with once the addict is cured, so the police can be discontinued once nova is removed.

installed radio transmitters and microphones in each bar," until "The Word broken pounded twisted exploded in smoke."

Late in the book, Burroughs quotes from Kafka's *The Trial,* as part of the dissociation of elements which is called the "Horrible Case," a section given over to the chaotic events wrought by the Nova criminals. Kafka's presence is evoked, not for the disorder he manifested, but for the control he was able to place over anarchy. Burroughs sees this as our condition. Kafka's use of courts, justice, legal arguments is transformed in *Nova Express* into aural assaults which allow the Subliminal Kid to control "the streets of the world" and to sweep up "sound and image of the city around faster and faster cars racing through all the streets of image record, take, play back, project on walls and window people and sky." Like a juggernaut, this display continues, until we explode into nova. Burroughs tells us he warned us. "Well that's about the closest way I know to tell you and papers rustling across city desks . . . fresh southerly winds a long time ago." He places the date "September 17, 1899 over New York," but the struggle is now, as he dates the book "July 21, 1964," from Tangier, Morocco, William Burroughs.

The Wild Boys: A Book of the Dead (finished 1969, published 1971) and *Exterminator!* (written 1966–73, published 1974) are very much outgrowths of Burroughs's sense of American culture in the sixties. The first—really a number of sequential episodes, a narrative—is presented as a film script. Cameraman, reels, angles of observation, characters who perform: all these are structural elements of the narrative. "The camera eye [Burroughs begins] is the eye of a cruising vulture flying over an area of scrub, rubble and unfinished buildings on the outskirts of a Mexican city." The first line has many of the images that will inform the book. The outskirts of the Mexican city are marginal areas of life which Burroughs draws together to become his "symbolic city." The "camera eye"— which structures "peep hole" chapters—becomes the observation post of the author as he charts the "wild boys," but it is also part of the sexual imagery, the target of all sexual activity, the anal hole, which is described as an eye, a target, a tube. The vulture prefigures the "book of the dead," a reference on one hand to the Buddhist document and on the other to its American counterpart: death without transfiguration.

Kaleidoscopic scenes of pleasures and pains, usually climaxed by wild and obsessive anal intercourse, are foreshadowings of the book's motif: the wild boy, dedicated to death without transfiguration. Burroughs's wild boys are not simply the generation of young in revolt sweeping the earth for victims, not only a sense of the sixties; but the young who have turned into vicious, merciless killers, intent only on their own group. They have moved outside civilization. Their culture is not a counterculture; it is a return to a primitive state of eat, screw, kill. The wild boys are "an overflow from North African cities that started in 1969," and they continue for the next two decades, which Burroughs foresees as the era of wild boys.

Burroughs himself, as controller of the narrator, is only one step from the wild boys. For he enters into the pain they cause, and he enjoys the pain they convey buggering each other. He borrows from Genet the miracle of the rose, which becomes the "rose of flesh," the areola around the rectum. All that degradation is part of the burden Burroughs must assume in order to "normalize" his observations. Since he is so close to the wild boys in their philosophy, even while reeling them in, he is able to convey their facelessness, their denial of alternative forms of life, their primitive desire for blood. They mutilate their victims, they eat flesh, they burn and slash and gouge. There are glider boys, skate boys, slingshot boys, blowgun boys, shaman boys, even "boys skilled in bone-pointing and Juju magic who can stab the enemy reflected in a gourd of water," desert boys, dream boys, and "the silent boys of the Blue desert." The wild boy *is* the new culture, not just urban but international.

The wild boys sweep through jungles, villages, and vast territories, bringing their form of death. They are, in semihuman shape, like the napalm used in Vietnam, which not only brings individual death, but kills an entire area for generations to come. Beyond their qualities as death-givers, the wild boys are feral images of sexual abandon. Their prime satisfaction after the kill is the mutilation of their victims, and often they cannibalize the flesh and boil the bones for soup. Their destruction of every taboo and form of civilization is complete. Their form of communication is not words, not language, not any form of civilized achievement. The "wild boys" are nothing less than a vision.

Burroughs structured *Exterminator!* directly on Brion Gysin's fold-in method, with each episode a "short story" or narrative prose element of differing material. The presentation is like that of a film, as in

"Twilight's Last Gleaming": "This film concerns a conspiracy to blow up a train carrying nerve gas." Like so many other Burroughs pieces, it concerns conspiracies, not politically but personally motivated. The conspirators are his usual collection (an "embittered homosexual," a Chinese cameraman, a lesbian, a "Negro castrated in his cradle by rat bites"), funded by an eccentric billionaire "perturbed by overpopulation, air and water pollution, and the destruction of wild life."

Like Kosinski's *Steps,* which employs a similar structuring of episodes, *Exterminator!* moves rapidly, the film technique creating fold-in, wraparound montage. Burroughs is also concerned with transformation. At one time, he considers himself as a "middle-aged Tiresias moving from place to place with his unpopular thesis." He plays numerous roles in the book, from exterminator in the opening sequence, to bartender, to someone who changes his very face by draining another person of his life's elements. The transformational qualities of *Frankenstein* and *The Island of Dr. Moreau* are never distant.

Even when film is not mentioned, the scene is still a "set," a scenario, a working out of a property. The world has become all theater. Late in the book, Burroughs describes episodes from the 1968 Chicago convention riots; and his presentation is of the city as a vast amphitheater, with the good actors (the rioters) and the bad actors (the police, the politicians behind them). The arena is like that of a morality play, in which violence, rioting, and planned brutality by Daley's police are filmed or staged. Like junk, the film goes on and on: "The more you use the more you need." The final episode, a prose poem, "Cold Lost Marbles," is a symbolic world of marmoreal deadness, where the "film is finished" and "City night fences dead fingers you in your own body." Comparably, Burroughs has played exterminator and other roles which allow him access to deadness, killing, sudden violence.

He flits from role to role, but essentially all roles are similar, part of the incoherent life which identifies our planet. In the episode in which he is a bartender, he serves commuters, all of whom have been psychoanalyzed and therefore have no fight left in them; while he saves his tips for a spaceship he is building on his Missouri farm. The confusion of roles, the sudden shifts, the lack of center, the black hole for a plot recall the Dada movement, in itself an adversary response to social/political intrusion into individual lives. Burroughs follows Kurt Schwitters in this movement, and his use of the fold-in method in his later work parallels some of Schwitters's ideas. The latter's collages were created out of rubbish and refuse: gigantic arrangements of diverse material in tribute to trash. A garbage society, for Schwitters, with memories of the First World War, is best manifested in a trash art.

Like Schwitters and his random compositions, Burroughs has attempted to find in the artwork itself some principle of incoherence which can be caught in words without loss of its essential irregularity. Burroughs fears order; and his drug-induced fantasies earlier were paradigms of his world. He presented such fantasies as cautionary tales—as part of the evil of drugs—but he also achieved literary coherence by way of these fantasies. Even as he attacked the drugs, they were essential to his powers of expression.

By working along paradoxes and contradictions, Burroughs is quintessentially American. Whatever he scorns, he ends up indulging as a form of imagination. Frontiers, distances, castles on earth and in the sky, even spaceships, are never far from his vision; but they are chimeras or illusions and, therefore, the greater reality. Fantasies and dreams, with their side effects of theater, film, reels, reeling, Dada manifestations, are really *the* thing: the way in which America can be captured in words. When Burroughs rages against those fantasies as punishment for drug hallucinations, then he rages, paradoxically, against what makes his art possible, what allows him his manifestation of America.

It would be a great mistake to read Burroughs as a "novelist," for he is, more broadly, a maker of visions, which are episodes in a vast history of his developing imagination. He is, also, a writer of epics, like Dos Passos in *U.S.A.,* wherein his U.S.A. is an internal journey and all roles are his. His body of short fictions is a remarkable achievement; for he became not only the greatest of the Beats, not only their finest poet, but a unique voice of America in the fifties.

Hawkes and Nabokov in the Fifties

For John Hawkes in the fifties, I include those works which lead up to *The Beetle Leg* (1951) and *The Lime Twig* (1960, 1961), and end with *Second Skin* (1964).* These fictions seem a singular phase in Hawkes's work, for with *The Blood Oranges,* in 1971, he appears to have entered another turn in his imagination. (This later stage leads up to *The Passion Artist,* in 1979.) These two phases are distinguished not only by differing visions, but by shifts in language, alterations in kinds and intensity of sexuality, different views of the "moment," of time itself.

Similarly, for Vladimir Nabokov, I take two works as indicative of his leap into American fiction in the fifties: *Lolita* (1955, 1958) and *Pale Fire* (1962). They, along with *Ada* (1969),† are Nabokov's chief American works, with *Pale Fire* straddling his several worlds and *Lolita* demonstrating his commitment to American themes, language, and visions.

"The Owl," written in the 1940s, "The Goose on the Grave," also from the 1940s, and "Charivari" (published 1950) are examples of Hawkes's "waste land" work, which foreshadows *The Beetle Leg* and *The Lime Twig.* The waste land image, while clearly recalling Eliot, derives from deeper reaches of Hawkes's own vision of postwar developments. In every respect except direct involvement, Hawkes responded to the 1940s (war) and 1950s (war's aftermath) in his language and point of view, reaching deeply into the imagination for myths, metaphors, images, phrases. In many ways, he presents the purest response of any of our novelists to postwar life, delving under surfaces to what remains after prosperity and success are washed away.

"The Owl" and "The Goose on the Grave" lead into *The Cannibal.* In the first, Il Gufo is an executioner, a hangman, a goof, who does his work in a mythical Italian province called Sasso Fetore, the time undetermined, perhaps medieval, perhaps modern, with Il Gufo a spoof of Il Duce. The hangman is called Il Gufo because the heart of his escutcheon "burst and became an owl: with wisdom, horns, and field rodent half-destroyed, hardly visible under the talons." The novella is remarkable for several things:

*For *The Cannibal* (1949), see Chapter Four, on the 1940s; *Second Skin* appears cursorily in the Introduction.

†Discussed at length in "Growing Up in America."

the prose, which sings; and the point of view, which defamiliarizes familiar things. The women of Sasso Fetore cannot find men to marry, and the hangman is a prize catch, although some feel he is married to the gallows. Playing through the hangman's role—he does hang someone at the end of the story—is the motif of marriage: how the marriageable women of the village will find a man, how Antonia will catch the owl. Il Gufo is clearly the source of all strength in the village, for his talons voraciously clutch all possessions.

Yet the power of Il Gufo could only be gained through Hawkes's experiments with prose. The citadel under a storm is described:

> Nowhere could a man walk without seeing through the rain the city's virginal design, the plan of its builders: the sheer blackness of stone intended to resist and put tooth to the howl and sluice of water, intact as it was, echoing, beset with the constant fall of the rain, unviolated and dark as in the Holy Day curfew of the year twelve hundred. No storm could dislodge those early grimly smelted chains but rather gave the city its victory in its architecture, fixed, steeply pitched, weatherbeaten. Not a bolt rang. As a prosecuted law with the ashes of suffering and memory carried off on the wind, Sasso Fetore was a judgment passed upon the lava, long out of date, was the more intolerant and severe. Only the absolute wheel is known, old as it is, and I looked for the first exacting laws in the archaic, listened for the skidding of an absolute machine on the narrow driving streets.

Faulkner's presence may be felt, but Hawkes is more precise, with a latent cruelty in his vision, which transfers to the phrasing. Obdurate objects dominate, a vision of intransigence, in which man is impermanent, yielding always to the ungiving nature of things. Human flesh, against inexorable stone, chain, and bolt, is more intensely frail, less able to withstand slash and beat. Hawkes's phrasing recalls Hopkins's poetry, that pulsing, driving vocabulary which informs "The Wreck of the *Deutschland,*" as the storm sweeps over the ship and wrecks hope and it: the "anvil-ding," the "flange and the rail," "sea flint-flake, black-backed." Hawkes sets up reverberations of noisy things amidst terrible silence, a conspiracy of silence with intrusions. A foot potential upon the stones will become thunder. Syntactical dangers also lurk for the reader, as in the sentence beginning: "As a prosecuted law . . . intolerant and severe." The subject of the final "was" is Sasso Fetore, but it comes to us while slipping away and is, therefore, more disconnected from human reality than if syntactically correct. Alliteration accentuates the hardness; and the vocabulary is crowded with parental figures dominating and subjugating children. The town is itself a stern judge, preparing us for the ugly, violent image of the owl.

The sole creatures that survive outside the owl's predatory strike are the four ganders. Only they escape being "lieges to Sasso Fetore's hangman." All others are a "chary parliament," the dead "with which he met at dusk, having no voices to raise and unable to tell which limbs were lost or which ribs had been staved in the process of death's accomplishment, what weight of marrow and gut given." The ganders' whiteness—"White and silent was their propulsion" —is a talisman for protection, as they move in formation, "pointing their sails, languid but regimented and stately despite webbed feet." But even they, with their purity, stateliness, untouchability, are brutally murdered, throats sliced evenly, "felled carefully, symmetrical and clean . . . the necks touching and torn, left in their severed lines and with their cold windpipes in this intimate unnatural pattern."

The killer is probably the prisoner, a spy, who had escaped the steep jail by having taken on flying powers of a giant owl, itself the product of a witch's brew. The prisoner, owl's prey and hangman's victim, is the living bait in Sasso Fetore, the reason for Il Gufo's existence. He is caught, and the ritual of execution begins, with skin from his abdomen becoming the skin of a drum which can be beaten for all to hear. When the prisoner drops, the hangman's noose around his neck, he drops into the void that characterizes the entire novella: a void filled with the momentary time and space of Hawkes's tale. Both prose and vision embodied in "The Owl" make all life tentative. The agony of Sasso Fetore becomes a miniature of vast emptiness, an enclosure of limited, restricted life, all against a cosmic indifference.

Tonally, "The Goose on the Grave" is an early version of *The Cannibal*, although the setting is Italian and the time the Second World War. The novella illustrates Hawkes's view of fiction: a lack of narrative, a vagueness or absence of traditional character, setting and language; a seamless totality or a prose poem recalling some of Pound's and Lowell's work in the early 1950s. But even Hawkes, in the purest of his works, must retain some connection with the conventional world, and this he accomplishes through the presence and image of the goose.

Adeppi, the wandering Italian orphan, everywhere meets aspects of corruption: cemeteries, dead or dying people, perversions, murderers, fanaticism, an entire universe of putridity which has resulted from the war. But set in, along with the corruptive forces, is that singular image of the goose: an old man, near death, accustomed to eating brambles, has, suddenly, a goose to eat. "A goose with a broken neck lay against his feet. . . . The goose's body—it was enemy to rodents and the pups of wolves—smeared blood from the old man's fore-flank to his collar-bone." A goose now dead—like the ganders in "The Owl"— nevertheless becomes symbolic of something else: art, softness, life, musicality; elements that forerun the "second skin" of Hawkes's novel and suggest the power of resurrection.

To define these objects is to make them appear more distinct than they are. Hawkes's achievement in his early novellas was to create a dim outline, like the lines of a palimpsest, that image which arises so frequently in postwar fiction. As one rereads it, "The Goose on the Grave" keeps "coming up" ever more clearly, but its resistance to clarity is part of Hawkes's effort at a unified artifact, a seamlessness which makes subject indistinguishable from object.

The following passage about a gondola, in which Adeppi finds himself, blends the boat with its myth:

> The totemic arms rising from the bows of the gondolas are striped around with bands of gilt and red paint, necks of the headless swans festooned by once rich color, pale and flaking as the groined vaults of a church with its peeling decoration and ancient quarrels. The gondolas have been hired for an evening on the lagoon bordered by apses and limpets dating centuries. Adeppi joins in the merriment and, for a night, is anonymous, as if he too is no more than a whelk glued among lichen and fern on the lower butts of a bridge, any moment in danger of being sheared away by an over-anxious oar blade.

Such grasp of language and such a desire to eliminate segmentation forced Hawkes to become a "montage writer," one who constantly slips away from his subject toward reverberations. He can never hold still. Thus, *The Cannibal* became for him a process, World War I turning into II, people telescoped, events clustering, that montage effect we experience in film. Since these early works lack traditional narrative and character, Hawkes found himself, like a chemist, applying an acid that would stress a hitherto invisible pattern. The aim was no less than a purification of fiction, a new direction for the genre.

"Charivari," a novella of discordant voices, is another of Hawkes's early efforts to slip outside plot, character, narrative (linear development), and even time and place. Once again, the goal is to capture consciousness and make language oblique: to make us see and hear language freshly, even in ordinary situations. Hawkes was toying with an American version of *l'écriture blanche,* Sartre's characterization of Camus's prose in *The Stranger,* and what Roland Barthes would later describe as "writing degree zero": neutral, colorless writing. The Hemingway–Fitzgerald–Dos Passos axis in fiction, still a powerful tug in the 1940s, is absent. By his twenties, Hawkes was an altogether different writer from his more popular contemporaries. Unlike Bellow, Mailer, Styron, Salinger, he had a view of language that would permanently remove him from the popular arena.

"Charivari"* is "about" Henry Van and his wife, Emily, and their parents, hers a general and a generaless, his father a parson. Although Henry is already married when the novella opens, the first section is "Courtship," the narrative plan being to incorporate all forward and backward experience in a single flow. Marriage involves the entire process of getting married and all the fears and anxieties one has about a permanent union. In a dream, an Expositor reminds Henry, at the start, that he is married, that Emily has a baby in her arms. He dreams, further, that he is drowning. He does not want the marriage, the responsibility, the baby, even Emily, certainly not the parents. As a man who confronts his feelings in a dream and then flees, Henry is gentle, sensitive, self-centered, fearful of sex, irresponsible, juvenile in his attitudes and reactions: a frequent figure in Hawkes's fiction.

He recalls Prufrock. "He inched his way into the darkness," Hawkes writes, while a party rages just beyond. He is incapable of action, smothered by his inability to focus on details, full of an "inward consciousness of his inopportune match with the little. . . ." He feels trapped by circumstances, by choices not really choices, by the presence of so many fully adult figures outside him (a general, a general's even more military wife, a parson), a social world insisting on action. He writes Emily, when he leaves, that he cannot be a father—Emily has announced the news, still in the "Courtship" section—that he is tired

of the "feminine role." Like Bellow's Joseph, he dangles in a situation partly of his own making, partly of circumstances; in limbo between adult and child. Such a state of being is a finely angled reflection of the late 1940s, when being and becoming were thwarted by circumstance, when one could not locate blame, guilt, or even problem.

When Henry leaves, he goes through, in his mind, bachelorhood, his own desire to drown, the wedding itself, the birth of the baby (though Emily's pregnancy has only just been announced). The mode is montage—events, people, fears, floating in and out of Henry's mind—a consciousness like a superimposed film. One recalls Sterne's way with *Tristram Shandy,* in which the whole is encapsulated in the small, the mind like a palimpsest of superimposed texts, equal though layered. By such means, Hawkes can move outside time and space, as Bellow attempted with Joseph; but Bellow, despite use of a journal and an external narration, was too strongly tied to realistic modes. With fewer inhibitions about narrative function and reader receptivity, Hawkes can destroy linear form as the enemy of consciousness.

All events, external as well as internal, are nightmarish, surreal. The novella, having opened with Henry's awareness of the coming event and Emily's announcement she is pregnant, then veers to Henry's attempt to escape this knowledge, to establish a different set of priorities for his life. Finding almost none, he is recaptured, returned to the beginning, to actualities that cannot be avoided. He has made a journey, half real, half dream, and the journey has forced him back to the start, neither wiser nor more accepting, just *there.* " 'All right . . . it's time to play,' " a friend named Gaylor announces wittily, play out the game, which is, merely, Henry's life. Thus the novella ends.

In *The Beetle Leg* (1951), the setting may be the American West, the language Faulknerian in its rhetorical reach, but the terms and textures are Kafkaesque. Hawkes has written a western in the Kafka manner. The central character of this brief novel is Lampson, who was buried ten years earlier in a dam: "A man lay buried just below the water level of the dam"—which may have been, under differing circumstances, the first line of *Metamorphosis.* Flesh and blood are intermingled with obdurate objects: "He was embedded in the earth and entangled with a caterpillar [tractor], pump engine and a hundred feet of hose, somewhere inside the mountain that was protected from the lake on one side by rock and gravel and kept from erosion on its southward slope

*A charivari, or shivaree, is a noisy celebration, a mock serenade to newlyweds, with kettles, horns, etc.

by partially grown rows of yellow grass." He was a victim of the "Great Slide," which is to Mistletoe, Government City, what the Depression had been to the country at large.

Lampson's grave site is Edenic in one respect, with earth, mountain, and grass marking his burial place; but he is also buried with the detritus of a modern civilization: hose, pump, big Cat. An act of chance or happenstance took him, and yet he becomes, because of that act, a central character in this ten-part novel (with a brief introductory chapter). All ten parts depend upon him. Yet human values hardly count, for land and landscape rule life as well as death: a silent, unmoving earth that is like the Great Slide itself, burying life in its very movement. The Great Slide is an apt metaphor for the entire novel, since Hawkes is working out patterns of life and death and landscape as they interact. A Great Slide is a natural occurrence of sorts, but also man-made, piles of earth and hard matter that exist from his doing. Yet such immensities refuse his dictates. They slide, and by sliding they bury and kill. The slide embodies a Hawkes metaphor for life and death.

Much of life around the dead Lampson—his brother, his wife, a sheriff, a motorcycle gang called the Red Devils, a former worker on the dam named Camper—moves in a sliding manner, in courses of action that pit flesh against desert, sky, landscape, aridity, ennui. Everything is slowed down, stilled; except the Red Devils, whose bursting energies of body and motorcycle break the stillness. Life is measured by "beetle's legs": "Leaned against by the weight of water, it [the dam] was pushing southward on a calendar of branding, brushfires and centuries to come, toward the gulf. Visitors hung their mouths and would not believe, and yet the hill eased down the rotting shale a beetle's leg each several anniversaries, the pride of the men of Gov City who would have to move fast to keep up with it."

Because of such movement, Lampson's grave is living, shifting with the dam's slide. He is, in a sense, more alive in death than in life, part of the diurnal motion of all natural things, and yet connected, by way of brandings and brushfires, to man-made events which measure the slide. The dam creaks along, the men move against a silent landscape; and only the Red Devils rev up and away, modern-day Lone Rangers. They are the "new," the direction in which desert and land are going once all becomes slide.

We never see a particular Red Devil; only a gang or a vague figure. The revved-up machine characterizes their being and becoming, as the slide characterizes the county. One critic has spoken of the slide as a movement toward entropy, a vision that connects Hawkes to apocalyptic writers like Barth and Pynchon. But entropy indicates a movement toward final things, whereas the slide is pure movement: the slide *is.* There is no sense that it will eventually level; that would be a consequence, even a resolution. All imagery in the novel supports the slide, discrete, disconnected elements joined in a common process.

Hawkes's style is manifest in his choice of landscape, which is never equivalent to place, nor is it setting in time. A mode of observation creates his particular sense of landscape, and what is remarkable is that no matter how vastly different each book is from the other, landscape remains essentially the same. *Second Skin,* as we shall note, captures that landscape in lighthouse and frozen waste. The landscape of *The Beetle Leg* may be the American West, but it is not West as we know it from movie or pulp story, or even from historians. Many critics have spoken of the hallucinatory or even Gothic quality of Hawkes's writing, but his landscapes, unlike those in hallucinatory visions, are firm, solidly grasped and placed; and yet at the same time, without recognizable qualities, lacking those elements we associate with places we recall.

The Beetle Leg contains numerous characters, and yet nobody inhabits its length. Perhaps the sole memorable figure, someone who refuses to blend with desert, sand, and vastness, is Cap Leech. Leech is a doctor whose practice has fallen to virtually nothing, along with the loss of nearly all his medical equipment, as a result of pulling a live baby from a dead mother. "Leech left his scalpel stuck midway down the unbleeding thigh, buried the wailing forceps in his shiny bag, stepped outdoors with the infant and disappeared, thereafter, through all his career, barred from the most fruitful of emergencies."

With most of his skills intact, he is an American wanderer, heading from one disaster to another. He pulls out a festering molar from an Indian girl and, in the process, outrages her body as well as her head, although the exact extent is vague. People and animals become the indifferent object of his observation. His practice is a montage of poking, pill giving, cauterizing, listening to irregular breathing, "stethoscope pressed upon the shell of a beetle sweeping hurriedly its wire legs," beetle signifying anything alive in animal or insect world. He is an "old obstetrical wizard who now brought forth no young, losing year after year the small lock-jawed instruments of his kit, chalking black prescriptions on the leaves of a calendar." Later, he will dissect a rooster, as the sheriff and his assistant fire on the Red Devils, hoping to kill as many as they can before they escape on their motorcycles, like beetles.

Even Cap Leech, however, disappears into the landscape. There is no room for characters, as there is no room for narrative or plot. The ten episodes, which occur ten years after the burial of Mulge Lampson, are connected only by landscape and language. Just as the former is a state of mind more than a place, so the latter exists more in Hawkes's imagination than in the ordinary resources of language. That is, he forces us to accept phrasing that does not exist in any formal sense: "singing scream," "pointed glowing of hidden skin," "each plaguing timeless yawl." Nearly every paragraph contains a phrase or sentence that suggests an extraordinary yoking, a yearning after limits of language that goes beyond what English allows, and yet expresses, nevertheless, whatever the landscape demands. Robert Lowell's own "singing scream" is a parallel development.

The Lime Twig (1960, 1961) is possibly the best example of Hawkes's early style, the most mature of his intense, unfocused narratives, without the moments of sentimentality that would mar *Second Skin.* The latter novel reaches out to broader themes and is Hawkes's fullest work; but *The Lime Twig* shows how he could manipulate that early manner as far as it would go. In a sense, it signals the end of the first phase of his development. *Second Skin* stands somewhat alone, looking ahead to the substitution of sentimentality or softer associations for that hard, intense vision which had been Hawkes's distinctive mode.

The Lime Twig recalls the work of Harold Pinter, especially *The Birthday Party,* as much as it does Greene's *Brighton Rock.* The Pinter play and the Hawkes novel emerged at about the same time. In common, they display certain modes of expression, attitudes, and oblique referencing. Both are oriented toward violence, with Pinter's more implied than stated. More apparently, both move into a "middle sex" area, where sexual potentialities of character are expressed in a variety of ways, or there is no clear focus. Hawkes's presentation of Thick and Larry has in it the fascination of male for male, muscle and strength and brutality as forms of sex. Yet sexuality remains potential, what is not stated or acted out more intense than what is expressed. Further, both writers can be witty about violence, incest, dominance. In the Hawkes novel, all varieties of sexual and social relationships are possible. In people under stress, normal modes of behavior prove only façades for disturbance.

Hawkes's manner of working is to bring together units or blocks, as he did in *The Beetle Leg,* whose juncture had been the buried man in the shifting dam. In *The Lime Twig,* the focal point is a horse race: the explosive quality of horses juxtaposed to man-made hardness, and greed. The horses with their hooves kill as do the men: a horse kicks Hencher to death, and racing horses trample Banks. The horses are, in nature, the equivalent of Larry and Thick, who are built, as we say, like horses. What makes Hawkes's world so complete—that is, what submerges the distinction between nightmare and actuality—is that seamlessness of experience, that continuity between what lies in nature and what lies in the man-made world.

In *The Lime Twig,* there is little uncertainty. Banks moves along the line of his fantasies: all the sex he can enjoy, the potential for a huge killing with Rock Castle, a fast, dangerous life in which he is central. All this appears within his grasp as a consequence of the horse race and the fact that he has substituted a ringer provided by Hencher. Hencher's name derives from *hengst,* male horse, which came to mean groom or squire—someone around horses—and then turned into a word meaning helper, used pejoratively. Hawkes's use of the name carries with it a mythical connotation; for Hencher is part centaur, but only part. A horse, finally, rejects him, and all his efforts to enter the world of horses are defeated by hooves, which pound his head to jelly. For the horse, he is only a man—he, who had attempted to be part of the horse's world.

The play of meaning attributable to the horse associates us with myth, the wild forces of nature. The centaur has such a grasp on our imagination because of its embodiment of an unblendable dualism, man and beast, man and natural elements. Rock Castle in the Golden Bowl at Aldington—with *its* connotation of the superelegant Henry James novel—becomes a mythical test, a chess piece: a horse returning from past great triumphs entered as a ringer by an amateur who discovers the stakes are different from those he had figured on.

Perhaps the central scene for the mixture of man, horse, hallucination, and actual nightmare is the lavatory setting, when Banks recognizes that he is caught in a spiraling trap. He enters what he sees as a cavernous, empty lavatory, row on row of toilets, one without a seat, a series of pipes with "great brass valves," a tomb of whiteness and flushing water and huge pipes leading to beyond. This is a mausoleum—no lime or lime twig here, no benevolent nature. A man steps beside him "with feet large as boxes and a slate strapped across his chest," "Rock Castle" printed on the slate. Soon a second and then a third man appear, all of them carrying these little slate boards. Their shoes slap against the latrine and squish in the water. "Banks held tightly to his clothes, heard them shuffle, breathe, splash loudly."

They are men from a nether world, dragged up to earth level by demons. "Dressed in rags, lean, fast as birds. These were the men who sat on the rails with knees drawn up and scraps of paper fastened to their lapels, soothsayers with craftiness and eyes that never stopped." They are called eunuchs: "while clacking within arm's length of the hoof-cut turf, each one sat in his astrological island, shabby, each figuring for himself with twitching cheek muscles and numbers on the slate," communicating with the crowd through slate and numbers. Squishing and rubbing are the sole sounds in the vast latrine. They whisper that Sybilline's in the Pavilion: Sybilline, the tart who offers Banks a fantasy of sexual pleasures before he runs under the horse's hooves. He has entered, by way of Hencher's deception, into a world in which all reality is refracted; and Sybilline, mythical doom, is transformed into a desirable sex machine. The latrine, a hellish place for the natural release of human waste matter, turns into the ultimate place of terror: nature is no longer God's world, but part of warped human nature. The three eunuchs warn Banks not "to run off in a scare," for they carry pellet bombs, enough to blow off a foot, a hand, an eye. They leave Banks at the broken toilet, sitting as best he can, while they stand close by, "making wet sounds with their boots and rubbers beside him."

Remarkable is Hawkes's ability, recalling Graham Greene's, to derive terror from muffled sounds, here of water and rubber, where water turns to poisons—another fact of nature contaminated by human motive. Commenting on some of this is another element of nature turned hateful and mechanical, the gossip columnist and handicapper as quasi detective, Sidney Slyter. Slyter introduces each section of the novel—there are nine, one of them being introductory—with a trendy line about the coming horse race and what he has discovered about it. He is all solicitude for his readers, full of false sentiments, a kind of Miss Lonelyhearts in control of his emotional state. He represents that sly, expedient, gossipy media world outside, in its values as parasitical and counterfeit as the crew within. Slyter frames, structurally, a story he is

really part of, although in his media role he can escape violence and nightmare.

Hawkes's area of maneuver is, in fact, rather small, far smaller than Greene's, and the question arises of how much dimensionality he can suggest. Is his violence restricted by a peculiar cast of characters, or does it maintain momentum beyond them? By making nightmare or fantasy and actuality seamless, Hawkes tries to suggest vast areas. And the prose works to disorient us; it jars, shivers, reverberates with fresh yokings of words and phrases, carefully modulated. Slyter speaks one language, Banks another, Hencher still another. The variety of voices, each with its own language bundle, creates the sense of a many-peopled world, well beyond the actual small cast.

Further, Hawkes includes many different kinds of scenes besides those concerning horse races. Early in the novel, Hencher lives with his mother, in circumstances strongly reminiscent of Beckett in his trilogy. Before the old lady is burned in a firebombing of London, there is, apparently, real affection, the sole reciprocated love in the novel. In another variation, we see Banks and his faithful wife, Margaret, in domestic scenes; she is later beaten with a truncheon and bleeds to death. We note the track crews, the jockeys—creatures from a half world, crooked, unable to function without drugs. Only violence suggests passion. Thick, a Dickensian creature of the subterranean world, reaches orgasm with his beating of Margaret. Hellish scenes and demonic characters provide variety, and suggest a much larger world than horse races, touts, handicappers, track.

Love is itself squashed, by violence, terror, greed. Further, all this occurs in a timeless world. The novel suggests "a time slipped off its cycle with hours and darkness never to be accounted for." The time of myth, shamans, ahistorical eras lends itself to seamlessness, giving Hawkes's constructed world a larger temporal-spatial dimension than the limits of the novel. Castle Rock, also, has a lineage that recalls Biblical begetting: "Draftsman by Emperor's Hand out of Shallow Draft by Amulet, Castle Churl by Draftsman out of Like Castle by Cold Masonry, Rock Castle by Castle Churl out of Words on Rock by Plebeian." In the background of Castle Rock, in that world of nature enhanced by genetic breeding, we have surging elements that complement and put in relief man's attempt at manipulation. The horse comes through, a winner in the past, a surger, a brutal force in the present. Man gives way, unless he matches equine strength with human brutality and cunning.

Yet the ancestry is not only Biblical, it is reminiscent of chess pieces—Castle, Plebeian or Rook, Emperor or King—so that within that world of disorder, Hawkes has located precision, exactitude, forms of order.

Fog, miasma, deception, intrigue, and brutality preempt the world of lime, which is cool, relaxed, of tropical leisure. Everything works to defeat the hope for lime or a lime twig; it is the distant Eden, which Banks and Hencher can never achieve. In *Second Skin,* Skipper reaches the land of lime and of lime twigs, but amidst a sentimental world, carrying associations well in excess of what he could ordinarily gain for himself. Despite its distance from a social or political world, *The Lime Twig* is connected to everything by way of images, yearnings, sense of self, loss of love, and enjoys a coherence missing from *Second Skin.* This novel that takes place in England is America in the 1950s; for it locates feeling outside feeling, situates deception and intrigue as focal points, and turns our more immediate political nightmares into actual lives. The lime twig is all cold war.

Despite the tremendous energy, his surges of swift power, and his sense of spatiality and mobility, Hawkes appears to fit readily into paralysis—certainly as a powerful countering force in his vision. In *Second Skin* (1964), we note his typically American reliance on space: a bus trip, an island off the Atlantic coast, a spice island, "a wandering island . . . located in space and quite out of time." In addition, there is Skipper's ship, on which Tremlow mutinies, the frenzied wedding night trip to the abandoned silver mine, and other locales which involve distances and spatial perspectives. Nevertheless, despite spatiality and obsessive movement, the novel is defined by an innerness that seems peristaltic. Space denied, like time stilled, appears to be the inner thematic line of the novel, even while spatiality and time passing seem connected to the outer narrative line. We note opposing drives, one inward and one outward, one attached to theme, the other related to narrative.

"I will tell you in a few words who I am": so begins *Second Skin,* with the epic "I," the picaro, the narrator of his own mock epic. We are carried within to a man for whom each locale has brought with it disaster, a personal loss. He sees himself, if not as Clytemnestra, then as the pawn Iphigenia, this hulk of a man, the Hamlet-husband of Gertrude, whose daughter, Cassandra, remains almost dumb while pointing toward violence and death. His father, his wife, his daughter suicides, his son-in-law murdered, his mother, having vanished, now dead, Skipper carries death in his wake, is victimized by others, blunted by circumstances. Like the scrambled literary figure he recalls, he is accompanied by bloodshed; yet he is a bringer of life, an artificial and a human inseminator. He plans new generations as rapidly as the past has wiped out those attached to him. Hawkes locates Skipper in a no-man's-land between life and death. Unable to control death, he is able to modulate some sense of life.

The novel is about conception, in all its punning, ambiguous potential. Hawkes works as hard at his conception of the novel—how to tell it, how much of character, event, plot line to reveal or exclude—as Skipper works at replenishing a world that drops away from him. There is a double agent here which enters into virtually every aspect of the novel: Hawkes peering down the ruins of his material and doling it out through Skipper's memory; and Skipper himself, peering down the ruins of his life and trying to find areas of meaning, not at all above distorting his own powers in order to shore up the past. Not unusually, in such a formulation of narrative, scene, and character, images of subterranean things dominate. The sole place where conceptions can come together is in burrows and lairs. Skipper roams from place to place, not unlike a wounded animal, or Kafka's mole, seeking a refuge, only to discover new threats to his existence. So much of Hawkes's view is oppositional that it is difficult to locate the center, except, finally, that island with the bovine Catalina Kate.

To begin, Skipper is himself the old man of the sea, a combination of a wandering Ulysses, a magical Prospero-Ariel, a desolate Menelaus, and the mythical Poseidon. As the latter, he is a man who threads his way through the deep, surfacing from depths. As Menelaus, he travels with Cassandra, his wife, Gertrude, having deserted him for others, as Helen fled Menelaus for Paris and as Gertrude moved to the bed of King Hamlet's brother. As Ulysses, he has his Circe-Miranda, his passage from island to island, his adventures with life-giving as well as death-bearing women. As one or another, Skipper (also known as Captain and Edward) is continually changing shapes and roles. He mothers Cassandra, grandmothers Pixie, acts as stud for Catalina Kate and artificial stud for the cows on his sweet island, has incestuous drives toward Cassandra, acts as faithful son to his suicidal father, serves loyally as husband despite (or because of) Gertrude's alcoholism and faithlessness, plays father-in-law to Fernandez and countenances the latter's ludicrous marriage to Cassandra. He plays all family roles, even as the members of his family, as in a classical tragedy, drop away through violence.

The tattooing scene in Chapter 2 recalls Kafka's "In the Penal Colony": Skipper is paying for unknown sins and being forced, by his love for Cassandra, into a pain beyond pain. With that experience, we have the external form of suffering which gains us narrative or scenic entrance into Skipper's world, that world or "overview" provided in the first chapter. There, by "naming names," he supplies a Proustian reverie, the past that his pen and memories will recapture. The tattooing is the first external act that gives us any approximation of his Hamlet-Odysseus-Menelaus inner life, as the "courageous victim." That scene is followed by the one in the bus, a tunneling into the velvet dark, a subterranean trip into unknowns. The bus journey is concerned with final things, where the "highway was a dead snake in the distance," where the desert contains "tiny cellular spines, dead beetles, the discarded translucent tissue of wandering snakes, the offal of embryonic lizards and fields of dead dry locusts." Skipper, along with daughter and granddaughter, must traverse this field of the dead in order to arrive at the death city in the East where he will find Cassandra's husband, Fernandez, a "little fairy spic," stabbed to death.

Interwoven with these scenes of darkness, death, paralysis, and suffocation are those on the sweet cinnamon island, where Skipper artificially inseminates cows. This island is Eden revisited, where, now fifty-nine years old, he writes down his memories. One of the false notes in the book is the ease with which Skipper achieves bliss. Granted that the novel operates at the level of myth, and that this island is part of the Eden–Golden Age legend; nevertheless the novel also functions at the level of unresolved tensions and conflicts. The sweet island of Catalina Kate, however, has no tensions: insemination, which was never Skipper's thing, now comes easily, and bread and fruit grow on trees. Hawkes has provided his Prospero with a retreat as if there were still no Lear, or Hamlet, or Coriolanus.

More accommodating to the novel's tensions are the scenes on the windswept raging isle off the Atlantic coast, where a different kind of sexuality obtains. On this other island, everything that had been sweet and spicy becomes charged, tense, anxiety-ridden, full of cruelty and brutality; sex is symbolized by men circling Cassandra, by a lighthouse off which the fated girl jumps, by a Circe-like Miranda, quite unlike her namesake in Shakespeare, by the ex-marine Jomo with his hook, by Captain Red with his drunken intensity and Bub with his willingness to do their dirty work. All is encapsulated dynamism, negative, disguised energy, potentiality; experience based on inertness and suffocation.

In the section "Cleopatra's Car," Miranda's hot rod is a multiple symbol of sensuality, phallicism, and eroticism, all played out against a snowy battleground. Fire and ice grip the characters, their responses so intense words are unnecessary. The scene passes like a catapult drawn ever tighter. The silent snowball fight in the graveyard, a scene of primitive intensity and covertness, is the "ice" equivalent of the "fire" of the bumping inside, with both suggesting an unexpressed sexuality, potential ejaculations, an entire life based on incompleteness. Despite intense sensuality, the key image is impotence.

Whereas Kafka's mole stuffed his burrow with provisions, Hawkes pours into his maze contrary feelings which cannot break out. We realize that except for Skipper, who is writing this narrative, almost no one speaks in Second Skin. It is a novel of great silences and interstices, like Robbe-Grillet's fictions, in which the work generates its own expression of sound and silence, isolated from what occurs beyond it.

Like Hawthorne with his historical material, Hawkes probes margins and seams, and explores "static silences." The reader struggles for connective tissue even as he is being borne along on the crest of violence and death. This method, which also appears intrinsic to The Lime Twig and The Cannibal, catches the undertow of American attitudes, that other side of a "city of words": an inability to verbalize, a need, concurrently, to express in violence what words fail to express. In the penultimate chapter of Second Skin's twelve-chapter quasi-epical structure, Hawkes carries us back to the cold island. Chapters 9 and 11 parallel each other, and both are sandwiched between "sweet island" episodes. Chapter 9 fills in the incomplete details of Twemlow's mutiny, Fernandez's hopeless, seedy death, and the suicide of Skipper's father while the boy played Brahms on his cello to still the older man's pistol hand. The chapter ends with the eschatological vision of final death for all. "Wasn't I myself, as a matter of fact, simply that? [Skipper muses] Simply one of those little black seeds of death? And what else can I say to Father, Mother, Gertrude, Fernandez, Cassandra, except sleep, sleep, sleep?"

The eschatological vision is already complete for Skipper, since he is writing a remembrance of things past, but we do not know as yet what he knows. He must carry us through final things. Chapter 11, on the "cold island," is the denouement of the "silent death" which accompanies Skipper's "first skin." Skipper is in almost constant activity which leads nowhere, first in the *Peter Pool* sail, then in the drag race on the beach, finally in his frantic footrace to head off Cassandra and Jomo at the lighthouse. The sail on the *Peter Pool,* a rotting little fishing boat, is something out of Conrad's *Typhoon* and also the scene for Skipper's assumption of a "second skin"—the oilskin he dons for the wet sail. A second skin usually signifies a rebirth, the snake's molting, seasonal change. Skipper, apparently, is going to enter a new phase without Cassandra, a revived life. Yet this second skin is not his, but something he must don as protection: armor-plating, not an element intrinsic to his growth or development.* Like nearly everything else in the novel, it is ambiguous: both protective and part of what will destroy. For the *Peter Pool* sail is the beginning of the end for Skipper's last possession, Cassandra.

The drag race follows, once again based on misunderstanding. Skipper races to head off Cassandra and Jomo, only to discover that he has been blocked by Bub, which gives them time to make for the lighthouse. Miranda, who accompanies Skipper in the hot rod, is a form of sexual torture, the possessor of the black, huge-cupped brassiere that appears throughout, a leitmotif of frustrated sensuality, voyeurism and/or masturbation. Skipper "drags" furiously, not to win anything, but to block, to impede, only to discover he has been tricked by Jomo's decoy. Frustrated by deception, tortured that someone with a hook has got to Cassandra, *his* Cassandra, Skipper frantically makes for the lighthouse, only to arrive after she has jumped. The horizontal spatiality of the race blends with the girl's vertical plunge; distance dominates, only to be muted by the containment of space within Skipper's experience. Cassandra's jump carries him back through memory to those other leaps into the darkness of suicide. The chapter ends with Miranda's presentation to Skipper of a box containing " 'Just a fetus, Skip. Two months old.

---

*I have merely touched upon the idea of a "second skin," with its sense of covering up, creating an inner space. It has multiple references. It is sheath material, evokes sexual connotations, and suggests a protective-destructive potential.

Human.' " A bit of living tissue enclosed in a box, it is Cassandra's reason for her leap, her posthumous gift to her father.

The novel teeters on melodrama, especially when the ironic tone is diluted. But because so little is devoted to talk, melodramatic events become part of the spatial and temporal substructure. With the line of development so close to night dream, or a day reverie, or a sequence of memories, Hawkes can just escape without sensationalism. Also, by having avoided linear development in the narrative, he can conjure up episodes which would, in a more normal narrative, have seemed extravagant, what we find in Mailer's *An American Dream.* By the early 1960s, Hawkes had discovered the way to present that mixture of violence and sentiment which has so dominated the American novel, and without forgoing the innerness so frequently sacrificed to spatiality.

The final chapter, titled "The Golden Fleas," brings Ulysses home. The seas are quieted, and he is enwrapped by his devoted, nonverbal Penelope, Catalina Kate, a prelapsarian Eve. Unlike Agamemnon on *his* return, he is not destroyed. On the "sweet island," having observed his former life slip away, like an old skin which no longer functions, he enjoys his "second skin." Molting, seizing control of his destiny with a pen, writing his way out of his death-dragging memories, Skipper finds a way of transforming entrapment into a new life: by turning it into the narcissistic circuitry of memory.

In *Lolita* (1955, Olympia Press, Paris; 1958, in America), Nabokov has written a "modest proposal" for the postwar years, with special reference to the counterfeit fifties. Instead of Swift's suggestion that the Irish eat their infants to relieve their hunger, a parody of English "proposals," Nabokov has suggested how American males can slake their thirst for sexual fulfillment by nourishing themselves on nymphets. Just as Swift could indulge his disgust for mankind in his work, so Nabokov could indulge his revulsion of women, physicality, and even passion by way of Humbert Humbert's obsession with Charlotte Haze and Lolita. Because, like Swift, he was dealing with both the indulgence of an obsession and its parody, Nabokov found a way of reinforcing his own hatreds.

In his *Griffin* essay upon the American publication of the novel, Lionel Trilling called it "about love," not "about sex but about love." But it would appear that the very basis of the novel is a parody of love, a replacement of it by passion and obsession, and in turn, a burlesque of that. Unlike many of his American contemporaries, who had no way of dealing with their female characters, Nabokov in this novel found a way.

The novel is, indeed, less about love than about food. Images of eating dominate. Humbert consumes, with his eyes, then his mouth and tongue and teeth; and while his mouth tours Lolita's narrow ridges, the twosome tour America's eateries. If packaged differently, the book could have been a guide to fast-food atrocities in the (then) forty-eight states; less a parody of America than a burlesque of Michelin and Kléber. Sex and eating are repeatedly equated, and in fact, Lolita's sex drive can be maintained only by way of her stomach. The novel is, in part, a record of her gain in height and weight; and one of the marginal benefits of Humbert's "nymphomania" is the fact that he enjoys a girl whom he can, literally, nourish. She starts out almost skeletal—her body as slim as a boy's—while Humbert probes her exterior and fills her interior. Sex is androgynous, and even here Nabokov was a decade ahead of the pack.

Everything about *Lolita* is parodic, a celebration of the counterfeit; its methods based on mirrors and reflections. By joining Humbert, a polyglot European (Swiss, Austrian, French, a "dash of Danube," and English from his mother), and Lolita, a prototypical junk-food American, Nabokov had a ready-made mirror that would always reflect the counterfeit. Each makes some effort to adapt to the other: Humbert to her indulgence in fast food, guidebook scenery and sights, movement and spatiality; Lolita to his indulgence of his child-passion of constant touch and sex, most of which she can barely tolerate. She becomes his Annabel and Virginia Clemm, his Beatrice, his Laura, his Sadean sex object, as well as his Undine and White Goddess, while he becomes her tutor in life and languages, her classical guide as they travel America's tourist spots; her Vergil in the underworld of the American substructure, as well as her sugar daddy, her dirty old man. Each role is defined by the others, and each exists by way of parody of more "normal" roles. Every reflection of the real reveals the counterfeit.

The idea is triumphant. Nabokov has caught the prototypical aspect of the American novel, its spatiality and constant movement, and yet he has been able to root it in fixed values, all connected to Humbert's nympholepsy, a disease to the Greeks and a source of great pleasure and pain to Humbert. This wedding of American themes and European tradition gave Nabo-kov the kind of weapon denied to American novelists. Whatever he shows with one hand, he can disguise with the other; put another way, the novel is a two- or three-ring circus, in which each ring resonates toward the other. This concept becomes fully elaborated in *Pale Fire*.

Despite narrative spatiality, movement from one boondock to another, *Lolita* conveys a claustral, enclosed feeling. First, the Foreword. This is a typical Nabokovian invention, one he would indulge more fully in *Pale Fire*. The Foreword by John Ray, Jr., Ph.D., the degree as significant as the name itself, gives historical veracity, as it were, to the Humbert fiction; for it locates the story within a real journal or confession. The nondescript commentator, an academic hack apparently, the flatness of his name, are in inert contradistinction to the tale itself, with its exotic title "Lolita, or the Confession of a White Widowed Male." Ray also gives us much significant information: that the author of the manuscript, Humbert Humbert, had died in prison while awaiting trial for murder; that his name is itself a pseudonym—Ray reads it symbolically as a "mask," a reflection of two "hypnotic eyes"; that Lolita's first name is the same as that of the real person, but "Haze" only rhymes with the true surname; that the entire story of the crime can be found in the papers for September 1952;* that Lolita has herself died in childbirth on Christmas Day—a Nabokovian touch to set up false trails for academic critics; that many of the other characters have continuing stories, all forwarded by Mr. Windmuller of Ramsdale.

The Afterword by Nabokov in his own voice, after the Foreword in Ray's voice, of course raises the question of which is the real Nabokov—an illusionary sandwiching effect that is in keeping with a manuscript based on "rays" and mirror reflections. Andrew Field describes the key image or situation as the prison: Humbert writes from prison, Lolita is imprisoned by her stepfather-lover, American motels are like prisons, and when Humbert decides to murder Quilty he first locks him in. But prisons are physical mechanisms, and the metaphor takes second place to

---

*More likely as a source was Nabokov's "The Magician," written in Russian in 1939. Here a magician spies a twelve-year-old girl in the Tuileries gardens and becomes obsessed with the sleek and vague ridges of her barely developed figure. In the story, once the girl's mother dies, the magician makes a sexual advance which is, apparently, unsuccessful. Ten years later, Nabokov, now at Cornell, would begin an expanded treatment of theme and scenes only alluded to in "The Magician."

ways in which the material is observed. The prison image, in fact, is subsumed in the question who is free, who imprisoned.

Humbert is, to some extent, liberated by his obsession with Lolita; whenever he possesses her, he embodies in sensation and release what is for most obsessed people merely an idea. Similarly, we may speak of Lolita as imprisoned—like Albertine in Proust—but she, also, gains considerable release from a suburban existence that is close to death. She learns French, she acquires the understanding of a large vocabulary and of an ironic-parodic sense of things; she becomes sophisticated enough to make a marriage to a decent, if impaired, young man. She has, in a perverse way, been lifted from a humdrum existence into something alien, and apparently she has not been damaged in the process.

If she had been destroyed by Humbert's attention to her, then Nabokov would have been dealing with a different range of moral-ethical issues. But she moves toward normalcy of sorts—marriage, enterprise, childbirth—to the degree that Humbert must work out his obsession by murdering her kidnapper, Quilty. In a sense, she has remained outside of what has required complete surrender for Humbert. He is doomed, whereas she blithely escapes—saved by space, American innocence and ignorance of the past, remote from history, tradition, custom, and their imprisoning effects; all part of Nabokov's condescension to his adopted country.

How much of this do we believe? The question of ambiguity of tone arises: whether the possibility of tragedy preempts comedy, or vice versa; or whether Humbert is a tragic hero of the bedroom or a comic antihero—cousin-german, Trilling calls him, to Rameau's nephew. If we accept the mirror image, then the tragic side of Humbert reflects the antihero, and the antihero the tragic; by which means we obtain Nabokov's multidimensionality. Connected to this is the chess problem, which we discover in so many of his novels. Field quotes a printed conversation between Nabokov and Alain Robbe-Grillet in which the former indicated that *Lolita* represented a certain problem he wished to resolve, as with chess problems, which follow certain rules.

Chess problems carried over to literature are cast as reflections and illusory images. Chess is a game of space and time: the board representing space; with time reflected by tradition and historical games which govern the validity of moves. Although such moves are infinite, one is bounded in any given play by a limited number of possibilities. These are, in turn,

connected to those historical games. Further, chess has its historical connections, to medieval and Renaissance royalty, its stress on ancient forms of power, its acquisition and retention. Through the actuality of play, the chess participant acquires great power, moving a queen, protecting a king, sacrificing pawns, using knights and bishops to consolidate situational power. In this respect, chess carries the mirror image to the player: turning a mortal into someone immortal, transferring moments and hours of greatness to the ordinary man. He upholds regimes or assassinates monarchs.

Humbert, then, moves in this world, and part of the chess problem is his manipulation of Lolita (pawn? queen?) across the chessboard of America. She is his sole piece (pun), but in this extended sense, she is all pieces, from lowest to highest. All is mirrored. The duplication of his name, Humbert Humbert, or variations on that, with its suggestion of Humbug, Humble, Humble Pie, Hubert Humphrey, even Hamburger, not only makes him a comic figure but gives us clues to his double image. He is always being turned inside out, role-playing to the audience in his confessional journal, playing up to Lolita to satisfy his obsession, while displaying a persona of stability to the rest, beginning with Mrs. Haze. Humbert tells us he once considered using the doubling Otto Otto as name, indicating an "in and out" or reflectional pattern. Nabokov's refusal to place his protagonist either within the chess game, where he could be tragic, or outside, where he would be comic, gives him the quality of elusiveness also conveyed by the name doubling.

A novel of such ambiguous goals is tested, finally, in its language. For a book based on nympholepsy and a multidimensional tragicomic protagonist, Nabokov needed a particular kind of prose, as, analogously, Borges developed a special language to present his world of archaeological excavation. Nabokov's strategy is to tell Humbert's story in an affected, Alexandrine prose rich in literary allusions, puns, double entendres: a prose, we assume at first reading, appropriate to a serious book. After all, Nabokov did not want to become mired in questions of pornography, although *Lolita* was immediately caught in censorship until American authorities released it in 1957. One way to circumscribe pornography was to provide a prose style too difficult for the reader looking for cheap thrills; at the same time, an exalted style could raise more salacious moments to higher levels of desire, rather than leaving them as pornomasturbatory. In another sense, an exotic style could convey the speciality of the relationship, bizarre by any count.

The virtues of such prose, however, cannot mask its excesses. Nabokov's self-love, his egomania, his need to point to his own cleverness are qualities we have accepted. They are not unconnected to his role as a perpetual émigré or to his living, always, as a foreigner with an accent. Humbert carries that strange accent across America; to some it sounds suave, but to most it verifies his alien status. Conrad recalls the same problem: indulgence in a profound egomania to compensate for a lifelong foreignness and alienation.

Phrases in French, classical allusions, reveling in bizarre and obsolete American words, rollicking in clever puns are all Nabokov's attempts to flaunt self; and, inevitably, they lead away from, not toward, the subject. Unfortunately, they become affectations, unbecoming in narrative and stylistic terms. The prose, in fact, sets up a geometry of its own, establishing lines parallel to those of the narrative, as if competitive rather than integral to meaning. Nabokov must indulge his virtuosity: on one hand complaining that he had to forgo his own rich Russian for an imperfectly learned English, and then dazzling us with his English as if to demonstrate what we are missing in his Russian. Nabokov's use of language is itself a parody of language, self-consciousness played back as self-reflexive fiction.

A typical passage: "We came to know—nous connûmes, to use a Flaubertian intonation—the stone cottages under enormous Chateaubriandesque trees, etc." Nabokov repeats the "nous connûmes" and calls it "royal fun." The parody is pointed, of course, the playing off of Humbert-Lolita against Emma Bovary and her lover; but it is also an indulgence, for there is no connection except authorial self-display. Flaubert's style is consciously flattened, relieved of excessive color and tone; Nabokov's is the opposite, supercharged with color and literary poses. Wedding the two makes little sense. Or else: Humbert repeatedly plays to the reader, becoming the actor in his own drama, committing the act and then commenting on it. We have, as it were, a cycle of Humbert. The address to the reader, the breakdown of tone, the intrusion of authorial voice by means of the narrator all suggest an author so contemptuous of his readers that he feels he can do anything and escape. The method often turns style into an affect of the author's needs, rather than into a tool of the narrative.

Although voyeurism is implicit in nearly every aspect of Humbert's life, from his spying on nymphets to his watching others observe him, he does not see himself clearly. By way of Nabokov's mandarin prose and his own feelings of superiority, he accepts his removal from criticism; and so his attitudes go unexamined. In justifying his attachment to nymphets, he argues well, but he fails to explain his disgust for mature women or his ungovernable hostility to psychiatry. This does not imply he must explain everything; but so many of his attitudes are based on denial of ideas and phenomena, including half of the human race, that we insist on the very kind of self-knowledge Nabokov fails to provide. His critics have, up to now, indulged his every whim and excess.

One argument supporting Humbert's lack of self-knowledge, even in a book where everything is analyzed and then reflected into double images, is that Humbert is an artist. In this view, his acts are only meaningful, ultimately, when they can be captured in some art form, i.e., his confessional journal. He makes a "book" from his experiences, and this final product justifies whatever went in—artistic license, as it were, permitting a careless moral life. It is also true that Nabokov has Humbert comment that "sex is but the ancilla of art," as opposed to Freud's idea of art as a secondary characteristic of sex. By locating art as primary and preempting all other considerations, this argument runs, Nabokov transcends child-love and child-sex, turning them into personal pain that art makes necessary. This is a romantic art, with the protagonist struggling through self-torture in order to become, himself, his art.

If we follow this argument, then we can see the mirrors, the layers of reflections, the double searches for Lolita and Quilty, the doubled-back images, the replay of scenes; the double and triple play, for example, on The Enchanted Hunters, where Lolita seduces Humbert, the shifts in focus of the camera eye. But what undercuts this idea is Nabokov's superiority to it, his mockery of the very mechanism that justifies art's transcendence of daily travail. His Humbert, even as he strives for an art of sorts, is a lunatic, a ridiculous man, a superfluous fool, an underground man, a madman, in line with those characters in Gogol, Turgenev, Tolstoy, Dostoyevsky. This is his derivation, and we recall that Nabokov wrote a revealing critical study of Gogol in 1944, stressing the outrageous and Rabelaisian in the Russian writer. If we locate Humbert in this line, and Nabokov's attitudes there, then the argument based on the artist is diluted.

Nabokov, actually, is more concerned with suffering, that peculiar kind of obsessional longing which characterizes both sufferer and victim, than he is with its product. The most compelling passages in *Lolita* are descriptions of Humbert's love-longing, in which he is a fool of love, a ridiculous man. "The hollow of my hand was still ivory-full of Lolita—full of the feel of her pre-adolescently incurved back, that ivory-smooth, sliding sensation of her skin through the thin frock that I had worked up and down while I held her. I marched into her tumbled room, threw open the door of the closet and plunged into a heap of crumpled things that had touched her. There was particularly one pink texture, sleazy, torn, with a faintly acrid odor in the seam. I wrapped in it Humbert's huge engorged heart."

This is truly Nabokov territory, the borders as well as the center of which he fully understands: where obsession and rationality meet, where folly bends reason, each to accommodate the other. For in this area, he can locate the risibility of human behavior; and here, despite a prose that infects rather than effects, Nabokov's art gains multidimensionality.

In *Timon of Athens,* Timon offers to the bandits examples of thievery that far outweigh the mere thieveries of their profession. While the sun robs the very sea, "the moon's an arrant thief, / And her pale fire she snatches from the sun," in turn being robbed by the sea, and so on. The world connects a circular thief, each element deriving something by stealing it from another. This is also a metaphor for art, beginning with the Promethean theft of fire from the gods, an offering to mankind for which he paid with his gut. Since so much of Nabokov's work is concerned with the making of art—that self-conscious process in which the given text is the outer shell of an art in the making—we should read *Pale Fire* (1962) as both the final product and the process of an artwork. The turn of Nabokov's mind—snobbish, aristocratic, anti–twentieth century, solipsistic—could never take him far from that subject, in which art circles back to itself: itself subject and object. Reading backward to *Lolita,* one can suggest such a view: Humbert's exaltation of the ordinary Lolita is based on his need to make her an art object worthy of his devotion, Pygmalion's own creation. Similarly, in *Ada,* Nabokov will raise incest to the textures of an art in the making.

To carry through the point above, *Pale Fire* is the obverse of *Lolita.* A more adventurous effort than the earlier book, it nevertheless picks up the self-love at the heart of Nabokov's conception of art. In an age of narcissism and solipsism, he outdistances his closest competitors, Mailer, Roth, and Bellow. Everything about *Lolita* is counterfeit, although details of food, sex, lodgings, travel, are real enough. Everything about *Pale Fire* is also counterfeit, and as in *Lolita,* counterfeit leads back to Nabokov, the creator. Humbert is an American tentacle, Kinbote a Russian. The landscape of each novel may be America, transcontinental in *Lolita* and New Wye, Appalachia, in *Pale Fire,* but the true terra cognita is Nabokov's tenacious memory. Into everything he floated Russia, an insistent juggernaut of a Russia. Unlike his American counterparts in narcissism, however, Nabokov could turn a self-serving image into self-parody. If *Lolita* is the reaching out of his Russian self into America, *Pale Fire* is a returning of that American soul (Shade) back to Zembla by way of the mad Kinbote.

Pale Fire is a fiercely unified work. The 999-line poem by Shade, the Commentary by Kinbote (which occupies three-quarters of the book's length), and the Index by, apparently, the author are interconnected. They are associated by Nabokov's insistence on being all characters and places in the book, however unorthodox the arrangement. *Pale Fire* is in the long line of self-conscious or self-reflexive novels beginning with *Tristram Shandy* and continuing in Beckett, Borges, parts of Joyce, Mann, Proust. Nabokov differs somewhat from the above in that he does not locate himself in a particular character, but spreads himself into halves and quarters: Shade here, also Kinbote, the King, Gradus-Grey (the assassin). By splitting himself off, he can probe his own consciousness, display himself, and still return to the process of making art. Nabokov is the ultimate mirror, and we must read him as a preening and primping verbal genius, having turned languages—Russian, French, German, English—into affectations worthy of himself.

In this view of *Pale Fire,* the poem becomes armor plating for the self. As noted above, Nabokov was the personification of the exile; the man who, having been denied by circumstance or personal taste the security of a refuge, chooses marginality. Nabokov's insistence on his fate or circumstance was not an attempt to "enter," even as a Cornell professor, but to stress his outsider's status. His development of *his* kind of English was a further insistence on difference: to master a kind of English as far removed from contemporary American English as was possible; to sound like a colloquial writer would suggest integration. As *Speak, Memory* amply suggests, Nabokov reveled in his outsider status because it called attention to his speciality; and in fact, his final work, *Ada,* becomes the ultimate in that posing of self, that use of incest as another form of self-love, and that deployment of prose more to obfuscate than to reveal. *Ada* is a brilliant transformation of modern life into Nabokov.

We must view *Pale Fire* in this light. The three levels or layers all lead back to Nabokov: the ridiculous poem, parody as much as verse; the Commentary; and the Index. Proustian time passing, time lost and recalled, encounters time present. Kinbote, the mad commentator, originally thought Shade would call his poem "Solus Rex," a title Kinbote suggested from his own life—the exiled solitary king, a chess reference as well as a description of the marginal artist.* Kinbote had expected Shade's poem, in fact, to be about his glorious past, as king, his life in Zembla, his lovely flower boys (the persistent homosexual theme), sunset castle, marvelous horse, stained windows. Instead, he finds a run-of-the-mill "rather old-fashioned narrative in a neo-Popian prosodic style— beautifully written of course . . . but void of my magic, of that special rich streak of magical madness which I was sure would run through it and make it transcend its time."

The poem takes the form of an indifferent social structure, one that perpetuates itself without regard for the splendors of Nabokov's memory, his nostalgia, the tight, incredible density of his past. The poem is, in a broad sense, part of that American indifference to time past, to memory; and Nabokov as Kinbote must resurrect history, whatever the madness of the act, or else perish in the effort. Unless Kinbote can make some impression on Shade—whose life and welfare have nothing to do with Zembla—then everything Kinbote represents is lost. Postwar America swallows and digests memory before it even has an opportunity to settle. Nabokov devised the commentary, Kinbote's memorial to his own *Speak, Memory,* as a way of countering the swallowing effect. Whereas in *Lolita* swallowing concerned food, here swallowing means being swallowed up.

Shade's poem is a catchall: of modernist mannerisms (Eliotic references, lines 617–20), pastoral nonsense (lines 272–5), Popian heroic couplets parodied (throughout), plain nonsense lyrics: "I had a brain,

*Solus Rex (royal solitude) turns up in *Pnin,* as the fantasy of a lonely king in the mind of Pnin's stepson, Victor Wind. Solus Rex is a great and lonely figure for Nabokov, a king without a queen to protect him, a prototype of the artist; but references to him derive from the fantasies of an American boy who comprehends nothing of the true meaning. Life is a form of vengeance for the exile.

five senses (one unique), / But otherwise I was a cloutish freak" (lines 133–4). It lacks coherence, and rather than being Shade's masterpiece, it is a mockery of poetry; the way *Lolita* makes a mockery of the strung-out, picaresque American novel.

The Commentary, then, will return the poem to what Kinbote feels is the proper theme: his state of being, his past, his nostalgia, the reconstruction of his world. What the poem lacks he will read into it, an academic exercise which has built within it the parody of the critical function Nabokov was so close to at Cornell. The Index will be icing on that cake: footnotes to footnotes. The assassin of Shade is Gradus, Russian for stages or degrees, and Gradus is a member of the Shadows, a regicidal organization. Gradus also poses as Jack Grey—Grey, Shade, Shadows, Gradus; and much of the work is done by mirrors. All this suggests that the work taken together is a self-enclosed artifact: art mirroring art, each part not only in itself but elements of a mirroring process. There is much peering, and in fact, Shade's poem begins with the lines: "I was the shadow of the waxwing slain / By the false azure in the windowpane." Shade is identified with the windowpane, reflections, peering in and out, the artistic function personified.

A correct assumption is that Shade was the original victim of the Shadows: to kill the poet rather than the king. For Nabokov's purpose, the poet—himself as artist, the artist as solitary king—is a truer target for assassination than a deposed king; on the analogy of Baudelaire's albatross, that "solitary king of the air" which becomes the butt of the ship crew's mockery. To kill a poet, however poor, is to threaten the true kingdom, not of a deposed king but of the memories that Kinbote carried from Zembla. Without Shade's bad poem, there would be no Commentary, no Index, no artwork, in fact. That skew relationship to the making of art is, for Nabokov, a perfect model for his own sense of himself: exile from Russia to England and Western Europe, exile from Hitler's Europe, now strangest exile of all in Ithaca, New York. Nabokov lacked the moral fervor of Conrad; he lacked, also, that intensity or fixity which gave Conrad his dense textures. Lacking these, he needed to turn exile, dislocation, sense of separation into something else; and for this, the role of artist, the process of art-making, the place of art as a crazy quilt (Quilty?), all served Nabokov's function.

Carved into pieces by exile, Nabokov's career is curiously like the careers of an American action painter, who after years as one kind of artist moved to another stage, as though in a different language. That sense of the protean, of constant change, of movable careers, which we find in Nabokov is prototypical postwar American; so that despite his discomfort as an Amerian, Nabokov proved, in some ways, typical. Dislocation for the European fitted well into America's constant reshaping of itself as a counterfeit culture.*

Some Pictures from an Exhibition

The fifties, apart from movements noted above, saw the beginning of several large careers, nearly all of them in adversary relationship to the more stable elements of the decade. An exception was James Gould Cozzens, a survivor from the thirties, whose *By Love Possessed* encapsulates the counterfeit as the real. One career, that of Flannery O'Connor, was conceived and almost ran its entire course during the decade. Other writers, such as Styron, Malamud, Updike, Vonnegut, Buechner, and Roth, began what were to be extended careers. Still others—Bellow, Wright, Porter, Morris, Bowles—were to continue careers begun in previous decades. In addition, Hemingway, Dos Passos, and Faulkner published well into the decade, although they had defined their major work in an earlier time.

Perhaps the most singularly unique voice was that of Flannery O'Connor. Her mixture of wit, irony, paradox, and traditional belief in the devil and God gave her prose a maturity that belied the age at which much of her fiction was written. Like Hawkes, with whom she corresponded during her last years, she early on discovered a voice that distinguished her from those influencing her. O'Connor's frame of belief was to be found within the Roman Catholic Church, which she saw as a church of great diversity, great paradox, and great profundity for the individual willing to give his/her life to it. As she wrote to Cecil Dawkins: "At the age of 11, you encounter some old priest who calls you a heretic for inquiring about evolution; at about the same time Père Pierre Teilhard de Chardin, S.J. is in China discovering Peking man."

Aside from providing her with the title "Everything That Rises Must Converge," Teilhard was for O'Connor a more pervasive influence than any purely literary figure. For she found, in Teilhard's ability to turn his face toward science and evolution without losing his sense of where pieces fitted into a spiritual plan, a view sympathetic to her own sense of suffering and achievement. O'Connor had to account for her affliction, a degenerative disease called lupus, within a framework of great creative energy. She came to identify with Teilhard's "passive diminishment," the phrase suggesting acceptance of an affliction which, while determined and unavoidable, is accompanied by a strengthening of the will. Thus, she becomes a battleground of diminishment and response, the affliction leading to a countering achievement which may not have been otherwise present. This grounding in suffering and increase makes her work far more than Southern or regional, as she suggests in her essay "The Grotesque in Southern Fiction." If she writes about freaks, she says, it is that she can see what whole man is. Being "Christ-haunted" and seeking her self in Teilhard's paradox has given her a vision not grotesque or peculiar to any region, but one which parallels that of Jesus himself.

Although anyone who writes intensely about the Deep South recalls the work of Faulkner, Flannery O'Connor is only superficially similar. Her type of Gothic or grotesque differs from Faulkner's in essentials, and her style, while less convoluted, is more unbending. *Wise Blood* appeared in 1952, but many of its parts—four sections were published as short

---

*Counterfeit recurs in Jerome Charyn's *The Tar Baby* (1973), which seems deeply indebted to *Pale Fire*. Charyn's wild, comedic novel takes the form, not of a poem and commentary, but of a magazine *(The Tar Baby)*, with commentary. At issue are angles of observation, the unreliability of witnesses, the nature of truth.

stories in *Sewanee, Partisan,* and *New World Writing* —were written just after she received her M.F.A. from Iowa in 1947. Thus, while the novel appeared in the very early 1950s, it signaled a talent breaking in style, content, and intensity from a somewhat more established group. In this respect, as in many others, O'Connor resembles John Hawkes, although she is far less experimental or daring in her arrangements and in her demand upon the reader.

O'Connor's antecedents in fiction, besides Faulkner, are not difficult to seek. We look to the obsessed and monomaniacal: aspects of Hawthorne and Melville, for example, are apparent. The vision of sin which keeps Hazel Mote alive and intense is one that not only hovers over the South but enters into writers as different as Purdy, Bellow *(The Victim, Seize the Day),* Walker Percy. But someone even more immediate—mordant, witty, parodic, deeply committed to loneliness and to questions of sin, sinning, and repentance—was Nathanael West, particularly in his *Miss Lonelyhearts* (1933). O'Connor could have taken as epigraph his ironic "Men have always fought their misery with dreams." In a narrow sense, *Wise Blood* picks up from West's work, especially the witty examination of sin and repentance in which Christ has failed. Hazel Mote's Church of Christ without Christ recalls Miss Lonelyhearts' advice to the defeated, the worn, and the exhausted, while all around them are the Shrikes, the Enoch Emerys, the Hoover Shoateses.

In the order of things, Mote is a mote, a speck, a blemish, or a particle of dust. His given name is ambiguous, male and female, as well as a tree, a nut, a piece of nature. Within religious parable, Hazel Mote moves well beyond a cartoon character or freak. Even his car, the virtually indestructible Essex, has magical qualities, the steed to his inverted-heroic knight, so that the image of Mote in his Essex is of a centaur. When Mote blinds himself and plays Oedipus, as against the false blinding of Asa Hawks, he is doing no more than working out his heroic motif in a setting of the false and artificial. The characteristic O'Connor theme is there: the individual who burns with passions that cannot find fulfillment, the "hunger artist," as it were, who is dying intensely while audiences seek cheap thrills.

Her character, here as elsewhere, is the creature who pours oil on himself and sets himself afire, while people ride by unconcerned or else take photographs for sale to tourists. Hazel's double is the Prophet, the man who tries to eke out a few pennies by fortunetell-ing, turning Mote's deepest feelings into salable items. When Mote kills him, he tries to kill off all "reproductions" of the truth; the truth may kill and the artificial may save, but in Mote's inverted idealism, he insists on the reality of sin, not on the saving qualities of redemption. Grace, perhaps, is all. Hazel Mote meets Wyatt Gwyon across vast depths.

The "hunger artist" does not bend. He is bent. His suffering is irredeemable because it goes unnoticed. Mote's appearance, like Miss Lonelyhearts', is that of a preacher. If the West character recalls the New England puritan without a beard, Mote resembles the grim visage of Calvin himself. His sense of sin, however, is gripped by wit. His pleasure is in seeking antipleasure; what is for others is not for him. And if Jesus has redeemed some, he knows he does not want to be saved. "He felt that he should have a woman, not for the sake of the pleasure in her, but to prove that he didn't believe in sin since he practiced what was called it." The blind man's child is so homely he assumes she is innocent. But the blind man is not blind, and she, in turn, with the Hawthornian name of Sabbath Lily, seduces Mote, who is the innocent one.

O'Connor has been accused, in terms reminiscent of those who once commented similarly on Jane Austen, of ignoring all the larger issues—war and peace, science and technology, the financial and industrial world, even normal family life. Granting that her view cuts deep, critics have cautioned that it is too narrow and provincial. But the argument is futile. Clearly, the breadth of her observations comes through her ordering of images, and by way of dreams, the presence of death, coffins, final things, the witty way she has with sin and redemption; she has, in these terms, created her own "war fiction." The combat in her first novel is a religious one, between those who easily accept Jesus as the redeemer and those, like Hazel Mote, who sense that sin lies outside of what can be redeemed, that the Church of Jesus must be without Jesus.* There is a small third group,

---

*Repeated in several stories, but especially significant in "A Good Man Is Hard to Find." O'Connor differs here from both François Mauriac and Graham Greene, with whose work her own may superficially be compared. The epigraph to "A Good Man" (1955) derives from Saint Cyril of Jerusalem, to the effect that the way to a spiritual life must pass by the dragons, who may devour you. The grandmother feels that the way into the spirit can be effected without the dragon; but the Misfit, who has no illusions about the spiritual life, is aware that dragons lie everywhere. Confrontation between grandmother and Misfit

those who run a confidence game within the interstices of sin and redemption, like Hoover Shoates and the Prophet in his pay. Within this sense of things, O'Connor has enclosed an entire world, in which Manichean elements clash, leaving little other ground.

One who attempts to achieve other ground is the extraordinary Enoch Emery, a zoo worker, a voyeur, a man who desires human contact. His career is completely within the world, but an artificial one. A worker with animals, he seeks an apeskin so that he can become the "ape" who shakes the hand of people at events and sideshows. He "experiences" women by way of a hidden area from which he can observe them swimming and sunning themselves. He is a more unbalanced avatar of Walker Percy's Will Barrett. He approaches history of sorts by stealing from the museum a three-foot mummy, which represents, in his absence of real belief, a kind of totem he needs to fulfill himself. Emery, if we can even define him, is patterned on what does not exist for Hazel. If Hazel is the intense negative of commitment, Emery is the intense positive of social artificiality. He tries to be saved by way of an apeskin, a mummy, compensatory sexual experience; his world is based on artifice which can never achieve belief. Mote's is founded on a negative of belief which is itself a form of devotion.

Like West in *Miss Lonelyhearts,* O'Connor celebrates oddities as forms of contemporary worship. Emery's "wise blood"—a means to salvation without sacraments—does not lead to any advantage at work or personally, but to indulgence in bewildering acts he cannot himself comprehend. Although cults and fanaticism in a larger sense had not as yet become public matters, we can see, through O'Connor's work, their potentiality for the 1960s and 1970s. By extrapolating from her own religious commitment, she could see both the positive and the negative, chiefly the intensity with which anything can be held. Mote's blinding of himself, the putting out of the

_____

—typical designations in O'Connor for benevolent artificiality and malevolent intensity of feeling—is postwar combat: false spirit meeting contaminated body, role reversals, quickening of feeling, alertness to potentialities, death around the corner. " 'It's no real pleasure in life,' " says the Misfit, and finds a form of salvation everlastingly denied to the grandmother, who seeks it in unfulfilling ways. Strikingly, O'Connor moves close to Gaddis in *The Recognitions,* seeking forms of authenticity in the recognition itself, even when embodied in vile creatures. Intensity carries the individual past the factitious. The Misfit is a prophet of sorts, a dark Jesus.

speck in the eyes of the Lord, is an act of belief. Asa Hawks's false blindness serves as warning to Motes of what he must avoid, or else he falls, in his view, into the worship of idols.

"Jesus saves," for O'Connor, but Who and What are Jesus? Is the redeemer necessary for those who seek redemption within themselves? Is sin something beyond Jesus' power to redeem? Is grace sufficient, without further intervention? As a Roman Catholic, O'Connor questioned, with Hazel Mote, matters of life and death which fall between religions. In her 1962 notes to *Wise Blood,* she described it as a "comic novel about a Christian *malgré lui,* and as such, very serious, for all comic novels that are any good must be about matters of life and death." The majority who believe in Christ, she says, dismiss these questions as of "no great consequence"; but they are everything. In this Manichean struggle, where the individual battles without support, she has structured her war analogy. Mote's battlefield, on which he dies huddled and alone, is different from that of Mailer, Jones, Shaw; but it is ground nevertheless on which wars are fought, won or lost.

The Violent Bear It Away (1960) takes its theme from Matthew II: 12, to the effect that the "kingdom of heaven suffereth violence, and the violent take it by force," or in O'Connor's phrase, "bear it away." In this her second and final novel, she has reassembled many of her by now familiar materials: the implicit and explicit violence of those who live intensely; the family that recalls the House of Atreus, lines of hatred and love which are indistinguishable; the preoccupation with baptism, damnation, redemption, which seems to enchant an entire society; bizarre, possessed people whom she makes familiar and apparently ordinary; a background society which seems diluted by contrast with her intense characters.

The structure of the novel is formed by a vertical line based on an extended family. The top of the line is a possessed great-uncle who lives with his young great-nephew, Tarwater, and instructs him in the ways of a God not unlike himself. Just beyond this line, slightly to the side, is another paternal figure for Tarwater, embodied in the stranger, a voice rather than a body. A countering parent, the stranger instructs Tarwater in how to escape the commandments of his great-uncle. But for the God-crazed boy, the stranger could also be a voice of the devil, and it upsets him because if he breaks from his great-uncle, as the voice counsels, then he isn't certain who and what he will be.

Directly in the vertical family line is the old man's nephew, Rayber, who is Tarwater's uncle. Rayber is a much more definite force than the stranger, in that he openly represents nonbelief and wishes to indoctrinate Tarwater in the ways of atheism; that is, in the ways of self-choice and self-appointed function. Rayber has himself fought to escape the old man, having been seized when he was seven and forcibly baptized. Further, when Rayber first tried to get hold of the boy, he went to the old man's farm, only to be shot in the leg and ear. In their vicarious roles, fathers and sons are competing with each other, by way of God's power, with death and damnation or salvation as the doom or reward. The conception is grand for a novel so deeply provincial: O'Connor's final effort to cut so extensively she could reach completely across the world by way of a thin line piercing the earth's skin.*

There is, further, another son, and this is Rayber's idiot boy, named Bishop. Tarwater's mission is to baptize Bishop, and Rayber's mission is to prevent it. Yet Rayber is ambivalent, full of terrible love and terrible resentment that his child is an idiot. In a situation in which he thinks he can trust Tarwater, he lets him row the boy out into the middle of the lake, where Tarwater does indeed baptize Bishop by drowning him. He insists he only meant to drown him; the baptism was accidental, a by-product. With that, Tarwater has fulfilled his great-uncle's mission for him; he has forsaken his own direction for the ways of the old man, and he must return to the property, where he will be in charge. He has become like Cain and Ishmael, outcasts who identify with all those who have committed a preordained act.

The structural images for this shriek of a novel—it never simmers, but boils fiercely—are light and darkness, fire, mirrors and other forms of reflection, and even rape. Between his fulfillment of his great-uncle's mission and his return to the property, Tarwater is picked up and raped by a passing motorist;

---

*J. F. Powers's *Morte d'Urban* (1962) is an urbane version of the murderous interplay between sacred and profane. A Catholic like O'Connor, Powers institutionalizes belief, removing it from those open areas where she locates wild and possessed devotion. He takes the struggle into church politics, his Urban a kind of King Arthur done in by deceit and petty corruption. An idealist, Urban tries to keep worship within an increasingly secular institution. But his doom is clear when the bishop's golf ball strikes him on the head during a match, and he succumbs, a knowing man who believed in the mission of God.

earlier, on his movement out to his mission—to baptize Bishop—he had been aided by a motorist named Meeks, who counseled success in the world. The mirrors, lights and darks, fires lead not only into Biblical metaphors but back toward the individual. For despite the religiosity of her material, O'Connor was very much a part of the 1950s. And her commitment to the self was typical, in that restraints, moral constraints, desire for expression warred with liberation, narcissism, inward turning. What is most striking, despite the intensity, fire, and heaving passions, is the absence of any sexual undercurrent. Everyone who might have been involved sexually is dead or has vanished. Rayber's wife has run off; Tarwater was born in a car wreck, in which his mother, often referred to as a whore, was killed. Not only do no women of any sexual viability exist in the novel; the men yearn for little but the completion of their mission: God- or hate-filled, they have eschewed moderate or normal relationships. The sole act of sex is the homosexual rape of Tarwater by the motorist.

This, too, is part of a 1950s vision: the self as fulfilled by a mission rather than by indulgence; indulgence as itself a form of demonry, damnation, a weakening of purpose. Malamud's *A New Life* and Philip Roth's stories, both at the end of the decade, were pivotal points in this ideology of self versus self. O'Connor has taken the 1950s sense of mission to its final point, to Tarwater's insistence: " 'I only meant to drown him.' " Here mission is fulfilled, a baptism by way of an ultimate act. Inadvertently or not, Tarwater works out the destiny of his great-uncle. The family line is completed by way of the mythical pattern of generational struggle and murder. An extended incest pattern is also apparent: all those wifeless and motherless men grouping, then consuming each other, culminating in the rape of the final scenes. That passing motorist, a surrogate father of sorts for Tarwater, also acts out the shadowy designs of fathers and sons. He drugs Tarwater, seizes him, as his great-uncle had, as Rayber tried, as he had Bishop.

By the time of her final lingering decline from lupus, O'Connor's vision had extended, although it may seem only as if her scalpel had cut deeper. The vision involved nothing less than final things, in which self-denial, mission, obsessive belief were aligned against letting go, release, liberation. Her bizarre, marginal outsiders are, for her, those whose feelings are central; whereas so-called normal society is diluted, pale, debilitated. Intermixed is a sense of social dialectics: a society that tries to hold together under onslaughts of the new. The new is less prejudicial, more enlightened, inevitable, and yet the old, the incestuous old, is like a vise, holding on to values deriving directly from Jeremiah, Matthew, Ecclesiastes, and even Job. One of the dangers in reading O'Connor is to stress her bizarreness, her Gothic strangeness, and to miss the social dialectic that is as much at her heart as it is at the heart of another writer once attacked for remissness, Jane Austen.

O'Connor's shorter fiction is remarkable. Not only have half a dozen stories entered anthologies; the very titles have entered the language: "A Good Man Is Hard to Find," "The Artificial Nigger," "Everything That Rises Must Converge." One of them, early in her career, "The Displaced Person," suggests large social and political currents; with this story O'Connor's more personalized symbolism opens up an area of change that would overtake the South in the 1950s. Here, her chess pieces are her beloved peacocks, in decline; blacks in a peculiar love-hate association with their employer; a "displaced person" from Poland who offers the "new"; and those marginal whites who represent a dispossessed Garden they still think of as Edenic. The story cuts deep and wide.

Peacocks here become symbols of the decline of everything but what they themselves represent, which is the transfiguration. The peacock's displacement from the natural world becomes the displacement of all things, except those that live, however shakily, in the eyes of God. The old, tired priest survives all the tragedies because, appearing to observe nothing, he has, like the peacocks, seen all. But even the birds must go, for the pastoral is a dispossessed Garden, based on forms of slave labor, and no perfect emblem of God can survive such deception. What remains then is that wrung-out form of belief which lies beyond land, displaced person, even peacock.

O'Connor has miniaturized a changing American South, and indirectly a changing America. Mrs. McIntyre, after the death of her husband, has had a succession of hired help; it is from Mrs. Shortley, of the present couple, that much of the first half of the story is unfolded. She and her husband are "poor white trash," although Mrs. McIntyre treats Mrs. Shortley at a higher level. Below them, socially, are the Negro farmhands, whom the Shortleys find reassuring, as contrast. When a refugee Polish family arrives—Mr. Guizac, wife, two children—the new order threatens. Guizac can work every farm machine, is indefatigable, efficient, clean. Mrs. McIntyre finds him a marvel, although she fears he will want higher wages. The Shortleys, however, see him, rightly, as undermining their position. They must ally themselves with the Negro help to regain the old pecking order.

The local priest, who brought the Guizacs to the attention of Mrs. McIntyre, makes frequent visits. His attention is taken up by the peacocks—a peacock and two peahens, the remnants of a much larger group. The peacock's grandeur recalls Hopkins's lines: "The world is charged with the grandeur of God. / It will flame out, like shining from shook foil; / It gathers to a greatness." Contrasted with the hired help, the peacock represents glory, indeed a past glory, an Edenic splendor before sin, when only beauty obtained.

Now, on Mrs. McIntyre's farm, the peacocks—their tails "full of suns"—are juxtaposed to scheming, barely surviving, nasty-minded Mrs. Shortley, the human representation of the present. As she resents the presence of the priest, and even more that of the Guizacs, the peacock plays out its determined role. "He had jumped into the tree and his tail hung in front of her, full of fierce planets with eyes that were each ringed in green and set against a sun that was gold in one second's light and salmon-colored in the next. She might have been looking at a map of the universe but she didn't notice it any more than she did the spots of sky that cracked the dull green of the tree."

The peacock suggests another world, or the transformation of this one, but Mrs. Shortley is intent on her own vision: not of God's grandeur, but of an invasion of Guizacs, "ten million billion of them," forcing their way to our shores and displacing the Negroes, then her, all people like her. Her concern for the Negro help is, of course, based on their inferiority. In the eye of the peacock, itself being phased out from the universe, everyone is displaced: except the priest, whose gaze is on eternity.

When the Guizacs continue to be so efficient, there is no need for the Shortleys. Hearing that they will be given thirty days notice, they leave suddenly in the night, but first they sow suspicion. Mrs. McIntyre watches Guizac carefully, and then comes that moment which brings around her revelation of breakup. Guizac has promised his cousin, a young blond girl, to one of the Negro farmhands, Sulk, backward, illiterate, barely balanced, if he will put up the money for her release from a camp in Europe. The farmhand will marry her, and they will, apparently, live together on Mrs. McIntyre's property.

This is, of course, against custom, society, nature, a desecration of life so ugly that Mrs. McIntyre knows she must release Guizac from her service. She now has justification for firing him, as she has had to fire every other hired hand before him. Only the Shortleys had lasted, for two years. The Guizacs, perfect in so many other ways, lack a moral dimension; furthermore, they do not begin to understand the color bar, the racial issue, the question not only of a white girl marrying an illiterate farmhand, but marrying any Negro.

The issues begin to take on an even greater complexity. For Guizac, himself no more articulate in English than the Negroes, sees freedom from European chaos as the first priority; whereas Mrs. McIntyre is horrified by the personal and racial element. She cannot begin to comprehend what lies behind Guizac's offer of his cousin to Sulk, for she cannot perceive the death camps, the stacking of bodies, the crematoria, although she has heard of such things. For Mrs. McIntyre, what matters is the survival of a way of life, even as it changes. She must preserve what can be saved.

The resolution is swift. Shortley returns, without his wife, who has died, and he is taken back on, all the time speaking of how he risked his life in the war, how he put himself in danger so as to preserve America for the likes of him. In what appears an accident, Shortley leaves a large tractor on an incline, the brake gives way, and Guizac is crushed to death. Mrs. McIntyre has a moment of decision, to warn the Pole of the slipping tractor, but she freezes, says not a word, and lets the machine do its job.

All are now displaced. Guizac, the refugee, is dead. His family, doubly displaced, leaves, as do Shortley, Sulk, and the old Negro Astor. Mrs. McIntyre sells the farm at a loss, retires in failing health, parts of her ceasing to function. What remains is the priest, who comes weekly to explain the doctrines of the Church, a Catholic attempting to convert her. The peacocks are completely forgotten as human lives preempt the earth, displacing God's grandeur. The South is leached out.

In the long story "The Lame Shall Enter First" (published in 1962 in *Sewanee Review*), we have a convergence of nearly all of O'Connor's themes. The "Lame" is a young boy, Rufus Johnson, with a clubfoot; and the totemic object is his shoe, a piece of junk laced high that forces him to walk incorrectly. His benefactor, Sheppard (the good shepherd, deceived by others and himself), puts his faith in obtaining for Johnson a new shoe; from his godless point of view,

the shoe will prove salvation for the boy.

One of O'Connor's last stories, "The Lame Shall Enter First" proves to be one of her most political, a reprise of the 1950s. The three elements of the story are the liberal do-gooder Sheppard; the destructive, God-fearing, satanic Rufus Johnson; and the stolid, fearful Nelson, Sheppard's son, who misses his mother and seeks her spirit amidst the dead. Sheppard's liberal faith is useless because it is based on misunderstanding of human nature; he expects to reform the damned Johnson by showing goodwill, providing healthy food, and giving friendly support. He places faith not only in the right shoe—the central emblem of the story—but in the good effects of science. He buys a telescope so that Johnson can view the wonders of space, the beauties of the universe, and thus move beyond his own tight circle of hatred. When this fails, Sheppard buys a microscope, hoping that vastness can be replaced by detail, depth rather than spaciousness.

But the depth and spaciousness that concern Johnson are located in a space well beyond Sheppard's comprehension. So while he buys a telescope and a microscope for Johnson "to see," he himself remains blind to the ways of both devil and God. When the great, good moment arrives and the new shoe is ready, Johnson refuses it, indicating that the old, rotted piece of footwear is his signature. With the new shoe, Sheppard will have bought him, and Johnson's vision of hell does not allow himself to be bought. The new shoe would enable him to walk better, but walking, a secular enterprise, is meaningless for one who wishes to "enter first," as scripture says the lame shall do. Sheppard thinks he's Jesus Christ, so Johnson indicates to Nelson; but he's a false prophet in Johnson's eyes, one of the many in O'Connor's stories who blur distinctions between God and devil.

Johnson's revenge on the man who attempts to reform him by means of good deeds is to win over Nelson. For Johnson, social values mean nothing; he steals, destroys property, moves in and out of the clutches of the police. Johnson insists on himself, as agent of the devil and agent of experience that moves outside liberal social and political faith. O'Connor does not respect or admire his integrity; rather, she uses Johnson's corrupted form of belief as a weapon against Sheppard's bad or counterfeit faith, grounded as it is in good deeds separated from broader belief. And in the working out of this struggle between two incompatible elements, she sees a human sacrifice is necessary.

Nelson's position between Sheppard and Johnson

is Isaac's between Abraham and the Lord; only in O'Connor's ironic, mordant way, the terror of sacrifice is completed when Nelson hangs himself from an attic beam "from which he had launched his flight into space." The final word is particularly ironic, since it was through spatiality that Sheppard hoped to reform Johnson. But Nelson's view of space differs from Sheppard's; he uses it in search of his mother, dead a year and apparently forgotten by his father. Nelson's hunger is for love, recognition, security; but Sheppard misses all this and moves to good deeds as a form of expression. He forgoes human direction while pursuing social and political. By the time Sheppard realizes the course of things and rushes up to embrace the boy, Nelson has hanged himself, launched into the space where, by means of the telescope, he had "discovered" his mother in heaven, Johnson having convinced him that his mother entered heaven if she believed in Jesus. Standing well outside formal politics, O'Connor has nevertheless written an intensely political fable, all well within the fictional elements she had pursued from the start of her career.

The reprise of the 1950s continues in "Everything That Rises Must Converge" (1961). Young Julian's mother wears a crazy hat which defines some aspect of herself trying to escape a narrow, hard existence. The hat, inanimate, and later duplicated on the head of a black woman, is a statement his mother must make despite her better judgment; for it expresses something she could never articulate. It is a form of life. Just as Julian's social egalitarianism, political liberalism, lack of racial prejudice infuriate his mother, so he is infuriated by the ridiculous hat. When he sees the same hat on a black woman who boards their bus, he thinks that his mother will be shamed into learning her lesson; but on the contrary, she is able to smile. Her will prevails. Her generation, slyly, gets back at his; but the means, as in so much of O'Connor, is an inanimate object that becomes charged with totemic power, usually ringing some change in the individual. It is not necessarily a form of salvation; but neither is it simply mechanical.

We find comparable objects in the "artificial nigger," the "plaster figure of a Negro sitting bent over a low yellow brick wall," an image of immense desolation emblematic of a waste land; or the artificial leg in "Good Country People"; or the tattoo in "Parker's Back" and the coffin in "Judgment Day." These inanimate emblems in O'Connor are in a sense her "Cherry Orchard," suggestive of the passing of time. In "Everything That Rises," Julian rightly feels

shame at his mother's patronage of the black woman and her child; yet the scene goes beyond that, to a world that is passing: not a good world, of course, but it is passing to Julian, who is uncertain of everything, whereas his mother was certain. The "convergence" of the title is somewhere outside Julian's philosophy, but there, in the world beyond his bubble, that achievement of values lies. Salvation? Redemption? Heaven? Perhaps, or else that invisibility which is the most intense of experiences to the dying Flannery O'Connor, who insisted on what remained beyond the eyes trapped within the bubble.

When Asbury in "The Enduring Chill" recognizes he will live, he awaits the new life that will come, the old life in him being exhausted. But he expects this life to arrive in the form of warmth, heat, something branding or emblazoning him. O'Connor then provides a finale that is, surely, one of the finest examples of prose in the entire postwar era:

It was then that he felt the beginning of a chill, a chill so peculiar, so light, that it was like a warm ripple across a deeper sea of cold. His breath came short. The fierce bird which through the years of his childhood and the days of his illness had been poised over his head, waiting mysteriously, appeared all at once to be in motion. Asbury blanched and the last film of illusion was torn as if by a whirlwind from his eyes. He saw that for the rest of his days, frail, racked, but enduring, he would live in the face of a purifying terror. A feeble cry, a last impossible protest escaped him. But the Holy Ghost, emblazoned in ice instead of fire, continued, implacable, to descend.

Published in 1958, these words, witty, religious, penetrating, go against the grain of nearly all major American fiction of the time and the ensuing decade. Had O'Connor lived beyond 1964 and continued to write, she could have been a major countering voice to the dominant tones of the period. For every "American dream" offered up by Mailer, she could have offered her own, that fierce bird which brings not release and personal excess, but the holy terror that, ultimately, lies too deep for words. O'Connor's religious emblems bridge the gap to the nonbeliever.

Flannery O'Connor commented on Styron's *Lie Down in Darkness* (1951): "To my way of thinking it was too much the long tedious Freudian case history, though the boy can write and there were overtones of better things in it." On *Set This House on Fire* (1960), she wrote: "I don't think concern with guilt has too much to do with the traditional Christian artist's attempts at the novel. It may have a good deal to do with Styron's." Unfortunately, O'Connor did not gloss his work more, for her own work belies any attempt to group novelists regionally and her views would have been a corrective to those "critics" like Granville Hicks who indiscriminately praised every Styron production. Another view of Styron's career is this: that each novel, located almost a decade apart, was preparation for a succeeding effort in which he would break free of something. We can perceive *Lie Down in Darkness* as purging Faulkner; *Set This House on Fire* as exorcising elements of personal guilt; *The Confessions of Nat Turner* as coming to terms, Styron's own intimate terms, with black-white relationships by way of the legendary rebellious slave; and finally, *Sophie's Choice* as Styron's apotheosis of his freedom: his choice as embedded in Sophie's.* Each work was like an act that had to be written, and while the earlier books are derivative, overly rhetorical for their basic weight, and full of artificial flourishes and feelings, they can be justified as part of a long development and reach for greatness in *Sophie's Choice.* For if nothing else, the latter novel demonstrates that Styron was straining for development and achievement at a time when many of his contemporaries had given up, either repeating themselves or reaching for popular modes. Whatever its

---

*"Long March" (no "The") is an interim piece, written between *Lie Down in Darkness* and *Set This House on Fire,* two highly rhetorical and ambitious works; it is analogous in Bellow's career to *Seize the Day,* located between *Augie March* and *Henderson.* A kind of Xenophon Persian Expedition applied to the Korean War, "Long March" (1953) seems to imply a good deal, but along the way dissipates its potential. The central consciousness is Lieutenant Culver, called back from a pleasant civilian life to serve in the Marines. He accepts his fate; and when the colonel orders a long training march of thirty-six miles—not to be confused with Mao's—Culver is only worried he won't be able to complete it.

A more complicated reaction derives from Captain Mannix, whose recall has brought on him much hardship. Mannix, who has retained his Marine attitudes while storming against the fates for *his* fate, gives the story its shape; for even as he determines to conclude the long march, he rails against its injustice. The object was a seamless story of war and civilian life, recalling *The Red Badge of Courage,* as represented by the lives of two men. But it required a deeper probe of subjects; and the ending, in which Mannix and a black cleaning lady meet in a kind of understanding, resolves elements for which we have not been prepared. Styron wanted some level of experience which passes into revelation, but he loses deeper meanings amidst the details of the march itself.

flaws, *Sophie's Choice* justifies the missteps we can observe in Styron's earlier work.

The war, as we have noted, created a crisis in the novel, ending the "old novel" by implication and pressuring the writer to explore a new sensibility. In *Lie Down,* Styron failed to catch the note of the new and trapped himself in a pastiche of the old. Either he did not perceive or did not care that his kind of novel had been written before, although not with such lyricism, except perhaps by Fitzgerald. *Lie Down* is an artificial book.

It is constructed out of other novels, not from any kind of life generated by a given set of characters or situations. Many novels of the highest quality in the past have been constructed out of others, but for satirical purposes. Styron's novel, however, is fully serious; it is at the highest levels of pastiche, where counterfeit and real yearn for each other. Gaddis's Wyatt Gwyon paints "lost paintings" that are so real they help to create a canon of their own. Styron paints his characters and scenes so artificially he makes us marvel anew at the brilliance of those he imitates.

Essentially, his models are Fitzgerald—his characters as well as Scott and Zelda themselves; Faulkner—whose presence is everywhere, in Helen Loftis, the lost Southern lady, frustrated and yet hanging on, in Peyton, the damned young lady, in Milton, who has no role in the new South and cannot handle a life without work or aim; Hemingway—the constant drinking, the need for masculine assertion, the lyricism of lost causes and lost generations. The models are excellent. To this Styron has fused a "romantic prose," in which words and phrasing are carefully modulated, what we call "good writing." It is a very studied language, but, then, so is Faulkner's. We are reminded of Faulkner's imitation of the romantic poets in his early attempts at verse.

The style is perfectly attuned to the characters: a lost family in the South which, despite war and vast social changes, remains fixed in the past. Its pastness comes to us in Helen Loftis, a woman who through religious belief tries to mold a family that no longer fits her sense of order; and her husband, Milton, who wanders from one drink to another. His passion, when not directed at his daughter, is aimed outside marriage. Peyton, whose dead body runs like a leitmotif through the novel, is the moving force, the catalyst of doom. She is the repository of this South which, while seemingly providing release, is really a source of final things. She is calculatingly self-destructive: within her family, with her mother, in her drinking and promiscuity. Unable to function in any orderly way, she forgoes the love and forbearance of the one man who tries to help her, Harry Miller, a Jewish painter.

As in Faulkner's *As I Lay Dying,* the chief image is of burial. In *Lie Down in Darkness* (the title refers to "lying down" with the devil, experiencing sin so that one can become cleansed), the corpse of Peyton arrives in Port Warwick, Virginia, at the beginning of the novel and is then transported, despite several breakdowns of the hearse, to the cemetery. Thus, we are always aware of Peyton's death as Styron reconstitutes her life, from childhood to death and original burial in New York's potter's field. Though her death dominates the novel, her lack of actual presence dilutes that stress. The structural conception—to locate all within flashback—creates a tightness which we associate, also, with Faulkner, especially in *Absalom, Absalom!* Although Styron handles the flashbacks well, the method as well as the content is by now more than a twice-told tale.

Styron provides no persona or external commentator beyond an omniscient narrator; thus, irony, narrative locationing, and objective comment are forsaken. The author, we assume, accepts Peyton's story, much as Fitzgerald accepted the stories of his protagonists in *This Side of Paradise* and *The Beautiful and the Damned.* All detail falls into familiar, unquestioned patterns. College is not for learning, but for drunken frat parties, football games, screwing in the woods or a distant motel. The question is not simply one of stereotypical locales, but of authorial acceptance of the fact that no other dimensions existed. With all its sophisticated prose, *Lie Down* is a very young novel.* Styron cannot escape from one point: lacking experience of the world, he created a world from literary sources.

Stereotypes close like a trap around Styron's ambitions. After their wedding, Harry and Peyton take a ferry; and of course, it is a ferry to hell, across the Styx and monitored by Charon. Their stay in New York's Greenwich Village is a descent into the Inferno, replete with Italians. When Peyton is unfaithful to Harry, she takes an Italian lover, who wants only to screw and treats her like dirt. Peyton's mother back in Port Warwick is religious and pious, whereas her husband is promiscuous and alcoholic. Milton Loftis, frustrated by an ascetic wife, looks longingly at the young body of his daughter and commits incest

---

*The early parts of *Sophie's Choice* are similarly damaged by young Stingo's revelations, filtered now through the older Styron, who serves as narrator and maker of his own life.

in his mind several times over. No matter how fine the prose, there is no way for an author to overcome the deadness such a pastiche creates. Worse, Styron is offering up, evidently, dangerous elements—incest, promiscuity, drinking bouts, extramarital affairs—as though this were a perilous and exciting life. Such characters are surely not ready for tragedy, maybe not for farce either; though irony, distance, repositioning might have created a novel that spoke *to* us rather than repeated things about us.

Although Styron hoped to gain Gothic breadth in *Set This House on Fire* (1960), it, also, is characterized by stereotypes, in characters, scenes, and narrative development. Every gesture appears in what was, by 1960, an exhausted form. Mason Flagg, whose murder remains the mysterious core that the narrator, Peter Leverett, must get at, fits Fitzgerald dimensions. His name, his Long Island background, his lovely but alcoholic mother, Wendy, his tycoon father all yield no new meanings. Flagg has been a typical dissolute youth: expelled from boarding schools, seducer of young girls, mighty drinker, hater of women even as he pursues them compulsively. To seek mystery in him is to look for diamonds in a swamp.

The narrator is himself like Nick Carraway in *Gatsby:* laid back, a lawyer (although how he achieved the discipline for that is a better mystery than Flagg), a footloose young man for whom nubile women are always available. The name of the game, for all, is surface cool, while below destructiveness looms. Another character who sets out to destroy himself is Cass Kinsolving, a Southerner like Peter, a painter who never appears to paint; but, withal, a prodigious drinker while he lives in Sambuco, not far from Salerno.

The novel moves from New York to Sambuco and then relocates in and around Cass's place in South Carolina. The conflict is old world versus new; and in this format, while Sambuco appears like the new Eden, it proves to be more evil than paradisiacal. Styron uses Italy for its great beauty, but a grandness that only barely disguises a terrible corruption, like Rappaccini's Garden. We are, already, entering that dispossessed Garden which looks ahead to *The Confessions of Nat Turner.* Along the way, Peter meets lovely women; of course, it helps that Flagg is involved with the making of films—his father became a film distributor and left Mason a fortune. The young ladies have marvelously developed bodies, as well as expressionless faces, and for depth they have all been hurt. Flagg's latent companion, whom he knocks around when he feels threatened, is a gorgeous blonde, who begins to confide in Peter. She recalls Flagg's mother, Wendy, herself a replay of Zelda Fitzgerald.

Given such materials, Styron can only generate further clichés. He tries innovation with frequent flashbacks, but they are perfunctory gestures: swinging mechanically between Sambuco and, mainly, Cass's South Carolina refuge. What is remarkable about Styron's treatment is his unawareness, as he fills in backgrounds, of how that material had been exhausted well before he got to it, or how his characters themselves undermine his claims for them. Early on, Flagg says: " 'Petesy, there's more twat up on this mountaintop [Sambuco] than a wise man could possibly handle.' " *That* is the man whose mystery remains at the center of the novel. His level of discourse hardly reinforces what Peter claims for him, his charm, intellectual abilities, his conversational talent, his interest in the arts. When Flagg speaks, it is platitudes: " 'Sex is the last frontier. . . . In art as in life, Peter, sex is the only area left where men can find full expression of their individuality, full freedom.' " Compared with this, the discussions of sex in Mailer's novels are metaphysical dialogues.

Potentially, we have compelling conflicts: the drifting, laid-back Peter Leverett (a hare of sorts, passive, yet filled with fifties Beat possibilities) forced to confront someone of tremendous evil charm in Mason Flagg, a man with qualities of a Dostoyevsky protagonist in his quest for perversion and self-destruction. At this level, the confrontation—alternating attraction and withdrawal—could be played out in several dimensions: individual, social, even political. In this scenario, Flagg would be a wealthier and more with-it Neal Cassady, attempting to flee internal demons. Peter Leverett would be a more established Sal Paradise. The novel would confront several of the issues we find in *On the Road,* which Styron in any event seems to replay. An implied political situation would emerge: the politics of individual behavior, the politics of varying ideologies, the politics of public and private, what we associate with the irresolvable conflicts of the 1950s.

Styron, however, dissipates these or similar opportunities, by confronting his characters with stereotypes and, even more, with a prose style that draws on platitudes. The language is stale—people are silent for a moment, specks of sadness predominate, scenes are dreary or marvelous, voices are modulated, mouths are foul or sweet, breasts are hard or luxuri-ous like melons, butts are bouncy; the very verbs are tired—people gaze, or wonder, or reflect. Dulled by language and perceptions, the reader cannot possibly respond to the depths Styron is leading him into. And yet his aim is to be a modern-day Vergil leading us, the readers, into the Inferno of Italy; not the Italy of travel posters or even of Rossellini movies, but an Italy of Dante's subterranean regions. Mason Flagg may have a palace set on a hill in Sambuco, but he is a man of depths. In *The Recognitions,* Gaddis has a somewhat similar young man in Wyatt Gwyon, although his painting ability provides a focus to his life, lacking in Flagg. Wyatt was far more likely to "set this house on fire," Styron's pretentious use of Donne's phrase, than is Flagg.

Another key in this triangular arrangement is the painter Cass Kinsolving, an extremely unstable young man, with a loving (Catholic) wife and several small children, all of whom appear angelic. He is self-educated, a terrible drinker, and a man who is drawn to scrapes. He gambles away the family's last money, or tries to, spends nights in the police station, and yet appears endearing to his immediate family and to Peter.

Part II of the novel works out what happened. Styron tells us from the start Cass has killed Flagg, and that creates the mystery not of killer but of why and how. The shift now is to Cass, whose life has several sides, and these unresolved aspects will provide the narrative substance. We do know Flagg has humiliated Cass, making him perform obscenely and demeaningly in front of gathered guests. Why does Cass do this? What is his relationship to Mason Flagg?

Cass is filled with guilt—as a teenager he was involved with a man who punished a black family severely for having fallen behind on radio payments—and he is, as noted, a drunk, unable to function as husband or father. Having entered the valley of hell, he must rise through Purgatorio to some glimpse of redemption. Appropriately, his ascent comes by way of temptation, a young and very appealing peasant girl named Francesca Ricci (riches). Cass takes Francesca into his household—although he does not sleep with her—and sells his soul to Flagg in exchange for medication for her dying father. Flagg now holds Cass's soul, and he squeezes by way of humiliation. Also, he indicates interest in Francesca. As Styron presents the dramatic conflict, there are several crossing patterns: Cass and Francesca, who poses for him and offers herself; Cass and Flagg, who is interested in a "sexual circus," including Cass's wife; Flagg and

Francesca, who eludes him until he corners and rapes her.

Cass's relationship with Francesca is, for him, a form of salvation, especially since he resists sex. It must be through her that he can reach beyond the nullity that defines him. And yet, once again, the prose fails. Language turns the unfamiliar to the familiar, and breeds contempt. In the reduction, she is his angel; he is the devil. Yet he must not defile her.

The demonic Flagg does, and Cass vows to kill him. But Cass also believes Flagg has murdered her, which was untrue; that the village idiot accomplished. Nevertheless, Cass kills Mason and reaches the end of the road " 'and had found there nothing at all. There was nothing.' " An Italian policeman lies for Cass—his deep guilt will be his punishment—and Flagg's death is recorded as suicide after his murder of Francesca. Cass is released; the Furies are appeased and he can free himself. He returns with his family to South Carolina, gives up booze, paints successfully, and tells his story to Peter. The latter is himself relieved of *his* guilt when a motorcyclist he had struck on his way to Sambuco miraculously comes out of his coma.

Peter's guilt over striking the motorcyclist, Cass's guilt over his past as well as his inability to handle his life, Mason Flagg's demonry—all must be exorcised or resolved. Francesca is the innocent means by which the demons are driven out, her destruction the precipitant. Angel and temptress, the peasant girl represents the part of Italy that is both saved and damned. A political fable lies here: Francesca ruined by the aristocratic Flagg, almost saved by the lower-class Cass; her fate somehow intertwined with the middle-class Peter. Flagg destroys her, Cass avenges her, and Peter is allowed to free himself of Italian-based guilt. Standing outside the two "great powers," Peter can avoid the destructiveness of each, working through in personal terms cold war choices. Salvation lies not in Europe, but in the healing life of a South Carolina Eden.

In *Cannibals and Christians,* Normal Mailer offered a sweeping critique of his contemporaries that was as much an assessment of himself, lamentation for his stalled career intermixed with hopes and plans. Jones and Styron were once considered Mailer's chief rivals for "Numero Uno" among American novelists, and his commentary on *Set This House on Fire* must be viewed within that context. Mailer speaks of being present at a Styron reading of excerpts from Jones's *Some Came Running,* the book itself a mixture of insights and tastelessness, at which Styron drew laughs for the poor writing. Mailer laughs, but detests his reaction, for a good novel from Jones would have forced him into serious competition, shaped him up. Much of this is posing, with Mailer using sports lingo, especially boxing terms, one-on-one competition; but it gets him musing about Styron and *Lie Down.* "A bad maggoty novel. Four or five half-great short stories were buried like pullulating organs in a corpse of fecal matter, overblown unconceived philosophy. Technicolor melodramatics, and a staggering ignorance about the passions of murder, suicide and rape." He adds that whenever Styron became stuck, he turned to landscape: "More of the portentous Italian scenery blew up its midnight storm."

Mailer's observations about *Lie Down* could well fit an assessment of his own *The Deer Park* (1955), his novel before *An American Dream.* With *The Deer Park,* it becomes clearer that *Barbary Shore* was not an aberration in Mailer's work. He was misjudging his talent by yearning to be a Jewish Hemingway, when, in fact, he could have aspired to be an American Kafka. Mailer, evidently, caught by the fifties, wanted to write in *The Deer Park* a vast, philosophical treatise of good and evil, virtue and vice, decency and corruption. Desert D'Or is his legendary place where Arcadian fantasies turn to tarnished gold. His epigraph on the historic Deer Park, where the innocent were thrown to the sexual lions, comes from a life of Louis XV, but his real meaning is derived from Dostoyevsky. The devils that lurk within are not only sexual but the demonic ideas that govern everything we do. One devil recommends *la dolce vita,* epitomized by Hollywood and its aspiring stars. Ratings are all, and they govern personal life, marriage, publicity, where outer and inner meet. Set against this is the desire of Mailer's protagonist and narrator, Sergius O'Shaugnessy, not to capitulate but, among the fleshpots, to discover himself and stay the route as a writer. Mailer's working out of literary problems involves as much masculine virility as it does literary talent.

Sergius, the central intelligence, Mailer's embodiment of innocence confronted with evil outside (Hollywood values) and within (his napalm bombing of Koreans), is a lackluster creation. His efforts at writing, which, somehow, will purify him, are almost afterthoughts; and his extraordinary appeal to Hollywood types—he is twenty-three and not overly bright—is forced. He would seem to be just another pretty face, Mailer's conception of the Gentile stud. His appeal as an innocent should have been handled ironically or parodically, but Mailer could not find the right tonal attitude for Sergius. At one point, Eitel mentions Joyce, and for the young man this could have been the name of a starlet. How can we have faith in a young writer who does not know Joyce, and how can Eitel, an intelligent man, treat him seriously after this? Yet Sergius, at the end, hears Eitel whisper to him, in his imagination, that he must go forth like Stephen Dedalus: "And with the pride of the artist, you must blow against the walls of every power that exists, the small trumpet of your defiance." Sergius, a refugee from Desert D'Or, not only runs a bullfighting school; he serves, at night, as a bull servicing the local talent. One, a Jewish girl with muscles, has never achieved orgasm, and Sergius's mission is to be her first, especially since he is a kind of landmark stud. To get Sergius in bed is a mission for young women: "I was one of the credits needed for a diploma in the sexual humanities." Mailer or Sergius had foreseen the "star-fucking" phenomenon: singles or groupies who gain their own notoriety by way of the celebrities they sleep with. After a good deal of dialogue about Denise Gondelman's shrink—whether he is purely Freudian or an eclectic who accepts Reich's category of "phallic narcissist"—Sergius begins to work, forward and aft. It turns out that aft does it, and she begins to float through an orgasm. Sergius proves here, with Denise, as does Rojack later with his wife's German maid, that the way to reach bottom is through the bottom.

Had Mailer, from the first, been able to evaluate his talents, he could not have gotten himself into *The Deer Park.* For any novel of this kind, which mixes cynicism and idealism in equal doses, characterization must be on target. Except perhaps for Eitel, Mailer writes around and around, words seeking a focus, and his attempts at females—self-discovery failing him here—fall into melodramatics. Lulu, the actress, is a throwaway—she performs, she is on stage, she plays roles we expect. Elena, who has no talents, is a noble effort, since she is a personal disaster, and anyone involved with her is drawn into her own inability to function well. When Eitel is down, he is drawn to her; but once he achieves success after he serves as stool pigeon for the congressional committee, he begins to move beyond her. Yet Elena fails as a character because Mailer cannot perceive her, except as a victim for men who temporarily find her desirable. Even her physical vitality does not move us; nor do we believe she could engage so many intelligent men beyond some sexual groping. If Sergius is an artificial Hemingway, then Elena is a retread Zelda.

In Eitel Mailer attempted to probe self-discovery, followed by self-deception, and then an effort to deal with both sides of an incomplete being. Eitel, however, is given away by his name—"I tell"—and long before he does tell the committee what he knows of subversion in Hollywood circles, we know he will give way and also fail Sergius, who believes in him. Eitel, then, becomes a cog in Sergius's education, when Mailer had apparently brought him along as a person in his own right. Just as Eitel and Sergius fail to connect, others strut without making a parade. There are characters and characters, actors and actresses, perverted young men like Marion Faye, or middle-aged women like his mother, Dorothea, homosexuals and bisexuals, swinging couples, swinging singles, the typical film mogul. There are also the inevitable scenes of gambling, coupling, drinking, and eating, little of it coherent.

Still another miscalculation is Elena's letter (Chapter 23) to Eitel, an attempt at an honest confession. The letter is just too old-fashioned; it recalls Tess's to Angel Clare in the Hardy novel—a curious device for a modish novel rejected by seven publishers. Further, the tone and style of the letter (barely literate—i.e., direct and honest) clash with the content, not as dramatic contrast but as something stupefyingly boring and misplaced. Mailer is trying to explain Elena long after the reader has slid away from her. In its way, the letter highlights Mailer's difficulty in finding an appropriate style for *The Deer Park.* She has one style, Sergius another, Eitel a third, none of them cohering, as if dragged in from other times and places. Trying to move outside the naturalism of *The Naked and the Dead,* Mailer attempted a Hemingway style, a Fitzgerald style, a Nathanael West style (Marion Faye, from *The Day of the Locust*), but nowhere is there a Mailer style. The hodgepodge of styles becomes a maze of mannerisms. Mailer's attempt to justify the revisions to the book loses sight of the frail base on which the alterations would be made.*

---

*In *Advertisements for Myself,* Mailer displays some revisions and their basis: "Now, after three years of living with the book, I could at last admit the style was wrong, that it had been wrong from the time I started, that I had been strangling the life of my novel in a poetic prose which was too self-consciously attractive and formal, false to the life of my characters, especially false to the life of my narrator who was the voice of my novel."

Before *The Deer Park,* Mailer had come to a crossroads and attempted to work through with "The Man Who Studied Yoga" (1952). He had achieved the great, and unexpected, success of *The Naked and the Dead;* he had charted new ground, so he thought, with *Barbary Shore.* The internal confusion was there, as it would be in so many postwar novelists who gained immediate recognition with a first novel. Mailer had to change directions in his work when his reputation depended on a kind of fiction he could not repeat. It was a difficult time, the most difficult for the novelist who yearns to be a great writer, a conscience for his age; and he recognized early on that reviewers would praise him for the meretricious in his work, not the daring. "The Man Who Studied Yoga" is, in many ways, a cover story for these internal struggles; for Sam Slovoda is selected by the nameless narrator as his prototypical writer, and Sam carries with him much of Mailer's own burden. Not that Sam is a famous novelist; he is a cartoonist who yearns to be a serious writer, but is blocked. Sam is settled into a bourgeois existence, sees a psychiatrist named Dr. Sergius, and has desire for a wife who is often cold and unresponsive.

The freeing process—that line of liberation in which Mailer was to explore the connections between sex and time—comes in the form of a home pornographic movie. Sam and his wife, along with two other bourgeois couples, excite themselves with the prospect and then with the movie itself. Sam is "disordered" by the experience, and he dreams of diverse responses. The devil, in the shape of the unnamed narrator, suggests: " 'Destroy time, and chaos may be ordered.' " Mailer's message to Sam is Mailer's message to himself: break through existing forms into disorder, where life is more intense, driven, energetic. This breakthrough Mailer would experience not in fiction, certainly not in *The Deer Park,* where he had placed his bets, but in his essay "The White Negro" (1957). In the torpor of half sleep, Sam repeats the message, but rather than awakening to its import, he reverts to sleep. In sleep, he will continue with his Dr. Sergius, he will avoid pain, so he thinks; but the devilish narrator, that infiltrator of the soul, knows that in avoiding pain he "succeeds merely in avoiding pleasure." Sam makes the compromise that Mailer vows not to make himself. In his fight to counter the Grand Inquisitor, Mailer makes Dr. Sergius into Sergius O'Shaugnessy, a desolate urban apartment into Desert D'Or, and the porno movie into actual life.

With *The Natural** (1952), *The Assistant* (1957), *The Magic Barrel* (1958, stories from 1950), and several short pieces collected in later volumes, Bernard Malamud seemed both a unique voice and a worker in the Bellow field of alternating guilt and release. Together, they appeared to have given shape to the "Jewish renaissance," or the "Jewish novel," as many critics tagged the phenomenon. *The Magic Barrel* became one of the three famous collections of stories of the decade, along with Salinger's *Nine Stories* (1953) and Roth's *Goodbye, Columbus* (1959).

In all three Malamud books, we can relate his desire for authenticity of feeling and response to his sense of the fifties. *The Assistant,* like *The Natural* before it, attempts to cut through layers of artificial responses in order to discover what men live by. It is this exploration of how men live which energizes Malamud's work, not any formal sense of Jewishness. Malamud's historical Jewishness is connected to its ethical sense, and how that dimension can be achieved in lives that must acknowledge other impulses, whether sexual, familial, artistic, or emotionally divisive. The ultimate line for a Malamud character is the way in which he (not she) responds ethically. In this respect, it is idle to compare Malamud to other "Jewish writers," such as Roth, Mailer, or Heller. Bellow of *The Victim* seems a natural forerunner, but Bellow had himself moved on into very different modes by the 1950s, with *Augie March* at the beginning and *Henderson* at the end.

The Assistant, far more than *The Natural,* will define Malamud's unique world: post-Holocaust ethics, Jews and Gentiles intermingling in universal suffering, guilt, and penance; that consciousness of miracle which derives from faith in something beyond the self; the despair that precedes a deepening of ethical belief. If all this is Jewish, then Malamud is a Jewish writer; but I would argue that except for certain intonations of his prose, overtones of Yiddish, and varieties of humor, Malamud is exploring themes that belong to all people, responding to 1950s counterfeit in a deeply ethical way.

The element that endures in *The Assistant* is the grocery store in a run-down New York neighbor-

*Discussed briefly in my Introduction. A novel like *The Natural* makes the author of this study realize how artificial categories are, for the Malamud book "fits" in several areas: as an example of pastoral, as part of the reaction to the counterfeit 1950s, and of course as an intrinsic work, part of Malamud's own development.

hood, a store that is a sign of Jewish failure for Morris Bober, his wife, and his daughter of twenty-three, Helen. That store is a symbol of persistence, survival, joyless days. It has its Kafkan implications as an enclosed space which, in turn, has elements of eternal time. Certainly the store moves through historical time, proving in a way immortal, whereas the individuals tending it die. The store exists in one temporal dimension, the people who depend upon it in another. But the store also has almost a human existence, for like the individuals dependent on it, it thrives, then becomes ill; it waxes and wanes, seems near rock bottom, recovers, wavers, offers hope, then falls back. It is, most of all, a repository of exhausted desires and lost hopes; recoverable only at moments, needing less a king to rule it than an Osiris, less a Job than a schlemiel.

The store, then, is both a living organism and a waste land for the Bobers, a frontier of despair. It is, in this respect, parallel to Kafka's castle, beckoning with possibilities but beyond reach, causing more pain than pleasure, and yet enriching because of its demands. Neither the Bobers nor Frank Alpine, the interloper, can let go of the store; the suffering it causes is universal. Frank assumes that suffering is only Jewish, but by way of his involvement with the store, he, an Italian Roman Catholic, moves toward conversion, first with circumcision and then with vows. In a sense, the store, a modern God, has transformed him from sinner to believer; most of all, from a young man doomed to seeking pleasure to a mature man possessed by suffering, pain, deeper meanings. For Malamud, transformation of Gentile to Jew comes when the former prefers pain and suffering—and the deep joy implicit in that—to cheap, unearned pleasure.

It is in this area that, as we shall see, the novel runs aground. The store, with the Bobers as its moles, is almost a subterranean lair. The neighborhood seems hooded or veiled, hardly alive, the city a Kafkan necropolis. The customers buy in small amounts; like tiny animals or insects, they seem marginal, eating little, their lives remaining out of sight. The Polish woman who spends three cents each day on an unseeded roll (seeds would be Jewish) is a relentless pressure, forcing Morris and then Frank to open before anyone else shops. By appearing inexorably each day regardless of weather, store owner, conditions, she is, in a sense, the external equivalent of the inner elements of the store.

Like the store, she must be served; for her and her type, the owner is a prisoner, although the store is also a refuge, without which the owners would float toward disaster. When Morris cannot sell, an arsonist offers to burn it and the house for the insurance; and although Morris is tempted to do it himself, he resists. The store, accordingly, is connected to the very real world—pressures, demands, insistence; but also to the supernatural, as a place where gods reside, associated with fire and air, with forces of life and death. Morris almost dies of gas—the store has elements of a tomb; people are buried in it—and he finally dies after sweeping snow in front.

The run-down grocery store is connected in American fiction to those earlier naturalistic symbolic places—Death Valley in *McTeague,* the summer resort and Bittern Lake in *An American Tragedy,* the small town in Sinclair Lewis or Sherwood Anderson. Such places ordinarily act as giver and taker of light: for those who fit, the place is supportive; for those moving against the grain, it is destructive. But the place, regardless, has elements of magic, of the divine, of something indefinable. Some people try to figure out the formula, and they discover it, like Morris's neighbor Julius Karp, the liquor store dealer, or the Pearls, whose son Nat pursues Helen. We recall Arthur Miller's *Death of a Salesman,* Willy Loman and Uncle Ben, one missing the formula, one always finding it. Withal, the store is a dismal place that barely sustains life, a waste land within a waste land. It demands not a Fisher King but someone who can bear varicose veins.

This view of small life is unassailable. Malamud captures the immigrant experience of many Jews and Italians, those who tended tiny stores and hung on, in the hope their children would fare better. Helen speaks of college, attends part time, reaches out for something beyond. But even for her, moving toward assimilation, the store betokens separation from the American mainstream; for her to escape the store would be to evade that undefinable identification as a Jew.

By falling for Frank Alpine, she subconsciously does just that. Her parents fear not only Frank's marginality but losing a daughter to assimilation. By accepting Frank, she would be rejecting Jewish family, store, the God of her fathers. Malamud stresses that Morris Bober is not a good Jew in any formal sense; he stays open on Saturday, he does not follow the dietary laws, he sells pork products. From the Judaic point of view, he has long since been lost. Yet as a sufferer, he is seen by Malamud as intensely Jewish, Jewishness defined as suffering.

The problem for Malamud was to fit into this

scheme a Gentile who is almost the opposite of what the Jew stands for. Frank Alpine begins with a name that stands "outside" or beyond the Jewish pale—Alpino, someone from the heights. He comes, however, out of violent depths, in reality a man who aids in a holdup of the Bober store and then repents. He returns to help in the store he wanted to rob, a samaritan to help Morris, who had been struck on the head by Frank's accomplice. The story of Frank is that of a sinner's redemption, the Christian won over by the Jew's suffering and persistence. Malamud introduces Frank to the store, for the store is like the Babylonian exile, something to be endured until a better life, somehow, appears. If Frank becomes attached to the store, the premise is, he becomes a surrogate Jew, eventually a Jew. In this very area, the novel falters; for the conversion of the Gentile—a revamping of the more traditional conversion of the Jews—takes place in regions of Frank that Malamud cannot plumb.

What he offers up is the persistence of Frank to better himself through associating with gentle, decent people, to transform himself as a result of his love for Helen. Helen is somewhat misnamed, since she is no seductress, although she dreams of romance. Frank, however, is not a Paris who can remove her from a dull life, and what she finds in him is difficult to comprehend. Malamud does not demonstrate what shines through, except his persistence in the store, keeping it going when it should go under.

Whenever the novel moves away from that intense underground location, the store, the line of reasoning weakens. The transformation of Frank into a suffering Jew remains beyond what Malamud can motivate. The relationship between Helen and Frank—which develops in the local library and park—remains shadowy because we do not see his magnetism for her. Is he no more than an exotic bird, a forbidden quantity? She is far more attractive than he, physically, intellectually, morally. If salvation of the beast is the aim of this beauty, then here, too, the novel falters. The intensity of the store subsumes all other dimensions. Malamud functions best here as a naturalist with Kafkan pressures; when he departs from that not so strange combination, he weakens. The insistence on the Jewish experience, which seems at the very heart of the story, proves to be a weak link; whereas the store, which lies in some mythical, universal land, is the source of strength.

Helen, for example, is the stereotypical naturalistic victim: an attractive young lady yearning for a better life, hoping through education to put distance between herself and her parents, whom she cannot reject. Her years, salary, devotion are all sacrificed to hanging on; by the time her parents die, she will be beyond help. Her choices are threefold: her parents; a young man named Nat Pearl, who is all aspiration; and Frank, who offers depths, not heights. Pearl and Alpine are contrasted: the smooth assimilated Jew in law school, the rough, uneducated Gentile whose life will always be a struggle. The parents are immigration victims—those who escaped so as to try a better life, which turns out to be sheer toil, without pogroms.

The terms of the conflict are conventional, as conventional as Frank's efforts to repay the money he has stolen. These are tricks of plot which lack freshness, and the result is that those involved in them lose dimension. What remains is that store, all ears, eyes, and voices, an accumulation of the sorrows of generations of immigrant losers. Such is its intensity that Frank Alpine, despite goodwill, cannot become a part of it. To the extent that it is so intense, it remains a force of its own, a repository, not a golden treasure trove but a Pandora's box.

In the collection *The Magic Barrel* (1958), the titular story is rightly the most applauded. It is, in its way, a miracle of storytelling and shaping, a magical presence, like the barrel filled with human hopes. But in terms of Malamud's own development, the Fidelman story, "The Last Mohican," is more important. Fidelman has links to Finkle of "The Magic Barrel," to Levin of "The Lady of the Lake," to S. Levin of *A New Life,* even to Alpine of *The Assistant,* certainly to Lesser of *The Tenants* and to Jakov Bok of *The Fixers.* By the time of *Dubin's Lives* (1979), Malamud had found different strengths; Fidelman, who sought "new worlds" in order to write about Giotto, has discovered Arcadia in order, as Dubin, to write about D. H. Lawrence. Like Styron, Malamud found room for development.

In this area, we have the peculiar Malamud protagonist: a man who seeks, who rarely finds, and yet who maintains some hope he will find whatever he seeks. His Jewishness does not extend, usually, to forms of belief, but to a point of view or a tone. A victim, marked for suffering (Fidelman, Lesser, Bok, Bober, Levin), he is a survivor. Malamud's definition of Jewishness is opposite to that of Roth, who sees Jews as ambitious, full of self-display. Malamud's Jews are strangely outside any economic system, beyond any political system that can touch them, outside careers or professions. If they pursue a profession, they are, like Fidelman, failures at it for one reason or another. While they have some sense of their worth, they cannot find containers for it.

Malamud has structured a unique world for his people. When they are store owners (Bober), or fixers (Bok), or writers (Lesser), or painters (Fidelman), or baseball players (Hobbs)—still they are not classed or classified. They move well outside the categories we associate with Americans. Even their Jewishness is not a form of belief or adherence. Leo Finkle in "The Magic Barrel" is perhaps indicative: a rabbinical student without fervor, uncertain of his vocation, a borderline believer. Yet being Jewish is intensely important to Malamud's characters, for it identifies them with a kind of forbearance which fills out their lives. If they deny their Jewishness, or question that of others, they are rejecting an ethical center.

Fidelman, significantly, runs like a leitmotif through Malamud's work of the fifties and sixties, culminating in *Pictures of Fidelman,* in 1969. The collection *The Magic Barrel* is full of such characters. In "Angel Levine," the long-suffering tailor Manischevitz (a matzo of a man) finds a double in Alexander Levine, the black ghetto "Angel." That doubling of characters, of a man trying to break out juxtaposed to a man trying merely to survive, is so weighted in Malamud because he perceives human nature as a conflict of opposites trying (unsuccessfully) to resolve themselves. A shaky reconciliation arrives in a moment of faith or belief, as part of a larger ethical response to human needs. Malamud's ground, like Fidelman's, is always uneven, sloping this way or that; and that unevenness is associated with dualisms in his characters that are far more complex than a dialectic.

Finkle-Salzman in "The Magic Barrel" are embodiments of Fidelman, the story itself an updated *Miss Lonelyhearts.* West's presence fills the narrative, from the female rejects paraded before Finkle's eyes to the fabulous grotesqueness characterizing all relationships. Salzman, the marriage broker, becomes Finkle's "double," the man who, while purporting to resolve the rabbinical student's needs, confuses resolutions with undefined desires. In an imperfect world, Salzman's rejects are, also, imperfect. Too old, or crippled, or not pretty enough, or malformed and maladjusted, they have not forsaken hope: the marriage broker is the last line of their hopes, their Miss Lonelyhearts. His "magic barrel" contains the discards, that overflow of names and photos and résumés of those who are no longer in the active file. When the active file does not satisfy, he dips into the barrel; and in that container—magical because it is bottomless with the hopes and desperation of the female world

—he sees reflected, as it were, his own misery.

For Salzman is not solely a broker, he is a man broken by a wild daughter, a living adversary to every Jewish principle. Salzman's daughter has escaped from the small, poverty-stricken flat, out from the world of Judaic law based on deception, disguise, and lie. She has moved into the open, run from the "magic barrel" in order to fulfill her own life—and she is feral, a whore, a woman whose photograph has by mistake gotten into the file. She is a figure of life—at the end we glimpse her, dressed in white with red shoes—although for the man who marries her, she will prove deadly. Leo Finkle, the rabbinical student fearful of doing his own choosing, is chosen; his choice will destroy him, and yet he is driven to it when he observes her photo. Salzman "chanted prayers for the dead."

The "magic" of the story comes from the juxtapositioning of antithetical elements, the massing of bright detail against demeaning situations, the contrast and conflict between opposing human needs. Central to it all is the "Miss Lonelyhearts" positioning of the marriage broker, that link between eternal loneliness and some human source, however imperfect.

But beyond "The Magic Barrel," *The Magic Barrel* is a shaped experience, the various parallels of Finkle and Salzman culminating in the titular story. At nearly every stage of the thirteen stories, Malamud reaches for a motif that will come together in the final tale. "The First Seven Years," about a modern-day Jacob, feeds into Manischevitz of "Angel Levine," that into Levin-Freeman, the loser in "The Lady of the Lake," that into a greater loser, Fidelman, ending with the magic of the barrel, whose bottomlessness evokes art as much as lost hopes.

The collection *Pictures of Fidelman* (1969) stresses doubling—double lives, selves split in two, elements conflicting without chance of reconciliation, a self withdrawing from its own experience even while trying to break out.* Fidelman thinks of himself as a perfectionist, and one reason he has failed as a painter is his inability to be satisfied with his work. Such dissatisfaction fills out an entire "picture" or episode, "A Pimp's Revenge." That dissatisfaction, however, lies at the heart of more than one tale. It is the cross of Fidelman's life, for, unable to choose whether to

---

*The epigraph, from Yeats—"The intellect of man is forced to choose / Perfection of the life, or of the work"—fits not only the Fidelman stories but the protagonists of *The Natural, A New Life, The Fixer,* and others.

perfect his life or his work, he does neither. He is, by all measures, a failure; except, for Malamud, he has tried to live. He has lived for moments—a great love, an image on canvas, a temporary revelation of brush stroke, object, result—and such moments add up to a life.

Fidelman comes to Italy to study Giotto, but that act sets off a complex series of internal pressures. Sidetracked early on by Susskind, he is forced to confront his function. Fidelman is in a way escaping his life for the year off in Italy: escaping his failure as a painter by becoming an art historian researching Giotto. That escape is pure Malamud: the individual tries to carve out a new life by evading the former one. Yet that effort at evasion only intensifies his relationship to what has been evaded, and he finds himself not drawn into the new life but caught by the coils of the earlier.

So Fidelman must confront his messy internal experience even as he expects to escape into the beauties of Italy in general and Giotto in particular. Malamud now has his basic structural concept: as Fidelman moves into his present life (evasion), he returns on another level into the past (which cannot be evaded). This past includes failures, Jewishness, his condition as a sucker. A secular individual, Fidelman finds himself becoming more and more a character in a religious drama, at least in connection with Susskind, who asks for help from a fellow human being, a Jew appealing to a Jew in what may be a hostile atmosphere. Susskind, who has nothing, asks for sharing, because Jews must share in the land of the Gentiles. Fidelman, who has enough (although little), does not view Italy as hostile, rather as salvation for his fragmented personal life. As he starts to pull together the pieces, he avoids the larger scene, what Susskind calls the Jewish "question" or "situation." Like Asa Leventhal in Bellow's novel, he becomes a victim. The inevitable outcome is the loss of Fidelman's manuscript on Giotto, for the manuscript has come to epitomize his evasion of what he is. Susskind, who has destroyed the manuscript, says " 'I did you a favor,' " by which he means that the work was poor or, more likely, that Fidelman has deceived himself by focusing on Giotto.

In the fourth episode, Fidelman works on a painting to get it just right—once again the desire for perfection in an imperfect world—while an eighteen-year-old girl streetwalks to support them. He is a man so committed to his work that no personal act can inhibit him. What will save him, and her, is the painting, which keeps undergoing transformations, from mother and child, to sister and brother, to prostitute and procurer, reflecting stages of Fidelman's own life. Yet even when certain he can obtain an excellent price for it, he is dissatisfied. The need to reshape it is there, to achieve the absolute painting, the perfect image which will express something in Fidelman, a truth beyond truth.

In the final episode, the sixth, he has sunk deep into Venetian life—working only intermittently, carrying people across rivers when the canals overflow, a Charon, except that he is closer to hell than are those he ferries. During one flood, he meets a Venetian woman who, dissatisfied with her life, forms an attachment to Fidelman. One day, her husband, a glass blower, surprises them, and he takes Fidelman. They become a couple, and the former Giotto researcher becomes a glass blower. He is unable to achieve perfection there, and Beppo, his lover, criticizes his work as no different from his failed paintings. Fidelman has hit bottom. In despair, he rows back to Murano to work on what will be be his masterpiece, a heavy red bowl. It was "severe and graceful" and reminded him of "something the old Greeks had done." But the next day, when he goes for the bowl, it is missing. Perfection achieved is not to be retained, and Fidelman leaves Venice, sailing for America, where "he worked as a craftsman in glass and loved men and women."

"Pictures of Fidelman" as a title resonates: as his pictures, as views of him, as observations of the painter. The book is Malamud's portrait of the artist as a middle-aged man: pictures and portrait blending with each other. At each step, Fidelman destroys something in order to achieve himself as a man, or else destroys himself in order to attain some realm of art. He encapsulates the two decades following the war.

Although Malamud and Kurt Vonnegut, Jr., seem light-years removed from each other as novelists, their two early publications (in 1952), *The Natural* and *Player Piano,* demonstrate compatibility. For both were responding to the overall pastoral theme in American culture, with Malamud using baseball as an alternative existence to systems, Vonnegut a farm. Later in the decade, John Updike would begin his productive career where most writers end it, with depictions of old people's lives; but underlying his novel is a "poorhouse fair" and the values such an event insist upon, forms of pastoral. The persistence of the theme, here and elsewhere in the 1950s, as we have observed, makes strange bedfellows.

Player Piano takes its name from the "mechanical piano" which plays off a punched roll, without the necessity of a player. It suggests a mechanical principle applied to an art object, and it stands, in Vonnegut's gentle allegory, for the region of Ilium, in upper New York State, where machines, having proved more efficient than people, have replaced their operators. Only a few individuals remain to run the plant, and these are Ph.D.'s—managers, technocrats, special persons. Their lives move along on clearly prescribed, Skinner-like lines, and any display of individuality is controlled by a rising series of laws. Loyalty to the machine is loyalty to the state, the direct forerunner of Vonnegut's novel being *Brave New World* or *1984,* although in *Player Piano* life for the chosen few is relatively pleasant.

Life is divided into three parts, one section for managers, engineers, and civil servants; another for machines; and a third, across the Iroquois River, for the people, in an area called the Homestead. Relationships between managers and people are few, since the latter are losers. For the first hundred pages of the novel, Vonnegut's protagonist, Paul Proteus, accepts this view of his society and anxiously awaits word of his transfer from Ilium to Pittsburgh, the major leagues. Paul's wife, Anita, is a true technocrat's mate, in that her ambitions often exceed his.

But Paul would not be Paul, nor would he be Proteus, if Vonnegut did not mean change. Like his namesake—a forerunner of Billy Pilgrim and other Vonnegut reshapers—he undergoes a conversion and decides to try on different forms, play alternative roles. Such a course of action jeopardizes his life twofold, as he tests his loyalties and challenges the state's premise that his energies belong to the machine. This is very much an early 1950s fable, disenchantment with the postwar years having already set it. On several occasions, his position can be redeemed if he will testify about others, the McCarthy syndrome. Ed Finnerty is the "Communist" in the novel, a man who has rebelled against the machine and who represents choice. If Paul will oppose Ed, he will satisfy his boss, Kroner (the crown).

The alternative to machinelike Ilium comes in the form of a farm, the pastoral mode as salvation. The farm is decrepit, Dickensian in its coziness. Nothing runs on machine energy; human endeavor is all. The idea of the farm, then its acquisition, finally its human atmosphere convince Paul that he must experience something besides machine life, a mechanical wife (they exchange daily vows of "I love you"), and pursuit of power. He attempts to gain Anita's sympathy

for the farm, but she is appalled. Paul then breaks with his former life and joins a group of the people, the Ghost Shirt Society. He comes to write its manifesto: Paul's Epistle to the People, intended to reach "ghosts," men and women exiled by the machine. The manifesto lauds inefficiency, as long as it is human. Perfection, as represented by machines, is rejected: "That there must be virtue in inefficiency, for Man is inefficient, and Man is a creation of God."

Several plants are destroyed, and the revolution appears won; but the mechanists remain in major control and impose a blockade. For Paul and his cohorts, the time (six months) can be used to create a model society. But as rapidly as machines deteriorate, the people try to repair them: they are wedded to the machines as to their own lives. Human mind and human hand are no longer of significance, and they fail the revolution. Paul, Ed, and the others head toward capture and death; the walls of Ilium have indeed been toppled, but the transformation they had hoped for is lost.

Vonnegut's allegory or fable of men and machines has minimal life. Anthony Burgess's *A Clockwork Orange,* which moves around similar material, has intense verbal wit and a display of violence which jars the reader's sensibilities. Vonnegut's novel makes obvious points: America is losing its most valuable asset: its people, their abilities, their very hands; and machines, having invaded our souls, are transforming us. Eden is rapidly becoming unrecoverable. To regain Eden (the past, the golden age, a vision of Walden, old America), one must repudiate what is corrupting us. Burgess, under the sword of *1984,* argued similarly for his violence-prone but music-loving Alex. When machines "cure" Alex, he loses his delight in Beethoven and Bach. But despite the greater impact of the Burgess novel, both works sentimentalize the "lost Eden." What the machine takes away, man can deplete as well; which is not a defense of machines, but an argument recognizing imperfect man.

Like Barth in *Giles Goat-Boy* half a decade later, Vonnegut used science fiction modes to write about America and its relationship to itself, its policies, its humanitarianism, or lack of it. Vonnegut's geographical areas may be, in addition to earth, places he calls Mars, Mercury, Titan, and Tralfamadore, but he is, like Barth with his gigantic computer, working over questions of how we live and how we quantify our lives. For all its gadgetry and spatial sweep, *The Sirens of Titan* (1959) accommodates 1950s modes of thought, especially the cold war. The slogan or motto Vonnegut repeats is "Chrono-Synclastic Infundibula," a coinage which suggests places (funnels) that fit together so that all forms of truth are accommodated at once (the curved surfaces meeting in time, chrono-synclastic).

The main place that locates the meeting of such different truths is an area between earth and Mars, which Vonnegut calls Titan. The largest of the nine moons of Saturn, Titan has a life-support system similar to earth's: e.g., oxygen and a temperate climate. On Titan, Winston Niles Rumfoord and his dog, Kazak,* reside, materializing only at intervals on earth, which become great happenings. Rumfoord has infinite percipience, and with his foresight he can arrange events, or he can simply wait for them to occur. He is a punisher as well as a rewarder. Vonnegut has created a "god" residing in a mechanical system, whereas other planets contain creatures without will, sex, flesh, or humanity—simply mechanisms.

The spatiality of the novel comes in the intercrossing journeys of Malachi Constant, a rich spoiled Earthling, heading for Titan, where he hopes to find the three exquisite sirens; and Salo, the messenger from Tralfamadore, who becomes stranded on Titan because his machine breaks down and he awaits a replacement part. That part arrives with Malachi, whose son, Chrono, has been playing with it as his good-luck piece. Titan, then, becomes the crossing point, between the mysterious Salo and the transformed Malachi, the once billionaire now living a primitive existence and seeking happiness. Salo carries a sealed message, which, when unraveled, says "Greetings," a communiqué not of war but of friendship. He is himself a mechanical contrivance, as are all such " people" on Tralfamadore: having relied on machines, they have been transformed into them. And they now control events on earth: "Everything that every Earthling has ever done has been warped by creatures on a planet one hundred-and-fifty thousand light years away."

The interplay of events on Titan, the ultimate destination, involves several layers of perception: the three sirens are sculptured pieces of Titanic peat, made by Salo—therefore a mirage, illusions of beauty; the earth is controlled by machines, by way of Tralfamadore, which means well—sends greetings; Constant, the wealthy, indifferent man, must become

sentient and conscious of himself and others; Rumfoord, now that Salo and Constant are on Titan, must move to another part of the solar system. He does not die, but remains "there," all-knowing, a godlike figure behind the vastness of systems. When Salo's replacement part is discovered and his space machine repaired, he takes Constant back to earth, to Indianapolis, Indiana, where he dies; Mrs. Rumfoord has died on Titan, and Chrono has adapted to bird life and remains. Constant's final vision—the result of a hypnotic spell put on him by Salo—is of his only friend, Unk, whom he had executed on Martian orders. The novel is then resolved with Unk-Constant lofted into a heavenly blend of friendship and love, the message of *Götterdämmerung*. Inventive and imaginative as the novel is, Vonnegut sentimentalizes all, expands in order to reduce.

The need to go "outside" or "beyond" 1950s categories and assumptions, which energized Vonnegut's science fiction work, can be found in Richard Wright's *The Outsider* (1953), his last effort to make a big statement about marginality, underground existence, alternative forms of life in a counterfeit society.

The Outsider, the product of Wright's Paris years, is his major attempt at a novel in the modern mode. But it is also an extension of *Native Son,* with Cross Damon a grown-up, intellectualized version of Bigger Thomas. The theme is insistent, the right of the individual to direct his own life. Yet Cross Damon is only given the chance to express himself in a situation fraught with deception. When his death is announced in a Chicago train accident, he seizes the moment to escape who and what he is. He assumes different identities in an effort to get out from under his former life, which has become a personal, professional, and financial trap. He escapes not only a bad situation, but his own bungling of it.

Yet to escape it, he must play a constant game of deception, taking the name and birth certificate of a dead man, Lionel Lane, and gaining the draft card of a man who, consumptive, is unable to serve. In every respect, Cross Damon struggles to assert himself under the banner of an aborted life. His new life, literally, begins in the cemetery, his name on a headstone. Wright apparently planned a large statement on counterfeit life, deceptive views, an artificial society.

Playing through *The Outsider* are diverse modern elements, none of them, unfortunately, integrated. Wright, in fact, wanted it all at once, the whole modernist movement packaged in a single fiction. One of

*Reminiscent, perhaps, of Franklin D. Roosevelt and Fala; Eliot Rosewater in *God Bless You, Mr. Rosewater,* is another FDR figure. Knowing this makes no difference, however, in either novel.

the major problems comes when he dissipates the powerful modern elements with speeches which, while essential for his need to express what few other novelists were stating, work against modernism. What Wright missed in the sense of the new was its elliptical elements, obliqueness of presentation, paucity of words, understatement, efforts to mislead so as to create ironies and paradoxes, its use of surfaces to suggest gigantic chasms. The modernist elements are, specifically:

1. Use of Kierkegaardian section headings: "Dread" and "Despair" for the first and final ones; "Dream" and "Descent," Freudian aspects, for the middle two. Such headings, however, suggest a more cosmic scale than Wright can convey. Cross Damon, at twenty-six, even with considerable reading in philosophy behind him, does not move beyond his situation. Wright's headings cannot propel him into larger size.

2. Idea of the "outsider," which derives from Camus's "stranger." What made the Camus novel and protagonist work, however, was understatement, leaving large holes. Wright fears holes and fills in at every opportunity.

3. Sartrean notions of freedom. Wright turns Damon's life into contingency—that is, into discrete, disconnected, unrelated elements, matrix of the absurd. Once experience is viewed as such, then all pressure upon it comes from individual choice— Damon's sense of freedom. He can be free, he assumes, only when all experience is shaken into chaos. The train accident provides the external factor for this. The weakness of the idea is that even while he moves Damon into this situation, Wright insists that human acts are interrelated, that each man is more than a particle in a field of force. Author and character pull against each other.

4. Gide's gratuitous act. Ely Houston, the district attorney, perceives in Cross Damon a man capable of great crimes because he will commit a crime without motivation, as an act of amorality. His experience as a crippled person and his reading incline Houston to observe Damon as concerned with making a statement: " 'That no ideas are necessary to justify his acts. . . . Our mythical killer is as lawless as the other two' "—the Communist and the Fascist who appear to have killed each other, when actually both were slain by Damon. What weakens this assumption is that Damon does have some motive—he kills, first, to protect himself, and then he kills not as a "free act" but as a means of preserving his idea of freedom.

5. The Houston-Damon jousting. This recalls, of course, Raskolnikov and Porfiry in *Crime and Punishment,* the police officer toying with the criminal. But Wright weakens this by making Houston into a hunchback, which puts him on a par with Damon: physical disability equals blackness. It does not really work because Houston sounds pretentious rather than sly, and Damon's fascination with him is, in turn, pressured from the outside, from Wright's desire to find relationships between men, not from the dynamics of the situation.

These five categories of the novel are not cohesive, although each remains of great interest. Wright indicates at the end of *The Outsider* that the writing took place in 1952; and there is a hastiness, not to the writing, but to the conception. The lack of consistency is particularly disappointing because Wright had here several natural subjects, and the intelligence working on the material indicates he had absorbed whatever he needed. But he demonstrates insufficient ground plan, lack of distance on ideas that took hold of him very rapidly in his French stay. If we view him as Harry Ames in John Williams's novel *The Man Who Cried I Am,* he was moving with frenzy, on several fronts; fiction was only one of the arenas.

None of this, however, should consign the novel to oblivion. It is of great interest, not only as part of Wright's own development, but historically in terms of how blacks in the early 1950s were reacting fictionally to their experience as postwar Americans. For *The Outsider* was written in the same year *Invisible Man* was published; and the two, like the obverse sides of a coin, give us sliding portraits of the black experience. Ellison moves us with irony and paradox, using mordant wit and Negro humor to deny spatiality to his unnamed protagonist; giving him a refuge, finally, in a clean, well-lighted place where his invisibility can burn brightly. Wright rejects irony for political and social statement. Strikingly, perhaps, he denies that Cross Damon's situation is the result of his blackness—"for he alone had been responsible for what he had done to Gladys [his wife] and Dot [girl friend]. His consciousness of the color of his skin had played no role in it."

Damon argues that his intense concern with himself had led him not "to cast his lot wholeheartedly with Negroes in terms of racial struggle. Practically he was with them, but emotionally he was not one of them." Part of the weakness of Wright's conception is here; for Damon's blackness, whatever his view of it himself, has helped to create him and not simply his own struggle "for the realization of himself." Ellison's unnamed protagonist is always reminded he is black; he would like to be more neutral, but he is never permitted that.

Two aspects of blackness lie here. One factor is that Ellison's protagonist is an innocent, almost a schlemiel. He wants to be simply an American, and to achieve the way white Americans do. Cross Damon, however, needs to break out—an imposed modernism, one senses, since Wright presents him as a rotter from the start. He lacks responsibility in every family situation, deserting his wife and three sons as well as his mistress, who is pregnant. He has not earned our interest in his freedom, and when he seizes it after his train accident, we have no real frame of reference for him. Ellison's frame of reference for his protagonist is secure: he is damned whatever he does until he becomes invisible—i.e., himself.

Damon goes to New York and becomes an avenger. As with most Wright protagonists, he contains within himself an intense desire to display violence. Having killed in Chicago to protect his identity, he acts out a Wright fantasy by eliminating both communism and fascism in New York, two Communists and one Fascist. But this does not clear the field, for now he must live with the idea that he loves the woman whose husband he has killed, a situation that leads into that of *Savage Holiday* and turns modernism into old-fashioned melodrama.

In one way or another, James Gould Cozzens, by now a seasoned novelist, Frederick Buechner, still an apprentice, and John Updike, a beginner in longer fiction, all found modes of conciliation with 1950s paradoxes and discordances. They touch on the counterfeit, but their responses are quite different from those of most of their older and younger contemporaries, in that they have discovered areas of compromise (Cozzens), religious faith (Buechner), and pastoral splendor (Updike) as alternative, viable forms of life. In Buechner and Cozzens, at least, I feel that the life they propose is part of the very counterfeit they hope to counter; that, in fact, they do not respond to counterfeit, they blend with it. Buechner's response in *The Seasons' Difference* (1952) is the purest, a revelatory experience by one Peter Cowley, a visitor to the summer house of Sara and Samuel Dunn. As the others put it, Cowley sees God under a tree, but rather than "observing" God, Cowley has had some presentiment of God's immanence. This experiences distinguishes him from the others, who

are there to have a good time; Cowley's experience, as any sacred experience in a secular society, is perceived as an intrusion, as artificial, as itself counterfeit.

Buechner insists on the validity of the experience, suggesting that those who view it as an intrusion are themselves counterfeit, that is, contravening human feeling. Yet the vision or presentiment is wasted unless shared. Attempts to share it fail, of course, and even lead to tragedy. Christ's simplicities become infinitely complicated in a secular society; so that the most innocent element appears corrupt.

Buechner's style is pseudo-James, a kind of religious version of Louis Auchincloss, and it does not lend itself to religious experience; nor to his efforts to make others feel guilt at their distance from such an experience. Characters caught in an essentially artificial style (pseudo-James is quite different from James) cannot have an authentic life, a problem Updike's characters will also have as they attempt to swim upstream against his tide of words.

James Gould Cozzens, in *By Love Possessed* (1957), on the contrary, had evolved a prose style that was perfectly coordinated with his sense of life as compromise. Yet despite that prose, *By Love Possessed* experienced one of the strangest passages through best-sellerdom of any postwar novel; simply to engage the book at *that* level is instructive in terms of 1950s counterfeit.

Except for Dwight Macdonald's vitriolic attack on the novel, it garnered highly favorable reviews which suggested that great literature was, finally, at hand. Predictably, *The New Yorker,* with its antimodernist bias in the fifties, offered Brendan Gill's assessment ("Summa cum Laude") that "No American novelist of the twentieth century has attempted more than Mr. Cozzens attempts in the course of this long and bold and delicate book." James, Dreiser, Hemingway, Dos Passos, Faulkner, and Fitzgerald are eliminated from contention. *Saturday Review,* also predictably, was lavish in its praise, with Whitney Balliett (of *The New Yorker*) calling the novel brilliant and Cozzens the most technically adroit American novelist alive. Ellison, Gaddis, Barth, Mailer, Styron were shot down here. The American Academy of Arts and Letters weighed in with its William Dean Howells medal for fiction, awarded only every five years. *Reader's Digest* bought condensation rights; film rights went for a quarter of a million. *Time* magazine entered with a cover story, and John Fischer, in *Harper's,* touted the book and its author as of Nobel Prize caliber, his argument being that Cozzens showed us, "more revealingly than did any other contemporary writer," how we live.

The novel has, in fact, dated badly. In some ways, the supportive critics—and especially Fischer—were correct: Cozzens had caught the small-town equivalent of the stodge and complacency that Eisenhower generated. His was a golf generation: a culture of small Americans (car dealers, insurance men, self-made millionaires) who entered government and disdained cities, blacks, urban problems; men whose conservative views reflected a routine of club dances, social drinking, swimming pools, children in college, suburban homes; whose sexual lives only rarely went beyond marriage; who firmly believed in a dispossessed Eden as a true pastoral, insisting on the fantasy as the real thing.

Arthur Winner, Cozzens's protagonist, is the small-town success story, the perfect counterfeit man: there is an Arthur Winner senior before him, then a solid education and law school, entrance into the family firm, an easy, comfortable existence; and most of all, passions that can be kept at low ebb, no trouble from his emotional life. Winner is so constituted that it would seem Cozzens had read Riesman on anomic man—someone ungoverned, maladjusted—and decided to create the other, a man who purports to be inner-directed but who really receives his message from others.

Winner is the perfect personal reflection of what Eisenhower hoped his political position would bring America: stultification at home, peace abroad. By his rejection of the entire introspective modernist mode, Cozzens has settled easily into an Edwardian type of fiction, although the self-consciousness of his style lacks the easy precision of those earlier writers, Wells, Galsworthy, or Bennett. Not untypical is the pseudo-Jamesian description of Mrs. Kovac, the mother of a young woman who claims she has been raped by Ralph, the brother of Arthur Winner's secretary: "Conceivably, the reaction would be that of Veronica Kovac's mother—fury at the author of, not so much perhaps Joan's [Ralph's fiancée], as his, shame. How dared she let fingers be pointed at her— his [Moore, Joan's father] child; bearing his name? Could a suggestion that some blame must attach to the parents be ventured, that someone's blind inattentiveness, someone's stupidities of disregard, someone's neglects of indifference, must have been chief factors in making this predicament of Joan's possible?" Punctuation should not blind us to Cozzens's point that the rape victim is more to blame than the alleged rapist. What is of cultural importance is that an immensely sophisticated audience viewed Cozzens as the great hope, the counter to modernist experimentation, or American modernism—which often meant obscenity, extremes of behavior, lack of respect for women, the elderly, and fools.

"Love conquers all," Cozzens asserts at the beginning, but while offering his theory, Cozzens seems unaware of his practice: that love does not conquer all but threatens all and must be conquered. Every form of it is a threat: sexual love (Marjorie Penrose, the wife of Winner's crippled law partner), love of God (Catholicism), love of child (discipline is preferred), love of wife (her body, not her person), love of self (only a public mask is recognized). Winner wins by exclusion, whereas Cozzens wants us to view him as winning by conquering temptation. "Agreed, agreed! Victory is not in reaching certainties or solving mysteries; victory is in making do with uncertainties, in supporting mysteries." Winner's stream of words here is a complete falsification of the book's thrust; not continuous with it, but continuous with the very modernist tradition Cozzens has eschewed throughout. Words and actions pull against each other. There have been no mysteries, but rather hard-headed decisions. When Winner discovers, from Penrose, that their partner has been embezzling funds for at least twelve years, he decides to keep quiet rather than ruin himself and Penrose. It is reason, not grappling with inexplicables, that motivates Winner. His words belong to another novel, another novelist.

So much is occurring beyond Cozzens's sense of what his material means—essentially an incomprehension so narcissistic that only self-love dazzles—that no observation can be trusted, and stylistic acrobatics must be viewed as cover. The style is aimed at conserving, at not giving an inch to all that modern muck threatening the golf (and Tory) generation; whereas the material grafted on is not a demonstration of aspects of love, but of that mucky life which must be put down. In a book that is almost contemporaneous with *By Love Possessed,* Gaddis wrote of the need for recognitions—revelations, insights, moments of truthfulness—even when forgery and counterfeiting are the means of arriving at them. Cozzens has moved in the opposite direction: toward recognitions not arrived at, toward forgeries (of feeling) which lead nowhere, toward counterfeit in its sense of disguise, not revelation. Cozzens's town of Brocton, in its disguise of the real, serves as a true reflection of the Eisenhower years, not as a flawed Arcadia, but as a counterfeit Eden. Those who overpraised the novel were messengers of cultural mediocrity, deceived by their own fantasies of America.

Unlike Cozzens, who had lost his bearings, the young John Updike in his first novel, *The Poorhouse Fair* (1958), knew exactly where he was. What we find, however, is that the prose came too readily, replaced spaces and connections where meaning should lie, and became at once both admirable and destructive. Applauded too young for his feats—and his use of language is a feat—Updike failed to reassess, and words plunged in when they had little to wrap themselves around.*

> The disc of the sun was no longer seen. Opaque air had descended to the horizon, hills beyond the housetops of the town. On one side, the northern, a slab of blue-black, the mantle of purple altered, reared upward; on the other, inky rivers tinged with pink fled in one diagonal direction. Between these two masses glowed a long throat, a gap flooded with a lucent yellow whiter than gold, that seemed to mark the place where, trailing blue clouds, a sublime creature had plunged to death. . . . Off to the south the rivulets of dark vapor left in the wake of the catastrophe broadened into horizontal pale by contrast to the deepening sky behind them. Upon the terraces of these ranged clouds blackish embryos of cumulus stood on their tails like sea horses or centaurs performing. As the patients [the old people of the poorhouse] watched, the golden chasm shaded, through faint turquoise, into blue, and clouds propelled by evening winds trespassed its margins.

Language moves on majestically, with a princely cadence of its own, somewhat "purplish," but firm and resonant for a very young writer. He can write. And he knows he can write. And the writing here has almost no connection to what the novel is doing, or where it is going. He is marvelous on weather effects, the way in which the climate will bear upon a "poorhouse fair." "The air turned white; a fork of lightning

---

*John Aldridge was particularly harsh on the novel, calling it a book "essentially of style and terribly oblique and opaque and tinily inward observations of people." He said it demonstrated Updike could work well in an outmoded convention, although one would expect that in a very young writer. Aldridge commendably refused to bend before the popular reviewers who lavishly praised Updike, as well as Cozzens, Styron, O'Hara, and several others.

hung above the distant orchards, shocking each spherical tree into relief. Seconds later the sound arrived. The clouds above formed a second contingent, with its own horizon; a bar of silver stretched behind the nearly tangent profiles of the farthest hills and clouds. Again lightning raced down a fault in the sky."

This is honest descriptive writing. It goes off here and there—"each spherical tree" or "a bar of silver stretched"—but it is not hollowed out, as some of Styron or Mailer, where pretentiousness overwhelms. It does share one element with them: it shouts to the reader that the writer can handle words. Updike here is writing about poorhouse people who are very old, Hook well over ninety, many of the others not far behind. Updike is the sole young thing around.

Here is an author in his early to mid-twenties writing not about parents or even grandparents, but greatgrandparents—another era, in fact. The people speak of Lincoln and McKinley and Grover Cleveland as contemporaries, not of recent politics. By the time of the Depression, they were already old. They are shrewd, but slow; careful of what they have, which is very little; aware of mortality, of how little time is left, of diminishing energies. Against them, the author is a demon of energy, with fifty years of life left. The excesses of disproportion emerge in the descriptive passages; the author, while sympathetic to the old, shines by contrast. Since he does not expect the old and poor to be anything but what they are—and the novel succeeds very well here—he puts pressure on himself; and the long descriptive passages, the reveling in words and phrases, are Updike's way of calling attention to himself.

He reveals, this early in his career, that his talent lies in the short short story (as against that which runs over 7,500 words); that he is, essentially, a *New Yorker* writer. There is nothing pejorative here; but if we attempt to get behind the extravagant praise of reviewers, we must cut to the nub. Even *Poorhouse Fair*—brief at 50,000 words—is a series of vignettes, short fictions given associations and continuity by way of the central image of the poorhouse and the fair planned for that day on which the novel takes place. With great skill, Updike moves in and out of the consciousness of a number of old people, being most successful with Hook, who is ninety-four but sane, and Gregg, who is a generation younger but going crazy. There are several others—Mrs. Mortis, who makes quilts but has no use for money; Lucas, who suffers from a blinding toothache. The old enjoy their dignity, and what is particularly appealing is their refusal to be romantic about their situation: they are old, close to dying, and poor. Nothing will alter that.

Updike has, in a sense, started at the end of his career. His characters, from another era, have nothing but shreds, and many of them have forgotten what they once were. It is all receding. One would like to see some allegorical resonance here—America as fading, after the war, into a form of kindly senility, power passing over, all supervised by a benevolent prefect, here Conner, a kind of Eisenhower figure. Updike's book refuses to be manipulated into larger significance. There are the doughty old, and there is Updike hovering along the margins with his typewriter poised for a beautiful passage here, a lovely phrase there. It is painted in, all the squares. And it is lovely, vignettes of a summer day that turns to rain and spoils the fair, and then becomes pleasant toward later afternoon and allows the fair to continue. It is just that.

A NOTE ON SEQUENCES

In comparison with their English contemporaries, American novelists do not have many second acts. This paucity of sequential novels is connected to our social expectations, associated with our need for movement and escape. The lack of second or third acts, no less fourth and fifth, goes deeper than its linkage with rapid change; it is tied to our optimism, our desire to break from predetermined forms, to free ourselves from the historical past, emerging into that purer atmosphere of the pastoral, which promises liberation. The sequence implies limited options, whereas the American writer offers unrestricted freedom. It may prove a chimera, but it is there. No wonder that the American character is doom-ridden, for he leaves behind him all the protections that sequences provide, relies on his own devices, and must, like Pynchon's rockets, eventually fizzle out after achieving his zenith.

Thomas Berger's Reinhart trilogy (*Crazy in Berlin,* 1958; *Reinhart in Love,* 1962; *Vital Parts,* 1970) demonstrates many of the traps facing a sequence. After a promising start, the novels have nowhere to go. Carlo Reinhart is a kind of precursor of Heller's Yossarian, a survivor in the army who finds himself in Berlin with the war just ended, the city in ruins, Americans as conquerors. Berger's plan is ambitious, more than putting an all-American boy into postwar Germany and letting him loose. The "crazy" in the title refers not only to the mad chaos of the scene, but

to going crazy in a situation that defies reason. Reinhart finds Berlin a crazy place, but near the end of the novel he, too, goes crazy or appears to after a violent run-in with two German thugs. Berger works on two levels: that of Reinhart amid the crazies; and Reinhart getting in his own licks. At the level of the latter, we find adolescent stuff, particularly when Reinhart attempts to make out with the gigantically breasted Veronica (Very) Leary. The other side of Reinhart, his delving into his German past, his efforts to discover roots, background, ancestral past, to make sense of history, is worthwhile, but unrelated to the first part.

With the second volume, it becomes apparent that Berger's protagonist is insufficiently compelling to be the focus of what will be one thousand pages of text. In the first volume, Reinhart is potentiality, and he may move in any direction; by the second, he is not only a loser, he is a boring loser; and by the third, there is no reason we should be interested in a forty-four-year-old who lacks wit, knowledge, even self-knowledge.

Reinhart returns to his little town in Ohio, to a completely indifferent society. His father and mother barely acknowledge his return; and the town itself barely knows anything of the war. A black named Splendor introduces Reinhart to Dr. Goodykuntz's correspondence course, offered as part of the "Universal College of Metaphysical Knowledge," which has strong resemblances to the program of study outlined in Barth's *The End of the Road.* The import of the program is its insistence on nonchemical cures, and in its crazy way it points ahead to biofeedback and all those other self-induced cures which have some legitimacy at present. It is, also, a state of mind: medical treatment as founded on the individual's sense of himself as a human being, a combination spun off from Gurdjieff and Thoreau.

Reinhart is looking for some form of quackery in which he can get his start, and from Goodykuntz he moves to Humbold, another confidence man. Reinhart sells raunchy properties, gets involved in shady deals, his biggest coup being a sewer construction company which has all the paraphernalia of a corporate enterprise, but without the sewers. As a fifties scene, enterprise intermixed with deception, guile, and counterfeit activities, the sewer company has validity as a social institution. Had he remained in place, Reinhart could have made his fortune.

By this time, however, he is married to Genevieve Raven, but Berger never gets her right: his females are either benevolent sexual objects or malevolent sexual objects—in both cases, objects. Besides, Reinhart is inconclusive; not only does he not know what Genevieve wants, he does not know any longer what he wants.

By *Vital Parts,* Berger has moved Reinhart into the 1960s. In the immediate background is the "scene": a son who is disaffected over political/cultural matters; a fat daughter who is a dropout; a wife who has rebelled and taken a self-supporting job. Reinhart is abandoned by his entire family—and yet is still passive, unable to discover what went wrong, a decent but ineffectual man.* None of it washes, however, and personal life fails to connect to history.

---

*A Jewish version of this is Bruce Jay Friedman's *Stern* (1962). Stern is a typical schlemiel, full of innocence and savvy, able to work well in his advertising firm as a label writer, but incapable of holding together as a Jew. He suspects his wife is unfaithful to him, he has visions of a Puerto Rican wife and untold sexual delights, his son sits on the lawn chewing his blanket, and his neighbor mocks him. He is a passive sufferer, full of fears, secret pains, then an ulcer, the Jewish disease. Hovering over all is the anti-Semite's perception of him as a kike. The novel is a variation on passivity, without being passive enough.

If Berger had wanted an Oblomov, he missed there; if he had wanted a dropout from life, he missed. No ideological or stylistic net catches Reinhart. He is now a blubbery 265 pounds, his business and personal life in shambles. Everyone around him is deep into his own thing: children are on the march; young women are bedding down with everyone (except him); Genevieve, now separated, plans to marry her boss, her junior by fifteen years.

Near the end, Reinhart begins to gain insight into how things go, how one can adjust, how he can throw off a "bitch" like Genevieve. He will join his daughter, just recently struck by a truck, her life a mess. Identifying with her, he becomes a father; and he aligns himself with the way things work, or thinks he does. Having promised another confidence man, named Sweet, that hc would permit his body to be frozen, now he chooses a natural death. He has come through. Yet the reader has no sense of having come through. As a trilogy, this does not build, nor unfold in intensity; only events, undifferentiated, unfold, without that thickness of historical and social detail which makes the sequence possible.

Chapter Seven

IIIIIIIIIIIIIIIIIIIIIIIIIIIIIIIIIIIIIIIIIIIIIIIIIIII

THE POLITICAL NOVEL:
1950S AND AFTER

Shapeless, colorless beings, sacks of guts stuck together carelessly, peopled the world all around us, without giving the slightest thought to what they should make of themselves, to how to express themselves and identify themselves in a stable, complete form, such as to enrich the visual possibilities of whoever saw them.

ITALO CALVINO, "The Spiral," in *Cosmicomics*

The large-scale political novel such as we associate with Mann, Musil, Malraux, Kafka, or even with Koestler and Orwell, has eluded the grasp of the American novelist, postwar or otherwise. If we expand our idea of political to include the metaphysical "how to be," then Bellow's *Henderson the Rain King* is our finest postwar example. In American life, questions of pastoral and space have always preempted purely political matters, whether relating to local or federal government or to ideas of the nation. Few postwar "inside" novels such as Henry Adams's *Democracy* (1880) have emerged; nor can we expect the appearance of larger theoretical novels, such as Malraux's *Man's Fate* and *Man's Hope,* and surely not anything on the scale of *The Magic Mountain.* The persistence of the Edenic myth has, I believe, dissipated our seriousness about politics; and the fact that the state has not intruded in our personal lives has kept the idea of government relatively distant from our fiction. Just as the American distances himself from whatever he cannot resolve, so he perceives the state as a distant body, not concerning him or his fortunes.

It would be possible to see the fictions of several black novelists as political in nature, their entire experience as political. Even when they focus on individual lives, the state as agencies, local power groups, the police, the community is authoritarian and totalitarian for them. William Melvin Kelley's *A Different Drummer,* for example, has a large political potential: the fleeing of blacks from a particular state, an exodus based on the desire for liberation. John Williams's *The Man Who Cried I Am,* like *Invisible Man* and *Native Son,* cannot be isolated from its political context. Yet except in the Williams novel such politics are not broad, but mainly personal, connected to blacks' invisibility in the eyes of whites and the law.

For that intrusion of state into personal lives, Malamud goes to czarist Russia, to the life of a Jewish "fixer." In a parallel sense, Lionel Trilling uses the pressures of Communist Russia in the background for his "intrusive" element into the lives of his characters in *The Middle of the Journey.* Mailer's *Barbary Shore,* similarly, stresses foreign political ideas as intrusions into American political life. Or else the sense of politics is found in particular issues, separated from any serious examination of the state. The best of these is Doctorow's use in *The Book of Daniel* of the Rosenberg case—also utilized by Robert Coover in his inventive (but overly frenetic) *The Public Burning.* In the Doctorow novel, we can respond to several parts no matter how we feel about the Rosenbergs' guilt or innocence, although in the fuller sense we are expected to react sympathetically. Africa serves Bellow for *Henderson,* a work of inventiveness, intricacy, and great maturity. We have in *Henderson* and *The Book of Daniel* our most accomplished political novels, although the label must be stretched to include both.

Africa also offered John Updike an opportunity to break from what he could do with his left hand, the suburbs, and move into larger literary territory. *The Coup* is to his career what *Falconer* was to Cheever's; having wrapped up the suburbs, they dared more, and Updike's achievement here is significant. Somewhat less compelling as political efforts are Philip Roth's *Our Gang,* with Nixon as the culprit, and Mary McCarthy's version of the McCarthy era in *The Groves of Academe.* In her most recent novel, *Cannibals and Missionaries,* she tries to touch all political bases, but despite the modish hijacking scene, her focus is still early 1950s struggles between liberals and radicals.

Since this section is mainly a celebration of *Henderson the Rain King,* it may be instructive to start not with an American version of Africa but with a foreigner's, Naipaul's *A Bend in the River* (1979), as counterpoint to Bellow's version. Even though Naipaul enters Africa as an insider, he is very much aware of the American presence; one of the finest episodes in the novel, in fact, is the Americanization of Mobutu's Zaire, with the shipment of a Bigburger franchise which the protagonist's friend Mahesh acquires. Naipaul's persona is Salim, an African with an Indian background, a storekeeper who wants to make a living in an African republic that is undergoing political and economic transformation. Stability is followed by tyranny, followed by another form of tyranny, in cycles of repression.

Naipaul has a location and a historical scene which no American writer can possibly deal with, rhythms and tones of slippery and desperate behavior which have as their model Conrad's *Nostromo* and *Heart of Darkness.* He shows how it is inside a village that, while enjoying prosperity under a new president, begins to deteriorate into anarchy as the president's power slips and he hangs on with totalitarian methods. African politics are Balkan, formed more by Europe than by Africa. The loser in all this, however, is familiar: the African. Ferdinand, taken in by Salim as a young boy, is educated and becomes one of the administrative cadres of the president even as the country begins to fragment. He saves Salim from detention and possible death, and explains how disintegration will affect everyone: they are all marked for death.

Naipaul clearly differs from Bellow and Updike (especially the latter) in his view of Africa from the inside. This is Africa at the village level, a more historical and a less mythical continent. Naipaul's Africa is subject to the laws of history, to generational changes that disallow any beginning countries from achieving stability. Temporary stability is always followed by decline; prosperity by terror and near-anarchy. Murder and looting occur nearby in the "beyond," and bribery is the sole way of doing business. With everyone on the make, as the country prospers, the task becomes larger, more ambitious. History is doom. While the African performs his job, his attention is elsewhere, in some inner region of the mind impenetrable by the outsider, perhaps not even understood by the individual. Bellow and Updike must work differently, more allegorically and mythically, within the "idea of Africa." Bellow, indeed, creates his own Africa, Updike his own country.

One of the paradoxes of *Henderson the Rain King* (1959) is that it is so fine a political novel because politics, narrowly, is not its base; we must extend the idea of politics to fit the book, rather than contract the novel to fit a political scheme. With this novel, Bellow could have taken off imaginatively, for *Henderson* has the vitality and surge we experience in Grass's *The Tin Drum.* But Bellow chose instead to withdraw to *Herzog,* a considerable achievement, but essentially a cul-de-sac, leading into Kafkaesque fiction unsuited for his talent. *Henderson,* however, pointed outward, toward the large themes *Augie March* suggested. Bellow has it all here: breadth, expansion, a heroic figure, and political ideas at their fiercest. As myth, legend, and allegory, *Henderson* observes twentieth-century America as Whitman's major poems reflected the nineteenth. The comparison is not an idle one.

Henderson was the beginning of an intensely political period in Bellow's career. Politics for him, as for many of his contemporaries, meant reactive politics, rather than any definitive position. Only Mailer had flirted with theoretical ideas, the socialism and Marxism of *The Naked and the Dead* and *Barbary Shore.* Yet even he, by the end of the decade, had abandoned labels, for style of life, modes of being, the sensation of becoming. Bellow's *Henderson* fits into this category of political thought, far indeed from labeled politics, reactive to dominant 1950s modes both ideologically and attitudinally. *Henderson* is concerned with becoming, more than with being; it has an existential grit to it, since it placed Henderson on the edge, much as Ellison's invisible man is brought to realization through trial and exposure.

Eugene Henderson in his natural habitat appears as a somewhat eccentric rich man: big, bluff, powerfully built, with large tastes and an infallible instinct to marry unsuitable women. This is a given in Bellow, the unsuitable wife, other women more accommodating. Henderson does not permit himself to be contained or halted. Beating within him is a gigantic Whitmanesque ego with a voice that cries: *"I want, I want, I want, oh, I want—yes, go on . . . Strike, strike, strike, strike!"* This voice insistently carries over into all his activities. While he remains in America, he suffers a loss of innerness, except for that voice. He cannot touch whatever he is, nor is there any opportunity for reaching out. Family and children, by the 1950s, do not work. Africa is the alternative.

When he comes upon the drought-struck Arnewi in Africa, the queen asks who he is, where he comes from. It is a simple question, with a complicated genealogy; for it seems to search out elements in Henderson that disallow a straight answer. He is confused, for can he tell her he is a rich man from America? "Maybe she didn't even know where America was, as even civilized women are not keen on geography, preferring a world of their own." Can he tell this old queen in a lion skin and raincoat (his incongruous gift) "That I had ruined the original piece of goods issued to me and was traveling to find a remedy"? "Grun-tu-molani," the old queen says: "Man want to live," and Henderson affirms her words fervently.

He immediately thinks of some way to repay her insight, and he decides to annihilate the frogs that are poisoning the cistern. He will blow up the frogs and make it possible for the Arnewi cattle to drink. If the Arnewi can eliminate *his* sickness, he will eliminate theirs—and in the process destroy their water supply, bringing drought on the entire tribe. Henderson takes from the Arnewi a sense of vital renewal and gives them, in turn, a 1950s practical solution to their problem, which brings them ruin. The reader knows Henderson's project will be disastrous, since it is based on the self he came to Africa to slough off. The knowledge he brings to the frog problem is gained from his military training, *Popular Mechanics,* and American know-how: the very political and social reasoning that had fed his emptiness. And even though he jeopardizes his own life, by holding on to his homemade bomb until the final second, his solution is doomed, suitable for American problems, disastrous for African.

Like the junkies and Beats of the 1950s, like Burroughs's searches, Henderson is reaching out for alternatives. Their drugs, Zen, "on the road" frenzy are his Africa. It is astonishing how Bellow has joined writers, seemingly moving on different planets, who are, in reality, associated very profoundly with each other: Americans responding to the 1950s through denial of self and seeking in drugs, Eastern religions and philosophies, constant movement, African and Negro life as alternative forms of existence. The way out, apparently, was the way in.

Henderson leaves the ruined Arnewi and heads for the Wariri, to see if he can discover missing links in himself. That insistent voice, "I want," still has no object, although it has a transitive force and requires completion. If he can find the objective form that will complete it, then "I want" becomes a true expression of himself. If he cannot recover that object, then the subject-verb expression is simply a manifestation of ego, of the very 1950s tone and attitude Henderson has gone to Africa to escape. The Africa of Bellow, incidentally, is neither Conrad's Congo—where enervation, ennui, and nihilism are the by-products of man's inability to find support for his regular ethical and moral systems—nor is it "kind nature" in, say, the Wordsworthian mold. To escape into nature is not equivalent to a purification of self. Bellow, unfortunately, does flirt a little with Rider Haggard's Africa, playing up the oddities of the Wariri ruling class: colors, size, massive bodies, and comical aspects. Ultimately, however, he avoids all this and creates his own kind of Africa, in which we find an adversary political experience.

One element does remain constant in Bellow's fiction, after its locus: women are the source of man's death, be it spiritual or physical. Dahfu, the Wariri king, explains to Henderson that as soon as he can no longer service his retinue of gigantic queens, he will be strangled, as his father was strangled before him. "King for a day" rings through our ears, not for a day, really, but for as long as the sperm holds out. Woman, in this scheme, is literally the receptacle of man's life force and has, inevitably, life and death judgment, by way of her sexual needs.

This is the physical foundation of Dahfu's throne, and it becomes, in turn, the metaphysical basis of his entire philosophy. He and Henderson trade philosophical ideas, but the essential fact of metaphysics is the way the throne is passed on. Connected to the succession is the lion. Dahfu must capture the grown lion that his father's spirit has developed into, and until he accomplishes that, he is not considered, fully, the king. When Dahfu dies, a lion cub grows from the maggots in his body, and that cub, when developed, is in turn to be captured by his successor, and so on into history. Dahfu's sin in the eyes of the rest of the ruling class is that he keeps a lioness, against the rules, for the sole lion he must possess is the huge male that is the reincarnated body of his father.

Henderson is taken in tow by Dahfu, who was trained at a Western medical school and speaks sophisticated English. He has rejected not the ideas but the practices of Western culture, in order to return to his tribe as instructor. Salvation, as he indoctrinates Henderson, lies in the lioness, Atti, whose shuffling, rippling, padding presence is that of a goddess, not of nature, but of becoming and then being. Henderson will, expectedly, achieve satori in the presence of the lioness, a kind of Zen master. Her smell is staggering, her perfume that of some other-dimensional force; her physical presence demands exact attention to protocol; and her claws and mouth remain reminders of the physical and political world she emblemizes. Bellow suggests Conrad when Dahfu remarks that men throw themselves into the sea while denying it is infinite, an intimation of Stein's dictum in *Lord Jim* that man should immerse himself in the destructive element and by the exertion of his own force keep himself going until the infinite claims him. But this is not the way for Dahfu, who counsels embracing the infinite, the lioness herself.

Henderson's encounter with Atti is central to the novel, and it does not, for the most part, fall into the usual platitudes of "born free" lion experiences. The lioness, despite her fearful physical presence, is very much "the other," which represents whatever it is that Henderson has yearned for. It is highly sexual, and yet beyond sex; we recall Balzac's "Passion in the Desert," even more Rilke's panther. Rilke: "The padding gait of flexibly strong strides, / that in the smallest circle turns, / is like a dance of strength around a center / in which stupefied a great will stands." When Henderson's hand touches the flanks of the lioness, the smell of the animal penetrates beneath the skin, and his "nails became like five burning tapers. The bones of the hand became incandescent." Through the lioness, Henderson recognizes that his existence has been defined by natural objects: he has married a "Lily," whom he still loves; he has raised pigs; he tried to rid the Arnewi cistern of frogs so as to provide water for their cattle; and he had once attempted to murder a neighbor's cat. Daniel's prophecy to Nebuchadnezzar comes to mind: "They shall drive thee from among men, and thy dwelling shall be with the beasts of the field."

Unfit for human companionship, Henderson discovers that his role is to loosen his self, since in his relationship to people he must dominate. He must learn to act like the lioness, to lose the restrictions of his "extremely contracted" state of being. Dahfu is the perfect guide, Vergil to Henderson's Dante, since Dahfu has absorbed the lion into himself. He is the cub grown up, and he will capture the lion that is the reincarnation of his father. Every aspect of his existence is tied to the life cycle of the lion; even his need to satisfy his retinue of gigantic women is connected to his role as a lion satisfying his pride, insatiable lionesses. He is the guardian of *his* pride, and once he cannot serve that function, he must be replaced by a younger male who has full powers. This is, for Bellow's males, one of the unbending laws of nature: the male must "act the lion," while the women are always poised to bring him down as soon as he shows a fault.

Henderson becomes known as Leo E. Henderson, Leo replacing Eugene: a replacement of "well born" by the lion of nature. Bellow's own point about male-female relationships—the male as lion of the pride, the female waiting to humble him at the first signs of weakness—is played out in Henderson's drama with Dahfu. The latter is killed by the giant male lion who is mistaken for his father's reincarnation; Dahfu is raked to death, claws penetrating to his very being. And Henderson is to succeed him. He escaped, however, taking with him a lion cub, in a sense carrying out his succession as king, but in the West. Henderson flees to America, stopping off in Newfoundland, where he leaps, "pounding, and tingling over the pure white lining of the gray Arctic silence." His home is ice as well as jungle, cold as well as heat. The lion cub is within as well as without. He adopts a Persian boy on the plane who speaks no English, is mute; with him, Henderson feels a sense of belonging. The "I want," which had been simply an ego shrieking to escape, has located an object, in the boy, and in the lion, now absorbed.

Henderson sprawls over the 1950s. Its hero escapes pure self-indulgence and narcissism, but barely; and for those who never connect, the "I want" becomes a complex "me." We can see how the "on the road" search for interior values led fluidly into the narcissism and self-seeking of the 1960s and 1970s; continuity, not discontinuity, is revealed. Personal and political ideas became profoundly intermixed, as in the political riots of the 1960s, out of whose turmoil came not the desire for a new political system but a wish for purification, conservation, personal integrity, internal satisfactions. Paradoxically, the entire process burrows deeply into an Edenic fantasy.

Bellow's novel suggests that in America every seemingly political movement ends up as a personal mission, with strong self-aggrandizing tendencies, the personal function eventually overriding the original political purpose. Remarkably, the "road" phenomenon, even as it glorifies the search for values not explicit in the system or the nation, illuminates self-serving. If we view "road" literature this way, we can see how much more complicated it is than simply rapidly changing episodes, quickie sex, or fleeting relationships. It is, like *Henderson* itself, at the very heart of American culture and fiction, in the tradition of Emerson, Thoreau, Whitman, and Melville, those early forerunners of that search for the connection between "I" and a suitable object of "want."

A more constrictive, more *Herzog*ian political follow-up to *Henderson* is *The Dean's December* (1982), Bellow's first novel since his Nobel Prize. Despite the fact that Bellow attempted a very difficult type of novel, the scale is smaller, the ideology more traditional, the ambition less audacious. He reverted to previous Bellow, rather than expanding his experience. This is a tale of two cities, Chicago and Bucharest, with Albert Corde the connecting link. Bellow's central consciousness in this book is of mixed Irish-French ancestry, an investigative reporter from Chicago who is now a professor and dean of students at some unnamed but important university there. With the news that his mother-in-law (Valeria), a person of repute in Rumania, is dying, Corde and his wife, Minna, go to Bucharest. As his name indicates, Corde is the linkage between the two cities and, by implication, between the two worlds, one free, chaotic, and depressing, the other ordered but imprisoned by Russian ideology, and equally depressing. Corde's name also suggests "heart"; this signals a dimension of feeling brought to political issues, a kind of phenomenology of politics.

Bellow has focused his attention on the values of each system, the American leading to rampaging blacks, poverty, superfluous people, the result of free enterprise; and the Communist, to a totalitarianism which disallows personal expression and instills daily fear. In Chicago, the individual is in danger from other individuals who have already been shunted aside into superfluity; in Bucharest, the streets are safe, but one lives in danger from the constant surveillance of the Rumanian KGB. Chicago is rough, a spawning ground for disreputable people, crowded

with blacks whose lives of crime fill the streets, a trap for an exposé journalist like Corde. Bucharest has, instead, secret police agents who monitor all calls, observe all bystanders, control every aspect of individual life.

Corde's mother-in-law was a personage, a former minister of health, someone who was familiar with the highest levels of the Stalinist government, but is now in disfavor. Although she receives modern treatment in a party hospital, the very hospital she had founded, she is closely watched. Corde and Minna are forbidden to see her more than twice (finally, a third time) by a colonel in charge. Valeria has been sealed off for her past errors, whatever they were—sealed off by her heart attack in the present, by the state mechanism in the past. The point about Bucharest is made in the hospital: a sealed-off dying woman who once served the state and its ideology nobly. If the hospital is the focal point of totalitarianism, Chicago is the focal point—in Corde's memory or in reports he receives from friends passing through—of the free world. Bellow does not romanticize Chicago, but it has a vitality and energy which contrast with the deadly atmosphere of Bucharest. Chicago is dangerous and alive, Bucharest safe and dead. It is in Bucharest that Corde rethinks his past, especially his relationship to a case in which a university student has died and the dean's nephew, Mason, is implicated as distant accessory. As dean, Corde became intensely involved in the case, helping to find evidence against street blacks who, supposedly, murdered the (white) student. Mason insists that the student, Rick Lester, had come looking for trouble and then fell from a window; Corde insists that street blacks cannot be glamorized and that Lester was murdered. Mason's 1960s sympathies run up against Corde's 1970s "common sense."

That was the Chicago Corde. In Bucharest, he begins to have doubts. Viewing a different scenario, he perceives that blacks have been victimized by a government which considers them superfluous. Exposed to totalitarianism, he comprehends what human superfluity is. Despite his privileged position as a visitor on an American passport, he understands he, too, is superfluous in such a country. Everyone is subject to the whims of a government whose rage is, not for justice, but only for control and order.

Bellow has written a "December" book, a novel of old age, in which wisdom dictates not positions but a questioning of positions. There are no Jews or Jewish issues here, no setting of "us" against "them." Even Rumania's checkered history in the Jewish final solution is bypassed. Bellow's aim is to turn around on himself, and in the December of his life to question what he wrote when he enjoyed May. Corde is a good deal of Sammler and Herzog. From the latter, we note the passivity, the lying in bed, that Oblomov-like quality which characterized Herzog's inability to make sense of all the questions he wanted to ask. Corde has that quality, but also Sammler's effort to perceive a rational universe under the anarchy which seems to have taken hold of America. However, unlike Sammler, the Jewish survivor, and Herzog, the Jewish renegade, Corde is a Midwestern Gentile, angry about corruption, superfluity, doing a turnabout on blacks and issues affecting them. Sammler saw blacks as magnificent, the males with big cocks, superb criminal types; Corde attempts to redress that unjust view and to see them as victims, just as citizens of Bucharest are victims of their form of government.

Corde has written articles speaking of "superfluous populations," "written off" groups, "doomed peoples." He recognizes that such talk doesn't go down well. One can speak of anomie, or underclasses, or "redundant peasantries"—all theoretical terms and, therefore, safe. "You could discuss welfare politics, medical and social work, bureaucracies, without objection. But when Corde began to make statements to the effect that in the wild, monstrous setting of half-demolished cities the choice that was offered was between a slow death and a sudden one, between attrition and quick destruction, he enraged a good many subscribers."

Bucharest, then, does not change Corde's mind— he has written these articles before coming to Rumania—but it unsettles him and forces him to doubt his previous certainties even about the guilt of the black "killers" of the student Lester. Emissaries—the journalist Dewey Spangler, Vlada Voynich, et al.— keep him in touch with Chicago, so that it rages fiercely in his mind. For Corde is in a kind of limbo as the result of his exposés, his threat to political careers, his involvement in the Lester case. The latter episode has tentacles which spread out into every seam of American life; just as the hospital scene with Valeria extends into every aspect of Eastern European life.

The plan is ambitious, and *The Dean's December* is possibly Bellow's most explicitly political novel. Where it can be faulted is in the very area where Bellow was brightest before, in his line-by-line work, in his paragraphs which delighted the reader even when the philosophizing was excessive. That onetime verbal brilliance is somewhat muted, as if the expo-

sure to Bucharest Oblomovism had taken the bloom off language itself. Bright spots are often buried beneath long-winded efforts to understand the two cities. Politically, Corde comes to the conclusion that while America has compromised every ideal, it is preferable to Bucharest; yet he is not enthusiastic about the comparison. He realizes further that "Reality didn't exist 'out there.' It began to be real only when the soul found its underlying truth. In generalities there was no coherence—none."

When Corde returns to America, he resigns as a dean, decides to become an active journalist, and accompanies his astronomer wife to Palomar Observatory, where he rises toward the stars and catches a glimpse of the heaven that can be. The moment is lovely, but it is disconnected from the rest of the novel. For it suggests an order of life and being for which Bellow has made little preparation, and it exists there solely as a revelatory moment, a "recognition."

Although the rich, burnished prose remains, *The Coup* (1978) is a serious attempt on Updike's part to develop new themes and locales in his fiction. Using African history of the last decade and a half, plus some basic literary texts—Waugh, possibly Conrad, Mungo Park—Updike has written a witty account of a small African landlocked country called Kush. Its president, minister of national defense, and commander in chief, Colonel Hakim Félix Elleloû—whose last name is Berber for "freedom"—is trying, like Libya's Qaddafi, to take his country into Islamic purity in order to avoid the "mongrelized, neo-capitalist puppet states" on his borders.

Kush is almost a deserted land, its chief product peanuts, its literacy rate six percent, per capita gross national product seventy-nine dollars, average life expectancy thirty-seven years. Its chief characteristic is emptiness, although its name locates it deep in Biblical history, named after Noah's grandson, son of Ham, father of Nimrod. It is, all in all, a land without definition, and its preponderance of languages, living styles, name changes suggest it is more a process than a country. Kush or Cush (Genesis 10: 6–8) comes in the Bible just before the description of Babel; a language and a people proliferate, and this is the process Updike describes for this African country. The mise-en-scène is one of constant redefinition, in which disguise, deception, counterfeit, imitation, and precarious survival are intermixed. Kush is like a shadow presence of America.

Elleloû is himself the prototype of a "new leader."

Having fought for the French in Indochina, he deserted rather than fight for them in Africa. He comes to America, to study at McCarthy College in Wisconsin, and there he meets Candace, who has a thing for black men. While moving toward his idea of African independence from colonial powers, and under the influence of Black Muslims, he forms an alliance with the very white and blond Candy, whose father is a bigot and racist who would kill him if he discovered the relationship. In these details, the novel becomes undone, for what Updike has accomplished is a suburban view of Africa: Ellelloû as little more than a lightweight confidence man; those surrounding him likewise—his Black Muslim friend at college, for example, becomes a policeman when he recognizes the Muslim leader is a lecher; and the country, Kush, little more than the source of fun. What we have is Waugh's "black mischief" updated into contemporary political terms,* but without any of the complicating elements. Updike strives to be witty, but one of the flaws of the novel is that it is insufficiently witty for the point of view it takes.

Updike's Africa is a curious place, although not simply because of the conflicts generated in a continent ideologically and culturally confused. It is curious because Updike has given us the "fun side" of it: nothing of the ambiguous commitment to freedom; little of the cultural mix which creates irresolvable conflicts and tensions; nothing of Africa that is not foreign-made. Ellelloû is himself a product more of Western than African culture. He fought for the French, was educated in Wisconsin, has an American as one of his four wives, speaks English and French better than his native tongues, and rides around in the ultimate symbol of affluence, a Mercedes. He is African only in the sense that he can be a big man in Kush, whereas elsewhere he is simply a small, plump, unprepossessing black man.

The novel, then, is about a confidence man who ends up as ruler of a doomed country. Typical of all undefined nations, Kush is a pawn: while the Soviets plan militarily for Kush, American culture is everywhere—a disposable culture in a country dependent on its peanut crop. Here Updike is at his best: African dress, speech, manner, style, even dreams give way to

a jeans subculture. Yet novelistic problems remain. Since the presence of Ellelloû indicates a confidence man, the novel should take its shape from that; and yet Updike's prose, which has rarely been better, works at cross-purposes with the need for wit, or lightness. The prose takes the high road. Here is Ellelloû's meditation before he executes the king:

> The handle of the scimitar, bronze worked to imitate wound cord, nearly fell from my hand, so unexpectedly ponderous was the blade. In this life woven of illusions and insubstantial impressions it is gratifying to encounter heft, to touch the leaden center of things, the *is* at the center of *be,* the rock in Plato's cave. I thought of an orange. I lifted the sword high, so that the reflection from its flashing blade hurtled around the square like a hawk of lethal brightness, slicing the eyes of the crowd and the hardened clay of the façades, the shuttered fearful windows, the blanched, pegged walls and squat aspiring minaret of the Mosque of the Day of Disaster.

This brilliant passage, which is not uncharacteristic, suggests the novel's overall uncertain tone. Ellelloû's flights of verbal fancy we can explain by way of his education, and also by way of his assumption of his role as a confidence man. He does know about Plato's cave and even the *is* at the center of *be.* Yet the display is really intellectual slumming on Updike's part; for Ellelloû's act, slicing off the king's head, is not supported by such existential bunkum. Nor does the passage serve any function in explaining Ellelloû; it neither opens up anything new nor suggests greater complexity.

Far more impressive are short passages which point up political incongruities. As Ezana, the Marxist, wittily exclaims: " 'I sometimes wonder, my President, if even the fruitful diagrams of Marx do schematic justice to the topology of a world where the Soviet proletariat conducts a black market in the blue jeans while the children of the capitalist middle class manufacture bombs and jovial posters of Mao.' " Or the amusing perception that the Kush peanut crop may go begging because Americans are pursuing low-calorie diets in which peanut butter has become taboo. The larger areas, however, remain unamusing. When Ellelloû—then called Felix, or Happy, by his friends—visits Candace's home, the patterns are stereotypical, as is the conversation: a bigoted father who pours out his animosity against American blacks, which Felix, as an African, is expected to agree to.

What we miss in this expertly crafted novel is some

---

*Waugh's Basil Seal, in *Black Mischief* (1932), is Minister of Modernization in Azania, a black empire off the coast of Africa; Ellelloû is a mirror image of Seal—an antimodernization force, a return to purity, a man who has a low estimate of Africans. Seal treats them as mass men whom anyone can lead, as savages only generations removed from the trees.

thematic presence beyond ideas generated by the daily press and weekly magazines. When Waugh wrote his vitriolic satire, he gave vent to all his hatred of lesser people; Africans were not only black, but lower-class, insignificant socially, political nonentities. Waugh could savage them as a type of vicarious English lower class. Updike has no such freedom of choice, nor does he want it. He is far more decent than Waugh, and he means well for Africa and Africans. He even shows pleasure in Ellelloû's confidence tricks, his deception of himself as well as others, his desire for comfort and pleasure, his ruthlessness in a country where acts of decency suggest lack of manhood or loss of power.

Updike needed a more philosophical novel than he wrote, and there are indications he wanted something larger, or more varied. He is, after all, toiling in heavy territory: Conrad, Greene, as well as Waugh. The patterning of the novel shows Updike at his most ambitious and expert: cutting back and forth between Ellelloû in Africa, then to his college days in Wisconsin, his visit to Candace's home, his journeys in Africa to visit his four wives, his political excursions, his attempts to salvage a career for himself where he is unrecognized apart from his Mercedes. If we add, to these, elements of name-changing (Kush, for example, was once Noire), language confusion (signs in Arabic, French, English, Russian; none in any tribal language, however), confusion of the people themselves (unable even to recognize the deposed Ellelloû), we have a different Updike from that in his previous fiction. He has taken upon himself the fictional ideas he writes about so well in his *New Yorker* reviews and elsewhere, those themes as embodied in Nabokov, Borges, Pynchon.

Just as Africa experienced by an American provided Bellow with one of the finest postwar political novels, so the Rosenberg case furnished E. L. Doctorow with far-reaching materials in *The Book of Daniel;* and, as well, Robert Coover, in *The Public Burning.* The Rosenbergs, the Hiss-Chambers confrontation (foreshadowed in Lionel Trilling's *The Middle of the Journey*), and aspects of Nixon-McCarthy (in Roth and Mary McCarthy) form the tripartite political axis of the postwar period. Larger political issues, matters of freedom, economic and social questions, are only rarely the concern of the American novelist—except marginally for the black writer, whose stress, as we have mentioned, becomes less political than a matter of identity, religious concerns often replacing politics.

It is safe to generalize that for our political novelists, profound questions of ideology, class, caste, party affiliations, and related issues are not viable. Even Warren's *All the King's Men,* truly a political novel, left behind politics as such to resolve itself on moral/ethical issues. Instead, state and nation are transformed into questions of "how to live," in which Edenic fantasies, transcendental spatiality, memory of a paradisiacal past, withdrawal and escape, even invisibility, become an American equivalent of the traditional political novel.

The Book of Daniel (1971) is a novel based on the Rosenbergs, seen from the point of view of Daniel, one of their two children; the other is Susan, who goes mad and finally kills herself. Doctorow's method is to use Daniel as observer and narrator, and at the same time have him refer to himself in the third person. The "I" may be Daniel, or the novelist as external narrator; plus the "he," who is Daniel. There are several texts, as it were, and the novel's effectiveness rests strongly on these parallel texts or subtexts. The novel at its best powerfully evokes past elements, which are themselves at several removes and several levels. It begins on Memorial Day in 1967, fourteen years after the execution of Daniel's parents, Paul and Rochelle Isaacson. Daniel is now Daniel Lewin, his name derived from the last of several people who took care of him and Susan after the FBI seized their parents.

Given the nature of the multilevel experience that Daniel has been exposed to, Doctorow needed the immediacy of observation that "I" can convey, as well as the historical perspective only a third-person narration can provide. Unlike Coover's novel on the Rosenbergs, which focuses directly on them, Doctorow's book eschews satire of the system in favor of perception, observation, understanding. Coover goes the way of a wild Orwell, an "Animal Farm" updated, with Nixon and Eisenhower instead of pigs and donkeys. Doctorow cuts, instead, into Kafka territory. That is, while much of the novel is concerned with knowing and observing, another large element is given over to discovering why things happen as they do.

By shifting half or more of the novel back to the young Isaacson children—to Daniel's perception of his family as he grows up—Doctorow has located the material in a kind of limbo or stillness that recalls Kafka's searching narratives. For the world of the children, while full of personally observed details, never contains the totality of experience; it is always partial, a search for missing elements. Accordingly,

Daniel can never comprehend, as a child, what is actually occurring; for his mother and father are to him full-time parents, and he cannot assimilate the fact of their having a life outside the home. Even in 1967, as Daniel hurls himself against the barricades, as Susan throws herself into self-destructive acts of defiance and rebellion, they cannot locate the missing elements. Rochelle as a housewife and Paul as a radio repairman appear unrelated to the terrible crimes they are accused of (and others that are suggested); the accusations open up the very chasm children are incapable of bridging. Those who attack Doctorow's sympathy for the Rosenbergs fail to see that the novel focuses far less on them than on how their children perceive them.

Doctorow moves on the margins of tragedy, conveying its sense of inexorable doom; and we can observe his Daniel and Susan as avengers, a modern-day Orestes and Electra. It is all written beforehand, and even as they change their names, their lives, their predilections, they are entwined no less than Laocoön in a terrible binding. They are the children of Isaac-(son), executed by the state (which poses as a nation), victims of a system that required tangible proof of Soviet insidiousness—sacrifices, so their children feel, to a state that chews up its small people to serve its larger interests.

Guilt or innocence of the Rosenbergs is not at issue in the novel; Doctorow is not parti pris. Although the children believe in their parents' innocence—and they must, to survive personally the transformation of their lives—their actions are not connected to innocence or guilt. Their actions are linked to necessity: what worked through their parents' bodies in the form of electrical currents is an energy transmitted to the children. They are marked out. Daniel, of the Book of Daniel, has a vision or dream of the four beasts, the fourth of which is a terrible beast indeed, described as "terrible and powerful, and strong exceedingly; and it had great iron teeth; it devoured and brake in pieces, stamped the residue with its feet; and it was diverse from all the beasts that were before it; and it had ten horns." And these horns have another come up among them, and it plucks up three of the others, which turn into the eyes of a man and a mouth "speaking great things." Daniel's vision of the fourth beast is a vision of the state, which, although it speaks of subversion and treason, has a human face. But the state is a beast, for it deceives; it accuses the Rosenbergs of conspiracy to commit espionage because it cannot prove espionage.

The issues are momentous and the levels several, all of differing intensities. First, there is the past itself, related by Daniel and the multiple "I," as Daniel and Susan grow up, observe their parents, their friends, their roles. The beginning of this childhood, however, does not come in chronological order; it arrives as flashback in Book One, "On Memorial Day in 1967," and Daniel Lewin (the adopted name) is hitching his way to Worcester, Massachusetts, where Susan is being kept under observation for having tried to kill herself in a local Howard Johnson's. The entire section hovers over the past, a kind of suspended shadow.

Doctorow spends much time here on the Lewins, establishing them as parents, until we learn more clearly that they are foster parents; the Isaacsons, like a palimpsest, emerge from beneath the portrait of the substitute parents. It is a brilliant strategy, for it establishes an immediate counterpointing within Daniel, and begins to explain—without there being any official explanation—why Susan has taken her present course. Doctorow, then, can work through substitutes—shelters, homes, temporary foster parents, the Lewins—back toward the Isaacsons, such figures of mystery to the adult Daniel and Susan. Through this, we gain insight into the levels of experience that turn Susan into a psychotic and Daniel into a self-destructive, often cruel and sadistic young man. In few postwar novels do we have such clear lines of motivation for people's actions; Doctorow's method is both a burrowing and an opening up. As a consequence, the children of the executed Isaacsons seek identities and meanings even as Doctorow divulges such information for the reader.

Book One, then, is siftings, fragments of lives which have not gained coherence. Daniel's "Book" is to "make book" on his life, simultaneously working out his own destiny and discovering what created that destiny; finally, trying to survive it, unlike Susan, who succumbs in anger, frustration, indifference. Daniel's "Book" on Rochelle, a version of Ethel Rosenberg, is particularly insightful; she is made visible. Rochelle is a woman of impeccable order, whose sense of organization and cleanliness give her feelings of superiority. Once on that high ground, she can see all human behavior as folly, except that which is directed toward social and political wrongs. As revolutionaries, she and Paul are tidy, lower-middle-class, struggling South Bronx Jews.

Actual events in Book One are sharply observed, especially the Peekskill riot during the appearance of Paul Robeson. In the aftermath, collusion between rioters and police leads to bloodshed, to terrorism on the roads, and to Paul Isaacson's single act of heroism: he helps to save his bus from being overturned, at the expense of injuries to himself. It is, in the eyes of his small son, his grand moment, a moment when greatness touched his father. It passes.

Still in Book One, as Daniel dips further into his background, he speaks of his grandmother, of her trials, which maddened her. But then when Daniel swings back to himself after this journey, he perceives a young man, a doctoral candidate at Columbia, married, the father of a son, but a nonperson in the government's eyes: both a nonperson and a special person. He is so fully documented, his life so entirely observed, that he is "deprived of the chance of resisting" his government. He could evade the draft, burn his draft card on the steps of the Pentagon, do anything, and it would simply become another entry in his file. He is a statistic: the son of the Isaacsons, not Daniel Lewin, not Daniel whatever. "There is nothing I can do, mild or extreme, that they cannot have planned for." He can receive no money from the government, nor serve it: he is Orestes seeking revenge in a vacuum.

The motto for the growing boy was: "I could never have appreciated how obscure we were," an observation made when the family has become internationally famous. Yet even as he makes the comment, he had felt, as a child, that they were the center of the universe. "I thought we were important people." His father seemed able to explain everything; his mother's orderliness offered solutions to incoherence. But even as he desires their importance—"what happened to us was important"—they were obscure, ants in an army of ants. Then when his parents are taken away, the boy perceives that "it was like the world had finally agreed to what I always knew—that we were important people." The narrative method of the novel leads to this curving back upon experience: the obscurity he senses, the importance his attitudes lead toward, then the meeting of the two in the arrest of his parents—an importance so disproportionate to what he had sensed that it disarranges his entire mode of perception.

By Book Two (after a little more than one hundred pages of text), all the subtexts have been established: the Isaacsons' line, the lives of Daniel and Susan as children, their present lives, Susan's suicide attempt, the various foster parents (not as yet fully fleshed out), the shadowy political background (from left and right), the South Bronx background. Doctorow's method is at the opposite end from the minimalists: a writer like Joan Didion, who also works intensely with past material as it presses insistently on the present, but with a minimum of strokes. While she calls attention to the spareness and blankness of her narrative, Doctorow provides a fully textured narrative; including, whereas she omits.

Book Two begins only a month after Book One—July–August 1967. We dip back to the moment when things happen; Mindish, the family dentist, turns informer, and the FBI begins to tune in on everything that concerns the Isaacsons. With the line "Mindish has been arrested," we have, for the children, the advent of fate itself. Docotorow then provides a perfect spatial metaphor to describe what is occurring. "Our lives are shrinking," he has Daniel say; but even as that occurs—as the FBI closes down radio store, family life, freedom of movement—an expansion is taking place. "While our life is shrinking, another existence, another dimension, expands its image and amplifies its voices." This is an apt assimilation of the Kafka method: to restrict freedom of movement and/ or thought, while opening up infinite vistas of potentiality. It can also be likened to what a hallucinatory drug can do: first inhibiting rational sequences, then opening up consciousness to other possibilities.

With that metaphor, Doctorow had his basic movement: the lives of the Isaacson children open to new experiences, while the lives of the parents are closed off. The high bail that keeps them from leaving prison necessitates the children's shift from one foster parent to another. But even as that is occurring, we observe Daniel in his present life, trying to come to terms with his hippie wife, Phyllis, his young son, himself. He commits uncontrollable acts, such as throwing his son ever higher, catching him, tempting fate, almost destroying his own son as a way of destroying sons, of getting at fathers, himself, Paul, the very idea of deceptive parentage.

That rage earlier has led to destructive role-playing when Daniel and Susan are placed in a shelter in a section of the Bronx they do not know. Here Daniel must compete against other boys, some of them stronger, more athletic and street wise. He has no talents, only a sense of survival. He thinks of "making it" with his mind, but he perceives that without the right attitudes and tones, a boy is mocked for his brains. He must find another way, and what he decides to do is his "imitation of the Inertia Kid," achieving a catatonic state, ultimately to gain an adversary position in the shelter that approximates his parents' adversary position in the larger culture. Daniel performs, clowns: "His tongue protruded and his eyes saw nothing. His hands lay as if broken at the wrists, the thumb of one in the palm of the other. ... He never closed his eyes to sleep. ... I did all these routines, becoming in one moment popular for them, a new thing in the society, a wit, a mime of affliction, a priest." What makes this imitation so appropriate is Daniel's awareness that once his parents are picked up, all he can do is play roles, perform.

The reason refraction functions so well with the political material is that in Books One and Two, we have a society that can be viewed best with mirrors, reflections, filters. We think of John Barth's metaphor of "lost in the funhouse" as a way of comprehending the diverse nature of experience: life contracting even as it expands toward infinity, American spatiality as doom and escape. When Doctorow moves from that sense of things, which is a vision of America in the fifties, his material thins out. For instance, Book Four has Daniel the hippie board a plane for Los Angeles, where he plans to seek out the old Selig Mindish, to discover what happened. His quest is reaching its final stage: to search, perhaps to forgive; to make himself, in manner, appearance, goals, a hostage to his parents' crime. The Daniel we meet in the final section is clearly some form of sacrifice: the son giving himself over to his parents' memory, Orestes to the end. Electra will soon be gone, a suicide, the victim of a "failure of analysis."

Daniel sees the Mindish daughter, who is now engaged to be married to a straight lawyer type. She and her fiancé take the high road, that Mindish suffered for doing his job, that evidence (suppressed) against the Isaacsons was so overwhelming that they were a menace to civilization itself. Daniel insists on seeing Mindish, who is observed finally, senile, at Disneyland. His favorite spot is the Richfield Autopia, toy cars that block out the larger culture. This image of Disneyland, Barth's funhouse, almost closes out the book.

Daniel returns to the Bronx, to Susan's funeral. There is no more, except for his Book, the Book of Daniel. He kept book on it all, and it is now submitted in partial fulfillment of a doctorate at Columbia, in all fields of study. His will be a composite doctorate, biology as well as cacophony and demonology, even eschatology. The novel ends with the Biblical injunction to Daniel to go forth, knowing that *his* fiction is indeed over. Doctorow's book, which is highly personal, now leads into Coover's, which is fully political.

The "public burning" of *The Public Burning* (1977) is the execution of the Rosenbergs, for betraying their country, in Times Square: recalling the kind of medieval ceremony in which Savonarola was burned at the stake. But "public burning" has an equally significant sense, of a public being burned by its officialdom, and the novel is as much about that.

The brilliance of Coover's formulation of his material—comparable in ways to Mailer's novel about the Vietnam War—comes in his interweaving of Richard Nixon's career with the lives of Ethel and Julius Rosenberg. Having been successful with his prosecution of Alger Hiss, having been selected as Eisenhower's vice-president, and having survived with his "Checkers" speech, Nixon sees his career as culminating with the presidency itself, the Great Incarnation. His constant companion is Uncle Sam Glick, whom Coover presents as a real person and also as emblematic of the country. Nixon plays golf with Uncle Sam, listens to his homilies, defers to him. Nixon and Uncle Sam will ride into the presidency together, once the grinning, almost idiotic Ike runs his course.

But Nixon is troubled by the Rosenbergs, for in his isolated, introspective way he sees parallels of the most unlikely kind between him and them. Nixon recognizes that the Rosenbergs' Communist slogans and even the "way the Russians wrote USSR," CCCP, approximated his own campaign slogans. His slogan was K_1C_3—Korea, Communism, Corruption, and Controls. "Or Costs—we never got that sorted out. The Great Crusade. Dean Acheson's College of Cowardly Communist Containment."

The Vice-President runs over his own background: his series of unpleasant jobs, his lack of stability, the often violent father, the two dead brothers, his humiliating courtship of Pat; and this demeaning sense of himself gives him temporary insight into the Rosenbergs' world. They become actual for him as the other side of America, the enemy, which Nixon perceives as bearing the mirror image of himself, New York as the reflection of Yorba Linda. This aspect of the novel is of extreme importance; for we can understand something of Nixon's America by understanding his mode of perception.

What both Coover and Mailer in *Why Are We in Vietnam?* recognized is that America is a "mode of perception," politically; the solidity and stability we once associated with the nation no longer obtains. What does matter is the way we view the country, and the modes of perception are infinite. Thus we have an infinite America, whose infinitude is quite different from the way Emerson perceived the country a century ago. His infinitude was based on the diversity of possibilities; it was a potentiality, an optimistic assessment. Our modes of perception, while possibly infinite, suggest a country that exists only in the imagination, not as substance. The nation now is fifty states, whereas before fifty states were the nation.

Nixon's America is the one he imagined from his lonely outpost in Yorba Linda, as a boy far more marginal than the Rosenbergs, who were active politically when Nixon didn't know the difference between Marxism and Martians. As Nixon reviews the Rosenberg case, which leads from Klaus Fuchs and atomic secrets to the flake Harry Gold, then to Greenglass, Ethel's own brother, a network of unlikely people betraying their country out of ideological fervor, he is led ever deeper into his own motives; and he senses that what they have done at their level to undermine the country, he is doing at his.

Coover introduces us to the scene on the eve of the Rosenberg execution. The way has been cleared for the Times Square spectacle, when, after William Douglas gives a stay, the matter is thrown back into the courts. Nixon meditates on the nature of reality, which is also the nature of theater. The public burning will be spectacle, in which the Rosenbergs have the role of traitors. America will be purged, the ceremony proving cathartic, like public beheadings in Arab countries. Nixon sees all as role-playing. His perception of his own life and career is that he is playing a role over which he lacks control, in the same way the Rosenbergs, once they began their lives at City College of New York, lost control of themselves.

But none of this paralleling could succeed without Coover's fictional strategy of turning real people into characters in a novel of their own making: in effect, reversing normal novelistic procedures. He starts with people we all remember from the recent past, people who have deeply influenced our political lives. His characters at the upper reaches of government, as well as the Rosenbergs, lost their "reality" in order to play roles in their own stories. Eisenhower, for example, is not the Ike of history, but Ike as perceived by Nixon, a fictional character; and behind Nixon, the Ike as perceived by Coover using Nixon as commentator on a person we already know well. This is an alternative structuring of political realities, not in terms of what gets done, or even how issues are decided, but in terms of roles and appearances.

Not unusually, Nixon mentions Arthur Miller's play *The Crucible* several times, and in fact, would like to take Pat to see it for their fourteenth wedding anniversary. *The Crucible* is the side of the political spectrum that is always a threat for Nixon and his colleagues; for it offers a view of government that is cautionary, even if it is not a direct gloss on the McCarthy-Nixon years. From Nixon's point of view, *The Crucible* is as much the enemy as are the Rosenbergs, for it provides observations about the political process by an Eastern intellectual that must undermine Nixon's view of government and his role in it.

Nixon's identification with the Rosenbergs, but especially with Ethel, culminates in his secret visit to Sing Sing Prison in Ossining, New York, just hours before the scheduled execution. He has just come up from Washington for the "public burning," but instead of heading directly for Times Square for the "pre-game festivities," he becomes the single passenger on the Ossining train. These scenes, in which Nixon wanders the streets of Ossining, false mustache misplaced on his face, his name given as John Greenleaf Whittier (who gave his name to Nixon's alma mater), his stomach growling and his bladder bursting, are fine political parody. As he edges toward the greatest crisis of his career, Nixon feels only he can save Ethel, for only he knows how weak the government's case was: files sealed, evidence withheld, witnesses sequestered and tutored, prejudicial judge, Jews railroading other Jews to demonstrate the loyalty of American Jews.

Just as Nixon became the scourge of the Rosenbergs, having given his support to their prosecution, now he identifies with them. Ethel has become the fantasy female of his daydreams. He imagines what it would be like, he a Westerner and a rural type, she an Easterner and an epitome of the urban type, to make it with her. He becomes a driven man. Even the outer security of the prison facility does not discourage him, and he pierces it, heading inside. He needs, before all else, a john, but one door he opens leads to the death chamber. Bladder leads to death, not love.

The mission to Ethel, he feels, can be his alone, because only he can appeal to someone within hours of death: he has himself felt those moments, which bridge East and West. Eisenhower can play golf on the White House lawn on the eve of the execution without being troubled by his decision to let the Rosenbergs burn, the Supreme Court having left it up to him. But Nixon burns with them; he must exorcise his vision of a desirable Ethel, and he can do this only by jeopardizing his own career in a secret visit.

The final 150 pages of the novel define the nature of American political life. Coover's vision becomes wilder, the language freer, the apocalyptic sense more intense. The "public burning"—observed from Ossining and then from the execution site—is great theater, a politician's dream of free publicity. The final sections begin with "A Last-Act Sing Sing Opera by Julius and Ethel Rosenberg." Ethel is the soprano, Julius the tenor, Bennett (federal director of the Bureau of Prisons) the baritone, the warden the bass; with choral effects taken from the *Congressional Record* and including some of the better-known congressional voices (Hale Boggs, Edward Martin, for instance.) The operatic line approximates Mozartian recitative rather than Brecht-Weill political drama. More appropriate would have been "The Rise and Fall of the City of Mahagonny," but Coover nevertheless picks up a "sing sing" line. The confrontations are between Julius and Bennett and Ethel and Bennett, climaxed by a love-death duet between the principals, evoking *Tristan und Isolde* as well as *Tosca*.

Into this Nixon intrudes, desperate for immortality. Early in his life, he had recognized that he had to create himself or else be forgettable; and even with his achievements through adolescence and young manhood, no one noticed him. Nixon arranges to see Ethel in her cell next to the death chamber, whose door remains open during the proceedings. He has become the existential hero of his own self-organized drama, and functions best in a nihilistic scenario.

Ethel is a fetching victim: Nixon in the role of savior, she female flesh waiting for his penetration. He inserts his tongue in her mouth, meets little resistance, and then must deal with her sexual aggression. For the first time in his life, he finds a woman melting for him, for him alone, in a true moment of passion. The death chamber door is nearby, but Nixon is too intent on finding sexual satisfaction to worry about Liebestod. Like the great aria in the Wagner opera, their movement becomes increasingly intense, inflamed; Ethel has been continent for two years, and Nixon has never been sexually fulfilled. He has the chance to be animal.

When Ethel starts to tear his clothes off and his pants are caught around his ankles, they are interrupted. The execution must go on, and she must be transported to Times Square. Unable to disentangle himself, Nixon is brought along, his ass exposed, with the words "I AM A SCAMP" lipsticked on it by the playful Ethel. Now he faces another crisis, for the audience in Times Square consists of acres of celebrities as well as the hooting, jeering, cheering crowd. Nixon must either face disgrace or turn it all into a triumph. With another "Checkers" speech situation, he succeeds by getting most of the dignitaries present to drop their pants after a rousing speech which intermixes God, patriotism, and democracy. "Pants Down

for God and Country," "Pants Down for Jesus Christ," "Pants Down for Dick." Down come the pants, everyone from Tom Dewey, Strom Thurmond, and Jimmy Byrnes, to old Joe Kennedy, Walter Winchell, Ralph Bunche; on to Elsa Maxwell, Bess Truman, and "all the ladies in the Mormon Tabernacle Choir." The scene becomes patriotic frenzy, an orgy of Nixon fervor. The crowd is now worked up for the next act: the public burning of Julius and Ethel Rosenberg.

Coover has turned these final sections of the novel into orgiastic "living theater." All politics in America, as we can observe from a "public burning," is a theatrical event, like Miller's *Crucible,* its burning playing parallel to the execution. Joe McCarthy is the leading actor in this spectacle, grabbing off the headlines with the best speeches; and it is with McCarthy that Nixon must compete. While the execution is being prepared, the crowd is provided with additional fare. Cecil B. DeMille uses the Paramount Building as a "giant magic lantern, the Claridge Hotel as a screen," and "has commenced to project Uncle Sam's documentary film on the Rosenberg boys," to augment the pathos and "to restore a certain monumentality to the event, a bit diminished by the actual human size of the principals."

Film is needed because the event is itself insufficiently large, the screen reflection becoming more significant than the actual episode. Within this mix of roles and reel, Nixon has found the seams; he is the man, not McCarthy, who can shape the big lines. The less apparent destructiveness is the more destructive.

In the final scene, Nixon is anointed by Uncle Sam. In one of the most disagreeable scenes in all postwar American fiction, Uncle Sam gives his approval to Nixon by screwing him in the ass, pushing in his seemingly endless weapon until Nixon is writhing in agony. First, Uncle Sam seems like a reincarnation of Nixon's father, who beat his sons mercilessly; then he becomes Uncle Sam, Nixon's adviser and confidant. And since he's fucked them all—Ike, Roosevelt, Hoover—so he fucks Nixon. ". . . it felt like he was trying to shove the whole goddam Washington Monument up my ass." For once Nixon has ingested Uncle Sam's prick and jism, he has been knighted, dubbed the successor; and Nixon responds as Sam knows he would: "*'I . . . I love you, Uncle Sam!'* I confessed." The way to Nixon's heart is through his ass.

The Rosenberg case returns us to the later 1940s and early 1950s, and this appears to provide the major political arena for Trilling, Mailer, and McCarthy. Since Nixon was involved in Hiss-Chambers, and indirectly in the Rosenbergs, he provides continuity, also giving Philip Roth the opportunity to join "his" later Nixon with Coover's in *The Public Burning.* Further, McCarthy's *Cannibals and Missionaries,* although a 1979 publication, reactivates many of the early 1950s controversies, in which Trilling was himself active. We have, here, almost a *Partisan Review* symposium, with novels rather than well-turned phrases offered up for delectation. Yet except for Trilling's novel, the fare is pallid; and this is true even when we include a book that breaks from this, to focus on the Jew as schlemiel holding off czarist authoritarianism: Malamud's *The Fixer.* Yet there is one constant in nearly all of the above, whatever their setting: pastoral considerations remain strong. Trilling's mise-en-scène is rural Connecticut, which suggests that political beliefs can be best examined not in the arena but as far from practice as possible, in an Edenic locale.

When the politics of the 1930s, with its varietal species of socialism and communism, met at the end of the Second World War, the political novel took many shapes. It might be purely a dialectic of elements, as in Mailer's *Barbary Shore;* or else a combat novel with a political dialectic, as in *The Naked and the Dead;* or a description of the army as a whole reflecting the political process, as in *Guard of Honor* or *The Young Lions;* or it could be a negative of the political process, a denial of it so strong that the refusal to confront it becomes counterpolitical, as in *The Adventures of Augie March.*

Lionel Trilling's *The Middle of the Journey* (1947) is somewhat distinct from the above by virtue of its attempt to be a novel of ideas without becoming purely a novel of dialectics. Except for Gifford Maxim, the characters embody the ideas—unlike, for instance, the personages in *Barbary Shore,* who exist solely to express particular shades of ideology. Furthermore, Trilling's novel is less concerned with purely ideological beliefs than it is with "how to live," "how to behave," how to bring political beliefs down to routine life, which is ordinary, insistent, inexorable. Trilling's observer is John Laskell, whose position in the novel is threefold: as the one through whom the experiential quality of the novel is sifted, a Jamesian post of observation; as a man attempting to rise from the dead after a near-fatal bout with scarlet fever; and as a person responsive to the intense political ideology that intellectuals in the 1940s had to confront, analyze, resolve, or reject.

Although the novel takes place one summer in an apparently idyllic Connecticut rural setting, at Crannock, where Nancy and Arthur Croom have a summer house, the issues are momentous. The setting is one of those Chekhovian places where the tranquil surface is continuously being broken by poisonous currents from beneath. In fact, the political themes are accompanied by that other aspect, of how the trivialities of ordinary life can surface as dramatic, intense events; how the trivial becomes mighty. The physical side of this is Laskell's illness, the scarlet fever which enables him to grow a second skin, after the old one drops away. Even his feet become different as the callus falls off: he walks differently, when he can walk at all. This acquisition of a second skin, part of the physical process, is a clue to Laskell's political development. The illness leads to his second life, death and resurrection. Near death, he has been brought back, transformed, at age thirty-three, that end of the journey for Jesus and the middle of the journey for Dante's modern man.

In his new life, Laskell can reexamine his political beliefs in the Crannock setting, where political involvement seems a distant consideration. Yet it is here, at the Crooms' summer place, that a potentially great drama will unfold, with various positions represented by the Crooms themselves, the transformed John Laskell, the resurrected Gifford Maxim (recalling Whittaker Chambers), and the liberal editor Kermit Simpson. Around them are various rural types: Duck Caldwell, a ne'er-do-well who captivates everyone; his wife, Emily, who has a brief fling with Laskell; their doomed daughter, Susan, who suffers from a heart condition and dies when her father slaps her; and the Folgers, representing stability among this ferment. The calm surface is roiled by undercurrents which can be murderous: Duck is no duck, no natural man, but a drunkard, braggart, and bully.

It is John Laskell's burden to separate one current from another, to thread his ideological and personal way through Maxim's conversion from Party-line communism to reactionism; through Nancy Croom's insistence on dedication to Party ideals despite repellent Party means; through Kermit Simpson's soft liberalism, which condones in the Soviet Union what it condemns in America; through his own efforts to locate a center when all ground appears to be shifting. Laskell's new skin affords him the opportunity to be reborn, but difficulties remain, since currents flow and eddy, are never stilled by his own will to come through. Compounding the novel's problems is Laskell's woodenness, the narrow range of his emotional responses, his traditional approaches to issues, and the complacency that attends upon his sense of himself, his ideal of order and rationality.

We enter the strategy of the novel, which was to observe Gifford Maxim from outside, to view his influence upon people different from himself, to reveal by slow degrees his disenchantment with the Party, his fleeing from it to law, status quo, indeed reaction and religion; his fear that as a nonperson, he might be eliminated by the Party. The unstable element in the novel obviously pertains to Maxim—his name indicates the degree of pressure he can bring—and yet for Trilling to have focused more directly on him would have meant a Dostoyevskian type of psychological fiction, quite different from what we have here. Yet ideology is transplanted from the "Grand Inquisitor" section of *The Brothers Karamazov,* the Crooms and their liberal ideas representing the Inquisitor (bread for the masses) and Maxim himself representing a threatening Jesus, the free individual who believes in man's responsibility and accepts God's grace. Laskell is Ivan Karamazov, who places himself in no-man's-land and hopes to locate a position between man and society. " 'Neither beast nor angel,' " Maxim mocks, reflecting Pascal's taunting of the man who tries to claim untouchability.

The novel, then, flirts with radical extremes, Dostoyevskian passions, but sifted through Laskell, the venture is becalmed. He is a good, decent man who pierces the false liberalism of the Crooms and Simpson, the fluctuations of Maxim, who appears to ride a pendulum from extreme to extreme, and even his own uncertainties. In seeking self-definition, he tries to be Spinoza's good man, but is without Spinoza's passion for great unknowns. Paradoxically, the novel's central intelligence, Laskell, is dull, whereas Maxim, whom we observe only from a distance, has the qualities of a fictional character, half sane, half mad, compelling.

Laskell is Trilling's intellectual hero, fully consistent with his ideas developed in *Matthew Arnold* and his brief study of E. M. Forster. In nineteenth-century terms, Maxim would have been Thomas Carlyle or else the spirit of Hebraism; whereas Arnold sought the Hellenic voice. In the twentieth century, Forster tried to discover the good man, who surrendered the center to warring parties while he moved along distant frontiers. What counts for Trilling is not only a position on issues, but the style and mode of resolving them. Manner, not matter, is the mark of the man.

Such a play of ideas works within biography and critical studies, but in fiction no writer can afford to throw away Maxim. Like Arnold, Trilling may feel that cultural balance (Laskell) outweighs political and religious commitment (Maxim) because the first is various and full whereas the latter focuses upon singularities; but for fictional purposes the obsessed man is more compelling than the reasonable one. On the margins of these two major combatants, the Crooms and Kermit Simpson are too pallid to provide dramatic differentiation; nor are the locals, the Caldwells and the Folgers, sufficiently "done." Only Duck Caldwell could be of interest, the Lawrentian character who consistently fails us and whose relationship to nature is, finally, antinatural. Yet Duck is of such little substance that attention lavished on him cannot create dramatic force. The interest Nancy Croom has for him is misplaced—we see that from the first; so that when she recognizes what he is, we are two hundred pages ahead of her. Trilling is very uneasy when he must write about characters who fall outside the dialectic of ideas, a kind of reverse of Mailer's *Barbary Shore,* where all the unease comes in the dialectic.

The attempt at a dialectic was Mailer's downfall in *Barbary Shore* (1951). It was unfortunate that he tried to write a solemn political novel so soon after the success of *The Naked and the Dead,* possibly deceived into thinking the Hearn-Cummings dialogues there were of value, when it was the narrative sequences that proved so compelling. Mailer erred in believing he could forsake narrative and still sound important, when his best work was to incorporate ideas into narrative or events. With this novel, we have Mailer's characteristic need to rush into print before his ideas can be assimilated to people, events, and narrative. *Barbary Shore* foreshadows those later difficulties in writing novels.

All elements remain shadowy and inconclusive. Mikey Lovett lacks a past, an amnesiac probably from the war; plastic surgery has created a new face for him. Thus, in his second skin, he is a tabula rasa, waiting to be written upon and given a function. In a Brooklyn boardinghouse owned by Guinevere, Mikey meets McLeod, a kind of Whittaker Chambers mutant: an ex-Communist, ex-capitalist, now a revolutionary socialist. "Barbary Shore" is a refuge of pirates, the end of the earth sheltering those on the run from the American system. But it is more like Harry's bar in *The Iceman Cometh,* a place where people indulge in boring talk: Guinevere, the nympho, and her tale of lost opportunities; McLeod, her husband, and his suggestions of a mysterious past, for which he is, mysteriously, murdered; Mikey and his talk of writing, which we never see; then the blather of other boarders, like Lannie, a truthful but drug-and-alcohol-ridden young lady, finally Hollingsworth, a government investigator, perhaps an FBI man. So inert is the material that Mailer's prose breaks down, loses touch with subject and object, like a batter in a slump who cannot "feel" the pitch.

Mary McCarthy's *The Groves of Academe* (1952) was written as an academic *1984:* the way the world ends at what should be a citadel of learning. McCarthy takes her epigraph from Horace's *Epistles:* One seeks truth among the groves of academe. But truth in her tale is hopelessly confused, becoming entangled in McCarthyite politics in the time of the Rosenbergs, Hiss, the Un-American Activities Committee, Nixon, and all the rest of the "wild bunch." Since truth has become suspect, the greatest truth becomes the biggest lie. To protect oneself, one must lie; the groves of academe are, very possibly, the best place for such lies.

When Dr. Henry Mulcahy (the sole Ph.D. in Jocelyn College's literature department) finds a letter from the president informing him that his appointment has been terminated, he desperately needs some strategy to forestall the event. The truth is he took the appointment knowing it might be for only a year, and he served at the pleasure of the president, Maynard Hoar (a name too broad even for satirical purposes). Like most of the students and faculty at "experimental" Jocelyn, in Pennsylvania, Mulcahy is unappetizing, though supposedly distinguished: Guggenheim fellow, Rhodes scholar, contributor to *The Nation* and *Kenyon Review*. Married, the father of four small children, he is, at forty-one, at the crossroads of a very checkered career. McCarthy, however, never makes clear why a former Rhodes scholar would find himself in such a backwater college. Mulcahy is apparently a loser, but even mediocrities in the academy are recognized for achievements such as his.

Mulcahy decides to use the political atmosphere as his weapon. Since Hoar poses as a liberal, has in fact written a pamphlet called "The Witch Hunt in Our Universities," Mulcahy decides to trap the president in his own rhetoric. By posing as a Communist Party member and claiming, further, that Hoar knows Mrs. Mulcahy is a dying woman, Mulcahy will gain sympathy and political support. The liberal college community will rally around anyone whose rights are being traduced. Mulcahy plans to create an atmosphere at Jocelyn that will make Hoar retreat, or else appear to be part of the very witch hunt he has con-

demned in his pamphlet. Like many of her *Partisan Review* colleagues in the 1950s, McCarthy directs her scorn at liberals, who, she assumes, pursue their politics unthinkingly. Mulcahy has taken into his confidence a young teacher of Russian, Domna Rejnev, suspecting that beneath her hauteur she is a conventional liberal whose sense of guilt can be played upon. ". . . she was a true liberal . . . who could not tolerate in her well-modulated heart that others should be wickeder than she, any more than she could bear that she should be richer, better born, better looking than some statistical median." Mulcahy has, of course, guessed correctly.

There is the potential here of a first-rate satirical comment, but McCarthy gets in her own way. Her depiction of faculty is undifferentiated, and her presentation of students as a swarmy bunch has all the condescension of a Vassar graduate. Vitiating the satire at every stage is McCarthy's own assumption of superiority, and that connected to the fact she is attacking liberals, *her own kind of people*. Of course, a novelist can choose her own materials, her own pressure points, but satire—unlike burlesque—presupposes balance, an awareness of several countering elements. And in contemporary satire, as against its eighteenth-century versions, the author is part of the process and needs greater sensitivity to contexts. McCarthy indulges herself and expects us to acquiesce.

Part of the problem with overkill is that we come to sympathize haphazardly with the wrong character at the wrong time. In terms of what college presidents are capable of, Hoar is not a whore. Also, we begin to feel sorry for Mulcahy, since his talents do seem more extensive than those of his colleagues. Even Domna, who should be pivotal, becomes murky. She's a lovely young woman who becomes Mulcahy's fool, a political foil, someone who, feeling used, should be resentful. But she fades from sight, and turns up only to remind us she was once important. The lack of coherent elements results from that constant need for overkill. No one can survive McCarthy, and after thirty years the novel catches almost nothing of our memories of the time. The academy in the 1950s was a far more complex, compelling, and, indeed, savage place.

Cannibals and Missionaries (1979) is Mary McCarthy's most ambitious novel since *The Group*, and in some ways it is more adroit. Yet it returns in its ideology to many of the controversies of the 1950s, between liberals and radicals, and their slightly updated varietals.

In his preface to *The Princess Casamassima,* James speaks of how the novelist should maintain balance between two elements: the intelligence every character needs to be interesting and compelling, and the bewilderment that same character must have to convey surprise and tension. McCarthy does not achieve that balance, for she drives hard on being in command. Only Lily in *Cannibals* seems close to that balance James suggests, her hard insights intermixed with a "water color" kind of personality. But for her main characters, McCarthy parodies anything less than intelligence, rejecting bewilderment.

Cannibals and Missionaries tries very hard to be a "now" novel." The hijacking of a plane en route from New York to Iran, via Israel, gives McCarthy three converging political elements. First, we meet a mixed group of liberals on their way to Iran to poke around in prisons and similar places to see what kind of shop the Shah is running. Their interest is in preserving the decencies of democracy. This group includes the rector of St. Matthew's, an old retired bishop, a senator, a college president (Aileen Simmons), a Jewish reporter named Sophie, a Dutch government official, Henk, and two others. First-class passengers include twelve millionaires, nearly all of them serious collectors of art. Separated by money and class from the other group, they run their own operation, much disliked by Simmons.

The third element consists of terrorists, who hijack the plane and fly it to Schiphol, in the Netherlands; there, they transfer to a helicopter and fly to a polder, a piece of land reclaimed from the sea by way of dredging and landfill. The terrorists, a mixed group —two Arabs, a South American (Carlos, but not *the* Carlos)—are led by a Dutchman named Joeren and a Dutchwoman, Greet. Their aim originally was to barter hostages for jailed terrorists, four of the latter for each one of the former. But when they assess the group, they focus on the art; the barter will be lives for art.

Joeren is a former art student, who sees that "terrorism was art for art's sake in the political realm." Disbelieving in the usual slogans, he feels all political solutions are quite temporary; the Palestinian question, for example, "was merely a parenthesis." He sees that art can prove transformational: merely take all those miserable millionaires and make them transmute themselves into masterpieces, through the exchange of their lives for their great artworks: "turn their base substance into pure gold."

The spatial area chosen for the caper is crucial to the enterprise: the polder is, for McCarthy, a perfect meeting place of terrorists, bourgeois capitalists, contemporary liberals, and that world of art and old masters. Before the group arrives, we are led into Holland as a place that "no rational mind in this century could believe in . . . as a real place." The prime minister is Mr. Owl; Henk is a deputy whose grandfather was a famous popular novelist; and the country—reclaimed land, dikes, a fantasy of antinature—is meaningful only to other Dutch. "Being Dutch was a comical predicament, more grotesque even than being Swiss." This description is an apt foreshadowing of the hallucinatory quality of the hijacking—a mythical country as backdrop for the twentieth-century fantasy played out in a hijacking. The polder is a nowhere ("Holland's Alaska") which spatially becomes everything.

Part of the problem with the plan, however, lies with the groups themselves, primarily with the liberals out to investigate the Shah's prisons. As McCarthy demonstrated in *The Group* and *Birds of America,* the very idea of grouping suggests a breakdown of the human spirit, which functions best in the individual. Within this group, she has several portraits: portraits rather than characters. Senator Jim Carey is based apparently on Eugene McCarthy, in the details of both his accomplishments and his personal life. Mary McCarthy writes about him fondly, but her insights are familiar to us from the columns of *The New York Times.* Also in the group is one of McCarthy's standbys, a refugee, as it were, from her Vassar College group. This is Aileen Simmons, petty, occasionally venomous, old maidish and yet desirous of some action, a driven liberal whose hatred for the millionaires focuses her. The problem with the Simmons portrait is that McCarthy is uncertain whether to laud or parody her. She is one of the two unharmed survivors, the other being Frank Barber, the energetic rector. Barber is a man driven to see good done—his campaign for equal rights has almost lost him his church—and he perceives the hijacking as not a tragedy but a test of faith. His Christianity is muscular, full of social substance, politically liberal to its core. He will take consequences. And yet McCarthy edges him with parody; the mere fact of him is comic fodder. Americans, for McCarthy, are people who cannot be presented without parody. The Dutch Henk, however, who is bourgeois, stolid, a man not above playing around when away from his wife, has a presence McCarthy can take straight. His fantasy sense of Holland dominates our imagination; we accept it, through him. His discussions with Joeren are reality itself. Joeren indicates what he wants, and Henk tells him what the Dutch government will give: art, perhaps, but no withdrawal from NATO, no break with Israel, no alignment with the Palestinians. Henk's centrality, unfortunately, turns Simmons and Barber into marginal figures, even as McCarthy devotes space to them.

Among the hijackers, the sole glimpse we get of a real presence is Joeren's. Poor, a struggling artist in his youth, a member of the Party, Joeren became disillusioned with all formal rebellion and turned to terrorism as a display of pure leftism. When the hijacking involves the millionaires, it is natural for him to think of offering their lives as ransom for their Vermeers, El Grecos, Cézannes, Giorgiones, watercolors. To acquire great art is for him the final act of revolution. The bourgeois Vermeer, his *Girl with a Guitar,* becomes for Joeren the focal point of his life, something he can finally love.

The idea is an excellent one, but McCarthy does not fictionally lead us to accept it. Her methods are insufficient; the hijackers escape her explanations. In *A Smuggler's Bible*—not hijacking, but smuggling is close—Joseph McElroy devised internal techniques or substructures which would approximate the subject. McCarthy attempts to locate the point of view in various characters, but otherwise her techniques are external. Yet we are, after all, in the midst of great despair—hijacking must be observed as such, not simply as an accomplishment—and Joeren in an act of despair blows up the house, the art, himself, and most of the remaining hostages and terrorists. The Vermeer, which goes up with him in the explosion, has precipitated the act: his love for it, for the girl situated in it, for the idea of a Vermeer. Here is his true revolutionary act; and yet we do not comprehend it or the despair that went into it.

The world goes out with a bang, but the effect is a whimper. The happening on the polder is over, already replaced in the media with another event, significant only to those who experienced it. McCarthy's novel appeared just when the fifty-two hostages held by the Iranian kidnappers were the focus of world attention, and as the novel faded from view, so did the world's concern for the hostages. Except for their families (and themselves), and the politicians who could make capital from their plight, interest waned.

Here the McCarthy novel reaches for a real contemporary response: our inability to focus attention for more than minutes. We are, she suggests, attuned to the media presentation of events, and we have replaced a sense of historical contexts with two- or three-minute presentations: all news occurs in fragments, or "cartridges," to use McElroy's term. The terrorists on the polder, like those in the American embassy in Teheran, could not exist without the insistence of the media. Yet the paradox: although revolutionaries and leftists wish to suppress television and press crews, they have their own dilemma; for without the presence of the media, there may be no revolution.

Although this is not a completely new cultural development, the advent of television in the 1950s created its own political culture, in which those who can least afford exposure are forced to rely on such means of communication to maintain their momentum. Here is an aspect of the novel which McCarthy only suggests; and it is, like so many other elements in *Cannibals and Missionaries,* inchoate matter; the substance of an extremely penetrating intelligence that has not informed its materials. For when we are finished, we do not understand the liberals, nor the millionaires, nor, least of all, the terrorists. All that remains is all that beauty, caught in the eye of the perceiver, for it has been blown sky high, art, cannibals, and missionaries together.

Whereas McCarthy seems uncertain of her tone, whether to head openly for satire or to settle for moderate parody, Philip Roth in *Our Gang* (1971) has opted completely for satire. Although the novel is slight, more or less a variation on a single joke, it does raise interesting questions about the very possibility of ambitious political satire in postwar America: something more profound, that is, than the one-liners of a stand-up comic like Mort Sahl. Roth intended a kind of *Gulliver's Travels* or *Animal Farm* in his treatment of Nixon and his presidency. Epigraphs from both Swift and Orwell appear, also a passage from "A Voyage to the Houyhnhnms" and Orwell's "Politics and the English Language." The latter is the key to what Roth had in mind: that "present political chaos is connected with the decay of language, and that one can probably bring about some improvement by starting at the verbal end." Orwell's point, which Roth reflects, is that political language, whatever the party or ideology, is designed to "make lies sound truthful and murder respectable, and to give an appearance of solidity to pure wind."

The trickiness of Dicky comes from his misuse of language. Words are for him always forms of doublespeak, the substance of four of the novel's six chapters. Two final chapters concern the assassination of Tricky, then his comeback trail—the final crisis he must confront—from his location in hell. Everything in Roth's book derives from Nixon's "Checkers" speech in 1952, when he used language as a way of disguising what and who he was, hiding behind his dog, Pat's cloth coat, his near-poverty.

The problem with Roth's formulation is that he did not find a conceit or metaphor as a vehicle for his satire. There is, in effect, no satire, since Tricky's words are predictable; by 1971, anyone who would be reading Roth's book had already written "Our Gang" in his own mind. The crux of political satire must lie in its use of exaggerations to limn the ordinary, or to make the ordinary appear extraordinary by way of distortion. Thus, *Animal Farm*—with barnyard animals as elements of the political state (whatever its precise ideology); or *Gulliver's Travels*—with distortions of size and space; or *Alice in Wonderland*—with its fantastic characters who embody aspects of royalty, diplomacy, affairs of state. Whatever the exact form political satire takes, it has shapes that alter our perception of what is being satirized.

Roth's problem is duplication, or imitation. The words in Tricky's mouth are actually little different from those in Nixon's. What we read is not the ordinary made extraordinary, or carried into another dimension, but a repetition of the known. Political satire must foster laughter, or else it sermonizes. Roth's outrage as a liberal and humanitarian turns his passages of Tricky's doubletalk into homiletics. War, sex, abortion, the political process all come under the hammer, but they remain as they were, unaltered by Roth's treatment of them.

Political satire in our era may be impossible for an American writer to achieve; that is, in fictional form. There are several reasons. As both Roth and Barth have noted, reality may have outrun our ability to imagine things. Nixon's real career had more wild swings than anything in Coover's novel. Also, in a free society, where everything is possible in print or orally, it may be impossible to find the fictional equivalents of what can be satirized. In oppressive societies, political satire can thrive because when the printed word is censored, words become weapons. Their use—and the ideas they shape—has a weight and measure denied to words that can be used and reused indifferently. To print words as an act of defiance is a step toward satire; when such words are placed in the mouth of an unlikely person, the satirical mode is born.

For the American writer, freedom of usage means language has lost its political significance. Unfortunately, the same casualness applies to shaping charac-

ter. The free society tolerates every eccentricity, whereas the less free sees such individuals as antisocial or, in some cases, pathological; in most parts of the world, as political enemies of the state. The individual in such societies is measured in terms of social contributions; whereas in the free society, success or failure remains a private matter, the individual's tragedy, not the state's. In those terms, satire becomes difficult to locate, for the agon has been lost. Antagonism between individual and state is diluted, or eliminated.

The final two political novels we will consider have a curious affinity: Malamud's about a Jewish schlemiel who defies the Czar, Kelley's about blacks who also "refuse" and silently depart rather than serve. In both cases, the state oppresses, and individual integrity becomes more vital than whatever is offered in exchange. Unlike Chamisso's schlemiel, who sells his shadow for worldly goods, Malamud's Bok becomes a goat in his stubbornness, refusing his shadow for a chance to live; similarly, Kelley's blacks demand the retention of their shadow—that is, their selves. In both novels, underdogs achieve stature by holding on to their shadows.

In *The Fixer* (1966), Bok, a variation on Gimpel, is accused of the ritual murder of a Christian boy, is imprisoned in a Czarist jail, and awaits an indictment. His period of waiting, unlike a prison sentence, has no limits. Like Kafka's protagonists, he is being tried for something he cannot grasp, but even more, he is unsure of the nature of the game being played against him.

Eventually, it becomes clear Bok is a piece in a political puzzle. His indictment, or admission of guilt, would draw interest to the Jewish question when the Czar needed relief from agitation. The period is after the 1905 revolution, before the buildup for the Bolshevik revolution. Bok is a pawn in the plans of the Black Hundreds (a virulently anti-Semitic organization), the Czar's own government, and those interested in agitation and further political unrest. His admission of guilt, then, becomes a national problem: if Bok holds out, he will foil plans; if he succumbs to his misery and admits guilt (in exchange for his freedom), then he opens up a bag of worms for other Jews. In either case, Jews get the worst of it: punished if he confesses, a pogrom if he doesn't.

Like Job when he refused to deny God's right to punish him without apparent reason, Bok is made to carry the entire Jewish race. The problem with *The Fixer,* or one of its problems, lies here. Bok's individual burden becomes indistinguishable from the burdens of his race, from the survival of Jews in Czarist Russia, and by implication from the entire Jewish movement. For Bok is accused of all the Jewish crimes: being a follower of Herzl's Zionists, belonging to various secret organizations, being a socialist. As in a Kafka novel, the persecution of the protagonist derives from a source indifferent to the individual case.

Malamud, however, is unable to make the transition from individual to society and back again. He stresses a man and yet reaches toward allegory. While Kafka pegged his narrative to a level of ambiguity, Malamud locates his narrative in detailed and realistic elements; Bok is very much part of his community. His wife leaves him when he becomes impotent with her; he drifts to an area beyond the pale and relocates in a section of Kiev forbidden to Jews; hiding his Jewishness, he is employed by an anti-Semite (a member of the Black Hundreds); he is almost seduced by the anti-Semite's crippled daughter; and then, after having been given a good position as a brickworks foreman, he is taken in by the police for the ritual murder of a twelve-year-old Christian boy. Each stage is particularized, so that Bok is far more of an individual than is a Kafka protagonist. For example, when the crippled Zina Lebedev entices Bok to her room, he watches her wash at her basin and sees a fine trickle of blood run down her leg. Bok, whose conditioning makes him consider the woman untouchable during her period, is disgusted, whereas Zina regards this as the best time, when pregnancy is all but impossible.

The sharpness of this image confers individuality on Bok, as it drives home to him that the disguised Jew is very much a Jew. Yet at the same time Bok is made to stand for all Jews: those who are hidden as well as those who profess their faith. Bok's secretive nature, his inability to connect to his Jewishness as a living faith—elements we considered peculiar to him —become symbolic, and he is transformed into a running figure in an allegory of persecution. Triumph over oppression supersedes Bok's individual suffering. The novel begins to come apart. Near the end of the novel, Bok has dreamlike interviews with the Czar. These take the form of visions, in which the two sit down to settle their differences. The Czar speaks of himself, of his hemophiliac son, of how the lack of coagulant in the blood of the young Alexis is connected to Bok's alleged crime, his having drained the Christian child's blood in order to make ritual matzos. When the Czar talks about his trials, of how he never wanted the crown, Bok interrupts to say that whatever his intentions, the Czar has made a "valley of bones" of the country. " 'You had your chance and you pissed them away.' " Bok adds that the Czar lacks in his rule what his son lacks in his blood, an essential element. The Czar attempts to defend the pogroms: " 'Water can't be prevented from flowing. They are a genuine expression of the will of the people.' " With that, the Jewish prisoner points a revolver at the Czar and shoots him through the breast. The vision ends, and Bok is back in the carriage that, after an explosion, is carrying him to court. The novel ends on Bok's defiance of a political state that oppresses the individual. "You can't sit still and see yourself destroyed." Bok becomes Israel, a pageant.

While the lines of allegory are misplaced, the idea of the "hidden Jew" is an excellent one, and it is connected to several related types in postwar American fiction. Most obviously, the disguised Jew recalls the invisible man. The hidden Jew can "pass" when he changes his name, has a national rather than a racial nose, and wears his hair like everyone else. In somewhat similar manner, Ellison's invisible man, before he chooses his kind of invisibility, hopes to pass into white society, for him by way of the work ethic, perseverance, attention to orders and detail. Thus, the hidden Jew will become part of the Gentile world; the black, part of the white world. Both become invisible as a consequence of their choices. Bok's invisibility is achieved deep in a Czarist prison, where day and night blend; Ellison's unnamed protagonist achieves invisibility as an act of will, in his underground stronghold, lighted only by hundreds of bulbs placed in the walls.

Within *A Different Drummer* (1959, 1962), William Melvin Kelley employs a Faulknerian strategy, locating a narrator, Mr. Harper, to fill in background on the "State" and to create interior dialogues. From that, Kelley proceeds to his main subject, the literal emptying out of all Negroes as they leave the State to go to neighboring areas or North.

The State is a south central region, bounded by Tennessee, Alabama, the Gulf of Mexico, Mississippi: in effect, the Deep South. Harper recalls the slave trade and reminisces about a particular African chief, his feeling being that Negroes in 1957 are leaving because their African blood is acting up. The African is a magnificent creature of size and determination, a man who refuses to be enslaved. Carrying a baby under his arm, he fights his way free of the slave traders, flees into the countryside, is cornered finally, and shot dead by the man who had purchased him and the baby for a thousand dollars. The baby survives, and begins the line that leads down to the present.

Kelley's development of the African has in it the mythical qualities that Richard Wright attributed to his "Big, Black Good Man": a man beyond men. He is, also, something like Faulkner's Sutpen, whose determination to clear and build his estate enables him to overcome all obstacles. But the African is not interested only in his own freedom; he sets out to free as many slaves as possible: "And up the front lawn [of Dewitt, the buyer], dressed in African clothes of bright colors, with a spear and a shield, comes the African, bearing down on the house like he was a train and it was a tunnel and he was going right through."

The African, then, is savior as well as mythical figure, Moses and Jesus leading Negroes from their bondage, Nat Turner as well. Kelley, we recall, was writing this book in the late 1950s, right on the cutting edge of major developments in postwar black history, when civil right groups were forming, Muslims were active, and the entire white South was in ferment, ostensibly over *Brown* v. *Education* but really over what it foresaw as the end of its way of life. Kelley's epigraph is from the Thoreau passage that speaks of the man who does not "keep pace with his companions . . . because he hears a different drummer." The application of this to the African chief, then to those who leave the State, is a brilliant perception of the 1950s.

When Tucker Caliban, believed to be one of the chief's descendants, seeds his land with salt, he is preparing it for destruction, the Biblical commandment to let things grow having been reversed. Caliban's action is the key one in the novel: the central mystery, the unraveling of which is the basis of the novel's development. Kelley uses a technique similar to Faulkner's in *As I Lay Dying,* which is to radiate out from a central event with several commentaries. Kelley also uses a family, the Willsons. Descendants of the general who fought under Lee and was first governor of the readmitted State, they have been deeply involved with the Calibans, from slaves, to freed slaves, now to the "free" Tucker, who still feels himself indentured.

The difficulty with the novel comes in the development of parallel and lateral actions, such as the involvement of the Reverend Bradshaw in the exodus. Necessary ideologically, Bradshaw weakens the structure. Having been at Harvard with the senior Willson, he comes to the town when he hears of the exodus. He rides around in a large, chauffeured car with young Dewey Willson III, in order to glean information from him. Bradshaw eventually becomes the scapegoat for town toughs who seek revenge on someone for the loss of their blacks. Bradshaw becomes a lynch victim, and Dewey barely escapes, and that only because the mob fears his father's power.

The lynching of Bradshaw, in Kelley's plan, will be the final act of desecration in the town and in the State. There will be no more blacks to lynch, and this last act of sacrifice comes as the result of both Bradshaw's mere presence as catalyst, and his interest in the exodus as leader of the Resurrected Church of the Black Jesus Christ of America, the Black Jesuits, an amalgam of Black Muslims and Panthers as they would later form. More confidence man than leader, Bradshaw has put together an organization that cites the Bible to prove black supremacy, believes Jesus was black, and attacks Jews as exploiters.

With him, unfortunately, the novel begins to lose coherence, even as it gains political meaning. The flashbacks, through Willson's diary, of the white man's friendship with Bradshaw at Harvard do not mesh with the Reverend's involvement in the town during the exodus. Bradshaw is too complicated a creature for the event; and our attempts to comprehend Tucker Caliban's act—one of independence, liberation of self and family—through the complex motives of Bradshaw are defeated. Kelley does not himself appear to know what to make of Bradshaw: a creature with a motor of his own, perhaps symbolized by a car that can take him anywhere. Bradshaw is too much a mix of black aspirations, spellbinding speaker, false prophet, black supremacist and anti-Semite for Kelley's brief glimpses of him to blend. The Willson diaries, the reminiscences of family life by the Willson children, Dewey and Dymphna, the flashbacks of Mrs. Willson about herself and her husband when young; plus political aspects, introduced with Willson's flirtation with communism, his being blackballed by the town and regional newspapers, and his return to the plantation as a result—all these set into motion far more lateral activity than a novel of two hundred pages can possibly contain. Not only the edges but the internal workings become incoherent.

The problem with this considerable first novel is that elements that should feed into the central tension spin away. Bradshaw is only one of the difficulties.

The device of the Willson diaries is artificial, since the novel's strength has been gained by way of oral, not written, language. One of the really fine moments of the oral tradition occurs when Bradshaw speaks to young Leland in educated tones, and the white boy simply does not comprehend the words. Bradshaw then puts his words into Southern talk, erasing his Northern education, and Leland understands. It is a moment of considerable wit as well as definition of character.

Drummer has a central structural concept such as too many novels lack: an idea that generates its own kind of historicity and symbolic action. Had Kelley stuck to that central motif—the exodus, the mystery of Caliban's decision, the overall desire for liberation —the novel would have been a literary event and a cogent political statement. The dissipation of energies, while understandable in a first novel, takes *Drummer* into social and political areas alien to the main development. Kelley was apparently torn, between the Ellison kind of statement, which is scaled down to the individual, and his concern with black aspirations, which uses the novel as a forum for social and political issues. Ideology derived from characters is far more compelling than characters derived from ideology.

Chapter Eight

||||||||||||||||||||||||||||||||||||||||||||||||||||||

THE 1960S: THE (WO)MAN WHO CRIED I AM

But since I [a mollusk] had no form I could feel all possible forms in myself, and all actions and expressions and possibilities of making noises, even rude ones.

CALVINO, *Cosmicomics*

Introductory

Certain novels, while not themselves great literature, often foreshadow a cultural or historical shift. The novelist senses a change in taste, attitudes, a new direction, or simply variations on themes. Such novels help establish a framework, which is then fleshed out by the truly great works that establish change, whether *Don Quixote, Madame Bovary,* or *Ulysses.* But those works in the minor mode notify us a new sensibility is arriving. Since change is so rapid in America, it may appear that such foreshadowings can come at any time; but between the late 1950s and early 1960s, we recognize that America was poised for a cultural revolution: an accumulation of shifts in sensibility that would affect not only the arbiters of taste but taste itself.

Four such forerunners are: J. P. Donleavy's *The Ginger Man* (1958), which seems to be the one book he would continue to write; Terry Southern's *The Magic Christian* (1960), a kind of "Animal House" with solid perceptions of the culture; Philip Roth's *Goodbye, Columbus* (1959), distinctive fictions which foreshadowed not only the sixties but Roth's own varied career; and Clancy Sigal's *Going Away* (1961), an excellent place to start, the sixties in embryo.

Going Away has been mentioned only infrequently in studies in the novel, perhaps because it does not easily fit into any slot. Subtitled "A Report and a Memoir," it is part nonfiction, part eighteenth-century picaresque, part a drifting act of liberation. *Going Away* focuses on one year, 1956, but it is an excellent junction of several elements, some of which extend back into the thirties and several of which adumbrate the sixties. The protagonist (let us call him Sigal) is a twenty-nine-year-old who has seen the world, and especially the United States, and discovered that it is dispiriting, dehumanizing, full of what Marcuse was to call "one-dimensional men," a 1960s catch phrase.

Sigal is crossing the country "to look at America and try to figure out why it wasn't . . . [my] country any more." His parents provided a background of radical politics, and his own beliefs maintain a radical politics is still possible despite the need to reject Stalinist Communists and academic liberals. Sigal is struggling against America as a mass, 1950s counterfeit. His trip, in 1956, coincides with several historical events, which he picks up on his car radio as he swings around the country: the Hungarian uprising and the invasion of Hungary by Soviet armed forces; the Eisenhower-Stevenson campaign for the presidency; and the Israeli invasion of the Sinai and Suez, along with French and British forces.

These political events work through as leitmotifs, so that we never forget political acts that go beyond direct American needs. Sigal is able to avoid the severe narcissism of Beat "on the road" narratives, and even that of Bellow's *Augie March,* by reaching out beyond the individual to the country at large, then beyond that to world politics. The immediate model for the book would appear to be Dos Passos's *U.S.A.:* the bums, the tramps, the road experiences, the desire to see America as large and vital, intermixed with poverty, expedience, political compromise. Further, Sigal's political sympathies seem attuned with the Dos Passos of that work: large, union-oriented, in the radical tradition of the Wobblies, but wary of formal designations.

In his travels, Sigal looks up former friends and acquaintances, trying to see how they have lived since the war, how they support themselves, what their political ideas are, what their lives are made of. He is interested in substance, not outward signs. He seeks that adversary relationship man has created between himself and the state or society which suggests the degree to which he has preserved himself; and to what degree he has something left of himself to give to ideas, beliefs, even ideology. Sigal observes self-betrayal or, more often, those who are confused and unable to define their own lives or their sense of the country.

A telling episode involves his stay in Cedar City, Iowa. The location is significant, for it denotes corn country, rural values, the meeting place of old and modern, the old favored by most, the modern supported by the university crowd. Sigal is the guest of Axel, a former army man whose job was as a graves registration officer, a man who dealt in bodies. Axel's wife committed suicide a week before he returned home, and he became a wino on skid row in the City of Angels in 1946. Then, in an unlikely move, Axel married Marie, a girl of seventeen who had spent the war giving herself to servicemen, but a tough young lady with strong survival instincts. Axel has brains, and they end up in Cedar City, where he teaches sociology at the university.

The classic situation is there. The individual has recovered personally and is prepared to indulge himself in everything America offers, setting up an adversary relationship to his own self, which recognizes that he has lost integrity, compromised his beliefs, lost all faith in the social process, and finally, is prepared to abandon those who need his brains and commitment to ideas. With few exceptions, this is what Sigal observes throughout the country: those who

mock Eisenhower, but buy Eisenhower's America; or those who support Eisenhower, but have abandoned any feeling for the country. At a party Axel arranges for his guest, the situation becomes focused, with Sigal attempting to demonstrate the growing one-dimensionality of the country. Man's subversive force, that potentially destructive character which suggests his vitality, has been lost. By seeking more, he has settled for less.

As Sigal observes everyone becoming more modernized—that is, compromising himself for the sake of goods—he feels he is becoming increasingly older, "not the son of immigrants but an eighth-generation American . . . [who] was sitting in a hard-constructed rocking chair on the porch of my house somewhere in Vermont and feeling terribly *old* American, as though I were some obscure but stern-souled Van Rensselaer or Cabot or Stevenson." He foresees that need to return to the land, to rethink the reliance on Thoreau and Emerson which characterized American youth in the 1960s and 1970s, or became part of the environmental movements. The son of Jewish immigrants, Sigal suddenly identifies with the most American parts of the American experience, that belief in individual action. He comments later that he was brought up to believe the single life took on meaning only because it derived from the mass; but one arrived at the individual by way of the mass. The other way, which he now embraces, is to see the individual life alone, that rural sense of people living by and for themselves, independent rocks. That, too, is a romantic, pastoral fantasy, since, as we know, drunkenness, madness, homicide, suicide are the other ingredients of these pastoral American communities; but they are, nevertheless, part of that dream which undercuts mass men and mass societies.*

The device Sigal uses to measure all this, besides the ostensible mode of the journey itself, is a personal crisscrossing pattern. For he has given up success as a Hollywood agent, divested himself of salary, pad, lady friends, advancement, in direct proportion to his former friends' acquisition of goods. The America he observes becomes increasingly an arena of what he senses is wrong with America and Americans. The power of Sigal's book, altogether missing from *On the Road* and other Beat-oriented fiction, is the tremen-

---

*Sigal also omits the provincialism, racism, anti-Semitism, and, often, fanatical right-wing sympathies of those rural Americans; pastoral, idyllic as their villages may be, they are desperate that America has left them behind.

dous weight of social and political fact; it is, also, the source of some of the book's sluggishness. Sigal overdoes the union conflicts, his friends' histories, the dipping into the past for ever more stories. Too much accrues, and soon all stories begin to sound similar, an unfortunate characteristic of picaresque narratives. The friends are insufficiently differentiated—they become part of the undifferentiated mass, at the very time the particularities of their experiences are the elements Sigal must depend upon.

The book Sigal writes—which wins a literary fellowship at his publishing house (Houghton Mifflin)—is the single function keeping him sane, as he observes America lurch toward varieties of lunacy. Sigal vomits his way across the States—Henry Miller tried to set a literary fucking record, but Sigal does it in puke—so that only the book remains after he has coughed up the rest. It is a record, an anchor, a force for truth, no matter how artificial or false the rest is, including his publishing house. The book records that he attempted to be honest, acted as a catalyst wherever he went. He recognizes his literary tradition is that of two writers he does not like, Whitman and Wolfe, but he'd known he "could write in no other tradition."

At twenty-nine, he would no longer be trusted by the new generation, just as he no longer trusted the generation he had grown up with. An outsider, a stranger, a believer in modes that no longer obtained, he leaves, just as Budapest Radio signals, in its final effort, "Help us, Help. Help. Help. Help." A cry to the world for help against Soviet tanks, it is also the cry that the 1950s were making to the succeeding decade.

Sigal's insurgent persona is paralleled by J. P. Donleavy's apolitical Sebastian Dangerfield. In its concentration on self-serving episodes and a solipsistic, hedonistic protagonist, *The Ginger Man* recalls two somewhat similar movements in America and Britain. In America, the novel has affinities to the Beats, although that movement had some loose ideology, which *The Ginger Man* lacks. In England, an even less focused group, the so-called Angry Young Men, tried to define a rebellion against bourgeois life, even while enjoying its creature comforts. In both instances, English and American, the phenomenon produced a picaresque protagonist: a drinker or drifter, or both, highly sexed (heterosexual in England, less defined in America), rebellious (seeking something in spatial America, more rooted in temporal England), an adversary element living by his wits,

using others as necessary, and treating women as objects with convenient orifices.

It was the kind of fiction that would run its course after the 1950s, when stodge and counterfeit led to real rebelliousness, whatever shape it took. In the 1960s, rebellion became more complicated, not only self-serving and solipsistic, but connected to issues. In Donleavy, there is no "other," there is only Sebastian Dangerfield. An American, Donleavy has donned an Irish persona, probing Joycean language to reinforce his own not insubstantial linguistic gifts. In locating Joyce's lyricism, Donleavy has also found a language suitable for his Sebastian, whose name as a martyr is belied by his hedonism. The basic pattern for Sebastian is that he comes upon a vulnerable woman, offers her a drink, commiserates with her situation (usually lower class, deprived, exploited by father and employer), holds her hand, which leads to seduction, then he abandons her with sweet words and moves on to the next. The level of action is comparable to that of a fraternity brother with the gift of gab.

Sebastian's success is partly the result of his good accent, partly the result of his intuition that everyone wants pleasure in his/her life. He does give pleasure while taking his own, although the question of his wife and child is a moral issue Donleavy evades. Part of the problem with this kind of novel—we also find it in Amis and Wain, as well as Kerouac—is the lack of a moral center: not morals, as such, but a center or pivot where we, as readers, can orient ourselves. Donleavy here foreshadows the next decade or more of writing, in that the reader is expected to shift around as much as the protagonist and, in the process, slough off usual expectations of morality, stability, even ethics. The moment, the episode, the happening is sufficient. In this fiction, the moment is earned with a joke or witticism, and Sebastian is full of old jokes, usually at the expense of women. Self-examination is brief here, as it must be.

This type of fiction—and *The Ginger Man* is excellent of its kind—liberates the reader from all historical considerations. Reviewers praised it as full of energy: Granville Hicks characterized it as a "wild and unpredictable outburst"; *The Nation* called it "an Irish comic masterpiece"—which, perhaps, freed it of ethical standards; the reviewer in the now defunct *Herald Tribune* praised it as "reeling, lurching, boozing, wenching . . . vitality is its keynote." The adjectives are toned up to praise the novel, although with a slight twist they could also have been toned down to bury it. In this light, the book and its protagonist are precursors of the 1960s, better written than anything in Kerouac, less extreme than Burroughs, more endearing than Amis's *Lucky Jim*.

One's nagging feeling is that this is a dead end for fiction: language, witty as it is, derived from Joyce; moral dimensions missing; picaresque protagonist set upon self-gratification; food, drink, and sex as the sole drama of life; and a convenient savior at the end—Percy Clocklan, an old buddy. Typical is Sebastian's fantasy life, which includes a harem, himself as center and supervisor, everyone serving him. Heartiness is insufficient for the reader who seeks some other pivot. In Kerouac, we sense the search for a value system; here one's livelihood comes from handouts, begging, sponging, seducing. As 1950s antibourgeois rebellion, Sebastian's breakout may be momentarily effective; but by the 1970s, two decades of issue-oriented rebellions have diminished it.

Like Donleavy, Terry Southern is interested in bringing down walls, exposing rotting foundations, and then fleeing. Throughout Guy Grand's often sadistic exploits in *The Magic Christian,* Southern's purpose is to expose the meretricious and counterfeit that lie at the core of our culture: films, television, newspapers, advertising, the automobile industry, the rich operators. Since every man and woman has his price, Grand gets his way—he MCs the world—by paying off people to allow him to indulge his outrages. He exists, this stout fifty-three-year-old, as a perpetual put-on. All his energy, sexual and otherwise, is expended in acting out roles and scenarios, creating happenings. One of his best pierces the solemnity and artificiality of the film *The Best Years of Our Lives*.

As we recall, the film features a young war hero who returns with hooks instead of hands. In the film's big scene, there is a seven-second pan of the hero and his fiancée sitting on the family porch swing. The hero is courting her within the ambiguity of his situation, his having hooks instead of hands. Yet despite his affliction, he is a shepherd, she a loving shepherdess. ". . . a scene which was interrupted by Grand's insert: a cut to below the girl's waist where the hooks were seen to hover for an instant and then disappear, grappling urgently beneath her skirt." The scene lasts less than one-half second, and is usually caught by only a few people in the audience, who cannot be certain what they have observed. "No one could believe his eyes; those who were positive they had seen something funny in the realism there, sat through the film again to make certain—though, of course, the altered version was never run twice in succession."

Southern's use of this Grand exploit has resonance, several layers of message. The film is originally a counterfeit experience, making us share certain feelings which the director insists upon by producing stereotypical scenes. Grand inserts the war hero's true feeling, to hook into his fiancée's body, despite his lack of hands, a noncounterfeit feeling which the film omits in favor of artificial virtue. But he does so rapidly, almost with the speed of a thought. Accordingly, even as he has inserted a "truth" into the counterfeit, he has done so in such a way that those who observed the truth now doubt it could have occurred, or else are suspicious of their observation.

In another effective episode (most episodes, I should add, rarely rise above the sophomoric), Grand becomes involved in the production of the Black Devil Rocket, a gigantic convertible. Mounting a broad advertising campaign designed to make the car sell, he offers power, sexual thrills, status, all the usual claims made for a car. *"Performance? Ask the Fella Behind the Wheel!"* or *"Getting the feel of this big baby has been one thrill, believe you me!"*—this latter from an Indianapolis car champion, whose figure is dwarfed behind the steering wheel of the mammoth vehicle. The campaign works, and models are sold from a display room on New York's Fifth Avenue.

When the cars hit the street, they are immediately too large for turns or for maneuvering. ". . . the big cars did prove impractical in the city, because their turning-arc—for the ordinary 90° change of direction—was greater than the distance between the street-angled buildings, so that by five thirty all four of the Black Devil Rockets were wedged at angles across various intersections around Columbus Circle, each a barrier to thoroughfares in four directions." Only cranes and derricks are able to break up the traffic snarl, and the city moves to ban the car, with one official calling it ugly and pretentious.

Nearly all these episodes, incidentally, take place between brief insertions of a family gathering of Grand and his two old aunts, who dote over him and his money. Interspersed with these domestic scenes of harmless chatter and meaningless dialogue are Grand's grand schemes, in which he plays Panurge to a settled, counterfeit society. Each of the exploits is intended to humiliate, often sadistically, those who are secure in what they think they may do. Grand buys and sells them, small people as well as officials or representatives of law and order. But his need goes beyond revealing individual greed; he needs to establish disorder as a way of expressing some response to the artificial.

The longest episode is one of the weakest, since it becomes predictable. The *S.S. Magic Christian* is lavishly outfitted by Grand and puts out to sea with a combined passenger list of the high and mighty, wealthy, outcasts, and freaks, a ship of fools. Everything begins to go wrong, deliberately, and the lavishly appointed ship becomes a floating nightmare. It is now Grand's plot to unsettle as much of the world as he can control. The ship at sea is his universe, which he can play with, bring to chaos and anarchy, as every form of human credulity is played upon and turned inside out. Eventually, the *Magic Christian* turns around and returns to New York, its plans aborted.

Grand, too, was intended as a "Magic Christian." He offers whatever he has, here vast amounts of money, and takes on the role of Christian samaritan and television MC; but his "magic" is to humiliate and tyrannize in order to break even. Whatever he provides, he takes away in individual freedom. Had Southern moved this onto a larger scale, he had a superb image of America in its postwar years: a benevolent-seeming figure who demeans and humiliates for whatever gains he offers. In 1960, Southern had no way of knowing Lyndon Johnson would become President.

As a cultural artifact, apart from its considerable literary qualities, *Goodbye, Columbus* moved right to a frontier, between our sense of the fifties as a tempting but imitational experience and our sense of the new, which remained shadowy, vague, even threatening. The "Jewish experience," such as it is in Roth, is part of that frontier, by which he can explore how Jewishness has become American and America Jewish. Merging, they have created a one-dimensional society which, while seductive, is also a form of enervation and death. That perception of spiritual deterioration amidst plenty, located in American Jews, becomes the young Roth's chief cultural freight.

One of the key images in *Goodbye, Columbus* involves not so much a change as a difference. In the titular story, Mr. Patimkin, a maker of bathroom wares, has kept his nose intact—"up at the bridge it seemed as though a small eight-sided diamond had been squeezed in under the skin. I knew that Mr. Patimkin would never bother to have that stone cut from his face." In contrast, his daughter, Brenda, had her "diamond" cut from her nose and "dropped down some toilet in Fifth Avenue Hospital." Patim-

kin is a hard worker and liver; he represents the work ethic, the Jewish version of the Protestant organization man, working as diligently for himself as the organization man does for a large corporation. His daughter, however, is the new generation, putting distance between herself and her parents by way of the straighter, more Americanized nose, and playing the role of Jewish-American Princess.

Yet her resistance to parental values is not based on any solidly constructed rebellion. It has to do with taste, tones, textures, embarrassment at their vulgarity. She is more refined, more country-clubbish and suburban, more prepared to enjoy the rewards of their position. She receives, others give; and she, a consumer and waster, has endless time for herself, while her father, a producer, is busy. She produces sweat, but at tennis and running. Although she attends Radcliffe, she never mentions a book, nor an idea, nor a moment at college; all her activities are self-oriented. Expecting only the best, she opens herself out to what the world can offer.

She is, therefore, open to Neil Klugman, not Harvard, but Newark College of Rutgers University (free), a young man who works in a library (but never discusses books), who has undistinguished relatives and undistinguished clothes (one shirt from Brooks Brothers). He is lower middle to middle meeting upper middle class. She is open to receiving, he to giving. What finally separates them is her diaphragm: when her mother discovers it—it was left where it would be discovered—Brenda uses it as a shield behind which she can rejoin her family and reject Neil.

In the working out, Roth recognizes extreme self-consciousness and self-indulgence as new cultural patterns, what would be that part of sixties rebellion without issues. The nose image—which Neil jokes about until he sees it is dangerous territory—suggests self-love, but even more, a generation preparing for expressions of ego, for placing distance between itself and its elders. Brenda is conveniently myopic. The separation is reinforced by the title. Brenda's brother, Ron, owns a record from Ohio State, a memorial to the college and town, "Goodbye, Columbus." He has gone out into the world stamped by Ohio State and Columbus. But the title extends, because of the place name, to a farewell to the America of Columbus in favor of the next millennium. In that, Brenda can indulge herself, even as Neil reaches upward, he seeking marriage, she a summer fling.

This pattern is quite different, of course, from Clyde Griffiths and rich Sondra in *An American Tragedy;* there the gulf between boy and girl is so great that the social issues preempt all else. Here the social gulf is more subtle: a question of values rather than status, although the latter counts. Brenda experiences narcissism, a reception of things and feelings; she will be a collector, and in many ways embody 1960s attitudes. Neil is willing to play the fifties game of "making it," if he can win her. The values of each are pulling in opposite directions. Columbus is the pivot: Neil sees Columbus as the traditional Eden, not the Columbus of Ohio State, but the one who discovered America. Brenda knows the era of Columbus is over; the era of self is ready to begin, self-assertion at its best and its worst. Pastoral confronts suburban. Brenda has the options, and she chooses separation, turning a diaphragm into a wall.

With this novella and the five stories accompanying it, Roth was assigned to the Jewish-American-writer phenomenon. But his placement there has little significance in broader cultural terms, other than the fact that he is Jewish and writes, mainly, about Jews. His issues, however, are not Jewish issues: not matters of belief or of exogamy, not connected to the state of Israel or related to language (except here and there a Yiddish word, but all urban America uses such words). The larger frame is quintessential American, from Columbus to Ohio State (where Woody Hayes fashioned All-Americans) to Short Hills, where the Patimkins live, one of those places once beyond the pale for Jews. The values are not those of Jewish life in America, not how one remains a Jew in Gentile territory, but of *adjustments* a family makes to American affluence: relationships of the young to that family, to rich suburban life, to subtle differences in class and, especially, caste. The main issue is how to live, not how to live as a Jew.

Neil asserts at one point, " 'I'm a liver,' " and since Brenda cannot respond in kind, she jests, " 'I'm a pancreas,' " which is close to being a parasite. Neil offers his doing and giving, even as a librarian, to her receiving; he stresses he is not a planner, not set, ready to go in any direction. Like Augie March, he remains open to life. He will, we can expect, demonstrate in the 1960s, be antiwar, support the civil rights movement, vote for Eugene McCarthy in the 1968 primaries, support environmental issues in the 1970s. She will cultivate her bobbed nose, her myopic eyes, her curvaceous figure. Hers will be a consumer society, that part of the narcissistic sixties; whereas he is headed for fulfillment. She will be his temptation, a decent young woman whose head is elsewhere, and whose values follow. She will be the type of matron the women's movement will attempt to reach, although they will probably fail. Values, not Jewishness, prevail; and the values pertain to all upwardly mobile assimilationists.

The remaining stories play with possibilities: If I were a practicing Jew, how would I feel about Jesus, Gentiles, Hasidic Jews, Jews who demand kosher food in the army, Jews who fall in and out of bed? Rather than showing Jews in the practice of their religion, Roth situates a narrator in his stories who must react to the Jewish experience of others. In "The Conversion of the Jews," the motif suggests really a plurality of religious beliefs, so that the rabbi is forced to recognize that Christianity is possible. In "Defender of the Faith," the narrator, Nathan Marx, a sergeant in the wartime army, must recognize that Jews are neither chosen nor privileged; Epstein, in that story, must try out things that are taboo for Jews —practice adultery, expose himself to venereal disease, and so on. In "Eli, the Fanatic," Eli, who is unstable to begin with, plays a Hasidic role, putting on the suit and hat to see what being a "real Jew" is like.

All the stories are concerned, then, with role-playing; not with Jewishness, but with the outer reaches of Jewish adaptation. These Jews are like Melville's confidence man: uncertain of their own identity, uncertain of the roles they wish to play, and therefore participants and spectators in their own drama. Theirs is not a question of belief, of Jewishness—compare Flannery O'Connor's characters for their belief in Christianity—but of locating themselves in America. They look toward the 1960s in their insistence on trying out selves, as Eli tries on the clothes of the Hasid, Tzuref. One lives one's religious life and experience through another, not directly; and it all becomes a matter of experience; which is, in turn, a matter of the self devouring all experience. The self does not develop in Roth; it consumes. Here would lie both the strengths and the excesses of his future work.

Makers and Seers

Although the 1960s will remain unique in American culture, having created lasting patterns of social and political behavior, the decade was also part of a large cultural revisionism that started well back in the fifties. In his influential study linking character types to population growth, *The Lonely Crowd,* David Riesman was concerned with authority, stress on the self in its relationship to society, and achievement, as matters of both pride (how one feels about oneself) and vanity (how one wishes to be seen). His "hero" among those who have adjusted is the inner-directed man, a goal-oriented person whose grip on himself was assured and whose aims were implanted early in life. The inner-directed man comes through despite his feeling that he "had constantly to fight against doubts concerning his state of grace or election." The terms of definition recall the Puritans, and inner-directedness is indeed a throwback to Puritan values: work, self-definition, discipline. Joining the inner-directed, among those adjusted, are the other- and tradition-directed, all of whom respond to their society at its particular stages in population growth, with other-directed in the ascendancy, as most responsive to elements of a mass, directed culture. Those who do not conform or adjust may be anomic or autonomous, and the latter, while few, are the least rigid, being capable of choosing but insisting on their freedom.

For the 1960s novelist, the other- and tradition-directed are unworthy even of description. It is the inner-directed man who is mocked and satirized, whereas the anomic—the maladjusted or ungoverned—becomes the new hero. The inner-directed individual is someone well beyond the organization man; he (she, in Kesey's *One Flew Over the Cuckoo's Nest*) represents systems, computers, mechanical devices that "stencilize" or steal our spirit.* He lies at the heart of the powers of entropy and disintegration, of which the organization or gray flannel man is merely the avatar.

Systems became definitive in the fifties. Not only Eisenhower's arteries hardened, but an entire culture's. Systems were the great legacy of the decade, and television immortalized them. Although the tube

hardly did it alone, it nevertheless created a significant cultural pattern that carried over into other dimensions. Television crept into every value system, since its demands for production and consumption were voracious: no less than the making of an insatiable consumer society. Although many factors were involved in 1960s prosperity, surely television's success in selling America to Americans was critical.

Television supported systems. News, communiqués, terrible events were all intermixed in that frantic selling process. When the Vietnam War became nightly television fare, it was trivialized in all its horror: little people shooting each other within a twelve-inch or nineteen-inch screen. Panoramic war became personalized war, and attitudes toward it began to alter. As Riesman foresaw, politics would become part of a consumer system; but everything did —films as reviewed, books as noticed, personalities as interviewed. Television announcers became coequal with what was announced. Everything was scaled down. The breakup of traditional power blocs into subgroups, which continued into the seventies, was connected to the influence of television, since it brought together coalitions of people who would never have seen each other before.

Television was the means, and systems the enemy. Yet within its systemization, its support of institutions and authority, its blind faith in capitalism and its benefits, television brought a new kind of tolerance for others' lives, other forms of behavior. Part of the paradox of selling America was that a consumer society needed to be more open about products, and if products were the game, then the message had to be tolerance. This shift from a moralistic to a tolerant society would gain momentum in the sixties, but the pattern was already set, even within the confines of the small box. One could argue that since the box was so small and so restrictive, the shift to tolerance became more acceptable; larger advocates of tolerance would be too visible and revolutionary.

Further, as part of the breakdown of larger groups into subgroups, we note a renewed identification with pastoral ideals; the communes and environmental agencies of a later time were becoming set even now. The idea of subgroups has the pastoral feel to it, the individual or community fighting against big-city central government, dedicated to "small lives" in a rural fantasy. This dispersal of power to subgroups is,

---

*The old novel of manners, focused on class and caste distinctions, has not faded away, but has been transformed into those fictions in which system wars against antisystem. *V.* and *Catch-22* are thus novels of manners updated, not phased out.

of course, a vital stage on the way to self-indulgence, shifts in discipline, inevitably some form of narcissism. Give the individual power, as Emerson advocated, and he will employ it anarchically. Thus, television, more than any other media, in finding consumers and selling its products helped to break down large blocs, and these smaller groups, in turn, would rebel against every authority figure television stood for.

The conflicts were there, and they would work out in the novel as attacks on systems, whether the campus in *Giles Goat-Boy,* the military in *Catch-22,* the asylum in *One Flew Over the Cuckoo's Nest,* racial areas in *The Man Who Cried I Am* and *Sula,* international politics in *V.,* or areas of male-female and parent-child relations in *them.* A parallel development is the fiction devoted to a minimalist scale; that is, fiction whose text is as much white space as words. Minimalist fiction would appear to be both a response to television's miniaturized scale and a mockery of those ideas and products sponsored by television and its spinoffs. Minimalists, a diverse lot, include Donald Barthelme, Joan Didion, Jerzy Kosinski, Rudolph Wurlitzer.

Similarly, the growth and development of another literary subgenre became apparent: the nonfiction novel, in which history, sociology, criminology, even autobiography, became matters indirectly related to the novel. This phenomenon is not a happenstance; it is profoundly connected to the proliferation of subcultures, and to the visibility and accessibility (via television, films to a more limited extent) of individual lives and subgroups that once, if noticed, were distant and strange. This familiarity with "others" via the media, aided by the Supreme Court's liberalization of obscenity laws, would lead into elements as different as nonfictional novels and opened-up personal attitudes. The latter, in turn, would lead to reshaping of couples and groups into variations, shifting of partners, regrouping with different partners and children—what Updike tried to grapple with in *Couples,* Roth in *Letting Go.* Although the idea was still inchoate, this breakup of large blocs would become the "female experience," the most powerful of late 1960s movements socially and literarily.

Established norms gave way to imitations of behavior, for which television and the printed word provided models. "The Age of Sensation," as Herbert Hendin titled the later consciousness of the 1960s, did not stop with the reshaping of subgroups into protean forms. The drug culture was part of the change, not distinct from it; peer-group pressure became more intense, whether to go to bed with one's partner, to share drugs with him/her, or to keep moving on in alternations of control and passivity. Role-playing became essential, as we see in Barth's *The End of the Road,* when Horner's doctor advises "mythotherapy," observing one's life as a series of dramas. Playing roles permits the individual to stay partially in his subgroup, yet feel free to step out. Being "spaced out" becomes a norm, and for the writer all aspects of this "presentation of self" are part of a counterfeit or imitational culture: i.e., the culture as itself part of role-playing. In Gaddis, Barth, Pynchon (his entire development in the sixties), Heller, McElroy, among others, the stress is on playing off a near-anomic individual against a culture given to role-playing: so that the maladjusted, like Calvino's mollusk, has no form, but can comprehend all form in himself.

In this area, all the forbidding interpretations of 1950s man come together: Keniston's "uncommitted," Lifton's "protean man," Fiedler's "new mutant," C. Wright Mills's "white collar worker" or "new power elite," Marcuse's "one-dimensional man," the familiar "organization and gray flannel" man. The most extreme statement of this changing phenomenon comes from Timothy Leary, who in *The Politics of Ecstasy* says that passions are forms of stupor, and only sensations, opened up through psychedelic drugs, can make us creative. The emotional life misleads, whereas the "sensational" life is fruitful; we must get beyond emotion, not to reason but to sensations. Norman O. Brown's astonishing address to the Columbia University chapter of Phi Beta Kappa at the start of the decade moved him beyond reason, beyond passions, into sensations. Called "Apocalypse: The Place of Mystery in the Life of the Mind," his address, with its apotheosis of Dionysus, helped anchor the decade at one end, while it would be secured at the other by Leary and like-minded "sensationalists."

The following six fictions represent the vast changes the 1960s heralded and helped to form. Together, they catch the main outlines of the decade: the attack on modernity, technology, everything having to do with systems, in Barth's *Giles Goat-Boy;* the concern with violence and disruption resulting from blacks' insistence upon constitutional rights, in John Williams's *The Man Who Cried I Am* (Toni Morrison's *Sula* focused more specifically on the emergence of black women); then the emergence of a woman, in Joyce Carol Oates's *them;* followed by two books which, in retrospect, form two parts of a hinge leading from the 1950s into the 1960s, Pynchon's *V.* and Heller's *Catch-22*. Not unusually, the latter two became cult novels, since their main thrust was not only to attack systems but to suggest rebellion, resistance, disruption. In a way, the self-indulgence apparent in varying degrees in all these novels was a factor in their importance; at their best, however, they raised self-indulgence to aspects of transformation.*

We start with systems, antisystems, pastoral, the whole American tradition caught up in an immense, self-indulgent, overbearing novel: Barth's summa theologica, *Giles Goat-Boy* (1966). In several ways, this novel is the most all-inclusive work of its decade, transforming the cold war of the fifties into the campus wars of the sixties, and subsuming under campus everything we associate with the American experience. Yet, at the same time, Barth has entered his own "new phase" or "new curriculum," in which a fiction can exist only as a phenomenological experience, as a self-conscious artifact, itself the subject of itself. Further, Barth perceived all human experience as fitting allegorically into technical terms: for the human body, we have the body of the computer; for human passions, the responses of the programmed material, etc. A brief quotation, from Volume II, First Reel, Chapter 7, is our paradigm:

> I *was* the GILES, I repeated, by WESCAC out of Virginia R. Hector [George is speaking to Virginia's father, Reginald Hector, who put George out to die as an infant]; rescued from the tapelift by G. Herrold the booksweep, reared by Max Spielman as Billy Bockfuss the ag-Hill Goat-Boy, and come to Great Mall to change WESCAC's AIM and Pass ALL or Fail ALL.

The elucidation of this passage is the subject of the novel, 750 pages, over 400,000 words. The book, like Barth's later *Letters,* is for survivors.

---

*Christopher Lasch's well-argued case against narcissism—as an intense fascination with self that leads to loss of self—does not account for its therapeutic value for the individual. While it may be circuitous, it does release sensations, states, attitudes, even obsessions; and this "release" is part of the creative process. Thus, while the narcissist may be socially negative, in Lasch's terms, he can be creatively positive. Lasch views narcissism as decadent, but he observes with the Puritan's eye, in which duty and discipline preempt creativity. A novelist of the sixties who works in and out of these very ideas is Walker Percy, whose *The Moviegoer* (1961) is a paradigm of self-indulgence, role-playing, rejection of authority, but, withal, full of ethical modalities.

Giles Goat-Boy is subtitled "The Revised New Syllabus." The title page, after various cover letters, is far more elaborate: "R.N.S. / The Revised New Syllabus / of George Giles / Our Grand Tutor," with further information that this is the "Autobiographical and Hortatory Tapes / Read Out at New Tammany College to His Son / Giles (,) Stoker / By the West Campus Automatic Computer / And by Him Prepared for the Furtherment of the / Gilesian Curriculum." But before we arrive at this elaboration of the book—and it is helpful to digest this material from the start—we must travel along a good deal of self-conscious material: a "Publisher's Disclaimer," followed by letters from four editors, including the publisher's son, who served as readers, and that followed by further disclaimers from the publisher. Each editor-reader offers reasons why the book should or should not be published, none of them on its aesthetic values (although the publisher's son hints at these), three of them on its pornographic qualities, its lack of coherence, its defiance of propriety in manners and morals, its association with anarchistic and nihilistic values.

In this section—still far from the beginning of the novel proper, unless this is the beginning—the manuscript, so the publisher tells us, has been altered, with passages deleted, all because the author refuses to respond to queries.† From there, we arrive at another prefatory section: "Cover-Letter to the Editors and Publisher" from J.B.—the author, we assume. He announces that the manuscript enclosed is not the one they had expected, *The Seeker,* but another one, put into his hands by Stoker Giles, a student at an unnamed campus (Penn State?); and the manuscript therein is his story as provided by his father, George Giles, printed out by the West Campus Automatic Computer (WESCAC) and itself a lengthy description of the Revised New Syllabus.

After forty-odd pages of text, we arrive at the subtext, which is the novel proper, the growth and development of Barth's latest picaresque protagonist, the goat-boy Billy Bockfuss, who became George Giles. As Billy, he was goat; as George, he was man. We enter Swiftian thickets, Horses and Houyhnhnms, or classical centaurs. Barth's elaboration serves a strong 1960s function in its presentation

---

†The text of *Giles* closes with the recipient of the text disclaiming the "Posttape," which had apparently ended the novel proper, unless the novel had ended before the "Posttape." In any event, the latter may be spurious, "an interpolation of later Gilesians, perhaps."

of life as existent only in the eyes of the observer, the solipsism Barth finds so distasteful in some of his contemporaries.

All he lacks are reviewers' and readers' opinions, but he has prepared for them by way of the editors' views, which suggest four ways to judge the book. And if Barth had been able to foresee the paperback edition of his book, he would have found his narrative surrounded by blurbs that provide reviewers' judgments, although these are proffered in the general terms of high praise that may mean limited (if any) reading. *Time* compares *Giles* to "perhaps Batman" and the *National Observer* suggests Barth as "The Rudolph Nureyev of Prose," while the *Times Book Review* compares him to Joyce, Proust, Mann, and Faulkner. These remarks, even if unincorporated into the Preface, complete the cycle of self.

For his "outer world" Barth has found another self, in computer technology. The computer is the ultimate in the narcissistic experience because it creates and completes cycles, from programming through completion, without interruption or interference. In his disdain for old fictional forms, Barth saw mechanical elements and technological means as ways to enter the new.* The WESCAC computer, under whose aegis the entire New Tammany College once fell, has taken on not only human functions but functions involving brainwaves. It is theoretically capable "of being intensified almost limitlessly, at the same amplitudes and frequencies as human 'brainwaves,' like a searchlight over tremendous spaces."

Barth then plays with military and other applications, which complement the computer's ability to EAT. The computer consumed people when Maximilian Spielman (minstrel, play-man), goat-boy's tutor and mentor, pressed the EAT button. Thousands of Americans suffered "mental burn-out" as a consequence, the severity depending on how close they were to the center, like victims of atomic fallout on Hiroshima. The losses were most severe at the center: instant death; then radiated out to catalepsy, disinte-

gration of personality, loss of identity; still farther out, inability to choose or act except on impulse, then suicide, madness, despair, hysteria, "vertiginous self-consciousness." In the very outer rings of affected areas we find "impotency, nervous collapse, and more or less severe neuroses." Damage was functional and, therefore, permanent.

New Tammany College has experienced apocalypse, and the society into which George is to be transformed from goat to boy is one contaminated by computer fallout. The context is, in a sense, not only the past apocalypse, as related to George, but present sixties chaos, campus riots, subsequent "fallout." In that present, the campus, as a reflection of the world, involves a deadly struggle between Student-Unionism and Informationalism. The codification of information has meant departments have absorbed human impulses: men's freely willed acts have been classified by psychology or anthropology and determined to be historical events, or by philosophy as matters of dissection. A moral vacuum has developed, which various movements have desperately attempted to fill.

New religions have proliferated, Barth's campus versions of the consciousness and political movements of the 1960s: the pre-Schoolers, the Curricularists, the Evolutionaries, the Ismists (ideologues), the neo-Enochians (Christers), the Bonifascists (Nazis), the Secular-Studentists (Communists), also called Mid-Percentile or Bourgeois-Liberal Baccalaureates, the Ethical-Quadranglists, the Sexual Programmists, the Tragicists and New Quixotics, the Angry Young Freshmen, the Beist Generation (consciousness-raising), East and West Campus (Soviet Union and America). They range from "good feeling" groups, to academicians who have forsaken teaching for worship of administration and their Kanzler (Chancellor), to pedagogues who offer various theories of learning (not learning itself), to those who return to old systems once they are labeled new.

With its East-West struggle, its computer wars, its tribalization of the student body, its ideological divisions, the campus is a disintegrative force—an educational institution which has collapsed as much as the society. It *is,* indeed, the society. Within this, the group that rules is the "Sovereignty of the Bottom Percentile." In the multiple confusions, proliferations, internal conflicts, tensions, struggles for power and control, the West Campus computer, WESCAC, is refined. Into it are incorporated other systems, those acronyms which Barth finds to be so dehumanizing: NOCTIS (for Non-Conceptual Thinking and Institu-

---

*Lost in the Funhouse (1968), some of whose pieces precede the publication of *Giles,* is an experiment with voices and "voice prints." Barth writes: " 'Glossolalia' will make no sense unless heard in live or recorded voices, male and female, or read as if so heard; 'Echo' is intended for monophonic authorial recording, either disc or tape; 'Autobiography,' for monophonic tape and visible but silent author. 'Menelaiad,' though suggestive of a recorded monologue, depends for clarity on the reader's eye and may be said to have been composed for 'printed voice.' " "Frame-Tale" is put together like a Möbius strip, one-, two-, or three-dimensional.

tional Synthesis) and MALI (Manipulation Analysis and Logical Inference).

None of this hodgepodge is idle information, for George's birth, as he will learn later, is connected to the computer and its functions. At this point, about one hundred pages after the start, George enters into his novelistic phase: that age-old attempt to discover who and what he is, his origins, parentage, tribe. Barth crosses with his own work in *The Sot-Weed Factor,* duplicating those early fictional efforts which stressed the protagonist's discovery of his origins: Tom Jones, Humphry Clinker, etc. These discoveries —social, personal, psychological—are connected to George's decision to forsake his Billy Bockfuss identity and assume his human one: " 'I don't want to be a *Billy* now or a *Bockfuss,* either one! I'm going to be a human student." His decision to become George cannot be dissociated from his desire to discover his parentage; and this, in turn, will draw him ever further into the innards of the computer, three Dantesque descents in all. The pattern is strikingly like that which Pynchon will employ later in *Gravity's Rainbow,* where technological patterns replace pastoral as forms of sustenance; where one is determined, not by association with life-giving elements, but by scientific complications lying beyond individual comprehension. The ultimate truth will be that Billy, now becoming George, was computer-born, fathered by a computer, and fated for his present course. George Giles is the GILES, the aggregate of all data fed into WESCAC. As he reaches toward the innards of WESCAC, he is named and then prepared to go forth to meet his maker. God's creation is now the computer's. The struggle is displaced Oedipal: animal son with father (WESCAC) a mechanical object; not pastoral but technology epitomized.

George's plan is to discover AIM—Automatic Implementation Mechanism—which determines, in the very innards of WESCAC, what the computer will EAT and when it will EAT. To be a hero, he must also be a Grand Tutor, a kind of Christian knight who will do good. Max, the specialist in psycho-protology (he should have been called not Spielman, but Scheisskopf), is dubious; for he wants George to have a normal life. Yet he recognizes the latter's situation as that of the classic hero, having apparently read Raglan, Campbell, Weston, Frye, among others. George enjoys the mystery of parenthood, the irregularity of his birth, the threat on his life and subsequent injury to his legs, the circumstances of his rescue by George Herrold, his namesake, the fact that he was raised by a foster parent (Max), disguised as an animal, and

bore a name not his own. Life takes after legend, fiction, and myth.

Struggling to emerge through this morass of exotic detail, acronyms, strange events, animal-human combinations, is a rather traditional picaresque-hero type of novel. Essential to Barth is the "adventure of life": that meeting between an innocent young man and what lies beyond, in which determinism and free will can struggle. One begins, like Laocoön, with a few coils encircling oneself; the next step is to break out, or succumb. Potential self-destruction overlaps with expression of function, with characters and elements extending from one book to the other.* Such a format has served Barth well, since he has perceived postwar America through the eyes of a minstrel or troubadour, a Spielman; all has been imitation, and the real, whatever it signifies, is buried beneath layers of deception. He is, like Gaddis, one of our writers of the imitational world. In *Giles Goat-Boy,* the computer world, as essence and terminology, serves what the counterfeit does for Gaddis.

Since George is a goat-boy, every new situation, event, even food, is, for him, a source of wonder. Each new figure he meets—whether Maurice Stoker, Max Croaker, or Eblis Eierkopf—has a dual purpose: to keep the narrative going by supplying the reader with new information and to provide context for George's wonder and innocence. For George is a rustic, Huck type coming to the big city; the West Campus and New Tammany College in particular are urban experiences for the farmboy-animal. George responds with innocence, but his innocence—like Cooke's in *The Sot-Weed Factor* or Horner's in *The End of the Road*—must turn slowly toward forms of knowledge, even at the expense of life. And just as Cooke must write his epic poem, George must justify himself by committing a heroic act: in his case, penetrating to the belly of the WESCAC computer and redirecting its aim.

His goal is, seemingly, an act of broad cultural dimensions, but it is also connected to his own manifest destiny. Barth has, in several ways, thrown himself back into a much older frame of reference—into Emerson counters, behind him Carlyle, Wordsworth, and Rousseau—and attempted to find amidst seeming 1960s chaos elements that join. And in personal

---

*In my discussion of *Letters,* in Chapter Eleven, I will bring together Barth's total work, as a mosaic of interlocking people and events. *Letters* received a very poor press, but it is, with all its excesses, an uncanny fiction, a capping of Barth's career and the entire postwar era.

heroism, of the parodied sort, he finds AIM. This heroism cannot be clear and free, that is, romantic, but must be immersed in particular American conflicts: pastoral versus urban, Garden versus technology, systems versus antisystems, history versus now. Further, Barth introduces large historical processes, allegorical elements at work behind campus activities: cold war, struggle against the Nazis, Jewish Holocaust, Nazi types remaining within the Western world, continuing ideological struggles between survivors of the free and less free worlds. Civil rights and black movements are still inchoate.

Holding the disparate elements of *Giles* together is Barth's sense of apocalypse: not the end of the world, but the termination of a way of life. It is, essentially, the end of the pastoral existence which George, in a more innocent world, could have represented. Within the imminence of apocalypse, the man who controls the computer controls life. Ostensibly, the chancellor of New Tammany is Rexford; but he is, like Eisenhower, whom he resembles, a figurehead. The real power, the emperor of the land, is the computer, WESCAC (with its suffix close to shit), and there Bray is king. As a false Grand Tutor—Secretary of State?— he has entered the belly of WESCAC, and from there his edicts control the college, the campus, the frontier, the clocks, all the details of Matriculation, Commencement, and Examinations. Since Bray is himself a confidence man—a man who traffics in masks and antimasks, in roles and counter-roles—elements behind the apocalypse are themselves distorted and disguised. There is no clear pattern, no straight road toward what we commonly assume is an apocalyptic end of things.

George gets a whiff of apocalypse when the Dean of Flunks, Maurice Stoker, takes him on a tour of the power area, one wing of the computer complex. They descend into the guts, passing guard dogs reminiscent of concentration camps. In this power complex, the allegories become mixed: camps, furnaces, guards, dogs. In the Furnace Room (Germanically capitalized), an emergency threatens to blow everything up, and a key valve must be turned. Amidst troops running everywhere, fire, hideous flames, heat, huge muscled women as well as men, Stoker is in his element: " 'Volcano with a cap on it!' " he exults. With his huge tool, he turns the valve where others failed, in the act knocking down men with his wrench, then spraying one of the women with a caustic fluid.

The scene, recalling Bosch, is all sadism. Stoker gains his satisfaction from humiliating and demeaning others; or from open acts of brutality. This is, in effect, George's introduction to the power center, to whose controls he aspires as Grand Tutor. If the computer is, ultimately, a form of the bomb (the struggle over which characterized 1950s science as much as the moon shot did in the 1960s), then to control it is to have at one's fingertips the means of apocalypse. This, then, will be the area in which George can test his aspirations for herohood: as the ultimate hero, the mythical savior not only of his people but of the world.

Bray explains the Examination. In the procedures of Matriculation, Placement, Graduation, and Examinations, Barth has located his apocalyptic vision; what will be for Pynchon rockets, what was for Gaddis imitations, for Ellison invisibility, for Heller the catch, will be for Barth the examination. It is both an existential and a metaphysical moment. Bray brays:

> . . . that while the questions are different for each Candidate, the Answer is the same for all; the other, that while the Question never varies, the Answers do. Whether, in either case, the variation is from term to term or Candidate to Candidate; whether it's a difference in formulation only, or actual substance; whether it's radical or infinitesimal; whether the matter or the manner of the Candidate's response is of more significance, the general tenor or the precise phrasing—these and a thousand other considerations are much debated among your professors, many of whom, one sadly concludes, are more interested in academic questions of this sort than in the ultimate ones which in principle they should prepare you to confront.

Apocalypse interlocks with other elements; for example, the three descents George must make into the belly of WESCAC. Each descent involves a different perception for goat-boy of the nature of his role and of campus reality. A sense of ending is imminent in each descent. To "go underground" is to explore the nature of death, or, if one is fortunate, to find signs that indicate prolongation of life. But such signs—as in the subterranean journeys of Vergil, Odysseus, Dante—can exist only alongside final things. So, too, with George; each descent has within it a potential shredding.

His first descent is based on his view that Passage (Passing) and Failure (Failing) are fundamentally distinct, each ideologically pure. While this applies directly to campus affairs, its apocalyptic potential applies more intensely to East-West political stances; such a firmly held distinction can lead only to nuclear war.* George's opinion, however, is naive, not strongly held, simply something he hits upon and then tries to work out. This descent is marked by his wearing the mask of Bray, so that, in effect, his philosophy of distinction is a lot of braying, a lot of wind.

For his second descent, George has leaped to the opposite conclusion. These choices, incidentally, involve brushes with personal death, as well as the opportunity to "kill" the computer. George has a perception of still another position while he chews on the old New Syllabus, that of Enos Enoch, the old New Testament of Jesus Christ.† This revelation shows George now that "failure is passage"; but while it seems to have relevance for the sixties, it is, also, pure braying. It is a witty way of saying the part is the all, elements being equal regardless of differences. The parody of 1960s compromise suggests a deeply conservative vein in Barth despite the radical structure of the novel and the original means of displaying the self. George's second passage underground is a failure, since the philosophy on which it is based is spurious. Further, in making the descent, George must deny his own sexual proclivities, deny distinctions between male and female; denying sex, he negates life. The passage, if successful, would be an ironical end of all things; for life to continue, George must move on to another descent.

For the final one, George must achieve wisdom: i.e., Dante in the *Paradiso.* The third descent arrives with George's sense of failure: his "paradoxes became paroxysms." He finds his reason constricted, himself fearful that his previous assaults upon truth have revealed only confusion. He feels his mind will crack. As he tells Rexford: "I'd come to understand that East and West Campuses, goat and Grand Tutor, even Passage and Failure, were inseparable and ultimately indistinguishable." George's perception of interconnection will save him, but it is, really, old, based on Emersonian unity of self carried into politi-

cal ideology. The "revised New Syllabus" sounds strikingly like the "original New Syllabus" of Enos Enoch, George's revelation not too distinct from that of Jesus: self-reliance for the individual, interdependence for the social body.

The larger mythical frame for the descents is the struggle between father and son, the Oedipal conflict which is the subject of a play by Taliped, the famous Dean of Cadmus College. The inset play, coming just before the novel's midway point, is a parody of Sophocles' *Oedipus,* adapted to deans, pot, and blind academics. It is the campus equivalent, on still another level of perception, of apocalypse: here generational conflict, which Barth sees as one of the keys to the sixties. Taliped has not just murdered his father at the crossroads, he has committed a pre-Manson butchering of the innocents. "First I cut the old man's throat and dumped him out to teach him manners. Then I humped his girlfriend as he bled to death, for sport. My policy, in cases of this sort, is first to stab 'em in the belly-button and then cut other things." He spends so much time "butchering and banging her" that the others almost get away, but he finds them hiding and dismembers them. Taliped insists he felt remorse afterward, saying that if he had not lost his temper he would have dispensed with the carving.

Like the original, Taliped's version is based on revelations which trap the seeker after truth, even crazy Taliped. When he is blind, Taliped "sees the light," as it were, perceiving he is thrice flunked—on his ID card, in bed, and at the crossroads. The "smartest dean that ever deaned" will never see the light again, although he has achieved awareness. The chorus then chants, "Here today and gone tomorrow," before breaking into an orgy of rhetorical terms which explain the movement of the drama. The final message, an "interruption of this catharsis," brings a news bulletin.

Parody of the Oedipal myth is essential to Barth's overall structural concept, which I locate in father (WESCAC, technology, mechanical, informational, progress) and son (George, pastoral, Pan, goatish, humanistic, compromising). The successive tests George must pass before he can descend into the belly of the computer—the goal being to replace *its* truth with *his*—are all stages in growth and development against the background of a generational conflict. The tasks all display some threat to his very survival and are, therefore, the way in which life itself is carried forth, by way of murderous conflicts. Since this appears to be the chief structural element of the novel, it brings us back to traditional forms, the epical quest,

---

*Barth began *Giles* in June of 1960, more research than writing, abandoned it for another novel, called *The Seeker,* or *The Amateur;* then returned to *Giles* in early 1962 and continued, with some starts and stops, until the end of 1965. Thus, he was able to incorporate 1960s events as he went along, and those descents of George seem keyed in directly to American-Soviet confrontations early in the decade.

†In an interview in *Wisconsin Studies,* Barth spoke of his desire to write a "new Old Testament, a comic Old Testament," which he called a "souped-up Bible." His Bible is the revised New Syllabus of George Giles, reached after descents and revivals, approximate to the emergence of the "original New Syllabus."

those attributes of the hero's life as laid out in Lord Raglan's *The Hero*.

If WESCAC is the emperor, not of ice cream, but of the land, then George—if he is indeed the GILES, the real Grand Tutor—must save the campus, the university, the land and world. The sick king has infected all forms of knowledge: whether it is Max Spielman's Hebraic humanism; Eierkopf's religious devotion to technology and positivism, reflected in his lenses and mirrors, all secondary means of "seeing";* Maurice Stoker's ability to change sides, as needed; Harold Bray's edicts from the belly of WESCAC, all misleading, because he is not the true Grand Tutor, but a poseur; Peter Greene's boosterism, his platitudes, his simplistic Americanism (behind which is much decency); Anastasia's inability to define herself through choice, her willingness to be used, to be a receptacle; Julius Rexford's lack of definition as Chancellor, his surface perfection which hides considerable confusion; Croaker's animality, which in another context might be a way of knowing, but which here is purely carnal chaos; Dr. Sear's polymorphism, which proves untenable. Even the Living Sakhyan, the campus god, remains sphinxlike, mute, giving out no vibrations, offering no solace, remaining stolid and neutral.

An acute paradox arises. For while all generational activity must derive from George, he is, to a large extent, hobbled by a doom assigned him. If he is chosen, if he is the GILES, that incorporation of the total university (or universe), then his task is to postpone the apocalypse, at least during his lifetime. That is, in a sense, his mission. And while it is a huge mission, of messianic proportions—he is to be the new Founder—he is, then, kept from individual development by the nature of his task. To establish the Revised New Syllabus, he must break free, as limned by his three descents; and yet freedom is not his, either. Task or destiny struggles against liberation.

Barth has attempted to manifest those 1960s tensions in formlessness struggling to escape from form, in the need for personal expression bottled up by destiny or function. The novel's structure follows George's own gait. Caught between four-leggedness and two-leggedness, George must carry a stick, especially when he moves from goat to boy. Like Oedipus

*With his "ire" head, his "I-er" head, his egg-head, his "eye-er" head, Eierkopf admits to being as blind as Dean Taliped without his lenses. In order to see, not only does he need lenses but he must "compensate for optical error, and for this he relied, in his own work, on the lens in his hand, which he knew to be accurate."

with his pierced ankles, George has legs that do not straighten out completely, and his slightly bent form, supported by the stick, is a physical manifestation of who and what he is. No longer goat, not quite man, he is a mutant of sorts—and as mutant, he has no clear identity. He is, in fact, merely a response to situations, utilizing a stick as a third leg when he forsakes his four legs. The gait created by this locates George in a physical limbo, and even his sexual tastes will be affected.

The mutant quality of George's condition, while permitting him to live in the animal-pastoral world, inhibits him in the man-made world. It disallows a clear identity, making him a figure of destiny, despite his descents to perceive the truth. Barth has caught that sense of the sixties which seemed all change and yet hobbled change. Through his first three novels, Barth had stressed quality of freedom—that ability of the individual to impose his own pattern on a contingent universe, connecting absurd fragments by way of will, or failing and needing support. Basically a rationalist's view of universe and individual, it has become, by *Giles,* ambiguous. Barth has been caught up by history; the great freeing powers of the postwar years, transformed into human liberation, have become restricted. The materials of *Giles* are concerned with frontiers, dualisms, competing campuses, ideological antagonisms and conflicts, confrontations between historical elements, generational struggles. George's innocence has lost its bloom. The picaresque hero, who is Barth's trademark, must become a statesman, ideologue, humanist, politician, social scientist, pedagogue, academician. The demands of the sixties turn us into polymaths, as George learns; and yet at the same time, we must not lose our original perceptions. For George, that is the stable, the company of goats, his Panish earlier existence.

Barth threads through a narrow course. Conflicts and decisions call for a mutant, and yet all intellectual mutants—Bray, Stoker, Rexford—betray themselves and the campus. George must resist that. The way he can do it is, chiefly, by means of sex. Sex should remain barnyard sex, which for Barth means honesty of feeling, direct expression of self, simple physical release. As soon as sex becomes part of other schemes—like Dr. Sear's polymorphism, Stoker's display of sexual bravura, Croaker's beastliness—it loses its primary function. Pure and simple pleasure is the sole form of salvation.

Barth's reliance on pastoral is curious, seriously out of phase with complications at other levels. The crucial segment arrives when George is ejected from

WESCAC for the third time. Sparks and flames reveal that the computer is shutting down and the time is out of joint, personally as well as ideologically. That ejection sets off the 1960s, so to speak. What, then, can George do? The verdict indicates that he belongs back in the barn. In that third descent, he has lost touch with himself; he has a blank ID and an uncertain sense of self. "I was not born George; I was not born anything; I had invented myself as I'd elected my name." That separation of name, self, presentation of self can only mean George's contact with the working universe is disjointed. Touching the barn—Antaeus with the earth—can restore him, and it.

Restoration in the barn simplifies one structural element of the book, the sexual motif. That simplification, which is essential for George's youthful work to be done (the establishment of the new revised syllabus to replace the Founder's Scroll), manifests how shaky Barth's interpretation of his own materials is. For while writing a vast critique of the 1960s, the most compendious work on a decade since Gaddis's *The Recognitions* on the 1950s, Barth has fallen back on sexual platitudes. He has honored the simplicities of barnyard sex, glorifying the pleasure principle of uncomplicated intercourse (goats or people), and epitomized in the sensations of sexual release the essential human factor. Whereas everything else is unduly complicated and caught up in irresolvable trappings, the sexual component of all this can be reduced to manageable levels. Renewed by the barnyard experience, George can complete his mission: "for though my youthful work was done, that of my manhood remained to do." In the so-called Posttape (a kind of Beckett Krapp), which Barth suggests may be spurious, George speaks of going forth to teach the unteachable, expecting to fail. The students will quickly forget who "routed the false Grand Tutor, showed the Way to Commencement Gate, and set down this single hope of studentdom, *The Revised New Syllabus.*" He, too, will end up "naked, blind, dishonored."

This is a good deal for sexual renewal to help bring about. The solution is far out of line with the ingredients. In *The Sot-Weed Factor,* Cooke's compulsive virginity—the other side of George's compulsive barnyard sexuality—was a source of humor, since he was barraged by those offering sexual favors and he burned with desire. His restraining himself for the sake of his poetic art carries a witty undertow. Here, in *Giles,* Barth has no such effective ploy; for issues, despite their parodic and even burlesqued presentation, are serious; and George's reversal of Cooke is

supposed to offer a viable alternative to counterfeit feeling. He is the real thing, life itself, the embodiment of vital principles; whereas the others are either moribund, dependent on lenses and mirrors, sexually frantic because incapable of sex, neurotically polymorphous, or remnants of a humanism that no longer functions. In this chaos of university and universe, George and his liberated sexuality are deemed valid. His sense of his sexual powers offers true liberation.

Thus, Barth is trapped, himself, by the very decade whose conflicts he has limned and intuited. For to believe in the sexual life as valid alternative to falsity is itself the kind of simplification Barth would otherwise bring against the people he parodies. One of the allures of the sixties was their offer of a sexual "coming out": be oneself, whether hetero, bi, or homo, or some exotic combination. The other side is sexual disability, and there is a sufficiency of that in the novel, in Barth as a whole. His fictions are filled with sexual cripples; from those impotent to those pansexual, there is barely a normally functioning individual: Todd, Henry, Ebenezer, Jake, Sear, Croaker, Max, Hewwig, Anastasia, Bray, Stoker. From the sexual point of view, Barth's novels are a circus sideshow, he the barker offering untold and fascinating effects from male and female, or from both sides.* The sexual cripples, the overachievers, the impotent, and others (mounters of mother or sister) seem more than social reflections, more than demonstrations of the body politic; just as George's rampant sexuality seems to move beyond simply "health." Barth's distaste for sexual definition, if these reflections of over and under are significant, seems part of his exhausted vision. He is not Swiftian enough to see sex as filth, as rooted in elimination; but rather as part of the exhaustion of the

---

*When George and Anastasia (really the stepdaughter of his mother) descend together into WESCAC, they do so as "twins," incestuous in their love-making, a family unified, a round robin enclosing sexual activity. A similar phenomenon had obtained in *The Sot-Weed Factor.* In *Giles,* the sexual play, keyed in by Taliped's Oedipal farce, is also reflected in loss of eyes, or in substitute eyes. We mentioned Eierkopf, whose "egghead" name also suggests "eye" or "I"; but we have, in addition, Sear, who loses his eyesight; Peter Greene, who sees with one eye and then loses that; also Leonid, the defector, with a single eye, then none. But besides natural eyes, there are the eyes of machines: fluoroscopes, lenses, mirrors, materials both lauded and feared. The presence of so many lenses, mirrors, and reflections leads Barth's characters into voyeurism, a substitute sexuality, a "funhouse" of perversities. Sear looks on, while his wife performs with male or female; and yet Sear is sere, eventually blinded. Within this tangle George must function.

entire Western tradition, whose depletion he has located as central to our culture.

"Reality" in *Giles Goat-Boy,* until efforts at resolution, had been on a mighty scale. Without making excessive claims for Barth's philosophical powers, we can observe him as trying to negotiate his way through highly difficult terrain. The terrain is divided between that which belongs to the practical world and that which belongs to the world of pure knowledge, roughly the Kantian division between reason and understanding. *Giles* is, in certain respects, Barth's equivalent of *The Magic Mountain,* that disquisition on reason and understanding within a world of sexual and other cripples. As a "magic mountain," New Tammany College has its sphinx (also its sphincter, since Max's masterwork is *The Riddle of the Sphincters*), its philosophical opposites, its disease in WESCAC, its appeal to the universal mind, its atmosphere of enclosure and hermeticism. Even the time sequencing—George spends seven years at instruction—has parallels, in that inner and outer time conflict: New Tammany and the magic mountain are both in and not in the world.

In that struggle of opposing elements, the pure world versus the practical, Barth comes up against what he cannot resolve; and when he attempts to do so in the person of George, and in George's sexuality, he denies a good deal of the complication promised the reader. To bring together the pure world of understanding, perception, and self-consciousness, and the practical world of ethics and morality, is to see ironically, even parodistically. To attempt a resolution, in a goat-boy or otherwise, is to reduce.

The disclaimer in the "Postscript to the Posttape" may then be validated. The entire enterprise is questioned, and the author is not even sure if the manuscript is by Stoker Giles or Giles Stoker—backward serves as easily as forward. Barth (signed "J.B.") questions the tragic view of himself with which George closes the narrative: "the hopeless, even nihilistic tone of those closing pages militates against our believing them to be the Grand Tutor's own." George's rejection of even his friends, of his son, his embrace of the mulatto boy Tombo, his sense of his own apocalyptic end, all, "J.B." says, throw into doubt the validity of the text. Then the editor, a voice beyond "J.B.," questions whether even the Postscript is valid, for it is in different type from that of the "Cover-Letter to the Editors and Publisher." The end note casts the entire enterprise into confusion, and Barth has negated—not through parody, but through denial—the book. He has thrown it back into a fun-

house and demonstrated in over 400,000 words the exhaustion of the very elements he has tried to perceive. He is, in his own admission, no more than a voyeur.

Giles serves as a cover novel for the other five books that chart sixties directions, for each is a response to a system: whether modes of political life in *V.,* authority in *Catch-22,* established racial restrictions in *The Man Who Cried I Am* and *Sula,* * and, finally, sexist lines in *them.* For nearly all, "system" is more a vague but threatening force than a definite organization. It is a felt presence, but no less binding for being unstructured. Ultimately, it is a restriction of human freedom and individual aspirations; to oppose systems is to seek not only liberation but life.

In *The Man Who Cried I Am* (1967), John Williams became trapped between writing an important document about blacks and writing an important novel about American culture focusing on black life. He tried to locate, in 120,000 words, every significant postwar development in black culture. His protagonist, Max Reddick, is a writer involved with Kennedy, Martin Luther King, Black Muslims, Richard Wright, the young James Baldwin, the CIA, an international plot called Alliance Blanc, an American plot called King Alfred, an international scene— New York, Amsterdam, Paris, Africa, with many intermediary stops—the emergence of African nations, and the appearance on the political scene of African leaders. Situated in this activity, much of it presented sharply even if hurriedly, is the personal side of Reddick. He is, apparently, a great cocksman, attracting black and white women like flies. He is a connoisseur of "pussy," a word that appears on nearly every other page, either from the author's point of view, from Ames's (Richard Wright's), or from another character's. Women, incidentally, *are* mainly "pussy." Only one doomed black woman, Lillian, ever moves beyond this designation, and even she remains something of a physical decoration for Reddick.

Yet the frantic quality to the novel, the scream deriving from a man crying out who he is, should not blind us to the fact that Williams was attempting to locate the important themes. He perceived, by the middle to late 1960s, that there had to be a novel which gave expression to what that decade had meant

---

*Published in 1973, *Sula* is not chronologically a 1960s fiction, but in attitudes and stresses it belongs to the earlier decade and I have taken the liberty of including it there.

that the "relationship between reality and the artistic image is not always direct and simple." He warns of a "vulgarized simplicity" as constituting the greatest danger in "tracing the reciprocal interplay between the writer and his environment." Writing has its own sense of autonomy. To achieve the greatest goal, the black writer must travel the most dangerous road.

Wright offers a two-step plan: the "ideological unity of Negro writers and the alliance of that unity with all the progressive ideas of their day." He assumed that such writers would be male, for his plan, which is utopian, is based on common ideas, without consideration of differentiation of sex in terms of viewpoint or stress. Also, there appears little likelihood of an ideological unity holding a group of writers together if each is to respond as an individual to the "progressive ideas" of his times. The first step is a social one, the second aesthetic, and except for the greatest modern masters—Proust or Mann, perhaps Conrad—the combination is virtually unattainable. Consider Wright himself, Ellison, Baldwin, Morrison, Williams—each going his or her own way, moving in and out of modernist motifs, stressing black themes on one hand, general themes on another, racism for some, society for others. Withal, Wright's thesis has a basic theoretical soundness. For it posits the black writer as living a dualistic existence, writing in a language that is part of the general culture, an American language, which carries forward traditional American themes, and still experiencing those elements which are more specifically black, or part of black life. These problems, these tensions, Williams addresses in his novel. Williams's book is, in a way, the perfect working out of Wright's formulation.

In a sense, all ethnic or minority writers—Jewish, Italian, Irish, as well as black—must work within a dualistic frame of reference: they are part of something external to America and yet they are, by virtue of language and cultural history, American. For blacks, however, the situation is more intense, because of the nature of their heritage, the weight of prejudice that is part of their cultural tradition, the difficulties placed in the way of those seeking change, all of which moves them arbitrarily in and out of American history, and affects their visibility. The weight exerted on the black writer, as Wright emphasizes and Williams reflects in Reddick, is enormous, comparable to that experienced by Carlyle's culture heroes. For he or she is not only the conscience of his race; he is also the conscience of his country. He may transmit the traditions of blacks, or explain them to themselves, but he must also, as a writer working at a particular time in a particular place, transmit a culture that makes contemporary sense. A purely black aesthetic that argues past injustices reaches few ears, dismissed before it communicates.

Written when Wright was still under the influence of the Communist Party and yet to write *Native Son,* "Blueprint for Negro Literature" remains a tremendously significant document, already demonstrating that he and the Party would separate. It is a call to action not only for black writers, but for all writers who come from an alien or "sub" culture and must move in a dual world. The new consciousness and responsibility Wright calls for may be directed toward "the people," if the writer wishes; but the tools must be sophisticated artistic patterns which open up consciousness. Representation diminishes; art stretches.

Williams incorporated certain modernist ideas of interrupted plot structure into his themes, using a shifting narrative line: time and place change at intervals, without regularity. Key dates are 1965 (the present), then mid to late 1940s and the 1950s; but these are rarely sequential, and often have tags or pieces which cohere only in later sections.* The aim was clearly to avoid any purely naturalistic, cause-and-effect narrative thrust; replaced by a mosaic of Reddick moving around New York, Holland, Africa, at different times. The thinly veiled historical and literary personages who come through are also attempts to introduce dimensionality into the material, to suggest a documentary but without reductionism.

Additionally, Williams has a central metaphor for black life: Reddick is suffering from terminal cancer, of the rectum. His pain is continuous and relieved only by pills and morphine shots. Reddick moves actively, but only because he is heavily dosed with narcotics; when he is found dead at the end of the novel, in fact, authorities will believe he was a junkie, dead of an overdose. Reddick's handling of his pain and his periods of exhaustion and daze (from the drugs) keeps the novel moving at the human level. All the while, however, he acts out a black psychodrama: the deeply wounded writer (a modern Philoctetes)

---

*Part I, for example, follows this pattern: (1) Amsterdam, 1965, Max at 49, all as memory; (2) Amsterdam, 1965; (3) Amsterdam, 1965; (4) Amsterdam, 1965; (5) Amsterdam, 1965, memory of New York, section called "New York"; (6) New York, Max at 24, 1940; (7) New York, 1940; (8) En route to Leiden, 1965; (9) New York, 1940?; (10) Italy, the war; (11) New York, 1946; (12) New York, 1946–47; (13) New York, 1947–48. Part II fluctuates between 1947, 1957–58, 1965; Part III is the 1960s; Part IV focuses on 1965, the present.

hoping to put it all together, trying to work through everything that has afflicted blacks since the war, attempting to be honest with himself and his people. If Wright's essay was a blueprint for Negro literature, Williams's book is a blueprint for black, a blueprint with black literally written over it. For Reddick's cancerous rectum, that ever-present black pain, is the way America views its Afro-Americans.

Another way in which Williams tried to break through the quasi-documentary nature of his material was by means of Moses Boatwright, who vaguely recalls Ellison's Jim Trueblood. Boatwright is a young black man who studied philosophy at Harvard ("'Howard?'" "'Harvard, Mr. Reddick, HARVARD.'") and is now in prison, accused of killing a white man—in fact, of having eaten the man. "I took the heart and genitals, for isn't that what life's all about, clawing the heart and balls out of the other guy?" Boatwright writes, sexually aroused as he relates to Reddick what it all tasted like. The Boatwright case never leaves Reddick's thoughts; for so deliberate an act of primitiveness casts into question the whole role of the black in a white society.

Williams has here a brilliant formulation—far more penetrating than Reddick's cancer (as an idea) —but he cannot work it through, given the nature of his material. Boatwright argues that his intelligence was always held in abeyance; that a black philosopher is a man shunned by whites and his own people; that he was too proud to teach in a black college and unhirable in a white. He wanted to be special, different, unique. "'I was born seeing precisely,'" he says, and the man without blinkers is the man doomed to a freakish life, if he is black. "'By my acts I decided how I would die.'" Boatwright says he went prowling along the edges of danger and death to remind himself "'that deep down we are rotten, stinking beasts.'" He figures that because of the hideousness of his crime, "'Someone will work a little harder to improve the species.'" Boatwright, in brief, works out a pattern he feels a superior black must fall into: moving beyond his background and heading for self-destructive acts.

What bothers Reddick, besides the crime, is the fact that Boatwright gets his sexual kicks from his story. "'It would be easier to jerk off.'" For the Boatwright case to be focused more definitively, it would need greater integration, and this Williams cannot do. It is an idea with French existentialist potentialities. The Boatwright in Reddick's consciousness would lead to some act or choice of his own. But that would have been another kind of novel,

more in the imagination and less in the sociopolitical realm where Williams wanted to go. Once again, documentary and novelistic materials pull against each other, one part moving Williams outward into spatiality, the other inward into "invisible man" concentration.

A major problem with the documentary level of the novel, despite the adroit cutting back and forth, is that characters beneath the roman à clef are captioned rather than developed. Even though much of the novel is reeled through Reddick's memory, and therefore subject to abbreviation, distortion, condensation (almost dream materials), it is nevertheless almost caricature. Harry Ames is never cogent as the literary father of them all. He seems more concerned with making out than with anything else. Everyone, in fact, is such a determined cocksman that the novel at times seems like a field guide to famous men and their sexual conquests. Ames's white wife, Charlotte, throws herself at Reddick when she wants revenge for her husband's philandering. And Reddick is himself irresistible.

This element of the novel is disheartening, for Williams appears to be acting out roles that undermine his novel at nearly every level; his Reddick in this respect a black Rojack, Mailer's cocksman supreme, or a more potent Sergius O'Shaugnessy. Reddick is fond of guns and hunting, as is Ames—scenes that recall, of course, Hemingway. But hunting has a sexual component, to conquer animals as one conquers women.

Except for brief moments between Reddick and Lillian Patch, there are no relationships and cannot be any, although Williams does not build the impossibility of relationships into his ideal of the novel. He takes the conquest of women as Reddick's right; his sexual prowess as signaling man's power. Ames, too, is constructed almost completely on sexual power, and this is unfortunate because Wright needed a more even presentation; *his* ideas, which rarely come through, would have been far more effective than Reddick's. Marion Dawes (Baldwin) is perceived as even thinner material, and yet the young Baldwin stood for a good deal, especially in his effort to share Wright's hegemony in black literature. Dawes, however, is merely glimpsed, a disreputable young man on the make, graceless, sponging, stealing linen from a hotel; helped by Ames, and then ungrateful, never at the level of his ideas.

Political figures, likewise, are thin. Reddick goes to work for Kennedy as a speechwriter and finds that his racial policies are mere tokenism, political ploys and strategies, not deeply held beliefs. One need not go to Washington for that. Malcolm X as Minister Q is only a spokesman, a mouth. Durrell, who is Martin Luther King, is presented unfavorably, as a bourgeois toady, not at all in the full richness of his role, whether one considered him a savior or not.

Toward the end of *The Man Who Cried I Am,* we find ourselves in a James Bond set. Before dying in the street, Ames gives Reddick the document about the King Alfred plan, one of America's deepest secrets, protected at every level. Now Reddick is a marked man, and two men he had trusted turn out to be CIA agents. There is a shootout; Reddick gets one agent in the groin, but the other injects him, first with a poison that creates the effect of a heart attack, then with morphine, and the game is over, another black junkie. The plan, however, will be exposed; the agents foiled.

The novel moves into an area of political violence that is in keeping, perhaps, with our sense of the sixties, but is at odds with our literary expectations. Williams is, of course, suggesting that the committed black—even the writer, or especially the committed writer—moves at a level of potential and real danger that is quite different from the calling of the white writer. (Williams caught some of this in his own life when he accepted an assignment from *Holiday* magazine, in 1963, to travel around the United States to gather impressions. The time was fateful, the year of civil rights demonstrations, and the trip could be fateful, a bourgeois black man driving a big white station wagon through the South, Midwest, Mountain states, and Southwest.) This element Williams conveys impressively. Problems accrue in *The Man Who Cried I Am* at the level of integration: attempts to connect black history with Reddick's personal quest for manhood, assertion, power. Parts do not always cohere, and we come to suspect that the frequent shifts in time and place are not simply inventive ways of connecting, but inventive ways of disguising fundamental incoherences. This may sound harsh, but Williams's novel is so clearly the prototypical fiction by a black writer in the 1960s that his achievement must be scrutinized carefully.

Toni Morrison's Sula (*Sula,* 1973) is, in many ways, the obverse of Williams's Max Reddick. If he is all activity and political passion, she is the woman who refuses to be used so that *he,* whoever he is and whatever the level of his success, can establish himself. Sula insists on Sula. Yet the black woman who attempts to be herself will be considered a witch by her people. The authors of that superb study *The Madwoman in the Attic* demonstrate the divisions into which male writers of previous generations located their female characters: as either angels or monsters (madwomen in the attic.). Sula is perceived as a monster, not by her author but by those, chiefly men, who judge her.

Unlike Alice Walker's Meridian, who functions within certain recognized systems, Sula breaks through all categories and insists on the same prerogatives that men obtain: sexual liberation, freedom of movement, irresponsibility, lack of social or familial commitment. Sula breaks from every expectation the black community has for a woman. She consciously damns herself in the eyes of others so as to prove to herself that a black woman can do what she does. At the expense of her reputation and any settled existence, she has achieved a form of personal liberation.

Morrison's point is not particularly new, although in the early 1970s it was something of a radical statement for a black woman. It foreruns the argument that Michele Wallace put together in *Black Macho.* Morrison's achievement is not only in limning liberation, however, but in making it part of a poetically evocative view of men and women. She does not vaunt Sula in order to pour hatred on men. Michele Wallace's delineation of black males is full of their sound and fury, their obsessive quest for sexual power. Morrison sees them as part of a context in which even as they seek their pleasure they are doomed; even as Sula is doomed as she seeks her pleasures. Tragically, life both allows and disallows personal choice.

Sula's childhood friend, Nel Wright, early on marries Jude Greene, who becomes involved with Sula. Nel meditates:

It didn't take long, after Jude left, for her to see what the future would be. She had looked at her children and knew in her heart that would be all. That they were all she would ever know of love. But it was a love that, like a pan of syrup kept too long on the stove, had cooked out, leaving only its odor and a hard, sweet sludge, impossible to scrape off. For the mouths of her children quickly forgot the taste of her nipples, and years ago they had begun to look past her face into the nearest stretch of sky.

By implication, the reverie concerns Sula, also; for the love that slips away from Nel was never to be Sula's

—life itself has slipped away from her. She dies of a cancer, literally, which is her fate, although her life has not been all pain.

Central to both lives is an incident that occurred when both were young girls. Playing in the woods with a little boy, Chicken Little, Sula swings him ever faster in her arms, until, clear of land, he arches out over a body of water and falls like a stone, where he drowns. The horror of the moment is preceded by moments of joy: "His knickers ballooned and his shrieks of frightened joy startled the birds and the fat grasshoppers. When he slipped from her hands and sailed away out over the water they could still hear his bubbly laughter." The sole witness is Shadrack, a crazed black, a man so deeply affected by his World War I service he has never recovered. He, in fact, can only exorcise death by having an annual holiday, which is called National Suicide Day. It takes place every January third, at first celebrated only by Shadrack, then gradually by the entire town of Medallion.

Sula grows up in Medallion in the Bottom, a piece of land originally promised to a freed slave, who thought he was getting some of the fertile valley land. But his master has said Bottom referred to "the bottom of heaven," the hills that intervene when God looks down on white folks in the valley. This dislocation of name and place is a metaphor for Sula, as for Shadrack, whose crazed presence runs as a leitmotif through the brief novel. Sula's choice in life, to liberate herself from stereotypical roles, is related to the location of the Bottom at the top, to being up in the Bottom—part of Morrison's evocation of the ironies and paradoxes she perceives as the very center of black life.

Morrison refuses to see these dislocations as forms of fate and doom; but rather as extensions of the peculiar existence all blacks must experience, places and events cohering in different ways than they do for whites. A young black girl growing up in the Bottom of Medallion has a textured experience that is unique. Sula's mother, Hannah, had serviced many of the local males, in joy, not doom; her grandmother, Eve, had poured kerosene over her beloved son, Plum, who had regressed emotionally as he grew older; and Sula is herself involved in the terrible mistake with Chicken Little. The rhythm of the novel takes its form from these unspoken events, not from economics, or politics, or any social stirrings.

Medallion is, indeed, closed off, as much as the Bottom is from the bottom, and the black worker from employment. No white world exists here, except for distant scenes of whites working on projects (roads, tunnel) denied to blacks. Blacks survive on their own, and there is a joy to it: "the streets of Medallion were hot and dusty with progress, those heavy trees that sheltered the shacks up in the Bottom were wonderful to see." "Maybe it was the bottom of heaven," and not the dregs.

Since Sula's survival rests with other blacks, she assimilates her blackness and attempts a reversal of expectations. She grows up in the twenties, leaves for ten years, returns in 1937, a new woman. The townspeople recall that when Hannah caught fire, Sula watched her mother burn, either too astonished to help or else caught in a fearful dream of expectation. They observe her as a witch, a role she has chosen to play. Sula has returned out of boredom, having found that life in the big cities is as undifferentiated as the men are. The men can speak only of love: "Whenever she introduced her private thoughts into their rubbings or goings, they hooded their eyes. . . . She had been looking all along for a friend, and it took her a while to discover that a lover was not a comrade and could never be—for a woman." Having discovered nothing in the larger world, she returns to the smaller, to seek in Nel, her childhood friend and secret-sharer, some kinship unobtained elsewhere.

"And like any artist with no art form, she became dangerous." She had expected Nel to comprehend what she was trying to discover, but Nel shares the perceptions of the townspeople, viewing Sula as a pariah and refusing to understand that the black woman is fated by these very perceptions; for those with husbands "had folded themselves into starched coffins, their sides bursting with other people's skinned dreams and bony regrets"; whereas those without husbands "were like sour-tipped needles featuring one constant empty eye." Once Sula returns, she and Nel become, for the time, opposites, the polarities of the black female experience.

Nel argues that as "a woman and a colored woman at that," Sula cannot act like a man, cannot be "walking around all independent-like." Sula responds that being a woman and colored is "the same as being a man." But Nel's trump is that Sula never had children, and if she had, she would be connected to a different set of coordinates. Sula responds by asserting that every man she knows left his children, and so her behavior would be consistent. She adds that the women she left behind were "dying like a stump," whereas she is "going down like one of those red-woods"; that her loneliness is connected not to some broken relationship but to her own making and being. "But my lonely is *mine.* Now your lonely is somebody else's. Made by somebody else and handed to you. . . . A secondhand lonely."

A man is not worth keeping, she tells Nel; what counts is that inner shout of being: "I am." She demands something that is hers, failing to perceive that Nel has not achieved the level of consciousness to understand that. Nel's hurt is linked to her Jude's getting into bed with Sula, connected to Sula's transgression into her marriage. She cannot see that Sula has tried to get beyond routine views, beyond ordinary relationships, into areas where legality, social sanctions, and possession do not prevail. She is seeking, somewhat inchoately, a level of communication and consciousness that transcends the ordinary; and because of this, she must fail. Only after her death does Nel gain insight into her friend's effort; only then does she invoke Sula's name, in the observation that their early friendship meant everything: " 'We was girls together . . . O Lord, Sula . . . girl, girl, girlgirl-girl.' " And then because of Morrison's location of the story in the Bottom, Nel can add with sad irony: "It was a fine cry—loud and long—but it had no bottom and it had no top, just circles and circles of sorrow."

The man who cried "I am" joins with the woman. Although briefly and inconclusively developed in many sections, Morrison's novel gathers its strength from its evocation. Morrison has moved outside relentless detail, beyond naturalism, toward another way of capturing what she perceives is a unique experience. In many ways, she is responding to materials like those in Shulman, Jong, Gould, Piercy, Alther, and others; but her points of reference are not by any means solely female. However significant she makes "female equality," she reacts to what is unique in the individual, to the ways in which a community can hobble that individual experience, can connect that experience to customs which, sometimes supportive, are often destructive. The individual life, she demonstrates, becomes more important, in fictional terms, than the social organism, or even the race. The narrow focus can evoke the whole, whereas frequently a broader focus loses all sense of life as lived.

However different in style and even attitudes *Sula* and Joyce Carol Oates's *them* (1969; later as *Them*) may be, they share a large middle ground of experience. For they have raised significant questions of breaking out, liberation, reshaping—all the traditional American themes brought to bear on particular female experiences. Further, in their intensity, they have moved beyond domestic scenes, taking their respective novels into broader areas for the "female experience," joining it to the human experience.

Sections of *them* devoted to Loretta, the mother of the main character, Maureen, seem to derive directly from Dreiser, an updating of Jennie Gerhardt, or reminiscent of Sister Carrie. Loretta's life appears caught by all the familiar elements of doom—poor neighborhood, petty crime of the young men around her, hopelessness of young women growing up resigned to their roles, "protective" older brother, who serves as a father surrogate, sudden crime (here a murder), marriage to a young man (Howard Wendall) who slowly descends into impotence. These elements serve as traps, and they are cyclical: what begins when Loretta is sixteen will recur when she is twenty-six, and after. Children appear regularly to ensure she can never escape. Thus, Loretta seems a person who will pass on to her children those same qualities of entrapment.

But like Dreiser's Carrie, although in a different style, Loretta is a survivor; and Oates's entire presentation is a tableau of survivors: how women, in effect, survive their men. In every way, the men are deadly creatures, and they dominate the lives of their women. But they do not triumph. The men are violent—for example, Loretta's second husband, Pat Furlong (a horse of a man), severely beats up Maureen and terrorizes the household. He is a successor to Loretta's own brother, Brock, who shoots Bernie Malin dead when he finds Bernie in bed with Loretta. Loretta's father controls his household by way of bouts of insanity and drinking; her first husband, Howard, sets the pace of the house by way of negative qualities: sullenness, potential violence, alcoholism. At nearly every stage, the men seem in control—either physically or by way of negative force; but the women survive them. Loretta marries to get away from her brother; Howard is killed in an accident; Furlong goes to prison; Maureen seduces a college professor in order to reestablish her life.

Modes of survival differ, of course. Loretta surrounds herself with similar women, proves tougher and cagier than her men, provides them with just sufficient services to control them. Young Maureen uses school and then the library as a way "out," as moments of peace, although the school situation is destroyed for her when she loses the secretary's book of minutes. But the library remains a sanctuary. Jane

Austen, among others, introduces her to alternative worlds where she can, temporarily, escape—and escape she will, even after the severe beating Furlong administers. Her means of escape is through prostitution, and Oates's handling of these scenes is expert.

As the novel shifts toward her, Maureen has felt herself emptied out. She has nothing but contempt for her situation, but mainly for Furlong, whose heavy, smelly, hairy presence is a desecration even of their minimal home. Her brother Jules had felt that way about their father, now she about her stepfather. "There was nothing in her but a hatred for him so diffuse that it was like her own blood, coursing mechanically through her. She ransacked her mind but there was nothing in it. Everything was emptied out, exhausted. She might have been inhabiting her mother's body." Even books can no longer stir her.

The image of emptiness is, by way of contrasts, a cogent one in postwar fiction. Not the emptiness of Hemingway's characters, who raise the quality almost to heroic terms, that in postwar fiction is sheer blankness, in contrast with rich life around: a negative element which works by opposites as well as by definition of an individual. It is not a condition that can be filled by the elements of life; nothing will sustain that emptiness. It is not even Kafkaesque, which has some morbidly comic dimension to it. It is close to anomie, to utter silence. It is outside space and time, in some dimension that lies in the sub- or unconscious; and it is completely countercultural. It cannot be reached by the culture, although on occasion that can be tapped by the individual. Maureen has to learn how to deal with emptiness; and her success or failure is, for Oates, a paradigm of what women must do— that emptiness, for her, defines in the main where women are. Loretta sinks into it; Maureen still has options, however circumscribed.

In the circumstances, Maureen feels something snap, which means she can control her emotional life, and she can use the one thing she has to make money: her young body. The man she sells herself to offers kindness, interest, and money, which she saves in a book of poetry*—a practice that leads to her undoing, when Furlong discovers her cache and beats her. In describing Maureen's physical reaction to a man's body, Oates is superb: "His skin was a man's skin, a

Poets of the New World is the name of the volume, suggesting not only "poetry" but Maureen's new world, which she is exploring and/or discovering by way of her body. The circumstances are, of course, paradoxical: Eden discovered by way of submission.

little rough. It felt almost sandy beneath her fingers. He himself was a little rough, and so she seemed to be guiding him with her hands on his back and her mouth near his. A man was like a machine: one of those machines at the laundromat where she dragged the laundry. There were certain cycles to go through."

By turning sexual intercourse into a laundry cycle, Maureen has discovered her way out: mechanizing feeling, she controls it, whereas the man will always be humbled by it. She has learned what Loretta also found, that men can be manipulated despite their physical power and their desire for domination.

For the sake of the novel's forward movement in real time and space, Oates has chosen to introduce the actual "Maureen Wendall." "This is a work of history in fictional form," she writes, "that is, in personal perspective, which is the only kind of history that exists." Maureen was a student in Oates's class at the University of Detroit, whose life seemed to be so absorbing—and, incidentally, internally similar enough to Oates's own to create interest—that the novelist felt: "This is the only kind of fiction that is real." The novel about Maureen became *them:* "Them" would heroize or memorialize; Maureen must ascend from a lowercase "them."

Two-thirds through the novel, Oates interrupts with two letters from Maureen. The technique serves primarily as the letter did in the Victorian novel, functioning for purposes of plot—like Tess's letter to Angel Clare in the Hardy novel—and giving the novelist another means of conveying narrative dimensions, however unwieldy. It is a deliberate way of introducing a naturalistic element—the cause and effect of the real world—while insisting on the prerogatives of the fictional world. It offers a good deal to the development of the nonfiction novel.

Maureen's two letters come in 1966, nine years after she has emerged from a near-comatose state, her depression after Furlong's beating so great she has grown enormously fat, pimply, unresponsive to stimuli. She has, in her withdrawal, become infantile, and her mother can handle her only by hand-feeding her and letting her settle into a childlike existence. What awakens her is the sudden appearance of Loretta's brother Brock, the man who had shot Bernie in bed. Brock is a terrible failure, but he encourages Maureen; and a letter from her brother Jules supports her further. Parts of her body begin to cohere; she feels connected, like a machine reassembled.

In the nine years since her awakening, as she tells

Oates, she has taken some control of her life. She has moved into a single room of her own, taken a position in an office, and started to pursue a degree at the university, where Oates had her as a student, and failed her. At twenty-six, she writes to tell Oates she failed her in the course, failed her out of the university, and in turn, failed *her*.

The letter is a remarkable document, for it suggests that Oates, while brilliant in the classroom, missed altogether what Maureen was—the student had asked for a dimension the teacher could not give, not as a woman, not as a person. "One year I lay in bed in silence and a few years later I was writing papers for you, trying to write. You failed me. You flunked me out of school." She says she does not condemn; she does not even judge. Oates gave her an "F" for "Lack of coherence and development."

What makes the letter so remarkable is the way it uses a "marking system," a classroom procedure which puts walls between people in the system (Oates) and those who must find their way outside it (Maureen). It is not simply well-to-do versus poor, or have versus have-not, or educated versus uneducated; it goes to the heart of democratic procedure, which in its egalitarianism is ruthless, uncaring, cold-blooded. This is essentially what Maureen accuses Oates of being: of existing so cocooned (her writing, her sense of "art from life," her husband driving her to the campus, her shielding herself from all intrusions) that she becomes impervious to touch.

Maureen says she has lived off hate of her former teacher, and we must not forget that Oates has chosen to include this damaging letter, her version of what Maureen wrote. "But yes. I hate you and no one else, not even those men, not even Furlong. I hate you and that is the only certain thing in me. Not love for the man I want to marry [her evening teacher at her next school] but hate for you. Hate for you, with your books and words and your knowing so much that never happened, in a perfect form, you being driven to school by your husband, and now there are even photographs of you in the paper sometimes, you with your knowledge while I've lived a lifetime already and turned myself inside and out and got nothing out of it, not a thing. . . . I lived my life but there is no form to it. No shape."

Everything Oates had taught about forms, shapes, and systems is questioned by the reality of a countering life, by the history of a single person. This is, as I have already suggested, a common theme in postwar fiction, reflecting as it does the American hatred of the very goods and materials supporting the culture. Bellow's Herzog in his Vermont farmhouse dreams of a simpler existence, despising the complications of the larger system, all the while drawing on services from that culture. Oates demonstrates Maureen's intense hatred of Oates's world, and yet her survival depends on her acquiring a piece of that world: a husband (any decent man!), her own house, a child, curtains on the windows, a settled and stable existence outside her Wendall background. She cannot speak of art forming life, because life has had no shape for her.

Oates's insight is so grand because it folds both sexes into a system-antisystem confrontation while showing how the conflict more directly affects the woman. Maureen's struggle is, I feel, the key "woman's life" since the Second World War, not only for its qualities of survival, but for thrusting into relief Oates's own very different, and very sheltered, existence. They were seemingly very alike, Oates says; and yet her intelligence and talent put her in a category of escape: through achievement in school, then through achievement with her fiction. Yet they were similar in their awareness of women trapped, forced to escape by bizarre means. Maureen's life, then, becomes prototypical because it is played off against Oates's, because of that one long letter which, while describing her, reflects the other.

One wonders how Herzog would have looked if Bellow had provided an external version of him: Herzog observed through others' eyes, not simply through his own perceptions of himself. A male writer does not consider such self-criticism appropriate. Since Bellow's acceptance of Herzog's self-indulgence does not permit this, the latter is given his own reins, drives his own team, and no one, except himself, judges. Similarly, we wonder how Mailer's American Dreamer, Rojack, would have looked from the outside, although Mailer's obsession with himself could not countenance this. Rojack remains in his own class or category, a fighter winning against his own shadow, not against an opponent.

A parallel movement to Maureen in *them* involves her brother Jules, and here we have a structural element that calls into question Oates's method. Jules is the footloose opposite of Maureen: as obsessively as she demands some stability for herself, he rejects it, becoming the archetypical American male, seeking spatial adventures and losing mightily in the exchange with America. At every turn, Jules is defeated by the country, its people, its size, its values. He is, however, a survivor; and even his love for the rich-born Nadine, who shoots him in the chest, does not doom him. He survives the wound, survives his obsession with Nadine, survives anarchic elements in himself. He apparently thrives on acting out the wildness that constituted his background.

Jules and Maureen are sides of Dreiser's Clyde Griffiths. They identify with his upward mobility, and they contain within themselves unidentifiable elements of doom. Jules branches off to become one type of Clyde, surely in his relationship to Nadine, whereas Maureen finally rejects that aspect of herself.* The hand of Dreiser lies heavily over *them* in that stress on ordinary detail which becomes, with art, the generality of the human condition. Oates is almost singular among contemporary novelists in being able to evoke the Dreiserian social sense without sinking into programmatic naturalism.

Jules represents Oates's opportunity to get beyond herself, to relocate the Maureen in her, and to explore a double or twin. Although Jules is older and independent almost from childhood, he is devoted to Maureen and, in his way, attached to the family; he sends money, he writes, he never fully deserts his mother or sister. While the other siblings fade into the background, Jules remains in Maureen's consciousness: as possibility, potentiality, ideas of escape. Still, Jules is caught by his own form of doom, in the person of Nadine, who comes from Grosse Point, is

---

*Maureen could easily have been Roberta; in fact, her relationship to men in general and to Furlong in particular made her a victimized Roberta. Roberta's death by water, accicental in one sense, purposeful in another, is an archetypal experience which underlies Maureen. The female motif is evident; Roberta lacks power, imagination, guile. She is well outside the male world of acquisitions and material things. She is a casual property who has only her own person to offer: shabby, faithful, obedient to social dictates. She is a victim well before she is victimized, her career in American fiction a constant as the abandoned girl friend, wife, mother. The man moves on, while she drowns. Her fate is to be sunk by some man—suitor, casual boyfriend, brother, stepfather, even father. This description from Dreiser: "And the left wale of the boat as it turned, striking Roberta on the head as she sank and then rose for the first time, her frantic, contorted face turned to Clyde, who by now had righted himself. For she was stunned, horror-struck, unintelligible with pain and fear—her lifelong fear of water and drowning and the blow he had so accidentally and all so unconsciously administered. 'Help! Help! Oh my God, I'm drowning, I'm drowning. Help! Oh my God! Clyde, Clyde!' " This is, with a change of venue, Maureen; before her, Loretta. The future is theirs.

obviously wealthy, and yet is herself foundering in some doom-filled sensibility. She and Jules run off, and he helps to support her by way of a series of petty crimes; then when he falls ill, she abandons him, unable to deal with giving. As a vampire, she does not lack victims.†

The Jules-Nadine relationship, although a dimension Oates felt was necessary, lacks center. It is full of frenzy, wild passion; but ultimately cold. Oates is not very effective in her scenes of erotic passion, imposed on us by a skillful writer who is outside her metier.

Oates is superb, however, with Maureen, focused, pitched, passionately sympathetic with Maureen's desire for identity and existence. This is one of the strongest presentations of character in postwar fiction not solely a woman writing about a woman, but an author writing about a character. She has the same intensity here that James Jones had with Prewitt and, especially, Warden; Oates as a writer recalls Jones: his honesty, his intensity, his centering himself in Dreiserian forms, and yet his recognition that he must break out into something less binding.

Unfortunately, Jules and Nadine become dead-end characters. That is, they heave and strain against each other or against their personal demons, but remain only possibility. Similarly, Oates's attempt at achieving a vision of Detroit—the typifying American city of the late 1960s—is not fully successful. As background for the Wendalls, once they move from the grandmother's farm, Detroit is always present: a discontinuous mix of whites and blacks living in fear and hatred of each other, white bigotry matched by black violence. This part Oates catches well: that sense of people in poor circumstances forced to live near each other and forming "tribes" or primal hordes as ways of excluding outsiders. Black imagination, white hatred, fear on both sides, a rising crime

---

†With her reliance on violence, and not simply fists or shoving, Oates breaks from any stereotype of a "female novelist." The novel begins when Brock shoots Bernie dead in Loretta's bed; we discover that Bernie had been shot before—by a store owner who waited for him one night. Loretta herself seeks a gun for protection. Then Jules is shot by Nadine. At various times, he carries a gun; in fact, he serves as protection for a rich confidence man, whose throat is slit. Finally, Detroit itself goes up in a race riot, a conflagration that appears like the end of city life, the end of the sixties. During the riots, Jules shoots a man full in the face. For people who are not primarily gangsters, the level of violence seems extraordinary, even if we grant Oates her terms.

rate, unsafe streets, casual violence, all characterize the Wendalls' world as Maureen grows up. Late in the novel, with Jules on the margins, she focuses upon a group of revolutionaries, led by Dr. Mort Piercy, a rich and successful young man who preaches revolution. The scene is an effort at sixties explosion, urban apocalypse, a sense of final things. Yet it appears tacked on; at least the riot does, although it existed in fact.

What partially vitiates the power of Maureen's tale is the aborted quality of other elements: Jules in nearly all his activities, although his presence does seem necessary for analogy, contrast, textual thickness; the finale with Detroit apocalypse, and the emergence of Jules as a figure of power; the linkage to constant violence, focus on guns, their use and presence; the subsidiary characters, who appear and then usually vanish without defining themselves. The line of strength in the novel lies with mother-daughter; then with Maureen's resolve to undermine her evening teacher's marriage. Oates does not show that plan in sufficient detail, only the resolve, even fore-shortening the meeting with the teacher's wife. That showdown, in which one woman survives by undermining another, is told in retrospect, Maureen to Loretta, after the fact. Yet the process of undermining, of subverting another, innocent woman's marriage, has potential interest, for Randolph's wife is as much a victim as is Maureen. Yet Oates was interested, apparently, in larger dimensions, and she dissipated the immense power of the primary line of development. Nevertheless, whatever deterrents we discover, *them* is a fitting capstone to the sixties: not only for women's issues, or for the sense of urban violence, or for the renewal of social and class values in American fiction; not only for these reasons, but for Oates's intense fidelity to a vision of life.

With Thomas Pynchon's *V.* and Joseph Heller's *Catch-22,* we enter more firmly into the modern mode, where the novelist is conscious of modernist techniques and attitudes and uses them as needed, while at the same time remaining solidly within traditional American themes: "Americanized Modern," we might label their works. *V.* is the more elusive piece of work and suggests a future development in Pynchon of even greater indirection, toward that self-consciousness of technique which has been associated with postmodernism. Heller's development toward *Something Happened* and *Good as Gold* would prove more conventional; *Catch-22* is his single modernist experiment to date, in which Joyce, Eliot, and Céline crisscross to alter considerably the terms of the war/combat novel.

The structure of *V.* (1963) is not of two legs attached at an angle, creating the letter V, but of a mosaic in which pieces do not quite touch: an asymptote, as it were, of converging elements. The novel is shaped something like a film in which rapid cuts do not give the viewer an opportunity to settle in; Pynchon's forte is the fast break, the ellipses we associate with a visual technique. He appears to omit everything in between, although, eventually, he cuts back to the lacunae. Meanwhile, he convinces us that as much is omitted as is contained. Our expectation for more is an element in the making of *V.;* as in a modern poem—Eliot's "Waste Land" an apparent example—we yearn for missing pieces, only to discover we do not need them. The novel is made up as much in our minds as it is on paper.

V. lacks narrative, but is full of stories; lacking true characters, it is overloaded with people; lacking place, it is full of locations, and one of them, legendary Vheissu, seems absolutely essential. It recalls Kafka's example: offering us so much we only slowly begin to realize how little is there. For all its five hundred pages, *V.* is minimalist fiction; and paradoxically, for all its half-million words, *Gravity's Rainbow* is not too much, but too little, a minimalist exercise. In each, Pynchon was aiming at only slightly less than a history of the twentieth century; and the two novels, we can see in retrospect, should be read together, as one book—in the way that Gaddis's *The Recognitions* and *JR* are really one book, or *Catch-22* and *Something Happened,* sequential histories of our time.

A book constructed like a mosaic has its advantages and disadvantages. One advantage for the author is that incoherence cannot be a factor, since disconnection except where edges touch is the rule, not the exception. At several junctures in *V.,* for instance, Pynchon moves to the crowd Benny Profane knew when in the navy, or else does navy scenes—the book begins with one such episode. Characters like Pig Bodine, Pappy Hod, and others move through these scenes, and they reflect the typical high jinks we associate with service personnel. Their fun and games are service equivalents of fraternity "Animal House" activities. Though they may serve some small function as parallel activities for the Whole Sick Crew in New York, they are in themselves amusing at such low levels they demean the book; Pynchon, usually sophisticated, insightful, and historically very mature, cannot resist such bouts of masculine play. The question is not of function, but of quality of scene itself, here and in *Gravity's Rainbow,* where several of the characters (Pig, Chiclitz, others) reappear, as do several incidents. German Southwest Africa, somewhat marginal here, becomes central there.

We could possibly argue that the high jinks are initially necessary, since through them we find the original connection of Profane and Paola Maijstral (Pappy Hod's wife), which leads him on to Malta, Valletta, etc. Also, we could further point out that the presence of such scenes—the final one in Valletta, as a capping event—reinforces Pynchon's idea of yo-yoing, in which everything repeats itself. That reliance on yo-yoing, taken from those who shuttle between Times Square and Grand Central, suggests all life as repetitious and cyclical.

We follow that lead, in our effort to connect yo-yoing to the repetition of even adolescent materials. The yo-yoing of alternating activities, along with the more general theme of entropy or things running down, provides powerful tensions: chiefly, delusive spatiality juxtaposed to dead, waste-land areas. Here, as later in *Gravity's Rainbow,* such tensions suggest how things of the world lead us toward death, no matter if will and function choose otherwise.

Profane, Pynchon's hesitating but operative man of life, can move between spaces, even between groups, and yet always end up in stagnation, much as the Times Square shuttle, that archetypal yo-yo. The movement of the shuttle through the labyrinthine underground maze is rapid, but its terminal points never alter. Movement alternating with "dead landscapes" characterizes *V.:* Malta under air attack of the Germans and Italians; Valletta, a dying, almost dead city; Vheissu, that mythical and legendary area which has died out except in memory; Stencil, a version of his father, seeking V., who may or may not be dead, who may or may not have even existed as Stencil imagines her; New York City underground, filled with dead alligators in caves and the Whole Sick Crew above; Southwest Africa, where Germans have systematically massacred the Africans, preparation for even larger-scale exterminations.

As part of this vision of suffocation, decline, passivity, and frantic activity leading nowhere, Profane seeks various refuges; and one connects with the Pig and Pappy crowd. To follow this: Profane moves in holes, rooms, subterranean mazes, tunnels, and in odd, marginal jobs—as a night watchman, for example, in a robot factory. The infantile crowd is just one such arrangement. He has decided against the world of dynamo and progressive energy (although not against life), and his literary points of contact are underground man, invisible man, Kafka's withdrawn victims, Beckett's bums and questors, all of them marginal, but still vital. To fit Profane's locale, Pynchon has devised for him a language of onomatopoeic sounds which punctuate the silence around him.

The mosaical arrangement sustains such connections and such scenes, since everything can touch. Withal, these juvenile episodes of fun and rioting, of using contraceptives as bombs, display a side of Pynchon that weakens his work. He locates Profane in an obsessively masculine tradition, insists he is okay, not "queer," and lets him drink and brawl in mindless parties among like fellows. Profane expends tremendous amounts of energy on producing disorder, in this respect the opposite of Herbert Stencil. From this, we perceive Pynchon's sympathies with energy and activity, *even when* they are recycled into waste.

Although Profane, as his name implies, is the antibourgeois principle in action, like Rabelais's Panurge, his rejection of a productive life is not a negation. By way of the groups Profane associates with—once again the mosaic principle—Pynchon arranges types of life around him: the Puerto Ricans with whom he hunts alligators, the Whole Sick Crew introduced to him by Rachel Owlglass, the Pig-Pappy crowd from his navy days, the people around Stencil involved in the V. quest, and so on. Profane wants an adversary life that no longer obtains; and he sinks into passivity when he cannot find it. Yet he does not succumb to total ennui. Pynchon here and Bellow in *Augie March*—both books products of the fifties and therefore not so dissimilar—are probing comparable malaises of character and event. And just as Bellow would not accept malaise, but had to seek some resolution in life, so Pynchon cannot desert Profane in the intensity of his countering existence. The dilemma seems characteristic of the postwar American novelist: to seek energy in areas that call for Kafka-like passivity and silence; to insist on the energy, and then to recycle it into waste.

Under these conditions we could close the circle of our argument and possibly view the infantile antics of the Pig-Pappy crowd as quite necessary. The navy crew are full of vitality, however mindless; they have not given up on life, though their quality of life is not high; and they represent the dynamic principle, however wasteful this sense of the dynamo has become.

Yet even if we grant this, Pynchon heads into confusion; for if Profane, who seeks life, is the antithesis of Stencil, who seeks repetitions or duplications, then one is hardly preferable to the other. Profane represents the familiar "making out" quality of American masculinity as a form of life spirit, a shaping of energy; when, in fact, it is also something dead. Profane's profanation is weakened, not defined, by his fun and games with Pig Bodine; and these sections loosen, do not reinforce, the mosaical arrangement.

Yet these episodes aside—and there may well be those more sympathetic to them—Pynchon's arrangements in *V.* occur at high levels of imagination. Points of departure are seemingly disconnected: the obsessive quest for V.; the legendary quality of a briefly glimpsed Vheissu, an Edenesque memory; the city of Valletta, capital of Malta, and Malta itself, emblematic of continuing life, despite conquests, bombings, conspiracies; the episode at Fashoda in 1898—France and England carving up Africa as a foreshadowing of World War I; the German conquest of Southwest Africa, leading to its extermination tactics in World War II; the Whole Sick Crew, a stencilized New York version of real art and artists, those who do not create but talk "about people who do." These are the major points of contact, the places where pieces of the mosaic touch; and the key element is the pursuit of V.

The quest for V., whoever she is, whenever she lived, if she did live, if she is still alive, is not linear. The brilliance of the conception of the novel makes V. into anything and anyone beginning with the letter, from Victoria to Valletta. It is, also, a sexual symbol of the female, the two legs of the V meeting in the great feminine mystery. Pynchon's V. as a legendary female appears to owe a good deal to Durrell's sense of Justine in his Alexandrian Quartet. "Disguise is one of her attributes," Stencil states; that is, she moves like Proteus, a legendary confidence woman.

Behind both Justine and V. is a long tradition of women in literature, described by Mario Praz in *The Romantic Agony:* merciless women, deeply sadistic and often masochistic, whose appeal is their ability to convey pain and suffering as sexual substitutes. Such a woman reappears as Katje in *Gravity's Rainbow.* The desirability of V., if she really exists as Pynchon makes her seem, is her elusiveness, her ability to be all things, her protean nature, her disappearances. All her movements transmit pain, first for the elder Stencil, then for his son, who must repeat the experience. Vera Meroving, Veronica Manganese, Victoria Wren —these are some of the guises of V., who ultimately is the pursuit of an idea, an ideal: like Vheissu, that paradisiacal vision, an Antarctic Shangri-la. The elements of highest value in Pynchon are intangible, in the mental or imaginative quest.

That everything remains beyond reach is significant; for the novel is a reflection, deeply so, of the 1950s. The present is 1955–56; and even background events, starting before the turn of the century and continuing into the twenties, are refocused in the mid-fifties. Pynchon's response to the decade is not unlike Bellows or Heller's. The Bellow I have in mind, besides *Augie March,* is *Henderson the Rain King;* an Africa of the mind, a politics of existence. Heller's Pianosa is similar, a place created rather than existing. For Pynchon, who is virtually our archetypal American writer, his background reaching deep into Puritan times,[*] America is beyond reach. The 1950s proved to be a time when America chased the chimera; it, not the sixties alone, split the country. In this respect, America became an unknown country, even as the media and some intellectual journals spoke of reconciliation. Pynchon's America is like Vheissu: the legendary Eden briefly glimpsed, lost, and then unachievable. One quests for it, as for a new Zion, but it remains elusive. Vheissu is, then, a larger vision of what V. might have been. Each is the lost vision.

Aspects of the 1950s mise-en-scène appear in several guises. The Whole Sick Crew—a stencilized version of real culture, a yo-yoing group of superficial talents—is Pynchon's (unjust) version of the Beat movement. Benny Profane is the dysfunctional man of the fifties, an oddball because of his inability to achieve affluence; *anti* force when everyone else is *pro;* a profanation not of God but of God's culture. The surrounding world, like Stencil's preoccupations, is dead, dying, diminishing. The search for V., attached to dead matter as it is, is somehow a countering movement to death, in the way Kafka's protagonists, caught in dying situations, struggle to maintain minimal life.

Profane is the schlemiel, a figure who plays a large

---

[*]Pynchon's forebears came to America in 1630, when William Pynchon became an influential and wealthy settler in the Massachusetts Bay Colony. He was also a magistrate who presided over witchcraft trials, and the family entered into Hawthorne's *The House of the Seven Gables* as the Pyncheons. Thomas Pynchon reproduced many family details and the general outlines of his background in the Slothrops, Tyrone's family, in *Gravity's Rainbow.* He also followed it, more loosely, in the description of Wyatt Gwyon's New England background in *The Recognitions.*

role in our postwar literary culture, who yearns after some form of unattainable purity.* The schlemiel is never far from the idealistic tradition, a counter to heroism (Mailer fights mightily against becoming or creating a schlemiel), an adversary force in American culture. Everything that the fifties in their larger sense came to represent is opposed by the schlemiel image: lack of achievement, dropping out, loss of direction, stress on some personal form of purity, an innocence which makes accomplishment impossible. The phenomenon need not be Jewish, although Jewish self-deprecatory humor and guilt lend themselves to the schlemiel tradition.

The schlemiel accommodates well a vision based on irony, self-deception, disguise. As half Jewish (half Italian), Benny Profane fits, in this respect, into Pynchon's ironic sense of America and American destiny. The irony is based on promise versus achievement, Eden (Vheissu) versus what is, the quest for V. versus what V. may turn out to be. Profane runs the gauntlet of 1950s ideologies. Hunting alligators in New York City's sewers and becoming a watchman in a robot factory are his means of achieving schlemielhood while everyone else is advancing or running down. He walks a treadmill until he returns to Malta, where he

---

*After a long tradition, the schlemiel reemerged in postwar fiction in Isaac Bashevis Singer's "Gimpel the Fool," in Saul Bellow's translation. But even before, Bellow had utilized schlemiel qualities with his "dangling man," his "victim," then of course with Herzog—although he struggled against the image with Augie March. In nearly all of his 1950s fiction, Malamud moved in and out, as did Roth in aspects of Portnoy. Heller's Yossarian is part schlemiel, especially since he was first cast as a Jew, not an Assyrian. Ellison's unnamed invisible protagonist is a prototypical schlemiel. Many novels about the female experience in the late 1960s and thereafter are based on female schlemiels. The counter to the schlemiel, among Jewish writers, is the figure of Benya Krik, who appears in Isaac Babel's Odessa tales. Krik is the "other" kind of Jew, the active man, a gangster, a man who makes out with Russian women, who does not respect authority, a man who defies social roles. Mailer builds his characters on Benya Krik types; Roth would like to embrace Krik, but is caught too tightly by the schlemiel; in *Dubin's Lives,* Malamud reaches out toward Krik. Remarkable about this figure is his lack of guilt, his refusal to fall into Jewish stereotypes, his insistence on being a new kind of Jew, an Israeli freedom fighter before Israel.

Pynchon's earliest publication, "The Small Rain" (in *The Cornell Writer,* March 1959), focuses on a Benya Krik type, Nathan "Lardass" Levine. At first a schlemiel, ready only to do his job at a crisis center after a hurricane, he changes, in three days, into a new man: from passive to active, from schlemiel to Krik.

can vanish: "Profane and Brenda [a college girl] continued to run through the abruptly absolute night, momentum alone carrying them toward the edge of Malta, and the Mediterranean beyond." Profane disappears into the night, as Yossarian paddles toward Sweden: both "resolutions" coming through the schlemiel's way of handling antiheroism, dislike of violence, a self-preserving effort at idealism amidst corruption. The schlemiel in contemporary fiction often serves the role of Thoreau at Walden: a refusal to enter the mainstream, to compete, to go for the prize. The schlemiel and the "insane" touch.

Further, the schlemiel in contemporary fiction has qualities of the "holy innocent," a divine dimension. Profane is not sacred; but he is, as a profane man, often more sacred than those who assert divinity—this condition will be one of the many themes of the 1960s. As antipower, he is the opposite of those in Stencil's past who quest after power. Like the Herreros in German Southwest Africa, who rebel only to be exterminated, Profane represents an inner function. And yet he cannot be sentimentalized; nor is he a viable alternative to Stencil, who represents the "world." He is not a solution to anything, but a more reliable part of the problem. He *does* work at robot testing, for Anthroresearch Associates, where SHROUD ("synthetic human, radiation output determined") and SHOCK ("synthetic human object, casualty kinetics") are being constructed, eventually, to replace man. He only loses the job when he oversleeps. Through work, he enters into the scientific dehumanization of man, Pynchon's major theme, and even feels a "certain kinship" with SHOCK, "which was the first inanimate schlemihl he'd ever encountered."

V. established Pynchon's position in mainstream modernism by exploiting those elements which originally made modernism possible. With his background in engineering physics and the humanities, he was uniquely equipped. The rhythms that underlie his work, the sense of opposites, the tensions and conspiratorial silences, derive from meetings between technology and humanism. The advent of speeded-up technology permeating the culture had its humanistic counterpart in opposition, undermining, in frantic and often useless attacks on technology's values. American politics often rest there, not in ideologies. Pynchon is in that tradition: seeing dynamo undermine virgin, technology destroy faith; and yet his strength lies in exploiting elements of the conflict. *Gravity's Rainbow* becomes our novel of the 1970s: where the self is minimized in the name of the self; where ego is reduced in the name of ego; where the individual is diminished in the name of the individual. The play of opposites, as in *V.,* gives Pynchon the drama of ironies and paradoxes that modernism affords only the best novelists.

There are in *V.,* repeated areas of disguise, hiding, layers of concealment. Only Profane is out front; the rest invade shadows to discover what lurks there. The outlines of the novel are concerned with questing after what cannot be clearly seen, no less found. The following is a tour de force of subterranean ordeals, all connected to Stencil:

> Not when a barbaric and unknown race, employed by God knows whom, are even now blasting the Antarctic ice with dynamite, preparing to enter a subterranean network of natural tunnels, a network whose existence is known only to the inhabitants of Vheissu, the Royal Geographic Society in London, Herr Godolphin, and the spies of Florence.

The lineaments exist to do the work of the greater element, which is concealment: Vheissu, V., myths, conspiracies. Every foreground action has its parallel of background elements; Pynchon is always busily working back and forth, individual and history, now and past, real and stencilized. Tensions and conflicts are all focused on trying to find what constitutes freedom, whether the individual lives skew to the rest of society or in frantic relationship to the culture. Surrounding him are all the factitious elements, from Stencil's nonproductive search for V. to the Whole Sick Crew as a carbon copy of artistic achievement. Neither is the real thing, which lies in murk. It may lie in alligator hunts, where Profane feels comfortable: underground, bizarre, himself against nature. Perception is *there.*

Yet even as Pynchon celebrates Profane's vitality —human energy as against technological, mechanical energy—significant elements of the novel do not lie with him. He is only tangentially connected to what matters, which is the quest for V. The concealed and disguised obtains, the conspiracy, not only the human energy expended in seeking. Stray elements of detective fiction—Greene, Chandler, Hammett—haunt *V.* Early in the novel, we gain some sense of how Pynchon intends to mirror elements: inner and outer, human and technological, etc., in a temporal image which combines many diverse quests—Profane, Rachel Owlglass, Paola Maijstral, and young Stencil. The time is 1956, when the earlier Fashoda incident of 1898 would reappear in the Anglo-French, Israeli Suez venture, a warmup for the new war, as Fashoda was for World War I. Rachel is described:

When she left, turning off all the lights, the hands on an illuminated clock near Paola Maijstral's bed stood near six o'clock. No ticking; the clock was electric. Its minute hand could not be seen to move. But soon the hand passed twelve and began its course down the other side of the face; as if it had passed through the surface of a mirror, and had now to repeat in mirror-time what it had done on the side of real-time.

Time, reflection, narcissistic impulses, the mirror image, all provide a transition from the Whole Sick Crew to Stencil and his quest. By way of the clock, Pynchon can move in and out, between real time on the clock face and mirror time, which is, as it were, a distorted version of clock time. In that reflected image of clock time we find Stencil—himself a copy of his father, himself a mirror image of the real one. The twisting and turning here are brief images of the alternations of display and disguise which characterize the novel's structure.

Because he operates in real time, Profane can speak of freedom, can free himself for whatever he wants to pursue. Unlike Rachel with her car, Esther Harvitz (another member of the Whole Sick Crew) with her remade nose, Stencil with his tracking of V., Profane is not part of the gallery of fools, malcontents, robotlike creatures. He is asked what he does and responds: " 'Kill alligators.' " He then defends his choice: "Because it [the myth of the alligators] wasn't born from fear of thunder, dreams, astonishment at how the crops kept dying after harvest and coming up again every spring or anything else very permanent, only a temporary interest, a spur-of-the-moment tumescence, it was a myth rickety and transient"—and therefore neither mechanical nor demeaning. When Profane is offered a clerk's job, he declines—" 'I don't go for that inside work too much' "—and he does not wish to move up or make something of himself. He glories in being a schlemiel —"A schlemihl is a schlemihl"—because of the choices involved. Even waiting for the interview at the employment agency sends him into a funk, and he runs out, to return to alligator hunting, which is itself winding down, like big-game hunting.

Pynchon, in *V.,* in 1963, was attempting to become a spokesman for the decade that had passed, as well as the one coming. For the decade that had passed, he saw a stencilized existence: the quest for a chimera in the person of V. and the search for a Shangri-la in the shape of Vheissu. Those searches paralleled in their intensity the exploitation of people and self that were the buildup for war. He observed diminution and exhaustion of resources in the quest for personal fulfillment which was little different from robotlike action. In SHROUD and SHOCK—as he would demonstrate in *Gravity's Rainbow*—he foresaw the mechanical personification of man's quest. And yet in those false efforts, he could not completely condemn the energy, the conspiratorial quality, the paradoxes of quest and discovery; in this, he entered mainstream America. Although his career is still young, Pynchon may be our quintessential American writer, the way Hemingway was for the two decades before World War II.

Much of *V.* depends on experimentation with forms of language; the languages—not *a* language—of the novel. With Profane's activities, we have current American, really Americanese, the slurred, slangy speech of the big city. Gesture, sounds, movement are more significant than words; the voice is emblematic of a life style rather than the desire to communicate. With Fausto Maijstral and Malta, deep in the conspiracy, we have Nabokovian parody; the description of St. Giles Fair, in Fausto's journals:

> Her rhythms pulse regular and sinusoidal—a freak show in caravan, travelling over thousands of little hills. A serpent hypnotic and undulant, bearing on her back like infinitesimal fleas such hunchbacks, dwarves, prodigies, centaurs, poltergeists! Two-headed, three-eyed, hopelessly in love; satyrs with the skin of werewolves, werewolves with the eyes of young girls and perhaps even an old man with a navel of glass, through which can be seen goldfish nuzzling the coral country of his guts.

Not only Nabokovian parody, but Nabokov; Humbert is located in here, as is Shade's fruity poem.

Describing the Whole Sick Crew, Pynchon is parodic in a lower key—not as witty, however, as he would like to be. Presenting Foppl's Siege Party and the German extermination of the Herreros in Southwest Africa, he is objective and clinical, only intermittently voluptuous. Foppl's Siege Party, the holding of Faschung while war rages outside the barricaded compound, is a more corrupt form of the parties of the Whole Sick Crew, Foppl's group sinister in their pleasures while massacres and mutilations proceed outside their walls.

Through levels of language, Pynchon was trying to find one that was suitable for him, an experiment that continued into *The Crying of Lot 49.* By *Gravity's Rainbow,* he appears to have discovered a voice, one voice with several variations. Here, in *V.,* there are several voices, a virtuoso effort: a voice for each element of the fifties, another for the sixties.

A NOTE ON PYNCHON'S SHORTER FICTION

While at work on *V.,* Pynchon published several shorter works, the most significant of which is "Entropy" (1960), in *Kenyon Review.* "Entropy" leads directly into Pynchon's three novels to date. (Two other stories are "Mortality and Mercy in Vienna" and "Low-Lands" (both 1959). Another, "Under the Rose," became, with revisions, Chapter 3 of *V.*)

The scene: degenerative, disorganized, discrete, urban. Time is running out, and things do not cohere. Tensions make life irresolvable at every level; so it diminishes, disintegrates. The epigraph is from Miller's *Tropic of Cancer,* to the effect that the weather forecast is so bad we can expect calamities, more death, more despair: "We must get into step, a lockstep toward the prison of death. There is no escape." The time: early February of 1957; the place: Washington, D.C.

"Entropy" warns of apocalypse, but with omens: temperature threats, heat-death as potential endings. Binary choice—the lot of those in *The Crying of Lot 49*— seems the reductionism of our time: survival, through wild parties, or doom, by way of disintegration, heat-death. Downstairs is the party, run by Meatball, called a "lease-breaking party," characterized by destruction, torpor, diminution of self; that aspect of the world Pynchon associates with Henry Adams's dynamo, the technological principle which upsets and disorganizes.

Upstairs, at another level, is Callisto and his controlled universe, a form of art which is, he hopes, impervious to Meatball's disorganization Downstairs. Upstairs is the organizing principle based on balance of elements, especially of temperature, that was suggested by Adams's Virgin. The proof of Callisto's plan will be whether he can keep a canary warm. His task is monumental, for in his sealed room, he is doing nothing less than attempting to preserve life.

The basic situation, however, is not this simple. For Meatball also attempts to create some organization; and Callisto is not quite sane, his sense of entropy being that all efforts to triumph over the phenomenon are doomed; he is doomed, we are doomed.

Callisto's efforts are apparently negated by what he already knows: that "the entropy of an isolated system always continually increases." As a result of knowledge, he has to forsake his idea of a theoretically perfect engine which runs at 100 percent efficiency—that is, Heaven, a perfect Upstairs—in favor of an alternate plan in nature: "the horrible significance of it all dawned on him . . . that the isolated system—galaxy, engine, human being, culture, whatever—must evolve spontaneously toward the Condition of the More Probable [less than perfect efficiency]. He was forced, therefore, in the sad dying fall of middle age, to a radical reevaluation of everything he had learned up to then; all the cities and seasons and casual passions of his days had now to be looked at in a new and elusive light."

Just as Meatball's desired perfect party cannot be obtained, so Callisto's plan of a perfect art or science is foiled by the constancy of temperature, which he sees as nature's plot to cause heat-death. The beauty of Pynchon's patterning is that no matter how paranoiac any particular idea proves, it can be reinforced by nature: heat-death or not, entropy or not, social decline or not. Upstairs and Downstairs are ever-changing; each is a system with its own flaws. Nothing brings balance or salvation. The canary, of course, dies, to prove to Callisto that his plans are invalid; and his girl friend, Aubade—a musical form connected to the dawn—smashes the window in order to disprove Callisto's obsession that the "transfer of heat" has ceased to work. While the breaking of the window will be no solution, it will return a momentary balance, 37 degrees inside and outside, and propel them both "into a tonic of darkness and the final absence of all motion."

The Pynchon vision is readily established. The pursuit of *V.* will allow for infinite choice of means and yet "stencilize" the pursuer. *The Crying of Lot 49* will reveal a bidder, but it will also reduce man's "lot" or choices to a binary system. And most significantly, the modulations of *Gravity's Rainbow* (the falling implicit in gravity, the harmony created by the rainbow) will reveal not balance in nature, but disharmony, apocalypse, rocketry as the end as well as the means. Pynchon's attempt to find an analogy for postwar life —the continuing process of human means against scientific ends—has led him into a "death alley," where no resolution is possible. Upstairs and Downstairs do not connect, but remain separate experiences, each reaching out to touch the other, but to no end.

The shaping of "Low-Lands" derives from a sea metaphor, and that in turn refers to a garbage dump which is gradually being brought up to sea level with fill. The center of these two metaphors, one sea, one land, is Dennis Flange, whose name suggests a way of connecting land and water by way of a juncture. Pushed out of his house by his wife for cavorting with male friends unacceptable to her, Flange is taken to a garbage dump whose watchman is a black named Bolinbroke. We have a typical Pynchon crew, whether the Whole Sick Crew of *V.,* or the rocket teams of *Gravity's Rainbow,* or even the mail teams of *The Crying of Lot 49.* Such crews are male-oriented, based on drinking bouts, buddy-fraternity routines, talk of making out, but not lacking in the poetry of masculinity and machismo. Pig Bodine, who keeps turning up in Pynchon's fiction, is present, but with a minor role.

The story focuses on Flange's exploration of "Low-Lands," his passage from bourgeois security in a house overlooking the sound to a lower-than-ground-level experience which leads to a further journey, either of fantasy or of waking dream. The latter involves an exploration of the tunnels under the garbage, led by a lovely, forty-two-inch young woman, Venus to his Tannhäuser. The discongruity between Flange's former life and his present exploration is Pynchon's theme: between his "large half-earthen mass at the top of a cliff" and a kind of prehistoric existence underneath rubble, with a perfectly formed midget who promises sensual delights.

The little group of breakaways—Flange, Bodine, Rocco—tell sea stories, although Flange recognizes that for him to tell a story is to alter the course of the sea that lives in his fantasies: "because you and the truth of a true lie were thrown sometime way back into a curious contiguity and as long as you are passive you can remain aware of the truth's extent but the minute you become active you are somehow, if not violating a convention outright, at least screwing up the perspective of things." The analogy is Einstein's relativity: observed data depend on the observer.

As fantasies and memories filter in and out of the speakers, a dreamlike atmosphere forms. Flange is possibly awake when he hears someone call for an "Anglo with the gold hair," although the sounds and sequence are dreamlike. He follows what turns out to be a great beauty, "roughly three and a half feet tall." Flange, who has no prejudices about short women, follows her through a maze of household appliances, then into a forty-eight-inch concrete pipe, finally through mazes of tunnels and entrances and exits which mark an underground city of gypsies: the alternative existence. The tunnels had been constructed in the thirties by a terrorist group known as the Sons of the Red Apocalypse, who were eventually caught by the FBI. The labyrinth remained; alligators would enter it in *V.*

In the earliest of his major stories, "Mortality and Mercy in Vienna," Pynchon was trying to get at his still partially buried talent. He was, as always, literary, sardonic, full of unusual lore, and secretive. It is, in fact, the lore that makes the story move: his knowledge of life among the Ojibwa tribe, and its association with the "Windigo psychosis." The key image, however, is not Indian, but Conradian. Cleanth Siegel (half Jewish, half Roman Catholic) as part of the joke of his name works out the meaning of Kurtz in the Western world. "Mistah Kurtz—he dead," is the parting shot of the host of a party as he hands it over to Siegel, and from that the latter must negotiate the Kurtz route.

Standing by himself at the party is an Indian, Irving Loon, who has become something special for one of the young ladies, Debby. Siegel begins to flip back his mental IBM cards for information programmed there, and he recalls a college anthropology class in which Loon's tribe, the Ojibwa, was discussed. Ojibwa Indians dedicated themselves to ideals of starvation, deprivation, self-extermination, a group and theme Pynchon would repeat in *Gravity's Rainbow* with the Herreros. While Debby goes on about how Loon was happy only in his tribe with his family, Siegel recalls the tribal ideology, which, based on a paranoiac fear of forces aligned against the individual, seeks release by way of a supernatural state achieved through starvation and deprivation.

In this state, the Ojibwa undergo a mass psychosis —the so-called Windigo psychosis—which makes them see "succulent, juicy, fat" beavers, and when that occurs they gorge themselves on members of the family, in an act of physical release and ideological fervor. Debby introduces Siegel to Loon, and the former whispers "Windigo" to the Indian, who nuzzles Debby's neck and murmurs "my beautiful little beaver." Pynchon now moves his opposites toward some potential conflict: the tribal, which has murder at its roots, and the modern, Siegel as guru, priest (literary, a Cleanth), disaffected party-goer, observer rather than participant.

As father confessor, savior, controller, Siegel recognizes he is playing Kurtz; that the host's parting comment was close to the mark: "that the man [now Siegel] really had, like some Kurtz, been possessed by the heart of a darkness in which no ivory was ever sent out from the interior, but instead hoarded jealously by each of its gatherers to build painfully, fragment by fragment, temples to the glory of some imago or obsession, and decorated inside with the art work of dream and nightmare, and locked finally against a hostile forest, each 'agent' in his own ivory tower, having no windows to look out of, turning further and further inward and cherishing a small flame behind the altar." Observing Loon take down an automatic rifle from the wall and dreamily begin to load it with .30 caliber ammunition, Siegel can warn everyone, or even wrest the rifle from Loon; but his decision is clear, and he walks slowly from the apartment, so as to avoid calling attention to himself. "At the first landing, he heard the first screams, the pounding of footsteps, the smashing of glass. He shrugged. What the hell, stranger things had happened in Washington. It was not until he had reached the street that he heard the first burst of the BAR fire."

The cultural potential here is enormous. For Pynchon is at the edge of Washington politics: the "Windigo psychosis" lies at the heart of American politics, almost a foreshadowing of the Vietnam adventure, the need to demonstrate ideological obsessions by way of great bursts of violence. The counterreaction may be an attempt at blockage, or retreat and escape, keeping oneself pure, the course Siegel chooses. In terms of Pynchon's own development, the story has almost limitless possibilities: at the least, the use of bizarre information makes Siegel into a kind of Ur-Slothrop of *Gravity's Rainbow,* for whom the working out of his destiny must be in terms of information he seeks. Pynchon peers out over the 1950s, looking back to the old decade of Eliot, Joyce, waste lands, frantic energies, forward to an automatic rifle spraying death on those who worship the primitive as the savior of life and fortune.

To perceive *Catch-22* (1961) and *V.* along parallel lines is not without profit. Both Pynchon and Heller make use of leitmotif, repetition as a way of shaping, narrative interruption for historical purposes, characters who slide in and out, unidentifiable, conspiratorial elements. Ultimately, Heller works through all his mysteries—the man in white in the hospital, Snowden's bloodbath, Nately's whore, for example—whereas Pynchon withholds.

The latter's is far more a "constipated vision," denying as much as is given out; information restricted as though the supply were finite. Heller's vision is more oral, the material withheld only so that its parodic and humorous elements can be better perceived. In the long run, the two novelists belong to different traditions: Heller in the oral tradition, the stand-up comic, the conventions of verbal barrage; Pynchon, for all his prolixity, connected to those who hold back, like Gaddis or Hawthorne. Yet despite their differences, both writers have tried to mirror the 1950s with a vision that owes something to film, but a good deal more to a network of modernists in fiction, whether Joyce, Nathanael West, Céline, or even Kafka.

Heller often works by defining or suggesting elements through the negative. His entire novel is an expanded litotes, that form of understatement and irony in which something is expressed by way of the negative of its opposite. Litotes is, also, a form of wit. One never says "not many" but says "not a few," creating a dialectical confusion as to how many or how few. "Catch-22" as a phrase which has entered the language is connected to its litotic function. For it expresses an underlining negative aspect: if you are crazy, you need not fly, but if you do not want to fly, that proves you're not crazy. The expression upsets our notions of what is, what is not, in the way a comic uses wit to express the opposite of what we ordinarily take for granted. It is a form of verbal irony, whereby what is stated differs from what is suggested—thus, in the phrase, Heller has a context for and expression of the military of the 1940s, the counterfeit of the 1950s, and the defiance of authority which would characterize America of the 1960s.

How, chiefly, Heller responded to modernism was through not irony but the interruption or displacement of narrative. The forward movement of the novel proceeds by means of brief character descriptions in which plot elements are embedded. Movement forward is slowed everywhere to allow for lateral movement, so that our sense of narrative is glacial—a large mass moving almost imperceptibly toward some resolution of the catch. As in a comedy routine, the resolution is not of what lies behind the joke, but of the joke itself.

Thus, Yossarian's movement toward escaping Catch-22 will resolve the irony contained in the phrase, not in the attitudes and intellectual assumptions that lie behind it. In effect, Yossarian works out a means by which he can counter Catch-22, not one by which Catch-22 is countered. He steps outside history, not within it, to resolve a historical dilemma. When questioned about what would occur if everyone felt the way he does, he responds by saying that if they did, he would be a fool not to. Part of what made this intensely fifties book so popular in the later sixties and then in the seventies was its glorifying of individual solutions, the sole way in which mass lunacy could be contained. Kesey's *One Flew Over the Cuckoo's Nest,* a far lesser novel, offers a similar play of events: crazy is sane when all else that is crazy is accepted as sane. A more subtle version of a comparable scenario is Walker Percy's *The Moviegoer,* with Binx Bolling's moviegoing resolving for him the episodic meaninglessness of his own existence.

Those early reviewers of *Catch-22* who saw it as formless or as running on failed to note how linguistic elements are wedded to overall plan: language based on negations juxtaposed to chapter segments based on interruption, dispersement of elements, undercutting of expectation. Early on, Heller has Yossarian react to language in ways that stress the structural concept of the novel itself. "To break the monotony he invented games. Death to all modifiers, he declared one day, and out of every letter that passed through his hands went every adverb and every adjective. The next day he made war on articles. He reached a much higher plane of creativity the following day when he blacked out everything in the letters but *a, an* and *the.* That erected more dynamic intralinear tensions, he felt, and in just about every case left a message far more universal." A good deal of the subliminal humor of the novel lies here, just below the surface of actual words and movement, in the interstices, as it were. This is part of Heller's borrowing from Céline, although it is also programmatic of modernist fiction —Kafka, Beckett, Camus. The publication date of the novel should not deceive us, for it is connected more clearly to Gaddis's sense of a counterfeit decade than to developments in the Vietnam decade.

That sense of the counterfeit which lies so close to Heller's linguistic and formalistic patterns is organic: that is, the unraveling of counterfeit within counterfeit, of hypocrisy and deception within further deception, is profoundly connected to method. For the method is predicated on ways of revealing by denying, on ways of unraveling by undercutting and dispersing. The wit of the novel moves well beyond the set joke—jokes often pursued well beyond their yield —into aspects of comedy delineated by Bergson and others; wherein the closer man can be made to seem mechanistic and inorganic, the more he seems a comic figure.

The mechanical line is a steady one: from Scheisskopf's insistence on uniformity to Cathcart's insistence on raising the number of missions. That is the one constant, and since this is a comic novel, it is a constant that constantly changes: numbers rise, so that each higher figure is an asymptote bringing the fliers that much closer to death. The novel in a real sense hangs on this line. It is "out there," uncontrollable, since it is part of Cathcart's need for personal glory, the sacrifice of his command. It is, also, characteristic of any large organization—and will be repeated, with variations, in Heller's *Something Happened* almost fifteen years later, as the company or corporation. It is intrinsic to any association in which the individual must give part of himself, that part ever increased and called upon. And it is essential to Heller's other peg, that of Catch-22 itself, the catch that catches all efforts to break out of what is systematically catching one.

In *The Moviegoer,* which also appeared in 1961—and was given the National Book Award over *Catch-22*—there is an equivalent form of strangulation. Walker Percy's is more undefined, what he calls a malaise. This malaise, which is not only existential angst, but Kierkegaard's fear and trembling and even his sense of dread, is a peculiarly American ailment; it lies in the character, but also beyond. And it is unconnected to personal success or failure. Binx Bolling suffers from it while he is quite successful as a broker and quite attractive to women.

It is, we may say, the Catch-22 of life itself, and it seems associated with the fifties: *The Moviegoer* takes place in the fifties, Binx has fought and been wounded in the Korean War, and the novel was written and rewritten throughout that decade. The period which more than any other in history allowed American affluence to multiply also produced a sense of doom and disquiet that was a Catch-22 or malaise; and since it did not roar like apocalypse or Armageddon, it was even more prevailing. It is embedded, in the Heller novel, in the "city of death," Rome, which had at one stage been the city of life—women, booze, freedom from missions. For Percy, it is New Orleans, with its Elysian Fields and lovely-sounding areas. Behind all the loveliness, or the relief, there lies a mechanical principle which is typically American. It is not clearly defined as destiny or fate or even doom; nor is it directly connected to history, the weight of the past, as it is for the European. It is, rather, connected to the very success that America brings, to that destruction which lies so close to success.

One reason *Catch-22,* both as novel and phrase, seemed such a penetrating exposé of the sixties was that, still in the fifties, it picked up all the paradoxes of affluence, success, media hype, empire-building. Milo Minderbinder is 1950s affluence run rampant, embodying in himself and his syndicate a multinational corporation. He is our own I. G. Farben, the

element that holds everything together and, at the same time, makes war desirable. Pynchon in *Gravity's Rainbow* points in the same direction, and Styron in *Sophie's Choice* touches upon Farben's need for slave labor as the glue that held the death camps together. Styron came to see the structure of Farben as a parallel to American plantation slavery, the work camps as something comparable to the enslavement of the black. Heller's Milo, while presented within a comic framework, is the 1950s wrapped up, the enterprise, energy, drive toward the top.

The military for Heller serves the function of any large, impersonal organization, not unlike Kesey's Cuckoo's Nest. Cathcart sets production quotas; the Chaplain, until he rebels, offers faith in whatever the boss decides; Milo assures the stockholders that profits will be maximized; the generals, Dreedle and Peckem, skim off the benefits in the form of perks; Korn vies with Cathcart, each jockeying for power and promotion to general. In the middle range, just below decision-making, are the officers who fly the missions; and well below them, like janitors, maintenance men, kitchen help, are the enlisted men, those already left behind by the corporate system. Once again, this is a 1950s vision, the manifestation of what James Burnham warned about in the "managerial revolution" and what William Whyte described in *The Organization Man.*

Within the organization, the leitmotif may be the man in white—an encased figure, which may or may not contain a human body. It may be the carcass in Yossarian's tent, a man who has fallen between assignments and is not even a statistic; or blood and guts spilling out from behind a flak jacket, Snowden's demise; or the mechanical raising of missions, so that formal release becomes impossible; or the setting of ever higher standards which the men, but not the senior executives, must meet. It may be the formation of a syndicate which, like a corporate office, takes precedence over any individual expression; or the offer of relief—whores in Rome, superb food, beach facilities, nurses—which, however, at every turn carries with it the whiff of death. Even pastoral becomes contaminated, for an idyllic day is interrupted by McWatt's buzzing of Kid Sampson, his miscalculation and, before everyone's eyes, the slicing of the Kid into two.

" 'I'm cold' " is the human response; and the only one who responds fully to Snowden's death, Nately's and Orr's disappearance, and the slowly dwindling supply of veterans fliers is Nately's whore. Her reaction to Nately's death is to try to kill Yossarian on several occasions. Her logic is clearly within the novel's frame of reference, linked to both theme and technique. For Nately's whore is life-giving—even more than Yossarian, who does his seventy missions, drops his bombs, destroys and kills—and the sole way she can avenge Nately's death is by way of her one connection to the mechanistic force that did it. Her reappearance in various military guises reinforces Yossarian's commitment to some form of escape; for wherever he goes, she follows, and he recognizes that his death is for her a form of life. When the novel ends with his jumping from her knife thrust, he is ready for the escape to Sweden.

Part of Heller's strategy of interruption, delay, frustration, repetition—all intrinsic to comic effects—is based on military procedures which allow little linear movement. Even the generals are impeded in their plans by ex-PFC Wintergreen. Wintergreen, who does not appear, is the key strategical figure in all maneuvers, for he has achieved the position in the enterprise that lies at the pivotal point: in the seams along policy and decision. Just as Wintergreen has positioned himself centrally in policy-making, so Yossarian, by refusing further missions, has located himself centrally in the carrying out of such decisions. The military must, in its way, work around both: Wintergreen at the comic level of the novel, Yossarian at the level connected, ultimately, to human survival.

In addition to their roles as characters in a scenario, the personages are used as technical counters. One recalls Nabokov's Humbert in *Lolita,* saying, when Quilty dies, "This was the end of the ingenious play staged for me by Quilty." There is the dimension in *Catch-22* of the Nabokovian sense of a play within a play, or a Borgean pseudodrama played out in a historically realistic setting. The Heller strategy, which he did not duplicate in his next two novels, was to keep turning the same people around, from one chapter segment to the next, so that even as we meet them as fictional characters they are functioning within the technical mechanism, playing out real roles in their fictional lives. The result is that a seemingly "open" narrative becomes, at a deeper level, quite cohesive, quite coherent. Fable (real settings for people playing out roles) meets realism (actual people dying in what appears a mythical place), to establish a structure that lies beyond narrative and scene.

Structurally, the two extremes Yossarian must avoid include the avarice and egoism of Milo and the innocence and naiveté of Nately ("newborn") and Snowden (pure, white). As Heller presents the alter-natives, a person must be in the know in all the particulars of life or else he cannot be true to himself. Only a fool walks in darkness. Yossarian tries to be an honest man through balance, but balance fails him, and he must assure his own survival without others' help. He must skip between Nately and Milo; the latter obviously stands for a base, commercial acquisitiveness, while the former attempts to be Jesus Christ in a situation that calls for an instinctive sense of survival.

Those who have felt the tragic overtones of the novel often find it difficult to place its tragic center. Clearly, *Catch-22* is not simply a comic novel full of puns, high jinks, slapstick, witty dialogue, and satirical asides. It has these in abundance—on occasion in overabundance—but its purpose and execution are fully serious. At the center of tragedy is Heller's awareness of a passing era, an era that perhaps never existed but one that might have if people and situations had measured up. This desperate longing for the great good past—what we associate with the pastoral tradition—becomes the body of *Something Happened:* how the past betrays those who believe fervently in its salvation. Heller's is the nostalgia of the idealist: such a writer's style is usually jazzed up, satirical, somehow surrealistic; the idealist who can never accept that moral values have become insignificant or meaningless in human conduct. This heritage, which we find in Nathanael West, early Céline, and a host of similar writers, derives from the tragic undertones of Ecclesiastes, with its monody against vanity, egoism, hypocrisy, folly—qualities that, unfortunately, have become the shibboleths of recent decades.

Heller's literary recoil from these false qualities takes the form of his attack upon religion, the military, political forces, commercial values—as C. Wright Mills indicates, the whole power formation of a country successful in war and peace. Yet with all the success of the assault, a value that falls victim to mockery is any semblance of feeling except self-love: what used to be called love. Orgasm replaces feeling in situations in which even male bonding fails man. Women are objects, desirable holes, but so are men, thrusting engines. In the name of life, all is mechanized. We have a curiously atomized society here, of a fable that goes beyond the confusions of war: an almost incomprehensible mix of nostalgia, sexual drives, fear of feeling, rejection of even companionship, all in the name of survival. Although the action is on Pianosa, the novel is really located in some undefined middle kingdom where every god, whether of waste land or of fertility, has died.

The nightmarish scenes of *Catch-22* which convey its tragic sense culminate in the cosmic nightmare of Chapter 39, "The Eternal City." Once glorious Rome is now a "dilapidated shell," as though modern Goths and Vandals had destroyed everything in their path; or as if a modern God had visited his wrath upon it. Monuments are shattered, streets contain surrealistic episodes, people seem the husks and shards of humanity. All values are overturned, all hopes and dreams made valueless; sanity itself becomes a meaningless term. Everything visible—an emblem of what lies beneath—is off balance, out of phase. The center of Western religion is godless. Here we have Heller's 1950s vision, a scene from Hieronymous Bosch's Hell, in which Aarfy can freely rape and kill while Yossarian is picked up for lacking a pass. Caught in such a dark world, Yossarian can only run. If he stays, he will —like Milo and the others—eat and sleep well at the expense even of those who share his ideals.

An early version of *Catch-22* was itself much more nightmarish in its development than the published book. Evidently strongly influenced by *Ulysses,* Heller had originally tried to make the narrative typically Joycean: that is, full of intermittent streams of consciousness and involutions of temporal modes. Further, he suggested the narrative through recurring symbols of devastation and doom, eliminating in several places all effort at orthodox plot structure, even the lateral movement that characterizes the revision. As a consequence, the reader who missed the significance of the symbols—and they were by no means clear, even peripherally—was lost in a surreal forest of words from which there was no escape. Added to the stream, the symbols, and the temporal involutions was an impressionistic treatment of characters and events, a half-toned, half-tinted development that seemed neither to go forward nor to remain still.

For the final version, Heller retained in its entirety only the first chapter of the original and then in part straightened out both narrative line and character development. Words themselves became a kind of language located midway between evocation and denotation. At its worst, language overextends itself, tries to become too many brilliant voices; but at its best it suits Heller's zany, absurd world. So often misunderstood, his language would not of course fit a rational theme; it is itself an attempt to convey a world beyond the logic of the word.

For Heller, the war is a perfect objective correlative of dislocation, as it was for Hemingway in *A Farewell to Arms.* Both, however, are war novels only in limited ways. The war gave Heller, even more than it did Hemingway, the community against which Yossarian can operate. The military becomes an entire society, looming so large it casts its shadow on the horizon and blocks out everything beyond. Such is the nature of the curse, and it is this—the indefinable character of what one is part of—that Heller can exploit. The war or the military (*not* the enemy) provides the conflict, makes anything possible. The norm is no longer any determinable quality: each action gives form to a norm of its own. Unlike the fixed roles that people assume in civilian life, in war they hide behind masks (uniforms) or rewritten parts, and redefine themselves, like the protean creatures in Ovid's *Metamorphosis.* Here, Yossarian—the ancient Assyrian, the modern Armenian, but really a wandering New York Jew—can give vent to his disgust and revulsion, and through recognitions show us that our better selves may still turn up in Sweden. In the 1960s, when the novel peaked, no one remembered that Sweden's "neutrality" favored Nazi Germany, or that its corporate barons sold high-grade steel for Hitler's war machine. In the 1960s, Sweden was our fantasy of Edenesque pastoral.

The Didactics

The fictions cited above followed the contours of what the sixties had already started to become, or else they proved prophetic of stresses and directions in the culture. But there was another kind of fiction, one that was "adversary" in the sense that it emphasized didacticism in the face of liberation and dissolution of self. If the sixties came to mean what we saw in *V.* or *Giles Goat-Boy* or *The Man Who Cried I Am* or *Catch-22,* there was a powerful counter, which I assign to didacticism: novels given over to ethical instruction, moral cautioning, homiletics on sexuality and race, joyless prophecies of decline.

Within this didactic function, we have strange bedfellows: dissociation and madness (Walker Percy), reification of all emotional patterns (Purdy), alternative forms of love (Baldwin), breaking away or letting go (Roth, Updike), the bourgeoisization of experience (Bellow, Mary McCarthy), racial crossing over (Styron). Without giving up typical 1960s themes, Kurt Vonnegut, Jr., was another writer who fit into didacticism, and not surprisingly, his novels became cult items. Even the advent of minimalism in Barthelme, Didion, and others had, indirectly, a didactic function; for minimalists are like stern Puritans, eschewing the flesh for essences.

It would be a mistake to overstress didacticism, since it is so intermixed with the new and now; but it should be given its place. Much of the fiction identified as "absurdist," because of its association with French existentialism, or with Husserl and Heidegger, or because of its "black humor," is frequently didactic, even allegorical in a medieval sense. The names, for example, given to innumerable sixties characters recall both absurdist fiction and medieval allegory, although they also have, as Leslie Fiedler noted, a comic-strip quality. Pynchon leads with Mike Fallopian, Stanley Koteks, Oedipa Maas, Pig Bodine, Genghis Cohn, Benny Profane, Bloody Chiclitz; but we also have Snow White, Billy Pilgrim, Scheisskopf, Billy Bockfuss, Dr. Hilarious, Eierkopf, Dr. Thomas More, Binx Bolling, Lancelot, Maurice Stoker, Snowden, and many others. While such usage of names is hardly unique—Hawthorne's Dimmesdale is a ready forerunner—it significantly shapes our responses.

These names, obscene and otherwise, give the author a two-way tool: to base his character in society and to undermine him (her) with a name that is antisocial. The name suggests a dialectic, of someone who can function and who will not function; direction and antidirection, definition and adversary role. The name also creates a certain stylization, making the owner an inhabitant of what critics have labeled an absurdist world. I prefer to see not only "absurdity" or existential contingency, but social role: the weirdly named character lives both in the world and outside it because of some obsession or compulsion. Such a character, while often mad, flaky, primitive, opposed to systems, also carries out duties and functions. That dualism I locate within a didactic frame of reference.

Instead of absurdity, we have the location of new moral centers. Burroughs, for one, so reorganized our sense of values, in terms of basic ways of perceiving, that if we take him seriously, as I think we must, we can no longer understand "instruction" in the usual ways. The didacticism of Burroughs (and the culture he foreshadowed) is ever present, although located in writers very different from him: Percy, Purdy, Bellow, McCarthy, Baldwin, Wallant. Percy and Purdy, for example, wish to sink us deep into despair and grim joy, where we can wallow in the slough of despond, and there, having given ourselves up to hopelessness, seek where our moral center is. In some mad ballet, Burroughs joins with medieval allegory to produce a modern ethics.

Sixties didacticism is discovered in wild swings of behavior and function. Purdy's style fits the vision, for it is a style of antimatter, pure corrosiveness devoid of information. If Pynchon is all information theory, Purdy is anti-information, fact, theory, befitting a writer who fears false sentiment and easy connections. The angularity and brittleness are forms of wit, and they reinforce Purdy's didactic aims: to alter our perceptions, make us aware of aspects of hell, and then leave us to rearrange ourselves accordingly.

The other side of this didacticism is the phenomenon Marshall Berman has shrewdly characterized as "Sympathy for the Devil," taking his phrase from the Mick Jagger/Rolling Stones song. Even here, however, we have a didactic function, in that Jagger, a persona of the devil in the song, tells us that he has been responsible for every human catastrophe from the French Revolution to the Nazi extermination camps and Kennedy's assassination. Neutral toward events, he will show us the same impulses within us —irrational, sadistic, unexamined—and leave us to deal with them as we wish. We can harness those impulses into social forms or we can let go and do the work of the devil, as did the Manson group. Implicit in the Jagger rendition are all the elements of 1960s letting go: drugs, sexuality, sorcery, religious needs, desire for a führer, contempt of bourgeois values, insanity that falls beyond clinical experience, vulnerability of the rich and famous to threats, blackmail, assassination, new social arrangements and associations, bisexuality and group sex as forms of experiment. Manson becomes, here, emblematic of extreme forms of what would be otherwise acceptable, the "crazy" version of something standardized.

Although Manson on one side and didactic values

on the other seem worlds removed, our novelists assimilated the decade as a unity, and we see even a novelist as controlled as Percy moving toward *Lancelot,* Cheever toward *Falconer;* Mailer already there in *An American Dream,* having arrived by way of *The Deer Park;* Bellow barely skirting it all in *Henderson the Rain King,* although safely removed to Africa; Styron trying out forbidden topics in the persona of Nat Turner. The point is that flirtation with Satan—the very soul of medieval allegory, the very heart of Burroughs's communiqués from the dead—becomes an intrinsic part of 1960s didacticism.

Walker Percy is very possibly our most graceful and inventive instructor. His five novels to date* demonstrate that he is, foremost, a teacher. However much he entertains—and he is witty and adroit—his primary function is to lead us into a deeper sense of ourselves, to make us perceive the nature of despair. In this respect, he is a litmus of reaction to contemporary American culture, the recorder of events by a man who refuses. We recall Melville's Bartleby. Percy must simultaneously restrain the forces of apocalypse and remain loyal to protagonists who are inert, disaffected, wrong in the head, unable to act or lacking in the will to act. The main character in two of his novels is Will, who lacks what his name suggests. Yet even the man without will owes something to himself and to his society, especially when God is dead and society is secularized. Golf and golf course become for Percy the emblems of such secularity: pastoral spatiality given over to effete shepherds and shepherdesses. Somewhere there lies a balance of inner and outer; to locate it is Percy's quest.

He makes certain all his protagonists have successful careers, or the potentiality of such success; for he wants them to have infinite choices. Careers, money, status, rich marriages—they have these, and yet they must remove themselves from climbing in order to descend. Binx Bolling in *The Moviegoer* (1961), Will Barrett in *The Last Gentleman* (1966) and again in *The Second Coming* (1980), Thomas More in *Love Among the Ruins* (1971), and Lancelot in *Lancelot* (1977) are men of substance undermined by ruins. They, their personal and emotional lives, are in ruins;

---

*The Second Coming (1980) will be discussed in the final chapter of this study. Prior to *The Moviegoer,* Percy tried a novel in the mid-fifties, "The Charterhouse", which he put aside. Then he started another one, about a pathologist and TB patients at Saranac, a kind of *Magic Mountain.* By 1958, he began his "third" novel," "Confessions of a Moviegoer," finished in first draft in 1960.

Will must be literally hoisted out to be saved. They are, all, more than Southern gentlemen, more than social or psychological misfits; they have been born too late or too soon, and their quest is for some ideological thread that can connect them to a center, however inadequate centers are. Binx depends on film for certification of reality; More must live in the shadow of his illustrious name; Lancelot is supported by modern novelties; and Will Barrett finds peace in a Trav-L-Aire camper, a complete environment which isolates him. When he reappears, fourteen years later, the camper is no longer adequate; only a pastoral greenhouse can help him survive. In common, they share the nausea of Roquentin in the Sartre novel, men out of phase, historically misplaced, emotionally dislocated, culturally discontinuous.

Binx Bolling comes out of the 1950s and with a somewhat different focus could have been a figure of the Beat movement. But he is attached to money, to making it, increasing it, and holding on to it; although his other sensibilities are in ways Beat. A Percy character does not surrender his bourgeois connections easily. He is a mental dropout, a young man (late twenties) who senses the malaise, personal and social, which lies at the heart of an affluent, energetic society. He is an Americanized Oblomov. The malaise he feels, which comes over him like a fog rolling over the countryside, is the adversary side of a rational society, a New Orleans that appears to work. Set into that malaise, as a real inmate of an inner, mad world, is Binx's cousin Kate Cutrer. Since her fiancé died in a fiery car crash on the eve of their marriage, this modern-day Miss Havisham has never been right, a young woman who moves from rationality to depression in almost imperceptible swings of mood.

Surrounding Binx is the inauthentic: those of false sensibilities, those who lack perception, or live in the past. But authenticity is difficult to perceive or comprehend. Binx tries to find it in movies, where the search for the authentic is available to the viewer; but the movies make a mess of searches because they must resolve elements. Movies have to end. Nevertheless, they have a reality and an authenticity life lacks. Early in the novel, William Holden strolls down the French Quarter and is spotted. "An aura of heightened reality moves with him and all who fall within it feel it." Yet even that "peculiar reality," which in itself is astounding, is a cheat; it eases but does not displace the malaise.

Moviegoing fits into the temperament of a romantic: one whose expectations of life are in excess of what it ordinarily supports. Someone may be a moviegoer—as is a fellow Binx meets on the train—without going to the movies. Because he places a value upon life it cannot meet, the moviegoer is an appealing person. He may be aware of Kierkegaardian dread, but he has an idealist's demand. Binx's aunt, whose tradition is Southern chivalric, is not a moviegoer, despite certain superficial resemblances. She argues for a conventional view of behavior, something based on the statements of "I'll Take My Stand." This is, curiously, a South Percy was himself to hang on to in *Lancelot,* where his protagonist kills to protect it. But such values, based on gentility, chivalry, gaiety, and hatred of outsiders, cannot work for Binx; are, indeed, part of the malaise he suffers from.

The moviegoer cannot be certain of anything. He lives on the edge, a parapet-walker who peers into the abyss. The ordinary becomes, for him, threatening. Movies provide temporary respite; they heighten and lighten, and offer an alternative reality. Binx refers to *Panic in the Streets,* a movie filmed in New Orleans about a cholera threat. Anyone watching it in a New Orleans theater, as Binx and Kate do, can locate the very neighborhoods of the movie. This, Binx feels, "certifies" the neighborhood, gives it a fixed reality. For that moment, for that glimpse of time and space, there is certainty.

Binx's sole reading is Doughty's *Arabia Deserta,* the only book in his library. That reading is part of his malaise, his own Arabian desert, defined as a sense of loss: "The world is lost to you, the world and the people in it, and there remains only you and the world and you no more able to be in the world than Banquo's ghost." The malaise makes one doubt one's existence, since, as in the existentialist's absurdist universe, the individual has lost all supports. One is like the denizens of Doughty's vast desert, lost amidst swirling sands, caught only by some inner purpose which becomes ever fainter as winds intensify.

The alternative to this, however temporary, is the movies. Percy's sense of the 1950s is quite apparent, in that only the temporary respite of moviegoing can relieve the emptiness of affluence. Binx repeats that his chief forte is making money, and he is good at it. And yet even that activity by contrast makes everything else seem so difficult. The movies are the single contemporary art form that can reach those who have entered the absurdist jungle. The marquees beckon, the movie "certifies," the performers pin down reality; all else is floating, evanescent, part of the swamplike malaise. Movies are part of the American collective unconscious, our primary shared experience.

Centered in that bog is Kate Cutrer. We can understand her appeal to Binx only because of his recoil from scientific humanism. It is the latter that has created "the great shithouse" where "needs are satisfied, everyone becomes an anyone, a warm and creative person, and prospers like a dung beetle . . . and men are dead, dead, dead." The malaise settles like fallout, "and what people really fear is not that the bomb will fall but that the bomb will not fall." Binx perceives that within the world of malaise there is really very little sin, not because of lack of desire for it, but because "nowadays one is hardly up to it." The malaise reduces, minimizes. Without it, Binx could not find Kate so attractive; and we, as readers, cannot understand his desire to have her. She drinks, takes heavy doses of pills, cannot cope with even the most ordinary or trivial moments, is always on the edge of collapse, and yet she is precisely, it seems, what Binx wants.

The alternative to Kate is Binx's secretary and assistant, and because she is there, he romances her. Sharon is all life, vitality, responsive to situation and sensation. Percy's presentation of her is the first of several such in his fiction, and they are great triumphs. He catches their confidence in their bodies and health, their awareness of their attractiveness to a certain kind of man, and their ability to handle their own reactions. They are rational, finely toned creatures, not overly intelligent, but bright enough to understand the main chance and to work their way through life. They minimize disaster by foreseeing possibilities. And while they are calculating—Sharon understands Binx's strategies for getting her into bed—they are fun. Whereas Kate represents the darker side of Binx's need, Sharon represents the life side. With her, and her successors, he can fight the malaise; with Kate, indulge it, recognize its proximity. With Sharon, all the feelings he sees as bogus when observed by way of Kate are still real, *there;* but as his mother, the prophetess, perceives, Sharon is not for him.

There is, nevertheless, vitality for Binx on the trip he and his secretary take to his mother's fishing camp. Water, beaches, fresh fish, an open life, offer alternatives, pastoral simplified to basics, adversary of the urban shithouse. Here Binx meets his numerous half brothers and sisters, the result of his mother's remarriage. This world touches him, but like the relief of moviegoing, it is temporary. Sharon falls back into her life and marries an unlikely sort, a mystery to Binx, who desired her flesh but not her life.

Kate and Binx come together, as they must, since only they comprehend the malaise. Their marriage will be like their courtship, full of swinging moods. Kate will try to function—the novel ends on that note as she runs a simple errand—and he will enter the malaise full-on under her influence. They will confront it, unlike all those surrounding them who counsel happiness. Binx Bolling's "search" remains unfocused. All he can do, as he moves across the 1950s, is to "plant a foot in the right place as the opportunity presents itself—indeed asskicking is properly distinguished from edification."

Williston Bibb Barrett in *The Last Gentleman* is an explorer of middle distances, a young man who through amnesia and a perpetual sense of déjà vu occupies territory that is his own. His sense of distance, of spatial arrangements, is first presented when we meet him, his eye behind the glass of a telescope. He picks up a "handsome woman" in the park who leaves notes on a bench for a very lovely younger woman, with whom, from a distance, Will falls in love.

Although a tool, the telescope has properties of magic. Within its short, compact space it is "jam-packed with the finest optical glasses and quartzes, ground, annealed, rubbed and rouged, tinted and corrected to a ten-thousandth millimeter." That small, toilet-bowl-shaped object contains a whole world of spatial arrangements, bringing into visibility what is otherwise unknown to the naked eye; opening up spatial dimensions Will has only dreamed of. It is also his Eden: the means of transcending his position as a dehumidification engineer in the subasement of Macy's, an easy night job in which he is buried deep in the bowels of the earth. The sole way Will can temporarily escape that urban blight, that denial of space, is through those magical lenses which create new relationships.

As the "last gentleman," Will is further disoriented by being a Southerner (from the Mississippi Delta), distinguished by spatial-temporal dimensions and by style. He is, like Dostoyevsky's Myshkin, positioned differently from other people: head filled with déjà vus, on the edge of amnesia, eye distanced by telescopic eye, body inhabiting a geographical territory alien to every attitude. As a consequence, Will lives hesitantly, poised between experiences, where things join. "What with the ravening particles [those elements which disorient] and other noxious influences, when one person meets another in a great city, the meeting takes place edge on, so to speak, each person so deprived of his surface as to be all but invisible to the other. Therefore one must take measures or else leave it to luck."

As he eavesdrops on the "handsome woman" (Rita Vaught), he fantasizes that if he saw her snatching a purse and then being pursued by the police, he would hide her in the park, in a "rocky den he had discovered in a wild section. . . . He would bring her food and they would sit and talk until nightfall when they could slip out of the city and go home to Alabama." The fantasy is, of course, of Eden, with Alabama as the place of refuge, where the urban "ravening particles" might not reach him.

The telescope makes it possible for Will to move from a world of pure possibility to one in which a chance event alters the course of his life. He goes from existential contingency to one of Christian potentiality, in which openness of experience is, through "revelatory" observation, transmuted into attachment to another. As one of the epigraphs puts it, "If a man cannot forget, he will never amount to much" (Kierkegaard). Will has in a certain sense to be reborn, the way Myshkin is resurrected each time he experiences an epileptic seizure. Will's life is experienced on the edge of this moment of near-extinction. Will must be translated into will, and sickness (ravening particles, urban blight, "last man" philosophy) transformed into social and personal engineering.

During Will's time in New York, his work as a dehumidification engineer places him in a "dead world," those areas also explored by Pynchon and Wright protagonists. His area of work is a chthonic place, inhabited by devils who attack his knee, his memory, his ability to face happiness without feeling sick or weak. As an engineer, he is not only out of phase with himself; he has placed himself outside any meaningful society. The telescope brings him closer to connections, for through the telescope he sees the female side of the Vaught family: Kitty, with whom he falls immediately in love; and her sister-in-law, Rita, the divorced wife of Sutter. Will is informally adopted by the rest of the family: the father, an automobile dealer and tycoon; his wife, a racist, an anti-Semite, a believer in the fading Old South; their younger son, Jamie, who is dying of leukemia; and the older son, Sutter, a physician, now forced because of malpractice into pathology and odd jobs.

The philosophical or ideological line of the novel becomes the opposition between Will, the "last gentleman," who is mentally ill, and Sutter, the man who has observed everything and now plays the role of devil. Sutter is a failed medical doctor, a pornographer, a man of great potential violence (he carries a revolver and threatens to end his own life), a man as out of phase with settled life as Will is out of phase with engineering and urban existence. Later in the novel, Sutter offers Will the choices a man may make: "Which is the best course for a man: to live like a Swede, vote for the candidate of your choice, be a good fellow, healthy and generous, do a bit of science as if the world made sense, enjoy a beer and a good piece (not a bad life!). Or: to live as a Christian among Christians in Alabama? Or to die like an honest man?" Will does not perceive that Sutter is being candid, that in fact he is offering choices gleaned from the words of Dostoyevsky's Grand Inquisitor when he confronts Jesus; or else the philosophical alternatives offered to the underground man, between exalted suffering (living on the edge) and cheap happiness (living like a Swede).*

Sutter's casebook, which he conveniently leaves behind so that Will can read it, is full of the rage of a man—patterned on D. H. Lawrence, Dostoyevsky, Nietzsche—who has refused to play the normal game, or to follow through on the expected route. Living at the edge, he is intolerable to those who seek a toehold on interfaces, as Will does. Sutter hopes to transform Will into someone more spectacular; whereas Will is desperately seeking some balance within himself, some cure for the ravening particles, amnesia, inability to face happiness in others. The two must clash, since interfaces and edges do not blend.

---

*In "The Message in the Bottle," Percy writes of a castaway who must sort out information that comes as messages in bottles washed up on his island. The castaway is well educated and not in need; he has the leisure to distinguish information and news. He is, in most ways, ourselves, cast away on a well-stocked island, receiving messages from everywhere. How we relate to these "messages in the bottle" defines our existence. Percy invokes what Kierkegaard called an "Absolute Paradox," which was that "one's eternal happiness should depend on a piece of news from across the seas." Or: "To put it briefly: When Kierkegaard declares that the deliverance of the castaway by a piece of news from across the seas rather than by philosophical knowledge is the Absolute Paradox, one wonders simply how the castaway could be delivered any other way. *It is this news and this news alone that he has been waiting for.*" Salvation comes, not through scientific or verifiable knowledge, but by way of a piece of news. Is this, then, simply a thunderbolt, a miraculous favor? Percy says Kierkegaard recognized that a category of communication was involved; that faith comes from hearing, that there is a news bearer. Such messages are in the "sphere of transcendence" and are therefore paradoxical; one need, however, only understand the message in the bottle. Deliverance lies there.

Intermixed in their conflict at both personal and structural levels of the novel is the presence of Jamie.† In some way, the dying Jamie is the sacrifice who can bring together lives that would otherwise fragment. His moments of illness, remission, dying are part of a process acting as a lens focused on the family's existence, serving to bring them face to face with more than their great wealth, their father's strange generosity (he gives each child a check for $100,000 at age twenty-one, for not smoking), their secular, uncaring way of life (the Vaughts live near the sixth hole of a golf course). Jamie's impending death threads through and becomes a religious presence, a potential "message in the bottle." He is the news bearer.

Like Graham Greene, another Catholic convert, Percy refuses a simplistic Jesus or a refined church. Jamie is in fact a Baptist and, therefore, someone who remains unbaptized until he is prepared to declare for himself. He has never declared, and now, on his deathbed, he remains out of touch with any formal religious support. Another sister, Val, has herself become a religious, a member of a Catholic order, and she ministers to poverty-level blacks in Tyree County, the end of the line for humanity. She insists that Will, the engineer, find some religious aid for Jamie before he dies, to ensure a state of grace. The sole man of religion Will can bring to Jamie's deathbed is a Catholic priest; and there, in a scene in which religious ministrations (conditional baptism) are intermixed with the release of Jamie's bowels, we have the best we can hope for in a secular society. A Catholic priest ministers to a Baptist, arranged for by the Episcopalian Will and attended by the atheistic Sutter: an ecumenical service of sorts. Jamie dies, a martyr somehow to their way of life; a brilliant mathematician who will never have a chance to become a man of numbers.

The idea of the book, as well as its beginnings, often promises more than Percy can deliver, especially in the middle 150 pages. The Vaught family, despite its diversity, is insufficiently interesting; and Will's love for the prosaic Kitty, essential though it

---

†Like Dostoyevsky, who profoundly influenced him, Percy uses a sick child or person as a double for the protagonist. Jamie is preceded by Lonnie, Binx's younger brother, deformed, in a wheelchair. Thomas More's daughter died of cancer, and Lancelot's first wife was a cancer victim. Such afflictions and deaths appear to give the protagonist energy or function, to proceed to the ethical stage of his life, where he assumes responsibility for it and his actions.

is, for Will's developing sense of unity with himself, diminishes his presence. On the other hand, the opening scenes, with telescope, ravening particles, eavesdropping and voyeurism, movement back and forth between street level and Macy subbasement, are visually and philosophically compelling. They have a witty view of life which has been translated into brilliant visual images. When Will puts his eye to the eye of the telescope and observes a peregrine falcon in its moments of hurtle, its own eye fixed on a pigeon, as Will's eye is fixed on its, we enter into a mixed urban image of technical mastery and natural need. Later, the novel's ideology dominates.

Percy's métier (for the secular reader) is his ability to interweave his medical knowledge with ordinary situations. Failed doctors, false curers, imitation shamans abound—in Sutter, in Will's psychiatrist (who of course cannot help), in doctors and nurses surrounding Jamie—as witch doctors fill *Love in the Ruins* and *The Moviegoer.* The presence of the secular doctor is, obviously, insufficient for Percy's religious sense, and when he begins to make his corrective moves in that area, there is a falling off. The reason is evident: what had once been complex becomes reductive; not simplistic, but resolvable, as at the end of *The Last Gentleman,* when Will and Sutter go off together. True, they go off in an Edsel, a doomed car, but Sutter's Edsel functions. Typically, he has a car that is an "end product," and typically, it works for him. Typically, he makes his peace with the "last gentleman," Will, a human Edsel.

Will's search for good environments, his rejection of bad environments seem possible, although still tentative. Sutter's view of such a search is mockery, and the novel hovers on this edge. In his casebook, Sutter has commented that Barrett's trouble is "he wants to know what his trouble is. . . . if only he can locate the right expert with the right psychology, the disorder can be set right and he can go about his business." Sutter understands Will is seeking salvation, some transcendent being who "will tell him how to traffic with immanence"—those environments, groups, associations, which will lead to happiness (cheap happiness, for Sutter). This was the way of his family. Sutter feels Will's condition belongs to the human condition, not to the individual, and Will would "do well to forget everything which does not pertain to [his] salvation."

Will reads all this—it has been left behind for his perusal. He perceives what Sutter says, and he rejects it as extreme advice, full of God and not-God, or else peeking under women's dresses one moment and blowing out your brains the next. Will views his problem as quite different: not to settle the universe, but to get through the afternoon hours of a Wednesday. His religious ideal is not to give up hope, not to accept despair, as the long empty hours march on. He leaves it to Sutter to attempt the merger of opposing elements: Will simply wants to still the ravening particles.

Ideologically, Percy moves between two worlds. One reason Kierkegaard so appeals to him is that the Danish philosopher cast into doubt the very elements that were essential to faith in them. An epigraph to "The Message in the Bottle," from Kierkegaard, presents a conundrum: "No knowledge can have for its object the absurdity that the eternal is the historical." Kierkegaard plays into Percy's sense of man and his associations when he asserts that no truth is established unless it is a truth for him: thus, the engineer must forgo the attraction of scientific fact for the messiness of human associations. Kierkegaard spoke of an *"imperative of understanding"* which *"must be taken up into my life,* and *that is* what I now recognize as the most important thing." As Will comes to discover, throwing himself into life is insufficient for discovery; exploration derives from within. Unity lies there.

Love in the Ruins is subtitled "The Adventures of a Bad Catholic at a Time Near the End of the World," or apocalypse almost now. It is an excellent follow-up to *The Last Gentleman,* creating a trilogy of novels, to be broken by *Lancelot* in 1977.* The protagonist is a very ill psychiatrist named Thomas More: "I am a physician, a not very successful psychiatrist; an alcoholic, a shaky middle-aged man subject to depressions and elations and morning terrors, but a genius nevertheless who sees into hidden causes of things and erects simple hypotheses to account for the glut of everyday events; a bad Catholic; a widower and cuckold whose wife ran off with a heathen Englishman." More's positioning of himself vis-à-vis his society and culture is roughly equivalent to that of his distant ancestor Sir Thomas More, who found himself a Catholic in a historical era shifting away from him. More held on by insisting on what he knew were individual and religious truths, and paid for his beliefs with his head; our contemporary More—a scientist

Lancelot, as I discuss it in Part One, is more tirade than novel, a polemic disguised as a fiction. Its sources are as diverse as *The Fall, The Good Soldier,* and the King Arthur legend; but its assault on the modern and new reduces and distorts all human experience.

who yearns after the Nobel Prize—has devised a Lapsometer, a machine that "can disguise and treat with equal success the morning terror of liberals and the apoplexy of conservatives."

More's machine, called More's Qualitative Quantitative Ontological Lapsometer, quantifies "angelism-bestialism," those wide swings of mood and temperament which make man subject to extremes of behavior. One of the machine's bad side effects is that even as it makes men happy (like soma in *Brave New World*), it produces a chain reaction in the heavy sodium deposits where it is situated. For all its value as a sedative and soporific—a great pill, massage, rubdown—the Lapsometer is a false guide, a solution from outside. It is, also, an imitation shaman, like so much of Pynchon's technology, which leads to decline even as it reinforces, a sign of entropic exhaustion even as it appears to support all systems.

The Lapsometer functions in a society that has exhausted itself on an Ecuadorian War of fifteen years standing—apparently our Vietnam War—and a racial war, in which Bantus and local blacks are slowly overrunning the countryside. Snipers are everywhere, and More's life is saved only because, as a doctor, he had befriended many poor people and blacks. The social fabric has been shredded; everyone is involved in a last-ditch effort to save himself, or else to continue as if nothing has happened, while the walls fall.

Percy has structured the novel carefully, with all but twenty pages of the narrative occurring in a four-day period, July 1–4. The plan, apparently, was to approximate the creation of the world with something of its decline: the fall to work within more or less the same terms as the rise. The opening segment uses July 4 (5 P.M.) as the date, and Dante's "middle of the journey" as the psychological equivalent. More muses: "I came to myself in a grove of young pines and the question came to me: has it happened at last?" July 4, traditionally Independence Day, now signifies dependence, for More lives in the "latter days of the old violent beloved U.S.A. and of the Christ-forgetting Christ-haunted death-dealing Western world."

The time is sick, the narrator, More, ill (hives, loss of breath, alcoholism, fall from Catholicism, fall from grace, purpose, function). Things fall apart. There only remains the Lapsometer, that measurement of one's fall—a scientific marvel of sedation which may win a Nobel Prize and which is sought for the military. Percy then moves us backward in successive segments to July 1, 2, 3, to an earlier time on July 4 (8:30 A.M.), then to a later time on July 4 (7:15 P.M.). The fourth is the key, like the sixth day of Creation:

"Two more hours should tell the story." The rise and fall of the Western world, as embodied in America, lies at stake. The time is now, but the world of the novel is future America, teetering. The sole one who can hold it back is a lapsed Catholic, an alcoholic doctor. If the territory seems Greene, Percy has enlarged it, so that personal frailties are associated with a global situation.

While More's long-range solution is the Lapsometer—he has had fifty machined in Japan—his short-term solution is a half-ruined Howard Johnson's, a fortress against the coming siege. The "oranging of America"—a locale for refreshment and relief of physical needs—has become an outpost of American civilization. More holes up there provisionally with three women. Percy's perception of the women's movement, in the late 1960s, does not mitigate More's need for more: three women to service one man, an ill man at that.* One, Lola, provides music, her chief attractions, besides her ability on the cello, being a strong set of legs and a powerful back. Her muscular structure seduces More, as he positions his body where the cello usually is. A second woman in his Howard Johnson's harem is Moira, whose perfectly formed limbs and healthy abundance—heaviness in small things—make him aware of what a marvel the female body is. Her cultural tastes, however, run to Montovani. The third woman (and More's fate) is the nurse Ellen, who caters to his ills. His attacks of hives and suffocation—an asthmatic condition—need ministering, and Ellen, a strict Presbyterian, is there. He does not sleep with her until their marriage—she wins the man by hanging on to her virginity.

More services his harem—Herzog's ultimate dream!—with more than affection. He stocks the Howard Johnson's with a six-month supply of food, runs in a water line from a nearby Esso station, supplies air conditioning, lays in cases of whiskey and a set of the *Encyclopaedia Britannica,* and is prepared to establish an alternative life to the guerrilla warfare that threatens to overrun this section of Louisiana. But more than guerrilla warfare is the "apocalyptic" fallout that is expected: a sickness unto death. "For I have reason to believe [More says] that within the

---

*Possibly, the presence of three women fits Percy's theory of rotation, which he develops in "The Man on the Train." In adapting Kierkegaard's term, Percy sees in true rotation—not merely repetition of routine events—that one snatches "freedom from under the very nose of the *ens soi.*" True rotation can lead to the search, which is transcendence. This is, surely, the direction in which More is heading.

next two hours an unprecedented fallout of noxious particles will settle hereabouts and perhaps in other places as well. It is a catastrophe whose cause and effects—and prevention—are known only to me. The effects of the evil particles are psychic rather than physical. They do not burn the skin and rot the marrow; rather do they inflame and worsen the secret ills of the spirit and rive the very self from itself." Whatever is unbalanced in man—rage, sense of separation of himself, terror—will be intensified by the fallout, and he will be driven ever further into isolation and solitary wandering.

The apocalypse will be both physical (from the heavy salt in the area) and psychical. The 1960s were, for Percy, the time when both of these conditions obtained: *Lancelot* measures his more violent response. The Lapsometer may "save" those who have fallen, but Catholicism—or any strictly held religious belief—might have equally saved, as More recognizes when he seeks absolution for his sins. Yet what really saves is not religion but the discovery of an alternative life, one that goes beyond the hospital, where the sick are well and the so-called normals are sick. In the Pit, where doctors perform for the sake of a student audience, More demonstrates that an allegedly psychopathic patient, Mr. Ives, is quite normal, simply rebelling silently against what society does to its aged citizens. The twisting of sick and well—here, Percy appears to have learned from Laing—is a pervasive sixties theme, perfectly tuned to the needs of the decade when abnormal and normal converged. Laing's clinical rather than theoretical evidence could only have been embraced at a time when sensations became at least as significant as intellect.

Percy's More does not choose to lose his head. He is impressed by countercultural possibilities, and considers moving in with some dropouts, in order to live "completely and in the moment the way a prothonotary warbler lives flashing holy fire." In effect, he salvages what he can, by marrying Ellen and carrying on a very low-key medical practice, while living in "slave's quarters." The novel shifts, and we move five years forward. We have the "new age," one that features "the new plague, the modern Black Death, the current hermaphroditism of the spirit, namely: More's syndrome, or: Chronic angelism-bestialism that rives soul from body." He still believes in his Lapsometer to save the world, but he cannot get it right; meanwhile, men have taken the form of beasts, blood-suckers, werewolves. More hopes that one day he will turn the corner and transform ghosts or beasts into men. The world now, for More, is a Bantu world,

achieved not through revolution but through their exercising their property rights. The old area, once called Paradise Estates, contained oil, and the Bantus profited; now they own 99 percent of Paradise. More adapts, unlike his namesake, who refused Henry's direction.

The lapsed Catholic is received back into the church. Although he cannot regret his sins, he has "perceived" his life and altered it. He has forsaken alcohol, has married and settled down with Ellen, has fathered a family, helps the poor for little compensation, and has made his peace with the one issue that was always the great sin of white America: race. As blacks form a new Hanseatic League of City-States (Detroit, New York, Chicago, Boston, Los Angeles, Washington, etc.), More stands fast. Without forgoing his body or his plans for the future, he contributes himself. But "now" counts. In the last age, men "planned projects and cast ahead" of themselves, hoping to reach goals. More simply lives.

The truly evil element in the novel is represented by Art Immelmann, who is ever present as CIA, FBI, military, government, corporate complex. He is the beyond. For him, the Lapsometer is a weapon, and he gets his hands on More's stock of them. He does not wish to cure, but to hold power. His curious name is emblematic. Max Immelmann, a German, devised for pilots a defensive maneuver—a half loop, followed by a half roll, then a level position—that allowed the pilot to gain altitude while appearing to fly in the opposite direction. The name is brilliantly applied to someone who represents bad faith.* But More's own "good faith" has hardly been pure. He needed his harem, his drug fix for hives, breathing difficulties, lows and highs; he required his cases of whiskey. Only when cultural and political changes occurred did he alter his style, and he feels like "Robinson Crusoe set down on the best possible island with a library, a laboratory, a lusty Presbyterian wife, a cozy tree house, an idea, and all the time in the world." Such is "love in the ruins," that mix of scientific humanism gone sour and Nietzsche's "last man" philosophy. Only irony wins.

James Purdy surveys the ground Percy retreats from, where the slough of despond branches off into hopelessness, transcendental boredom, and eventual madness as a form of escape. Percy has chosen to be

---

*Immelmann is a modern-day Mephistopheles, offering art for cures, offering trade-off rights and "more altitude," a "last man" philosophy.

ironical and flexible, whereas Purdy has decided to stonewall against all normalizing values. *Cabot Wright Begins* and *Eustace Chisolm and the Works,* Purdy's novels of the mid-1960s, are the fictions by which, ultimately, he must be judged.* They have the distinctive Purdy mode: self-hatred, dislike and fear of women, desolation of the gay scene, need for love even when it means self-destruction and physical torture, masochistic immersion in mental torture as a means of intensifying otherwise meaningless experiences, stress on antiaction, antilife, failure as a mode of success.

Purdy is our novelist of the "anti," far more than Pynchon or Barth. Everything in his vision of America runs counter; even his vision of gay love is not romantic or satisfying. It is, simply, experiential, existing for itself. Yet within that negation of pleasure, that refusal, lies a stern didacticism. Behind nihilism is a Calvinist preacher who suggests the greater sin as the greater show of belief. Purdy has attempted, by shattering morality, to be our archetypal moralist; much on the order of Burroughs, who broke the ground for Purdy's work in the sixties. In this vision, the repressed, suppressed life, once it emerges, can only be a source of mockery even as it displays its pain. Purdy chooses to be our Saint Sebastian.

In *Cabot Wright Begins* (1964), Purdy makes by far his most complicated statement about a side of America he understands quite well: that part of life which is always seeking an outlet for its energies, but in vain. Cabot Wright, the quintessential "old American," finds his outlet in rape, over three hundred victims. Perversely, rape becomes the norm for a society which Warburton—Wright's boss at a brokerage house—characterizes as, having begun as a focus "of men with plans, confidence, and good blood in its veins . . . ended in a shambles of scrofulous obscenity and barking half-breeds in which nothing worth selling or connecting is hawked, barked and exposed in its inadequate meretricious shine to a nation of uninterested buyers. Young and old have suffered and are suffering a series of consumer hemorrhages from a non-attendant civilization that has only noise, confusion, pumped-up virility and pornography. It is a nation of salesmen, imbeciles." It is the familiar litany of a pastoral America undermined by immigrants, sellers, and senseless consumers. What makes it different is that rape becomes the means by which one breaks out.

---

*In the section "Growing Up in America," I discuss his two earlier works, *Malcolm* and *The Nephew.*

Rape as an escape from societal boredom and madness, even when such rape is unaccompanied by brutality, violence, or even coercion, could only occur in a fictional and cultural setting in which women are either puppets or figures of mockery. For even if, for the moment, we discount Purdy's rape victims, his female characters are sexually voracious (Carrie Gladhart, working on her fourth husband; Gilda Warburton, who "uses" her black servants) and voracious consumers, like Zoe Bickle. Although the novel as a whole may be viewed as satirical, the way in which satirical elements are maneuvered reveals a good deal.

The central figure is Cabot Wright, a "suppositious" child, an orphan of the modern era. He is sick unto death, rootless, full of fear and trembling, uncertain of his sexual powers, incapable of relating to other people. He is the paradigm of the secularized sick modern man, the subject of a thousand treatises. Not only has the sacred disappeared from the world, but even the profane has emptied him out. The sole element which might help is therapy, and toward that end he visits Dr. Bigelow-Martin. The latter's treatment is to hang Wright on a gigantic padded iron hook, until "everything hangs out," literally. His center of gravity descends toward his genital area, and he becomes a sexual athlete, demanding variety, constant activity, and prolonged sensations. He is a Priapus of the modern era, and since rape is his sole way of gaining satisfaction, he rapes. An unpardonable sin becomes no different from a routine activity.

One way to read the novel is as a treatment of a literary subject: a burlesque of writers like Henry Miller, Norman Mailer, Terry Southern, and those others who take heterosexual activity seriously. Read in this way, *Cabot Wright Begins* becomes a gloss on the sixties just as they begin: Cabot Wright begins, with rape; the decade follows. Reading the novel as containing a gloss on writers and novels is appropriate, since Cabot Wright is the subject of a novelistic treatment by Bernie Gladhart, revised and added to by Zoe Bickle, nourished by Wright's own memories, such as they are, and expected to be a massive bestseller under the direction of Princeton Keith, a hugely successful literary agent. Thus, the story as it comes to us has the counterfeit feel of a ghosted presentation several times removed from the original event: sifted through and added to, finally readied for a commercial market which is jaded by way of both normal and abnormal events.

If extended, the satire spreads to the entire culture.

Princeton Keith is a voracious man, needing a success; and the publisher, Al Guggelhaupt,* a riffraff of a man whose tastes suggest several New York publishers, editors, reviewers, past and present, establishes the cultural level. " 'Do you realize,' Al Guggelhaupt said, 'and I see you do not, that if he says the book can't be sold, it cannot. Do you see, sir, the death-warrant in Pepscout's last sentence? *Indelible Smudge* [the novel based on Cabot Wright's exploits] is dirty *and* well written. Do you get that? That's the combination means no Fifth Avenue bookstore will take it, no book club, no book award group even will touch it. You've again violated protocol and produced a dirty *hard* book.' " Further, Talcum Downley, an important critic, who some years ago established the Flat-Foot School of Writers, regards the book as "morally loathsome." Downley wants to bring bloat back into the novel, eight hundred pages, with war as the best subject.

In defining the culture, Purdy is also arguing his own case. His books are well written and "morally loathsome" in the marketplace. He wins few awards, is not selected by book clubs, is judged unacceptable by the New York market as represented by the Fifth Avenue stores. While "dirty," his books are unacceptable as pornography. Also, they are brief, in the two-hundred page range, not bloated; and they are not about war—the kind of novel on which nearly every young American writer cuts his literary teeth. Also, behind it all is the sense that taste and markets are controlled by Jews—Guggelhaupts, of course—who reject books about loathsome Cabot Wright types written by the likes of James Purdy.

Part of what hurts *Cabot Wright Begins* is its involvement in a mixture of elements, many of which do not cohere. Cabot Wright's career in itself is of interest. The man who rapes, who commits an unspeakable violation, and yet who is not criminal in any other way; the man who has no self except what he can discover by violating another person; the man who considers women such trivial material that they exist only as a warm, wet orifice—such a creation, in 1964, *is* of significance. Although the individual symbolizes the culture, more than isolated pathology is at stake. Large issues are suggested, for Cabot Wright's sickness unto death manifests its cure through acts of vengeance on women. Implicit here at its extreme is the male-female relationship of our most famous and successful serious novelists, where rape is sublimated to forms of hostility, aggression, condescension, usability, disposability.

Purdy uses "frame materials," however, that do little to enhance the interior story, which is Wright's. Diversionary are Bernie Gladhart and his shrewish, voracious wife; the Bickles; and the self-serving material about New York publishers and agents. To a limited extent, they may be relevant, since they help establish the moral arena; but the various activities used in getting the novel written are supernumerary. The essential stuff is embedded in the following, a shrewd mixture of outcry, satire, mockery, and ideology:

> Now Cabot was alone again with his non-self. Loneliness feels so good after the mythic contact with the social. Dreams become clear, and nightmares are no longer attention-getting. One sucks eight or nine aspirins and allows his calloused thumb to rest on a quilt. The trauma of birth, life and death pass as shadows on the moon. Mother Nature goes right on keeping house even though nobody is to home.

Here is the nub. Cabot Wright is the man born to a particular kind of America, which hears, "but they don't get it," which sees, "but the image is blurry. The rain is falling on their TV screens." These American cannot tell the difference "between General Roosevelt and Captain Truman or Professor Eisenhower from Grover Kennedy Johnson." Out of this comes a respectable rapist.

The satire itself is established by way of Purdy's unique use of a flat, cliché-ridden language. Someone speaks of Wright's "better-half in a mental home." Cabot Wright tells an elderly psychiatrist: "The older the hen, the richer the gravy." "Middle-aged women are in," etc. Like Barthelme, Purdy works over phrases that are obsolete—the comics as "funny papers"—or else puts an edge on a cliché, calling TV Tuesday "gaze-night." The use of platitudes within Wright's own desperate condition mixes matters, giving Purdy's verbal mockery a larger cultural satirical thrust. But despite the inventive language, the advent of a style, the problem remains, which is that the satire is unfocused, too much of it unexamined. Purdy

---

*Obviously Jewish, by name and by stereotypical statements and actions. Purdy, an outsider to the literary establishment, manifests something of the paranoia outsiders have. His Jews, like his blacks in other roles, lack dignity, do not command respect as individuals, demonstrate a shabbiness of character and ethics. Both groups fit into racial stereotypes. Blacks are servants, the butt of jokes, and not only in the eyes of disreputable people, but in the voice of the author speaking to the reader. Purdy travels along the opposite side of Mailer, who makes blacks into cocksmen, intense primitives; and Bellow, who sees the urban black as a threatening, criminal type.

erations and lacking Jewish instruction; a teacher, however, in his own way.) Of them all, Wallant is our most transparent instructor, in a career cut off at thirty-six and seemingly boundless in its potentiality.

As an intensely Jewish writer, Wallant is concerned with survival. But the survival of his characters depends on a small-scaled experience, not the kind associated with war or combat, nor the Hemingway variety; not even the type that calls attention to itself. Wallant's terms of survival are all internalized; physical threat is far in the past. Suffering of the most intense kind cannot be avoided. If it is confronted in full intensity, then one may come through, or not.

Wallant's Joe Berman, in *The Human Season* (1960), is a man in his sixties who lost his wife to cancer and his son, long before, in the war. He has two daughters left, one of whom wants him to live with her and her family. Berman, whose fortunes Wallant catalogues from 1907 in Russia to the present, is a plumber, a solid family man who had always felt in his veins the joy of living. Now bereft, he rejects his rabbi's traditional argument that God is testing the suffering man. Berman counters that God was just another power-hungry individual: "He tried to show off to the Devil, to prove He was stronger. . . . He is cruel and takes pleasure in demonstrating how powerful He is, like Superman."

Rejecting God, and himself, Berman exists in a no-man's-land. He takes refuge in his spotlessly clean apartment, but while it offers physical comfort, it is a reminder of his loss. Every encounter with the apartment gives him superficial strength, but at a deeper level enervates and depresses him. It is like the cleanliness he so prizes. As a plumber, he is engulfed in muck on the job, and to compensate he is meticulous about his person. Wallant stresses scenes of washing, changing of clothes, water pouring over Berman's skin—as though each time he cleansed himself he was baptized into a new life which he could not recognize.

The novel is a dirge, Berman's lament for himself, his Job-like experience, but without Job's belief in God. Yet everyone around Berman is understanding. His partner, Riebold, shrewdly tries to take him out of himself, although his devices become too transparent. Berman's daughter Ruthie pleads with him to leave the apartment and live with her. He even tries taking boarders, for company, but each boarder proves disastrous—more depressing, if possible, than Berman himself.

The "human season" must, however, pass. Suffering must end in either suicide or a recognition of life.

Like Morris Bober, Berman is a survivor of disappointment. Like Asa Leventhal, he realizes that his victimization is not the end of life, but a beginning. The beginning for Berman comes when he suffers a deep electrical shock from his television set, and that shock, like therapy, clears the fog. He recognizes that "there was no Enemy, no Betrayer, no bearded Torturer." He was indeed alone. "How could death measure up to that blackness!" When he rises, uninjured, from the litter of tubes and wires of the set, "he was conscious of a greater courage than had ever existed in him before."

There is, clearly, an existential component here: the mingling of Berman's childhood European experience with his adulthood in America, suffering that runs like a motif throughout, and the infusion of courage lying very close to that suffering. Berman can overcome death by realizing that blackness within is more significant than an impersonal end. When he recognizes death, life begins, and he is able, finally, to accept his daughter's pleas. He must forsake the apartment, since it is associated with a past that no longer works; all that matters is life. Existential despair, the American experience, aspects of Kafkan enclosure all join in Wallant's book, as they do in the Malamud and Bellow novels.

His work is Jewish to the extent that in need Berman calls on God in Jewish languages: Yiddish, Hebrew, Russian. God, if He even exists, exists for Jews to appeal to. Berman views himself as Jewish, but he lacks belief in Jewish ways and rejects a specifically Jewish God. Berman wants the American dream: six rooms, an enclosed porch, a decent street, a month at the seashore, freedom from persecution.

When we call Wallant a "Jewish writer," therefore, as when we assign such a label to Bellow, Malamud, or Roth, we must note how their Jewishness passes into other forms of experience. In Wallant's case, the presence of postwar existentialism is very clear, wedded to ideas of Job. We also note how the novel plays with other modernist notions, particularly of temporality. The present is 1956, but much of the novel is part of a tunneled past. Wallant retrieves memory by way of receding years, each chapter of the present accompanied by a journey into the past. Although the method is transparent, it is an effort to impose a modernist technique on somewhat traditional material; once again the Jewish experience becomes associated with fundamental European ideas.

Further, Berman's shift is upward, from ghetto experience to a mobile American one. Early in his career, he has a life-and-death fight with the Irish foreman of his work gang, in which he bashes in the foreman's face with a rock and himself loses a finger. The point of the fight, however, is not who wins or loses, but the fact that it starts Berman's upward mobility. The Irishman remains what he is, but the Jew will rise. Here, too, the American experience preempts a distinctly Jewish one. As we shall see in *The Pawnbroker* (1961), Wallant is concerned with suffering and how an individual can accommodate its intensities. That containment of suffering becomes a universal quality, embodied in the Jew, but not restricted to him. Pain becomes, in this respect, its own instructor.

The Pawnbroker is Sol Nazerman, whose family was exterminated in the camps. Nazerman is without feeling for himself or others, having suppressed his emotional life as a way of dealing with the past. To feel is to relive what happened. Once in this country, he lives with his sister, whose family is typically American, as though the Nazi past had never occurred. Nazerman moves between his pawnbroker's shop in Harlem and his sister's home in Mount Vernon, with occasional stops at Tessie Rubin's. Tessie's husband died in the camps, bitten by dogs and burned to a crisp on the wire.

Nazerman is a survivor rather than a victim; or, rather, he is a victim first, then a survivor, and he cannot understand why he alone survived. His world is inexplicable because his wife and two children died, while he came through, an event incomprehensible in the nature of things. His world is "absurd," in that all is contingency, all open to questions and answers distinct from a coherent universe. Although alive, Nazerman has found no reason to live, except that his body, misshapen and broken, continues to live on. Nazi doctors had removed pieces of his hipbones and ribs, experimenting with his anatomy to see how he would walk minus several crucial bones. Both his mind and his body, then, have been conditioned to crippling. He has been divested of everything associated with civilization, and yet he lives on. How does a man live?

His pawnbroking establishment, the embodiment of his own existence, is a clutter of unrelated objects, bits of people's lives, fragmented as is his life. The people themselves, flotsam and jetsam of decaying neighborhoods and destructive lives, seem extensions of camp inmates. "On and on they came, shy, sullen, sweating, guilty, paying in fear for tiny crimes they had done and were doomed to do, striking out with furtiveness and harshness, sickened with their heredi-tary curse, weary and ashamed of their small dreams and abandoning the cheap devices they had dreamed with. . . . They packed in one kind of glitter for another, haggled in soft, furtive voices, each ashamed and desperate and hungry, each filling the Pawnbroker's spirit with rage and disgust as he smelled and saw their ugliness." Their ugliness, of course, is an extension of his own; he is as ugly to them as they are to him. For he is twisted, unable to comprehend them, spiritless and emotionless. They seem to him vampires, ready to suck his blood. He senses that "they were all making a profit on him, that they found ease from their individual pains at the sight of his great aggregate of pains."

Behind Nazerman's shop is a Mafia type, who uses the pawnbroker as a means of laundering dirty money. When Nazerman discovers that the money derives from a brothel, he tells Murillio, the gangster, he wants to end the arrangement. At this, Murillio threatens to wipe him out, gangland-style. Nazerman comes around, then stands his ground, for death holds no fear for him. Murillio cannot understand this, since for him life is everything, and because he cannot understand, he relents. This situation coincides with another, the robbery of the pawnbroker by three local blacks, a job planned by Nazerman's assistant, Jesus Ortiz. This is a relationship that Wallant tries to develop very carefully, and it is of some interest since it is a very rare one, of Jew and black (Jesus is black despite the Hispanic name) forming a close tie. From Jesus's point of view, Nazerman belongs to a magical world: the tattoo on his arm, his deadness of spirit, his ability, withal, to make money. Jesus admires the Jewish penchant for profit, and he connects his own future success to learning the business. Nazerman, for his part, slowly teaches Jesus tricks of the trade.

In a sense, Nazerman permits Jesus to take on a son's role, although without any expression of feeling. He believes there are things Ortiz will not do, and this expectation is rewarded when the holdup occurs, and Ortiz takes a bullet intended for the pawnbroker. "Jesus saves" indeed, but the grandiose symbolism is misplaced. What he saves is his father surrogate (his own father is gone), Nazerman the old Jew as Abraham. This takes us into Biblical thickets which the rest of the novel does not support. After Jesus is killed, Sol calls his nephew, Morton, an artist who is a pariah in his Mount Vernon home, and asks him to replace Jesus. The pawnbroker will now gain the son he has lost, first in the camps, then in Jesus.

Wallant is superb at depicting the man who lives

in deadly silence with himself, but the recovery of Nazerman to humanity is less sure. One source of recovery for the pawnbroker is the pink-skinned, hopeful, and cheerful Marilyn Birchfield. A Gentile, she is, at thirty-seven, a spinster, screwing on her hope each day, forcing herself to meet the dawn with humanity. She strives to make contact with Nazerman, and despite his withdrawal from her overtures, she succeeds in touching him. This, too, is somewhat weak. Wallant's talent is for the bottom, not recovery, the same problem he faced in *The Human Season*.

Nazerman, Berman, Leventhal, Bober, Sammler: these middle-aged to elderly men are versions of Hemingway's defeated and undefeated. While they are intensely Jewish in their associations and attitudes, they are equally connected to America; in the way that Ellison's invisible protagonist is an American outsider and stranger, as much New World as Negro. Even the men who suffered in the camps— Nazerman and Sammler—are touched by American values, by associations with Americanized families, American spatiality, and, in Nazerman's case, the quintessential American woman, Marilyn Birchfield.

What is distracting about these Jewish types in their American setting is that they have so little connection to Judaism. Even one of the most intransigent, Bellow's Sammler, is more seduced by H. G. Wells's rational view of the universe than by Yahweh's. What they all feel, however, is guilt, which in literature at least seems to be a Jewish experience; a guilt which plunges deeper than words can explain. They are pursued by types who instill guilt, and even when guilt is not personified, it exists—in Sammler for having escaped, in Bober for his failures. Yet Jewish guilt, even if definitive, is balanced by other elements, not specifically Jewish, which have assimilated these "Jewish types" to American mores.

What this means, for Nazerman, among others, is that American traditions have preempted what appear to be ethnic types. When Nazerman employs Jesus Ortiz, then his nephew Morton, when he toys, however tentatively, with Marilyn Birchfield, he has moved from Europe to America. As her name suggests, Birchfield is not only from a different culture and history, she represents spatiality, not time. For Nazerman's memories in time, she offers an excursion up the Hudson, where he observes the beauties of America, fields of birch. While her sense of space can never efface his temporal trap, and while neither Jesus nor Morton can replace his own children, nevertheless Nazerman is embracing the New Zion. Wallant's instruction in how to live is how to live American.

A NOTE ON *THE TENANTS OF MOONBLOOM* (1963)

The tenants of Moonbloom Realty are a cross section of humanity, the kind of amalgam we associate with a squad or platoon in war and combat novels. They are, however, older, in the main, and desolate, with few expectations. Whatever dreams the tenants have, they come up against the fact of their crumbling buildings, mortality itself. Wallant has an acute sense of final things, of small endings; and the buildings are his medium. In a sense, the way in which the tenants relate, not to themselves, not to others, but to the buildings, suggests who and what they are. They are a typical crew: a boxer who is scrupulously clean, a young German woman who tries to control anti-Semitic feeling by becoming a Jew, a pair of high-flying musicians, a whorish blonde who is babied by her father, a "candy butcher" who hawks candy on trains, an old, filthy man with memories of his life in Russia, a black homosexual writer, reminiscent of James Baldwin, a teacher of Italian whose insides have turned cancerous.

Besides the buildings, another source of their misery is Norman Moonbloom, the collector of rents, a weekly torment he imposes on them and himself. Norman, a typical Wallant creation, feels directionless, has no center or focus; urban, deracinated, secular, he perceives his life as measured out in empty coffee cups. Despite his many attempts, Norman lacks a vocation. He is a Jewish wanderer, the eternal student: of art, dentistry, the rabbinate, accounting, podiatry—fourteen years of education until his thirty-second year. "He felt an unusual self-disgust, which puzzled him, and as he ate with the newspaper opened before him, he pushed down the faint disturbance. When he washed the pot and the dish, he had an image of himself, thin, dark, idiotically placid, sealed into a hermetic globe whose thinness gave him only the flickering colors of the outside."

He is reminiscent of Nathanael West's Miss Lonelyhearts, distant from others' pain at first and then gradually drawn in. In time, Norman tries to become a Jesus among the tenants. Against his penny-pinching brother's advice, he will make essential repairs. The people are too far gone to be made happy, but he will give them decent accommodations. He will, like a sleeping or sick king, renew a waste land.

Wallant's great novelistic gift is that within a routine frame of reference—no experimentation, no narrative adventurism, few tonal and textural modulations—he can convey desperation, anguish, flatness, the desolation of undifferentiated days. His great triumph, more than Norman himself, is the "candy butcher," Sugarman, who plies his wares on trains running to Grand Central. His métier calls for clowning, but he is a dour, morose person, full of the past, aware that the future lacks meaning for him. His name, Sugarman, was his doom. Sugarman identifies with Norman because he, too, is "essentially humorless and unalive." " 'I have spent my youth no place, in transit. I am a wraith, Moonbloom, I doubt my existence.' "

The souls of others enter Norman as if he were a dybbuk, turning a "very sensible and efficient person" into an obsessed man. His ultimate goal is to repair Basellecci's wall. The teacher of Italian has complained that the pain in his gut was the result of chronic constipation aggravated by the thought of a bathroom wall bulging with waste matter. This wall of shit becomes Norman's fixation, also; and he saves it for the final repair. By then, Basellecci knows his pain is cancerous, not wall-related; and yet the wall has come to stand for everything. Norman tears at it with a pickax, until it collapses and covers him with liquefied waste matter, baptizing him with shit. Norman has succeeded. The wall is down, and he is, at least for the moment, a new man. Even Basellecci, drunk and carried away, is happy.

Of course, Norman's action brings only a limited happiness, for his obsession with repairs guarantees his loss of job. Sitting in his office, waiting for the end, he sees the erosion of the *m* in Moonbloom, so that the company sign is an endless progression of *o*'s; the Joycean croon "Moonblooo-ooo . . ." ends the novel. Norman Moonbloom joins Leopold Bloom in some timeless, endless, measureless existence. He has broken down the wall, exorcised some of his demons, asserted himself, brought temporary happiness to miserable people.

Theme and treatment seem sentimental, but Wallant infuses his presentation with such sincere feeling that we are, rarest of things in postwar fiction, forced to react emotionally. He will not let us escape. Wallant is a man of great moments. We are not swept off our feet, as in larger fictions; we keep our feet and our heads. But traditional fiction can still touch us, unless, like Norman earlier in the novel, we have cut ourselves off from all sources of feeling.

Seize the Day (1956) makes us realize what an aberration *Henderson the Rain King* was in Bellow's development. For *Seize* joins with his work in the sixties and seventies to establish Bellow as our most renowned instructor. He has indeed set himself firmly "against the grain," not only in moral and ethical terms but in his refusal to enter more adventurously into modernism. The award of the Nobel Prize to him —rather than to Borges, Márquez, Grass, for example—indicates that the novel as a *developing force* was considered dead, at least by the prize committee. In every work except *Augie March* and *Henderson,* Bellow has fought against the prevailing culture; and those who bracket him with Mailer as "Jewish writers" have to resolve his distinction from Mailer in every possible way except their common rejection of literary modernism.

Seize the Day fits curiously between *Augie March* and *Henderson,* one of the strangest placements in postwar fictions, in terms of a writer's canon. Questions of how it fits in Bellow's developing career are potentially as compelling as the quality of the novella itself. It is a middle-aged man's lament for his lost youth, his lost opportunities. Tommy Wilhelm, at forty-four, is a man standing among the ruins. He is built like Samson, and like the Biblical hero, he has brought down the temple; but for very unheroical purposes. In point of comparison, he is more like Arthur Miller's Willy Loman than Samson, both protagonists of the indeterminate middle class.

Miller's play, together with his justification for his protagonist, comes to mind, since both it and *Seize the Day* are appropriate fictions for the 1950s. Both, also, are developments of a Depression ambience. Like Willy, Wilhelm had been a traveling salesman, a commercial cowboy, possessor of a piece of territory for Rojax, until a son-in-law was moved in ahead of him. But behind that story, possibly all of it a disguise, is another story, that of Wilhelm's philandering and his own failure in the job. For Wilhelm, like Willy once again, lives amidst dreams, of a career as a movie star, a rich man, a vice-president of Rojax, achievements well beyond his powers. He has befouled everything he has touched. His movie career was a farce— he barely became an extra; his marriage fell to ruins when he left his wife for a Catholic girl who loved him. His job as a salesman followed.

Now, like a child, he lives in a hotel (separate rooms) with his father, whose expense he cannot afford. To establish his independence, the son has changed his name, from Wilhelm Adler to Tommy Wilhelm, part of the falsification of every aspect of his life; he has also claimed to be an alumnus of Penn State, when he had only got through his freshman year. He is a self-invented romantic hero, part of that tradition which extends from Don Quixote to Lord

Jim. But since Bellow is writing bourgeois, not romantic, tragedy, Wilhelm's reach exceeds his grasp in small things, as does Willy Loman's.

In Bellow's own canon, Tommy Wilhelm is the obverse of Simon March, in *Augie March.* Both are big men, physical, Gentile in appearance, and clearly dependent on striking at the right moment to gain their advantage. Simon strikes, and forms a contrast to Augie, who waits out his chances. Wilhelm strikes at all the wrong things, and despite a hardheaded father, a doctor, he never learns. His farcical movie career becomes continuous with, most recently, his investments with Dr. Tamkin.

Part Houdini, part confidence man, trailing legends, Tamkin is *there,* inside and outside, living off the misfortunes of a man like Wilhelm. Tamkin makes himself into shaman, scientist, psychologist, doctor of souls, magician, confidant of the rich and famous; and he may be telling the truth or he may be lying, or he may be expressing partial truths. He is an imitation Eugene Henderson, a teller of tale tales, an extravagant figure in American fiction, now living in a hotel, playing the commodities market, and awaiting his chance. It does not really matter how much truth resides in Tamkin's assertion; for a confidence man has no existence except in association with those who confide in him.

Wilhelm is a middle-class, broken-down Faust, willing to sell his soul for whatever relief he can gain from his monetary and personal misery. In a display of subtle wit, Bellow has Wilhelm place his remaining cash in Tamkin's care. His future depends on the commodity market, on margins, mainly in lard, a fit commodity; for as he turns to lard, his money, based on lard, becomes increasingly less.

Tamkin's philosophy is to "seize the day," not to wed oneself to a life of suffering. " '. . . don't marry suffering. Some people do. They get married to it, and sleep and eat together, just as husband and wife.' " Some people stick to suffering, he argues, because they fear that without it, " 'they'll have nothing.' " All this appeals to Wilhelm, because he is a man who always tried to cheat suffering; and he recognizes that Tamkin speaks the truth. But it is a half-truth, because it embodies the very kind of advice Wilhelm cannot heed, as well as a type of advice that had proved disastrous to him in the past. Tamkin repeats that only the present is real: one must grasp " 'the hour, the moment, the instant.' " Wilhelm is hypnotized by such words; yet he has nothing with which to seize the moment, the day. Even his father wants no part of a son who has made so many mistakes, and Wilhelm's desire to regress to small son protected by gigantic father is rejected by Dr. Adler.

The archetypal situation for this in modern literature is, of course, Kafka's "Letter to His Father," the letter never sent, but in that the son seems victimized by a general need the father has to humiliate and confuse him. In Bellow's novella, Wilhelm has given his father more than sufficient reason for rejection of his financial and personal disasters. Everyone in the novella, in fact, acts toward Wilhelm as he deserves. Part of the problem in locating the value system Bellow is suggesting derives from Wilhelm's own faults, much as we find Willy Loman so flawed Miller's compassion for him is stretched beyond what literature allows an author.[*] Miller argued that Loman's situation was so general a quality of American life that he was victimized by our being what we are—and as a consequence, we must pay attention to the Willy Lomans.

The argument is itself a trap, as well as self-defeating. Bellow wants both Wilhelm's failure and our attention. Yet Wilhelm had his chances, he followed the dream, and the dream led to disaster. He let down everyone who touched him. When Conrad dealt with this in *Lord Jim,* he surrounded Jim with commentators, with irony, and finally, with a warning that Jim must pay. Bellow suggests Wilhelm deserves our attention because he is human, because when he weeps at the funeral of a strange man at the novella's end, he is transformed into Niobe, and weeps for himself and for all mankind. By that act, he has joined himself to all of us, and we must not judge. Yet in his every dealing, Wilhelm has proved imitational—name, college degree, marriage, as a son. Although we might respond favorably to the presence of a big, blond, blubbering forty-four-year-old, he has so few redeeming features, except self-pity, that fictionally the presentation falls between stools.

We swing around to our original proposition, which questioned what place this work had in Bellow's canon between two "open" fictions, *Augie March* and *Henderson.* We are tempted to associate Bellow's sympathy for Wilhelm with personal causes; but this type of connection is weak, and frequently beside the point, as will also be the frequent autobiographical parallels in *Herzog.* More likely we are wit-

---

*Bellow's uncertain mixture of elements here may be located both in the naming and the situation. The father is "Dr. Adler," the follower of Freud; the son is Wilhelm, the crippled Kaiser, a loser despite his strutting; and the association is Kafkaesque. Elements struggle against each other.

nessing a crucial shift in Bellow's sense of fiction, what he spoke about much later in his *Paris Review* interview, as part of that restraint of style which characterized his later fiction. Although in Bellow's own view *Henderson* appears restrained, it is indeed open, centering on a brisk, picaresque character who is out to gain experience. It is life-oriented, *Seize the Day* death-oriented. All aspects of the novella are connected to death, the death of Wilhelm's opportunities overreaching all. The long scenes at the commodity market are for life substances—rye, wheat, grains, lard—yet for Tommy they signal an end, of his money, his chances. Marginal, they stress his own marginality. *Henderson* is the opposite, all potential death situations turned to life.

Seize the Day apparently signaled a literary crisis, in which Bellow either sought another style or had lost his bearings. It is tight, unadventurous; everything occurs on a single day, indicating a closing down. *Augie* and *Henderson* sprawl. In a curious way, *Seize the Day* curls back upon Bellow's earlier career, suggesting *Dangling Man* and *The Victim*, whose styles he tried to escape in *Augie March*. *The Victim*, with Asa Leventhal and Kirby Allbee, particularly comes to mind, here transformed into Tommy and Tamkin.

The real question, then, comes with how we should read this novella. It is the most problematical of Bellow's fictions, and yet many critics have cited it as among his most successful work. By "successful," they mean shaped, consistent in its details, and full of compassionate humanity. Yet it is pinched, and Wilhelm is of little interest; so little, consequences are reduced. His humanity is insufficient, *fictionally,* to be built upon in Bellow's terms. His tears at the end may signal a connection to others, a recognition that someone besides himself deserves pity; but it also signals tears for himself, that circuitry of self which is so stifling. Bellow has constructed Wilhelm on too obvious a scale; given his romantic nature, his lack of restraint, his inability to curb his overreach, his failures are transparent. His separation from his wife, Margaret, is stereotypical in its details; his movie career, farce that it is, has no surprises; his failure at work is little else than the fact itself. Willy Loman succeeded because he was present, on stage, with the gestures and expressions of a fine actor. We were drawn in by the physical man. On the page, he is flattened out, less appealing, the play shrill in its insistence. But Miller wrote the character to be performed; Bellow wrote him to be read.

The Dostoyevskian and Kafkan type of novel is characterized by an ironic surface beneath which life drops off into endless tunnels of torment and anguish. Those tunnels of pain are areas of grotesqueness which we recognize as modern equivalents—that is, psychological melodramas—of Gothic subterranean passages and underground dungeons. The trick for the novelist who attempts to utilize Kafka's insights is to bind together what seem disparate elements, fragments of wit and irony with portions of true tragic awareness. The result must be tensions between the surface and that which lies beneath, what we find more suitable for poetry simply because such tensions would appear to function more effectively in short rather than long works.

The idea of opposites pulling against each other leads us into Bellow's work in the sixties, to *Herzog* (1964) and *Mr. Sammler's Planet* (1969–70), in which he achieved his most mature style, having worked out of the picaresque episodic nature of his earlier fiction and become the novelist of synthesis. He had found, if we use his own comment about his work, a method whereby he could blend a witty, mocking, ironic sense of modern life with a more didactic, ideological position which derives from the old rabbis and judges.* Some of the text could have been derived from Jeremiah's "Oh that my head were waters, and mine eyes a fountain of tears, that I might weep day and night for the slain of the daughter of my people!" The arena was to be a huge one, since the surface disclosed a deep antagonism to contemporary life, an antibourgeois intensity that seemed akin to Kafkan disgust. But beneath that ironic tone was an intensely bourgeois soul, trying to reach back past the contemporary style toward a Biblical injunction for the good man and the good life, all defined, curiously, by a materialistic society.

Contradictions appear to abound, and this segment will be devoted to how Bellow—taking on some of the most compelling themes in contemporary life—attempted to join two very disparate views. If he failed to succeed, he failed at a high level: not at the level of imagination, but ideologically. A novelist praised for thoughtfulness, Bellow is often least imposing there, most impressive where wit, irony, and mockery meet. Hoping to be Conrad or Malraux, Bellow is closer to Céline. The most satisfactory part of his work is the surface, at the level of wisecrack and ironic counterpoint; the least satisfactory where a tra-

*Herzog's full name is Moses Elkanah Herzog; Elkanah was the father of the prophet Samuel.

dition-bound, didactic ideology wars with the surface anarchy and passes itself off as a thinking man's critique of modern life. The worst excesses of this occur in *Mr. Sammler's Planet,* although the resolution of *Herzog* is equally tenuous. We can try to pinpoint how this happens; for to do so is to provide a critical tool for assessing not only Bellow but large cultural questions that developed from the sixties.

The chief technical device in *Herzog* and *Sammler* is tunneling, so that we gain the sense of material coming to us from deep within caves and grottoes, a method that is, apparently, Proustian, but which recalls, among others, Dostoyevsky and Kafka. Herzog's experiences are cyclical; as one critic points out, in his end is also his beginning. The memories, reveries, and daydreams dredged up at the novel's opening join with the same material filtering through Herzog's mind at the end, Proustian settings both, with overtones of Oblomovism and Sartrean nausea. Bellow evidently aimed at achieving a balance between inner and outer, between a solipsistic sense of the self and a perception of the whole person turning outward toward others, society, community; what is culturally known as *agape.*

Herzog is located on ground shared by the underground man, Oblomov, Nietzsche's "last man," Sartrean nauseated man, Camus's stranger, Ellison's invisible man, Kafka's K. or Joseph K., Proust's Marcel, and Beckett's gasping, weary warriors. The structure of the novel is circuitous, leading Herzog into narcissism, self-reflection, and the mirror image of a self indistinct from a soul. There is little "distancing" in the novel; that is, we learn nothing which is not Herzog's apperception. Other characters are emanations from his sensibility; and we only rarely (and marginally) learn how others see him. We know they respect his learning, but we do not know what he is like to live with. He appears attractive to dependent women, but again, that is from Herzog's perception; we never learn of his rebuffs. As *we* see him, we do not find him magnetic except in some funereal, morbid sense which seems to be precisely what Bellow wishes to avoid.

Bellow has spoken of the need for man to be freed from "shameful and impotent privacy," freed from the intellectual privilege of his bondage; but the very strength of *Herzog* appears to lie in the protagonist's suffocated sense of life. The novel falls into unreconcilable elements because Bellow does not sufficiently pursue the Kafkan mode which is his evident line of development. When the novel opens with Herzog alone in the "big old house" in Ludeyville, we seem to be immersed in that dryly comic ("ludey-ville"), morbid, circuitous self which derives from Kafka. The novel is based essentially on self-analysis, with little relationship of Herzog to others; his "sickness unto death" will not be relieved. Ramona may tinker with his genitals, and with her full breasts, deep thighs, and Carmen sultriness give him enjoyable erections, but the very point has to be that sex and food—twin commodities of the comic sensibility—cannot reach his self or soul. He remains embedded in himself (not in her), and the novel follows the random curve of his movement from place to place, house to house, although in terms of inner space and time he never leaves the Vermont enclosure. That house is his area of decision, his locale of soulful struggle, the true battleground of Apollo and Dionysus. Despite rampant nature outside, it incorporates innerness—a distinctive space and time, terror, collapse, paralysis, inertness—comparable to the treadmill, static quality of the Kafkan arena.

Reinforcing this stress on the sick, enervated soul is the letter-writing. Letters never sent, they are full of self-love, self-entertainment, solemn parades of undigested learning. Quotations from Pascal, Tolstoy, Hegel, et al., are misplaced, as in a Woody Allen film; they should be comic and parodic, but Herzog uses them didactically. True, he indicates he will cease the letter-writing, but he is still narcissistically immersed in that house, tended by Tuttles and others, infantile in his attachment to the umbilical cord: telephone wires, electric lines, wells, cisterns, all hooked up and connected by others in order to "feed" Herzog. He has exchanged letters for tubes. At the other end are those who make life possible for him, give him air to breathe, water to drink, food to eat.

The imagery and shaping would appear to contradict the parodic elements underlying the book's conception. The arrangement of objects and scenes turns Herzog inward; the novel is a matter of memory, and most of the shaping is internal, toward room and house, books, mirror reflections. How, then, do we reconcile Bellow's insistence on self moving toward community, a comic resolution, when the novel seems to be self in eternal, fixated love with itself, as part of an intense adversary existence which is anarchistic and even nihilistic? Can Herzog avoid becoming Nietzsche's "last man," that expedient survivor on the bourgeois dung heap?

A paradox of the novel is that Bellow is best with characters such as Valentine and Madeleine, whose instability gives them life. Herzog's sensitivity and humane sanity, however, make him the most dangerous of all fictional characters to place: a self-loving, romantic, would-be Don Quixote; a man who while yearning for the spirit insists on the things of this world; one who, critical of others' amour propre and hypocrisy, yet exists as a parasite, with infantile wishes for women, food, and drink; a man who does not have the honesty of Oblomov, but proves to be a bed warmer who ventures out to lay claim to objects personally unearned.

Herzog's view of himself as the eternal sufferer is reinforced by Bellow's apparent identification with him, and yet the reader who moves outside this circuitry sees Herzog as the maker of his own suffering. In the traditional story, the comic fool or sufferer, whether Gimpel or the Don, is miserable while others are joyous and prosperous; he suffers for their earthly gains. Herzog, however, makes others unhappy; they do not bounce off him or move free of him. His lack of foresight and his infantile self-centeredness do not expose hypocrisy, cant, or worldliness. His letters, with their sophomoric response to world conditions, are not criticisms of politicians, philosophers, world leaders, but continuations of his own failings; not correctives but parallel follies.*

The failure here is the lack of intensive inwardness which would have carried Bellow dangerously close to the very things he has attacked in recent American fiction.† That tunneling into caves and grottoes of the past, into the subconscious, into that spatial and temporal frontier between waking and sleeping, between life and death, Bellow blurs because no coordinates beyond Herzog's are available. A good case in point is Madeleine, presented through Herzog's eyes as the classic American bitch, the emasculator of men, the feminine parasite and vulture so familiar in American fiction.

She is caricatured and "mad" because in Herzog's eyes she is everything out there which has victimized him. Yet Mady, whatever her other qualities, is the sole female in the novel who does not cater to Herzog's infantilism. Unlike the Japanese Sono, the His-

panic Ramona, the Polish Wanda, and numerous other mistresses and admirers, she has gained strength from Herzog's very weaknesses. Rather than exploiting him, she has refused to accept his failure and helplessness as attractive. The demands she makes on him focus on his being a full person, not an incomplete man. Unlike Ramona, she has apparently not desired a child-mother relationship with the man she marries. Unlike Sono, who babies Herzog in warm bathwater and defers to his needs, she has demanded something which evidently he cannot give. All this is apart from whatever madness, quirks, eccentricity reside within her, as such qualities surely do.

The dissolution of the Herzog-Madeleine marriage, then, is not quite what Bellow presents it as being; for, if seen from beyond Herzog's own self-absorbed view, the relationship helps to pinpoint not Madeleine's failure but his. If Bellow had stressed Herzog's innerness, rather than his puerility (which often passes in the novel for intensity and introspection), then Madeleine's deficiencies would have gained more balanced perspective. We would not be offered the false sense of Herzog's victimization by a castrating bitch, which is what we are led to expect, but a relationship that ceased to work at a much higher (or lower) level of failure. Very possibly Herzog's "innerness" would make any relationship fail, as is apparent with Dostoyevsky's underground man; but in any event, we would not have to accept solely his view of things. Bellow's identification with Herzog lets the major line of inner development slip by, while the comic surface and anguished subsurface irresolutely clash.

Almost the first third of the novel is taken up by Herzog's Vineyard trip to visit the Sisslers. This section ends when he decides to find alternatives to Ramona's companionship, without altogether rejecting her or her comforts. Like so many other women drawn into Herzog's life, Libbie Sissler has found him appealing, and they "had once considered having an affair." Now, in his need to escape, she offers a haven, motherly care for his insulted and injured self.

The train trip is itself a long enclosed section of memories, a collage of Herzog's past and present life, a fragmented, skew sequence of remembrances. The shaping of the material is particularly apt, since Herzog's memories are caught in timeless time. They are part of the Herzogian mythical past, and they are tunneling experiences shaped even as the train tunnels through New York's cavernous streets into New England openness. More appropriately, the train

---

*Mailer described Herzog as having unoriginal ideas: ". . . his style as it appears in his letters unendurable. . . . Like all men near to being mad, his attention is within, but the inner attention is without genius."

†In 1971, Bellow wrote that what "we have now is a great public with small-public attitudes." Adding: "But the interests of this great-small public are not at all aesthetic, they are social, and what it wants is not art but art-tinctured ideas and suggestions for the conduct or misconduct of life. Art is its wardrobe, literature its scenic background. Its own glorious self-realization is what really counts."

rushes into space, moving forward at great speeds, even as Herzog has fallen into the past and rejected space, stopped time, negated all dimensions except involuntary memory.

The actualization of these segments brilliantly uses novelistic materials, very Kafkaesque and Proustian in the author's insistence on sealed-off matter which resists outside pressure. The external image is of rushing, the world in motion; but the internal scene, the one dramatically necessary, is of stillness, the still point in the moment of chaos which Bellow stated it was his intention to capture. Spatiality, which we are aware of, nevertheless flattens out; time becomes an endless tunnel, an enclosure housing both comic detail and past and present anguish. This same sense of muted time is particularly effective in *Mr. Sammler's Planet,* which is bound by memories as they resist the incursions of the present.

As Herzog prepares for the journey, which will be a trial—for he expects Libbie to introduce him as "her professor"—he moves rapidly through familial scenes, succeeded by experiences with Wanda in Poland (which has little organic function in the novel). Then, in a cab to the station, follow thoughts of the Pontritters, Madeleine's family, and so on to a collage of Madeleine herself, Park Avenue traffic, his flight from Poland, a family vacation when he was a child in Montreal; so that travel and trips surfacing from the past parallel the present excursion to the Vineyard. Important here is the shaping of materials to imprison Herzog in a circuitry from which there is no escape. The Kafkan mode is explored, and Bellow, without Kafka's terrible intensity, is nevertheless able to see Herzog alternately trapped and attempting to find a refuge from his entrapment. The antipodes appear to be Madeleine at one end, his childhood memories at the other. At stake is Herzog's existence.

As memories proliferate, Herzog zigzags in time, as though the train trip were itself a "privileged moment" setting off the entire train of childhood thoughts, moments of joy intermixed with periods of acute distress. The dash and whoosh of engine coincide with the rush of Herzog's thoughts, a mélange of interrelated, interdependent, sane-insane memories, frontiers between this world and another, in time and beyond. Midway through this reverie, the hurtling train throws together another mélange: people, events, defenses, the flotsam and jetsam of a life that has achieved forty-seven years are regurgitated as the train moves inexorably toward the ferry slip, toward water and ocean, which for a Jew means freedom.

The trip, then, is composed not only of outward scenes or sights, but of inward realms of gold. This section is very possibly the last time the novel is true to the interiority that Herzog and *Herzog* demand. That the trip out is capped by an almost immediate journey back completes the circuitry of form and content; mind and memory are matched equally by external movement. End and beginning have the same function, to seal mind and memory in an inescapable capsule of conscious, sub-, and unconscious matter, *from which there is no escape.* Mothering, ministering women cannot be the means by which Herzog comes alive or achieves completion between man and nature. The train whooshing through the tunnels of New York, the man encapsulated in that train, memories trapped within that man—*they are all.* Herzog's condition is life itself, and it needs no excuse. His fate is to be an underground man, notwithstanding Bellow's stated intentions to the contrary.

Later, Herzog moves into further self-reflected episodes, peering at others from behind closed windows, sizing up situations from a distance, watching others watching him even as he watches himself, the circumstance of the mole in Kafka's "The Burrow." This is Herzog territory, and Bellow should have given him more room in which to maneuver than this hothouse atmosphere, that borderline between comic movement and tragic stasis. There is much one can do in this area: write books, become an artist, plumb paralysis and inertia, seek further labyrinths in the tunnels and caves, explore ever deeper into motives, and, finally, achieve the balance between private and public which is impossible in the world beyond. Yet Herzog, speaking Bellow's lines from his numerous essays and reviews of this period,* reiterates his belief in brotherhood: "The real and essential question is one of our employment by other human beings and their employment by us."

When Bellow, or Herzog, wishes to ridicule the private man, where subterranean intensity lies, he does so by caricaturing "isms," especially existentialism, for its call for a leap into some kind of belief. The question, however, is not one of a leap, existential or

---

*From, for example, the *Encounter* piece, for 1963, "Some Notes on Recent American Fiction"; from "Where Do We Go from Here: The Future of Fiction," 1962, in which he feels Joyce and Proust have overexploited the "single consciousness" so that the writer's art dominates everything; from, also, *The Living Novel: A Symposium,* 1957, and "The Writer as Moralist," 1963. In the latter, Bellow explicitly rejects the passivity and inertness which appear to be winding the novel down; he offers comic affirmation of human values and cites the need for love and the play of the imagination.

otherwise; nor of the disintegrative effects of modern life which one must resist. At stake is the sense of what the self can do, given the nature of Herzog's self, and whether or not he can make the very leap Bellow ridicules. Herzog refers to Kierkegaard, among others, for making us play "shivery games," without which life is hard enough. "Praise of suffering" takes us in the wrong direction. Suffering must be an antidote to illusion, Herzog states, and this "needs no doctrine or theology of suffering." None of this ironic mockery of serious ideas, however, can change the fact that Herzog has not earned the words he is writing or mouthing. He has earned, instead, what Dostoyevsky's underground man and Kafka's protagonists have known all along: that if one has the sensibility to suffer, one must suffer, and there is no leap for such a man into nature, no relief between a woman's legs, no palliation of what one is. In that circuitry of self, Herzog might have found his glory. It was precisely what Bellow with his ambiguous comic ideas and movement toward community could not entertain.

Although *Mr. Sammler's Planet* answers some of the objections to *Herzog,* it also involves us in further unresolved tensions. Here, Bellow the social realist is still hanging on to reason as the sole humane course, swimming dexterously in the destructive element even as the current carries him ever farther from shore. The method crackles with contradictions, both aesthetic and ideological. Comic seems to rule, anarchy is glimpsed, and then homiletics takes over to settle what is irresolvable.

Artur Sammler is a brilliant creation to carry forward Bellow's enclosed, subterranean idea, the "lower half" of his vision. He has, evidently, earned his point of view in a way denied to Moses Herzog. As a survivor, he tries not to be Nietzsche's "last man"; as a chance remnant of the Holocaust, he has been underground and has risen from grave and tomb to New York in the late 1960s. Sammler's narrative, like Herzog's, is based on memory, here in a man of "seventy-plus," whose life is a cultural review of a past era. Very little external time passes—in fact, a matter of days—and yet the novel conveys the sense of historical epochs by way of Sammler's memory, which roves back, through the Holocaust and through his association with Wells, to a nineteenth-century awareness of human progress and development. As a "Sammler," he is a collector, an accumulator; he has soaked up the past.

The narrative method is based on memory and tunneling, with external space and time (moon exploration, swirl of outside events, Wallace Gruner in his plane, Angela Gruner in Acapulco) as the comic alternative to Sammler's grave-tomb, *his* planet. Reinforcing Bellow's juxtaposition of outer space and time with innerness is Sammler's own sense of encapsulation, which he has gained from experiences denied an American "dolphin-torn," "gong-tormented" younger generation. Sammler is, indeed, Yeats's "tattered coat upon a stick" who seeks a Byzantium of the spirit; his Byzantium, like Yeats's, is in a different cycle of existence and in an opposing era. Yet that era, for Sammler, also contains the Holocaust, so that memory for him is never unalloyed, never affirmative in Yeats's sense. Sammler must first find affirmation in the past and, at the same time, avoid the graves and tombs the past also offers.

Bellow's stance is precarious, for Sammler's memories of his nightmares in Poland are almost equaled by American madness, characterized by the Gruner children. The rational mind has been superseded in both past and present. Cultural survival, either in holocaustic Europe or in nihilistic America, is the prize which Sammler must somehow collect.

We appear, then, to have located Bellow's primary fictional tensions in the 1960s. He is caught between alternatives: on one hand, the enclosed, labyrinthine nature of his imagination, which includes the type of inward-turning protagonist he feels most comfortable with, the shaping of tunneling narratives, and memory-laden imagery and scenery, all of which finds parallels in Proust, Kafka, and Beckett. On the other hand, Bellow intellectually and in comic method has rejected this kind of narcissistic flirtation with consciousness as neurotic and counterproductive to good fiction and to a good life. Bellow's ideas, as he has developed them over this decade, indicate a need to locate man in a community, a society, even a world, certainly to have him respond to phenomena outside the circuitry of his own self-reflected image. He fights against the sixties. Contrary to the absolutism of enclosed man, Bellow man must seek order in himself —what, I assume, the author would call a personal godhead not too different from Freud's superego. Sammler perceives only id flourishing in America, and where that is, he cautions not ego but superego. As he tells Govinda Lal, the Indian scientist, "Perhaps the best is to have some order within oneself." This tension between the passivity of the buried protagonist and the authorial need to make him react to vibrant externals Bellow never satisfactorily resolves. It haunts *Herzog,* and it splits *Sammler.* It will prove equally unresolvable in *Humboldt's Gift,* Bellow's sense of the mid-seventies.

Specifically, Sammler's reaction to and rejection of life in New York is based on the caricature of ideas and people, for Bellow never tolerates any kind of "opposing" culture. Sammler wins all the bouts because his antagonists are freaks or confidence men. He wars against Angela Gruner's short skirts, her sexual profligacy, her indulgence in fellatio, her swapping of sexual partners, even her uninhibited income. He sees Wallace Gruner as a "high-IQ moron" and as an infantile product of a none too happy home. Sammler judges the younger generation of students on the basis of Lionel Feffer, who is neither representative nor, indeed, particularly reprehensible; like everyone else, including Sammler, he uses the culture for what it can bring him personally. Racially, Sammler sees the "black prince" (an elegant pickpocket) as a big cock, and is impressed by the splendor of the person and by the strength of the cock. Sammler parodies all modern ideas, with Bellow speaking (through Feffer) of Genet as someone supporting "pure Christian" angels who commit murder and then "have beautiful male love affairs." Sammler views the younger generation, and particularly the females, as stinking together "in defiance of a corrupt tradition" and he fears a "loss of femininity, of self-esteem." He fears, further, that in their "revulsion from authority they would respect no persons. Not even their own persons."

If anyone should recoil, Sammler should. Rejecting and caricaturing everything outside—failing indeed to distinguish what is vital from what is shoddy and meretricious—Sammler is left only with memories.* He cuts himself off from any comprehension of, or sympathy for, America, except as promised land, and he is disconnected by history from that reservoir of the past which is, for him, tantamount to order. In New York, Sammler can understand and accept nothing; all experience becomes black cock, fat, exposed thighs, sexual excess, misused intellect, stinking, shabbily dressed young people, rude, phony-

---

*A parallel to Sammler is Willis Mosby in "Mosby's Memoirs" (1968), an exile of sorts living in Mexico. Since he told people what they did not want to hear, Mosby is acceptable to no one, and relegated to memoirs. He had tried to bring ideas to areas where they are anathema, somewhat like Feller with the Gonzaga manuscripts in Bellow's 1954 story "The Gonzaga Manuscripts." Mosby is a man out of his era, a man of ideas in a coarse world, who is left only to traffic with ruins because he is himself a ruin. *"Yo mismo soy una ruina."* This should be Sammler's epitaph, also.

revolutionary students. He is impressed, however, by Old World Gruner, extending to his Rolls-Royce and his masterful chauffeur, who insists on knowing about cousins, uncles, distant genealogy. Apparently, only the Jewish experience holds meaning, and the essence of that experience for Sammler is embodied in memories of Europe, since New York offers caricatures even of Jewishness. Yet that Old World Jewishness is bounded by the Holocaust, by images of grave, death, starvation, repression, terror, by a fence of recurring nightmares. All this should lead to paralysis, not to society, and it appears Bellow has separated Sammler from the sole area which could be his: the caves, tunnels, rooms, labyrinths, graves, and tombs where his kind of life is possible.

Sammler's sympathetic view of Govinda Lal, the Punjabi scientist, alone breaks the cycle of European memories held up as a barricade against New York crudity. Only Lal lets anything foreign penetrate into Sammler's tunnels and caves. And even Lal has meaning solely because their common ground is H. G. Wells: Sammler's connection to London and to his recollection of a past culture which offered social values. Their discussions are important, but not crucial, since Sammler reveals little to Lal that we do not already know about him and his world. To Lal's defense of moon exploration, Sammler offers the mixed nature of all new experience, ambiguities of individuality, the hopeless condition of the earth itself, the negative aspects of any incursion into the unknown when the known remains only partially explored. These are all meaningful arguments—they recall, in fact, the reasoning of Kafka's mole—and they locate Sammler solidly in his tomb, if only Bellow had permitted him to remain. The fact is, by rejecting Lal's moon exploration and by insisting on Bellow's planet, Sammler is left with a web of untenable arguments; so that the issue is not whether Lal's position is valid or invalid, but whether Sammler has any ground left to stand on, given Bellow's rejection of inertness, defeatism, neuroticism, negativism. Below the level of community, there is, for Bellow, only a nihilism to be refused.

Where, then, can Sammler go, except back into the grave? He is a brilliant collector of old ideas, the best culture can offer. Despite his dehumanizing experiences, he has a residue of feeling, his judgments are sane, his advice is wise. But he has rejected all new experience, or else turned it into a caricature of itself, into thighs, black cock, and rude expedience. He never sees around his caricatures to root causes; he grasps only manifestations. If only Bellow had permitted him to sink into Kafka's burrow, where he could have used his negative energy, and had not attempted to make him bridge old and new or forced him to attack avatars of the new and now. Like Herzog, Sammler is soggy to the touch because manipulated from without and related unnaturally to society and community. Although he has earned his attitudes in a way denied Herzog, he is not permitted the full run of the labyrinth, where his personal sense of space and time could rule and where he could measure refuge against trap in alternating experiences of inertness and wariness, rejection and response, paralysis and awareness of self. Essentially narcissistic, Sammler is not left to his own earned vision of doom. He must, for ideological reasons, become Bellow's intelligent survivor, society's last hope, the philosopher's good man, the author's baleful response to Nietzsche's "last man." Sammler cannot sustain the burden, nor can *Sammler*.

Just as Bellow came to insist on the priorities of Jewish life, and turned fiction toward homiletics, so did Baldwin, with his insistence on the priorities of black life. This has been true of his fiction and theater since *Another Country,* in 1962. The two essays in *The Fire Next Time* (1963) in a sense pushed him toward black life as the basis of his work. Yet as a novelist he presented the clichés of that existence; truisms of Harlem life are repeated and tirelessly explored, in music, sex, degradation, and/or forms of relief. Intertwined as they are with black life, these are all powerful fictional themes. But Baldwin, curiously, rarely develops them; they remain as stationary elements.* We have no sense of other vital forms in Harlem, little sense of those who move on, of political events which grip the imagination, or social forces beyond family, neighborhood, general degradation/exploitation. Baldwin is fixed at the level of young men growing up, where he started with *Go Tell It on the Mountain:* the unexamined anti-Semitism, disintegration, violence. Themes repeat themselves: need for love; hunger for sex, whether male, female, or both; the individual caught by self-destructive attitudes; stress on family and church; music, either gospel singing or jazz.

The themes are intrinsically valuable, but they are

---

*He has, however, undergone some changes of idea, in specifics and generally. In *The Fire Next Time,* he said that "the Muslims do not help matters," locating them as part of the problem; whereas in *Just Above My Head* (1979), Muslims are forms of salvation.

hermetic. Even as Baldwin argues for great openness, his novels become more strident, increasingly didactic. If we compare his recent work with *The Man Who Cried I Am,* we perceive how Williams moved his protagonist beyond Harlem into broader themes, while Reddick still carries Harlem or its equivalent in his head. The point is not the simple one that Baldwin cannot move past those early years in Harlem, but that as a profoundly traditional storyteller, he has exhausted his method of handling those themes and experiences. He cannot break free so that his rhetorical gifts are matched by his novel-making.

One problem is that he uses homosexuality repeatedly as "another country," by that means hoping to locate his protagonists in new territory. But homosexuality has become a well-settled issue, having lost the literary weight Baldwin attempts to derive from it. In the black community, it may be more difficult to perceive it as acceptable, since it calls up, historically, the idea of male "weakness," of the master-slave relationship, and of a "deviation" which debilitates black power. But Baldwin uses it, also, as a way of thrusting guilt upon the reader, white and black, testing or daring us. Yet "white guilt" no longer is elicited by sexual arrangements, cross-racial or otherwise; nor even by scenes of injustice to blacks. The field has shifted, and with it novelistic themes must shift, toward new levels of relationship. That Baldwin sees homosexuality as liberation is a more serious miscalculation: it is a style of life, no different from any other in which love is sought, gained, rejected. Its pains do not convey uniqueness. And if Baldwin is trying to educate blacks about homosexuality, he has miscalculated once more. They have already rejected the premises of his fiction of the last twenty years.

Another Country purports to be a novel and does have novelistic features, but it more closely approximates Baldwin's essays on race and identity—*Notes of a Native Son, Nobody Knows My Name, The Fire Next Time*—than it does fiction. *Another Country* is, in reality, a series of interconnected essays or extended statements by various characters on being gay, black, white, male, female. For the first time, Baldwin attempted to probe identity in women, in a white woman (Cass) and a black woman (Ida Scott), who is the book's most effective character. The central personage is Rufus Scott, Ida's brother, whose early suicide in the novel serves as focus: just who was Rufus? what made him, a former jazz musician of great promise, kill himself? what racial, sexual, other characteristics were functioning in his despair?

The sexual axis tends, also, to be the color axis:

Rufus and Eric (a kind of white Baldwin) in the background, Vivaldo (an unpublished writer) and Ida in the foreground, and Eric and Cass (both white) in the foreground, with Eric as predominantly gay-oriented. All relationships are incomplete, or cut across racial and sexual lines. Eric is the sexual focus of foreground action: we meet him first in Paris with Yves, then in the past with Rufus, then in New York with Cass, and, finally, with Vivaldo, who considers himself straight. Eric, insisting on his sexual tastes, his abilities as an actor, his sensations and pleasures, is the magnet—his beauty, his compassion for others, and, possibly, his availability to both sexes.

Part of the problem with the novel, as distinct from the meditations on sex and race, is that Rufus, the source of everyone's love, does not seem lovable, or compelling, or even appetizing. Like so many of Baldwin's central characters, he has become caught in Baldwin's didacticism. Only Ida stands solidly within the novel; the rest, including the much-described Vivaldo Moore, provide less than meets the eye. In Vivaldo, Baldwin attempted a white man in depth, a sympathetic, wounded man, an unpublished writer who desires love and has great love to give. Yet Vivaldo is curiously stolid, lacking in intellectual depth, a hanger-on of no great interest.

Similarly, Eric, Baldwin's "other country," with his homosexual lover and bisexual capabilities, does not communicate the charismatic qualities other characters attribute to him. He appears selfish, childish, narcissistic, a man dependent on sensations, without regard for consequences. His portrait is, for Baldwin, part of a freeing process: he is an American, lives in France, finds a young French lover (Yves), and enjoys a budding career as a stage and screen actor, roughly analogous to Baldwin's own beginnings as a writer living in self-imposed exile. Eric's early affair with Rufus, his later affair with Cass, his brief interlude with Vivaldo give him points of contact in a society that seems to be in perpetual deflation.

His counterpart in the black world is Ida, a waitress eager to develop into a successful jazz singer. Her color, ambitions, personal likes and dislikes all come together in her affair with Vivaldo, the first man to treat her decently—but white, powerless, dependent on her. She seeks not only identification but the sources of power she can plug into, and this comes in Ellis, a promotor of talent and himself. Like Vivaldo, Ellis is white, but he maneuvers authoritatively in the world, and he can provide a focus for Ida's ambitions. If she is to move from waitress to singer, she must forgo Vivaldo (love, decency) for Ellis (unpleasant sex, power).

The alternative to Ida's quest for power is Cass Silenski, who, after a dozen years of marriage and two children, finds herself without an anchor. Baldwin's portrait of Cass is remarkably perceptive, for her type of woman was still rare in American fiction, rarer yet in work by male novelists. She represents someone who, having failed to travel to "another country," has chosen the safe way: early marriage, children, identification with her husband's career—Richard strikes it rich with a poor but commercial novel. Her life shadows Ida's: Ida seeks that "other country" where she can become not a mate for someone but the power base for whoever mates with her. To that end, she must learn to control her feelings, manipulate men through her beauty, make her blackness a positive rather than negative factor. She must overcome the fact that white men see her as a whore, while black men see her as a useful tool.

In most of this, Rufus is forgotten and lost. Although we are aware of him as a former lover of some of the characters, he plays little role in the novel which he dominates for the first fifth. Baldwin saves him, however, and he does reappear as Leo Proudhammer in *Tell Me How Long the Train's Been Gone* (1968) and as Arthur Montana in *Just Above My Head* (1979). But the structure of *Another Country* cannot accommodate him, and what begins as Rufus's book turns out to be quite different; also, what seems to be interesting structurally, the use of a dead character as a motif running through a long book, ceases to function. Ida speaks of how Rufus meant everything to her, but her remarks seem perfunctory, that in some way Rufus can be used as a weapon against Vivaldo. The flatness of her language reflects, I think, an uncertainty on Baldwin's part as to what Rufus did mean; or else suggests he needed Rufus literarily, for the novel's structure, without any clear conception of him as a character.

Another Country is, in one sense, a paradigm of Vivaldo's own blocked novel. It moves into Baldwin's new staked-out territory, into areas of his essays, especially of *The Fire Next Time;* but it dissipates energies which he seemed novelistically capable of in *Go Tell It on the Mountain.* While nothing is pure miscalculation, much is spun out, filler made into content, ideas offered as structural and then withdrawn. Vivaldo's long-awaited novel, blocked through the entire Baldwin novel, seems our archetype: the book which would not come is made to appear, regardless, and published. Even the epigraphs for each of the three sections of *Another Country* display confusion. The first has an epigraph from W. C. Handy, on "easy riders," which seems suitable for Rufus; the second has as epigraph Lena's plea to Heyst in Conrad's *Victory* that he carry her out of "this lonely place." The third, entitled "Toward Bethlehem," has lines from Shakespeare's Sonnet LXV, "How with this rage shall beauty hold a plea, / Whose action is no stronger than a flower?"

The three epigraphs, if we take them seriously, move the novel in three different directions. The Handy applies to Rufus, who disappears early on; the Conrad applies to Ida, whose relationship to Rufus is spelled out in words which rarely come alive; and the Shakespeare applies generally to the power of love (beauty), which must prevail despite differences: gayness, color, adulteries, et al. Each element is applicable to that section, but no more. For if love means more than anything else, then Ida's quest to leave behind her victimization as a black woman is vitiated; Cass's movement toward freedom and/or independence is frustrated; and only Eric is fulfilled, with the arrival of Yves.

The novel becomes more a plea for homosexuality than for racial tolerance—despite Ida's fierce protests; or for a woman's right to freedom—despite Cass's complaints about Richard. Stress on homosexual love preempts everything, even when love does not appear as a solution, even when love, in fact, appears as a trap. For if we accept Ida's protestations about being victimized, then we cannot accept her love for Vivaldo; her quest for a power base makes more sense. If we accept Cass's description of her suffocating married life, then we cannot validate her acceptance of Richard after he has bloodied her face. Only Eric becomes acceptable. If that is Baldwin's final point, it cripples the novel, for its "lesson" applies only to one-third of the main characters, one-third of the book's relationships.

With *Another Country,* Baldwin moved into a period that would see his career moving out of focus; a great intelligence and verbal talent unable to find equivalent fictional expression. It was not unique to Baldwin, but was paralleled by Bellow, Mailer, Styron, Updike, and several others. The reasons are of several kinds: too easy acceptance and early fame, surely; the sheer complexity of the 1960s for writers nurtured on the 1950s; their failure to have developed sufficient philosophical/ideological bases for future development; careers that were overpraised to begin

with. *Tell Me How Long the Train's Been Gone* (1968) *If Beale Street Could Talk* (1974), *Just Above My Head* (1979) were Baldwin's major achievements for these ten years, but none caught either the language or the coherence of his earliest work.

Tell Me begins with a disaster for the main character, which gives Baldwin the opportunity to relate the novel as a playback (not flashback). Leo Proudhammer, a well-known black actor, suffers a serious heart attack during a performance, and spends most of the novel on his back in the hospital, recalling incidents which brought him to where he is. Suffering the loss of his "proud hammer," he falls stricken, the black no longer acting out roles but giving way to natural causes, the accumulation of grievances.

The conception is sound, perhaps recalling Ellison's beginning of *Invisible Man,* with his narrator already having chosen an existence that is the accumulation of what he was and now must be. Proudhammer's first name is Leo, the lion of action and intrepidity—yet even a lion is struck down when so much pain has accumulated at the heart.

Though Leo Proudhammer is an actor, however, Baldwin fails to play off the various potentialities of his situation. Proudhammer's roles are rarely examined, except for one, near the end of the novel, when he acts in a black version of *The Corn Is Green.* But even here, Baldwin never explores the dimensions of acting; he is more interested in racial matters and sex. In race, Proudhammer is continually humiliated by the white world, as well as hassled by his own people. In sexual matters, Baldwin provides yet another of his men who seem ideal as bed partners.

The central section of the novel, which is the major part of Proudhammer's playback, is his training or apprentice period with the San-Marquand company, which is rehearsing in a small town. It is an almost unfocused episode, running on well over fifty pages, full of young people talking and screwing; but primarily, it serves as a racial weapon for Baldwin, who shows Proudhammer's humiliation with townspeople, police, etc. It achieves its effect several times, with repetition, not development, creating its length. And since it is clear that small-town people will not accept black-and-white (Proudhammer's liaisons with Madeleine and Barbara, actresses), we find pages turned into acts of injustice. What ceases to work as literature functions as propaganda.

Connected to Proudhammer's racial problems, which are real, intense, degrading, is an element that seems relentless in every Baldwin novel except his first. Even at nineteen, Proudhammer is sexually irresistible to males and females, and he charms whoever can advance his ambitions. Only Caleb, his brother, turned reverend from street tough, resists Leo's charms. These charms are not presented, however, nor are Leo's qualities as an actor. We do not understand what makes him special.*

These Baldwin characters—Proudhammer, Rufus Scott, Arthur Montana—we recognize, are ego trips, personae for Baldwin or some sense of himself: acting, loving, bisexual, racially proud as lions. And while they are very vulnerable, they are full of performance. Disaster may claim them—Rufus's suicide, Leo's heart attack, Arthur Montana's stroke—but they have achieved great love before the apocalypse. Fictionally, the strongest elements of the book have to do, not with acting, not with loving, not with race, but with surviving: Leo's family in Harlem, and especially his relationship with his older brother Caleb. Caleb is a street person transformed during the war into a believer, then a preacher who uses his Harlem constituency to gain not only moral heights but financial security. Baldwin has a fine sense of how blacks, rejected on the outside, are able to climb on each other's backs by way of religious activity. Like Malcolm X on a different scale, Caleb discovers his personal transformation fits the needs of his Harlem community; and he enters the black world of nationalism and religiosity with a vengeance, turning on Leo as an actor and a man neglecting his family. Momentarily, Baldwin regains his touch, and the love/animosity of a family relationship returns us to *Go Tell It on the Mountain.*

Styron's *The Confessions of Nat Turner* (1967) is distinctly a part of the 1960s; for black-white confrontations on civil rights, questions of job equality, relationships between the sexes are reflected in this account of the 1831 slave rebellion led by the Reverend Nat Turner. We must perceive the novel as Styron's ruminations on the sixties, as that decade, in turn, reflects our past, black reflecting white, white reflecting black. In racial terms, the 1960s were as significant as the 1860s. Calling his work a "meditation on history," rather than a historical novel, Styron made his goal a grand one; an effort he would repeat in his novel of the 1970s, *Sophie's Choice.* In the later novel, he meditated on World War II; in the earlier, on the background to the Civil War. Because Styron was attempting something so difficult in *Nat Turner,* he made several strategical mistakes, which seriously affect the ideological level of the novel. The response of ten black writers to the novel is revelatory:† for while it pinpoints Styron's errors, it also establishes several assumptions, part of a black aesthetic, which are destructive for fiction as a whole.

One of the basic assumptions of all the writers except John A. Williams is that a white author should skirt black themes. Only one of the ten suggests that Styron's Turner is a tragic figure almost on the scale of Othello, and that his murder of Margaret Whitehead in the fields, by piercing her side twice with his sword and then smashing her head with a post, has the power and feel of Othello's murder of Desdemona. The errors Styron made—the worst of which is to have an unmarried Turner lust after white flesh, when his own Confessions indicate no such thing—do not affect many of the powerful segments of the novel. The buildup to the insurrection itself, the rationale for the slave revolt, and Turner's own hesitation—these do not demean blacks, but, on the contrary, give great weight and thrust to black aspirations. Rather than justifying the "kind master" theme, Styron makes us accept that the slaves under Turner would murder even the kinder slave owners—Travis, for example—in order to assert their own

---

*Barbara, who is white, has been going with Jerry, also white, both members of the acting company, when she suddenly informs Leo she loves him: " 'I told him how much I love you.' " From a rich Kentucky family, Barbara is open and flexible; and yet her "love" for Leo seems nothing more than the platitude that Southern white women yearn for the black man. Further, this view of the arrangement runs counter to Baldwin's larger plan, for Barbara is a person in her own right, not stereotypical.

†A very valuable document printed in 1968 (Beacon Press), *William Styron's Nat Turner: Ten Black Writers Respond,* edited by John Henrik Clarke. These black responses are significant not only for their antagonism to Styron's presentation of Turner, but for their particular ways of viewing black-white relationships in the novel. I will take up their various points later, but I am concerned throughout with the pressure such a response puts on any writer, black or white, who tries to write about racial relationships, or generally about blacks. In the decade and more since then, whites have written only rarely about blacks, chiefly Malamud in *The Tenants* and Updike in *Rabbit Redux,* the latter a noble effort at understanding which touches upon no reality. One point the Nat Turner "ten" fail to respond to is why no major black writer has tackled the Nat Turner rebellion. Baldwin, Williams, Morrison, Killens, Demby, and others all passed up the opportunity, as did the most obvious choice, Richard Wright. Since the subject was also a 1960s theme not preempted by blacks, the implication that white writers should leave black subjects alone is not well taken.

humanity. One must read the book this way.

Styron's novel is concerned, broadly, with the tragic destiny of American history wherever it touches on black-white relationships. His assumption of Turner's voice as his narrative device was, I think, an attempt to bridge the gap between black and white, by ingesting the slave experience within himself and then manifesting the result in literary terms: exaggerating or distorting here, following Turner's Confessions there, allowing himself the play of interpretation fiction permits. He would do something similar in *Sophie's Choice,* ingesting there the concentration camp experience.

Yet the crux of the matter is that that assumption of Turner's voice, whatever Styron intended by it, was a strategical error. For the very reasoning that led Styron into attempting an "I" narration in the voice of Turner should have dissuaded him: questions of language, mentality, point of view, and motivation. As soon as Styron used Turner as his "I" he became involved in questions of verisimilitude beyond the distortions a literary genre permits; he became involved in his own credibility, which is one of the very areas the black critics questioned.

If Styron made strategical errors in assuming Turner's narrative voice as the novelist's own, he also erred in matters of sex. Turner's Confessions reveal a Christ-obsessed young man, someone who senses he has been chosen and awaits the call, a God-driven man swollen with pride and consciousness of his separation from others. Turner, in fact, equates himself directly with the crucified Christ, at least as his words are conveyed to us by Gray's transcription. Question: "Do you not find yourself mistaken now?"—that is, after the failure of the insurrection. Answer: "Was not Christ crucified?" Jesus speaks directly to him, having even told Turner things before his birth, so that he appeared as a prophet, embodying certain stated truths. He combines Old and New Testament qualities: the sternness of the prophets and the insistence of Jesus urging his mission.

There is no stated sexuality here, certainly none of the lusting after white flesh that Styron makes part of Turner's masturbatory fantasies. "It was always a nameless white girl between whose legs I envisioned myself—a young girl with golden curls." This is repeated in response to a particular white girl, Miss Emmeline, "whose bare white full round hips and belly responded wildly to all my lust." Later, just before the rebellion starts, Turner sees Margaret Whitehead as a rape victim, although the young girl shows some willingness. "I could throw her down and spread her young white legs and stick myself in her until belly met belly and shoot inside her in warm milky spurts of desecration."

None of these episodes has any basis in the Confessions, and one wonders why even for fictional dimension Styron inserted them, since they serve no function in his development of Turner. In actuality, Turner was married, his sexuality contained. Styron even provides a mild homosexual episode, in which Turner and another young black friend mutually masturbate. The black-white fantasies appear a serious miscalculation, although Styron's critics appear as equally intent on castigating any mixed sex as attacking Styron for fictionalizing the record. But they are essentially correct in stressing that the episodes above fall into racially derogatory patterns, based as they are on the myth that the black lusts obsessively after white flesh. Connected to this is Styron's repeated suggestion that several of Turner's followers saw the rebellion as a means toward raping white women—although Turner's Confessions contain no such implication.

Styron's miscalculations here—and they are serious racially, as well as a subversion of Turner's reality—are connected to the initial point above: to his assumption of Turner's voice. For once he did this, he became involved in terrible inner tensions: his own Southern background, its values still held, together with those transcended, his need for historical distinctions, all of which involved him in several false steps. Here the body of the novel is seriously affected. Questions of language arise immediately, for Turner has been given two languages in the novel, that of the self-educated slave, and the approximation of Southern black dialect, used when he speaks to the other slaves. Neither is authentic; neither could be.

When Turner speaks with Styron's accents, the voice has such literary echoes from the Southern novel, with particular reference to Faulkner and to early Styron, that Turner's sensibility is drowned in a rhetoric not his. The rhetoric is often noble and very moving—this is a beautifully crafted and written novel. But from the first, authenticity is lost. Very few of Styron's black critics are responsive to how strong many passages are, and how sympathetically these passages present Turner because they are so well written. But in the larger sense, Turner drowns in another man's language; and when Turner speaks in his "common voice," there is little that is distinctive.

Once we move beyond language, to details themselves, Styron's use of Turner as narrator created several inconsistencies, some of them racial, some literary. In Turner's Confessions, there is no indication of slaves who fought and killed for their masters, although there is mention of Joseph Travis as being a "kind master" to him. Once the insurrection begins, Styron makes much of loyal slaves who fired at Turner's army, kicked wounded blacks, and served their masters with zeal. Although Styron is not bound by Turner's words, this phenomenon appears once again like a miscalculation in literary terms, for it derives more from Styron than from any necessary fictional need. It would appear to serve as little literary function as Turner's masturbatory fantasies over white girls. Whether these are racial slurs or not, they make the novel fall into racial stereotypes: in this instance, the idea of the loyal slave. The only "loyal" slave would be the brainwashed slave, and to make that real literarily involves a different perspective from Styron's. A comparable analogy, appropriate for Styron's next novel, would be the concentration camp inmate who fights alongside the camp commandant. To show that literarily, one must make deep preparation; to state it without explanation is a desecration.

There is still another voice floating around, that of Thomas R. Gray, the lawyer who elicits Turner's confession. Gray's voice plays throughout the novel, very subtly intertwined with Turner's at certain points, the seams expertly closed up by Styron's skill in handling the narrative. Yet Gray's voice could have been the commentary. Styron might have used his narrative as Conrad did Marlow's in *Heart of Darkness.* Conrad chose not to tell Marlow's tale directly, but inserted an "I," who in turn related Marlow's story, so that it becomes the inner voice.

To avoid the narrative miscalculations already cited, Styron's positioning should have been by way of Gray, whom he could have distorted as he wished in terms of language, observations, response to Turner. As a Southern white lawyer, Gray would have spoken in Faulknerian terms. He might have imagined whatever he wished about Turner as a result of his confession, and he could have displayed whatever racial sympathy or animosity Styron wished to insert. Such a distancing of author from main event, by way of Gray, would have permitted Styron an additional voice, his own, which now is lost. So much is moving in *The Confessions* that "rewriting" becomes a temptation. A more acute awareness of modernist techniques would have served Styron well literarily.

Paradoxically, Styron's sexual inventions regarding Turner, while suggestive of racial platitudes, pro-vide one of the most compelling scenes. In his Confessions, Turner speaks matter-of-factly of his slaying of Margaret Whitehead; it takes only a few lines, some repeated blows with a sword and then a further blow to the head with a fence rail. In Styron's recreation, Turner's resolve to continue with the insurrection is sorely tested by his need to slay the sympathetic young girl. There is less sexual memory here than humanistic consideration: To what extent can children of slave owners be held responsible for their parents' deeds? Can the sacrifice of innocents be justified by the need to eradicate a poisonous social and economic system? Can revenge against children compensate for the misdeeds and personal horrors suffered under even kind masters? Is there, indeed, such a thing as innocence, when the very system is poisoned? Even the sexual motif makes sense here, since Turner's piercing of Margaret's side with his sword has sexual connotations. As he runs after her, he cries: *"Ah, how I want her,"* an ambiguous phrasing which suggests his dualism. The episode pulls together a great deal of the novel, since this murder is the sole one Turner commits, the only one he is able to commit.

His compassion here gets Styron and us into thickets of problems, most of them concerned with novelistic license. How does one see the Negro in general: as a tragic figure or as a man with characteristic frailties and desires? Was Turner a larger-than-life figure of tragedy, someone who moved amidst slavery as Greek tragic heroes moved among their people, doomed and liberated by their mission? If we view Turner as tragic—that is, so intent on his function that all other considerations fall away—then Styron's portrait is a disservice from nearly every aspect. If, however, we observe him as a man with a mission who was also riddled with human frailty, then his pathos and hubris can be granted. Then we can possibly even accept Will, a man so driven by hatred of his cruel master that his mind has been warped. Styron presents Will as turned bestial by repeated whippings and inhuman treatment. Will is beyond the pale and makes Turner fear for his own leadership; for Will kills readily whereas Turner vacillates. If we seek heroic figures, then Will is not animalistic, but a man driven to another level of existence by ill treatment. If we seek less than tragedy, then Will has become a crazy man, intent on nothing but destruction as retribution for his own destruction. The question is one of Greek tragedy or modern psychology. Such questions, which apply as much to a slave situation as to a concentration camp, apparently led Styron into his next book, *Sophie's Choice,* where the camp experience of Sophie (the inner story, her "Congo") relives the slave experience of Nat Turner.

Historical detail is another matter. In the Author's Note, Styron indicates that Turner's revolt is "the only effective, sustained revolt in the annals of American Negro slavery." The black critics responded the way Jews react to those who claim European Jews went to their deaths without protest. The "ten" cite other instances of revolt, Cato's in 1739 or Denmark Vesey's in 1822 as examples, but there are many others mentioned in documents, either incipient revolts or rumors of plots.* Their point is that Styron has assumed the docile Negro slave, almost happy with his lot under masters who were often kind, a bourgeois "Sambo" disinclined to upset his situation. In their view, Styron's Negroes would fear freedom more than slavery.

Once again, Styron seems to have gained nothing by citing this as the only sustained revolt, unless he was prepared to demonstrate fictionally that the slaves were happy with their lot, which he does not do. His portrait of slavery is not of happy Negroes, his critics notwithstanding, but of a horrible institution which sucks spirit, mind, vitality. Yet by claiming Turner's revolt was singular, Styron left his flank open, and the charge that slaves therefore accepted their lot inevitably followed. One can understand the attack, but the novel is not quite what the attackers claim.

From a sixties point of view, Turner should be heroic; not a man torn by human doubts but a fiery, retributive figure leading the slave revolt against inhumanity. The black critics take a social-political position on Turner, claiming him as their own; whereas Styron took an almost purely literary position, claiming him for both whites and blacks. Styron's Turner is not the black Turner; and for that reason the author should not have personalized his protagonist, but should have located him in the mind or imagination of a contemporary of Turner's, such as Gray, or even the judge, Jeremiah Cobb, an interesting but undeveloped secondary character. By such location, Styron could have presented the black Turner as well as the Turner who fitted his own literary conception. Instead, he lost distance, and his Turner loses credibility, neither the Turner of history nor the Turner of an imaginative recreation.

*Styron's exclusionary point is difficult to explain since he did review Herbert Aptheker's *American Negro Slave Revolts* in 1963.

From his first conception of his character to the reception given by both the black and the white press, Styron's writing of this novel took on extraliterary dimensions. Whereas the white press was almost universally approving—views often based on ignorance of Turner's own Confessions and black history—the black reception from the start was antagonistic. Although these responses must have been painful for Styron, they did expand the novel's social relevance. That is, they stirred up, far beyond the novelist's apparent intention, the issue of race, whose agonies the novel was to reflect. In a sense, the response, antagonistic and virulent in turn, was part of the dialogue of the 1960s; and the "black aesthetic" which the ten black writers manifested was directed toward creating a "social literature" rather than a "literary literature."†

Whenever the Styron novel departs from Turner's own Confessions, the critics consider it racist—quite a fearful catchall term of criticism in the late 1960s, which consequentially soon lost its force—especially since most of the ten believed that for Styron even to write about a black hero was potentially racist. Yet many of their criticisms, as we have seen, pinpoint ideological and racial difficulties in the novel—some of them not even fictionally important to Styron and, therefore, perhaps unconscious reflections of stereotypical attitudes. Even so, the critics on one hand did not allow Styron sufficient literary license; whereas he, on the other, undermined his own position with poor narrative decisions and unexamined racial attitudes.

Still, the book is a powerful statement—for blacks perhaps only to the extent that it called for such a virulent response, comparable to the Jewish response

†That social literature implicit in a black aesthetic, however broadly defined and applied, would seriously hobble black writers in the 1970s. For it defined modernism as white elitism, and discouraged black writers from moving outside naturalism and realism into more imaginative modes. It tried to enforce a code of literary behavior, not in any formal sense, but as a racial pressure which was very powerful. As a consequence, no black writing of the seventies equals in ambitious reach John Williams's *The Man Who Cried I Am* or Richard Wright's early work. Toni Morrison and Ishmael Reed achieved striking effects, but by pulling in, not reaching out. It is unfortunate that at the time blacks gained so much in legal reforms (as apart from practical effects), their writers did not reinforce that image with advanced imaginative fiction. All of Baraka's posturing, in turn, as a separatist, an anti-Semite, a pan-African, and a Marxist would have been more effective in literary form; as rhetoric alone, it blew away.

to Hannah Arendt's book on Eichmann's trial; for all readers, however, for its attempt, often moving and compelling, to enter into a black consciousness that black writers themselves had been reluctant to assay. There is, unfortunately, only one black equivalent of this, Arna Bontemps's *Black Thunder* (1936), a large-scale effort to catch the slave revolt directed by a leader named Gabriel. Bontemps's novel aside, it is a curiously empty area. Williams in *The Man Who Cried I Am* (published in 1967, the same year as *Nat Turner*) wrote his own gloss on the black protest novel, in the person of a very modern black who is still trying to reject the label of slave imposed by a white world. But the Nat Turner material, nevertheless, has been revealed only by a white writer, and one must sharply disagree with the black critics who find sympathy for slavery or its institutions in Styron's novel. More than nearly any other work of fiction since *Uncle Tom's Cabin,* it makes slavery come alive, removes it from statistics and history into a vital area of universal concern, foreshadowing *Roots* and a whole series of studies devoted to black history. That Styron, with all the flaws we have noted, could do this is to suggest that his novel had its impact, painfully for him, painfully for his black critics and readers, but also painfully, because of its content, for all readers.

With *Player Piano,* in 1952, Vonnegut established his literary mode as comic didactic. The use he makes of satire and of science fiction techniques reinforces his performance as instructor. His role is avuncular, kind, sweet, the opposite of Mailer's menace, Bellow's heavy preaching, or Pynchon's sense of flashing doom. Since *Mother Night* (1962), Vonnegut's work has been characterized by a declining regard for fiction and an increasing regard for an audience. In a rather unfortunate interview he gave to *Playboy* in 1973, when he had just completed *Breakfast of Champions,* Vonnegut said: "My books are essentially mosaics made up of a whole bunch of tiny little chips; and each chip is a joke. They may be five lines long or eleven lines long. If I were writing tragically, I could have great sea changes there, a great serious steady flow. Instead, I've gotten into the joke business. One reason I write so slowly is that I try to make each joke work." Connected to this is an earlier statement: "This is a lonesome society that's been fragmented by the factory system. . . . I want to be with people who don't think at all, so I won't have to think, either. I'm very tired of thinking. . . . The human brain is too high-powered to have many practical uses in this particular universe, in my opinion. I'd like to

live with alligators, think like an alligator."

Except for *Cat's Cradle* (1963), Vonnegut's work is not poorly defined by these offhand remarks. He has, in fact, joined several other writers—Updike, Mailer, even Bellow—who have capitalized on the fact that a few others have kept the novel alive while they fiddle and garner prizes. With others doing the real work, Vonnegut can continue to publish his fictions under the protective mantle of the novel without really writing anything but "prose fictions." He is, then, free to come into the novelistic tent and cash in on the proceeds without contributing to the genre. This has become an increasing trend since the 1970s, in that many (most?) of our most lauded writers are still considered serious—they have assimilated certain "serious" modes—and yet they no longer provide a serious forum for fiction. *Mother Night* is characteristic of Vonnegut's sixties work, with only *Cat's Cradle* emerging as something not drenched by sentimental whimsy.

In *Mother Night,* Vonnegut has produced a stand-up comic routine based on the Hitler years, the Holocaust, and the immediate period thereafter. The way to make it work, as Vonnegut recognized, was to keep moving fast, using flip lines as a way of avoiding real issues, shifting to new elements of deceit within deceit, veil within veil. Despite much wittiness, one is troubled by a certain moral and intellectual mush—too many alligators, in fact. Vonnegut's own base outside the material he presents seems especially lacking in the control which would give him the right to try something so dangerous. Put another way: he has so insufficiently based his routines, technically, ideologically, philosophically, that he comes very close to vulgarization of his material.

One dislikes being solemn about a witty book, but Vonnegut surrounds his reductiveness with solemn statements and moves. In the Editor's Note, he turns himself into the editor of Campbell's confessions (as Campbell awaits trial in an Israeli prison) and roves in and out of what he kept, tampered with, altered. He cites from Goethe's *Faust* Mephistopheles' claim that he originated from the darkness of the universe where all was Mother Night, before there was light. The literary maneuvering, the title, even the dedication (to Mata Hari, another whore in espionage) all suggest not a comic routine but something weightier. Elements pull against each other.

Campbell broadcasts hate messages from Nazi Germany during the war, devises slogans, posters, and strategies for focusing Nazi hatred of minorities (i.e., Jews). He works under Goebbels, and he and his wife are amply rewarded for their diligence. When the Allies invade, his broadcasts become a combination of Lord Haw-Haw and Tokyo Rose, but far more virulent and original. He is, however, also an American counteragent, using his broadcasts as ways of getting information out of Germany, by way of pauses, silences, coughs, hesitations during his delivery. Only three men in the United States know of this, one being Roosevelt (Rosenfeld, in Campbell's broadcasts) and another an undercover American major. At the war's end, Campbell's disappearance is arranged—he is relocated in Greenwich Village—but the Israelis want him at the same time they have plucked Eichmann from Argentina. It turns out the Soviets also want him, to parade him as a war criminal shielded by the Americans. Campbell is a cold war victim, on one hand; a real victim, on the other: a pawn in the historical process. Vonnegut has his "American fool."

In his Village existence, Campbell is supported chiefly by right-wing groups: the Reverend Jones, a would-be dentist, whose researches have shown racial minorities give away their inferiority through poor teeth; Jones's entourage, composed of the paranoiac right; and the black Führer of Harlem during the war, who accepts Jones's racial policies because he believes that eventually blacks will rule the world. McCarthyism, the John Birch Society (founded in 1958), anticommunism, Father Coughlin's anti-Semitism of the thirties, black power—a mélange of conspiracy theories come together in Campbell's attic. One of the highlights of Jones's career is his book *Christ Was Not a Jew,* in which he demonstrates that in his examination of fifty famous paintings of Jesus, not one revealed Jewish jaws or teeth.

The comic routine has moved us back and forth. Gags are interwoven with serious comments about totalitarianism. Craziness can operate with impunity behind the circumference of order. The "banality" of Eichmann is just such a working out of the totalitarian mind, as are American adaptations. We learn Campbell will be saved by his American major, now retired to Maine; that the Israelis will release Campbell when they receive word of his true activities. Campbell, however, has come to feel nauseated by events, by his sense of what people believe and how they act, and he plans to hang himself for his "crimes."

The problem is not that Vonnegut moves heavily, but that he is too deft, damned by his own balletic grace. Campbell will go out lightly—his own suicide to become part of a musical comedy routine, perhaps with "White Christmas" as background music. Vonnegut picks up and drops all the detritus of a wacky culture, but he tells us little about it we did not already know or suspect. The outline or the line or the brief episode is the thing. In a book of some two hundred pages, there are forty-five chapters, some half a page, a page, two pages long. Rapidity is the key to the episodes, as it is the key to the language. Sentences are very brief, the words familiar and conversational. Dialogue is of the rapid-fire type—two or three words back and forth down the page, themselves contained in brief episodes, Woody Allen routines. We are not expected to pause, for if we do, the entire structure fails. If we ask questions, the book is doomed.

God Bless You, Mr. Rosewater, Or Pearls Before Swine (1965) is, ideologically, a spin-off from *Mother Night.* While that was something of an allegory, this book is a parable of sorts. It lines up the greedy of the world (law firms, government, fathers, Norman Mushari—an enterprising young Roy Cohn) against someone who, while generous and self-sacrificial, is also insane: Eliot Rosewater, Roosevelt/Goldwater. Eliot's purpose in life is to give away to the needy his vast fortune, which produces nearly ten thousand dollars per day. Although he is surrounded by misery in the small Indiana town where he has established his Rosewater Foundation, he tries, like a modern-day Jesus, to create an atmosphere of help, dispensing uppers—wisdom, pearls, optimism—to drunks, suicides, the hopeless, swine.

Eliot's two great passions are to help the downtrodden and to serve in a volunteer fire department, and he sits by his telephones: red for fire calls, black for those seeking help. Eliot, seeking martyrdom through devotion to others, is deemed insane; and many of his actions are out of control, except for his singular desire to help. He is personally filthy, lets his wife crack up for lack of concern, and has no interest in money. The young, pushy lawyer Norman Mushari thinks he can gain the Rosewater Foundation for another branch of the family, in Rhode Island. The novel plays off Eliot in Indiana against Fred in Rhode Island: Eliot, crazy, doing what he wants; Fred, normal, immersed in a routine of waste, his spirit exhausted by a life he does not comprehend.

The problem with the novel, as with so much of Vonnegut's didacticism, is obviousness. Fred's life has no interest, is simply the givens of a stereotypical suburban life: a hysterical, useless wife, a business in insurance offering few rewards, a home life characterized by sterility. To this Vonnegut applies some arch phrasing, some hoked-up activity; in brief, examples of tired novel-making.

Eliot's great influence is Kilgore Trout, in whose work Vonnegut for the next fifteen years was to implant seemingly great wisdom. In fact, Trout spouts platitudes about American life: " 'Americans have long been taught to hate all people who will not or cannot work, to hate even themselves for that. We can thank the vanished frontier for that piece of commonsense cruelty.' " While full of pity and compassion, Trout's sentiments are old clichés hauled up for Eliot's delectation as if themselves pearls. Trout, indeed, either in person or in his books, demonstrates little to substantiate Eliot's (and Vonnegut's) elevation of him into guru.

The mere presence of a guru type in a 1960s novel was sufficient: that is, Trout—with his magical name from nature, his recalling of pastoral truths, his connection to a pure existence—did not need development. Anything he said was wise because *he* said it, the voice a guarantee of the content. How curious that a decade of people devoted to so much activity was so uncertain as to need such dubious leaders! How shaky everything was! In this respect, Trout represents what is generally true of Vonnegut and his work: Lovely sentiments are sufficient.

The meeting of *Slaughterhouse-Five* (1969) with a particular time, its date of publication, was auspicious; for it had assimilated all the strands of the sixties and positioned them literarily to ensure its success, without itself being a literary moment. The refrain of the novel is "So it goes," a phrase borrowed by Billy Pilgrim from the Tralfamadorians, who use it to comment on dead people. It embodies a shrug and a valedictory, and it suggests that conditions will improve for that person at another time, in another place. Even death, for the Tralfamadorians, is not final. "So it goes" becomes the way Billy, and Vonnegut, can comment on the worst.

Billy gained this knowledge when he was kidnapped by a flying saucer in 1967, taken to Tralfamadore, displayed naked in a zoo, and mated "with a former Earthling movie star named Montana Wildhack." Billy Pilgrim is the chief character in a book narrated by someone who sounds very much like Vonnegut. The novel he writes, the interior novel, is about looking back, and while he does not, like Lot's wife, turn into a pillar of salt, he does create a character who becomes "unstuck in time," Billy, the Christian of Vonnegut's allegorical "Progress."

The narrator, who has, among other things, had Vonnegut's own wartime experience in Dresden, poses as the old codger, a combination wise old man of the woods, Will Rogers, and Mark Twain. The pose is the opposite of the confidence man image projected by several of Vonnegut's younger contemporaries in the 1960s, Barth, McElroy, Pynchon, Coover. Vonnegut presents himself, and his internal novel, with great sincerity:"You can believe *me.*" When the wife of a former war buddy disapproves of still another war novel glorifying combat—a vehicle for John Wayne or Frank Sinatra—the narrator promises her he will call it "The Children's Crusade."

"So it goes," then, becomes the reassuring rallying cry of those who refuse to accept finality. Billy says in a letter: " 'The most important thing I learned on Tralfamadore was that when a person dies he only *appears* to die. He is still very much alive in the past, so it is very silly for people to cry at his funeral.' " Despite tragic potential, we are assured by "So it goes" that fate is kind, especially when a character is named Billy Pilgrim. Much of Vonnegut's appeal derives from his suggestion that while human imbecility will always be with us, one can still maneuver in the interstices. In Vonnegut's secular religion, great evil is balanced by those who refuse to let it direct them. From Vonnegut's point of view, evil can be turned into something laid back, trivialized. The result is that even when he is witty and his parody is working, he has achieved his effects from a confusion of large and small, a leveling of experience. Vonnegut's incorporation of science fiction stratagems into realistic fiction—another source of his success with the young a decade ago—minimizes the realistic in order to incorporate the fantastic.

Example: Billy Pilgrim's experiences in the Dresden slaughterhouse during the Allied firebombing of the city embodies a multilevel effect: politics, humanity, personal experience, universal caring. Yet their significance *in the novel* remains diluted, for Vonnegut's moral frame of reference, first of all, disallows distinctions; and he is eager to group the Dresden bombing with others, i.e., the napalming of Vietnam and the atomic destruction in Japan. Billy's ability to rove into time past and future enables him to combine wars, as well as personal experiences.

Such generalizations—popular in the sixties, when American insanity in Vietnam required some historical basis, and Americans were compared to Nazis and other butchers—make sense at political rallies but doom fiction. He speaks of American robots dropping napalm on Vietnam: "Robots did the dropping. They had no conscience, and no circuits which would allow them to imagine what was happening to the people on the ground." The image is an excellent one, as connected to Vietnam, where there was no association between pilots thousands of feet above the ground and the people they were destroying. Such men *were* robots: volunteers well trained for random destruction. The Dresden firebombing, however, no matter how grotesque, was part of a different war and moral pattern. Arguments may be for or against the bombing, but the act was itself quite distinct from napalm bombing of Vietnam, whose civil war was not threatening America, whereas Germany had become a threat to the very idea of humanity. One's goal here is not to score political points, but to demonstrate that moral softness and flatulence in *Slaughterhouse-Five* have become part of the problem, not the solution. Billy Pilgrim is not simply a victim of a capitalistic, politically greedy, militaristic, money-grabbing society; he is not simply a good Christian being consumed by war and materialism, forced to defect to Tralfamadore to gain perspective. He is the product of Vonnegut's unquestioning attitude toward extremely complicated historical elements, which, for the sake of a "morality play," he simplifies.*

The Tralfamadorian experience enables Billy to "gain perspective" on Earthlings and Earth affairs. " 'How the inhabitants of a whole planet can live in peace! As you know, I am from a planet that has been engaged in senseless slaughter since the beginning of time. . . . So tell me the secret so I can take it back to Earth and save us all: How can a planet live at peace?' " Its intentions pure, its morality innocent, its attitudes beyond ethical reproach, *Slaughterhouse-Five* nevertheless turns human behavior and history into molasses.

Billy Pilgrim is himself an optometrist, successful as the result of having married the ugly daughter of a wealthy man in Ilium (a spin-off from *Player Piano*). He is set for life, but despite his vocation—and despite a breakdown, a near-fatal airplane crash, and a close brush with death during the Dresden firebombing—he does not *see*. That sixties need to zero in on one's centers of being will elude Billy until he is kid-

*One should not be too solemn, however. Billy as a prisoner of war grabs whatever clothes are available and ends up in a Cinderella costume: blue togs, silver shoes, fur muff. The clownish image he casts is an excellent metaphor of America at war, and his reception as an example of American power reduced to travesty is visually very effective. Here, Vonnegut is at his most appealing.

napped and taken for a six-month stay to Tralfamadore. There he can couple with a movie starlet, father a child, and enjoy sexual bliss with the porno fantasy of his dreams.

Even though Billy is exhibited in a zoo, as an animal to their human, Tralfamadore represents paradise, offering an alternative to Earth and Earthlings. Since on Earth the weak cannot make the powerful even hear them, the Tralfamadorian experience allows a breakout from implacable forms. Yet that experience has no substance; that is, no conflicts or tensions. It is part of Vonnegut's old codger advice. Empty air, not an idea, surrounds Tralfamadore, even more here than in *The Sirens of Titan,* where the magical place is introduced. It is sentimentalized, a golden age, the Edenic place, all to give Billy an alternative experience; and yet not substantive, simply a magic carpet into fantasy.

Vonnegut uses *Slaughterhouse-Five* as a reprise not only of his own life but of his professional writings. Kilgore Trout, the science fiction writer, is reintroduced; Eliot Rosewater surfaces; Howard W. Campbell reappears; a Rumfoord, from the Rumfoords of *The Sirens of Titan,* has a brief interlude. All these appearances and reappearances are in keeping with the time shifts that characterize the novel. Since Billy has the ability to move backward and forward in time, he can reenter Vonnegut's fiction, personal history, even world history. He foresees what is coming, and yet, like Cassandra's, his warnings go unheeded. He sees doom, including his own death; but he also sees salvation, the result of being a pilgrim, a "Billy," an eternal youth. He is a figure of universal significance. As an optometrist, he can devise strategies by which seeing is clarified; his business is observation, perception, foresight. He magnifies, as a microscope, and diminishes, as a telescope; near and far are available to his devices. Thus, Billy, like Barth's Billy or George Giles, is a man for all seasons.

In *Rabbit, Run* (1960), his second novel, Updike has written a moral fable for our times: about the self-absorption of a young man who lacks wit, charm, and intelligence. He does have consciousness, a sense of something missing, and a physical desire which transcends occasions. Harry Angstrom, or Rabbit, as a former star basketball player on his high school team, has conditioned himself to run. Those years in the limelight are his lost Eden. At the very beginning of the novel, he comes upon a group of boys playing a pickup game. Dressed in his business suit, now twenty-six, married, the father of a son, a demonstrator of vacuum cleaners in a local store, Rabbit is dying; but the game gives him vitality. "That his touch still lives in his hands elates him." When he's with his wife, Janice, who is also dying, he "tries to think of something pleasant. He imagines himself about to shoot a long one-hander; but he feels he's on a cliff, there is an abyss he will fall into when the ball leaves his hands." Rabbit runs to recapture the Eden of those days, and yet each move to discover it turns sour.

The novel is clearly a response to 1950s malaise, a political statement at the level of small-town life, with people gasping out their lives, a Sherwood Anderson scenario. *Rabbit, Run* overlaps with Malamud's *A New Life,* Roth's *Goodbye, Columbus,* Donleavy's *The Ginger Man,* some of Salinger's stories, Vonnegut's *Player Piano,* all of which have in common a character who has refused his role, or who is attempting to rediscover himself by running.* Each novel is based on the feeling that to escape is to live, or try to live, whereas to remain placed is to accept death. Since the point is quintessential American and hardly original by the 1950s, the novels which focus there must themselves contain an original point. Malamud's is witty, full of the ironies of a Jew in the Northwest amidst Gentile enemies. Roth's titular story has the uneasiness of younger Jews located amidst the affluence and expectations of their elders. With this as pivot, he sees how "running" prevents suffocation, and he is quite prescient about the newer Jew of the 1960s, the Jewish activist and radical (American style). Vonnegut's protagonist must struggle for life against his organizational role in a machine-made world. For him, a farm is Eden.

Rabbit moves more constrainedly. The sole way he can replay those basketball games is in bed, apparently: orgasm itself, the warmth of flesh, and plenty of it. The most successful parts of the novel occur in Updike's descriptions of Rabbit's desire, his pleasure in the tactile sense of flesh. Whoever satisfies this aspect of Rabbit will hold him together; he moves from his wife to Ruth, a part-time prostitute, back to his wife, then to Ruth, each move creating chaos. His desertion of Janice leads to her excessive drinking and the death of their infant by drowning; he gets Ruth

pregnant, and wants her to have the child but without marriage.

Updike is striving for a vision based on juxtapositions, some insight into Rabbit's need for freedom even as circumstances and the paltriness of his own desires draw him back. He is not a bad man; he is, however, hollow, and hollow in ways Updike does not recognize. The dread he runs from is undefined. While he has demands upon life which life cannot meet, he brings nothing to it. One could argue that Updike meant to present a cipher with a huge appetite —but then what is the point? Where does the author take his stand? Even emptiness must assume significance. Updike gives us no resting place; the tone of the novel is neutral. Rabbit does not seek our approval, and we should not disapprove. If neutrality is the aim—that is, we simply observe—then where do we locate ourselves morally? Rabbit is charmless, witless, a young man full of disaster, but even that on a small scale. Is he the archetypal American male?

As he tells Ruth, after one has been first-rate at something, the second-rate is a form of death. Yet he is himself a form of death and has not earned the right to express that. The problem, once again, lies here: Rabbit expresses feelings and ideas beyond him. The Reverend Eccles, who tries to help him and only creates muddles, says he can always redeem himself, that circumstance is not the master. But Rabbit understands only lust; like many other Updike protagonists, he is too shallow to investigate matters of will and chance. Such a passage as the following is far in excess of the character: "His [Rabbit's] life seems a sequence of grotesque poses assumed to no purpose, a magic dance empty of belief. *There is no God; Janice die* [in childbirth]: the two thoughts come at once, in one slow wave. He feels underwater, caught in chains of transparent slime, ghosts of the urgent ejaculations he has spat into the mild bodies of women." Not only is this excessive to what Rabbit can comprehend, it serves no function, for he cannot act upon what is, really, Updike's, not his, perception of events.

The language rings false: "ghosts of urgent ejaculations," "spat into the mild bodies," the water images. There is, throughout, an inappropriate adventurousness with language.† For Janice, a real twit of

---

*The male dominates in the late fifties and early sixties; the female plays an increasingly important role by the end of the decade. See "The Female Experience" for new aspects of "running."

---

†In that mixture of good nature and viciousness which characterizes his evaluations of his contemporaries, Mailer speaks of "one thousand other imprecise, flatulent, wry-necked, precious, overpreened, self-indulgent, tortured sentences. It is the

a young woman, Rabbit's female equal, Updike uses a modified stream of consciousness, modeled apparently upon Joyce's Molly Bloom. And he repeats the method for Ruth, a woman of no interest, no charm, no qualities except the ability to draw breath and spread legs. Her mind meanders in the stream. She thinks of her clients: "After all it's no worse than them at your bees and why not be generous, the first time [fellatio] it was Harrison [a former teammate of Rabbit's] and she was drunk as a monkey anyway but when she woke up the next morning wondered what the taste in her mouth *was.*"

Language regurgitates trivia. Rabbit sneaks into his house for his clothes, and every item he takes is listed. Boring food is described in detail. Yet trivia, unlike its use in Joyce or Oates, does not intensify into thematic importance or into stresses which highlight certain motifs. Experience itself is so trivialized that Rabbit's moments of glory—the remembered dream, intensity of orgasm, succumbing to abundant female fleshiness—are diminished. Running on the basketball court produced scores and winning games; running in society, as Rabbit learns, produces no results, merely a sequence of disasters.

This is a very significant American theme: fleeing a static or enclosed life, a form of suffocation. From it derive all the elements novelists mock: gray-flannel-suited man, loveless marriage, importuning children, sexual frustration, boredom. The 1950s are located here. Rabbit foreshadows 1960s "opening up," the tryings-out which characterized the decade, even the solipsism and narcissism which demanded voices. One of the most effective episodes occurs when Rabbit sits with Harrison in a run-down bar, and he recognizes that Ruth, *his* prostitute, has probably committed fellatio with Harrison. Rabbit then demands she do it with him, to humiliate her and let her know who is master. By degrading her—he has also spoken of his love for her—he will relieve the emptiness in himself; but the act proves disastrous for both. He gains no victory, only her humiliation; emptiness remains. He returns to his wife, only to desert her again, and that, in turn, leads to the drowning of the infant.

Rabbit Redux (1971), or restored, is Harry Angstrom's life ten years later, when he is thirty-six and the country, in 1969, is experiencing the moon shot, street riots, racial disturbances, and a general convulsion in morals. Rabbit is caught in the middle, back in Brewer, the small Pennsylvania town which is, apparently, a microcosm of America, just as Rabbit is a miniature of American life. Rabbit ten years later is a ranting, warmongering, frustrated individual coming into heaviness, gloom, and right-wing paranoia. Again, the strategical problem is that Rabbit's opinions, trials, erections, preference for large fleshy women have little significance.

Playing around Rabbit are the various phenomena of the sixties. Jill, a rich eighteen-year-old, has run (in a Porsche) from her Stonington, Connecticut, wealth to find new life among blacks, drugs, danger. She seeks new states of being by way of Zen, sex, which she does not appear to enjoy, and threatening associations. She also seeks humiliation. After Rabbit's wife leaves their home to live with Stavros, a Greek car salesman, Jill moves in with Rabbit and his son; later, the household is joined by Skeeter, a ghetto black.

A demonic element, Skeeter offers all the temptations which heighten life while destroying it: drugs, brutality, sex, and jive talk about race which finds Rabbit half sympathetic. The patter Updike has derived for Skeeter, however, lacks authenticity; Skeeter himself is simply words, failing to embody anything more than an idea. What makes this part of the novel so unconvincing, even embarrassing, is that Skeeter is what Flannery O'Connor called "an artificial nigger." He is the idea of a ghetto black, just as Jill is an artificial rebel. These two allegorical figures are set off against Rabbit, who is real, and styles clash. Talk, actions, responses are all efforts to mix what does not blend. Set into this is Rabbit's son, Nelson—in love with Jill, possibly even having sex with her, turned on by the excitement—but lacking resonance. The point of view is all Rabbit's, his ego, needs, solipsism.

Rabbit's basketball days are only a memory. Now heavy, he is short of breath, and only his hands are still graceful. He drinks after work, he sleeps around, he rants that the Vietnam War is necessary—if we must fight, we should fight *them there*—and yet he is attracted by the new. He is a mutant of sorts. He agrees to his wife's affair, is fascinated by Jill and sympathetic to Skeeter. But it is all in a frame of reference as a registering consciousness. Rabbit listens, responds, but cannot comprehend. The background is moon shot, moon walk, moon talk, but that, like everything else, passes him by. Updike has little

sort of prose which would be admired in a writing course overseen by a fussy old nance."

sense of dread, personal disaster (beyond the grief of the moment), none of the intensity Joyce Carol Oates applies to a situation or character who is down.

Jill at one point conveys her Zen view, which is strikingly nineteenth-century, that the universe is a clean place once we can efface our own egos: ". . . all the animals and rocks and spiders and moon-rocks and stars and grains of sand absolutely doing their thing, unself-consciously." With Emersonian stress, she says "matter is the mirror of spirit." Man destroys the sense of things by thrusting ego and self into things. Rabbit is entranced by her talk, but it passes him by, for whatever did register could not matter. Jill is for him little more than a number of willing orifices, and it is fitting that while Rabbit is away playing with another woman, Jill is burned to death in his house, the fire set, apparently, by local people objecting to her and Skeeter. In the first novel, the infant is victim; here, Jill: one drowns, one burns, water and fire claiming the sacrifice. Janice and Rabbit reunite amidst the ruins.

Like Malamud with *The Tenant,* another effort to capture the "scene," Updike has little ear or sense of things when he moves from what he does know; and his use of Rabbit Angstrom as a registering consciousness in a long novel was an error. In another format, Skeeter's attempt to explain himself and blacks to a frustrated, conservative, even paranoiac white audience may have had significance; but Rabbit has so little of our faith that the stream of talk is only embarrassingly tedious. " 'Baboons, monkeys, apes: these hopeful sweet blacks trying to make men of themselves, thinking they'd been called to be men at last in these the Benighted States of Amurri-ka' "— so Skeeter goes on, mocking blacks who try to fit themselves into what whites want, only to be mocked in turn. Skeeter's barrage, which could have been meaningful if dramatized differently, if dramatized at all instead of sermonized, is verbal disaster.

With the publication of *Rabbit Is Rich* in 1981, it becomes clear that the three Rabbit novels should be read as a trilogy. A trilogy assumes that there is interwoven material, that each novel is a slice of the pie, not the whole of it. If we view the books in this way, *Rabbit Redux*'s weaknesses can be partially papered over by the stronger novels on either side, and *Rabbit, Run* takes on a greater cultural urgency. If three, why not four? *Rabbit Is Rich* seems to foreshadow a fourth book, a kind of Brewer *Ring;* for Rabbit must begin to pay with his health for his excesses, and *that* is a subject. His heart will go bad, he will find himself

losing his virility, he will be replaced, gradually, by his son, Nelson. Everything in *Rabbit Is Rich* suggests that Rabbit, now forty-six, has peaked, in an allegory of America itself in the later 1970s and early 1980s. What Rabbit represents as a piece of America is being transformed; and his own life, so much a microcosm of middle America, must undergo a similar transformation. It is a sign of Updike's achievement here that he has found, as Lewis did with Babbitt, a real voice for the country, or at least for the part of the society that would vote for Reagan and continue to support him.

Carter is President, the gas lines have lengthened, the Iranians have just taken their hostages, gold and silver are rising in price, inflation is rampant, and Rabbit is rich, the co-owner of a Toyota dealership in Brewer. He is now cozy with his wife, Janice, having accepted his fate after the disasters of *Rabbit Redux,* in which his affair with Jill ended with her fiery death and Janice had gone to live with Charlie Stavros, who now manages a division of the Toyota dealership. Rabbit is heavy, successful, a country club man, a golfer, faithful to Janice, but torn by doubts and intimations of mortality. The person who is the locus of his doubt is Nelson, his troubled son, who decides to return to Brewer after three years at Kent State University. Nelson returns with one young lady, Melanie, and then another appears, Pru, who is pregnant and whom he marries against his will. He, also, intends to get his start in the Toyota dealership, forcing Rabbit to acknowledge him. Although Rabbit fits well within his cozy life, he finds himself in a constant struggle with Nelson, who has Janice and her mother (the other co-owner of the dealership) on his side.

Nelson reminds Rabbit of all his own messes—in his disregard for property (he bangs up one car after another), in his moving from one girl to another, in making a marriage that seems doomed even before the ceremony. He is bitten by some disgruntlement which also gnawed at Rabbit and made him run. Unlike his father, Nelson has had no successes, only bad memories. He is a young man of the sixties, remembering the doomed Jill and Skeeter, the black revolutionary of *Rabbit Redux,* holding his father responsible for Jill's death. Skeeter, too, is now dead. The sixties have vanished. Nelson has nothing to hold on to but these recollections, since he senses intense hostility in his father and has nothing of his own to sustain him. Updike is very successful in making Nelson appear as unpleasant as he is supposed to be. Janice is sympathetic, but she is a heavy drinker, under the sexual sway of Rabbit, a woman seeking her own pleasures. Rabbit is still incapable of being a father, although he wants some closeness and pays heavily for Nelson's mistakes.

Rabbit Is Rich is the most effective of the three Rabbit books, the one with the most sustained tone. The now familiar characters have all reached a turning point, well illustrated in the book by the army of Toyotas, like gigantic ant colonies, which are overrunning America. American convertibles, cherished by Nelson, are now antiques, virtually fossils. The comfortable American car is a gas guzzler; the Toyota, while economical, has little inside space for large Americans, and yet Japanese cars are the cars of the present and future. They have made Rabbit rich. American cars, suitable as collectibles, are now a side item for him. The symbolism seems obvious, and yet Updike works it exceptionally well. He has always been compelling on cars as intimate cogs of American life, and even in a book as miscalculated as *The Centaur,* one recalls the aching grind of a car on a frozen night. Like Cheever with railroads, tracks, small-town stations, Updike shapes cars to the form of the American dream or nightmare. No passage in his other books matches the loving care with which he opens *Rabbit Is Rich:* the Toyota itself, Rabbit's showroom, the demonstration Rabbit gives to a young couple. The observable detail and intense attachment to the artifacts of decline compete favorably with a similar kind of thing we find in John O'Hara, Sinclair Lewis, Wright Morris. The passing of the American motorcar—that paradise lost—is, ironically, inversely related to Rabbit's growing girth.

Rabbit is, in many respects, an updated Babbitt. Updike does not work the town for its yokels and foibles, however, but uses a more modern post of observation to reach somewhat comparable conclusions. He is not a satirist, rather a historian of contemporary mores. Lewis put Babbitt into a context of social connections, so that he reflected Zenith and Zenith mirrored him. Updike, the heir of half a century of modernism, filters the town more restrictively through Rabbit, with occasional excursions into Nelson's consciousness. There is really a narrative dualism: the omniscient Updike, the Rabbit post of observation. The book's limitations are, in fact, directly associated with that intense, almost claustrophobic stress on Rabbit's consciousness.

The problem lies there: not in what Updike does, for he performs very well, but in what he does not do. Inevitably, with a character like Rabbit—and after three views of him, one thousand pages—his ordinariness transcends his performance. The accumulation

of sexual thoughts and performances, the emphasis on women's bodies, their inner parts and protuberances, cannot hide the fact that sexual activity is being used as a tease. Updike conveys delight in the female form, in the joys of heterosexual connection, in the varieties of sexual excitement a man and woman can conceive of—as experienced by the man. Even the return of Ruth—the part-time whore from *Rabbit Redux,* who bore Rabbit a daughter he has not seen—now fat and gray, brings back to him her heavy, sweet body. Rabbit not only performs well, he remembers well. All this is to be praised, since good sex has become a rare commodity in the American novel.

There is, however, a sameness to the performance, too many adolescent fantasies; the sex never achieves eroticism. Although Updike is aware of mortality—Rabbit comes close to heart attacks when he runs, and the birth of a granddaughter is, for him, a sign of his own imminent death—the indulgence of his body outpaces deeper thought. Rabbit's views are of little interest; his inner life, when not associated with sex or hostility to Nelson, is a waste land. Not even his dimmest ideas have content. Rabbit is something of a trap for Updike, as he must have recognized. For Updike had to exalt the ordinary without falling into the tedium that many naturalist novels repeat.

Part of the problem derives from the people around Rabbit; while he continues to perform, they more or less stand still or are frozen into roles. Janice remains a warm, trim body, full of alcohol and sexual desire, but little else. A cipher, she goes nowhere, except deeper into the marriage. Nelson's two girl friends are hardly defined; they are "the younger generation," symbols of what is growing up. The social set, in and around the local country club, cannot say anything that interests the reader; so that the latter, if male, must wait for the sexual action.

A vacation trip that three couples take late in the novel is predictable: it must lead to wife swapping. With his eye on the well-filled-out Cindy (she is only flesh, not life), Rabbit is more than willing to trade off Janice in order to get his hands and mouth on her opulence. But he ends up with slim, prim Thelma, who turns out to be sexual dynamite. What is disturbing is the predictability of the strategy; good sex is not being used as part of something else, but as a diversion, and yet Updike cannot maneuver into something significant because he has established such limited actors—whose movement is, indeed, best in bed, or thinking about the possibilities.

There is a hermetic quality to *Rabbit Is Rich*

which derives not only from what is created but from what is omitted. For the ordinariness of ideas and conversation manifest in Brewer, in small-town Reagan territory, is a literary blind alley. Sinclair Lewis was able to sustain his vision of Zenith because, first, he got there before anyone else to establish the mode, and second, he saw George Babbitt as being slowly dehumanized by the rounds of clubs and meetings, the demands of business. Lewis was at ease with naturalism, and in its mechanisms he found images of Babbitt's decline even as he prospered. Updike is a less enthusiastic naturalist, and Rabbit remains on top. Decline will, of course, come, and there are, as we have seen, foreshadowings. But personal—as apart from social—decline is not a felt quality of the novel, and it does not work out in performance. Even the Oedipal struggle slips away, for Nelson runs off before Pru gives birth, and Rabbit is left as king of the hill.

He and Janice move into a new house, with money from the dealership and from his appreciated Krugerrands. In the new home, Rabbit rules the roost—more rooster than bunny—and even if Nelson does return eventually, even if he can learn to stop running, he will live not with Rabbit but with Janice's mother. Thus the potentially deadly struggle—deadly because Nelson flirts with death by car—is muted. Routine remains triumphant, and yet this evenness, this acceptance of values, this desire to keep the present going indefinitely—all of which are the novel's victories—are also the source of its limitations. Those intimations of mortality are little more than window dressing.

Piet Hanema's is the central intelligence of *Couples* (1968). His name suggests *anima,* a word with rich classical connotations, meaning air or the breath of life, soul, intelligence. It is one of the basic words in the Western vocabulary. His Christian name is not idly chosen either, Dutch for Peter, connotative of the Pietà (Mary mourning the dead Jesus) and of Pietism, the seventeenth-century Lutheran movement which stressed personal piety (another reference) over religious orthodoxy. Piet's Pietism is a form of rebellion. His wife, Angela, is angelic, holding her body as her own, to bestow as a rich gift or treasure on rare occasions. Built like Mother Earth, massive below the waist, she is both Earth and Angel to Piet's Life and Soul.

The subject of the novel, accordingly, is a moral lesson based on adultery; adulteries, multiple and casual, of a large number of inhabitants of Tarbox, not too far from Boston. Tarbox is a seething box, as it were, into which new bodies are thrust and sacrificed almost weekly. Among participants, the most active is Piet. But before we arrive at Piet and his triumphs, failures, slightly sourish marriage, we come through two epigraphs, one from Paul Tillich, to the effect that if we give too much to fate and not to choice, we compromise the idea of a living democracy; and from Alexander Blok, that our love of the flesh and its pursuit even with "gentle jaws" often crack the fragile bones beneath. As in so many Updike books, epigraphs point toward multiple dimensions, many-layered experiences. And *Couples* does reach for this kind of dimensioned reality; for historically we are in 1963, with Cuban missile crisis, Vietnam, Diem, Pope John, airplane crashes, earthquakes, and, finally, the Kennedy assassination as background.

In one respect only, Updike's pretentious epigraphs, naming of characters, and use of historical background work—he is extremely prescient about certain aspects of the 1960s. Piet plays golf during the missile crisis, and a party at Freddy Thorn's is held on the night of Kennedy's assassination. These people insist on their sexual lives, on their need to be cosseted, nursed, and psychoanalyzed. They are representative of one segment of American life in the sixties: narcissistic, self-serving, lacking political or social commitment. They have relocated in Tarbox on the wave of 1950s affluence, a professional class by and large—dentist, money managers, contractor and builder (Piet). Only the men work, while the women wait around, for someone to crawl into bed with them.

Updike has chosen not to satirize but to celebrate them. The confusion of realms here involves matters of tone. For he cannot justify why Piet should earn our attention for 200,000 words, when he is less a character in a large novel than a small creature in a porno nursery story. The problems of the novel become overwhelming when we try to read it seriously. If adultery is the pastime of the suburbanite—what *Time* magazine called "their glue"—then the lower half of the body preempts all other interest. Updike rarely misses out on a large ass, a wide pair of hips, earthy thighs, a good muscle here, a sexy development there. Breasts, also, can matter, but faces and heads not at all, except for mouths, which can perform fellatio or cunnilingus. Blow, blowing, blown have replaced pillow talk, in what has been labeled "an intellectual Peyton Place."

Besides the problem of tone in the presentation of Piet, we note the lack of coherence between foreground and background. Updike is always there with delicate touches and his verbal brush, but these people have no substance, and therefore their adulteries do not extend from meaningful lives. They perform in a porno fantasy. No Emma Bovarys, the women are merely orifices, even after dozens of pages devoted to them. The men are little different. Only Piet takes any interest in his work, but part of that concern is connected to the time it gives him with available housewives.

At the beginning of Chapter 2, Updike fills in what has made this generation: depersonalization, an affluent and indulgent economy, a "climate still *furtively* hedonist," a sense of freedom. If into this you put people who are determined to be liberated, but without a commitment to duty or work, you find a preoccupation with fun and sensory experience. Yet the lists of personal and historical-social elements do not connect people to their era; they remain disembodied, not as part of some overall plan (as in Beckett, for example) but as examples of deficient development. They manifest the quicksilver of figures in a news story. Their adulteries have a certain sensual patina, but without the moral tensions that make adultery interesting. If their superificiality is to be stressed, then how can we explain anima, Tillich, Blok, and other heavy allusions? Updike strains after resonance, significance, but achieves neither distance nor tone.*

Marry Me (1971–76, 1976), made up of bits and pieces left over from *Couples,* is a 1960s book catapulted into the 1970s. The perfect example of a writer's publishing the kind of thing he knows he can do in order to maintain an appearance, it signaled to Updike that he could not continue to do this kind of novel, and led to *The Coup,* in 1978. *Marry Me* is an expression of 1970s "open marriage": endless dialogues among two couples, who exchange (heterosexual) partners; and it had its usual admirers in *Time, Newsweek,* et al. (Admiring adjectives for Updike are held, possibly, like an arsenal of words ready to be applied whatever and whenever he publishes: "witty," of course, "perceptive," "sharp," "honest," "stunning," "exuberant," "famous style," "best yet.")

As a counter to a tired novel like *Marry Me,* we turn to "The Blessed Man of Boston, My Grandmother's Thimble, and Fanning Island" (in *Pigeon Feathers,* 1962), a startling piece of fiction. The "Blessed Man" is an old, fat Chinese sitting in Fenway Park, upon whom Updike wishes to lavish great effort, spending thousands of pages on trivia, capturing the slightest details of this person; but given the limitations of the writer, he recognizes his reach is shallow. "We walk through volumes of the unexpressed and like snails leave behind a faint thread excreted out of ourselves." "My Grandmother's Thimble" is a silver, engraved heirloom, the sole item of worth left to the narrator by his grandmother, whose tale he considers telling—

Bech of *Bech: A Book* (1970) existed before the book did. He is an Updike persona—as a middle-aged Jewish writer hanging on after some badly received work, but still internationally famous—heading out from his Riverside Drive apartment to discover something beyond or in himself. The "book" is a sequence of interrelated stories linked by Bech: in the Soviet Union, Bulgaria, Rumania, at a girls' school in Virginia, on a Massachusetts beach, in England; finally, Bech apotheosized as an academician. Bech is, in some respects, the working out of the career of the American writer: "His reputation had grown while his powers declined. As he felt himself sink, in his fiction, deeper and deeper into eclectic sexuality and bravura narcissism, as his search for plain truth carried him further and further into treacherous realms of fantasy and, lately, of silence, he was more and more thickly haunted by homage . . . by election to honorary societies, by invitations to lecture, to 'speak,' to 'read,' to participate in symposia trumped up by ambitious girlie magazines in conjunction with venerable universities." Even the government has asked him to travel "as an ambassador of the arts."

While the artist in Bech strives to survive, the man has been swept away by the stream of public relations and hyperbole. When his English publisher invites him to London to be lionized, Bech says he prefers to be "lambified," but telephone reception is poor and the word is not heard. He *is* lionized. Like Matthew Arnold's poet, grown old, his talent withered, he

---

the tale of a "woman in a Vermeer," recalling George Caldwell's love of Vermeer in *The Centaur.* Like Borges, Updike has reached back to a real literature (his own), and whereas Borges forged something he has passed off as a historical present, Updike refuses to rove further into the past. Fanning Island, in the third tale, is a place where, Updike speculates, some men were cast adrift. And since they could not propagate, they became fewer, until only one remained. He would be, if the tale were written, Updike's narrator. The tale would have been the days, the tasks, the story "full of joy." Updike cites Pascal to the effect that such a tale suggests men in chains, awaiting their end, illustrating the human condition as they confront their condemnation.

The story is so compelling because Updike found a formal structure for it, without wrenching the material out of the traditional modes he is comfortable with. If the story as a whole is about the death of the short story—it concerns material never to be formed into tales—then the untold stories themselves build into episodes leading toward death, Pascal's finality. Updike proves loyal to his vision of Vermeer and Chardin, miniaturists who enclose us, who squeeze out the beyond. They are all foreground, which is, apparently, the area where Updike can himself excel.

watches while the world screams his praises. Bech is caught in perpetual irony: that the public man must sustain repeated assaults against the private man; that once he is public, he is lost in circumstance; and that only he can comprehend the melancholy of a gift drying up while his fans applaud the past.

"Bech Panics," the fifth of the seven stories, and one that did not appear in *The New Yorker,* seems the fullest expression of Updike's talent. It is a masterly description of Bech's journey to Virginia at the invitation of a girls' school, three days, two nights. Bech, a bachelor, has moved from one woman to another, is currently with Bea, who shares his bed with her small son, the son at the breastworks, Bech at the buttocks. It is not enough. He accepts the invitation, is picked up by two girls in a convertible, and as the car rushes toward the campus, the girls giggling, the smell of horse manure in the sweet air, Bech "panics." "Along with the sun's reddening rays and the fecal stench a devastating sadness swept in. He knew that he was going to die. That his best work was behind him. That he had no business here, and was frighteningly far from home."

The panic intensifies as he enters into the activities planned for him. The "massed fertility" of the young women, the fact that their young bodies were broadening and deepening and giving off liquids which would, later, produce new bodies from their own cells, that "mackerel-crowded sea" in turbulent unrest, all convince Bech of his superfluity. Nature is working on a scale which leaves no room for Bech, and his immediate role recedes in significance against the terrible immensity of eternity. A short, somewhat angry exchange at lunch with a black student, who objects to "Negress" in his work, takes him out of his panic. A Southern white girl tries to mediate and demonstrates an opening sensibility, and Bech speculates: ". . . that for this excited young convert to liberalism anthropology was as titillating as pornography." All the while, Bech observes the "munching females . . . as pulpy stalks of bundled nerves oddly pinched to a bud of concentration in the head." Even as Bech is aware of their consciousness, he is cognizant of chemistry and biology working themselves out inexorably; and from that he is excluded. He is cells, not a famous writer.

Bech's bedroom is in the dormitory, separated by a wall from the "harem." He feels, strangely, asexual, and his mind roves to his mother, whom he let die in a Riverdale nursing home, to his own artistic impotence, and to his dependence on mere routine functions. Since the art has withered, he stresses elimination: long periods in the bathroom, promptness with letters, compulsive emptier of wastebaskets. His panic is the recurring recognition of decline and death, even as the walls themselves breathe with the pulsing cells of young women.

He meets a Jewish teacher, Ruth, who seems to be living amidst alien corn; but she is levelheaded, takes her job and the students seriously, and offers to sleep with him his last night. She also requests that he judge a poetry contest. He accepts both, performs, and flies off the next morning, touching his pocket to make sure his check for $1,000 is there. The present closes over him. He feels there is little of him left to share, that his resources have been exhausted, which is to say he is back to himself. The panic is part of the ordinary, not the extraordinary. End of segment.

The entire sequence of Bech pieces demonstrates Updike at his best. He has a congenial subject—himself transformed into a Jewish author—and a witty, ironic style. He has forsaken the flights into referential work and backgrounding, and he has let the social forces implicit in the 1960s enter naturally. His exchange with the black student over "Negress" and "Jewess," the statement that sociology/anthropology is more titillating than pornography, is suggestive of all. It is remarkable how close Bech seems to Malamud's Levin, in *A New Life;* but not so remarkable if we realize Levin is a persona of Malamud, the New York Jew who panics even at joy. *Bech: A Book* does not suffer that clash of styles which Updike frequently offers as a sop to modernity, and which, in point of fact, suggests he merely plays at it. Long after the steamy couplings, broken marriages, and suburban exchanges are forgotten, *Bech: A Book,* its brio intact, should remain.

While *Bech: A Book* seemed natural and unaffected, *Bech Is Back* (1982) is a bore because it becomes forced, an act of duty. It is in this respect, like much of the 1982 crop of novels by famous authors, a perfunctory production, performed for an audience, meeting imagined expectations. It's as if our writers were acting out Barthian roles on a publisher's stage, primping and preening for the camera, then expelling the requisite words. The new Bech—which will form part of a trilogy, like the Rabbit group—is such a production.

After fifteen years of fallowness, Bech marries his Gentile Bea, becomes fertile, and produces his fourth book, its title going from *Easy Money* to *Think Big.* The success of the new novel thrusts Bech into fame, even as he recognizes he has lost whatever talent he had; and now, in his early fifties, he goes through the motions, waiting for a frisson. Midlife crises require fresh sensations. He is still an obsessive womanizer, approaching each encounter with recognition that it solves nothing and yet it is a form of life. But Bech is unexamined, inspected solely for inadequacies, and his sense of being carried along by market and expectations—a potentially notable theme—is not given context. That he recognizes the plaudits are false confers no distinction, exerts no influence. Updike offers no alternatives. To stress these aspects of the book is another way of saying it is insufficiently diverting. Even Updike's mockery of a strained, George Steiner review of Bech sounds hollow, missing the true Steiner vainglory.

Updike dissipates several episodes. In "Three Illuminations in the Life of an American Author," a Rimbaudian lark, Bech is paid $1.50 per signature to sign 28,500 tip-in sheets for an edition of his *Brother Pig.* For this he can choose his mate on a Caribbean vacation, his quota being two thousand signatures per day for two weeks. What begins as a lark becomes, predictably, a nightmare, as Bech loses control not only of his signature but of his identity. The blankness he has experienced as a writer now comes home as blankness with his own signature; but the episode, potentially witty, loses energy and direction. Several of these skits appeared originally in *Playboy* magazine—"Australia and Canada," "Bech Third-Worlds It," and "The Holy Land"—where amid cheesecake they may have seemed in keeping with the context. As part of a book, where reader expectations rise, they are curiously flattened out: vaudeville skirmishes, not chapters; performances for one's audience, not aspects of Bech's progress. "Australia and Canada," in particular, seems exhausted, perhaps a verbal reflection of Bech's own extended journeys from Up Above to Down Under. Women pop up as a given of Bech's life, but they are lifeless, his response lifeless; on the page, they all look alike.

"Bech Wed" is the longest and most worked episode, providing Updike with a familiar suburban setting, in Ossining, where his friend John Cheever lived. He is very good on the town as a backdrop for blacks, a kind of Southern village on the Hudson, once "filled with ice cream and marching music," only now sliding into somnolence. Tucked away at the top of a huge Victorian house, Bech is prodded by Bea to write and he does. But the writing of *Think Big* and its unexpected success exacerbate the differences between Bech and his Gentile princess. Marriage, suburban life, WASP friends, young people and their problems are not for Bech, and he breaks the marriage by sleeping with Bea's sister, his onetime lover. Yet the quickie in bed as well as its aftermath really fails to matter; Bech is so paper thin by now that nothing surprises or amuses. He is back in New York when the episode ends, ready for the inevitable cocktail party, "White on White." Here a female mud wrestler catches his eye. In every aspect, Updike has been here before. *Bech Is Back* slides into perfunctoriness—first some rabbit, then some Bech, then more rabbit, now more Bech. At this stage, Updike seems to receive reviewer plaudits for any fare. They do his real talent a disservice.

In *The Group* (1963), Mary McCarthy characteristically provides a society within a society: here with 1930s Vassar graduates; in *Cannibals and Missionaries,* several liberals setting out for Iran, accompanied by millionaire art collectors; in *The Groves of Academe,* the English Department of Jocelyn College; in *Birds of America,* a flock of birds. While this group functions within the larger society, it never really stands for that society, since McCarthy's grouping is so special. By working within a group, her equivalent of the squad or platoon in a war novel, she can exert control. Yet such focus is also a disadvantage, for it implies that nothing eccentric or unusual will penetrate, only what reason dictates. Here, McCarthy has measured her talents, recognized she cannot bend, and controls by forbidding expansion beyond the group.

McCarthy's work is characterized by two dimensions, both of which help to curb excessive individuality. The first is the idea of the inner society, whose other members act as pressure. Mere acquiescence to the group idea reinforces some form of social behavior. The second method is by way of wit, traditional notions of comedy used to contain excessive individuality or ego. One thinks of George Meredith in his novels and in his "Essay on Comedy," where he defines comedy as that element which seeks out egoism and vanity, driving people toward norms of behavior. But McCarthy is interested in rooting out egregiousness. What has been called maliciousness in her wit is really not that, but a strong sense of what in the nineteenth century was known as propriety. McCarthy had the reputation in the thirties as daring and adventuruous, even wicked, but overall she was taken with mediation, proportion, classical virtues. She was appalled by excesses surrounding her, politically most of all, but also socially and culturally. Her method may be Meredithian, but her didacticism derives from Ecclesiastes: the world as a vanity fair.

In *The Group,* Harald Peterson and Kay Strong—she of Vassar, class of '33, he of Reed, '27—marry on the first page.* Certain of their lives, they plan every detail of their future years. She will work at Macy's; he will progress as a man of the theater until he becomes an internationally known director. They will live in a certain kind of apartment, in a certain kind of neighborhood; and they will apportion their time down to minutes and hours. He will cook, when he has the time; she will learn from him. The background, we recall, was the Depression years. But even poverty is treated as something they could manage. As McCarthy comments: "Great wealth was a frightful handicap; it insulated you from living. The depression, whatever else you could say about it, had been a truly wonderful thing for the propertied classes; it had waked a lot of them up to the things that really counted."

Harald and Kay are not heroical creatures in McCarthy's treatment. Their ego has supplanted common sense, and like ancient rulers riddled with hubris, they must be reduced. The marriage occurs at the very beginning, and the rest of the novel charts its dissolution. McCarthy's wit does not destroy them, but diminishes their expectations. Even the spelling of Harald's name is an affectation.

The structure of the novel is such that the Depression recalls everyone to some kind of reality, despite the expectations Vassar has raised in them; despite the wealth and status that many of the eight young women continue to enjoy throughout the economic slump. The point is significant: even those who have been relatively unaffected by the Depression's enormous disruptions are forced to seek different proportions in their lives. When Harald and Kay try to escape from all historical entanglements, McCarthy can identify them as among Meredith's vain and egoistic creatures. They must be shot down, as later, in a kinder way, Peter Levi is shot down in *Birds of America,* or in a more vitriolic way, Dr. Henry Mulcahy in *The Groves of Academe.*

Pulling against the Depression, the "now" experience, is the memory of the Vassar years. As the young women head out into jobs, marriage, affairs, trips abroad, their collective memory of Vassar is of some archetypal paradise, the Eden which lies deep in their

collective unconscious as the kind, good place. The exchange of one society for another is vastly uneven, for Vassar raised expectations no society beyond it could satisfy. Unlike Rugby or Winchester, Vassar was not continuous with or a preparation for life; it deceived about life. Here is McCarthy's entering wedge: to present a walled-in Garden and then to eject her young women from it, Eves turned out.

This very conception, of Vassar as Garden, the world as unfamiliar and even alien, helps to support McCarthy's mockery. Yet so persuasive is her satire that little remains; the young women, *apart* from the ways in which McCarthy can mock them, are not persuasive. What they do, how they think, how they respond to stimuli outside the walls of Vassar College might have been of greater interest if McCarthy had been able to write about them in the thirties; but by the sixties, their pursuit of independence, romance, jobs had less thrust. In a real sense, McCarthy was trapped by her own sense of the material: not daring enough for the sixties; not sufficiently varied in her characters to permit them to break from her satire; too committed to her satirical means to provide alternative modes of existence.

Even the Depression recedes as a compelling phenomenon. We never observe its true deathlike effect: a nerve gas, spread by winds, which enters into every breath. Thus, the idea of the group within a larger body—social, economic, political—rarely works; Roosevelt enters only occasionally, and toward the end we hear of the war in Europe. The decade is spanned: Kay is buried at twenty-nine when France has fallen and the Luftwaffe is bombing England. That is, in effect, the end of the Vassar years, the final ejection from the Garden: Kay's fall from the window of the Vassar Club and the Depression winding down because of war.

With *Letting Go* (1962) and *When She Was Good* (1967), the sixties became for Philip Roth a period of stylistic interludes. The danger, which he was only partially able to overcome, was his desire to reflect the fifties, an effort which led particularly into *Letting Go.* Also, his probe of moral themes in both novels took him into areas of didacticism and earnestness which were unsuited to his more feral verbal talents; so that in a real sense these two novels led nowhere in his development. *Portnoy,* in 1969, indicated the breakthrough which has, at this writing, culminated in *Zuckerman Unbound.* What Roth more than anything else had to overcome was the tremendous success of his first volume, and his strategy was (1) to

---

*The final section is devoted to Kay's funeral. The progression is from Vassar as the one-time Eden, then to marriage, ending in death after ejection from the Garden. Her death: a "fall" from the twentieth floor of the Vassar Club.

respond to those who attacked him for anti-Semitism in *Goodbye, Columbus;* and (2) to provide a more balanced view of America poised to leap into a new era.

The choice of a title, *Letting Go,* suggests his dilemma. In one respect, to let go is to drown, as in Conrad's phrase about immersing oneself in the destructive element and then letting go when one can no longer hang on; but at another level, it offers the prospect of a new self, leaving oneself open to new experience, letting go of the old, embracing the new. In this regard, it becomes valedictory of the Eisenhower decade. Roth wanted both aspects of the phrase, and his two young men move alternately between one level and the other. The problem arises in that swing between "savagery and impotence" which both reject as unsuitable, and yet whose choice would have brought them out of passivity. Three of the four characters in fact have names with "heart": Paul and Libby Herz, and Martha Reganhart, whom Gabe Wallach chases. The stress on hearts, the rejection of savagery, the reaching toward impotence and passivity are all characteristic of the 1950s; but they do not adequately translate into viable fiction.

By avoiding extremes—neither impotence nor savagery—Gabe, as well as Paul, hopes to find a civilized center; but as the Eisenhower administration demonstrated, the rejection of extremes leads to deadening passivity. Such is the young man Paul also turns out to be: an emblem of the decade. Once he leaves Harvard, he lacks forward drive. Charming, serious, he has little focus or will, no positive energy or goals. Bellow's Augie March seems a shadowy presence; Oblomov the archetype. Paul attaches himself to other people and tries to discover how they can use him. An innocent in a savage world, he waits to be ground to dust. In linking his fortunes with Libby— a Catholic who becomes a Jewish convert—Paul falls into all the stereotypical disasters of the young: a mismatched marriage, no money, sexual problems, an abortion for her, an academic career which goes nowhere because he does not complete his dissertation. The latter is in creative writing, and while he insists on integrity, his English Department sees writing as a technical matter apart from style or feeling, or even form.

The more centrally located intelligence of the novel is Gabe, or Gabriel, a messenger of sorts, who fears throughout that the willed human being can fall into savage choices. He seeks honesty, and when he meets Libby Herz, toward whom he becomes very attached, their common love is Henry James, especially *The Portrait of a Lady.* Gabe, though, not

Libby, is a kind of Isabel Archer, the person who sacrifices and yet insists on choices: caught between a desire for martyrdom and a certain function. Lucy Nelson in *When She Was Good* is another version of Isabel Archer.

Roth then follows Gabe's career in great detail, but the array of detail does not add up to definition. He pursues Martha Reganhart, his opposite, a sloppy Gentile with two children. She is also sought after by a Jewish lawyer, Sid Jaffe, although her charms— except for a heavy sensuality—are difficult to discern. While involved in this no-win relationship, Gabe attempts to help the Herzes adopt a child. With this, we have several elements working, including the backgrounding of Martha as a victimized woman. In some way, Martha is seen as a foil for Libby; the former large and messy, the latter thin, ill, anemic. Caught among all these forces, Gabe dedicates himself to helping others: Martha and her children (one of whom kills the other), the Herzes in their disintegrating marriage, the adoption of a child for them, his own father, ad infinitum.

In a long letter to Libby which closes the book, Gabe indicates that he has lived as an indecisive man "on a hook." His own decisive moment came when he helped the adopted child, Rachel, and settled that issue for the Herzes; all of which he observes as an act of self-sacrifice. He does not want Libby to think that as a result of his efforts he is off the hook: "I'm not, I can't be, I don't even want to be—not until I make some sense of the larger hook I'm on." Gabe closes with "Yours" and admits a guilt which Roth has not made fully plausible. There is in this intelligent novel a reaching for a grand theme which we only occasionally arrive at. In part, Roth's inability to perceive his way derived from his failure to find suitable voices for this kind of novel. But even if he had, I feel the voices would have proved to be the wrong kind of language for his talents, which lay elsewhere.

During the period 1962–67, from *Letting Go* to *When She Was Good,* Roth was, in fact, incubating very different voices. In "How Did You Come to Write That Book, Anyway?" he speaks of the origins of Alexander Portnoy, which started as "The Jewboy," then merged with a play never produced, called "The Nice Jewish Boy," Dustin Hoffman *(The Graduate)* destined as a vague Portnoy type. "Jewboy" was aggressive and marginal, Cain, whereas "Nice Jewish Boy" was socially acceptable, Abel; the two sides of the eventual Portnoy. Meanwhile, Roth labored on "Time Away," "In the Middle of America," "Saint Lucy," all early versions of *When She Was*

Good, a book which would pay his moral debts. Before the latter's completion, however, he worked on a long scatological monologue, a Lenny Bruce routine: a slide show of the private parts, fore and aft, of celebrities: "President Johnson's testicles, Jean Genet's anus, Mickey Mantle's penis, Margaret Mead's breasts, and Elizabeth Taylor's pubic bush." Fortunately, except perhaps for the latter, this project was abandoned, including the several thousands of words on adolescent masturbation. Tandem with all this furious projection was an autobiographical fiction based on his own upbringing in New Jersey, called "Portrait of the Artist." Upstairs from his family lived the Portnoys, and they gradually became blended with a family Roth had described five years earlier, called "Some New Jewish Stereotypes." He had the basic ingredients for his *Portnoy* stew, added the analyst, started "A Jewish Patient Begins His Analysis," discovered *his* voice, Portnoy's, Spielvogel's ear: "Now vee may perhaps to begin. Yes?"

With this, Roth had the major line of his next decade of work, running from *Portnoy* through *My Life as a Man* (where Peter Tarnopol relates the adventures of Nathan Zuckerman) to *The Ghost Writer*

(more Nathan Zuckerman) and *Zuckerman Unbound* (1981), which reaches back to 1969 and *Portnoy. Zuckerman Unbound* charts Nathan's overwhelming success and notoriety as the author of *Carnovsky (Portnoy).* Success brings more than money; it threatens every aspect of Nathan's life, most of all his ability to work. It displaces his center, turns him into a celebrity, and exhibits, both wittily and with much cultural detail, how America destroys while it celebrates. It also returns Nathan to his family, for his father dies, with "bastard" on his lips, intended for the author of *Carnovsky.* Nathan must pay and pay, for even his younger brother turns on him: "To you everything is disposable! Everything is exposable! Jewish morality, Jewish endurance, Jewish wisdom, Jewish families—everything is grist for your fun-machine. . . . Love, marriage, children, what the hell do you care? To you it's all fun and games. . . . And the worst is how we protect you from knowing what you really are!" The novel ends with Nathan returning to the old Newark neighborhoods, now in disarray, the past effaced. Zuckerman is unbound, liberated from *Portnoy.* The book is an ending and a beginning.

Versions of the New

Although we perceive the 1960s in retrospect as a decade of innovative thought, of novelty in our cultural as well as in our political and social life, its examples of the new do not necessarily supersede those from the previous decade or from the earlier sixties, before real change was apparent. Hawkes's 1950s fiction, Gaddis's *The Recognitions,* Pynchon's *V.,* Heller's *Catch-22* to a limited extent, Barth's *Giles Goat-Boy* in some ways, Barthelme's *Snow White* and stories, Wurlitzer's minimalist fictions, Kosinski's *Steps* are all indicative of the modern influence, with most of them coming well before that "cleaning of the stables" which characterized the decade. In their way, they helped that opening out culturally, joining with comparable developments in poetry, art, sculpture. Hawkes, Gaddis, Pynchon, Barth, Barthelme were the tribunes of the new, well

before we fully recognized the new was upon us.

By the end of the decade, with additional Pynchon, some Robert Coover, a novel by Robert Stone, work by Ishmael Reed and Steve Katz, two startling novels by Joseph McElroy, we observe that the new in fiction has taken hold, bucking the more popular serious novel as practiced by Bellow, Mailer, Roth, Styron, etc. Thus we had clearly for the first time in postwar American fiction a branching off of two kinds of serious fiction: that which eschewed the modern, often passionately (as with Bellow and Mailer); that which, just as passionately, attempted to find in modernism ways of keeping the novel going as a developmental genre. Questions of entertainment arose, for critics and most general readers were attuned to the first group, who gathered in the larger share of the favorable reviews that not only generate sales but win awards, although such reviews are often from the very people who cannot adjust to modernism or the new, failing to comprehend it or finding it lacking in entertainment value.

The modernists (or postmodernists) who set themselves against "accessibility" in favor of stretching the genre—for good or ill—found themselves working in five major areas, any one or two of which suggested their stance: areas of innovative language, which has always distinguished between traditional and new; areas of subject matter—once again a separating point, although less obviously so in the new era of print freedom; areas of technique, that withdrawal from traditional narrative and character development, that stress on abstract forms—once again a characteristic distinction between traditional and new; areas of "usage" made of Kafka, whose influence pervaded both kinds of novelists; finally, areas concerning Borges, whose fabulations, narrative strategies, and inversions of reality have threaded their way through American fiction, traditionalist and modernist alike.

Pynchon's *The Crying of Lot 49,* which seems slight because of its brevity, is a major modernist achievement: a novel to be read not so much as one would read other novels, but as a work which serves as an experimental development of a major talent, whose flowering would occur in *Gravity's Rainbow.* Pynchon bridges most of the five categories cited above, owing more, perhaps, to Gaddis than to Kafka, but otherwise creating new voices, cutting through standard narrative devices, establishing different principles of observation. In his way, Robert Coover in the long story "The Babysitter" and his first novel, *The Origin of the Brunists,* attempted breakthroughs in both technique and subject matter; as did Robert Stone in *A Hall of Mirrors,* which functions through reflections instead of expected realities. Such visual deceptiveness became emblematic of 1960s culture: the self mirrored, remirrored, refracted, fragmented, reconstituted. With Steve Katz, we have the obverse of minimalism: a stress on spareness, but presented with fullness, so that our perception is disoriented. Similarly, with Ishmael Reed and, to some extent, George Cain, the use of a specialized language disorients, which is to say that linguistic modes approximate subject.

One of the failings of the more traditional novelists has been their rejection of language that would accommodate their subject matter. Thus, Bellow's characters fall apart, but their linguistic medium remains the same as when they are whole; there is little aware-ness that forms of expression must change to reflect altered states of consciousness. In our more modernist fictions, this sense obtains, and very possibly language, voices, linguistic modes more than anything else separate the traditional from the new; although narrative experimentation—sharp cutting, montage, unclear arrangements and sequences—is not to be discounted.

Besides Pynchon, Joseph McElroy best represents the new. His debut in the sixties with *A Smuggler's Bible* and *Hind's Kidnap* carried forward a career concerned with positioning and locating. McElroy has learned all the lessons of modernism and has moved beyond assimilation to extension. He explores not only the disorder beyond order—which any contemporary novelist can do—but the patterns of order which lie beyond disorder, a transcendental potentiality. Film, its usages and dimensions, is brought to bear upon fiction, and phenomenological resonances become not magical but central. Further, time/space expectations are disrupted, so that McElroy's novels locate themselves in an intermediary zone of consciousness.

The Crying of Lot 49 (1966), a novel of fewer than 50,000 words, alters our perception of seemingly stable institutions. Here, Pynchon works the new with confidence that his readers will follow him, although this novel has not caught on in the way of *V.* and *Gravity's Rainbow.* Like Oedipus, Oedipa searches—not for ancestral background, but for a worldwide conspiracy, an alternative mail system operated by a group called the Tristeros. She is Oedipa Maas—mass, bulk, existence, presence; or *más,* Spanish for "more," as Tristero in one of its incarnations is "sad" or "bereaved." But *The Crying of Lot 49* is really a brief statement about the 1960s. It was for Pynchon an interlude, a valley between a very long work about the fifties and another about the seventies—all three trying to comprehend America in the postwar years. Pynchon is an interpretive novelist, obsessively seeking meaning in metaphors: in *V.,* the Edenesque Vheissu; here, the mail conspiracy; in *Gravity's Rainbow,* a technological paradise which squeezes out individual choice and freedom.

The Crying, an auctioneer's term, is also a shriek; Oedipa's metaphor is one of "stripping":

> They are stripping from me, she said subvocally—feeling like a fluttering curtain in a very high window, moving up to then out over the abyss—they are stripping away, one by one, my men. My shrink, pursued by Israelis [for acts committed in the camps], has

gone mad; my husband [a disk jockey], on LSD, gropes like a child further and further into the rooms and endless rooms of the elaborate candy house of himself and away, hopelessly away, from what has passed, I was hoping forever, for love; my one extra marital fella [Metzger, a lawyer] has eloped with a depraved 15-year-old; my best guide back to the Trystero [Driblette, the director of Wharfinger's *The Courier's Tragedy*] has taken a Brody. Where am I?

Oedipa, like Oedipus, is lost amidst patterns she cannot understand. Without knowing why, she has been made the executrix of the estate of Pierce Inverarity, with whom she had an affair before her marriage. Carrying out her role leads her deeper into conspiracy, the most mysterious aspect of which is W.A.S.T.E.—"We Await Silent Tristero's Empire." A peculiar knotted or muted post horn, first seen by her on the wall of a latrine, suddenly begins to appear everywhere. It is at the heart of the conspiracy of Tristeros, who have dropped out of America, suicides or would-be suicides. Having given up hope not only of the mail services, but of America itself, they use counterfeit stamps, and mail letters in waste containers.

Pynchon probes deep into the 1960s, when the literary need was to find some fictional equivalent for inexplicable events. Oedipa's quest for knowledge, which forms the entire narrative of the novel, is an attempt to derive sanity and order from incoherent experiences. Everyone she knows has gone underground, split off, divided: her husband wild on LSD, her shrink paranoiac, her associates severed from normal patterns, herself near the brink. Her search for the meaning of the muted post horn, which takes her ever deeper into Tristero mysteries, is her search for America. It is fraught with deception.

The Crying of Lot 49 is a meeting point of Pynchon's concerns, that linkage he sees as contemporary America: running down, laws of conservation fighting against diminution; individual choice struggling to remain viable; and words themselves traduced, as symbolized by the manipulation of the mails. The way into all this seemingly disparate material is by way of Pierce Inverarity's estate; to execute his estate is to explore America of the 1960s. Oedipa achieves "recognitions" only by undertaking the quest. Had she remained indifferent or had she settled for surfaces, not probes, she would have become as counterfeit as those around her. By digging in, Oedipa becomes *más* or Maas.*

With all his disguises and brilliant management of narrative strategies, Pynchon has in part fallen back on picaresque narrative, which allows Oedipa to have sequential encounters. Coherence derives, ultimately, from the search itself, which continues as the novel ends and she awaits the actual "crying of Lot 49" and its bidder. Metzger, a glamorous lawyer, explains how roles shift, how deceptive our appearances are; until the nature of all activity becomes blurred, like the Tristero stamps later. "But our beauty lies . . . in this extended capacity for convolution. A lawyer in a courtroom, in front of any jury, becomes an actor, right? Raymond Burr is an actor, impersonating a lawyer, who in front of a jury becomes an actor. Me, I'm a former actor who became a lawyer. They've done the pilot film of a TV series, in fact, based loosely on my career, starring my friend Manny di Presso, a one-time lawyer who quit his firm to become an actor. Who in this pilot plays me, an actor becoming a lawyer reverting periodically to being an actor." The film can itself be repeated endlessly, replicating convolutions and deceptions.

This confusion of roles begins Oedipa's "California scene," the emblem of America. At a motel, Echo Courts, she has met Miles, who patterns himself after the Beatles; then the Paranoids, a rock group recalling the Whole Sick Crew of *V*. She is now in San Narciso, "holy self," and she has observed Yoyodyne,* a giant of the aerospace industry which Pierce owns a piece of—we recall the Yoyodyne logo from *V.,* where Benny works in the shadow of SHROUD and STRIKE. Oedipa is being readied for that succession of weirdos, creeps, and crazed scientists strewn across the path leading to Lot 49, for (she thinks) the ultimate uncovering of the conspiracy. Along the way, even she alters shape, for to prepare herself to play Strip Botticelli, a form of strip poker, she dresses in endless rounds of undergarments, dresses, slacks. Whatever is revealed to her, she reveals little to others. Unlike Oedipus, Oedipa remains a mystery.

One of the most bizarre elements is offered her as "Maxwell's Demon," the result of an encounter with a Yoyodyne executive, one Stanley Koteks—Pyn-

*She also becomes a modern, 1960s woman, who refuses to collapse while all the men around her are succumbing.

*Literally, "yo-yo power"—part of that world of mass (Maas), thermodynamics, and other scientific elements which become a grid for *Lot.*

chon's names often become too cute. Koteks, who seems to Oedipa a step toward the disclosure of the horn symbol, explains the Demon's workings: it is essentially a sorting machine, and therefore a preparation for the Tristero operation, based on sorting. James Clerk Maxwell postulated a tiny intelligence whose aim was to violate the Second Law of Thermodynamics by getting something for nothing—once again a key to the Tristero fraud. The Demon, sitting in a box among air molecules that moved at different random speeds, sorted out the fast ones from the slow ones. Since fast molecules have more energy than slow ones, a concentration of sufficient fast ones gives an area of high temperature. By using the difference in temperature between the hot region of the box and the cooler part, one can drive a heat engine. "Since the Demon only sat and sorted, you wouldn't have put any real work into the system": it is perpetual motion, antinature, self-perpetuating, the ultimate for San Narciso.

Koteks explains further that John Nefastis, at Berkeley, perfected a Nefastis Machine, based on Maxwell's Demon; in that, mental work provided thermodynamic energy. It was possible by intense concentration upon a photo of Maxwell, to make the Demon work either the right or the left cylinder through raising its temperature; this would expand the air in that cylinder and push a piston, activating the entire system. The idea works, however, only for "Sensitives," those "with the gift." Oedipa lacks the gift. Pynchon's figure for the sixties is not simply zany, but a combination of science and pseudo science, what he would elaborate so intricately in *Gravity's Rainbow* as symbolic of the last half century.

Pynchon now begins to enter territory familiar to us by way of Borges and Nabokov: that use of words, literary texts, and subtexts as means of verifying something which may have existed in history; although the very ambiguity of a text may create an ambiguous history. Oedipa now needs some verification in literature of what she senses has been occurring in life, in the historical development of the Tristero conspiracy to defraud the mails. The chief clue comes in the performance of Wharfinger's *The Courier's Tragedy,* directed by Randolph Driblette. In the fourth act, Gennaro, played by Driblette, utters these lines: "No hallowed skein of stars can ward, I trow, / Who's once been set his tryst with Trystero." That sets Oedipa on the trail of how those words came to that performance, since they are a corruption of the established text. She pursues the lead from one source

to another, and reaches the expert on Wharfinger, one Professor Bortz, whose life style is that of a Hollywood star. The pursuit of these lines, played out in Borgean-Nabokovian terms, leads back to Yoyodyne, where an executive who had been fired had decided to "fire himself" with gasoline, as he had seen a Buddhist monk in Vietnam do. When the effort failed, he noted that the gasoline had turned some of the stamps in his pocket white; and when he peeled off a stamp he observed the image of the post horn.

The intricacies increase: worlds within worlds, deceptions and fantasies within fantasies and deceptions. The suicide having failed, the executive, who had discovered his wife on the rug with an efficiency executive, swears off love. " 'From this day I swear to stay off of love: hetero, homo, bi, dog or cat, car, every kind there is. I will found a society of isolates, dedicated to this purpose, and this sign, revealed by the same gasoline that almost destroyed me, will be its emblem.' " This society, of failed suicides who have sworn off love, an archetype for California's self-help groups, keeps in touch through the secret delivery system, W.A.S.T.E. Oedipa now begins to see the sign everywhere; it is as though, once she is keyed in to the symbol, the conspiracy has become public.

What troubles her—and here she is a typical Pynchon protagonist—is whether or not she has fantasized the entire matter. It is this stage which is essential for Pynchon; for while he shares the sense of an incomprehensible America with a dozen other writers, he differs in his ability to call into question whether America really exists. Here, once again, he joins with Gaddis, who through layers of alternating counterfeiting and recognitions tried to penetrate to the real. Under all those layers of clothes when she plays Strip Botticelli, Oedipa is America herself, somewhere to be touched and penetrated, if one can find her.

To reify what she has discovered, she seeks out her analyst, Dr. Hilarius, who, in a role reversal, is now the patient. Oedipa finds herself trying to save him. In his belief that the Israelis are after him for acts he may have committed in Buchenwald, on "experimentally-induced insanity," he has become violent and destructive. Hilarius, "put in charge of faces," had developed a look which can drive a man insane, and now he feels the Israelis have caught up with him, like Eichmann, and will charge him with complicity or kill him on the spot. Oedipa finds his world has split, even as she seeks help about hers.

When she turns to her disk jockey husband,

Mucho Maas(!), she finds he has split off from reality on acid. She returns to Bortz, for at least his guidance is connected to hard information. He discovers his own edition of Wharfinger has been bowdlerized by the publishers, K. da Chingado ["Fucked"] and Company. And what about the Vatican's pornographic *Courier's Tragedy?* Gradually, she learns more of the origins of Tristero, but information about its founding, in the late sixteenth century, only leads to further questions, and all "could be traced also back to the Inverarity estate."

If the estate is all, is America, then Tristero—the symbol of fraud—is America as well. There are several possibilities: either she stumbled onto a network in which X number of Americans are communicating secretly, while "reserving their lies . . . for the official government delivery system"; or in some paranoiac way she perceives that a plot has been mounted against her, down to forged stamps and ancient books. Or she is hallucinating. Only the first possibility is "real": Americans are so distrustful of government institutions that they communicate secretly with each other, creating an alternative form of "communication," which is a way of life.

There remain, however, the Tristero forgeries, the stamps the mail fraud had used since the late 1840s, when the U.S. government carried out postal reform and cut away independent carriers. The Tristeros organized and maintained their own mail systems; and the stamps they used then and later are to be sold as Lot 49. The bidder, whose presence is expected at any moment, will indicate to Oedipa where the trail will lead. "The auctioneer cleared his throat. Oedipa settled back, to await the crying of lot 49."

There is another aspect to *Crying,* which is the parodic, the names, activities, use of language; the mockery of language itself in the use of an alternative mail system, a way of bringing words to us. Connected to this is Oedipa's discovery that each effort at creating order leads only to further disorder, each discovery of disorder has behind it order. The identification of the bidder for Lot 49 will not close the issue, but extend it in further spirals and cycles. The Demon in Maxwell's plan will not settle anything; although it seemed to Maxwell to decrease entropy, in actuality it may increase it. Rather than contradict the Second Law of Thermodynamics, it may verify it; and order and disorder, rather than being sorted out, are even more intensely intermixed.

Further associated with the Demon is the quantification of information: the fact that the more the Demon seems to sort, the more disorder seems to be created. A scientific metaphor of orderings turns out to be Pynchon's way of suggesting ever-increasing disorder.* His use of language, as parody, as semblance of disorder, as pure rhetoric, and as repetition, is to discover the artistic component of the entropic state, of Maxwell's Demon. Besides the sorting of mail and correspondents according to W.A.S.T.E. or according to the regular mails, there are innumerable linguistic situations. Oedipa's husband, Mucho, is a disk jockey whose words are redistorted in transmission—thus, he calls her Edna Mosh on the air, to approximate what will come out as Oedipa Maas. Oedipa herself hears and mishears the two lines about trysts and Tristero, first in the Quarto edition, then in the Whitechapel, finally when she observes a group of children at jump rope: " 'Tristoe, Tristoe, one, two, three.' " In the Tristero form of communication, W.A.S.T.E., letters are mailed in wastebaskets. The "Thurn and Taxis" from *The Courier's Tragedy* also comes out distorted, formed and reformed, even in Joycean lines such as "Turning taxi from across the sea." Pynchon transforms words even as he distorts them, a Joycean plot.

Oedipa's search for information, like Oedipus's, is strewn with riddles; in her pursuit, the divulgation of additional information only adds to her confusion. Knowledge does not clarify what she is seeking. In the classical use of such a search, self-discovery was the goal, although it could mean destruction. For Pynchon, where parody is more apparent than tragedy, seeking leads not to coherence or order or wholeness—which is the same as self-discovery—but to further reaches of distortion and misinformation, behind which order may lurk. Each time Oedipa senses herself on the edge of more knowledge, she is really

*In an excellent essay on the novel, called "Maxwell's Demon, Entropy, Information," Anne Mangel demonstrates the relationship between entropy or disorder and information theory. She asserts that the more entropy or disorder there is, the greater is the need for information. I think she is basically correct in linking disorder and information, but I disagree with the finality of the association as she describes it. I connect the entropic vision in Pynchon more to a rejection of 1950s philosophies which vaunted America than to any purely scientific accounting, without discounting the latter. The problem with pursuing technological underpinning is that each scientific system carries a different meaning: Maxwell this, Slizard's correction of Maxwell, and so on. More to the point, it seems, is to seek Pynchon's cultural roots in the fifties, where the matrix of his ideas was formed.

staring into the abyss. Her desire to seek order with Dr. Hilarius, for instance, simply throws her into a deeper quandary. Every meeting, in the Greek Way bar, for example, creates further smoke screens, there into the Inamorati Anonymous Society, those committed to nonlove; or else into memories of Inverarity, whose last vocal contact with her was a series of shuffles from Slavic tones "modulated to comic-Negro, then on to the hostile Pachuco dialect, full of chingas and maricones [fucks and faggots]; then a Gestapo officer asking her in shrieks did she have relatives in Germany and finally his Lamont Cranston voice."

This confusion of voices, as if from the dead Pierce, becomes continuous with vocal confusions and misleading signs. Pynchon has dragged up postwar counterfeit, words which must be distorted to sound right, signs which have multilevel meaning and confusion, voices which say this or that, imitation at every level, organizations which represent whims, people floating through an existence which lacks anchorage, which reflects only fancies. This is, in its parodic insistence, a very condemnatory book, much more moralistic than *V.* Under the mod, hyped-up writer is a stern teacher. *Lot* was, for Pynchon, a way into America of the previous decade, a critique not only of word fumblers but of those receiving the word; takers as well as givers. In this respect, Pynchon follows the lead taken by Gaddis, for whom confusion was the sole way to unsettle, to lead to recognitions.

Pynchon uses order and disorder as tensions. It is incorrect to see him as an advocate either of entropy (disorder) or of order gained through technology. His area of play is dualistic. Mass (Maas) man is the result of both technology and free choice, of ordered society and disorder. The disorder that lies beyond in all Pynchon fiction is also a concomitant of the drive toward individual liberty. Oedipa may be snared by Pierce Inverarity's will, but she also opens herself up to life and possibilities by following the leads in Pierce's acquisitions. She enters history, crime, terrible passions, deceptions, imitational feelings; and through these tests out tensions between hallucination and reality. Experience is its own reward! As a critique of America of the previous decade, *Lot 49* demonstrates opening up. "Entropy," which Pynchon has latched on to and popularized, is not simply running down; it is also running, process. As he says in his story "Entropy," there are closed circuits in certain word usages, but there are also words in-

volved that contain "Ambiguity. Redundance. Irrelevance, even. Leakage." This "noise" may, as he warns, "screw up your signal," but it is also a form of life; diminution but not the end.

With Robert Stone's *A Hall of Mirrors* (1967), and with the first of Robert Coover's and Joseph McElroy's fiction, we begin to see firmer outlines of the Gaddis-Pynchon generation. Such writers are committed not only to exploring modernism but to removing themselves from the established and popular line associated with Mailer, Bellow, Malamud, etc. They have been vilified by many reviewers as "academic writers,"* but then a far greater group of writers, the first wave of modernists, suffered more intense vilification from comparable reviewers wedded to outmoded literary traditions. Each generation of innovators must undergo a similar "martyrdom." This generation is fortunate in that a university audience is there to read and understand what the reviewer would like to bury.

Stone's novel suggests a life experienced in reflections: love as self-love, Pynchon's San Narciso embodied. What makes the novel new is that mirrors reflect the system one is attempting to escape. They proliferate systems and selves even while reflecting or distorting them. Stone's chief character, Rheinhardt (whose name recalls Rinehart of *Invisible Man*), is a mirror image of the Harlem numbers man, the "cool cat" hipster, albeit a failed one. A former music man, Rheinhardt had his greatest moment when an audition for which he played the Mozart Clarinet Quintet was successful. But for every "high" he achieves, he must seek a "low." Rheinhardt is a man who has assimilated and embodied doom; personal destruction defines him, and the vehicle is alcohol.

Unlike Malcolm Lowry's Firmin, he is able to function, though in reflected ways. His journey to the bottom takes him to the most run-down and bumstrewn sections of New Orleans; but his background

---

*The wittiest critic is Gore Vidal, who refers to such fiction as "American Plastic," including Barth, Barthelme, Gass, Pynchon, all of whom he considers to be deep "into R and D (Research and Development) as opposed to the old-fashioned R and R (Rest and Recuperation)." Vidal's instincts may all be to the good, but he is so intent on eliminating the kind of fiction which threatens his own that he condemns before understanding. His essay on Italo Calvino shows how he can enter into a great talent alien to his own; so that his assaults on the modern and new would seem to be focused mainly on American models. *Plus ça change . . .*

—he is educated, well-spoken, articulate—gets him work, first in a chemical company, then as a radio announcer. As an announcer, he is a disembodied voice that reflects the empire of Mr. Bingamon, whose politics are racist, reactionary, completely opposite to everything Rheinhardt in his more sober moments represents. The job gives him some status at the same time he becomes a "hall of mirrors." Whatever integrity he had no longer exists, and when free of Bingamon he loses still another self in drink.

Parallel to Rheinhardt are others whose careers are reflections, or else journeys into distorted images. Morgan Rainey is a Harvard graduate who attaches himself to lost causes. A welfare investigator in New Orleans, he thinks he is doing a vital job—helping needy blacks—but is actually the agent of a conspiracy to move these people from the welfare rolls. He is an innocent in a highly structured world of deception, a hall of mirrors that contains the deluded blacks themselves; Lester Clotho, a black who works for the white agencies; and the agencies, out to make political capital from padded welfare rolls. Rainey moves like an innocent fool, a Prince Myshkin in his sweetness and decency, and of course he stumbles at every turn.

Geraldine is another denizen of the lower depths. Horribly scarred by an oyster knife wielded by her gangster boyfriend, Geraldine has drifted down to New Orleans, the victim of male persecution. She is interviewed for a whorehouse, but rejects the opportunity; she then becomes, literally, a marked woman: marked by her scars but also by warnings that she never hustle in the city on her own. She meets Rheinhardt at Bingamon's chemical plant: the scarred Geraldine, a victim who reflects the woman's position, and Rheinhardt, a victim of his own self-destructiveness. In the building they move to, they encounter Rainey, another loser in the sweepstakes.

Rheinhardt has obtained the chemical job by way of a former friend, Farley the Sailor, a failed confidence man who is now a preacher, running the Church of the Vision of the Power of Love. With him, we are back into the world of O'Connor's *Wise Blood,* or those stories of demon preachers obsessed with conversion. In his earlier career, Farley recalls that crowd of crazies in *V.* who run from enterprise to enterprise, hoping to evade systems.

The young Farley, Rheinhardt, Geraldine—all those, ironically, who come under the umbrella of Bingamon—are on the run from systems. Self-destruction is preferable. Farley has thrown himself away on Natasha Kaplan, a waitress at the Italia Irredenta Coffee House behind Carnegie Hall. The crowd they run with, as well as the names, are reminiscent, once again, of Pynchon, and Rheinhardt at this stage resembles Benny Profane.

In New Orelans, overshadowing all is the bulky figure of Bingamon. His radio station, WUSA, is dedicated to patriotism; it is system itself, as is the chemical plant where Rheinhart first finds work. Bingamon represents America as it moves ever closer to a totalitarian state; his conception of a free world is one with a benevolent tyrant as ruler, himself as model. But Bingamon is not alone. He is part of a larger political structure which aims to purify, purge, and restructure America along truly Christian and military lines. Bingamon's culture is really a counterculture of sorts, one that runs marginal to the main structure in Washington and is, in a sense, its mirror reflection. Taking cues from Washington, it intensifies the image, as if microscopically magnified. In Stone's broadly satirical treatment of this reactionary counterculture, the book at times loses its momentum in childish mockery.

The narrative moves inexorably toward the climactic renewal jubilee, a gigantic outpouring of religious revivalism, patriotism, and dedication to American principles. It will reflect the racism, nationalism, and ethnic exclusiveness of the true American. Present are military men of the highest rank, a movie star named King Walyoe (a broad representation of John Wayne), and various assorted figures from the artistic, political, and religious community. The jubilee is nothing less than Armageddon, where the elect will be separated from the damned (blacks, Jews, ethnic minorities, those on welfare, outcasts). By implication, someone like Geraldine, marginal at all times, is doomed by such an outpouring; as will be Morgan Rainey and Rheinhardt, whose feelings are the true enemy for these people.

The jubilee, then, is a meeting of several key forces in America: it is, for Stone, a pageant of the country, a hall of mirrored images of America linked in the stadium. The stadium is itself ringed by police, and the revival becomes a paramilitary exercise, as much controlled by armed strength as by religious fervor. As early as the mid-sixties, Stone, writing the novel, saw that the American role in Vietnam was held together not only by the military but by religious elements which saw in anticommunism a form of military resolve. Armageddon, the battle between the forces of good and evil as described in The Book of

Revelation, is the location for America: the meeting ground of apocalypse through the bomb and potential for renewal through religious revivalism.

Intermixed with these elements are several others: the countering forces of marching blacks, protesters of every stripe, and the working classes, represented by S. B. Prothwaite. Sitting in a truck filled with dynamite, Prothwaite waits for the gates of the stadium to be opened so that he can drive in and blow up everyone within reach. His is the true vision of Armageddon, in which souls are joined, the death of all assured. What occurs thereafter will be up to God. Prothwaite will take his chances there, if he can take with him all those who have oppressed the workers. He sets out under a sign of his own: "YOU SHALL NOT CRUCIFY / S.B. PROTHWAITE UPON / A CROSS OF GOLD." He borrows Bryan's motto in order to establish his own credentials as part of that class kept under so that military and religion can rule. His natural allies are blacks; his natural enemy is Calvin Minnow, the local district attorney and spokesman for every oppressive cause. Joined by Morgan Rainey, who is unaware of the dynamite, Prothwaite will destroy everyone.

Rainey frustrates the main objective of the mission, although he and Prothwaite are blown sky high. Minnow remains, a small fish who leads the large. As violence increases and the revival gets out of control, Rheinhardt breaks from his role as spokesman on WUSA for Bingamon and his cohorts. Farley the Sailor, forgoing his disguise as a man of religion, beats Bingamon into insensibility, rifles his pockets and those of others (including King Walyoe), and makes off. Geraldine, who has been roving the stands, also attempts escape, but fails, the victim represented in the melee by Prothwaite and his sense of crucifixion. Sought out by the police, by men of all sorts and systems, once she loses Rheinhardt's protection she is snared; and her sole resource is suicide, with the chain of her jail bunk bed. "Mistake, mistake, she thought. Nobody could want this. But she knew there was no mistake. It was very familiar." Geraldine experiences remorse as she strangles, but she has little to repent, except having been.

Rheinhardt, escaping the jubilee and his role in it, comes out from under his disguise and exchanges Bingamon's message for his own form of self-destructiveness. When he hears of Geraldine's suicide, he sinks into an alcoholic fog and tries a personal Armageddon in a local bar. " 'They killed my girl,' " he intones as he threatens to " 'bust up the bar.' " His

final social commitment comes in his avowal to destroy; the hall of mirrors will, in a sense, be cracked, while the main arena, what has been reflected, will remain.

Earlier, Rheinhardt had tried to reflect what he felt, when he was searching for Geraldine. As he explains to a hooker named Nicaragua, he was going to pull off a trick. " 'I'm going to insert my cupped hands into my mouth and gripping my innards firmly, I am going to pull everything up until I am completely inside out. This is a very easy trick for me because I am what is known as an invert.' " Rheinhardt then elaborates on his trick, saying that when he is completely inverted, he will spread himself at her feet as a "gray ill-smelling film." He will become ectoplasm, with the smell and consistency of old Camembert. In the middle of this ectoplasm will be "a lot of crap-colored blue." This mess of blue will have little suckers on it, and these suckers, constantly hungry, must be fed at all times. Rheinhardt continues, in this manic description, that everything connected to his ectoplasmic structure is hungry, sexual, demanding. Chiefly, these blue suckers eat love, and he slurps his lips next to Nicaragua's ear.

Rheinhardt's crazy monologue, a Lenny Bruce routine, is all a matter of reflections, of inner and outer exchange, with inner given the functions of outer. His craziness is identified in his clairvoyance, his ability to perceive in this manic moment that whatever is outrageous can have as much truth as what is routine. That perception is for Rheinhardt, and for Stone, his awareness of the hall of mirrors. We see distorted images in the hall; we grope for reality in these distortions. And yet reality is truly mirrored in the distortions: it is precisely what they tell us. Barth called it being "lost in the funhouse." What we see exaggerated is not the distortion of reality but the very aspect of reality to which we must relate.

Like *A Hall of Mirrors,* Robert Coover's *The Origin of the Brunists* (1966) posits a modern society turned insane by its religious convictions. The Coover novel is not modernist in the sense of Pynchon and McElroy, but its angulation, its montage effects, and its shifting point of view help create the aura of modernism, more apparent in his books on baseball and Richard Nixon, his stories in *Pricksongs & Descants* (1969).

Giordano Bruno was an Italian philosopher, heretic, and cosmologist of the sixteenth century, who challenged virtually all dogma, holding to a physical explanation of the universe. His cosmology was a primitive form of what we now know from Einstein: what is knowable is relative to the perception of the knower. Bruno, however, was not completely an individualist, for he posited certain fixed physical laws, in which individual elements, monads, were governed by irreducible ties, themselves governed by an infinite principle. Bruno's pantheistic deity was manifest in all His work. For the Inquisition, Bruno gave too little to God, too much to man, and he was burned at the stake in 1600, in Rome.

Coover's Bruno is Giovanni Bruno—"Chonny"— an unnoticeable coal miner who, mysteriously, survives a mine disaster that kills all his crew. Bruno is extracted from a holocaust of fire and coal dust, and survives, having seen a white bird in his visions before he fell unconscious. That white bird, or the way in which it is interpreted, becomes the basis for the Brunists, a heretical cult which believes it is privy to the exact hour and day when the end of the world will arrive. They are chiliasts with a vengeance.

Each of Coover's novels is shaped as an extended metaphor of American life, here in *The Origin of the Brunists,* later in *The Universal Baseball Association* and then in *The Public Burning.* His stories fit as interstices between novels. The longer fictions have, in their neat formulation and their incorporation of real people and events, something of the quality of allegory. What Coover has anticipated in this sharply angled, rapidly shifting narrative is the fervor of a heretical cult, the readiness of normal people to give themselves over to something that will pour meaning into their lives.

The novel is intensely political as well as religious; many of its elements reflect the McCarthy hysteria of the previous decade. Bruno is a dark, gaunt, spectral figure; he speaks hardly at all, and when he does it is in parables which all point to Armageddon, in which possibly only the Brunists will be reborn. Bruno's gloss on reality recalls Kinbote's in *Pale Fire,* a madman's message which gradually comes to replace sanity. Bruno carries the community with him, only town officials and the newspaperman Justin "Tiger" Miller remaining outside as nonbelievers. Town officials, however, oppose the Brunists less for their beliefs than for fear of a "lower-class" rebellion, a shifting of power.

The allegory posits an America, embodied in West Condon, which has gone religiously mad; as later, in *The Public Burning,* Coover focuses more directly on political madness. The religion of the Brunists is based on a destructive idea, Coover's entropy: that

aspect of Revelation which indicts the present in order for us to prepare for a future life, if we are fortunate enough to be reborn. Bruno is a superb technician of this cult because he says almost nothing, has represented nothing in the past, is unnoticed until his resurrection from the mine. He is, for the cultists, a modern Christ, risen, prophetic. He may be McCarthy of the 1950s, or Malcolm X in the 1960s. The allegory fits sixties images. The madness of that decade was its power to move us to thoughts and actions which often opposed our own interests. Coover's Brunists come alive under their idea, and for some, like Eleanor Norton, Bruno represents the connection with the apocalypse she has been searching for all her adult life. Whatever Bruno's deficiencies, he touches something vital, and the cult will not go away. Even suspicion that Bruno's own sister, the innocent and perhaps martyred Marcella, was sacrificed for the sake of the cult cannot dissipate its appeal; in fact, it reinforces it, for many believe that in her death throes, she had pointed to heaven "and then, miraculously, maintained this gesture forever after. This death in the ditch [she is thrown from a car], the Sacrifice, became in the years that followed a popular theme for religious art, and the painters never failed to exploit this legend of the heavenward gesture, never failed to omit the bubble of blood. Which was, of course, as it should be."

The sane voice, like Marlow in Conrad's narrative, belongs to Miller, a journalist who savors the cult for its newsworthy potential. Having prepared a series of articles and a sheaf of photographs, he releases them at the right moment to news services all over the country. When the pieces appear locally, he is ostracized and nearly murdered at the huge rally honoring the end of the world. Left in a ditch himself, he is brought back to life by his nurse friend "Happy Bottom," whose presence as a woman takes second place to the felicities of her rump. She is, for Miller, what Ramona is for Herzog, a comforter, a sexual kitten (though tigerish on occasion), a security pillow (that rump), one who cossets her man.

Although the design of the novel is of strategic interest—first the sacrifice, then the "white bird" of the mine disaster, followed by the formulation of the cult and its effects on this backwater town—the working out involves problems intrinsic to allegory. In such fiction, no person can develop; what develop are incidents or events, which draw in fixed people. Internal development, if any, gives way to external events, which preempt choice and growth. Thus, we have a monolithic structure, either for or against, such as we find in much utopian or dystopian fiction: *1984, Brave New World, A Clockwork Orange.* The Coover novel falls into those fictional traps; whereas Nabokov in *Pale Fire* avoids the traps through a constant shifting back and forth from sanity to insanity, undermining the very ground on which his political allegory is being played out. Coover's use of Miller cannot serve that function, for his journalist is too stereotypical, his attitudes too perfunctory. A drink, a good lay, a timely story, and he is satisfied.

All that remains is the development of the cult itself, by basically flat townspeople, individuals trapped by their own superficiality. Except for their involvement in the Brunists, they are slobs, raising children who are little different. West Condon (condom?) owes a good deal to Sinclair Lewis's "Main Street" towns, with sexual mores updated to the 1960s. Lack of variety drags the book down, since after a while one miner seems similar to the next, one town leader little different from the other.

From the first, Coover sought American myths—here a cult or sect with political overtones; then baseball as the pastoral myth of America; after that, the Rosenberg case as the expression of postwar America. Despite successes in each, there is still a lack of fulfillment. America keeps slipping through his lines. Part of the problem is his sense of relationships in America. Fighting didacticism and homiletics, he is basically a "with it" sermonizer. Technically, he strives for novelty, but is pulled back by concerns which require more traditional resolutions. Intermixed with that, he relies on the masculine tradition, to the extent that his men and women are stereotypical. His men lose focus because they can be played off only against other men, who are similar; whereas the women spread their legs or whine or rage. Only Ethel Rosenberg proves different.

In *Pricksongs & Descants* (full of point and counterpoint), "The Babysitter" is a distinct 1960s piece, evoking the world of young people and their ideological separation from an older generation; but accomplished within overlapping worlds, not in appearances on opposite sides of the barricades. In babysitting, we have that meeting ground: parents and small children, a babysitter, whose age falls between parents and young children, and her boyfriends. Intermixed is whatever occurs on a television set, which never goes off: detective action, love stories, maniacal violence, all sexes and age groups blended without regard for coherence.

The aim of the Coover story is simultaneity. He has arranged the scene as a montage, very brief sequences involving several layers of experience. Past, present, future, television changeovers, as well as fantasies and plans, are alternated. Like a porno movie, the story revolves around the unnamed babysitter, whose nubile body attracts Tucker (the man for whom she sits) and two young friends, Jack and Mark. Viewing her body, touching it, penetrating it: these become the conflicts for the story. But other pressures appear: two small children who insist on their rights (peeing, bathing, eating, watching television), and a baby who until near the end remains offstage, that ever-threatening dirty-diapered baby.

In a sequence near the end of the story, the babysitter is sitting in a sudsy bath; Tucker has been in and out of his house, looking; the small boy, Jimmy, is up and around; sirens go off on a television program; Jack, a boyfriend, is probing the scene; Mrs. Tucker calls to inquire about her husband, all the while she is being shoved back into a tight girdle at *her* party; and the baby seems to have drowned in the bathwater. All this is presented as fact, but in the nature of the story, very little is fact, most imagined; and the evening may have gone smoothly, or else been the nightmare the facts make it seem. Coover has intermixed a possible evening with an actual evening and withdrawn the boundaries. Everything that is potential in a babysitting evening is blended with what does actually happen; so that the entire experience is transformed into a television program. We perceive a film of the evening, with almost infinite possibilities presented simultaneously, each overlapping others. The babysitter takes a sudsy bath for nearly the entire time we see her, and yet the bath is only one sequence. Intervening in each reference to the bath is a telephone ring, a child appearing, an imagined friend or act, a manifestation of violence.

As a cultural commentary, the story establishes a generational struggle, but within the framework of a shared experience. Even if sitter and friends are paired off against Tuckers (he balding and she fat), they are still not completely free of each other, for the children serve as common ground. The children are, in turn, unruly, demanding, incapable of giving up their needs in the face of older pressure. We have, then, a triple-layered sequence—three distinct age groups, each with its own demands upon life, each at its own level of sex: children with constant toilet activity; sitter with nudity and bathing, touching herself, weighing her breasts, peering in mirrors; boyfriends insistent upon making out with her; and the Tuckers into their own sex thing—he hoping to get at the sitter, she, drunk, using her girdle to gain attention. As in minimalist fiction, all is incomplete; or else completed only at one layer of experience, with the end of the babysitter's tour of duty. Far more than in *Brunists,* Coover has angled into the modern mode, moving along the line of film, piling up images and words not *for* meaning but *as* meaning.

Like several of Barthelme's "city tales," Steve Katz's *Saw* (1972) is an urban fantasy, a spaced-out view of city life, and, accordingly, its leading male character is an astronaut—The Astronaut. The city is Leroy, which could be a borough as well as a city. The leading female character is Eileen, who serves as toothsome flesh, little soul or aura.

The narrative comes as a series of reports—cf. Kafka's "Report to the Academy." In the Preface, Katz shrugs off the meaning of the reports and how they got to him, although he vouches for their veracity or validity.

> The order of these "reports" is arbitrary although their accuracy is strict. . . . The natural number and order of words in each report has been strictly regulated by universal laws that are presently being studied, and the events accounted for within each individual report are arranged in a sequence and system according to a code that isn't yet deciphered. . . . I am not yet at liberty to divulge the manner in which these reports got to me, but I can freely reveal that some of them seem to be missing, though I don't know which ones. There may be more reports than presently meet the eye. Other languages are a distinct possibility. . . . One can speculate about the veracity of these contents and decide for him, but whatever the conclusion it is still a matter of mystery that they exist at all, and in a form that can please or amuse us.

Once these points are established, or put into question, Katz reveals that all the major questions remain: the addresses of The Astronaut's reports, how they were deciphered, what they mean, and what kind of danger they foreshadow. Katz says that whenever these questions arise, he smiles, shrugs, contemplates the roaches in his apartment, observes accidents in the street. Information may be complete, or incomplete, or even illusory.

We are located, then, in middle ground between regular fiction and science fiction, what we will see later in McElroy's *Plus.* The Astronaut is all command, from another planet, a kind of mutation; Eileen is all vulnerability, flesh and holes awaiting pene-

tration and a "new life." (One problem with experimental fiction is the females, embodying quivering desire.) Eileen copulates with a sphere, one of the major characters (others are a fly in a bottle and a cylinder), and, for the first time, feels completely surrounded, penetrated and stroked on all parts, yet not threatened. The sphere "seems to get naked from within, its most intimate substances seeping to the surface." Eileen's life is a series of receptions in which she experiences alternative feelings—spheres, cylinders, The Astronaut, earlier a talking hawk.

We are in a fiction of infinite possibilities, in which elements never before mixed are now combined into relationships, copulation, associations of soul, spirit, and body. Early on, Eileen hides a puppy under her coat, rides the subway to Van Cortlandt Park, and there lets a hawk swoop down and eat the puppy. The hawk thanks her for "bringing me those tender pups," saying life in a city is very tough on a hawk, and only the endless pleasure of circling—" 'We're up there for the circling, making the circles, that's where it's at' "—justifies the life. The hawk knows how to live, and informs Eileen she exists in a box. From this point, she attempts to leave the box.

It is necessary to escape, or else headaches and other ailments lead to complete malfunction. This is very much a résumé of the 1960s, a warning that bourgeois life is more than tedium, it is illness. Garbage dominates. Katz quotes from one Blathinger—who could be Pynchon—whose theory of garbage is presented in *Waste and Rebirth.* "Life persists, according to Blathinger, in a metabolic era such as the present until wastes reach cataclysmic proportions and smother all life in their own garbage, at which point everything rests for uncounted centuries until the new, antimetabolic forms appear spontaneously, an era of hydrocarbon breathers, munchers of minerals and plastics, with open sores that work like muscles, who communicate by coughing." The Astronaut expounds this philosophy, and we recognize we are living in phases of the garbage age, until death by garbage occurs and the world goes into a recessive phase, when a new era emerges.

The narrative becomes "reports" of these moments of death interpenetrated by moments of life; all related by a self-conscious narrator who mentions his first book, *The Exaggerations of Peter Prince* (1968), his friends, life in Leroy. At one point, the narrator, who is Steve Katz in several places, admits to being The Astronaut. "The only proper explanation of what has preceded, at this point, is to admit to you that I am The Astronaut. This book is an autobiography." He then proceeds to provide some details of his personal life, but his account has more vacancies than hard information. "This doesn't give the whole picture. . . . I am The Astronaut. I believe that the things that happened in my life never happened to anyone else."

Episodes, confessions, incidents, characters from a geometry course, from nature (the hawk, the fly in the bottle), from city life, are all manifestations of disconnectedness. Unlike the minimalists, whom he superficially resembles, Katz describes matters in full, to the point of tedious detail. His aim is to suggest phenomena that are only spots in a void; behind them all is the vast nothingness of a life which is isolated, discrete, dissociated. In such a life, any kind of event, person, or shape is a form of experience, for it moves one from routine to concern with whatness. Eileen is foundering until she releases the madness of experience bottled up in herself—even the fly recognizes that in its bottle episode. Thus, Katz has written not a novel, really, nor even a narrative, but a series of "reports to the academy," without Kafka's irony. It is a parable rearranged in tough modernist prose, disconnected elements and sharp angulation fighting against familiar subjects: urban solitariness, wasteland environments, pastoral salvation.

In *The Free-Lance Pallbearers* (1967), Ishmael Reed forged a language for the jazz idiom of the black, intermixing it with the traditional, standard language. Both are spoken by Bukka Doopeyduk, Reed's "holy innocent," a duped duck until he comes alive and takes charge of his life. He reminds us of Ellison's invisible man, constantly hoodwinked by the establishment, here embodied in Harry Sam, son of a self-made Pole, a former car salesman, and a "lowdown, filthy hobo infested with hoof-and-mouth disease" of a mother. Sam has taken over the territory around Buffalo, eighty percent Polish and Roman Catholic. Bukka, an apprentice to the Nazarene belief, is an innocent black prepared to learn Christian beliefs at the feet of the master, Harry Sam (Hare Krishna?).

Harry Sam's motel is like Kafka's Castle, a mysterious, inaccessible place. "The Harry Sam Motel rose so high that it pushed the clouds aside. The helicopters whirred above, dipping in and out. They were marked with the symbol of the Great Commode. . . . It stood there harsh and forbidding in the moonlight." Bukka does arrive there, and is almost killed;

he swims the poisonous bay only because he has a secret liquid which clears the way of sea monsters. In his motel-castle, Sam sits on a john and his wastes pollute the bay. Everything Sam stands for (sits for) is shit to the Negro, a color inversion of Coptic White for Ellison's protagonist. "What sort of commode should HARRY SAM be sitting upon? Should it be a pink plastic one or one made of mahogany? Should it be done in lavender with a beautiful ring of fur on the seat? I didn't even want to get into the subject of tissue; that one stumped the best scholars in the movement."

Bukka is duped by Entropy Productions, which pays him two hundred dollars to enter into a Becoming. The Becoming consists, in part, of his being hit in the face by baseballs thrown by a robot, while a tape informs the white audience, which applauds and cheers, its days are numbered; the scene recalls Ellison's Battle Royal. The time is 1945, but the atmosphere and references (to JFK, RFK, et al.) suggest the 1960s. This is very much a performance for that decade, attuned to the freeing process of the novel, in language, attitudes, tones, and to the idea of the black as dupe.

Bukka tries to make his way as a hospital attendant for loonies; as a husband, with a wife who is into lesbian relationships; in college, where he does not fit. His professor is U2 Polyglot, who writes a paper on "The Egyptian Dung Beetle in Kafka's 'Metamorphosis' " and prepares by pushing a ball of dung with his nose. Everywhere Bukka turns, he is done in—by wife, job, school, his desire to be a Nazarene. What remains are a black's menial tasks, dressed up to sound better.

"Your name is Doopeyduk, ain't it? Where dat name come from, kiddo, da Bible or somethin'?
"No, sir. It came from a second cousin of my mother who did time for strangling a social worker with custom-made voodoo gloves.
"I see. What do you do for a living, Mr. Doopeyduk?
"I am a psychiatric technician.
"What precisely does that involve?
"I empty utensils and move some of our senior citizens into a room where prongs are attached to their heads and they bounce up and down on a cart and giggle.
"That must be engaging work.
"Yes, it is. I'm learning about the relationship between the texture and color of feces and certain organic and/or psychological disturbances.

As part of this same hyperbole, "Free-Lance Pall-bearers" are those who will carry off Sam as soon as someone swims the bay, that is, passes the test and replaces the king.

The triumphs of the Reed novel come in its mixture of styles, languages, references—all muddled as if in some television news broadcast which moves from murder to commercials for panty hose back to war or rape or nuclear blasts. Reed has tuned in to the cultural muddle that passes through us each day; intensified for the black, who lives in twilight zones —duped, confused, made a fool of by one confidence man after another, befuddled by religion, hexed by the very voodoo he professes. For blacks, all life is a tall tale.

In *Yellow Back Radio Broke Down* (1969), Reed continues the tall tale. Here, Loop Garoo Kid, a black cowboy hero, brings Hoodoo to the West. Hoodoo is a form of black power which prevails over a series of villains. Hoodoo power will recur in *Mumbo Jumbo* (1972), and its expression is a manifestation of the black's specific needs and his language.* The gang, a Western Mafia, has taken over Yellow Black Radio, setting up a showdown with Loop Garoo Kid, a combination of Billy the Kid, voodoo priest, and Gary Cooper. The showdown, however, is chiefly a matter

---

*George Cain, in *Blueschild Baby* (1970), conventional in its narrative line, attempts a break with standard English for thought processes. His chief method is elimination of the subject, beginning with a verb. "Knowing enough of the game he [Roger, a white man] insisted that he accompany me. Explained why he couldn't, a white in Harlem is a tip." This shorthand, effective for speed and offbeat rhythms, is used only internally. For narrative purposes, Cain is quite obviously literary. There are, also, occasional words which reflect nonstandard speech: "Shouldn'tve," for example.

Other than the experiment with "thought language," Cain's rhetoric, like Baraka's, is accusatory. Leaders are convicts; whites get blacks high on drugs so they can dehumanize and emasculate them; prisoners are a power base for blacks, in that all prisoners are political; the greatest crime for a black, in white eyes, is awareness. Truths and half-truths intermix in a rhetoric that is distinctly 1960s. Like Baraka, Cain marries a white woman, has a child, and then, nauseated by his wife's whiteness, seeks salvation with a black mate. His use of junk, in fact, is connected to his need to identify with the most destructive of black conditions, where he feels his "brothers" really are. Yet all this passes when Cain decides not to be an outcast (rejects "Cain") but to reenter, purified of the heroin in his veins. He "withdraws" in seventy-two hours of dedication to self and suffering, refocusing on self after concern with larger issues. The novel is a sometimes powerful statement, distinguished by daring use of language.

of words, as the Kid's job is to close down all signals from the radio, to block communication. In the language of hype and dipseydoodle, Reed catalogues the confrontation. He has broken free of restraints of realism, naturalism, expressionism. The following passage indicates the direction, Loop speaking:

> Didn't you say something about spade poets having gone up in tinder when I walked into the party the other night? Come on preacher don't start your thing, I don't want to hear anything about Matthew Chapter and Verse in ditty bop talk. I get sick of "Soul" sometimes. All right then, Loop said.

He lashes the preacher.

> (CRACK!) Whenever you say something like that. (CRACK!! CRACK!!) In the future. Check out some sources. (CRACK!! CRACK!!) Motherfucker!! (CRACK! CRACK!) Ask you mama. (CRACK!) Yo wife. (CRACK! CRACK!) Guillaume Apollinaire. (CRACK! POP! CRINKLE! SNAP!) Anybody you want to ask. (CRACK!) But get your information right next time (NICK!) O.K.?

In *Mumbo Jumbo* (1972), Reed explores Pynchon territory, a conspiracy in which the "Jes Grew" movement is proliferating. "Jes Grew" is a code word for black power or the black movement, in some sense; and the novel becomes a series or sequence of mysteries based on Neo-Hoodooism, which is to explain why "Jes Grew" is growing. Reed's language retains its hyperbolic quality but is toned down somewhat to narrative, since the novel takes the form of a crazily patterned detective story. "The Wallflower Order attempts to meet the psychic plague by installing an anti-Jes Grew President, Warren Harding. He wins on the platform 'Let's be done with Wiggle and Wobble,' indicating that he will not tolerate this spreading infection. All sympathizers will be dealt with; all carriers isolated and disinfected, Immuno-Therapy will begin once he takes office." One problem with a novel even as lively and inventive as *Mumbo Jumbo* is its hyperactivity. Every moment must be a throb, every act a leap; so that the reader is allowed no base or stance; like a stand-up comic who keeps coming, not even desisting to allow for breath between gags.

JOSEPH McELROY

Just as in the 1950s Gaddis saw counterfeiting and forgery as the symbolic shape of the era, so McElroy in *A Smuggler's Bible* (1966) perceives smuggling as the indicator of the 1960s—indeed, of the postwar era.* At its most literal, the emblem is a hollowed-out Bible which smugglers used for transferring goods illegally. It is a particularly apt mixture of secular and holy, of devil's work and God's representative. A smuggler's Bible was something to swear by, and it was based on deception, a sanctified deception. The phrase moves us ever deeper into levels of imitation; for the Bible was indeed "hollowed-out," its message erased in favor of an object or objects. And yet its presence gave the smuggler a sense of kinship with the protection afforded by a holy or magical object. For appearance' sake, the Bible was magical, whereas the smuggled object for the smuggler or counterfeiter was the truer "magic."

In the modern mode, McElroy arrives at his metaphor indirectly, in somewhat disconnected leaps, though the novel is tightly organized—in every way a "modern construct." It is a piece of verbal architecture: an entrance, a large interior with the potentialities of the hollowed-out smuggler's Bible itself, and various exits, any one of which the characters may take. They wander through the structure as if in a maze, whose paths are as central to this novel as to McElroy's next, *Hind's Kidnap.* But while they wander, McElroy has maintained a tight grip on them, by means of several control points. The structural archetype is Joyce's Dublin in *Ulysses:* the maze of streets, the threading through, the apparent lack of control, ultimately an impacted, tight organization and direction.

David Brooke, McElroy's protagonist, is the "keeper" of eight manuscripts, which he later refers to as his "pieces of eight," smugglers' and pirates' money. He and his wife, Ellen, are on board the *Ar-*

kadia bound east, that is, heading East of Eden. His "keep" is the eight manuscripts "in the East Lite Box-File (with Lockspring) on the stateroom table." These manuscripts are his own work, we learn, stories involving himself and those around him: they are, literally, the texts establishing his existence. He has a week, later extended to eight days, to assemble the manuscript fragments, one day more than God needed to create the world. They allow him to be smuggled into life from what would otherwise be a form of extinction. There is, also, a mirror image to David, a narrator who observes him and is "in him and behind him." This narrator is a hovering presence, and he serves in the segments between the manuscripts.

The novel's structure consists of the eight manuscripts, each disconnected by a brief separation, or entr'acte, no more than a few pages of personal matter. But there is a further system of arrangement. At the top of pages in the entr'actes, sequentially, small letters *a* through *z* run through the novel twice. Each time a manuscript appears, the sequence of letters is broken. In an attempt at disorder, the first letter *(a)* of the second sequence comes just before a major break, Manuscript IV. This letter seems, in fact, to serve as an eliminator from the sequence of previous *u-v-w-x-y-z,* as well as of *a* itself. The asymmetrical arrangement is such that *a* is isolated from the rest of the alphabet, as if its own design. The function, which is ambiguous, is to upset organizational rigidity and to give the "mirror image" or narrator the power to take away: literally to delete the alphabet from his arrangement.†

David's "pieces of eight" work on a dialectical pivot: as much as he puts in, he must smuggle from his own life. He must feign amnesia, finally, in order to regain some stability, which comes when he can enter into the life and mind of his dying father, Halsey. As submitting and withdrawing become the

---

*McElroy comments on this: *"A Smuggler's Bible* was praised for some wholeness or totality in the midst of disintegration. I'm content with that estimate, especially when it includes comparisons with Malcolm Lowry and William Gaddis. But that hugely intriguing book [*The Recognitions*] with which it was often compared—and which I at last read in '62 when I was well into *A Smuggler's Bible* and which encouraged me to see how far I could get with the smuggling metaphor I found in the emptiness of a tacky old hollowed book in a museum in Cornwall—was a feat that I deliberately aimed to fall short of. *The Recognitions*—as I scanned it then (even hunting up Clementine materials in the British Museum)—follows its networks of forgery so as at last to organize itself into a convincing grandeur of completion and faith. And this is reflected not so much in many instances of truth imitating imitation and imitation coming true, as in a recognizably pleasurable and old-fashioned yarn. My story in *A Smuggler's Bible* was designed to fracture."

†The *u-v-w-x-y-z* cast aside, as if letters in an alphabet soup, are part of a sequence of therapy deeply embedded in memory: "reflex therapy, or what bruder didn't say." The narrator furnishes David with a variety of dreams, but David must handle them, organize them as he has organized his memories for the manuscripts, those fragments he has smuggled out of himself and others' lives to provide an art form. Bruder is a therapist who cannot help David, yet insists that he not go to another doctor: remain with his memories, then, whatever the outcome. Experiencing memory and entering into others' makes David into a smuggler; and this passage takes place in memory on board the *Arkadia,* with the blond smuggler never far from his presence. Even Eden is traduced; original sin nags.

theme of the book, we can perceive how the smuggler's Bible works. For, inevitably, the Bible replaces the manuscripts; David's East Lite Box-File is subsumed in the Bible: "he is seeing what the smuggler-man [a ubiquitous blond fellow, a shadowy presence] promised. A Bible? Black, magisterial, stipple-grained imitation morocco and, shining across the top, these gilt-tooled letters: HOLY BIBLE." Inside the Bible's cover, a label identifies the article: "A Smuggler's Bible. Used by smugglers on both sides of the Atlantic in the early nineteenth century to conceal small objects of value." This discovery, not unusually, leads David into "Symptoms of Fugue," or how "in a sense [David] faked amnesia." At about the same time, Walker Percy's Will Barrett was suffering his "ravening particles."

This is the kind of thing Barth used later in *Letters:* characters from his books act out a gigantic scenario which recalls them and Barth's relationship to them, including his own role as letter writer in the script of his life. McElroy uses two extended chain letters, in which David indicates who is to respond and in what sequence. The chains lead away from him and back, so that he is shackled by the letters yet freed from his feigned amnesia by way of the memories other people recall to him.

The regaining of ourselves, as David recognizes, is an act of smuggling. "Do you see how people try to smuggle themselves out of life? To pretend to sneak across the mortal frontier—when in fact you stay right here after death." And the contrary holds: one must attempt to smuggle oneself into life. The sense of the sixties is clearly present, a dialectic seemingly the sole way for the individual to achieve bearings: by a precarious hold on contraries. Pynchon had moved along the same track in *V.* and *The Crying of Lot 49.*

Beyond the individual lies a cat's cradle of relationships, and apparently no association among these people occurs except in the single life that holds them in a personal balance. Here we see McElroy, through David, and through David's mirror image, the narrator, turning his life into an art form: creating relationships which are artificial and imitational, and yet are necessary in art for the sake of structure and organization.

McElroy has created such a book: not only a book about itself (a familiar genre in the postwar era!) but one that enables the characters to learn about themselves. In other words, a smuggler's Bible, with its potentiality to be filled with anything precious, except the words it was intended for. The metaphor grows as we observe it. For that smuggler's Bible exists as a "free space" once the Biblical text has been removed; and what charges it is, in a sense, a "recognition" of what we are. David will stuff it with memories, that accumulation of materials embodied in the seven-level screwdriver utilized by electronics engineers for various tasks. Their use of such hardware has its counterpart in his seven-day journey (extended to eight at the last moment) and in his seven manuscripts (plus the one in which he enters his father's sensibility). When David places the multipurpose screwdriver in that Bible, he is smuggling a valuable tool and his memories; once that occurs, he will himself be bereft of memories, that is, amnesiac.

Who makes up David's recollections? It is a seemingly diverse group with little associational value. There are the people centered around a rooming house in Brooklyn Heights, where everyone "has a shelf" in the refrigerator. But before that there is Peter St. John, who owns a rare-book store and whom we meet when he is being shadowed by a young man who says Peter resembles his father. The first manuscript or memory is, in fact, called "The Shadow." In many ways it is a prefiguration, for everything is perceived as shadowed, shadows, shadowy, from people in their lives to smuggling.

Shaped thus, McElroy's characters are removed from a realistic format, although they do realistic things—they eat and drink, work, teach, speak to family and friends. Another aspect of the novel, also prefigured in that first manuscript, is the resemblance among people, what we see in pop art objects of the mid-sixties: Peter St. John reminds the young man of his father; and characters always recall someone else, smuggled personalities.

There is even intellectual smuggling. David, living in a trailer in New Hampshire and doing odd jobs around the university, once met Duke Amerchrome, who built a national reputation as a historian on spurious work. He forged sources and blew over his opposition in order to disguise his piracy. He is to history what many literary men are to fiction—Norman Mailer is suggested by Tony Tanner; but I suspect Duke Amerchrome (like his name) is the "tarnished metal" of those who smuggle themselves into position: men who live off reputation rather than work. He is the American confidence man, an archetype of many postwar novelists who manipulate celebrity to disguise hollowness.

Duke becomes one of David's memories, as do Duke's long-suffering family: Mary, his third wife, twenty years his junior; and Michael, his son. Within David's memory, Michael relates the tale of his father, in "The American Hero, or the Last Days of Duke, Mary, and Me." While Michael is the ostensible witness here—*he* learns of Duke's having counterfeited details of the Battle of Ticonderoga—David's memory co-opts the incident and the relationship. And beyond David is the smuggled-in narrator, himself commenting on David and his memories, a shadowy existence as a mirror image. There are layers of relative commentaries and, thus, layers of relative information. Duke's forgery lies within such layers, themselves as shadowy as is his exposition of an event two hundred years old.

Furthermore, Duke is a creature of the decade: McElroy's dependence on a deliquescent consciousness does not exclude deep political implications. We would be in error to see Duke only in literary terms; he is also Lyndon Johnson, or a figure like that. Johnson "stole" his Senate seat in a last-minute shift of votes, which remained suspicious until his death; and his movement in the decade, as shadow to Kennedy and then as the Cecil B. De Mille of Presidents, has its counterpart not in Duke himself but in the conception of a creature whose frauds and good deeds are indistinguishable. Behind Duke's bluster and overblown language may be a complicated man, or nothing at all. Part of the advantage of the shadowy method is that everything becomes imminent, potential. As in *Lookout Cartridge,* all activity lies "between" or "among."

Before we encounter Duke, we meet the rooming house people, one of whom is an old man, Pennitt, who deals apparently in rare coins and has a coin press in his room. David also, in the rooming house episode, is interested in coins and speaks to Pennitt about coin appearance and duplication,* so that there is suspicion of illegal coin smuggling or dealing. When we seem on the edge of something tangible, Pennitt becomes annoyed, or else the narrator breaks off. The use of coins and objects, hard, material things, is always juxtaposed to the shadows in which they exist; the world beyond becomes curved into the imagination.

The episode "Anglo-American Chronicle" is apparently a reflection of Angus Wilson's *Anglo-Saxon Attitudes.* In New Hampshire David links up with Harry Tindall, an Oxford graduate who has come to the university as an instructor in history. They room

together in a house on the property of an eccentric squire. Their lives seem unremarkable, as are their contacts with the locals, except for Wanda, an older student who pursues Harry. But the key element in this otherwise lackluster segment is Harry's compulsive recital of the story of Jaro, a Jewish-Czech student.

After emigrating, Jaro becomes a student of overwhelming brilliance at Oxford, an expert on the Thirty Years' War because of his interest in "how, physically and emotionally, [people] go through the last process of dying." With his knowledge of seemingly everything and his mastery of numerous difficult languages, Jaro becomes an expert in death, dying, dying cultures. He is fascinated with a Peruvian artifact called a quipu, a counting device the Incas "webbed by knotting bits of rope or string in many different ways." Since history is his doom, the quipu is Jaro's destiny, and he hangs himself, letting the quipu slowly strangle the life out of him, without any jump. Jaro's tale prefigures other dark matters, such as Wanda's attempt to ax her way into the forbidden chapel, an episide in which the squire is badly wounded.

In the weakest episode, David and Ellen take a vacation on an island outside the Bay of Naples, where a local rich man insinuates his life into that of the Brookes. But elements do not cohere meaningfully, and the episode is like a dream McElroy placed here but could have dispensed with altogether. It is followed, nevertheless, by the very significant entr'acte *(n* through *t)* called "the black box," which introduces the smuggler's Bible.

Then comes the episode of David's amnesiac condition, part of it self-induced, part uncontrollable. Having smuggled so much of himself into his manuscripts, he has nothing left for himself. We cite lines from Mark Strand's poem "The Remains" to suggest such a personal and cultural condition:

> I empty myself of the names of others. I empty my pockets.
> I empty my shoes and leave them beside the road.
> At night I turn back the clocks;
> I open the family album and look at myself as a boy.
> What good does it do? The hours have done their job.
> I say my own name. I say goodbye.

McElroy's relationship to Brooke and his need to arrange, "keep," and smuggle is solidly within traditions of a culture of aesthetics. For while David loses

---

*The idea of coins and coinage, as part of the counterfeit idea, also seeps into theater, with David Mamet's *American Buffalo,* in part a 1970s version of this theme, coins as emblematic of a shifting America.

his self in his work, and has little left over for wife or associates, that "lost self" nevertheless is in the interest of a creative impulse. It demonstrates both the best and the worst of himself; withal, it allows something to be made, but, of course, at the expense of the maker. The cultural weight here seems a direct heritage from the sixties, in which whatever was given was also taken away. One threw oneself into activities —antiwar demonstrations, civil rights marches, free speech movements—only by becoming blind to several of their aspects. In political terms, one pushed on with the knowledge that, culturally, the younger generation was responding with a "greening of America" which was superficial, even meretricious. To support anything meant, then, either a suspension of self or a withdrawal into the status quo. David's "hanging" between elements is, in this sense, his cultural response, where no response can be simplistic. Jaro hangs himself with a Peruvian artifact, choosing in his self-destructive way a cultural simplification; returning to the primitive, he has used it as a solution. David cannot accept that solution, though it is attractive: the Peruvian artifact must remain not a guide, not a direction, just a compelling object. Subjects lie elsewhere. The point is disconnection, not destruction.

The mirror image McElroy projects in and around David—what Tanner calls the "machine-voice"—is not solely mechanical and objective; it also allows David to design his structure, keep his manuscripts, give them coherence. It is a voice of warning, the devil in the machine, as well as the God of creativity. God and devil, in effect, as in so much modern art, fit together, a dialectic and ultimately a unity, each incapable without the other. Mann's *Doctor Faustus,* the classic of such a dialectic, seems well within David's dilemma. For David's choice as a maker of art is not simply to describe; he has taken upon himself some of the devil's own work, which is to enter into the lives of others to inform their existence. That thrust is toward remaking his characters. He is, to use the contemporary vocabulary, not only a programmer but a re-programmer, and he is interested in change: to disconnect, enter, redirect, reorganize. He is, then, both God and devil. The aim: to relocate the self after dismemberment.

The prose is both God and devil: descriptive, narrative in many of its functions; but also packed and impacted, ready to break out or explode in other guises. The refrain of "Follow the Drinkin' Gourd" trails through the text, a slave song which suggests the possibility of freedom in the North while one is enslaved in the South. The message there is clearly the one David must pursue, for he is enslaved and yet seeking freedom, which he does achieve when he passes over into his father's sensibility, smuggles himself into it and out of himself.

That release comes after a particularly Joycean passage of liberation, in which David both advances toward maturity and regresses into *Winnie the Pooh:*

> "Ellen [David's wife], once I thought of killing myself—to get out. But instead, I chose another way of leaving myself—projecting into the lives, the consciousness of others." (Kaa-kaa: remember the day we spent in Harry's mind? and saw him thinking we —i.e., *you*—were, in his favorite phrase, 'too light for heavy work'? And remember *all* our *friends*—e.g., Mary Clovis, chosen one of the 1376 people to tape-read twenty-five verses from the Bible (any version) for WFME-FM, Newark!) (Please! Don't you know me? I'm Yore Old Eeyore Yore Ol' Gay Donkey, egomorphosed so as to pass unnoticed in that low-lit stable tableau. David! Davey! Aieee! DB—)
> "Ellen."

The final section is "Smuggler's Harbor," the implanting of Halsey Brooke before his bay window, looking out on New York Harbor from his vantage point in Brooklyn Heights, and in turn, David Brooke taking up residence in his father's mind. After disconnection and fracture, we have the final act of juncture, like Bloom and Stephen outside Bloom's house on Eccles Street. The harbor, New York's, is also Halsey's—and David sails into it, as smuggler, giver, resident spirit, hanging on until Halsey, ill with cancer, dies. At Christmas, David gives Halsey *Atoms and People,* with its description of a chain reaction of neutrons, ready to blow as the hemispheres in the experiment neared each other. David has scribbled two "mad equations" in the gift book:

(HEMISPHERES) Unite = Disperse
Heart of Matter = Heart of Person
Atomic Bomb = Discovery of Apartness
Epistemological
Impotence

The dialectic is there: reaching the heart and impending explosion, or moving apart, avoiding the blowup and also connection. But even with that neat formulation, there is a further equation, heart of matter and heart of person: an additional choice, within choices. And an equal danger, that of epistemological impotence: words may themselves prove hollow, insufficient, metaphysical danglers. The perils are all implicit in making art of one's memories and in smuggling oneself out of art into the thing itself. What remains is the dialectic, not the resolution.

With all its novelistic qualities—and McElroy is a writer's, not a reader's, writer—*A Smuggler's Bible* is but a warm-up for *Hind's Kidnap* (1969) and *Lookout Cartridge* (1974), two difficult novels which represent the true McElroy world of "middle states" or "neural neighborhoods." *Hind's Kidnap* is more compelling as idea and as structure than it is line by line, page by page. McElroy moves right along the frontiers of modernism, having assimilated both its European and its American practitioners. Among European writers, he is most indebted to the French: Proust, as the massive figure behind his conception of time and memory; then Michel Butor, especially a novel such as *Degrees;* finally, Robbe-Grillet, with *Jealousy* and others. American models are, very possibly, Pynchon, but mainly Gaddis. The theme of imitation, forgery, counterfeiting, applied to the realm of ideas and memory, is a key to McElroy's method.

Hind's Kidnap revolves on a kidnapping which obsesses Jack Hind, the six-foot-seven-inch protagonist. When Hershey Laurel was four, he was kidnapped from his rural home, and he disappeared—no ransom note, no clues as to where he was taken, by whom, for what reason. After seven years, there is still no trace of him. Hind's obsession is never clarified, but he cannot live peacefully until he checks out every possible lead.

What gives the novel its energies is that Hind begins to seek leads where none, realistically, exists. Unlike Robbe-Grillet's protagonist or narrator, who clue by clue begins to uncover a crime, Hind builds up a sequence of clues which do not lead to any crime. He creates a labyrinth of great complexity, which only he can negotiate. Every nuance reflects the crime: General Hershey, the chocolate bar, certain trees all lead to Hershey Laurel.

People move in and out of Hind's life solely as clues. At the outset, a "tall old woman" has left him a note: " 'If you're still trying to break the kidnap, visit the pier by the hospital.' " What gives the novel structural underpinning is that Hind uncovers sufficient leads to support his pursuit of the kidnappers. Thus, at the very stage we may think he is pursuing illusions, and is himself fragmenting, something will support his suspicions of conspiracy and crime. The external world buttresses the schizoid mentality.

Hind's life becomes a maze. He is separated from his wife, his obsession with the kidnapping no small cause; he visits friends, but less to see them than to pursue leads, voice suspicions; and he revisits old haunts, to seek out new information after all these years. Each time he visits or revisits someone, the tale of the kidnapping is retold, kept fresh through repetition. Hind sees a young woman named Laura, whose name recalls the Laurels, and the kidnapping by association now comes between him and Laura as it did between him and his wife, Sylvia—even her name, with its pastoral connotation, having suggested Laurels. The novel's subtitle is "A Pastoral on Familiar Airs."

For Hind to find peace, he must "de-kidnap" friends, even strangers—for all are implicated until relieved of complicity. But as long as the kidnapping remains unsolved, there can be no relief of suspicion. The labyrinth is circular, and Hind is trapped in what his own ingenuity and concern have created. Application to an artwork is apparent: Hind creates, discovers motives, pursues, and is wound in his own bobbin of creativity. The Proustian mise-en-scène is rejuvenated in American backgrounds—a pier, a rural setting, a golf course, a university, and so on: memory works in a circular fashion, molding conscious and sub- or unconscious, creating a continuous narrative from disparate materials.

The idea of de-kidnapping is one of McElroy's most exemplary structural discoveries—a counterpart, I think, of Gaddis's stress on counterfeiting. As a structural element, it means that every time characters appear, in present and past, they become implicated in the Hershey Laurel kidnapping. They become part of Hind's "kidnap," and work through their own lives even as they are working through their role in Hind's sense of their implication in the crime. Every act, every activity, becomes dualistic, even multiple. Characters, as in *The Recognitions* and *V.,* move on the level of their ordinary life, while something additional has been invested in them: for Gaddis, their part of a vast forgery ring; for McElroy, their possible role in the crime which has lasted for seven years.

Proustian temporality plays a large role here. For even as people work through their own linear lives, they are involved in a very different temporal sequence in Hind's mind. There is movement beyond, stasis within: the static element always connected to Hind's memory of the crime, which remains within him like the "vase filled with perfumes, sounds, plans, and climates" Proust speaks of in *Le Temps retrouvé*. Proust calls "reality" a certain relationship "between these sensations and the memories which surround us at the same time." Gaston Bachelard, defining dimensions within a Proustian frame of reference, used "reverie" to designate the act behind a poem or artwork, something part of the topology of the imagination; and this, too, is close to McElroy's sense of the "presence" which overwhelms Hind's quest. He does his seven years as Jacob did to win the hand of his beloved; and he must see, as did Jacob, a pattern in everything that leads him toward his goal.

That kidnapping is the "ecstasy of the moment" Proust associated with the release of memory; not through a denial of objects, but as an ordering of them into their artistic potential. Unlike Mallarmé, who had to void or "whiten" what he needed, to efface what he presented, Proust reinforced those textures and tones which evoked memory. The tea and madeleine of the narrator's initial moment do not become for us mirages or hallucinatory elements, or even ecstasies; on the contrary, they become solid, everyday objects which possess, within, infinite extension. Thus, for McElroy, the kidnapping does not itself become hallucinatory; it is a solid event, which becomes more definable as it shapes Hind's adult life. For through it, he has discovered a way of comprehending himself, his childhood, his dead parents, his guardian, his early loves. Lost places as well as lost times are recovered. Poulet writes: "Creation or re-creation of space, the phenomenon of the madeleine has thus for its consummation the integral reconstitution of place."

Whatever is inside, is. That insight McElroy conveys through his blending of various layers of consciousness. The surface of Hind's life is rarely undisturbed for long without the interference of several pasts: the past of the kidnapping; his childhood—divided into life with his parents, then his guardian; his marriage and his career in the university; details of the post-kidnapping period. Each past, moreover, is presented as coexistent and coequal in intensity with now. McElroy has learned how to swing back upon Hind, negating time and space while at the same time displaying them.

Like Marcel in his quest for artistic unity, Hind must dissolve the self and personal ambition as an act of greater achievement of self. The larger self comes through effacement: a paradox of the modern quest, so different from the nineteenth-century expression of self as an experience in itself. Hind must first die within himself. Once reborn, he has greater resources, his quest that of the artist seeking materials which will justify the quest.*

Such novelists, McElroy, Gaddis, Pynchon, will always work within paradoxes. Through memory, their protagonists can make themselves, to use Proust's words, the "master of two worlds." The kidnapping for Hind has its alternative reaction in de-kidnapping, whose dynamics keep the original act alive. Once Hind's memory functions, de-kidnapping becomes coequal to kidnapping. He gains clues to clarify the maze, and the same clues entrap him in that maze. The ingenuity of McElroy's method poses a phenomenological conflict: actual events have become so absorbed in the internal workings that events and imagination become a total reality. Hind can experience nothing without working it through to his obsession: the artist making all elements cohere. Yet the product or artwork which results is quite different from Proust's, in that McElroy gives Hind nothing but a mental structure, whereas Proust has his long novel as his achievement. McElroy has taken a truer phenomenological path, by subsuming all external evidence (a novel, a legal case, clues) to the internal workings of Hind's imagination. He has achieved something close to Bachelard's "reverie," that act settled deeply behind whatever the imagination makes of it.

As noted, "A Pastoral on Familiar Airs" is the novel's subtitle. It seems curious, until we recognize it is associated with Hind's mission in life, which is to become a shepherd for his circle of friends; and further, to act out his role as shepherd in regard to the disappearance of Hershey Laurel. If four-year-old Hershey is a "laurel," then the sole way to aid him—if help is still possible in the light of official indifference—is by becoming, literally, a shepherd, a pastoral being. The idea is not at all farfetched, since country matters are relocated in the city, whose streets become a grid in Hind's mind. The grid provides locations and, at the same time, becomes the maze con-

---

*Ortega y Gasset argued quite differently, associating this type of analysis, chiefly in Proust, to paralysis. By forgoing dramatic action, Ortega believed, writers like Proust reduced narrative to "ecstatic stillness without progress or tension." This "ecstatic stillness," which characterizes McElroy's novels, would have been for Ortega a source of weakness; but for those who accept it, it becomes a principle of art and transcendence. One criticism of the McElroy method may be annoyance at being forced to witness his struggles to achieve the reality which will become his novel. But "stories" are no longer stories, narratives no longer narratives; the very validity of sequence is at issue in the post-Heidegger world.

nected to New York neighborhoods and their rapid changes from street to street.*

Further, we have the names of the characters: Hind himself, the female of the deer in one respect, or a rustic or a farm laborer in another; and then the parade of "rustics," from Hershey Laurel and the Laurels to Sylvia to Oliver Plane (whose "double" Hind often becomes), Dewey Wood, Ivy Ash, Maddy Beecher, and so on. They are all friends of woods, inhabitants of rural and city locations which blend into the singular act that obsesses Hind. Further, at six feet seven, Hind is himself a redwood among normal people, a man whose growth spurts were proportioned to trees more than people. As doubles of Hind, trees are proliferating objects, in names, acts, symbolic stories, parallels. In myth, men marry trees. Hind is, for children, a kind of tree, a pastoral skyscraper.

How is this related to kidnapping, smuggling, counterfeiting, imitation, all of which seems to be McElroy's territory? They are linked, but not directly. In Part II, McElroy moves from the surface narrative into a kind of reverie of materials, Hind's background: the idea is to thread through the kidnapping to earlier years, and to try to observe how Hind became a person obsessed with kidnapping. In other words, the aim is to turn Hind from object to subject, and then to relocate him as object. The section which dominates the entire middle of the novel begins in Joycean stream terms: " 'Vanilla for your ice cream cone comes from a bean on a plant. And once upon a time they thought it was magic medicine—once upon a time before tractors and billboards.' "

Hind's mother is explaining to him "pastoral airs" when he is six years old, legendary days when all were shepherds or pastoral people. The section is difficult, and, in parts, inaccessible—but its function, if read aloud, is to create the rhythms of a childhood which must be constantly retrieved by the adult Hind. We recognize that his quest for the kidnappers of Hershey Laurel is associated with the need to discover his background: his true paternity, the nature of his parents, and of his guardian, who disguises all things in ambiguous phrases or linguistic distinctions in which content is difficult to fathom. The long dip into the past (almost one hundred pages) is Hind's way of discovering himself. And so the obsession with kid-

napping is also a journey into self: to separate real from counterfeit, actuality from illusion. Hind has been "forged" by way of duplicities and deceptions, himself "kidnapped" from his parents by a guardian. Parts of himself have disappeared, smuggled away from him to areas he cannot quite locate. Such smuggling has left him hobbled and without energies for actual events; he must, therefore, travel the grid of memory—like a New York subway map, written over, defaced, misleading—and try to discover his position vis-à-vis past and present.

Something of Stephen Dedalus hangs over Hind. Joyce's Dublin is, of course, a maze and an actual route; McElroy's New York has similar qualities. Whatever is, is also not quite that.† The labyrinth is of one's own making, and yet it exists. A figure of the mind—the maze of one's own memories, the place into which one has been kidnapped—it is a literal site: skyscrapers as trees, people as potential shepherds or flocks. Hind's vocation is to shift back and forth, uncovering what he can as he journeys in and out of locations, memories, sights, and recollections. Everything becomes grist for his mill: an obsession.

"De-kidnapping" is Hind's way of releasing people from his flock; reversing his role as shepherd, he frees the sheep of his memories. At the same time, he is freed of some of the past by discovering new elements in it. He was himself kidnapped in the past, in memory, by parents (right ones and wrong ones) and guardian. He was misled by language—a weapon used by his guardian for control and subservience—and yet simultaneously, in the present of his life, he attempts to release people from their imagined role in the kidnapping of Hershey Laurel. McElroy parallels young Hind and Hershey, past and present, pastoral and city. Dualities make the novel somewhat inaccessible; in much the same way, John Barth in *Letters* moves along past and present, using his own fictions and "internal funhouse."

All maps are defaced, the map of New York City subways and that leading us into our own lives. To locate the alternating possession and dispossession which are the subject, McElroy has forged (duplici-

---

*The grid prepares us for the opening of *Lookout Cartridge:* "It is a silent flash there in the city's grid, and as I happen to look down [from a helicopter] at that precise point I am thinking of real estate prices."

†In an essay, "Neural Neighborhoods and Other Concrete Abstracts," McElroy speaks of a pastoral about a city; so that city—its disguises, reifications of people, defacements—is only one half of the dialectic. The city is also revelation; and from that we recall Calvino's "invisible cities" of twin purposes: the visible city and the invisible city, each recalling the other. In *Ancient History,* his next novel, McElroy removes that city space to a mental function, internalizing grids and transforming all into a tunneling journey.

tous word) a prose that hides as well as uncovers, that must be refocused in the reader's mind before it registers. There is style and stylistics here, as in the following passage, which concerns Hind's relationship with his guardian and simultaneously creates suspicion that things are different from what they seem:

Precisely because in certain dreams the guardian was telling Hind point by point that (and how and where) he was his adopted son, Jack would think—in the middle of dividing practice, or on the early morning local express under the river taking the paste-work dummies to the printer's on Twenty-Third Street the night after putting the school paper to bed, and even then at the instant of confronting rather proudly the brusque stocky printer in his long fifth-floor shop seemingly filled only with the unresonant cross-cut slug slug of the linotype—Hind would think that the guardian had never actually spoken of the adoption in so many words. This strange possibility—like a dive so well sprung you thought you lay out indefinitely in the higher volume near the wire-basketed roof-lights—turned you down into reaches and reaches of special kinship accumulated under the knowledge of the guardian's foster-paternity. That inviolable understanding grew up as a tiny shell imperceptibly forms, or a great impossible suspicion, or, one day on your beach (after you and he laughed at the waving Portagee Chief offshore there in his Coast Guard picketboat he called "waterborne logistic craft") a sympathy made of need and habit you are surprised to see alive in the vectors of your limbs as the almost naked guardian straightens up to show you a palmful of (very common, *Nucula Proxima*) Near Nut Shells.

The prose is off center, and yet not precious or affected. Nor is it inaccurate; it has focus. But it swings wide of our expectations. It is not a narrative prose, but a meditational one suitable for inner voices, whence it emanates. McElroy is always coming at us from within, even when his focus is external objects. His language mediates between subject and object and captures the innerness of things we do not associate with internality: shells, a dive, a boat. The prose works to "kidnap" qualities from elements in the way that the movement of the novel moves to see all activity as forms of kidnap, that smuggling of bodies and souls which connects to counterfeiting and forging: the imitational violence of the postwar era.

McElroy's third novel, *Ancient History* (1971), is based on a spatial arrangement and leads directly into *Lookout Cartridge,* his most distinctive fiction to date. Here, space is not a component of escape or being "on the road," but of a different kind, space set deep into a version of Robbe-Grillet's or Butor's mental substructure. The movement is inward, tunneling; the narrator, Cy, discovers himself while burrowing into another's life. Cy enters Dom's apartment immediately after his body has been carried out, after an apparent suicide. Dom is a disappearing body, but withal a powerful presence, embodied by way of his possessions, his apartment, his pervasiveness.

The narrator speaks of two men, Al and Bob, whom he has known since childhood, but who are unknown to each other and to Dom. We now enter into several spatial considerations, some involving a place, some inner journeys, some the distancing of characters. Using Bob and Al, one a city man, the other from the country, the narrator sets up coordinates by which we can comprehend associations. Once these coordinates are positioned in relationship to the narrator, we begin to learn of his life, and by indirection, of Dom's. The novel becomes a substructure of revelations, all of which depend on spacing.

The pattern is a "field state" or "field theory," in which one can plot mathematically the distribution and movement of matter under the influence of one or more fields. In such a field of force, a particle or matter as soon as it is situated has several pressures on it; it accelerates, moves, jumps, reacts. What makes it react, in physical terms, may be gravitational, electric, or magnetic. The gravitational field accelerates particles or masses like us; an electric field accelerates protons, electrons, and masses which have a surplus of protons over electrons—miniature aspects of us; a magnetic field accelerates magnetic particles such as a north or south pole, huge elements beyond our comprehension. All three types of field exert energies which move us beyond our own self-control and which, accordingly, belong to a world of both spatiality and magic. They can also be scientific equivalents of philosophical and theological notions of fate or destiny or doom; and they are ever-changing, from very complex to very simple, from strong to weak.

From McElroy's suggestion of this patterning, we can observe how the narrator enters into his own life by way of these coordinates; then as he discovers himself, he allows Dom to recede. Yet as he establishes his coordinates, he opens up Bob's and Al's lives, and by so doing enters ever more deeply into Dom's. Although Al and Bob and Dom cannot meet, they begin to approach each other in the field of force exerted by the narrator; they enter into overlapping lives by way of a narrator who is discovering himself. Spatially, they move around each other; temporally, they cannot meet, since they are distanced from each other and Dom is dead. But pressure exerted in one place, as in the field of force, creates movement elsewhere. Receding and foregrounding can occur simultaneously, and the novel reveals its "ancient history" by way of a suffocating apartment, people who have never met, and a narrator who not only discovers himself but discovers he has played a key role in Dom's life (and by indirction, in his death). The inner journey among Dom's objects has opened up an external world of almost limitless space. We enter a tunnel with a small opening and, like Alice, locate spatiality.

In *Lookout Cartridge* (1974), the helicopter descent—the computer is in trouble, having lost part of its functioning power—prefigures, on the first page, the descent into the maelstrom which will characterize the novel. The pace is frantic, even when frantic matters do not press; and the line of narrative lies somewhere between conscious and subconscious. McElroy tries to discover a realm of narrative line which lies both within and without, one that describes external events, but always in the whisper and hesitation of an observer who is uncertain of what he has perceived. Uncertainty of observation foreshadows the uncertainty of all systems; suggesting that antisystems, by analogy, may mirror survival. *Lookout Cartridge,* like *Gravity's Rainbow* of the previous year, is a reprise of postwar motifs.

The play on "cartridge" which is the crux of the novel is an attempt on McElroy's part to write a "total novel." This is Garcia Márquez's phrase, and it suggests a complete world made possible through artifact: a world of its own. Such "total novels" would include, of course, Márquez's *One Hundred Years of Solitude,* possibly Grass's *The Tin Drum,* Pynchon's *Gravity's Rainbow,* Gaddis's *The Recognitions,* Barth's *Giles Goat-Boy,* with some hesitation Barth's *Letters* and McElroy's *Lookout Cartridge.* The "total novel" phenomenon is not new, since in the nineteenth century Dickens, Dostoyevsky, and Tolstoy pursued it. But in the twentieth century, except for Joyce's two major works and Conrad's *Nostromo,* the total novel has not enjoyed much vogue. Apparently, it thrives on adversity, and the Second World War was a watershed for its development. *The Naked and the Dead* and *From Here to Eternity,* as their titles indicate, were efforts to develop total fictions or a totality of experience. But despite the fineness of Jones's novel and Mailer's ambitious reach, they were distinctly limited.

McElroy moves toward a total fiction not by direct inclusion (of life, death, eternity, marriage, divorce, love affairs) but indirectly, through metaphors of existence: the filming of episodes, the loss of the film, the attempt to recall it, the threat to the film-maker, the very questioning of what is. Episode headings indicate that frontier between "real life" and "filmed life," the two halves of a hallucinatory world. By moving along the edges of hallucination (montage, cutting, linkage, interrupted development, and related techniques), McElroy creates life by suggesting its opposite, even its denial; as in *Ancient History* he created spatiality by enclosing it. Since a film is a record of events, events do remain when the film is lost; on the other hand, events have a greater reality on film than in life, and therefore the disappearance of the film does affect vitally the sense of life caught on the reels.* McElroy uses another ploy or strategy: the film in Cartwright's mind is not precisely the film made. At least, that is what we think, since no absolute knowledge of either the film or Cartwright is attainable. All information of a "lookout cartridge" is arbitrary, neutral, or shifting. As Cartwright himself says midway through the novel: "A lookout stays in one place. But what of a moving lookout with a stationary trust?" Or somewhat earlier: "With the distance between me and the Druid [part of the filming of Stonehenge], as well as my growing need to trust fewer people [because he recognizes that there is a conspiracy against him] with the weight of my private inquiries [to chase down the missing film, to perceive who is following and who is seeking], this lookout cartridge [himself, his role, his placement of his concerns as an insert] narrows from the walls of its slot. But it enlarges too so that that which lies between, crowds that between which it lies."

The novel becomes something of a detective fiction, in which vague clues lie around, if one chooses to pick them up. The sole urgency is that Cartwright knows someone is after him as he seeks the film; for early in the novel he has been pushed down a nonmoving escalator. That "fall" has been a "Fall," an

---

*"Clearly Phil Aut had been shooting parallel footage to which ours might have been added as cut-in or complementary expansion; but Claire must have given Jack the idea that the Bonfire had been shot by Outer Film, not Dagger and me. . . . It seemed to me they knew different things, and this might be why or how they were going round in circles." Profusion of names is part of the hallucinatory sequence.

abrupt descent altering his state of mind, disrupting his state of being. "So I placed my plunge two-thirds of the way before slowing enough to do two, then one at a time, then stop, get the hands and fingers free [of his trench coat], and twist to look back up to the top. . . . I had somewhere in my head why Dagger DiGorro's film [Dagger is his partner in filming sequences in Corsica, Wales, etc.] got destroyed. I saw almost none of the film itself and shot only a few minutes of it; but no one saw more than I and I was there when Dagger shot the bulk of it."

That fall provides near-destruction and insight, coming on like a fit; it enables him to "see," and what he perceives is the film made by Dagger and hitherto unobserved by him, Cartwright. The fall serves as did the tea and madeleine for Proust's Marcel, jogging memory, shaping memory into a historical artifact which can be transformed into the artwork. Midway through the novel, Cartwright reminds us of the fall.

But you've been here before and you're looking back and forward, so you know the escalator wasn't running. All those grooved steps dropping away in front in a noise like motion weren't moving, but the new steps behind me were. . . . But I could only look ahead. . . . Yet when I began this story did I think this momentum mine? I think I did. But it was my pusher's first, then mine, which I see now is like that I, if not (no surely not) Dagger, saw us doing in the film, taking other energy in process and using it for our own peaceful ends. But was not the end there that of my pusher?

Cartwright suggests a reordering of our perceptions, based on a film made passively, literally pushed into existence by others' activities. One films what is, instead of creating tableaux or movements. The film crew has shot ordinary things: a commune here, a house there, Stonehenge at different angles and times, people in their routine functions—long sequences of passive elements. The question, of course, is why these reels should be of interest to anyone, why they have been stolen (if so), why Cartwright must make such an effort to recall them, why his diary of the events, which carries us along in his memories, is missing, so that he must reconstruct that as well.

In any process of reconstruction, space and time are altered, since they become internalized. In McElroy's novel, all objects become subjectified. Very little has objective existence once it is turned into material for (1) film, (2) diary, (3) memory. Tucked inside, made into an insert or a cartridge, objective data have taken on a different function. Lodged away, they can swell and contract. They are, also, a sexual metaphor: the enlargement of the insert within the walls of the container clearly works within the space/time of the sexual act. Time/space, as in the artwork, stands still; the sexual function takes over while the performers are passive, waiting for the act to be completed.

One problem in particular, we should mention at the outset, is that *Lookout Cartridge* is all dimensionality; unlike most "total novels," it has little matter at the core. McElroy moves immediately toward dimensions, levels, layers. Reality, as I suggested above, lies in the intermeshing of elements, not in the elements. The novel—a vast detective story in which victim, crime, and victimizers all work behind a screen of memory, doubt, and projective imagination —recalls one that is almost an exact contemporary, Gaddis's *JR*. In both, empirical knowledge is transmitted only through a world "out there"; information is fed through mind, memory, imagination, and that information, once sifted, becomes our informational world.

This is another way of saying that *Lookout Cartridge* is often more compelling as idea, as the idea of a novel, than as performance, dazzling as its elements may be. McElroy is interested in information theory, and he conceives of the novel as a form of computer which plays back information. In that novel, there is a different language (as in the computer), a different sense of space and time (banked, cartridged, enclosed, housed, inserted), and a serial-like source of materials which will make up the narrative. McElroy writes with characteristic oblique eloquence:

Information and the prospect of more dragged me toward some final grid no grander than this one here and stuck to it the regular driver's two signs declaring a man's cab is his cab and he would move it any distance for a price: a final grid-like this protective mesh that had changed the New York taxi not to a London cab class-comforted hackney carriage but to a squad car's compartmented coop: the wipers now slowly swinging against a film of rain.

The question arises: "Information theory? I had none. Only these circuits of addition two by two." Cartwright himself, like the figure in the cab, is only data in other people's minds; existing through their plans for him, yet unwilling to forsake his own sense of himself. He struggles to escape the computerized predicament: encased as a cartridge in cab or information bank, struggling to be something other than a "lookout cartridge," a wary insert. Cartwright struggles to be more than plugged in.*

Although the organization and prose of the novel are deeply original, the narrative metaphor is familiar: the need for the protagonist to move outside systems, whatever they are, and to establish his own forms of experience and identification. Cartwright struggles with and against not only computer-program schematics, but against (and with) all forms of determinants. McElroy offers us large chunks of material based on Mercator projections of maps (how we can turn vast space into manageable areas by way of the god Terminus); Mayan calendars (how we can enforce limitation on vast spans of time); Stonehenge (the vastitude of worship brought under Druid control); filming itself as the motif (how experience can be reeled in, made parallel to itself through replication); survey maps (which, like Mercator projections, give boundaries to demarked areas); the Standing Stones of Callandish in Scotland (like Stonehenge, containers of vast forms of religious worship); the computer, as already described, the basic form of information theory. All such systems, whether mechanical, religious, or scientific, are forms of entrapment as well as of experience and release.

Later in the novel, Cartwright begins to repeat the Yiddish word *shtip* (which he picks up from Tess, a Jewish refugee, his mistress for a time), which can be translated as "stab" or "push." It may be broadly

interpreted as "one's thing," being oneself, while at the same time it suggests something being done to one: one is released and yet enclosed by one's *shtip*. The *shtip* is associated with the computer existence into which we are plugged:

> For my *shtip* exemplifies the multiple and parallel sorties which raise our brain above the digital computer to which it is akin: the digital computer works its yes and no operations faster than the brain yet is confined to serial single-file one-quest-at-a-time circuit seeking; but the human natural Body Brain (as my Druid terms it) sends countless of these single files not one at a time but all at once circulating down the deltas, through the gorges and moving targets and . . . athwart the axes of all pulsing fields.

Here is, by way of a marginal science fiction, the archetypical American theme. In his perverse way, Cartwright is working through what we observed in Wyatt Gwyon, Gaddis's doomed artist: breaking away from systems through art, yet entrapped by imitation, however glorious his counterfeits. But McElroy suggests that exploration is the thing, not resolution, of which there is none. His exploration of new space/time dimensions, his forging of an original prose style, his use of a "lookout cartridge" as a metaphor, all indicate that living out one's *shtip* must occur whether one is plugged in or plugging in. The novel is a hymn to life even though it involves encasement, hovering vague boundaries, the god Terminus, huge chunks of "dead matter" (Druids, Stonehenge, the stones of Callinash, Mayan calendars), and an organization which is slowly eliminating people.

The polarities of the novel, life versus antilife as basic metaphor, can be observed in chapter headings, even when they are not located at the top of the page, but encased. Some are: Yellow Filter Insert, Slot Insert, Dagger-Type Cassette, Unplaced Room, Love Space, Corsican Montage, Lookout, Hinge, and Cartridge (the longest, which ends the novel). These named chapters are set into more conventional numbered chapters, which run consecutively through seventeen. Nearly all the named episodes are spatial in nature, whether inner or outer, space given or taken away, and they work against the narrative of the numbered ones to some extent, providing layers of internality. Named and unnamed elements work at layers of consciousness. There is an indeterminacy, such as we discover in the layered consciousness of a character like Geoffrey Firmin in Lowry's *Under the Volcano;* but there the layered consciousness derives

---

*The "terminal" idea in computers—one's ability to plug into the main computer by way of the terminal—arises in that helicopter scene at the beginning of the novel and now more significantly at the end: New York observed from the failing helicopter, all elements inserts or cartridges. ". . . it's as if my optic nerves . . . are now tuned to that tiniest muscle that operates the stirrup bone in the middle ear's drum—itself a slot in the temporal bone guarding the inner ear's semicircular circuits that compute my balance [man as helicopter hovering above a fall]—and so lower Manhattan bulges, or bulges in some inflationary sign to me that weightlessness may make those canals come unplugged and Terminus the god of boundaries and property may be subject to Mercurial delusions because of insecurity arising from the fact that his post was created to take some of the work-load and even responsibility off Jupiter's back but the liquid stir of that city aggregate there below may be my post-Terminal sense that I'm at the center but overcommitted and unconnected. A plane makes its way above our new tempo and can it be we cannot go forth and back now?" All the elements are present: the hovering but failing helicopter, Cartwright encased as cartridge, enclosed, and his awareness of existence beyond as a computer terminal into which all life, including his own, is plugged.

from an alcoholic fog, which creates its own terms of system and antisystem. Cartwright is more purely conscious than Firmin, more capable of being both less and more than a cartridge. Yet despite broad distinctions of character and personality, both seek a space/time continuum which differs from ordinary or normal. And both yearn after a linguistic medium which can express such layered consciousness: Firmin closer to Joyce's inner stream than Cartwright, who moves in and out of narrative modes.

The elements of the novel, often diffuse, full of layered characters who refuse identity, peopled by figures from Cartwright's imagination, do come together in that hovering helicopter flight. Hovering, like inserts and hinges, is a spatial metaphor for a defiance of gravity. McElroy has many such defiances structured into the novel. At one point, Cartwright remembers when a friend, Ned Noble,* threw a baseball in the air near Cartwright's apartment, The passage is a magnificent one, the moment of defiance of gravity, the identification with a deed that locates one in still time and space:

> Ned turned toward my apartment house and unfurled a monumental throw almost straight up, but the ball never quite reached the bricks of my house, yet came so high it came just up to my level past the silence of the watchers but perhaps three and a half feet out from my window and as it came to rest in a moment of equality [slicing "between gravities"] that I'll never forget, I lunged with one strange half of my body, and my mother who had felt a draft and come into my room shrieked behind me, and I took that white sphere out of the air at the instant it stopped rising and stopped spinning so it might have been a knuckleball in space and facing me as I took the ball was the name of Ed Head [pitcher for the Brooklyn Dodgers, who had only one great moment, outside gravity] whose steady no-hitter one day was a mercurial once-in-a-lifetime he never survived.

That vertical throw more than defies simply gravity; it seems to distinguish between gravities by establishing an association with something which lies undefined. That vertical throw is, more than anything else in the novel, a whiff of art, Ed Head's "privileged moment," identified with Proust's Marcel.

In its main thrust, the novel aims at working through those two gravities. By moving along interfaces, McElroy can justify his elliptical methods. For the novel is inaccessible in any ordinary way; and it remains a private code in large passages, which work through mediational modes, what we find in difficult poetic expression. John Ashbery's poetry comes to mind.† Necessary in reading such material is gaining the point of view, finding out what the narrative derives from. McElroy is a master of disguises and deceptions: the prose unwinds at its own pace and it enforces an experiential mode, forgoing direct narrative. We move along, but not ahead, rather like that vertical throw symbolized by Ned Noble's noble knuckleball.

Part of the disjointed nature of the narrative line, the discontinuity of fragments in a very long book, derives from the film and reel-like replication. But more than that is involved, although the concept of a diary helps to inform every element. More, also, is involved than that montage, called Corsican montage in several segments, which provides discontinuous juxtapositions; although montage is an inescapable component of the book. More, even, is involved than the reliance on the cartridge idea—lookout, enclosed, dreaming—although the cartridge is one of the major symbols of the novel. All these elements are profoundly significant, as is a reliance on a kind of verbal stream which drops into private meanings and subsidiary characters who remain unrevealed. More is involved even than memory, although recollection is a profoundly important controlling factor.

What McElroy is after is nothing less than a complete defamiliarization of our normal expectations, whether data, information theory, linear accessibility, spatial and temporal dimensions. The novel ultimately gains its power and significance not from its ability to move us—it rarely does that—but from involving us in a labyrinthine experience, far more elaborate than anything else in contemporary American fiction. Compared with *Lookout Cartridge,* Pynchon's two major novels are accessible and identifiable. For McElroy, we must constantly confront that

---

*Noble refers to himself as Nobel; this recalls the Nobel Prize, funded by the discoverer of dynamite; and this keys in to the explosion Cartwright sees from the helicopter at the beginning, which—an explosion, explosives—braids itself through the novel. Cartwright fears being exploded and is himself suspected of carrying explosives.

†One thinks especially of a long poem called "Europe" in *The Tennis Court Oath,* divided into 111 brief passages, some incantatory, some narrative, some even in prose. Section 104 has a marked-out grid, with words placed in different rectangles. The aim is montage: not the "Corsican montage" of McElroy, but a European montage. Deeply indebted to surrealistic techniques, the poem nevertheless has content; the problem, as with McElroy's novel, is to find a coherent point of view.

question which modernism long ago posed: Is the trip worth the effort? Are the demands made worth the diligence required? The response here is a qualified affirmative. McElroy inserts us, like one of his cartridges, into an experience; discovering the way is our satisfaction, for we are never there; we never arrive.

Halfway through the novel, in a section called "Lookout," Cartwright ponders what would happen if he "found the source of my undreamt lookout dream." If he could do that, he would have answers to what happened to the film, to who was looking for him, to who was stealing film from him, to the way in which a baseball thrown into the air did not return to the ground, and, finally, to the reason why someone pushed him down those unmoving escalator stairs. He would, in brief, have some insight into why things happen the way they do.

The entire novel, then, is a labyrinthine exploration of the way things happen; not why they happen, but how. The "why" remains buried deeply in the stream of existence, impenetrable except by way of journeying itself. Cartwright enters into the computer bank of his own life and ponders where it is taking him. At that point, as Walker Percy's Binx Bolling also recognized, existence is little different from a film of it: metaphysics, which seemed relevant to our forebears, is what shadows us as a reflection of ourselves.

McElroy's America is so severely disturbed because it has become so elusive. It is, at every stage, undermined by dissociation of reality, space fighting space. His vast format suggests an America which is an amalgam of "invisible cities," grids which, once shaped, become places where people may live. All is malfunction within function, great energy expended on the thrust itself. He has become a master of the fade-out, of the negative which disappears as we apply chemicals: a kind of reverse Polaroid.

Plus (1977), McElroy's fifth novel, was a spin-off from *Lookout Cartridge:* the ultimate in insertion and discovery now reflected in Plus, a disembodied brain, orbiting the earth in a capsule called Imp. The aim here is to test out structures, distances, movement, in their pure states. The prose is itself an attempt at a new voice: "And the wendings in the solid of their spiral up and down yet as well under the full reach of multi-sight that Imp Plus relented into, gathered

radiance of motion into a fixity like his own orbit: or, beyond his orbit, a possibility he wanted not to think of." Isolated passages such as this create the sense of an inventive voice, one mediating the situation of a disembodied brain, and accommodating the physically bizarre. But an entire novel filled with such passages is difficult to assimilate even in small doses; parts displace the whole.

McElroy has written articles on Apollo 17 and Skylab, showing interest in man-made machine systems which carry over into *Plus.* We perceive he is attempting to go beyond Barth and Pynchon into interfacial areas which border man and machine. Interfaces are imaginary locations where information and power are exchanged, by way of a man-machine system which feeds in information. The problem is a hardware one, of fitting two systems together, human and mechanical. Barth had reached for such a system in *Giles,* Pynchon in *Gravity's Rainbow.* In this respect, *Plus* is our novel of the seventies: an orbiting disembodied brain so connected to its mechanical systems that it functions as system; until, inevitably, its brain function begins to work, as if against the systems. And once that occurs, the brain begins to put together sensations, memories, extensions of itself in a real world.

In a way, the brain is an embryo which gains consciousness slowly; in fact, McElroy has structured his floating or orbiting brain as embryonic matter, but with memory, past consciousness, and sensations; a kind of Wordsworthian preexistence. In "Holding with Apollo 17," he speaks of writing about technology and people "in accord with some virtue of vision to be found in technology." Space systems somehow have to be incorporated into our view of human life; there cannot be the novelist's bias against that machine world, that dismissal which McElroy suggests is a rejection of human qualities as well.

This fascination with machines as extensions and embodiments of man can be discovered in shapes, and here we enter the world of *Plus.* Plus orbiting in Imp is nothing if not shape, a blob here, then extension of that in memory and in feelers, until we have something human which is also mechanical: the two meeting in some transfigured orbit. McElroy's motto: "The real action is in the movement that inheres in relations." Otherwise, everything is "invisible cities."

Chapter Nine

||||||||||||||||||||||||||||||||||||||||||||||||

THE POSSIBILITIES OF MINIMALISM

Elsewhere is a negative mirror. The traveler recognizes the little that is his, discovering the much he has not had and will never have.

CALVINO, *Invisible Cities*

Minimalism in fiction seems to have followed closely on the pop art that characterized the latter half of the 1960s. Pop art functioned as a way of camping up familiar objects or else by stressing the obvious until it seemed freshly structured, and minimalism could simulate some of these characteristics. In pop art, everything is there, nothing omitted, and part of the effect on the viewer is his recognition that he is staring at what is there. The trick with minimalist fiction is a variation of this, tipping off the reader that the artist is conscious of what is being omitted. The minimalist writer must assure the audience that he, the writer, knows far more about the subject than he is including; that beyond him, in some spatial realm, there is the rest, undefined perhaps, but *there*. Often, the writer makes as his point of reference not the line he develops but the beyond; what is not is as dominant as what is, and possibly more significant.

The 1960s and 1970s have produced a small body of minimalists, of whom Donald Barthelme is the most practiced, and his *The Dead Father* the most expert example. The group includes the novels (and essays) of Joan Didion; at least one novel by Jerzy Kosinski, *Steps;* the work of an experimental novelist, Rudolph Wurlitzer; the novel *Panama* by Thomas McGuane; *The Adventures of Mao on the Long March*

by Frederic Tuten, a combination of fiction, history, parody, and myth; *Sleepless Nights* by Elizabeth Hardwick and Renata Adler's *Speedboat;* Susan Sontag's two meditative fictions—*The Benefactor* and *Death Kit.* Much minimalist fiction tries to be innovative: Wurlitzer, Tuten, Sontag, McGuane, Adler (to whom we could add Richard Brautigan). Sequential narrative line and routine characterization, as well as plotting, are either diminished or undermined altogether.

The two finest examples in modern fiction of minimalism are Camus's *The Stranger* and Beckett's trilogy of *Molloy, Malone Dies,* and *The Unnamable.* In such works the reader is aware of the spaces between words, the pauses between breath, the silence between noises. Everything is intermittent. The narrative of these works relies on spurts which barely penetrate as decibels. The author brings us close to boredom, withdrawal, rejection of the work itself. Further, minimalist fiction is nearly always based on a pessimistic view of life, where all the normal goals or controls no longer obtain. It depends heavily on irony, itself a form of negation. In Camus's *The Fall,* depths dominate over heights; narcissism, self-regard, self-indulgence are norms.

Beckett attempted to replace words with silences,

and silences, as we shall see, are leitmotifs in minimalism. The prototypical author of silences—and thus of minimalism—is Mallarmé, in "A Throw of the Dice Will Never Abolish Chance," where whiteness dominates our reading of the poem, space bleaching out language in favor of surrounding blankness. In the Beckett universe, the shrinkage we become aware of is emblematic, not of man's effort to survive, but of the margin of survival itself. By contracting, by nearly silencing, he isolates individuals from objects, nature itself becoming a residue or remnant. Yet forms of salvation come in language, voices, speaking to oneself, mainly—what we also see in Barthelme's stories and longer works. Since all that remains is words, it is necessary to locate language in a new frame of reference, where it becomes not Babel but the typology of a modern world. The true self is unknowable, that is a given; and one is thrust into a Husserlian world of reductive consciousness, separated from familiar objects, feelings, et al. Even ego, which we consider the last line of defense against the engulfment, is insufficient, itself manipulable by some transcendental element. With the self unknowable, then all knowledge—even *us*—is unknowable.

Echoes, mirrors, images based on reflection and doubling become like a "second voice" in the novels of minimalism. If echoing is the means, revelations are the end, irony the middle ground. The irony may be muted, but it must exist, or else minimalist fiction can easily fall into pure self-indulgence, as some of Didion's work does, or some of Barthelme's briefer stories. Every truly minimalist work is an act of great daring: an effort to reveal or expose by way of negating the real.

The Dead Father (1975), along with *Steps,* is our representative American minimalist work, an audacious cultural document as well as a dynamic and original fiction. Although a mid-seventies publication, it follows sixties "death of" and caps *Snow White* (1967), Barthelme's only other novel. Unlike most dead fathers, Barthelme's can speak. What he speaks of is what most fathers would speak of if they could after they were dead. They speak of mortality—of what it was like to be a father before they became a dead father. Barthelme's Dead Father is a collective voice, like those collages which characterize other aspects of Barthelme's work: a father bigger in death than in life, because he is the accumulated fathers of our life and literature, the fathers of myth and legend. He is the collective hero as a father figure, Lord Raglan's and Joseph Campbell's hero with a thousand faces and innumerable attributes.

To be a father, one must have children, and children are more than the sum total of siblings one has fathered. "No fatherhood without childhood," Barthelme writes. "I never wanted it, it was thrust upon me. Tribute of a sort but I could have done without, fathering then raising each one of the thousands and thousands and tens of thousands, the inflation of the little bundle to big bundle, period of years, and then making sure the big bundles if male wore their cap-and-bells, and if not observed the principle of jus primae noctis, the embarrassment of sending away those I didn't want, the pain of sending away those I did want." Fathering is the historical, mythical, overall caring for the race; and when the father is dead, the procession of dead may go on, but the living need guidance, or seek it, or hover indecisively without it. The young may kill their fathers, but they cannot exorcise them.

The father takes on a multitude of sins, becomes the one burdened by historical necessity, which is another way of saying that fathering is a fate and not simply a role. "I never wanted it, it was thrust upon me. I wanted to worry about the action of the sun fading what I valued most, strong browns turning to pale browns if not vacant yellows." Every father is thrust into the role of a hero—whether with a thousand faces or the twenty-two attributes of Raglan's heroical figure. That thrust into heroism is a condition of being a father to sons, daughters, mankind, and it involves such a burden of life, history, and convention that one finds solace in death.

So that the "dead father" does not spill over into emotion, Barthelme retains his basic pattern of the questionnaire, that device which turns all information, feeling, emotional values into data. This pattern fits Barthelme's flattening out of experience to a funeral procession, the way in which Faulkner leveled the characters for *As I Lay Dying,* giving the procession a universal rather than a specific application. Barthelme, of course, abstracts his characters more than does Faulkner, taking them beyond easily definable roles, making them commit deeds that do not fall into discernible patterns. The son Thomas sneaks off for a brief interlude of breast sucking with the daughter Julie. "They retired from the Dead Father's view, behind a proliferation of Queen Anne's lace. Julie seated herself on the ground and opened her blouse. Two bold breasts presented themselves, the left a little smaller than the right but just as handsome in its own way." " 'Nothing like a suck of the breast. Is there more?' " Thomas asks, and she responds that there is always more while she lives. The interlude has overtones of a surrealistic escapade, told deadpan; but it is also part of the reasoned structure of the novella. For Thomas and Julie are now orphaned, the father dead, the mother long since gone or unknown, and all they have, besides the other members of the procession, is each other.

Nearly every story told or retold derives from myth. "Tell me a story," the Dead Father requests of Thomas, who then proceeds to unfold a very lengthy tale right out of the Raglan series of the hero, the riddle, the mythical role, which Thomas could not tell to the live father but which can be related to the Dead Father. Thomas's answer to the riddle, which is "What do you really feel?" is "murderinging," which he has read about and simply repeats. He wins, for that is the answer, a play on murder, but with an extra "ing," to suggest a long-drawn-out process. When the Dead Father calls that a tall tale, Thomas responds that all tales are distorted in the telling, but "the moral is always correct," which is "murderinging"; to which the father objects that the "sacred and noble Father should not be murdereded," the past tense drawn out into a continual murder.

Was the father a good one when he was alive? Did he deserve to die? Was Thomas the *murdererer?* How did the Dead Father die, since his qualities seem perpetual? Who are in the funeral procession of nineteen, besides Thomas, Julie, the Dead Father himself, and one Edmund (Lear's bastard?)? Barthelme creates the Dead Father as two beings: the natural one, who fathered real children; the mythical or ritual father, who flits in and out of the heroic categories that accommodate legendary fathers. When the Dead Father is asked to make a speech, he delivers several hundred words of nonsense, non sequiturs of science and pseudoscience. When asked what it meant, he answers that "it meant I made a speech."

Behind literalness lies ritualized speechifying: his words enter history as a speech given at such-and-such time in such-and-such place. The words are less significant than the fact of the speech. Words, in fact, do not count at all, since the Dead Father has always been making speeches, which cannot be distinguished from each other. Those he made as a person and those he made as a personage merge: speechifying is the ritualized process of Dead Fathers becoming legendary figures.

Although the Dead Father—the dying, dying, dead father—fits many of the categories we associate with the hero, he is, in actuality, a Victorian father, full of prohibitions and admonitions, making the son tremble in his presence. As a huge body being hauled by nineteen helpers, he is a process: the novel as idea is embodied in this great figure being brought ever closer, through enemy territory, to his burial ground. Thus, the father and the novel—the Victorian father and the type of novel in which he was central—is being hauled to extinction. Before he is buried, the father must be dismembered—a leg here, an arm, his balls there—in order to satisfy enemy chiefs; this piecemeal destruction of the Dead Father suggesting, once more, his parallelism to the novel. As elements drop away, as the novel moves through enemy territory (readers? critics? reviewers?), it changes its form somewhat, becoming ever more truncated, lacking in parts, shifting from narrative to sensation, as Barthelme's own tale does. With his loss of limbs, the Dead Father reaches toward minimalism.

The introduction of the long section called "A Manual for Sons" gives us the opportunity to extend our metaphor of the Dead Father as representative of the novel itself—the haulage, extension, transformations, the dying, dying, dead aspects—and the son setting forth his ideas, an author outlining his sense of the medium. The son outlines twenty-three points, one more than Lord Raglan's twenty-two for the birth of the hero, and he ends with "Patricide a poor idea." Much of the list, each item of which is given a paragraph, sometimes a page or more, concerns ways in which sons can locate the father's power and try to control it.

It is a manual for survival for sons as well as their fathers. The list proceeds from mad fathers, to fathers as teachers, to the "leaping father," who is not encountered often but exists. "Two leaping fathers together in a room can cause accidents. The best idea is to chain heavy-duty truck tires to them, one in front, one in back, so that their leaps become pathetic small hops. That is all their lives amount to anyhow, and it is good for them to be able to see, in the mirror, their whole life histories performed, in a sequence perhaps five minutes long, of upward movements which do not, really, get very far, or achieve very much."

The core of danger in the leaping father, unhampered by heavy-duty tires, is ambition, the father's for himself and perhaps for his son. Relief from this can come from open liver surgery, at the seat of the humors. The son finds "something very sad about all leaping fathers, about leaping itself." The son prefers to keep his feet on the ground, although he must be wary of the tunneling father in that situation. The father is dangerous, in fact, from any angle, for faced front to front, he may hurl his javelin. Although he may miss, he may not; one should be able to twist this way or that to avoid its flight. If a son has paneling in his house, it may suffer a hundred wounds from javelin tosses.

These episodes of survival for the son parallel episodes of power for the Dead Father, and are Beckett-like in their oblique wit. They are compounds of fear, but also expressions of awe at the natural order of things, which produces a father. While the generations may clash to the death, with a Dead Father refusing to die and children eager to bury him finally, the son has fond memories; and the father, ultimately, is the goal, is the son's destiny. Sons grow up to be like fathers, although they are not truly fathers until their own dies. Once freed of fathers, they can achieve fatherhood.

In naming: fathers fill every letter and combination of the alphabet. The son lists only a partial *A* and *B,* but each is so full that we recognize the father preempts all alphabetical combinations: A'albiel, Aariel, Aaron, Aba, Ababaloy, Abaddon, etc. After twenty-seven names, the son has reached only Albert. Similarly with the letter *B,* although *B* goes more rapidly since it lacks the possible Hebrew mixes of *A*'s. All letters inevitably lead back to the death of the father, who then passes back to where the alphabet came from, an "All-Father, who is the sum of all dead fathers taken together." Such transfers of power, with the son yearning for the Dead Father's control, are marked with ceremonies, rituals of transference, after which the son must deal with memories, which can be more potent than the presence of the father. The Dead Father becomes a living presence, an inner voice in the surviving son(s), full of commands and harangues. The son is trapped: "you are always partly him. That privileged position in your inner ear is his last 'perk' and no father has ever passed it by."

Parricide follows, but it is a foolish move, since "time will slay him" and save the killer the trouble. The duty of the son is not to kill the father but to reproduce "every one of the enormities touched upon in this manual, but in an attenuated form." He must become a paler copy of him, a weaker imitation. He calms fevers by doing less well what the father did with booming command. He should aim toward a "golden age of decency, quiet, and calmed fevers." If he attempts to meet the father on his ground, then he carries out the former's revenge upon him.

Before the book returns to the Dead Father in the final passages leading to burial, we can see how Father-Son duel applies to Novel-Author duel. The ways in which the father can be controlled, the de-

cline of his power, the fear the son has of his leaping and hurling, the gradual loss of the father's powers so that his world is debilitated, the fact that the son remains a paler copy and must live with memories of the father all cohere in the relationship of the author to contemporary fiction. If the Dead Father is the dying novel, the heritage is enormous, and the son is obligated to make an effort to continue. Like a Beckett protagonist, a dying gladiator himself, the Son-Father must reshape what is left him, the consequence of memory, lost power, declining control; and the result will be bulldozers for the dead (the final passage) and continuing life for survivors. Thomas is indeed literary, as a speaker or from his words transposed into nondirected free associational Joycean verbiage. Beneath the narrative, another kind of fiction is poking out, the detritus and debris of the novel itself, and Thomas is struggling to achieve it; or else to achieve some kind of voice against the overwhelming weight of the past.

One of the problems, among many, is that fathers' penises are so well hidden, lying dormant under overalls, aprons, ordinary suits, dress clothes, and so on. They are the mystery, and unless the child can work through the mysterious placement of the sexual organ, he cannot break through to his own life. Let him or her look, even touch; but the erect penis is in a world by itself, and the power it conveys is metaphysical, far greater in fathers than in nonfathers. The size and weight do not matter so much as the "metaphysical responsibility"; the penis goes beyond impregnation to the very heart of the universe, to a universal penis. To comprehend this power is to enter into the highest mysteries; where the penis lies, so lie clues to the father's achievements. The penis is, in one of its variations, the archetypal pattern: the author must become a father or else he cannot attain the father's power. And although sons are stressed, some of this rubs off on daughters as well. Yet the mother appears only briefly, and she is consigned to household areas; this is, indeed, a book of fathers and sons: of Dead Fathers and Manuals for Sons.

The partially disembodied Dead Father moves inexorably toward his grave, a huge burial ground hollowed out for his bulk. When the children bury their father, they bury the entire historical era, freeing them for their own forays into history, but conveying also the terrible fear of the unknown. The Dead Father had explored the past for them and given them direction. Without his presence, they enter an incoherent world, or one to be made coherent only by their own moves. "Bulldozers" are called for even as the Dead Father asks for one more moment. Bulldozers end it.

In his second book, after the collection of stories *Come Back, Dr. Caligari* (1961–64), Barthelme first ventured into a longer fiction, *Snow White* (1967). Not only did it help lay out the terms of Barthelme's subsequent career, but more importantly, it established the Barthelme mode of minimalism. *Snow White* defined a style based on parody, self-reflexive parody, collage, echoes, reflections, yards of white space, silence, boredom.

Barthelme transformed the fairy tale of Snow White into an avatar of the women's movement. But even more, he reshaped the traditional persecuted maiden into an American woman of the 1960s; further than that, into a type of American woman who has peopled our literature, her prototype Hester Prynne. Yet the background of Snow White is, also, the equally tortured Lady Brett. " 'Snow White,' we said, 'why do you remain with us? here? in this house?' . . . Then she said: 'It must be laid, I suppose, to a failure of the imagination. I have not been able to imagine anything better.' " This satisfies the questioners, although she adds to that: " 'But my imagination is stirring.' " She gives as analogy the long-dormant stock lying in a safety-deposit box, suddenly stirred because of new investor interest.

The juxtaposition of elements here is apt: a stirring Snow White; seven baffled and impotent dwarfs (joined by a narrator, who is part of the dwarf crew and yet separate, an "eighth," as it were); and a stress on goods which have a life of their own. The dwarfs are quite prosperous as window washers and as makers and packagers of Chinese baby food. They stir the vats, or else they dangle from windows, drinking beer and swabbing glass.

Their tone is set by Bill, who in the first line of the book "is tired of Snow White." They are accustomed to enjoying her in the shower, but Bill has defected because he does not wish to be touched anymore. Human contact, even in the shower room, has broken down, possibly because of the change of spirit in Snow White herself. She is exhausted by tired words, tired sights, and, apparently, tired sensations. As she awaits her prince (a less than princely Paul), she is depleted by her lack of positive feeling, and her role as shack job for the dwarfs is winding down. " 'Oh I wish there were some words in the world that were not the words I always hear!' "

Barthelme's role is to orchestrate the new sounds by mocking worn-out voices. He will not create new sounds, or new words, or whatever else is new; he will make the old sound depleted. He will attain this in several ways, and *Snow White* remains his chief achievement until *The Dead Father,* which was to define for the seventies what *Snow White* meant for the sixties.

Part of what Barthelme sweeps out is false sentiment. The fairy tale of Snow White (not the Disney version) has, like all tales of distressed maidens, elements of real pathos. We respond to Snow White's plight because she is deserving of our caring. She is not an independent woman prepared to march on her own, but a victim of everything the world brings down on a young girl and woman. Reviled by other women, she knows her fate is a perfect young man; but in between, she must find acceptance, which can come only in the "fairy tale" world of dwarfs. She must slave for them, her female functions the mark of her existence, and although these functions may lead toward happiness as well as misery, she lacks control.

Barthelme's Snow White is disillusioned, dissatisfied, disaffected from the role she has to play in the fairy tale, even the modified version of it. " 'Which Prince?' " she ponders while brushing her teeth, and then runs through a representative number from life, literature, music. " 'Well it is terrific to be anticipating a prince—to be waiting and knowing that what you are waiting for is a prince, packed with grace,' " but it is waiting nevertheless, a "darksome mode," and she would prefer to be doing. The passage becomes, in retrospect, vintage Barthelme: the witty list of likely and unlikely candidates; the setting of a scene which is parodic of life, tale, hopes; the definition of real aspirations; the shaping of all into a pattern on the edge of reality-fantasy.

Preceding "Which Prince?" is this announcement: "The value the mind sets on erotic needs instantly sinks as soon as satisfaction becomes readily available. Some obstacle is necessary to swell the tide of the libido to its height, and at all periods of history, whenever natural barriers have not sufficed, men have erected conventional ones." Such announcements or communiqués from the world of psychological reality occur at intervals, in a sense, political banners. The slogan may be Marxist, Freudian, or pop theological speculation. While it has the edge of self-parody, coming as it does in a mockery of Snow White, it also has the edge of actuality, suggesting that while power has shifted, people's consciousness remains untouched by the new. This Snow White is not what the dwarfs expect anymore, nor is she such a fine young woman as Disney portrayed. She plans, in phenomenological fashion, to redefine herself beyond the tale.

The dwarfs are themselves not Marx Brothers, but fat capitalists, seven young men pulling in different directions, unsure of themselves despite financial success. As a tribe or gang, they are beginning to disintegrate. Sexually, they have depended on Snow White while she awaits her prince; but now this, like everything else, is collapsing. Bill's disaffection, his request not to be touched, his need to avoid "human speculations," all point to dissolution of the band and of the idea. The fairy tale is altered to modern life, marriage, breakup, the inability of any individual to continue as part of a bloc.

Barthelme utilizes an ingenious narrative device to shape this tale of cultural dissolution, breakdown, impotence, disaffection. The narrator seems part of the dwarf band and yet is separate, a comrade so close to them he can speak as a part. " 'We were all born in National Parks,' " says Bill, and names one for each, the Everglades for himself; none mentioned for the narrator, who may be a composite dwarf. They are, as part of the parks, an indissolvable part of the country: as the country is connected by national parks, so the dwarfs; and the narrator has a voice that emanates only from them. The point is deliberately unclear: for we hear the narrator coming from "us" and from "we," the corporate experience, but unidentifiable.

Part of the evasion of naming and identification is connected to the parodying of conventions, until conventions vanish, leaving only the parody. This device, which is Barthelme's strength, proved in later years to be a disadvantage, for he tended to perfect the talent to the exclusion of others; and even sympathetic critics—who called his style the most influential in American writing—found him repetitious, failing to yield. Of course, in *The Dead Father*, Barthelme found range, depth, and significance for the method, demonstrating to both literary radicals and to the center (reviewers and other literary hangers-on) that his methods could prove more flexible than some of his stories indicated.

Although an actual questionnaire appears about a third of the way through the novella, questionnaires as a structural mode, as a strategy, dominate. This type of questionnaire is not of the conventional sort, for there are questions for which no answers can be supplied; and conversely, answers for which there are no apparent questions. The mode of the questionnaire is appealing because of its reductiveness. If "Snow White and her Seven Dwarfs" (plus narrator and sub-

sidiary characters) are a society, then it is a community reduced in all its elements: family, individual, class, and caste, all brought not only into decline but into minimalism. While increasing our methods of tabulating feelings about things, the questionnaire is noted for its elimination of feeling, for its transformation of attitudes into statistics.

Here, too, the medium is the message, for attempts to make more of tabulations than the tabulations themselves involve a leap which the questionnaire cautions against. By posing the questionnaire form, Barthelme has (1) a device for parodying our way of responding to feeling; (2) a method for containing a life of passion, compassion, pathos; (3) a means of expressing a minimalist response, joining him with Didion, among others, in fashioning a strategy that signifies both a commentary and the limits of one's talents, which is to say a style.

Barthelme's type of minimalism takes somewhat different turns from Beckett's, and by contrasting and comparing them we can see that even within a reductive form, different goals and methods exist. Only basic drives continue to exist in Barthelme's world—we note how his minimalism, mockery, and reductionism are familiar aspects of American naturalism.

The dwarfs' disaffection from Bill, when he no longer wishes to be touched, derives from their perception that he no longer can lead them as they wish to be led—toward business success and satisfaction with Snow White, their long-haired, beauty-spotted young waif. Bill is, inevitably, executed, for the crime of hurling two six-packs of Miller High Life through a windshield; but his more serious crime is his illusion of leading without providing the substance of leadership. Barthelme is right there, in the mid-1960s, with a view of the President, of leadership in general, with mockery of heroism in every heroic act. The people, the dwarfs, want only goods, accept their destiny, dispute only details; anyone threatening goods must be eliminated.

Beckett minimalizes, defuses, deglamorizes in order to point up elements of heroism that lie in small acts, indefinite decisions, wavering choices. Hovering on edges, vacillating over abysses, split by inaction, enervated, Beckett's characters demonstrate the potential or possibility of action. Through their vacillation, we can perceive unleashed energy; whereas in Barthelme, the opposite is true. Through energy, we can see the enervation, exhaustion, the played-out quality of life. Didion is closer to Barthelme in this respect than she is to Beckett, whereas another minimalist, Rudolph Wurlitzer, identifies with Beckett, suggesting that within waste lands, fructification is potential.

A great deal, of course, depends on language. No American author has discovered the magic of Beckett's minimalist prose. The combination of wit and wisdom, of casual irony, is unique. What Barthelme has found for himself—and it is distinctive, a logo—is a language of dislocation. Such a voice is always "moving off" even as it describes. It is, as a roving language, more suitable for short fiction and the novella than for longer works; and one reason Barthelme has stuck to the shorter forms may not at all be a failure of imagination, as some critics have suggested, but a recognition that his type of prose—unlike (say) Bellow's or Styron's—works only in briefer units. The Barthelme linguistic mode is geared to bursts, not expansions. He has developed the rapier, the frequent dislocation, as ways of evading what he calls a "stuffing" quality. He is never endless—thus, the short burst; and never like sludge—thus, the hit-and-run quality.

Midway through the novella, Barthelme has several sections based on responses, or lack of responses, to Snow White's hair. Like Rapunzel, another imprisoned young woman, she lets her hair down, so that it hangs over the window, long black hair that signals (sexually) that she is ready for some form of escape. One such response or lack leads to a discourse on language, to what he calls the "blanketing effect of ordinary language." This effect comes from language that fills in—such as "you might say" or "so to speak"—and it may also be called stuffing. Stuffing has two salient qualities: (1) that of being endless; (2) that of being like sludge. The endless quality of stuffing means that "it goes on and on, in many different forms, and in fact our exchanges are in large measure composed of it"; the sludge quality is "the *heaviness* that this 'stuff' has, similar to the heavier motor oils, a kind of downward pull but still fluid."

But as we have noted, the method goes beyond any particular scene. It figures in Snow White's own puzzlement as to her situation: her decision to rebel against cooking, cleaning, picking up after the dwarfs. Even the wicked witch Jane, or the anti-Prince, Hogo, or the Prince, Paul, are caught in questionnaire procedures: unable to find the long movement or action, they are reduced to limited areas. Jane maneuvers, despite her powers, in such a small turn that nature, forests, life itself are beyond her control; and while mismanaging her effort to poison Snow White, she kills off Paul instead, with a poisoned vodka Gibson. No one escapes the questionnaire. The Xerox copy would be another such device: caught in the copy of things, one is limited by imitation, like Pynchon's Stencil. Barthelme mocks human aspirations for freedom, choice, selectivity, by way of forms people have themselves developed as ways of limiting such freedom. Desiring this or that, we develop forms and elements which work in the opposite way.

Still another way of locating Barthelme's "aesthetic" for such a retelling of the Snow White legend is to see the questionnaire as a verbal equivalent of the layout, that design which turns words and ideas into pattern. This is a form of minimalist art in itself, in which words or stuffing becomes unnecessary. A good layout has a minimum of stuffing, of both kinds, either endlessness or sludge.

The layout is apparent in *Snow White*. Part I begins with a graphic device, the six beauty spots marking Snow White's body, all more or less in a row, up and down. Each is a marker, each more or less equidistant from the next. The book ends with a pattern of headlines, something that occurs at intervals throughout the novel. "The Failure of Snow White's Arse / Revirginization of Snow White / Apotheosis of Snow White / etc." These headline sequences are like telegrams to the reader, layout materials, and also shorthand forms of narrative.

The vehicle is the layout or collage—to give the page the look of something new: different type faces, different sizes, differing spacings, and no follow-up. That statement is the message: "Snow White rises into the sky / The heroes depart in search of / a new principle / Heigh-Ho." Or else the headlines come as free-associational materials: "Snow White thinks: the house / . . . walls . . . when he doesn't / . . . I'm not . . . in the dark / . . ." Such materials create different pacing or timing for the reader, serving more as dislocation than as stability. Barthelme's free-associational material has little narrative or communicative value; it is disruptive, aimed at creating a new association of words and people, a synesthesia of sorts. It fits the layout principle: to spread out only to take away. Barthelme's vision is entropic: systems are indeed running down, becoming exhausted; but he saves as much as he can by patterns—salvation without stuffing.

SHORTER FICTIONS

As a 1960s writer, Barthelme produces in *Come Back, Dr. Caligari* (1964), not only landscapes of exhaustion but staging areas where one seeks—in vain—modes of renewal. Wherever Barthelme looks in his search for renewable territories, he finds only discarded junk heaps—trips to the moon to locate rocks. His creation of a Barthelmeian language was a way of circumventing the exhausted, turning it into something meaningful by stressing its platitudes. Through that distinctive voice, he separates himself from sixties pop art, which also exploited the well-known.

Peterson in "A Shower of Gold," for example, wants to win money on a program called "Who Am I?" one of the many quiz-and-tell programs of the late 1950s. Once Peterson enters that world of the program, he is, in a sense, programmed into absurdity. His life is reeled before him, and he seems to be in a film about himself, even while he observes the unrolling of the film—a double and triple play characteristic of Barthelme, shared with Barth and Pynchon. What had been a planned, ordered, dull world now splits into contingent fragments. "I was wrong, Peterson thought, the world is absurd. The absurdity is punishing me for not believing in it. I affirm the absurdity. On the other hand, absurdity is itself absurd."

The "shower of gold," which betokens wealth, goods thrust upon one, has sexual connotations, too, and can signify being pissed upon—a shower of golden drops. Peterson feels the latter, although he yearns for the former. There is also a mythical dimension, for Zeus visits Danae in the shape of a shower of gold and impregnates her with Perseus, each of them condemned to death. Peterson in some manner or means is moving toward a death sentence, even as he hopes to change his fortunes.

In "Hiding Man," A. L. Burlingame enters a movie house that features exotic themes—"offscreen rapes, obscene tortures"—and finds it occupied by only a well-dressed black man, Bane. They talk across the theater, Burlingame desiring anonymity, the black insisting on talk. The former seeks some meaning in the situation: desire for solitude and being lost, while the screen pours out images of disconnected scenes. "On the other hand, perhaps antagonist is purely, simply what he pretends to be: well-dressed Negro with dark glasses in closed theater. But where then is the wienie? What happens to the twist? All of life is rooted in contradiction, movement in direction of self, two spaces diagonally, argues hidden threat, there must be room for irony."

It is not that the theater is empty; it is not empty enough. It is not that the black is a threat; it is that he represents a formula one cannot derive. It is not that Burlingame has chosen to hide; it is that once confronted, he must hide everything: even what he is not certain of must be hidden. The Barthelme "location" is present: the individual is thrown off his line of direction, even one that is itself not quite sane or stable; and once thrown, must grapple with the new, the Joseph K. of the ordinary. Barthelme must now develop a language, a commentary, with which to pursue him into incoherence, absurdity, a misaligned universe.

Like Ellison's invisible man, Burlingame has discovered a pattern of existence which can be defined only by a hole or an underground experience; there, he can live through an intensified terror which makes distinctions between sanity and insanity meaningless. That he is insane, or moving along a new definition of man, is not the point. He may be some protean man—capable of innumerable changes as reality shifts—or else a man who has passed into a schizoid condition. But neither is significant. What is significant is that he has assimilated role-playing, that he has absorbed films into his system, that he represents on the individual level a culture whose meaning accrues from images, scenes, reflection, reels. Life is a film, and in a curious way Barthelme's story returns us, via Kafka and Ellison, to Delmore Schwartz's "In Dreams Begin Responsibilities," life as a self-induced film.

The leitmotif of "Me and Miss Mandible" is disproportion, appetites, situation. In a rough way, this story foreshadows *The Dead Father*. The narrator, a huge adult, has been placed in a public school class for eleven-year-olds, the result of a computer error. He is an army veteran and has worked as a claims adjuster for the Great Northern Insurance Company, a position that suggests Kafka's own work, and is a clue-in to the size motif. For the protagonist-narrator has, except for Miss Mandible, found himself a giant among children, a reversal of the Kafkan mode, a Swiftian conceit. Miss Mandible, the teacher, yearns for the narrator; he, in turn, prefers the female students (of eleven), Humbert rejecting the mother for the daughter.

As her name suggests, Miss Mandible will chew up the narrator if given the opportunity, as she does, bringing on the disaster that ends the story. But the narrator is Barthelme's prototypical man: we can, very possibly, speak of Barthelmeian man. His job as a claims adjuster had made him spend his working day amidst "the debris of our civilization: rumpled fenders, roofless sheds, gutted warehouses, smashed arms and legs." After a decade of this, he tends to see the world "as a vast junkyard." Hoping for reeducation, the narrator is mislocated in the sixth grade, with no way of correcting the error. Attempting to be salvaged, he is lost in the system; reprogrammed to grow up, he is accepted by all, except Miss Mandible, as a sixth grader. His culture becomes the culture of the children sitting around him. "Who are these people, Debbie, Eddie, Liz, and how did they get themselves in such a terrible predicament?" He peruses the young girls' magazines, which they tempt him with, all filled with Debbie losing her man, Eddie unable to make the break, Liz coming on strong, all run together in headlines such as "Eddie's Taylor-Made Love Nest" or "Debbie's Dilemma." Seeking salvation, the narrator is "lost in the funhouse" of pop culture, yearned after by young girls, lusted after by Miss Mandible, straining his knees at his desk, unable to straighten out, wary of attack from either small or large, and surrounded by Eddie, Debbie, and Liz. Ungrowing has proved as difficult as growing.

In *Unspeakable Practices, Unnatural Acts* (1968), Barthelme's second volume of short stories, the most notable pieces are "The Dolt," "Robert Kennedy Saved from Drowning," "The Indian Uprising," possibly "Edward and Pia," "The President," and "History of the War."

In "Robert Kennedy Saved from Drowning," Barthelme tries to observe politics by describing trivial details of Kennedy's life—at his desk, with his secretaries, at the level of his attitudes. Through this, Kennedy is reduced, minimalized, humanized rather than politicized. The method is also satirical, because it eschews the heroic aspect in favor of the ordinary. When Kennedy speaks, it is in platitudes. When Barthelme speaks of his qualities, it is in clichés: "The thing you have to realize about K. is that essentially he's absolutely alone in the world. There's this terrible loneliness which prevents people from getting too close to him." As a result of such methods, which turn all into trivia, Kennedy seems to be in a vacuum, or else at sea, drowning in Robert Kennedyness. When he speaks, we hear only echoes: "The world is full of unsolved problems, situations that demand careful, reasoned and intelligent action. In Latin America, for example."

Or else, Kennedy poses as someone with intellectual interests, and he attempts clarification. He speaks of Georges Poulet, the philosopher of time: " 'For Poulet, it is not enough to speak of *seizing the moment* [Kennedy parodying Bellow?]. It is rather a question of, and I quote, "recognizing in the instant which lives and dies, which surges out of nothingness and which ends in a dream, an intensity and depth of significance which ordinarily attaches only to the whole of existence." ' " Kennedy goes on, an echo of an echo: drowning in words and thoughts lacking significance. The final segment of the story has Kennedy in the water—although he has been drowning all along—and the narrator, unnamed, pulls him out, gasping. " 'Thank you,' " he says, and the story ends.

"The Indian Uprising" moves along like reels from a Godard film: the quick jumps, lack of connectedness, assumption of a different reality, exploration of boundary between real and fantasy, talk of actualities when the scene is itself distorted. The aim throughout is to disorient the viewer or reader, so as to force new perceptions. Attacks come from Comanches; as in Godard's *Weekend,* guerrillas work along the countryside, Indians of sorts. "We defended the city as best we could. The arrows of the Comanches came in clouds." Guerrillas from the countryside have moved toward the city, and Comanche war clubs "clattered on the soft, yellow pavements." What follows is a sequence of disassociated phenomena, the detritus of a culture self-destructing, or reverting to the Indians: the South Bronx as a microcosm of all cities. "The Indian Wants the Bronx" was Israel Horovitz's response to this cultural condition, his Indian from India, but with the connotation for the American of our Indian wanting the Bronx back.

With *City Life,* in 1970, Barthelme achieved his sui generis style. He was striving, as before, for the perfect collage, that ordered and coherent expression of anarchic materials which, when verbalized, will express a visual, aural, imaged reality. That mélange of materials reordered for synesthesiac purposes is Barthelme's way of presenting America: a design of our life, in arrangements that recall layouts. In *City Life,* the expression of this view contains the sharpest, as yet, cuts and breakaways. Barthelme has become merciless in his input into the collage, unhesitant in his confidence to manipulate the reader, as we see in the key piece, "Kierkegaard Unfair to Schlegel." The perfection of the Barthelme method comes with his expression of confidence, and contempt: confidence in his ability to present his antiseptic vision; contempt for the reader who misses connections or cannot leap gaps.* Whereas earlier, his ear had been his glory,

---

*Efforts cross, and while Barthelme disdained the reader, he also had, in the mid-seventies, to disclaim work submitted to magazines by authors using his name; work which, ironically, seemed an almost perfect imitation of his. Not only did he have

now he must get beyond the ear and move toward another dimension. *Great Days,* at the end of the decade, reaches for new expressions and structural arrangements.

As *City Life* indicates, brain damage lies everywhere, like trout fishing in Brautigan. "This is the country of brain damage, this is the map of brain damage, these are the rivers of brain damage, and see, those lighted-up places are the airports of brain damage, where the damaged pilots land the big, damaged ships." Brain damage permits new arrangements, sanctions lack of coherence, justifies Barthelme's constant revisions of the new. With brain damage, people plug flowers into electrical outlets so they will grow better, waiters tip each other, a dead waiter is poached in wine and herbs. Barthelme can move into the seams.

The epitome of brain damage is "Kierkegaard Unfair to Schlegel." With this, Barthelme has forsaken all "narrative line" for skew elements—a riddle of sorts set into a questionnaire of sorts. But the answer precedes the question, and the line of the story is the analysand, a writer, relating his methods, attitudes, or lack of them to the analyst. This is an abstract of Portnoy to Dr. Spielvogel. The narrator speaks of a type of image he uses, a girl on a train, then his tastes, politics, his ironic mode. He has complex ideas about irony, and these shape the rest of the narrative.

First, he views government as ironic, in that it sells surplus uniforms and other military paraphernalia cheaply. This leads to youngsters' wearing pieces of uniforms, creating with their military look a parallel street army, which is a mockery of the real one. "And they mix periods, you know, you get parody British grenadiers and parody World War I types and parody Sierra Maestra types. . . . and of course the clown army constitutes a very serious attack on all the ideas which support the real army including the basic notion of having an army at all." From this confusion of realms, the narrative proceeds to questions, which lead into the central question about irony.

Having rented a house in Colorado belonging to a ski instructor, the narrator discovers in the closets "all kinds of play equipment," every kind of game and mechanical contrivance to postpone boredom. From this, the narrator tries to find jokes to deal with such monomaniacal attention to play as a way of displacing boredom; and in his jokes, he perceives irony as a form of negation. Kierkegaard's *The Concept of*

---

to be careful not to imitate himself, he had to take care not to imitate his copiers.

Irony is part of the ski instructor's haul, a book in which the Danish theologian disapproves of irony because it becomes "an infinite absolute negativity." Irony according to Kierkegaard produces both estrangement and poetry; and with that insight, he attacks Schlegel's *Lucinde* as an example of making the whole of existence "alien to the ironic subject." For the sake of irony, Schlegel has forsaken reconciliation. That can come about only through religion, and Schlegel's ironic method has undermined a religious prescription.

The narrator concludes that Kierkegaard was unfair to Schlegel, but all the while he recognizes he was "fair," only unfair in his, the narrator's, mind. This is represented by a large black square set into the center of the argument. The square emblemizes all we fail to understand, synapses that reach toward but do not touch each other. The remainder of the story is a return to questionnaire and response, a collage of materials, including a zoo trip, Hitchcock's *Psycho,* Pasteur, a method that recalls a running commentary of gossip. End. That narrator has minimalized all experience, but touched upon absolutes and infinitudes. The Barthelme method, which was becoming more refined, could now reduce to such levels, without forsaking contact, that even irony, the mainstay of his method, can be questioned and undermined. Barthelme has upended his own modes in order to comment upon them, established a riddle, and transformed life into an infinite analysis session.

"Views of My Father Weeping"—foreshadowing *The Dead Father*—is cryptic, as fits the volume. But its layout is familiar: an act or event, disconnected activities which move toward the central event but can never resolve it, and finally, a confrontation which demonstrates how effort and event can never connect. How, in effect, individual effort runs up against events or circumstances and, in some ironic ways, fails to achieve anything; that is, Kierkegaard unfair to Schlegel.

In the story, the narrator's father is run over by an aristocrat in some Scandinavian country; the time is undifferentiated, but medieval rules cover relations between aristocrats and subjects, who live in highly restricted areas. When the narrator finally traces the livery, he must deal with the owner's driver, Lars Bang. The meeting comes at the Lensgreve's house, in the servants' quarters; the narrator has brought a gift of expensive wine, which the servants drink. Bang offers his version of the story, which is that the father, half crazed by drink and impelled by some anger which could end only in destruction, threw himself against the Lensgreve's carriage. With that, a dark-haired girl says: " 'Bang is an absolute bloody liar,' " as we assume from the regularity and coherence of his story.

But the main thrust of the story is not the revelation of detail or even how the father met his end; for set at intervals are refrains of the dead father weeping, scenes from the narrator's childhood, and scenes of the dead father as imagined by the narrator. The dead father "lives" in those memories or fantasies even while the narrator pursues the senseless murder and listens to Bang's invented story. Those cuts or collages of the dead father—weeping for himself as Niobe wept for her children—set against his death under horses and carriage of an indifferent aristocrat, are scenes of "city life." This is how we have organized ourselves, characteristic urban images. Juxtaposition, counterpoint, the fugal play of opposites—Barthelme has accepted his fictional destiny.

With *Sadness* (1972), Barthelme has turned the conceit or extended image into the whole. His short fictions, no longer stories in any formal or even informal sense, have lost all beginning and end. They are all middle, prose narratives without any apparent structure; dialogues of modern life, language, mores. They are "inserts" into life, and both their virtues and their occasional vices can be attributed to something of the format of *The New Yorker,* where so much of Barthelme's work has been published. The "insert" conception is an adaptation of *The New Yorker*'s more formal story, where middles run on and simply terminate. Also, the brevity of the Barthelme story fits into the magazine's idea of a short fiction: a civilized comment, followed by an ambiguous withdrawal. The lack of personal violence, the absence of contemporary epithets (sometimes inserted into the book version of the story), the paucity of sexual references all fit *The New Yorker*'s conservative or genteel literary ideology. Barthelme works, then, within a particular frame of reference, and the tendency is repetition of attitudes and forms which become formulaic. The singularity of his magazine publisher reinforces the singularity of his work.*

---

*Barthelme has spoken of the freedom of *The New Yorker*'s publishing policies, with Borges, Singer, and Nabokov, added to Cheever and Updike, appearing there regularly. Yet the latter two long ago entered formula fiction: doing well what they could do, and doing it repeatedly. Publishing there almost exclusively in the flush of their careers proved as much a disadvantage as an advantage for their development. As for Nabokov, Singer, and Borges, no one would suggest that the best of their work appeared in the magazine. On the contrary, their

Sadness is concerned with performance, especially in "A Film," "The Flight of the Penguins from the Palace," and "The Rise of Capitalism." We live vicariously by way of acting out roles others have created for us. We have devoted our lives to an "acting company." In "The Party," King Kong returns, now transformed into a new role as "an adjunct professor of art history at Rutgers, co-author of a text on tomb sculpture." Kong is indistinguishable from us.

In "A Film," everything that occurs in the shooting of a film can become part of the story line. Vandals dog the making of this particular film, and even kidnap the child of the star. "But might not this incident, which is not without its own human drama, be made part of the story line?" If we exist within a film, then all is film, the accidents of our life as well as those planned or determined by the scenario. The larger scenario, in effect, may contain accidentals as well as determined events. At the outer reaches, which is where we live, there are few distinctions.

Film-makers can call up or group all emotions: "Today we filmed fear, a distressing emotion aroused by impending danger, real or imagined. . . . We filmed the startle pattern—shrinking, blinking, all that." The director is good "in demonstrating the sham rage reaction and also in 'panting.' " Such emotional reactions appear meaningless unless under the eye of a director and film crew, unless filmed. In the filming of ourselves, we can see the reflections; and we are, then, like the denizens of Plato's cave, watching for glimpses of ourselves reflected, eschewing whatever reality exists outside of or off the film.

One day the crew films the moon rocks. They set up a "Moon Rock Room, at the Smithsonian." The moon rocks preempt all other experiences, all colors, all loud sounds: "They produced booms, thunderclaps, explosions, clashes, splashes, and roars." The rocks also perform: "The moon rocks whistled *Finlandia* by Jean Sibelius, while reciting *The Confessions of St. Augustine,* by I. F. Stone." They are the ultimate "turn-on."

Living by way of the film collapses time and space, in favor of unrestricted temporal and spatial experiences. A doll is murdered; who murdered it? "We

---

careers were established elsewhere, earlier, with far stronger works; magazines picked up names, not significant fictions, when it published them. To break free of *The New Yorker* may be necessary for the writer when still in the flush of his career, at a time when the magazine has itself lost much of its former sharpness, in its feature articles and its book, theater, and film reviews.

pressed our inquiry, receiving every courtesy from the Tel Aviv police, who said they had never seen a case like it, either in their memories, or in dreams." Restrictions of help, support, location are removed. Inevitably, we live only in the film, our personal lives having been suppressed and/or sacrificed. "A Film" suggests that Barthelme has deepened his vision of America by turning his material into Borgean frames of reference. Film here approximates the Borgean duplicating literary structure, where alternative and, sometimes, enhanced life exists more in the artifact than in the fact. The "sadness" of the book title is the sole true feeling left after we have surrendered all to alternative processes.

The most ambitious story in *Guilty Pleasures* (1974), "And Now Let's Hear It for the Ed Sullivan Show!," continues the theme of roles and performances. The MC may be Ed Sullivan, but Sullivan is a persona for Nixon, and the show is the "fun festival" he has made of America. The performers are stand-up comics, dancers, singing groups, great actresses. Each plays the role suggested by Sullivan's introductory remarks. Sullivan is himself described as combined MC, religious leader, and confidence man: "Church of the unchurched. Ed stands there. He looks great. Not unlike an older, heavier Paul Newman. Sways a little from side to side. Gary Lewis and the Playboys have just got off. Very strong act. Ed clasps hands together." Sullivan's bulky body, so lacking in poise and grace, picks up its rhythms from those swirling around, the talent he has marshaled, which reflects his view of America and its culture. His performers are, so to speak, his cabinet; none breaks from the routines Sullivan demands, and none, therefore, can move outside the magic circle he has drawn for his program.

Unlike Pynchon or Barth, with whom he has been compared, Barthelme moves around edges and margins, prowling his targets, working corners and perimeters. Unable to discover any overview of American culture, he began to locate his arsenal of tricks in the seams of our cultural life, not in the big areas of staging, action, forays. In *Amateurs* (1976), "The Reference" involves the selling, by a friend, of an engineer–master builder McPartland, to the Arkansas State Planning Commission. " 'Very much a team player. You get you your team out there, and he'll play it, and *beat* it, all by his own self.' " But McPartland is really a "warp," and goes off in his own direction, and some of these directions—as we find from suggestions—may be disasters, individual projects which went wrong. As his friend says:

" 'McPartland worked on the kiss of death, did you know that? When he was young. Never did get it perfected but the theoretical studies were elegant, elegant. He's what you might call a engineer's engineer. He designed the artichoke that is all heart. You pay a bit of a premium for it but you don't have to do all that peeling.' "

McPartland may well be an "amateur" being pushed as a professional, which is one way of moving the seams out into the reality. He has the "warp to power," and is clearly the man to get "the troops back on the track or tracks," since Arkansas is, "at present, pure planarchy." In this very brief fiction, Barthelme, from the vantage point of a seam,* not the main angle, is able to illuminate business. Reality is reflected, by way of references, so that the principal remains hidden, full of secrets, power "warps," and other independent means. The significant element is that presentation by way of the "other": an entering wedge, so to speak, into the main arena by means of something almost always neglected, the reference.

In the interview Barthelme gave Klinkowitz, he mentions rejecting collage in favor of perspective: shortening forefront so as to deepen what lies beyond the line of the story. We can speculate that perspectives were so significant for Barthelme because several of his shorter fictions began as novels and then remained stories. "Flying to America" was "twice cannibalized, since I have drastically cut it and combined it with another story to make 'A Film.' " This movement from short fiction to novel, then back to story length when novel fails, is all a matter of perspective. Forefront, back detail, angles of vision, obliqueness, and clarity become of primary importance under such circumstances. Barthelme has not so much forsaken collage for perspective as intensified his sense of the latter while lessening his grip on the former. This is clearly the direction for the stories in *Great Days* (1979).

Great Days is more formally arranged than Barthelme's previous collections, being given over to three dialogues, followed by ten fictions, ending with four further dialogues. More than one of the dialogues may be a monologue. In the key fiction, "Concerning the Bodyguard," Barthelme locates himself, as Kafka did, just beyond the characters. His observa-

*In a mail interview with Jerome Klinkowitz, Barthelme, not unusually, lists Kafka among his favorite writers of the past. He also mentions Rabelais, Rimbaud, Stein, Kleist, who offer, collectively, lists, montage effects, prose inventiveness, and irony.

tion is that the bodyguard is emblematic of American life; the eminence or "principal," as he is called, is followed and succeeded by an entourage. Once this entourage was admirers, but now it is a body of guards, the Renaissance prince surrounded by cutthroats and mercenaries. The fiction is structured mainly on what life looks like from the vantage point of the bodyguard; how he perceives the reality around the principal, rather than what the principal sees. We enter the seam and peer out.

Barthelme poses many questions, some related to the bodyguard's association with the principal he is guarding, some to his connections with other bodyguards, some to his observations of the world he must guard the principal against. In that world, everything is of potential danger to the eminence. Does the bodyguard speculate on world matters? "Does the bodyguard know which foreign concern was the successful bidder for the construction of his country's nuclear processing plant? Does the bodyguard know which sections of the National Bank's yearly report on debt services have been falsified? Does the bodyguard know that the general amnesty of April coincided with the rearrest of sixty persons?"

The bodyguards' perceptions here shift from the seams onto the main stage, where their moves become the arena. At work, the bodyguards must avoid certain restaurants which are "packed with young, loud, fat Communists," they must move carefully through crowds which surround their Mercedes, stopped for a light or sign, they must deliver children of principals to schools with other children of other principals —and they must fear kidnapping. All is in vain, however, for the story ends: "Is it the case that, on a certain morning, the garbage cans of the city, the garbage cans of the entire country, are overflowing with empty champagne bottles? Which bodyguard is at fault?" The country is celebrating the death of the principal, possibly also of the bodyguard(s). We never learn the relationship between principals and guards, we never learn about tipping, courtesies, and other details of boss-employee associations; these all remain questions when the principal's removal is celebrated.

Also, the principal never appears, is never individualized. He is like the official Kafka's K. is seeking, just beyond reach of the questor, despite his diligence. The principal is all principals: the Shah of Iran, Kissinger, the Kennedys, Nixon, Castro, those who need protection for what they are and/or for what they have done.

This is one of Barthelme's more conventional fictions, far more regularized than the seven dialogues (some of which could be monologues) that begin and end *Great Days*. The more experimental dialogues appear similar to what Beckett has done in his recent stage works, reaching back to *Krapp's Last Tape* and continuing to *Monologue*. The dialogues—and we cannot be certain of two voices in many, since they could be, like Prufrock, a single self split into two or more voices—are aspects of "great days," voices coming at us in stereo, male and female intermixed, the world of dead matter, news items, personal relationships all reduced to the snippets by which we assimilate them; there is no continuity.

The dialogues, whose content is deliberately murky, recall Gaddis's *JR*— that paean to voices and sounds deriving from every direction. The idea is that "voices" in themselves go beyond communication; we hear sounds, but are not concerned with their meaning. Sounds are sufficient. Prototypical are noises on a street now that portable stereos are abundant: huge orchestral arrangements or vocal groups available to teenagers, who tune them high, and compete with other stereos, traffic noises, sirens, people's voices. The result, from both Gaddis and Barthelme, is "voices" without direct communication, overhearing without hearing. These, too, are the great days that are coming, the politics of noise.

Joan Didion's career has shown her gaining steady strength from minimalism as she develops from novel to novel. Although self-pity continues to dominate, she has, by *A Book of Common Prayer,* found a way of integrating it into a larger context. As she works out the elements of what is an ever intenser version of minimalist techniques, of white space becoming ever whiter, of silences becoming ever more deafening, she shapes our responses to a developing capacity for suffering.

The essays in *The White Album* (1979), although coming after her three novels, lay much of the ideological and stylistic groundwork for those works. These essays, along with those in *Slouching Toward Bethlehem* (1968), are observations of the 1960s, when Didion herself started as a novelist, with *Run River,* in 1963. She writes the roving essay, short scenes or episodes that catch the California sense of sixties history: a mother who places her five-year-old daughter on the center divide of Interstate 5; Didion herself disintegrating and "kept up" on Elavil; Didion meeting and interviewing Linda Kasabian, star witness for the prosecution in the Manson trial; the band called The Doors, the "Norman Mailers of the Top Forty," whose music insisted that "love was sex and sex was death"; vignettes of Huey Newton, whose presence in a play about Huey Newton seems to characterize his role-playing; scenes of Eldridge Cleaver, whose presence is so great that every visitor to his house must stand in the middle of the street and be recognized;* the disorder at San Francisco State College, which "was its own point," where the white students fooled themselves that they were living like revolutionaries; Didion's silk dress, whose presence seems to clothe her sense of historical moments. Didion intermixes her history and California's, as well as the nation's. What occurs is associated with what she feels, how she feels, what she wears. The 1960s may have ended for most when Manson committed his murders; but for Didion, the decade ended officially when she left one house for another, and history appeared to move with her.

The personalized history-journal-memoir is a conceit from Mailer. Didion's White Album is a female's, Westerner's, introverted version of "The White Negro." She is the obverse of Mailer, withholding, whereas he attempted to expand; fearful of historical change, while he devours change; conservative to his radical; foreseeing chaos, while he thrives on confusion. She morally condemns excessive freedom, longs for authority, whereas Mailer posits a society in which Mansons may indeed result from ultimates in personal liberation. She harbors sanctions; he abhors them. The anarchy she senses in society she arrives at by way of her own breakdowns, akin to Mailer's solipsism. She describes it as an "increasing inability of the ego to mediate the world of reality and to cope with normal stress. . . . It is as though she feels deeply that all human effort is foredoomed to failure, a conviction which seems to push her further into a dependent, passive withdrawal. In her view she lives in a world of people moved by strange, conflicted, poorly comprehended, and, above all, devious motivations which commit them inevitably to conflict and failure."

Didion's short piece called "The Women's Movement" seems to be an exercise in self-deception; or else she is simply obtuse when it comes to dealing steadily with larger units or historical moments. One suspects that her immersion in herself and her ability to fight her way through to sanity, stability, and perception have led to a conservative vision of society, a desire to hold elements steady; and, also, disallowed her sympathy for people different from herself, or given different qualities. She takes isolated aspects of the women's movement and treats them as the whole; as if the movement were singular, or women were singular. (*The White Album* was published in 1979, and a footnote would have dissipated the period feel of the essay, published in 1972.) "To those of us who remain committed mainly to the exploration of moral distinctions and ambiguities, the feminist analysis may have seemed a particularly narrow and cracked determinism." Didion fails to recognize that the tensions and conflicts in the women's movement reflect those tensions and conflicts in the larger society; that women in making their decisions have to explore the same "moral distinctions and ambiguities" she allots to herself.

She takes, also, statements from women who speak of remaking their lives, of redoing themselves, and relegates them to "converts who want not a revolution but 'romance,' who believe not in the oppression of women but in their own chances for a new life in exactly the mold of their old life." This is disingenuous and perhaps dishonest, for if women united sufficiently to want a revolution, then Didion would also oppose them for that. She uses a measuring rod that makes them losers no matter which way they jump: toward political and social revolution or toward personal change. She misrepresents the women's movement as (1) a singular affair; (2) concerned with trivial personal change; (3) resting in a historical vacuum. By 1972, the elements that made up the women's movement were quite differently located; and even Didion's claim for "romance," not revolution, could not be well taken by then. Like Mailer's stress on male ego, her perception of women's roles will somewhat hobble her fiction.

In *Run River,* Didion's subject is a doomed family, the McClellans, who live on a ranch in northern California. The McClellans recall the Tyrones in Eugene O'Neill's *Long Day's Journey into Night:* they tear and rage, but are unable to break out of a destiny that dooms them. Although her characters play with tragedy, their platitudinous lives seem more the stuff of Fitzgerald dilettantes. Her main voice is Lily Knight McClellan, who marries a man she is only vaguely interested in, has two children by him, carries out

---

*Unfortunately, Didion could not complete the Cleaver story. A convicted rapist, Cleaver became an eloquent revolutionary leader; labeled James Baldwin inadequate for the black revolutionary cause because he was a "faggot"; jumped bail and fled to Algeria; tired of exile and plea-bargained to return to America; turned born-again Christian; and in the 1980 election, announced support for Ronald Reagan for President. Pure Californian? Pure American! The latest development is that he has opted for the Mormon Church, perhaps to blacken its Optic White.

repeated adulteries when he goes off to war and even after he returns, is sustained by reveries, drugs, and headaches, and manages to control nearly everyone around her by way of weakness, not strength. Always ill, pitifully thin, almost wasted, fragile in every respect, Lily is a typical Didion survivor; all the strong ones, like heroes, die away, while she holds on.

Lily's one memorable experience was a primal act in the woods, in a watery stream bed, with her future husband, Everett, as they play a somewhat soiled Adam and Eve, a pastoral romance which she never regains once they marry. Since Lily is named after a flower—fragile, pure, white—her essential experience is pastoral, although life on the McClellan ranch is for her a form of death. But Lily is a representative Didion woman: she may function minimally, but overall she has lost direction, identity, will. She attaches herself to seemingly strong people, who live and die for her. While her lowest depth is migraines, theirs is actual suicide, drift toward it, alcohol.

In *Run River*, Lily's closest friend is Everett's sister, Martha, who resents her sister-in-law for being inferior to her brother. Incestuous feelings, at least on Martha's part, boil beneath the surface. When Everett chooses Lily, Martha takes up with Ryder Channing, a Tennessean of mixed charms. After Martha's suicide, Channing and Lily engage in an intermittent affair, until Everett shoots him. This action begins the novel, Everett's murder of Channing, and the rest of the book, in flashback, explains why.

Like Maria in *Play It As It Lays* or Charlotte in *A Book of Common Prayer,* Lily is a woman without a vocation. College, books, mental or physical activities, marital duties, housewifely duties, parental responsibilities are tests Didion's women fail, as well as their being unfit for any vocation in the larger world. They go beyond being victims, to being strangers, anomic creatures whose hold upon reality depends solely on a will to survive. They are frail in every respect, virtually anorexic—we never see Lily eat, although there are dinner and restaurant scenes. They barely hang on to sanity, suffering nightmares, bad daydreams, needing support during storms, although shaping up during emergencies. Lily's finest moments comes when life depends upon her. "What eluded her was the day-to-day action. She would not buy a dress without his [Everett's] approval, but she had driven into the hospital without waking him the night last Christmas when they called to say that Julie [their daughter] had been in an accident after a dance."

Didion's women are spatial creatures, expert drivers, using the car not to get anywhere, but to put distance between themselves and whatever they want to escape. Home for them is a refuge, but it is also a double bind, signal of their enthrallment to a type of life in which they are alien creatures. To escape, they drive recklessly into the country, the next town or city; there they simmer, until someone comes to get them or they feel able to drive back. They are always being picked up or called for, like schoolchildren. Their role is to make a man father them; husbands who cannot be fathers provide disastrous marriages if they marry such women.

Didion's page is like those medieval pageants in which figures move across the observer's eye, standing for this or that. It is not that the characters move within a hallucinatory world, although some of that is present, but because they are types who rarely become individualized. Everett is *the* wastrel brother, as in Faulkner or O'Neill, moving in a world undefined by anything we can grasp. Ryder Channing is *the* somewhat charming, somewhat disreputable Southerner who gets nasty when things go against him. Martha is *the* young lady simply waiting for the right moment to kill herself, a born suicide.

The two fathers, Knight the philanderer and McClellan the reactionary Californian, are both "Western" types. McClellan, in particular, is a throwback to pioneers, full of himself as a northern Californian, xenophobic, so full of hatred it runs over into self-hatred; yet protective of values that have long since passed. All of these people fall back on tradition because they cannot live in the present, although Didion appears sympathetic to their delusions, like Faulkner in this respect.

Questions of point of view arise. Didion has positioned herself with Lily without informing the reader how to relate to the character. Lily appears to deserve exactly what she receives, yet we feel Didion nudging us to observe her as victim, as done in by importuning males, a pressuring society, inadequate fathers. The author's presence is so significant because she is moving us in ways the presentation has not fulfilled.

When Camus presented his "stranger," he created for him an ideological position, a philosophical stance, in which anomie and alienation of self and society were central. In Didion's novel, there is only the floating free, the reflection of a person moving outside herself and others. True, men who desire power and dominance circle around her, but why her? We can sense that such men need a helpless woman, but our knowledge of that derives from outside the novel. Although the prose is not minimalist, Didion locates herself in minimalist terms. *Run River* waits for camera and action to fill in where words fail.

In *Play It As It Lays* (1970), Maria Wyeth, formerly married to a movie director, Carter Land, is in a state of disintegration; everything she does pulls her away from a balanced life. When we first meet her, she reviews herself for us, as Jean-Baptiste in *The Fall* attempted to do. While he paraded failure as success, she parades whatever successes she had as failure. She is the voice of the lower depths, the sense of the Kafkan mole or beetle close to her sense of herself. Maria is in a hospital or institution under doctor's care, divorced, her daughter Kate a vegetable and under shock therapy in another institution.

In this, the first segment, where she begins the review of her "career," Maria is only a voice. One of Didion's triumphs in the novel is to make Maria's voice disembodied, as if it were prerecorded and the tape played quadraphonically. She explains her sense of life: "I am what I am," and as in craps, one must let it go "as it lays," or play it as it lays. Her father, we learn later, had told Maria life itself was a crap game: "don't do it the hard way" was one of the two lessons she learned. This lack of resistance to what is, to the lay of the craps, does help to flatten out Maria, which is to Didion's advantage; but that lack of resistance disallows any other voice, any textural variety, and, ultimately, any sense of the outside. Maria may be so terminally narcissistic that the world is miniaturized in herself; but from the novelist's point of view, in such minimalist art, there must be an "other."

After Maria's segment comes a brief episode with her sometime friend Helene and then an equally brief one with Carter, her former husband. Each speaks of her selfishness, her inability to live normally. Then follows the rest of the novel, divided into eighty-four brief segments. The effect is of a kaleidoscope, each segment being an image that plays off and back upon Maria. Holding it all together is her instability, her skew relationships to everyone else's "reality," her adversary movement to their artificiality. The first person of the first segment gives way to the more impersonal third. At the start, Maria speaks of herself; then the authorial voice speaks of her. A first-person narrative running throughout would have thrown Didion's plan off, by personalizing what were to be voices coming from the dead. The dead Maria!

The eighty-four short chapters are concerned with running. The novel fits into our notions of the American as a spatial creature; although for Maria all spatiality is trap as well as escape. The road leads to death rather than to a dispossessed garden or a "world elsewhere." When internal pressures are unrelieved by sex or drugs, Maria takes to the freeways, driving from L.A. to Santa Monica, to San Diego, back and forth, like the human yo-yoing in Pynchon's *V.:* to create the sense of movement even when it is tied to nowhere. Her Corvette, that emblem of American success, becomes a mechanical extension of Maria's sense of herself; as do the freeways, which end up as they began. They are the central metaphor of the novel: free-ways offering speed and destruction.

In *Slouching Toward Bethlehem* (1968), an assortment of personalized journalism, Didion in minimalist terms wrote of Haight-Ashbury in the 1960s. The titular essay has become a model for sixties reporting because it works by arrangement of information rather than by information alone. It captures the voices of the young, damned, and doomed. What Didion needed, and found, was a prose equivalent of being spaced out: doing to reportage what acid did to Haight-Ashbury. Since the essay is brief—and pretends to no more than what it is—it works; but when the method is carried over into *Play It,* we are troubled by the lack of resonance, the failure to locate context.

Everyone around Maria in the novel is lost, but only she recognizes it; she refuses to delude herself as they do. Everyone is spaced out on drugs, sex, self-regard, artificiality. Fake is norm, counterfeit the mark of success. Maria marks herself as a failure, because her inability to "play it as it lays" labels her as one of the crazies, excludes her from their games. The problem arises when we recognize that everything we know about her, and are expected to respond to, derives from the people she rejects.

Didion's choice not to provide another voice or dimension locates us so fully in Maria's consciousness that it is like Narcissus's circuitry of self-love. Her self-hatred is in actuality self-love, which is not what the novel is really about. Superficially, Maria recalls Jean Rhys's victimized females; but more substantially, Mailer's Sergius O'Shaugnessy and Rojack, prototypical ego-tripping males. Maria uses space to fill herself, but what she experiences is less a spatial dimension than a vacuum. She is the devourer of space, not so that she can fill it, but as a method of evading whatever she is.

Didion's use of "play it as it lays" is connected to Maria's ingestion of space. Rather than making coherent the interconnection of environment and being—what Camus did, minimally, in *The Fall*—Didion, failing to distance herself, provides no interchange, and being, here, is nothingness.

The Possibilities of Minimalism 399

The reviewers praised Didion's prose in extraordinary terms, calling it "dead-on dialogue," or full of "plastic ironies," or "capsuled brilliance," or "scrupulous, exact in understatement." The paragraph that begins the novel, set off from the first segment and then repeated in Chapter 52, reads: "Maria made a list of things she would never do. She would never: *walk through the Sands or Caesar's alone after midnight.* She would never: *ball at a party, do S-M unless she wanted to, borrow furs from Abe Lipsey, deal.* She would never: *carry a Yorkshire in Beverly Hills.*" There *is* great economy here, and the sentence closing with "deal" is beautifully cadenced. Apart from this, though, the passage is all tinsel, smart-alecky, a world without resonance, yet one Maria is serious about. Examined, the prose lends no meaning. Does one indict the counterfeit at that level? All the key factitious elements are there: the hotels and gaming places in Las Vegas; S-M, a relatively new social phenomenon in 1970; a frivolous event in Beverly Hills, whose mere mention is calculated to set off fireworks. In "Slouching Toward Bethlehem," Didion mocked just this kind of talk: " 'But I'm holy on acid,' " someone says. " 'We're just gonna let it all happen. . . . Everything's in the future, you can't pre-plan it.' "

Part of minimalist strategy is to omit background, history, even choice. It goes beyond existentialism, naturalism, supernaturalism, freeing the author from tradition. Didion has pursued this method, providing a scenario, a shooting script. But a script is later filled in by images, figures, gestures, angles. Here we stumble for reference, and we suspect that while the novel pretends to be everything, it is merely disguising nothing. Maria is a shell which she cannot fill, which Didion cannot, either; and the play on the determinism of craps is part of the disguise. A throw of the dice will never abolish chance, as Mallarmé wrote, which suggests universal design, not Southern California chic.

Maria's emptiness, her own feminine mystique, her sense of herself as victim and victimized, her instability even as she observes sanely are vitiated. The novel pulls away from itself; expressing its own emptiness, it empties out. Maria has a moment in which she seeks an apartment, 2-D, once lived in by Philip Dunne—" 'Excuse me, it was Sidney Howard.' " Dunne is the surname of Didion's husband, and Sidney Howard did exist. But the "dream moment" has no significance, only the shock value of seeing Dunne's name. It is a name that holds no sense for Maria, only for Didion, who is not there. Preoccupation with death, depression, the death of small children, the tragic end of innocent beings, fire and burning and apocalypse are of course valid concerns. But the fictional reference must be more than a woman who cannot deal with her own life, while she drives a Corvette, lives in expensive homes, props herself with drugs, occasional sex, and acts of humiliation. The banishment of self, here, is the equivalent of the vaunting of self, a twisting of meaning Didion seems unprepared for. There is, also, the sense that by being wounded severely enough, one can become one of the elect. Not by faith or by determinism is one elected, but by virtue of one's self-centeredness and being among the insulted and injured. By giving her body and mind over to male exploiters, and their female flunkies and whores, Maria rises above them; or so the narrative would have us assume. Her superiority is based on her ability to suffer, to endure their slings and arrows; her pain marks her as saint, martyr, sacrifice to modern artificiality. In this respect, Maria joins all the phonies she screens through her own sensibility; she becomes not the whore of Babylon, but of Narcissus.

The Book of Common Prayer, not Didion's title, but the Anglican service book, was produced in 1549 as a selection and translation from the breviary and missal, and included some additional materials. After a tortured history, it became the official "prayer book" of the English church. It has almost no connection to Didion's novel, which is not religious; therefore, it must be perceived as an emblem, or else ironically. Didion apparently views her tortured protagonist, Charlotte Douglas, as part of a vast modern service. In this service, for which she, Didion, provides the prayer book, Charlotte is a victim (a familiar victim by now) and the society is itself pulling apart in a myriad of ways. The society is Boca Grande, an equatorial Latin American republic, caught in the middle of a revolution, reminiscent of Conrad's Costaguana in *Nostromo.* The revolution, however, is offstage, with bombings, murders, arms shipments, tapped telephones.

A Book of Common Prayer (1977) shows Didion's talent at its most compelling. She has undertaken a larger task than before, moving into materials associated heretofore with Conrad, Greene, García Márquez, and other ambitious novelists. She has, also, attempted to move beyond her intensely narcissistic female victims, gaining distance through a narrator; at the same time, she uses sharp and rapid cutting to produce a novel of kaleidoscopic brief scenes. Although the novel becomes fussy—excessive cutting, too little establishment of thematic material

—it reverberates impressively.

The narrator is Grace Strasser-Mendana, sixty years old and undergoing cobalt treatment for cancer. She had married into the ruling family of Boca Grande and after the death of her husband became a dominant voice in the country's affairs. But she is not fictionally developed, far less than Conrad's Marlow, whom she superficially recalls. The real subject is not Grace but Charlotte, who is a doomed woman, doubly doomed by her attraction to men, triply doomed by her lack of control over her life. She has been twice married, first to a sometime academic, Warren Bogart, a confidence man consumed by an inner rage to destroy whatever he touches, and he tries to touch everything. Her second husband is a Jew, Leonard Douglas, a radical activist lawyer who is always in transit. He and Charlotte are two people in orbit around each other.

The great tragedy of her life, however, is not the two senseless marriages—she could make no other kind—but the defection of her daughter, Marin. At eighteen, Marin is a 1960s revolutionary on the run from the FBI. She is a blend of several young ladies who became "wanted" in every post office across the United States, and she also has elements of Patty Hearst, whose case was so well publicized during Didion's writing of the book. As presented, however, Marin is simply a viperish young lady from whom we obtain slogans, not substance. She tells Grace that " 'Tennis . . . is just one more mode of teaching an elitist strategy. If you subject it to a revolutionary analysis you'll see that. Not that I think you will.' " Or: "Birth control is *the* most flagrant example of how the ruling class practices genocide." Her disaffection runs into Didion's distaste, and the revolutionary content of Marin's underground experience becomes comic book stuff: guns, bombs, explosions, running.

Grace has established herself as Charlotte's "double": "I will be her witness." In an extraordinarily fine beginning page, Grace speaks of her own function as witness—she will intone a "common prayer" over Charlotte—and runs through the latter's disastrous career, as someone who "dreamed her life," yet who died hopeful. There is pith and wit in these lines, but they are unsustained. We are led into Márquez territory, but the values of each group or set are parodied *before* they are clarified. The problem we experience with Marin later—she is mocked before she is made sufficiently substantial for mockery—occurs with nearly every element. What Didion does is to rely on our received information instead of her own spade-work. She expects us to know what banana republics are like, what rulers are, how revolutionaries function, what bomb-throwing young ladies are. She assumes we have read the same newspaper and magazine articles as she. With that assumption, she can cut from here to there, each chapter being a page or two, at the most four or five pages. Minimalism exists here as a challenge or dare to the reader to make connections.

Except for aspects of Charlotte, there are few specifics of behavior, motivation, or working out. The two husbands always act in the character of what they are, no different in their consistency than is the ruling party of Boca Grande, represented by Victor. Grace's son, Gerardo, is a male version of Marin, always within the role. No one is permitted divergence from type, or development. Charlotte's doom is forever, until her death by shooting when the country is torn apart by guerrilla warfare. Part of this reliance on the typical and type could be Didion's desire to create an allegory of modern life, Boca Grande as a state that shadows our existence, the young people in the novel as mockery of the new—and this our "book of common prayer."

All that is implicit, and it does help to make the novel an ambitious, moving piece of fiction. Despite the weakness of typicality functioning at every level, we are in the presence of something strongly created. The movie technique of fast cutting, of a montage of brief scenes, of constant moving in and out kaleidoscopically all help reinforce the unreality of Grace's inner story. Those people in Grace's tale are both intense and evanescent, alive and yet puppetlike. Without comprehension of events or themselves, they move within terrible historical forces, driven by inner needs which preempt all other experience. They are more than doomed; they have lost all connection with others or themselves, which even doomed literary characters have. Didion has advanced well beyond Maria Wyeth, although Charlotte is implicit in that protagonist of *Play It As It Lays*. While the same victimization is there, Charlotte's role is now on a larger scale. She moves as a ghost or ghoul once her daughter has dropped out, but even before that she lived in a daze. In Boca Grande, to which she comes after Marin goes underground (or, possibly, has been blown up), Charlotte finds a national embodiment of her own state of being.

Didion created in Boca Grande and the chaotic activity therein a perfect emblem of what she had written about in her essay "Slouching Toward Bethlehem" ten years earlier. America was spaced out there, symbolized by Haight-Ashbury, and now it is an entire generation, America and its values on the run in Boca Grande. Yet Didion's distaste for the new—destructive, lacking substance, filled with its own narcissistic doom—disallows ideas to penetrate; she catches disgust, as does Greene, but she lacks his broader ideological base. As a consequence, even as she enlarges with her frenzied cutting back and forth, she diminishes whatever she touches. Either her disgust with the new narrows her vision, or else her disgust is not profound enough; she needs more of it on a larger scale of reference, more particularized within its types.*

Although when compared with Joan Didion or Donald Barthelme, Susan Sontag hardly seems like a minimalist, her fictional versions of "against interpretation" and "the aesthetics of silence" are minimalist experiences. Silence, white space, intervals, anti-action, reverie, subliminality predominate. Undertones and middle states of being are reified; Sontag's characters, like Barthelme's, live just to the side of normal spatial-temporal dimensions, thus calling into question "normal." His "dead father" could have been her Diddy of *Death Kit,* and his "Snow White" her Hippolyte of *The Benefactor,* allowing for differing circumstances in the respective novels.

Sontag in the 1960s attempted to confront in her fiction and essays a crisis in the novel in particular, the arts in general. In this respect, she fits well among minimalists, who offer the dissolution of content in their pursuit of new forms. In "Against Interpretation," she argues a personal view of that crisis: "If

---

*Although her young career is still to be fashioned, I think Ann Beattie is deeply indebted to Didion and to minimalist fictional ideas in general. Her *Head Over Heels* (originally called *Chilly Scenes of Winter,* in 1976), for example, is an attempt to pick up all the detritus of 1970s culture and spew it out in neurotic and antiproductive behavior. Although the main character, Charles, is male, he could as easily be female. The central principle is movement, really yo-yoing—going out to eat, to bars, people coming and going aimlessly, incomplete conversations: Pamela has returned East from California, and Charles asks why; she answers, " 'Oh, I . . . started to feel I was expanding too quickly—that I'd end up like stretched taffy or something. I came back to compress.' " As in Didion, we have a spatial and spaced-out culture, with Charles and his sister Susan as "orphans," despite friends, connections. Beattie's sense of the decade is of people disconnected from each other, their lives, any fruitful activity; like Maria Wyeth, they are almost anomic, although they function at jobs. The prose is spare, elliptic, an effective weapon for people who doubt they will ever become whole again.

excessive stress on *content* provokes the arrogance of interpretation, more extended and more thorough descriptions of *form* would silence. What is needed is a vocabulary—a descriptive, rather than prescriptive, vocabulary—for forms. The best criticism, and it is uncommon, is of this sort that dissolves considerations of content into those of form." Her fictions are a gloss on her critical ideas.

The Benefactor (1963) is the beneficiary of a long European tradition in the confessional mode. In this type of fiction, all experience is centered in the head of the protagonist, usually a first-person narrator, whose function is to confess all and turn data into subjective experience. Variations on this type come in *Notes from Underground, Diary of a Madman, Diary of a Fool, Monsieur Teste.* What Dostoyevsky, Gogol, Tolstoy, Valéry, and others in confessional fiction do is to question lines between subjective and objective, thereby questioning the line between sanity and insanity. Sontag goes further, blurring the line between not only sanity and insanity (which is not really her point), but real life and dream. The epigraph for Chapter 1 is: *"Je rêve, donc je suis."* In this respect, her most immediate predecessor is *Monsieur Teste,* in which Valéry's protagonist generates the world from within his head.

Sontag's chief character is Hippolyte, the country (never named) is France, and the time is thirty years or so in the past, continuing toward the present. Hippolyte is writing his memoir; the diary or journal that he keeps and that becomes the narrative is completely enclosed within his making. He encircles himself: "If only I could explain to you how changed I am since those days!" he begins. The change, almost imperceptible, enables him, in his later life, to separate his real self from his dream self; in the past, dreams and waking life were aspects of an inseparable fantasy.

Sontag has, in effect, turned her back on American fiction by denying spatiality in favor of the inner world which stretches in French fiction from Proust through Butor. Self-containment, being caught within severe limitations, self-serving intensity of experience, are the major considerations. When she came to write *Death Kit* a few years later, she carried over the preoccupation with a contained self, with narcissistic looping, but extended her territory to include a trip, a distant place, a railroad—examples of a spatial journey, as well as the inner one. In *The Benefactor,* we are hardly aware of movement, except within the severely demarked area of the protagonist's mind: Hippolyte is her Teste.

Hippolyte must distinguish between waking life

and dream, and yet dreams command. They appear at intervals, and while their details are indistinct, their commonality appears clear. They involve ambiguous sexuality, confinement (physical and otherwise), attempts to teach him something, uncontrollable emotions of humiliation, surprise, and the desire to please. The dreams seem to work against the grain of Hippolyte's waking life, which is highly controlled, independent, heterosexual (except for one episode). In neither, however, is he quite sane, and what he fails to recognize is that the controlled decisions of his waking life are sane only when identified with his own immediate needs. He sells his mistress, Frau Anders, into captivity to an Arab merchant; he attempts to burn down her house with her in it; he gives her a large house he inherits. Each action, a kind of benefaction, is an effort to provide her with what she wants, but it is what he thinks she wants.

In a sense, by trying to carry out his dreams and to break from them, Hippolyte confers life and death. When Frau Anders is sold to an Arab merchant—because she is dissatisfied with her life—she enters a world in which women are property, are humiliated, branded, and tortured if they resist. That is the way of Islam and Paul Bowles. But the way of Christianity is not much better, because when Hippolyte thinks she is tired of her life after she returns, he attempts to kill her. But she suspects he will, and observes him pouring gasoline on her house and flaming it. Then he turns benefactor, and she gains his father's house. The externals of the narrative, those elements which characterize objective events, are all the result of Hippolyte's plan, what Wittgenstein meant by "the meaning is the use."

One person he cannot control is Jean-Jacques, a character based apparently on the writer Jean Genet. Jean-Jacques is a former boxer, a thief, a prostitute, and a writer who gains ever greater fame. He is concerned with masks, with life as games, with the variety of play which a serious life permits under its cover of respectability. "Because he was absolutely committed to his work, writing, he could afford to be unreliable in every other way—and to ornament his life with games, strategies, and artifacts. These strange rites he practiced . . . were not mine." Jean-Jacques practices almost absolute detachment from himself—the modern man who can separate subject and object so completely he is always a witness—and can, therefore, hold himself ready for success deriving from his talent. Hippolyte wishes rather to be himself, and as a consequence, whatever his talents, he has little to show for his career. His vocation is to work out the

being in himself; whereas Jean-Jacques's is to gain the world's rewards, in his case a place in the French Academy for his literary efforts, despite rumors of his collaboration during the war.

Hippolyte enjoys acting, and he gains roles in films, mainly minor ones. Acting, he feels, is useful because it gives him "a sense of being absolutely used, deployed—and this I knew was the model of my salvation." By disappearing into his film roles, he can remain what he is; whereas in theatrical performances, he would have to relive the role each time he played it and, accordingly, give himself to it. What matters is only his "dubious pursuit of wisdom" through his dreams.

Hippolyte cannot rest easily, nor can he devote his energies to anything else, until he coordinates his waking life with his dreams. He and Jean-Jacques are opposites, one representing dreams, one achievement. They recall, in this respect, Oblomov and Stolz in Goncharov's novel, the one seeking something in his inner life, the other devoted to works. They are subject and object, and their friendship, however full of hostilities, is their attempt to interpenetrate each other. It is, of course, a futile effort, since each represents something very distinct. Jean-Jacques, nevertheless, offers an alternative to Hippolyte, and the latter even attempts to enter the writer's world—thus, their single sexual episode. But there are no others, and they remain opponents as much as friends. When Hippolyte marries, he does not introduce his friend to his wife until she is very ill; and then Jean-Jacques carries on so madly that the young woman dies shortly afterward, her disease apparently intensified by his antics.

The novel, in its farthest reaches, becomes a meditation on a minimalist middle state: that world between complete subjectivity (Proustian memory) and complete objectivity (the world of time and space). Sontag reaches for no-man's-land, where there is a waking life, but one given over to dreams, reveries, fantasy. *The Benefactor* is a curious novel in that it has turned away from American models in favor of continental ones, especially French, and yet it flirts with American ideas within that frame of reference. It is as if Sontag had fictionalized Gaston Bachelard's ideas of fire, reverie, and dream in terms of American violence.

Still, Hippolyte is not really Bachelard's inner state or Valéry's Teste; he must express himself in action, even while he struggles with dreams. He yearns after reverie as a form of existence, as salvation; but he works out his waking life in acts of benefaction, an attempt at murder, marriage, an affair, a homosexual episode, visits to his dying father. And he is dissatisfied with his dreams; he wants to transcend them once he understands their significance. He hovers at the edge of potentiality. As in her essays, Sontag views America from France, France and Europe from America.

Death Kit (1967), written during the height of the Vietnam War and the protests against it, turns America into a symbolic crypt, a necropolis. The central burial place is a train tunnel, where Diddy (Dalton Harron) changes the course of his life. Sontag's purpose is to take the average sensual middle-class American man and alter his life by way of a dramatic event; in this instance, the drama is connected to Diddy's murder of a worker in the tunnel, while the train is stalled because of an obstruction. On the way to a business conference upstate, Diddy leaves the stalled train, sees a worker hacking away at an obstruction, gets into an altercation, and smashes his head. Yet the act is so hallucinatory he is not certain he has committed the murder. Because the circumstances have confused him as to what is true, what untrue, what is subject, what is object, he needs external proof. The line between himself and his former self, as well as between himself and the dead worker, becomes the compass point of the novel. Sontag's area of movement is a Robbe-Grillet substructure.

Death Kit is a phenomenological novel, most of it taking place within Diddy's head, or within the head of the young woman he goes with. Hester's internality is forced by way of her blindness, an ailment that operations cannot help. Diddy's "blindness" is his exclusion from the vital centers of his own life; and the crime he commits, almost indifferently and gratuitously, gives him insight, makes him alive to himself. Further, Sontag makes the experience of the crime so confusing to Diddy he must work out his dilemma without really knowing what he has done. This gives Sontag the authority to use a shorthand language—fragments, phrases, pieces of information, synaptic elements—rather than a fully fashioned prose. While not experimental, the language is an attempt at a mental state, translated into words. She is particularly good on aspects of blindness:

> How does an inexpressive face age? More slowly, one would suppose. A sightless face, one that's never learned to be consistently expressive by watching other faces, probably remains unlined many years after the exertions of expression have creased and wrinkled seeing faces of the same chronological age.

Maybe Hester isn't as young as she looks. With another rhythm of use, another rhythm of aging.

Because the event in the tunnel remains so ambiguous to Diddy, he must research his own crime. The murder itself cannot be uncovered, for flesh and bone have been obliterated by the train. Diddy reads up on the death in the local paper, once he arrives at his conference, and then attends the services at the funeral home. After that, he visits the widow's house and almost lets her make love to him. Intermixed with these acts of detection, which can only implicate him in his crime, Diddy pursues his professional career. The conference is aimed at increasing business for his company, which makes microscopic-camera equipment. As the rational part of Diddy's life, the conference is set against the irrational element, his detective work.

A third line of development concerns Hester's hospital stay, in which there is a final effort to give her her sight. The operation fails, and Diddy and she leave to live together. He quits his job, so that his pursuit of a new reality will be unencumbered by extraneous circumstances. To discover the truth of his act, the truth of his blindness, the essence of his being with Hester overtakes all other considerations. His life becomes pure quest, channeled through compulsive sexuality with his blind partner, followed by his retracing the steps that led to the tunnel murder. Diddy and Hester reenter the tunnel and there they encounter another worker, who looks just like the murdered Incardona. Diddy repeats his act, killing this double of the murdered man, perhaps a brother, perhaps simply a reincarnation of what was then a dream. Hester is still blind to the crime, since she cannot observe, just as she was blind to the first crime when Diddy attempted to tell her what he had done. As before, there is no objective witness to the murder.

With only himself as witness, the murderer now enters his own death journey. This trip toward death has been implicit in Diddy's entire life, as he drifts down from an unlived existence, through business relationships that have no meaning, into a marriage that has broken up when his wife left, through sexual encounters that are trivial, indifferent, or crude. Nothing has touched him. He is, in effect, a stranger to himself, although fully capable of functioning within a normal social or professional situation. He loses and gains weight with alarming rapidity; so that we see his body as either small or large, as going this way or that, without rationale or direction. Only his head counts. And it is his head he must set in order when he starts on his final tunnel journey.

After the second murder (or the first, if the first never occurred), he props Hester up in an alcove and moves along the tunnel. The tunnel becomes a necropolis, a series of interlinked rooms, large and small, which serve as crypts. The dead of all sizes and shapes, all ages, both sexes, young and old, civilian and soldier, lie here; some orderly, some strewn around. Many are in coffins, many others stood up. Before he arrives at the crypts, however, Diddy makes his way through a tunnel of detritus, the junk of a civilization that has never cohered. We find the discrete, anarchic, object world of American culture, neither lending itself to understanding nor able to be brought under control. It is a world of the absence of real things, filled with items of junk.

Then come the burial grounds. Here is the house of death Diddy has chosen to enter. America is a necropolis, the tunnel experience man's identity: angry, savage, murderous, intent on extinction and obliteration. Diddy is that man, otherwise harmless except in a tunnel situation. "Diddy is exploring his death. Cautiously, thoughtfully, diligently. He wills to know, he will know all the rooms in this place; even if it's the house of death." The inventory is complete when it catalogues Diddy's death. He moves to fulfill himself. "More rooms. Diddy walks on, looking for his death. Diddy has made his final chart; drawn up his last map. Diddy has perceived the inventory of the world." Minimalism meets apocalypse.

Not unlike the worlds of Barthelme, Didion, and Sontag, the Kosinski world is a lunar landscape inhabited by an ego capable only of narcissistic impulses. For Kosinski, the observer observing comes as close to reality as reality permits. And therefore, for the world's anarchy, Kosinski has only himself to offer as an antidote. The observer acts as witness, as the photographer acts as camera. The dimensions of *Steps* (1968) are the worlds of the photographer, snapping at each act of imbecility, bestiality, self-indulgence, as it passes before his camera. *Steps* is not a departure after *The Painted Bird,* but essentially a refinement of a fictional process already functioning there: the young boy as observer, even as he participates, observer and/or participant doubling himself.

Steps is a series of forty-nine very brief episodes* held together by that watchful camera eye, the photographer's art operating at its most intense, rather

_____
*Some as short as two lines, one running as long as ten pages, most in the two-to-four-page range.

than the novelist's. That dualistic, bifurcated observer comes up in an early episode. The observer-narrator sees a woman, her face thickly painted, her dress large and ill-fitting, hiding her figure. They go to a room, where the narrator undresses, while the woman remains clothed; she caresses him, and her hands feel familiar: "I looked again at her dress and suddenly realized my partner was a man. My mood altered abruptly. I felt the longing for pleasure and abandonment inside me, but I also sensed that I had been accepted too readily, that everything had suddenly become very predictable. All we could do was to exist for each other solely as a reminder of the self."

The circuitry of self which defines the narrator remains constant no matter how involved he becomes. In a scene that almost duplicates episodes in *The Painted Bird,* the narrator is young, back in the war years, unable to find work. A vagrant, he becomes the victim of the peasants he works for, and to gain revenge, he decides to get at their children. He collects discarded fishhooks and kneads them and crushed glass into balls of fresh bread; these he feeds to his employer's youngest child, a little girl, then to others. All die in horrible agony. The peasants are bewildered, blaspheme God, curse a cruel world. "Others insisted that Death had come to dwell in the villages to avoid the bombed cities, and the war, and the camps where the furnaces smoked day and night."

The economy of this might mislead us as to how much is suggested, and perhaps only Kosinski among contemporary novelists could create it—before his English became more supple, more aware of itself. The very starkness of his language, the English of a foreigner, allowed an understatement that conveys its own grotesqueness. The image winds from personal injustice to the unjust world, the Holocaust in the distance, while death stalks in the foreground: a Europe of death, while the young boy observes, enters it with his fishhooks and crushed glass, then steps back.

Steps is stages, movements, moments of ballet. Its most immediate visible component is balletic, that ability to move expertly through the anarchy of cruelty, barbarism, appetites, which constitute modern life. Without steps, the narrator, either youthful or older, would be only victim; whereas with steps, he can command his own presence, counterattack, and above all, observe. *Steps* is also stages, however. Each step leads to a new stage in which the narrator can play roles. The connecting element in the entire

Kosinski display of self here is role-playing: the key here and in all his fiction.*

To extrapolate the character of the undisclosed narrator from Kosinski's book is to draw out the quintessential Kosinski experience. The narrator's chief characteristic is loneliness, which can only be turned into passion by way of domination. The narrator wanders—like the boy of *The Painted Bird*—and his wandering, when devoid of domination, is like a continuing suicide. He always moves alone, whether in the park, at a ski resort, as a new immigrant, as a member of the army or the Party, most of all in a sexual relationship. Yet his inner tensions, whatever his conflicts, do not permit him to remain solitudinous; he demands connection and expression, but his means is not based on equality of expression. He must triumph, demonstrate superiority; he must have, if not the last word, then the last feeling. He must, in order to express his emotion, prove his ability to resist emotion. Every act of connection is a contest, a competition; in bed with a woman, he must prove as combative as he is when winning a bet, or testing his courage and driving skills.

In one episode, a longer one, he drives in a contest on the city streets, in which books are taped to the

*In a critical piece Kosinski wrote to "explain" *Steps* (for *The New York Times Book Review* and later published as a pamphlet), he speaks of the novel as metamorphic. "The leit motif of *Steps* is metamorphosis. The protagonist changes his external appearance and plays all the characters. He is a tourist, archeological assistant, skiing instructor, a deserting soldier, a sniper in the army, a photographer. His metamorphosis follows his design even when it is involuntary. . . . His entrance often leads to the metamorphosis of others." That is, other characters change when he is present. I prefer the term "role-playing," which allows disguises, masks, the counterfeit, an entire run of imitational devices, all used to allow an incomplete identity to hide behind a multitude. Kosinski quotes from Milton for his epigraph: "O What a mask was there, what a disguise!" True metamorphosis involves reshaping, whereas in *Steps,* the narrator plays at himself to gain advantage or dominance, or else to survive. Changes are only in his mind.

Narcissism and solipsism are implicit in both method and manner. The language Kosinski forged, so different from the English that Conrad, another Pole, worked out for himself, is one of exclusion; only the self can be paraded in such a language, for the reader is neutralized from the start. Kosinski's distrust of others, whether gentle and compassionate, brutish and violent, cannot be bridged. It would be folly to say he sees women as objects; he sees all mankind as objects, which is the sole way in which a writer who seeks dominance can go. That is his strength, incidentally.

bumpers of parked cars. ". . . none of the drivers knew in advance on which cars the books were taped. Then the drivers, waiting in their cars two blocks from the course, would be waved in one by one by the referee. When signaled, a driver had to drive over the course at a minimum of fifty miles an hour and keep close enough to the cars with books taped to them for the bumper of his own car to dislodge as many of them as possible." The winner was the driver who dislodged the most books and held to the minimum speed.

The contest is at night, creating problems of visibility. Headlights pick up strange shapes; parts of the car intrude. Drivers who come too close smash into parked cars and are immediate losers. The narrator negotiates the course and knocks off twice as many books as his competitors; he moves on to the next stage of the race, and continues to win. He drives with a stereo tape of music pitched to his own tension, and his nerves "gauged the steering, the speed, and the distance." He always wins; for the test is made to order for him—purely competitive, a night contest, and without meaning except the money and the control of nerves. The competition ends when, one night, a couple sits in one of the parked cars and the man gets out to investigate the noise just as a speeding car goes by. "The body disappeared. Only the head remained outside, as if balanced on the knife-edge of the door; then it rolled down and hit the asphalt like one more book that had been struck off." An intensive police investigation will, of course, turn up nothing.

The finale to the competition suggests that the man opening the door was more than unfortunate; he was a fool. He had let life conquer him; instead of being wary, he had been curious. Anyone victimized allows himself to be a victim; one must conquer. And the way one does that is by role-playing, intuiting what is necessary to survive in any given situation and then devising a strategy for overcoming it. The narrator, late in the book, plays a deaf-mute—once again a carry-over from *The Painted Bird* and Kosinski's own condition; for the role of deaf-mute allows him to locate himself in alien surroundings, permits him to retain his language, his manner, his belongings, without giving anything away. He travels to a country where there is a revolution, and since he does not speak the language, he plays dumb. As such, he moves with either side, each group convinced a deaf-mute spastic will "fight for the future they envisioned for their country." Once, when captives are taken and are to be executed, he must behead them or be executed himself; and that, too, he justifies. The passage is one of Kosinski's best; but more than the lyrical nihilism it suggests, it expresses a Nietzschean contempt for anyone who fails to play his role all the way:

It was inconceivable, I thought, that I would have to slash the neck of another man simply because events had placed me behind his back. What I was about to do was inescapable, yet so unreal that it became senseless: I had to believe I was not myself any more and that whatever happened would be imaginary. I saw myself as someone else who felt nothing, who stood calm and composed, determined enough to stiffen his arms, to grasp and raise the weapon, to cut down the obstacles in his path. I knew I was strong enough to do it. I could recall the precision with which I had felled young trees: I could hear their moaning and creaking, and see their trembling, and I knew I could jump aside as they cracked and fell, their leaves brushing my feet.

The narrator, already playing a role as a deaf-mute spastic, must readjust to still another role, of not being himself, of not feeling what he would feel if he killed someone. And he can do this by turning human bodies back into natural objects—not into the pastorality of trees, but into the downing of trees, the destruction of nature in this respect indistinguishable from the destruction of man. By reifying the captives, the narrator is able to transform them into "objects" suitable for his domination; he has, after all, little choice. But within that area of little choice—a Camus bargain with fate—he finds justification by way of role-playing: stepping out of himself, in itself a step in *Steps,* and rearranging the stage components.

For Kosinski, there is always the void to fill—what makes him an Eastern European writer, no matter how fluent his English or Americanized his experiences. That void is the emptiness of the displaced person, changing place and language for another. We find it in Conrad, Kosinski's countryman, whose displacement was less radical but no less dramatic. Even when survival is at stake, the void remains; and a good deal of Kosinski's work must be concerned with transformation, of which role-playing is a critical element.

To extrapolate experience from the larger world and present it with a maximum of bare space around scene, character, episode, even expression; to let speech trail off into emptiness, so that it loses weight and texture and becomes evanescent; to relive memories by destroying them with reductive responses are all minimalist techniques. They are, also, modes of being for the sixties, like Didion's "nerves" and Sontag's phenomenology. The greatest expression of self is its intense effacement.

A key episode is located about halfway through *Steps.* In a dialogue marked by italics to internalize it, an architect is described whose first assignment was to draw up plans for a concentration camp. A camp was a complex assignment, since it had elements of school, hospital, funeral home, prison, public building, all intermixed to gain maximum efficiency. Its function would be the opposite of a maternity hospital, which sees more people leave than arrive. The goal is always hygienic, as when one exterminates rats. One speaker asks the meaning of this, and the other responds that one does not lose one's love of animals just because rats are exterminated. So elimination of rats for hygienic purposes "is empty of all meaning." In the camps, "the victims never remained individuals; they became as identical as rats. They existed only to be killed."

Such nihilism is commensurate with the subject. But such nihilism also means that character must alter to accommodate it. For dialogue, Kosinski uses unidentifiable speakers. Unnamed, undescribed, they are part of the void, reliving the camp experience as gossip. If life is that void, then role-playing is the sole form of survival: integrity, identity itself are senseless to counter a void well beyond Nietzschean nihilism. This is a deadness beyond God's deadness, because it is a world that never accommodated God. Kosinski becomes one of the men Nietzsche called "preachers of death," those for whom even lust is a form of self-laceration,* men who have begun to die even as they are born.

Not unusually, such a man as the narrator wishes to bring down an entire city, to destroy the old and leave open the consequences. Near the end of the book and in a frame apocalyptic in its potential, the narrator speaks of doing away with his ordered world, liberating himself from "birth certificates, medical examinations, punch cards and computers . . . the world of telephone books, passports, bank accounts, insurance plans, wills, credit cards [with which the "steps" began], pensions, mortgages, and loans." For the greater the order, the greater the sense

---

*Or what Herbert Marcuse in *Eros and Civilization* called repressive desublimation, in which sexual release is so arbitrary or reductive that it weakens erotic energy. Lust would be one such mode, as would be promiscuity.

of death, Marcuse's argument in *One-Dimensional Man.* Who can destroy the world of usage, consumption, ownership, and credentials can possibly have a world that "would begin and die with me." The city is a "mutant among the wonders of the world," mixing pollutants with priceless objects; and the narrator "would wage war against this city as if it were a living body." Kosinski is in lockstep with the decade.

In his war, he would explode the city, literally, using the night—"sister of my skin"—as his protective shield. What he cannot bomb away he will destroy, knifing doormen, suffocating the rich, pinning down bodies with broken statues, slashing family portraits. Highways and speedways he can make inaccessible with bent nails; bursting tires and screeching brakes will indicate the end of travel. His work done, he can sleep in the morning, its light his enemy. The void here is the narrator's need to empty out, to put himself inside by way of destroying others. Kosinski was never more apparent: that cleaning out before beginning. Yet Kosinski's narrator is not that positive; the void remains, and only he, not his works, survives.

He has placed a miniature microphone, which also functions as a transmitter, in some unfinished apartments, and as voices filter in, he tries to discover whose they are, carrying on casual conversations with everyone in the building until he can match microphone voices. One woman in particular interests him, and he monitors her apartment carefully. Once he knows her, he comes to meet and date her; and his purpose is to tailor his presentation of himself to her: "Now I could manipulate her: she was in love with me." A little later, that young woman overheard on the microphone (or one like her) tells the narrator: "Then, all you need me for is to provide a stage on which you can project and view yourself, and see how your discarded experiences become alive again when they affect me. Am I right? [She does not know of his microphone.] You don't want me to love you; all you want is for me to abandon myself to the dreams and fantasies which you inspire in me. All you want is to prolong this impulse, this moment."

The narrator's "steps" provide not movement toward anything, but a hovering presence over himself. He is no closer to self-definition at the end than at the beginning; if anything, he is further, because the nature of himself has escaped him. Attempting to fill the void, he has defined it more than himself. Kosinski's response to the sixties is implicit here; they are, for him, a continuation of the war years, time stilled.

There is only space, spatiality, frantic movement. Skiing and horseback riding are part of that movement: overcharged motion to return, eventually, to the starting point. But foremost is the camera eye: that need for double and triple observation. Self is projected on self, and so on, in Chinese boxes of spatial extension of selfhood. With *Steps,* Kosinski defined his terms and reached, in minimalist modes of expression, their highest form. The void inspired him.

As a pure response to the 1960s within minimalist terms, Rudolph Wurlitzer's three remarkable fictions (novels?) are hardly for the casual reader. Wurlitzer is the most uncompromising of minimalists, using the novel as a depressed medium. Not for him the "middle state" of consciousness we find in Sontag; or the witty and ironic play we discover in Barthelme; or the self-pitying flagellation of Didion's characters; or the extensions of self in Kosinski. With the solidity of pianos and organs in his family background, Wurlitzer seeks to abstract: to enfold himself into a declining state, going from objects toward deobjectification, to zero.

The central presence of *Nog* (1969) never appears, but exists insistently in the imagination of the narrator,* who is himself named only once. Orin Carmele is the name on the Oregon driving license he carries; it may not be his, however, and his name may be something else, but we will never learn that. Nog is a prospector of sorts, an adventurer, the symbolic American strongman, the roustabout who makes it to the gold fields, who works on the railroads, and who seems, like the Indian, representative of an America now passed. Nog is of Finnish extraction, "one of those semi-religious lunatics you see wandering around the Sierras on bread and tea, or gulping down peyote in Nevada with the Indians. . . . His face was lean and hatchet-edged, with huge fuzzy eyes sunk deep in his skull like bullet holes. He kept complaining about a yellow light that had lately been streaming out of his chest from a spot the size of a half dollar." Nog is the mythical vanishing American.

Since the narrator must confront the Nog in himself, he is more Nog than he is Orin Carmele. But since Nog does not himself appear—and remains enigmatic, perhaps unreal—the narrator deals with another presence, that of Lockett, who turns up with a young woman named Meridith. Meridith and Lock-

---

*The subtitle on the cover of the paperback is the portmanteau word "headventure": head-venture, he-adventure.

ett take the narrator on a journey, which is less spatial than a reduced level of consciousness. The vision of Nog (the land of Nog, Nod, Nodding) is a drug-induced vision, the entire book a hallucination. It may or may not have occurred; and it may recur. Lockett is shot, later in the novel, and the narrator moves into his identity, traveling with Meridith as Mr. and Mrs. Lockett.

The intermixing of characters and sensory experiences is foreshadowed by an image, at the beginning, of a latex octopus. The narrator buys the octopus and a truck from a man in an Oregon logging town—that is, from Nog. The octopus, which looks real, is housed in a bathysphere, carefully fashioned out of a butane gas tank. Nog had traveled with it throughout the West and Midwest, charging children a dime, adults a quarter, to see it. The narrator readily admits the whole thing may be a put-on, that he is inventing the octopus and may be inventing even Nog. But truth is not the issue, rather the reflection of it in whatever mirror the narrator is using at the time to measure experience. In his reduced state of consciousness, all experience is reflected experience, all sensation vicarious.

Meridith, in her silence, indifference, quiet frenzy, and spaced-out manner, is the perfect complement to his laid-back fatigue. The Wurlitzer emblem is of terribly fatigued people doing very energetic things. The result is a tremendous tension of opposites: kinetic energy matched against the negative energy of malaise. The octopus, if it exists, is symbolic of that: bottled up in the bathysphere, struggling to escape; yet it is inorganic, merely latex rubber waving about in a discarded butane tank. In the reduced state of consciousness Wurlitzer captures, subject and object interpenetrate so that neither seems to exist.

The narrator follows Meridith and Lockett as they work through heavy underbrush, hills, valleys, difficult countryside, toward some town where they have a commune, or expect to have one. Yet even as they move around obsessively and insistently, they are barely aware of movement. Along the way, they steal a doctor's bag in a raid on a hospital, and that bag, with its morphine and other supports, becomes a totem of their journey. As we shall see in *Flats,* space is almost always contained, although it stretches out. One must achieve certain distances to get there, and yet one arrives by way of tunnels, caves, bags. "I descended. I am involved in an uncontrolled stumble. I fell, it is difficult to enter narrow passages with steep walls on either side. It is darker. The darkness is oppressive, as if it has been trapped here for centuries. I have delayed the dawn. The ground is uneven and rough. . . . The walls press in, and the more I touch and fall against the walls, the more the walls press in."

What characterizes a Wurlitzer novel, besides its estrangement and disaffection, is its pitilessness. People act, they are acted upon; they do, or are done to. Everyone is involved in a subject-object duel, and winners and losers feel the same, having abided by the same rules. Within that definition, Meridith is the perfect young woman. In a fog, whether drug-induced or not, she moves through a very controlled kind of existence—doing whatever is necessary to satisfy herself sexually and make her way. The narrator meets her as both are stealing from a supermarket, outrageously, entire fish, steaks, jars, and containers stuffed into clothing. Yet she survives without distinguishing between subject and object, between herself and what she stuffs into her. Mouth, vagina, asshole —it's all the same to her.

Meridith is a young woman of the communes, a product of the sixties, like Lockett; the two pursue their obsessive vision of estrangement and alienation, while utilizing whatever bourgeois America furnishes. Wurlitzer's presentation is neither judgmental nor approving. The neutrality of his style is the making of the novel. Without mockery or parody, he has caught a mechanical line in American culture, and the mechanism applies to both upper and lower routes. Everyone moves as a zombie, whether drug- or culture-induced. The humorless narrative is a meditation on a mode of consciousness: American culture, whatever, wherever, whoever.

Flats (1970) is a meditation on space. As a title, it is used in many ways, but primarily to represent a piece of level ground, recalling Pynchon's title "Low-Lands." The novel is cast as a Beckett-like drama, drawing heavily on the trilogy and *Waiting for Godot,* in phrases such as: "Wichita can't go on. I have to go on"; or in lists, as of items in the narrator's pocket: " 'Two used three-cent stamps. One pebble. One ticket stub directing the bearer.' " But it is both less and more than a Beckett dramatic representation. Wurlitzer is trying to limn a personal America. His character(s) are named after cities, and yet they are little more than a single character with a succession of names: Flagstaff, Fairfax, for one set; then Memphis, Omaha, Abilene, Wichita, Duluth, Cincinnati, Houston, Mobile, for another. The latter group of cities seems to represent the one character whose movement is essential for the thrust of the novel. But even movement is not the key, nor is dramatization; spatiality given and denied is. The novel is a fore-shortened version of America's spatiality, something like Jasper Johns's map of the United States, where some states are exaggerated, others almost lost, still others abbreviated.

The meditation exists in a temporal vacuum. Cities come and go, but activity, as in Beckett's trilogy, is minimal. Language itself is minimal. The beginning: "I walked a far piece. I'm sure of that. Not that I remember the old ways, signed directions. I stopped. I would have crawled farther but the road gave out or I gave out. The horizon is limited, as if to say, I'm resting in a hollow or crouching in a man-made hole. These are the usual impedimenta against nodding off: a dead oak, sticky tufts of brown grass. Two bricks. More, certainly, a garbage can, a complete list except that fatigue strangles my concentration." The prose narrative chronicles tremendous effort made against equally tremendous enervation: one force advancing Memphis (or, later, other cities), fatigue restraining him.

The "flats" of the title are emblematic of his movement in space and time. In music, a flat is a tone half an interval lower than another; and in life, one feels flat, or suffers from a flat tire—elements of being lower, down, flattened out. All movement, such as it is in the narrative, is along the flats, made by cities which are suddenly bunched against each other. "Call me Memphis," Memphis says, but he (only identified as "he" by a cock) is also "I." Wurlitzer uses a shifting narrator, who moves from "I" to "he": involved in his own quest, and yet commentator upon it. "Omaha keeps sinking into the first person like warm mud. He's always rescued in time, as if I set that up without letting myself in on it. The third person handles the changes, keeps me from getting popped. I don't want to knock the third person. I like to travel there. It avoids stagnation and the theatrics of pointing to myself." The self-consciousness of Memphis, of "he" and "I," recalls the self-reflexive novel, as *Tristram Shandy,* which Wurlitzer's novel abstracts from: that roving in and out of participation and commentary.

The minimal narrative in Wurlitzer's hands, what we find also in *Nog* and *Quake,* is an expression or presentation of self; but self abstracted by an impersonal, nonrevealing prose. In this minimal dramatization, every act and nuance of the self, its slightest movement in space, its smallest response to time, is catalogued. Character no longer exists, only a purified, alembified self. As: "Flagstaff gathered the objects that were spread out in half circle. Abilene watched. Behind Abilene the trunk was wrapped in flames. Flagstaff put the objects in his sack and sat down. He flipped the knife forward, so that it landed on the rain slicker. Abilene picked up the knife and held it in the palm of his hand. He stepped over the narrow end of the trunk and scratched a line toward Halifax. Abilene sat down and looked at Flagstaff. Flagstaff met his gaze and then stared at the ground in front of him." It is all there: the exchange of small items, the cataloguing of one's pockets, the map of America daring one to move, cities congregating, marking off their boundaries; movement offered and denied.

All parts are, apparently, replaceable, since all segments emanate from a single self. Conceiving a 1960s version of the 1950s "on the road" narrative, Wurlitzer has taken Kerouac's basic situation and turned it into a drugged version: the movement of Kerouac's speeders is transformed by speed itself, into aborted movement, constipated action, spatiality as an idea, not an actuality. In Kerouac, reaching a destination had some significance, whereas in Wurlitzer it has none. "It's true, since Wichita came on the scene, Memphis, Omaha and Halifax have receded. In fact, even the circle has grown dimmer. Flagstaff and Abilene no longer exist. They have their pull, to be sure, but I have been able to pull back."

At issue is not the actual space of America, but the map of the States, the flattened-out space into which a map fits. It is a foreshortened version suitable to a drug-induced sense of the country, all pulled together here, all spread out there—but flats everywhere. We read: "Portland is not able to handle the edge. And yet he can't return to the ragweed. He has to take a step farther into the field or continue along the edge. The voices from the ragweed don't engage him. They seem banal and predictable. But Portland is unable to hear anything else. He is threatened by gravity so that I could easily nod off and never make it back. He needs a shape to embrace." The narrative ends with Mobile, a city whose name suggests movement; but Mobile walks only to end boredom. Nothing happens. "The journey is already over or it never happened. Let Mobile crawl on."

The narrator, now as "I," questions what happened to Mobile. "He must have dropped away. I didn't hear his breathing recede. There was no sound, no whimper. There was nothing to mark his separation from me. There is no one, not even me, to take his place. That is a final relief. He is gone although he never arrived." All that are left are questions, and "there are no questions to ask." What remains is light, or the lack of light. Wurlitzer's narrator, caught on the flats, is like Ellison's unnamable, trapped by light, or relieved by it. "I can recognize separations as they arrive," says Mobile, or once-Mobile. The narrator drifts off as light slowly covers him.

Repeated readings indicate the coherence of the brief paragraphs that make up the 159-page narrative. Some are only a few lines, others a page, most half a page. The narrative comes, then, in short bursts, like sections of a lyric poem. By flattening out his language, giving it minimal texture, Wurlitzer makes sure the prose poem does not become "poetic." Yet it coheres as a vision of America, embedded in its period: closer to the map of America than to America.

Like Walker Percy's *Love in the Ruins, Quake* (1972) is apocalyptic. The scene is Los Angeles, and the event is, apparently, an earthquake which has devastated the immediate area, perhaps the entire state, possibly the whole country. The narrator of Wurlitzer's novel, laid back, waiting for his money to run out, is staying in a hotel when walls, ceiling, floors heave and ho; and people begin to die, screw, play with each other, scream, run, sit, wait.

Nearly all apocalyptic fictions and films have one thing in common: the disaster permits people to display their real selves. In *Quake,* roving armies round up innocent people, strip them, maim them, kill. California has become a battleground, not only of rescue squads but of those who have awaited disaster in order to seize power. The most immediate analogue of the novel is Godard's film *Weekend,* apocalyptic, but heavily political. A couple starts out on a typical French weekend and must struggle to make its way through murderous traffic, wrecked cars, dying people, endless blockades. The background is screaming klaxons, police cars, ambulances, the sounds of war. Like Wurlitzer's quake, the weekend reveals people as savages, killers, rapists, cannibals. On their way back to Paris, the couple encounters a guerrilla band of Maoists, who are eating a barbecued Englishman, an innocent tourist, a parody of the bourgeois cookout. The couple split up as the woman chooses to remain with them. In this parodist's vision of France, the weekender is little different from the Maoist; only the ingredients are different.

Once the quake occurs, the way to survive is to flow with it. The narrator, unnamed, moves along the contours of disaster. Wurlitzer, like Godard, posits a world in which all assumed order is broken. The quake is like a nuclear strike, or a drug vision in which connections collapse. Survivors are those who can adapt themselves to chaos. The innocent are stripped of their clothes, marched along roads to general areas, then marched to new meeting points. Their captives are themselves sniped at by other captors, each group involved in a death struggle with other roving bands, hard hats, right-wing groups, police, rescue teams.

Captors are in as much danger as victims. There is no available food, except for scraps tossed into the crowd. The victims have no sense of who is controlling them, lack of information being one of the disarming factors of disorder. They also have no sense of the scope of the disaster, whether immediate, statewide, or national. The naked individual loses all sense of himself, and he must function as part of a herd; sheep, cattle become the suitable metaphor. Every aspect of civilization has broken down, far more than in Percy's *Love in the Ruins,* where a partially destroyed Howard Johnson's is a haven. All perspectives, as in a drug-induced hallucination, are altered; time and space as we ordinarily experience them are meaningless.

Within this vision of present life, all aspects of civilization become detritus. We recall Marlow's observations of the Congo in Conrad's novella, the artifacts of civilization rusting, decaying, rotting, falling apart, useless. The Africans are themselves detritus, wasted-out bodies, shades and phantoms. America is a Congo. In *Quake:* "The side of the road was completely devastated and we had to crawl over trees and work ourselves around deep cracks that sometimes stretched for a hundred yards. We passed bodies, some of them burned beyond recognition. Four men had been hanged with clothes lines from a sagging telephone pole. We walked past the remains of small expensive shops. Brightly colored clothes lay scattered on the street among paper back books and bronze bathroom fixtures. The chop-chop of a helicopter approached from the east. We dove for cover, crouching behind a pile of twisted metal outside of an antique shop."

Bodies, objects, limbs—a white German shepherd is calmly gnawing on a human arm—are all thrown together. But unlike Marlow, the narrator here makes no moral judgments, himself finds no value in life or death. There is only survival; one tries to live, but gives oneself up completely to the captors. The death camps are evoked: arbitrary acts, brutality, everyone at the level of animals. Wurlitzer presents what occurs in an even, flattened prose which simply relates.

People are not named, only places here and there, freeways and cities in California, streets in the Los Angeles area. The country has emptied of all value systems, people are reified, objects themselves of no worth. The captors char meat over a fire, living like cavemen.

One of the lengthiest scenes occurs in a football field, which becomes a prison ground. Football is evoked by some of the victims, O. J. Simpson, Jim Brown, et al. Just beyond the field are expensive shops, caved in, glass everywhere, a looter's paradise. People are snorting or shooting up, whenever they can get their hands on drugs. The narrator is captured and given the modern version of tar and feathers: catsup and mustard, whiskey poured over him, a severed head tied to his stomach. He escapes and enters a warehouse area, where Red Cross women serve cold coffee and candy bars. The candy bar becomes the food of the future. Flames tear at the warehouse, and the narrator barely escapes. He finds himself at a wall, guarded by one gang. Another gang decides to build its own wall. Each will fight the other to protect its territory. The struggle for control is on, and after constant firing of rifles, there is a lull, which ends the novel. " 'Oooooooooh,' I prayed before I passed out. 'Oooooooooh.' "

In one sense, *Quake* is an epitaph for the 1960s; the natural disaster as a manifestation of human upheaval. One can catch the sixties only in terms of explosions of human feeling, a decade of violence capped by the moonwalk, the result of ten years of national purpose. To capture that sense of incongruity—assassinations, demonstrations, topped by moonwalk—one needs quakes, nuclear wars, holocausts, a world of captors and victims. Although not directly related, Wurlitzer's three novels are interconnected by their fidelity to that sense of the decade, the sixties as unearthly. Nog is mythical America; flats are legendary areas of land set between cities; and quake is the way the world goes out. Obviously, in order to achieve his vision, Wurlitzer omits a great deal of what we consider to be novelistic reality. There is no love—only sex, and that usually public; no community—only grubbing around, survival itself; no family life—if families appear, they are screwing each other, or fighting generational battles; no organized, or even disorganized, society—people are discrete beings; no government—it is not even in the distance. There are, also, no warmth, sympathy, compassion, pity, books, leisure, entertainment. Yet not everyone is an animal. There are "considerations," alternative forms of relationships, mutations created.

Feelings have been deflected, so that a different kind of kinship is created. To survive that different world is to survive.

SOME BRIEF TAKES

Godard's films also lie heavily behind Frederic Tuten's *The Adventures of Mao on the Long March* (1971), especially *La Chinoise* and the Maoist bands of *Weekend*. More than a particularized influence, Godard's presence lies heavily because he linked the 1960s years as a series of fragments both witty and tedious, narrative segments intermixed with long disquisitions, characters roving in and out of roles, where everything is undefined and contingent, all caught within a radical fervor, often gone sour. Such ironies are also Tuten's concern, for his Mao is both the heroic adventurer of the long march and a consumer-oriented Westerner, caught up by fads and movements. If Godard is the pivotal figure behind the novel, then pop art serves a secondary, but not inconsequential, role. Warhol, Barthelme, Johns, Lichtenstein (who designed the cover illustration) have combined to turn energy into nonenergy or into nonheroic acts: as adversary response to the Vietnam War, American military and industrial energy, waste itself.

Similarly, Thomas McGuane in *Panama* (1978) writes of many things that are not Panama or Panamanian, and the place may not even exist in the novel. *Panama* takes its themes from its locale, Key West, which recalls to us the Southern California settings of Didion's fiction or the city landscapes of Barthelme's short stories. Waste matter is a key to all, key to Key West, to Far West, to East. Like Wurlitzer in his three novels, McGuane works by what we may call "negative accretion." Instead of gathering facts and feelings, the minimalist novelist doles them out. The more that accumulates, the less there is.

Comparably, Renata Adler's *Speedboat* (1976) and Elizabeth Hardwick's *Sleepless Nights* (1979) are minimalist adventures, in that the narrator in each attempts to limn a city or a life by way of snapshots. Minimalism takes upon itself a heavy burden. For at its outer reaches, it challenges a genre: it is, often, the novel as a form of poetry. Hardwick strives to be lyrical; and in fact, her book depends on a lyrical note which moves fiction off its pivot as narrative.

Frederic Tuten's method is to juxtapose aspects of our culture—objectless art, matters of verification, a beauty contest, optional art—with Mao's struggle to survive against the massive forces of Chiang Kai-shek in the late twenties. The culmination of Mao's struggle is his decision to go on his "long march," which meant breaking out of Chiang's encirclement, fighting through successive layers of resistance, and then walking on to a distant province. The long march becomes, as a historical act, equivalent to other long marches, such as Napoleon's in Russia, Washington and his men crossing the Delaware, the Lewis and Clark expedition, the Armenians' flight from genocidal Turks, Moses and his followers fleeing across the Red Sea, Castro's retreat into the Sierra Maestras.

Mao's journey is a central document of our time, made all the more transcendent by its juxtaposition with a self-conscious and self-regarding culture, such as our own. It itself, Mao's march needs no further explanation; but in contrast, it gathers up the resolve, idealism, heroism, and direction that, in 1971, our own culture has dissipated. For Mao's long march has many qualities in common with events in early American history: his forging of a country by way of extreme adversity recalls our own striving to carve out territory, establish a life, create a culture. Yet such greatness passes. The revolution is the thing itself: the breakout, the escape through encirclement, and then the march. After that comes the inevitable decline, a pop culture transcending heroism.

The Adventures of Mao recalls Barthelme's *Snow White,* chiefly in the use of fairy tale material in the way myth was once represented. The aim is to create contrasts between memory or fact (of Mao's march) and the development of a given culture. Since the literary method is minimalist, the line of development lies in the contrast or in the juxtaposition itself.

The march is not without its unexpected elements. A tank stops near Mao and Greta Garbo steps out, the device familiar from surrealist art and, more recently, from Godard's films. After initial resistance, Mao succumbs to Garbo and instructs her "in the Chinese Way, the Five Paths, and the Three Encirclements." Since the long march is, in one sense, Mao's "poem of life," it is possible for certain images to be introduced which function at the poetic level. As a poem, as distinct from its function as a military and political maneuver, the march has adversary elements which grow out of it at random. Holding it together is Mao's resolve to break through, to attain a safe haven; but the path is strewn not only with enemy dangers but with internal turmoil.

Mao is torn between his political/ideological journey and his inner world: poetry, desire for lovely women, need to transcend the routine. He wants to identify with other things, as the final interview shows. He admires abstract and minimal art. The work of such artists is "like The Long March, a victory over space and time, a triumph of the necessary over the unnecessary."

Even while caught in the struggle to emerge as a viable Communist threat to Chiang, Mao has moved to other grounds. He perfects his breathing so that he can stay under water; he dreams of other cultures, and he subscribes to dozens of American magazines; he wishes to be a Renaissance man, not simply a warrior or leader of his people. He aspires to a poet's vocation, which means he wishes to enter adversary worlds. He seeks "perfect stasis and equilibrium," what he identifies as the "Great Harmony." He wishes to break out, not only of Nationalist encirclement, but of all bonds. He is our man of the 1960s, trying to remake and transcend everything, seeking the ultimate, dissatisfied with human limitations, reaching toward Promethean powers. Mao embodies the counterculture, already dissatisfied with his own cult, ready to oppose it.

Panama takes place in Key West, the new frontier where bizarre events, lost memories, drug-induced hallucinations come together. Adding to that sense of a paradise irrevocably lost is McGuane's prose style: a terse, almost epigrammatic pithiness, rapid cutting, acts of violence juxtaposed to diminution. "When I'm tired and harmless, I pack a gun, a five-shot Smith and Wesson .38. It's the only .38 not in a six-shot configuration I know of. How the sacrifice of that one last shot makes the gun so flat and concealable, so deadlier than the others. Just by giving up a little!" The six-shot .38 turned into a five-shot weapon is emblematic of the situation: take something away, make it flatter, easier to conceal, and we have the lost paradise of Key West. Featured is Chet Pomeroy, the once famous, now lost protagonist, full of violence, capable of martyrdom (he nails his hand to the door of his ex-wife's house), and possibly of murder. McGuane, like Didion, another specialist in spare parts, is excellent at catching the deadness of flesh. " 'I am a congestion of storage batteries. I'm wired in series. I've left some fundamental components on the beach, and await recharging, bombardment, implanting, *something,* shall we say, very close to the bone.' "

The strongest parts of the book derive from Pomeroy's descriptions of himself as someone close to waste matter, rotting along the edges of a failed career as stunt man, acrobat, performer, in the waste lands of Key West. The novel is of flotsam and jetsam, lost souls well below the lostness of Tennessee Williams's characters. (Williams, who had a home in Key West, hovers over the novel.) The Panama of the title has little to do with any of the activity, but with the felt sense, with the possibility Pomeroy and the woman he considers his wife may have been married there, which he only dimly recalls. A land mass made meaningful solely because it houses a thin trickle of water between two continents, Panama is a dim place. The nature of *that* in the past, like the nature of Key West in the present, negates certainty.

The novel as method or structure, most of all as prose, is more interesting in part than as a whole. One problem with minimalist fiction is that a protagonist, or even minor characters, may seem pallid, thin. McGuane can generate no positive energy in Pomeroy, since the novel terminates before we learn much about him. He is like Camus's Meursault, moving asymptotically toward total negation; but Meursault has around him a large ideological presence. Pomeroy has none; he moves without a net, as he admits. As a "walk-through" or a "simple occupant," that unnamed resident, he has no "affect," as in a Didion novel. Minimalist techniques drag characters toward cipherdom. Thus, minimalism establishes an atmosphere in which nothing can live, no less thrive; and we find no empathetic relationships, no associations, nothing but mechanical responses. Comparably, Warhol's *a* thrives in such a milieu, for it is already tape-recorded, outside human connection, part of a mechanical process, *Krapp's Last Tape* without remembrance of things past.

Renata Adler's *Speedboat* has several possible meanings, connoted by a boat that speeds through, leaving only glimpses. This fits the idea of the narrator as a tabloid reporter whose life is made up of glimpses, as she, the reporter, speeds by. But "speedboat" has other suggestive meanings: of speed, LSD, rushing into someone's psyche and creating a montage of sensory experiences, sensations, unconnected to each other or even to the person experiencing them. These two "speedboats" are the most reasonable. A third is the way we may call someone a speedboat, a flashy show-off.

Information is emitted into an indifferent world, and there it must be picked up by a consciousness that can or cannot interpret it. This example is a witty "sensation," embodying what we find throughout the narrative: short episodes like Kosinski's "steps," only briefer, less ego-centered, less manipulative. Yet they are ego too—part of the "me" demonstrating its ability to hold in balance that montage of disparate sensations and experiences. The narrator, Jen Fain, does take the pose of knowing all; she moves everywhere, sees everything, reports what she sees, enters into the lives of her friends.

There are six sections, all involving movement, defensive and otherwise; and yet all movement appears to be like the voice giving the Series scores: lacking any hold upon the experiences unless one picks up the right signals. If one misses them, then experience remains incoherent. As in McElroy, information theory is chaotic; as in Pynchon, it is overcharged. Information pours out, and no one is prepared to receive it.

Within the catchall of the reporter's consciousness is a sorting mechanism called language, although language itself is part of the confusion and incoherence, often only voices. It is the vehicle for information and yet a part of the information theory which must be decoded. Language both serves and disserves, a Wittgenstein conundrum. "While people tagged up on these public codes and incantations, baby talk took over private conversations—naughty and cranky in particular. Personal treachery and acts of violence were naughty. Citizens in the middle of small betrayals or murder trials described themselves as in a cranky mood. Murders, generally, were called brutal and senseless slayings, to distinguish them from all other murders; nouns became glued to adjectives, in series, which gave an appearance of shoring them up." Everybody lies, words lose meaning. "The jig was never up. . . . In every city, at the same time, therapists earned their living by saying, 'You're too hard on yourself.' "

Language and knowing surface when Fain becomes an instructor in a branch of City University, and she must teach those who have neither precision nor awareness of words. Fain is very hard on these students, turning their errors into mockery, seeing her supervisors (chairmen and deans, the president himself) as part of a vast rip-off of city funds: making believe they are educating people when no one can handle language, the basic tool of knowledge. Here knowledge and information theory serve the narrator's social/political intolerance, where she fails to distinguish between those who cannot handle language and those who learn it minimally so as to improve their lives.

Her arrogance here is not isolated. The consciousness behind the tone assumes the world is a rational place filled with irrational people; and that if we can get behind the irrationality, we can structure sanity and stability. It is, in brief, a young person's sense of the world, where experience of order deceives her about the nature of disorder. Adler is excellent when she provides examples of disorder: for instance, course offerings, where groupings allow *The Brothers Karamazov* to be listed in the English department, Ibsen and Strindberg in the German department, where Swinburne, floating around, is also offered. Chekhov turns up in Classics, and Drama has added Film. The seizing and misplacement of courses are metaphors for the world outside, in which seizures force the temporary coherence of elements basically incoherent; and the university system, rather than disentangling, helps to abet the confusion.

Similarly, the male-female split is well taken. Adler mentions many of the "contra-fifties" people, braggarts, among the men; whereas the women are suicides. The formulation is simplistic at one level, profound at another. "All those unendearing braggarts and, on the distaff side, the suicides."

Elizabeth Hardwick's *Sleepless Nights* is not really a novel, but a sequence of episodes controlled only by the narrator's consciousness. They are "dream" sequences which are the by-product of sleepless nights: night dreams presented as waking dreams. That is, there is no attempt to capture the language or flow of dreams, no effort to approximate the dimension of sleeplessness in fragmented or disjointed images. Language is controlled, instead, by a lyrical literary consciousness: a metaphor, as it were, for sleepless nights.

Observations rove back and forth between layers of the past. Hardwick announces on the first page: "This is what I have decided to do with my life just now. I will do this work of transformed and even distorted memory and lead this life, the one I am leading today." Observations are disconnected, associated only by way of her ability to evoke them. Many of them are patently distorted, memories heaped upon memories. She speaks of cafeteria food in the Automat, commiserating with herself for the vileness of poverty. She speaks of "watery macaroni, bready meat loaf, the cubicle of drying sandwiches; mud, glue and leather, from these textures you made your choice." Yet the Automat was quite different; the macaroni, actually, was a superb dish for the price, the very opposite of mud, glue, and leather. Her memory of the past is impeded by a kind of romanticization of poverty; by inverting her suffering, she makes it seem heroic, all for art.

Billie Holiday is evoked, her elusiveness almost captured. Hardwick cannot fully succeed, because Holiday staged herself, and elusiveness became part of her genius as a performer. She was always far more than the parts, and Hardwick's "segments" can only suggest the whole. The Hardwick passage locates Holiday in the dark, as a dim personage, perhaps trafficking with satanic elements; emerging only to sing, and then creating her own dark around her. But this is only the physical presence. There is no sense of Holiday as a person, only as a personage, and this is where minimalism fails; it depends almost entirely on the physical, on the presence. In many of his brief minimalist tales, Kafka could suggest the inner being of things because he moved directly toward "souls." Hardwick's minimalism accumulates external details, and by way of them attempts to strike through to essences. Sleepless nights do not produce profundity, but flashes, presences.

She films, in her mind, a woman whose news is all bad, "and so her talk was punctuated with 'of course' and 'naturally.'" Her son is a mess "naturally," and "of course" she had got married very young, before she knew what she was doing. "Now? The boy's just sitting around, actually living with a couple, both psychiatrists, and it's supposed to be therapy. They hate me, naturally. When he was with me a few months ago it was a nightmare." Since the woman is not famous, unlike Holiday, Hardwick can contain her brilliantly; the woman's phrases resonate from a world she has had to accept without comprehending her place in it. "Naturally" and "of course" carry the freight of her bewilderment. We know her soul; whereas Holiday's soul—because so famous, so much part of the performer—remains buried ever more deeply the further Hardwick tries to penetrate it.

She is best with people who do not reverberate, who can live in phrases: small-town men who seem so appealing, but who, upon examination, provide "death traps" for women who marry them. "I know what the men are like, but I do not know what she is like, with her washing of clothes, her baking, her dangling shutter never mended by the husband-carpenter, the broken lamp never fixed by the household electrician, the flowerless, shrubless plot of land of the town gardener." She catches the appearance of the men, who appeal with their manly ways, their mastery of their type of life; while their women toil in the home, live beyond the charm, in the life itself.

The Dutch scenes, with Dr. Z., work not at all, neither as an evocation of the place, nor of the Doctor and his philandering ways; nor of his wife, their visit to New York, their dependence on familiar objects and ways. Similarly, Maine scenes, which make up the latter parts of the book, only intermittently convey the bleakness of life there; or else Hardwick cannot get into the style of the people who barely survive, or who, like Josette and Ida, survive through commitment to work. Yet at least one passage conveys superbly the landscape, a "lunar landscape," without people:

> The winter came down upon them. The suicide season arrived early. The land, after a snowfall, would turn into a lunar stillness, satanic, brilliant. The tall trees, altered by the snow and ice, loomed up in the arctic landscape like ancient cataclysmic formations of malicious splendor. The little houses on the road with their stoves and furnaces blowing heat, their lamps glowing, trembling there in the whiteness, might be settlements waiting for a doom that would come over them silently in the night.

The problem with minimalist art is that supporting evidence for such passages, brilliant when isolated, is not forthcoming; for the very technique provides only thrust and withdraw. Such a passage as the above is right in particulars and should be the centerpiece. Hardwick attempts to follow it up with Ida, a washerwoman, and Herman, a drifter, a half-crazed, isolated man. But the passage becomes lost, or else drifts out of sight—like Herman, when he runs off. Her minimalism is for the landscapes of life, not for life.

Chapter Ten

THE FEMALE EXPERIENCE

Much madness is divinest sense
To a discerning eye;
Much sense the starkest madness.
'Tis the majority
In this, as all, prevails.
Assent, and you are sane;
Demur,—you're straightway dangerous,
And handled with a Chain.

EMILY DICKINSON

A phenomenon such as "female fiction" does not exist, but in the 1960s there began to appear novels about the "female experience," by both male and female writers. It is necessary to separate these books from anything called "female fiction," which would suggest that the culture bifurcates into two distinct experiences, one male and one female. That such experiences differ, there can be no disagreement; but that such experiences overlap among American modes of escape, spatiality, pastoral fantasies, and opposition to systems, there should also be no disagreement. I concur with Elaine Showalter's statement:

> Women writers should not be studied as a distinct group on the assumption that they write alike, or even display stylistic resemblances distinctively feminine. But women do have a special literary history susceptible to analysis, which includes such complex considerations as the economics of their relation to the literary marketplace [in which they overlap with some men]; the effects of social and political changes in women's status upon individuals [which they share with some male black writers, also some Jewish and other ethnics], and the implications of stereotypes of the woman writer and restrictions of her artistic autonomy [which, once again, she may have shared

with some male black writers, at least until recently].*

There is by now a sizable body of fiction which focuses on female experiences or conditions, in which women must find their way personally, professionally, socially, in what is basically a patriarchy. The latter we may define as any society in which men control authority and determine what roles women should or should not play. Adrienne Rich adds that in a patriarchal society, "capabilities assigned to women are relegated generally to the mystical and aesthetic and excluded from the practical and political realms." This approximates what Betty Friedan

---

*The question may arise that if I can isolate something called the "female experience," then why not similarly isolate the black experience, the Jewish experience, et al.? The reason is that the former was conceived of as a distinct grouping by a number of novelists, whose similarities in subject matter and treatment give their work commonality. The black experience, on the other hand, is dispersed among every kind of mode, and so is the Jewish experience. For blacks and Jews, being American preempts other considerations. For the women in this grouping, being female supersedes all else. This, too, will change in time, and the novel of female experience, as we can already see in Didion, Oates, and Morrison, will no longer be the separate body of material it was in the late 1960s and early 1970s.

had several years earlier referred to as the "feminine mystique," that order of being, or quality of life and feeling, which gave women special and distinct powers in order to keep them "progressively dehumanized."

An example of the female imagination at work comes in the following way. In *Jane Eyre,* Bertha, the "madwoman in the attic," is presented as the element that must be eliminated in order for Rochester and Jane to complete their destiny together. Imprisoned in the upper reaches of Thornfield, she is a threat to foreground order and stability, a principle of chaos, in fact. Since Charlotte Brontë was writing a romance, Bertha could become expendable. In a society more oriented to the overall female experience, Jean Rhys in *Wide Sargasso Sea* perceived in Bertha the characteristic victim of a male-dominated society, a woman moved around as an object, living out others' sense of her experience, not her own, and becoming mad as the sole way of breaking through an unyielding situation. In this view, Bertha's plight is more archetypically female than Jane's, by far, since Jane is moving in a fairy tale of sorts where elements yield to her, whereas Bertha has moved in the real world of power. There is, I feel, no male novelist who could have picked up the thread of Bertha's existence and turned it into an emblem, as Jean Rhys did; and here alone we note how the female novelist can perceive aspects of experience which remain (at least in our era) outside the reach of the male writer. Reading back from Rhys, we experience *Jane Eyre* differently.

The major literary documents for the women's movement of the 1960s are curiously spread out. Simone de Beauvoir's *The Second Sex* (1949) is the single book to which all paths, rightly, lead. In that anatomy of women's lives against a background of a corruptive capitalist system, de Beauvoir spoke of the need for women to struggle to achieve a better society. In such a society, one based on socialist principles, women would be able to liberate themselves from the fundamental patriarchy which corporate capitalism imposed on them. De Beauvoir perceived the almost infinite ways in which women were prevented from developing as human beings, but she associated their ameliorated condition with change in the society itself. She would, later, in a *Ms.* magazine interview, speak of a shift in her views, to the extent that women would have to take their own lives in hand instead of waiting for social change. She recognized that even in socialist countries—and we should add, in most 1960s radical groups opposed to corporate capitalism —women have not fared so well as she had hoped once a change of mind took place.* In her talk at the 1976 Brussels International Tribunal on Crimes Against Women, she further withdrew from her earlier position about changing society and exhorted women to become decolonized.

But despite her shift in tactics, de Beauvoir has remained absolutely faithful to her original assertion that "One is not born a woman, one becomes one."† In a kind of literary embodiment of many of de Beauvoir's ideas, Doris Lessing wrote in *The Golden Notebook* (1962) what is still the finest of contemporary novels about the "female experience." Her point, too, was that women would emerge or have a greater opportunity of liberation when society itself is altered. Lessing asserted she was not a feminist in any narrow sense, since she saw "women's issues" as connected to larger sociopolitical questions. In her subsequent fiction, she moved even more intensely into those areas of change, where dehumanization of both sexes has led to an apocalyptic explosion and society must change or confront its demise. Yet despite her disclaimer of being a feminist, her sense of female life in *The Golden Notebook* is intense, varied, and cogently presented. Through flashback, she was able to find coordinates for Anna-Ella in a diversity of experiences, deeply political as well as personal, and through past–present focusing to suggest a range no other postwar novelist could offer in this area.†

The more immediate source of inspiration for a literature about the female experience was Friedan's *The Feminine Mystique* (1963). Besides the cogency of her arguments, we must remark the astonishing

---

*Frantz Fanon's eloquent examination of how women progressed during the Algerian War is belied by postwar developments, when traditionalism and Moslem fundamentalism prevailed, reestablishing women, with few exceptions, in their historical roles.

†Behind de Beauvoir, Virginia Woolf, and others lies Margaret Fuller's *Woman in the Nineteenth Century,* both a personal quest for self-fulfillment and a more general plea for women's rights. We should, she wrote, "have every path laid open to Woman as freely as to Man."

†In an amusing *Commentary* round table discussion ("Culture and the Present Moment," December 1974), the participants saw the vulgarization of modern culture in the fact of a Modern Language Association "annual seminar devoted to Doris Lessing." Hilton Kramer disagreed with the ridicule cast upon Lessing (by, among others, the editor of *Commentary*), asserting that "Her books deal with serious and often difficult experience." Nearly all the participants, some of them refugees from *Partisan Review* symposia, sound like creatures freeze-dried since the 1950s, then brought forth into a not so brave new world for which they are, simply, too fine.

timing of the book; for it attempted to bring women into the mainstream of professional and political life just as civil rights, antiwar sentiment, and other forms of "rebellion" were emerging. Surely, part of the resistance to Friedan's statements was connected to the entire matrix of adversary ideas which were being disseminated in the sixties; and women's issues in the eyes of many became indistinguishable from other, far more radical matters. We note how unradical female issues had been when we consider the popularity among women in the late 1940s and early 1950s of *Modern Women: The Lost Sex* (1947) by Ferdinand Lundberg and Marynia Farnham. Offered the view that women may achieve sanity and balance through passivity and subordination, it presented itself as a vehicle for female liberation. This appeared two years before the French edition of *The Second Sex,* and well before that book had any influence here in translation.

Friedan's support for the emergence of women contains the most gentle of arguments. Neither anti-male nor overly focused on larger social issues, she offers evidence of what later appeared to be obvious: that women without career choices languished in a doll's house, their abilities curtailed, their mental (and physical) health threatened, their roles as wives and mothers debilitated by their lack of focus and power. Friedan argued that "the core of the problem for women today is not sexual but a problem of identity—a stunting or evasion of growth that is perpetuated by the feminine mystique." To desensationalize her thesis, she separated "sexual" from "identity," although indeed the two are intricately interconnected. Later discussions of orgasm—how, why, when, with whom—would link sex and identity. Nevertheless, Friedan did not at that time wish to be sidetracked from her main point, which was to provide for women the same guidelines in their development as obtain for men. ". . . why have theorists," she wrote, "not recognized this same identity crisis in women?"

Her analysis covers a good deal of ground, not so familiar then as it is now, as the result of feminist writings. Of particular interest, almost two decades ago, was Friedan's analysis of Freud's theories as connected to women, and her printing of some of his devastatingly demeaning letters to his wife-to-be, Martha. Friedan does not sufficiently distinguish between Freud's theories—which could be potentially as liberating for women as for men—and his practices, which were fixed in Victorian attitudes. Yet her points on Freud are valuable, as they also are on

Helene Deutsch and Margaret Mead, who later was considered a spokeswoman for feminism but who, in actuality, waffled on nearly all the big issues.

With its timeliness, its distillation of many of de Beauvoir's more complicated positions, its application directly to American women (mainly, but not exclusively, white, middle class, educated), Friedan's book was the impetus behind two decades of change. She points out, however, how easy it is for such issues to die, for after women obtained the vote in 1920, there were decades of neglect, indifference, "dead history" for feminism. Feminism, careerism, the independent woman, were all used synonymously with lesbianism; such women were called "Lucy Stones," after the nineteenth-century feminist who helped to open educational and professional doors for women. Marriage and children were the destiny for women, whether uneducated or graduates of Friedan's own Smith College.

More recently, Virginia Woolf has become a powerful influence in analyses of the female experience by American writers. Not only her fiction and literary essays, but a book such as *A Room of One's Own* (1929), have served to reinforce what many women writers were already saying. Woolf offered, also, something of an aesthetic, in that she asserted women had to develop a prose of their own. After mentioning Newman, Sterne, Dickens, Thackeray, among others, she says: "The weight, the pace, the stride of a man's mind are too unlike her own." She quotes a typical early-nineteenth-century sentence and adds: "That was a man's sentence; behind it one can see Johnson, Gibbon and the rest. It was unsuited for a woman's use." She sums up: "There is no reason to think that the form of the epic or of the poetic play suits a woman any more than the sentence suits her. But all the older forms of literature were hardened and set by the time she became a writer. The novel alone was young enough to be soft in her hands."

With such remarks echoing in her head, Kate Millett suggested in her Introduction to "Prostitution: A Quartet for Female Voices" that if "we are saying something new, it does seem to me we ought to say it in new ways." She mentions women's ability for oral communication and advocates that some kind of seamless verbal communication take place, a form reminiscent of Woolf's own practices. Her argument for a new female linguistic mode is also political. For if the media are in the hands of those who govern, then those out of power (females, blacks, the poor) "must settle for talk." In the past, she says, women's talk has been trivialized, or considered trivial by those in authority. Yet, she adds, there is "a new cogency and direction, a clarity and rising consciousness in the speech of women now."

While accommodating the sense that women have an outlook which calls for different ideological responses from those of male writers, such suggestions lose sight of the commonality of language, the mutuality of goals in the American experience, and the ways in which the culture shapes both sexes despite individual differences. There is no escaping the larger role of the American experience, especially since liberation, freedom of choice, escape into spatiality, and pastoral fantasies are associated male/female properties. The "how" will dominate, not the "what."

In the public sector, the 1965 President's Commission on the Status of Women reported in statistical detail what everyone had known: that women at every level of the public and private sector were earning far less than men for comparable work—about one-half in some areas; that women could not enter many fields, which were deemed male preserves (sciences, mathematics, professorships in most disciplines, banking and finance); that women had to be encouraged to enter professional life through child care centers, counseling, reeducation. Even before that report, however, Title VII of the Civil Rights Act of 1964 had banned sex discrimination in employment along with racial discrimination. Incidentally, that statement, along with the words of the presidential commission, became like a long-buried time bomb: almost forgotten and then reactivated in the seventies. These legislative acts became the background for the now stalled Equal Rights Amendment.

Friedan then started National Organization for Women (NOW), the feminist organization with the longest reach. In its early issues, *Ms.* magazine offered valuable articles on women's bodies, on male-dominated medical practices; and the proliferation of publications and organizations was on. Since this is not a history of the feminist movement but an examination of some of the fiction it produced, we can obtain a better indication of the movement as it is reflected in feminine experience in fiction. Although women predominate here, feminism has been taken up by several male writers, with about the same mixed results we find in female writers.

What characterizes nearly all such fiction—whether depicting female subservience, or rejection of the male, or lesbian relationships, or attempts at marriage and children, or efforts at careers, whether de-structive or self-destructive—is a naturalistic/Darwinistic determinism. Liberation, if it does come, must emerge from a clearly deterministic pattern, understandably so given the nature of the feminine quest in a mainly patriarchal society. Instead of the former counters of doom and destiny, we have the male, as an active agent or even as an invalid. The male, as a kind of reincarnation of Heathcliff and Rochester or a Gothic presence, hovers over all female experience, and that constitutes the nature of her deterministic doom.

Spatiality is something women must earn very dearly. They are not, by the nature of society, the ones to gain much by space; and in older fiction, the woman who cherished space usually became an outcast, or suffered dearly for her desire for release: the heroines of Hardy and Eliot immediately come to mind. But spatiality, that intrinsic American experience, remains relevant for women, although they do not achieve it with leaps. Their "on the road" is measured not in hundreds or thousands of miles, but often in streets and neighborhoods, one exchanged for another.

Joyce Carol Oates's fiction is in one form or another concerned with the female experience—best achieved in her novel *them,* which I see as a key text of the sixties. *Do With Me What You Will* (1973) has a spatial plan in it, for Elena is kidnapped by her father, removed from *her* life and reconstituted in his. Under her father's control, Elena is almost inadvertently neglected and forgotten; her "doom" is clearly her father. To survive, she must escape, back into her own life, and assume some semblance of control. Replacing her father with Marvin Howe, Elena finds herself "re-kidnapped," made subservient to still another male and his life. She must escape that, as before. Salvation, indeed life, for her depends on spatiality, distancing herself from men who seek authority over her. Her potential male savior is Jack Morrissey, whose father was literally a killer, whereas Elena's father and husband are only indirectly so. In his anti-authoritarian activities, in civil rights, the antiwar movement, Jack offers a model for Elena. But she is insufficiently developed as a character *outside her victimization* to gain our attention; and the novel, as a whole, trails off.

In the earlier *Wonderland* (1971), Oates has a typical "orphan" in Jesse Hart, a male, whose father one day murders the entire family but only wounds Jesse. The main section of the novel concerns Jesse's life with Dr. Pederson and his family in the Niagara region. By way of the male, we glimpse female life:

subservience, self-destruction, dehumanization, lack of mature development. The Pederson family is ungainly, fat to the point of pathology; and the fattest of them is Hilda, a math genius, but a bottomless container for food in a family in which Dr. Pederson has full authority. Mrs. Pederson chooses to revolt against his control, and when Jesse attempts to help her, he is thrust out by the doctor. Oates's plan is to see the family's females as a reverse image of Jesse: he skinny, withdrawn, foodless; they fat, empty, unable to function.

In their care, however, Jesse becomes as bloated as they, as obsessed with eating. Escape, withdrawal, survival often take the form of losing the weight one piled on during empty periods. Maureen in *them* becomes monstrously fat after her stepfather's murderous assault on her, and when she moves toward survival on different terms, she must lose weight, take care of her looks. Mrs. Pederson wants to escape the "concentration camp" atmosphere of her husband, but she cannot do it because she remains obsessed with food; food has replaced all control that should be in her hands, and she is filled instead of fulfilled. By being so grotesquely fat, she has made herself repulsive to her husband; but even more, she has gained revenge for her lack of control by becoming repulsive to herself. In *Expensive People* (1968), Richard Everett, who as a boy murders his mother, is a small hippo at eighteen, his weight an emblem of inner chaos.*

While men as well as women can be monstrously heavy in Oates's work, it is the women who suffer more: as a form of self-punishment for their inabilities. Connected to this is the women's feeling that men are more in control of their lives than they; this is not true to the degree the women want to believe it. Ultimately, Jesse must live out his father's pattern: as the older man killed, so must the son. Jesse discards his goods, all forms of identification, his money, and, as the ultimate authority over his daughter, goes after the seducer of his daughter. Jesse has passed through all the wonders of Wonderland—the modern world, the American Eden—and has become the

---

*In *The Necessary Blankness,* Mary Allen makes the excellent point that since Oates's sympathies are primarily with the poor, "she makes abundance particularly gross." I would add that fatness is for her another sign of violence: an emblem of internal disorder which is the coordinate of the terrible crimes that occur throughout her novels and stories. Overeating is, I suspect, an aspect of the "female experience," though Thomas Mann in "Little Lizzie" used fatness as an entire critique of a bourgeois society.

atavistic protector of his daughter's virtue. She, in turn, is wasted away, by drugs and experience, a zombie. Wonderland reduces to this: the male as victim, but even in his victimization encountering women who are more dehumanized. Oates's point is not to separate men and women as distinct victims, but, to repeat de Beauvoir's stress in *The Second Sex,* to perceive that American life can itself be a form of doom.

For a writer like Oates—and we can add several others—characters are female versions of Clyde Griffiths, as we observed in *them.* They are part of an American tragedy, programmed to bad marriages and imprisonment, able to escape into pastoral, or spatiality, by metaphorically "drowning" their husbands or boyfriends—thus the women of Jong, Rossner (in *Goodbar*), Alice Walker, French, Gould, Shulman, Piercy, Morrison (to a lesser extent), and others. If they succeed in "drowning" the man in their lives, they break free, often into a lesbian relationship, or into another cycle of dependency, sometimes into doom like Rossner's Theresa Dunn. This is their rite of passage. Clyde struggles against class and caste; these women struggle against the destiny of sexual coding. The breakthrough, surprisingly, has little thrust toward successful careers. Characteristic of most of this fiction is not professional achievement, but achievement of self: finding oneself preempts other considerations.

We recognize how in much black and Jewish fiction, so called, this same consideration holds: the rite of passage, the breakthrough, the form of survival or destruction connected not to "success" but to personal salvation. In this respect, women writing about women are in the mainstream of American fiction. We do not find in serious fiction by Jewish writers any young people training to be doctors or lawyers or professors; rather, they are struggling to achieve themselves in some metaphysical realm of pure being, Portnoy with his whang, Augie March with his running, Alpine with his conversion, Herzog with his sanity. The point about Ellison's invisible man is achievement of some balance of self and society, which, ironically, he can discover only underground, in pure invisibility lighted by 1,369 bulbs. Baldwin's characters, similarly, do not achieve: they struggle to find a self which must emerge.

For the woman writer, there is a circling back to Hester Prynne. In the dispossessed Garden outside the prison, Hester begins life in the most dire circumstances a woman can find herself in: reviled for adultery, unmarried with a child, lacking status in her community, isolated by way of an act of love, forced to balance herself between her womanly needs and social deprivation. Update this and we have a dozen or more 1960s and early 1970s novels by women about women. We find elements of Hester in Morrison's Sula, Walker's Meridian, Rossner's Theresa, Gould's Julie, French's Mira, Piercy's Beth. Although Hester's intensity is lacking, and Hawthorne's historical sense, these novels are attempts to depict women in dispossessed gardens, whether of marriage, motherhood, or personal relationships.

As we observed, Morrison's Sula breaks out, damning herself in the eyes of the black community in order to discover herself, pursuing the same rite of passage as a Baldwin character. For both, the pressures from the black community are far greater than for a white protagonist, male or female; and the harking back to Hester and the repressive Puritanism of her culture is not an idle comparison. Alice Walker's *Meridian* (1976) charts many of these struggles for self. Meridian, entrapped in early marriage and motherhood, is by seventeen socially doomed by her personal life. But when her husband, Eddie, deserts her, she gives away her baby boy in order to develop herself, first in voter registration and then at Saxon College, in Atlanta. Saxon is a finishing school for black women, but it does heighten her sensibilities, even as her physical being deteriorates.

Walker has not written a simplistic novel; it is neither a traditional rite of passage nor a political diatribe. Her point lies elsewhere, first in the liberation of Meridian, but also in a depiction of the trap that awaits the black woman. Michele Wallace in *Black Macho and the Myth of the Superwoman* (1979) picks up from here. Although the situation of the black woman differs from that of the white, we recognize an archetypal male as doom. Lessing had, in a very different context, caught the same point. For Walker's men, while kind, are infantile in their need for wife/mothering, incapable of sustaining anything that does not gratify their senses and well-being. ". . . she became obsessed with the horrible thought that Eddie, like his name, would never be grown up. She thought he would always be a boy." This is a figure not unlike the boy-children we find in the Jewish literary experience.

Several elements give this novel its resonances, evocative and poetic at their best. Walker runs brief sequences with longer ones, uses an interrupted narrative line, insists on the extra dimensionality of the black experience. This dimensionality is located not

in the social arena (she breaks with naturalism here) but in energies devoted to thoughts which have no outlet, sensibilities which lack resolution, psychological states for which no language exists. Meridian's life is pieces, just as the men in her life are episodes. Although there is a strong social commitment to poverty-level blacks, Meridian is only a borderline revolutionary, until she sees a young black clubbed to death. Then she feels she might kill, although she knows she could not.

Walker finds an apt metaphor for Meridian's faltering sensibility in a "wild child." A girl of about thirteen wanders the landscape as an unloosed dog would. She wears cast-off clothing, eats garbage and refuse, smells like a pig, and becomes pregnant. She is found in the slums near Saxon College, and Meridian takes her in, bathing her and feeding her at the table. The girl cannot adapt to civilization, escapes from Saxon, and is struck down by a speeding car, "her stomach the largest part of her." As a girl/-woman, the child epitomizes the pure victim, deemed by men to be a piece of meat. She emblemizes the bottom rung, what the fate of every black woman in society could be. Meridian sees her future rewritten by virtue of the wild child, and her life takes on commitment.

One large area of difference between the black female experience and the white lies in this area of commitment. For while most white female novelists attempt to locate the female identity in the individual, the black seeks verification also in relationships to others—the poor, the deprived, the have-nots. White experience leads ever inward, black experience both inward and outward. And when white men write about the female experience—Alan Friedman, William Gass, Ivan Gold—they stress individual identity; the "mystique," whether subservient or liberated, is the thing, not social commitment.

"Life change," which so characterized aspects of the 1960s, filtered into every aspect of the female experience. Role-playing, conscious or not, was a form of politics; the American tires of the script and changes according to some internal pressure. The "female experience" accommodated this view, since women had been involved in playing roles, social, political, professional, personal, as forms of experience. Reading the correct signals, for them as for Jews and blacks, enabled them to achieve sanity, or else they became "madwomen in the attic." But we should stress that change of life styles, which so nourished the women's movement, touched every aspect of the culture. LeRoi Jones leaves his white Jewish wife and two half-white children, becomes Baraka; next he takes on an African heritage with an African-dressed wife, becomes a black power advocate, hates whites and Jews; then he becomes a socialist, a Marxist, and woos blacks and whites (presumably Jews) for political support. Mailer, his counterpart in many ways, moves through various wives, stabs one, pleads he is undergoing profound changes, moves through various ideological shifts from "White Negro" to suspicion and fear of black activities, runs for mayor of New York City, makes films, speaks of his long-awaited blockbuster novel, and writes books about astronauts, Marilyn Monroe, Henry Miller, and Gary Gilmore. Stokely Carmichael coins "black power," marries a rock singer, and departs with the ruins unshored. "Black Is Beautiful" becomes the name of a perfume. Eldridge Cleaver goes from rapist to macho culture hero, once imprisoned, to exile abroad, to born-again Christian supporting Ronald Reagan and the Moral Majority.

The point of all these bizarre changes suggests that female aspirations and changes of status must be perceived within a context of role-playing as much as one of personal yearning for something better. The culture was itself opening up toward innumerable acts of role-playing (Lifton's "protean man" comes to mind); and it was this cultural matrix—which allowed Mailer and Baraka, among others, to relocate their selves to suit the moment—that also accommodated the women's movement. Personal liberation became possible mainly because the larger culture was expanding; and then, in the kind of reciprocal action every large movement entails, the women's movement helped to make that culture more accessible to alternative life styles.

This is one way to explain the female experiences described by Judith Rossner in *Looking for Mr. Goodbar* (1975), Erica Jong in *Fear of Flying* (1973), Marge Piercy in *Small Changes* (1973), Lois Gould in *Such Good Friends* (1970), Marilyn French in *The Women's Room* (1977), Lisa Alther in *Kinflicks* (1976), Alix Kates Shulman in *Memoirs of an Ex-Prom Queen* (1972), Cynthia Buchanan in *Maiden* (1972), Diane Johnson in *The Shadow Knows* (1974), Maureen Howard in *Before My Time* (1974). All are representative novels focusing chiefly on the female experience.* Toni Morrison's *The Bluest Eye*

---

*Against these, I include three books by male novelists about the female experience: Gass's *Willie Master's Lonesome Wife* (1968), Gold's *Sick Friends* (1969), and Friedman's *Hermaphrodeity* (1972). The latter two are not solely about

(1970) and *Song of Solomon* (1977), like her *Sula* and Alice Walker's *Meridan,* move in and out of traditional feminist themes, but are also associated with ingredients of a social/community commitment.

Rossner's Theresa Dunn is doomed by her pursuit of alternative life styles, even though that pursuit is a necessary part of her liberation of self. Theresa is doomed by the way the novel is arranged, since she is murdered on the first pages. Rossner's aim was to remove the suspense of the crime and move the action to what Theresa is. Once her death is established, the point is to see what brought her to her death, and it is clearly a search for a life style; both what she is and what she seeks are forms of doom, the old naturalist formula claiming yet another seeker. The film of the novel dispensed with the early murder. Films apparently still play on our Edenic fantasies.

Like Shulman's Sasha and Oates's Maureen, Theresa must find constant reassurance that she is attractive, fate for the female. A victim of childhood polio which left a slight curvature of the spine, she is less than perfect; and therefore as a complement she obsessively seeks, however self-destructively, the perfect male, Mr. Right, the candy bar with the memorable flavor. She feels most desirable with Tony, who, while he bullies her, makes her alive sexually. Doomed by her preference for rough sex, she neglects the side of herself that is fulfilled by working with children. The two sides do not quite cohere, but Rossner's point is a complex one. For unlike many of her contemporaries, she does not see all of Theresa's problems as female-based. Some of her conflicts are personal, individualized; and they derive not only from a woman's weakness but from a particular woman's weakness. Since her values are doubly and triply twisted, she will use sex as aggression until she meets a man who will murder her rather than submit to her hostility. Theresa's relationship to Tony—reminiscent of Oates's women and their obsessed relationship to food—focuses her anger, aggression, masochism, and yet gives her a sense of superiority. She feels better with such men, needing their sexual excitement to turn her on. These unresolved elements will doom her as a woman, trapped by her sexuality—and, additionally, her spinal affliction—into seeking out the very men who will destroy her.

Alix Kates Shulman, in *Memoirs of an Ex-Prom Queen,* reduces that complex point to a single

---

women's experiences, but focus on them sufficiently to make their inclusion here valid.

counter: Sasha Davis's experiences are forms of doom connected to her extraordinary good looks. Sasha has apprenticed herself to Ralph Waldo Emerson—she has considerable intelligence and, as a man, would have been a professor—who offers possibilities of choice. For Emerson, America is a vast emptiness which the individual can fill. The "fat" theme recurs. If the young open themselves to experience (female experience?), they can gorge on riches. Sasha wills herself to Emerson's sense of individual destiny, although at every turn her destiny is not Emersonian, but her face and body. Even as she masters philosophical systems, it becomes apparent she cannot master her own. Like an Oates character stuffing herself with food, she stuffs herself with knowledge which bears no application to her.

Sasha is destined to become a statistic in Friedan's "feminine mystique." Before college, before marriage to Frank, a graduate student, Sasha has experienced the "doom" of her life as a form of celebration: her election as prom queen. As much as Theresa Dunn is fated by "non-good" singles bars, Sasha is doomed by her achievement at graduation. She falls into the archetypal situation: suppression of her talents, subservience to a male, a marriage that proves unrewarding; and then the repetition of it in her second marriage, to an enterprising engineer. With Frank, she worked so that he could achieve in his history department; with her second husband, she keeps house while he achieves in his business. Brought home to her is the dictum of Bayberry High School, the location of her prom queen success: It is a sign of weakness for a man to need a woman, whereas it is a sign of strength for a woman to win a man. That, not Emerson, will define her.

Sasha's form of revolt against Will, her engineer, is to cut her hair, hoping to interrupt the rhythms of a destructive cycle, his success and her appearance. At thirty, she finds herself under a hair dryer, turning the pages of a women's magazine, entrapped by children, her husband away on a business trip; and she senses that her life has been the "fulfillment of a curse!" Her form of revolt will only presage another round in a doomed cycle; if not Will, than a third husband, a lover, another man. In her next novel, *Burning Questions* (1978), Shulman presents a different female experience, that of Zane IndiAnna, who eludes her doom in the Midwest and seeks Emersonian freedom in a lesbian relationship and the women's liberation movement.

This pattern becomes paradigmatic: the need to break away in order to survive; defensiveness toward men, the sense of being taken, the consciousness that men will always triumph on their terms; the growing loyalties to women's movements, and with this, the movement toward lesbian relationships. We note this in Marge Piercy's *Small Changes* and Marilyn French's *The Women's Room,* among numerous others. Several problems remain, however, as much in the conception as in the execution. One premise is that lesbian love runs smooth: once Ms. Right is found, all experiences open to Eden. A second premise is that once a woman locates these feelings, she can drop out, fulfilled by love or common bonds. This is an abdication of power, leaving the larger world to men, the smaller one to women: simply another version of the formula that while men do business, women keep house.

What is incredible about such novels is that their authors settle for so little for their female protagonists. Their women, once freed of some of their doom, do not move out into the larger world and use their newly discovered power, the way their authors have. On the contrary, they seek out that small world—the "women's room," in another sense from French's— as a haven. Having discovered small forms of happiness, they settle for so little. Oates's *them* is representative: Maureen's aim is to find a stable marriage and then curl up in a cocoon; except that Oates does see it as pure destiny, the irony of the woman's condition. The women of French, Piercy, Shulman, Jong, among others, have broken with destiny, and yet they, too, wish to curl up. Mary Allen asks an obvious question: "But why is it that women's natural need for many kinds of development has not worked its way into our literature? Is it only because writers of the sixties [her book was published in 1976] lag behind the general culture in their awareness, or do they see a truth that will outlive current fads about women? . . . No major author of the sixties, to my knowledge, male or female, gives us heroines whose jobs have any meaning for them, in the few cases where they work at all."

Only Lisa Alther, in her excellent *Kinflicks* (1976), has created a protagonist who prepares herself for the larger wars, in that having come through forms of death, including her own spiritual demise, she perceives a world lying outside herself. It is toward this world, for good or ill, that she begins to move. For most of the other writers, there is the sense of "licking their wounds," refusing achievement because it is so tainted by masculine values. This way is another form of death, since achievement in the larger world, in any mode, is the sole way the cycle of doom can be broken. It is at least as important as self-fulfillment in love. The nature of the love bond may be male or female, but it cannot be the end of the journey; and yet our novels of the sixties and seventies repeat that theme: love, bonds, common sympathies are fulfillment. If for men they clearly are not, why should they be for women? The authors cannot argue that since women are such cripples they are incapable of larger fulfillment, for their characters have broken free.

Piercy's *Small Changes* and French's *The Women's Room* are instructive here. But before I discuss these two novels, another issue seems appropriate, and that is the form or shape novels about the "female experience" take. I think that the lack of experiment, the paucity of narrative daring, the stress on traditional storytelling—except, perhaps, in some of Didion and Morrison—is connected to the failure of the women's experience to be projected onto the larger world. That desire to resolve old wounds through love and bonding, that forsaking of achievement in the larger world, is reflected in the unadventurous use of narrative, plot details, character. The "female experience," like all other experience, must be handled in modern or postmodern terms, and yet repeatedly novels limning this experience are old-fashioned in structure, based on Edwardian models. Only Cynthia Buchanan had tried to break with realism, opting for fabulation of sorts, transforming realistic detail into social fantasies.

Piercy's *Small Changes* is a paradigm of the solid Edwardian novel updated to fit the female experience. The rite de passage for the young woman (here Beth) at the end of the sixties goes something like this: conventional upbringing, marriage to a local boy (lower/lower middle class), great love for him and hopes for the future with him and his children, his growing indifference and/or his reversion to his male chums, intensification of the split in sensibility between him and her, mechanical sex and lack of satisfaction for her (and for him), her growing dissatisfaction with marriage and subservience—terrible feelings of hostility as she increasingly becomes his handmaiden. Even if she works, he expects her to cook for him, serve him, as if her job were nothing; further, he is resentful if her earnings approach his. She begins to fear him physically, and blows may be struck when she confronts him on some issue, whether cooking, chores, his desire for a child, her resistance. His physical violence, potential or actual, creates a "rape situation," even though marriage sanctions forcible penetration. The pattern becomes ever more intensive when he will not or cannot change: their relationship reflects jailer and jailed.

The young woman's marriage often duplicates the family situation she grew up in. When the young woman, Piercy's Beth, sees the pattern, and how she fits as prisoner, she duplicates the marriage her mother made and solidifies the jailing. This is the "primal situation" for the young woman of the sixties and early seventies novel. If she stays, she relives her mother's world; if she leaves, she confronts in her marriage the same choices her mother faced. Finding herself brutalized in such a situation by an importuning husband, when he wants a child, Beth runs. Piercy then enters into that typical American theme the Emersonian option: the opening up of the individual and the resultant experiences as good in themselves. To be free is a given of the good life, a birthright, not a privilege. What counts is escape, even though what follows may be miserable or threatening. Liberation has within it the possibility of change, choice, self-definition.*

Piercy parallels Beth with Miriam, less typical as a victim but nevertheless victimized by men. Despite her achievements (brainy, MIT, career-oriented in math and computers), Miriam falls into the same traps as Beth. The latter, the weaker woman, comprehends her situation better, and when her marriage sours, she moves into a "women's house," where women recover from bad marriages by gaining support from other victims. Gradually, Beth comes under the influence of a particular woman, Wanda, who becomes for her a viable alternative, although not exclusively. Miriam, on the other hand, attempts to orchestrate her stifling marriage—she is the proto-type of Friedan's housewife—while her husband, Neil, stifles all initiative.

Piercy's description of Miriam as she attempts to survive is quite poignant: "Out of such connections [past and present friends] she could weave no security, no protection against her worst fears. But of such connections were wrought an end to the slow relent-

---

*In *Goodbar*, Rossner shows some of the ambiguity in the shift toward independence. Freedom may move Theresa Dunn outside the limits of an imprisoning family situation; but the "scene" beyond is threatening and even, as it proves to be, destructive. Thus, the young woman is doubly trapped: enclosed in a stifling family situation and doomed by the world beyond of predatory males. The archetype is Richardson's Clarissa.

less dying back she had known, and the slow undramatic refounding, single thought by small decision by petty act, of a life: her life. That life shone too, dimly but with considerable heat, banked coals in the dark." Miriam's attention to her husband really does not matter, since he begins an affair with another woman, who hopes to win him away from this hausfrau. She, too, will be a victim.

While Beth achieves liberation through Wanda and her new life with women, Miriam toys with her "secret work." Using her computer knowledge, she compiles secret files of access to computers across the country. With her secret codes, for which she has no present use, she will regain her pride. Her present is circumscribed, but she has not forsaken the future, although it is connected to machines, not people.

Like so many novels limning the female experience, *Small Changes* assumes that the Edenic vision can be realized, even if the road to it is mined with obstacles. The "American dream" remains, in different modes and forms. Essential to women is love, bonding, and since that cannot be found with men, it must be sought with other women, where it can be achieved without the potential of violence and domination. It is that level of experience which remains to be examined, that assumption which remains to be questioned. Far too many novelists impose a resolution of problems, dilemmas, and choices which love in itself, whatever form it takes, cannot satisfy. To stress love is to close out the rest of the world, as a protagonist finds bliss with Wanda or someone else.

The pattern we have been describing fits Marilyn French's *The Women's Room*. The frame of the novel comes in the voice of an unnamed narrator, who walks a Maine beach and is writing about her friends.* One of them is the prototypical Mira Ward. Mira is first found hiding in the ladies' room—"la-

---

*Her disclaimers about her ability are intended to undercut criticism. Near the end of the novel, she excuses herself for lacking art: "I give up. I can't think anymore. All I can do is talk, talk, talk. Well, I will do what I can. I will talk, talk, talk. I will tell you the rest of what I know, take it to as much of an end as it has. It is not over. It will never be over. But I am finite. That is the only reason this account will end." Such loose writing suggests strongly that all that counts is subject matter, the nature of Mira's oppression as a miniature of women's oppression; that the artfulness of the narrative must be secondary. This is pure ideology, reminiscent of the arguments for social realism, and it sounds curious coming from an author who has written on James Joyce, *Ulysses: The Book as World.* In order to write about women, why must she discard everything she learned while obtaining a Ph.D.?

dies' " scratched out and "women's" substituted—at thirty-eight, in the year 1968. She hides there feeling "stupid and helpless," unable to function, and then finally washes her hands and heads for the classroom. Mira's background becomes something of the feminist movement in miniature.

As the narrator focuses on her, we learn that Mira had a conventional female upbringing, married Norm when young (and watched as he advanced from medical student to successful doctor), became enclosed and suffocated in the "American dream" of upward mobility, clung to a circle of friends who are equally doomed by their lives but who, in the main, accept them, however tedious and superficial. Mira cannot accept her routine; Norm, however decent, does not begin to comprehend the cycle in which his wife is located. She discovers that her only sustenance comes from her circle of female friends, who share her dilemma and have come to terms with it. Female bonding is the sole way of dealing with a male-oriented world which assumes domination.

This is, of course, a powerful political statement, suggested earlier by Lessing in *The Golden Notebook;* but French, unlike Lessing, does not examine the politics of the problem and its resolution more than superficially. That is, it could be a viable political argument *if sustained literarily.* But French has overloaded her circuits with stereotypical men: her forms of doom, while not monstrous, have few individual traits. Each man is men, whereas each woman is a woman. As a political idea, female bonding is meaningful if male consciousness is investigated as particulars, not as a generalized condition. If men are perceived as what exists "out there," a mass, the enemy, then French has joined with Mailer, who perceives women as indistinct.

Along the way, French recognizes that she must protect her literary flanks, and comments on her male contemporaries in two places: "Maybe the men are worse off than I think. Maybe they're going through all kinds of inner torment and just don't show it. It could be. I'll leave their pain to those who know and understand it, to Philip Roth and Saul Bellow and John Updike and poor wombless Norman Mailer." But this is only momentary. French cannot have it all ways: she cannot put down Mailer for his stereotypical women and then vaunt her own narrative, whose men are stereotypical. Also, she hardly seems willing to assume that female bonding with other women is the sole sign of their independence, and yet this is what comes across in her rejection of that larger world. For that larger world must be met head-on, not through women's houses, or in women's rooms, or through female bonding; except as very temporary arrangements, as escapes from violence. French's women abdicate power in favor of personal peace; and yet acquisition of power over themselves is what they want. Such power, however, cannot be achieved by erasing one-half of the world, just as Mailer's men cannot will themselves into power by demeaning one-half of the population. French dangles her women, first, in demonstrating how, puppetlike, they are strung along in a male society; then she repeats the process by failing to treat them within a holistic world.

Nevertheless, her insights into the deadening life for both sexes in most present arrangements are entirely valid. The women wait for their men to arrive home, dreading it and at the same time looking for some diversion. The men think of their home as refuge, but they really want narcosis. They perceive the home as order (when order is obtained only by means of a female servant), but then their inability to function satisfactorily in sex indicates that they, too, come from a deadened world. Sexual malfunction derives from an entire society. We are, accordingly, forced into a political world, where inner torments and malfunctions are emblematic of the larger malfunction. Yet once French provides this diagnosis, and joins Lessing in this respect, she dodges the issues involved and opts for a female solution. It is like the solutions the male novelists she mocks often take, offering male bonding as a temporary solution to deep divisiveness. With French, the female situation becomes an ideological one, as it should. But even while shaping the issue, she evades it literarily, and here she becomes of a piece with those male writers who perceive the problem and also evade it. French's females are as much "prisoners of sex" or of "their sex" as Mailer ironically labels his men.

Kinflicks, by Lisa Alther, is a distinguished book, characterized by wit and precision of writing. Alther does not fall into clichés, but is able to handle the stereotypes of growing up female by turning them inside out. The consequence is a witty apprenticeship-to-life novel, a kind of female *Huckleberry Finn* or *Catcher in the Rye.* But her witty tone precludes her accepting her protagonist's innocence as a given, as Salinger does; she does not see certain elements as still trailing heaven's glory, or as leading back to Eden. Her Ginny Babcock rejects nearly all that pertains to Hullsport, Tennessee, although in the moments when her life is collapsing—when her husband

kicks her out and keeps their small child, Wendy—she sees Hullsport as a possible place for stability. There is, always, a realistic assessment of things, a most delicate assessment. This is a novel of the 1960s as much as of a female growing up in the decade, the two parts inescapable.

Much of the early wit pertains to sexual matters. Ginny, a flag twirler at high school athletic contests, is like Shulman's ex-prom queen, but tuned in to feelings other than beauty. She has been raised by parents obsessed with death, so that thanatos and sexuality are constantly at war. Her father, the major, is in charge of munitions production, and his preoccupation with impending disaster leads to his building a bomb shelter. In that shelter, Ginny "goes all the way" for the first time. Her chief sexual focus, however, is not the boy with whom she does it, but the boy with whom she does not do it—except for hand jobs in the school lavatory or in the trunk of a friend's car.

The novel functions at several layers of experience, and is possibly the most ambitious of the attempts to understand the female psyche since *The Golden Notebook.* Lessing, incidentally, gave *Kinflicks* one of her few blurbs, calling it a book "no man would have written," although agreeing it was "very far from being 'a woman's book.'" She adds that it "is the size and scope of the territory Alther claims which is impressive." The several layers result from Alther's structuring. The motif of death comes from the start, with Ginny's "fear of flying," the consequence of childhood instruction in how death may strike at any moment. One must be prepared to meet not life, but death. The fragility of the human being is always present as a reality, even when enjoyment seems more indicated.

There is, also, the level of the "kinflicks," those scenes of growing up which Ginny's mother, addicted to home movies, has caught on film. These are the "stills" of life, Mrs. Babcock's lifeblood. The kinflicks are the reality of her work as a mother, whereas the children—all disappointing—are slippery, movable, and uncertain. Whenever Ginny acts out something with her mother in mind, she thinks of being on camera for the home movie, which will fix it forever. Her mother's tragedy as a woman is her reliance on the "flicks" for her substance, when, in fact, the movement beyond them locates the real world. She cannot follow, however; once out of the darkroom, she is doomed.

Another level, of course, is Ginny's effort to float free of her death-oriented, small-town existence and find some meaning for her own. The novel, in fact, begins with her return to Hullsport, and that "return" dominates, since it brings her back not only to a dying mother but to the destiny of her formative years. Implicit in her sense of childhood is her awareness of how and what a female may contribute to society. Joe Bob is a great football, basketball, track, and baseball star, whereas she is a flag twirler. At first, she hopes to be a defensive left tackle for the Oakland Raiders. But "that was before I learned the bitter lesson that women led lives through men. In short, that was before I became a flag swinger on the sidelines of Joe Bob's triumphs." This awareness that she will never become a "woman warrior" is connected to Ginny's passivity: her inability to have an orgasm or to turn her education into a career, to reject Ira Bliss, the Sno-Cat salesman, even to make contact with her mother or to teach two tiny birds, deserted by their mother, to fly.

Her passivity is not only juxtaposed to Joe Bob's athletic triumphs, but positioned in relation to Clem Cloyd. Clem is a doomed young man, with a twisted leg from a tractor accident and a twisted personality bent on self-destruction. Ginny has her first sexual experience with him, in the bomb shelter, and almost meets death in a motorcycle accident in which Clem speeds recklessly. The accident transforms him, and he becomes deeply religious, a model husband and father, and an excellent farmer. His leg, also, miraculously improves; so that he is a normal man, after being a stunted youth. He, too, is a male model for Ginny, and she tinkers with the viability of his beliefs, living in a commune and farming with other women, and so on. But her passivity, however charming, precludes her completing whatever she begins.

This is a crucial point. Ginny does not lack in energy; she lacks focus for it. Whatever her enterprise —as daughter, bird-keeper, lover of men or women, farmer, wife, mother—she is an incomplete woman. This is Alther's point: to demonstrate how a bright, personable, attractive young woman can be defeated by the decade of the sixties; and if not defeated, then baffled in her enterprises, until she fulfills no given role. Ginny's greatest success would appear to be as Miss Head's student of philosophy at Worthley College, a stand-in for an Ivy League women's college. Miss Head, unfortunately named, as is Worthley, is a tightly organized woman who has excluded from her life everything unmanageable. Her specialty in philosophy is Descartes and Spinoza, rationalists; and her bêtes noires are messy nineteenth-century savants like Nietzsche and Schopenhauer. Miss Head has arranged her life around maidenhood, collects lovely

articles for her apartment, plays the cello, goes to operas and concerts, and she captivates the young Ginny. Her student becomes a student of her type of life.

But like most of the novelists of her generation, male and female, Alther must make Miss Head represent something desiccated and exclusionary, and therefore the embodiment of lifelessness. She is damned for gaining order by excluding life, not praised for confronting and then arranging it. She falls into the same category as Ginny's husband, Ira Bliss, whose version of bliss is based on arrangement. As the army deserter and hippie Hawk says of Ira, his is "order achieved by exclusion, rather than order achieved through combating and subduing the chaos." Miss Head's exclusion of all but head finally alienates Ginny, who comes to see the other side through her suitemate Eddie, a lesbian, revolutionary, radical feminist, a young lady conceived when her mother, at fifteen, was raped. Here, the novel becomes much too symmetrical, even smug, and loses that odd wit which tilted everything slightly.

The problems are several. We are never permitted to see how Miss Head reached her conclusions; she is given a damning role without the backgrounding that would make her comprehensible. Possibly *her* mother, at fifteen, was raped. She is set up—as are so many of her type in postwar American fiction—in order to be shot down; although her own formation into a "Miss Head" could be instructive. Also, Ginny's relationship to her is built up only in order to be squashed; what Ginny learns from Miss Head never enters her figuring after she leaves Worthley. She apparently does not read, does not think in either Descartian or Nietzschean terms; and her only bout with thought comes in Hawk's instructions about transcendentalism, which is not so much intellect as abandonment of it.

Further, the alternative to Miss Head is Eddie. The latter, stereotypical sixties, must be everything Miss Head is not. She is the principle of disorder, playing Nietzsche to Miss Head's Descartes and Spinoza. Miss Head practices on her cello according to the metronome, and lives accordingly; when Ginny, under Eddie's tutelage, rebels against her teacher, she first destroys the metronome, that marker of temporal exactitude. The critical ideological moment comes when another suitemate, Bev, attempts suicide, after Ginny has rejected her offer for a meal together. Ginny surveys the dying girl, slumped over in the bathroom, and thinks of suicide as an intellectual act; meanwhile, Eddie, the non-thinker, rushes in and saves Bev. All Ginny's "headmanship" becomes questionable if her ideas cannot respond to a human life ebbing away. All her studies in microscopic life as well seem pitiful; what are particles filling an infinitude of space compared to Bev dying of an overdose! Ginny responds, then, to what Eddie offers: the disorder which saves, while order condemns. The novel becomes "framed," categorical.

What may be quite intentional is also injurious to the book. Eddie's background is the opposite of Ginny's, which has been privileged. Eddie is the principle of contradictions, nihilism, defeatism, attempts at personal salvation. She travels extremes in order to locate some role for herself, and these extremes become for her like suits of clothes she can put on or take off. Underneath, however, she is very frightened, possessive, intensely jealous. She wants Ginny to enter into a true marriage and suspects that she considers their arrangement only temporary, until the right man comes along. It is during one such moment of jealousy and desperation that she races off in Ira's Sno-Cat and strikes the barbed wire the women had themselves strung, cutting off her head.

Interspersed within these 1960s frames of reference (radicalism, growing feminism, commune life, the rejection of men and marriage, the inability to achieve orgasm except with a female lover) is the more traditional theme of the generational struggle. Here, Ginny must grapple with her mother, whose own passivity has been transmitted to the daughter; so that despite her privileged upbringing, Ginny is unfitted for life. Her parents' obsession with death, slow and lingering as well as sudden and disastrous death, has sapped Ginny's energies from the start. Like the rest of the family, she is caught in a curious series of tableaux associated with the "kinflicks" her mother prizes, those scenes of children and home life which suggest passivity, enervation, entropy of a sort. With her mother's terminal illness, Ginny must come to terms with this aspect of her life. Although while her mother is dying she tries to revive two parentless birds, she must ultimately forgo the birds and try to revive her childrenless mother.

Mrs. Babcock's slow death is accompanied by the death of nearly everything. Ginny's entrance into Hawk's transcendental state is terminated not in divine intercourse but by the intrusion of Ira. Ira points a rifle at Ginny and orders her from their Vermont home. Ginny's role as mother dies when her daughter, Wendy, is kept from her. Hawk is himself caught in a sense of death—which he defines as forces " 'going to suck all the heat from my body before I have a chance to get out of it. I'll be trapped in it and will die.' " He crawls back home, and is hospitalized as a paranoid schizophrenic, the diagnosis used to explain his desertion from the army. The Home Encyclopedia which Mrs. Babcock has been reading throughout her adult life reaches its final entry, then that, too, "dies." The second bird, which Ginny taught to fly, beats its wings around the room and dies when it strikes a solid surface. And Mrs. Babcock, all bandaged like an Egyptian mummy, dies. The era dies slowly behind Ginny, and she attempts suicide, by drowning, then by shooting herself, finally by cutting her wrist. Nothing works. Her blood, unlike her mother's, clots.

Ginny had entered the sixties defenseless, a vessel for Joe Bob or Clem to fill, while she awaited the orgasm which would not come. Joe Bob never enters, but she relieves him; Clem enters, but produces no result; Ira pushes away, strokes her like a cylinder block, and elicits no satisfaction. Only Eddie produces satisfaction, but that is only a phase for Ginny; she is heterosexual. Caught, ensnared by her sex and by the decade, she has come through, barely. The final words are an epigraph from Idries Shah, to the effect that one must be prepared for the "transition in which there will be none of the things to which you have accustomed yourself" and attachment to "the few things with which you are familiar" will "only make you miserable." Her mother dead, Eddie dead, the old house and properties sold, her ties with the past unraveled in every way—the letter Z achieved in the encyclopedia—Ginny is ready to move out.

Kinflicks is one of several novels, all written early in the seventies, which perceive more than grimness in the female experience, although there is plenty of the grim and morbid, especially in Lois Gould's *Such Good Friends.* Cynthia Buchanan's *Maiden* is characterized by the fabulous and the fantastic, an attempt to break away from realism, into romance, myth, legend, the irrational. Since Buchanan's mise-en-scène is Southern California, she has immediately entered the world of fabulation: realistic social modes turned into forms of fantasy; stereotypes transformed into fabulous clichés.

The basic plan is a dialogue between Fortune Dundy, Buchanan's thirty-year-old maiden protagonist, and Bert Parks, the master of ceremonies, best known (until recently) for his work with the Miss America pageant in Atlantic City. Bert is her imaginary double, a kind of twin, who knows her mind and heart. Fortune knows who she is, what she wants, but it remains to tell the world, which appears indifferent. Bert becomes a device of hers: "He knew who she was. He lurked in her vapors. 'Bert' stood for any emcee, any interrogator, any reporter, any judge or juryman, any person or thing whose sole interest was her. Whose sole purpose was to examine her, discover, present her, and venerate her. 'Bert' meant the way things should be. 'Bert' was the voice of her playful, high-strung narcissism."

Not only does Fortune "talk" to Bert Parks; all her actions are measured against what she thinks would be his ideal. Shulman's ex-prom queen measures herself against Emerson; Buchanan's, in a different mode of satire, against Bert Parks. She must somehow measure up to his expectations, which are based on generations of Miss Americas. As a consequence, Fortune becomes the plaything of "fortune." She awaits courtly love, an "awful, abstract, improbable lover! Someone on whom she might test her disdain." She carries her maidenhead like a burden, wishing to unload it, but incapable of discovering the right target.

Fortune tries all the usual gambits: Datamate (which uses the IBM 360 for its match-ups) and Dionysus West, an apartment complex for singles. She seeks a roommate, and a young woman named Beverly "Biscuit" Besqueth responds. Beverly plays the "female game" from the other side, thinking every moment is right. She goes after unsuitable men; she tries to make herself physically attractive (she has a breast lift); and she moves from man to man, in the hope of making a marriage (her second). Fortune has set an impossible standard; Beverly has set none, except the altar. Each young woman becomes the polarized half of one person.

All activity in Dionysus West is hyper. People exercise, swim, screw, mate and remate, couples and singles in constant reformation, everyone on the make. Bodies are exposed, either parts or whole, as if slabs of beef, a gigantic meat market. Only the youthful appear: no one over thirty and no one under fifteen. The action is in between, as Fortune, at thirty, sorrowfully recognizes. Her unlikely focus is a dentist, Beverly's first husband. He is slothful, apparently incompetent, obvious and crude as a lover, a man lacking all the qualities Fortune had prided herself on seeking. But her fortunes have been such that the dentist seems a possibility.

Fortune has arranged a blind date with Rusty; over the telephone, his great quality is his ability to listen. He comes to pick Fortune up; the hair she had expected to be rusty is black. He takes her to a bar on Sunset Strip, where they sit in a booth with his friends. The group exchange pornographic photos from Sexpo 70, in Copenhagen, with people strapping on plastic phalluses or holding Pepsi-Cola bottles between their legs ("the Pepsi generation"). One friend is called Frank, but Frank is a woman, as is Rusty. Rusty is a nickname for Ora Russell, and Ora Russell, among other things, is organizing "Butches for Peace." Fortune's blind date!

Fortune has something of Candide in her makeup. She is seeking an innocent existence in a world of the fabulous, which has as its traps sexual snares of every variety. Fortune considers the word "maiden" a designation for a single woman, whereas Beverly's boyfriend indicates it means " 'You ain't neveh made it with anybody, Champ.' " He offers to lend himself to the task. By insisting it means "unmarried," Fortune plays her own form of fabulation against theirs. Her "maiden" condition becomes the last outpost of sanity in an insane environment, but such is the nature of the commodity being held out, Fortune is the fabulous one. As Campbell says, " 'Still cherry? Camp. Very high camp.' " The environment poses only extremes: Fortune's denial as against everyone else's accessibility, the "real" nowhere to be seen.

Since extremes rule (Beverly and Fortune), there must be a showdown. The meeting occurs in a motel on Highway 101, where the dentist (Skip Fritchey) takes Fortune. They choose the Safari Suite, where "even the telephone was painted in zebra stripes." The television set "peeked out of foliage," and the shower "in one of the bathrooms was made of flat rocks." The scene is of hunter and hunted, a corrupted paradise, an obverse of Miss Havisham's. The dentist begins his moves, but Fortune remains unviolated. As he gathers her in the shower and approaches his goal, a "whump! whump" is heard. Beverly has pumped bullets into his back, in the act shooting off the tip of Fortune's finger. Hitchcock's *Psycho* redux! Earlier, during their marriage, Beverly had stuck a knife in him. Fortune seizes one of the African spears—this is the Safari Suite—and stabs Beverly to death; she and the dentist are joined in "carmine pools." Fortune lies down on the floor, "as if she were listening for a heartbeat in the cold, wet tiles."

She has, in any event, broken from the Bert Parks dialogue. The extremity of her condition has been resolved: the virgin has killed the whore, just as the whore has murdered the man who deceived her. The level of fabulation has been raised to grand opera. The end is pure Verdi. Implicit in Fortune's comedic quest for a connection between her inviolate self and a suitable container for it is a tragic potential. For the society or indeed the culture has gone crazy. Fortune keeps seeking a center, in a territory where all is margin; where artificial has preempted all other considerations. But even Fortune, as her name suggests, has lost her center; her dialogues with Bert Parks indicate that she seeks her fulfillment in the very artificiality which consumes her.

In the phrase "fear of flying," Erica Jong has encapsulated her sense of being a woman. The book posits Isadora Wing's inability to choose between security (represented by the safe, but silent and censorious, Bennett, her Chinese psychoanalyst husband), and those men who represent "flying," men who offer the possibility of the "Zipless Fuck." Such a man is Adrian Goodlove. The "Zipless Fuck" becomes Jong's existential quest: it means sex with a man one hardly knows, coming together where only mouth and organs count in a frenzy of desire, jeopardizing whatever else the moment might have created. It is the opposite of a secure life offered by marriage, and its sexual content has a dangerous quality not to be found in Bennett's excellent but predictable screwing methods. It is like shooting up, the rush, the sensation, the calm.

The frame is a psychoanalytic conference in Vienna, which Isadora attends with her husband, surrounded by shrinks who have treated her and her friends. Having offered herself up as fodder in two marriages (the first to a psychopath, who had visions of Christ-like control of the world), she has personally retreated from the analyst's world even as the conference drives her closer to it. Her "fear of flying" to the conference is connected to the land as well as the air experience.

Isadora is the prototype of the urban, Jewish, "with it" young woman, close to thirty, deracinated, her Jewishness more a matter of her hatred for the Jews' oppressors than love for Jews or the religion. Living among the Germans when Bennett serves in the army, she works out some of her hostilities in articles about Heidelberg and its efforts to evade its Nazi past. But her ideological likes and dislikes are merely background for the personal struggle. As a budding poet, she feels the need for experience; and yet as a vulnerable young woman, she feels, equally, the need for protection. She possesses a boldness when she is being protected, which vanishes as soon as she must operate alone.

Since nearly all the narrative occurs during the conference, Isadora can put an analytical interpretation on everything. As she delves into the past for Adrian—they tell each other stories, he being a Laing disciple of sorts—she sees her years in the coils of analysts, herself a denizen of Dante's circles, where the torturers are shrinks. Her first husband, a mad genius named Brian, began the cycle, although Isadora had picked up conflicting forces from her mother, a woman who strove for perfection in style, manner, furnishings, and personal dress, and yet achieved nothing more than that. With three sisters who early on chose to breed prolifically, Isadora lacked a sufficient, strong female model.

Her schooling, where she excelled, proves insufficient to pin her down; religion, social purpose, even her career as poet are inadequate to define her needs. Rooted in one respect, yet cut off in another, Isadora Wing, as her name suggests, is isolated, unable to connect. Thus, her fantasy of the "Zipless Fuck" moves well beyond the sexual, into areas where sex, body, needs, organs themselves, blend with each other into the perfect moment. In many respects, her desire for the "Zipless Fuck" has within it her mother's desire for perfection: updated, of course. Her great desire is to feed herself, to nourish her needs on what is out there. Her British lover, Adrian, seems fixated on Isadora's "great ass" and comments on all the food she must have stuffed into herself in order to create that monument.

While it all seems perfect, Adrian can perform well only when danger, exposure, is imminent. He may be more attracted to Bennett than to Isadora. But whatever his condition—and his attractions remain somewhat remote to the reader—he is predatory. Adrian is an existential moment for the woman who wants to have her illusions of freedom. And illusions they will prove, for Adrian makes the rounds with Isadora until he is ready to meet his wife and family. Beneath his pose of existential errantry is a man comfortable with order, needing balance. He, too, acts from desperation and depression, although, unlike Isadora, he can dress up his feelings with philosophical trappings.

Yet after all is said and done, we are left with Isadora's ego: her celebration of the self. We get the shape of every part of her, the look of her menstrual juice, the sounds of her peeing in the pot, her squatting and spreading and sucking. Although, so she says, she fears to be by herself, she has no fear of speaking of herself in endless roles and poses. True, she seeks some center, some pivotal point; but in the search, she is as self-seeking as any Roth or Bellow protagonist. We think, in fact, of Roth: simply trade his mother-wounded young men for Jong's mother-wounded young woman. Roth's men often seek the perfect lay; so Isadora, the perfect fuck. Their imagination is frequently set on adolescent masturbatory fantasies; or else such fantasies are so powerful they drive out other passions—in Spinozan logic, a greater passion driving out a lesser.

A further consideration, one that also arises with Roth's young men, is whether or not the tribulations of a middle-class white woman can generate so much anguish. Why, we ask, should we invest our interest in a young woman who is born with all the advantages of money, family, brains, appearance? Her difficulties in the scale of problems seem minimal; her needs less than pressing; and her satisfactions possibly acts of childish demand. She has been propped up with analysts, supported by a decedent father, is a victim of neither violence nor incest, the daughter of an ordinarily misfocused mother. In such circumstances, she has started out more advantageously than 99 percent of the world's population, and her inability to be happy may require little attention.

That is a frequent criticism of such fiction, of such protagonists (male or female). The perfect fuck, an enjoyable masturbatory fantasy, the release of sexual tension: such are middle-class indulgences. In the early sections of *Soul on Ice,* Eldridge Cleaver speaks of how he set himself to rape white women, and we suspect he had in mind these women, located in *his* mind as parasitic, self-indulgent, entrappers of innocent blacks like Emmett Till. Isadora, then, would fit perfectly that image of femalehood which Cleaver rages against: on his part, a pathological answer to a real question of female roles.

Our response is connected to the type of society we have structured, the type of society we embrace. If that society is strong, willed, directed, then Isadora is a self-indulgent princess, seeking her satisfaction while everyone else burns. But if the society stresses egalitarian principles—the right of each individual to pursue his/her own pleasures and needs—then Isadora can follow her self wherever it leads. Bennett Wing represents that first type: inner-directed, in his self-control Chinese, ordered and organized, basically moral and decent, chiefly career oriented. Bennett is also maddeningly silent, unable to express whatever is disturbing him, incapable of connecting in any emotional way to his mate. His sexual powers are considerable, but they derive from that same, silent person; he screws like a piston rod, enduring, holding back, giving satisfaction, but seeming to gain little. He is all "systems."

Adrian Goodlove, also an analyst, but more indebted to Laing than to Freud, represents the other kind of society. Not only is he the existential fuck, he is also the opposite of the piston rod, for Adrian's rod (unlike Aaron's or Wing's) is rarely stiff, unless under conditions of danger and jeopardy. He goes soft with Isadora, but since he says he is the antihero and represents no heroic pose, she finds his soft rod more endearing than Bennett's rigid one. Except for the bourgeois streak in connection with his family, Adrian appears systemless, part of that society which counsels indulgence. Bennett is named "wing," and the name suggests the directed purpose of Mercury; Adrian is named Goodlove, and while he gives less than that, he does offer release, abandonment, the embracing of self-indulgence as a form of therapy.

Adrian, however, is not the answer, although Isadora's delving into systemless life is necessary for her. She returns to Bennett at the very end of the novel, returns, that is, to his room in a London hotel, in a chapter headed "A 19th-Century Ending." Her liberation has both ended and not ended: she returns to home base, as it were, but has given herself the opportunity to choose. "Fear of flying" has diminished for Isadora. She has entered the mainstream of indulgence, experience of self, ego needs—the full thrust of the sixties—and while discovering it to be liberating, she decides to terminate it.

If we give Jong the benefit of every doubt, we can glimpse the ambiguities of the woman's situation: dependent on male support even while flouting it; so that beneath the inner urgency for liberation there still lies the attractiveness of the male world, for its support and security. If we still give Jong every benefit, we perceive Isadora as a bad girl returning to her family (husband now, mother before), the prodigal daughter/wife seeking safe return. She expects forgiveness, as we forgive a small child who transgresses rules made for others.

Jong, accordingly, refuses to see liberation as the "final solution," however attractive the "Zipless Fuck" may seem theoretically, or even in practice. Her refusal, however, is not connected to her lack of enthusiasm for liberation itself; it is associated with a recognition that women, however freed, must still deal with dilemmas liberation in itself cannot resolve, at least not for the present generation.

If we do not give Jong the benefit of every doubt, then we see her resolution of Isadora's emotional life as a failure of nerve and perception, an act of coward-ice in her attempt to give her protagonist the best of both worlds. In such a scenario, Bennett indulges Isadora as he would a child, and he offers a broad male acceptance that she, as a female, can trade upon in her digressions. In this scenario, Isadora has not even begun to grow up; she expects to be cosseted, kept, accommodated. Infantile to the end, she is a receiver of goods, incapable of making a mature effort at adult connections, a reduced Herzog hooked into life-support systems.

In *Such Good Friends* by Lois Gould and *The Bluest Eye* by Toni Morrison, both from 1970, we discover common ground for two very different protagonists, both victimized. One is urban, one rural; one sophisticated, one innocent and untried. One moves in circles in which she could possibly have learned a different way; one is caught in a coil of circumstances which disallows emergence. Yet later, by *Song of Solomon* (1977), Morrison would demon-strate ways in which female strength could be exerted in areas that ordinarily might bring stiflement and disintegration. The difference here is more than be-tween black and white; it extends to differing forms of experience in country and city. Both may create victims, but the city pulls with a naturalistic sense of doom, whereas country, allowing for distancing and integrity, makes provision for growth. The distinction between the experiences of the two writers is rooted deeply in the tensions of traditional American fiction, and their heroines are located accordingly.

At the beginning of *Such Good Friends,* Richard Messenger is caught in a situation usually reserved for women: bound and wired to a hospital bed, dying after a minor surgical procedure. As a male, he has been put in a completely dependent situation, admin-istered to by a small army of doctors and by a "freed" wife. Julie is able to muster support for her husband, and to take over an independent role, but only after, like Laocoön, he is tied up by tubes, with everything being done for him.

Richard's dying and finally his death should theoretically free his wife from their relationship, which had made him clearly master and herself clearly subservient to his wishes and whims. Yet Julie cannot be free, for a variety of reasons, one of them her discovery of Richard's diary, with its coded com-mentary; and her "journey" through his dying days is to discover what the diary means. The end of her marriage is the beginning of her knowledge.

As she works her way into the diary, through evidence supplied by a friend, suggestions of still an-other friend, and her own insights, she finds Richard has been sleeping around with many women she knows and keeping "score" meticulously. MGM is not, as she finds out, Metro-Goldwyn-Mayer, but Miranda Graham, a statuesque model, one of Julie's "good friends" in the hospital vigil. An entry may read: "WEDNESDAY Nov 6 26J dinner 7:30–10:30, 2x (reg; or)"—which indicates a three-hour session, with Richard performing twice, once regularly (vaginally), the other orally. Oral dominates in the entries, since Richard finds vaginas smelly and prefers the bondage of the female sucking him off. Once Julie begins to decode the diary, she lives amidst Richard's con-quests, or imagines she does. All females in their circle become suspect.

But more than that, Julie becomes, by way of the diary, as much a mistress of Richard's life during his dying as she was while he lived. Her so-called free-dom from him, about which she is very ambivalent, takes on an intensified thralldom; for the diary dic-tates she must relive the marriage under different terms. Her discoveries are revelations which turn the marriage into another kind of experience, even as she finds herself "freed" of that marriage by Richard's inexplicable reaction to an anesthetic, which has set off a complete disordering of his bodily functions.

The book is expertly structured in its use of paral-lel situations, something we do not find in many late sixties or early seventies novels. Gould has not poured out an anger, but has found a way of shaping it into the needs of fiction. She has located a reversal situa-tion, in which the woman can transform a death into a liberation; yet at the same time, the woman is frus-trated in her very quest for freedom by the discovery of something which undermines her married years.

The reversal of situations involves nearly every-one. For "such good friends" become, in virtually every case, potential enemies, or else become agents of Richard, watching her every move. Her "circle," both hers and Richard's, can enlighten her and, simultaneously, lead her astray. What could be an act of freedom becomes a further act of suffocation. The hospital, where she attempts to discover what the doctors are doing to her husband, becomes her prison, as revelations pour out. Her futile attempts to gain revenge on Richard, by sleeping with his friends, do not amount to self-discovery. She remains Rich-ard's wife, even when the revelations come, encircled by him in life and death.

Part of the problem with the book's thematic development occurs outside the shaping, which is masterly. It comes in Julie's thralldom to Richard. Here we are on delicate ground, for part of Gould's purpose is to show how an intelligent woman transforms her neuroses to her marriage and permits her husband to trample on her while she rationalizes the process. Accordingly, Julie's terrible weakness in dealing with the living Richard suggests how even a bright woman becomes servile in the male-female relationship, or else loses her ability to deal with life when confronted by a stronger force, the male. This is clearly one aspect of the novel, and Gould is able to "excuse" Julie's weaknesses as an aspect of having been born female. The female grovels, commits debasing acts (oral sex with Richard, who is repelled by her vagina), and then reasons she has held her man.

Yet this very point is partially vitiated by the nature of the relationship between Julie and Richard, which in retrospect takes over the movement of the novel. The dying Richard has preempted the novel. In life, he was often absent, whereas in death, in the hospital bed, he is very much the center of attention. Instead of having his wife minister to him, he has a team of willing nurses and a host of medical experts. Every part of Richard is tended to—kidneys, liver, lungs, heart, blood. He is drained of his own blood, and it is replaced by the blood of his friends. Tubes replace sex. And the doctors even plan to describe his condition in a monograph, attacking the anesthetic that has put Richard in this condition.

Nevertheless, the center of this attention does not seem to have one saving grace. Richard in marriage, as a roving single, as a friend, as a father, at work, is self-serving, infantile, a human being at his worst. Thus, his appeal for other women and men is as inexplicable as his appeal for Julie. For if we assume that his appeal for Julie is based on her weakness, her need to be servile, and a masochism that is only partially clear to her, we must find other reasons for his appeal to his friends. But Richard's qualities remain obscure.

Richard's lack of appeal and Julie's generalized masochism in her relationship to him, and to other men, cause the novel, despite the masterful structuring, to lose some of its drive. Once the situation develops, Julie has opportunities which she forgoes or fails to perceive; and while her failure may be connected to her own deficiencies, they do turn the fiction (as apart from life) into predictability. As friends pour in, to pay respects to the dying Richard, or to give blood for transfusions, or to sit with Julie, the narrative line loses variety; and Julie herself becomes curiously static even as she experiences revelations. The discovery of the code makes insufficient impression on her, for she is so prepared to receive pain and humiliation, her reception of the information is insufficiently intense, or insufficiently broad. Once again, this may be Gould's very point: that Julie has been so conditioned to masochism as a woman she cannot deal more definedly with the revelations. But then masochism, which is a general condition, becomes the explanation of a particular woman; and her experience goes over into the universal, when the novel calls for something more individually distinctive.

For the black Pecola, at eleven, in *The Bluest Eye,* the goal of her life is to have blue eyes—that is, to be white, blue-eyed, golden-haired. She does gain these qualities, by substituting for actuality the "movie" version of herself.

Real life is something else, for Pecola serves as witness to a marriage distinguished by its disintegration. The Breedloves define themselves by their hostility and combativeness, in a union founded on physical aggression. Until she is made pregnant by her father, Chollie, who has intercourse with her twice, Pecola is ignored. In Morrison's presentation, Pecola has no way out except in fantasy. At eleven, her life is fixed.

The novel is more a series of vignettes than a coherent narrative. One vignette concerns the sadistic Louis Junior, whose mother "did not like him to play with niggers. She had explained to him the difference between colored people and niggers. They were easily identified. Colored people were neat and quiet; niggers were dirty and loud. He belonged to the former group." Although Morrison is writing about how blacks perceive themselves, we note how this distinction applies, also, to other groups. German Jews saw themselves as "colored," while they perceived Eastern European Jews as "niggers"; with Italians, the distinction was between those who came from north of Rome and those from Naples, or between Neapolitans and Sicilians. In an earlier period, the English applied a comparable image to the Irish when they immigrated to America. Louis Junior is only ironically a member of a super race, for he turns out to be pathological, injuring his cat severely and then accusing Pecola. Another vignette concerns Elihue Micah Whitcomb, who seems an outgrowth of a Carson McCullers or Flannery O'Connor character. He is a freaky young man who likes young girls and yet is asexual, an outcast with repulsive qualities. It is to him that Pecola comes for her blue eyes, and he writes a long letter to God, in which among other things he speaks of the breasts of little girls. This man "causes a miracle," and Pecola will have her blue eyes: "No one else will see her blue eyes. But *she* will."

The book as a whole is a youthful piece of work, a novelist trying out some images and episodes which will locate her young characters and which, later, will deepen and intensify. The scenes all shift into and out of Pecola, demonstrating victimization by her immediate community (parents, neighbors, friends, cruel boys) and by a culture beyond which she never observes, that of the white world. She is, in effect, given a role whose control comes from a direction she cannot begin to perceive. Unlike Gould's Julie, she has no codes to decipher, only the fantasy of blue eyes.

Song of Solomon is Morrison's most ambitious work, and it endeavors to present a full rather than a narrowly based view of black life. The novel runs in several directions, with multileveled themes, not all of which cohere. Basically, this is a search for roots, in Milkman Dead's effort to discover his great-grandparents and, through them, to learn about his grandparents and parents. Milkman has had to fight against his name: "Milkman," because someone saw his mother nursing him when he was almost a teenager, and "Dead" because of a mistake in registry. The name was entered as Dead, Macon—Milkman's grandfather.

Naming is an important element in the novel, Dead providing many puns: I may be Milkman, but I'm not yet dead. Milkman's aunt Pilate has a daughter, Reba (for Rebecca), and a granddaughter, Hagar; Milkman's sisters are First Corinthians and Magdalene. Solomon enters in several ways: as the name of the man whose bones in the cave become significant for Pilate; as the name of a store in Virginia; and most significantly, as the name of Milkman's relations in Shalimar, pronounced "Shalleemone." The Song of Solomon in the Old Testament speaks of the eventual union of the bride and bridegroom in invincible love; and Morrison's novel is concerned with the union of beings in love which transcends hatreds, divisions, misunderstandings. Black people must love each ther, a lesson Milkman learns even when he is being hunted by Guitar Bains, a close friend who thinks Milkman has double-crossed him.

The "heroes" of *Song of Solomon* are mainly female, heroines: old Circe, a Faulknerian black lady who inherits by default a white estate; Pilate, who offers love and help when Milkman's father has almost disowned him; Hagar, who gives herself unrestrictedly to Milkman, and then dies when rejected; First Corinthians, who finally rejects her "Pauline"

austerity and seeks fulfillment in sex and love; Ruth Dead, Milkman's mother, who lives in fear of her husband, but insists on her own sense of things. Milkman's quest for his roots, which locate him in the Blue Ridge Mountains of Virginia, forces him to strip himself of his illusions. He must see himself as he has been, as a strutting peacock insisting on male prerogatives. Milkman is a pleasant young man, not a heavy egoist; but he has always assumed he was there to receive, others to give. Deep in the mountains, hunting bobcats, being hunted in turn by Guitar, he recognizes that in the field he is nothing except what he is: ". . . where all a man had was what he was born with, or had learned to use." When Milkman learns that, he can move back from ego to recognitions.

Running parallel to Milkman's quest for self-knowledge is Guitar's desire for revenge. In the group calling itself The Seven Days, each member has a day assigned to him, and a job to kill a white person in revenge for the murder of a black. Guitar is Sunday. If four black girls are killed in a Birmingham church, he will seek out four white girls to murder. Milkman feels Guitar is mad, perpetuating the white man's violence. But Guitar's is the heritage of violence: justifiable in the light of what has happened to blacks at white hands; unjustifiable in the sense his victims had nothing to do with the original crimes. Guitar never changes, whereas Milkman Dead seeks resurrection.

One major point of structure is the dualism implicit in Milkman and Guitar. Close friends, they are like twins who break off so as to represent different elements of the black experience. One problem is that Milkman, though expected to carry some of the ideological freight, is one-dimensional. Morrison's real triumphs are the women, many of them extensions of Faulkner's Dilsey, in that they endured and prevailed. These women sustain a deep relationship to life; even Ruth Dead, who periodically goes to the cemetery late at night so as to lie on her father's grave, fights for life, against Macon Dead, her husband, who has learned how to live on the white man's terms. Guitar Bains is also flat, a man whose entire adult life is defined by his desire for revenge. As a consequence, the ideological level is flattened out, whereas the level of vitality is full.

Morrison is able to intensify her narrative by way of enriching images or symbols, such as the peacock which looms up halfway through. Milkman "saw a white peacock poised on the roof of a long low building that served as headquarters for Nelson Buick. He was about to accept the presence of the bird as one of those waking dreams he was subject to whenever in-decisiveness was confronted with reality." Milkman thinks it is a peahen, but Guitar knows a peacock when he sees it, for its tail is full of jewelry that weighs it down, and Guitar is a man infatuated with gold. The gold he hopes to gain by robbing Pilate joins with the "jewelry" of the peacock's tail, the cock of the walk, their masculine assumption that they can al-ways receive; and we have a moment, as in Flannery O'Connor, of a transcendent life, a bird from the zoo in all its glory juxtaposed to two blacks on a seedy mission.

But despite it all, and the prose which "sings" and hums, the parts do not quite cohere. Morrison is at-tempting to gather in too much: a display of black family life, the search for roots, a play on invisibility and visibility, the examination of black male-female relationships, the transformation of a "typical" black man under the influence of enduring women, the struggle between two ideological lines in Milkman and Guitar, an exploration of black violence in the Seven Days group. Politics, caste, class, sexism, genealogy are too much for the scale. What works best in the arena Morrison has selected is the male-female association, parts of the search for roots, parts of family life. The ideological struggle between Guitar and Milkman for the black man's soul is not well integrated into the other elements, and, as a result, Milkman as a character suffers whenever he is under threat. He works best as a man who must grapple with his own life and with the women in it; and those women are a triumph: old Circe, ancient as her name implies, living with her Weimaraners in the white man's dispossessed Garden; Pilate, whose strength belies her name, who makes a happy home, while the Deads' is repressed and sad; Reba and Hagar, who give themselves, despite consequences.

Three novels by male authors cut across this swath of the "female experience": William Gass's *Willie Master's Lonesome Wife,* Alan Friedman's *Herma-phrodeity: The Autobiography of a Poet,* and Ivan Gold's *Sick Friends.* Although the Friedman novel is about male/female and the Gold book has a male protagonist, they reverberate, directly and indirectly, with aspects of the female experience.

As the women's movement began to shape itself, Gass responded, and helped to shape its literature, with plaints from a lonesome wife. Willie Master's wife has no name and is "owned," but she does not fit readily into any of Betty Friedan's categories. Nevertheless, she is part of that "feminine mystique,"

a woman whose passivity and desire to please veil a multileveled sensitivity.

Gass's method is really a verbal fugue. He has many topographical arrangements which amount to voices: a voice coming from each kind of typeface, from each kind of cartoon, as well as from the nude photographs of the "wife" which accompany the text in the Knopf edition. Even without the photographs, we would have the import of a fugue. The wife is presented in soliloquy form, reminiscent of Molly Bloom's at the end of *Ulysses.* Molly's plaint, how-ever, is more a triumph of the flesh than it is an attempt to understand her as a woman; whereas Gass's involved method is an effort to get at the wife through various levels and dimensions of voices.

The novella would be best served on records, ac-companied by a "film" flashed on the screen: car-tooned words, comics blurbs, photos, et al. Accord-ingly, the experience of the reading is a form of diminishment. In his use of "voices," he foreshadows in many ways Gaddis's great oral novel, *JR,* which is fugal in almost every respect.

The wife of Gass's Willie is aging, abandoned, lonely, full of self-pity, passive, yet willing to serve, seeking direction from a missing husband, full of con-trapuntal desires of her own which match the coun-terpoint of the presentation. I assume Gass's aim is not to fix her in time and space, but to release her from temporal and spatial limitations by way of the fugal arrangements of the materials. She is, as it were, swayed this way and then that, as the elements move around; swept up in the dialectic, becoming part of the voices which swirl in and around her.

Willie Master's wife is going soft. Her great body, which Gass celebrates, is beginning to sag; and her pneumatic bust, which was her triumph as a younger woman, is, she feels, becoming less attractive. She must fall back upon resources she has not developed, but she can only reminisce about days when she served male wishes, when she played Ramona to Wil-lie's Herzog. For example, in one passage, where the type goes from a very small face, which is a conversa-tion between two stage characters (one of whom is the wife in a role), to a newspaper headline face, and then grows gradually smaller, she thinks of gears and pis-tons and cams as sexual objects.

Meanwhile, on the stage, where a comic soft-por-nographic scene is being enacted, one Ivan, while making up to one Olga, discovers his penis in a break-fast roll he is cutting into. This scene plays as a coun-terpoint to the wife's lament. The commentary:

Now a fellow finding his penis baked in his breakfast roll like a toad in a biscuit—that's a naturally humorous finding, the very heart of a naturally humorous situation, and he could say: say, I think I've found my penis baked in this roll like a toad in a biscuit, and ever/yone would laugh; . . . A fellow losing his dick somewhere, of cour/se, that could be tragic, anyone can see that could be tragic, but finding it again, in his billfold possibly, or lying across his co/rnflakes, or coiled in the bottom of his tackle box, that would be comic, sure as shooting—comic as Christmas—a fundamentally funny fix.

Yet even as the wife pours out her heart, amidst all these distractions of other voices, events, blurbs, cartooned words, she feels she is unheard, not reaching us because the very nature of the page works against her. The lack of pagination of the piece disallows her any specific point of departure; the lack of name makes her Willie's woman, not hers. Without page numbers or name, she is obliged to wander through the narrative without any focal point, a voice among voices, an unclear identity amidst several roles she has played, as younger woman, wife, subservient female figure. *Her self has been dismembered or eradicated,* the archetypical female situation. This conception of the wife—a voice, unnamed, unpaged, unidentified—is Gass's triumph in the novella. He has, in this respect, helped to shape a conception of a plaintive woman; not a Medea but a modern-day Niobe. The pouring in of other voices, on the other hand, is often arbitrary, lacking in associational value, full of clichés meant to call attention to themselves as platitudes but that, lacking wit, fall flat.

The self-consciousness of the enterprise, not in itself a bad thing, has preempted the work. While the wife laments her abandonment by the stupid creature "whom I favored with my charms, a bosom born but thirty years ago and plump as ever, round as a pair of pies when I lie down," she is superseded by the author circling around her with demonic intensity. The strain to achieve something profound is too evident, for the material defies profundity, just as large parts fail to be witty, when only wit could have supported them. Joyce's Molly has the magical other-dimensionality of language; Gass's conception is there, but neither content nor verbal dexterity lifts the wife. The shaping serves as an alternative to the words themselves, but the self-consciousness of the conception returns us, always, to the author, not to the wife. We experience a curiously divided attention, a sense of pieces, a lack of cohering elements.

Superficially, *Hermaphrodeity: The Autobiography of a Poet* would appear to be part of that fictional world in which the novel is gamesmanship, what we associate with *Giles Goat-Boy, Ada, Snow White* and some of Barthelme's short stories, or *JR:* fiction as fictional game, part of what Richard Poirier called "a literature of self-parody." In this, we have a sport in which words, narrative, and technique are subsumed under playfulness, burlesque, extreme self-consciousness. Friedman's novel, then, could also be viewed as parodic, in line with *Pale Fire, V., Portnoy's Complaint,* only more outrageous.

In still another sense, we can view it as a burlesque of Mailer's "American Dream," book and idea. Simply a list of the narrator's triumphs, the achievements of M. W. Niemann, turns 1960s narcissism into a complete life style: Niemann preempts male and female sexuality, and very possibly fathered and mothered his/her own daughter; he/she is a deity of sorts, worshiped by Sardinians, who remain pure, like Lawrence's Etruscans; he/she develops a thriving business based on a chicken sauce whose ingredients are divulged to her by Puddu, the Sardinian insurrectionist; he/she is a poet who will eventually receive the Nobel Prize; he/she produces a new cigarette concept, called Fica ("cunt" in Italian and Sardinian); and he/she is instrumental in the progress of the Sardinian guerrilla movement for independence from Italy.

Anarchy, chaos, and abnormality become the norm in business life, archaeological digs, sexuality, and, especially, poetry. Dependence on the outrageous turns the novel's episodes into a kind of circus sideshow. Characters are brought on—and this includes the protagonist, Willie-Millie, the so-called M. W. Niemann—for their curiosity value. They are all oddballs. And strangely enough, they are nearly all bisexual, overjoyed when they find their loving Niemann possesses dual sexual characteristics, or as Friedman says, she has a male addendum to her female pudenda. Yet, somehow, sexual revitalization is insufficient; Niemann wants to find a center, whether in the navel, the vulva, the womb, or the "zero-point out of which . . . life pulses." That center, which Niemann expresses but which is never really clearly fashioned, recalls to us Gaddis's "recognition," which is reached, not sexually, but artistically. Friedman's stress on internal fire, centers, pulsing life, the lower half, the flame of life, the division between Self and Being, satori is all Lawrentian territory, even the long scenes on Sardinia. Sardinians are mythical creatures, using a language heavily indebted to Latin forms, passing outside history; in its prehistorical mode, hermaphrodeity is godlike. Niemann is worshiped as a sexual deity, and a good old rousing gang shag becomes a form of adoration of his/her dual sexuality.

Yet once we grant the outrageousness, the novel as game, the verbal witticisms, the burlesque of the American dream, the parody of bourgeois sexuality, the novel is still insufficiently "created." That is, it becomes a mirror image of the sixties in its striving for excess, and at the same time a reflection of those needs associated with the fifties: financial success, acquisition of goods, accumulation of power. In a sense, Niemann achieves the goals of both decades, summing up their value systems. But he/she does this without sufficient loss, pain, or suffering. Like a modern-day Moll Flanders, he/she keeps coming at us with sexual changes—from female to male, back to female, accepting both. Also, we can locate a curious deceptiveness in the sexual element, which vitiates what Friedman is driving at. While he is superb at detailing what problems the female encounters in her drive at financial and scientific goals, he plays a strange sexual game. For Millie in her final shape is offered for sexual titillation, as a woman with curled-up penis and scrotum; and so we have a not so mild pornographic stress to the book. This is a male writing for other men and giving us a sexual machine, a porno fantasy, yet at the same time insisting on something beyond sex, that "center" where recognitions can occur.

Friedman is not alone, of course, among 1970s writers in this kind of presentation. Several women have done the same, using their female characters to titillate the male reader with their sexual availability and expertise, while the author claims a deeper meaning, a "center" which no male can comprehend. Quite probably it is impossible to expect writers to emerge from the ambiguities of the sixties with sexual balance or integrity. As a male writer, Friedman presents the "new woman"; Millie is nothing if not liberated (in business dealings, in handling Sardinian macho), and yet how much is the result of her male equipment! She is also a sexual performer, aimed at a straight male audience; and in fact, some of the most amusing passages describe the sexual act in mechanical terms—driving, clutching, braking, accelerating—or in musical lingo—strumming, pizzicatos, fiddling, octave stops, repetitions, rousing choruses. As a sexual machine—with all holes accessible, plus that extra set of male gear—she is, like one of Portnoy's ladies, hardly liberated.

The novel, then, falls betwixt and between, a witty and amusing metaphor for 1960s sexuality, an attempt to reintroduce mythical resonances back into sexuality, a desire to bring commitment to vapid lives —Niemann's devotion to Sardinian independence; but all the while it is a kind of soft porno, full of dirty jokes, like Niemann's titles for his/her poetry: *Snatches: For the Left Hand Alone* (cf. Mailer's *Poems and Short Hairs*). Tones and textures lose their substance; lines of thought are undermined by the need to amuse at any level. The parody which superficially seems to ally Friedman with Nabokov, Barthelme, Barth is traduced by different lines of development. Sexuality is given some Lawrentian solemnity, orgies turned into mythical events, sexual disturbances played for both humor and seriousness, all of which give the novel several levels of experience which do not and cannot cohere.

The protagonist of *Sick Friends,* a combined novel-diary-journal, is Jason Sams, reminiscent, perhaps, of Jason of the Greeks and Samson of the Hebrews. His career is remarkably similar to that of the author, Ivan Gold: a volume of stories *(Nickel Miseries),* a bachelor life, grants and advances on a new novel, the effort to write, which runs throughout the book. The career is also, more generally, "the life of a writer."

Yet despite stabs at wit, it is essentially an artificial book. It is, too, a pretentious book, because Sams, despite almost four hundred pages of introspective analysis, never even gets close to a self-examination. He takes his pleasures, seems to give them, but lacks center. Moving in a bachelor's world, he uses his small downtown apartment as a fortress, a snug garden apartment into which he retreats, licks his wounds, drinks steadily, tries to keep at the typewriter (lots of sweat there, but little sense of the writing man), brings in women, from married friends to prep school girls, screws them to their delight, corresponds with his male friends, mainly about how they are making out, screwing, getting in.

Sams is an educated man, and he even offers a course in creative writing to a small group. But the dimension of intelligence, knowledge, learning, application of ideas is missing. Except for certain cultural freedom, there is no world beyond Sams's preoccupation with his penis. This could be a theme—Lois Gould uses it very wittily in *Such Good Friends*—but Gold does not provide that inner intensity which justifies such focus on self, ego, personal need. Sams does not earn his feelings. He is, after all, well into his thirties, and we expect dimensions of maturity: he is a New York sophisticate, a published author, moving toward another book. Yet his attitudes and ideas are all so self-serving that his demands on himself are infantile. This, too, would be acceptable, if he were conscious of it. The focal relationship is between Sams and an Armenian young lady of twenty-six, named Christa Sarkissian, a name that suggests she is an avatar of another kind of existence. The physical aspect of this relationship takes up some three hundred pages; but beyond descriptions of her appetizing breasts, belly, thighs, and rump, we are told almost nothing about her. But she is not a complicated "mysterious woman"; no V., she is, despite all the penetration, an unpenetrated woman. One reason is that Sams lacks perception. His sense of women falls into every possible stereotype, as for example: "In mind or in flesh, I suspected that pain [for women] was a part; and that virgin or no, in their lives as in their fantasies, rapee was a role they lusted after." The theorizing here recalls Mailer at his worst, as in parts of *An American Dream,* where male forcible penetration represents the forbidden, the taboo, the slide into hell. Sams labors under comparable misapprehensions about every aspect of life.

Except for drugs, Gold reviews the decade in its forms of cultural release; yet curiously, nearly everything of complexity is missing. Here is a New York City in the later 1960s denuded of all activity. Nothing happens. This isolation of the self from all else could have been movingly egoistic; instead, it is merely self-indulgent.

A FEW WORDS ON FEMINIST LITERARY CRITICISM AND AMERICAN FICTION

The critical battles which have raged in this country over Barthes, Bloom, and Derrida, or the influence of Heidegger, hermeneutics, and deconstruction, have bypassed feminist literary criticism. Postmodernism and even modernism have not yet entered into female discussions of the feminine experience; these French derivatives are exclusively male preserves, at least as of this writing (1980). Feminist literary criticism has been more concerned with marking out the arena where woman can survive; it has developed slowly in the seventies as a mode of discourse which seems to establish literary criticism by and for women, on the assumption that previous literary discourse was almost solely by men for men. In the latter type of discourse, the female writer failed to be understood. An exception to the above divisions is, obvi-

ously, Susan Sontag, whose works reflect a sensibility that very clearly does not identify as male *or* female. Her criticism is male/female, which is to say it is holistic.*

For other female critics, however, the deconstructionist tenet that the ego must be eradicated or dismembered, that the text is all that counts, and that discourse must be at the level of language alone would be a form of death for the female experience; as such criticism is indeed for many, if not most, male critics. Who but those most staunchly devoted to literary theory will accept Barthes's definition of writing now as "the zero degree of writing," or "neutral modes of writing," or "colorless writing"? The latest modes of hermeneutics and deconstruction, which *can be* very significant, are by no means a reflection of where most critics, male or female, are located. In the universities, the New Criticism of the 1940s and 1950s still reigns, and it is this very old and established tradition which feminist critics are struggling to deal with. For New Criticism stresses texts—as deconstruction emphasizes tropes and language—and here the feminists feel the cultural matrix for the female experience becomes lost. Thus, although dimensions have been enlarged, battles are on quite old ground. At its best, feminist criticism, like all criticism which establishes itself, will prepare us to be more careful readers. Adrienne Rich locates this point:

> Such a criticism will ask questions hitherto passed over; will not search obsessively for heterosexual romance as the key to a woman's artistic life and work; will ask how she came to be for herself and how she identified with and was able to use women's culture, a women's tradition; and what the presence of other women meant in her life. It will thus identify images, codes, metaphors, strategies, points of stress, unrevealed by conventional criticism which works from a male/mainstream perspective. And this process will make women artists of the past—and present—available to us in ways we cannot yet predict or imagine.

We might add that such critical insights may also point up flaws, failings, incoherences, as well. Criticism must cut both ways.

---

*For example, her remarks in "The Aesthetics of Silence": "In the light of the current myth, in which art aims to become a 'total experience,' soliciting total attention, the strategies of impoverishment and reduction indicate the most exalted ambition art could adopt." While such "minimalism" is a defense of Sontag's own kind of fiction, it has broader applications, in that it denies "content," the first line of defense of feminist criticism.

Probably the best example of historical criticism in this area is *The Madwoman in the Attic: The Woman Writer and the Nineteenth-Century Literary Imagination* (1979). The authors, Sandra M. Gilbert and Susan Gubar, define their goal:

Both in life and in art, we saw, the artists we studied were literally and figuratively confined. Enclosed in the architecture of an overwhelmingly male-dominated society, these literary women were also, inevitably, trapped in the specifically literary constructs of what Gertrude Stein was to call "patriarchal poetry." For not only did a nineteenth-century woman writer have to inhabit ancestral mansions (or cottages) owned and built by men, she was also constricted and restricted by the Palaces of Art and Houses of Fiction male writers authored. We decided, therefore, that the striking coherence we noticed in literature by women could be explained by a common, female impulse to struggle free from social and literary confinement through strategic redefinition of self, art, and society.

But in the decade preceding, of particular importance because of its "best-seller" status was *Sexual Politics* (1970). Kate Millett's analysis of Mailer, Miller, Lawrence, Genet, among others, gained some of its impact from its timing. In 1970, when feminist literary criticism was still relatively inchoate,* it served as a corrective. Several critics took it to task for its excesses—Irving Howe being the most noticeable—but the study of particular authors and some of the theory loosely behind them made deserving points. Millett rightly located male attitudes toward women in the above writers' fiction as infantile, hostile, contemptuous, or filled with disgust. She saw that "sexual combat" was rarely between equals, but was based on male need to define female inferiority and then to be contemptuous of women for demonstrating inferiority. Theirs was essentially a circular reason-

---

*Mary Ellmann's *Thinking About Women* (1968), with its phrase "phallic criticism" (that which uses masculine standards as the measure of praise), broke new ground. With her measure of "phallic criticism," she could demonstrate how the inferior and negative were reserved for what could be labeled feminine. Also, often forgotten among other considerations is that in *The Second Sex,* Simone de Beauvoir included feminist analyses of five writers: Montherlant, Lawrence, Claudel, Breton, and Stendhal, joined together as aspects of "The Myth of Woman." Her conclusions are those that would become very influential, for her negative view of Lawrence became the standard female response. Only Stendhal, of the five, sees female independence not only in the "name of liberty in general but also in the name of individual happiness."

ing, for women could not break out: if they deserved respect by way of achievement, they were no longer attractive women; if they acted in a "feminine way," they were figures of sexual contempt.

Mailer, who responded in *The Prisoner of Sex* (1971), defined sexual experience as a form of combat. As he learned from Wilhelm Reich, or from his own predilections, the orgasm was not simply a mystery into which two people entered, but a resolution of (male) problems. In the early story "The Time of Her Life" (1958), Mailer's Sergius must achieve an orgasmic response from the New York University student who defies him, or else he will be unable to define his own masculinity. The orgasm will save him, not her. Further, we can read Mailer's "The White Negro" by way of his attitudes toward orgasm, sexual combat, and women. For in identifying the Negro with a prodigious sexuality—as well as with other "antisocial" tendencies—Mailer could measure himself (perhaps literally) against Negro sexuality; he could enter their women, compete with their men. In *An American Dream,* Rojack plays out a comparable fantasy; the existential attraction of the black is his big whang.

Millett is able to perceive that the females in Miller, Lawrence, and Mailer are part of that "feminine mystique," a role Lawrentian women in particular play. The more deeply a woman can enter the mystique in Lawrence, the more womanly, and submerged, she becomes. She is associated with the tides, moon, earth, the Great Mother, and so on. Simone de Beauvoir has an apt passage for this transformation of natural woman into mysterious woman:

In a way it is a good thing that a woman is no longer ashamed of her body, of her pregnancy, of her periods. But one must not make too much of it and believe that the female body gives a fresh vision of the world. It would turn it into a counter-penis. Women who share this belief descend to the level of the irrational, the mystical, and the cosmic. They fall into the trap of men who will then be able to oppress them more easily and even to keep them away from knowledge and power. The eternal feminine is a lie, for nature plays a minute part in the development of a human being: we are social beings. I do not think that woman is naturally inferior to man, nor do I think that she is naturally superior to him.

Great Mother theories are, ultimately, as anti-woman as "ass 'n' tits" theories.

In this context, Mailer's response to Millett on Lawrence and Miller is instructive. He argues that Miller's seeming put-down of women is meaningful within a context of women as figures of such wonder and awe that the male can respond to them only by appearing to demean them. Responding to what he cannot comprehend, the male turns the woman into someone mythical and legendary: that is, he responds to the "mystique." Further, Mailer sees in the relationship of the sexes an antagonism which sharpens "our resistance, develops our strength, enlarges the scope of our cultural achievements." The loss of sexual polarity, he says, is part of that "larger disintegration, the reflex of the soul's death and coincident with the disappearance of great men, great causes, great wars." Yet Mailer sidesteps the point that such causes and wars, such reflexes, are perceived by his authors, by himself, as male-oriented and male-dominated. Miller's very base of meaning is masculine, not the "wonder-ful" women who worship his greased pole.

Mailer's point is, in fact, a longing for an Eden in which Eve supports and reinforces the great plans of "her man," in which Mailer is reincarnate as Adam and greatness is still possible. Much of Mailer, despite his New York tough guy stance, is naive pastoral romance, and in that fantasy world female shepherdesses bow to masculine prowess.

To Mailer's credit, he entered a fray which, whatever his arguments, he could not win. He could only further reveal himself, and what he revealed would be tangential, not central, to the feminist argument. There has been, in the following decade, no comparable debate. Male-female discussion has become, in a way, like black-white: separatism has ruled where discussants fear to tread. Once that is said, we must recognize that Mailer's points are not responses, but restatements. In his famous defense of Lawrence against Millett's attack, Mailer perceives Lawrence as a man who "had become a man by an act of will . . . [who] was bone and blood of the classic family stuff out of which homosexuals are made . . . he had lifted himself out of his natural destiny which was probably to have the sexual life of a woman, had diverted the virility of his brain down into some indispensable minimum of phallic force—no wonder he worshiped the phallus, he above all men knew what an achievement was its rise from the root, its assertion to stand proud on a delicate base."

The words are more elegant than Millett's, but Mailer seems unaware that every phrase is a put-down of female sensibility. A man "lifts himself out of" what is below, i.e., femininity. What is female is lower. What is the lowest of all is the homosexual, i.e., the female man; not to be homosexual is to have received a form of salvation. The import is that

women and homosexuals are located in some lower depths, from which Lawrence, to his credit, says Mailer, elevated himself.* Further, Mailer offers pop psychology to diagnose Lawrence's condition: a genteel, worshipful mother, a tough, distanced father, the stuff out of which homosexuals are made. But also, we should add, many heterosexuals; and by 1971, this deduction simply will not do as explanation.

Despite her excesses, flourishes, and overkill, plus many passages which simply do not read, Millett's basic points remain. Her earnestness is grist for Mailer's mill (puns here are unavoidable), but when he comes to Ellmann's witty and irreverent *Thinking About Women,* he circles her arguments and backs off. A mocking, witty woman cannot be put down with mockery. The entire *Prisoner of Sex* is, in fact, cast in a flirtatious, condescending rhetoric: Mailer splitting himself into roles, each of which has a voice. We have Mailer as prizewinner (Pulitzer, not the Nobel he had expected); Mailer as acolyte, finally Mailer as prisoner—the three Mailers responding to Kate Millett, Ph.D., Columbia.

Several studies have attempted more formalized historical evaluations of women in their society: Ernest Earnest's *The American Eve in Fact and Fiction, 1775–1914;* Elaine Showalter's *A Literature of Their Own,* based on British women novelists, but full of material which can be applied to their American counterparts; Mary Allen's *The Necessary Blankness,* which focuses on contemporary American novelists, male and female; parts of Josephine Hendin's *Vulnerable People;* the section on "Women's Literature" by Elizabeth Janeway in *Harvard Guide to Contemporary American Writing;* the chapter "Female Identities," in Patricia Meyer Spacks's *Imagining a Self: Autobiography and Novel in Eighteenth-Century England;* some essays in Adrienne Rich's *On Lies, Secrets, and Silence,* especially on the Brontës; the collection *Contemporary Women Novelists,* edited by Spacks (essays by Bradbury, Oates, Karl, Spacks, Kuehl, Mailer, among others); *Literary Women: The Great Writers* by Ellen Moers, a highly influential work; Hazel Mews's *Frail Vessels: Women's Role in*

---

*Cf. Baraka (Jones): "Most American white men are trained to be fags. . . . the purer white, the more estranged from, say, actual physical work." Baraka completes the circle by locating women with "fags," in some lesser area, as "behind the lines" where they are supportive of their black warriors. Is this simply loose 1960s rhetoric or more deeply held? If the latter, it is a form of female genocide.

Women's Novels from Fanny Burney to George Eliot; Spacks's *The Female Imagination;* Elizabeth Hardwick's *Seduction and Betrayal;* Françoise Basch's *Relative Creatures: Victorian Women in Society and the Novel;* an attempt at consolidation in *Feminist Literary Criticism: Explorations in Theory,* edited by Josephine Donovan; and numerous essays in magazines devoted to women's studies.

Earnest's *The American Eve* stresses that fiction did not do justice to how women were actually performing in the real world; that most literary figures —female as well as male—held to modes of thought in regard to women that belied the facts, in the face of overwhelming evidence to the contrary. Earnest deduces four types of women after the Civil War: (1) the college girl; (2) the titaness (the social dragon— Mrs. Jack Gardner, for example); (3) the office girl; (4) the Gibson girl, who appears later in the century, the product of Charles Dana Gibson. From diaries, memoirs, and biographies, Earnest gleans statistics which "show that a large number of women did not fit into the nineteenth-century stereotype of the fragile, timid innocent, with little learning but a heart of gold."

Some historical studies—Earnest's is itself sketchy in its reach—are invaluable, since they will help to create a cultural matrix in which women characters in older fiction can be more accurately perceived. The more clearly we observe how social and cultural needs determined the facts of fiction, the more clearly we can disentangle the complexities of roles as presented, the ways in which details and nuances may trigger counter responses, the modes by which "seeing" itself takes place. Many of these issues are at stake in the essays making up *Feminist Literary Criticism: Explorations in Theory.* Several female critics have zeroed in on Kesey's *One Flew Over the Cuckoo's Nest,* making it a kind of test case in which male readers observe one thing, female readers another. Basically, the reading depends on where the emphasis is put.

Male readers may emphasize that Kesey is speaking about forms of freedom, that Chief Bromden's escape is the key to the ideology of the novel; that McMurphy's martyrdom is the sacrifice of human values to those of the machine, the system, the computer; that within this formulation Nurse Ratched represents everything America has become technologically; that in her person she emblemizes the dehumanizing factor not only of institutions but of life itself (of the Indian within us). Female readers have perceived the novel very differently, observing that Kesey's presentation of Ratched is an act of pure hatred for women; that by making her represent everything detestable (she is, by name, a mechanical principle), Kesey has created a male world castrated by an overpowering female. True, he has created a "successful" woman, but her achievement consists of dehumanization, castration, ugly authority. She becomes a monster through her success, and by implication she represents what occurs when women get out of line. They cite the primitive nature of the male-female relationship in the novel, and to that I would add Kesey's romantic innocence about the prostitutes, who service the male idea and offer bliss. The course of bought love runs smooth!

The neutral reader may feel that the truth, whatever it is, lies somewhere in between; but the female reading of it makes us aware of elements that go to the heart of any description of the novel. The female reading, which sees the creation of a fantasy world in which women are subhuman, to cite Shulamith Firestone, points up Kesey's infantile observations of male-female sex; and by extension, leads us to perceive the infantilism of many of his contemporaries.*

Female criticism, however, cannot consist mainly of attacks on male points of view; it must establish grounds on which women writers can perceive other forms of female experience. In that respect, female criticism can serve as guidepost and support for the female writer who may feel diffident or uncertain. The best of such criticism, in the recent *The Madwoman in the Attic,* the comments in Elizabeth Janeway's chapter in the *Harvard Guide,* some of Elizabeth Hardwick's remarks in *Seduction and Betrayal,* parts of Kate Millett's *Sexual Politics,* some essays in Adrienne Rich's *On Lies* and Ellen Moers's *Literary Women,* can pinpoint areas that accommodate such female concerns. Janeway offers two major areas: (1) female writers can observe data of ordinary life as evidence in which some significance can be found; and (2) they can create a new order of values that suit the lives and purposes of women seen as women. Eventually, these values may become transcendent and help to demonstrate a "new life" for women.

The first order of business must be a broadening, not contracting, of female sensibility, a movement out

---

*Several female writers have demonstrated a comparable infantilism. When they write of lesbian bliss, they transfer Kesey's simplification of male-female relationships to female-female associations. The simplification falsifies human experience, diminishes it, and derives from a desire for a paradisiacal fantasy, an element of an infantile wish fulfillment.

for themes, conflicts, encounters. Novels by women must go beyond the traditional female world, into areas of great achievement, into the largest of worlds. Women may not fight wars, and thus we may not have the female novel of combat, but women fight significant other battles. That escape into spatiality, which involves so much adventure and discovery, must become part of the literary female experience. The second need is for female novelists to "educate" the male writer toward a more varied order of perception. American male novelists with their fear of rootedness run up against an area of traditional female experience: to gain rootedness, even at the expense of self and sanity. To alter that male perception of the woman—as the archetypal keeper of the hearth, the domestic castrater, the force that offers complacent order for creative disorder—is almost as important, literarily, as it is for the female experience to move out into larger space.

The male/female exchange must become a dialectic, for antagonisms and distinctions will always remain. If we perceive the order of business from the female side, it is more significant for the range of female experience to grow broader literarily (it is already deep) than for male writers to be educated away from violence. Women writers must establish their own ground, which is one thing they can be certain of. The female can always try to negate the male view

of her, an act which is in itself of considerable value; but she must also control her own territory both within and *beyond* the traditional values associated with women and their literature. The rearrangement of one's emotional life and internal pressures to relieve incipient madness through release and liberation can all be played out in a larger scale. Lessing demonstrated that in *The Golden Notebook* and *The Four-Gated City,* as did Woolf and George Eliot in earlier eras.

For the black female writer, the situation is social and political as well as personal. According to Michele Wallace, in her *Black Macho and the Myth of the Superwoman,* the male perspective of black women keeps the latter in bondage. She cites the usual sources of contempt for women—Cleaver, Baraka, etc.—but I think she gives too much weight to what was 1960s rhetoric. When Baraka spoke of women as "supportive units for their men," he was flexing muscles, trapped in his own rhetoric, uncertain of his direction and mindlessly "using" women. Female writers like Morrison, Walker, and others paid little attention. The black female writer is in the strange situation of feeling both a social and political commitment and a commitment to her sex—a duality that can prove either fatally divisive or something more challenging than what white female writers confront.

Chapter Eleven

THE 1970S: WHERE WE ARE

For the listener, who listens in the snow,
And, nothing himself, beholds
Nothing that is not there and the nothing that is.

WALLACE STEVENS
"The Snow Man"

Pynchon and Barth

The major problem for the novelist in the 1960s was that there seemed to be too many realities. In the 1970s, the problem has shifted, in that it has become difficult to determine what, if anything, reality is; where it lies; what shape it takes; where, if anywhere, it is heading. The seventies have become a time when we have reintroduced realities whose actuality we had not yet established by the end of the sixties. Robert Frost intuited our situation: "He thought he kept the universe alone; / For all the voice in answer he could wake / Was but the mocking echo of his own / From some tree-hidden cliff across the lake." With the ground shifting to some middle area of undefinable experience, where not even the certainties of 1950s counterfeit are verifiable, our leading novelists are younger men who do not insist on reality or realities. The major voices of the 1970s have become writers whose difficulties of presentation return us to the earlier days of modernism, when "serious fiction" split off from more popular fiction, when Joyce, Proust, Mann, and Woolf, or Eliot, Pound, Rilke, and Yeats, sheered off to form their own readership. I have in mind Joseph McElroy, whose fiction I have already examined, as well as a swelling of work by Barth and Pynchon. I have in fact, except for *Giles,* held off Barth for this section, since his *Letters* is a summa,

his collected works, so to speak, in this one novel. As for Pynchon, *Gravity's Rainbow,* whatever failings it may have as literature, has become the *Ulysses* of the seventies: a work whose difficulties, abstruse references, and historical sweep recall Joyce's plan of the twenties.

The 1970s in fiction have a very different feel from the 1970s in reality. In fiction, the decade appears turbulent, contradictory, unresolved, looming; whereas in life, we appear to have forged links, however tentatively, and to have become quiescent, compliant, self-absorbed. Narcissism has become a symbol of our withdrawal; conservative politics our badge of honor. Yet massive issues boil, the culture is rent at every level, and the quotidian existence we prize provides threats of varying intensity. On this stage, fiction plays less bizarre, more realistic roles. At the beginning of the decade, *Gravity's Rainbow* seemed an aberration; at the end, it is a traditional novel. At the end of the decade, Barth's *Letters*—immense, overdrawn, self-indulgent—seems to be a form of literary masturbation, whereas at the beginning, it would have appeared prophetic. The novelists are not out of step; they are moving to different coordinates. The Pynchon novel is a summation of the sixties; the Barth a summation of the seventies. Both are invaluable as cultural documents, although their difficulties and self-indulgences restrict audiences.

Part I of *Gravity's Rainbow* is called "Beyond the Zero," and it establishes some of the interconnections of rocketry and human fallibility: technology as deeply embedded in the individual as well as the culture. At the very end of this section, Roger Mexico, one of the agents working with "the White Visitation" which is attempting to decode Slothrop's magical awareness of the rockets, meditates about his friend Jessica, and the connection of things:

> It has begun to reveal itself: how easily she might go. For the first time he understands why this is the same as mortality, and why he will cry when she leaves. He is learning to recognize the times when nothing really holds her but his skinny, 20-pushup arms. . . . If she leaves, then it ceases to matter how the rockets fall. But the coincidence of maps, girls, and rocketfalls has entered him silently, silent as ice, and Quisling molecules have shifted in latticelike ways to freeze him. If he could be with her more . . . if it happened when they were together—in another time that might have sounded romantic, but in a culture of death, certain situations are just more hep to the jive than others—but they're apart so much.

Pynchon's world of clashing cultures is limned here, not so much through juxtapositions of adversary elements ("maps, girls, and rocketfalls") but through levels of language, jive associated with a "culture of death." The outrageous, the tall tale, the poignant, and the technological interpenetrate; *the culture Pynchon describes has no profile or silhouette.* All elements are skew, and yet they appear to cohere because his individuals are protean. Characteristic of most of them is their ability to reshape themselves, alter their attitudes and perceptions, achieve new boundaries; thus, they are truly people from the 1960s intruding into the 1970s, although caught in a way that recapitulates "ancient history." As characters, they are analogous to the rockets, for each rocket development precedes a new stage. The rocket in its developmental phases is always changing, adapting itself to a new context; so, too, the men and women involved in rocketry. The passage above catches the multilevel dimensions of life as it switched decades, so that even while a quieter time was augured, still implicit are all those elements which had exploded and remained hot.

Both Pynchon and Barth in their immense novels work through not only human themes juxtaposed to technological; not only the human insistence on direction against technological chance, entropy, sudden death or maiming; not only choice and will moving against random events (the fall of the rocket, or the inner workings of a cosmic computer, a programmed existence); not only man as he attempts to overcome contingency, a seemingly endless and irresolvable mass. They further load the dice, especially in Pynchon's case, by intermixing a pop culture with a serious event, creating cultural levels which intersect without touching. Pynchon, for example, uses personal names that also fit rock groups, then he thrusts his characters into situations with tragic implications, comic names involved in deadly games. The names suggest people with platitudinous personalities and pop responses reacting to random events which are nothing less than cosmic: fall of rockets, knowledge the Germans are preparing a knockout blow for England, awareness that events are narrowing down to Armageddon.

Part II's title, "Un Perm' au Casino Hermann Goering," refers to the Allied laboratory set up to investigate German rocket plans. The epigraph is pure pop: "You will have the tallest, darkest leading man in Hollywood," words spoken by Merian C. Cooper to Fay Wray, indicating that her suitor will be King Kong. Into the deadly game of rockets Pynchon inserts Kong, the idea of Kong. Behind Kong lies the idea of Tarzan, and behind both is a witty sexual pageant. For disguised by all the mumbo-jumbo about Tarzan are unspoken questions: his sexual capability, his prowess as a man, his virility as a jungle lord (son of an English lord). But while Tarzan is easy to accommodate—he is a "jungle dreamboat" —King Kong presents problems of race, size, and suitability.

The Kong motif, juxtaposed to cosmic rockets, life and death situations, deadly games of conspiracy and counterintelligence, is a key to Pynchon's world. For Kong works at significant levels, ludicrous yet probing. The Kong experience, presented as the black jungle ape and the very white young lady, serves as a useful gloss on the sixties; one need read only Cleaver's *Soul on Ice* to perceive that he saw himself as a Kong rapist, his victims white women as helpless as Fay Wray. Behind his early conception of himself Cleaver saw not Tarzan but Kong: the ultimate terror weapon, a huge black penis, the shadowy presence in every white woman's nightmares.

The end game with all Kong references is the idea not only of rape but of the size of his weapon. Since it is supposed his penis is enormous, he becomes a threat by virtue of that: he is, in this respect alone, made to order for Pynchon's mixture of sophisticated and sophomoric humor. Behind the "animal house" antics here is a great cultural divide: black energy placed in a rocket of its own, as against white yearning for the unspeakable. Since the latter is still taboo, even in the sixties, Kong becomes a victim of what he is and what he stands for. Played off against the huge dong is Fay Wray's virginity: at stake, veritably, a culture.

Further, if we keep the 1960s firmly in mind, Kong represents that Dionysiacal principle suggested by Norman O. Brown and others who sought liberation in orgiastic abandon: sex, drugs, groupies, etc. Against Dionysus, it is not always Apollo who is arrayed, but an unresolved, often shaky cultural value system with no clear lines of demarcation. Here we have Fay Wray's virginity and society's need to protect it, intermixed with the ultimate threat from Africa, the third world, a politically unsatisfactory creature with legitimate claims. Racism, imperialism, colonialism, sexual repression, creative energy, repression of ultimate desires all come together in a duel to the death, which Kong must lose. He becomes, in this pageant, our sacrifice to the unresolved issues he raises, our modern-day Frankenstein's monster; and he enters our imagination not as a tragic figure caught in a shoot-out, but as a pop figure brought back repeatedly to fill television screens and sell products. For Pynchon, the "tallest, darkest leading man in Hollywood" serves as a gloss on his novel.

Barth is less radical, but as his work developed through the 1960s, with the fictions of *Lost in the Funhouse* (1968) and *Chimera* (1972), he found himself deep in issues which Lionel Trilling outlined in his Norton Lectures at Harvard in 1970, and collected as *Sincerity and Authenticity.* Earlier in his career, in *The Floating Opera* (1956) and *The End of the Road* (1958), Barth had worked along the lines of what Trilling called "sincerity." Behind sincerity lies a culture in which individual and social elements form a comity, a union of needs. Although sincerity allows for great latitudes of individualism, it makes use of self-knowledge in order to bring the character into association with others: self-knowledge brings to others what one has perceived about oneself. Dickens and George Eliot are great exemplars of a fiction based on sincerity.

Beginning with *The Sot-Weed Factor* (1960), which was pivotal in Barth's exploration of self and society, and then continuing through *Giles Goat-Boy*

(1966), Barth moved from a vision of society based on sincerity to one based on authenticity. Trilling perceived authenticity as a quality in which exploration of self preempts other considerations; in which ideas of the common good or commonwealth are replaced by needs of ego or self. From this develops a culture quite different from one connected to sincerity. For the latter, imagination was a means of bringing the individual's knowledge of himself to the consciousness of others; imagination was itself a socializing power, and on its dramatic qualities rested class, morals, culture itself.

Authenticity creates a different kind of culture, which Trilling doubts is culture at all. This "movement" began in the eighteenth century, and Trilling cites Diderot's *Rameau's Nephew* as a key document in its development. With authenticity as the goal, the individual becomes paramount; what we observe in *Letters* become possible. For Barth is interested not only in justifying the qualities of his characters—in returning them from a quasi-sincere quest to one involving authenticity—but in making them insist on their own existence. Trying to defy their creator, they argue with him about the roles assigned to them. As maker or God, Barth must deal with the "souls" of his creations long after they have been put to rest; resurrected, they revolt, demand their own voices, reject earlier senses of comity, however slim. By reopening his own work in *Letters,* Barth has provided a reinterpretation of his times by way of shifting his creations from one cultural base to another. The heroism of *Letters* is that he has tried nothing less than a restructuring of the world.

Todd Andrews and Jacob Horner, respectively of *The Floating Opera* and *The End of the Road,* had always been on the margins of comity, uncertain of their relationships to a social ideal; so that Barth's subsequent shift to exploration of self is not acute. In his lectures, Trilling was not particularly interested in showing how the shift from sincerity to authenticity was a concomitant of democracy, or that the imagination which works to create elements of authenticity is also an imagination freeing itself from restraints.

Trilling's definitions are a response to the 1960s, especially to student-faculty-administration struggles at Columbia, and they fail to account for that radical shift to egalitarian democracy which helped shape the decade. Trilling was concerned with "loss of control," whereas Barth, as a novelist, is concerned with how that shift of cultural values affected fiction and fictional ideas. Trilling was seeking elements to conserve, his own political and social ideas shaken by events; and his role as a humanist to save what was necessary led to his distinction between a culture of sincerity and one of authenticity. For Barth, the question is not of conserving, but of observing the self as it functions in a culture whose values have already shifted, where realities have already become indefinable, or where things are eradicated or dismembered.

In *Gravity's Rainbow* (1973), Pynchon positions scenes and characters somewhere in a void or in middle areas beyond touch. In this respect, he picks up from Gaddis's *The Recognitions,* where the method is similar, although the latter floats less. Pynchon's people lack a context, but not for reasons of impersonality or indifference on the author's part. His object is to find in people and scenes the correlative of the rocket, rockets incoming, apocalypse not portended but in the making. Once we meet the people and see them acting and interacting, they have sufficient energy; they are not Oblomovs or Beckett-like creatures.

The archetype for Pynchon's form is the idea of *progression d'effet* developed by Conrad and Ford Madox Ford at the turn of the century and refined in succeeding decades. What was once a means of developing a society is now a method of dismembering it. Pynchon's modernity or postmodernity is the exploration of a seventy-five-year-old strategy by which elements float into being without ever gaining direct access. The method introduces people and matter by way of accretion of detail, in the manner of accumulation, until pieces, as in a puzzle, fit. The work shapes itself in the reader's mind. The reader *makes* the novel. Conrad said it was to make you *see,* and the method is a mode of perception, although difficult and, in Pynchon's case, even perverse. Bits and pieces replace lines; characters shape their present and past very slowly, obliquely. The rocket falls, we have pieces, and then we must fit the rocket together to gain the novel. The mode for Pynchon is dismemberment, whether V., Vheissu, Slothrop here, London, or the novel itself.

The opening passage on the evacuation is a typical strategy. All London seems on the move, to escape the buzz bombs, then the V-2 rockets, which hit before their sound arrives. "The Evacuation still proceeds, but it's all theatre." No light, girders looming overhead, glass from somewhere: he (later identified as "Pirate" Prentice) fears a collapse and a spectacle.

The people moving out, the imminent fall or collapse of structures, the "screaming across the sky" of the buzz bomb, the smells of past and present all create that unsettling of the senses and dislocation of temporal and spatial elements which characterize the incoming novel. Like that "screaming across the sky" of the approaching projectile, the novel will shriek across, theater and spectacle in a buzz bomb of elements.

Shortly after that, the novel shifts to Pirate's ability to turn out "famous Banana breakfasts." Bananas—which are like eatable rockets, or rockets called "steel bananas"—become "banana omelets, banana sandwiches, banana casseroles, mashed bananas molded in the shape of a British lion rampant, blended with eggs into batter for French toast, squeezed out a pastry nozzle . . . tall cruets of pale banana syrup to pour oozing over banana waffles . . . banana croissants and banana kreplach and banana oatmeal and banana jam and banana bread, and bananas flamed in ancient brandy." A life-giving fruit becomes a mythical element, saturating Pirate's breakfasts the way the Germans are saturating the sky with rockets; and while men flock to his repasts, the world of London is filled with "steel bananas," death kreplachs either buzzing in or soundless.

Added to Pirate's ability with bananas—which recalls Milo Minderbinder from *Catch-22,* the ultimate forager—is his extrasensory qualities as a "fantasy-surrogate," by which he "had known for a while that certain episodes he dreamed could not be his own." This is not madness, because one day he meets the real owner of one of his dreams. Pirate recognizes this ability could be valuable for someone who discovers it, and he has a fantasy of his own in which he would be "abducted by an organization of dacoits or Sicilians, and used for unspeakable purposes." From this, he goes into an episode that occurs outside any known condition of sleep, in which he communicates with a gigantic Adenoid slowly consuming all Europe. The episode is a fantasy replica of the German monster, now using rocketry to savage London; and we foresee Pirate's gift as crucial to the working out of the narrative.

In this, the fourth episode of the novel, Pynchon opens up his hand slightly, and bananas become steel bananas. An American, Tyrone Slothrop, keeps in his makeshift office a map of London which has on it silver stars labeled with girls' names, indicating rocket drops. The map will become a focal point, because it is of interest to young Roger Mexico at the

White Visitation office;* that map is photographed by Teddy Bloat, transferred to Pirate Prentice, and delivered to Roger Mexico, a double-play situation. The White Visitation is a catchall agency known as PISCES: Psychological Intelligence Schemes for Expediting Surrender. Just "whose surrender is not made clear."

The novel, barely begun, has developed into a multilevel mystery. Besides Pirate's ability to dream episodes not his own, there is Slothrop's extrasensory ability, Pavlovian conditioned reflex, to sense incoming bombs: "He can feel them coming days in advance." Slothrop, who derives from an old family reminiscent of Pynchon's own (the Pyncheons of Hawthorne's *The House of the Seven Gables*), has sensory antennae which pick up what others are too coarse to sense. The question is what Slothrop experiences in this "transmarginal leap"—a kind of abreaction, in which he leaps toward a resolution of neurotic elements. His talent is a military weapon; he is a human radar station.

Slothrop's unique talent is revealed in a scene which permits Pynchon to display his virtuosity: his scatological sense of subject-object, in which the agent is human, but the environment is shit. He explores fantasy worlds by way of ordinary elements— a men's john, a shoeshine boy (who happens to be the young Malcolm X), a toilet bowl—all juxtaposed to a much larger plan, which is to determine whether Slothrop under the needle can divulge the way his special gift operates. The "test" comes in the Abreaction Ward of St. Veronica's Hospital (linkage of Abreaction and Veronica, of the veil, is itself a conceit), a scene Pynchon introduces the way Gaddis brings on many of his scenes: we back in by way of an exchange of seemingly meaningless letters, the focus of which is the needle slipping into Slothrop's arm, followed by the toilet fantasy, which is itself preceded by a brief tour of black Boston. In all, a poor man's Inferno.

In the men's john, Slothrop goes in pursuit of a mouth harp, which drops into the toilet. As he

plunges in after it, the scene takes on the wildness of a homosexual nightmare intermixed with the water imagery of a birth. At one end Slothrop is offering his buttocks for rape by a black gang led on to racial violence by Malcolm X; at the other, he is moving down through the world of excrement toward some birth or rebirth at the far end, if he can reach it. Along the way, he reads the "toilet world" as one reads road signs: "Burma-shave signs of the toilet world, icky and sticky, cryptic and glyptic." He finds that traces of shit are identifiable, and in some instances he can even identify what was eaten: "There's bean sprouts around here someplace and even a hint of that wild plum sauce." In the fantasy, Slothrop looks for signs of Jack Kennedy: "say, where the heck is that Jack tonight, anyway? If anybody could've saved that harp, betcha Jack could." Kennedy was a classmate of Slothrop's at Harvard, and part of the Burroughs-like journey through the toilet world is a tracing of Harvard excrement, expelled in black Boston!

Eventually, Slothrop emerges into a new world, inhabited by one Crutchfield or Crouchfield; and what follows from that is a montage of images of Indians, Mexicans, et al. The scene then shifts to a short quotation which ends with the name Dr. Laszlo, and we begin to move toward the central mystery of Slothrop and his gift, which, in turn, will help to unravel the mystery of the rockets. The point about Slothrop is that he may have achieved a reversal of cause and effect; that is, he may be a perfect case of Pavlovian psychology, but in reverse. As a result of Jamf's work at Harvard, Slothrop is known as the "famous Infant Tyrone." The mystery is whether Jamf merely deconditioned Tyrone's hardons—that is, waited "till the infant showed zero hardons in the presence of stimulus x"—or ignored the "silent extinction beyond the zero," which would allow the adult Slothrop to intuit the incoming rockets before their presence is apparent. If the latter is the case, then Slothrop can, by way of his erection, plot the rockets, according to a Poisson distribution, before they fall. The map he keeps in his office, with a record of his female conquests, is actually a map of rocket strikes according to that Poisson distribution: hardons, girls, and rockets all interconnected in Slothrop's "gift."

There is, here, Pynchon's penchant for sophomoric amusement, which is never distant from his work. But his working of the conceit takes it beyond fraternity house bawdiness into that world he explored as early as *V.*, between the younger Stencil's ordered and imitated existence and the messy and

---

*The White Visitation is a kind of Bedlam, an outpost of pseudoscience in a context of scientific study. It serves as a counterthrust to real science, and yet cannot be discounted. It is, in fact, like Barth's West Campus computer in *Giles,* the potential panacea. The key to the White Visitation is the thrust of the maniacal and irrational into logical and rational plans, that infusion of madness into sane schemes which Pynchon sees as not only the basis for the Allied winning of the war but a schema for the workings of the world, whether in war or in peace.

"lived" one of Benny Profane. Here, on a larger scale, Pynchon emblemizes how technology (rocket) and human reaction (or abreaction) can interconnect. The aim is both sexual and countersexual, both fraternity humor and gallows humor. Pynchon presents the view of a famous Freudian, Dr. Edwin Treacle, who thinks Slothrop's gift is psychokinesis:

> . . . Slothrop is, with the force of his mind, *causing* the rockets to drop where they do. He may not be physically highballing them about the sky: but maybe he is fooling with the electrical signals inside the rocket's guidance system. However he's doing it, sex *does* come into Dr. Treacle's theory. "He subconsciously needs to abolish all trace of the sexual Other, whom he symbolizes on his map, most significantly, as a *star,* that anal-sadistic emblem of classroom success which so permeates elementary education in America. . . ."

The V-2, then, is a weapon aimed at destroying English morale, but one which, at the same time, gives Slothrop's genius an opportunity to manifest itself: as an erection working backward from explosion to sound.

What makes it all possible is the rocket, the new V-2, which embodies chance itself. The most advanced kind of chance developed by man, it challenges nature itself as the guide of man's fortunes. It is, by virtue of its chance element, a para-category, something ejected not by the Germans but by some force, malevolent or not, which exists distinct from human life as we know it. Even those who eject the rockets, as Captain Blicero recognizes, are not free of its randomness; they, too, are as much target as launching site: ". . . they were all condemned. The house lies west of the Duindigt racecourse, quite the other direction from London, but no bearing is exempt—often the rockets, crazed, turn at random, whinnying terribly in the sky, turn about and fall according each to its madness so unreachable and, it is feared, incurable."

In Mallarmé's "A Throw of the Dice Will Never Abolish Chance," the artist-captain, even with his hand on the controls, is himself at the mercy of chance. Pynchon has found in rockets and rocketry a perfect example of a central dilemma in postwar culture, already foreshadowed by midwar discoveries. The world Pynchon describes makes the rocket king, which in turn embodies man's greatest fears: not sexual, but those concerning chance, randomness, and exposing desire for control, selection, choice. When the V-2 exemplifies first explosion, then sound, it re-

verses our conditioned reflexes, as Jamf's experiments on infant Slothrop revealed. That reversal of normal conditioning is, in one sense, a great form of consciousness. We have entered a new world, a variable culture. With our expectations no longer sustained, we perceive the rocket as forcing a reordering of experience: as we find in art, familiar is defamiliarized.

Thus, the rocket with its disruption of our expectations has something in it of the artistic process, in which all becomes contingency, randomness. But behind that chance is some pattern, some way of positioning ourselves in relation to randomness, whether art or rocketry. But where? How do we penetrate to it? Is it even discoverable? Behind art is the artist; behind the rocket stretches the vastness of chance, perhaps behind that some guiding hand is an oceanic universe, an unfathomable cosmos. Disruption, indeed, seems to be all; except that, like art in the hands of a consummate artist, the rockets do fall into a pattern. Slothrop, unconsciously, is that artist: embedded somewhere in his reflexes is the sensory perception of the rocket pattern. To discover that is, like writing a great fiction, an act of art, whose working out becomes *Gravity's Rainbow*.

The locale for working out that world of rocketry —the artist's studio, as it were—is the White Visitation, described before as a Bedlam or Charenton. The White Visitation is man's opportunity to abolish chance: a throw of the dice in this instance is the mixture of science and pseudoscience which characterizes the Visitation experiment. For example, a film is made to deceive the Germans, a film in which everything is placed so as to create the illusion of being real, when it is, in fact, a prop. The chance is appropriated to counter or abolish it: for props, like the element they are expected to counter, are infinitely expendable. *The culture of the 1960s Pynchon reflects is one that cannot accept randomless patterns unless its individuals can also indulge in random experience themselves.* The Pynchon paradox is apparent: chance by way of the cosmos is unacceptable, while chance by way of individual choice is accommodated. The two, of course, must conflict, in a reordering of experience whose glory and doom pull us apart.

Pynchon speaks of a "culture of death," which goes further than the rockets; but he is not writing of the fashionable and romantic preoccupation with death, that sense of an ending, which has overtaken the late sixties and the seventies. In that view, death is to be postponed by innumerable individual acts— cosmetic surgery, drugs, magical and mysterious rites —and, at the same time, is romanticized by death philosophers like Kübler-Ross, who see in it our "final choice." Death in these opposing views, postponement and embrace, is associated with all the quasi-religious, mystical groups which have characterized the later postwar era. Despite enormous differences, everything from health food addicts to Moonies, from vegetarians to Hare Krishnas, is involved here. Pynchon has not entered the culture from these fashionable angles. His "culture of death" is the inescapable fact that human rationality cannot obtain in a world of infinite chance; that rationality is absorbed into the irrational, or into forms of doom, as rapidly as it asserts itself: that the two are like Siamese twins, so joined that separation is itself a form of the culture of death.

As Pynchon begins to develop the rocket theme, with an episode set in prewar Germany, when rockets were still little more than bombs which exploded unexpectedly, he writes of Walter Rathenau, the financial wizard and planner, a Jew, who was assassinated in 1922. Rathenau was a German who helped to guide the German war effort, and after defeat, he became a spokesman for a general democratic rehabilitation of Germany and the rest of war-devastated Europe. His ideology found middle ground between socialism and democratic capitalism, what, in effect, the West German government now practices. With his training in engineering, philosophy, physics, and chemistry (Pynchon's own background, in some part), he seemed ideally suited as the man who would guide Europe's destinies after the war. Further, his family background—his father, Emil, started the German electric utility company—gave him luster, personal fortune, and social position. But he was, also, a Jew, and German nationalists found in him the epitome of everything they felt had led to their defeat in 1918 and would lead to future defeats. His assassination was set. Further, according to Pynchon, Rathenau ran afoul of I. G. Farben, the cartel that in a sense controlled every aspect of the German political and military position.

Paralleled to that is the White Visitation's need to discover what Slothrop's unique gift is: he becomes for them an object, as Rathenau had been for the German nationalists. A good deal of the second part of *Gravity's Rainbow* is devoted to the plot to find out what Slothrop knows, through the agent and counteragent Katje and a linguistics genius named Dodson-Truck. But these sections, which take place on the Riviera near the Casino Hermann Goering, involve more than the manipulation of Slothrop; they take us ever deeper into the labyrinths of chance, random-

ness, human choice (or lack of it). As Slothrop is explored, so he explores; an updating of the search for V.

Slothrop suspects that "Something was done to him, and it may be that Katje knows what. Hasn't he, in her 'futureless look,' found some link to his own past, something that connects them closely as lovers?" He ponders on the nature of their love, which has within it that mysterious sense that it is not an end in itself: ". . . all in his life of what has looked free or random, is discovered to've been under some Control, all the time the same as a fixed roulette wheel—where only destinations are important, attention is to long-term statistics, not individuals." Slothrop is under a sign or curse, that parabola. "They must have guessed, once or twice—guessed and refused to believe—that everything, always, collectively, had been moving toward that purified shape latent in the sky, that shape of no surprise, no second chances, no return." It is inescapable: "Yet they do move forever under it, reserved for its own black-and-white news certainly as if it were the Rainbow, and they its children." The pastoral mode of benevolent or idyllic nature passes over to the terror the rainbow now suggests. Behind the buzz bomb lay the V-2; and behind the V-2 lies the still mysterious A4s. London is slowly being reduced to rubble; a new beast waits to slouch toward Bethlehem and somehow Slothrop may be the source of its existence. What he and Katje do is, like the croupier's roulette wheel, fixed.

In writing about Pynchon's novel, we must stress the larger scheme, which is of a size that few other contemporary novels have equaled. Pynchon is moving the novel back into spaciousness, into full systems, although his inability to write about love (as apart from coupling and sex) hobbies his achievement. Nevertheless, he has located the novel in that world where we find Grass, Garcia Márquez, and, in an earlier generation, Mann. This is the novel, not only of war and peace, but of "Other Kingdoms," beyond frontiers or borders. "Doomed lovers" working through a vast fate of parabolas, destruction, cosmic occurrences are actors in a drama extending from the individual to the larger mysterious elements which control all life, beyond technology into magic and legend. By way of chance and randomness, Pynchon penetrates into fate and destiny. What is the nature of our doom, if it is doom that is our nature? Although many passages are adolescent posturing— the sex, for example—the overall drama makes the lapses acceptable.

How, we ask, does Pynchon achieve both spaciousness and temporality, within which he presents not only teams of doomed lovers but hordes of characters all caught within a cosmic scheme? Would conventional means, which would have made him more "readable," has served as well? He gives us some clue to his own novelistic methods when he writes about the development of plastics. In tracing origins of Imipolex G, that mysterious material which seems connected to the rocket mystery, a mystery which concerns a plastic as much as a weapon, Pynchon moves into du Pont's discovery that it could rearrange nature. Chemists "could decide now what properties they wanted a molecule to have, and then go ahead and build it. At du Pont, the next step after nylon was to introduce aromatic rings into the polyamide [the chain made up of polymers, essential to plastics] chain. Pretty soon a whole family of 'aromatic polymers' had arisen: aromatic polyamides, polycarbonates, polyethers, polysulfanes." Once this was achieved, Jamf, among others, then "proposed, logically, dialectically, taking the parental polymide sections of the new chain, and looping *them* around into rings too, giant 'heterocyclic' rings, to alternate with the aromatic rings." The development and modification of these chains led to Imipolex G, that insulation material for the rockets now being fired with the aid of a transmitter on the roof of Dutch Shell headquarters.

We have, here in this cellular makeup, the archetype of the novel's own structuring. The cellular expansion into different forms, by way of changing the molecular structure of each cell, afforded Pynchon a method of accretion and slight modification. Just as each modification of the cell created a different molecular structure, and that in turn a new product, so Pynchon is able to hold together his basic cell—the juxtaposition of rocketry and human fate—while tampering with each unit so as to create a differential of incident.

The method differs from more conventional novels in that Pynchon is concerned with constant process. Most novels remain static while the writer dips ever deeper into whatever he is describing or plumbing. Pynchon is attempting the novel of flow, of spatial and temporal process—what we catch in Joyce's desire to create process of time and space by way of one day in a fixed place. Joyce used an enclosed spatial and temporal unit in order to create its opposite; whereas Pynchon moves across the cosmos, gravity's rainbow, for much the same effect: to join individual fortunes with those vast temporal and spatial empires which, by contrast, make human life minuscule. Pyn-

chon found in the cellular method of accretion and modification, of putting a "different face" on that unit, the means by which he could repeat, cross over, dip back.

Characters assume different guises, even different shapes, in order to work along the model of the cellular structure. About one-third through the novel, Tyrone Slothrop has taken on a new name (Ian Scuffling), a new role as an English war correspondent, and a new function, to enter a different time and space medium. He will work out the cellular structure of Slothrop by posing as another, then slowly move back toward what he was: his quest to find out. Thus, the novel is poised: Slothrop and rockets, individual and gravity's rainbow.

Cellular structure has advantages over more traditional picaresque, which is episodic, linear, somewhat formless around the edges. The disadvantage of such a narrative is its lack of coherence, its inability to hold ideas intact, and its total reliance on space. Pynchon's cellular structure allows for change within constants: he utilizes spatiality with almost abandon, and yet the cell holds the nucleus or clue. I mentioned above that Tyrone Slothrop (T.S., himself) becomes Ian Scuffling, and yet the new name and new role as correspondent are not a nuclear change, only a cellular one. The center or nucleus, the identifying element, remains, while the actual molecular structure is altered to allow for narrative progression.

In still another way, the cellular structure takes on a crucial role, in the association of those gigantic cartels with individuals, whom they control. The cartels are an essential element in *Gravity's Rainbow,* since they supervise chance, as it were. Whatever their precise role, they serve the function of Zeus in ancient drama, and their presence, even when not felt directly, is a hovering shadow. That configuration which Slothrop senses—"that *smell* again, a smell from before his conscious memory begins, a soft and threatening smell, threatening, haunting, not a smell to be found out in the world"—lies, actually, within the provenance of the cartels. These international monopolies develop by horizontal and vertical accretion, acquiring not only the means to peddle their product but virtually every aspect of what their product is made of: forests for lumber, ships for transportation, steel to make the ships, pulp mills, hotels and restaurants. The cartel, like the cell, contains the nucleus (what it originally was) and yet it transforms itself by way of changes in its molecular structure.

Slothrop's choices in reentering his past, to discover shadows and configurations, are all ultimately controlled by cartels, which have used him since infancy in the Jamf experiments. Slothrop is a victim of capitalists at the highest level, a tool in Marx's sense, but also in Pynchon's, a tool which hardens and erects in patterns Slothrop cannot comprehend. "He is also getting a hardon, for no immediate reason." That hardon, which we consider to be an element of personal choice, is related to cosmic control: the cartel's conditioning; and so Pynchon has connected, by way of cellular molecularity, the individual and fate or destiny. Sex itself is controlled by some cosmic computer.

It is, I believe, the cellular method which permits Pynchon such sweeps of space without disruption of controlling line. This novel of seemingly endless chaos is, in reality, tightly organized. Pynchon extends the molecular makeup of the cell to language itself: "How alphabetic is the nature of molecules." Like the polymers in plastics, our words "too can be modulated, broken, recoupled, redefined, co-polymerized one to the other in worldwide chains that will surface now and then over long molecular silences, like the seen parts of a tapestry."

Furthermore, Pynchon uses chess as an analogy to the molecular theory which underlies cells, putting the association into the mouth of Wimpe, a super salesman for a Farben subsidiary. The chess pieces, Wimpe demonstrates, can be observed as though "each molecule had so many possibilities open to it, possibilities for bonding, bonds of different strengths, from carbon the most versatile, the queen," whom he calls " 'the Great Catherine of the periodic table,' down to the little hydrogens numerous and single-moving as pawns."

We observe how chess randomness works out within characters, in the strange sibling relationship of the Russian Tchitcherine and the African Enzian, who heads the Schwarzcommandos. Tchitcherine's father, a sailor, had deserted from his ship and lived with an African, which resulted in Enzian, half-brother to the younger Tchitcherine, left behind in Russia. The two are like a single cell broken off, or like movable molecules in a given cell, thus creating combinations analogous to those in plastics or in a given chess game. Tchitcherine, preparing a rocket of his own, is working the seams of a zone caught in the German vacuum—a role which fulfills his compulsive need to annihilate the Schwarzcommandos and his "mythical half-brother Enzian." Not to be confused with the Tchitcherine who helped negotiate the Rapallo Treaty with Rathenau, this Tchitcherine is nihilistic; there are in his ancestors "any number of

bomb throwers and jubilant assassins." His heritage is those students who threw themselves under the wheels of carriages or died in the Czar's prisons. Tchitcherine, whose needs will intertwine with Slothrop's fortunes, is a driven man, propelled by the need to gain power so as to destroy. His ruthlessness is equaled only by that of Enzian and the Schwarz-commandos, those strange Herero Africans caught in the interface of cultures. Everyone is a spin-off, a molecular peculiarity. Tchitcherine can rightly be seen as a supermolecule, Enzian as a property in himself, an enzyme.

In still another combination, Pynchon uses characters and scenes suggested by his own earlier work, V. and The Crying of Lot 49, as if Gravity's Rainbow were itself a molecular change from the basic cell structure of Pynchon's canon. Bodine from V. appears briefly, but more importantly, the long episode at Foppl's villa in V. is alluded to, an episode of considerable significance in both novels. Here, Pynchon uses Weissmann, a key organizer of the rocket construction project, in conjunction with Mondaugen, both of whom occupied the villa during the siege in the Südwest. Once involved in the desecration of the Hereros, they are reunited for rocket work, which is to desecrate Europe. A little further on, while discussing general rocket background, Pynchon introduces Maxwell's Demon, which is so instrumental in an understanding of The Crying of Lot 49. At the university, Kekulé, whose research made Farben possible, comes under the influence of Liebig, a great professor. Liebig serves as a conduit for Kekulé's talents, serves, in fact, as a kind of "sorting-demon," in which energy is concentrated into one "favored room of the Creation at the expense of everything else."

Suggested here, as in the references to V., is a universe as a huge, indifferent space, into which a favored few, by way of Clerk Maxwell's sorting mechanism, are introduced to do the thing they can do best: here, the rocket. Although Pynchon is not really clear about his idea—or else has so embedded it in other matters it lacks definition—there is nevertheless the interaction between destiny (the huge space) and individual fortune. A motif in Gravity's Rainbow, it remains inchoate in its specifications. Pynchon plays with it, makes individual destiny and spatiality meet on interfaces, but leaves the matter as uncertain as Maxwell's Demon, a sorting mechanism for human as well as material fortunes. It is, in one sense, his overall motif, in another the theme he slides away from. In still a third way, that interplay between individual and destiny is secondary to sensations, acquisition of power, sexual gratification. Although Pynchon has his share of doom and apocalypse, they are manifested within contexts of enthusiasm, enjoyment, even gratification, however bizarre. The play of sixties roles looms large, a spread of splendor.

Role-playing, the duplication and triplication of characters, the assumption of new names and identities, the element of theater (not only roles, but stages, staging areas, arenas, poses, postures, developing ironies of character and motives)*—these, and more, are connected to plastic molecules and the cellular structure they represent. "Each plot carries its signature," Pynchon writes. "Some are God's, some masquerade as God's. This is a very advanced kind of forgery." Though not the first introduction of imitation into the novel—Slothrop, in fact, can be viewed as a forgery in his own right—it does suggest that Pynchon is picking up Gaddis's theme in *The Recognitions*.

Forgery is a style of life as well as an act of dissembling another's signature. The black marketeers who thread through the novel—Springer offers to sell Slothrop the Imipolex secret for £10,000—are part of the forgery theme. The largest of the black marketeers are the huge cartels, which stand to win whatever the outcome of the war. Pynchon suggests the great German depression of the 1920s was artificially forced, so that Germany could avoid paying reparations and then recover free of debt. Whatever the historical validity of the idea, forgery in its largest sense serves as ideological underpinning. Just as we can speak of Marxists, Social Democrats, Communists, Fascists, so Pynchon can speak of Forgers, a party, a class, a profession, an attitude.

From one point of view, Slothrop is a man involved in a forgery not of his own doing. He has been forged by Jamf, conditioned, not reconditioned, and left to function with imposed reflexes. Even when he is being himself, he is acting out the role Jamf created for him. Theatrical roles and forgery connect.

Pynchon speaks of the feeling of pain and relief, in a context of the discovery of the perfect medicine, one that can "kill intense pain without causing addiction." Yet that puts one up against a basic law of nature, which Pynchon compares to Heisenberg's sit-

uation. Heisenberg posited the law of uncertainty, or the indeterminacy principle, which questioned absolutes in nature. By demonstrating that we could locate a subatomic particle without being accurate about its velocity, or else its velocity without accuracy about its location, he introduced relativity into areas assumed to be absolute. The idea has profound implications outside physical nature itself, since it suggests an entire mode of existence. "The more pain it [medication] takes away, the more we desire it. It appears we can't have one property without the other." That is, either location or velocity, but not both. Prolonged relief brings addiction; addiction is itself the idea of release from something else, as well as an entering into. Every act calls for a shifting role, reinforced by Heisenberg, plastics, chess, nature itself.

Once we have insight into associations, we can perceive how Pynchon's mind works, on that network of balances which are never balanced, on that dipping in and out of chance, randomness, contingency, which offer as many uncertainties as certainties. The Hereros, led in post-Nazi Germany by Enzian, are an excellent example of an entire people caught in the Heisenberg principle. For in their struggle for independence against German rule of South West Africa in the early twentieth century, as we saw in *V.*, they were virtually exterminated. As a foreshadowing of German extermination of Jews, Slavs, and Gypsies, we have the Hereros. The Germans treated them like so many slugs clustered on plants, not people, not even bodies (except for the women), but inorganic matter.

Yet the Herero response to the failure of their rebellions from 1903 to 1907 was a kind of suicide. "They want a negative birth rate. The program is racial suicide. They would finish the extermination the Germans began in 1904." The Schwarzcommandos—Hereros the Germans were training as "black juntas" for the eventual takeover of British and French colonies in Africa—are filled with that sense of sterility and death. Called the "Empty Ones," they have chosen tribal suicide (their own form of death) over Christian death (dying for any other cause). These "Empty Ones," now exiled in the Zone (an interfacial area), "calculate no cycles, no returns, they are in love with the glamour of a whole people's suicide—the pose, the stoicism, and the bravery. These Otukungura are prophets of masturbating, specialists in abortion and sterilization, pitchmen for acts oral and anal, pedal and digital, sodomistical and zoophiliac." Their goal is the day when the last Zone-

---

*The theatrical element is apparent in several ways. Pynchon is very fond of slapstick, often with adolescent wit not far behind, and he is obviously tuned in to the Keystone Kops, Laurel and Hardy, early Chaplin, etc. The use of chimps for parodic effect is such a device right out of early movies; also his references to King Kong.

Herero will become a "final zero to a collective history fully lived." It is against this that Enzian must struggle to carry out his plans of leadership, revenge, revitalization of sorts.

More than a simple motif, the Hereros are thematic: a people who respond to extermination (pain) with an analgesic of their own (suicide) and an addition to it (the death principle). Here Heisenberg's principle of uncertainty in nature has become embodied in a race: its desire to survive in its own perverse way against the perversity of those who would exterminate it in their way. By choosing tribal suicide, they make procreation itself the enemy. The addiction for death enters into the sexual act: anything which avoids penetration is sanctioned. They guard against nature's uncertainties by countering with one unavoidable evidence of nature: procreation cannot follow nonvaginal intercourse.

The Hereros catch Pynchon's imagination both here and in *V.* because they focus on forgery, analgesic and addictive medication, balances, playings-off: areas where Pynchon can search for certainties amidst indeterminacy. He reflects the 1960s intensely: that striving, not for existential authenticity, but for some human principle in which the addiction (drugs or otherwise) is not worse than the analgesia (however powerful). The Hereros, an ostensible play on "heroes," are the Jews of Africa, hunted down and yet refusing to buckle under. Their choice of extinction is like that of the besieged at Masada, preferring tribal suicide to death at the hands of the conqueror.

Yet the group that splinters off when it is taken to Germany, the group that reforms as the Schwarzcommandos, asserts a new feeling, like the Jews who fought to establish Israel against overwhelming odds. Instead of contending with British and Arabs, the Hereros have to deal with the occupying forces immediately after the war. The Hereros have their own form of Israel in the making, a tiny beachhead formed in the interfaces of the established zones: "Oh, a state begins to take form in the stateless German night, a State that spans oceans and surface politics, sovereign as the international or Church of Rome, and the Rocket is its soul. IG Raketen, Circus-bright, poster reds and yellows, rings beyond counting, all going at once. The stately Finger twirls among them all."

The Hereros, of course, are not the only ones working in that zonal interface, or creating a zone of their own, zones within zones. Parallel to them, as enemies to all and to each other, are Nazi remnants, Russians, Americans, and English. All the powers who as allies fought the Nazis are now divided over the rocket, and a separate war—a postwar, so to speak—is occurring. The Hereros, that group marked by the Nazis for black power, are now struggling for just that, with Enzian its leader and ideological mouthpiece—the ultimate Black Panther.

In another way, the rocket has parallels to the struggle to create nuclear weapons. That Zone Pynchon refers to as a separate state is an appropriate representative of the state created by the bomb, the bomb as a state of mind, a political and ideological concept. The rocket, then, the one Slothrop spends most of the novel searching for, is a power base within itself. To enter that rocket world would be like Slothrop's unusual sensation, while with Bianca, a child sex object, of being *"inside his own cock"*: activator and spectator. Within, he activates the organism which is also enveloping him: ". . . his arms and legs it seems *woven* among vessels and ducts, his sperm roaring louder and louder, getting ready to erupt somewhere below his feet. . . . He is enclosed. Everything is about to come, come incredibly, and he's helpless here in this exploding *emprise* . . . red flesh echoing . . . an extraordinary sense of *waiting to rise.*"

By way of this extended conceit, Pynchon connects the Rocket State to the individual situation: because of his unique gift, Slothrop experiences the sense of the rocket rising, the result of Jamf's conditioning of erection and coming. Slothrop here is both launcher and what is launched, outside and inside his own organ, as the rocket is both within and without our experience. There is, by way of association between individual and rocket, an effort to consolidate the various meanings of the novel.

Not the least of these efforts at consolidation comes near the end, when Pynchon repeats his image of the Rocket State as our state of the future, which for Americans and the rest of the world is America herself. The Rocket State has already taken over, in that Pynchon blend of immediate postwar rocketry with America of the sixties and seventies. The Rocket State becomes a giant "factory-state," rather pleasant, but with a villain, "serious as death": it "is this typical American teenager's own *Father,* trying episode after episode to kill his son. And the kid knows it." Pynchon is referring on one level to the Vietnam War, in which a boy who had a father (and mother) supporting the war was doomed to fight and possibly die in it, with sons reliving war exploits for their aging fathers; but on another level, a form of death embodied in what Pynchon calls the "Radiant Hour," a form of mechanical and technological death suggested by Slothrop's quest to seek himself within the sheathing of Imipolex G.

For Pynchon, America is "a City of the Future full of extrapolated 1930s swoop-façaded and balconied skyscrapers, lean chrome caratids with bobbed hairdos, classy airships of all description drifting in the boom and hush of the city abysses, golden lovelies sunning in roof-gardens and turning to wave as you pass. It is the Raketen-Stadt." Within this city-state-country, Slothrop must seek the "Radiant Hour," that technological solution which sets him and Pynchon off on a manic quest for some essence amidst pop culture. No writer, not even a with-it poet like Allen Ginsberg, can catch the popsicle nature of pop culture as devastatingly as Pynchon, perhaps because he derives his humor from its banalities. A song: "My Doper's Cadenza"—"If you hear, a 'box' so sweet, / Play-in' tunes, with a peppy beat, / That's just MY DOPER'S CADEN-ZA-A-A-A!" "Ass backwards" and "Shit 'n' Shinola" become linguistics tests, acts of Wittgensteinian authenticity. At the heart of it is the statement: "Well, there is the heart of it: the monumental yellow-structure, and there in the slum-suburban night, the never-sleeping percolation of life and enterprise through its shell, Outside and Inside interpiercing one another too fast, too finely labyrinthine, for either category to have much hegemony any more. The nonstop revue crosses its stage, crowding and thinning, surprising and jerking tears in an endless ratchet": America.

America as an endless revue is a conceit of cultural depravity, but also a source of great energy, wit, and enterprise. One perceives the sixties as a revue: words, theatrical roles and poses, vaudeville acts, mechanical chess players, Nazis moving around in unidentified U-boats, waiting to regroup in "shipboard tribunals against enemies of the Reich," streets and toilets full of transvestites, violence everywhere, bombs going off even in the plumbing. All the while, as a parallel action, there is King Kong, a persistent motif, hanging off the Empire State Building, a "sacrificial ape." Love in the West is between the blond, rather dull girl and the beast too fine for her, too devoted, with a love that "passeth understanding."

Working all sides of the monologue and dialogue, like a novelistic Lenny Bruce, is Pynchon, the self-conscious, intruding author, unable to leave his artifact alone for more than moments, bubbling with commentary, one-liners, words directed at both characters and audience. Bruce's dialogues with his audience seem the basis of many of Pynchon's short bursts: brief vaudeville or stand-up comic routines. Unlike Bruce, however, who martyred himself to the audience's own desire for guiltless scatology, Pynchon drifts off, thrusting out a line or dare, then withdrawing. "You will want cause and effect. All right," he throws in at a time when the narrative line has become chaotic and he wants to convey the semblance of a plan, or to assure us there is order. Bruce sought to convey ultimate disorder, whereas Pynchon's energies are devoted to creating patterns, distribution curves, parabolas.

Particularly brilliant (inevitable pun) as an insert is the tale of Byron the Night Bulb. As we shall see, its brilliance derives from its presence as a saga of endurance. In a controlled state, whether socialist or capitalist, it creates panic because it is a perfect technological feat. It will burn forever, and therefore it is destructive of the market. The cartel which created it, Phoebus (Apollo, the sun personified), monitors the Bulb and tries to destroy it. The attempt by Byron to survive against repeated efforts to blacken it is the epic of a survivor and rebel. Byron is a hero trapped in the confinements of a bulb: observing the world, suffering from neuroses of confinement and isolation, seeking some way to put his energies to positive use. Meanwhile, he suffers one indignity after another, monitored, harassed, hounded almost out of existence. "The cartel had already gone over to Contingency Plan B, which assumes a seven-year statute of limitations after which Byron will be considered legally burned out."

Furthermore, Phoebus has viewed Byron as merely providing light, restricting the "Bulb to this one identity." Yet " 'there are other frequencies above and below the visible band. Bulb can give heat. Bulb can provide energy for plants to grow, illegal plants, inside closets, for example. Bulb can penetrate the sleeping eye, and operate among the dreams of men." The Bulb can, in a sense, take on as many shapes as the city itself, which it illuminates, heats, and dreams its way into. We recall "Der Raketen-Stadt," the Rocket State, which resembles Lang's Metropolis or Calvino's "invisible cities," for there are cities throughout the novel with as many functions, guides, forms of endurance, as those of Byron the Bulb. In Pynchon, cities form and reform, taking on the shape of dreams as well as being technological actualities. We may be in London being struck by buzz bombs and V-2s, in a destroyed Berlin, or in places that are projections of men's minds; or in cities which spring up in the interfaces of the occupied zones.

For if the city is mainly a shape emanating from our imagination, forming our perceptions of its systems, so the rocket is a representation of the All, a Jungian archetypal image. The rocket "must answer to a number of different shapes in the dreams of those who touch it—in combat, in tunnel, on paper—it must survive heresies shining, uncountable . . . and heretics there will be: Gnostics who have been taken in a rush of wind and fire to chambers of the Rocket-throne . . . Kabbalists who study the Rocket as Torah, letter by letter—rivets, burner cup and brass rose, its text is theirs to permute and combine into new revelations always unfolding . . . Manichaeans who see two Rockets, good and evil, who speak together in the sacred idiolalia of the Primal Twins (some say their names are Enzian and Blicero) of a good Rocket to take us to the stars, an evil Rocket for the World's suicide, the two perpetually in struggle."

Pynchon's premise with cities, rocket, and Rocket State is that every creation is based on existing systems but profoundly altered by the one who perceives; thus, technology remains the stable element, whereas the individual introduces the human, variable ingredient. Central to Slothrop's dilemma is that in order to discover his identity, behind the Jamf conditioning, he must escape all systems of thought and action. His quest, however, is impossible: systems claim all, and even Slothrop's perception of himself as unique cannot exclude him. He is scattered to the winds, a kind of Osiris, whose pieces will be hunted down by Isis.

Only Byron the Bulb, who can slip outside the system, will survive. But he must do so at great personal cost, for his transcendence was "clear subversion. Phoebus based everything on bulb efficiency." Yet Byron in his subversion of the system makes contact with other kinds of electric appliances, in homes, factories, even the streets. "Each has something to tell him. The pattern gathers in his soul (*Seele,* as the core of the earlier carbon filament was known in Germany), and the grander and clearer it grows, the more desperate Byron gets." For the more he learns, the more impotent he will be to impart that knowledge; he will, like Cassandra, have the gift of foreknowledge which no one will believe. Knowing the truth of things, he will be powerless to alter them. He will grow into a "poor perverse bulb," full of anger and yet enjoying the frustration. He will take on human limitations even as he transcends his role as bulb.

Pynchon stressed the Byron insert because it represents a tour de force of his ambiguous world: that race to transcend diminution, that technological element or shaping which passes into human life, affects it, becomes indispensable to it, and yet refuses to play its predetermined role. The Bulb personifies the interplay of technology and humanity in which everything is given life, yet is based on systems which move outside our control, even as we hope to control them. Systems split off functions into separate roles—Tchitcherine and Enzian, half-brothers, personify this. In the Pynchon world, the search for roles goes on compulsively, the only certainty being that no role will be found even when the search seems completed. He is so intensely American.

Rilke is the poet of the what-might-be, of transformational potentialities: "Earth, isn't this what you want: an invisible / re-arising in us? Is it not your dream / to be one day invisible? Earth! invisible! / What is your urgent command, if not transformation?" Or in the same Duino Elegy, he captures at the very beginning the paradox of the Rocket State, which lives in the interfaces of the zones: "Why, when this span of life might be fleeted away / as laurel, a little darker than all / the surrounding green, with tiny waves on the border / of every leaf (like the smile of a wind):—oh, why / *have* to be human, and shunning Destiny, long for Destiny?"

Slothrop's stars on his distributional map, which indicate his sexual conquests, his life "amidst laurel," is also a distributional map of the rockets' fall on London, both settling into a perfect Poisson distribution. Thus, his conquests, suggesting pastoral moments amidst war, are also deeply associated with Destiny: that of Slothrop himself and Destiny in still its larger sense, of London, England, the wartime powers, sanity perhaps. Slothrop needs to work out his Destiny, through his search, which will, as Rilke prophesies, elude him. He becomes, as do all the other major characters, an acrobat in a farcical drama, a performer in a vaudeville revue, in the theater of war and death. Rilke senses all this in the opening passage of the Fifth Elegy:

> But tell me, who *are* they, these acrobats, even a
>   little
> more fleeting than we ourselves,—so urgently, ever
>   since childhood,
> wrung by an (oh, for the sake of whom?)
> never-contented will? That keeps on wringing
>   them,
> bending them, slinging them, swinging them,
> throwing them and catching them back; as though
>   from an oily
> smoother air, they come down on the threadbare
> carpet, thinned by their everlasting
> upspringing, this carpet forlornly
> lost in the cosmos.

Laid there like a plaster, as though the suburban
   [outskirts, margins]
sky had injured the earth.

The Rilke spiritual quest always ends up in recognition of what may hobble or frustrate the spirit. The acrobats who seem so sure of their fate by way of self-control are being swung, wrung, bent, as much by another will as by their own. Even their carpet has been thinned by its repeated use as support for their falling and rising bodies; so that it is ambiguous: necessary to cushion them, yet diminishing at every cushioning. Comparably, the men who engage themselves with the rocket had found a destiny, a carpet, as it were; but their association with rocket and Rocket State sucks out their destiny even as it supports them. One never eludes systems.

For Barth, too, systems have become all. It is not a question of existential freedom, but of liberation from systematic control. And like Pynchon, he has devised a technique by which he can present systems literarily as well as ideologically. Instead of describing Barth as he has developed from the mid-1950s to the present, I have decided to observe him the way he has perceived himself. Except for *Giles Goat-Boy,* discussed in Chapter 6, I have subsumed all his work under *Letters,* which he has seen fit to offer as a recapitulation of his career, as of 1979. Using *Letters* as a post of observation, we can peer back into the reaches of the career, much as Barth has done, and offer parallel comments to his own.* The method is somewhat unorthodox, but then so is a writer's use of his own works as the structure of a new book. What he claims to perceive from within, we may observe from without.

Letters extends Barth's fictions of the previous decade, beginning with *Giles,* continuing through *Lost in the Funhouse* and *Chimera.* The goal was to create fictional strategies rather than "novels": that is, to explore the resources of the genre rather than to provide traditional forms of storytelling. Barth is obsessed with narrative modes—his interest in the old-tale cycle, particularly of the frame variety—but he is also aware storytelling belongs to a fictional type that no longer reflects who and what we are. Exactly who and what we are Barth never defines; but his

fictions are efforts to involve us in media experiences, and since his mode is linguistic, dazzlingly verbal, he must explore means by which he can convey what we experience through radio, television, recordings, film.

Strategies are stressed over conventionalities. When Barth is linked to other writers as a black humorist or fabulist, or whatever, he is wrenched from his unique mode. He has delivered us from the story—for good or ill—and thrown us into a maelstrom of words, crossovers, exchanges of information. His model is not the reader sitting down to enjoy a good book, but one caught in the gigantic coils of systems he must negotiate. Barth's fictions are computer retrieval systems; not for nothing is *Giles* our novel of 1960s technology.

In the first fifty-odd pages of *Letters,* Barth offers his program. As befits a computer program, the system is balanced and delicate, as well as intricate, the very thing that enraged many reviewers. On the title page, there is a rectangle at the top which indicates a coded message to the reader. It is an anagram, or parts of a crossword puzzle, outlining the seven-part arrangement of the book, each part standing for a letter of LETTERS. In some parts, a given writer of letters will provide more than one section, often as many as four. The sequence of letter writers, however, will remain the same, in this order: Lady Amherst, Todd Andrews, Jacob Horner, A. B. Cook, Jerome Bray, Ambrose Mensch, the Author (to the reader as well as to the characters). All are familiar from previous Barth works, or are spin-offs from characters therein, except for Lady Amherst, a 1960s feminist.

The characters write to each other, although the great majority of letters are directed toward the Author, the "Clarissa." But *Letters* differs radically from *Clarissa* as a fiction; for while the Richardson novel drives toward moral and ethical concerns, *Letters* is propelled toward fulfilling its own pattern: it is self-enclosed, not moral, ethical, or even social. It is the ultimate narcissistic artifact, for at the center, always, rests Barth—maker, doer, director of letters, receiver of letters, all concerned in one way or another with Barth's previous fiction. This is the beginning. "Their several narratives [Barth writes in the pre-letter phase of the book] will become one; like waves of a rising tide, the lot will surge forward, recede, surge farther forward, recede less far, et cetera to its climax and dénouement." But there is a far more intricate ordering of material, modeled possibly on Joyce's patterning of *Ulysses* on Homer.

Barth tells us he has been enamored of certain types of fiction on the order of *The Thousand and One*

---

*My plan is to intrude with extended commentary on each previous volume, except *Giles* (1966), as Barth himself stresses it in *Letters.* Thus, we will note *The Floating Opera* (1956), *The End of the Road* (1958), *The Sot-Weed Factor* (1960), *Lost in the Funhouse* (1968), and *Chimera* (1972).

Nights, the *Pent-, Hept-,* and *Decameron, The Ocean of Story,* all frame-type fictions already explored in *Chimera.* Barth indicates that by 1968, instead of told stories he wanted to use documents: "texts-within-texts instead of tales-within-tales," a wedding of frame fiction to Richardson's epistolary method in *Clarissa.* What engaged him about the early novelists, Defoe, Sterne, as well as Richardson, is that their fictions were often concerned not with "life 'directly' " but with its documents. Fiction about fiction, all connected to historical documentation, is not new, but was the beginning of the novel in the eighteenth century.

Barth's documents were, in a sense, already there, for they existed in part in his own creations; by putting his characters back on the page and having them correspond with each other and with the author, Barth was simply extending the idea of the document —which is false, an artifact to begin with. "Thus Art [Barth writes] is as natural an artifice as Nature; the truth of fiction is that Fact is fantasy; the made-up story is a model of the world." Barth justifies his method by saying that "fiction has become a pleasure for special tastes, like poetry, archery, churchgoing. What is wanted to restore its ancient dominion is nothing less than a revolution."

There is little modesty here, and it grows worse. The letters add up to eighty-eight, piano keys, perhaps played by a dissonant author-performer; and if we turn back to the anagram on the title page and read across, as though surveying a calendar from March to September, we find this: "An old time epistolary novel by seven fictitious drolls & dreamers each of which imagines himself factual." The pattern overall is sevens, caught in LETTERS, seven letters for seven parts, the magical seven of Mann's *Magic Mountain* and traditional and folk fictions. If seven cannot save (or doom), nothing can. This extreme self-consciousness about fiction and fiction-making leads back to *Chimera. Letters* is, as it were, plagiarized from parts of *Chimera,* for two sections of the latter ("Perseid" and "Bellerophoniad") were even to appear in *Letters* before being expropriated for *Chimera.* What Barth has revealed is the anagrammatic quality not only of a given work but of an entire career.

CHIMERA

Like the mythical Chimera itself—a fire-breathing monster whose fore part was a lion's, hind a dragon's, and middle a goat's—Barth's Chimera consists of

three interrelated yet differing elements: fore, Dunyazadiad; hind, Bellerophoniad (Bellerophon not only tames Pegasus, he kills the Chimera); and middle, Perseid.* The Chimera itself, and its disparate but connecting parts, is an emblem for storytelling: that is, for a narrative which collects data in the foreground and recedes into a bizarre shape in the background. Barth's image or symbol of storytelling is the so-called "Maryland marsh snail." This snail, like Calvino's mollusk, makes its shell as it goes along out of whatever it comes across, using its own juices as cement, always selecting the best materials possible. It carries its history on its back, lives in its shell, as snails do, and adds new spirals from those already existing. It literally creates itself, its development matters of choice, its materials always at hand.

The emblem of fiction growing from itself, self-started and self-generating, nourishes the first of the novellas in *Chimera,* "Dunyazadiad." Although its materials are associated with the younger sister of Scheherazade, named Dunyazade, the quest for ultimates in fiction telling and retelling links the Barth work with Gaddis's (later) *JR,* that most extended of oral narratives shaped out of themselves, fiction generating fictions. The key to such a process is the vanishing author or controlling hand; ultimately, he is there, but so distanced from the fictional process he is like the Genie whom Barth introduces, a voice out of the whirlwind. There must be a storyteller somewhere, obviously; but the movement in twentieth-century fiction as a whole has been to disguise the teller of the tale by moving the latter to the forefront, the former to the back. God paring his fingernails was Joyce's image of the writer, echoing Flaubert; Conrad and James, in their use of a registering consciousness, pursued similar goals. Woolf located her narrator in some middle area of consciousness, an undefined place only fiction sanctions.

The apparent reasons for the shifts in narrative

---

*Before his publisher (Random House) suggested a shifting of elements, the original order was "Perseid," followed by "Bellerophoniad," concluded by "Dunyazadiad." The original arrangement makes more sense thematically, although it does locate the more spectacular "Dunyazadiad" at the end; whereas the less accessible "Perseid" begins the volume. With the alteration, failure concludes the book, whereas before, a "revelation" on Doony's part had ended it, a considerable shift in fictional process and ideology. Barth's motives in changing the order— when he was an established author—make less sense than his willingness to alter *The Floating Opera,* when, at least, he was unknown. Was he yearning for that elusive popular success with such recalcitrant material?

method are social and political as much as literary. We can say modern narrative functions respond to a broad cultural sense, away from fixedness toward relativity, rejecting stable forms for fluidity and indeterminacy, moving from straightforwardness toward forms that reflect the unconscious and the unknowable. The chief movement in narrative is for it to discover some role in unstable and volatile materials. Fixed narrative is inappropriate to voices uncertain of what they are saying, or aural reception unsure of what it is hearing. To find the treasure in the treasure is the Genie's counsel; which is another way of saying to find a voice that matters, that can be heard or comprehended.

For Barth in "Dunyazadiad," the treasure is the treasure trove of stories the Genie tells to Scheherazade, which keep her alive; in Gaddis, it will be the Rheingold which sets off the narrative line, that school version of the play which establishes the treasure as lying there for anyone who can retrieve it. Scheherazade seeks the Genie's stories in order to stay alive. But she does so also to help her sisters, women who would ordinarily be raped and then killed the next morning by Shahryar, the evil king. The cleverness of Barth's story is concealed within layers of deception. The key element is a response to the women's movement in the late sixties and early seventies; for his Scheherazade is, ironically or not, a heroine of that movement. Like the Biblical Esther, she takes on the role of savior; for every night she holds the interest of the king, she saves the life of a young woman. Her enemy is not only the king himself, but the arbitrariness of life, in which women can be sacrificed to the whims of men. " 'The only pleasure I'll take in that bed is the pleasure of saving my sisters and cuckolding their killer,' " she tells Dunyazade. When the stories run out and Scheherazade must decide what to do, she tells Doony that while they saved a thousand from a quick end, there is another thousand who suffer protracted violation at the hands of fathers, husbands, lovers. She adds: "For the present, it's our masters' pleasure to soften their policy; the patriarchy hasn't changed.' " She counsels castrating Shahryar and his equally evil brother, Shah Zaman, under pretense of providing a new sexual thrill.

The frame of the entire narrative is Doony unraveling Scheherazade's narrative technique, to Shah Zaman. Doony is herself now the repository of everything known in the world of fiction and fictional narratives, as well as of erotic techniques; she has been witness to both in her sister's efforts to stay alive.

Scheherazade's peculiar role in her relationship to Shahryar had been to provide sexual satisfaction as well as literary interest. She has retained her traditional female function, as a sexual service station for her man, but she has also become an author: fed stories by the Genie, the voice out of the whirlwind, the imagination in its peculiar function.

The spectacular brilliance of Barth's performance derives from the fact that he has something fixed against which he can work: *The Thousand and One Nights* as mortality itself, which is present whatever one may do to elude it. Mortality is allied to suicide, a state of mind many of his characters live with; yet there are also life, love, work, countering propositions. Withal, one cannot penetrate too far into either life or suicide, or one discovers the paradox "the treasure *is* the treasure." Barth concurs with modern linguists who argue, from Wittgenstein and others, that what is, is. Words are what they are; things are exactly what they appear to be. The beyond of words and things is simply more of what the word and the thing are; no more. "Aesthetically, the miracle is that the world exists. That what exists does exist," Wittgenstein notes. Or he locates existence in behavior: "The act of the will is not the cause of the action but is the action itself." Wittgenstein tortures the idea and question: "But is *language* the *only* language?" which Barth answers affirmatively, that words are the treasure from which we draw the treasure; that the universe and all its stories are a verbal universe which can be penetrated only by words. And here lies the limitations of man, his mortality. He arrives at the frontiers of experience, which give power to the writer and, at the same time, shackle his desire to expand. Exploiter of words, he is trapped by words.

Although Barth, Gaddis, and Pynchon are all intensely wordmen, they differ considerably in their sense of language. Both Gaddis and Pynchon believe in the word as a way of expanding our sense of the universe, giving it dimensions we would not ordinarily observe. In *JR,* in particular, Gaddis's verbal universe is virtually ubiquitous. In *Gravity's Rainbow,* Pynchon unfolds in infinite sequences. Barth is far sadder about the role of words; they are the means to elude suicidal impulses, but they speak, too, of limitations and mortality. They lead back to themselves, the way Doony's story leads back to her own fate. She does not escape, as her sister does, by way of words; she uses them to circle around to mortality, a stable boy-girl relationship. Doony and Shah Zaman will try out his plan, to be equals among equals and to live the good life; as well as to die at the end of it.

Scheherazade had put herself in touch with the infinite universe, the Genie supplying powers which not only delayed her demise but gave her intimations of immortality. But her sister, the titular character, has the first and final word; she frames Scheherazade's attempt at immortality, and she prevails. What triumphs is stability, existence, a decent life—all desirable, but quite ironic given the nature of the quest. We return to the desire for life and stability, but we forsake existence at the edge.

That use of the frame into which the story is set was the perfect technical means for Barth; for frame provides limitation, while tale within can expand, until, asymptotically, it reaches toward frame. Standing outside as wizard, magician, verbal Houdini is Barth. He controls the Genie, who releases his own writer's block by providing stories for Scheherazade. The Genie, incidentally, looks very much like Barth in midcareer, tall and balding. Barth, further, controls the stories Scheherazade will tell the king, controls not only the beginning, but places to pause, and the end, in a fluid sequence. Then he controls, still further, how these stories will be put to use when Dunyazade's turn comes—and he can foreshadow that by making her part of the tale come first, as the frame for her sister's thousand and one nights. He can even "ensorcell," or enchant, everyone by way of words, as the prince in the tales of Scheherazade is enchanted.

All roads lead back to Barth. Just as the "Perseid" in the volume is concerned with glass, reflections, shields, reflected light, as Perseus endeavors to kill Medusa, so, too, by way of words has Barth created the glasslike circle, that perfect expression of narcissistic impulses. The frame stories which he suggests as models, those by Boccaccio or Chaucer, for example, were means by which the author could release the material within. For Barth, the frame story leads him back to himself.

The final say in *Chimera* was originally to be the author's words to the reader at the end of "Dunyazadiad," which in the alteration ends only the first part. Here, he reminds us that *The Book of the Thousand Nights and a Night* "is not only the story of Scheherazade, but the story of the story of her stories." The way these stories end is with the "Destroyer of Delights" and the "Desolator of Dwelling-places": that is, with houses fallen into waste, palaces into ruins, and previous kings into dust. In Barth's version, the Arab storytellers have their way, but, then, so does Barth, who reminds us, ever so softly, that "The key to the treasure is the treasure." These are the words

that signaled the appearance of the Genie, who so strongly resembles JB himself. The thirty volumes of tales that Scheherazade relates come back to us, finally, by way of Barth. As the Genie, he has the power, the imagination, and, ultimately, the narrative strategy. With this as given, we see how fiction has been turned self-consciously by Barth into the author's voice, almost literally—whether taped as in some pieces in *Lost in the Funhouse* or here orally transmitted.

Barth's Perseus is now middle-aged, fattening out, without any direction to his life, a 1960s loser. He is also henpecked by a wife who is interested in liberation—she needs space in which to breathe and develop; and the women he meets are also independent. His days as hero are finished; by forty, most mythical heroes have had it anyway. The Perseus we meet is all memory, almost impotent, in what he thinks is heaven, with the boylike Calyxa. His adventures and antics are now embedded deep in memory and recalled by a panel of his deeds, a mural of Perseiditis, as it were. By reviewing the panel, he can recall the deeds, the order, the way in which Perseus became a legend that lasts "longer than men."

The Perseus story gives Barth the spiral-like frame against which he can measure words, actions, contemporary deeds. His Perseus is transformed into an oral tradition, as he explicates his past to Calyxa. Adventure is turned back upon itself and revealed as words: panels in "Perseid" have much the same fictional weight as film in *Letters*. It is the "echo of an echo," the reflector which permits events to be changed into reflections. The nub of the thing remains out of sight; all we have, as in the reflection of the shield which protects Perseus when he slays Medusa, is that reflection. Words cannot retrieve the thing, only the memory, which becomes the substitute for the thing itself. Barth's Perseus, therefore, is not the mythical or legendary hero, but a ceaseless talker, a worrier about his own misfortunes, a cuckolded husband who desires revenge on his torturers, a man whose inner life does not begin to match the achievements of his outer life.

The basic story is the familiar one of the man programmed to enter a salvation myth, a man whose grandfather puts him out to die, since the oracle indicates death will come by way of the grandson. First, Acrisius tries to close up his daughter, Danaë, in an enclosure made of brass or stone; but Zeus visits her, impregnates her by way of a shower of gold, and the result is Perseus. The latter is, therefore, the golden one, often referred to as *aurigena.* Acrisius then puts mother and son in a chest and throws them into the sea, but Zeus once again arranges to save them. The king of the country where they are washed ashore falls in love with Danaë, and tries to get rid of Perseus, who has, by now, grown up. He sends Perseus to gain the head of Medusa, one of the Gorgons. Protected and guided by Hermes and Athene, Perseus gathers the necessary articles for survival against Medusa's petrifying glance. The key article is the shield which enable Perseus to observe Medusa without a direct look, which would have turned him to stone. The helmet he wears makes him invisible when the two other Gorgons chase him.

Having been saved, Perseus now saves. He heads for Ethiopia and rescues Andromeda, who is chained to a rock because of Poseidon's jealousy. In saving Andromeda, whom he later marries, Perseus also saves the country from a sea monster, which is devastating the countryside. Perseus must also rescue his mother from the violence of Polydectes, the king who sent him for Medusa's head. The legend is completed when the oracle becomes fact: Perseus, taking part in public games, heaves the discus, which strikes and kills his grandfather. Perseus now has fulfilled every event he was programmed for, and the rest is middle age.

With glory behind him, even sex for Perseus is part of memory. His most glorious memory, in fact, is of Medusa, about whom he has always felt guilty. In Barth's telling, Medusa is revived, and Perseus finds refuge with her, for only she can understand his tale. Perseus becomes an acute, self-conscious observer of his own acts. As he tells Medusa, "It wasn't you who discovered your beauty to me, but I who finally unveiled it to myself." Perseus finds himself reflected in her eyes in two ways: as "a reasonably healthy, no-longer-heroic mortal with more than half his life behind him, less potent and less proud than he was at twenty but still vigorous," and as stars that suggest "blinding love, which transfigured everything in view." Perseus is not in heaven, as he had thought, but in a seashell-like temple: back in the sea, despite his being a constellation which showers meteors.

We are now deep inside Barth's myth-making, his taking the old myth apart, reversing it so as to derive its storytelling qualities, and then recreating it as a contemporary myth of the ordinary. *Letters* was to be the next project when Barth began to spin out these tales; and indeed, the tales are "oral equivalents" of the "writing surges" (transformed orality) which characterizes *Letters.*

Perseus is now relegated to words; and yet through words he can find rejuvenation. In "Bellerophoniad," the final novella in *Chimera,* Barth will speak of one's being transformed into the story of one's life: "I wonder how many voices are telling my tale. It seems to me that upon my first being transformed into the story of my life, at best a sorely qualified immortality, the narrative voice was clear and objective." As he comments, Perseus is caught in a narrative dualism: while addressing the reader from heaven (where he is a constellation), he most immediately tells his story to his mistress Calyxa in Egypt; and that retelling is for him a way of discovery. In the process, he has discovered the fountain of youth now lost to him in middle age, and has opened up potentialities of renewal. He is being recycled by his own words. We can see how the principle of *Letters* is already at work: reappearance as an act of recreation.

If not for the retelling, Perseus would be fixed in the heavens, without freedom, except as a constellation. By way of the tale and the outpouring of talk, he can move beyond recapitulation to renewal, can reenter his life, hitherto denied him by immortality. Time itself is at stake. When Perseus explicates the panels Calyxa displays, he perceives that he is covering his life in such rapid moves that days will replace years. The time shift between panel and tale is equivalent to that involved in any fictional handling of an event or a series of events. Perseus worries about coming to an end: "What I meant, I explained when we [he and Calyxa] returned to bed, was that given on the one hand my rate of exposition, as it were—one mural per day—and on the other the much rapider time-passage between the scenes themselves, we had in six days rehearsed my life from its gold-showered incept to the nearly last thing I remembered. It followed that soon—any day now, perhaps—the marmor history must arrive at the point of my death and overtake my present transfiguration."

Caught up in the possibilities of his own tale, like the spider spinning out its web and finding itself almost snared in the silken threads, Perseus wonders if he is entrapped. What once seemed like immortality is now rapidly approaching the end of all things: his life and the climax of his tale, himself and words. But he has been placed by Barth in a spiral, and Perseus speculates that perhaps his life will approximate the inward turn of the spiral "and forever approach the present point but never reach it. . . . the story might be presumed to be endless."

Perseus's return to the living, as it were, derives from a revived Medusa, who still loves him. The resurrection of the dead—Medusa has been "scalped, rebodied, and revived" by Athene—is of course basic to the conceit of *Letters;* and Barth's discovery, in 1969, of the method that would nourish that massive novel was a perception leading to great personal triumph. For he had an insight into his own career, finding the absolutely correct movement along the axis of his own development.

His sense of the sixties is very firm, for he feels middle age, is outgrowing his first wife, is being pumped up by a different set of juices; the individual (Barth?) must take the opportunity to move on, that is, recycle, or declare himself dead. The entire culture of the sixties, which Barth ridicules in both *Giles* and *Letters* as either pretentious or mad, is really integral to his work, verbally parodied but intensely there. Barth agrees: growth derives from the death of something.

Perseus has his opportunity with the revived Medusa. Athene has withheld some vital information: whether Medusa still has her withering glance. She is allowed a "one-shot glance," and if the man whom she gazes on is her true lover, then both will become "ageless as the stars and be together forever." But she does not know if she is still a Gorgon, and her glance —intended as love—may petrify. The man who uncowls and kisses her must chance either immortality or petrification. The choices of the 1960s are at hand for Perseus: safety or bliss, control or chance, bourgeois immortality or Parnassian contingency. By choosing Medusa, Perseus can reclaim his youth; Calyxa brightly tells him he wants to be twenty again. Reliving his life, Perseus can redirect it, and his entrance into sensation will be Medusa.

By the time of *Chimera,* women are keys to everything, and with *Letters,* so strong is the need for female clarification that Barth invented a new character, Lady Amherst, and gave her the broadest presence in the correspondence. Barth's women, like Bellow's, fit extreme roles: as either fatal temptresses or sex kittens. One reason mythical women fitted so well into Barth's work in *Chimera* is that such extremes were ready-made. The women could be, on one hand, tricksters (Doony or Sherry), or Gorgons (Medusa), or Andromeda (seeking a middle-aged life change); on the other hand, the adulteresses and sex kittens of "Bellerophoniad." In Lady Amherst, Barth's most considerable invention of this period, we find a new stage or mutation: a woman of considerable accomplishments who puts herself at the disposal of Ambrose Mensch, who uses her, wants her (at fifty) to bear his child, and cheats on her openly. A feminist

in some respects, Lady Amherst defers to the man she loves, waits out his excesses, and considers herself lucky to gain him in marriage. The pattern begun with *Chimera* continues: Lady Amherst is the sex kitten, not the trickster; the Penelope who allows her Odysseus to wander.

Except for *Letters,* which this novella interrupted, "Bellerophoniad" is the most self-conscious of Barth's fictions. It is, in fact, so self-reflexive that Barth cannot avoid interrupting it with segments of *Letters*—bits and pieces which must have seemed opaque to readers who did not enjoy the knowledge of a book published several years later. In one way, Barth is torturing the reader with Barth, creating that Barthean cyclical universe in which the various forms of heroism and mythology are transferred to the writer, who then must convey his methods, although not transparently, to the reader. The way in which Barth can overcome the difficulty of having Bellerophon speak directly to the reader, while at the same time confusing his tale with Barth's self-conscious techniques, is to cast the novella in the form of a bundle of letters floating in a Maryland marsh: "Loosed at last from mortal speech, he turned into written words: Bellerophon letters afloat between two worlds, forever betraying, in combinations and recombinations, the man they forever represent."

Bellerophon is, in one guise, a man who had a glorious career that went up like a burst, as he rode Pegasus to victory after victory, but who is now "shot down," suffering "hero's block," so to speak, as Barth explains his own writer's block. Bellerophon is the writer who enjoyed success in an earlier phase and is now old and forgotten, lame and even blind, a seer without the seer's powers. Having failed as a hero— Bellerophon thinks of himself as a failure—he has returned to Barth's own grounds; his presence in letters foreshadows *Letters,* and in fact, several items of those later *Letters* are included. Part of Bellerophon's difficulty as a hero is that he is doomed to repetition. Through his persona, Barth admits storytelling is not "his cup of wine . . . my plot doesn't rise and fall in meaningful stages but winds upon itself like a whelk-shell or the snakes on Hermes's caduceus: digresses, retreats, hesitates, groans from its utter et cetera, collapses, dies."

The Barth retelling of the Robert Graves retelling of the mythical story is one series of "spirals" after another, tales within tales: Bellerophon telling the reader what he once told his mistress Melanippe, the Amazon he captured; what he told of his earlier life to his wife, Philonoë; then what he will tell of his life to his children and to students at Lycian University. The arrangement, as far as we have gone, suggests the patterns of *Letters,* where historical detail, events, personages, heroic or villainous acts, all forms of data are turned into correspondence, bounded stories that can be told, retold, cross-referred, speculated about in words. But in "Bellerophoniad," Barth moves us along even further, and suggests that Bellerophon is not a true mythical hero but an imitation acting out his life as if it were true. Barth simply keeps tightening the narrative screw, giving us another twist of the writer's potential in turning a persona from his own life to the fiction of his life.

Bellerophon's wife, a student of mythology, expresses some of the fictional potential: "I quite understand . . . that the very concept of objective truth, especially as regards the historical past, is problematical; also that narrative art, particularly of the mythopoeic or at least mythographic variety, has structures and rhythms, values and demands, not the same as those of reportage or historiography. Finally, as between variants among myths themselves, it's in their contradictions that one may seek their sense." Barth's use of the seer Polyeidus as a wild-card joker, taking on any number of roles and shapes, places him inside the tale, seer analogous to author. With his protean improbabilities, Polyeidus allows Barth time changes, space switches, foresight. It even permits Bellerophon to "write letters" in an era before writing; and it allows Polyeidus to recover Napoleonic material from the distant future for purposes of comparison and contrast.

Even more, Polyeidus gave Barth the equivalent of a magic wand. Polyeidus can be everywhere: he is the document called "Perseid," as well as the explanation in twenty-two steps of the mythic hero we find in Lord Raglan and in Joseph Campbell. Polyeidus has turned Bellerophon himself into a document. Carrying the conceit further, Barth has made it possible for Polyeidus to both carry messages and be the message.

In another respect, the seer, one of Barth's most fruitful experiments, serves the function here that the computer served in *Giles* and that letters will come to serve in *Letters.* By way of Polyeidus, Bellerophon becomes not only a document but an imitation of someone playing the role of Bellerophon; while that may seem tricky, even deceptive, for the reader, it does approximate the fictional dimension of any tale retold. For any character who supposedly has a fictional life becomes "dead" on the page, part of words. The words *are* the character; the document

is his life. Bellerophon can exist only by retelling his story, within other stories; and he exists only because people listen to him. Poor Bellerophon! He has been so associated with the Chimera that the tripartite monster has rubbed off on him. He may not even have killed it, for if his life is a counterfeit, a sequence of tales rather than an actuality, then all his deeds might have been imagined. If he is a character in a tale conceived of by Polyeidus, then we have no salient reasons for believing his assertions.

Barth has, as it were, turned the hero into a truly "mythic" creature by mythicizing the myth: turning it into something we can believe only by suspending our judgment, and even questioning the nature of the reality the myth is supposed to explain. Polyeidus was also the "Perseid," but he allowed Perseus some independent existence; with Bellerophon, he has made the mythic creature into a forgery. When Bellerophon laments he is a middle-aged failure—like Perseus, doomed to tell and retell his story in order to resurrect his deeds—he is in one sense entirely correct; for he owes everything to the seer who has undermined his every act. He is not even certain he is Bellerophon, for he may be his brother, the one he has accidentally killed—or did he?

The main cultural implications of Barth's choice of narration are acute. He has, in many senses, joined with Gaddis's vision of the counterfeit and with Pynchon's presentation of stenciling, deception, conspiracies within conspiracies. As much as they, Barth has discovered technical means for concealment, forgery, imitation, by exploring the fictional labyrinth and exploiting the potentialities of narrative. Gaddis, Pynchon, and Barth have become a cyclical trio: Gaddis in the mid-fifties with *The Recognitions,* then Pynchon with *V.* in the early sixties, Barth with *Giles Goat-Boy* in the mid-sixties, Pynchon with *Gravity's Rainbow* in the early seventies, Gaddis with *JR* in the mid-seventies, and now Barth intertwining with *Chimera* and, in the later seventies, with *Letters.* Each novel is a capstone of previous efforts; each, with faults, warts, and terrible excesses, is larger than nearly anything else in American fiction.

Culturally, they are all exploring what remains in the largest sense unexplorable and inexplicable. They are, through literary techniques, attempting to penetrate into cultural diversities that underlie innumerable subcultures. What has steadily characterized American culture since the 1950s has been the proliferation of subcultures, the replacement of any main culture (or idea of it) by alternative modes which drift off from main lines. The country can no longer be defined in terms of major developments; rather, it can be comprehended only in stages, episodes, spirals (to use Barth's favorite literary conceit), or individual "letters"—missives found here and there, correspondence sent out or not in the hope of an answer (Herzog's unmailed letters). Gaddis sees in this proliferation of subcultures endless varieties of forgery and counterfeiting; Pynchon perceives in it an infinitude of imitations, the flattening out of individual life approximating, in the physical world, the process of running down. Barth partakes of both, granting authenticity nowhere, observing imitations in even our holiest texts (our myths and legends), perceiving the counterfeit in every act of history (especially the War of 1812), so that history itself becomes a fiction which can, or cannot, be turned back into history.

These are not just deep social and political statements, but broad cultural reflections: Barth's sense of echoes, his transmission of information as reenactments, as recycled materials which move, spiral-like, nowhere, except back to beginnings. *The reason Barth cannot tell a story straightforwardly anymore is not that every story has already been told—as Borges has asserted—but that every story has become sidetracked by the claims made upon it.* The story no longer has meanings in traditional senses; it has meanings in its diversities, in its marginalities. We must, therefore, seek the teller of the tale as much as the tale, for the teller has altered our perception. If the teller thinks he is Bellerophon, but is not; if the mediator is a seer who can locate himself as both narrator and tale; if the material related may or may not be actual—then all is an act of perception. Like modern physics, the Heisenberg principle of uncertainty, we slide from absolutes. All is questionable.

BACK TO *LETTERS*

Barth, then, becomes an anagram. His life, work, development, progress, failures are to be mined. He is the ultimate document, the maker and conceiver of all seven characters, all eighty-eight letters, every detail of the anagrams and calendars. His novel is, further, a huge historical datum, for every date in his 1969 calendar, from March through September, has detailed relationships to these dates in the past. If the text or documentation of the novel is six characters (plus Barth) in search of an author, the documents are also deeply embedded in history. Literary figures as well as historical personages move in and out of the characters' lives; and since Lady Amherst's back-

ground, together with Jerome Bray's, involves real historical figures, among them Napoleon, we are thrust backward as much as forward.

Barth's recounting of one dream, on March 9, 1969, the 157th anniversary of President Madison's "disclosure of the notorious 'Henry Letters' to Congress in 1811," illustrates the knotty method. Such history, Madison or otherwise, is constantly paralleling, replacing, substituting for, elements of personal history, all intermixed with the history of Barth's characters. The megalomaniacal desire for control, of one's own work as well as of the historical world, is caught in the following passage:

Just as Eben Cooke put aside his *Marylandiad* to write *The Sot-Weed Factor*—and the "editor" of *Giles Goat-Boy* put aside his novel *The Seeker* to edit *The Revised New Syllabus,* and J. Bray's LILYVAC computer put aside its *Concordance* to propose the revolutionary novel NOTES—so I put aside, in 1968, in Buffalo, a *Marylandiad* of my own in favor of the novel LETTERS, whereof Mensch's *Perseid* and Bray's *Bellerophoniad* were to be tales-within-the-tale. Then, in '69, '70, and '71, I put by LETTERS in pursuit of a new chimera called *Chimera:* serial novellas about Perseus, Bellerophon, and Scheherazade's younger sister. Now (having put by Buffalo for Baltimore) it's back to LETTERS, to history, to "realism" . . . and to the revisitation of a certain marsh where once I wandered, dozed, dreamed.

Unlike Richardson, Barth uses letters and characters as ways of commenting on fiction; not, as in the eighteenth century, as a way of displaying female behavior under testing. Richardson's aim is to have Clarissa triumph over Lovelace on moral grounds, when in any other area of competition (lineage, family, fortune) she might have lost. Barth is not concerned with such matters, for his letters do not help to create characters so much as resurrect them. And his characters are clearly fictional elements, reminding us and themselves that they are playing at being real, even while they insist on self-identification. Barth *is* concerned, as we have observed in *Giles,* with systems: how people define themselves as part of a system, then how, with equal fervor, they attempt to evade that system. Part of the historical resonance of *Letters*—for example, the stress on the War of 1812—is to put the weight of the past on every present activity. The War of 1812, although remote, and not much of a war as wars go, may well be the major clue to American history, the linchpin in our understanding of ourselves as a nation and as individuals. Yet that war is only one aspect of the "systems" or histories which pull at us.

As part of Barth's vision is that counterpulling of individual against what weighs him down: history, systems, dates themselves. To pull free of systems is to assert individuality and freedom—as Giles the Goat-Boy must do, or else the WESVAC computer wins by default. Whatever we fail to throw ourselves against in the Barthian world—whether computer, history, or even the darker side of our own selves—will pull away to conquer. To prevent that default, we must always be ready to surmount our desire for acquiescence. Henry Burlingame, the *Sot-Weed* character whose descendant returns in *Letters,* is the prototypical figure here; the protean man appearing in guises and disguises, reshaping himself, able to defy systems or fate. Giles is another such figure, moving between animal and human world so as not to be identified with systemic elements.

Concealed deep in the epistolary texts are intimations of other worlds. Although one must keep changing for survival—that is, play with the world and its activities as if each element as met is the sole obstacle—there are counterforces or concealed devices which make change almost impossible. Such human efforts to break free into a noncausal, nondetermined universe, a Wittgensteinian world of discrete experiences and events, are all partially doomed. Early in *Letters,* Barth quotes and requotes the Latin *Praeteritas futuras stercorant*—"the past fertilizes the future." Barth translates this differently each time, as "the past turns the future into shit" or "manures the future," etc. The motif is apt; for it accommodates the Barthian universe, and it brings together his human and literary efforts.

For that sense of past beshitting future is at the heart of Barth's literary beliefs, as well as his static sense of human activity. He is basically a static writer—despite shapings and reshapings, devilish literary devices and tricks—because he seems struck by the futility of change even as he perceives need for it. Whatever the reader may make of his two difficult texts, he is such an excellent guide for the 1960s and 1970s because while he picks up on our sense of liberation, he refuses to accept it as definitive. *Letters,* which appears so modish, is an expression of profound countercultural passions. It helps negate the very freedom Barth himself may yearn for, for such notions of freedom go against the nature of character (and characters). All that remains, in Barth's formulation, is old characters attempting to redefine themselves, refusing previous roles; and yet still caught in new systems, new histories, new roles as limiting as former ones.

Wittgenstein makes the act of will and the cause of whatever ensues comparable: "The act of the will is not the cause of the action but is the action itself." This is a concomitant of "The will is an attitude of the subject to the world." One cannot will without acting, and if one needs an object in the world, then it can be the intended action. Things exist discretely. Whatever is, is created by an individual will bringing it into existence. Barth holds to this almost obsessively, and then must counter it with his sense, defined in his essays and interviews, that literarily all has been defined. There is little room for such will, only for rearrangements.

The Barthian world, then, becomes one of desperate rearrangements. A passage from Ortega y Gasset's *The Dehumanization of Art* is instructive, for the entire argument in these linked essays can be viewed as reviling the kind of novel Barth would come to write. Ortega poses a conceit, of an observer peering through glass at the scene beyond, a garden. "The clearer the glass is, the less (of the glass) we will see. But then making an effort we may withdraw attention from the garden; and by retracting the ocular ray, we may fixate it upon the glass."

By forsaking the glass, we see the reality beyond; by forsaking the reality beyond, we can see the glass—which Ortega identifies with the art object when we look at it and try not to see beyond it to the "other." As soon as we move toward that other, we make believe the glass is not there. Consequently, glass and "beyond" are incompatible. Most observers do, in fact, forsake the glass in order to "wallow in the human reality," as Ortega puts it. Barth, however, tries to play a double game, by fitting himself into the interstices of Ortega's argument: offering both glass and "beyond" for our perusal, refusing the selection of one or the other. Bellow, for example, clearly chooses the "beyond"; as do Roth, Styron, Updike, Malamud, Percy. On the other hand, Pynchon, Gaddis, Hawkes, McElroy, as well as Barth, find themselves caught: while incapable of forgoing the garden, they desperately want us to see the glass.

The complications are formidable. An author who attempts both glass *and* beyond will find himself in a Wittgensteinian world of possibility. Elements in fiction are connected by way of what one sees in the beyond; they are disconnected if one attempts to see the medium by which the beyond is observed. By attempting to see both, the novelist may fall into what Robert Scholes calls fabulation, or else he may simply become a distortionist, concerned with how glass refracts as well as with what it reveals if one looks straight through it. Wittgensteinian possibility derives from disconnectedness of elements, and that comes when one wants more than the beyond. If one chooses disconnectedness, despite contrary pressure from the culture, then one is thrust into a different verbal universe, where I locate a novel such as *Letters,* or, in different contexts, *JR, Gravity's Rainbow,* part of *The Recognitions, Giles Goat-Boy,* Burroughs's and Hawkes's early fiction, McElroy's *Hind's Kidnap* and *Lookout Cartridge.*

The recurring passages on the War of 1812, which are enfolded in *Letters* as a leitmotif, are Barth's way of focusing on the glass. The war, although murky for the reader, is a way by which one can read America. Beginning one-seventh into the novel, the ancestor of Ebenezer Cooke of *The Sot-Weed Factor,* one A. B. Cooke IV, writes two very long letters to his unborn child (Henrietta or Henry) about his heritage. The first of these letters is dated 2 April 1812, the second 9 April 1812; and while they relate the unborn child's background in Cookes and Burlingames, with a side look at Castine (who will figure in Lady Amherst's own personal history), the real thread running through is American history leading up to the War of 1812, when the letters are being written. The 1812 repetition is a code of sorts, very possibly a commentary on the Vietnam War, which was ongoing when Barth was writing *Letters.* Compare 1969 and 1812: the latter as our world, with its misunderstandings and confusions, as much as the former, which *is* our world.

THE SOT-WEED FACTOR

Behind all the artifice and contrivance of *The Sot-Weed Factor* (written 1956–59) are themes familiar from Barth's two earlier novels, *The Floating Opera* and *The End of the Road.* He may have contrived a style from the eighteenth century to say something about the late seventeenth century, but he has, nevertheless, written a novel based on the 1950s. At one time, perhaps carelessly, he referred to the novel as an allegory; and it is, indeed, at one level an allegory of the 1950s. The politics of Maryland, which will be the source of Ebenezer Cooke's crowning achievement, are very close to those of Washington in the fifties; and Cooke's journey from innocence to experience is

close to what Americans would undergo in their journey from 1940s optimism to 1950s realities. The allegory is an American story, full of Barthian choices, Mythotherapy, Scriptotherapy, cosmic dimensionality, et al. It is as much a part of the counterfeit decade as *The Recognitions,* not only in its political implications but in its assumptions about individual behavior.

Barth has written a gloss on the fifties from the vantage point of a young man coming of age, Huck Finn, Holden Caulfield, the virgin(al) American: location Maryland, politics based on deceit, personal behavior based on choices which prove destructive, key image one of disguise, dissembling. Primarily, we carry away from *The Sot-Weed Factor* the sense of role-playing, most dramatically so on the voyage to Maryland aboard the *Poseidon,* with Ebenezer Cooke, the master and laureate, playing servant to his own servant, Bertrand, who plays the role of poet and master. The reversal of roles, as in Genet's *The Maids,* is a constant throughout; so that the individual is not only choosing a way to pin down his identity, he is choosing an identity in order to determine the course of his life.

Assumption of disguises in order to achieve an identity has its obverse side. Disguises, masks, concealment, can undermine even as they confer distinction. Like Moll Flanders, Cooke becomes increasingly what the external world demands. All energy is concentrated on the role rather than on the unraveling of one's destiny. Moll shows little or no interest in whatever does not directly concern her (survival is all), and Cooke commits acts antithetical to himself because his particular roles call for such behavior. The protean character survives because of his or her ability to shift roles, but the character also loses definition. The satirical mode cannot disguise that.

Cooke is only one role-player, and the episode on the *Poseidon* is only one episode. Ebenezer plays the role of others almost to the novel's end, not only as Bertrand, but as the servant of Cooke, his bitter enemy, and as others (Sir Benjamin Oliver and Edward Cooke). But his real teacher in role-playing is his former tutor, Henry Burlingame 3rd, who acts out nearly everyone in the novel, including Eben himself. Burlingame is a consummate actor in his own drama. He is the ultimate narcissist, which is what role-playing is about, since all disguises lead back to self: Burlingame as Coode, Peter Sayer, Lord Baltimore, Bertrand Burton, Governor Nicholson, Cooke himself, besides minor characters. Sexual encounters are profoundly affected by imitation. Whenever Eben, the fierce virgin, is close to a sexual encounter, it is with Joan Toast, the prostitute; but he never gains *her,* only someone like her in disguise.

Even the title of the book, which is also the title of Eben's poem, is shrouded by ambiguities and roles. This is fitting for a narrative itself always reshaping: counterfeit and actuality so interchanged one feels one is in a dream sequence, a "floating opera" rather than anything as realistic as parody of the eighteenth-century novel. The title refers to a merchant of "sot-weed," or tobacco, someone who sells or factors it. But "factor" can also mean a point of circumstance, the influence of "sot-weed" on this or that. A "factor" may, additionally, be a maker of things, a manufacturer. Factoring, further, reduces or increases something mathematically by way of its functions. Thus, by factoring, one has elements which when multiplied provide the product. A factor here is elements or components, parts of the whole: that is, the disguises which eventually add up to the full person, the pieces which must be brought together. There is a still further function, that of the factotum, the person who performs all jobs, someone who role-shifts as necessity demands. The "sot" in the sot-weed helps create this crazy jumble, a besotted factor, a term which fits well into the drug-induced experience of 1950s Beats.

The pattern of disguise and divulgation demonstrates that *The Sot-Weed Factor* is only superficially related to the picaresque narrative of the eighteenth century. It is more substantially connected to the "fool" narratives that we associate with *Don Quixote, Simplissimus, The Idiot, The Good Soldier Schweik,* looking ahead, in its strange fashion, to *Catch-22.* In itself, it clearly defines, as we have suggested, an area of the 1950s concerned with deception and ideological confusion. Eben feeds into this mix his own sense of values, based on virginity and poetry-making, very clearly the opposite of Tom Jones, for whom poetry is alien and virginity is to be shunned. Eben does share something with Tom, however, in his involvement in what Northrop Frye calls the "birth-mystery plot." But such a plot is concerned with Burlingame's attempt to discover his ancestors, and Eben is part of it only to the extent that his fortunes depend on his former tutor.

Eben's withdrawal from sex unless love is involved is a source of ridicule, even though his stated values depend on a purity of self.* But that negation of sex,

while it feeds into his sense of his mission as a poet laureate, as a priest devoted to his craft, is associated with his lack of identity. Barth writes: "Ebenezer was yet a virgin, and this for the reason explained in the previous chapters, that he was no person at all." As long as Eben remains a virgin, he has no self, and he must work at mythotherapy, the role-playing necessary for persons who have to adapt themselves to shifting situations. That lack of sexual identification means that Eben, having taken on so many selves other than his own, is submerged in theirs, is more persona than person. It is part of Barth's method, as well as the brilliance of his execution (despite tedious stretches which try even the committed reader), that in such a long novel he can connect different elements, making each a conduit for another. The picaresque episodic narrative does not hinder the cohesion of parts, since all depends on an ideology running parallel to what we know of the 1950s. That is best expressed in the scene between Eben and Sayer (really Henry Burlingame in one of his guises): " 'Ye can never know [Sayer says], especially in Maryland, where friends may change their colors like tree frogs. Why do ye know, the barrister Bob Goldsborough of Talbot, my friend and neighbor for years, deposed against me to Governor Copley? The last man I'd have thought a turncoat!' "

This allegory of Washington and, by extension, the country perhaps explains the tedious insert on the history of Maryland (in Chapter 10). Possibly the only way to read this mishmash of incidents, deceptions, historical detail (all apparently culled from the *Archives of Maryland* as well as from Lawrence Wroth's biography of Cooke), is to see it as a potpourri with reference to Washington or the country. Then what we read is not really history but a comic record of human duplicity, in which only a long poem, Cooke's projected *Marylandiad,* will have a semblance of truth.

Such a characterization, of insane infusing normal, occurs in the voyage over on the *Poseidon.* Eben is about to be buggered, as an initiation of sorts, when a pirate shallop comes alongside and seamen board the ship. Intermixed in this is Eben's desire to get hold of a historical document which he thinks will provide Burlingame's background, *A Secret Historie of the Voiage up the Bay of Chesapeake;* the secret diary of Captain John Smith, it is also much wanted

---

*All of Barth's major characters up to this point suffer from sexual malfunctions (Todd Andrews's infected prostate and bouts of impotence, Jacob Horner's indifference) or from a malaise. Although his characters run the range of sexual expression, I sense he is unclear as to how sex can be used fictionally beyond simply a personal outlet.

by Lord Baltimore, whose delegate Eben is. As the external action intensifies, the internal machinery heats up; Barth's method, in fact, is to speed up externals so as to make internal events seem even more subversive and confused. We find something similar in Pynchon, that working within and without, so that intensification of conspiracy outside creates internal cells even more arcane. In the given situation, Eben's life was already in danger, even while he was still playing the role of servant to his servant, Bertrand. The pirates pose another threat, and Eben's efforts to get hold of the diary will further expose him to a violent end.

But then still a further development builds upon the existing complications. The *Cyprian,* a whore ship, full of women coming over to America for a six-month stint as prostitutes, pulls alongside, not knowing pirates have commandeered the *Poseidon.* A fearful scene ensues, Bosch's vision of hell. In a mass rape, the pirates violate and brutalize the women, including one pursued by the barbaric mate Boabdil. "In the moonlight, from the present distance, she bore some slight resemblance to Joan Toast, the recollection of whom had fired his [Eben's] original desire." The scene is hallucinatory, since Joan is Eben's "Beatrice," the whore whom he has refused, whom he hopes to purify with his love. Her reappearance in several guises stresses Eben's attitude toward his virginity, and by extension toward his mission as laureate; at the same time, it allows Barth to move in and out of fantasy without losing his hold on reality. Intermixed with this Boschean scene on the deck of the *Cyprian* is Eben's discovery of Captain Meech's portion of the John Smith diary, with its clues to Burlingame's background.

The scene ends with Cooke and Bertrand Burton walking the plank, only to find themselves in a few feet of water. But the significance of the previous segment, one of the most forceful in the novel, depends on Barth's mixture of elements: that confusion of the senses intermixed with straightforward narrative which pulls the story along even as it is interrupted. Fantasy becomes permeated by reality, or the other way around. Visions of Joan Toast float in and out of Eben's vision, as she flees Boabdil's evil; and Eben is himself caught in something that can destroy him, the manuscript which will divulge Burlingame's ancestry.

Innocence hovers on the edge of betrayal—Eben almost "lets go" and rapes his Joan—and man's desire for harmony is counteracted by Darwinian struggle and chance. Man struggles, says Burlingame, against elements he can never comprehend. As he tells Eben when the latter wonders who he is and where he stands: " 'What is't you describe, my friend, if not man's lot? He is by mindless lust engendered and by mindless wrench expelled, from the Eden of the womb to the motley, mindless world. He is Chance's fool, the toy of aimless Nature—a mayfly flitting down the winds of Chaos!' " The juxtaposition here of Henry's cynical realism and Eben's desire for knowing himself and his mission is, once more, prototypical of the American fifties: that sense of chance having claimed us once again even as we hurtled along in what we thought would be meaningful choices.

Despite his resolution to devote himself to his great epic poem of Maryland, Eben compromises at every stage: the epic of Maryland becomes the eventual *Sot-Weed Factor,* a cynical diatribe. Among other things, he marries the syphilitic Susan Warren; he ineptly loses Malden, at Cooke's Point, the ancestral home; he finds himself indentured to the man who gains Cooke's Point; he prostitutes his wife to gain money for the passage out; he sees Malden turned into an opium den. As he moves toward knowing about life and himself under the tutelage of Henry Burlingame, his tale becomes full of temporizing about the truth; so that we sense the parallelism to America's postwar passage as a whole.

As part of disguises and role-playing, there is a Kafkaesque dimension at the edges. People who are of the greatest significance remain invisible, or have a questionable existence. This ploy becomes evident when Burlingame reminds Eben that neither of them has seen Lord Baltimore. Eben received his commission from Baltimore, he thought, but it turned out to be Burlingame; and the latter admits: " 'I ne'er have met the man who hath seen John Coode face to face, nor, despite his fame and influence and the great trust he hath placed in me, have I myself ever seen Lord Baltimore, any more than you have.' " All Burlingame's dealings with Baltimore have been, like K.'s with the Castle, through messengers. Eben's former tutor, in fact, has given up all hope of ever seeing Baltimore and has concentrated his energies on seeking out John Coode—if *he* exists, if he is not Baltimore.

Besides the split between those who act and those who direct, there is the preponderance of conspiracies, several of which reinforce the Kafkaesque atmosphere. The journey of Eben from innocence to experience comes not only in his compromising of his own intentions but in his growing awareness of conspiracies, which preempt all action and planning. In the circular world of conspiracy, Burlingame is the key figure, and Eben is never quite certain of his former tutor's role. Further, Captain Mitchell may well be Coode's functionary, and Coode may be Baltimore's —if the latter two exist. Or else Mitchell may be calling the turns, so as to gain access to Cooke's Point, an essential element in his empire-building. All of the above can, also, be Burlingame, who is not Tim Mitchell, as we know, but may be Coode, as Bertrand informs the horrified Eben. The entire conspiracy, which may not even be a conspiracy, is masterminded by Burlingame or by his personae.

As part of this process of "recognitions," Eben comes to see what counterfeit values he has lived by; or else, how his values, once thrown into the hopper of human experience, are not different from counterfeit values. The Barth novel reaches for a certain grandeur here, comparable in some ways to Don Quixote's recognitions in the second part of the Cervantes novel, especially when he counsels Pancho that each must honor the other's secrets. As Eben delves into Burlingame's background, he finds an increasing ambiguity; for Burlingame is the son of a savage, Chicamec, and is a partaker of the dual worlds of English gentleman and American savage, old and new, civilized and primitive. And he is not alone, but has two brothers, one (Mattassin) a murderer, now dead, the other (Cohunkowprets) more savage than civilized. The family trait for this savage race is a dwarfed penis which makes normal intercourse almost impossible. Barth has his fraternity joke: the primitive man with his intense sexuality has a member that is almost sexually dysfunctional.

In this inordinately long novel, with longueurs and compelling sections of about equal stress, Barth attempts to aid the reader by frequent recapitulations, in the epic manner. These summaries usually take the form of Eben's telling his story to some new character. But unlike the epic form of narrative summation, Barth's method allows Eben to reshape his summary according to his gained insights. Although Barth does not appear fully aware of the potentialities of this method—some of Eben's retelling is rather casual— the recapitulations do permit him to bring along his protagonist without actual authorial interference. The method is ingenious and has affinities to some of the technical experimentation we find in early Hawkes or in McElroy, or in Robbe-Grillet and Butor abroad. Chiefly, we are in the presence of a registering consciousness *as it perceives* the events that are themselves altering that consciousness.

Even Barth's experimentation with language, the attempt to reflect Shakespeare as much as the eighteenth century, is a response that finds parallels in the deliberate flatness and directness of the French writers. Barth has been accused of indulging an ornate prose, but rather than ornate it is clipped, almost epigrammatic in places. It is an attempt, only partially successful, admittedly, to create a language within a language: to forge a literary expression within the formed language, much as Robbe-Grillet in his "colorless" or "zero degree" prose attempted to register a different perception of objects.

Barth's forms of language—"wight," "rent," "'tis," "e'en," et al.—are not attempts to return to outmoded means of expression, but efforts to defamiliarize the familiar. One reason Barth is not always successful is that he offers too much abundance. He writes in waves of words—at such length, in any given scene, that we resist. Even for the careful reader, it is almost impossible not to skip, once the sense is clear. And with his frequent recapitulations, there is little chance to miss anything significant. It is as if Barth, by way of repetition, has taken into narrative account the reader's skipping of words and paragraphs.

Very possibly the recapitulations, repetitions, duplications, overlapping identities, paralleling of scenes and dialogues feed into that thematic presence as defined by the following exotic chapter heading, in Part III, "Malden Earned": "THE POET WONDERS WHETHER THE COURSE OF HUMAN HISTORY IS A PROGRESS, A DRAMA, A RETROGRESSION, A CYCLE, AN UNDULATION, A VORTEX, A RIGHT- OR LEFT-HANDED SPIRAL, A MERE CONTINUUM, OR WHAT HAVE YOU. CERTAIN EVIDENCE IS BROUGHT FORWARD, BUT OF AN AMBIGUOUS AND INCONCLUSIVE NATURE." One could add to the list: whether it is, perhaps, a shot of sperm, an act of nature which continues life and means no more than a combination of chemicals. A man who has attempted to remain pure, as Eben has, must wonder what the world is made of if it rejects his gift. Barth (through Ebenezer) mentions the legendary Ouida bird, which reputedly flew in "ever-diminishing circles until at the end he disappeared into his own fundament."

Barth, then, has shifted the Emersonian sense of innocence and nature. Writing amidst the woodsiness, forest areas, and mountains of the Penn State main campus, Barth no longer admits Adam can regain his innocence or be resurrected in the American Zion. The American in the 1950s is the Adam who *must* learn, whose sin derives from trying to avoid knowledge of self and role. In the Postscript, Barth argues that we all remake our past, and therefore it is valid for him to remake history, which is simply an "invention" on a larger scale of what we do on a smaller. ". . . we all invent our pasts, more or less, as we go along, at the dictates of Whim and Interest; the happenings of former times are a clay in the present moment that will-we, nill-we, the lot of us must sculpt." Not God but Man is the potter. Then Barth carves his most compelling monument: "Thus Being does make Positivists of us all."

What holds this enormous book together is a growth pattern in Eben that leads from his desire to write an idealistic *Marylandiad* to the actual historical writing of the cynical history of the colony in *The Sot-Weed Factor*.* The writing of that work, instead of the original one, parallels Eben's own advance. Although he retains his virginity until his marriage to Joan Toast, the dying whore, virginity has become not a weapon, as in medieval tradition, but a burden, as in the modern. Henry Burlingame has been a true tutor and guide. Implicit in the development of Eben is the discovery of Burlingame's background; for the piecing together of this past history will, in a sense, help complete Eben's awareness of himself as well as the details for his history of Maryland.

As Barth develops this point, a key detail in the first Burlingame's history is the way he and Captain John Smith avoid death at the Indians' hands. It is one of the weakest elements in the novel, and some of the ploys are extended sophomoric jokes. The Indian princess Pocahantas is noted for tough hymen that no man's penis can penetrate. And yet Smith's life, as well as Burlingame's, depends on such penetration. The Captain devises a huge eggplant, cut to shape and affixed to the groin, as the weapon—the way an invading army might fashion a battering ram to knock down defending walls. With this, he gains entrance, saves his life, and wins the affections of the princess. So goes the John Smith–Pocahantas story.

Burlingame's presence at this "egg-plant trick" reverberates to the grandson, the Burlingame line being noted for its tiny member. The wit of the novel lies elsewhere. Barth's energies flagged in many of the inset stories, but waxed in the prose itself, a clipped middle ground between affectation and epigrammatic appropriateness. The real value of the novel lies here, in that page-to-page prose; as well as in its placement

as an allegory of the immediate postwar years. In this respect, the 1950s are not some anomalous, eunuched years, full of accommodation and acceptance, but a decade filled with noisy negation, a refusal to bow easily. The 1960s, in turn, would be a period of virginity reconsidered, equivalent to Cooke's sequel to *The Sot-Weed Factor,* which he calls, in 1730, *Sot-Weed Redivus, or The Planter's Looking-Glass.* Barth would pick up the new sexuality in *Giles Goat-Boy.*

BACK TO *LETTERS*

Barth was attempting to provide the glass or medium as well as the beyond or garden. He perceives associational material everywhere, but, with Wittgenstein cautioning him, he refuses to make final connections. To insist on discrete particles of experience, to hint at their association, to draw back before final connections are made is to practice precisely what Ortega called the dehumanization of art, and what Barth and those like him see as forms of salvation for fiction. Disaster for the Spanish philosopher is salvation for the American Ahab.

But such dehumanization is only the beginning. Barth goes after elements with a vengeance, not only dehumanizing but catching the process in innumerable ways. One way is to film it. He makes the process seem a living one, by locating in his narratives characters who creep out of his books to insist on a life of their own. But then he circumvents the living process by putting it all on film: by making lives into filmed lives, he fixes them historically as well as visually. Reg Prinz, a rather raffish young man, has been engaged by Ambrose Mensch (of *Lost in the Funhouse*) to write a screenplay from Barth's fiction and to film it. Prinz is to turn everything into theater, including a student demonstration, which he takes over, directs, and films; then he removes all political content by transforming it into a historical act before it can become a contemporary one.

Operating against freedom in Barth, as we have suggested, is this sense of binding: the culture dehumanizes every human impulse, Barth argues, not he, the author. Mass cult operates as much as mid and high cult to transform everything into performance. Even his characters, struggling to escape their fictional fate and to establish their personal credentials, are conscious of severe limitations. No one breaks out, or for long. Part of the dryness and tediousness of the novel derives from this. Often the prose reflects the claustrophobia: paragraphs that portend playfulness die in the word or sentence. Writing, for

---

*The 1708 publication: *The Sot-weed factor: Or, a Voyage to Maryland. A Satyr.* In Burlesque Verse. By Eben. Cook, Gent.

example, about Reg Prinz ("Prince Regent"), Barth says: "One hears that he is scornful of esoteric, high-art cinema as unfaithful to the medium's popular roots, which however bore him. Political revolutions, he is said to have said, are passé, 'like marriage, divorce, families, professions, novels, cash, existential *Angst.*'" The passage purports to be witty, or should be, but the list is not, and the verbal twist of "is said to have said" misfires. Satire is deflated because the words flatten out conventionally. *Letters* may be Barth's *Ada,* but the language is not Nabokovian.

Lady Amherst, the one character not represented in Barth's earlier fiction, moves among his cast, sleeping with this one, flirting with another, roaming among friends' husbands, becoming the wild card or joker. When we meet her, she has been taking in Ambrose Mensch in multiple ways, and he is her current mate. As she says, she is not one to remain celibate for long. Her role, however, is not solely to provide convenient orifices for the men she favors but to furnish integument for the beehive; as cover for all, she serves as queen bee, consolidating their activities, making them all interplay. In her buzzing, a metaphor for incest is implied, even historically. Her one-time affair with André Castine, whose presence she sees everywhere, connects her to the past, since Castine of Castine's Hundred is interrelated with the Cook family, themselves descendants of Ebenezer Cooke and his twin sister, Anna. Since Burlingame fathered a child with Anna, and since this child has been passed off as Eben's and Joan Toast's, the development of the Burlingame-Cook(e) line involves a near incestuous connection; brought further along by André Castine's presence as an offshoot of a Castine-Burlingame-Cook(e) linkage. Thus, Lady Amherst, also known as Germaine G. Pitt (née Gordon), is located historically as well as contemporaneously, a catalyst for each layer of the novel.

Yet that is not all, for she is also a kind of incestuous figure in modern letters, having chalked up affairs with everyone from H. G. Wells (who seemed to have engaged an entire half-century of female volunteers) to modern writers such as D. H. Lawrence and Evelyn Waugh, whom, presumably, she meets at conferences. As a historian, the writer of elegant articles on eighteenth-century figures, life, and morals, Lady Amherst is herself caught in the incestuous politics of a third-rate state university in Maryland, where she serves as provost. Marshyhope is, in fact, a step up from what it was only seven years before, when it was Tidewater Technical College, having grown from a private vocational school with thirteen students to one that projects 50,000 by 1976. Like the university in *Giles,* this one recalls Barth's Penn State, an agricultural school with pretensions to more serious academic pursuits.

Lady Amherst is, demonstrably, overqualified for the job; but her role gives her access to the lines of power, mainly putting her in touch with the author and giving him the opportunity to lean on her as a character in his novel. She writes to him; he writes to her; Todd writes to his father (a suicide); Jacob Horner writes to himself; Jerome Bray writes to Todd; the author writes to all of them, they to him. The round robin, conceived of in the *Clarissa* pattern, is incestuous. By reviving his characters in one fictional mass, Barth is able to re-seduce them into his imagination, to re-present them as his various children, and to reorganize them along different familiar lines. To borrow Donald Barthelme's phrase, he has refused to play the Dead Father.

Barth traps them in the labyrinth of plots and plotting. He plays both Dedalus, who must devise the labyrinth, and Theseus, who must unravel it; he is also Minos, the king of Crete, husband of Pasiphaë, who orders the labyrinth. As we saw in *Chimera,* Barth has so enfolded his creation in plots, subplots, counterplots, plots subsumed in other plots, that the labyrinth has no entrances or exits, unless those at the beginning and ending of a letter. The method accommodates Barth's larger fictional plans, which are to mock plots and plotting while exploiting them. That circuitry fits well into his sense of literary exhaustion, in which the very weapons of exhaustion, here plot, can be used as a means of attack on that concept.

What contributes to unreadability of long sections of *Letters* is Barth's self-burlesquing, his unwillingness to forgo the last word. The play on false royalty, for example, is full of longueurs. Harrison Mack, with whom Lady Amherst has a twilight affair, conceives of himself as George III, who was mad some of the time, and whose shadow fell across both the American Revolution and the War of 1812. Harrison Mack is the man cuckolded by Todd Andrews, with Jane, in *The Floating Opera.* This occurred thirty-seven years before, and now Harrison is posing as George III, the antic half. Barth exploits the metaphor: Harrison believes himself to be a mad George, George believes himself to be a sane Harrison. Who is mad, who sane? And why George III? Why does Lady Amherst have an affair with him while Jane is away? How much American history is the result of a mad king of England, whose career fits that of Lyndon Johnson? "Harrison *suffered* from the duplicity of reality, as it were; events and circumstances that he could not 'decipher' into Georgian terms and thus deal with on their own, alarmed him, lest he mishandle them." Substitute Texan for Georgian and we move up to 1969, when Johnson in *his* madness recognized he could no longer rule.

But Harrison's condition extends further than providing a gloss on both a modern and a historical era; he entices others to play his game, so that Lady Amherst, normally rational, plays Lady Pembroke to Harrison's George because that Lady was the woman of his dreams. In his incarnation as George, Harrison can play out George's (not his own) infatuation, and by so doing create a drama that cuts between states of being as well as historical eras. The point is not the ingeniousness of this—nearly everything Barth touches is ingenious—but the belaboring of it. This interplay of elements is not a thread in the novel; it *is* the novel, it and hundreds or thousands of parallel materials, most of only peripheral value.

The War of 1812 clearly serves as focus for much of the internal activity in the novel, and it will become the point of reenactment for Prinz's film crew. It was a war that served little purpose and was won by America because England decided to lose it. It does, however, fit a historical idea Barth finds parallel to America's war in Vietnam. The scheme of *Letters* calls for individual missives to be dated 1969, except for the few from A. B. Cook IV to his unborn child, and those are dated 1812. The year 1969 then becomes a pivotal time, when thoughts of the useless War of 1812 can be used to support thoughts of the wasteful Vietnam War. Such parallels allow Barth's fiction to coalesce, as some huge grab bag secreting fact and fiction.

Barth uses the reenactment of the War of 1812 as a means of commenting on the intertwining of myth and legend with the novelist's ability to reflect them. By setting the film in a fictitious place, while holding to historical accuracy, Prinz mirrors a typical Barthian ploy.

Prinz's Barataria is itself a general-purpose set, a series of shanty fronts on an island used by the U.S. Navy for gunnery practice. The set is a flimsy reality which the reenactment, a fiction, will turn into the process we associate with fiction-making, creating its own legends, myths, successions. The Baratarians who follow will be, in Barth's mocking analogy, like the followers of Jesus, who claimed miracles for their leader so that prophecies could be fulfilled. Once Barth gets into that process or procession, we can see how central to his vision was that outline of purposes in *Chimera.* * Barth's analogy there was the snail, creating itself from itself, and the speaker was the Genie, a persona for the novelist with a special mission.

That analogy with the snail in "Dunyazadiad" is a clue to *Letters* and Barth's sense of himself as a novelist.† Part of Barth's problem as a writer is his repeated need to justify his type of fiction. Unlike most of his contemporaries, he has eschewed a narrative line; he has designated himself, as John Hawkes once did, one of the martyrs of fiction. Such martyrs are more concerned with "making" than with showing, and their role is like those theoretical mathematicians whose work lies deep out of sight, until, at some moment, it emerges in a practical application from someone more "reality-oriented." Barth has been associated with exhaustion of literary modes, but misunderstood. He has not described the death of the novel, but the death of the kind of novel most reviewers favor. The "Tower of Truth" erected fraudulently on marshy ground in Marshyhope College is emblematic of this: the tower as symbolic of the fiction that lies on fact, of fact that lies on fiction. All may well be blown up by the younger generation, who question all received truths. We are, after all, in 1969, and no "tower of truth" can remain standing as it was once conceived.

The Tower of Truth—or its archetype the Tower of Babel—built on shaky ground, with shoddy construction and short-lived expectations, is the linchpin of Barth's fictional world. He is attempting a tower of truth, but must undercut himself, as Mensch Masonry undercuts the tower with shoddy materials. Barth does it for self-conscious reasons; but he also erects the tower so we cannot easily elude his grasp. The Barthian universe has become a gigantic tower,

---

*Or this, from "Night-Sea Journey," in *Lost in the Funhouse:* " 'One way or another, no matter which theory of our journey is correct, it's myself I address; to whom I rehearse as to a stranger our history and condition, and will disclose my secret hope though I sink for it.' " The "I" is a spermatozoon on its route toward fertility.

†Although Lady Amherst is now an administrator, at one time she established herself as a critic and scholar, and her master's thesis was entitled: "Problems of Dialogue, Exposition, and Narrative Viewpoint in the Epistolary Novel." Her letters to JB (John Barth) are consciously styled for their connection to her thesis, to the tradition of the epistolary novel, and, in turn, to Barth's current project, which is a remaking in modern terms of *Clarissa*. Although directions are often murky, permutations are clear.

the Barthian letter like a clutching claw which discourages escape. *Letters* is a receptacle for the past to such an extent because Barth's characters insist on their historical dimensions. Todd Andrews at one point even measures his own life (fictional to begin with) against the fictional representation of it in *The Floating Opera*. Column against column, he insists on his reality, even though he is dead. Everyone insists on living, whatever the circumstances. Todd, whose life has been spent within the shadow of death, writes insistently to his father, a suicide. The dualism and parallelism are intrinsic to the novel, in that Todd, near dead of a cardiac condition at nineteen, experiences his father's death at thirty, contemplates his own suicide, then dies as a character when Barth concludes *The Floating Opera,* and only comes alive again when *Letters* resurrects him in the years after 1954. His Inquiry into himself is, in a sense, continued when Barth pursues *his* inquiry into Todd in *Letters.*

THE FLOATING OPERA AND THE END OF THE ROAD

The Floating Opera (written in the first three months of 1955) is the first manifestation of Barth's interest in the eighteenth century, especially in its fiction. For this first novel, written when Barth was twenty-four, is heavily indebted to the idea of fiction as a narrative already fixed for mockery. Like Tristram Shandy in Sterne's novel, the protagonist is a self-conscious first-person narrator, and his story is based on interruptus, coital and otherwise.* What interrupts his coitus is a history of prostate trouble, which gives him an unpredictable off and on again potency. In a "floating opera," Barth can play on the waterworks of his protagonist, for till Todd Andrews was thirty-two, his instrument was apparently good only for leaking, not for pushing.

"Tuning my piano," the first chapter, begins like Sterne. The "I" in 1954 (at age fifty-four) asserts that his literary activities since 1920 have been relegated to legal briefs and his Inquiry. The latter is devoted to explaining a crucial day in 1937, in itself begun as

---

*Barth has disclaimed Sterne's influence, but the tradition of self-conscious narrative is clear. In this tradition, the purpose is to present a shimmering reality by way of a central character who is deceived and who deceives, whose consciousness plays tricks on him. Machado de Assis, cited by Barth, was a modern practitioner of this, especially in *Epitaph for a Small Winner* and *Dom Casmurro.*

a story in 1938, a job that required nine years. Intermixed with this, by the second chapter, is Todd's plan for suicide and the introduction of Jane Mack, his mistress, the wife of his best friend, Harrison Mack. The third chapter, mainly an interrupted explanation, is designated "coitus." Then, in Chapter 4, Barth jumps back seventeen years, to 1937, to his discussion with a Captain Osborn and a Mister Haecker, two very old men whose firm grip on their lives contrasts with Todd's slippery grasp and uncertainty.

These major time fixes are only part of the temporal juxtapositioning. Barth returns Todd to 1917, his birthday, when his initiation into sex with Betty June, reflected in a mirror, changed his life, turning him into a giggling, braying ass. The temporal sequence jumps forward to a scene in the army a year later, when Todd kills a German sharing a shell hole with him. These two events—one associated with life, but a farce, the other with death, and also a farce—are the twin nodes of his life, his slippery connection to reality. Both reveal an animality of nature that would become turned inside out in Barth's next novel, *The End of the Road,* which in a sense completes this one.

To the Sterne presence we must add a general existential flavor, Camus more than Sartre. For Todd (in German, "death") lets suicide inform his life, dictate its meanings as well as its possible end. He asserts that unless religion determines man's morality, there is no question more pressing than "whether or not to commit suicide . . . before he can work things out for himself." He adds that, of course, he is speaking only of people who choose to live rationally. Since most people do not, the question never arises. These words are spoken to a seventy-nine-year-old man, Haecker, who insists that life itself "has a value, under any circumstances." To which Todd counters: " 'Nothing has intrinsic value.' "

Implicit is the idea that everything must prove itself, which means that life must be filled in or else it has no more value than any object. Once it loses its quality, as in old age, it is discardable. Todd expresses a view of life in a brief chapter called "a premise to swallow," which not only fuels his own work but catches that sense of a counterfeit decade already apparent by 1955. "Quantitative changes suddenly become qualitative changes. . . . Water grows colder and colder and colder, and suddenly it's ice. The days grows darker and darker, and suddenly it's night. Man ages and ages, and suddenly he's dead. Differences in degree lead to differences in kind." This is not entropy; nor is it a reversion to pure naturalism of cause and effect. It is too witty for that. Under the eye of eternity, all is insignificant. Todd can never forget the circumstantial aspect of his existence, its relative minuteness contrasted with the beyond.

Todd argues he is no philosopher, no thinker, only a "mean rationalizer." Since he cannot formulate the philosophical argument for such a rational belief, he offers two contrasting voices. Because they lead to such different premises, Barth introduces them similarly. The left-hand voice (positioned not by tones but by the dictates of print) in this counterpointed fugal structure sings the music of the calliope, the steam whistles of "Adam's Original & Unparalleled Floating Opera." Todd, the lawyer, thinks of a client's case, a nonsensical court case, while the calliope plays "Oh, Dem Golden Slippers" and then shifts to "What You Gon' Do When de Rent Comes 'Round?" This voice is the quotidian one, court case, simple songs, a "floating opera" or divertissement. The *other* voice repeats Camus's question about suicide. Todd considers Hamlet's indecision about life and death and rejects that as basing suicide on too flimsy grounds. Bad luck, feelings of inferiority, choice of an unknown evil for a known one, inability to face social pressures are all inadequate reasons for self-destruction. They are escapes, merely negations. One must be positive about suicide. Todd's father had hanged himself after running up huge debts in the market crash, and the son feels such a suicide was frivolous, lacking any "valid reason." "I merely hold that those who would live reasonably should have reasons for remaining alive."

Sterne and Camus become wedded to Kierkegaard and to Hume, the Scottish skeptic. Todd doubts we can ever know anything—thus, the interminable nature of his Inquiry—because as soon as we try to go from what we perceive to what we think, we have created inferences for which we have no evidence or justification. That "leap" requires an act of faith which the man of reason does not have. In the Kierkegaardian sense, the act of faith is the leap, if one can make it. In the Humean, skeptic's sense, such a leap would be based on false thinking. Todd does not go as far as Hume, however, since the Scot argued against empirical evidence because it is based on man's reason, which is itself uncertain since it is an inference. With both man's reason and his acquisition of empirical data held invalid, Hume offered only a skeptic's awareness of the world, a view which common sense alone could undermine. "Let's talk sense," said those who countered Hume in the mid-eighteenth century, and it is there, in common sense, that Todd finally works out his desire to live.

On all its several levels, the Inquiry is to be Todd's explanation of himself, linking, in fact, several selves or voices. It is, in somewhat capsule form, the key to much of Barth's present and later literary thinking. It embraces deep skepticism, what we see stated in "The Literature of Exhaustion" fifteen years later; the need to locate a technical means for several parallel and seemingly independent voices, as in *Letters;* the desire to justify writing itself, an act which had fallen into the seams of his skepticism, as in *Chimera* and *Lost in the Funhouse;* the reliance, if not on Sterne, then on Sterne's response, which moved in circles without ever arriving, the point of arrival suspect; the stress on exhaustion and enervation, which force innovation and defamiliarization. By his first novel, Barth had almost bypassed Scott Fitzgerald's comment that American lives have no second acts, by emphasizing that they have no first act either.

The Inquiry was originally begun to delve into the life of Todd's father, Thomas T. Andrews, who hanged himself in 1930. This would be, in the Sterne fashion, a complete study from birth to death, from the "umbilicus that tied him to his mother to the belt that hanged him from the floor joist." By searching deeply, Todd hoped to discover the causes of his father's suicide; and the decision to study the life came only after he had resolved to examine the death. Those two inquiries now lead to a third factor, a "letter to my father," in the Kafkan mode, and that, in turn, to a "Self-Inquiry": four parallel inquiries, on life, on death, on self, and the letter to his father— three peach baskets of material and a cardboard tomato box.

Todd Andrews's life is, in a sense, four boxes full of research into life, death, relationships. All parts of him are seeking answers to questions he knows will be unresolvable. Here is, fundamentally, the shape of Barth's career, the reason for both the energy and the enervation which characterize it. Long before he analyzed the literature of exhaustion, he observed life as something which could end before one even got to it. The circular manner of *The Floating Opera* is a manifest of this "end in my beginning." The central point in time is a day in June 1937, the day when Todd Andrews has decided to end it all. His life no longer justifies itself; ergo, he must end it. He looks back on this day from 1954, obviously not having carried out the resolve.

For us to understand this decision, he provides us with the Self-Inquiry. The narcissism of this act is not lost upon Barth, who mocks it even as he indulges it. Barth states the adversary nature of the self and its relationships: "The connoisseur . . . requires of a paradox . . . that it be more than a simple ambiguity resulting from the vagueness of certain terms in the language; *it should, ideally, be a really arresting contradiction of concepts* whose actual compatibility becomes perceptible only upon subtle reflection"(italics mine). In poetry, such incompatibility was found in some seventeenth-century metaphysical work, that yoking of such dissimilars that the eventual resolution pulls apart our common notions of compatibility and establishes its own terms of compliance. Although *The Floating Opera* is centered on a day, month, year, with a Sterne-like sense of anarchy, Barth throws up all kinds of dates and acts, moving the narrative back and forth, interruptus. The fundamental point is that nothing can be completed, a corollary of Todd's idea that nothing can justify a life with no meaning. Barth keeps us on this philosophical plane, so that narrative function, meanings, characters are subsumed under life and death concepts. This is very much a young man's novel, an apprenticeship-to-life, Todd as Holden Caulfield under the aegis of Camus, Kierkegaard, and Sterne.

Barth was attempting to avoid the counterfeit, but was suspicious of the literary means to achieve the evasion. The key image or "fix" for the novel comes early, when he speaks of a play performed on a moving boat. The audience sits on both banks of the river as the boat passes by. "They could catch whatever part of the plot happened to unfold as the boat floated past, and then they'd have to wait until the tide ran back again to catch another snatch of it, if they still happened to be sitting there." What they missed would have to be filled in by imagination or word of mouth. They would be the makers of the drama passing before them, their own lives being the model of their creation once essences or basic premises are established. While this seems "poetic" or even philosophical, Barth plays on it as witty, a form of mockery of expectation, continuity, settled opinion. It would, in miniature, be like the self-conscious novel that was to follow, pieces, scenes, bits of dialogue which float past as part of the floating opera that is life's minstrel show, spectacle, and melodrama.

But Barth is rarely simple, and his novelistic ideas always generate several levels. He seeks dimensions, by way of either technique or ambiguous statement. His protagonist is a madman of sorts, the first of Barth's protagonists who exist in a space of their own, young and not so young men who, while trying to control their destinies, are self-serving, even sadistic. Todd is also murderous, for (in the original conception of the ending) he would be more than willing to blow up the floating opera with everyone on board, including, possibly, his own daughter. "I considered a small body, formed perhaps from my own and flawless Jane's [his mistress's] black, cracked, smoking." The bilge of the boat fills with gas, but nothing blows, not even Todd's own weak heart.*

Considerations here go beyond the comedic, becoming part of a grotesqueness Barth treats as normal. The lack of commitment to human feeling or sympathy his protagonist experiences is not a fault; nor is it something to be resolved. Only life matters, and that only if one can make something of it, whatever the nature of the act. Barth is trying, under somewhat desperate conditions, to find equations for human behavior, by way of eliminating the ones we accept. Since traditions are not useful—e.g., Harrison Mack, the millionaire with his liberal support of Communist causes, is a foil to Todd—the world is open-ended. Once that is accepted, any form of behavior is possible. Barth recognizes that the *acte gratuite,* as suggested by Gide, involves a broad frame of reference: gesture, narcissism, as well as ethical commentary. It embodies a philosophy of self in relationship to a society skew to all traditional notions. It frees the individual from moral or ethical considerations, which are rational dimensions, and locates him in the area of ego and self, matters of irrationality. Todd's monstrous act of potential arson is a testing of his personal need for expression, and since it is an extension of something unreasonable, it falls well beyond any traditional ethical mode. Once the self is vaunted, it expresses only the self.

The relationship of an unpredictable self to "others" carries over into the discontinuous narrative: interruptus *is* the theme, what Barth describes in that early image of the play performed on a moving boat. The fixed point is that June day in 1937 when Todd plans his suicide and then changes his mind. It is, also, the period of the Spanish Civil War, and Barth uses the politics of that era to limn the 1950s: the way, for example, in which Harrison Mack's inheritance is settled is based on political considerations, his sympa-

---

*All this changed in the first printed version by Appleton-Century-Crofts, after the manuscript's rejection by several publishers (who felt, rightly, that the book would not sell). Todd decides only on suicide, not the big bang; but when the child who may be his daughter is carried backstage ill, he chooses to live. "Things needed explaining; abstractions needed to be straightened out. To die now was simply out of the question, though I hated to spoil such a perfect day." When the book was reissued by Doubleday, eleven years later, Barth restored the original ending and made several rearrangements.

thy for the Loyalists. Writing in 1954, Todd Andrews, as Barth, moves the political climate of the 1930s into the 1950s; as later, in 1979, Barth writing as seven characters in search of a novel will relocate the War of 1812 in the period of the Vietnam War of the 1960s.

If *The Floating Opera* was a comedy of nihilism, *The End of the Road* (written in the last three months of 1955) is a tragedy of nihilism. Jacob Horner relates his own story, from the unnamed Black Doctor's newly located farm in Pennsylvania, where the fugitive confidence man has gone at the end of the novel. "Terminal," the final word of *End,* indicates Horner is going to remain with the Doctor, as part of his bargain for an abortion the latter performed. Horner is writing his story on Tuesday, October 4, 1955, at 7:55 P.M. He has moved from Mythotherapy, which involved his taking on a succession of roles, and which failed to work, to Scriptotherapy, the working out of problems or conflicts by writing them down. Horner is writing about the fall of 1953, when he took a position as a teacher of prescriptive grammar at Wicomico State Teachers College, in Maryland, at precisely the time when Barth took a position at Penn State as a teacher of composition and grammar.

Instead of sitting in a corner, Barth's Jacob Horner sits in a rocker, like Beckett's Murphy. Also like Murphy, Horner is activated by "others," and particularly by a doctor, a shamanistic figure who directs his life for him. Once again, in this companion novel to *The Floating Opera,* we have an enervated Barth protagonist with energies for all kinds of devilry. The passive "I" narrator seems tied to the Eisenhower decade, someone who prefers the placid aspect of life and denies the dark, the shadows. But then, once activated, this light figure is capable of moving in shadows, taking on different colors and appetites. One constant: sexual energy is low, almost depleted, partial more to ideas than to performance. Never far is the idea of suicide. "Only the profundity and limited duration of my moods kept me from being a suicide," and even "this practice of mine of going to bed when things got too awful, this deliberate termination of my day, was itself a kind of suicide, and served its purpose just as efficiently."

Barth was struggling against the Laocoön pressures of the 1950s, a decade that strangulated in slow measure. Barth asks in multiple demonic ways what occurs when the enervated individual seeking to avoid choice is slowly squeezed, like the figures in the *Laocoön.* It is a very American question, echoing the queries of Melville and Hawthorne more than a hundred years before. As we can expect, Barth uses the sculpture as one of the key images in the novel. Horner has a version of it on his mantel, a statuette of Laocoön's head alone, sculpted by an uncle now dead. Its "blank-eyed grimace" and ugliness confront his every choice, so that Jacob is aware of his limbs being bound, of his very spirit pressed inward by the twin serpents, Knowledge and Imagination, an inescapable pressure which compresses him ever tighter with anguish. The gaze of the awful head, like Medusa, fixes on him his fate; everything pressed in, nothing oozing out. At the end of the novel, Jacob leaves behind the *Laocoön,* along with the debris of his life at the college, with Joe and Rennie Morgan; but while he may free himself of the head, he does not rid himself of his fate, expressed in the final word to the cabby: "Terminal."

In still youthful fashion, Barth is trying to get at final things. He does not, however, have sufficient context for it; he has mainly reactions and early experiences. Jacob and Joe Morgan, an instructor at Wicomico ("why comic?"), have lengthy discussions of the "life style" variety. Their archetype is that long-running discussion between Naphta and Settembrini in *The Magic Mountain,* which attempts to dissect the world into two ideological camps. The major dialogue comes in the novel's center and is introduced by Morgan's question: " 'Horner . . . why in the name of Christ did you fuck Rennie?' " The question startles Jacob with its abrupt fashioning of the fact, but it has a witty base which vitiates the ideological fervor that follows. Joe Morgan, antipodal to Horner, is a boy scout instructor, a man who has put it all together, who insists on truth in word and performance, and a man who is leading his wife, Rennie, along to a full understanding of herself. He is the teacher, a man whose devotion to duty derives from his belief in rationality. On the surface, he appears admirable, especially in contradistinction to the flabby, vacillating Horner.

But as we know from a long tradition of writers, from Molière to Ibsen, the man who insists on truth is a fool. Life will baffle him at virtually every turn. What occurred between Horner and Rennie—their act of screwing when neither particularly liked the other—establishes a principle well beyond comprehension. Yet Morgan insists on understanding it, expressing it verbally. Language, of course, fails; all that counts is what is. The shamanistic Doctor explains his theory of Mythotherapy, which is that life allows no major or minor characters; the sole truth is that everyone is the hero or heroine of his own story. This view is therapeutic for Horner, who was will-less, motionless, catatonic, when the Doctor picked him up.

In his desperate dialogue with Morgan, Horner has to try to explain a position which drifts away even as he argues it. He asserts that "conscious motives" are insufficient to explain people's actions; that nonchalance is as important as energy, that what they cannot account for can be as significant as what they can. Morgan responds that each person must accept responsibility. Although we are in the mid-fifties, the argument foreshadows the sixties: the drifting energy which sparked confrontational politics and the stonewalling of those who insisted on dubious reason, first the Kennedy and Johnson crowd, then the Kissinger and Nixon gang. Morgan insists on throwing himself as "hard as possible against the facts." No matter how much it hurts, one must never forsake the problem. Horner can offer only the arbitrary nature of behavior and glance up at Laocoön, whose "agony was abstract and unsuggestive."

The affair with Rennie is foreshadowed in the brief meeting between Horner and Peggy Rankin, who seduces the reluctant young man even as he finds her somewhat repulsive. She is much older, desperate for attention, love, and sympathy, and not at all subtle. Horner obliges, but refuses romance; sex is all. The initial intercourse with Rennie develops from her position in the triangle between Horner and her husband. Morgan is constantly testing her, so she can find herself, and this involves exposure, not protectiveness. Rennie has a lot of negative energy which Morgan hopes to divert into selfhood. Put on this course, she goes horseback riding with Horner, and their negative selves attract each other. The consequences are Morgan's inquiry (a Barthian genre!) into causes, while Horner is exasperated with consequences, has tired of the experience, even the memory. The real consequence is far in excess of what either bargained for, the bloody, futile, grotesque death of Rennie, choked by her own vomit while her vagina squirts out blood and guts under the knife of the abortionist. The baby may be Horner's or Morgan's, and Rennie is the sacrifice, the female as first bait, then victim.

The problem throughout the novel is Barth's inability to find sufficient context for the high level of discourse he suggests. *The Floating Opera,* with its marvelous "operatic ending," its play on moving scenes and characters, its built-in arbitrariness, its screwball protagonist, fitted Barth's kind of talent

much more than the terminality of *The End of the Road.* He floats, as it were, far better than he finalizes. *The End of the Road* has no structural irony working for it, and the repetition of the Laocoön presence does not add sufficient dimension. Also, many of the points are themselves juvenile. Horner as an instructor in prescriptive grammar, a locked-in kind of language, is not an effective context for his own arbitrary nature. Irony is singular; it does not last. His triumph in the classroom may be in verbals, but that ironic detail carries little freight. Even the Doctor, who has potential literary size, is one-dimensional. We need only compare him to Bellow's Dahfu (in *Henderson*) to note how witch doctoring and shamanism can become significant.

There is an excess of despair, of talk of suicide and murder, too much Kierkegaardian apparatus set into a story basically burlesque. Barth was ready to turn to burlesque and parody in *The Sot-Weed Factor,* his next book, and we find *The End of the Road* caught between tones and textures. Although the latter helps to complete the first Barth phase, begun with *The Floating Opera,* it does not propel him into the areas yet to be explored. He was turning against the idea of the novel even as he was preparing it for grand drama. All that remains is the fact of Rennie's butchered body. If Barth's point is that her victimization was the result of arbitrary action—the end of the road for her and those involved with her—then he has a dubious point, not fully substantiated. For at the novel's finish, Morgan has recuperated. Horner is once again "without weather," that is, in a vacuum, without a self, but he does leave in a taxi, toward the terminal, still "on the road." While he has gone nowhere to get there, he *is,* poised to reappear in *Letters.*

BACK TO *LETTERS*

Unlike mad Horner, who writes letters to himself and lists historical events as forms of support on any given day, Todd Andrews in his letters to his dead father describes an ongoing life, especially his continuing love for Jane Mack, she sixty-three, he sixty-nine. Also, he serves as a commentary on other characters: Lady Amherst and Ambrose Mensch, Reg Prinz, Jane's daughter "Bea Golden," Cook, Drew Mack (Jane's son). Despite his morbidity, he is a reliable guide.

By about one-third (or 200,000 words) through the novel, Barth has created a narrative constructed like a tidal wave. There appears little overall direction —this is not a directed story or plot line—but a rolling, flood effect. To make certain nothing is lacking, Reg Prinz films events even as Barth recollects them through letters. That demonic need to include is paralleled by an equally obsessive sense that all is incomplete. Like Pynchon, Barth accumulates waste matter to be certain nothing is wasted.

One area in this mélange of fact, fantasy, and historical possibility is Cook's letters to his unborn child. Cook becomes involved with nearly every historical personage of significance, in France and America, in the years between the Revolution and the War of 1812. He suggests possible fatherhood by Aaron Burr, he moves among Jefferson and Hamilton, he will marry a woman promised to Tecumseh, he meets celebrated literary figures—Joel Barlow, James Fenimore Cooper, others. He is involved in one conspiracy after another, sending messages, carrying them, intriguing with Madame de Staël as well as the Spanish royal family.

With such a large historical era to fill in, Barth puts Cook near the center of events. Moving along the contours of power, he becomes an important ingredient in the making of the United States as well as a mover in the coming war between America and England. Yet as Barth has Cooper say, "the acceptance of 'historical' documents as authentic is also an act of faith—a provisional suspension of incredulity not dissimilar, at bottom, to our complicity with Rabelais, Cervantes, or George III's beloved Fielding." Here are the seams in which Barth moves so well. Where fact and fiction meet, we have relatively unexplored territory, as long as the author can avoid allegorical equations.

With Barlow, Cook romps through a fantasy history, yoking three countries and the fortunes of the Western world. As a consequence of his activities, Cook considers himself an archetypal American: the move from Napoleon's France and George's England "show'd me what Barlow & Tom Paine had been talking about; I understood I was not European." Cook's political journey from Europe back to America, written to his unborn child in 1812, about a crisis between the new colonies and a European state, relocates Barth back in the 1960s. Cook's use of his fantastic political journeys is, at one level, his attempt to encapsulate the American journey in terms of a single life; and then to transmit this information to his son or daughter, who will inherit Cook's world. We are situated, by means of a dubious historical journey, in the generational struggles of the 1960s, especially as they peaked in the latter part of the decade, when

Barth was writing and dating the letters in *Letters.*

We enter several dimensions: Cook's fantasies, which become intermixed with historical fact; historical fact, independent of how Cook handles it; personal journeys, apart from history; and the contemporary condition. Each narrative, however interrupted, looped, interpolated, is a version of these dimensions: fact and fiction against the contemporary 1960s, more focally, 1969. We see this mix in one of the most impenetrable and disagreeable series of letters, from Jerome Bray *(Giles).* His letters are an indulgence on Barth's part, because they lack anything of what we can call content; they continue, in fact, Bray's obsession with a computer, at whose core he lay in the earlier novel. In *Letters,* where Bray's letters are mercifully few, and usually brief, his aim is to find the key that will "turn Lilyvac's numbers [Lilyvac II, printing out Lilyvac's Leafy Anagram, located in Lily Dale, New York 14752] into revolutionary letters," which can be used by Drew Mack for his radical plans. Drew is son of Harrison and Jane, brother of Jeanine (Bea Golden). Drew is Barth's representative young man of the sixties, utterly obsessed by radical politics, idealistic, humorless, driven.

Bray sees codes in everything. He uses the Hebrew alphabet as some way of breaking the Leafy Anagram, and at one point, he even finds his secret in the final paragraph of Vladimir Nabokov's *The Vane Sisters,* "which also mentions en passant the Fox sisters of Lily Dale." Bray is self-conscious about his quest, recognizing the Nabokov "code" may fail, and even comments that he digresses "like an old-time epistolary novel by 7 fictitious drolls & dreamers, each of which imagines himself actual." He goes off in different monologues, gathering together information from the world outside and merging it with his own fantasies of breaking the code. In Bray's obsessions, we have Barth's reach, a verbal stream that engulfs past and present.

The Remobilization Farm (from *The End of the Road*) is a base for the characters. For when Lady Amherst and Ambrose arrive there for Reg Prinz's filming (of the reenactment of the War of 1812/of a version of Barth's fiction), they find Joe Morgan, now a bearded guru; Jacob Horner, half mad and half administrator; Bea Golden, one of several names of Harrison and Jane Mack's daughter, Drew's sister; the Black Doctor, who had advised Horner's Scriptotherapy in *Road,* but who refuses to act in the film. His place is taken by André Castine, the man Lady Amherst has been seeking (himself a combination of

André/Andrew Burlingame/Cook/Castine). There are also secondary characters who have not appeared earlier, such as Ambrose's former wife, Marsha Blank. In the filming of *Road,* Bea Golden will play Rennie Morgan, who dies during the abortion performed by the Black Doctor; Marsha Blank will appear as Peggy Rankin, the schoolteacher; Castine will play Dr. Schott, who interviews Horner for his position at Wicomico.

The point, apart from the word games and the detailed interplay of characters, is funneling inexhaustible energy into the blurring of boundaries. With Joyce receding into the past as a "classic," Barth has offered himself as our most representative literary magician. For even as he spoke, in 1969, of exhaustion and depletion, the death of old modes, he was embarking on the intricacies of *Letters,* which demonstrates a full engagement with the literary life. Far more than many who have written "nonfiction novels," Barth has truly broken down boundaries between genres.

Lady Amherst, for example, new to the cast, plays roles that interact with characters already fixed in Barth's novels. Yet such is the nature of her "acting out," she assumes a reality, as (1) someone new; (2) someone already integrated; (3) someone playing a role in Prinz's film of Barth's fiction; (4) someone caught in historical destiny—her search for André Castine, the descendant of Cook/Burlingame; (5) someone searching for herself—as a real person caught in absurdist roles—a fifty-year-old woman being impregnated by Ambrose, a titled Englishwoman serving as provost at Marshyhope State University; (6) someone who, by appearing the sanest member of the crew, must disentangle others' insanity without becoming tainted. In brief, she moves along a perimeter between fact and fiction. Remarkably, she falls into the crevices of Barth's fiction, even while her letters detail their nature.

One of the by-products of this massive novel is Barth's commentary upon fiction, a belying of the 1969 "enervation" theory. Barth himself comments on such theories, his own and others', and through Lady Amherst, says: "A. [Ambrose] assures me that you do not yourself take with much seriousness those Death-of-the-Novel or End-of-Letters chaps, but that you *do* take seriously the climate that takes such questions seriously; you exploit that apocalyptic climate, he maintains, to reinspect the origins of narrative fiction in the oral tradition."

LOST IN THE FUNHOUSE

One of Barth's central documents, although not necessarily his best work, comprises the pieces that make up *Lost in the Funhouse* (written 1963–68). Here, he appears to associate his fictional ideas with those of Borges, Calvino, Nabokov, and others who have mined the self-conscious, self-reflexive forms, of which *Tristram Shandy* is the archetype. Most of the fictions in this collection serve as conceits for the author's imagination as it grapples with its material; and they will culminate in Barth's very influential but misunderstood "The Literature of Exhaustion," in 1969. In that article, Barth described the death not of the novel but of now outmoded forms of fiction, stressing how another kind of literature can thrive. Probably the key piece in *Funhouse* is "Echo." Less a story or even a fiction than a "meditation" (Borges's designation for that frontier between fiction and nonfiction), "Echo" is a fiction about fiction: Barth's fundamental problem and dilemma. It will be recreated later, in *Letters,* in his reenactment of an enactment, the reflection of a reflection.

In "Echo," intended for "monophonic authorial recording, whether disc or tape," we meet several "reflectors." Chiefly, there is Echo herself, punished by Hera, so that it is impossible for her either to speak first or to be silent when anyone else speaks. Then comes Narcissus, who dies from self-love and is loved in vain by Echo; and Tiresias, who has a voice for all occasions. As the center, Echo is nothing but a voice, a device Barth repeats in "Menelaiad": "this voice *is* Menelaus, all there is of him." But we need not seek out individual Barth works for voices, since the idea of disembodied words is crucial for nearly all his work from the 1960s on.

Echo is described: "Afflicted with immortality [before punishment by Hera for her persistent chattering], she turns from life and learns to tell stories with such art the Olympians implore her to repeat them. Others live for the lie of love; Echo lives for her lovely lies, loves for their livening." Hera, however, is doggedly in pursuit of her, and since Zeus cannot be punished for his misdeeds, Echo pays. Unable to speak for herself, she is a voice which "gives delight regardless of hers." How, Barth asks, is this related to Narcissus or Tiresias? Like theirs, hers is a story of shortcomings, although she never purely reflects or repeats. Instead, she "edits, heightens, mutes, turns others' words to her end." Narcissus and Echo would appear to be opposites: "he perishes by denying all except himself; she persists by effacing herself absolutely." Nevertheless, they come to the same end, for each is a teller indistinguishable from the tale. Narcissus really craved only himself, "the Echo of his fancy," as Barth puts it. Self-knowledge is fatal for all, and there is no future for prophets, not even for Tiresias, who remains blind.

Voices, like a multitude of television sets gone amok, are everywhere. We drown in a sea of voices. Bellerophon in his story is not even himself; he is the product of Polyeidus's voice, which intervenes between everything that may be Bellerophon and his adventures. With comparable acts of intervention, we have Narcissus's gaze, Echo's repetition, Tiresias's doomed and dooming prophecies. "Night-Sea Journey," the second piece in *Funhouse,* is a classic form of vocal exploration, analogous to the writer taking on multiple roles to probe his material. Echoing Ginsberg's "Howl," Barth says: "I have seen the best swimmers of my generation go under." The swim is the test, and for the young it seems like a lark: "in our ignorance we [spermatazoa en route to fertility] imagined night-sea journeying to be a positively heroic enterprise. . . . to be sure, some must go down by the way, a pity no doubt, but to win a race requires that others lose, and like all my fellows I took for granted that I would be the winner. . . . We milled and swarmed, impatient to be off, never mind where or why, only to try our youth against the realities of night and sea." Even their skepticism died and went unmissed.

"Night-Sea Journey," published in 1966 (in *Esquire* magazine), was a conceit not only for the writer —Barth had just come through *Giles,* no mean survival course—but for the country. He feels purged of everything by "dull dread" and a kind of "melancholy, stunned persistence." The skeptic in him, not quite dead, cautioned him that he might be the sole survivor of his generation, "tale-bearer of a generation." Makers are themselves divided into two types: those who create sea and swimmer (destiny); and those who give rise to the night which contains the sea and whatever waits at the end (destination). The night-sea journey has as its purpose the making of something: *"consummation, transfiguration, union of contraries, transcension of categories."* Creation requires voices, but voices without creation are Echo's echoes.

"Menelaiad" is cast in terms of voices or narrators, so that at some stages the line begins: " ' " ' " "— suggesting four or five layers of speaker, set deep within each other. The central voice is established as

Menelaus's, the sole presence he can command being his voice. He has returned from Troy with an unrepentant Helen, who knits, pouts, and frets. Menelaus is himself confused by events: while he was away his wife's sister murdered his brother, while she committed adultery with Menelaus's cousin Aegisthus. Her son, Menelaus's nephew, killed them both, "bless his heart," but Menelaus would do anything to have them all back. "Menelaiad" is itself a plaint, a caustic commentary on the futile events of the Trojan War, with its toll of the dead.

The narrator, Menelaus, informs the reader how "one night he told the sons of Nestor and Odysseus how he told Helen how he told Proteus how he told the daughter of Proteus how he rehearsed to Helen how he destroyed their love." His insistence that Helen respond to his question why she loves him leads to her running off with Paris. The concealment of voices within voices is, somehow, an approximation of Menelaus's own bewilderment as to what he has done, all about "getting laid." He is, like so many of Barth's heroic figures, now far less than heroic, middle-aged, worn out, disillusioned. "I'm not the man I used to be," he laments along with all the other tragic heroes. He is a "transitional" figure caught, like Perseus and Bellerophon, between heroic deeds in the past and a dying or dead body, epitomized by his being a voice which will itself be phased out. Barth delves into another aspect of the tragic vision, which is that not even these great tales remain. They fade like everything else, and all we have is the persona of the writer struggling to get his tale told and then himself dipping away into ultimate oblivion.

Barth's vision in the 1960s was of stories which needed to be related, whether on the page, on tape, or through microphones, while the author is shunted aside. As *Lost in the Funhouse* proceeds, narrators become older, moving closer to immortality even as they fade out. When they reach the final stage, they become "Anonymiad," the last fiction in a collection which began as the journey of a male sperm toward its goal of fertilization, its hopes all full of love, love, love—its destination to become "anonymous," like the writer who after giving everything remains unknown. One of the paradoxes of creativity is that the greater the accomplishment, the less the author matters, the more he or she becomes anonymous. Barth was particularly uneasy about the role of the writer, rejecting the label of "experimental"—which *Time* used—as "cold technique" or "heartless skill." He added that "passionate virtuosity's what we all wish for, and aspire to. If these pieces aren't also moving, then the experiment is unsuccessful."

The titular "Lost in the Funhouse" (1967) recalls Delmore Schwartz's "In Dreams Begin Responsibilities," Joyce's "Araby," Salinger's *Catcher*. The three Ambrose Mensch stories—this one, "Ambrose His Mark" (1963), and "Water-Message" (1963)—move his character toward adulthood, when he was to play a central role in a Barth novel. The funhouse is for Ambrose a place of "fear and confusion," as the movie house was for Schwartz's child. On an outing to Ocean City with other Mensches (including his brother, Peter, fifteen, and the enticing Magda, fourteen, later of *Letters*), Ambrose (thirteen) gets lost in the funhouse: caught in the labyrinth of his own development and his relationship to Magda and the external world. Barth has sought a structural equivalent of writing, and "Lost in the Funhouse" concerns itself with the growing up of Ambrose within a testing out of Barth's fictional process.*

On the way they look for the Towers, an allusion to the steeples in Proust. But as they move toward Ocean City (a magical presence), Barth intersperses comments on fiction writing with the narrative of Ambrose's fortunes. He speaks of the ordinary narrative, with its beginning, middle, and end, and speculates that "if one contemplates a story called 'The Funhouse,' or 'Lost in the Funhouse,' the details of the drive to Ocean City don't seem especially relevant."

Barth's strategy is to fill us in on what traditional fiction would do, and then to counterpoint to that his fiction, a mélange of inners and outers of the funhouse motif. He peers into his fiction, even as Ambrose peers out from his vantage point in the interstices of the funhouse. Barth worries that he has come so far without displaying a theme, and "a long time has gone by already without anything happening." He questions whether or not he should relate in the first or third person, but feels first-person narration would be poor if the author identifies too closely with the narrator. But point of view is not the only important matter; another question concerns how long "our hero" will remain in the funhouse. Will his skeleton be found someday and attributed to the original funhouse materials? Why don't the others outside miss Ambrose more? Thrusting itself into this is Ambrose's yearning for Magda, and her association with

Peter. Sexual sweat permeates the story, even when Ambrose is lost.

Yet even before the threesome moves into the funhouse, Ambrose is trapped, "off the track, in some new or old part of the place that's not supposed to be used." Barth comments with his favorite conceit, that of spiral and shell: "Even the designer and operator have forgotten this other part, that winds around on itself like a whelk shell. That winds around the right part like the snakes on Mercury's caduceus." The fiction lurches forward into Ambrose's future as a married man with children, then back into his present, to his fears of being found out, or of finding out. Discovery of himself, in both senses, confounds him.

As the fiction moves into its final pages, Barth begins to intensify his methods: first, Ambrose finds a name coin, lost or discarded, with "Ambrose" on it, "suggestive of the famous lighthouse [in New York harbor] and of his late grandfather's favorite dessert [ambrosia]"; and second, he becomes caught in mirror reflections that make it impossible for him to see himself. So reflected is he, so caught in proliferation of images in the mirrors, he is lost as an eye, and maintains only aural contact. He hears voices, and the disembodied voices, unconnected to eye contact, become one of Barth's most acute conceits.

With this, he can stress the geometric structure of his story, based on coordinates from A to B to C to D: exposition, conflict, rising action, conflict and climax, denouement or resolution. The imposition of this geometric pattern is not to turn Ambrose into stone, although it does suggest the Medusa syndrome, but to bring him into line with all those other stories of adolescents. The geometric shaping suggests archetypal patterns, what in *Giles* he associated with Lord Raglan's mythical hero. Barth, we should emphasize, is always moving in and out of a formalistic or structuralist sense of fiction, in which the fiction is itself a paradigm of a fiction. Lost, Ambrose will tell and retell stories to himself according to patterns Barth has imposed on his own story, until Ambrose's skeleton is discovered, part of the funhouse debris.

Ambrose's imagination wanders the landscape of his childhood, moves forward, returns; catches itself in the shape of fiction, bursts out toward some future life; then fades back into Barth's story, where he wonders if he will be a "regular person." He imagines "a truly astonishing funhouse, incredibly complex yet utterly controlled from a great central switchboard like the controls of a pipe organ." He could, he feels,

---

*Barth's "funhouse" recalls Borges's labyrinth, Gass's "in the heart of the heart of," Stone's "hall of mirrors," Pynchon's Valletta and Vheissu; it looks ahead to Barthelme's "city life" and McElroy's "cartridge."

design such a place himself, although he is only thirteen; and of course we have a vision of Barth's own *Letters,* which this "funhouse" description fits very aptly. "Therefore [Ambrose concludes] he will construct funhouses for others and be their secret operators—though he would rather be among the lovers for whom funhouses are designed."

This fiction is a tour de force, a 1967 turning point in Barth's sense of himself. Abandoned by Barth in his incomplete novel *The Seeker* or *The Amateur,* proposed between *Sotweed* and *Giles,* Ambrose becomes the seed for *Letters:* not only as a character, who himself writes along the contours of Barth's fiction, but as someone who rewrites Barth, as it were. Ambrose Mensch of *Letters* seems all ego and dominance, not nearly good enough for Lady Amherst; but if we reconnoiter among his adolescence here, and in the other two stories, we find him learning to be a character in Barth's craft.

In "Water-Message," the middle story in the Ambrose sequence, he is in primary school, his father the principal. He lives in a web of sorts: fearful of his peers at school, who bully him; considered a sissy by his schoolmates, needing protection from his older brother, Peter; excluded from the older boys' Den, where sexual high jinks have occurred. Ambrose confronts elements which never appear to cohere. He is, in effect, caught in a tunnel, a funhouse in which there is little play and no fun. He must walk with his eyes toward the rear. His childhood is a labyrinth of others' making, into which he must run and then find the thread out. He imagines a future, has romantic desires, finds himself in love with a student nurse who has been caught in the Den with a local tough, and substitutes with dreams what his present life cannot provide.

Living in a maze or jungle, Ambrose wanders to a beach, finds a bottle with a message, later referred to in *Letters.* He breaks the bottle and reads the "water-message": "To Whom It May Concern   Yours Truly"—unsigned, messageless. The missing space, evidently, must be taken up by Ambrose in whatever shape Barth will provide for him, at whatever length. In effect, the fiction called "Water-Message" fills that space, or else suggests how that space may be filled. The blank there foreshadows some future emptiness: the Barthian existential mode, in which the individual attempts to fill in the blank, even as it remains unfilled. Ambrose makes some commitments to himself, mainly for self-discovery: "for though he was still

innocent of that knowledge, he had the feel of it in his heart, and of other truth."*

BACK TO *LETTERS*

Barth is concerned with the ways fiction can remain alive. Basic to his practice is recycling: what he discovers in historical moments and movements is also true of the literary process. In such passages he sounds like Harold Bloom and the misprision of influence. Barth writes that "every firstborn son in the line [of Cooke, Cook, Burlingame, Castine] has defined himself against what he takes to have been his absent father's objectives, and in so doing has allied himself, knowingly or otherwise, with his grandfather, whose name he also shares!"

Such reordering of historical lines carries over into Barth's reordering of literary history: his dipping into the eighteenth century, use of the epistolary method, sharing of techniques not only with the moderns but with their fathers and grandfathers. It also justifies his reuse of his own characters. When A. B. Cook VI writes to the author, he outlines how Barth works: Lady Amherst gives him (Barth) the general conception of the project, "an old-time epistolary novel"; Todd Andrews offers the tragic view of history; Jacob Horner suggests the possibilities of letters "in the alphabetical sense, as well as what you call 'the anniversary view of history.' " Each character, originally created by Barth for a particular function, can be resurrected to offer back to the author what he once gave them, which he is free to reuse, freshen up with further dimensions, then cast back into literary history at a later date. This is, despite the tight controls, a good use of Heisenberg's principle of uncertainty. Associations, not absolutes, are all we can know.

---

*David Morrell in his study of Barth speaks of the original version of "Water-Message," which left Ambrose confused and lacking commitment. The bottle does not contain the blank letter but a note, "It Was Bill Bell," whose triviality is a letdown for him, for he had expected something more commanding. He lacks the desire to know more about himself or sex, in the original version, wanting only further truths of a general sort. "It Was Bill Bell" signifies the nothingness out there, what Barth calls Ambrose's "sweet melancholy." For the revision, Barth reworked the end passages so that the empty space can be Ambrose's own story, the story within the bottle which Ambrose is himself the actor in. Barthian nothingness passes, in the revision, into Barthian Chinese boxes, his later and more mature mode.

Prinz creates film tableaux which are themselves extensions of the reenactments, with a life of their own. They become, in this sense, something of a novel-film, a parallel or substitute film which uses Barth's characters for *its* own functions. The Chinese boxes multiply, but instead of receding, they move increasingly to the forefront. The Barthian narrative device is not miniaturization, but progressive enlargement of what once receded. Barth disallows depletion, refusing to allow what is dead to remain fallow. He must refertilize it, using for himself his leitmotif: the present manures the future. In the moment, deep in the seams, is located freedom or restriction.

Barth has his own sequencing, mocking the Richardsonian format and yet delving deep into it.* In one of A. B. Cook VI's letters to his son, he speaks of Cook IV's five posthumous letters. Thus we have a sequence that is from VI to VII about IV, who is himself writing to V and II. It is a tale of sons without fathers, or of sons held together not by parental presence but by letters. In his way, Barth has duplicated the situation of *Clarissa,* wherein the young lady must function in a world surrounded by father figures who have abdicated as parents. Lacking a "live father," she turns for protection to Lovelace, who turns out to be the incestuous father / brother / uncle figure. Translated into *Letters,* Barth has fathers and sons (no mothers and daughters here) connected by letters, not ties; and these letters are often written to unborn children or to children once removed by the disappearance or death of the father.

Central to Barth's fictional consciousness, as noted above, is the idea of "echo," in which the fictional dimension reflects a factual dimension, which in turn is problematical; so that echoes do not merely reflect reality, whatever that is, but play off reenactments of reality. Analogously, the great length of *Clarissa* creates its own temporal dimension; in adapting to Richardson's demand upon us, we fall into the patterns of the fictional world, accepting that temporality rather than our own. The result is that we become, in time, an echo of the Richardsonian dimension. This is, apparently, what occurred with contemporary readers, who responded so realistically to Clarissa, Lovelace, and Harlowe that they saw in those inner lives echoes of real lives, not echoes of fictional characters.

*When Ambrose and Lady Amherst go to the top of the Tower of Truth, they carry with them all four volumes of *Clarissa* (as well as a six-pack of beer, beach towels, suntan lotion).

In *Letters,* characters are requested by Barth to enter into his new fiction, and some agree, others rebel. Horner is involved in a *Wiedertraum,* a play back of his episodes with Rennie and Joe Morgan, in which he must bring Rennie back or Joe will kill him. Bray is attempting to find the key to the computer which will produce the revolutionary novel that can, in turn, help to foment the Second Revolution, a replay of the first. Characters play roles in their own lives, or under assumed names. Andrew Cook VI acts out his previous life as Andrew IV, while producing the letters of IV for his, VI's, son; and is himself a transfer from André Castine, a 1953 name and person changeover. Lady Amherst, although new to Barth's fiction, spends most of her time relating a shifting past, creating echoes of not only her own life but the lives of previous Barth characters with whom she is interacting. Ambrose Mensch, this Mensch from *Lost in the Funhouse,* is writing tales which smack very closely of Barth's own work in *Chimera,* so that his use of echoes from *Chimera* is, in itself, a kind of transference of techniques from one to the other.

Characters also revolt against Barth, refusing to be used as he wishes, or demanding different roles from the ones assigned to them. In Barth's letter to Jerome Bray, the Author denies Bray's allegations that he, Barth, plagiarized Bray's work. Barth bases his defense on the old conceit that the "fiction is not a fiction," that *Giles Goat-Boy* pretends to be a computer-edited and even computer-authored transcript of tapes, turned over to the Author by Giles's son for further editing. Thus Barth, as Author, has taken a fiction in hand, transformed it into something else, and Bray's charges that he "pirated an extraterrestrial scripture" and then published a "distorted version of it as fiction" is quite false, part of the very satire Bray has missed.

Entanglements never cease. Barth argues with Bray; Bray alleges Barth has plagiarized his work; Barth denies it, his defense based on the way fiction can be turned into nonfiction. Barth thickens the plot, so to speak, by turning to Bray's inchoate work and finding there interesting parallels with his own: "But your passing invocations of Napoleon, George III, Mme de Staël, Bellerophon and the Gadfly—these echo provocatively, not to say uncannily, some concerns of my work in progress; and I am intrigued by your distinction between the fiction of science and the science of fiction." Thus Bray is creating something which may (1) be either an echo of Barth's work; or (2) be echoed in Barth; or (3) parallel Barth. The

Author is interested in seeking the etiology of this circumstance and suggests Bray get in touch with him at his university office at Buffalo. At the same time, the Author informs Bray that he, Barth, is finished with the "transcendent parody" and "*sophomoric* allegory" of *Giles*.

Barth is entering the seams, exploring boundaries, trying to turn up territories that have gone unexplored in fiction. His exploration carries further than Borges's, while lacking the latter's elegance and polish; for Barth is not content simply with fiction-nonfiction paradoxes, but wishes to swing back and reclaim for fiction vast areas which have slipped away. While we explore Barth's explorations, we should not lose sight of his desire to conserve. The experimenters in fiction have all been conservers of the past, not squanderers of it.

Barth's conservation, however, goes further: in replays, filming, computer storing, reenactments, echoes. The letters of Andrew Cook IV, especially the group called the posthumous five, once again exemplify Barth's method. Here, the method seems somewhat miscalculated, for Cook's narrative (in Cook VI's 1969 paraphrase) of endless machinations in and around the War of 1812 is stultifying. These details form large sections of the novel, provide a narrative (unlike other parts of *Letters*), establish some action, and are historically based; but they are essentially circular, as the following summary will demonstrate.

After Jackson's great victory at New Orleans over the British forces (once the war had ended) and after Napoleon's great loss at Waterloo, Cook is at loose ends. Having been reported killed, he is free for undercover work. He links up with Jean Lafitte, the pirate whose aid was essential at New Orleans, and he concocts a plot to kidnap Napoleon from Saint Helena. But he is dissatisfied with a simple kidnap plot. Cook needs a scheme that parallels Barth's conception of the fictional process, "a multiple or serial imposture." He would, he says in letters related by Cook VI, also known as André Castine, "go ashore at St. Helena and by some means arrange to have *himself* doped and smuggled out as Napoleon and Napoleon left behind as himself (whose rescue he would then, as Napoleon, forestall, forbid, or thwart). Deceiving then even Jean Lafitte, he would continue to counterfeit the aging, ailing emperor long enough to mobilize the French Creoles, the free Negroes, and the 'Five Civilized Tribes' of Southern Indians for the Louisiana Project." Further, as Napoleon Bonaparte, he will marry Elizabeth Patterson Bonaparte so as to turn her family fortune to his purposes, and if that does not work out, he will reveal his true identity to her, "die again as Napoleon," and carry on the Second Revolution as André Castine.

Amidst such potential chaos, Cook represents coherence. For he is of course a writer, different in degree from the others who write letters. They "correspond," whereas his letters are extended diaries or memoirs, part of literature, and historically based; a kind of narrative history, intermixed with fiction, Mailer's "true-life novel." As a writer, he is mindful of the need for roles, plots, and counterplots; and these he provides so as to further the so-called Second Revolution, which will be in time his "great novel." For what we have outlined is by no means the whole. Once Cook carries out his scheme and returns to the ship as Napoleon, he has no way of knowing if the others are convinced, or whether Lafitte has himself penetrated the disguise. "He feels his way carefully: 'wakes' as if uncertain himself who and what he is; is greeted politely but ambiguously by Jean's body-servant, by Lafitte himself, whose ironical courtesies fit either hypothesis." Caught up by his failure to sustain an illusion, he "begins to suspect that Lafitte believes him to be neither Napoleon Bonaparte nor Andrew Cook, but the imposter alleged to have been substituted for Napoleon in January 1820—and that this state of affairs is for some reason acceptable to him."

Barth by now has spun seemingly endless variations on role-playing and unraveling. Here in somewhat tedious miniature is the fictional process, never mimetic or direct, but deceptive, along the lines of the imagination as it carves out its subject. Even more self-consciously, Barth pursues a similar deception when he has Ambrose Mensch correspond with him (Barth) to offer his views on the Perseus myth, which is what Barth had written about in *Chimera*. In a sense, Mensch's view of Perseus is parallel to Cook's measuring of himself: each reads himself into his structure, and each can only interpret according to his own plotting. First, Mensch outlines the features of the typical mythic hero, drawing on Lord Raglan, then Joseph Campbell. After that, he follows with still another pattern, which demonstrates how arbitrary our concepts and categories are. Finally, he comes to his own plan, a personal interpretation: Perseus falls from favor, his marriage fails, he suffers general stagnation, or "petrification," he desires to be reborn or rejuvenated by a "revisit to the scenes of his initial triumph."

Each stage of Perseus's career can then be linked to Mensch's. The goal is liberation of the artist within oneself. In typical Barthese, Mensch rhapsodizes about the possibilities: "Just as the Hero (at IF6) [within Plan I, Point F, section 6] finally terminates his tasks by exterminating his taskmaster and (IIF6) discovers in what had been his chiefest adversary [Medusa] his truest ally, so such an 'artist,' at the Axis Mundi or Navel of the World, might find himself liberated—Old self! Old Other! Yours Truly!—from such painful, essential correspondence as ours." The sole way to escape, even provisionally, from the restrictions of one's life is by way of a fiction which provides endless tunnels, roles, alternatives. The labyrinth is not a form of entrapment, but a locale of endless exploration. The labyrinthine experience is incremental, not belittling. Barth has so taken the novel.

The going has been extremely difficult, and the reader of *Letters* has every right to wonder if the effort was worth it. The response must be that Barth has, in a sense, offered himself up for the reader's wrath, which, for this novel, he richly deserves. He is not simply working out fictions about fictions; nor is he demonstrating the enervation of the genre, or the exhaustion of the author. He has, in a way, turned that entire fictional world around. By trying to explore the other side of narrative, that side away from mimesis, he moves us from representation as we ordinarily observe it operating in a fictional impulse. It is as if, to use an analogy from electricity, he had exploited the residual electricity not in the wire but in the insulation. That would not mean he was forsaking the main current, but that he was seeking alternative forms of current, marginal areas where the activity might be considered minimal. *Clarissa* appealed to him so intensely because Richardson, by way of dense, profound interweaving, was able to take the novel to its outer edges, and then by way of margins lead the reader back to centers, which always remain implicitly if the novelist is certain. Barth does not forsake that narrative center; rather, he leads us back to it by other means. If we stick with him, we are guided by a confident hand, although the way along is indeed often distressing.

By way of illuminating the fictional potential, Barth has located himself in several places in *Letters*: in characters, types of scenes, themes. As a "character," he identifies most strongly with Ambrose Mensch, Lady Amherst, and Todd Andrews. Mensch represents the fiction-writing self; Lady Amherst, the academic side, also a concern with the eighteenth century; Todd Andrews, the fatherly figure who has gained distance, wisdom, some ideas about dealing

with all the wandering son figures in the novel. Yet none is very confident of himself or herself: Mensch is egomaniacal, lacking discipline; Lady Amherst lets herself be guided by fortune and also lacks a strong will; Todd, often on the edge of suicide, is unable to break his allegiance to his father's memory.

Mensch, perhaps, represents Barth's interests most of all. As a writer, we have seen, he is involved in Barth's work, writing the stories of *Chimera,* even rewriting them according to personal needs. Mensch offers instructions to Barth outlining six steps which will take the Author to his seventh enterprise—which will be to "unlock at once the seven several plot-doors of your story!" Getting to the "seventh" is a huge obstacle in *Letters,* for seven is not only the number of Barth's works to date, but the number of letters in *Letters,* as well as the number of correspondents, including the Author. It is not by chance that the "Second Revolution," if it ever does take place, will be fomented by Henri (Henry) Cook Burlingame VII, son, very possibly, of Lady Amherst by Andrew Cook (André Castine). Before his disappearance, or death, Andrew Cook speaks of a Seven-Year Plan in which the Second Revolution would have occurred, and failed to do so. Within that fear of seven, Mensch offers Barth his work, continuation of the Perseus/ Medusa story and the Bellerophon/Chimera legend, plus a third which will help link the three. Barth could call the result a novel, and then proceed to his epistolary work.

In another way, Lady Amherst explores Barth's work, by reading his fiction as she corresponds with him and thus becoming not only a confidante but also an intimate of characters on the page as she meets them in her own life. Her relationship to the book's other characters is ingenious, since she is the sole correspondent who has not appeared before. Thus, she must play a dual role, as a person meeting already familiar characters, and as herself a character who must gain her bearings by becoming acquainted with Barth's novels. At the same time, she must relate herself to Barth in her capacity as a creature in a drama not so much of her making as of his.

By way of continuing his Inquiry into the life and death of his father, begun in *The Floating Opera,* Todd Andrews must work his way back toward the center. His continuing association with Jane Mack, with his possible daughter Jeanine (with whom he has an incestuous affair late in the book), his involvement with the Mack Estate all bring him into contention with the entire cast. Yet he moves on their margins, affording Barth a post of observation he lacks with the other characters. By means of his post, Todd offers Barth not only a personal listening device but a "mature" political and social observation post. In a long talk with Drew Harrison, the young radical activist, Todd establishes his "Tragic View of Ideology," which is a mix of antiwar politics and conservative caution. He acknowledges to Drew that the antiwar movement has had its practical effect in Washington, but looking beyond it, he did not "otherwise take the sixties very seriously even as a social, much less as a political revolution." In hindsight—and Barth is peering down from the later 1970s, while dating Todd's letter in 1969—the decade will fit in as any decade does. The Second Revolution, whatever its form, will never take place, for once the Vietnam War ends, the counterculture will become another absorbed subculture. Todd offers as an example Drew's estranged wife, Yvette, a black woman, who has left her husband and moved to Princeton, so as to give her boys Groton or Andover and the rest.

Todd has earned the "Tragic View" because at one time in order to commit suicide he would have blown up the floating opera, killing even his own daughter. Thus he knows both the intensity of violence and the ways in which violence drifts off into stodge and middle age. All passes, and he senses that the counterculture, once its main objective is obtained, will also pass. Yet Todd's "Tragic View" neglects social and political process. The absorption of countering views has altered stratifications, and it has led into what are new movements, among women and gays, as well as among blacks. The sixties may lead, as Cook VI suggests to his son, to the Ice Ages of the eighties and nineties, but not all Ice Ages are the same, even when so labeled.

One of the failures of *Letters,* in fact, despite its literary ingeniousness, is Barth's inability to assimilate the larger sense of the sixties. His caution restrains, even while he attempts to radicalize the genre. Fictional ideas and fictional content do not connect. Barth is a tinkerer, a mechanic, a technician. When he must assimilate and synthesize, he is left with a thin ideology: Todd's "Tragic View of Ideology," which is a conservative's fear of change, despite daring personal attitudes. Todd may contemplate suicide, violent death, even embrace it near the end, but he lives and thinks conservatively. Barth is indeed a conserver, as we saw in *Giles Goat-Boy,* the significance of which stopped short of the main thrust of the sixties. Perhaps one reason why Barth's work stays so close to the academy is that the academy, however mocked and satirized, represents that conserving ele-

ment—not only home of serious fiction, but refuge for those who dare to write it. Only the academy tamps down the elemental forces of anarchy, and in that respect Barth is an academic writer. Nevertheless, whatever our disclaimers, *Letters* will be to future generations a landmark fiction. Eventually, critics and other readers will confront Barth's achievement here, a path into the 1980s.

Subtitled "A Romance," *Sabbatical* (1982) takes its idea from a line Barth adapted from Henry Kissinger: "Our business is fiction, not lies." Like *Chimera* and *Letters, Sabbatical*—its title referring to time spent renewing oneself—is concerned with making fictions. The novel is a series of stories which are self-consciously arranged by the chief characters with the connivance of the author to create another historical pageant; this one, however, is romantic, not self-defeating. Barth has discovered the delights of the body and even the language for expressing feeling without parody. He has retreated from the mockery of emotion and moved to self-expression, although, still uneasy, he must inhibit the thrust of romance with devices which, in part, negate it.

One such device is twins, whether true twins or twinning. Barth entwines both Susan and Fenn, his main characters, in deep relational associations. Although not blood related, they are uncle and niece by a complicated series of marriages which are a Barthian contrivance to play variations on coincidence, storytelling methods, and incestuous narrative possibilities. Susan has a "sororal twin," Miriam, and Fenn has a fraternal twin, Manfred, who beds down with Susan's mother. This makes Manfred—the Byronic connection is not lost—both Susan's common-law stepfather and her brother-in-law, while also creating the uncle-niece association between Susan and Fenn. These are, however, only the beginnings of duplication, doubling, doppelgängers. Barth is seeking stories that have been told before, people who overlap their roles as relatives and in their professional life, episodes that can be duplicated in fiction after occurring in life (as reflected in the media).

In a number of footnotes, which come often in the early pages, Barth provides a running gloss on such relationships, giving the reader what he needs to know so that the story can go forward. The forward part of the story concerns Susan and Fenn and their sabbatical (she is an assistant professor on the rise, he a onetime CIA insider on the decline) on a small boat in the waters of Chesapeake Bay. Part of the "romance" of the subtitle relates to the affection Susan and Fenn feel for the *Pokey* (Poe-Key) and the Chesapeake waters, its bays and inlets, even its terrible sudden storms. Surrounding their shipboard life is historical pageantry: among others, Fort McHenry, the reincarnation of Francis Scott Key in Fenwick Scott Key Turner, the proximity of Edgar Allan Poe (Susan's sister has taken up with the Vietnamese Eastwood Ho; their child is named Edgar Allan Ho).

The background to all this, however, is conspiracy, another dimension of the twinning theme. Stories for Barth cannot come to us free of entanglements, of course, and here the linkage is to plots, counterplots, conflicting stories about CIA activities, sudden deaths, including those of Fenn's brother, Manfred, and Susan's half-brother, Gus. Those conspiratorial plots swirling around the Baltimore area are full of leads which go nowhere: they are simply the present historical pageant against which the sabbatical romance can be played out. Spies play roles, get killed or disappear, or become doubles and triples, even moles; but these games have no more essential meaning than any other historical activity. The real action lies in Fenn's weak heart (earlier an attack, now a minor seizure) and in the tubes beneath Susan's navel (she becomes pregnant and aborts twins); finally, in the relationship between the two as they steer the *Pokey* from one Edenesque spot to another. We see, then, that a sabbatical is really a mythical search for Edenic renewal, even while the rest of the world crumbles.

About two-thirds through the novel, Barth makes a shopping list of what has failed—not merely God, of course, but the entire world of culture: existentialism gone, Angries now "middle-aged and petulant," Nabokov dead, Beckett silent, Borges "turned into Rudyard Kipling," the literary world dominated by structuralism, deconstructionists, semioticians. The world has become unrecognizable, and the conspiracies swirling around Fenn—and his own possible role in them—are emblems of the times; part of the uncertainty, deception, enervation which a sabbatical romance can counterbalance. The question arises of what one should do with one's life confronted by choices that involve professional deceit or personal integrity and lead to dropping out, sailing, taking further sabbaticals. Barth has mellowed so that Susan's and Fenn's "story"—they are always writing/telling their story, or even dreaming it—involves doing what makes them happy. All that life offers is a sabbatical; the rest is conspiracy, sudden death, suicide or murder, CIA machinations, all emblems of what lies beyond the individual in present and past history.

A "romance" seems a holding pattern for Barth, the author restraining himself while he revs up for something that will capture larger stories, a bigger bite of the world, more intense narrative strategies. Or else it suggests a permanent departure, a recognition that strategies alone are inadequate, and he must venture out in his own *Pokey* to take new chances.

The Mid–1970s

By focusing on two aspects of the 1970s, the mid-decade and, later, the turn of the decade, 1979–80, we can concentrate on the novel as it presently turns. The mid-1970s demonstrated something of the malaise of the overall culture, a period in which conservative political and social considerations preempted openness or adventurousness. Consolidation rather than moving out was common in our national life, and not surprisingly, our literature at mid-decade demonstrated something of the same tendencies. Our cultural response was not only to a Nixon presidency, to the winding down of the Vietnam War, to a rejection of New Deal liberalism; nor even to the sequence of violence which had become part of American life. Rather, consolidation became apparent when the nation began to feel that little mattered. Disillusionment was part of every process—political, social, racial, economic. Nothing had worked except individual affluence, and those who had gained withdrew behind their walls to hold on. Contraction, retreat, holing up, became a mode of life.

Despite individual achievements—Bellow in

Humboldt's Gift, Heller in *Something Happened,* Roth in *My Life as a Man* and *The Professor of Desire,* Vonnegut in *Breakfast of Champions* and *Slapstick,* Kosinski in *Being There, The Devil Tree,* and *Blind Date,* Malamud in *The Tenants,* Hawkes in the trilogy of *The Blood Oranges; Death, Sleep & the Traveler;* and *Travesty*—all demonstrate a compression of their talents, a loss of exploratory nerve, a rejection of many salient aspects of modernism. We note a reduction in size, a lessening of tension, a loss of texture and thickening agents. They have come to expect less of their readers. None of this would in itself be a source of grief except that all of these significant writers have begun to repeat themselves, or else to retreat from forms that expand the genre. In some instances, these new works herald not renewed energy in fresh areas, but turning points in careers and, apparently, decline. Initial energies and inventiveness have been exhausted in favor of narrative ease and a relaxation in prose and attention to detail. In several, the sloth of the overall culture has infiltrated and overcome.

As against the established novelists, we find a few, still at mid-decade, who are attempting to develop new approaches. Much of this is mixed and unsatisfactory work, some of which will remain inconclusive until we can see their later work, in the eighties. For example, Toni Morrison's *Song of Solomon* is an effort to move on in terms of her own development after *Sula;* Doctorow's *Ragtime* is an attempt to find new areas of the novel, closer perhaps to musical comedy than to traditional fictional forms. Ronald Sukenick's burgeoning career is, in fact, located directly at mid-decade, with *Out* and *98.6,* and we can say the same of Paul Theroux, with *Saint Jack* and *Picture Palace.* Others include Thomas McGuane, Stanley Elkin, and Ann Beattie.*

Besides these efforts, personal or generic, often unsuccessful, the novel was being explored and expanded by less popularly received writers, whose roots lay back in the fifties: Gaddis, Barth, Pynchon, and McElroy. By the end of the decade, it was clear that the fate of the novel lay not with establishment authors—even when they are as intelligent as Bellow or Mailer—but with those whose work cannot find a broader audience. This is, of course, as it has always been in twentieth-century modernism. Conrad, Law-

*McGuane: *Ninety-Two in the Shade* (1973); Elkin: *Searches and Seizures: Three Novellas* (1973); Beattie: *Head Over Heels* (1978), discussed briefly in "The Possibilities of Minimalism."

rence, and Joyce lacked readers even as sales for Bennett, Wells, and Galsworthy skyrocketed. In the mid-seventies, the novelistic ground was double-layered: occupied by those who either sought or found popularity by contracting their inventiveness or by repeating successful earlier formulas; and those who retreated into adversary positions, became high priests, and offered an art that the larger culture could comprehend or not. We seem back in 1915–30, when the same battles were fought, and "high culture" (however defined) broke off from more popular culture.

In 1973, Raymond Federman tried to define a new fiction, which came to be known as "Surfiction." In this view, everything will be shaken up—reading, basic materials, character presentation. Federman posited fictional anarchy: "All the rules and principles of printing and bookmaking must be forced to change as a result of the changes in the writing (or the telling) of a story in order to give the reader an element of choice (active choice) in the ordering of the discourse and the discovery of its meaning. Thus, the very concept of syntax must be transformed—the word, the sentence, the paragraph, the chapter, the punctuation need to be rethought and rewritten so that new ways (multiple and simultaneous ways) of reading a book can be created."

What will be the shape of fiction? "The shape and order of fiction will not result from an imitation of the shape and order of life, but rather from the formal circumvolutions of language as it wells up from the unconscious." The materials of fiction will be made of fragments: "disassociated fragments of himself, this new fictitious creature will be irrational, irresponsible, irrepressive, amoral, and unconcerned with the real world, but entirely committed to the fiction in which he finds himself, aware, in fact, only of his role as fictitious being. Moreover, not only the creator, but the characters (and the narrator, if any), as well as the reader, will participate in the creation of the fiction."

Finally, what will fiction "mean"? "Since, as stated earlier, no meaning preexists language, but meaning is produced in the process of writing (and reading), the new fiction will not attempt to be meaningful, truthful, or realistic; nor will it attempt to serve as the vehicle of a ready-made meaning. On the contrary, it will be seemingly devoid of any meaning, it will be deliberately illogical, irrational, unrealistic, non sequitur, and incoherent. And only through the joint efforts of the reader and creator (as well as that of the characters and narrators) will a meaning possibly be extracted from the fictitious discourse."

A good deal of this, however, echoes early-twentieth-century theory, in Vorticism, Dadaism, Surrealism, and found its expression decades ago in Gertrude Stein and Samuel Beckett, a hero of Surfiction.* Federman's own fiction, *Double or Nothing* (1971) and *Take It or Leave It* (1976), while intelligent and heroic efforts to put himself on the line, are really dead ends: old-fashioned or exhausted content rearranged typographically as voices, entrances, departures. The fate of fiction cannot possibly lie here. Federman's error is in trying to transform fiction into a broader medium, with borrowings from television, film, recording equipment, while forgoing the dynamics of fiction. Burroughs and Barth have shown how such borrowings can be accomplished while a fictional presence is maintained.

If midcentury work, even at its best, seems exhausted, what about the turn of the eighties? Endings and beginnings have their own energy, and we find in the year 1979–80 a quickening of purpose. Nearly every major American novelist except Bellow came forth with a novel. We have already examined Barth's *Letters,* whose longueurs could prove discouraging to even the most devoted reader, but whose considerable fictional values are deeply embedded in its method. Barth was only one of several writers who used his work as a means of connecting to the past. Styron in *Sophie's Choice,* Roth in *The Ghost Writer,* Doctorow in *Loon Lake,* all dipped into their pasts to extrapolate possible contemporary meanings. Styron and Roth, like Barth, draw on previous characters in their books or on a previous persona. They have attempted, with considerable success, to create a *roman fleuve* of sorts, a continuing artifact. So, too, Malamud in *Dubin's Choice* has recreated earlier lives, his own and D. H. Lawrence's, to make a statement about the passing decade. End-of-decade fiction—the above plus Oates, Mailer, Hawkes, Kosinski, Didion, Abish, and others—suggests creative vitality in the novel, although traditionalism outscores modernism. With Pynchon and McElroy yet to appear, it is hard

*Comparable efforts to take account, fictionally, of who and where we are come in Ihab Hassan's *Paracriticisms: Seven Speculations of the Times* (1975), more attuned to criticism than to the fiction it services; and Jerome Klinkowitz's *The Life of Fiction* (1977), with graphics by Roy R. Behrens. Klinkowitz is concerned with locating certain writers—whom he calls Superfictionists—in the mainstream of postmodernism. He has in mind Vonnegut, Sukenick, Barthelme, Sorrentino, Abish, Baumbach, Steve Katz, Russell Banks. Yet except for Barthelme and Abish, the fiction drifts away into indistinguishability; there simply is not sufficient creative weight for Klinkowitz to lay such significance on it.

to see what the fate of modernism or postmodernism will be in the eighties. As we turn the decade, we have several B's—Burroughs (now restirring), Barth, Barthelme—and Pynchon and McElroy, possibly Abish, as those writers most able to explore and extend the genre of fiction.

The mid-seventies begin with *Humboldt's Gift* (1975). In some senses, Charlie Citrine, the narrator and chief character of the Bellow novel, is an older version of Moses Herzog. Although Citrine is still vigorous, he is already heading toward that bafflement of the soul which is Herzogoria: boredom (which will be the subject of Citrine's "grand essay"), entanglements with complicated women, flirtation with elements (savory and unsavory) completely foreign to him, dependence on the ministrations and cosseting of sacrificial ladies. Despite a busy and successful career as playwright, biographer, and all-purpose journalist, Citrine is moving inexorably toward the ennui and anomie of the soul that characterized Herzog's condition.

Bellow, however, has tried to create another dimension from what was available to Herzog. He has attempted a more ambitious novel, a reworking of earlier materials expanded by way of the presence of Von Humboldt Fleisher, whose career roughly parallels that of Delmore Schwartz. Fleisher's career rises and falls precipitously; in clinical terms, it is manic and depressive, as is his life with broad mood swings, often succeeding each other. At an age when most writers are still feeling their way and hoping for a first strike, *Fleisher had* established himself, through *Harlequin Ballads,* published in the 1930s. This coincides, again roughly, with Schwartz's volume of short fiction, *In Dreams Begin Responsibilities* (1938), which gained him instant recognition. Charlie Citrine is a student at the University of Wisconsin when Fleisher's volume appears, and he heads east to meet the great man. Fleisher likes what he sees, and the two begin an intense, often symbiotic relationship, which inevitably goes sour when Fleisher's gifts wane and great, disruptive energies feed his paranoia and manic swings. Meanwhile, Citrine gains fame of his own as a playwright, with *Von Trenck,* whose title broadly suggests Fleisher's given name.

Bellow's aim, however, is far broader than counterpointing these two; he is interested in dipping back into the Chicago of the first parts of *Augie March.* His ambitious portrait of Citrine is, in many respects, a gloss on cultural and intellectual America: what it is, what it should be, where it can go. For Bellow is trying to lift not only the novel but culture itself from the doldrums of indifference, disbelief, ennui, anomie, and "pop" aims. He is responding to a fiction represented, in part or in full, by Pynchon, Barthelme, Barth, Burroughs. The future lies elsewhere, Bellow suggests, and Citrine's career is a last hurrah to that distant territory Bellow feels is still attainable. The numerous references to Rudolf Steiner and his diagnosis of spiritual malaise is an effort to move beyond the material, pragmatic body. Bellow hopes to be our Socrates, creating a dialogue of countering elements, suggesting an adversary culture which brings us back from fragmentation toward wholeness. Citrine is a "lemon" of many colors, wears many different coats, colored and otherwise, and strives to break away from what he is, whatever that is.

Various elements struggle for Citrine's soul. The novel is in large part an atomization of those forces, past and present. Citrine's mind is also a great catcher of information, much of it now being marshaled for his essay on boredom, accompanying his thoughts of sloth, his drift toward anomie. The sole element that provides possible salvation is Steiner's "anthroposophy," which posits a world in which man's spiritual nature moves beyond his senses, beyond pragmatism and materialism. Steiner's philosophy was once called Theosophy, and he was himself the founder of the German Theosophic movement, which he abandoned for the more encompassing anthroposophy. Although the Theosophist's presence is felt throughout the book, much of the narrative, like that of *Herzog,* is filled with delectable items, whether rich foods and drink, or succulent breasts and thighs, meaty buttocks, nostril-expanding skin odors. Citrine is almost cannibalistic in his association of taste, smell, and visual delight with human flesh, his movement from food to sex almost indistinguishable.

Citrine enjoys being cosseted; and his choice of women, again like Herzog's, is full of the doom of a man who swings to extremes: selecting women who can minister to him and those who will threaten his very existence. He recognizes his situation, and his response is that he needs the wildness and anarchy, the freedom to choose destruction as well as salvation. Without that element of threat, his life grinds to a halt, and in fact, ennui creeps up even more rapidly.

In that swing to extremes we can locate Rinaldo Cantabile, whose name suggests both a musical composition (grace and flow) and sinister connections. He glides in and out of Citrine's life like a musical motif, threatening, offering deals, disappearing, resurfacing. His hold on Citrine begins in a card game, but quickens in a scene in which he has made Citrine his prisoner. Cantabile's bowels give way, Citrine must share a commode with him while he lets go, and that unpleasant scene seems to cement their relationship. Cantabile becomes Allbee to Citrine's Leventhal, part of that "choice" Citrine insists upon, the wild side associated with Chicago.

Cantabile, Chicago, Citrine's former wife, Denise, his present woman friend, Renata, the ministering Demmie Vonghel are aspects of Citrine's secular life. They tear him apart, along with various lawyers, who have their hooks into him; the IRS, which investigates him the length of the novel; alimony and child support payments, which bleed him. And yet they are essential to his well-being, for Citrine is nothing but a dialectic of struggling elements. Steiner's philosophy must always contend with those wild or anarchic elements which claim Citrine's body and soul. We have here, then, a Manichean contest of secularity and spirituality, materialism and soul.

Von Humboldt Fleisher fits neatly into this pattern, since he is himself possessed by wild swings between material and spirit, between being and Being. He embodies both his phase (the secular, money-making, postwar years) and its antiphase (the Renaissance, when poetry, art, and imagination flowed). Fleisher considers himself a Renaissance man, quoting from the cultural heroes of every era, functioning as a Platonic element in the lives of those he meets; and yet he is continually on the make, for grants, scholarships, professorships, money. His "gift" to Citrine after his death is the rights to two schemes the two had worked up as parodies of screen scenarios, wildly commercial projects which demonstrate Fleisher's instinct for the material side of culture.

Closing in on Citrine are Cantabile (representing the anarchic side of Chicago), Fleisher (emblemizing the life of the imagination, the poetic soul bent on its own destruction), various women (demonstrating the ways in which Citrine can dig his grave), and the "world beyond" (representing that real world of lawyers, IRS audits, scams). Citrine's wealthy brother Julius represents still another aspect of Citrine, like Augie March's brother, a man devoted to acquisitions; this, too, is Citrine's heritage.

The main problem, however, is that Citrine is a voyeur in the realm of ideas; he sees an idea, finds it attractive, like one of his women, and then discards it. Boredom, which has great potential, is one of these ideas, already surveyed in *Herzog,* discarded for other territory in *Mr. Sammler's Planet,* and now revived for Citrine. It does not fit him, and if we get behind the glib description of tedium, ennui, "boredom experts," we perceive Bellow has no genius for this kind of thing; it is, very possibly, antithetical to his talent.

He poses with ideas, grabbing them from his vast reservoir of reading, and thrusts them into his work. Literary and historical allusions succeed each other rapidly. Citrine's passage—and he is all journeys and yo-yoing—is from boredom to spiritual regeneration. He moves so precipitously, Bellow wants us to believe, so that he can return to his beginnings: from raw Chicago, to literary success, and then back to his roots with Waldemar and Menasha at Humboldt's new grave site. As Humboldt is reburied, Citrine is resurrected, his spiritual quest completed (as far as it can go) with the simple ceremony at Humboldt's grave. The play of ideas is to demonstrate a proud, ego-ridden Citrine, a man given over during his most lavish periods to deep boredom, who comes to comprehend where his beginnings are and returns to them, spiritually regenerated, filled with Steiner's apocalyptic apothegms.

It is heady stuff, full of Bellow's messianic fervor, which we first saw in *The Victim* and then in *Seize the Day*. When Tommy Wilhelm finds himself at war with Tamkin's philosophy of "seize the day," he for the first time finds tears for another. This is the beginning of Bellow's search for values beyond the ego, beyond narcissism, both of which he feared for the constrictions they placed upon the individual. But the messianic idea is not incorporated in the right structure; it fits only in *Henderson the Rain King*, because Eugene Henderson is committed to "becoming," not "being"; whereas Citrine, Herzog, and even Tommy are all being, pretending to becoming.

Tedium as an idea or ideology does not fit into Citrine's life, no more than does spiritual regeneration. Seeking a way out of the culturally doomed fifties and sixties, Bellow wants his character to be the battleground of extremes which seem beyond conscious resolution. Within these large movements of time, space, ideologies, Citrine moves to assert his individuality even as he is caught by elements (fates, destinies, doom) he cannot control. The familiar Bellow dialectic is there: that play of will (consciousness) and the pull from elsewhere (sleep, determinism, unresponsive individuals). Citrine will fight back by way of "ideas," and yet his true fight comes by way of his lavish manner with things, that immersion in objects and materials. This is the man we believe in, if we believe at all. He sports with ideologies and alternative roles.

He is truly fascinated by female knees that touch as they slide by each other (Dommie), little fatty deposits on fingers, thighs, the neck (Renata), arrangements of features which create special kinds of beauty (Denise). Delighted by sensuality, he is immersed far more in flesh than in ideas. Cantabile has trouble focusing on Citrine because he shrewdly sees a man devoted to lovely objects who insists on digressing about tedium and spiritual regeneration. Cantabile suspects that Citrine is a spiritual brother not to Steiner but to himself: devoted to larks, pleasures of the flesh, marginal scams. The struggle between them for the control of Humboldt's "gift" is a contest of likenesses, despite verbal and stylistic differences between them.

One reason for the many dead spots in the novel is that Bellow has reached broad seams. These seams fall between the different roles Citrine attempts to play; and Bellow has discovered no way to go from one mask to another. About one-quarter through, Citrine and Humboldt have lost their thrust, with the latter going on about his schemes to be a Princeton professor. His plan—a form of sorcery, Citrine calls it—is full of longueurs. The novel stands still. Stasis is achieved, however, not only because of loss of forward movement, or uncrossable seams, but because Humboldt has lost his glitter. Bellow must insist on the infinite variety of Humboldt, his presence, power, witty and profound sayings, imaginative thrust, and self-destructiveness; so that he appears a virtual god. Yet he is not what Citrine thinks he is, and his presence in the novel, while important for the regeneration of Citrine, means something different for the reader.

A persistent seam in the novel, that split between expectation and actuality, accompanies Humboldt's presence. His pouting, his thrust for greatness, his scheming, and finally, his disintegration do not reach the levels of distinction Citrine's pleas make for him. The dead spots accrue, almost incrementally. Humboldt becomes one of Citrine's "innovative bores," which would be part of a study Citrine might make with Thaxter's backing. Thaxter, incidentally, is the confidence man of culture, a creature whose charm and style barely disguise a shark's soul. Thaxter, too, loses his presence for the reader, although Citrine cherishes him, for values we fail to perceive.

The dead spots emerge because Citrine and his world have come to mean something for Bellow they do not signify for the reader, who recalls great textual paragraphs that have far more of the world in them than does the play of ideas or ideologies. Kathleen,

Humboldt's wife, is a great triumph of Bellow's art; clearly based on Schwartz's second wife, Elizabeth Pollit, in both personality and physical presence, the portrait goes beyond affection and sympathy. For Kathleen, as for few women in Bellow's fiction, male ego gives way to "seeing" the other sex. Bellow's description of their New Jersey hovel ("Eden!") has the revelation of something fully observed:

> Big fair wan lovely pale-freckled Kathleen with that buoyant bust gave friendly smiles but mostly she was silent. Wonderful things are done by women for their husbands. She loved a poet-king and allowed him to hold her captive in the country. She sipped beer from a Pabst can. The room was low-pitched. Husband and wife were large. They sat together on the Castro sofa. There wasn't enough room on the wall for their shadows. They overflowed onto the ceiling. The wallpaper was pink—the pink of ladies' underclothing or chocolate cream—in a rose-and-lattice pattern. Where a stovepipe had once entered the wall there was a gilt-edged asbestos plug. The cats came and glared through the window, humorless. Humboldt and Kathleen took turns letting them in. There were old-fashioned window pins to pull. Kathleen laid her chest to the panes, lifting the frame with the heel of her hand and boosting also with her bosom. The cats entered bristling with night static.

To condemn contemporary life, Bellow needed to examine the "other," those phases of experience, of life itself, which move the contemplative (and narcissistic) soul beyond itself. That "other," for Citrine, is Cantabile, threatening women, a destructive wife, an overbearing brother, Humboldt himself. They are all antagonists, and like Steiner in Citrine's reading, they must be confronted. The reach is Dostoyevskian, lacking only that violent presence which the Russian writer could situate at any point in his fiction. Bellow hoped to introduce the violence in Cantabile, but once Citrine sees that the gangster obtains his kicks from threats, not deeds, that dimension is not achieved. Bellow's effort to move Citrine onto this huge stage —Dostoyevsky seesawing with Kierkegaard, Steiner in the wings—is dissipated in mismatched equations. Sloth has its uses, but Citrine does not represent sloth; boredom may be innovative, but Citrine does not mix well with boredom; Humboldt may represent great genius gone to seed, but Humboldt seems as much confidence man as genius. Textures and surfaces of great intensity remain long after ideas and ideologies vanish. Bellow reaches for the universe and comes away with America.

Like Yossarian, who in *Catch-22* had to deal with the contradictory impulses of the fifties, Bob Slocum in *Something Happened* (1974) must attempt to resolve the irreconcilable impulses of the sixties. Slocum, in Heller's later novel, is a "white-collar" Yossarian. And since he is not equipped emotionally or psychologically to remain coherent within these contradictory impulses, he must express himself. Modeled apparently on the narrator's confession in Dostoyevsky's *Notes from Underground* and on comparable monologues, the narrative is a record of Slocum's journey through the 1950s and 1960s to his present situation. He is falling apart, and what he needs is others' support in his collapse. With everything centerless, the society surrounding him is little different. Not only is his rueful face reflected everywhere he peers, but society, office, home are all facets of the same look. If he is Narcissus, society is a "funhouse." Like *Catch-22,* the book is about individual and cultural madness.

In responding to such challenges upon his ego, Slocum must carry along everyone for support. He comes out of the fifties affluent: a house in Connecticut, two cars, a live-in maid, a nurse. He also has a wife who, he says, drinks too much, as well as three malfunctioning children, one of them medically an idiot. In the midst of plenty, he suffers the agonies of Job; although, unlike Job, he is not part of God's plan. His confession comes at us in waves of guilt: tunnels of confessions and inner urges, where parentheses indicate responses beneath his stated responses.

Slocum is a minimalist, a reductionist, for his narcissism and egoism make it impossible for experiences other than those servicing him to function. In this, he is an updated extension of Bellow's Herzog, although even more self-pitying. Part of what Slocum does in his need to embrace and devour is to transform everything not himself into an object: he reifies his children and wife, and he does the same with all women he goes with or dreams of, turning them into protuberances or fruits for his feasts. He can handle only an undifferentiated world.

What, then, is he? Not actually Jewish, Slocum is a New York Jew in his sensitivities, fears, assailability, sense of guilt.* Even with his drinking and phi-

---

*Just as Slocum in his precarious positioning in an organization looks back to Yossarian, so he looks ahead to Bruce Gold, his Jewish prototype in *Good as Gold* (1979). Slocum also shares many cultural resonances with the twin protagonists of John Cheever's *Bullet Park,* Eliot Nailles and Paul Hammer.

landering—which may be considerably less than he brags of—he could be Jewish, for old stereotypes of Jews as nondrinkers and good family men have vanished. Except in their consciousness of vulnerability and their eagerness to embrace guilt, Jews are not now much different from anyone else. Heller's strategy was to illuminate his protagonist from several angles, creating a saturation effect. We see Slocum in his first job, in a car accident liability company (shades of Kafka!); then in his present job; at home, with his wife, daughter, son; in his free associational ramblings with his idiot son; finally, in his memories of sexual paradise, almost gained, now irretrievably lost.

We know a good deal of him, along with much he has not revealed. While he presents himself as the average sensual middle-class man, the man without belief, hope, or direction except self-promotion, he also suggests qualities not in his monologue. Although he is a persona for a particular Godless, nonintellectual or anti-intellectual New Yorker, a philandering "nobody," he is profoundly deceptive of himself. He rarely recognizes, for example, how all life must be rerouted to accommodate him, or how destructive his embrace may be. In his arguments with his daughter (almost sixteen, faceless), he always wins, and while he boasts how easy it is to overcome her impetuous attacks, he cherishes these victories, no matter how he demurs or feels pain for them. Every act is calculated to give pleasure or pain, to enable his ego to sustain itself. What he needs, through argument or sexual act, is attention; whether with wife, child, mistress, or colleagues, he cannot tolerate being ignored or going unattended. He fails, however, to register his infantilism; and yet it is primarily infantilism which makes him reduce or reify all experience. It is not solely narcissism, as Christopher Lasch defines it in *The Culture of Narcissism,* that dominates the 1970s, but infantilism acted out in forms of obsessive behavior.

Heller's irony cannot disguise that Slocum leaks out in ways not prepared for in the narrative. We are not expected to pity him, although there are touching scenes; we are expected to recognize ourselves in his pathology, even though Slocum has achieved his own state by negating everything except his sensations. The difficulty lies here because he does not perceive the extent of his infantilism and narcissism, while at the same time he offers them as a universal human condition. Dostoyevsky attempted precisely this in *Notes from Underground* and succeeded because his corrosive irony was contained in an intense hatred of the modern world. Method and matter connected.

Slocum goes through a strange condition which, in a very different context, has been called a "sort of narcissistic *Liebestod.*" In this, the self is constantly reenacted, and with such passion and intensity that without its unfolding, it would die; and yet despite that continual unfolding it is still incapable of fulfillment. The process is one of continuous reaffirmation of the individual's identity while, in reality, he cannot affirm or reaffirm himself. Although Slocum is an extreme example of this condition, we find it also in several "heroes of our time": Mailer's Rojack, of course; Barth's Horner and Todd Andrews; Hawkes's Skipper; Gaddis's Wyatt Gwyon; Pynchon's Benny Profane; Roth's Portnoy; nearly all of Barthelme's characters.

The phenomenon reflects the central paradoxes of the American experience: the desire for personal choice in every area, and yet the capacity for wrong choice; the stress on intellect (Slocum is proud of his brains), and yet the need to emphasize will, experience, pragmatics; the insistence on presentness, and yet the parallel burden of lost chances, lost Edens, lost opportunities; the desire for confession as a means of relieving guilt, and yet openness as an admission of weakness, a denial of one's masculinity. Slocum can only confess with such intensity and glee because in his mind he has turned the weakness of confession into an act of strength; he is asserting the primal therapy of the scream, reveling in a putrid self. Through some inner chemistry which Heller does not explore, Slocum has reached the position that confession and admission are manly, expressive, acts of strength. Whoever he is and whatever he has thought and done, he deems himself, nevertheless, one of the elect. While he may be Emerson's representative man, he is also a key to the universal; what he has done, is doing, thinks is common to all men. In some oddball way, this is precisely what the Puritans believed, each man as a microcosm; without, however, the Puritan stress on a microcosm touched by something divine.

The subject of this 1969 novel is family pathology, with Nailles suffering from a sick son, and Hammer unable to work through his own malaise as a young man and now as an adult. As hammer and nails, they are caught in a spiral of intense responses to each other, with Nailles's son at stake. Heller crosses into Cheever's territory not by way of common structuring—Heller's novel is far more ambitious—but through his use of an extended pathological family situation. Slocum is far more self-indulgent than Nailles, but less so than Hammer, occupying a middle ground of destructive and self-destructive behavior that stops just short of Hammer's insanity.

Slocum's sense of his own importance, while intensely American, is nevertheless a delusion, based as it is on a pathology he fails to recognize and lacking any view of phenomena except as they touch on him. Heller has created a man without a shadow whom he offers as representative.

More than halfway through the novel, Slocum is still thinking of the lost Virginia, the young lady who teased him when he was seventeen and whom, he believes, he could have had. That lost opportunity filters through Slocum's adult life, an insistent motif, a manifest of lost Edens. Virginia in a sense becomes the prototype of the possible, and Slocum blew his chance. Yet Virginia *for us* is nothing but Slocum's fixation: "What good tits I could have been nibbling on all those months, instead of those soggy canned salmon and tomato or baloney and mustard sandwiches my mother made for me." Yet Virginia becomes indistinguishable, for us, from all other young women, older women, wife, mistress, prostitutes, by virtue of Slocum's memory of her. She is an object in his memory, a mythical loss, part of Slocum's reification of everyone connected to him.

A similar problem, we saw, accrued in *Herzog.* Herzog is a more subtle fellow than Slocum, but his relationship to women makes them all sensual creatures offering food or thighs. He needs ministering to, and yet what he offers is never observed from the woman's point of view. Comparably, we have only Slocum's sense of himself. We never perceive what his attractions are; they seem rather minimal, although he considers himself witty, mature, a "catch." Part of the problem with the modern confessional tone is that it cannot manage the devastatingly subversive irony of Dostoyevsky's underground man, the archetype of this genre. We see precisely what the underground man offers: a nervous, doubting, farcical, intensely sincere, terribly dangerous kind of existence. He proffers hope, hate, love, and their opposites in equal dosages; and his appeal is to the underside of events, to the vulnerability of people. Where does Slocum pitch his tent? Like Yossarian, what dead men does he have in it?

Heller attempts to advance beyond the infantile needs of a man seeking help through confession. He is concerned with stopping time, momentarily, in order to locate directions, place, sanity. "Who *am* I?" Slocum asks, about three-fifths through the novel. This is the knockout question, asked by Emerson, Thoreau, Whitman, Melville, Dickinson, beyond them the Puritans. His answer—"I am a broken waterlogged branch floating with my own crowd in this one nation of ours"—is connected to his later observation: "I have so many people to cope with at night. Many are made of varnished glass wax. There's no such thing. Ghouls are there, and midgets. Carcasses." If he could discover who he is, he might dissipate these images. As the sixties and seventies joined, this is precisely the issue, a large cultural moment to which Heller is witness.

Yet even when Slocum confronts enormous questions, Heller has diminished the response by virtue of the diminished inquirer. By now, 150,000 words into the book, Slocum has established himself, he thinks, as interesting simply because he is revealing himself: confession is all. Yet what he has revealed is often only dead matter. His solipsism comes without irony: "A vacuum cleaner that works well is more important to me than the atom bomb, and it makes not the slightest difference to anyone I know that the earth revolves around the sun instead of vice versa, or the moon around the earth, although the measured ebb and flow of the tides may be of some interest to mariners and clam diggers, but who cares about them?" That is the *beginning* of perception for a fictional character. If Slocum's indifference here is not the start, but the end product, then he is so common as to lack discriminating marks.

The decline of the past, the past held in memory like a fragile solution, the past as an Edenic memory of a lost existence are all standard themes, persistent for two hundred years of American fiction. Slocum observes that all gain is loss; all happy falls are really falls; all tastes, sights, sensory impressions reductions of the ideal. Our age, in his eyes, is witness to constant and steady loss. Yet the perception deserves more solidity than the perceiver provides. The mark of *Something Happened,* its brilliance as a witness, is the shrewdness of what is perceived, even as we doubt Slocum's perception of it. As in *Herzog,* it is not the experience that is called into question, but the one experiencing it.

The problem may lie in Heller's use of a narrator who seems to derive from *Catch-22,* for military life is like a suspended existence, caught outside real life. The sense of the military in all major novels concerned with it is that service life is distinct from everything else, in texture, content, and even sensory experience. If we leave the military and return to the world, our observations of phenomena cannot be identical. Slocum observes as if he were Yossarian, but Yossarian was special, as military life is special, not the real thing. In that "real thing," Slocum's perceptions reduce whatever he perceives.

Even the family, where so much dramatic tension is created, is faceless: an unnamed wife, daughter, son (not even "son," but "my boy"); only a named idiot son, Derek. In the office, nearly everyone is named after a color, Green, Brown, Black, to suggest their interchangeability. An unnamed family can become intermixed in Slocum's perceptions with barely named office colleagues. The point is established: Slocum exists within an undifferentiated world, in which moments and obsessive memories are the sole forms of relief. All else is dross, diminution, nothingness. Yet the very excess of this creates Slocum's lack of interest for us because he is, also, only an undifferentiated mass of zeroes, and lacks cultural weight, historical density. Even the great dramatic moment, when he accidentally(?) smothers Derek, is almost lost, an undifferentiated moment because Slocum has already managed to smother everything.

The circle of infantile ego is complete. Slocum, who seems ordinary, a nobody, becomes extraordinary by the amount of control he exerts on every aspect of his life, even to controlling every observation of himself. Whatever is gained, lost, or processed in the world out there has no intrinsic value beyond what it seems to him. There is little question Heller has caught the moment of malaise, indifference, ennui, even anomie, characteristic of the late sixties and early seventies. But he has also forgone the significance of objective elements, the excitement of passing moments, the sense of vitality of things not himself. Deadness is all, except Slocum's erection. If all sensation is, ultimately, to create an erection, then Slocum is, synecdochically, a prick and the confessional becomes a cock-and-bull story.

"A minute's serious thought to being reunited with those who used to love me, or simply knew me, and I am panic-stricken. . . . The panic of the escaped convict who imagines the authorities have picked up the scent—only I am the authority as well as the escapee. *For I do want to go home.* If only I had the wherewithal to extradite myself!" This is Peter Tarnopol writing about Nathan Zuckerman—who reappears five years later in *The Ghost Writer**—in a story called "Courting Disaster (or, Serious in the Fifties)." It is one of two stories by Tarnopol about Zuckerman in the volume; we are told in a Note that he is the author of the pieces. The first is called "Salad Days," and both are included in a section named "Useful Fictions." After them, we enter directly into Tarnopol's life in the chief section of Philip Roth's *My Life as a Man* (1974), called "My True Story."

For *My Life as a Man*—begun after *Portnoy* but interrupted by *Our Gang, The Breast,* and *The Great American Novel*—Roth started to use his own work as a resource: characters, situations, scenes. It demonstrates Roth's efforts both to include and to move beyond himself, to find art forms for life forms, to discover to what extent art must disrupt life or to what extent life breaks through art. In many ways, this book more than any other is preparation for Roth's finest work since *Portnoy, The Ghost Writer.* Several false starts had led to revaluation.

The three segments of *My Life* taken together display Tarnopol writing about himself through a persona, Nathan Zuckerman, then about himself directly. The quotation above promises a potentially tragic theme of advance and withdrawal, of the self in a panic reaction to what it wishes to handle but cannot; of a man who feels chased and who yet wishes a haven, which he will inevitably detest. The entire book shows Roth reaching out to important themes, some of them, however, unreachable because his female characters are parodic: voracious (Sharon Shatzky) or hideous (Maureen) or helpless and hopeless receptacles (Susan) for whatever Tarnopol wishes to shove in.

Like Bellow's Herzog, whom he recalls, Tarnopol-Zuckerman must measure himself against women who are unsuitable for him, all the while wondering about himself in deep metaphysical terms. The advance in Roth's conceptual ability comes in *The Ghost Writer* when he moves between older and younger writer and can work through the conflicts by way of an astringent sense of art. Roth's personal life, if formed into an art object, can then be reflected in one of his protagonists, there Nathan Zuckerman. Tormented by a woman, Amy Bellette, he can turn her into a literary figure, Anne Frank, worship her as a writer as well as a person, and forego the repetitions that his patterns force him into.†

In *My Life,* whether Zuckerman is the subject, as in Tarnopol's two stories, or whether it is Tarnopol

---

*Then again in *Zuckerman Unbound,* in 1981. With Zuckerman, Roth has a loose persona, a figure sufficiently like him so that he can be witness to the culture Roth has witnessed, but sufficiently unlike him so that Roth has distance on him.

†The later book is foreshadowed in several ways. Tarnopol writes a short story in journal form, entitled "The Diary of Anne Frank's Contemporary," published in *The New Yorker* and concerning an incident in which the young Tarnopol comes home to the wrong house.

himself, in the main segment, the rising crescendo belongs to women. Roth is women-obsessed, needing an exorcist more than a psychiatrist. Zuckerman has Sharon (a female slavey) crawl on her knees toward his penis and carry out his every whim, and then Lydia, and finally, her daughter, Monica. None are real challenges to his misogyny, since their emotional range is small. They either want him or simply agree to get on with it.

Not until Maureen, castrator, woman of rage, deceived and destroyer, does Tarnopol become fully engaged. The contest between Maureen and Tarnopol becomes the central act of "My True Story," the final section of the novel. And it is precisely here that the book in part founders, in narrative functions as well as ideologically. For behind Roth's rage, as reflected in Tarnopol's rage, we have a shadow existence, worked out in the relationship with Maureen, but presented too explicitly, even too derivatively. Missing is that act of imagination which transforms Amy Bellette into Anne Frank in *The Ghost Writer*. Here is displayed openly and reductively Tarnopol's preoccupation with himself. His account of his antics, related to his psychoanalyst, Dr. Spielvogel (who flew in from *Portnoy*), is not an act of imagination, but one of pure narcissism. He hopes to unnerve the doctor by telling of his exploits in marriage: " 'And I put on Maureen's underwear. I pulled open her dresser and I put on a pair of her underpants—I could just get them up over my prick. Then I tried to get into one of her brassieres. . . . And then I just stood there like that, crying—and bleeding.' " The blood comes from razor cuts, made when he intervened in her suicide attempt.

He relates how he deposits small amounts of his semen in friends' homes, in the library, and elsewhere, what he calls "Tarnopol's silver bullet." Also, he has sealed it in an envelope and mailed it with his bill to the telephone company. These admissions are made when he senses he is out of control, which Spielvogel interprets as being "in control"—Maureen's. Maureen is herself an emotional basket case, a woman who seeks men who can exploit her physically and emotionally and whom she can, in turn, enrage into beating and degrading her. Once Roth has engaged us in this heavyweight slugging match, we find an unequal contest. On one side, a hopeless woman, made repugnant through Tarnopol's eyes, never seen in her own right, and finally a suicide—the embodiment of every female disaster; on the other side, the male world of achievement and point of view, with a male psychiatrist. The consequence is

that Roth must keep us involved in a contest of unequal parts: Maureen, avenger and destroyer, observed from a distance and from her antagonist's point of vantage; Tarnopol, the protagonist, the man of accomplishment, the budding writer eager to complete his book, *A Jewish Father*.

The dialectic becomes a monologue that permits no interference. Tarnopol is not only the narrator of his own story; he is writing a book about his "story" with a Jewish father; he is telling his psychiatrist his story; he creates scenarios about his own work, as viewed by his students, especially one Karen Oakes, with whom he is having an affair. We are caught completely within the circuitry of Tarnopol's emotional and intellectual life, and yet—while this could be promising as a Kafka ploy—it is insufficiently textured. Roth relies—too much, I think—on echoes from his previous work, *Portnoy* and *Goodbye, Columbus* in particular, but also *Letting Go* and *When She Was Good;* so that when a larger hand is needed at the controls, he falls back on tested formulas. He is touching upon significant cultural moments, but only partially realizes them because life bulls through when shaping should be more incisive.

For example: Roth very shrewdly builds into the novel an assessment of Tarnopol's narcissism and solipsism. In the person of Dr. Spielvogel, we have an "antagonist" to Tarnopol's need to structure the world around his immediate needs. An important scene is developed when Spielvogel writes an article called "Creativity: The Narcissism of the Artist," and uses Tarnopol's case as one of his histories. In the article, Spielvogel (a "talking bird") attacks the patient's narcissism, which, he asserts, has made him unable to accept anything threatening his idea of himself. Tarnopol carries on a dialogue with Spielvogel, first as he reads the article and then in the doctor's office; and the result, while implying an attack on narcissism, is in effect an even greater act of narcissism. Tarnopol is given, in Roth's handling, a second and third opportunity to justify himself, to display himself, to reflect his inner needs; and all Spielvogel's explanations of a threatening and castrating mother, an ineffectual father, a doted-upon son are swept away in Tarnopol's reentry into his life as victim, as victimized. The article is simply more data featuring Tarnopol. He is reflected in everything: in a bookstore he visits, where he is recognized, in psychological history, in the mirrors Roth provides everywhere. The indulgence is emotional masturbation, fitting into Spielvogel's view of Tarnopol as a man who must turn all women into masturbatory sexual objects.

The fictional problem is there, even in Spielvogel's antagonism; for it pulls in even more of the world's weight and makes it all focus upon Tarnopol. He becomes a center of gravity. That *is* the point; that is also the weakness. "To be a man" is the quest, and Maureen's trial for Tarnopol is the test of his manhood, which he fails. Toward the end of the main part, Roth apparently had insight into the cornered existence he had described for his character and attempted to alter his angle of vision. The novel turns parodic, parody of Tarnopol and his conflicts as located in America of the mid-sixties.

Tarnopol's agonies are now played out against civil rights marches, social and political disturbances, assassinations. He hears Martin Luther King speak of his "dream" in Washington and muses that King can plead for him when he goes to jail for nonpayment of alimony. "Tarnopol Shall Overcome," his brother suggests. A week after Spielvogel's article appears, the Warren Commission's findings on the Kennedy assassination are issued: Oswald was the sole murderer, while Spielvogel finds Tarnopol "suffered from 'castration anxiety' and employed 'narcissism' " as his primary defense. Tarnopol discovers that his agony is not lessened by its juxtaposition with more universal agonies; it is, in fact, intensified because he recognizes its insignificance. Here Roth has room for maneuver: Tarnopol suffering, the world beyond, the scale not diminishing but increasing his pain, a parodic display that works well.

It is, however, short-lived. We return shortly to one of those ghastly scenes which in postwar fiction are relegated to domestic areas. They are, in effect, the domestic novelists' equivalent of the combat scene.* Maureen comes to Tarnopol's apartment, tells him she will never divorce him, and then appears to seduce him into beating her, while her sphincter lets go and she has a huge bowel movement in her panties. The scene is less powerful than Roth intends. It works only as shock, as a marginal distaste for Maureen, as a more centrally located disgust Tarnopol has for women. It is a scene that would be more fitting for a novel moving on a different scale, where

the shadow life of the novel was more defined. By "shadow life," I mean areas where irony gave full play to Tarnopol, where there were some objective criteria for judging his character, where elements of the novel derived from locations other than Tarnopol's own observation of them. Roth falls into the same pattern as Bellow with Herzog and Heller with Slocum. That "shadow life" of either Herzog, Slocum, or Tarnopol would dispute the presented data, or at least call it into question. Roth, like Bellow, establishes the world within Tarnopol, and then never lets go. The reflection of the period's narcissism is too complete.

In *The Professor of Desire* (1977), we meet university professor David Kepesh before he has changed into a breast, in *The Breast* (1972). In the earlier novel, Kepesh undergoes a transformation that seems borrowed, on one level, from Gogol ("The Nose"), and on the other, from Kafka ("The Metamorphosis"). Roth's plan to transform Kepesh was: "In *The Breast* my approach to the outlandish seems to me to be something like a blending of the two methods [in Gogol and Kafka] that I've just described. I want the fantastic situation to be accepted as taking place in what we call the real world, at the same time that I hope to make the reality of the horror one of the issues of the story."

Kafka assumes the transformation has occurred, part of the natural phenomena we live among, and the individual must respond to that. Gogol insists on the horror of the loss, whereby he questions the reality of it and suggests a dream sequence. To blend the reality principle of Kafka with the dream principle of Gogol was Roth's plan, and to give that plan some historical development he needed *The Professor of Desire*, Kepesh's life before the transformation.

Kepesh here is, in actuality, a replay of Portnoy. The familiar triangle is present: the protagonist (Kepesh, Portnoy, et al.) and his analyst and, the third leg of the triangle, the protagonist's women, either whores or madonnas. The whores, here, are Helen and Birgitta, the young Swedish girl, and the madonna is Claire. All parties except protagonist and analyst are Gentile, and all the young women remain marginal or shadowy. By making Kepesh a professor of comparative literature, Roth integrates literary transformations into Kepesh's life.

Kepesh teaches Chekhov and Kafka, and visits Prague to tour the various Kafka shrines. These two writers help define Kepesh's needs. Chekhov, the quiet tragedian, shows the humiliation and failure of

*In this respect, Roth was a "war novelist." For *Something Happened,* Heller turned *Catch-22* combat into domestic combat; Mailer moved from violence in *The Naked and the Dead* to domestic violence in *An American Dream;* Bellow assimilated the physicality of the war novel to the rage of marriage, divorce, and alimony. James Jones, unfortunately, never found a suitable domestic transformation of his combat scenes, certainly not in *Some Came Running* (1957) or *Go to the Widow-Maker* (1967).

those "who seek a way *out* of the shell of restrictions and convention, out of pervasive boredom and the stifling despair, out of the painful marital situations and the endemic social falsity, into what they take to be a vibrant and desirable life." Chekhov, like Flaubert, recognizes that a life lived according to natural dictates must be even, tedious, without events; whereas those who wish for more are risking imbalance and damnation. This is, we may add, a meaningless pursuit for Kepesh, and his quest for Chekhov's ideas seems chimerical. Similarly, his deference to Kafka, his worship of the Kafkan idea, seems misplaced; for Kepesh's needs—and Roth cannot convince us to the contrary—are at the level of physical desires, sensations, sexual longings. That he recognizes his infantilism does not mitigate the fact that he operates at that level. Kepesh may make Kafka meaningful to his students; but outside the classroom, he and Kafka part ways.

The success of *Portnoy* was connected to Roth's relatively simple line; Portnoy's needs did not involve him in literary dimensions. There was a vitality to his needs, and there is no question he put masturbation on the literary map. *The Professor of Desire* also seeks literary dimensions in masturbation, fellatio, multiple sex, Jewish-Gentile sexual polarities, and seeks them in writers as sober as Chekhov and Kafka. Yet here literary detail works against personal quest. Kepesh's visit to Prague with Claire, the Gentile madonna, on his arm is particularly revealing; for he worships intellectually what cannot possibly be significant for his life as he describes it to Klinger, the analyst.*

In Prague, Kepesh meets a Czech dissident professor, and for the first time recognizes the distance between himself and Kafka. The professor is translating *Moby-Dick* into Czech, an enterprise that is futile, for a good translation already exists and no publisher will touch his since he is a nonperson. The professor justifies it with penetrating Kafkan reasoning, and my point here is that Kepesh cannot in any significant way enter into this world: "I am able to undertake what I would not otherwise have dared to do, without having to bother myself any longer worrying whether it is sensible or not. Indeed, some nights when I am working late, the futility of what I am doing would appear to be my deepest source of satisfaction."

Very shrewdly Roth has captured the futility of the Czech and Eastern European world, but by doing

so he has put Kepesh's own needs in relief, to his character's detriment. Kepesh's interest in Kafka is not futile; the book he is writing on Chekhov is not futile. In neither instance is he doing a "translation" that is unneeded and will never be published anyway. The Czech senses this, for he turns to Kepesh and asks: " 'What draws you to Kafka?' " Kepesh is embarrassed, for he is conscious of the disparity between his despair and the Czech's. He attempts an analogy, that while he is not on intimate terms with totalitarianism, he does understand the dictatorial claims of the body: "Its single-mindedness, its cold indifference and absolute contempt for the well-being of the spirit . . ." He adds that one can petition the body and still receive no message back, as he did with his psychoanalyst. Even in defense, Kepesh reveals his distance from Gogol, Chekhov, and, most of all, Kafka. He wallows in self-pity, makes fun of himself—as someone trying to "outfox impotence"—but also takes his needs seriously.

Serious they may be, but the scale of reference makes Kepesh appear adolescent. His search for fulfillment, his sense of loss of Birgitta and her friend Elisabeth, his distance from Claire and her orderly perfection all make up a life, but not a Kafkan life. One problem with the novel is that Roth could not find a correlative in Kepesh for the literary dimensions he suggests; nor for the level of feeling he wishes to impart. Kepesh is a somewhat older Portnoy, but he has learned little; and even his insight into his situation does not mitigate its triviality. He depends on ministrations and cosseting, is attended to by his mother, and after her death, by Clarissa-like Claire. His mother's specially prepared food is replaced by Claire's deep and full breasts: Kepesh needs a nipple, on which note the novel ends. So badly does he need the nipple that he becomes the possessor of one, as *The Breast.*

Roth's need was to find in Kepesh some divisiveness, some demonic or satanic element which made it impossible for him to choose a rational life. He sought some way of ingesting the mid-seventies, when rational and irrational lost all vestige of their traditional senses. Roth is almost always on the edge of mockery and burlesque, of the self and others; and the tragic needs a more sustained sense of self than he is inclined to portray. Kepesh's squirming is suggestive of tragic capability, but here the novel lacks reinforcement. His fear of the future with Claire, in which he foresees the loss of passion, the decline of vitality, the breakup of his feelings, is all strained through a narcissistic impulse; and yet we are expected to respond to such

---

*Unlike Roth himself, who has written sensitively about Kafka and at present serves as general editor of a series of Eastern European novels in translation.

feelings at a more sustained level. Her sacrifices for him—she aborts their child so as to free him of responsibilities—are useless given the nature of his selfish needs.

Clarissa-Claire is a fantasy woman, whereas Helen, the worm in the apple, makes more literary sense. Like the Monkey, in *Portnoy,* she is a mixture of demonic forces: a person of terrible conflicts in which she must alternate between slave and castigator. She exists in Roth's imagination far more profoundly, as the Gentile prototype, than the sweet victim type, like Claire. When Helen returns to Kepesh, at the country house, she is ready to leave her present husband, abort their two-month-old fetus, and take up again with Kepesh—if he will reciprocate by leaving Claire. She asks implicitly for an elopement, like Helen with Paris, so that they can divest themselves of respectability and responsibilities in a daring dash for self-destructive freedom. What she offers is the temptation Kepesh has spoken of in the Chekhov stories he idolizes. There, the desire for something different must clash with the routine organization life demands, and the tragic situation between personal need and actual fulfillment is developed. Kepesh rejects her offer, sees her off, stays with Claire through his father's visit, peers somewhat more deeply into his needs, and hangs on to a thread. He will, shortly, turn into a breast. Perhaps Roth has represented the country: in the face of adventure, exploration, possible damnation, it has turned to titty.

Kurt Vonnegut, Jr., was apparently attempting to reach with *Breakfast of Champions* (1973) the same audience that the "Breakfast of Champions," Wheaties, reaches. The story is not for children, yet the profusion of pictures, drawings, and diagrams suggests a children's book. At the same time, the definitions of many objects—yeast as living in its own excrement, for example—swings us back to a child's view of reality: its simple components rather than its complicating factors. Vonnegut had in mind, perhaps, an "Alice in Wonderland" or "Through the Looking Glass" for the 1970s. There are numerous references to looking glasses, mirrors, reflections; and a point is made of equating mirrors with leaks, "looking" with making or doing. Vonnegut's Alice would be Kilgore Trout, whose naiveté and fey qualities recall the childhood of man. Yet despite the evocations of childhood—Huck Finn and his world also come to mind—the tale is not for children, although childish. The following dialogue suggests the novel's problems:

The driver mentioned that the day before had been Veteran's Day.
"Um," said Trout.
"You a veteran?" said the driver.
"No," said Trout. "Are you?"
"No," said the driver.
Neither one of them was a veteran.

Many interchanges are as minimalist as this.

A kindred passage, repeated as a motif, is the penis size of every male adult we meet in the book. "Dwayne Hoover, incidentally, had an unusually large penis, and didn't even know it. . . . The world average was five and seven-eighths inches long, and one and one-half inches in diameter, when engorged with blood. Dwayne's was seven inches long and two and one-eighth inches in diameter when engorged with blood." Men's penis size is complemented by women's bust, waist, and hip measurements. This breakdown of people into their vital measurements is accompanied by the breakdown of all matters into statistics: what happens during an erection, what occurs when whiskey is made, how chemicals in the body work, what occurs when waste is dumped into a river. Each process is collapsed into its components as part of a parody of the scientific mind; thus, people are observed not only as actors in their sad dreams but as chemical and physical reactors.

What Vonnegut grants, nature withdraws; that is the balance. And what Vonnegut grants, he insists, must include him.* Dwayne Hoover, the unbalanced car dealer, and Kilgore Trout, Adamic man, finally meet at the Midland City arts festival; but by the time they do, each has been making a journey which Vonnegut insists upon as a fiction of his making. Vonnegut locates himself solidly in the center of the novel, not as narrator, but as author. "I had come to the Arts Festival incognito. I was there to watch a confrontation between two human beings I had created: Dwayne Hoover and Kilgore Trout." He carries on a dialogue with himself: " 'This is a very bad book you're writing,' I said to myself behind my *leaks* [glasses]. 'I know,' I said. 'You're afraid you'll

---

*He tells Joe David Bellamy that putting himself in his books was an inner urgency. "You probably get to a point where you can afford to do more self-indulgent things." He says his publishers have told him he will sell whatever he writes, and thus he feels he can do whatever that inner urgency tells him to do. That same flexibility affected the original ending of *Breakfast of Champions.* In that, Hoover and Vonnegut are both in an asylum, but when his publisher disliked the resolution, Vonnegut decided to change it. Such randomness characterizes much of the novel.

kill yourself the way your mother did,' I said. 'I know,' I said."

Vonnegut justifies his intrusions by telling the reader he plans to cleanse himself of his characters. He introduces himself to Kilgore Trout in Midland City and informs him he was created for use in his books, and that he, Vonnegut, knows Trout's future, a Nobel Prize in medicine. Like Barth in *Letters,* Vonnegut, at fifty, is opening himself out to new experiences: "I am cleansing myself and renewing myself [he tells Trout] for the very different sorts of years to come. Under similar spiritual conditions, Count Tolstoi freed his serfs. Thomas Jefferson freed his slaves. I am going to set at liberty all the literary characters who have served me so loyally during my writing career."

Yet Vonnegut's "literary crisis" does not connect with the "crisis" of his characters, two middle-aged investors in America: Dwayne Hoover, for whom a materialistic America works beautifully; and Kilgore Trout, who rejects everything America ostensibly stands for and represents the forgotten writer, unsold and unread. He is a kind of mirror image of the younger Vonnegut, who toiled unrecognized until the sixties, when he gained a youthful readership. Trout's books, like Vonnegut's, are hybrids, "other worldliness" based on solid social criticism; he is a man for all seasons, rather than a specialist. The strategy is a potentially brilliant one for Vonnegut, to liberate his characters, but in episode after episode they stumble over each other like clowns; once free, they run down.

Located in these seams of American life is space for large-scale parody. Vonnegut has wedged himself into these interstices, but what has become increasingly clear since *Cat's Cradle* in 1963 is that he has failed to find sufficient form for the fun-making. Vonnegut carries on a kind of meditative dialogue with himself, to his own amusement, and then transfers it, untouched, to the page. His mind is full of such nonsequential moments, each of them with fictional potential, but untransformed, they remain the sensa of the novelist, not of the novel.

Vonnegut's forte is connecting the disconnected, turning our order into disorder, probing the layers of chaos we have created within our organization; and yet such probing can only function for the adult reader within some organizational principle or mold. In *V.* and *The Crying of Lot 49,* early in his career, Pynchon found such forms. Although his zaniness is no less than Vonnegut's, it is informed not by a lazy meditation on self and others, but on arrangements in which it can thrive and blossom beyond the moment.

Similarly, Barth has sought such forms in funhouses, crazy houses, colleges, and his career has been not to display personal zaniness but to find forms for containing it, the better to display it. This "wacky" view is itself quintessentially American: from *Moby-Dick* and *Huck Finn* to *Giles Goat-Boy* and *Gravity's Rainbow,* there is a clear line of continuity. Yet form is necessary. Vonnegut's formlessness does not approximate the formlessness of his views, but exposes them. Only shaping and orderliness can reveal disorder.

Much of this leaves us where we began, with questions about Vonnegut's audience. His predilection for certain code words or phrases reduces, not enhances, his appeal. In *Breakfast of Champions,* he has discovered "beaver," described as a large rodent which likes water and builds dams; also as the female vagina (drawing on page 23) which everyone from construction workers to firemen try to get a glimpse of. "Beaver" recurs regularly, and the joke lies heavy—it becomes a fraternity house image, yielding little enough even in its first manifestation. Trout looks at "beavers" in New York porno shops, although his activities there seem to have little bearing on anything else. For whom is this intended?

"Hi Ho" (Disney's Snow White?) replaces "So it goes," as *Slapstick: Lonesome No More* (1976) replaces *Breakfast of Champions.* "I have called it 'Slapstick' because it is grotesque, situational poetry —like the slapstick film comedies, especially those of Laurel and Hardy, of long ago. It is about what life *feels* like to me." What life feels like to Vonnegut in the mid-1970s is a vaudeville show consisting of brief episodes, little set pieces, each with its attempt at joke and whimsy. He has devised a fiction even more minimal than that of Kosinski, Didion, or Barthelme. His minimalism is not only of brevity, fleetingness, but of evanescence.

After an autobiographical introduction—himself, his extended family, his now dead sister and her husband, his scientist brother—Vonnegut comes to the narrative proper, the memoirs of a hundred-year-old man, Mel Brooks's thousand-year-old man reduced. Vonnegut's "survivor" of apocalypse (New York is stripped of nearly all its functions, and the country of all but bare living) is called Dr. Wilbur Daffodil-11 Swain, and before it was Daffodil-11, the middle name was Rockefeller. His twin sister is Eliza Mellon Swain. Besides Mellon and Rockefeller, characters are Fords, Paleys, Rothschilds, a naming conceit which, incidentally, connects to nothing else.

Wilbur and Eliza first appear in public as drooling,

idiotic children, but in private they are highly cultivated, learned, almost geniuses when they combine their intelligence. They work as a team, rather than separately, although Wilbur goes on to become a medical doctor, a senator, and President, excelling at none of these. The twins, who recall Ada and Van in Nabokov's novel, are part of that fashionable postwar incursion into incest and incestuous relationships. Although their connection is not primarily sexual—they are, rather, intellectual halves coming together— there is a strong sexual undertow, and on occasion they couple. They undertake the idiot pose in public because their extreme ugliness and ungainliness made their parents reject them. They have been established in great luxury in a house of their own, with servants and all their needs attended to, and their parents visit once a year.

The most effective sections of the book are the "slapstick" elements of their early lives. They throw food around, they slobber, they live in specially designed rooms; their behavior is tolerated, and their private physician, Stewart Rawlings Mott, does no more than check on their bowels and other visible signs of health. Wilbur and Eliza perceive that their parents, faced by such monsters, with twelve fingers and toes, extra nipples, et al., wish them to die. They are excrescences, but they enjoy perfect health, and of course, behind their pose, they are brilliant, although only together.

Vonnegut is taking on an entire aspect of the decade: its egocentricity, in the parents' disregard for their children; its irresponsibility and groveling before material things; the breakdown of family life, which Vonnegut resurrects with his idea of families extending across the country; a self-indulgence which is based not on greed, as it was in the past, but on a desire to avoid unhappiness and unpleasantness; the decline of family life as a signal of America's decline (the further America declines, the more tenacious and powerful become the Chinese); the lack of power felt by the individual, who needs another person for completion; the disintegration, akin to apocalypse, of American ideals, once again associated with neglect of the family, the needs of children. Vonnegut has stationed himself solidly in the children's camp, an updating of the "Children's Campaign" of *Slaughterhouse-Five.*

The subtitle of *Slapstick,* "Lonesome No More," is the motto for Wilbur Swain when he runs for President. It is his campaign idea that what America wants more than anything is an extended family. Swain, as he recalls in his memoir, tells people their "new mid-dle name would consist of a noun, the name of a flower or fruit or nut or vegetable or legume, or a bird or a reptile or a fish or a mollusk, or a gem or a mineral or a chemical element—connected by a hyphen to a number between one and twenty." Something from nature replaces something from the material world, as Rockefeller. All people with Daffodil as part of their middle name would be cousins, and those with Daffodil-11 would be even closer. Everyone is assured of perhaps 200,000 cousins in America and is to be "lonesome no more."

Vonnegut has positioned himself not only in the commune world but in the world set against the debased material, God's world of flowers and legumes. Whatever is natural is good; unnatural, bad. The mid-seventies stress, especially among the young, on antipollution and anticontamination feeds right into Vonnegut's fiction, becoming the "heroic" element as against the villainy of polluters (parents, advocates of progress, materialists). Connected to this regard for environmental matters is the presence of another kind of gravity, a lighter gravity, and the apocalyptic notion of "The Green Death," a plague on Manhattan Island. Within this altered country, Swain (our country lad) holds sway, although his presidency is hardly imperial, rarely even being recognized. Decentralization has occurred. The President must deal, for example, with the King of Michigan, the grandson of Stewart Mott the family physician.

Paralleling these developments is the rise of the Chinese into positions of power and knowledge. The Chinese have grown much smaller—part of a concerted effort to save materials in clothing—and yet as tiny men and women they have organized most of the world for their own use and benefit. Vonnegut, once again, has introduced a 1970s theme, here Nixon's opening to China, and from this expanded the Chinese into a race that knows all, even how to speak to the dead.

So it goes! After promising, in *Breakfast of Champions,* to cleanse himself of his characters, Vonnegut resurrects a couple here: Norman Mushari, the corrupt lawyer from *God Bless You, Mr. Rosewater,* now somewhat repentant for helping only the rich; and Captain Bernard O'Hare, Billy Pilgrim's sidekick in *Slaughterhouse-Five.* We are saved, fortunately, from Kilgore Trout and his platitudes.

In its helter-skelter way, *Slapstick* fits into the novelistic scheme we see as characteristic of the late sixties and the seventies: the autobiographical writing which allows the older writer to make contact between his later and earlier years. Vonnegut's Swain is 100; Nabokov's Van Veen is 97; Styron's Stingo is in his fifties; Roth's Nathan Zuckerman in his late forties. Barth at fifty resurrects his previous characters, cleansing himself, although in quite different fashion from Vonnegut. Fiction appears to accept the 1970s as a recapitulation: not a reaching out, but a gathering in. Culturally, it suggests we are grappling with retention, with holding on; and that the decade represents an attempt at consolidation of whatever we have, are, where we fit, if we fit. The decade has, in a sense, been sacrificed, at least in these authors, to an ingathering of goods and values, demonstrating both a failure of nerve and a desire to take inventory. Although *Slapstick* promises an outrageous turns of events, it delivers on little; it becomes, in fact, embedded in conservation: conserve the self from extremes by reforming one's egoism within extended families. Control the self not by self but through consolidation. With all his chic, Vonnegut has taken a step backward.

The Painted Bird and *Steps* (see "Growing Up in America" and "The Possibilities of Minimalism") are the two coordinates of Jerzy Kosinski's fiction. After these works, we find not development but a refinement of issues and conflicts already outlined. Kosinski achieved so much in *The Painted Bird* and then attempted something so daring in *Steps,* it seems ungrateful to maintain he has not developed beyond them. But there is no denying that his later work, whatever the interest of individual books or the power of certain scenes, does not surpass earlier achievements. One reason, I think, is that Kosinski moved too rapidly into a literary and cultural scene, became too rapidly his sole subject matter, and then found he could not distinguish between subject and object. Egomania dominates the later Kosinski canon, but it is insufficiently perceived by him to become a metaphysical principle. He remains so connected to himself that he functions with masks and personae which lack differentiation or variety, associated as they are with overlapping obsessions. With all his European sophistication and historical awareness, he became American too rapidly.

Kosinski's titles have increasingly taken on a character of their own: metaphysical, insistent on natural sweep, ambitious to the utmost. He is involved rarely with a name or person, but typically with an idea: *Passion Play* (1979), with its Easter motif, being the latest. *Blind Date* (1977) suggests a fated existence that only personal will can intrude upon; *Steps,* as

outlined before, explores a metaphysical notion of elements closing in, approaching, or as stages in development or resolution; *Cockpit* (1975), maintaining control, using temperament and skill to be a mover; *The Devil Tree* (1973), entering nature's magic associated with the baobab, the tree of life and knowledge. *Being There* (1970) has its Candide-like protagonist, whose words are meaning; *The Painted Bird,* its image of art versus life, its brutal transgression against the very order of things.

The titles seek essences, not individuals, and help prepare us for Kosinski's basically unpeopled world. People become fleeting images in his episodes, or else individuals who can be maneuvered and manipulated, as the inmates of the camps were checkmated by guards and officials. The world of Kosinski's novels, as signalized by the titles, will lack normal or routine affections. *Being There* is distinct from being alone. *The Painted Bird* is not a bird of nature. *Steps* are for moving toward, not arriving. *The Devil Tree* is a reversed tree, with its roots as branches, its branches as roots, the work of the devil. In this arrangement, whereby people take a secondary role to the idea of them, Kosinski can locate himself as the controlling element, the rising God in the passion play.

By suggesting such sweep in his titles, and by omitting names and people, he can magnify the insignificance of others while increasing his own role. The titular devices are suggestive of megalomania, but of a depressive sort. The man who controls all—a kind of godly presence—is frequently described as in ill health or as needing injections of energy and vitamins. He travels, often, with paraphernalia which will keep him alive, and he has sudden reactions to simple drugs that require emergency treatment. He is dark and frail, a demonic presence as much as a godly one. The will to power keeps him ill.

Connected to the allegorical nature of the titles are allegorical characters. Chance in *Being There* is the most obvious, but Kosinski plays on names throughout to suggest roles beyond realistic lines of development. Levanter in *Blind Date* is "Easter"; he will rise, and he partakes of something like the passion. Fabian, in *Passion Play,* is a *faber* or creator; his name suggests a godlike role for himself, and his polo playing transforms him into a centaur. References are to mythical experiences between man and horse, placed in a tableau of a "passion play," an Easter event of sacrifice and redemption. Tarden, in *Cockpit,* is a man who is late, or tardy, his survival depending on his ability to settle situations after they seem lost. In

Steps, the narrator is unnamed, as is the protagonist of *The Painted Bird.* By omitting names, Kosinski moved toward the anonymity of allegory; and by using names that suggest types, he also contravenes realism. He gains, as well, a dimension of abstraction, advantageous in *The Painted Bird* and *Steps,* miscalculated in his later fiction.

The minimalist structure Kosinski began with *Steps* continues in *Being There.* More a novella than a novel, it is a parable of sorts, although the basic elements are all variations on one joke: if you say something without elaboration, it will be altered along the way to mean something very different. The media will turn every phrase into an event, the event into a historical moment, the moment into a crisis. Thus, all public activity, as Kosinski measures it, is empty: a hole disguised as a pregnancy.

Chance, the protagonist of *Being There,* is a gardener on an estate, a man who exchanges his labor for his keep. There are no records of his employment, and he has failed to acquire any documents. Without a driver's license and credit cards, he is a nonperson. His life thus far has been spent cultivating the garden of the Old Man and watching television for endless hours. All he knows of the outside world derives from television. His knowledge is a reflection of the real, and he is, in fact, like Plato's denizens of the cave who think of the outside world as shadow, their reflected world as real. Chance, furthermore, is illiterate, a blank page on which television images can make their imprint.

As an antihero, Chance is expected to carry a good deal of freight. With *Being There,* Kosinski uses his fiction for the first time as direct social commentary, what he had already done in his two earliest books on collective behavior: *The Future Is Ours* (1960) and *No Third Path* (1962). Here his critique is not of socialist states but of America and American culture. Chance is his vehicle: a tabula rasa, a man without any sense of life except gardening, an illiterate who views everything in terms of television modes and pastoral images. As an orphan, he has floated free of everything that connects a person to society or a body politic. Here is Adamic man, and he is a blithering idiot.

Kosinski's conceit is to turn Chance into a man of significance. By way of an accident, he comes into contact with Rand, the ailing chairman of the board of the First American Financial Corporation, one of whose programs is to assist businesses harassed by riots, inflation, high taxes. Rand's wife, a young and frisky thing, renames Chance Chauncey Gardiner, and once he has a suitable name and connections to high places, he is taken seriously. His words, with their repeated analogy between country and garden, are pondered, dissected, examined for wisdom. Chance meets the President and impresses him; he meets heads of states, ambassadors, UN officials, and all come away convinced his is a new spirit at large in the world. Yet everything is a variation of what he tells a television audience: " 'I know the garden very well. . . . I have worked in it all of my life. It's a good garden and a healthy one; its trees are healthy and so are its shrubs and flowers, as long as they are trimmed and watered in the right seasons. The garden needs a lot of care. I do agree with the President: everything in it will grow in due course. And there is still plenty of room in it for new trees and new flowers of all kinds.' "

Kosinski is moving along some very gripping 1960s ideas. Yet while the novella is an attempt at a social/political critique, it is curiously exhausted. The brevity, the repetition of situation and comment suggest the course his work would take after *Steps.* Minimalism in execution becomes a reflection of authorial exhaustion, not an artistic statement. Chance is a short-story character, and *Being There* is not even a novella in its development. It is an extended single metaphor, so that even repeating episodes do not bring additional insight. Each gullible person, from the President to the Soviet ambassador, is an image of the same person. Once Kosinski establishes his situation, he brings no variations to it. Chance is a modern-day Candide, but without the witty context of Voltaire. He is an imitation of Candide. Kosinski has not given us the parable of being, or of being there, but a television script, slight, singular, exhausted before it begins.

Kosinski's vision beginning here is not modest. *Being There, The Devil Tree, Cockpit, Blind Date, Passion Play** are all brief titles with metaphysical resonances. All are concerned with existence, nature, control, with elements of chance, individual will, determinism. As executed, unfortunately, they have neither the solidity of *The Painted Bird* nor the truly metaphysical dimensions of *Steps.* That novel was Kosinski's entrance into formlessness—steps or stages, roles or acting, where theater dominated. Even *The Painted Bird,* in its image of the bird first painted and then turned loose to be pecked to death

---

**I discuss *Passion Play* more fully in a later segment.*

by its own kind, has the sense of an intrusion into nature. Kosinski's vision has become a refinement and reduction of that basic idea: life in nearly every form is an intrusion into existence, which is alien and foreign.

After *Being There,* Kosinski entered a period of consolidation, with three novels at two-year intervals, their episodes and protagonists interchangeable. These are great anal sagas, dominated by confidence men, with attitudes derived from James Bond adventures, capable of great cruelty, otherwise somewhat exhausted; men with endless wealth and other resources (apartments, houses, goods), all concealed. As we can expect, they manifest extreme contempt for women, and their stress on female allure is part of a porno fantasy which Kosinski presents as romantic love. His women are all viewed through the eyes of his men; nor do we ever gain any view of his male protagonists through their women's eyes. The men define the moral action of the novels; whereas the women fall into position as playthings, torments, goods, orifices.

What has occurred in these last three novels—and one can add most of *Passion Play*—is that Kosinski has discovered a workable formula, an extension of the method in *Steps,* where it was original and fresh. That book dominates: in method, the brief scene, rarely connected to previous episodes; in moral outlook, an amoral, neutral world into which a male may pour whatever there is of himself. Kosinski has become so carried away by the potentialities of individual freedom that he has failed to give either individual or context a valid container. More significantly, he has lost all touchstones for behavior: his characters are so driven by narcissistic impulses that there is no sounding board, no norm, nothing to measure them against.

In *The Devil Tree,* Jonathan Whelan is caught in a series of brief episodes, even less defined than those in *Steps.* He is, in some way, connected to the "devil tree," the baobab, whose branches and roots are reversed, the result of the devil's entanglement in its branches. The "devil tree" is a reversal of nature but in nature's pattern, part of the rule of anomalous elements. Whelan is also such an anomaly, part of nature and yet beyond it. Wealthy beyond dreams, he wanders a Kosinski lunar landscape, moving in and out of relationships, the briefness of each dictated by the brevity of the episode in which Kosinski screens him. The technique is that of a camera panning the landscape and picking up transitory images, a montage of this or that, in which Whelan moves without enthusiasm. The resultant novel is a narrative based on an ego meditating with itself. Whelan admits to a divided self, a part that deceives and destroys and a part that craves love and acceptance.

Karen, Whelan's "love," affords him an in-and-out sense of himself and her: subject and object intermingling and separating. Whelan meditates: "I still dread the thought of anyone being important to me." But since Karen is undeveloped, except physically, we know nothing of what that means. Whelan's meditation at the conclusion is characteristic not only of him but of the novel: "He sensed only surfaces. Forms became empty figures without gravity or weight. He closed his eyes, blotting out the flat shapes that used to have dimension and meaning in his life, and the sounds that used to have resonance." The very effort of hoping tires him.

By the time of *Cockpit,* Kosinski's fifth novel, patterns are clear. While the picaresque, episodic narrative returns him to his first two novels, he is also moving laterally. The influence from pop culture, whose values he parodies in *Being There,* has intensified. For his narrators are becoming urban James Bonds, men who revel in modern technology and maintain their superiority because of it. Tarden in *Cockpit* never leaves one of his several apartments without paraphernalia that can cripple an opponent. He eschews firearms for needles, drugs, sprays—contemporary killers rather than old-fashioned violence. He is fully urbanized, wandering the streets, picking up whores, soliciting aid from strangers; and his apartments are always high up in modern buildings. His devices are such that he conquers in all situations, this small, dark, unmuscular, sickly, almost emaciated Bond.

In other ways as well, the Kosinski protagonist, and we can include the narrator from *Steps,* borrows from pop, trendy culture. He is a typical wanderer, an urban cowboy, and his satisfactions, sexual and otherwise, derive from turn-ons. He is never far from sensationalism induced by drugs, and, in fact, the characteristic Kosinski narrator often seems hooked on medication, prescribed for his failing health. Tarden is an assumed name, given to him and barely mentioned again in the book. As his name suggests, he is a man who arrives when everyone else is settled and who then captivates, conquers, outdoes. Luckily, he never loses, for the games he plays are almost always with death. Once more, in the pop mode, he plays with apocalypse, sudden endings, death-defying decisions. His life is like the final moments from *High Noon*.

Such a hero has tremendous potential, but he must be tempered by wit, and here Kosinski fails us. Although much is fantasy and obsession, Kosinski works out the novel as reality. Wit comes into play only once, in a short section devoted to uniforms. Tarden has quit the "Service" (the CIA?), and he is under a cloud. Since he cannot surface, he lives for a few weeks at a time in different apartments, assuming different identities, always moving along edges and margins. We never see him in a normalizing situation with family or friends, or attending a concert or an opera simply for pleasure. All his activities are under cover, though he is no longer an agent.

Disguise and role-playing are all. "I've come to look upon disguise [Tarden says] as more than a means of personal liberation: it's a necessity. My life depends on my being able to instantly create a new persona and slip out of the past." This need extends well back, into *The Painted Bird,* where it is continuous with the decisions the young boy makes to survive. He can never be himself, because "himself" is reviled and marked for torture and death; he must become "others" in order to survive his own self. Kosinski has at his disposal a wicked cultural weapon.

In *Cockpit,* Tarden, although he is a nonperson, decides to move at the highest level, and in a Florentine military uniform shop he orders two outfits. His stipulation is that the uniforms be "easily recognizable, distinctive. Just make it undefinable." His costume becomes an ecumenical combination of German-Soviet-American-Nato-Chinese features, and it draws respect from the highest officers in their real uniforms. It opens all doors for Tarden, makes him beloved by the police, and affords him privileges usually drawn only by heads of state. The man remains Tarden, but the image sparks the imagination. Carlyle's *Sartor Resartus* is well illustrated. Effective though it is, the episode is almost the sole one in which parody and self-parody connect.

Elsewhere, Tarden is repeatedly the victim of Kosinski's obsession not to lose control. Scenes of sadism and physical cruelty abound. When Tarden is crossed by a woman who becomes his slave and then retreats, he devises a fearful death for her by radiation. Before that, he humiliates her sexually with three bums who are given carte blanche to maul and soil her as they wish. Many of these episodes are pornographic fantasies, for they involve master-slave relationships, not real people. Veronica is such a slave, given money to submit to Tarden's bizarre wishes. Similar scenes involve two lesbians who are paid well to accompany Tarden to his isolated estate and to perform for him. Tarden's expertise in photography fits the porno-fantasy impetus of the novel. He deals in lenses, scopes, and film, and often his interest is as a voyeur. Behind his camera, he can record, use his photos for blackmail, or else for his solitary pleasures. The camera is, for him, masturbatory, a form of self-performance, the zenith of control.

Despite the presence of so much gadgetry, Kosinski rarely shows us how things work; he displays only a narrator whose solipsism is pathological. *Cockpit*'s title suggests the dominant image: the pilot in the cockpit in control of the plane, the man behind the camera, Tarden controlling his fate across continents, manipulating anyone who might threaten him. These are the visions of the boy in *The Painted Bird,* endless repetitions of revenge—but with an urgency that consolidates the episodes. After several novels, such episodes can exist only by virtue of parody, not solemnly. Those obsessions have not found a sufficient literary medium, and they exist as raw materials, notebook jottings, not form.

The "blind date" in *Blind Date* is a compelling episode somewhat defused by the fact that Kosinski cannot quite fit it into a larger context. Even the perpetrator goes unexamined. The novel, nevertheless, is Kosinski's effort to draw together his materials, to review the terrible past, to find some metaphysical foundation for his middle career. A "blind date" occurs, in one sense, when a rapist enjoys his victim without her ever seeing his face. Levanter is coached in the technique by Oscar, at a youth movement camp in an unnamed Eastern European country. Oscar has perfected a technique whereby he can grip the victim from behind, keeping his face from her: thus the "blind date." Levanter attempts it, in a particularly brutal rape, and succeeds; his victim fails to recognize him, and Oscar, in fact, is picked up for the crime and sent away. Levanter's sole punishment comes when he meets the victim later, and she intuits that he is the rapist, at a time when he is romantically interested in her. The scene fades out on a note of nostalgia, rape-style.

Levanter's act, an invasion of an innocent, powerless person, floats within a neutral universe. Oscar is convicted, although Levanter volunteers that he was the rapist. The young woman seems none the worse for the brutal act, and Levanter simply loses out on a "blind date" that would have returned further dividends. Kosinski's failure to provide a social context for an obsessive power play disallows feeling for the protagonist, a lack which *he* may have encouraged, and feeling for the event. It occurs as if in the camera eye or in a porno fantasy. A very different kind of "blind date" occurs later, when Levanter, in planning to meet the woman who he thinks is the wealthy Mary-Jane Kinkaid, meets instead her secretary, who, in turn, proves to be her employer. This "blind date" turns out differently; since Levanter is irresistible, he makes a suitable marriage, along the lines of Kosinski's own marriage to a wealthy widow.

The "blind date" is further connected to something we have already suggested, Kosinski's concern with "blind chance," a concern he underlines in the meeting with Jacques Monod, author of *Chance and Necessity* (1971) and winner of the Nobel Prize in 1965 for his work in genetics. Monod's theories have made him a kind of philosophical outlaw, and Kosinski's interest in the man, which is intense, is paralleled by his interest in the ideas. Monod's theories all derive from evidence he has marshaled that man is the product, not of pattern or plan, but of chance genetic mutation. This suggests the necessity for a new philosophy of self, for if we deny the old theories of destiny and plan, we cannot continue to maintain old beliefs based on them. The entire philosophical tradition associated with Plato, Hegel, Marx, among others, no longer obtains. When man continues to accept philosophical systems which make him "animistic"— that is, with a soul and with a life distinct from his genetic inheritance—he becomes schizoid, split between a system that explains nothing and a materialism which also explains little.

That man needs to forge a new sense of himself appeals to Kosinski, who finds in this "new sense" a reinforcement of his own experience as a man moving outside pattern or plan, outside "blind chance" and life's plots. Roaming a neutral universe, controlling everything carefully, allowing himself all weapons, defining no moral or ethical areas, a Kosinski protagonist works within Monod's definitions of what is authentic. The only difficulty is that Kosinski's protagonists judge authenticity only for themselves, never for their partners, mates, women friends. Authenticity becomes a closed-circuit narcissism, with space only for one.*

---

*Kosinski has replayed the terms of the Camus universe, but has stopped short of Camus's insistence on some ethical accounting. A Kosinski protagonist is like Meursault of the first part of *The Stranger;* it is the second part which gives him trouble.

More than any other of Kosinski's novels, *Blind Date* introduces real people and real incidents. Besides the brief outlines of his own marriage and the meeting with Monod, he also limns the Sharon Tate massacre by the Manson gang. Since Levanter was not present—because of a mix-up in his luggage, which is what happened with Kosinski on that fatal day—he can only imagine what occurred; and this Kosinski recreates from accounts of the scene: the pregnant Tate, the Polish friend, the violence of what he calls the "Crabs of Sunset," the bloodthirsty massacre. In another "live" scene, Levanter meets with Lindbergh and chides him for his America First activity, which helped to keep America out of the war while Jews were exterminated in Europe. All these are "chance meetings," or chance events, part of the underlying ideology of the novel; but brief vignettes, lacking texture or even meaning.

Levanter defines himself, in part, by his juxtaposition to important people and events, but Kosinski misses the disproportion. Levanter is not scaled down, but is allegedly their equal in ways not demonstrated. Everything he does is noticed. When he writes on chance in creative investment—he calls himself an "investor," in life and ideas—this piece is recognized at the highest levels. It leads to his introduction to a wealthy widow and his marriage. He slides through the seams of life, and yet personal need, blind chance, contexts fail to cohere. Caught between allegories and realities, Kosinski has not integrated his materials. His scorn for the entire postwar era stops short of the philosophical statement he hoped to achieve.

With *The Fixer* and *The Tenants* (1971), Malamud became a political novelist, taking his themes and ideas from contemporary life. Whereas *The Fixer* focused on more general ideas of freedom and the state in areas of law, civil rights, concern for the individual, *The Tenants* zeroes in on the black "revolution" of the sixties. Once again, the stress is on how these changes in social and political thinking affect the Jew, here Harry Lesser. The Jew becomes, in a sense, both conscience and victim of all social/political change. Malamud's novel recalls Saul Bellow's *The Victim,* where Jew and Gentile form a symbiotic relationship in which the Jew becomes the keeper of the social torch, by way of Gentile blackmail of him. Here, in *The Tenants,* white Lesser becomes the holder of black Willie Spearmint's talent: Spearmint offers it up to Lesser, Lesser judges, makes suggestions, and, in effect, offers him ways in which he can improve his work. But Spearmint perceives that to follow Lesser's suggestions, to alter his manuscript according to white-Jewish recommendations, is for him to sacrifice some of his blackness, to sell himself to a Jewish way of thinking for the sake of possible success.

Lesser is trying to complete his third novel while living in a condemned building. The conditions under which he labors recall the setting of *The Fixer* or the apartment in *The Victim* where Leventhal must deal with Allbee. Lesser's first novel was an artistic triumph, his second a disaster. His life as a novelist is now on the line, for he must produce something significant with this third, or be relegated to the world of has-beens. He knows his first will sink away unless he can repeat something of his triumph, and for eight years he has labored in the wilderness.

He has become a monk, his personal and sexual life having come virtually to a halt. The abandoned apartment building, which the owner has been able to empty except for Lesser, is his monastery. At thirty-six, he is at the threshold of the most important few months of his life, when he can either bring off the novel or else watch it extend, incomplete, into the limitless future. Poised on the edge of a personal abyss, desperate for completion, he is yet unwilling to finish the novel until he feels he has got it right. There is in Lesser something of what Conrad put into Razumov just before Haldin appeared, in *Under Western Eyes*. The scenario is familiar: one person is moving toward a dramatic moment in his life (Razumov has decided to enter an essay contest which will give his life direction), when another person with a completely different set of coordinates appears and acts as disrupter and/or conscience. Personal considerations then become intertwined with social/political considerations, as well as with matters of conscience.

The theme is considerable, especially when Lesser's interrupter is Willie Spearmint, called Bill, trailing clouds of Shakespeare (not chewing gum) in his assumed name; but also a proud black man trying to achieve his kind of fiction. Spearmint holds to the black aesthetic of the 1960s, rejecting artistic ideas which will traduce the pure revolutionary quality of his work. What comes first, for him, is not form, but the content, the raw material of ghetto life: violence, brutal interactions among people. He seeks a direct representation of black life, not some artistically conceived mirrored refraction. He moves into one of the empty apartments and types away obsessively, his working hours coinciding with Lesser's. They are two gladiators, each in training against the moment when

the inevitable confrontation will occur.

Malamud poses the confrontation in terms of literary values. Social/political/personal dimensions are subsumed under aesthetic considerations. When Spearmint argues black aesthetics and Lesser counters with the aesthetics of form, their dialogues take on the elements of revolution versus status quo. No matter how much Lesser sympathizes with Spearmint's portrait of ghetto life, he must criticize the manuscript for lacking artistic distance. Spearmint has not assumed any persona, and the resulting material is too raw, too unshaped for Lesser's taste. This assessment, of course, infuriates Spearmint, who feels Lesser is trying to make him over into a white-Jewish writer, enemy values lying as a trap. Spearmint is convinced the Jew is the black's oppressor, and when Lesser offers suggestions, Spearmint takes them as victimization: the Jewish writer, like the landlords and store owners in Harlem, is trying to take over the black's imagination.

The ground is now prepared for the gladiatorial battle. There are, however, softening features. Spearmint reads Lesser's two published novels and greatly respects the first. His admirations lead him to agree that Lesser may have a point about distance and form. And Lesser, for his part, likes the women in Spearmint's camp, the black Mary, who travels with a friend of Spearmint's, and the latter's own white woman, Irene. When Lesser sleeps with Mary at a party of radical blacks, and is discovered, Spearmint saves him from violence. But when Lesser takes over Irene, who is feeling abandoned, Spearmint tries to kill Lesser by throwing him from a window.

The terms of the relationship intensify. Spearmint will indirectly pander for Lesser by offering him parties; Lesser will, in return, offer literary advice. It is an exchange which cannot function for long, since Spearmint will find himself back in the very role he has rejected; and Lesser cannot hold up his end, for Spearmint's work interferes with his own. Spearmint in revenge for losing Irene has his gang destroy both copies of Lesser's manuscript. Lesser must rewrite from the start. In his own form of revenge, he destroys Spearmint's work place. The two begin to circle each other, symbiotically; for neither can work without remaining obsessed with the other.

They take to sneaking around the abandoned apartment house, reading each other's work discarded in trash cans on the street. Their lives are completely intertwined, black and white, black and Jew, duplicating what Spearmint feels is a master-slave relationship. They are now real gladiators, each out to destroy the other in order to avoid self-destruction. "They trailed each other in the halls. Each knew where the other was although the terrain had changed. The trees in . . . [Spearmint's] room had moved off the walls onto the dank floors in the flat. Taking root, they thickened there and spread into the hall and down the stairs." The setting for the confrontation is now jungle: a "grassy clearing in the bush." Emotions are atavistic, and the battle begins. " 'Blood-suckin Jew Niggerhater,' " Spearmint growls. " 'Anti-Semitic Ape,' " Lesser responds. "They aimed at each other accurate blows. Lesser felt his jagged ax sink through bone and brain as the groaning black's razor-sharp saber, in a single boiling stabbing slash, cut the white's balls from the rest of him. Each, thought the writer, feels the anguish of the other."

In a hallucinatory scene of primitive survival, they have found their targets. Symbiotic to the end, they must destroy what each has felt as a threat. The black feels undermined by Lesser's "white" novelistic doctrines; Lesser feels threatened by Spearmint's raw scenes of violence unshaped by art and pointed directly at Jews and whites.

Lesser is, in a way, S. Levin, now returned from the West and dedicated to fiction writing. Lesser's devotion to his novel preempts all other experience; but it curiously connects him to Spearmint, whose subject matter and racial hatred would ordinarily mark him as an enemy. Like Levin, however, Lesser has a vision of a pastoral existence, which for him is the salvation of the writer. Nature, somehow, both saves and, later, destroys. "Lesser explorer. Lesser and Clark overland to Manifest Destiny. Or maybe Mississippi steamboat with blooming, spashing paddlewheel, heart-rending foghorn, and other marvelous inventions. Not a bad metaphor, boat. Lesser in short-masted bark with a pull of wind in its sail on the Galilean Lake, trying to spy on the apostolic shore what it's all about. Lesser sculling on the Hudson . . . or rowing to music on the sweet-flowing Thames. . . . Better still, the artist as broad swirling river, flowing freely amid islands of experience, some dense green, luxuriant, treeful; others barren, soft sand with wet footprints."

Many traditions connect here: Lesser as Huck Finn, but also as Robinson Crusoe, with a strong whiff of Leopold Bloom. Sitting in his room in the abandoned apartment house, he envisions kingdoms he can inhabit, for writing his novel has located him in "realms of gold." Explorer, discoverer, pioneer, he tries to create a world. Lesser's world, unfortunately,

is far less than what he envisages, and the novel he outlines is pure self-love. In his novel, to be called *The Promised Land* (America? Israel?), the writer-narrator creates a character who is something of a persona: "What it may come to in the end, despite the writer's doubts, is that he invents this character in his book who will in a sense love for him; and in a sense love him." He conceives of his theme as tragic, for he will append to it an epigraph from *Lear:* "Who is it who can tell me who I am?"

The book sounds like the biography of D. H. Lawrence which Dubin will write in Malamud's next novel, eight years later, the length of time Lesser has spent so far on his novel. Yet we see very little of Lesser's novel: even though he devotes himself to its completion, it seems the lesser part of him. Also, its narcissism does not convince us Lesser can move in those large areas of pastoral and heroism which his fantasies and visions provide for him. There is a profound split in him which Malamud does not account for. Like Spearmint, he is incompletely observed.

In *The Tenants,* Malamud reached for a very large statement about writing, race, human relationships, all caught in an urban waste land. Yet these large areas remain to be filled in. Spearmint does not ring true as a black writer, and his association with Lesser lacks meaningful levels. Further, the abandoned building, potentially a great emblem, does not take on sufficiently symbolic importance. We sense there are strong feelings and undercurrents seeking form. Lesser's advice to Spearmint that his ideas need form and shaping can be applied to Malamud's own working of his novel: themes here are in search of the correct structure, or else are projected on a scale which the novel (too brief) cannot sustain.

The structuring of a sensual paradise is Hawkes's goal in *The Blood Oranges* (1971). The place is Illyria, the ancient Adriatic country of legendary qualities, somewhat like Yeats's Byzantium as a place of the imagination. In Illyria, one can taste the sweetness of that citrus fruit which seems to have the ingredient of the life force. "Blood orange" is a contradiction, since fruit and blood meats are separate, and yet Hawkes has combined them. That combination suggested by both title and fruit is intrinsic to the combinations of the novel: the fruit as something to be eaten and yet an element penetrating deep into life itself.*

---

*In his interview with Robert Scholes, Hawkes spoke of "blood oranges" as part of a paradox: "it means that no sweetness is ephemeral but on the contrary possesses all the life-drive

If we add to the above the epigraph, from Ford Madox Ford's *The Good Soldier,** we have, even before the novel begins, a sexual drama of point and counterpoint. The epigraph, however, is misleading, since Ford's concern throughout is to put everything his narrator says into question, to underline his veracity at every turn; whereas Hawkes's narrator, Cyril, establishes the "truths" on which the novel can be based. In his solidity and fleshiness, he is not to be questioned, while Ford's Dowell is dubiety itself.

Cyril is the strongest figure of a quartet: Cyril and his wife, Fiona; Hugh and his wife, Catherine. Cyril calls the turns, and when he decides on wife-swapping sessions, the round robin commences and continues. Cyril lives for the moment, for the sensation; and he harbors no jealousy. Having entered a cycle of self-indulgence in which sexual dalliance defines him and his circle, he has liberated himself from the concerns of the average bourgeois man. All four are middle-aged or close to it; all four are hardly one's picture of "lovers" or of passion artists. They are, in stature and age, past their prime, and yet they insist on living out the fantasies of the sixties. As Cyril comments: ". . . we were a quartet of tall and large-boned lovers aged in the wood. Too big for mere caprice, too old to waste time and yet old enough to appreciate immodesty, we were all four of us imposing in height, in weight, in blood pressure, in chest expansion."

Beneath their sensuality lies potential tragedy. Hugh will die—not from the squeezing of the "iron hand" in his chest, but at the end of a self-knotted rope—and Catherine will be institutionalized. Cyril will end up visiting her on his bicycle, and living chastely with Rosella, a peasant woman who once posed in the nude for Hugh. Their indulgence lasts only for a season; Illyria, like the ancient place itself, passes. The novel, in fact, opens with the tragedy of their lives; not with the joys of Illyria, but with its demise as paradise. Cyril's spirit is not broken, but the quartet has been disrupted. In this respect, the situation of *The Good Soldier* is repeated: Ashburnham a suicide, his young admirer mad, Dowell's wife a suicide, Ashburnham's wife and Dowell the sole survivors.

In Illyria, the language is "croak peonie" or "cre-

spi fagag," or whatever the local people say when they speak.† The quartet of lovers, isolated by language from the place, are as though cast back to the ancient Illyria, with only themselves to consider. We have here, then, both the strength and the weakness of *The Blood Oranges*. For Hawkes has isolated his quartet for pure self-indulgence. Although Catherine and Hugh have three children, these only rarely intrude. Sensuality is the rule of the night, or even of the day; and the peeling off of a brassiere or the tightness of slacks around the buttocks provides the kind of voyeurism one associates with adolescents, not middle-aged couples. The preoccupation with sensual pleasures, with these heavy and large-boned people (Cyril describes himself as immense), to the exclusion of all else, makes the novel into a kind of family porno film. Also, the stress on fleshiness—thick thighs, rolls of belly fat, muscular buttocks, Cyril's love of mass—brings us into another dimension: one in which mother is as important as wife or mistress. And yet mother, big and fleshy, middle-aged, hardly suits the sensual atmosphere. Hawkes must consolidate several discrete elements.

The galvanizing force is Cyril. Like the others, he has only a Christian name, and his nationality is not given. Hawkes's attempt at a breakthrough into a different order of experience involves floating his characters through a social, political, and even geographical vacuum. In their isolation, they become Crusoes of the sensual world, with Cyril as guide and goad. His pansexuality, clearly, draws distinct lines, for his aim is to bed down only with women; he and Hugh, while sharing each other's women, are not ostensibly attracted to each other. The quartet never becomes a commune or orgiastic.

Also, pansexuality is derived from the male point of view. Cyril is circus-master: he seduces Catherine, he makes Hugh tolerate an intolerable situation, he thrusts Fiona off on Hugh, whose puritanical nature struggles against what is occurring. After Hugh gets hold of a medieval chastity belt lost in a cave, he puts it not on Fiona, as a mark of his possession, but on his wife, to keep Cyril away. The "belting" of Catherine by Hugh, followed by Cyril's removal of the belt, suggests that the sexual directive makes women into objects. Catherine, apparently, sways to each in turn,

---

seriousness of the rich, black flow of blood itself. It suggests wound invading desire, desire 'containing agony.' "

*"Is there then any terrestrial paradise where, amidst the whispering of the olive-leaves, people can be with whom they like and have what they like and take their ease in shadows and coolness?"

---

†"Croak peonie" and/or "crespi fagag" occur nine times in the novel, seven of which are in the first third of the book. "Croak peonie" appears to be an approximation of how the language sounds to the foreign quartet, "crespi fagag" an attempt to spell out what they hear.

permitting the belt as long as Hugh wishes it, then allowing it to be removed when Cyril dominates. Pansexuality as an idea has limited qualities, serving not as a breakthrough but as an adolescent fantasy of abundant female flesh, a mass which acquiesces, a motherly figure who is seductive.

A good deal of the problem lies here, not only with the execution of the novel but with the model. For the model appears to be a liberation of the self: Cyril sings of breaking free. He is willing himself into the sixties, striving to be young and virile. He warns Hugh that "it's something else again to try to tether your own wife the first time her natural instincts reach out to another man." Cyril encourages Hugh with Fiona, to ensure his own easy access to Catherine. Yet Cyril's plan or model is to allow himself freedom with both women. His breakthrough consists of his rearranging affections to give him an abundance of flesh; a pornographic fantasy is palpable, not real liberation. For the women are themselves unliberated. They simply move with the stronger force, which is Cyril; and Hugh, who couples with Fiona only once, is forced to go along. Cyril's integrity as a liberator is considerably compromised by the fact that he seems an actor in a porno film of his own making.

After Hugh commits suicide, Catherine is institutionalized, and Fiona goes off with Catherine's three children, we may find it difficult to comprehend Cyril's lyrical tone at the book's beginning. The events have already occurred, but he sees the past as Edenic, a bucolic frolic. In Ford's *The Good Soldier,* Dowell makes the past, also a series of tragic events, into an effort at "knowing." He is the very opposite of Cyril, of course, an asexual being caught in a hothouse atmosphere, very possibly drawn more to Ashburnham than to the women. Yet the success of Ford's novel is that he shows each individual as part of his/her own schemes. No one is manipulated by Dowell; and none of the essential quartet (later five) is isolated from a social context.

That isolation of the quartet in Illyria throws everything back on language and individual act, and there Hawkes strikes several wrong poses. Tones become uncertain. Prose reaches for significance where little or none is present. Cyril ponders Hugh: "Perhaps he was as indifferent to the male principle as he was to me, and was not searching for some sexual totem that would excite a little admiration in his wife and mine, but was instead determined to subject all four of us to the dead breadth of denial. Who could tell?" Or Cyril's motto: "Need I insist that the only enemy of the mature marriage is monogamy? That anything less than sexual multiplicity (body upon body, voice on voice) is naïve? That our sexual selves are merely idlers in a vast wood?" Or as an extension of that: "To young detractors I will say only that if orgasm is the pit of the fruit then lyricism is its flesh. Marriage, or at least the mature marriage, is the fold that gathers in all lovers nude and alone." Yet Cyril also insists that he stands for "sensuous rationality," the singer who spent his life "quietly deciphering the crucial signs of sex."

Cyril's pretentious claims for multiplicity and the breakthrough into alternative experiences seem based less on philosophy than on gaining access to a friend's wife. In his interview with Robert Scholes, Hawkes protested the vulgarity of the phrase "wife-swapping," but his vision reduces to that, little different from Updike's suburban "coupling." Hawkes's Cyril pretends to Pan—goats abound in the novel—but he is closer to Piet Hanema in Tarbox; and his puritanical Hugh recalls Updike's Angela Hanema: a suburban couple with an itchy male and a nay-saying wife.

Hugh is potentially more interesting, simply because he remains an enigma. Cyril defines himself repeatedly with his pleas for sexual release, and the two women are agents, not initiators. With his nude photographs of peasant women, his burning intensity, his inability to do with Fiona what Cyril is doing with Catherine, Hugh suggests a character whose sensations are more compelling than Cyril's. But Hawkes has chosen Cyril, and the novel moves according to his directives.

In this the first of his breakthrough novels into another type of sensibility, Hawkes seems ill at ease. The sunny novel, already suggested by the final pages of *Second Skin,* does not employ his strengths. The prose itself wobbles and strains at a lyricism which is unconnected to other elements. Even though macabre events occur in *The Blood Oranges,* the main line is the lesser one of heat, blood, sun; not art, sex, or the death of Hugh. Allert of *Death, Sleep, and the Traveler* will be an extension of Cyril, as if Hawkes had to rid his system of that type in two overlapping roles. Then in his recent two fictions, *Travesty* and *The Passion Artist,* he will try to move sensuality and sensation back toward forms with which he is more comfortable. The integration of all these new elements has not yet occurred in Hawkes, and as I write, in 1980, I sense he is still in a formative stage, either moving toward an integration of new insights or else incapable of finding the right modes and prose for that integration. Such exploration is compelling culturally, for American writers are so prone to repeating themselves that a fresh start in middle age holds a promise of its own.

For *Death, Sleep, and the Traveler* (1974), Hawkes has adapted the tale of the Flying Dutchman, transforming it into a modern tale of marriage, betrayal, passion, and death—all ingredients, as well, of his other three books since *Second Skin*. In the legend, the Dutchman sails the seas in a ship which anchors every seven years so that he can seek the love of a woman and end his wandering. His ship has a large red sail, a warning to other ships. Isolated by some undefined crime against mankind, the Dutchman is doomed to death, sleep, and traveling. The key to his recovery is a woman's faithful love.

Allert Vanderveenan is Hawkes's Dutchman, now in his fifties, fat, almost without direction or identity, a mass of sensuality seeking a focus. His most prized possession is his collection of pornographic albums, which provide satisfaction when his wife or another woman is unavailable. No woman, except those in the albums, is faithful to him; and he is condemned to journeys. When we observe him, he has begun a sea journey, which will end with the death of a young woman, of whose murder he is accused. Allert asserts his innocence, but as the Dutchman who flees all contact with humankind, he has guilt, a man condemned to be without identity, full of passion and yet incapable of focusing it. His wife, Ursula, dallies with Allert's best friend, Peter, with Allert's acquiescence; in fact, with his insistence—he on occasion watches. Ursula sometimes shares both men, all three acting out and observing. When Allert goes on his journey, he meets Ariane (Ariadne?), who shares him with the ship's wireless operator and other officers. Allert in a sense is in a worse situation than the Flying Dutchman, who is defined by wandering; Allert is uncertain even of that.

Hawkes has grafted the legend of the Dutchman onto Camus's Meursault, and then transformed both into a modern American tale, an epic of undetermined movement. The journey motif, begun in *Second Skin,* becomes extremely important in Hawkes's later work, connecting life and death. In *Death, Sleep, and the Traveler,* the journey serves both; in *Travesty,* which follows, it is a death journey, a coffinlike car speeding off to its destiny against a solid stone wall, incineration for the occupants. In *The Passion Artist,* in a role which Allert foreshadows, Vost takes a "static journey," moving frantically like Kafka's K. without arriving, or without even certainty of his des-

tination. Wandering, a form of destiny, may turn into a form of doom.

Despite his bulk and the bourgeois ring to his name, Allert is a phantom, like the legendary Dutchman. Hawkes plays off bulk and volume against a ghostly presence by way of a temporal sequencing, which helps to convey to this brief novel a sense of far greater length and extension. "Time Passed" is an illusion, since all time has both passed and not passed. The novel has three texts or main elements: the fact of Ursula leaving; the voyage out, during which Allert is suspected of having killed Ariane; and the past life of Allert, Ursula, and their common friend, the psychiatrist Peter. The smoothness of the technique derives from Hawkes's ability to make all three pasts appear present.

The novel begins with Ursula leaving Allert; but not, he assures us, because of what occurred on the ship or at the trial. He was, apparently, acquitted, although the novel's final line suggests he will always have to protest his innocence. The narrative moves almost immediately to the sea journey, which becomes the main aspect of the novelistic present, although in Allert's telling it is well in the past. During the ship sequences, Allert also tells us of the "circular red rash" he suffers from. "At first a few isolated splotchy areas of pebbled crimson, it now consists of a broad red welted ring completely encircling the little untouched island of the navel. The fungus, which is what it must be, surely, is textured like the outer livid flesh of a wet strawberry, and is spreading. Soon its faintly exuding and yet sensationless growth will blanket the entire surface of my global belly." The rash, while interesting, is one of those phenomena in the novel which seem to have an existence independent of any of the texts, serving, perhaps, as examples of guilt or conscience.

Further in the past, well beyond Ursula's leaving and the journey which leads to Allert's trial, is the three-way affair, which turns Ursula into an object and is a refinement (or vulgarization) of the arrangement in *The Blood Oranges* between the two aging couples; to be continued in *Travesty* in still another arrangement, the sharing by mother and daughter of a common lover. By *The Passion Artist,* a mother watches her son brought to "passion" by a large-bodied prison inmate. Except in *Travesty,* the women are fleshy, large-limbed, with thick, quivering thighs, massive buttocks: sexual fantasies which go unrealized literarily.

The triad of Allert, Peter, and Ursula engage in several dreamlike sexual excursions: in the smoky air of a sauna or in an outdoor picnic which features mussels and then slippery, buttery sex. These sequences are matched, as if in one endless present, by similar scenes during the cruise: for example, on a nudist beach, where Allert, Ariane, and the radio operator land for the day. The description is Edenic, with resonances from the final passages of *Second Skin:* "I concentrated on the sensation of the pale water against my skin and on the sight of the young woman who had thick black hair to the small of her back and who now was standing beneath the leaves of a tropical tree and waving. The island, or what I could see of it, was empty except for the eager girl beneath the tree and a far-off cluster of golden figures."

Hawkes has accomplished an almost seamless meshing of narrative elements, in that the three texts are made part of the present and yet can still be seen in retrospect. Hawkes is becoming both more and less experimental: while he has forsaken the narrative disruptions of his earliest work, in which time, place, and narrator were difficult to locate, he is still exploring ways in which narrative moves beyond ordinary sequential forms of knowledge. Without forgoing structural experimentation, he has forsaken earlier difficulties. He has, in a sense, smoothed out his technique.*

Although he has rejected the linear line of his more popularly accepted contemporaries, or the simplicities of flashback, his exploration of technique has been accompanied by a weakening of prose. "Weakening" is perhaps a loaded word, for Hawkes has deliberately set a different course for himself. As he explained in an interview by Robert Scholes, his vision has altered as part of a midlife change, and this has led to exploration of a different prose. Since the vision is one of breaking out, of movements beyond matrimonial convention, of developments in individual sensibility, Hawkes has attempted to discover a prose equivalent. The line is a thin one between a "sensual" prose and one that sounds overblown and affected. For we are speaking of a prose that demonstrates love of the body, respect for the "other" (usually a woman), and yet feelings that go beyond sex and sensationalism to deeper areas of fulfillment and satisfaction.

If we speak of a weakening of prose, then, we must do so within the context of Hawkes's attempting what is extremely difficult for an American novelist to accomplish. In his recent fiction, Roth seems to be moving in this direction, away from masturbation and fellatio toward a more mature sensuality; and Styron in *Sophie's Choice* has attempted to move beyond sexual posturing and toward love. But Hawkes's aim is even more ambiguous. For he wishes to explore a world now full of feelings that run counter to the American experience. (Hugh's puritanism in *The Blood Oranges* indicates where the American psyche was, before the changes of the 1960s.) He is trying to blend American pastoral, with its bucolic dreams, its hopes for paradise, its memory of an Edenic existence, with something close to its opposite: the sensuality and sexual love which led to the expulsion from Eden. The countering here could only be resolved by a prose short of miraculous.†

As first-person narrator, Allert becomes the novel; the prose represents the quality of his mind. Yet Allert seems pretentious and overblown, his prose like his huge body. His thoughts recall those huge welts which circle his lower body, ringed by something unnatural. "At that moment [Allert narrates] Ursula, my wife, entered the room and sprawled in a white leather chair in such a way as to reveal to my friend and me the tender fat of her upper thighs as well as the promise of her casually concealed mystery." This continues: "She rested her cheek in the palm of her hand, allowed the other to fall against the full white barely visible crotch of her underpants, and looked across the room at me with heat in her eyes. Even from where I sat I could smell the soap and sourness between her heavy legs. The mere thought in my mind was making her moist."

These are representative passages, and so much peering and smelling suggest an adolescent voyeur rather than a sensualist. The details create a different tone and a different observer from the one Hawkes takes seriously. His Allert in other respects is a most serious man. He dreams repeatedly of death, he is accused of murder, he arranges various lives as well as his own; he is spoken of as a man without identity, lacking substance, a phantomlike creature. To take him seriously in these areas, we must see him sexually as more than voyeur, masturbator, fantasy-maker.

---

*As a professor at Brown University—where he is a colleague and friend of Robert Scholes—Hawkes, like Barth at Johns Hopkins or McElroy at Queens College, has remained in touch with the latest developments in prose narrative.

†Updike in *Couples* falls afoul of the same problem. The prose purports to explore deep sensuality but ends up fulfilling adolescent fantasies. For both Hawkes and Updike, sensuality seems associated with heavy or thick women, so that the depth of the prose is often its ability to describe flesh.

Bellow's Henderson, who vies with Allert in bulk and volume, is a truer sensualist, although his sensuality is discovered not in America but in Africa. Allert stares at crotches, is fixated on buttocks, and peers around to catch glimpses of breasts; all of which is valid enough, except that it dates the perceiver. Further, and more significantly, sensuality becomes identified only with the body, negating a more profound sensibility.

Allert as a "passion artist" remains an adolescent at heart. Ursula, who serves Allert even as she mocks him, says: " 'Allert's theory is that the ordinary man becomes an artist only in sex. In which case pornography is the true field of the ordinary man's imagination.' " Ursula's comment comes near the end of a long section on her husband and his sex albums, in which his tastes run to "couples rather than singles," lesbian arrangements, scenes between animals and women.

While some of this becomes gentle mockery or ironic, it does undermine our acceptance of Allert as narrator, and in ways that Hawkes is unaware of. With Allert's total imagination submerged in sexual fantasy or practice, there is, apparently, little left over. When such values are translated into prose, we can understand Hawkes's wavering, with language caught between conflicting visions of reality which the author cannot control, no less resolve.

Travesty (1976) is the final volume in a triad of novels, with *The Blood Oranges* as the acting out of sexual dreams, *Death, Sleep, and the Traveler* as a descent into crime, and *Travesty* as a rush toward suicide and murder. This trilogy, however, should be seen as having developed into a quartet, with *The Passion Artist* as the fourth: a meditation on the previous three, in which sex, myth, imagination, death, suicide are all caught up in Konrad Vost's descent into experience.

Travesty is Hawkes's attempt to write a French *récit,* the kind of fiction Gide refused to call a novel. Hawkes's friend and former teacher at Harvard, Albert Guerard, has worked expertly within that mode, and part of the neglect Guerard's fiction has suffered is the result of the alien nature of the *récit.* The form requires a kind of sensibility few American writers possess. It demands wit (not comedy, not fun or amusement), a deft, concise, lean prose style, a textured view of human nature and individual character, a sense of historical dimensions.*

---

*Philip Roth's *The Ghost Writer* is an excellent example of an American adaptation of the *récit.*

By entering into this area, Hawkes is continuing his exploration of varying fictional modes, experiments not only with prose and structure, but with the nature of the genre in its American phases. The controlling metaphor of *Travesty* is an automobile speeding through the night, its three occupants all ticketed for a violent, fiery death: the narrator, his daughter (Chantal), and her lover (who is also the lover of the narrator's wife, Honorine). The locale, in France, is unnamed, as are the narrator and the lover. The narrator considers himself a "privileged person," someone who contains within himself "the seed of the poet." His greatest poem will be an act of murder and suicide, for the fiery crash of the car against a stone wall will be his statement: the poem written in violence, but not despair. He "creates" his act, only partially gratuitous, only partially willed, as an act of joy; for he savors the moments remaining before the car entombs its occupants. He speaks of the calm which has overtaken him even as terror overtakes the other two.

The narrator's sense of joy derives from his "static movement," that rush toward nothingness in a perfectly running car which will, in time, become a coffin. The meeting of a perfect machine and its fiery end is a conceit for the way the narrator locates our world, emblematic of the mode in which we live: between the machine and its destructiveness, between ideas of perfection and sudden endings. The narrator may be mad, although nothing in his manner, except exaltation and perfect fearlessness, suggests a lunatic. He does not include his wife in the "sport," because he wishes her to contemplate the result: death of husband, daughter, lover. It is the prospect of her memories that fuel the narrator's resolve.

Part of the sense of the novel is connected to "knowing." Since only the narrator speaks, or responds to the occupants' words, we learn of situations, people, conflicts solely from what he reveals. Yet he reveals only a little, working in the seams of the past rather than the main events. As in a Robbe-Grillet novel, we peer through the slits of "jalousies" or venetian blinds; everything we see is shaded by the presence of a slat which disguises. We are, almost literally, in a "blind." The narrator recognizes that "knowing" is tainted by what we can know: "In this sense there is nowhere I have not been, nothing I have not already done, no person I have not known before. But then of course we have the corollary, so that everything known to me remains unknown, so that my own footfalls sound like those of a stranger, while the corridor to the lavatory off my bedroom becomes the labyrinthine way to a dungeon."

Familiar becomes unfamiliar. The car is transformed into a tomb, the road into a path toward apocalypse, a perfect machine into a trap, the presence of loved ones into a deadly game of life and death. The narrator explains that while both he and the lover are Leo, the narrator is also part Scorpio, "a little dark river of Scorpio." Added to the lion is the scorpion, and it is that combination which has resulted in the plan of murder-suicide. Hawkes turns this into a Kafkaesque image: if the lover is the blustery Leo, then the narrator is "the powerful bug on the wall." That bug is the "ordinary privileged man" who turns out to have the deceptiveness of the artist; and it is the bug which is engineering their demise. Scorpio, not Leo, rules.

The monologue, inevitably, recalls that of Camus's Jean-Baptiste in *The Fall,* but the sensibility is different. Hawkes strives for but does not achieve irony, whereas Camus's irony is devastating, the chief modal effect of the novella. That insufficiency of irony undermines Hawkes's effort to create tensions where none existed before and diminishes from his "scorpion" the sting intended. Hawkes works hard at attaining irony, but he achieves it only in isolated passages, not as integral matter. He matches design and debris, the car as perfect machine against the garbage it will become: "nothing has disturbed the essential integrity of our tableau of chaos, the point being that if design inevitably surrenders to debris, debris inevitably reveals its innate design." The narrator will be the poet of debris.

In another passage, he meditates on an apocalypse without fire, a perfect expression of their lives; a passage, incidentally, which shows Hawkes at his most insistently perverse. If fire could be eliminated, then the crash would be a true travesty, an emblem of their selves: "Yes, it seems to me that if we preserve this scene in all its magnitude and with all its confounding of disparate substances and with its same volume of sound, but remove from it the convention of fierce heat and unnaturally bright light, so that this very explosion occurs as planned but in darkness, total darkness, there you have the most desirable rendering of our private apocalypse. Announced by violent sound and yet invisible, except for the glass scattered like perfect clear grains across an entire field."

Such passages, ironical and witty, define a novel Hawkes cannot sustain. As its title implies, *Travesty* must be a "travesty," and since passion—lover and wife, lover and daughter, narrator and all—is the subject, *the* subject of Hawkes's later work, then its opposite, deadness, lack of passion, must be conveyed by a suitable ironic mode. Hawkes reaches for it, but integrated irony eludes him. His narrator may speak with the accents of Jean-Baptiste, but Camus's dimensionality is unattainable.

Paralysis, entombment, concealment, enclosure, time and space turned static, speed countered by a silent car heading toward doom are all elements of Hawkes's vision of passion neutralized by its opposite. In *The Blood Oranges* and *Death, Sleep, and the Traveler,* he had explored sensuality; in *Travesty,* he has emerged into its obverse, as if from the sixties into the seventies. There lies irony, only irony; for all else would be passion. *The Passion Artist,* Hawkes's eighth novel, will be an attempt to cap this entire phase, in which the erotic, the artistic, imagination, and death all clash in a world of "static movement."

MORE MID-1970S: DOCTOROW, SUKENICK, THEROUX

Ragtime (1975) is like those musical comedy entertainments turned out by MGM and RKO in the 1930s, with Busby Berkeley settings, and perhaps held together by Fred Astaire or Gene Kelly a little later. Such entertainments had a story line that existed solely as cement for the musical numbers, dance sequence, or spectaculars. They had, in a sense, some linkage to circuses, to Barnum & Bailey's three rings. Such entertainments catered to nearly all tastes, since if one number bombed, there was quickly another. *Ragtime* is of this kind, the narrative serving as a kind of glue for all the sideshows: Houdini, J. P. Morgan, Henry Ford, Evelyn Nesbit, Stanford White and Harry Thaw, Emma Goldman, Henry Clay Frick.

Some of the "headliners" remain on stage through much of the novel, but most do their act and then depart: Freud, Zapata, Ford, and a few others. Also, there are brief scenes between some of the characters who never met in actuality, and whose relationship is not, of course, developed beyond the meeting itself. Evelyn Nesbit and Emma Goldman, for example, have a sexually charged scene together, as Emma, the political firebrand, rubs down Evelyn, the kept woman of rich and half-crazy men.

To hold the circus together, Doctorow uses an intense social and political sense, an irreverent view of the American past, updated to justify contemporary cynicism. Morgan is the most powerful man in the world, but his real interest lies in eternal life and transcendence, like the ancient pharaohs of Egypt.

Unable to settle only for power now, he needs assurance that it will not all be dissipated after death. Opposite him is Henry Ford, intent on consolidating what he has, uninterested in the afterlife, and satisfied by a reading a twenty-five-cent copy of *An Eastern Fakir's Eternal Wisdom*. There, he finds a simple explanation of reincarnation. "I explain my genius this way—some of us have just lived more times than others. . . . And I'll tell you something in thanks for the eats, I'm going to lend that book to you." To which Morgan rejoins: "Mr. Ford . . . if my ideas can survive their ultimate attachment to you, they will have met their ultimate test."

Much of the book is set within that parodic frame of reference, although not all. Harry Houdini runs through the entire length of the narrative, and he is, like Daniel in *The Book of Daniel,* a poignant figure. In his legend, Houdini creates the semblance of conquering man's destiny. But Doctorow's Houdini is a deeply obsessed man who knows all his feats are tricks, aware none of them is connected to the real world. He, Houdini, must create an artificial situation, which he can then overcome; his feats, accordingly, are heroic solely as reflections, not as realities. He is obsessed with creating greater tricks, confronting death as a way of forcing the reality which eludes him. Houdini competes with gods, and yet life restrains him from that ultimate transcendence of himself.

The central artifact of the novel is a family living in New Rochelle at the turn of the century. The narrator of the novel is ostensibly the son of this family, which consists of Father, Mother, Younger Brother, and the Boy, none of them named. They are the "Family," an allegorical mix. Father and Mother remain solid and balanced, but Younger Brother, using his knowledge of guns and explosives, becomes part of a black radical group. Doctorow's plan was, apparently, to move some of the politics of the sixties back to the turn of the century; as earlier he had worked through the politics of the Rosenbergs and the fifties by way of *The Book of Daniel*.

What upsets the harmonies of the family is the sudden appearance of a deserted baby, whom Mother takes in; followed by the mother of that baby, whom Mother also takes in. She is succeeded by Coalhouse Walker, Jr., the father of the baby, who wants to marry its mother. Walker is a ragtime pianist, a protégé of Scott Joplin; but he is also a man who insists on the letter of democracy, applied equally to all people. When his Model T is manhandled by the local fire department, he tries through every legal means to right the wrong, to have his car restored and the mischief-doers called to task. But as he discovers, there is no redress for blacks, even when liberal Father intercedes. Walker, then, takes justice in his own hands, and bombs the firehouse, bombs a second one, organizes a gang which terrorizes the city. His crew eventually takes over the J. P. Morgan Library, mistaking it for the Morgan residence, and demands restoration of the Model T and justice for the fire chief who mocked Walker's pleas for justice. It is this gang that Younger Brother joins, and to which he brings his knowledge of explosives.

Black rights are born amidst terror and destruction, and of course, the violent death of the leader, Walker. Younger Brother drifts off to join the Mexican revolution, and is killed. Morgan dies, convinced he has perceived the signs that he will be called back on earth, especially since he foresees a war coming, and a war without Morgan would be unthinkable. Freud returns to Europe, certain that America is a second-rate civilization. Houdini dies and is reborn, dies once more, is reborn, but is still unable to respond to the real situation, being doomed to react only to his own devices. Evelyn Nesbit, after having driven men mad with her seductiveness, loses her looks and drifts into anonymity. Political activity becomes increasingly senseless as the world drifts into a war; one of the final scenes shows a Serbian national at Sarajevo.

Like a ragtime musical bit, the novel turns on its variations. It is a light but expert job, with the sound of Scott Joplin tinkling through episodes and variations, always returning to the same rhythms and undertones. History is everyone's destiny, Morgan and Walker alike. Only acquisitions differ, Morgan with his wealthy artifacts, Walker with his beloved Model T. The individual life, consumed by goods, rolls on. This is hardly profound, but history is like ragtime, full of variations on certain common assumptions about mankind, and just about as certain.

Ragtime, like *Loon Lake,* five years later, is Doctorow's effort to discover another beat or tone to American life. The novel as musical comedy, lightly parodic, an entertainment: these are his adaptations. They are, apparently, ways of responding to the sixties, modes that assimilate music, television, film, the stage, on which famous people perform. In *Loon Lake,* with its overtones of Dreiser's *An American Tragedy* and Dos Passos's *U.S.A.,* Doctorow tried to deepen a similar kind of novel; but there is a pretentiousness that subverts his attempt at lyricism, that undermines his effort to restore radical politics.

Ronald Sukenick has eschewed entertainment for experimentation. As a writer of the 1970s, with his most significant work in the mid-decade, he is struggling against 1970s assimilation and enervation, attempting to define a distinct voice while expanding the genre's potential. His work has nothing to do with that of Doctorow, Hawkes, Vonnegut, Kosinski, et al. of this same period; it is, in fact, a negation.

Up, a Novel (1968) is a book of many voices, realistic assessments of life and fantasies of "other selves." This is a fiction that seems to offer objective data, which become, in the process, part of the fiction achieving itself. Further, the main character is Ronald Sukenick, and the development of the novel depends on his ability to finish his novel, which is the resolution of the voices.

Up is a summation of fictions whose themes have been a failed college professor, a young man obsessed with masturbatory fantasies, and a person trying to make his strong intellect square with his irrational bodily drives. The problem is that, retreaded, these themes seem exhausted, even in Sukenick's upbeat and often resonant prose. Sukenick has tried to undercut this attack by writing his own review of his first novel, *The Adventures of Strop Banally.* "This first novel by an obviously talented and intelligent young writer is another one of those tales in the manner of what has been aptly termed 'rebellious farce,' introduced with so much success by such as J. P. Donleavy and Joseph Heller." To whom one may add Philip Roth, J. D. Salinger, Saul Bellow, Bernard Malamud and, most recently, Gilbert Sorrentino. Sukenick's friend Bernie comments on the "screwed-up" chronology of the manuscript, although this manuscript is not *Strop Banally,* but the book we are reading, *Up.* Sukenick offers in his defense that " 'It's just a sequence of words. The only thing that matters is the order of revelation in print.' "

Technically, the idea is valid, but the episodes are themselves no longer fresh. Like his friend Raymond Federman, Sukenick can rearrange his material to create interesting sequences, but once the reader begins to examine what lies within, he is repelled. For the sequences are tired macho stuff: masturbatory fantasies which by 1968 are not sufficiently witty (Roth would hold this ground), "use" of women for sexual purposes, licking of lips over conquests, infantile glee over "making out," all taken seriously as novelistic materials by protagonist and author behind him. The future of American fiction may lie in new arrangements or new sequences of words, but those sequences must demonstrate more maturity than "getting laid" indicates.

Up, however, is a young man's book, and with *Out,* in 1973, Sukenick becomes more confident. *Out* is not a novel in any traditional sense; rather, it is a prose narrative, wherein the narration is broken down into segments which may or may not cohere. This is a spatial fiction, the idea being to conquer space so as to convey the sense of moving on, fragmentation, things breaking up and never cohering. This is, also, a fiction about instabilities, the individual's and the culture's.

Sukenick wanted some way to convey the spaced out dimensions of the sixties: spaced out in terms of those who move counterculturally as a consequence of drugs or radical politics; spaced out in the alternative sense of those who move continually. The archetype for this narrative is Holmes's *Go* or Kerouac's *On the Road,* or any of Kerouac's longer narratives in which movement preempts any social or community idea. Sukenick's characters belong to a loose organization that blows things up; they carry explosives and move across the country according to certain plans which develop at the last moment. The point is that at any given time, they do not know what they are supposed to do, who their cohorts are, or where their next move will come from. They are lost in space, spaced out, and yet they must move in it. The distance is America: the staging area for any given blowup.

Sukenick provides a good deal of white space around the print. The plan of the novel is to progress with gradual diminution of words on the page, a diminishing narrative, a growing minimalism; until the final pages are almost entirely white space, the last page containing only the letter *O.* Following that, *Out* contains several blank pages, so that the end is whiteness. Final things are, in this conceit, space itself as the reader slides off the whiteness of the page back into whatever world contains him.

Mallarmé's "white abyss" is suggested, although Sukenick's prose lacks the poetic dimension which can make whiteness a metaphor for man or his culture. Sukenick is aiming ambitiously at a "hymn to America," with that whiteness emblematic of the nation; his blowup experts as victims seeking their destiny in a reactionary culture. At one point, the narrator, who at times identifies himself as Sukenick, meets Empty Fox, who expresses the wisdom of culture as well as the future of the novel. Empty Fox asks Sukenick about his plans: "I want to write a book like a cloud that changes as it goes," an evocation which fits the spatial conceit of *Out.* Empty Fox replies, with what was by 1973 a platitude: "I want to erase all books. My ambition is to unlearn everything I can't read or write that's a start. I want to unlearn and unlearn till I get to the place where the ocean of the unknown begins where my fathers live. Then I want to go back and bring my people to live beside that ocean where they can be whole again as they were before the Wasichus ["fat-takers," or white men] came."*

Out is characterized by good passages that are diluted by a stereotypical primitivism, as Kesey's wonderful *Cuckoo* scenes become enmired in that adolescent ideology of the "mentally lame" or of the superior marginal Indian. Even the central idea— agents coming together for blowups, what are called "meets," an attractive metaphor for radical explosions—becomes fudged in the prose, which rarely attains the level of the subject. One of the problems, and it carries over both into and from the language, is the relationship between men and women. Not a single woman in the book, and several float through, is anything more than a receptacle for "her man" or "her men." The lack of maturity here, where women are will-less and subservient to willed men, corrupts the language, which describes their clutching and heaving. "Carl [one of the author's personae] pulls her out of the cabin shoves her into the back of the camper and unzips his fly suck it he says. That's enough he says after a while she comes up he busts her right in the mouth she bounces off the wall of the camper blood on her chin. What's that for she says holding her lip you forgot to say thank you he says take your clothes off I oughta walk right outa here."

He punishes her by forcing her to polish his shoes between her legs, then pushes her down, his boot against her breast. With this, she manifests love—a masochistic love object, all the while her husband is driving the camper. Not only does the prose express contempt for the very material it is describing, but the material is a dead end: spasms from the male, masochistic desire from the female, and we are back into pornography. This may be what Sukenick wants, but

---

*Jerome Klinkowitz sees this, also, as a crucial passage in the wandering book, but he fails to note, among several shrewd comments, that Sukenick has transformed a poetic idea into a platitude. "Unlearning" and returning to the "before" are poses; perhaps meaningful in a very youthful writer, they are unforgivable as the visions of a mature novelist. Empty Fox's message may have been a prescription for a new social arrangement—communes, social brotherhood, the virtues of individual labor—but as a prescription for a "new fiction" it is empty foxiness.

if so, he must discover some irony or comic pullback or means of stepping outside it.

It is true Sukenick refuses to remain still; that he believes devoutly the writer must reinvent and keep moving on, or else he experiences the "death of the novel and other stories," the title of his 1969 collection. Yet achieving the whiteness of the page has its problems unless the writer reaches toward the level of fantasy/dream/nightmare the subject demands. Empty Fox's attacks on American pop and schlock culture do not suffice; nor is his defense of primitivism satisfactory. They are one-dimensional statements of preference, lacking tension or conflict, or even accurate history. It is not that they are untrue; it is that a partial truth comes with the force of edict, of worship. Sukenick's effort to subvert ordinary fiction, whether realistic or romantic, is commendable; but it is bound by its own limitations of vision, language, and form.

The title *98.6* (1975) suggests normality, but it can be found only in the so-called counterculture, the communes which make up the land of Frankenstein. Frankenstein, however, is not simply the communes that settle in it; it is the country itself, America, Amerika, the land of the living dead. Sukenick's conceit for America plays upon the common conception of Frankenstein as the monster, not its creator. The land of Frankenstein is a territory the Aztecs would have recognized, death-oriented. The narrator, Sukenick, dates his dreams and nightmares, then matches them up against the reality, and there is little distinction. "The landscape of nightmare," Jonathan Baumbach called it; and Sukenick shifts the metaphor to a physical one. What is normal is 98.6, but what is abnormal is everything not that, which is practically everything.

The three parts of *98.6* are cryptic: "Frankenstein," "The Children of Frankenstein," and "Palestine." If Frankenstein is Amerika, then its children are doomed, but unaware of it. For in their communes, they play out their lives as children, getting high, having group sex, bleeding out their guts in childbirth, being threatened by townspeople or by truck and motorcycle gangs. They survive, and Sukenick finds their life full of lyrical wonder, but they survive despite what they are and what the country offers. As a section, "Palestine," however, is more elusive, for here we have a land of violence and death which seems like the solution, the commune that works.

The first part, sixty pages long, is essentially a collage: Sukenick's mind, his dreams, his imagination working on the materials of America, which are mind-boggling, the actuality rarely lagging behind what is imagined. These dated "dreams" and "actualities" are the most evocative parts of the novel, expressing a sense of the country moved to the margins, beyond social and political power thrusts. The second section, on the "Children" of all this, has sequences of vitality and vibrations; here, we find the reader thrust into rapidly changing scenes and images, paralleling Kosinski's *Steps*. Sukenick, of course, rejects Kosinski's yearning for an audience, making his own "steps" inaccessible, inward-turning, part of a flow. Note, in "Frankenstein":

> 4/30 he sees a strange thing in St. Patrick's Cathedral. A boy comes in with his arms full of large spools he's maybe fourteen blond skinny. The spools turn out to be spools of bright ribbon each one a different color which the boy unreels one by one as he walks around the aisles leaving behind streamers festoons of yellow green red purple all over the church. He assumes the boy is in some way connected with the Cathedral but three swarthy men are grumbling ominously near the entrance. When the boy goes out they come on with him very tough now he assumes it's they who are connected with the Cathedral.

As part of the underworld, the three men are very protective of the cathedral. They follow the boy, abusing him, beating him up, and even the presence of a cop does not stop them. The boy dies, while the cop lines up the three thugs at pistol point. The narrator goes to a restaurant for dinner. He cannot pay for his dinner, and then takes a taxi, which almost crashes on the ice. End of segment. Such scenes, and there are several, do cohere as part of a collage of America, or at least of New York City.

They are, however, insufficiently controlled by a larger imagination. In the section on the "Children" of this country, on their commune, Sukenick indulges his own unexamined fantasies: available women, raped women who come to enjoy the act, incest (which proves fun), blown-out minds, group sex, and all the "highs" which, unexamined, prove juvenile. While it is true the commune becomes increasingly like the Frankenstein beyond, Sukenick misses out on the irony.

The commune becomes the "Monster," as it is described by Paul, a former civil rights lawyer during "The Dynasty of the Million Lies." Paul merges at times with Ron, Sukenick's persona, who is attempting to write a book about the commune and his role in it. We have, then, within this spaced-out narrative,

the traditional fictional presence spinning out his tale self-consciously, the maker making. But Ron, also called Cloud, to identify him with a higher dimension, cannot "make" his book. The only synthesis comes with Israel, the "Palestine" of the third part; but even this resolution is a subjunctive contrary to fact, an "as if" fantasy in which "Robert" (Kennedy) is President.

"Palestine" suggests Yeats's Byzantium, where resolutions occur not in actuality but at the level of art, in the artwork. Everything else fails, except that structuring of an entity which stands outside time: thus, Palestine. Like his novel, Sukenick says, Israel is based on the Mosaic Law, "the law of mosaics or how to deal with parts in the absence of wholes." Israel resolves what is wrong with the novel, with the death of the novel, now revived in mosaics. This section become wild and dithrambic, virtually incoherent, as the narrator attempts to discover linguistic metaphors for coherence and resolution.

The "Moment of Luminous Coincidence" arrives, and it brings a temporary resolution, an imaginative collage: an alphabetization of scrambled language is followed by a concatenation of sound. A particularly acute line states that when you "try to sew Orpheus back together what you get is Frankenstein." Man is submerged in the monster; the Monster is still Amerika.

As a survey of America immediately after the 1960s, Sukenick's novel is more compelling in the retelling, at the level of its skeleton, than in its textures, which are often coarse and obvious. The matter is frequently mundane or trivialized, as in the following passage, which is not atypical:

> They decide to have a ritual basketball game maybe that'll clear the air. How is a ritual basketball game different from a regular basketball game it isn't. It's just that they decide to call a basketball game a ritual basketball game when they feel they need one and that in fact makes it different. The men decide to call one when they feel there's something to be cleared up among them even though they don't know what it is especially when they don't know what it is.

The prose is lax, the paranoia banal, loss of control or interest evident.

This kind of passage is matched by several others. Sexual content is undeveloped, and since sex waxes and wanes for a good part of *98.6,* it becomes the level of content. Real confrontations are rare, and when they occur, as in the scene between George Lance and his visiting father at the commune, we find all the clichés of the uptight father and the rebellious son. Lack of communication is frequently as much a platitude here as the kinds of communication.

These practices seem endemic to a certain type of fiction, in which the "new" does not mean breaking from platitudes. "New" often means changing arrangements on the page, but otherwise the page remains undeveloped. Passages do suggest a different order of business, but are insufficiently sustained. The following has a witty potential missing from most of the book, where frolics and orgies are solemn matters: "The children of Frankenstein are not psychological creatures they are creatures of biology and chance. First the parents create the children according to their dreams then the children create the parents in their image. The parents it turns out are probabilities of the cosmos acting through nature."

There remains to be written the countercultural novel, although in more conventional terms Pynchon has preempted some of the territory. Various minimalists, the linguistic experimenters, the white-pagers, the blank- and skipped-liners have all attempted through arrangements to convey what are difficult spatial metaphors. Yet inevitably, we must seek a sense of a distant, cosmic America—whether close up microscopically or distant telescopically—in matters of content, in relationships, in historical textures. Porno fantasies for relationships, hang-ups for behavior, personality quirks for character are insufficient. America eludes Sukenick in these intensely American fictions. Except for arrangments on the page, which neither enhance nor detract, we are no further along a spatial America than in Kerouac's yearning fictions, or Kesey's sense of a spaced out country. Being spaced out still means more than most American novelists have been able to fill in.

That same frenetic reach for expressiveness characterizes *Long Talking Bad Conditions Blues* (1979). There is an *Alice in Wonderland* quality to this novel, in that Sukenick juxtaposes states or conditions, contrasting "this world" and "that one." Black holes lead to that one, as Alice's exploration of the hole introduces her to another country. For Sukenick, the hole "gapes," and ever more people will disappear through it,

> till people learned how to control the hole to go through it and find out what was on the other side the only way to find out what was on the other side was through prediction and the medium of prediction was the written word there the achronicians [those who, denying time, favored distance] were correct the writ-

ten word coexists coexists with what coexists with the written word all written words comprise a vast and growing coincidence extending into past and future doubling and redoubling complex reflections not so with spoken words which disappear into the air into the ear into the gaping hole even the written word of history emerges at the fine edge of the future prediction of the past the word written only for the future never the moment telling the way was and is will be the written word pregnant with prophecy . . .

At every level, Sukenick's inhabitants are exiled: men from women, each from the other, as individuals or as people seeking, however tentatively, a community. Sukenick tries to wrap these meditations in stylistic equivalents: mainly interior monologue, paragraphs that occupy only a fraction of the page, endlessly run-together sentences which become coils and wraparounds, phrases and sentences interrupted by white space, removal of punctuation so as to approximate consciousness.

Yet the point remains. The issues are familiar, as are the diatribes against collectivization, the thwarting of individual expression, the movement toward ever greater bytes of data. We are, indeed, controlled, and exile does not mitigate a universal cultural condition. The writer must start there, seek the tensions in that clash of individual and culture, probe faults and seams, seek out weaknesses. Simply to rail against it all is to repeat what the early moderns said more lyrically. Put another way: we know nearly everything beforehand that Sukenick will tell us, and however blues-oriented or modernized his techniques, they cannot disguise familiar content. Familiar, finally, overcomes; unfamiliar fades away.

Paul Theroux's *Picture Palace* (1979) is about modes of perception. The novel focuses on a photographer, the seventy-year-old Maude Coffin Pratt; and since photography, the camera eye, is central, we are involved in something familiar in contemporary fiction. Most evident is the influence of film, whether reels of camera film or movie reels. Recalled are *The Moviegoer,* several Barthelme stories, the film crew in Barth's *Letters,* the film ideas in Pynchon. The significant elements are angles of observation, and the idea accommodates multiple realities, one of the major concerns of postwar fiction. Theroux has shrewdly targeted his book. This stress on angles of perception also fits into the self-consciousness of much fiction. It is not distant, either, from Burroughs's contention that we have entered an aural universe—for him, ear replaces eye as the characteristic mode of perception.

Although ear and eye create distinct dimensions, they are still aspects of observing, stressing the doer rather than what is perceived. *JR,* of course, fits into Burroughs's sense of an aural universe.

This may appear a long way from photography, but it is interconnected. When observer preempts object, the seer becomes paramount. In the scene in which Pratt enters Alfred Stieglitz's office, makes believe she is an amateur, and gets him to pose for her, she, the observer, is far more significant than the great Stieglitz. What she sees through the old-fashioned camera eye is what she puts into it, not what he gives; she catches him in a giveaway expression, one that she has created by what she says to him, by disarming his suspicions. Although Theroux cannot sustain such a scene in the structure of his novel, the passage is a strong one for its recognition of ways in which subject-object shifts once we relocate modes of perception.

The novel is itself structured on the way Maude's life differs from her photographs. She indicates repeatedly that while the photographs reinforce an image of herself as glamorous, well-traveled, fulfilled, the life behind it is ordinary, full of unsatisfied desires, rather miserable, in fact. The weakness of the novel is in that life behind the photos. It is, in the way now fashionable, concerned with incest: Maude feels a lifelong passion for her brother, Orlando, discovers that her sister Phoebe does also, discovers further, along with a photograph of their activity, that they sneak away to enjoy a physical fulfillment of that passion. When Orlando returns on furlough during World War II, Maude creeps into his room at night, but draws the wrong bed, that of Orlando's buddy, Woody, her incestuous passion never consummated. Orlando and Phoebe are drowned at sea, possibly suicides because of that photograph.

The novel opens with a quirky scene in which Maude, at seventy, has flown to London to meet and photograph Graham Greene. The scene between two old survivors establishes a level which little in the novel really comes up to again. Theroux then moves into a retrospective of Maude's life; the Greene photo, which she does not take, will be her last, she vows. The review of her past is counterpointed with an exhibit of her photographs arranged by Frank Fusco, a young entrepreneur who represents the "new." All the while the novel moves forward, so that there is sequential as well as lateral distancing. Technically, it is an excellent idea and works well, the main difficulty being in the relative insignificance of Maude's life.

The most notable of Maude's triumphs is her series showing circus performers doing their act in the nude, while below them, the circus management and friends dine and watch. It is a porno show turned into a circus performance, and the spectators include Maude's father (whose presence there loses him his broker's business). It is this series which thrusts Maude into celebrity as a photographer: one aspect of the "picture palace." A "picture palace" is also the repository of images in the mind: the mind as a vast gallery, reflecting what is out there. Everything is potential for the camera, which is both within and without, what Joseph McElroy meant, in part, by a "lookout cartridge."

Yet excellent as the ideas are, adroit as the techniques prove to be, Theroux seems indifferent in crucial scenes. The retrospective of Maude's "picture palace" is too pat. Maude, the artist, slips in unnoticed, no one pays any attention to her, and she remains a stranger at her own celebration, as if attending her funeral. All credit for the show goes to Frank; the entrepreneur wins the plaudits while the artist is ignored. Maud is superfluous. ". . . a man in a dress spoke volumes, while a woman with a camera seemed to have few secrets. I was merely a spectator, stinking of chemicals [artist as demonic?]. I had to be seen to be believed." She slips away, presumably, out of the retrospective, back into the camera eye. The organization wins out, whereas the artist has no face; only her photographs count, and even those less than the event itself. Celebrity has become its own measure. Such a resolution reduces both ideas and techniques, since it minimizes friction in its romantic view of the artist.

What has become apparent is that Theroux is more a "writer" than a novelist, as he demonstrates in his travel books. He has mastered the encounter, the scene, the techniques of blending past and present. Yet he turns casual when intensity and gravity are needed. He chooses "writing"—clean prose, good approaches, readability—over the true angulation his material calls for. He retreats from pressures. In *Saint Jack* (1973), Jack Flowers does not probe himself, nor are other presences examined. The result is a novel at the level of adventure, whose interest derives from exotic settings, sensual surfaces (no love, no pain, inflicted or received), and wisecracks which often suffice for conversation. This is the world of travel books, journeys, chance encounters.

Erwartung, not Götterdämmerung: 1979–80

The turn of the decade proves to be a gala of American fiction. By contrast, mid-decade manifested the doldrums of general American culture, drift and enervation in the arts as a reflection of political and social indecision. Barth, McElroy, Barthelme, and Pynchon seemed to resist this vacillation, but the fiction we examined that is clustered around mid-decade suggests undirected energy, ideas seeking form. The end of the decade, at least in fiction, indicates a renewal; awakening and expectation, not the end of things. Nearly every major American novelist weighed in with a contribution, and in some instances with ambitious work: Styron, Roth, Malamud, Oates, Percy.* A new writer of great promise emerged, Walter Abish, with a book that deserves attention, *How German Is It*. We await novels by Barthelme and Pynchon, and McElroy is preparing a saga-like book titled *Women and Men:* "a man and a woman who never actually meet but divide the action and its population in sundry ways between them." While publishing a documentary and labeling it a novel, Mailer continues to promise his novel, which also appears to be a saga. Hawkes and Kosinski published novels which demonstrate, especially in Hawkes's instance, efforts to move into fresher territory. Yet Baldwin, Doctorow, and Vonnegut disappointed with their work, in particular Baldwin, whose recent previous fiction needed an infusion of new ideas and techniques.

Modernism flourishes apparently only in those who adapted to it in the fifties and sixties, having gained few new converts except for Abish and Sorrentino. Oates's *Bellefleur* suggests, for her, a more adventurous technique, although she resists the angular disruptions and dislocations we associate with modernism. As the 1980s begin, it appears that serious fiction, as we have suggested, has settled permanently into two distinct schools, with little shifting from one to the other. On one side are those who pursue technical experimentation which locates them, in the terms of American fiction, in the avant garde, and for whom audience appeal is not an immediate goal. Here we locate McElroy, Barth, Pynchon, Barthelme, Gaddis, and the more radical experimenters. On the other side, we have those who sense an audience for their work and who do little to disrupt its expectations: we find here Mailer, Bellow, Roth, Heller, Malamud, Baldwin, Vonnegut, Styron, Percy. Hawkes has attempted to straddle both camps, but his transition has been, so far, incomplete. At his best, he must forsake readers. Oates suggests a writer who may go in several directions, as may Didion, if she can build upon her *Book of Common Prayer*.

Numerous establishment careers appear over, among them the most richly rewarded. There is, as yet, little sign of younger writers who can move the novel forward; we depend for that on those nearing fifty or past it. Fresh life is not feeding into the novel, but that I attribute to the disastrous, indecisive drift of general culture in the seventies. Robert Coover, if he can control excesses, has potential as a major satirist; a writer of proven wit, he has lapses of discretion, and loses direction, as we saw in *The Public Burning*. Our literary culture desperately needs a satirist of the first rank. The more purely experimental writers—Federman, Katz, Sukenick, for example—are to be congratulated for their perseverance, but their materials are not sufficiently created. Their experiments remain just that, laboratory efforts, without that ability to leap into credibility. Nevertheless, since there seems little chance reviewers and critics will become less establishment-oriented in their tastes—and of course, many establishment writers *are* deserving of the highest praise—the experimentalists are to be encouraged. While the future of American fiction may not lie solely with them, as they and their supporters feel, their efforts prevent the genre from languishing, from becoming fat on its own successes. We need fewer celebrities and more novelists.

The major traditions of American fiction recur here, at the decade's turn, as if in a continuing line from the nineteenth century. The sense of American power counterbalanced by the desire to withdraw into pastoral or Edenic fantasies is still strong. The clash between individual, the source of anarchy, and society or community, the source of order, remains intense. The attractions of space and spatiality preempt logic or reason; redoing one's life, seeking transfor-

---

*Like Barth's *Letters* and McCarthy's *Cannibals and Missionaries,* several 1979–80 books appear in other sections of this study. One of the obvious problems in breaking up the old groups—"Black Writers," "Jewish Writers," "Women Writers"—or viewing entire careers isolated from the culture, is an achronological arrangement. Pieces do not necessarily turn up where one wants them.

mation of self and ego are paramount. *One must always be becoming.* The dream of America, although no longer credible, is still pursued. Science and technology are no longer so apparently enemies. The presence of Emerson and Thoreau is as strong as ever, but the limits of power, change, and transformation are major elements in our novelists' consciousness.

Although trends are difficult to perceive in a culture which defies generalizations, perhaps we can venture that American writers have achieved a plateau. There is, as in their nineteenth-century forebears, an acceptance of an America which would have been anathema in the fifties and sixties. Rebellion here, in several of our writers, gives way to the urgency to understand. The press of American life is less severe, or less destructive; the need for personal expression more intense. But unlike what we observed in the sixties, personal expression is not just "I" or "me"; it is self-knowledge, based on achieving levels of comprehension. Society, culture, and history remain elusive elements, still, for the American novelist; but if generalizations signify anything, we can say 1980s fiction will be increasingly historical, socially oriented, more accommodating to the matter of America. There is no way we can foresee a "we decade," but we can envisage a reluctant assimilation of who we are, what we are; with spurts of modernism making the edges sufficiently jagged and angular so as to create continuity with the best traditions of twentieth-century fiction.

NONFICTION AND FICTION IN COMBAT: *THE EXECUTIONER'S SONG* (1979)

By subtitling this immensely long book about Gary Gilmore, the murderer who demanded his own execution, "A True Life Novel," Mailer fudges the generic lines. He gives himself a novel, but he provides something weak as novel, strong as documentary. For the very element the Gilmore story lacks is material we deem novelistic. Mailer is *not* there in the seams, where a novel needs its author; and he is missing in those areas of character—motivation, direction, intensity—where the novelist leaps the gaps from subject into object. By trying it both ways, documentation and fiction, Mailer feels he can drop out of Gilmore's life when documentation takes over, and then jump into his life when novel makes its demands.

While Mailer's methods are of interest, no single method is fully justified in the text. He first divides the novel into two sections, or books, of comparable length, the first called "Western Voices"; the second, "Eastern Voices," refers to the American East Coast and to the Far East, for Gilmore believed in reincarnation, in his return as a better person. Each of these books is divided into seven parts, with compelling titles: "The Shadow of the Dream," "Death Row," "The Fading of the Heart," et al. These parts are subdivided into chapters of varying length, usually ten to twenty pages; the chapters, in turn, are made up of segments, numbered up to ten, a few more than that. Then the segments are broken down into brief paragraph-like units, some of the paragraphs no more than a sentence or two, a few running to slightly greater length.

The pages display considerable white space, the result of Mailer's having located all his material in paragraph units, which build to the segments, which, in turn, build to chapters, the chapters building to parts, the parts fitting into two evenly divided books. The two books become the Book. The arrangement recalls that of the Bible, an easy breakdown into chapter and verse. The result, for Mailer, is great ease of narrative, great clarity as to where the book is heading; for even the most dreadful information—the two Gilmore murders—is located in a brief paragraph which looks just like every other. In no previous work, including his earliest, has Mailer so eschewed devices or strategies. He has provided a narrative the laziest reader can respond to, without fear of dislocation or interruption. Mailer may wind in and around, but he does so with his fingers firmly on the reader's elbow, guiding at every turn.

The method is workable at the documentary level, each paragraph like a burst of film reel, existing in itself but carrying the viewer forward to the next unit. The method works least well at the level of novel, where greater sophistication is called for. This is 1979, and our expectations have been raised. Such sophistication need not be of the less readable kind which some of Mailer's contemporaries have reveled in during the decade in books of comparable length. But Mailer should have given us a more complicated sense of Gilmore to sustain the overall presence of a character who dominates over one thousand pages. Gaddis's Wyatt Gwyon is an "outlaw" who can kill out of some innerness which defies comprehension—the same dead spot in Gilmore Mailer keeps butting his head against—and yet we see the potential of Gwyon's center. Gaddis provides the novelistic coordinates for his character in a way Mailer does not.

Part of the trouble lies in the protagonist. Mailer has blurred boundaries between fiction and nonfiction in order to disguise the thinness of Gilmore. He quotes letters from Gilmore, chiefly to his young girl friend, Nicole, and the letters demonstrate some literacy. Gilmore is judged by prison psychiatrists to be well above average in intelligence, with an overall IQ of 129, a man who has done considerable reading in prison (more than half of his thirty-five years). But the letters cannot disguise the triviality of the man, *unless* the novelist can work out coordinates which strengthen and support him. He must be reinforced by the very elements Mailer has eschewed by moving along documentary lines. For surely Mailer could have built Gilmore up—penetrated that dead center, those piercing blue eyes, that stare which equaled Medusa's. Mailer relies on the fact of Gilmore's physical impressiveness, but what we see is a punk.

In interviews, Mailer very shrewdly tried to explain Gilmore as a complicated man, as anything but a punk. A punk has no depth, no great reasoning ability, no sense of himself; he does not comprehend what he does, and he acts according to needs serving immediate self-gratification. Gilmore is a punk, not at all the figure in what Mailer posits as a Raskolnikovian drama of power, needless crime, repentance. And Provo, Utah, is no staging ground for drama such as Dostoyevsky's Russia provided; Mailer does not even fully develop the Mormon scene here. People endeavour to understand and even aid Gilmore after the senseless murders of a gas station attendant and a motel manager; though both of them were young and exemplary in their lives, they do not provide drama, delineation, or definition for Gilmore beyond the fact of their own law-abiding nature in contrast with his outlaw's mentality.

The more Mailer tells us of Gilmore—the more we are exposed to his sense of personal doom, his contempt for life, his hatred of himself, his inability to believe in anything more than immediate sensation— the more we observe him as a punk. For even before the murders, he is involved in petty crimes: ripping off, lying, dodging work, wrecking cars, hitting Nicole. Part of his appeal for Mailer is his outlaw nature, so far out of control it seems in another dimension. He is Mailer's "White Negro" of another time and place; really Provo's "White Negro," someone as difficult for it to understand in its territory as the original was for urban dwellers.

Yet Mailer's Gilmore cannot sustain this vision of himself. The more we try to understand him, the more he withdraws; not because he is so complex, but because he is so simple. He is, in the long run, merely a punk posing as a real criminal, whereas Mailer wants him to transcend two brutal murders to become something else. Exactly what he is supposed to emblemize we cannot perceive. He seems very much himself, a small-time petty crook who moves into big crime because the moment is passing and he has not made his move. Mailer's efforts to sustain some vision of Gilmore as reaching for power or even possession of himself are futile, since he lacks the substance.

About a third through the book, Mailer starts to quote extensively from Gilmore's letters to Nicole. They are the beginning of his display of his inner self, and they are supposed to suggest a man of sufficient complexity to support Mailer's exploration of him. Gilmore writes:

> I'm not a weak man. I've never been a punk, I've never been a rat, I always fought—I ain't the toughest son of a bitch around but I've always stood up and been counted among the men. I've done a few things that would make a lot of motherfuckers tremble and I've endured some shit that nobody should have to go thru. But what I want you to understand, little girl, is that you hold my heart and along with my heart I guess you have the power to crush me or destroy me. Please don't. I have no defense for what I feel for you.

Pleading weakness, Gilmore wants Nicole for himself, even though she is roaming free and screwing around, and he is imprisoned, awaiting, in fact, a death sentence. And yet none of this works: it has potentiality, but only if Mailer had supported Gilmore in those novelistic areas he claims for himself but does not provide. Gilmore's two murders are, in fact, so brutal, so lacking in human rapport, so needless—for neither victim threatened him during his robberies—that only a great woven context could have led us back to Gilmore. He is lost, novelistically speaking, when, in two brief paragraphs, Mailer has him murder. When that occurs, Gilmore goes down the drain, and all Mailer's efforts, either in the book or on interview shows, to sustain him are wasted. We do not care whether he lives or dies; he is an object.

Mailer desperately wants us to perceive this as an "American story," the Clyde Griffiths story from Dreiser's *An American Tragedy,* with different twists. Mailer is as interested in the exploitation of Gilmore, in which the author himself plays no small role, as he is in Gilmore. The "American dimension" here is the selling of tragedy to the media. Gilmore's conviction has significance only in Gilmore's insistence that he wants to die, which catapults him into national fame; and which brings to Provo the hucksters with something to sell: Boaz, a lawyer; Schiller, who merchants in death; and David Susskind, who turns everything into *Weltschmertz.* Thus, the Gilmore story, unlike that of Clyde Griffiths, has its "tragic" dimension not in the criminal act but in the way it is marketed in America. We all become voyeurs and participants in Gilmore's murders. That is the book's cultural freight.

But even before Mailer explores that aspect of his tale, the "true-life" part, he must establish Gilmore more firmly as a man worthy of such attention, as bearing sufficient interest to make him the cover story for *Time* and *Newsweek,* the cynosure of legal and media attention. Gilmore's letters to Nicole, which become the cornerstone of Schiller's "take," have within them passages suggesting a superior sensibility. We are struck not so much by anything intrinsically valuable Gilmore displays, but by the fact that he is distinct as a criminal. It is like the dog playing chess: the fact of playing, not the level of game, is the thing. "Nothing in my experience [he writes Nicole] prepared me for the kind of honest open love you gave me. I'm so used to bullshit and hostility, deceit and pettiness, evil and hatred. Those things are my natural habitat. They have shaped me. I look at the world through eyes that suspect, doubt, fear, hate, cheat, mock, are selfish and vain. All things unacceptable, I see them as natural and have even come to accept them as such."

This *is* sensitive as a description of what Gilmore has been immersed in; he can describe his condition. And as long as he is the focus of his own words, he remains sensitive; but his words never convey an understanding of how he has responded as an individual to his "natural habitat" or made himself what he is. The very thing Mailer conveyed in his other nonfiction, where he was himself so active, is missing in Gilmore's story, in which Mailer is a hovering presence rather than immanent.

Gilmore's lack of introspection keeps his level of response low. Similarly, while we are taken by the kind of reading he does—Hesse's *Demian,* Kesey, Alan Watts, *Catch-22,* "Death in Venice," J. P. Donleavy, as well as Irving Stone's *The Agony and the Ecstasy* and *Lust for Life*—nothing in his talk or letters suggests he has gained much, apart from vocabulary, from such reading. His discussions of reincarnation are popularized versions; his attempts at ideas always circle back to his own condition. Most of all, those deeply introspective readings have not brought him insights into himself or his condition. Gilmore before the reading is similar to Gilmore

after. One of the shills, Dennis Boaz, a well-educated lawyer, recognizes as much: "Dennis wasn't hearing ideas that were new to him," but "was impressed that Gilmore was actually this familiar with the consciousness stuff."

We are left, then, with many loose strands, each in itself potentially significant: Gilmore himself, who rarely becomes larger than his punkish life; his reading and his letters, which suggest some greater dimension but lack self-knowledge; his young girl friend, who seems bent on self-destruction—attempting suicide in a pact with Gilmore—but who also lacks sufficient self-knowledge; a Mormon community, which remains shadowy and vague; a large cast of characters who surround and/or support Gilmore, yet lack clear definition; a small army of shills who want to sell the story to the media, and invade Provo offering contracts, television and film exposure, to those who know the murderer, to the murderer; Mailer himself, hovering undefined, gathering evidence painstakingly, so that he is like a gigantic vacuum cleaner eager not to miss a particle.

Surfaces, all surfaces. Mailer mentions, in passing, *In Cold Blood,* which was required school reading for Gary's brother; and we are, of course, directly clued in to the kind of murder drama Mailer is exploring. Capote, however, had one great advantage over Mailer: he spent a great deal of time with the murderers, and he empathized with them, especially with Perry Smith. Mailer had to settle for secondhand and derivative information about Gilmore. The blue eyes of the latter and those of the former never had the opportunity to measure each other. Perhaps Gilmore would have revealed something to Mailer the others could not fathom.

A dramatic meeting of several areas of feeling comes with the struggle between the execution and anti-execution forces, while Gilmore has gone on a hunger strike to protest opposition to his execution. At the same time, with Gilmore only in partial possession of the facts, there is a broad scenario being played out in the world beyond: the media have taken over, and various exploitations are being readied. The television channels, several newspapers (Murdoch's *New York Post* and *The Village Voice*), and individuals such as Lawrence Schiller (who saw a package deal: *Playboy* interview, overseas sales, a book). Schiller is, in fact, secretly selling the Gilmore-Nicole letters, though he knows "the shit . . . would certainly hit the fan if Gary found out."

The man at the center of this maelstrom, Gilmore, has already attempted suicide once, in his pact with

Nicole, who has smuggled in drugs by way of a balloon shoved into her vagina, which he transfers to his rectum. The volume of drugs is insufficient; he nearly dies, but he recovers rapidly. He will, shortly afterward, make a more serious, attempt. At this crossroads of mixed motives, this boundary between life and death, Mailer has a character of considerable complexity, *if he can penetrate*. But commentary takes the following diluted form:

> After lunch, when Ron Stanger [one of Gilmore's lawyers] saw Gary again at the prison, it was like talking to steel. Worse than the pits of the hunger strike, Gary was as cold and hard and icy fevered as Ron had ever seen him. It burned your eyes to look into his rage. Man, Gary was triggered. Call it possessed.

This is Mailer speaking through Stanger's observation; but what Mailer offers is a steel wall separating himself, the consciousness of the piece, from the object of his perception. All he can produce for us by way of explanation is what Stanger's less trained eye would also see. Mailer fails here because his tools as a novelist come to naught, and he admits as much when he speaks of that wall around Gilmore. For the novelist's task is to penetrate the wall, or if not to penetrate it, then to create a web of explanations which are the verbal equivalent of penetration. Here, Mailer retreats, noticeably so; and his claims for the "novel" aspect of the "true life novel" are belied by the stance he must take.

What occurs in the book, in fact, is that the selling of Gilmore to the media becomes more compelling as a story than Gilmore is. Manipulation of an individual by the media, while that individual, in turn, manipulates the media by way of controlling his life and/or death, is now the subject of the drama. Mailer's withdrawal as a novelist leads to loss of inner dimensions and, at the same time, shifts the focus. The two parts of the book, then, do not mesh, even though Mailer has attempted a mix by joining "Western Voices" and "Eastern Voices," the voices of the Utah arena with those of the commercial East Coast and Gilmore's belief in karma and reincarnation. Instead of blending, they underline the confidence game.

The sell is expertly done. Mailer perceives the vulgar side of America as well as any living novelist, and these parts of *The Executioner's Song* vie with *JR* and its view of America as a gigantic market. We come to understand Schiller—his desire for respectability, his scorn at being labeled a merchant of death, his need for solidity by way of his association with Bill Moyers, representing CBS. And through it all, we observe Schiller meeting his match in Gilmore, the latter manipulating the manipulators by offering up his life and death. As Schiller slices more deeply into Gilmore's privacy, with interview questions that penetrate cruelly, Gilmore coughs up bits and pieces of himself, as, later, he will offer up his organs after his death. What remains, however, is Gilmore's secret, his wall, his impenetrability. No matter how close Schiller comes, he cannot replace the novelist's work; and Mailer's guiding hand beyond Schiller cannot find any point of entrance. The wall circumscribes. Gilmore goes to his death without having revealed the "real thing."

There is still the question of Mailer's participation in the "selling of Gary Gilmore." Schiller is presented with many of his warts, and he is well described; but Mailer sidesteps the entire question of his own commercialization of a man's deeply personal life. He only castigates the more obvious attempts at commercialism,* but leaves open the morality of the wheeling and dealing itself. Mailer was deeply indebted for information to Schiller, and we suspect his acceptance of this area is connected to his loyalty to his source. For where are Mailer's typical scorn and contempt? The title "The Selling of Gary Gilmore," more effective than *The Executioner's Song,*† would have located Mailer in the mainstream of his work, his dissection of American culture at its various levels of materialism and commercialism. He fails to define the shill in Schiller, and lets him off far too easily. By titling his book as he does, Mailer has suggested a lyrical solution to a contemptuous act: a callous and brutal murderer who becomes the focal point for American greed. Mailer missed where his true vocation lay, not only as a novelist but as a messenger of American culture.

---

*Such as the *National Enquirer*'s desire to establish a guessing game based on two objects to be put in Gilmore's possession and a twenty-five-word statement he would give to a bonded messenger; then various seers and clairvoyants would try to guess what those objects and the message are, the winner receiving up to $100,000. Schiller rejects this deal.

†The title of a poem Mailer published in *Cannibals and Christians,* which states Mailer's desire to "become an executioner"; and if we apply the sentiment to the book, we see him as part of an America that sings of death, of executions, in order to fulfill media needs. In a sneaky way, the poem underscores Mailer's ambiguous role in the Gilmore story, his uncertainty whether Gilmore should be sold as romantic outlaw or vicious murderer.

THE AMERICAN AS OUTLAW: HAWKES, VONNEGUT, KOSINSKI, PERCY

Mailer's book, where America and Gilmore as her prisoner blend, is indicative of several 1979–80 novels, in which the outlaw defines American themes. This has been, of course, a continuing theme in our fiction,* yet at the turn of the decade, actual prison scenes dominate, as we see in Hawkes and Vonnegut. But the prison as metaphor extends to authors such as Kosinski and Percy, for whom "normal people" become outlaws to prevent their own death. "The American as Outlaw" could, in fact, be applied to much of the fiction published at the turn of the decade; and it is a good indicator for the novel, certainly after the adjustments to exhaustion which we observed at mid-decade. The stress on outlawry suggests a return to fierceness, to opposition, to adversary roles, which is precisely what 1980s fiction needs. If fiction is to be large, it must derive from writers who station themselves outside and beyond, their weapons irony and satire, scorn and contempt. The leveling off of American fiction has come from accommodation.

For Hawkes in *The Passion Artist* (1979), Konrad Vost—a name suggesting a predatory creature—is undertaking a journey that will encompass his passion, as will the journey's goal. He is Hawkes's modern knight and outlaw, a man of bourgeois tastes (a pharmacist, father of a daughter turned prostitute, mourner after his dead wife) who is also the son of Eva, who is imprisoned in La Violaine. La Violaine dominates the town where Vost works and lives, like the Castle in the village Kafka's K. visits. Unlike K., however, Vost gets inside, as a civilian armed to suppress the women's revolt. But the revolt succeeds, and women come to dominate Vost's life: as potential saviors, castrators, Amazons with ultimate power.

Hawkes's eighth novel-length fiction is a meditation on a modern passage. It recalls a good deal of twentieth-century literature: Kafka, of course, his hunger artist and his two K.'s; Mann's Aschenbach in "Death in Venice," a conventional man turned into the subject of passion; Camus's "stranger" as well as Jean-Baptiste from *The Fall;* Gide's early wanderers, whose lives become clotted with alien and passionate feelings. In Hawkes's version of the modern journey and ultimate sacrifice, La Violaine, the name of both

the prison and the bar which awaits those released from prison, dominates. It is the emblem of the world, that world in Hawkes's vision which has been increasingly overrun by women.

Hawkes's sense of female domination goes well beyond anything associated with recent women's liberation. It is a mythic view of existence, reverting to a time before the Greek tragedians when scholars posit a matriarchy. In such a society, women not only wielded power, they infused their values into every aspect of life. Such is La Violaine, and its women are willing to fight for their power, to fight as barbarians against men who are also barbaric. Hawkes has attempted to return us to a kind of prehistory, where clashes take place in night and fog, and men attack women with heavy sticks, while the women defend themselves with homemade weapons which cut, slash, stab.

In this world, Vost becomes a "stationary traveler," Hawkes's symbol of the man who journeys subconsciously everywhere and yet fails to move. "He understood that what had occurred in La Violaine was both far and near, and that now, like the stationary traveler, he was listening to the sounds of awakening made by people who could not move." That tension between movement and stasis becomes part of the "meditation" which characterizes *The Passion Artist.* Hawkes is continuing the line of imagination we found in his previous novel, *Travesty,* in which a hurtling car becomes as static as a coffin, a car within which the inhabitants will be sealed in an accident that simultaneously will terminate the journey and their lives.

We note that departure in Hawkes's work from pure stiflement into new tensions, foreshadowed by *The Blood Oranges* and carried here into forms of journey and sacrifice. The aim is release, liberation, whatever the pain. If death remains a central symbol of Hawkes's work, it is not a "constant death," but a shifting view of it. Vost sincerely believes nothing is ever lost, that the world is one of change, multiplication, interpenetration. Hawkes finds structural examples of this by roving back and forth between Vost's present, which is like waking dream, and his childhood, which recalls reverie. If dreams and reverie interpenetrate, then all life is mosaics of varying proportions. Hawkes views Vost as both individual and historical presence, as a unique man undertaking the journey into his life which characterizes all men. His dead wife, Claire, expresses from the grave her view that "no life disappears, that nobody dies, that the person you have lost today reappears tomorrow in a

---

*As H. Bruce Franklin shows in his comprehensive *The Victim as Criminal and Artist: Literature from the American Prison* (1978).

different place, in different circumstances." Nothing is lost. Entropy in the larger world is undermined by everything which is saved in the human world.

As an example of loss, in the prison riot Vost seemingly loses his right hand, and yet he gains another one. This apparent severance—later, he discovers the hand was not amputated—is part of Vost's loss of nearly everything: wife, daughter, pharmacy (which burns), mother. For the missing hand he finds a black glove, inside of which is a silver hand. "He was both maimed and adorned. His character was now externalized in the gloved hand. Inner life and outer life were assuming a single shape, as if to conform with one of his theories. He was crippled, he was heraldic, soon the rest of him would follow the way of the hand until he could be mounted upright on a block of stone." Vost moves inexorably toward the outlaw's martyrdom: the "passion artist," the man who dabbles in women, becoming, like Kafka's hunger artist, an exhausted subject; now only an object for derision, yet somehow inviolate.

There is, in Hawkes's formulation, an interconnection between the "passion" of Vost and the demands of art; although his context nowhere duplicates those great meditations on sacrifice, martyrdom, passion, and art we find in Mann or in Kafka himself, where economy of means establishes its own ironies. Hawkes expresses his ideas in a heart of darkness. Vost stumbles toward his final passion as if under an archway of jungle branches which exclude light and warmth, leaving only stagnant air for the traveler to breathe.

His apotheosis as a passion artist arrives when he is a prisoner in La Violaine, the sole man ever to penetrate its depths and to communicate with the multitude of females imprisoned there. In this respect, he is privileged to be the only man permitted to observe what women have experienced. It is, for the first time, an experience which he can fully engage in, his previous life having been lived repressively, either at margins or superficially. He had not known he was fit only to live in darkness, and he had fought it as something alien, rather than as his natural milieu. Release, if it comes, will derive from fetid, rank, sexual darkness.

In the bleakness and grime of La Violaine, now the emblem of Vost's world, he is reunited with his mother, a woman who had poured volatile fuel over Vost senior and set him on fire, a woman who during her pregnancy had tried to expel the dead matter that would be Vost. After birth, the doctor tries to "seize the tiny creature and to crack its neck against the edge of the basin, as does the farmer who wishes to destroy the malformed newborn animal." Vost, accordingly, has a miraculous birth of sorts; everything after that moment of birth is deemed unnatural, and his mother refuses to say his name.

Their meeting in prison, where she is the leader of the revolt, is accompanied by Vost's helplessness before the seduction of a gigantic woman, whose massive body smothers him in acts of sexual passion. Eva is witness to their acts; having killed her Adam, she is now trying to "release" her son from his malformed life. The woman manages the act, playing upon Vost's filthy and exhausted body and liberating from it the final sense of "femalehood," which in turns transforms him into a "passion artist."

As a passion artist and an outlaw, Vost has acquired magical powers, although they are not to be enjoyed for long. He will die, shot by his friend Gagnon. But in the brief period of his passion, he will accommodate the experiences of a hitherto concealed world; and his powers will be great, as shaman, magician, artist. He has, in a sense, achieved the Byzantium of Yeats's vision, attained it not by way of art, as in the poem, but through passion and outlawry. His union with the gigantic woman has united him not only with his mother but with the dead Claire, his drifting daughter, the very idea of women.

Hawkes's visionary work inhabits a strange territory. The unnamed land, the unfamiliar landscape, the meditation on death, ice, and hard materials, the passage through pain as a form of renewable experience, Vost as a very flawed saint are all elements suggestive of allegory. Hawkes has moved toward this with his last three books, especially *Travesty*. Eschewing routine lives, he has tried with very different content to reestablish his earlier mode of exploration: working the seams of existence, concealing what he has discovered, denying the outward experience in favor of some inward communication which is itself incomplete. The following passage from *The Passion Artist* is not the end for Hawkes, but the beginning, not a moral lapse but the place where life is to be found. He is now a novelist not of ends, but of beginnings, honest beginnings:

> Innocence leads inevitably to ice and iron: to bones that become iron, to skin that freezes gradually into a blue and glittering transparency, and then cracks and refreezes until the entire surface of the body is encased and encrusted in scales and broken mirrors of ice, frozen in place.

He is trying to discover where life can be intensified with such fervor that it passes almost into death; so that whatever one seeks must be accompanied by its opposite. The greatest joys are balanced by pains; all passion is perverted, and yet passion, like art, saves. Vost is revived from exhaustion by the gigantic woman who plays on his body; and then he is prepared to die. The margins Hawkes moves along are very tenuous, for his themes and treatment could easily fall into romantic poses, into cries of pain a child emits. Like Barth, in his recent *Letters,* he takes great chances with his fiction. Attempting to return to the great modalities of his early work, he has forged a lusher and richer prose which begins to function in *The Passion Artist.* He has also shifted his vision, dealing now not with apocalypse and doom, but with what comes after. There is this: a refusal to settle in and repeat himself. Hawkes here, Barth, Roth in *The Ghost Writer,* Malamud in *Dubin's Lives,* Styron in *Sophie's Choice* have tried to move along the lines of their talent. Barth and Hawkes are the most ambitious, willing to experience the poor reviews and chancy reception of works that cannot please. Yet Hawkes's development, which seemed stalled in his previous fictions, has revived. We need, in the future, some large integrative work, in which the outlaw, violent, erotic, and artist—the ingredients of Hawkes's stew—come together; as they did in the writers he emulates in *The Passion Artist.*

Virginie: Her Two Lives (1982) is a curious successor to *The Passion Artist.* It is, clearly, in the same vein, an examination not only of passion but of the ways in which it may be created. *Virginie* is divided into two alternating parts, with the longer sections devoted to Seigneur, a mid-eighteenth-century "maker" or artist. With obvious links to de Sade's devotees of passion, he defines his art as that of creating women who will rise to the summits of their trade, submissive and subservient to whatever their master requires of them. When they are ready for this role, they ride off as perfect, having achieved "Noblesse." Seigneur himself never touches these women (he uses dogs and pigs instead), since part of their training is to make them subdue their sexuality when it is most intense. They must deny all to achieve an absolute state, an artwork. Virginie's role, as sister and daughter of Seigneur, is to represent purity, of body and spirit, even while present at all degrading ceremonies.

The other, alternating segments of *Virginie* are concerned with a 1940s "Sex Arcade," operated by a French taxi driver named Bocage, whose name signifies a grove or wooded region. His establishment provides a sensual Garden for prostitutes and their followers. Here, two hundred years later, we have a resurrected Virginie, once again an observer and as symbol of purity, until Bocage claims her. This, like the other section, ends in disaster. In the first, Seigneur, the hunter, becomes hunted, and the women he has "created" through degradation first mutilate and then burn him; in the second, Virginie's Maman torches Bocage's establishment. The eleven-year-old survives to write her journal, which describes the voyeuristic experiences of her two-phased life.

The lush prose we found in *The Passion Artist* here becomes Hawkes-Virginie's effort at heightened expression suitable for archaism, parody, and retread pornography. The novel begins, more an affectation than parodic: "Mine is an impossible story. My journal burns. My body burns. Child with no past, child forever denied her passing time, her maturation, her future realm of womanhood which justifies all our course of indentured innocence and is the golden glow that rewards the mere light of the female's purest youth: thus I lie asleep, awake, unmoving beneath Bocage on my little bed, bed from which I shall never arise, fixed as I am forever in the very center of my flaming nest, the true child poised once and for all, for a mere moment, in the throes of love while yet and always ignorant of that mysterious adult she too must have been destined to become."

With the 1740 segments juxtaposed to those in 1945, Hawkes was trying, apparently, to explore some historical sensibility, or continuity of sexuality, and then to express identification with those who rebel against degradation and passivity. Yet it is difficult to find where the integration of ideas takes place. The novel delights in so many repulsive scenes, bestiality in the earlier segments, male domination in the later, that Hawkes dissipates significance or else plays a double game of condemning what provides enjoyment. The eleven-year-old Virginie as voyeur only adds another repellent dimension. The novel seeks to make a large statement about passion and sensuality, perhaps, but it descends to degrading levels of pornography: reification of women, the deadening of sexual response, the titillation of voyeurism. That the women rebel is a late development which does not alter the fact that Hawkes is stretching after meaning at another dimension: to present Seigneur and Bocage sympathetically while they act vilely, to provide sexual kicks for the reader while debasing the performers. Perhaps the ultimate moment comes when Seigneur has his butterfly emblem tattooed on Finesse's buttock—so that her every movement makes it "fly." If this is art or even the parody of art, it is very close to shit.

Vonnegut's *Jailbird* (1979) is the news of the last few years rearranged as fiction. Most of its story line comes from Walter Cronkite or headlines of *The New York Times*. Walter F. Starbuck, narrator and chief character, is a minor Watergate casualty, doing time in a minimum-security prison. RAMJAC, the company run by a Howard Hughes-like old woman named Mrs. Graham, a former friend of Starbuck's, is the giant conglomerate which swallows up everything, including the *Times* and *its* subsidiary, a cat food company. Roy Cohn appears briefly as a lawyer for Starbuck, to gain his release from a padded cell which the police have forgotten about. The Communist scare of the fifties streaks through, embodied in Richard Nixon's early years as a House investigator. Starbuck, in fact, gives away a good friend to the Nixon committee. Vonnegut's narrator is himself Nietzsche's "last man," the one who adapts to any situation or condition and comes through, a Mother Courage of sorts, without the courage of Courage. As he says himself, he has done nothing to aid mankind, and he is, like most Vonnegut creatures, carried along by events and chance.

One of the other prisoners in the Federal Minimum Security Adult Correctional Facility, on the edge of Finletter Air Force Base near Atlanta, is a naturalized Italian, Dr. Carlo di Sanza, who holds a doctorate in law from the University of Naples. More Don than Sancho, Di Sanza is a promoter of Ponzi schemes; he insists he will start his third Ponzi pyramid as soon as he is released. The Ponzi scheme is a confidence game in which high interest is promised to subscribers, some of whom are paid, while most are bilked. It works on trust, and is intrinsic to capitalism, connected to it so closely that Vonnegut can observe: "every successful government is of necessity a Ponzi scheme," for "it accepts enormous loans that can never be repaid." After making this shrewd assessment, Vonnegut lets it dribble away in a lot of sentimental talk about lost opportunities, lack of basic necessities for the poor, the railroading of Sacco and Vanzetti to the electric chair by types who paralleled the WASPs who ran the Vietnam War. The structural idea for the novel lies here, in Ponzi schemes, but Vonnegut has preferred a loose narrative based on Starbuck's drift.

The crux of Starbuck's fate is that rich people direct his life. He is, first, the protégé of Alexander McCone, a young man so unnerved by his father's labor tactics he becomes a helpless stammerer. McCone makes it possible for Starbuck to become a Harvard man. Harvard runs as a leitmotif through the novel. Many of the prisoners at Finletter—bilkers, confidence men, former government officials—are Harvard men; so that much of the world's misery can be attributed to the "Harvard man" who sticks with his fellow graduates. There is a joke here, but it has been made long ago, when Kennedy was President. One of the disadvantages of history as sifted through Cronkite is the presence of stale jokes, which, transformed into themes, create stale themes.

From McCone, Starbuck gains his education, becomes co-chairman of the Harvard chapter of the Young Communist League, wins a Rhodes Scholarship to Oxford, and works for Roosevelt's Department of Agriculture, all the time drifting, without a vocation. He knows nothing about agriculture, nor does he, in fact, know anything about any of the positions he holds. He is *in government,* which in Vonnegut is similar to what *making a speech* means in Donald Barthelme; one works in government or makes a speech, and in neither is there any content, nor the need of any. Vonnegut suggests, but does not assimilate into *Jailbird,* that Starbuck is a "jailbird" long before he becomes a minor Watergate casualty. An archetypal American outlaw in his drift, he is incapable of controlling his own life; in fact, being a Harvard man has marked him for further drift, since he can never escape that "branding" which disallows independent thought.

At the war's end, Starbuck finds himself holder of considerable power, owner of a white Mercedes, originally an anniversary present from Himmler to his wife. While involved in setting up the Nuremberg trials, Starbuck meets *his* wife, Ruth, a former concentration camp inmate. Here, Vonnegut's sentimental, slippery method of narrative services him well, for his brief portraits of Ruth are superb: a woman who learned languages in order to survive; a woman whose vocation as a wedding photographer was brief because there "was always an air of prewar doom about her photographs," as if the "entire wedding party would end up in the trenches or the gas chambers"; a woman who lives without any beliefs in mankind. She is, when Starbuck finds her, much like Kosinski's young boy in *The Painted Bird,* in fact, Starbuck believes her to be a boy. Harvard men, however, materialize everywhere, and she obtains the best of American medical care, so that her plans to be "like a bird in flight" are altered to becoming Starbuck's wife. She then fades away, until her death from cancer. Vonnegut brilliantly characterizes her as "one of millions of Europe's Ophelias after the Second World War," her fate to be salvaged from the slag heap by the future Watergate criminal.

Starbuck's bailiwick is a unit called Down Home Records, which includes *The New York Times* (where his unpleasant son is a reviewer), Barnum & Bailey, Universal Pictures, Dell Publishing, et al. The juxtaposition is the joke, of course, and much of the novel is given over to that: set pieces which while amusing are structurally anomalous. Vonnegut's aim, apparently, was to convey that American sense of wandering through life—eighteenth-century picaresque as analogy and perhaps model—but it also permits destructive indulgences. When Barth and Pynchon indulge themselves, the act is an aberration; they return us to the main line of development. When Vonnegut indulges, it becomes the thing itself. Starbuck and his former wife, whose background is very different from his, can never overcome their dissimilarities, he lower class, she middle to upper; so they paper over dissension with joke routines. The insight is excellent: a couple who couple only by way of stand-up comic routines, bad jokes which disguise lack of communication. Question: What is the difference between an enzyme and a hormone? Answer: You can't hear an enzyme.

Such routines may be fun as marginal stuff, not as everything. Multiply them and the novel is based on routines. In prison, Starbuck meets Dr. Robert Fender, a writer who has published under the name Kilgore Trout, Vonnegut's science fiction friend from several previous books. The first line of *Jailbird,* in fact, announces that Kilgore Trout is back—"He could not make it on the outside." Trout is mentioned a third time when Fender plans to write a "science-fiction novel about economics under the pseudonym of Kilgore Trout." The introduction of Trout, and the outlines of some Fender-Trout stories, serve as linkage with Vonnegut's other books and, apparently, with his army of readers. But in every respect the linkage is marginal to the novel, an indulgence, a telegraphing to readers that Trout-Vonnegut is back with another one.

Marginal material fills pages, and pages end up as the novel. By turning all into whimsy—no one suffers very much in Vonnegut despite pessimism and a negative presentation of America—he reduces and simplifies. He really aspires to minimalism, for his method is to return to fundamentals. The force for good in Vonnegut's world is the Sermon on the Mount: Starbuck's very reason for ratting on his friend to the Nixon committee. Vonnegut wants us to take the Sermon literally; it is a good piece of advice, personally, but insufficient to build postwar fiction upon, unless one has the powers of Tolstoy. The index at the end of *Jailbird* contains strange combinations: Caryl Chessman, the executed murderer, Maurice Chevalier, Winston Churchill, with Clyde Carter, a prison guard, juxtaposed to Jimmy Carter. Just above is Al Capone. The index is, like several other postures, a whimsical trip: a documentary of our time intermixed with fictional elements.

Buried in all this is a real feel for the American as outlaw: that sense of our culture as resting on a thin line between respectability and criminality. Postwar fiction has delved deeply into the theme, its vitality as well as its contradictions; and Vonnegut is superbly equipped to probe it. Considerable satirical gifts, however, have been sacrificed to casualness, whimsy, and sentimentality. Not since *Cat's Cradle* in the early 1960s or parts of *Slaughterhouse-Five* later in the decade has Vonnegut taken the trouble to provide structures for his shrewd perceptions of a culture which slides away from definition even as we observe it.

Our response to Vonnegut's next novel, *Deadeye Dick* (1982), depends on what we expect. If we look for a book in its fullness and density, then we will consider it frivolous and trivial. But if we look elsewhere and see it as a series of sketches, a kind of verbal *Wisconsin Death Trip,* then we agree Vonnegut has become a bellwether of the 1980s in America. Vonnegut has developed into perhaps our most American writer, our Twain, but much of his America has been frittered away in whimsy and trivia. Even the jacket photographs of the author were designed to turn the shrewd observer into the old codger, to pull his claws before they scratched. In *Deadeye Dick,* he zeroes in on middle America, white, Protestant, middle America, where even the sane are loony. He has recognized, and he convinces the reader, that the most extraordinary act can be assimilated into seeming normalcy. His Deadeye Dick—Rudolph Waltz, whose stray shot kills a pregnant woman—is called and prefers to call himself a "neutral." A neutral or neutered creature is not interested in sex; but Rudy means more than that by the term. The neutral person is not anomic, nor a mere loser, although he does suggest those conditions. The neuter has, in a sense, succumbed to Americanitis, to the crisscrossing patterns of zaniness which make will, direction, ambition, goals, further aspects of lunacy. It is better to be neutral, to let America—here Midland City, Ohio—flow over one; not to struggle but to become a passive counter.

By the time Rudy Waltz tells his story, Midland City no longer exists, or at least Midlanders don't; a neutron bomb, called a "friendly bomb," since it was one of ours, has killed everyone. Property, apparently, remains, although Vonnegut in the preface suggests the bomb was not so surgical as it seems in the book. Rudy now hangs out in a Haitian hotel, which he and his brother, Felix, bought with money from the government. The latter coughed up a large sum to compensate the family for having permitted radioactive cement from Oak Ridge, Tennessee, to get into a mantelpiece adorning the Waltz home. The circuits of American madness are endless, leading from one destructive act to another, from Rudy shooting the pregnant woman so as to become, for one and all, Deadeye Dick, to the government murdering on *its* scale. America kills, as Michael Lesy illustrated in *Wisconsin Death Trip* (1973), only now it kills differently. In Lesy, the death trip was suicide, alcohol, random murder, to which we can now add drugs, police brutality, government genocide. Yet Rudy's parents, born rich, are indifferent to everything, even to their children; their family life is dominated by the Hitler-loving father, who dresses like a Hungarian Life Guard, in busby and panther skin. His most prized possessions are a gun collection of considerable historical value, and it is this embrace of a gun culture which leads to Rudy's fatal use of the Winchester one night.

In a sequence of brief sketches, further subdivided into even shorter segments, with some inset playlets, Vonnegut catches the fall of man in America even as the country expands, develops, struts. He has swung back to the themes of his earlier work: expulsion from Eden, man's lapse from grace, loss of religious meaning in secular man; he catches it all as the Waltz family waltzes toward its own fall in Midland City and resurrection in Haiti. Why Haiti? Because while Rudy and his brother survive in Haiti, Midland City, a miniature America, is becoming a refugee camp for Haitians. Processes reverse as readily as they go forward.

Deadeye Dick is *Player Piano* and *Cat's Cradle* rerouted, the fifties and sixties rerun at a faster pace perhaps and with less hope for unfolding, definition, and transformation. Rudy feels "neutrality" is his only defense against insanity, and he foresees thousands coming out of the closet to march in a parade

under the banner "Egregious," those who live outside the flock or herd. Yet even if the neuters will in fact inherit the earth one day, Vonnegut seems to pass over that one of them rather blithely did kill a pregnant woman. A moral issue lies somewhere in there, ignored, and yet such is Vonnegut's touch that we, too, forget moral issues and ride his rocket of doom to doom. By playing on the black keys, as it were, Vonnegut has leapfrogged over America and touched more vital issues than many writers who play the whole keyboard.

Fabian, a polo player, is Kosinski's nomad and outlaw in *Passion Play* (1979). The title is deliberately ambiguous, referring to the passion of play, the passion of competition in one-on-one field play; but also to Fabian's suffering, his own passion, and to the play of passion in him that neither horses nor women satisfy. It is a complex conceit, an excellent title and direction. Added to that is the promise of the epigraphs, one from *Don Quixote,* that some knights-errant "have been the salvation not only of one kingdom but of many." There is, also, an epigraph from *Moby-Dick,* that for the prisoner, Ahab, the beyond beckons, and for him the white whale is the wall between him and the outside. "Sometimes I think there's naught beyond."

Fabian is built loosely on the Don metaphor, a knight-errant of sorts; and at one point he rides competitively a horse called Captain Ahab. He is associated, by way of epigraph and suggestion, with both the innocence of the Don and the willful destructiveness of Ahab. But Fabian, in Kosinski's conception, aspires to more; he is also a modern centaur, using either horses or his VanHome as vehicle. He is, as well, an Odysseus of modern fabrication, a "nomad of the highway." In his VanHome, he shuns communities where other drivers gather to exchange tales of engine failure and sewage troubles.

As a nomad who travels in great comfort, Fabian insists not only on his privacy but on the singularity of his name. His first name, he says, is too difficult to pronounce, so he uses Fabian, which has the ring of Plato, and suggests a maker or creator of his own self. Fabian's plan is always to be recreating himself through play; in play's passion, he comes alive. His aging, aching, wounded body gains vitality, and he is able to surge. As a maker of his own destiny, a denier of chance, and yet a negator of life's easy plots, he is dedicated to himself. He bathes, preens, and luxuriates in his VanHome, which closes out the world; there are his horses in the rear and he, himself, in front. Since polo involves only establishment people, Fabian's touchstones are the extraordinarily wealthy, such as the Stanhopes, several of whom enter and reenter Fabian's life, even after he kills one of them, Eugene, in a contest which becomes less a game of polo than an opportunity for revenge. Fabian pursues Vanessa Stanhope, Eugene's niece. Some sequences resemble the television series *Dallas*.

Part of the appeal polo has for Fabian is that it is a life outside of life, with its own rules, which exist only for players. The rest of life—justice, roles, legal balances—is left behind. The intensity of play preempts life, makes life without play meaningless. The nature of Fabian's game is such that he has gained a reputation for revengeful shots; as a result, no one will give him team play. Unnerved, Fabian believes his distrust of team play derives from some fear of being trampled or from his distrust of the collective spirit. "Later in life, he decided that the spirit of the collective and the team bore for him another implication less ominous but equally disturbing: collective responsibility diluted one's faults, but it also diminished one's achievements, took away from them stature and consequence." Play must derive from the force of his own will, from "his unique instinct to survive." Polo has become a political statement.

Forsaking team play for individual effort, Fabian revels in his isolation: "he could claim no constant place as home, summon no assistance as he sought to make his way again." He drifts in his VanHome, a Don of the plains, although in Fabian's case, all his adventures reward the self, either monetarily or in access to power.

One-third through *Passion Play,* Kosinski begins the string of events which become the basis of the strung-out narrative. These episodes, familiar from his previous books, feature a wandering, Odyssean figure and a morally neutral world. We note the focus on sensation: a transsexual love affair, passion amidst horses à la Lawrence, a succession of pornographic fantasies. Many of the descriptions of sexual activity are not distant from descriptions of murder. When Fabian possesses Vanessa as a virgin and her vaginal blood flows, he withdraws his penis and strokes her face with it, leaving bloody streaks; he then licks the blood from her cheeks and neck, holding it on his tongue, and kisses her, "tasting the gift of blood he brought to her from her own depth. As she plunged beneath him, her eyes staring, her mouth trapping a scream, he moved into her again, a reeling of ebb and flow pulling her apart, buckling her in quivers of desire."

After such a passage, or others similar to it, the reader simply cannot accept Fabian as a valid witness of his own experiences. A curious bifurcation occurs, between Kosinski's Fabian and the reader's, who is parodic, a figure the author should mock for his solemnity, narcissism, solipsism, megalomania. Our Fabian is a self-conceived monster of self-deception. Whatever Kosinski accepts as Fabian's suffering, need, expression of will becomes for the reader egomania. By the time of Fabian's bloody sex with Vanessa, closer to the Manson murder of Sharon Tate than to romantic passion, the reader has long since rejected Kosinski's reach for metaphysical dimensions.

Fabian's quest is a traditional one, of a narcissist in pursuit of his image, the quest Kosinski has pursued for his last four books. The writing of *Passion Play* shows a fuller style, a more confident embrace of the language; but it is the lush prose a foreign-born writer is prone to—the English Conrad used in his early novels and later pruned. For all Kosinski's modern touches, protagonist and story remain rooted in the era of *Vathek* or a fin-de-siècle romance.

Only at the end does language come together with narrative and character to create a magnificent moment. In the final scene, Fabian decides to go after Vanessa, and he rides his horse onto the airstrip where her plane is about to take off. "He started along the runway, Big Lick [one of his two horses] unrestrained, whipping the withered grass to a fine dust. Fabian came abreast of the plane and glanced at the windows, a row of one-way mirrors. Its engines roaring, the plane started to roll for takeoff. . . . Vanessa, her forehead bent to the cool glass of the window, would catch sight of a man on a horse, streaming along the black strip of runway, the man's helmet, shirt and breeches all white, his horse black, the run of the horse unbroken, the rider tilting, as if charging with a lance in combat with an enemy only he could see."

Horse and plane rush along the strip. The proximity to the Don and his windmills, in this fine passage, only points up the greatness of the Cervantes conception and the flaws of Kosinski's "passion play" as a container for Fabian, the maker, the Don, the Captain Ahab of his own drama. Lacking a social context for his outlawry, Fabian has too readily fallen into self-indulgence and narcissism.

In Percy's *The Second Coming* (1980), Will Barrett, from *The Last Gentleman,* has traded his earlier sense of "middle distances" for a disorientation that involves loss of attention span and present moment; a condition that increases pressures until he is deemed mad. Will Barrett is now a generation beyond the young man of *The Last Gentleman,* having married and fathered a daughter, become a successful Wall Street lawyer, and then felt it all fall apart. The key image here is one of disintegration, which is the first stage toward some wholeness. Will seeks unification of self, if possible, by way of a cave and greenhouse, which is inhabited by Allison, the daughter of a dentist and Kitty Vaught, Will's former love from the earlier book. To pull disintegrative elements together before they destroy, Will has become an outlaw; not so much to express himself as to deny the world. Denial is the initial step toward recognition.

Around and above, Will views a world of fragmentation, incoherences. He is obsessed that the Jews are pulling out of North Carolina, and this is a sign, a Biblical warning, that the world is moving toward Armageddon, without any chance for redemption. Poised on the edge of madness and sanity, feeling first one and then the other, Will cannot accept a world that is godless and empty. Percy writes wittily and yet with foreboding:

> Did the growing madness have something to do with the Jews pulling out? Who said we could get along without the Jews? Watch the Jews, their mysterious comings and goings and stayings! The Jews are a sign! When the Jews pull out, the Gentiles begin to act like the crazy Jutes and Celts and Angles and redneck Saxons they are. They go back to the woods. Here we are, retired from the cities and living deep in the Southern forests and growing nuttier by the hour. The Jews are gone, the blacks are leaving, and where are we? deep in the woods, socking little balls around the mountains, rattling ice in Tanqueray, riding $35,-000 German cars, watching Billy Graham and the Steelers and M*A*S*H on 45-inch Jap TV.

A gloss on the above: The Jews are somehow a conscience, not exalted, in their presence a balance for Saxon madness. Golf is a key metaphor of the novel —Will and his "sane" colleagues all play and derive from it a focus for their lives. Tanqueray gin and Mercedes luxury cars are backgrounds for parties and daily survival; and Sutter Vaught, the Ivan Karamazov figure from *The Last Gentleman,* is now a television addict.

Such arrangements of life indicate to Will that we are a society devoted to the love of death: "The name of this century is the Century of the Love of Death. Death in this century is not the death people die but the death people live. Men love death because real death is better than the living death." Kierkegaard's caution that connection to something other than self must be preceded by the loss of all faith is well heeded. Will is "rotating," in Kierkegaard's sense, moving from one position to another while he seeks direction; even seeking death in the cave beneath the golf course as a way of finding something or forsaking it all. If routine life—little balls, Tanqueray, German cars, Jap television—is a form of death, why not seek the real thing? "Bad as wars are and maybe because they are so bad, thinking of peace during war is better than peace. War is what makes peace desirable. But peace without war is intolerable. . . . Men either kill each other in war, or in peace walk as docilely into living death as sheep into a slaughterhouse."

Will's pursuit, then, as the novel trails his rotation, is for something that is not living death, while he evades the madhouse in the process. For to others, kind as most are, he is mad. Similarly, to others, Allison, Kitty's daughter who lives in a greenhouse, is mad, an inmate from a mental institution who should not be left to herself. Yet she manages, with her twin talents as singer and "hoister." Percy has a marvelous insight here in Allison's ability to work ingeniously with block and tackle, first hoisting an eight-hundred-pound cast-iron stove, and then with her knowledge hoisting Will when he "falls into" her greenhouse from the cave. He falls, she hoists; together they are in balance in an imperfect world.

The hoisting turns Allison into both a craftsperson and a godlike creature. Will "falls into"—he really "falls up" from—the cave, and he is saved by Allison's craft and belief in herself as hoister. Her ability to lift is counterpointed to Will's golf, and while the golf course features strangely dressed men hitting a tiny ball with a variety of clubs, all aiming for distant holes, she plays out a life-and-death game in hoisting a cast-iron stove so as to heat her greenhouse. It is a miraculous juxtaposition, fully integrated into the mature Percy's vision of life: hoisting, an old stove, the ability of a woman to save herself, counterbalancing golf, gin, Mercedes.

The eighty-five-year-old stove is part of a pastoral vision which is an aspect of salvation; as is the greenhouse, penetrated by light, turned into a glittering diamond by lightning: a form of vitality as against the dead glitter of wealthy people playing golf around it. Will has inherited perhaps forty million from his "fat wife," a woman devoted to good works and to eating herself to death. She became so fat she was able to move only in a wheelchair, for her polio-weakened hip could no longer support her. While Will was happy with her, it was a conventional, unexamined happiness: he married her not for her money but because she wanted him to. He brought her pleasure, but himself only passivity. His "first coming" was a neutral existence; his "second" will be active, or not at all. If no lift is forthcoming, he prefers extinction in the cave.

Pastoral, however, is not an undifferentiated or sentimentalized form of salvation. For another, earlier, pastoral experience is, in part or full, behind Will's bouts with madness. That pastoral experience involved Will's father and *his* desperation, his hunting trip with his son, in which he planned to shoot the son (Will) and then kill himself. The mystery is why four shells were found, and Will finally figures out the reason: "One shell for the single [bird], two for me [Will], one for you [Ed Barrett]." Barrett, however, only grazes his son and misses himself; later completing his own death in a Mississippi attic. Will has escaped death in the Georgia woods by a chance he cannot comprehend, but he considers himself "already dead." He is an expert on dying, near dying, death; and he contemplates both barrels in the mouth. Percy writes:

> And what samurai self-love of death, let alone the little death of everyday fuck-you love, can match the double Winchester come of taking oneself into oneself, the cold-steel extension of oneself into mouth, yes, for you, for me, for us, the logical and ultimate act of fuck-you love fuck-off world, the penetration and union of perfect cold gunmetal into warm quailing mortal flesh, the coming to end all coming, brain cells which together faltered and fell short, now flowered and flew apart, flung like stars around the whole dark world.

Yet such death, attractive as it is, is masturbatory: one sucks off the Winchester and in the process blows out one's brains. Will then contemplates doing it with a Luger, which he carries in his Mercedes. He also keeps a hunting rifle handy, and moves, half-mad, among rifle, car, golf, and Luger, all forms of death. At this moment before he enters the cave to extinguish himself or to discover some living element, he is, this man worth forty million, an outlaw on the run from America, a Gary Gilmore of self-destruction.

The greenhouse saves; not only energy, but life itself. Alive by chance, Will seeks out Allison, first in his golf clothes and then naturally, in the nude, when she bathes and nurses him after his suicidal venture into the cave beneath the golf course. Arising from the cave, he achieves, finally, the second coming, an Easter. Unlike the first, it is a form of mutuality, not an aspect of masturbation. The second coming is not Yeats's rough beast slouching toward Bethlehem, but, for Percy, the turning of a death-oriented situation into a living one. Will plans to use Allison's property and his money to turn the land into log cabins, into forms of living things. It is still possible to exchange a passive death for an active life; and their combined madness—she an inmate, he an outpatient—will be productive.

Although Will Barrett derives from *The Last Gentleman,* he is really more attuned ideologically to Percy's 1977 novel, *Lancelot.* In *his* "first coming," Lancelot had brought death, and when we meet him he is a madman in his cell. He lives in a nuthouse, falls in love with a psychotic girl in the next room, and confesses all to a priest or former priest named John. He has destroyed the worthless society of his first coming, having murdered his wife and her lover. The mystery there is a matter of genes, by which he discovers his wife has been unfaithful to him; whereas here the mystery is shotgun shells, which Will unravels to discover his father intended to murder him, then himself. Common to both novels is hatred of the new, the modern, that which passes for life in a death-oriented society. It is preferable to kill off the old, even to kill off oneself, than to abide by rules of living death.

Percy is writing now at the end of his tether. Seeking a moral center, he recognizes it cannot be discovered in formal religion. In *The Last Gentleman,* the Catholic Church is little different from "the Sweet Baptist way"; in this novel, the local reverend is indistinct from the local shrink (Cupp and Duk), and they, in turn, no different from the local con man, Ewell McBee. They all represent a disorientation of values, and they are equally useless as guides. Allison discovers something of value in the greenhouse (mucky, dysfunctional for growing things, rotting), in hoisting (challenging God, lifting things that go beyond one's strength), and in singing (which she can do well when there is no audience). It is to learn how to experience these values that Will enters the cave, where he almost loses his life in trying to gain it. The "second coming" can be achieved only at the expense of the first, and the real question for Percy is whether anybody is willing to jeopardize the first in order to gain, possibly, the second.

The outlaw in America, if Percy is our evidence, is no longer the picaresque hero roaming the frontiers; nor is he the murderer Mailer describes in Gary

Gilmore, although that kind of outlaw seems to be proliferating. He or she is, more likely, the seeker after some way of life, a search which creates similarities among the very dissimilar Barrett, Fabian, and Vost. A characteristic of turn-of-the-decade fiction is that need to find ways by which a person can live, fulfilled only outside community, society, or state. We are returning, slowly, toward 1950s and 1960s rebellion, but not to change things; rather, to change oneself or be changed. In the next section, on the uses of memory and history, we do not depart from this theme. For different as they are, Styron, Roth, Malamud, Oates, and Baldwin are all involved in dredging the past for ways of understanding; revealing a growing sense of history—both personal and social—as a means of entering the self.

THE PAST RECAPTURED: STYRON, ROTH, MALAMUD, OATES, BALDWIN

Consciously or not, Styron in *Sophie's Choice* (1979) tried to write a *Doctor Faustus* for our era, emulating the Mann model as a way of delineating evil, guilt, and redemption for American audiences. The effort is of such overwhelming ambition that any reservations we may have—and they are numerous— must be weighed against Styron's reach, his attempt to move beyond any previous undertaking. That desire to move beyond himself is clear even in the narrative patterning. For the older narrator, clearly reflecting Styron's own career as novelist and man, is writing about an earlier period in his life when he received from Sophie Zawistowska the information that becomes the bulk of the novel. The narrative device is a circling one, enabling Styron to comment upon the younger Stingo's reactions at the same time he can present him receiving the information which will alter his life. In *Doctor Faustus,* we have a rough equivalent in Mann's fictitious narrator, Serenus Zeitblom, telling the story of Adrian Leverkühn, a man whose virtual double he becomes in the intimacy and intricacies of the narration.

Styron's use of music in his novel echoes virtually the entire play of music in the Mann book; for Styron sees music at every turn connected to life and death, whether in the pink house which is young Stingo's home or in the concentration camp which is Sophie's. The musical motif—Mozart, Schubert, Lehár—accompanies every phase of the novel, and more often than not is associated with a death theme, as a *Liebestod.*

In Mann's novel, music becomes the reflection of a culture and a civilization. Styron strives for this, but the nature of *Sophie's Choice* disallows his moving more precisely into the theme, although by juxtaposing music to death he does question how one of the highest examples of civilization can exist so close to pure forms of evil. For Mann, the music of Leverkühn —the name signifies "to live daringly"—must break with traditional modes. If music reflects a civilization's values, tones, textures, then the harmony on which all previous music rested can no longer be mirrored. The Mann novel, by way of music, becomes a critique not only of Germany in the Hitler era but of the entire contemporary world. The music of the spheres must become the disharmony of the world; Leverkühn is the man marked, doomed, fated to express what must be expressed, and his means is music. *His* music will manifest the new, but it will be a novelty associated with illness, with the adversary nature of art.

Through this mechanism, of a doomed and fated Leverkühn creating a new kind of art, a music based not on harmonies but on twelve tones, Mann tries to comprehend the absolute evil which has invaded the world; more absolute in its means and ends than anything encountered previously in civilization. This is, in one sense, what Styron has attempted to penetrate in his novel, an Americanized version—and, in part, a reductive version—of the Mann thesis: that in man's highest gifts one can discover the greatest areas of evil, or that man's highest gifts lie closely associated with the lowest forms of human behavior. Art is itself a trickster, for in offering beauty it also disguises the very worst man is capable of. Implicit in creation are the rot and decay which go into its shaping. Great music is a bourgeois art which can never leave behind the terrible evil lying at the heart of the placid, banal bourgeoisie.

Styron's young Stingo, at twenty-two, is involved in writing his novel, which sounds exactly like *Lie Down in Darkness,* when he meets Sophie in a Brooklyn boardinghouse. Yet the nature of that novel is not disturbed by Sophie's story. He proceeds with it, and offers sections to Nathan Landau, Sophie's savior and lover, as if he had not heard her story. It is Stingo at fifty-two, having written Styron's novels, all clearly alluded to, who guides us through Sophie's story of her life in Poland and then in Auschwitz.

The distinction is quite important, for Styron is filtering the experience, not allowing it to change the younger Stingo sufficiently so as to alter his art; but giving it resonance by way of memory. Stingo keeps a journal in his younger days, but it is mainly through memory that the older Stingo, or author Styron, recreates the story of Sophie. Some of the major problems in the novel develop from this superimposition. For we often find matters, sexual and otherwise, related by the fifty-two-year-old writer that seem adolescent, but that would suit the twenty-two-year-old. The rhetoric of the older voice establishes one kind of reality; the expectations, needs, and longings of the younger person establish another. And since Styron has so clearly intervened with his own work—repeated references to *Lie Down in Darkness, The Long March, The Confessions of Nat Turner* (Stingo plans to do research on Nat Turner on his trip south with Sophie)—we have still another voice, that of the "external" Styron, the Styron of history who has written several successful books and is an established literary figure.

The elements, then, are very consciously conceived. Styron evidently did not wish to disguise, but to manifest. The nature of Sophie's tale is not to be buried in novelistic trappings, but to be made palpable through several voices: the young Stingo, the older Stingo, the novelist Styron. Sophie's choice, the point where good and evil cross, is the choice all must face, either in actuality or in the ethical demands they make on themselves and others. Here the ambitious nature of Styron's book becomes apparent. For he has tried no less than to pick up the enormous questions forced on us by Nietzsche, Dostoyevsky, Kierkegaard, and Mann about the nature of good and evil in a godless universe. Sophie's story, climaxed by her choice, is the testing ground for civilization itself. In Mann, the testing ground was music, in all its manifestations; for Styron, it becomes the camps, specifically Auschwitz. How, quite simply, do we deal with Auschwitz in reality and in our imagination? By forcing the experience on the young Stingo in 1947, then on the older Stingo in the 1970s, when he writes this narrative, Styron is forcing a response to a thirty-year span of lingering evil. At stake is nothing less than our sense of our culture and civilization.

Sophie Zawistowska, when Stingo meets her in the pink Brooklyn boarding house, is thirty or so, living with the highly unstable Nathan Landau, an intellectual, a manic-depressive of such swings he speaks with several voices at different times. The boardinghouse is itself bizarre, the result of war-surplus pink paint; and, therefore, an apt accommodation for an almost hallucinatory experience. Stingo is most vulnerable: attempting to make headway on his novel, lacking a job or direction, hungering after female companionship and sex, unformed except by intelligence and ambition. Sophie and Nathan reveal themselves to Stingo by way of thumps on his ceiling. Their coupling sends vibrations through the room below, and Stingo's introduction to them derives from fantasies of their sexual encounters. This stress on Stingo's sexual needs—fantasies, gropings, masturbatory episodes—demeans the novel; it is Styron's accommodation to the American marketplace, whereas the theme is his attempt to enter high European seriousness.

The sex is very American, almost completely at the physical level of thrust, plunge, and suck. Fellatio, the great revelation of the sixties, is every young man's hoped-for experience, and Stingo yearns for it as part of that impossible dream. Fellatio, in fact, is the final sexual experience he has of Sophie, the climax of their one night of sexual plunging and heaving. Doomed lovers in the present, Sophie and Nathan; doomed Sophie in the past; the doom of all the camp victims, Jews, Gypsies, Slavs; doomed Europe, its civilization, its veneer of culture: all are reduced by Stingo and his sexual yearning. Sophie's agonizing existence at Auschwitz has as its counterpart Stingo's desire for her lovely person; while she speaks of the unspeakable, he feels lust. Although this may be the norm for the younger man, it establishes tensions which cannot function for the older Stingo. Disproportions exist, and what the older man wants us to see as the crisis of civilization the younger man sees, at least in part, as the crisis of his virginity.

Here the voices play Styron false, part of it connected to that circular narrative. Yet even here, the weakness of conflicting voices does not subvert the power of the internal story; nor does even a certain shallowness in Sophie hide the sense of what she reveals.* She reveals the essential duplicity of all human behavior, the fact that civilization is merely a veneer for overwhelming individual needs for power and domination; that the Nazis struck a chord in everyone, victim and conqueror alike. An individual must, in a sense, define himself by how he would react to the camp situation, a point Bruno Bettelheim suggests. All existence was distilled in the camps.

---

*One reviewer called Styron's creatures "weightless characters," by which he meant they lack a moral center: "They may have a past, a parentage, a repertoire of characteristics, but they lack in any defining sense, *character.*" The charge is not quite fair, since Styron's characters are assailed for lacking a center that is missing in most postwar characters, not to speak of most in the twentieth century. What is the moral center of Joseph K. or of the night creatures in *Finnegans Wake*?

Midway through the book. Styron notes several commentators on the camps, one of them George Steiner, who, in *Language and Silence,* counseled silence. Yet Steiner, who was not a witness, went on to speak about the camps as a phenomenon so beyond the imagination of those who were not involved in them that their commentary could only demean what they had not experienced. Yet Steiner's caution is pure presumption. The camps can be demeaned, of course, as can the entire Nazi experience, by a marketplace version; we saw this in the 1979 television production of *Holocaust,* beamed out not only to America but to much of the Western world. The real question is quite different from the one Steiner poses; and that is the issue Styron faces: whether or not one can find ways of describing and dealing with the experience, whether or not one can define the phenomenon without reducing it. The camps become a great artistic challenge, as did the Christian Passion, the Trojan War, the Crusades, the Napoleonic era, and other momentous historical events.

Ultimately, all descriptions may be reductive, but so are all descriptions of faith, or love, or the sexual act, or murder, or great terror. All of these are, in some final sense, unachievable; just as in any final sense, neither Styron, nor Sophie, nor Stingo can really capture the camp experience. But, then, neither can the witnesses. Eloquent as are Wiesel, Schwarz-Bart, Jean-François Steiner, Borowski, Bettelheim, and others, there is no reliving the experience in the written word; and in fact, it is probably the non-Jew Tadeusz Borowski who comes closest by turning the camps into witty episodes of horror. Yet he, too, gives only a semblance.

What Styron tries to do as Sophie's tale unfolds is to find a moral equivalent, and that he discovers in American slavery. Since Sophie is not Jewish—and, therefore, representative of all European "slaves" in Nazi eyes, not just Jewish scum*—Styron winds back to his own Southern background for the injustice historically done to blacks. He cites slavery itself, and his own guilt at having received money from a fund that derived from the sale of a slave. He points to the

Mississippi racist Bilbo, the Nat Turner slave revolt, the Emmett Till case, and others. "Bobby Weed," whose death reflects Till's, runs as a leitmotif through the novel: the victimizing of a young black for "leering" at a white woman. Styron works very hard to find moral equivalents for the camps, and he notes how the worst scoundrels often begin as social reformers [Bilbo, Huey Long] and then play on fear and hatred to consolidate their power. ". . . for each of them in the end, to one degree or another, was forced to play upon and exploit the poor-white redneck's ancient fear and hatred of the Negro in order to aggrandize what had degenerated into shabby ambition and lust for power."

Yet shrewd as this strategy is, it tends to reduce and even simplify the camps, to the very degree that it attempts to become an equivalent. For there are no equivalents, *only the artistic challenge itself.* Nothing Sophie says about her horror can characterize what happened there and what she felt. This is Styron's dilemma. It is as if he recognized this and attempted to finesse the point by the narrative strategy. We have, essentially, throughout the main segments of the novel four temporal tiers. In the forefront, with interruptions for Stingo's other activities, we have Sophie and Stingo: going to the beach, eating, talking and drinking, on occasion with Nathan present. Then we have, in the immediate past, a year or so back, Sophie's story of her relationship with Nathan: how he saved her in a library when she fainted, how he brought her back to health, how he tried to kill her in one of his insane rages. Further back, in the depths of the novel, is the "real" story, Sophie's narrative of what occurred in the camps, her "choice," which is climactic; and behind that, her childhood in Poland as the daughter of an anti-Semitic and anti-female autocratic professor.

The narrative method is tunneling, recalling a Faulknerian or Conradian narrative. In *Heart of Darkness,* for example, the interior story is furthest back, the final point that Marlow reaches when he encounters Kurtz; and then the experience returns to us in relays of information, as if Marlow had had to fight his way back through swamps and miasmas which interfered with memory itself. Styron's method works through a continuous clearing away of underbrush, giving the choice an element of suspense, since it lies so deeply embedded in other memories and can only be retrieved by way of hundreds of other divulgations. Before we reach the choice, it is essential that we wind through Sophie's tale, especially the direction of her childhood with a father whose racial poli-

*Yet Styron develops a weak point historically by lumping Jewish victims together with Slavs, Gypsies, and other undesirables. Hitler's plan for *Judenrein* was an essential part of his appeal, not only to Germans, but to other nationalities as well. Persecution and subsequent systematic murder of Jews were keys to his program, even when such actions interfered with his war effort. Nearly all Europe connived in the elimination of its Jews. Slavs and Gypsies, inevitably, were marginal matters.

cies had been to exterminate the Jews before the Nazis thought of it, her own anti-Semitism at various points in order to survive, her disastrous first marriage, her humiliation in the camps under Höss, the commandant of Auschwitz. Buried deep in her consciousness, and the guiding element for everything she does, is that terrible choice. So that when it does come, the choice must be of such immense proportions it governs the novel's entire moral perspective.

Sophie's choice is that when she first comes to Auschwitz the doctor who determines who lives and who is gassed tells her to select either her son or her daughter for life, the other for death. If she fails to make the selection, both die. " 'You may keep one of your children,' he repeated. 'The other one will have to go. Which one will you keep?' " This is the phrasing she cannot believe she is hearing, but it is repeated. As a "Polack, not a Yid," she has the "privilege" to choose. And for this moment, she has the terrible, unspeakable power of life and death that the doctor himself has. She pleads she has two racially pure children who speak German—perfect representatives of the Aryan policies of the Third Reich; that she is herself a Christian, a "devout Catholic" and not to be confused with the scum of Europe, racially impure Christ-killers. The doctor is like granite, for he is, according to Stingo's reasoning, working through his own moral dilemma, testing out his own sense of good and evil. Sophie chooses, and her small daughter, Eva, is carried off to be gassed. " 'Take my little girl!' " For the time being at least, she has saved her son.

The scene is unbearable, since the choice is of such moral rottenness there can be no equivalent for it. Even in the horrors of slavery, the "choice" for separation came from the master, not from the slave; nor was it direct consignment to death, and not for moral reasons, but because a slave was a valuable property. Yet unbearably moving as the scene is, does it work fictionally? We draw a large distinction between what moves us because of its ugliness and what functions within a literary text. The two are not comparable, or else sensational events could keep stunning us in a third-rate novel. Styron has worked exceptionally hard to bring us here, and he has taken tremendous risks: given us a non-Jewish victim, making her voice anti-Semitic remarks, trying to find equivalents in his own heritage, and attempting to explain the doctor as having replaced God with his own sense of himself as a god. He has even worked in the musical motif, that music always so close to death and final solutions.

Yet, at any of the highest levels of literature, the effort fails. And why it does is embedded in what has come before: Sophie herself, her relationship to Nathan, and most of all, the way in which the younger Stingo has related to her. For by observing Sophie in such explicitly sexual terms, Stingo has established certain terms which inevitably affect how we receive Sophie's past as Stingo himself receives it. If forefront is a form of sexual comedy, then background must be tinged, even though the two are not formally connected. Sophie's tale is being related to a young man with a perpetual erection. As she speaks of the unspeakable, of what has constituted her life, of her having been witness to the greatest crime in mankind's history, the receiver of that story should, somehow, be commensurate with what he is hearing.

By Styron's very narrative strategies, Stingo must be less, at twenty-two: a virgin, perpetually hard up, just starting out. This places a disproportionate burden on the older Stingo, who is writing of that earlier period; and in a sense, the older Stingo must bail out the younger. Yet it is the latter who receives the story, not the older man, who is removed by time and focus; and that presentness in 1947—what is being related —constitutes the major segment of the novel.

There is an additional set of factors besides the literary awkwardness created by the receiver. Sophie's relationship with Nathan, which parallels the narration of her story to Stingo, never coheres with the elements relating to her past. Styron works harder over Nathan than over any other character in his fiction except Nat Turner. Nathan is the prototypical New York Jewish intellectual: allegedly a scientist, a reader of poetry and fiction, a brilliant analyst of politics and social thought; but also mad, a bogus scientist, a man protected from himself by his brother and family friends, sufferer from wild swings of temperament which can turn into murderous impulses. Once again, Styron has tried something very ambitious, to capture a cultural phenomenon which requires considerable artistry; but Nathan does not ring true, from the first. He encounters Stingo in the boardinghouse and he parodies the Southerner: " 'We could have talked about sports. I mean *Southern* sports. Like lynching niggers—or *coons,* I think you call them down there. Or *culture.* We could have talked about Southern culture, and maybe could have sat around here at old Yetta's listening to hillbilly records. You know, Gene Autry, Roy Acuff and all those other standard bearers of classical Southern culture.' " All this is far too pat, Styron working too close to stereotypes; and this is what is wrong with Nathan Landau. He is the stereotypical New York

Jew, brilliance tinged by madness, insights complicated by obsessive personal needs. He always goes at Stingo as Northerner to Southerner, Jew to Gentile, urban sophisticate to untutored hillbilly. Nearly every interchange rings false, for ultimately Nathan speaks not like the character but like the type.

Once more, the narrative strategy which seemed necessary for one reason is wrong for another; for it juxtaposes hostile materials. No matter how sympathetic Nathan is to Sophie's past—although he does not know of her choice—his very presence in the forefront jars what we hear of her past. It is, yet again, too pat that after all her denials of Jewishness in the camps, after her intermittent bouts of anti-Semitism, after her upbringing by an intensely anti-Semitic father, she should find her good samaritan and savior in a prototypical Jew. This formulation combined with other narrative factors works on us almost subliminally to weaken the real story, that interior tale sunk in the hellish past.

The final factor is Sophie herself. She must function under terrible burdens. One of these is her intense physical beauty, so that she has movie star appeal, even though she is presented as a great tragic being, Antigone, Medea, Clytemnestra. We recall she first comes to Stingo's attention from thumps on the ceiling of his room, her sexual acrobatics with Nathan. With such physical assets, and they are necessary in her survival, she is nevertheless hampered as a tragic figure. Her present must, in some way, manifest the entire German nightmare. As a non-Jewish Pole, she stands for all victims, not only six million but double that number who went up in the crematoria. And her final choice, the personal level of the final solution, is the great tragic act of our time. The scope of the attempt, once again, is undermined by elements enveloping her. Stingo's sexual longing for her is reductive; Nathan's abuse of her is reductive, as are her own physical qualities. This is not to suggest that Styron had other options; very possibly he had none. What he attempted was so large, so ambitious, so compelling in human terms that he faced failure in whatever conditions he posed.

Perhaps that is not all. There are several aspects to the novel which jar, several irrelevancies. The details of Sophie's employer, a chiropractor, his wife's decapitation in an accident and the search for her head, the references to Styron's own career, even the research on Nat Turner, make the major elements less cohesive. They may have served in Styron's mind as buttresses for key points, but they weakened the latter because they are diminutions. The problem with such a mighty theme is that everything is reductive, unless scaled up. In *The Magic Mountain,* Mann had to scale up at every level to accommodate something as supernatural as a "magic mountain"—characters, events, conversations. Sexual longing finds its manifestation in bizarre forms of expression, not in tits and ass; he was watchful for anything that would demean or reduce his major elements.

In nearly every respect, the ways in which *Sophie's Choice* stumbles are connected to the ambition of the effort. Even Styron's prose, quite toned down from the excesses of *Lie Down in Darkness* and *Set This House on Fire,* does not always function as it might, given the level of achievement he strives for. Yet in this novel he has found a distinctive voice. As Nathan Landau says when he reads parts of Stingo's first novel, he, Stingo, has copied others (Faulkner, etc.) but has developed his own style; so, too, has Styron forged his own style from all the Southern streams flowing into his earlier work. Still, there is some jarring. For the older Stingo lays on with words and voices linguistic modalities which seem doubtful for a twenty-two-year-old and which, additionally, echo Styron, not the character in the novel. Stingo, too, often, speaks like Styron, and his thick rhetoric often works against, not with, the starkness of the internal story related by Sophie.

For example: young Stingo is dressing down Nathan for his blind prejudice toward the South: " 'Could it be because you Jews, having so recently arrived here and living mostly in big Northern cities, are really *purblind,* and just have no interest in or awareness or any kind of comprehension whatever of the tragic concatenations of events that have produced the racial madness down there? You've read *Faulkner,* Nathan, and you still have this assy and intolerable attitude of superiority toward the place, and are unable to see how Bilbo is less a villain than a wretched offshoot of the whole benighted system?' " Not only is the language unlikely (could it be parodic?) for a twenty-two-year-old to reach Nathan with, but it inevitably clashes in tone, texture, stress, and phrasing with Sophie's story. The clash is not that kind which results in harmonious blending of dissimilars, as in a fugue; but the kind which takes our sensibilities in several directions, unresolvably.

Withal, the novel is a tremendous advance for Styron, a book of immense ambition and achievement, a work that helps to close out the 1970s encouragingly. Except for Gaddis's *JR,* Pynchon's *Gravity's Rainbow,* Barth's *Letters,* and perhaps one or two other novels on a large scale, fiction had scaled down for the decade. *Sophie's Choice* raises our expectations, forcing us to span the forty-year period since the Second World War and reviving a topic of greater moral importance than anything raised in those four decades. Having tried nothing less than a *Doctor Faustus* or a *Magic Mountain,* Styron failed in his cultural grasp only by reason of a theme that lies too thickly and intensely within history for any but a Dostoyevsky, Mann, or Kafka. Whatever, *Sophie's Choice* shows that a large postwar fiction, however flawed in its execution, can assimilate history, morality, and individual experiences as great novels of the past were able to do.

Like most good writers, Roth in *The Ghost Writer* (1979) reproduces his central fictional intelligence. In this novel, his narrator, Nathan Zuckerman, owes something to the Jamesian central consciousness, to Conrad's Marlow, and to the magicians whom Borges delegates as "I." The method creates a circularity, forcing the writer to move back and forth between his latest work and his earliest. Like Styron in *Sophie's Choice,* Roth has circled back, here twenty years, when he was still an apprentice writer and looking for models. Styron's Stingo, as we have seen, returns even further, to the days when in a Brooklyn boarding-house he was attempting to fill notebooks with a novel; while upstairs pounding, knocking, and swearing fill his consciousness with an alternative existence. Roth's Nathan, too, finds himself filled with that alternative experience, although his is self-made, an act of creation, a bubble of potentiality. The crafting of this potentiality is Roth's most elegant statement thus far.

Not without flaws of pacing, *The Ghost Writer* nevertheless has an authority and a weight which suggest Roth's maturity. The persistent question for him, the basic metaphysical and ontological issue, is that of Jewishness. His investigation of this does not make him a "Jewish writer," but an intrinsically American one, his quest comparable to Baldwin's search for blackness, Didion's for the nature of the female. The "ghost writer" of this novella is neither Nathan Zuckerman nor E. I. Lonoff, the older writer at whose feet he comes to worship. It is Anne Frank, who in Nathan's imagination has not died in Belsen, but has lived on in the spirit and shape of Amy Bellette, who may be Lonoff's mistress. Anne Frank's presence, like Franz Kafka's in so much other recent Roth, swells to fill the second half of the novel. She is the gray eminence who will connect Nathan to his past, as much as Lonoff is connected to his present.

Nathan's search for her associates him with large cultural issues that both manifest and preempt the individual. The method is temporal layering.

The novel embodies a journey: a spiritual, creative, as well as physical journey. And since it is a journey which involves a young writer presenting himself to an older, established one, the novel is never far removed from a Jamesian hovering: the story "The Middle Years," which is cited, as well as "The Lesson of the Master," "The Death of the Lion," and others. Lonoff is himself a Jamesian presence, a Jewish savant of the Berkshires, and a counterpoint to the type of Jew Nathan has left behind him in Newark. The dual touchstones of the novel are the Jewish experiences Nathan has grown up with and the "Jewish experience" Lonoff typifies: the lonely, isolated, anxiety-ridden artist who must polish his work until it achieves gemlike perfection. Nathan swings between the two, that which stultifies with its Jewish identity and Jewish aims, and that which, universalizing, beckons as part of the creative life Nathan yearns for. We observe Roth reviewing his old novelistic material and then pushing it forward, into new areas of consciousness.

Lonoff himself never really comes to life; he is more a presence than a reality, more an ideal for the young Nathan than a breathing human being. His edges are chiseled in marble. He is the alternative to Nathan's father, to Judge Wapter, and to all those other Kafkaesque "judges" with whom Nathan spent his childhood. The elegance of Roth's short novel becomes apparent in his time sequencing: offering us Lonoff in his present, moving Nathan back, as "Nathan Dedalus," to a time when he needed to express himself, playing off layered experiences.* The Zuckermans are Jews first. Everything in their sense of life feeds into their pride as Jews as well as their fears. They live in the shadow of pogroms, a paranoia understandable even in America. While Nathan grows up, the Jews in Europe are being tagged for slaughter. But he also recognizes his father's attitudes as a generational matter: what is a valid feeling for the first generation does not necessarily hold for the second. The individual expresses himself or herself, and once he or she enters that arena, then all possibilities obtain. Nathan wants to open up even as his father suggests that he close down. Mr. Zuckerman, like Kafka's father, represents the enclosure of authority, whereas Lonoff in the expansive Berkshire woods

---

*In *Zuckerman Unbound* (1981), Nathan returns to Roth's midcareer, right after *Portnoy,* another layering of experience.

represents open potentiality, Emerson's counsel. That Nathan dreams of his father and of Newark while he rests in Lonoff's study is literarily felicitous, part of that novelistic shapeliness which makes *The Ghost Writer* function.

Settings count. Newark is urban, of course, a place of authority, enclosures, and limitations. By remaining narrow, one can succeed. Judge Wapter represents for Mr. Zuckerman the ultimate in Jewish responsibility. In thinking of those early experiences, Nathan is parodic; the Roth of *Goodbye, Columbus* and *Portnoy* revives: "Wapter lived with a spinster daughter—one of the first Jewish students at Vassar College to earn the esteem of her Christian teachers —and his wife, the department-store heiress whose philanthropic activities had given her family name the renown among the Jews of Essex County that it was said to have in her native Charleston." Newark is stuffed with Wapters and Zuckermans, all striving to impress Gentiles while beating their breasts over their Jewishness. Lonoff, however, lives in the open, pastoral countryside; his house and surroundings are described with Norman Rockwell precision. Lonoff is an immigrant who married into a well-placed New England family and lives, now, in Gentile territory. "Beyond the cushioned windowseats and the colorless cotton curtains tied primly back I could see the bare limbs of big dark maple trees and fields of driven snow. Purity. Serenity. Simplicity. Seclusion. All one's concentration and flamboyance and originality reserved for the grueling, exalted, transcendent calling. I looked around and I thought: This is how I will live."

A Jew can also live in pastoral splendor, the locale recalling Malamud's house near Bennington College, where he teaches; a detail repeated in Lonoff's schedule, that teaching at an all-women's college. In an uncanny way, if Malamud was perhaps a partial model for Lonoff,* Roth's novel parallels aspects of Malamud's own 1979 novel, *Dubin's Choice,* in which an older writer very much like Lonoff has an affair with a young woman who splits him off from his wife. And to complete the literary coincidence, Nathan lying in Lonoff's study and listening to sounds from above recalls Styron's Stingo lying on his bed and imagining the activity between Sophie and her Nathan. The past recaptures several cultural moments.

This cross-referring, all in 1979, is perhaps not so coincidental as culturally induced, although one could not have predicted it. It is based, with Roth's novel in mind, on both a sense of cultural revisionism and a continued need to explore new relationships. What we find at the end of the decade, if these novels are valid reflectors, is a mixture of revision and exploration, of reaching back (Holocaust, marriage, permanent attachments) linked with sixties and early seventies need to range over unknown territory. Roth's own obsession with Anne Frank, alive and reading her work in anonymity, while posing as Amy Bellette, Lonoff's student-mistress, contains both possibilities. We find that circling back to the Holocaust —Roth's Anne a Jew, Styron's Sophie a Polish Catholic; that need to understand a "Nathan" (a prophet who serves as the Lord's messenger to David)— Roth's Nathan a surrogate for the author, Styron's Nathan a mad pseudo-scientist; that obsession with self-expression, a 1960s pursuit, but tempered now by history, craft, responsibility.

The three novels, Roth's, Styron's, and Malamud's, capture a cultural crossroads experience. There are, of course, many detours; when we account for them, we can add Oates and Baldwin to the above list. Malamud's Dubin has his Fanny, but does not wish to forsake his wife. Broader experience within restrictions is his goal. Stingo is very young and has no attachments, but cannot find approaches to Sophie because of Nathan's presence, his maneuvers limited. Roth's Nathan longs after Amy Bellette, whom he imagines as Anne Frank grown up, a lovely young woman; while she, Amy, comes between Lonoff and his long-suffering wife, Hope—who has little, her name dooming her in Hawthorne territory. Hope, at the end, runs off into the snow, with Lonoff chasing her; a parodic chase, because we know he will catch her and bring her back. She is, after all, "Tolstoy's wife," and her role, while demeaning, is part of her need.

Culturally, these almost balletic groupings and regroupings suggest a restricted field of maneuver. Here are not Homeric wars or Paris stealing Helen, but domestic battles, which substitute for the spatial movement of an earlier generation of novelists. These protagonists journey but do not go "on the road," nor do they drift; spatiality is subsumed in their domestic activities. Nathan Zuckerman is on his way toward fulfillment and achievement as a writer, and Lonoff will be a stage in his development, as will the encounter with Anne Frank. But he must work through his needs not in terms of a large-scale development, but in the restrictions of domestic longing, familial divisions, historical awareness. Limitations confront the

---

*The setting also recalls Salinger, but only a selected few of the details fit. Lonoff is a mosaic of writers and attitudes.

American novelist; the slam-bang postwar era has ended. This is not solely a Jewish theme, although Malamud, Roth, and Bellow have played a consistent tune here. For even Styron, despite the exploration of holocaustic choices, makes the chief area of combat a domestic one, Stingo, Sophie, and Nathan Landau in that Brooklyn boardinghouse.

This cutting back to a contained self aware of constriction is, I believe, part of that circular, self-reflexive movement in the novel: that is, method is culturally induced. Like Bellow, Roth has always displayed his protagonists as reflectors of self—the self staged and restaged, a puppet of the writer, asked to perform, but nevertheless playing variations on the same role. In *The Ghost Writer,* Roth has found the perfect expression of that performing self; but now it not only reflects, but imagines itself an "other," a performing self with Anne Frank for partner, another performing self. For virtually the first time, Roth has provided his protagonist with a female counterpart who is not a castrator, nor a servicer of his genitals, nor a Gentile fantasy.

This is not to say he has made peace with his Jewishness. Roth's attitudes have always been part of a generational conflict and a distaste for bourgeois forms of Jewishness. His dedication here to "Nathan Dedalus," the artist as well as the man, has thrust him into a new relationship to himself and allowed him to transcend earlier stances. When previously he wrote about self—as Tarnopol in *My Life as a Man,* he wrote two stories about Nathan Zuckerman—he conceived of little but a solipsistic world reflecting that self. Now the reincarnate Anne Frank has her world, her wishes, her needs. Amy Bellette—"Little Beauty," connected to one of the "Little Women"—has a world of her own, far more significant than Nathan's, in fact preceding him into fame.

What gives *The Ghost Writer* its thrust and weight is the shaping. Nathan's journey to Lonoff, the novelist savant living in pastoral simplicity, is paralleled by Amy Bellette's journey to Lonoff after she was his student. Nathan's search for his craft, whether with Lonoff or with James, or in his own background, is paralleled by Amy's expression of self as Anne Frank and her diary of events leading up to her capture and death. Anne is imagined by Nathan, but his act of imagination gives Amy Bellette a mysterious form in the past; just as Nathan's restructuring of his parents' opposition to the kind of writing he does gives his past a form. "Nathan Dedalus" has his female counterpart in Anne Frank; and Anne Frank in her life recalls Franz (another Frank) Kafka in his imaginative acts.

". . . everything he [Kafka] dreamed in Prague was, to her, real Amsterdam life. What he invented, she suffered." The first sentence of *The Trial,* with the substitute of a name, applies to Anne.

In *her* world, Nathan can reconstruct a new depth of feeling. Once again his probe of such feelings is not uniquely Jewish—not even his amusing note to his parents that he would bring them a Jewish girl, Anne Frank, no more shiksas—but demonstrates an effort to justify his sense of fitness and proportion. Anne has moved in silence, even though she sees her father's photograph in *Time* magazine. "I was the incarnation of the millions of unlived years robbed from the murdered Jews," she intones. A lovely sentence and a sentiment of great emotional depth: Roth has entered upon new modalities. She is a saint, which means it is too late to be alive. What she also recognizes, in Nathan's reconstruction of her history, is that no one cares what happens to the Jews. Her book, which can retain its power only if she remains dead, is a monument not to Jewish survival but to Europe's and the world's indifference. Regarding the latter, the Jews created their own problems, and the few things, she says, that turned the Franks into Jews —their Chanukah songs and exchanges of presents, lighted candles, few Hebrew words—made them the enemy. "It did not even take that much. It took nothing—that was the horror. And that was the truth. And that was the power of her book."

Through Frank, Nathan connects himself, as we have observed, to Franz. " '. . . she's like some impassioned little sister of Kafka's, his lost little daughter —a kinship is even there in the face, I think. Kafka's garrets and closets, the hidden attics where they hand down the indictments, the camouflaged doors—everything." This dimension, which carries through the final two of the four parts, gives incredible resonances to *The Ghost Writer.* Nathan's trip to the pastoral Berkshires becomes a journey into the darkness, not of Africa, but of modern European history. In Anne Frank and her experience, and her refusal to die, Nathan reconstructs correlations with the fictional world he wishes to penetrate, that Eastern European world of Kafka,* that experience which thrusts the

---

The Ghost Writer is dedicated to Milan Kundera, the Czech writer, and reflects Roth's editorship, as we have noted, of a series called "Writers from the Other Europe." This immersion in Eastern European fiction parallels the abundance of references to Kafka in his recent fiction and literary essays. Roth rightly has seen Kafka as the most influential writer of the postwar era.

writer into Judaism only to make it broader than a uniquely Jewish experience. Anne's presence in Nathan's life will reconcile him to his parents and to Judge Wapter; but since his observation of this is parodic, she will also provide Nathan, and Roth behind him, with a new well of emotion to draw upon.

The overall elegance of the novel should not blind us to certain errors of taste, or to certain tactical missteps. Roth provides the obligatory masturbation scene: Nathan masturbates on the daybed in Lonoff's study as he imagines Amy upstairs unclothed, cavorting, moving around. He then balances this with James's "The Middle Years," reading it as an act of atonement. The inability to avoid parody remains; even James cannot escape. Although Roth has a theme and development of great intensity, he still fears high seriousness. While these moves into his vaudeville act—parody, mockery, burlesque, lists of words—are often amusing, they do tear the texture and rarely rise to true wittiness.

Roth's parodic sense can, in fact, clash with his purposes. In the novel, it is essential that Lonoff be matched against another writer of stature, and Nathan drags in Felix Abravanel. Abravanel, Lonoff's opposite, as if Saul Bellow were matched against Malamud or Salinger is described as being something of a heartthrob, with "Bombay black eyes." Nathan continues: "Beautiful wives, beautiful mistresses, alimony the size of the national debt, famous friends, famous enemies, breakdowns, public lectures." He has great charm, but it was "like a moat so oceanic that you could not even see the great turreted and buttressed thing it had been dug to protect."

Lonoff, on the contrary, is withdrawn, a man with one wife, a writer who dabbles cautiously in female students; a man whose dedication is not to life but to work and books. Yet by contrast with the burlesqued Abravanel, Lonoff becomes almost a parodic figure— the Russian-Jewish immigrant with the New England wife named Hope, the perfect pastoral retreat, the manner of a sage and guru, the reticence of a Jamesian character. If Abravanel moves close to phoniness, Lonoff insists too much on "true art"; and the manner Roth uses is so mocking as to undermine even the man whom Nathan worships. Intensifying the parody are those ingredients of the past: parents, Wapters, life in Jewish Newark.

Elements must clash at a tonal level, especially when Anne Frank is recreated, since there is no way Roth can parody her. She is a monument; she was *there*. Thus, while Roth has found his way into matters of structure that serve him well, we still meet some clash below the level of direct narrative. In a less carefully crafted book—that is, in one that was less elegantly self-reflexive—these tonal discordances would be more serious. Roth's movement onto new ground here reflects such maturity and mastery of novelistic techniques that any unresolved elements become not central but marginal.

Malamud's *Dubin's Lives* (1979) is the work of a fully mature writer which is, at the same time, a very old-fashioned novel. It is a work keyed in to modern modes while it is concerned with ethical and moral questions associated with an earlier period. Even Malamud's fashioning of his protagonist into a biographer (of Twain and Thoreau, among others, in the past, D. H. Lawrence in the present) has an old-fashioned ring, since to give such a solid profession to a modern character is itself a commitment to more enduring values than we normally associate with a contemporary work. Malamud has tried to reflect the current scene while bringing to bear upon it a nineteenth-century sensibility.

The reach is ambitious, and there are so many ways in which the novel can go wrong that we marvel at its successes. Dubin lives in Center Campobello, near the New York–Vermont border, but it is less a specific place than it is a "rural area," with a small village attached. The stress is on a rural experience, what Malamud had tried earlier in *A New Life*. But rural values are not mocked here; they are the substance of Dubin's life with his wife, as befits the biographer of Thoreau. Malamud is not eager to turn real events into fantasy or real areas into sources of parody or mockery. William Dubin is very earnest about his life, his work, his pleasures, the condition of his long marriage, his relationships to his stepson and his daughter. Except for a preponderance of vicious dogs and a stereotypical anti-Semitic farmer, the rural experience is almost Edenesque; whatever dysfunctions exist in it are the result of human habitation. The locale itself is blessed by magic: the seasonal flow, the overlapping of warm and cold, the ever-presence of growth, vegetation, fruition.

Dubin's present project is a biography of D. H. Lawrence, whose existence and message are so dissimilar to Dubin's that the confrontation must create a crisis. In a sense, the critical meeting of Dubin and Lawrence is the meeting of 1960s and early 1970s sensibilities with an earlier and older generation's attitudes. Although a figure belonging to the early part of the century, Lawrence is used by Malamud to point up what Dubin has submerged or repressed in himself. His biography of Lawrence will be more than a literary endeavor; it will involve an ideological struggle, in which Lawrence challenges everything Dubin represents, as biographer, husband, man. Fanny Bick, a footloose former college student who comes to work as a maid in the Dubin household, plays Lady Chatterley to his unlikely Mellors. What Dubin has to do, in his passage through experience, is to avoid being Gerald Crich, the ice-doomed figure of *Women in Love,* and grow toward the condition of Mellors, who can savor his sex amidst natural splendor. Much of the novel is taken with cocko-mania: the rigid member not as defiance but as Dubin's salute to his new being.

But Dubin is also married to a loyal woman, Kitty, who has longings of her own, a somewhat unshaped ego, a need for support from the local psychotherapist, which culminates in a brief affair. Kitty has particularly sensitive antennae, which pick up every shade of Dubin's movement toward and from her. Their relationship is balletic, so carefully choreographed by Malamud that it is, very possibly, the strongest single element in the book. The focus of the novel is really more the anatomy of a marriage than the sense of an affair, or the connection between a biographer and his subject. Whenever she is nervous, Kitty smells the gas burners, or else she plays the harp, "her hands moving like birds flying at each other." She is a creature who hangs on, eager to survive, and yet she flirts with what she knows could be extinction. One husband dead, her second withdrawing, preferring solitude to her presence, she moves between two objects, gas burners and harp.

Her anxiety over the burners is ostensibly to make sure no gas is escaping; but it is also a suicidal gesture. The harp, on the other hand, is her desire to please him, to turn the household experience into a form of art, or else to lead it toward an angelic, heavenly level. It is her love offering, as the gesture toward the gas burners is her offer of an alternative, her death and that of the marriage.

Playing through all this is the theme of Lawrence, his almost physical presence, and his work, which is embodied in Fanny Bick. Although her placement between Dubin and Kitty is of course necessary for the dramatic play of the novel, she is a source of considerable difficulty for Malamud. Even her religious affiliation indicates an ambiguity in his treatment of her, since she wears both a star of David and a cross; Dubin is himself Jewish, Kitty a Gentile. In the balletic movement between Dubin and wife, Fanny—among whose attributes one seems to have provided her name—intrudes as Venus; not so much love as temptation and alternative for the man in his middle to later fifties. Her attractions are mainly physical: a cello-shaped figure ("abundant, though not voluptuous"), a seductive walk, a braless top, and an attractive face with "loose fair hair."

Malamud's main problem in this far-ranging novel is to make Fanny Bick into more than a seductive body. Since Dubin is entranced, she must, in one way or another, be sufficiently substantial to justify his attention. Malamud has in mind nothing less than the passage of a middle-aged man to the fountain of youth, a sense of the 1960s as they passed into the 1970s, before enervation set in. While Lawrence's life and message are parallels, the guide must be Dubin's own need for expressions of sex, entrancement, magic; he wants to live within himself as well as within his subjects' minds and bodies. Fanny will, supposedly, fill that need. Much of the book, accordingly, depends on her ability not only to entrance but to hold. She must be more than Venus; she must have qualities of Athena.

Malamud tries very hard in this area, making Fanny a college dropout, giving her a thoughtful cast even as she is promiscuous and flighty, then providing her with a return to college classes. Yet what he cannot furnish is more than the *idea* of a hippie Fanny who wants to be more than a seductive body. A good part of the novel's stalling quality results from Dubin's seeking something not really there; nor can it be. Fanny is too much a part of the marginal sixties —communes, Zen masters, alternative life styles—to embody what Malamud is attempting to make her.

If Fanny had remained merely the sex object Dubin wants as signal of his own sexual liberation, the novelist could have avoided the ambiguities of turning a sex object into something more. Very possibly, Malamud was strongly affected by the women's movement, so that his presentation of Fanny was to be of someone striving hard to find the level of her own identity. But this very honorable desire to make her something more has interfered with the novel. For despite all notable efforts to "thicken" Fanny's experience, Dubin's regard for her is connected chiefly to her sexuality, even while ideologically the novel pulls in another direction.

Dubin is attempting to absorb Lawrence's full message. As he explains it to both Kitty and Fanny, Lawrence detested promiscuity and sought a far more complicated level of experience, a more conflicted association, between man and woman. It is this level which Dubin is striving for in his relationship to

Fanny, but unfortunately, she does not embody the substance of the attempt. Her speech pattern is 1960s at its worst, full of jargon, and her desire is for life lived at the moment. "Seize the day" informs her desertion of Dubin as much as her return to him in Center Campobello.

Whatever the novel's flaws, however, they derive from Malamud's considerable ambitions, which move *Dubin's Lives* far beyond many 1970s efforts, which attempt little so as to achieve something. The introduction into the novel of such a strong sense of nature helps turn the American novel back to what was once its most compelling elements. Malamud captures the seasons, but is especially good on winter—not just heavy snowfall, but the treacherous aspects of winter, which almost doom Dubin. He is saved from endless wandering in a blizzard by his wife; but winter has almost claimed him, a frozen corpse, like Gerald Crich in the iciness of a ski resort. Nature for Malamud also includes descriptions of places—Venice and Stockholm, New York City. He is aware of the physical aspect of things, as suitable for a man writing a biography of Lawrence.

In this respect, Lawrence infuses the novel. To get at the earlier writer is to recapture the past as a projection of the future. Lawrence's blood consciousness, which Dubin attempts to assimilate, is the very crux of the problem; for in ingesting Lawrence's message, Dubin must endow Fanny with qualities alien to her. That part of the novel falls into slackness. In fact, before she returns, Malamud treads water in the repetitious scenes between Dubin and Kitty. Yet so closely are elements worked and reworked that Lawrence's presence serves a thematic function, which is the sense of dying, of a universe perishing, only to reemerge like the phoenix: death and transfiguration or resurrection; the dying God, in the form of the phallus, rejuvenated. When Dubin is blocked on his biography, he is impotent with Kitty. When Fanny reappears, Dubin can move along on his Lawrence once more. Some of this may be too pat, but it does work, as that aspect of Lawrence well integrated into both the personal and the natural parts of the novel.

In his conception of *Dubin's Lives,* Malamud touches on other points of interest to the student of the novel, displaying here a far more ambitious reach in purely generic terms than in any of his other long fiction. Every novel has, of course, its subjective elements, autobiography distorted and transmuted into the fictional material suitable for this or that experience. By making his protagonist a biographer, a spender of enormous amounts of time in which he "lives" with dead figures—Thoreau and Twain, Lincoln, various "brief lives," as well as the centrally located Lawrence—Malamud has struck several chords.

There is, in fact, such potential richness in this formulation that one can only be grateful that Malamud, himself a conventional narrator in the past, has attempted so much. All biography is in good part displaced autobiography. Dubin, as we see, has learned a good deal from each of his subjects, once from Thoreau, now from Lawrence. The initial choice of subject, immersion in the style and routine experiences of the subject, collateral study of the period and surrounding figures, the delving into personal, even intimate details all involve an initial sympathy and then a continuing one. The best biographies suggest a strong subjective appeal from which the biographer can just barely keep his distance. From the point of view of the novelist whose protagonist is a biographer, the distancing and perspectives take on double qualities. Dubin's "lives" are manifold, but then so is Malamud's life in the life of the novel. Further, Dubin brings to his biography of Lawrence the lives he has written about and lived through before.

We are presented with a complicated process: Lawrence as observed by a man strongly influenced by Thoreau; Malamud, in turn, writing about a man, Dubin, who is writing about Lawrence; Malamud having researched both Lawrence and Thoreau so that he can produce Dubin's observations of them; Malamud bringing to Dubin whatever autobiographical details an author normally reserves for his major characters; Malamud, finally, disguising his self sufficiently so that Dubin's "lives" can live. Malamud is, in effect, changing autobiography—whatever the precise details—to both narrative and biography, himself influenced by Lawrence, the subject of his protagonist's study. Inner and outer are potentially very complicated, and Malamud through Dubin suggests many of these contrasting and competing elements; much as Conrad, in his use of Marlow, had been able to insert himself at different locations within his own narratives and then move in and out as necessary.

The strength of the novel, and it is considerable and compelling, lies here, in those interconnections which create dimensions. The interworkings of nature are linked to this "inner and outer" dimensionality. The novel stumbles only in Malamud's attempts to introduce more of the sense of the 1960s and early 1970s than he needed: for example, the parallelism between his daughter and Fanny, both hippie types open to the "new"; or the brief scenes with his adopted son (Kitty's by her previous marriage), who has deserted from the army and fled to Stockholm. Further, the references to Kitty's former husband, a doctor, are perfunctory, not really observed because he has died and left Kitty a widow before the novel begins. These episodes and parallels are either forced or incompletely detailed, fictive nuisances rather than enhancements. The power of this very strong novel lies elsewhere, in Malamud's recapturing of a particular time period in a particular marriage, in the detailing of a rural village, in natural scenes that are memorably observed, and, technically, in that association of biographer and subject. He has well avoided what had seemed to have become an obsession in his last few fictions, the Jew as victim, a theme that was yielding less and less for his formidable talents.

In Malamud's next novel, *God's Grace* (1982), a short story is struggling to escape from a narrative of man and apes. Chaucer had his "Parliament of Fowls," and now Malamud has his "Parliament of Apes." His aim, also, is allegorical: the making of a community on an Edenesque island after the Second Flood (a nuclear holocaust), then the breakup of that community. But there are other dimensions here, nearly all of them miscalculated. There is Calvin Cohn, the sole survivor of the Second Flood, who was working on the ocean floor when mankind was destroyed; Cohn plays the role of a Jewish Robinson Crusoe. There is his chimp mate on the island, Mary Madelyn, who gives birth to Cohn's daughter, the beginning of a new race, half human, half chimp. There is Esau, the bad chimp, who refuses to defer to Cohn and who becomes in his pride (his anti-Semitism?) the Lucifer of the piece. Besides the background of the Crusoe experience, there is, in fact, the whole allegorical smorgasbord of Western literature, beginning with the Old Testament. In our minds throughout, as a key allegory, is Abraham's sacrifice of Isaac, the note on which the novel ends—which is another way of saying that God dices with man's existence even while man attempts to understand the ways of God.

Malamud's chimps speak, go to school, understand long disquisitions on Darwin, Freud, evolution, sublimation, the good of the community. They are not converted to Judaism, but led to it by Cohn's sermons, by the recorded voice of his rabbi father, by the "Seven Admonitions" which he posts as the Mosaical Commandments. Malamud has structured this island community (Jewish chimps) for some pur-pose which may be serious or may be very close to satirical: is he mocking the whole range of Jewish experience? is he bringing down the temple on Cohn's head? is he aiming at a catharsis in which the Jew is perceived as no different from the amoral and power-hungry Gentile? If Frank Alpine can convert, can a chimp?

It is difficult to know what to make of *God's Grace* because so little is Malamud's. The chimp and ape lore is acknowledged as secondhand, but so are the ideas, the literary contexts, the language, even the few jokes. What seems clear is that this fifty-thousand-word novel is too long by far, that it dissipates whatever meaning is put upon it. We find it, instead, drawn out into a tedious school for chimps (a trendy topic now), into sexual union between man and chimp which has holy overtones—perhaps from this will come the Messiah (the real one).

There *is* continuity with Malamud's earlier work —with the witty fantasies of his first stories, even with *The Assistant,* another tale of conversion—but it has been diverted into undigested allegory and given longueurs beyond tolerance. The man who will spread the new religion, Calvin Cohn, possibly the "Jew-Gentile" of the future, is unexamined: power-hungry, sex-hungry, desirous of creating his own empire, and yet Malamud's voice. There is, at the center, moral as well as literary confusion, best exemplified by the staleness of language, the loss of that energy and verve which graced *Dubin's Lives.*

In *Bellefleur* (1980), Joyce Carol Oates has written a historical novel in order to make a large, episodic comment on the present. Her purpose is not didactic, but reflective, refractive. In part, she is rejecting modern Oblomovism; for if nothing else, her Bellefleurs are activists, project-makers, grander than life in many respects, in their grossness as well as their energy. The family extends to a time before the American Revolution, and it continues to the near present —when Gideon attempts to destroy its vestiges with a kamikaze attack on the Bellefleur castle—by way of guile, energy, and the embracing of a rough, often crude, existence. Although padded by the family wealth, individual members must come through marked dangers: a general curse which puts the sign of Cain on each of them; a melancholy and depression which is the obverse of Bellefleur energy and enterprise; passions which can prove obsessive and, in several instances, destructive; a compulsive need for inner expression which negates community or society and reveals ego, self, self-love; an antisocial drive which makes each member somehow marginal, even while the family is celebrated. We have, in effect, a contemporary family, reflected in this huge Bellefleur presence biding its time in the Adirondack forests, its home a huge castle, its enterprises wealth accrued in the past by Jean-Pierre.

The Bellefleur curse—which has its manifestations in Lake Noir, in various crimes of violence committed by the family as well as to it, in the presence of numerous bizarre elements (a gigantic spider, a dwarf and hunchback, an oversized cat)—both enervates and demands response. The curse is a phenomenon about which they are not even certain; but they feel there *must be* one if there is a large family, wealth, comforts. It is that curse which, inevitably, dooms the family, as if in some great tragic design. Children disappear, poor marriages are made, and Gideon, the instrument of the curse, brings it all down. Like the House of Atreus, the House of Bellefleur grows and destroys itself from the same seed.

Yet despite a curse, a Gothic castle, a region which recalls Gothic isolation and solitariness, vendettas, omens, and prophecies, *Bellefleur* does not reach for Gothic elements so much as for mythical ones. Oates's plan, if I unravel her multileveled novel correctly, is to present nothing less than a myth for our time. She uses a family, with numerous branches and a two-hundred-year-old history, as her wedge; so that the doomed, accursed Bellefleurs have something of the Kennedys in them, allowing for all the obvious cultural distinctions. That is, Oates has developed a family whose fortunes, like those of the Kennedys in a broad analogy, emblemize the country. Bellefleur as a word itself—lovely or pretty flowers—has the pastoral quality of America; and since the family, with the original Jean-Pierre, extends back before the Revolution, we are in the presence of the country in its full historical sweep. It recalls, in this respect, the Gwyon family in *The Recognitions* and the Slothrops in *Gravity's Rainbow.*

The events of the past are enveloped in mythical shrouds. The progenitor, Jean-Pierre, is murdered with one of his two sons, and the second son marries the widow of his brother. The first son's children are also murdered, and the second son then has three children by his brother's widow, which keeps the family going. But such beginnings are only a small part of the family's development. For successive children are named after ancestors, so that young people come on like waves recalling their namesakes. The second son (Jedediah), who marries his brother's widow, Germaine, has a son, Raphael, who later turns up in

another Raphael, son of Ewan, brother of Gideon. Jean-Pierre, who was murdered with his son, turns up as Jean-Pierre II, who is a murderer of terrible ferocity and suddenness. For several generations, with siblings either dying off or refusing to marry, one person continues the line precariously. One of the last in the line, little Germaine, who is born near the beginning of the novel, is herself magical, with special powers of divination. Although Gideon's final act destroys the castle, the curse seems to have ended with her, the youngest of the Bellefleur clan; for she turns the curse into prophecy.

In addition to Bellefleurs who live at the castle or in the region, there are those who are settled in other sections of the country, who visit, and who help to fill the castle with Bellefleurs. While branches of the family propagate and while Leah, Gideon's wife, attempts to reacquire the family's fortunes along the lines of Jean-Pierre's original possessions, Gideon is seized by demons. His demonic streak reveals to him that all activity, acquisition, pride in family are forms of vanity, that little is worth his energy; and he gradually declines, with drinking, womanizing, loss of self-discipline. Before he decides to annihilate the accursed Bellefleur castle, he deposits young Germaine in a safe place, gathers up his latest mistress, a doomed flier in her own right, and then heads out for his mission. The final chapter of the novel returns us to the beginning of the line, when a messenger comes to Jedediah in the woods to tell him his brother and father have been murdered, that he must return, marry his sister-in-law, and ensure that Bellefleurs can continue. "Your sister-in-law Germaine awaits you, the young man said evenly, watching Jedediah with the same pitying expression. You must return and marry her: you must continue the Bellefleur line: and you must exact revenge on your enemies. . . . I don't know what to believe, Jedediah cried aloud."

Just as myth returns us, after a journey, to our beginnings, so does the Oates novel wind back. As the Bellefleurs are ready to end, they are just beginning: their presence as mythical creatures, as a mythical family, lives on. What is further remarkable about them is that the group who live in the Adirondack region do no meaningful work. Gideon, his brother, Ewan, and others, as well as their wives, do little more than breed and take advantage of family holdings. Their lives are predicated not on achievement but on existence only. And nearly all of them suffer from terrible acts of violence: Gideon's kamikaze end, Ewan shot several times (a favorite Oates device), Raphael's disappearance, Vernon (Gideon's cousin) bound and tossed into the river, Louis and his father butchered, along with their children, Jean-Pierre II a murderer of numerous people in both past and present. While their deaths are not tragic in any classical sense, they provide us with a family of tragic events, nearly all connected to Bellefleur destiny or doom. An allegory of America is perhaps in the making.

The rivals to Bellefleur prosperity are the Varrells, Adirondack white trash, dirt farmers, hunters, mountain people, who see their destiny as the killing and harassment of Bellefleurs. Well beyond class distinctions, the two families form rival dynasties: Bellefleur prosperity and progress counterpointed by Varrell violence, brutality, drunkenness. Each act of one is met by a countering act of the other. Louis and his children are slaughtered by Varrells, who in turn are shot by Louis's avenging brother, Harlan. Later, Harlan is shot. Jedediah is then sent for, to revenge himself on the avengers, like the House of Atreus playing out its deadly games. As Oates writes: "The living and the dead. Braided together. Woven together. An immense tapestry taking in centuries." She has in mind chiefly the Bellefleurs, but in a sense the words are her subject: "braided together." The language, the conception, even the chapter headings are pointed toward interconnection of all things. For Oates, this novel is a *summa,* a cojoining of all her previous works. In that respect, for a novelist still well in mid-career, it is a remarkable achievement to find linkages. Barth tried something similar in *Letters,* and *Bellefleur* moves along comparable lines.

The chapter headings, indicative of the sharp cutting Oates will do from one to another, suggest many facets of the novel. Several of them evoke rather than describe: "The Arrival of Mahalaleel," "The Bellefleur Curse," "Powers," "Great Horned Owl," all from Book One, called "Mahalaleel." Subsequent book headings are also evocative: "The Walled Garden," "In the Mountains," "Once Upon a Time," "Revenge." Playing through nearly every phase of the novel is Jedediah's attempt to reach into the very soul of things by way of pastoral experience; set deep into the forests, he becomes the spirit of the Adirondacks, and, indirectly, of America. Having forsaken Bellefleur fortunes, having forsaken civilization itself, he attempts to get beyond even Cooper's Hawkeye into some realm of ultimate communion. But, Oates stresses, even he is not immune to the ways of the world, even he, who is reborn, cannot escape; and the novel ends with his being brought back to his civilized responsibilities, to make certain the Bellefleur line does not become extinct. Jedediah's experience is ar-

chetypical, illustrative of the extreme tensions of opposites, with his family burden overweighing his desire to be Adam, first man, a wanderer in the forests of the New Zion.

Oates has surrounded human life with all sorts of animal, insect, and subhuman life. Her stress on grotesques in her previous fiction finds more suitable expression here; for she has established such a feral society that grotesques become natural. The gigantic cat (Mahalaleel), the gigantic spider (Love), the hunchback (Nightshade), the eagle that snatches Gideon's son by Garnet, the "Room of Contamination" (itself a kind of Rappaccini's garden), the drum made from Raphael's own skin, the murders committed by Jean-Pierre II are all connected to Oates's basic motif: that struggle between civilization and savagery in a feral society and history. Violence fits into a necessary mode. When Gideon feels that the spider is a rival for Leah's affections, he knows he must eliminate Love. The spider's death is lovingly retold:

> The thing made a high shrieking noise, not unlike a bat, and stabbed repeatedly at him with its mouth (which contained teeth, or teethlike, and very sharp, serrations in its jaw), and kicked wildly at him with its many legs (which, though scrawny, were really quite elastically strong), and thrashed about so violently that Gideon nearly lost his balance and stumbled backward. He had not calculated exactly how to kill it—strangling was impossible, it hadn't a neck—but in the excitement of the moment his gloved hands acted as if by instinct, as if, in the dim Bellefleur past, they had killed many a Love, just by holding it fast, gripping it fast, and squeezing.

Death is celebrated with as much affection as is life. Jean-Pierre's murders, through rapid slitting of throats, dozens of them on two occasions, is almost gleeful, suggesting that he has within him an enclosed space civilization cannot touch. In that area, he is death personified. So, in his way, is Gideon. Although he does not kill, he is capable of killing; but instead of taking others' lives, he takes his own, and that of his mistress, whose dour sense of doom fits his prescription exactly. Gideon—who recalls Faulkner's obsessive Sutpen—internalizes all Bellefleur violence, just as Leah, from a lesser branch of the family, represents its acquisitiveness. Although drawn together by powerful physical attraction, they are mismatched, as they discover once Germaine is born. After giving birth to twins, Leah is delivered of a monster. It is killed by Leah's mother, and no more is heard about the incident. But the monstrous flesh is a reminder to

Leah and Gideon that not only have they lost touch, but the family is itself becoming monstrous, is moving toward disintegration.

As parable, legend, myth, *Bellefleur* dispenses with routine feelings and psychological causes. Instead, Oates stresses large emotional patterns, huge passions, life and death elements. She has broken free of realism and naturalism into new lines of force. Mythical patterns permit her indulgence in modalities her previous naturalistic fictions could not quite contain. *Bellefleur* is a remarkable breakthrough, an indication Oates is still searching for the large themes to accommodate her immense reach; that she is dissatisfied with more contained fiction and that she needs, now, a territory as big as the Adirondacks, the size of entire countries, for her area of maneuver.

Just Above My Head (1979) is James Baldwin's first novel since 1974. It occupies familiar ground, in which he returns to the evangelist experiences of his own youth and intermixes with those homosexual love, love as a general idea, and an effort to convey the feel of black life in Harlem and in the South. The vehicle for Baldwin's involvement in these deeply felt black experiences is Arthur Montana, a singer in a gospel group that moves from North to South and then back North. The narrator of Arthur's tale— Arthur is dead when the novel begins—is his younger brother and admirer, Hall. The form of the novel is a reminiscence, Hall's of his brother, but also stressed is political activity in the 1950s and 1960s, by Hall and Arthur.

The novel begins with intense scenes of family life in Harlem, the coming together of two families, the churchgoing Montanas and Millers. Julia Miller appears headed for a major career as a gospel preacher. She is tyrannical about the Lord and his ways, and she has conquered her own family by way of her words and presence, this before she has even reached puberty. Her younger brother, Jimmy, will become an accompanist for Arthur in the gospel group. Julia is precocious, right on the edge of madness with her fervor and intensity. When her mother dies, her father wants her to continue as a gospel preacher because it has brought a good income for them—he now depends on her. And he also comes to depend on her, at thirteen, for sex. The old devil incest is introduced in what is becoming a perfunctory act in contemporary fiction. Julia, needless to say, is shattered by something tantamount to incestuous rape; and she loses her faith, her desire to preach, and, apparently, her salvation. The novel is ready now to shift to Ar-

thur and his first love, Crunch; then to tilt further to his activities as a gospel singer on the move.

The ground plan thus far is promising, but as Baldwin has admitted, he has no interest in the angular modulations of the modern novel and considers himself an old-fashioned storyteller. The difficulty is that his storytelling is ponderous. He has tempered his earlier high rhetorical style—what sank *If Beale Street Could Talk,* in 1974—but nevertheless we are aware of being surrounded by words, phrases, clotted passages, verbal avalanches. The distinctions words define are often lost, simply because they come on without regard for the story itself. The first page is instructive. The novel begins with Arthur's death by hemorrhage: blood pounding through Arthur's face and emerging at the mouth. Baldwin passes from that to the press release of an " 'emotion-filled' gospel singer, dead at the untidy age of thirty-nine." From that to: "I: sat by the telephone. I looked at the marvel of human effort, the telephone. The telephone beside my bed was black—like me, I think I thought, God knows why I thought it, if I did. The telephone in the bathroom was gray. The telephone in the kitchen was blue, light blue. The sun was shining that morning, like I've never known the sun to shine before." Then the narrative returns to Arthur, found lying in a "pool of blood" in a men's room in the basement of a London pub: "why does one say a pool? —a storm, a violence, a miracle of blood: his blood, my brother's blood, my brother's blood, my brother's blood! My blood, my brother's blood, my blood, Arthur's blood, soaking into the sawdust of some grimy men's room in the filthy basement of some filthy London pub."

Part of the difficulty, apart from the flatness of the prose, is Baldwin's effort to gain sympathy for someone, Arthur here, who does not as yet exist for the reader. By way of rising language, by means of pitching words to an intensely emotive level, he strives to locate the narrator's feeling for his brother, with neither narrator nor Arthur having any significance for us as readers. The problem, once more apart from the prose itself, is that the pitch starts so high, with such intensity, it establishes its own climax. The actual Arthur, as well as the narrator Hall, must be less, and whatever either says or does is anticlimactic. But more deleterious than that is the fact that the calculated impact is really none at all: we sense a curious withdrawal of the narrator from the very event he wants us to enter into. The description of the telephone, as if we were suddenly catapulted into a Robbe-Grillet novel of things and thinginess, has no significance; none, unless Baldwin were working along not a narrative novel but a more experimental one full of clashes between people and objects. But such a method is distant indeed from *Just Above My Head,* from Baldwin generally.

The basic structure depends on four characters, all arranged in a semi-incestuous way, incest implied throughout though only actual between young Julia and her father. Julia and Jimmy are deeply involved with each other, as are Arthur and Hall, Millers and Montanas like the quartet in *The Good Soldier.* Arthur and Jimmy have a long affair, Arthur's final one; and Hall and Julia have an affair, which terminates, although Hall wants to marry her. Julia, having begun as a gifted gospel preacher, becomes a prostitute, a model, finally the mistress of an African chief. Parallel to her career—from sacred to profane—is Arthur's success as a singer with a gospel group that tours through many dangerous areas of the South when the civil rights movement was just beginning to gain momentum.

Their professional lives are more clearly focused than their personal lives. And here the intertwining of Millers and Montanas intensifies: in Jimmy and Arthur, Julia and Hall; in the disguised love of Arthur and Hall, Julia and Jimmy. Arthur's initiation into homosexuality comes from Crunch, another member of the gospel group, along with Red and Peanut. The group is itself covertly incestuous, with two members having an affair, the foursome seeking outlets in each other. The oldest of them by several years is Hall, and as elder statesman he moves with a seemingly perpetual wound. Baldwin writes repeatedly of Hall's pain: "Our love [his with Julia] was the beginning of my reconciliation with my pain." The reiteration of pain seems to be connected simply to being alive, or being black, or as suffering through an era: not associated with any particular wound. The Montana parents are decent, understanding; Mr. Montana is quite different from the father Baldwin presented in *Go Tell It on the Mountain,* which *Just Above My Head* resembles in its Harlem setting. We attempt to account for Hall's pain, his inability to connect, his Odyssean wanderings through life seeking meaning. Baldwin does not provide the significance; he presents details, not coherence.

Part of the difficulty with the novel is Baldwin's insistence on touching all bases. Since this is his first novel in five years, he understandably sought comprehensiveness. For behind the personal entanglements is a history of black involvement and activity for the last three decades, beginning with the Korean War.

Baldwin hits all the themes, as if redeeming himself for past omissions. Fifteen years later he is responding to Cleaver, now a born-again Christian Reagan supporter. Further, he moves us into all the fashionable literary areas of the last decade. Besides the theme of incest, which is sweeping through not only fiction but film and television, we have some fashionable black anti-Semitism, placed in the mouth of Red, a sympathetic character.* There is the standard African adventure, here Julia's, and related to us secondhand and briefly as a "different experience" from being black in Harlem, in New York, in America. There is, also, the explicit homosexual love, handled tenderly, but almost obligatorily now: Arthur and Crunch, Arthur and Jimmy; almost Arthur and Hall. There are the masturbation scenes, the civil rights scenes, the angry white crowd scenes, the night terror scenes in a Southern city, the taunt scenes; and the introduction of the Black Muslims, through Sidney, Hall and Julia's friend.

The novel is a kaleidoscope of our literary and social/political landscape of the last decades: the postwar past recaptured, as it were. Yet many of these elements are not integrated; they are excrescences. Sidney's Muslim beliefs and desire for separation, Julia's African venture and two-year affair with a chief, even the civil rights scenes—which are quite moving—do not and cannot cohere. Conveying little urgency, they exist simply by the fact that they have been put into words and spread out on the page.

Connected to these points—Baldwin's compulsive need to touch everything that has happened while he was away from fiction—is the question of love. Love is the impetus for all the characters. Even Joel, Julia's father, needs love, in his perverse way, and seeks it, after his wife's death, in his daughter's bed. Arthur is a huge receptacle awaiting love, and Hall is himself wounded by love or lack of it. Julia has sought love in God and in evangelical revivalism, rejected that,

---

*When Bellow has his sympathetic Mr. Sammler think of blacks, he thinks of huge cocks; but Baldwin draws out the antagonism further: " 'You [Red tells his mother] want me to peddle my ass to them Jew crackers? That's why Black people is where they is today! Always sucking around the fucking Jew! Them bastards had my ass in a vise one time and they can't have it no more!' " Peanut, who is narrating this passage, says that Red "knew better than that"; but the point is that a sympathetic character has voiced what was once the rallying cry of Baraka and has now become a cry of manhood for young blacks: Get the Jew. In response, Jewish critics, especially in *Commentary,* work more by innuendo, citing "achievement" as a way of putting the black down. Baldwin gives it to us in one big gulp.

and now seeks it in Africa. Nearly every character is motivated by his or her search for love. And yet love —of male for male, at least—seems little more than a swollen cock. Arthur sees Jimmy and falls in love at first sight, when Jimmy is not much beyond childhood. Crunch does the same with Arthur, when the latter is just reaching manhood. Hall sees Julia, as a model, and falls in love. None of the characters earns love, is developed as a loving or lovely creature; the need is for sexual relief. Since the novel is narrated by a male and from a male point of view, a heterosexual one, we have no sense of what the women feel. Besides Julia, whose deeper qualities are rarely observed, women move only fleetingly through the book, and they disappear early through death or neglect.

For a novel of five hundred pages, there is a curious lack of character depth, although there is a good deal of detail. Baldwin spends huge chunks of space on getting people in and out of rooms, walking in hallways, trudging up and down stairs, wandering through streets, whether Harlem or Paris, rolling sleeves up and down, putting on and taking off clothes. People also spend a good deal of time greeting each other. Quotidian quantities multiply, and they consume large parts of each page. We are thrust into such routines so intensely, so insistently, that we come to feel Baldwin is writing a domestic novel, not the tour de force suggested by broader elements of civil rights, Muslims, Africa.

The prose lends itself to the domestic novel. It is talky, hortatory. Since the novel returns to the fifties and sixties, Baldwin feels he must tell and retell what it was like, blacks in the South, northern blacks visiting the South, Muslims and their desire for separation, white antagonism at any sign of black vitality. Baldwin's treatment of all this, however, is perfunctory, except for the sounds and smells of a Southern city, as experienced by a Northern black. The prose grinds all larger dimensions, since it moves from domestic detail to preachiness. "No one called the late J. Edgar Hoover a terrorist, though that is precisely what he was: and if anyone wishes, now, in this context, to speak of 'civilized' values or 'democracy' or 'morality,' you will pardon this poor nigger [Hall] if he puts his hand before his mouth, and snickers—if he laughs at you."

The reader is positioned thus: if he rejects the rhetoric, he is accused of rejecting the sentiment. Yet while the sentiment is true, it is devalued by the rhetoric; precisely because Hall preaches, he is dismissed literarily. To whom does he think he is speaking? Who is Baldwin's reader? Does he think he is writing for racists or for government officials and corporate executives? He is writing for the convinced, for the most liberal audience, black and white, that exists anywhere in the world. And he preaches to them the routine details of race! Miscalculation lies everywhere: in charged rhetoric that goes nowhere; in themes touched upon that do not cohere; in attitudes and activities which have already become platitudinous; in inflammatory statements which are no more than fashionable poses; and in a presentation of love that is indistinguishable from a hard cock. It is very unfortunate, for now, in 1981, with racism revived and even trumpeted abroad, with all the code words returning, a black writer who wishes to enter the arena needs not a club but a delicate instrument. Baldwin loses the very people he might have touched. His "past recaptured" no longer obtains.

SOMEWHAT EXPERIMENTAL: ABISH, SORRENTINO, DOCTOROW

Although the novels that follow are not experimental in the sense of *Pale Fire* and *Ada,* or *The Crying of Lot 49* and *JR,* or *Letters, Lookout Cartridge,* and *The Dead Father,* or other recent Barth, Pynchon, and McElroy, and certainly not Federman, Sukenick, or Katz, they do indicate an experimental option. They keep open lines to modernism and postmodernism, with Abish's novel (and stories) the most fully wrought. This first long fiction by Abish also introduces a new novelist whose potentialities in language, technique, and reach seem considerable.

With mixed results, Gilbert Sorrentino has attempted to enter the modernist fray. He works very hard to touch all bases, touches some meaningfully, but misses often out of untargeted cleverness. Doctorow, with mixed results also, refuses to be stereotyped, coming off *Ragtime* with a more ambitious effort at pure novel-making, eschewing the musical comedy aspects of that earlier commercial success. But while the reach is there—to capture a whole chunk of America—the grasp of materials falters and elements remain disconnected, even skew.

The immediate literary background for Walter Abish's *How German Is It* (1980) is his story "The English Garden," which appeared in 1977 in a volume titled *In the Future Perfect.* * Although the col-

---

*All Abish's titles are deliberately ambiguous, giving us several levels because of diverse meanings of a word, lack of punctuation, or groupings of words. *How German Is It,* lacking a question mark, is turned into a dubious assertion. *In the*

lection has several fictions not associated with Germany, the title suggests a world that "would have been" if German values had prevailed. The "English Garden" of the story is borrowed from John Ashbery's *Three Poems,* in which he speaks of the English Garden effect as that which gives "the required air of naturalness, pathos and hope." The narrator of Abish's story speaks of Germany as a gigantic coloring book: "Nothing is intrinsically German, I suppose, until it receives its color." The narrator's desire is to establish the reality of Germany. "The question one keeps asking oneself is: How German is it? And, is this the true color of Germany?" The coloring book metaphor is so significant because everything one sees now in postwar Germany differs from what existed before.

> Formerly, on this exact location there had been a rather large camp, built along the lines of a city, with a post office, a library, medical facilities, a bakery, offices, tennis courts, recreation areas, trees, all enclosed by several barbed-wire fences. There were German signs all over the camp with arrows pointing in one or another direction. The signs are gone, the camp is gone. It no longer exists. Some of the people in Brumholdstein [which figures largely in *How German Is It*] remember playing in that vast camp, by that time completely run down, windows smashed, telephone wires cut, expensive equipment missing, toilets vandalized. The camp was called Durst. It is not represented in the coloring book.

Durst concentration camp has been demolished, for it proved, after all, only a second-rank camp. "It would not attract a sufficient number of tourists to warrant the extensive repairs that were needed. Furthermore, the camp had only two gas ovens. For the price of rebuilding and maintaining the Durst concentration camp they could build 2,500 apartment units. A lot of kids from the neighboring townships regretted the decision. They used to play soccer and other games on the grounds of the former concentration camp."

Germany is like a massive palimpsest, in which lower layers of life are struggling to be seen beneath colors piled on top. One tries to see as deeply as possible, but objects block the way; entire cities have emerged as differing radically from what preceded them. All is cover-up, conspiracy, glossing over. Brumhold, the philosopher of German ideals and idealism, has been honored in the naming of Brumholdstein; yet he represents a thinker like Heidegger, who retreated from moral and ethical considerations in order to do "meditative thinking" which indirectly justified the German past. "The city is named after a German philosopher, who, like so many of his predecessors, inquired into the nature of a *thing*. He started his philosophical inquiry by simply asking: *What is a thing?* For most of the inhabitants of Brumholdstein the question does not pose a great problem." To probe the nature of a thing is another way of asking, How German is it?

In *How German Is It* (a statement, not a query), Abish tries to discover how a society effaces its past, how it remakes itself by way of loss of memory. Technically, the novel owes a great deal to French methods, especially to Michel Butor and his novel *Degrees*. Rapid cutting, seemingly disconnected segments, several narrative layers, introduction of new characters without warning, the use of a particular place as metaphor characterize both novels. Butor uses a school and its curriculum, students, professors; Abish moves on a large scale, attempting to encompass a country, its history, its sense of itself as it shuffles off past, memory, its former roles.

The novel takes the form of a journey, of Ulrich Hargenau, back from Paris, where he is a novelist, to Würtenburg, near Durst, now renamed Brumholdstein. Ulrich, however, is not an ordinary German, but one whose father was executed in 1944 for plotting against Hitler. That is Abish's control point, for while Ulrich is famous by way of his father, the incident in the past has fallen outside memory, into an area the Germans have eradicated. Further, Ulrich's brother, Helmuth, is an architect; he represents the new Germany, the master builder of a new society which bulldozes the past as if it never occurred. Helmuth is all energy, purpose, work ethic. He has no moral or ethical sense, only the need to accomplish.

Future Perfect indicates a tense with both future and past temporality, each pulling in a different direction. An earlier collection of fictions, *Minds Meet* (1975), suggests a competition of diverse mental efforts. A first novel, *Alphabetical Africa* (1974), plays on letters of the alphabet, beginning with A (Africa), rising to Z; then returning down the alphabetical scale and ending with Africa. Even the title of a collection of poems, *Duel Site,* plays on the ambiguities suggested by "duel" and "site."

These ambiguities are connected to Abish's flattening out of his prose. As he explains in his interview in *Fiction International* (4/5): "In my writing I try to strip language of its power to create verisimilitude that in turn shields the reader from the printed words on the page that are deployed as signifiers. Writing as close as possible to a neutral content, everything, the terrain, the interiors, the furniture, the motions of the characters are aspects of a topography that defines the limits of the situation being explored."

He can live quite well without memory: "Helmuth rose each morning at six-thirty. By seven-ten the entire family was at the table having breakfast. No one was ever late for breakfast. . . . The children listened intently. They were seeing at first hand the life of an adult world unfold. It was a real world. They were aware that each day their father contributed something tangible to that world. Each day a number of buildings all over Germany rose by another few meters and came closer to the completion that initially had its roots, so to speak, in his brain." Germany is being recolored.

While Helmuth's life proceeds on tight schedules, at home and in his professional career, Ulrich's is messy, especially since his former wife, Paula, is involved in radical activities. Paula is somehow connected to a young woman named Daphne, who moves into Ulrich's building. A network seems in the making. Abish's sense of proportion is magnificent, as past and present combine, in Daphne now, Paula in the past, the elder Hargenau executed by Hitler in the previous generation. Time is layered and yet continuous. Furthermore, even as Helmuth designs and builds, radical groups bomb and destroy, sometimes the very buildings erected by Helmuth, like the new post office. As even as this is occurring, Ulrich receives letters threatening him, for he had testified against the radical Einzieh Group in the recent past.

Abish gains broad historical dimensions from his groupings. For at the same time the new Germany emerges, in Helmuth and those like him, and the former Germany is effaced, as Durst concentration camp has been eradicated, another Germany is also present, that of the radicals eager to annihilate whatever the new Germany represents. Ulrich leaves for Geneva, possibly to see Daphne, or to see Paula, or to collect material for another book; and while he is away a second bomb goes off in Würtenburg, destroying an entire floor in the fingerprint section of the new police station, also designed by Helmuth. As he thinks of Switzerland, the land where Musil, Rilke, and Keller died, where Rousseau was born, where Nabokov recently lived, Ulrich sees it as a prisoner of the past, as much as he is a prisoner of the present.

There is still another line of development, that connected to Franz, the waiter at the elegant Pflaume restaurant. Franz lives in Daemling, not in Brumholdstein, where the restaurant is located; and he regularly takes a bus, whose precise schedule indicates how this Germany works. But Franz, while deferential and servile in person, has something of the maverick or madman in him, and in his spare time he builds a replica of the Durst camp.*

After all Durst was, so to speak, Brumholdstein's antecedent. However, there are no books to be found on Durst. And Durst, accordingly, has no official history; that is to say, no one has as yet taken the trouble to assemble it in any coherent form. Not that anyone has tried to hide or conceal the fact—a futile task really—that it had been a forced labor camp for God knows how many thousands of foreigners, aliens, prisoners of war, political detainees, and other undesirables, including, of course, Jews, who presented a clear threat to the continued survival of Germany.

All these events, however, are muted, part of Franz's replica, perhaps, part of the coloring book of Germany, but dim and faint in outline. In the present, Helmuth continues his assault on power, sleeping with the mayor's wife, running his household like a camp, never doubting his capacities to build. He represents the unthinking vulgarity of the emerging nation, the power that can let memories slip away, the materialism which enrages those who seek a different way. Juxtaposed to this are merciless radical groups which destroy whatever Helmuth attempts to build, totally nihilistic as a response to epidemic materialism. Germany, possibly, is our model of the future, or of the future perfect, the perfect future.

Ulrich, meanwhile, tries to negotiate his way. He is, like Hanno in Mann's *Buddenbrooks*, the sensitive element, as against Helmuth's insensitive success. Ulrich is a novelist, part poet, a dreamer, a man who wants to sort out his memories. He lives with language, and language for him refers to things; it is not simply words which serve to efface things. Egon and Gisela, friends of Ulrich's, stand for the new Germany in other ways, through acquisition and harmony. "Clearly the Einzieh Group [Egon explains] intends to overthrow our system of government by destroying Germany's newly acquired harmony. For harmony spell democracy, if you will, but democracy, alas, is a word that has been depleted of its meaning, its energy, its power. If anything can be said to represent the new Germany, it is the wish, the desire, no, the craving to attain a total harmony."

*"He was not merely replicating in every detail, and to scale, something that in its day had been as familiar to the people in Daemling as the cows in the barn. What he was doing was to evoke in the people he knew a sense of uncertainty, a sense of doubt, a sense of dismay, a sense of digust. . . . In his case, to strive for bad taste was to strive for revolution."

The perfect philosophy for this "harmony" is Brumhold, whose theories of German life and language aim at forging a national spirit. Brumhold, who refuses to visit Brumholdstein, wrestles with eternal metaphysical questions: "What is thought? What is being? What is existence?" Brumhold prefers to remain in his forest hut, from which he utters his spiritual message: "For in the forest are located our innermost dreams and desires. In order to re-establish our roots and our purpose and return to a simplicity of life that can no longer be found in the German community, we turn to the forest . . . confident that in what we are doing, we are coming closer to our past, to our history, to our German spirit." He combines Heidegger's retreat from issues into *being* with Johann Gottfried von Herder's call for a national culture. He becomes part of the coloring book.

If *Alphabetical Africa* was Abish's attempt to deconstruct narrative by means of reducing all ideas to letters of the alphabet, *How German Is It* moves in the opposite direction. Here, he reconstructs Germany by way of its misleading use of language. Through metaphysical questions, Brumhold evades all discussion of the past, of German history, of Germany as the embodiment of modern death, a culture of death. He universalizes Germany, whereas Ulrich is endeavoring to comprehend it as a specific place at a particular time. It falls to Helmuth, not Ulrich, however, to make a speech on Brumhold at an outdoor memorial ceremony honoring the philosopher's death. Helmuth, the embodiment of the new, will pronounce on Brumhold, the defender of Germany's soul: Abish has his perfect coordinates. Helmuth stresses the German language, as the only way to understand the Teutonic *Dasein*.

> But how can they [foreigners] possibly understand Germany without appreciating the richness of its language, for only the language will enable them to comprehend the nature of that German restlessness and that intrinsic German striving for order and for tranquility as well as for perfection. . . . It must also be pointed out that although Brumhold clearly had a universal *being* in mind, what emerges from his metaphysical quest, from his deliberations, from his intense exploration of the German language and its roots, is a shape of *being* that cannot be divorced from the German passion for exactitude and abstractions.

Such a passion, Helmuth asserts, reached its apex in Bach, Grünewald, and Hölderlin. Helmuth bypasses how language goes with history, or how the German spirit has gained other, destructive and self-destructive outlets. He ignores the entire question how German is it.

Abish achieves many of his most compelling effects through rapid cutting. He dashes not only from scene to scene, but from person to person; or from event to event. These cuts occur like sequences in a Godard film, or a Butor novel, without preparation; as if all life were composed of nonsequential elements which succeed each other too rapidly for us to settle in. The verbal irony, the understated comments which carry such sarcastic thrust are complemented by shifting around, which has its own witty dimension.

Following the prolonged ovation for Helmuth's speech on Brumhold, Abish cuts to the photographing of the event; then to the mayor's young daughter, who asks why Brumhold lived in a cabin; after that to an evening at the mayor's house for refreshments; and then to a sequence which is at a different time, with Ulrich standing next to the mayor at the Pflaume restaurant while a mass grave has been uncovered. In the interstices, Ulrich is searching for Anna, the schoolteacher with whom he is having an affair. With the rapid cutting creating the opposite effect of Helmuth's building, Abish technically has a countering principle, whereby elements fall into disorder and anarchy even as juxtaposed events seek order. Musil and Mann come to mind as Abish's masters.

Violence is never far. A man with a rifle appears, a game warden, but instead of shooting Helmuth, he hits Ulrich in the arm. Threatening letters continue to appear. Ulrich heads for the East Frisian Islands, and an ominousness seems to accompany him. The East Frisian Islands, although east of Mann's Lubbock, do strengthen the *Buddenbrooks* association; for north is now juxtaposed to south, the two brothers distinguished from each other. Ulrich's visit with Egon and Gisela coincides with a terrorist group's activities, which are to blow up a bridge that will disrupt traffic, more an antibourgeois act than a political attack. They politicize the bridge-keeper, an indicator of their ability to win over those who are antithetical to their aims.

The drawbridge blows, two policemen are shot dead, the bridge attendant is wanted: all the details of a terrorist act. It drops, disconnected, into a vacuum; life continues as it always has. In the sequential follow-up, Ulrich discovers he is not the son of the man executed in 1944; the dates are wrong, and he is a bastard. He tells this to a doctor and indicates he is not who he is, that he was on his way to see a woman when the drawbridge blew, that all his coordinates are in question. The doctor asks him if he has ever been hypnotized, and when Ulrich says no, proceeds to put him under. The novel ends with Ulrich hypnotized: "Is it possible for anyone in Germany, nowadays, to raise his right hand, for whatever the reason, and not be flooded by the memory of a dream to end all dreams?" The true state for Germany is hypnotic: the sole condition where all else has been turned into a coloring book.

A mulligan stew is a potful of meat, potatoes, and whatever else the cook may throw in. Gilbert Sorrentino's *Mulligan Stew* (1979) is the literary equivalent, a potpourri, a big jigsaw puzzle with the pieces heaped one on the other. The chief ingredients of the "literary stew" are literary parodies and satirical thrusts at authors, editors, publishers, the entire industry. Sorrentino's central figure is an author, Tony Lamont, who is becoming increasingly paranoiac at what he sees as loss of critical and popular attention. He is the aging writer who has lost faith in himself and in his work, except to defend it obsessively, and whose sanity is slipping away from him as he sees so-called lesser authors praised and popularized. The theme, then, is a very American one, about failure and success, about loss of powers, about the vaunting of the self. Not unusually, two characters, Daisy and Tom Buchanan, walk out of *The Great Gatsby,* the archetypal novel about American success.

The basic line of *Mulligan Stew* is simple. Tony Lamont is working on a new novel, tentatively called *Guinea Red,* and his characters in that enterprise include Ned Beaumont and Martin Halpin. Both would like to escape Lamont's novel, since they feel he is uncertain about his aims and will make them do things they prefer not to do. During a lull, when Lamont seems distracted, Halpin murders Beaumont, although this is not a final action, since Lamont still controls them.

Desperate for recognition, Lamont writes a critic, Professor Roche, about his new work: "another first-person narrative, but this one with a real *persona,* a man who doesn't know what he is doing, or, for that matter, what he has *done.* I'm afraid that I am having trouble getting on with it, and am casting about for the correct 'tone' to give this voice." The novel is, indeed, his search for a tone, which is another way of saying, for a novel. While Sorrentino provides Lamont with materials, they never coalesce—since novel and author are doomed to failure—and the

enterprise, with lists, parodies, satirical thrusts, becomes the novel *Mulligan Stew.* The level of parody comes early when Lamont speaks of his sister's article, in *Object Review,* called "643: The Double Play in Malamud's 'The Natural.' "

Sorrentino, unsatisfied with the multileveled reality suggested by Robbe-Grillet's work, ingests that author's principles of uncertainty and turns even them into parody, of Robbe-Grillet himself and all those "new wave mystery writers" who feel they have captured a reality by evading it. Sorrentino's Lamont is more hazardously located than they, for his characters are themselves struggling to break away from what they think will be a second-rate production, or from acts they do not wish to commit. Embedded deeply in their activities is Ned Beaumont's infatuation with two whores named Corrie Corriendo and Berthe Delamode, who perform all kinds of tricks, magical and sexual, as forms of entertainment and whose marvelous bodies send Ned into paroxysms. Ned is himself involved with Daisy Buchanan, who is tired of Tom; but when he meets Corrie and Berthe, he ditches Daisy for their charms. At one point, he takes Daisy to them, and she, seeing all that succulent flesh, cannot resist either. Part of Sorrentino's novel, incidentally, is devoted to sexual thrills, woman on woman, two women and a man, masturbatory fantasies offered up as novelistic material. Although he mocks Ned's attachment to the whores, Sorrentino derives some of the novel's entertainment value from it, a kind of men's club blue film.

As soon as one looks within the novel, at male-female relationships, at attitudes that reach beyond the parodic, one perceives an unimaginative inquiry into the nature of things. Despite all his inventive lists —such as the books Halpin finds in an old barn,* where he "kills" Beaumont—the underlying premises are fraternity house male-female antics, men acting like boys, women as sexual objects, presented not as parody but as titillation.

The most effective sections come when the characters discuss their roles in Lamont's books. Occasionally, in fact, they encounter characters running loose from other novels by Lamont, or even other authors. Characters must also fear revisions, where their roles will be altered or even eliminated. "You can even end

---

The Truth About Vegetables by Harry Krishna-Rama, *Myth and Methodology in the Albanian Novel* by Julius Naranja, *It's Great to Be Champeen* by Gorman Sailer, *Negroes with Buns: The Story of the Harlem Cooperative Bakery* by Rose Towne Drug, *Born to Be Italian* by Myles na gCopaleen.

up in boys' books, as an old man who comes out of a secret door or a gypsy on a mountain. Ned knows one man who wound up playing trained *bears!*" Thus, Lamont's anxiety about his ongoing novel is equaled by the anxiety of his characters, who stand to lose as much as he if he falters. Yet while they have some freedom—they can move around when he is not using them—they are limited by their designated roles. Here the book opens up to a larger metaphor.

The shape of the novel is such that the interior narrator, Halpin, is a man uncertain whether or not he is a murderer; a man who has so lost touch with his life that he is caught in an "absurdist murder mystery." Although the narrator is trying to sort out what is certain from what is uncertain, he is still under the control of the larger "narrator," who is Tony Lamont, himself slowly sinking into paranoiac fantasies concerning his career. In another dimension, Halpin's Journal, in which he works toward some sense of himself, is part of Lamont's novel, which is itself part of a "new wave murder mystery."

Sorrentino has now provided part of the stewish mix. He has prefaced the novel with several letters from editors and publishers rejecting *Mulligan Stew,* including one from the general counsel of "Hasard House" that it will not even distribute the book under its agreement with Grove Press. The letters all point to the general worthlessness of aspects of the novel, or to its overall presumptuousness. With these lengthy rejections in hand, Sorrentino has solved several problems: he has provided a summary of characters and scenes, as well as themes, and he has undermined potential criticism. He has become, in his paranoia, someone very close to Tony Lamont in his letters to critics and friends.*

But while these locations of characters and author are adroit, Sorrentino's real talent shows in lists. Lists provide him with several aspects of his craft: parody and burlesque, of course, but also a restricted area to work in, a way of relating himself to his contemporaries; most of all, a means by which individual paranoia can be transmuted into a more generalized cultural madness. For no item on a list is too crazy to be possible. Reviews of Lamont's earlier novels are included, all demonstrating reviewers as assassins and

hitmen. A list of nude photos is offered to Beaumont by Corrie: "JUST RELEASED!! THE ULTIMATE IN BIZARRE BEAUTY!! NUDES IN LEATHER * HIGH HEELS * CORSETS * ETC. Yes mens! Fantastically proportioned Blonds, Brunets and Redheads in exotique costumes of shineing Leather, gleeming Satine, formfitting Rubber, vice-constricting Corsets, spikeheeled Shoes and high Boots, and MORE!!" The book ends with a list, of gifts for various people: "To Chichi Guffo, a tin zeppelin . . . to Obie, an overlapped seam . . . an empty ashcan for Toro Frank . . ."

Such lists are slightly tilted reproductions of segments from television or advertisements in local papers; that mixture of names, gifts, birth dates, and events, none of which has any significance for the viewer or reader. Yet these giveaways, announcements, promises, are all part of the culture, ongoing while we watch, accepted as part of a phantasmagoria. Sorrentino's lists are, of course, parodies of the original, in which paradise is promised but little delivered. Sorrentino turns America into a cornucopia, chock full of anomalous goodies, in the way that television presents an America lacking cohesion except through such giveaways. Sorrentino's "stew" is the matter of America, a later version of what de Tocqueville, Melville, and Thoreau had spotted in the mid-nineteenth century.

Doctorow's *Loon Lake* (1980) is America not as a stew, but in one. On the final page, we learn that Joe of Paterson, the novel's hobo hero, is really named Joseph Korzeniowski—Joseph Conrad's name before he Anglicized it. So we are dealing with "Joseph Conrad" here, a young man who does not go to sea but rides the rails, works for a road-stop carnie show, is almost bitten to death by wild dogs when he first approaches Loon Lake in the Adirondacks, is employed by Bennett Autobody Number Six, where he is almost killed in a union-police fracas, and ends up a war hero and a member of the CIA, in a long career well after the novel proper has ended.

The touch is a good one, that final transformation of Joe into Joseph Conrad, via his Polish name. But it is, like so much else in this ambitious novel, a disconnected element, meaning nothing more in the working out of the book than if Joe had been Allen Ginsberg or William Carlos Williams, also of Paterson. Further, the career subsequent to the end of the novel, when Joe returns to Loon Lake as a Bennett protégé, means little, since it suggests a kind of all-American success which has not been Joe's direction;

---

*Since 1975 is the completion date on the final page and the novel was not published until 1979, the rejections and paranoia may have been realities. An earlier publication, in mid-decade, would have helped Sorrentino, in fact, because his book is literarily topical and its subject matter has peaked.

the irony is a throwaway. Within the novel, Joe has been impulsive, a young man willing to chance all for love. The wealthy Bennett at Loon Lake has offered Joe a place in his organization, but Joe rejects the offer and then runs off with Bennett's mistress, the very lower-class Clara Lukács. Perhaps there is some kind of literary consortium here, with Joseph Conrad, the critic György Lukács, and the novelist Arnold Bennett. The names, in any event, point in directions not taken up by the narrative itself. Joe is not a producer of anything, but a consumer: he takes off with Clara and then ends up working in Bennett's Autobody Shop in Jacksontown, Indiana.

The novel begins with Joe on the road from New York to California as a hobo: armed "only with his unpronounceable last name," which is not divulged. This section is interrupted by a layout suggesting a poem: "Come with me / Compute with me / Computerized she prints out me / Commingling with me she becomes me." The poem introduces us to Warren Penfield, standing on a dirt street in Ludlow, Ohio, scene of labor violence. We then return to Joe and his job in the Hearn Bros. carnival, which features freaks, including a six-hundred-pound lady who after hours spreads for the local trade. This description is interrupted by an interlude about Warren Penfield, all within the first twenty-five pages. The biographical interlude is followed by a section devoted to Warren and his family life. Dos Passos's *U.S.A.* method is apparent. The rapid shuttling, intermixed with biographical inserts and pieces of information, creates a constantly interrupted narrative: metaphors for America.

We then have a large time shift to Joe leaving from the Pine Grove Motor Court, onto a road, then to railroad tracks, where he has a vision of "incandescent splendor." This vision of splendor, like that evoked by Proust's tea and madeleine, will be his insight into another kind of life. We shift abruptly to Ludlow and Warren, whose checkered career in the past parallels Joe's in the present,* then return to Joe

---

*Penfield's life opens the book, although we do not know who he is, where he came from. Then Doctorow picks up his background and future, long before he lives through those years. He becomes a war hero as the result of an accident: having semaphored Wordsworth's "Intimations Ode," he is decorated for having sent a message for help. After the war, he becomes a poet, then partakes of Zen training in Japan, is deported from Japan on a morals charge, becomes poet in residence at Bennett's Adirondack establishment, and disappears with Lucinda Bennett, in 1937, on a round-the-world flight.

and his vision of a girl standing "in front of the mirror and holding up the white dress on the train gliding past me out of sight." This is Gatsby's vision of Daisy. Joe heads for the area where he hopes to have another glimpse, is attacked by wild dogs on Bennett's property and barely escapes with his life—chewed out in every part of his body, a sacrifice to his vision. When he recovers, he is taken on as outdoor help; Warren Penfield is already there as poet in residence.

One of Warren's poems is "Loon Lake," an annotated text. The poem is reproduced, and set into it is a biographical frame on Bennett, whose middle name is Warren. The poem is then allowed to continue. It establishes Bennett's predilection for low-life company: a group of gangsters and their girl friends visit, people he uses in his vast holdings.. He pries off Clara from one Crapo. Set further in the poem is a biographical insert on Lucinda Bailey Bennett, based on Amelia Earhart. These inserts in the poem are really Warren's annotations; but as they are presented, they are set in as interrupters of the poem itself, in the Dos Passos manner. Still another insert or annotation is Clara Lukács, born in New York's Hell's Kitchen. She is eighteen, and Joe of Paterson will steal her from Bennett and the gangsters, and run off with her.

Loon Lake is itself thirty thousand acres of magic in the Adirondacks, where Oates's Bellefleurs also reside in their castle. For Doctorow, the lake is partially ruined by the presence of people who are out of step with nature; for Oates, the region eventually overwhelms its inhabitants. Every magical vision of the loons, the land, or the trains passing in the night is undermined by the avidity of the people there; only Lucinda, the flier, lives in a world commensurate with the grandeur of the locale. Doctorow is splendid when he writes about Loon Lake, a kind of Bittern Lake from *An American Tragedy:* lower-class boy works for rich man and covets his goods; comes there, in fact, to kill him. But the pattern differs from Dreiser in that Joe has a yen for Clara, who is also lower-class, lower in her thinking and speech than he. Nevertheless, Loon Lake, as a region, holds class interest, an enclave of wealth amidst the Depression (Joe arrives in 1936). Both writers perceive the place as mysterious, as having incandescent qualities. Doctorow: "The wind rose in a sudden gust about my ears, and as I looked back to the lake, a loon was coming in like a roller coaster. He hit the water and skidded for thirty yards, sending up a great spray, and when the water settled he was gone. I couldn't see him, I thought the fucker had drowned. But up he popped, shaking and mauling a fat fish. And when the fish was polished off, I heard a weird maniac cry coming off the water, and echoing off the hills."

Once Joe is located at Bennett's establishment, the narrative moves forward, after many leaps, and we find all the major characters present. Warren introduces Clara to Joe, and he recognizes she is his destiny. As an act of bravura, while he is still marginal at Bennett's, Joe signs the guestbook, filled with famous names: "Joe of Paterson. Splendid dogs. Swell company." The novel sputters when Warren's long poem "Child Bride in a Zen Garden" interrupts the narrative. Then it picks up with numerous interruptions and loopings in time. Having rejected a position at the establishment, Joe runs off with Clara in Bennett's old Mercedes, aided by Penfield. The novel swings into the deep past of 1923, Warren at the Zen monastery as retold to Lucinda. Then there is a sudden switch back to Joe at Hearn's carnie show. Fanny the Fat Lady is heaving and dying, while men pile on and screw her in every fleshly fold, a scene whose unpleasantness creates a tonal clash with the rest of the novel. Joe heads out with Hearn's wife in a Model A, this trip paralleling his present running off with Clara in the Mercedes. He deserts Hearn's wife and throws to the winds all the money she has taken with them; this is followed by more on Warren at the monastery.

We return to the present, as Joe and Clara start driving across America, to end up in Indiana, at the Bennett autobody plant. In Clara's story (she is the daughter of an undertaker), Doctorow attempts a lyrical description of an archetypal America, its orphans on the run: "in the dream life of the road the hours sitting next to each other and facing in the same direction brought things out we might not have otherwise said. We told each other about our lives, we gave each other our lives while we looked at the road backward into ourselves. Even though afterward we didn't remember what we said, or were too proud to admit we remembered."

Modish interruptions continue into levels of the past, but the working out of the basic narrative is Joe's involvement in a police-labor fracas, the death of a police spy he had been friendly with, and his own near-demise in the battle. With this, he claims to be Bennett's son, and returns to Loon Lake. "You are thinking it is a dream [Doctorow writes]. It is no dream. It is the account in helpless linear translation of the unending love of our simultaneous but disynch-rous lives." That last phrase is the key, America as an accumulation of lives out of step with themselves and each other.

The technical effort is to put it all before us at once. Past, present, and looping characters are part of a curving mural, somewhat like Oates's *Bellefleur*. Linear narrative would distort. Yet one problem with *Loon Lake* is that the cutting back and forth, the layered temporality, the interruptions and insertions, the poems intermixed with biographical segments give an ambitious feel to elements the novel cannot hold together. The reach is extraordinary, the achievement less. Joe of Paterson as Joseph Conrad, in disguise until the final page, is a typically pretentious aspect. What precisely does this mean, since Joe is not preparing to be an artist or a writer, but a member of the CIA? Conrad went to sea as preparation for something else, for a transformation; but Joe goes to college, becomes a member of the OSS, then the CIA when it forms after the war. He also becomes master of Loon Lake, succeeding Bennett. Was there some ironic transformation intended that paralleled Joseph Conrad's successive lives?

Further, Clara, the love of Joe's life before she returns to Crapo, has little significance, since she represents a vision, not the reality in which he lives with her. None of the characters has the magic necessary to transform them from singular, one-dimensional people into the symbolic presences Doctorow's method demands. The enchantment of the lake region clashes with the petty realism of the characters. Doctorow needed more symbolism than realism, what Oates was able to achieve in the Bellefleurs, *her* Adirondacks, *her* Noir Lake. Bennett himself remains unexplained; with all his wealth, he favors gangsters, hobos. If he is old Henry Ford, what do we make of that? Little of this is brought into line with what we see. His wife, Lucinda, also remains shadowy, an elegant lady with her own form of doom intact, who throws herself into the skies as an act of transformation. She has that symbolic aura, but it jars against everything else.

The object, apparently, was to create a fleeting vision of American life: of class and caste struggle, of those in power holding on against the powerless, of a Dreiser world in which the rich live fantastically in their own cocoons while others serve. Doctorow's political and social sympathies, to his credit, have remained constant. But with all its modernistic techniques, his novel does not serve him well. The cuts and shifts cannot disguise the fact that the novel is many discrete pieces; that by hanging them together out of sequence, he is merely taking advantage of the experimental novel, using its techniques without giving them substance. The realities caught within the experiments are ordinary: Joe as drifter, hobo, carnie worker; Bennett as a rich man with a taste for slumming; Warren as a crazy poet; Clara as a poor girl using her sex appeal to gain upward mobility. Even Lyle James, the worker who befriends Joe and Clara, is a setup, the union man who is really a police spy. Behind the looping and time shifting are tired forms.

Chapter Twelve

‖‖‖‖‖‖‖‖‖‖‖‖‖‖‖‖‖‖‖‖‖‖‖‖‖‖‖‖‖‖‖‖‖‖‖‖‖‖

THE NONFICTION NOVEL

"And out of what one sees and hears and out / Of what one feels, who could have thought to make / So many selves, so many sensuous worlds, / As if the air, the mid-day air, was swarming / With the metaphysical changes that occur, / Merely in living as and where we live."

WALLACE STEVENS, *"Esthétique du Mal"*

The nonfiction novel is misnamed. It should be called "non-novelistic fiction," since it transforms fact into fiction without using the full dimensions of a novelistic sensibility. The stress in this form of writing— whether one labels it "new" or "higher" journalism, "nonfiction novel," or some other variant—is on the self of the author intruding into work that is factual. That "self," which coincides with the disruptive element of self in nearly every 1960s activity, introduces novelistic potentialities into a given work; since the self is the voice we associate with a novelistic sensibility. But no matter how much self there is—whether in Tom Wolfe, Whittaker Chambers (*Witness* fits here), Tom Wicker, or Norman Mailer—still lacking is a full range of fictional techniques, the failure to transform character, event, even language, into fiction. We are speaking, then, of fictions quarried out of fact, presented with novelistic techniques so as to intensify fictional dimensions, but not turned into novels: rather, into "near-novels." "Nonfiction novel," however, rolls off the tongue more readily than "near-novel," certainly more so than "non-novelistic fiction;" and thus its apotheosis.*

I stress the self in all its varieties as the impetus behind the outpouring of such a high order of fictionalized journalism. Although *The New Yorker* had pioneered in the mid-1940s in giving over an entire issue to John Hersey's *Hiroshima,* the 1960s saw the development of many new kinds of personalized magazines and journals, so that even more traditional ones broadened their offerings. Several magazines had folded or were close to bankruptcy: *Liberty, Woman's Home Companion, Collier's,* then *Saturday Evening Post, Look,* and the seemingly indestructible *Life.* The magazine and newspaper industries were reshaping themselves, for inroads of television into their audience forced competition. Films had not been a threat, but rather a parallel entertainment. But the intimacy of television interfered with more impersonal magazines, even newspapers, as increasingly

---

*"Nonfiction novel" is Truman Capote's coinage in connection with *In Cold Blood* (1965), and his appropriation of such

an incestuous phrase could well have been connected to his difficulties in writing fiction. (Mailer's use of "A Real Life Novel" as descriptive of *The Executioner's Song* fits into a similar context: the need to be perceived as a novelist while writing, however valiantly, about other things.) "New journalism," incidentally, seems to have been a coinage of Pete Hamill in the mid-sixties. Inevitably, the two phrases merge, although matters of fact may differ from one practice to the other.

larger numbers of people took what was offered as news directly from the tube. The pictorial ability of magazines was neutralized, and magazines with human interest and other such stories found themselves on a collision course with television, especially as color was introduced. We have, then, a struggle not only for survival but for some way of reaching a reading audience. The culture did not simplify because of television; it became infinitely more complex. Television influenced every aspect of it, not the least our authors, novelists and nonfiction writers or journalists alike.

That reshaping of the media to allow for different kinds of experience and different ways of fashioning them was part of what was occurring in the larger culture, which, in turn, was influenced by what was happening in the media. The sixties saw widespread transformation, in the larger culture and in areas touching upon the individual. With television and satellite communications, a global audience was being prepared for new messages.

In this context, we locate a stress on the "new," whether "new journalism" itself, "parajournalism," "nonfiction novel," or variations thereupon. Little of it was precisely new, however, since aspects of new journalism can be discovered in the late nineteenth century, with Stephen Crane and Mark Twain, among others, and the rise of the Hearst newspapers. There are clear antecedents to Wolfe, Mailer, Talese, Didion, and others. Yet we find in the 1960s a distinct effort, defined by Tom Wolfe,* to fill the slack of what the journalists perceived as a loss of nerve by novelists; or else a national loss of novelistic talent. I think they erred in their estimation of the novel—the sixties were a particularly strong period for fiction—and were carried away by momentous events, which seemed to occur too rapidly for novelistic treatment. Journalism, even the nonfiction novel, was closer to

an "instant event" in print. An exception would be *In Cold Blood,* in the making as long as any carefully wrought novel. Also, several of the writers who turned to this form were having trouble in working through novels or were novelists manqué.

In this competition for an audience, we see editors in tune with the sixties seeking the new, even at staid places like *Atlantic, Harper's,* and *The New Yorker. Esquire* reemerged from dormancy with a flurry of novelties, including Tom Wolfe and Gay Talese. Willie Morris, at *Harper's,* encouraged Mailer to write about the Pentagon march. *New York* magazine became viable once the *Herald Tribune* folded and its Sunday staff needed jobs; these joined with Wolfe, Gloria Steinem, and others to make that magazine exciting for a brief time. *The Village Voice* was receptive to the new journalism and developed its own stable of writers, as did many underground papers, among which the *Berkeley Barb* was one of the best. The reshaping of the print media here provided audiences for writers coming mainly from the left, with strong sympathies for underdogs, marginal people and scenes, hitherto invisible aspects of America. In this respect, they were perfectly attuned to the developing decade, and their perceptions of America helped to shape the antiwar movement.

Three major anthologies appeared, in this order: Harold Hayes's *Smiling Through the Apocalypse:* Esquire*'s History of the Sixties* (1969); the most influential *The New Journalism, with an Anthology Edited by Tom Wolfe and E. W. Johnson* (1973); and Nicolaus Mills's *The New Journalism: An Historical Anthology* (1974). All three celebrate the emergence of the self into what had been considered to be factual writing. The transformational quality in all definitions of new journalism was the intrusion of the reporter. And this is as it should be, since many of the reporters were novelists, like Didion, or would-be novelists, like Wolfe and Talese. No matter how they twisted and turned, the standard for what they did came from fiction. The novel was the glamorous item, and they primped as novelists even when unable to write novels. Wolfe may have asserted that the new form would replace fiction as our most significant print medium,†

*The 1960s will be remembered, Wolfe says, "as the decade when manners and morals, styles of living, attitudes toward the world changed the country more crucially than any political events." Looking back, he asserted that novelists failed to capture the manners and morals of the sixties; that the parajournalists or new journalists rushed in, and what the novelists missed, they captured. Wolfe outlined four major areas of the "new" as: (1) scene-by-scene description, with little historical narrative; (2) dialogue in full, as part of a full scene; (3) presentation of the scene through the eyes of a particular character, putting the reader inside that character; (4) recording of attitudes, tones, gestures, manners, customs, styles, furnishings within a given scene, conveying a person's "status life," the way in which he expresses himself.

†Warner Berthoff (in *Fictions and Events: Essays in Criticism and Literary History,* 1971) believes *The Armies of the Night* and *The Autobiography of Malcolm X* are central documents in the traditions of American literature. Such work compares favorably, he says, with any fiction of the last quarter of the century. This level of enthusiasm, however, blurs the focus, as if film and television were to be treated as the same experience because both depend on visual images and voices.

but whatever he did is finally measured in fictional terms, by fictional standards.

Wolfe in *The New Journalism* demonstrates how fictional techniques may be adapted by journalists, to create the new form. Historical sequencing is eschewed in favor of dramatic scenes; quotation is out and dialogue is in, some of it even invented. A context is constructed, so that people in a situation come to us with the thickness of background, status, behavioral patterns. The reporter must describe events as they unfold, and therefore needs a point of view, a voice. Since these open up the full range of fictional techniques, we may add: roving back and forth in time; interior monologue, even stream of consciousness (all invented by the writer); composite characterization—the use of types to produce an individual; simultaneity of event (employed most effectively by Capote in *In Cold Blood,* where killers and their victims are paralleled); the invention of a supporting cast as filler.

Paramount, of course, is that individual voice of the writer, the "self" intruding everywhere as witness. Mailer, for example, in *The Armies of the Night,* is set in as novelist, historian, activist, and observed from without by a narrator, also Mailer. Mailer watching Mailer, all only slightly distanced from Mailer the writer of the sequence: what succeeds here is precisely the overwhelming concern with self and ego that makes it difficult for Mailer to succeed as a novelist.

The real question revolves around whether a new genre has emerged from the work of the last fifteen years. The argument for the new genre is, I believe, hyperbolic, overly ambitious, and neglectful of critical issues. Defenders argue that the polarities of fact and fiction are insufficient to delineate a fragmented, noncontinuous, seemingly incoherent reality. New realities require new perceptions, new forms. They suggest a new genre founded on its own terms, its own categories, movements, narrative devices, characters, plot. The old "totalizing perspective"* no longer obtains. According to this argument, an older society was coherent enough to encourage an epistemology which "views reality as an objective and knowable entity governed in its behavior by rational laws discoverable by the reasoning individual." This type of

---

*The term comes from Mas'ud Zavarzadeh's *The Mythopoeic Reality* (1976), the most organized of the studies of the new form, one that attempts a "Poetics" of nonfiction novels, to give to this form what Frye and Auerbach have defined for older forms.

novel is "closely related to the bourgeois liberal outlook." Under such conditions, we have a "totalizing modern novel—in which the fictionist interpreted the 'human condition' in the light of a comprehensive private world view." This must give way to a "supramodernist narrative with zero degree of interpretation."

In such a "zero degree" era, what worked as plot in the old fictional forms can no longer function, and we have instead something suitable for nonfiction forms, *aplotic,* which lies between plot and nonplot. A similar vocabulary can be worked out, something along the lines of Brooks and Warren's work in *Understanding Poetry* a generation ago or at present in the definitions of deconstructionists at Yale. The aim is to support the coming generation of nonfictionists who, "through a neutral registration of experiential situations, have captured the fictive nature of technetronic culture." This new breed is distinct from the "transfictionists," those like Barth, Barthelme, Pynchon, and Steven Katz, who have also repudiated the "totalizing novel."

In this general view of nonfictionists, the goal of the writer—to recall Conrad's words—is to "make you see"; but the goal is better achieved, it is felt, by film and television than by the traditional novel. The popular media have introduced such powerful means of "seeing" that the novel must rely on other forms which can bring back "seeing" to the printed word. The nonfiction novel becomes the new form, the new way of observing. The latter begins with "zero degree of interpretation," and it is not unusual that in this realm Andy Warhol's *a* (1968) is heroic. Warhol reduced all to zero by way of the small first letter; minimal beginnings are all we are capable of. Warhol's tape-recorded words are *aplotic, acharacter, anarrative,* and they reflect our world more validly than the old plotted, character-filled novels.

Part of this vision of the new involves what has disappeared. Barthes's "writing degree zero" becomes significant in that it covers the disappearance of elements. Wallace Stevens's "sovereign image" has vanished, giving way to secondary and tertiary elements. Joyce's epiphanic presentation is no longer valid, for it presupposed an ordered universe; whereas the present universe is so enormously complex no system can encompass it. Only a neutral "fiction" can approximate the contrasts, conflicts, and contradictions.

This is the argument for a "new fiction," which the nonfiction novel seems to meet. Yet one weakness of this defense is that its supporters view the past as ordered and perceive older fictions as "totalizing," or fully coherent. We need seek only as far as *Ulysses* to observe Joyce recreating our experience within terms now given over to the nonfiction novel. Joyce's use of a single day indicated we can comprehend only a day, not a year or a life. He removed himself from the consciousness of his characters and refused to embody any "totalizing" experience. He focused on a daily routine as a signal that coherence was impossible to achieve. He shifted from a dominant or "sovereign image" to secondary and marginal elements. He eschewed social and political controversy in any larger sense and remained neutral in most other areas —zero degree neutrality. His use of a freely associated stream has its counterpart in the tape recorders of present nonfictionists like Warhol and Oscar Lewis.

A good example of the weakness of these distinctions comes with Oscar Lewis's use of real people in *La Vida* and *The Children of Sánchez*. Lewis's defense of his methods took many forms, one of them being that his people were "real people" and therefore one could speak to them about their roles in the respective books. They reinforced the idea of the nonfiction novel in that they were only themselves, not part of any larger coherence or superimposed structure. Yet proponents of the method, and it works well in Lewis, forget he indulged in novelistic practices. He edited the tapes, excised material as repetitious and irrelevant, chose what to include or exclude, decided how much space to give to a character, translated, since his characters spoke in Spanish. These are not, as we are led to expect, neutral maneuvers, for they involve the most profound elements of novelistic practice, including the use of language.

Further, in transcribing these tapes, Lewis turned an oral tradition into written words, and that in itself involves a vast reordering of experience. For he lost movement, gesture, tone, rhythms, pacing, anger, joy, indifference. This is not even to speak of translation, which in itself changes the nature of the culture of the original. Lewis transformed illiterate or semiliterate speech patterns into an ordered, systematized, linear pattern. He did the very thing accomplished by the bourgeois novelist: turned apparently neutral data into a system, into an ordering.

Still further, while Lewis desired a multiple point of view, at a certain point he had to decide on a limited number of referents. Multiplicity is infinite, but space is restricted. Lewis controlled this flow:

space, number, questions, cutoff points. Similarly, on a more trivial project, Warhol in *a* made many critical decisions about his tapes. He chose his participants, mainly or exclusively homosexual, a choice which influenced everything that would follow; he decided to use a Bohemian quarter in New York City —quite a different atmosphere would have developed from, say, Indianapolis, Indiana. He allowed a duration of twenty-four hours. A week or a month, or more, would have provided more tapes to edit and, perhaps, a greater swing of mood and pace. So far, all the results, which may appear arbitrary, are made up of choices, and many of them are choices also made by novelists.

Suppose we praise the book's arbitrary character: its lack of a central narrator or a shaping experience, its notational method, which Zavarzadeh calls "narrative pointillism." Thus, the lack of conceptual relationships and ordering is a sign of Warhol's innovative exploitation of the nonfiction novel. We see Warhol as "surprised" by his material, as much as is the reader; and in this, the two are equated. Yet every distinction made here is in a way false; for Warhol created this setting, these characters, this time span. He turned on the tape, turned it off, spliced as he wished.

The writers of so-called transfiction achieve far more profound results. Gaddis, Pynchon, and Barth have let the tape run—especially Gaddis in *JR;* but they have not abdicated their roles. Whether writers or splicers of tape, they are in control; and to argue that they are not is to seek an excuse for them. Warhol perhaps wanted a book at the level of his Campbell's Soup cans. The cans can "work" in the plastic dimension because they are the visual equivalent on paper or canvas of what we are already familiar with; the transition from market to studio work calls up a familiarity, which we can then relegate to mockery, reinforcement, or nostalgia. This is painting following from television. But when Warhol tries to put the soup cans into words, which is what *a* is, then he has moved laterally across media which do not accommodate each other. The verbal level brings with it certain expectations, precisely as the plastic level does; and Warhol's flat-out transcription, like his films, does not come into any verbal focus.

We should stress that the best nonfictional works gain their qualities from how closely they use novelistic devices. That is, the novel remains the standard, and the nonfictional work is asymptotic. The finest works in the nonfictional subgenre do not define their own territory; they define an area, as we shall see, contingent on what the novel purports to do. And such works are judged not by separate values or criteria but by the way in which they can assimilate the novelistic tradition. Mailer's *Executioner's Song* fails to the degree he abdicates the novelist's responsibility: that is, when he confronts what he cannot interpret in Gary Gilmore, he backs off and describes Gilmore's "fixed look." The very things we want to know about Gilmore—how he was motivated, what made him run—are missing, and these are novelistic qualities. Mailer tried to create Raskolnikov without internal motivation, without depth psychology. The result is a paper-thin Gilmore whose existential life is far more nasty, even without the murders, than Mailer seems to recognize.

Tom Wicker's *A Time to Die*, which is one of the very finest works in this subgenre, touches all bases. Wicker is modest about what he can do, and what he accomplishes is astonishing. At a near comparable level of achievement, we can include Tom Wolfe's *The Electric Kool-Aid Acid Test*, Capote's *In Cold Blood*, Whittaker Chambers's *Witness*, parts of *The Armies of the Night*, segments of Oscar Lewis's *La Vida* and *The Children of Sánchez*, *The Autobiography of Malcolm X* (arranged, edited, and written by Alex Haley), and Maxine Hong Kingston's *The Woman Warrior*. Simply to list these examples will suggest how varied the subgenre is: from reported events to autobiography written by oneself or by another, to tape-recorded "history." Clearly, the only literary linkage among them is their common pursuit of novelistic techniques which will reflect their particular form of experience.

Even when such works buck against the novel, they are testing out its resilience. The nonfiction novel or new journalism is not satisfied with unadorned reality, simple story fact, traditional reportorial effects. In this respect, it opposes mimetic representation, opposes conventions of reality, opposes the event itself—whether Wolfe's journey into disorder, Mailer's Pentagon march, or Wicker's Attica Prison insurrection. Such works move against clear and defined meaning, against sharp delineation of subject and object. The revolt here is not against fiction but against simplistic ways of perceiving: which is to say that the influence of the modern novel is everywhere. The nonfiction novel is the beneficiary of those techniques which have always informed fiction and which, in particular, characterize postwar fiction in its modernist phase.

AUTOBIOGRAPHY AS NONFICTIONAL NOVEL

Maxine Hong Kingston's *The Woman Warrior: Memoirs of a Girlhood Among Ghosts* (1976) could be termed a female version of Henry Roth's *Call It Sleep,* a nonfictional counterpart of "growing up," in which a personal memoir uses nearly every device of postwar fiction.

The narrator is the girl "among ghosts," and she controls her story. The narrative depends on the various roles she must play: in her imagination, as she fits herself into the ghosts of her parents' background, and in the reality of her life as a Chinese American, caught between two cultures. Her mother offers ghosts, and American life offers only actuality. Trapped between the "warrior" status of her cultural past and the "student" status of her present, she must grow up, a girl in a society that places little value on its girls. As a swordswoman and heroine of her people —that is, as a warrior—she would count for much; but as a student, she must insist on her identity at every turn. And her mother, despite her medical training, insists on a Chinese culture completely antithetical to science and to the narrator's childhood.

Forward movement depends on a young girl growing up and trying to find her identity; but her test comes, not in her ability to make A's in school or to achieve anything, but in her ability to overcome the ghosts of the past. Despite the mother's own achievement as a medical student, she stresses the dysfunction of girls, the lack of value placed on them and on women. From birth, a girl-child was virtually doomed. "I hope," says the narrator, "this holeless baby [one born without an anus] proves that my mother did not prepare a box of clean ashes beside the birth bed in case of a girl." For midwives or relatives would turn the face of the newborn girl-child into the ashes. There is always the suspicion that her mother was no different, and that the survival of the narrator resulted from her birth in America, not in the China of her mother's past.

Such ghosts may kill as well as entertain, bind as well as exorcise the present. The ghost stories have great charm, especially the early one about the swordswoman who sets forth to save her people from evil landlords; but these stories also fix the past as a prison. A Chinese-American girl must not only negotiate the infinite varieties of the American present; she must somehow blend with that past as expected of her by her parents. If we compare her with the Mexican girls in Oscar Lewis's studies, we see how Mexicans move into the present, with few restraints, even religion; whereas the Chinese girl must straddle cultures: present one face to the past (Chinese culture, history, parents, ancestors), the other to herself, her own future.

A sixteen-year-old slave girl, purchased by the narrator's mother for $180—twenty dollars less than doctor and hospital fees at the narrator's birth—has been trained as a nurse, although she could have been kept as a slavey. The narrator senses: "My mother's enthusiasm for me is duller than for the slave girl. . . . Throughout childhood my young sister said, 'When I grow up, I want to be a slave,' and my parents laughed, encouraging her."

Spells, ghosts, phantoms, shamans: these control the narrator's mother, who sees the cultural past as missing pieces in a puzzle, without which her world would disintegrate. Her scientific background is grafted on, never integrated. Against this, the young narrator must emerge as her parents' child and as her own person. The emergence of the youthful girl is, then, the subject of this memoir, one steeped in images and metaphors of life and death. For those ghosts must not be minimized; they are forces for life, although for the American girl they may seem more matters of death. Yet she dedicates her book to her mother and father, indicating that her college years at Berkeley and her marriage to a Caucasian have not completely exorcised the ghosts.

For the non-Chinese reader, those images of the past cannot be written off as charming or culturally enriching. Many of our critics, especially when speaking of Jews, sometimes of Italians, describe the growing-up period with nostalgia, arguing that life is strengthened through hard work and commitment to principle. What the critics neglect—and what novelists provide (Philip Roth, especially, or Malamud)— is a recognition of how individually devastating such "charm" or "enrichment" can be. Kingston's life could easily have been destroyed by the cultural past.

The narrator's loss of voice, precisely the image Jerzy Kosinski used in *The Painted Bird,* emblemizes her traumatization. Her vocal cords damaged by her mother, she speaks in barely a whisper, even worse, in squeaks and quacks—a Peking duck. Cultivating either silence or a voice less than human, she melts into the woodwork at school, and only one other girl, who refuses to utter any sound, carries silence further. In one of the most moving scenes in the book, the narrator corners the silent girl in a washroom and batters her, to induce an utterance; but the girl remains silent until her sister rescues her. That use of

silence, which gives the narrator a "zero IQ" in the first grade, is both a weapon and a devastating trauma. Her outlook turned to silent observation, her language neither English nor Chinese, the narrator must deal with ghosts in a way not perceived by those who find the past culturally charming.

The book is ingeniously organized, so that the main part of the young girl's observations come in early childhood, or seem to. Although the ultimate voice is that of the grown woman, a retrospect, the narrative involves mainly stories she heard as a child. She begins to emerge quite late in the book, and then only in glimpses and brief sequences, except with the silent girl at school. One of the loveliest passages comes when she is still very young—she is born in the middle of World War II—and she perceives America as full of ghosts, the ghosts of her mother's tales transferred to these shores. "But America," she observes, "has been full of machines and ghosts—Taxi Ghosts, Bus Ghosts, Police Ghosts, Fire Ghosts, Meter Reader Ghosts, Tree Trimming Ghosts, Five-and-Dime Ghosts. Once upon a time the world was so thick with ghosts, I could hardly breathe; I could hardly walk, limping my way around the White Ghosts and their cars. There were Black Ghosts too, but they were open eyed and full of laughter, more distinct than White Ghosts."

But these ghosts are only the beginning. What frightens her most is the Newsboy Ghosts: "Carrying a newspaper pouch instead of a baby brother, he walked right out in the middle of the street without his parents. He shouted ghost words to the empty streets. His voice reached children inside the houses, reached inside the children's chests. They would come running out of their yards with their dimes." She and her sister pretended they were Newsboy Ghosts and collected old Chinese newspapers and shouted around their yard that they had papers for sale. When the real newsboy arrived, they would hide under the stairs or in cellars.

The ghosts carried everywhere. In the supermarket, she had to traffic with the Grocery Ghost and ghost customers. There were the Milk Ghost, who delivered without being seen; the Mail Ghost, Garbage Ghost, Social Worker Ghost, Nurse Ghost, even "two Jesus Ghosts who had formerly worked in China." The enumeration only reinforces her sense of America as a ghost-land, with people performing ghost functions, slipping in and out of our lives unobserved. Most jobs we take for granted are ghost jobs, roles without a performer. For the narrator to achieve herself, she must sort out these ghosts, not only of the recent past, but of her present, of her life.

The Woman Warrior is so successful, and so nearly erases boundaries between fiction and nonfiction, because Kingston has been able to find images (ghosts, silence, loss of voice, the weight of a discordant cultural past) which help to define her narrator. She can define her life only with her emerging brain, achieving A's at school, learning to write English well (even while not speaking), catching the eyes of her teachers. And yet all the while she is defining the way in which she can emerge and escape, her mother is preparing her for a different role, even to matching her with a mentally retarded young man who seems rich. From her mother's point of view, she is fit only for this young man; if he is a suitor, then she might think of accepting. He comes to the laundry and brings gifts, toys, devotion. His presence causes the narrator to find her voice and express her emerging self: "my throat burst open. I stood up, talking and burbling. . . . You think you can give me away to freaks. . . . I may be ugly and clumsy, but one thing I'm not, I'm not retarded. There's nothing wrong with my brain. . . . I'm smart. I can do all kinds of things. I know how to get A's, and they say I could be a scientist or a mathematician if I want. I can make a living."

How similar to this is the ranting Philip Roth protagonist, who screams out his independence from the cultural past in, usually, self-destructive acts; or Henry Roth's David Shearl, who prefers death and transfiguration to home. Kingston protests, but as a Chinese girl, she is not full of hateful rebellion. She seeks herself, not the destruction of what the past means for others. Once she recovers her tongue, words are all she needs. She can already write; now she can speak. She has broken free, liberated to pursue her own ghosts. The liberation is her version of the sixties generational break; like the protagonists in *Goodbye, Columbus,* she strives for survival, on her terms.

When, earlier in the book, we see her return home, a grown woman, she can barely stand her mother's ways. She develops a splitting midday headache, she has the makings of a cold, her health begins to go. Her illnesses are her response to the roles her mother's talk-story had insisted on, from her aunt who kills herself after giving birth to a bastard child to the "woman warrior" who wanted to use magic to overturn the emperor. All these "roles" are implicit in her mother's presence, and they evoke not only the magic of the past but its inappropriateness. Her weapon for response is illness, the signal to her of how she can deal with her mother's world: suffer for it, and yet reject it totally, without rejecting her mother. A "woman warrior," she supports all necessary roles.

By shifting the focus slightly, we can move to a work that may seem diametrically opposite, *The Autobiography of Malcolm X;* and yet, despite vast cultural differences, we have "The Woman Warrior" now become "The Male Warrior," the self-made hero of a picaresque novel. The model for Alex Haley's novelistic treatment of Malcolm Little's story was Richard Wright's *Black Boy,* and behind that lay the picaresque novel of the eighteenth century, in which a young man sets out to achieve himself against any number of adversary elements. His progress toward achievement is made through land mines, and defects in his own character contribute as much grief as others' opposition and hostility. Such is Haley's story of Malcolm, from Little to X, in which Haley is writer, editor, splicer of tapes, final arbiter of his subject's life as it is to be presented. Haley shapes Malcolm X in the book as much as the latter has shaped his own life in order to present it to Haley. We have, then, that novelistic dimension associated with *The Woman Warrior,* although in that book subject and object are one. Because Malcolm X's story is so large, he has become fixed in our imagination as one of the great literary figures of the past—Raskolnikov, Pierre Bezuhov, Stephen Dedalus, Joseph K. Our points of reference are novelistic.

Malcolm X's story is of sin and redemption, a black version of the Faustian legend; at the same time, it is very much a 1960s story. When we see Malcolm X historically, in the development of the Nation of Islam, we may forget how much he was a figure of those final years before his assassination, when he assumed several roles and became a tragic person. As the most representative figure of the black revolution, or what passed for it, Malcolm X embodied nearly every aspect of the decade; and with his death, black factions bickered and split, or dissolved altogether. He was, as we see him, both real and fictional: the Malcolm X of this or that position, and the Malcolm X who has become legendary, the sixties spirit, the conscience for whites and blacks.

Put another way, if Richard Wright had lived into the 1960s and been able to capture the decade's spirit by way of black aspirations, he would have written the story of Malcolm X, who lived out the violent, on-the-edge existence Wright's various "underground men" either survived or succumbed to. In his person and aspirations, Malcolm X refused the role of Ellison's invisible man and chose the roles of Wright's characters. He refuted, however, Wright's early (1944) position—in a passage already cited—that the danger to the white majority would come not from blacks who rebel, but from "those who no longer respond to the system in which they live." Wright continued, in what has become commonplace for the 1970s: "I would make it known that the real danger does not stem from those who seek to grab their share of wealth through force, or from those who try to defend their property through violence, for both of these groups, by their affirmative acts, support the values of the system in which they live. The millions that I would fear are those who do not dream of the prizes that the nation holds forth, for it is in them, though they may not know it, that a revolution has taken place and is biding its time to translate itself into a new and strange way of life." He concludes: "They [the white majority] never dream that they would face a situation far more terrifying if they were confronted by Negroes who made no claims at all than by those who are buoyed by social aggressiveness."

Malcolm X's rejection of this paradox—that a black on welfare is more of a threat to a white society than a black wielding a gun—does not change the fact that he acted out in life what Wright's characters pursued in fiction. Although there are aspects of Bigger Thomas in Malcolm X, a closer affinity is with Cross Damon, "the outsider." Damon's life lacks the integration Malcolm X acquired by way of the Nation of Islam, but parallels are so evident we marvel at Wright's grasp of a black archetype.

Pivotal in *The Outsider* (1953) is the dying of the old and the beginning of the new: that transformation which permits Damon to move out from under his cross, but not entirely. The transformation, in fact, brings with it other aspects of the cross, as Malcolm X's change carried with it, under the Muslims, a different kind of danger and potential death than he had experienced earlier as a street kid. Damon is reported dead in a Chicago train accident, and he seizes that opportunity to reappear with a new identity, Lionel Lane, the name from a cemetery; Malcolm Little "dies" and reappears as Malcolm X. But while Damon must deceive and lie in order to become Lane, Malcolm X opens himself up to what he considers to be the truth. Nevertheless, in both instances, the transformation permits a second chance, Damon toward further forms of deception, Malcolm X toward revelation. In another way, *The Autobiography of Malcolm X* is kin to those picaresque novels in which the rogue achieves self-knowledge and, finally, acceptance of sorts. With the modern and black version, however, whether Wright or Malcolm X, there is only process, not acceptance, peace, or resolution.

Wright's conception of Damon's life as discrete, disconnected events is very similar to the way Malcolm X saw *his* life before he discovered Elijah Muhammad. Wright views Damon in Sartrean terms, in which dissolving phenomena can be made coherent only by way of the individual's imposition of himself. The fact that experience is chaotic—and once again we see parallels with Malcolm X—gives the outsider the opportunity to impose himself in infinite ways.

Malcolm X accepts the discreteness of forms until he creates order by means of his religious beliefs; but then, when he discovers Muhammad's sexual profligacy, that world breaks into fragments, and he must, once more, choose freedom. That is, he must reshape himself through choice or else become enslaved to deception. When he was assassinated, he was attempting to choose his way into other forms, refusing slavery, which meant thralldom to easy resolutions. His misunderstood remark when Kennedy was shot in Dallas, that it was a case of "the chickens coming home to roost," suggested a formless, violent, contingent world in which anything was possible, in which men did not have free choice to create their own worlds.

The remark at the time suggested vengeance, even pleasure that someone as mighty as the young President had suffered what blacks had long suffered.* But the remark was not anomalous; it was continuous with Malcolm X's desire for freedom for himself and for blacks, in that area of choice suggested by Wright in *The Outsider* and Ellison in *Invisible Man.* Existentialism has more or less run its course in contemporary fiction and we have tired of its application, but exhaustion with its ideas should not blind us to its appropriateness to black life. Within that frame of reference of formless experience and discrete events, Malcolm X had the potential for passing into ever greater slavery. His inability to evade the police for his burglaries served paradoxically, by way of prison, as his means toward freedom. Prison gave shape to his life for the first time, and from that, as Cross

---

*In *The Autobiography,* Malcolm X explains the remark by asserting that hate, which led to the murder of so many blacks, had spread into the entire culture. "Allowed to spread unchecked, [it] finally had struck down this country's Chief of State." He cites Medgar Evers and Patrice Lumumba as comparable victims of such hatred.

Damon from his trials, he was able to perceive ways in which he could assert choices. By associating himself with an organization requiring decorum and fixed forms of behavior, Malcolm X found that paradoxical freedom described in Kierkegaard and others.

The Autobiography touches upon fiction, but then retreats. For Malcolm X's motives are more interesting than what he reveals of them, and Alex Haley does not intrude as an author would to explain motives. But we would like to know how significant Elijah Muhammad's sexual acts were in Malcolm X's break from the Nation of Islam, as measured against his desire to assert *his* kind of Muslim belief, *his* perceptions of black-white relationships, *his* sense of black separatism. All of these were reshaping themselves in his mind just before his death, and they are as significant in his break from the Nation of Islam as its leader's flaws.

One memory that haunted Malcolm X in his last months was his response to "a sweet white girl" who followed him to ask what *she,* she alone, could do to alleviate racial tensions; he had answered, "Nothing!" It was, he recognized, a smart-alecky response, and he had in a sense forfeited his freedom by disallowing hers. What became an increasing perception on his part was that individual black freedom was connected, in some tenuous way, with white freedom. Like Cross Damon in his fencing with Ely Houston (whose hunched back supposedly gives him insight into Damon's blackness), Malcolm X fences with ideas of whites and those blacks (like Martin Luther King) who associate with whites. This movement toward other perceptions, which a novel could have developed as paradox, irony, or simply textured process, remains unfulfilled in *The Autobiography,* especially since Malcolm X was assassinated while these ideas were still formative.

Alex Haley's commentary in the long Epilogue (almost eighty pages) carries along the narrative but does not clarify areas of thought and motivation, which would have been novelistic. Not that *The Autobiography* needed to be a novel; but Haley's presentation of Malcolm X's background suggests a novelistic treatment. The early family life, subsequent developments, life in Boston and its environs, and other activities all suggest the career of the picaro. That forward movement continues for ten chapters, until the chapter called "Saved," in which Malcolm, caught between Little and the soon-to-be X, bends his knee before something he accepts as larger than himself. At the time, the principle of Islam is not so much religious as ethical; by bowing to it, he acquiesces to

a moral order suitable for him. His previous life had been a denial of the bent knee, for he could, like Wright's Cross Damon, have found some niche and remained hidden away as a slave. The deference here, however, is not slavery but a greater expression of self within limitations. Acceptance of this role, which is the epitome of the book, has the quality of a novelistic climax, a moment of truth, the point of revelation.

At this stage, less than halfway through, the novelistic treatment implicit in Haley's shaping of the book gives way to political and historical considerations. It is just here that we need some sounding board. Once Malcolm X defines himself and becomes a worldwide character, we do not see, until the very end, any measure of doubt, any measure of conflict. Only his split with Elijah Muhammad creates that conflict and doubt; and at one point, he frankly and courageously tells a reporter he had no real position but was open and flexible. At the very time he began viewing whites not as devils but as themselves nourished by a racist society which "brings out the lowest, most base part of human beings," we have a dramatic novelistic moment: when tragedy is potential because intense choices are at hand.

Revelation, divulgation, confession, redemption, freedom: all the great themes coalesce in this area; and Malcolm X was on the edge of them. At the time he intuits that his immediate future is full of inexplicables, even death itself, his narrative is at an end; another ten pages concludes the book. Haley cannot recover the internal tensions, nor the tragic moment implicit in great choices. Malcolm Little had once aligned himself with Nat Turner and John Brown; but now he was on the edge of a different intuition. If anything, he was more humble than when he deferred to the Nation of Islam; humble enough to admit he was open and flexible, not didactic, not the angel of vengeance. The book should at this point soar, but it ends; and Haley's commentary can only fill in political details and the assassination.

Once Haley had completed his draft, Malcolm X wanted to redo parts, and since he had broken with Elijah Muhammad, he wanted to change his account of his former master. But Haley convinced him to remain true to the way it was, not to the way it had become.* Yet if Malcolm X had written his own au-

*For example, Malcolm X asks Haley whose book it was, his or Haley's, and the latter responds, " 'Yours, of course.' " This gives Malcolm X the right to change everything: "I was heart-sick at the prospect that he might want to re-edit the entire book into a polemic against Elijah Muhammad." Al-

tobiography, without outside aid, he would have revised the draft to fit his current state of mind; or he might have restressed elements so as to realign them with his current thinking. No one, except himself, would have known of this, and the revised draft would have become the book. In this respect, then, Malcolm X would have projected a different involvement with Elijah Muhammad, a different Nation of Islam, and a differently weighted commitment. The emphasis of the entire account would have shifted.

This is of great interest, since it demonstrates how shifting are matters of personal history as they feed into fiction. As history, we feel we have here the truth of Malcolm X's conversion to Islam and his relationship to the temple in Chicago. Yet we have this sense of truth only because Malcolm X did not have the time, or literary gifts, perhaps, to write his own autobiography. When he brought in Haley, he passed the "truth" of his story to another; and we have this version only because Haley prevailed to prevent alterations. How clearly we see where nonfiction and fiction touch, how embedded they are in each other! Malcolm's "story"—which he sees as "fact"—becomes Haley's version of that fact in *his* novelistic treatment; and yet the factual Malcolm would have fictionalized his account if he had not passed it on to Haley, who, as the novelist of the material, insisted on keeping the factual accuracy (or what he assumed was factual accuracy) of the original events. We reach back toward *Don Quixote!*

Another turn and we move into *Witness* (1952), Whittaker Chambers's version of his life, that of an existential and picaresque hero, a man who moves through underworlds and undergrounds as much as Malcolm X and who exists among ghosts of the past. Just as Malcolm X becomes a fictional character in Haley's presentation, as well as being the historical personage who went from Little to X, so Chambers sees himself as a literary figure in a drama created by the gods and as a historical personage acting out one of the great political dramas of modern times.

Although events and emotions in *Witness* purport to be truly autobiographical, and therefore valid, they are also the product of a powerful novelistic intelligence. Chambers views himself as a character in a Dostoyevskian drama, torn by emotions so powerful he has moved to the extremes of human behavior,

though Malcolm X let the account remain, Haley comments he never again gave him chapters without being present to forestall possible changes.

where light and dark interpenetrate and the individual moves along margins. Here, at the edge, the individual observes his distinction from the average run of men, a Nietzschean superbeing, and revels in both his suffering and his difference. He is made superior by pain. In this respect, as well as others, *Witness* fits into the 1950s, a decade dominated by counterfeit selves and the need for "recognitions."

What Chambers has witnessed, moreover, becomes, in the novelistic sense, less significant than the impressions these observations made upon him. The distinction between fiction and nonfiction lies here. In nonfiction, the matter at hand is the object being observed; in fictional handling, the important element is the impression or emotional reaction of the registering consciousness, whether an author outside or a surrogate figure inside. By becoming a witness of his own story, Chambers has sufficiently muddied the distinctions, playing an object in a drama observed from without by a man who has risen from object to subject.

The plan of the autobiography is novelistic. The line of personal reportage is a narrative, with the climax coming in Chambers's confrontation with Alger Hiss in the courts. But hundreds of pages before that confrontation, Chambers fills in with numerous Hiss stories. Like a novel, and unlike the more chronological movement of autobiography, Chambers roves back and forth, giving us glimpses of Hiss as we are moved toward the great climax. Hiss and his wife, Priscilla, weave in and out of the Chamberses' lives, as close friends, as the former owners of their car, Hiss as someone who brings home his briefcase so that the contents can be photographed by the next morning. All these details, as Chambers presents them, are historical facts, elements of his autobiography, and details which propel a suspense novel.

Chambers's father cannot bear to be around his two sons; he cannot tolerate affection; and, apparently, he cannot bear family life. He lives by himself in their home, so that the family's only feelings of freedom come when he leaves. He returns, however, and daily life is such that Chambers runs away to find work after high school and his brother enters a pattern of self-destruction that leads to suicide. As Chambers writes: "Beneath our quiet, we were wretchedly unhappy. My mother was not a mother. She was nothing. She was trying to be both father and mother. She dominated through her love, which was genuine, tender and sacrificing, but was dangerous. . . . 'My mother does not want me to grow up,' I thought." His family life had no mind, he says, only activity; no plans, only a few hopes.

But for the young Chambers, the family malady, while a powerful influence on his development, is not all. Although he did not understand it then, he came to see that the personal malady was connected to a larger one, to the materialism and godlessness which prevailed outside: "the disorder that overtakes societies and families when a world has lost its soul." He views his life as a quest for the lost way, and he sees himself, somehow, as messianic; through personal suffering and redemption, he will discover a world now lost. Thus, Chambers prepares us for his entrance into the Communist Party. For not only did it hold out the paternalism and need for blind loyalty he failed to find in his family; it also offered some exit from the malaise, from capitalistic materialism and selfishness, toward some "purification" of self in the service of others. Of course, this idol, too, proved tainted.

His hatred of the modern has long roots. At the turn of the century, such hatred was focused in Max Nordau's *Degeneration* (1895, 1911), which traced increases in abnormality and degeneration to the growth of aesthetics and decadence in both art and life. Nordau had many followers, and one of them, Francis Warrington Dawson, tried to form a Fresh Air Art Society, whose charter member was to have been Joseph Conrad. The idea of a healthy art and healthy life has Ruskinian roots, as well, and its manifestations in the twentieth century have been particularly virulent. It resulted in the banning of modern art in Nazi Germany and the Soviet Union, the fixing of state standards for all the arts, in fact. Chambers's reaction to the malady of modern life looks back to this and to Dostoyevsky, forward to Solzhenitsyn: the aim, purification by way of suffering and redemption. Like Alyosha Karamazov, Chambers holds as his highest goal a state of grace.

In these terms, Chambers's involvement for thirteen years in the Communist Party, above ground as well as in its underground, makes sense. So does his break with it when he recognized he had sadly misplaced his trust. Chambers is a man who had to live at the extremes. When he breaks with the Party, he speaks of the fear in which he and his family lived, of writing with a revolver at his side. But this fear is something he seeks. He may exalt peace and tranquillity, woods and farming, but he needed to sense life at the edge of the abyss. To make up, perhaps, for a silent childhood, he sought circumstances whereby he could embrace adventure. Other young men went to sea or war, or joined the foreign legion; Chambers joined the Party.

His "feminine" given name, Vivian, caused nothing but pain in school. Chambers revels in the name changes he experienced in the Party—Bob, Carl, George Crosley, others. He was secreted under layers of disguises. Most Communists who met him were certain he was not an American, but a Russian with a good American accent. His ability to move among several foreign languages—nearly all his communication as a Communist was done in German—was a further form of disguise. The boy Jay (after his father) Vivian Chambers, born in Philadelphia, growing up in Lynbrook, Long Island, yearned to bury that life for one that provided excitement and danger. The later confrontation with Hiss could be viewed, in the novelistic sense, as Chambers's need to push himself still closer to the edge: to jeopardize all in order to bury the dull self of his childhood.

While working at *Time* and then during the hearings, when the pressures were almost unbearable, Chambers returns for restoration to his small farm near Westminster, Maryland. With its animals and plowed lands, the farm represents for him all that is best in America; and it is precisely this type of America the Communists were devoted to destroying. Chambers's value system becomes clear, derivative as it is from nineteenth-century America. Communists are filthy urban dwellers, parasites; Chambers's descriptions of them in his earlier years locate them in subways and subway stations, on downtown streets, amidst the detritus and rot of modern cities. They move out of shadows; they lurk and peer, like criminals and pimps. They not only deceive and cheat their country; they lie to themselves. Much of the time they are little stunted men from Eastern Europe, frequently Jews. Although Chambers shows no overt anti-Semitism in the book, the cast of his mind in pitting the stunted urban type against the farmer is a traditional way of exhibiting the Jew as an outcast who fouls his own nest.

In this struggle, Chambers repeatedly casts himself as a heroic type. He views himself as David taking up "my little sling," or as Samson bringing down the temple on the Philistines. The whole cast of his political thought falls into the stereotypes of urban man pitted against the land, against the farmer, even against birds. Hiss, who could have represented the best, becomes demonic; God and the devil cast the dice, and mankind's fate lies in the balance.

It is not exaggerating to stress Chambers's messianic role. The political ideology of Chambers cannot, really, be separated from the messianic Chambers. What makes *Witness* so compelling, despite its risible political stance, its admiration for Richard Nixon, J. Parnell Thomas, Karl Mundt, Henry Luce, is the way in which Chambers maneuvers himself; like a chivalric medieval knight, he tilts against enemies of good, exposing himself to destruction. For Chambers, the New Deal was not a means by which Roosevelt could help to save foundering capitalism, but part of an international socialist movement. While the mass of those who supported the New Deal were sincere, by their support they gave themselves over to a drift toward socialistic control. Begin with the New Deal and end with Stalinism: "For men who could not see that what they firmly believed was liberalism added up to socialism could scarcely be expected to see what added up to Communism." We can better understand how Chambers embraced the Un-American Activities Committee, since its members—Thomas (who later went to prison), Nixon (who went into exile), Mundt (who fell into senility while representing South Dakota)—built political careers on exploiting these fears.

We are not here interested in politics, nor, certainly, in who was vindicated, Hiss or Chambers. We are concerned with Chambers's literary self-portrait, which, in turn, is based on his play of political ideas. It was not by chance that Chambers moved up the ladder at *Time,* to become a senior editor; for Henry Luce, too, had seen himself in the messianic role. *Time* gave Chambers his forum. Vivian Chambers, reviled in school, the outsider for many years, had found his destiny. Role-playing had paid off. Chambers's political ideas during the Second World War and just after—essential here in order for us to observe how he structured his roles—were predicated on the Soviet Union as the real enemy. ". . . the Soviet Union . . . was a calculating enemy making use of World War II to prepare for World War III. . . . The Chinese Communists were not 'agrarian liberals,' but Chinese Communists, after the Russian Communist Party, the Number One section of the Communist International."

The game was power, whether in the world or at the editorial level at *Time.* "It is all but impossible to convey briefly the special pressures that can be brought to bear upon a man who finds himself almost alone in a struggle for control of an important political department of the news." Chambers is clear that the winner of the struggle may control what the free world will think. If he, Chambers, loses out to the weak liberals or pro-Communist sympathizers at *Time,* then the free world may spin out of control. Chambers invests his every move with this sense of destiny; the marginal boy in a household with no love, no reciprocated feelings, will help lead the free world toward its rightful destiny.*

The last third of the book is concerned with the Hiss case. Again, what is of most interest is not the historical development (or nonfictional aspect) of this riveting affair, but Chambers's (novelistic) perception of his role in it. Now he is no longer simply the Don tilting at those who will not listen; he is a victorious Hercules who has finally completed his onerous tasks. His words, he says, called upon men to save themselves before it was too late. With that, "a segment of the greatest conspiracy in the nation's history heaved through the slick of public indifference, at the moment in history and the place where its disclosure was most relevant—in the shadow of the Capitol it threatened." Neither the President (Truman), nor the Secretary of State (Acheson), nor any of Chambers's antagonists are conscious of this threat; he must carry the burden while the rest are out to lunch. Hiss—so well named, the serpent of the underworld myth—is the man of glamour; Chambers, pudgy, with poor orthodontia, possessor of lesser credentials, the informer and betrayer of confidences, is almost forgettable. Yet with the help of a Nixon, a Mundt, a Thomas, he will prevail.

Although written at the very beginning of the 1950s, *Witness* links up with books written by an author with very different political views, Norman Mailer. *Witness* is contemporaneous with *Barbary Shore,* but in particular looks ahead to Mailer's fine essay "The White Negro" and, still further, to *An American Dream,* in the mid-1960s. Both authors are writing forms of dramatized autobiography, in which the self is the most significant character. Although Chambers argues throughout that his mission is to reveal and help destroy the world communistic movement, we could argue that he has created a self-serving role, more personal than political. The name-playing, the scenarios, the dangers (actual or implied), the calling attention to himself, the unraveling of plots within plots, the bringing down of a high public official are all fantasy desires, the young Vivian Chambers finally demonstrating his worth. Chambers testifying before senators, queried by FBI agents, seeking out Under Secretary of State Berle, tele-

---

*Chambers's mantle has now passed on to *Commentary* magazine, in a transformation that began a decade ago. America must be saved from itself by a handful of "neo-conservative" zealots, and history must be rewritten to make this possible: thus, nonfiction is turned into fiction in life as well as in books.

phoned by Nixon, courted by Henry Luce has entered the areas of power that life in Lynbrook with a non-communicative father never allowed.

At one point, Nixon asks Chambers if he has any grudge against Hiss: " '. . . anything that he has done to you?' " Chambers responds: " 'I do not hate Mr. Hiss. We were close friends, but we are caught in a tragedy of history. Mr. Hiss represents the concealed enemy against which we are all fighting, and I am fighting. I have testified against him with remorse and pity, but in a moment of history in which this Nation now stands, so help me God, I could not do otherwise.' " What a fantasy come true for Chambers to be able to focus his personal feelings and his political ideas, as well as his keen sense of martyrdom, on this single act! To bring Hiss down, although consciously motivated by patriotic zeal, fitted every aspect of what we know about Chambers: shabby, a college dropout, awkward, unpleasant to many; as against the sleek, genteel, well-educated, and highly placed Hiss. Who could resist?

What we must recognize about the Chambers who dramatizes himself in *Witness*—who turns the historical Vivian into the fictional Whittaker—is the terrible anarchy of the man, as well as the nihilism which bubbles beneath the surface. By living with a revolver on his desk, his eyes wary for attack, protecting himself from sudden assault, Chambers is living out the life of Mailer's hipster, his "White Negro": "So there was a new breed of adventurers, urban adventurers who drifted out at night looking for action with a black man's code to fit their facts." Or: "One can well wonder if the last war of them all will be between the blacks and the whites, or between the women and the men, or between the beautiful and ugly, the pillagers and managers, or the rebels and the regulators." Mailer's words limn Chambers's territory, as he moves back and forth between the rebels and the regulators, the beautiful and the ugly, the pillagers and the managers. In Chambers's vision, everyone is "overwhelmingly against me." Opposed to him were marshaled the major forces of contemporary America: the Communist Party, the American President (Truman and his "red herring" theory), the Justice and State departments, and all those in the upper classes who rallied behind Hiss. Confronted by such opposition, Chambers becomes a "White Negro," prowling the streets silently so as to avoid notice, moving in shadows, victim and target for all.

What sustains him is his sense of mission: " 'I am a man who reluctantly, grudgingly, step by step, is destroying himself that this country and the faith by which it lives may continue to exist.' " How well this fits into Mailer's Rojack, who reaches out for all experience—professor, representative in Congress, television personality, stud for beautiful women: the "American dream" in its ways the equivalent of Chambers's vision. All politics begin and end with the self. All acts are acts of solipsism and narcissism. Mailer recognized this early in his career, and it is the impetus behind his characters' careers and, of course, the driving force in Chambers's actions. The latter contemplated suicide, but before turning his revolver on himself, he walked into a little woods in the middle of his farm. The woods surround him, but the scene is all self: *he* this, *he* that, *he* something else. He recognizes he is doing God's work, that "the weight of God's purpose" was laid upon him, that he must "continue to bear a living witness." The penalty is that he will be destroyed "by slower means." The fate of the country rests with him.

What is authentic for Mailer is inauthentic for Chambers, and vice versa. But each needed an extreme kind of reality in order to find the right expression of self. The 1950s were hardly bland. Great conflicts of self and "other," displays of ego, explosions of nihilism were occurring just beneath the surface. There were intense adversary relationships which parallel the "normal" level of Eisenhower golf, gray flannel suits, student conformity, desire for goods and comforts. From Chambers's point of view, the parallel lines were ideological: those who believed in the country and supported it; those who tried, for whatever personal reasons, to subvert it. As is usually the case with someone who moves along the margins, he was privy to something very important. Real subversion, however, did not come from those who supported Communism, but from those—with strong affinities to the sinister, underground Chambers—who moved outside all systems, who thought of themselves as personifiers of the new, and who lived along the edges in order to savor a type of life not proffered by Eisenhower-Dulles prosperity. As it evolved, Nixon as congressman and then as President was more of a subverter, anarchist, and nihilist than Chambers had met in his political underground.

THE CULTURE AS NONFICTION: WOLFE, WICKER, CAPOTE, MAILER

Chambers's journey from under to above ground took him most of his life and was achieved only through the House Un-American Activities Committee. In this body he found his mode of respectability; and his fears, paranoia, sense of himself and country found their form, as by the technique a novelist uses to bring together all the disparate materials of his imagination. For Ken Kesey's Merry Pranksters, the subjects of Tom Wolfe's *The Electric Kool-Aid Acid Test* (1968), the medium was not a committee of Congress, but a painted bus, a drug trip, a canvas dripping in Day-Glo. Wolfe conceived of a film as his form for the journey the Pranksters took; and their "trip" was as quintessentially 1960s as Chambers's was 1950s. For while Chambers enveloped himself in counterfeit to achieve his version of integrity, so the Pranksters became theater in order to attain what they felt was authenticity. Between fifties counterfeit and sixties theater lies a huge cultural gap.

We can see the entire structure of *Electric Kool-Aid* as film within film: the Merry Pranksters exploiting their lives for a film which will be the film of the sixties; and Wolfe exploiting the Pranksters for *his* version. What is of primary concern is the desire to preserve every act, gesture, scenic effect, sound.* The bus on which the Pranksters travel the country is an engineer's delight. It is "on the road" with features of Kon-Tiki: every move chronicled and charted, as if it were entering unknown waters and had to prepare the way for the next explorer.

Not unusually, the driver of the bus is Neal Cassady, whose manic exploits Kerouac used in *On the Road* as Dean Moriarty's and who would stand in for Ray Hicks in Robert Stone's *Dog Soldiers.* Stone himself moves on the margins of Kesey's group. What Kerouac pioneered in the 1950s, and what the Pranksters manifest in their 1964 cross-country trek, was the desire to capture the Now. "Now" became so important because it cut through all the social and political detritus of the postwar era. It enabled the individual to become his own god, and it embodied the idea of all the various forms of "salvation" and "sensationalism" emerging from the fifties: the drug culture, the offshoots of psychoanalysis and psychology, the body cults, soul cults, screamers and boomers and gymnastics. What Kesey, a well-established

novelist by the time of the trip, hoped to accomplish was the ultimate journey, in its way the earth equivalent of the moon shot at the end of the decade.

It is important to view the Merry Pranksters and their Day-Glo, psychedelic, hallucinatory bus trip as part of the same environment that led to the moon shot in 1969. Wolfe cannot make this point, of course, in 1968. But the novelistic dimension is here, to contrast Pranksters and astronauts. Wolfe demonstrates that many of the same clean-cut, athletic, all-American types who went into the astronaut program were drawn to Kesey's exploration.† Kesey himself, Babbs, Hagen, Walker, even Cassady, are muscular, prototypical Americans who inspire confidence. Yet they are dropouts, even Kesey, who no longer believed in fiction after having published *One Flew Over the Cuckoo's Nest* and *Sometimes a Great Notion.*

Both groups believed in spatiality, in the journey archetype, whether crisscrossing the country or shooting to the moon. The astronauts stood in for the country, and to revive its flagging spirits, Kennedy promised a moon shot within the decade. It was to be like a great war victory, and the young candidates (white, male, no Jews) who went into it represented a privileged group who were indeed America. They were intelligent, courageous; they inspired confidence, and they seemed fearless. Although several had had to struggle in their youth, they represented the affluence of the fifties and the desire of America to remain in front of the pack in the sixties. They would compensate for the Bay of Pigs fiasco and the general inability of Kennedy to advance American power abroad. Both the moon shot and Vietnam were to be demonstrations of muscle.

The Merry Pranksters were also appealing young men—a novelist, a cameraman, a soundman—who wanted Now instead of Future. Explorers, they put their minds and bodies on the line. They, too, had the "right stuff." A good trip under acid *was* an adventure, perhaps more spatially oriented than the moon shot; certainly more unknown, possibly more dangerous. Yet what characterized the acid trip was not only its Nowness, but its antiestablishmentarianism. The astronauts used their considerable talents and courage to express the national will; there was little question they were our new missionaries and conquerors.

---

*This was, of course, a decade of sound: rock and roll, the Beatles, Jimi Hendrix, Janis Joplin, Chuck Berry. The point about the sound was that in most cases it was din, massed noise; and this, I feel, was an aural equivalent of the visual effects of television—blurred sight, undifferentiated images. The younger generation, caught between din and blur, understandably had difficulty with words. Benny Profane's "Wha—" was the new language, which fell between aural and visual.

†In *Of a Fire on the Moon,* Mailer calls the moon shot a WASP enterprise with Nazi brains. And Wolfe will pick up the astronaut role in *The Right Stuff,* a superb evocation of A. E. Housman's and Rupert Brooke's "lads" who embrace glory and death, American version.

Their adversaries were not African natives or strange tribes, but the scientific unknown. For the Merry Pranksters—also white, Christian, mainly men, a few harem women—it was not the national will, but the personal will. One motif that ran through their trip was that each could explore himself as he wished, as long as he didn't miss the bus. A bad trip on acid was supported by the rest; only one person was asked not to return. The national will was the enemy; Now was in.

While the astronauts represented the external, successful, spatially oriented country, the Pranksters represented where the country's soul was going, into internal trips, into Now and Me and I Am. We see this vividly in Kesey's conception of nature. For the astronauts, it was transcendental, Emerson's nature on an even greater scale; and the moon shot was a transcendental experience, religious, awesome, bringing one closer to God in every respect. For Kesey at La Honda, nature was simply a backdrop, a place where he could locate his sound equipment. Wolfe describes "the Nest":

> *Dusk!* Huge stripes of Day-Glo green and orange ran up the soaring redwoods and gleamed out at dusk as if Nature had said at last, Aw freak it, and had freaked out. Up the gully back of the house, up past the Hermit's Cave, were Day-Glo face masks and boxes and machines and things that glowed, winked, hummed, whistled, bellowed, and microphones that could pick up animals, hermits, anything, and broadcast them from the treetops, like the crazy gibbering rhesus background noises from the old Jungle Jim radio shows. *Dusk!* At dusk a man could put on something like a World War I aviator's leather helmet, only painted in screaming Day-Glo, and with his face painted in Day-Glo constellations, the bear, the goat, a great walking Day-Glo hero in the dusky rusky forests.

Day-Glo is preferable to nature's colors; sound equipment to birds; amplification to actual noises. Artificial has preempted natural.

Wolfe's effort here differs from fictional treatment in that he never penetrates into Kesey, nor does he really attempt to. Kesey is the novelist, the organizer, the athletic, bull-like, charismatic figure whose inner toughness impresses even the Hell's Angels. Yet we never begin to discover what he is, what made him throw over his fiction, what drove him into Prankster exploits when he is obviously more sensitive and intelligent than the others. He is grouped with Cassady, and yet he and Cassady are worlds apart—simply by

virtue of Kesey's ability to write two well-received novels.

The same is true of Wolfe's other characters, the other Pranksters. He presents an external view of "Mountain Girl," a young lady of considerable distinction who travels with the Pranksters and becomes Kesey's girl; but interesting as she is, Wolfe rarely gets closer to her. Fictional methods are eschewed; Wolfe revels in journalism. He explains in his Author's Note at the end that he tried "not only to tell what the Pranksters did but to re-create the mental atmosphere or subjective reality of it." This he attempts by way of a hyperbolic prose and an "acid test" obliqueness. He strikes from off center in superb clusters of prose. The "mental atmosphere," however, is not there, the very dimension fiction provides.

The Now experience may lend itself only to inventive journalism, since it has little of the resonance and texture fiction needs.* The Merry Pranksters, in this

---

*We can say the same of Wolfe's *Radical Chic* (1970), a nonfiction influenced by a particular kind of fiction. For Wolfe's method locates his tale of the Leonard Bernstein party for the Black Panthers in 1966 in a Donald Barthelme routine, in which words fly forth in no coherent pattern. The result is an accumulation of words which lack overall meaning, language separated from a society or a culture, caught, perhaps, solely in the egoistic needs of the speaker. The Bernstein party is related like *Snow White*, especially the sections devoted to dialogue. Richard Feigen (owner of the Feigen Gallery) rises to leave—he is only passing through on his way to a more socially important affair—and asks: " 'Who do you call to give a party?' " a line which cuts at a skew relationship. And yet, incorrect grammar and all, it is what everything is all about—the party as a way of becoming part of *it*. But the real sense of the Barthelme ploy comes in the dialogue. When Bernstein speaks to Don Cox, pressing him about relationships between Black Panthers and the established black community, Otto Preminger in his heavy Middle European accent tries to clarify issues. He never gets through, not a single line without interruption by either Cox or Bernstein. The dialogue—with Bernstein pressing, Cox attempting to sidestep a touchy black-Jewish area, Preminger concerned about Jews and Israel—becomes something of a vaudeville routine; but also something more, a social issue of great importance brought to its logical conclusions as parody, what Barthelme and Wolfe excel at.

There is a point in *Radical Chic* when fiction and nonfiction have to meet, a visible seam which occurs almost exactly at the halfway mark. Wolfe has to account for the Radical Chic phenomenon, and he has to account for why society in New York was so avid about courting anti-Israel, Jew-baiting Panthers. Wolfe starts by defining what he calls *nostalgia de la boue* (nostalgia for mud), that romanticization of the primitive: food, people, dance, clothes and hair styles, social and political types. It was, he says, part of the pop and camp movement of the

view, are what they are: a phenomenon with no further dimension, a happening. Wolfe becomes a Prankster for the sake of his "film," but is unaltered by the experience. One of the essential ingredients of the new journalism is that the author offers himself as an equivalent of the subject, or takes on a vicarious persona: Wolfe here; Capote for the killers in *In Cold Blood;* Wicker as poor and black, a prisoner; Haley as a slave in *Roots;* Hersey as a victim of the Hiroshima blast. This is the new journalism written by those who stand outside: comfortable, bourgeois, relatively untouched by their subject. There is also the new journalism by those who are within the subject; they are the material the outsiders are approaching, as Malcolm X in his *Autobiography,* Eldridge Cleaver in *Soul on Ice,* Claude Brown in *Manchild in the Promised Land.* But whether the experience is vicarious or lived, it reaches us by means of explanation, or exposition, not by way of imaginative or creative development.

Kesey and the Pranksters lent themselves to journalistic retelling when Wolfe found a language that would provide some equivalent in journalism for what development and creativity would mean in fiction. He used language as a way of creating what the novelist presents in terms of perspective, image, compression, and condensation. *In Cold Blood,* on the other hand, despite all its critical kudos and Capote's vast claims for it, would have come to us better as fiction. We can speculate that Capote did not feel sufficient creative gifts to bring the murders and murderers to us as a novel, and then found a way of disguising that. Mailer's choice, on the other hand, seems right; even the moon book, the lesser of his journalistic enterprises, would have been a disaster as fiction. To find an "inner life" in the astronauts would have led Mailer to parody, when they do not deserve

___

sixties, what Susan Sontag had already tagged in her famous 1964 piece on camp. This interest in the obviously second-rate, the poorly made article, the manifestation of bad taste was connected to a new society no longer rooted in social pretensions, and this society was heavily infiltrated by Jews. Wolfe then must retrace his steps and demonstrate how Jews have maintained a more liberal political tradition than the rich have as a whole. Now Wolfe has several ingredients: left-leaning Jews, Radical Chic and its love of *la boue,* camp art and style, the romanticized black and Chicano movement. He then goes into questions of sincerity and grants that while Radical Chic could be sincere in its concerns, it insists on its creature comforts. He winds back to Panthers, poor blacks, Chavez's farm workers, Indians. The elements do not cohere, and Wolfe is left with loose ends.

to be parodied. Wicker's *A Time to Die* is also in the correct medium, although Wicker miscalculates somewhat by making himself more central than some of the prisoners, who seem like fictional dynamite.

The Kesey phenomenon, finally, is not a film, although the film could have been a great piece of Americana. Even the Acid Tests—those large outdoor events, with acid replacing baseball or football—are typically American: a huge audience, now participants and not spectators, insisting on all the riches of the world, attainable in the hallucinations and trips of LSD. It is a marvelous image, part of Kesey's "plan" for a new America, part of his inchoate film of America. He apparently turned away from fiction because there was too great a separation between audience and author. In the Acid Test, there was no gap: Kesey and audience were one, "with all the senses opened wide, words, music, lights, sounds, touch—lightning—" Emerson's desire for an independent, thinking individual comes to this. In a sense, Kesey is Emersonian, carrying the tradition to its conclusion, while ignoring its warnings. Fritz Perls, a Gestalt psychologist at Esalen, had carried forward Kerouac's idea of the Now trip, which Kesey had hooked into. The Now trip was the philosophy for now: no past, no future, no fantasy—only Now, one's senses open to everything, one's life pivoting on information incoming at the moment.

Kesey put it as the way to defeat the lag of one's senses, and to explore what lies outside the lag. With lag, we are always within the film of the past, even if only one-thirtieth of a second behind. That fraction separates us from Now. What is needed is a personal breakthrough, beyond self, history, society. Zen, Blues, Acid are the means. God is there, Emerson's old transcendental experience, waiting for those who can get beyond the lag into the thing itself. Wolfe's book is a splendid evocation of the Prankster lens as it records on film this aspect of "American history."

In *A Time to Die* (1975), Tom Wicker turned a news story into autobiography. By shaping the nightmarish events at the Attica Prison riots in 1971 into a personalized story, he was able to create something very close to a fictional treatment. And yet the occasional weaknesses of this powerful book are in those areas where fiction and nonfiction try to connect and cannot.

Wicker's plan was to tell the Attica story as a journalist, but also to manipulate it so that its events would be perceived through a man whose conditioning had been to reject everything Attica came to mean. As a white Southerner, carefully brought up, bourgeois, successful as a *Times* writer, Wicker was taught by background and self-determination to rely on law and order once the uprising occurred. Yet the opposite came to pass. As he saw more of the prison and the prisoners, as he felt what it meant to be put away, he found himself becoming radicalized, although he rarely forsook his belief in logic and the workability of institutions. ". . . a thief or a murderer or a rapist, however reprehensible, retained his tiny share of the human predicament."

Even more, Wicker found himself drawn to people, on *his* side, whose views he would never have "seen" before. Those who came as invited observers were a mixed group: moderate (Wicker, Herman Badillo, Clarence Jones of the *Amsterdam News,* State Senator Robert Garcia, State Senator John Dunne, Herman Schwartz, a lawyer at SUNY–Buffalo); radical (Assemblyman Arthur Eve, clergyman Franklin Florence, Lewis Steel of the National Lawyers Guild); very radical (those who felt complete sympathy with the rioting prisoners, their demands for penal reform and personal amnesty for what had occurred during the rioting: William Kunstler, Bobby Seale, Thomas Soto of the Prisoner Solidarity Committee, Jaybarr Kenyatta, a Black Muslim and former Attica inmate, two members of the Young Lords). The observer group was a cross section of 1960s men of goodwill and those who felt society had to be overturned so as to function for its underclasses. These issues, of how a society is dysfunctional for so many, Wicker had never clearly faced, although he was liberal, humane, had even taken a good deal of flak for his writings on civil rights. As a Southerner, he had fought his way out of routine anti-black sentiments to broad support of everything blacks were striving for. But now, in a sense, came the acid test: blacks who had killed, raped, robbed at gunpoint, and who argued that they were political prisoners, human, little different from those outside who evaded the law.

Wicker had to confront the major question of the sixties and seventies in regard to race: whether or not blacks could claim their social situation made them political prisoners or whether they were, like everyone else, individually responsible for their acts. As political prisoners, they argued they had been programmed by the system from birth to be criminals; that the cycle of home, education, public attitude, victimization, lack of jobs or opportunity, had made criminal activity their sole choice. They were shaped to be what they had become; therefore—and this is

what Wicker found so difficult to accept—the system, not they, was responsible. They were victims as much as their victims were *their* victims.

The townspeople—rural, economically depressed, ill-educated, resentful—considered them as little more than human scum. The observers were counted as turncoats, and vilified. Wicker found all his respectable trappings dropping away; he was exhausted, filthy, hungry, verbally assaulted, almost lost in a crowd action. He had to think about himself and what he intended to do under conditions that invited easy solutions, not the difficult choices on which life and death hung. Not unusually, Wicker cites Joseph Conrad's work, for he found himself making moral decisions in rapid order under deteriorating conditions. The Conradian ethic, of forming moral decisions regardless of the inhuman pressures on one, strikes Wicker, as he comes to fear his own side as much as he does the prisoners and townspeople (guards and state troopers armed to the teeth and massed around the prison).

What intensifies the irony of the situation is the idyllic setting. Wicker points out how New York State located its prisons in lovely rural areas, not for pastoral delights but to isolate black prisoners from the area of their crimes; and as well from their lawyers, friends, families. While most prisoners came from big cities in the state and had committed their crimes in and around urban areas, they were imprisoned in lovely-sounding rural areas: Attica, Dannemora, Green Haven, Green Meadow, Auburn. Pastoral has been transformed into imprisonment: the walls of prison rising like those of great fortresses which swell up in Edenic settings, keeping out as much as holding in. Gothic prevails.

Wicker also had to face blacks who viewed Martin Luther King—Wicker's own heroic figure—as the white man's black, and who found even Malcolm X insufficiently radical. He had never recognized the hatred blacks had for whites, even for those who had tried to help them. The prisoners had asked for Wicker's presence, and he was treated decently, but they looked to Kunstler, Seale, and others for solutions. The advent of Seale—Kunstler requests his presence, and everything remains in limbo until his arrival—will be the great moment, the arrival of the ultimate Panther. Although Wicker has great respect for many of the most radical (Herbert Blyden and Roger Champen among the prisoners, Jaybarr Kenyatta of the observers), he does not sense Seale's appeal. Seale is for him a disappointment, especially when the Panther leader refuses to make decisions he feels only the inmates can make. Wicker believes Seale evades the main issues in order to protect his own political constituency, sliding off on matters of "free choice" when, in effect, the inmates want to be led.

The dramatic turns are all present: Wicker fighting himself, his past, his own conditioning; the observers themselves divided, trying to paper over rancorous distinctions; the situation itself, time passing while the inmates repeat their demand for amnesty, a rush on the prison inevitable; pressures on Prison Commissioner Oswald to storm the prison, regardless of the toll on hostages; pressures on the inmates to keep some order among themselves as anarchy threatens; attempts to lean on Governor Nelson Rockefeller, incapable of comprehending levels of human misery outside his background; pressures on the townspeople, whose husbands, sons, brothers, friends are being held hostage and threatened by the inmates. The issues were clear: the inmates for the first time had political power, but if they killed the hostages they lost their power. If they kept the hostages alive, they could bargain for more power. Yet, Wicker recognizes, their trump card is not their own. It derives from the state which imprisoned them, and as soon as they relinquish that element, they are back at square one.

The drama is a powerful one, and Wicker exploits it masterfully. The sole weaknesses derive from that shaky line he draws between fiction and nonfiction: the very area where novelistic means could have heightened drama, where nonfictional means diminish it. The flaw lies in his presentation of himself, necessary so that he becomes a witness, as a novelist establishes a fictional character as post of observation. Yet Wicker's "character" becomes an encumbrance once the actual prison story gets under way, and his life seems trivialized by contrast, the very effect he does not wish. The dual method does not quite cohere.

Just midway through the book, Bobby Seale is picked up in Buffalo and given a ride to the prison; there, when Oswald refuses to let him enter the compound, Seale leaves, only to have Oswald relent. A police car is dispatched after Seale to return him, to try to handle the inmates. The observers joke among themselves about Seale's response to the police car: "suppose, observers asked each other, Seale and his bodyguard chose to shoot it out when the police car tried to pull them over? How would Herman Schwartz [a moderate lawyer] perform as a getaway driver?" The moment is a fine one, great drama re-lieved by momentary high comedy with potential tragic consequences. Then Wicker intrudes as Wicker. He tells us about an incident, while he was in the navy, when he was sent on a troop train in charge of an unruly group, mainly of blacks. It is only a brief intrusion, and it does help to establish Wicker as a man who has earned his credentials. His decisions did require some loss of pride, some loss of face. But the segment trivializes, as do the other intrusions when they occur. It is not so much that we lose the thread of the narrative—fictional devices frequently require that—but that there is such a different degree of intensity between foreground and background. Background is never really threatening; it can be turned into humor; foreground is life and death, the American equivalent of the death camps, and Wicker is witnessing *that,* not himself.

He was, in a real sense, caught between methodologies. Fictional demands pulled one way, nonfictional another. Had he chosen fiction—and Wicker has a background as novelist—the details he introduces could have been stream, internalized, freely associated, or located so that they blended rather than intruded. Then the full potential of the story within a story might have been exploited; and instead of trivializing the whole through interruption, Wicker could possibly have heightened the whole. In pure nonfiction, on the other hand, Wicker should have deleted much of the background, given some essential facts about himself at the beginning, and then let the story tell itself. It is such a compelling story, with such intense characters among observers and inmates, that we want more of Champen, Blyden, and Kenyatta, less of Wicker. This may sound ungrateful, but it testifies to his considerable artistry in unfolding this dramatic moment in American social history.

Wicker conveys with great insight and humanity the terrible waste society and individuals suffer when men like Champen, Blyden, and Kenyatta, regarded as scum, are lost to it. Champen and Blyden have organized the inmates, Champen as a self-taught jailhouse lawyer of compelling presence; Blyden as an orator, a man also of considerable presence and leadership qualities. On the conference side, Kenyatta appears in a long robe, with a turban wrapped around his head, a rug over his arm, huge sunglasses across the top of his face—everything calculated to turn someone like Wicker against him; and yet Kenyatta emerges as a man of great intensity, insightful, passionate, and sincere. Wicker perceives all kinds of new things: a different order of men as leaders. His own moderates—the persistent Badillo, whose poignant words gave the book its title, and the courageous Jones—pale in comparison to the radicals; and even Kunstler, who has struggled against his own comfortable background, comes through as a man passionately committed to justice, even when Wicker cannot agree with him. Meanwhile, the governor's army is poised for what will be a murderous and senseless attack.

A Time to Die makes Capote's *In Cold Blood,* despite its fine writing and careful attention to detail, seem clinical and insignificant. What is doubly painful about Wicker's story is that the seventies killed all meaningful discussion of these issues. Instead, Moynihan's "benign neglect," whatever the original intention of the phrase, became prophetic. The 1971 revolt was a cul-de-sac, leading neither to significant prison reform under Nixon and Ford, nor even to recognition under Carter.

Capote's *In Cold Blood* (1965) falters whenever the author comes up against novelistic reference points, succeeds best when it withdraws toward journalism. This is another way of saying *In Cold Blood* is least what Capote claimed for it, more if we forget his remarks and read the book neutrally. He created a considerable stir in the mid-sixties when he labeled this book about the murder of a Kansas family, the Clutters, a "nonfiction novel." He meant he had written a novel without "affect," perhaps on the model of Robbe-Grillet, Sarraute, and Butor. The nonfiction novel would be based on fact, here the brutal murder of the entire Clutter family on November 15, 1959, by Perry Smith and Richard Hickock. It would not contain authorial commentary or analysis, and it would be meticulously researched and presented dispassionately. Its "novelistic" quality would be a matter of arrangement. Overall, it would fit into what Sontag called "against interpretation."

To take the latter point, the arrangement, first: The book has as its plan the same conception that went into Thomas Hardy's great poem "The Convergence of the Twain." As the *Titanic* prepares to sail with its glittering passenger list, an iceberg is slowly forming in the North Atlantic. Two seemingly isolated facts will bring destruction and death. Capote has provided dual convergences. The first is the description of the Clutters in their everyday, highly successful lives, with the author intruding to tell us it was their last day; this is followed by a description of the killers preparing to make the journey which will result in the Clutters' deaths. The family moves to-

ward its hour of doom, while the murderers race their car to bring it about. Once the murders have occurred, the next convergence has to do with the killers racing away, to other states, then to Mexico, while the police begin to pick up clues. As part of the convergence, we learn of a prisoner who knows the killers and why they sought out the Clutters; based on information he supplied as to the layout of the farm, they hoped to break into a safe holding considerable cash. This part of the convergence, then, involves three elements rather than two: Hickock and Smith moving away, the police inching toward them, and the third party with crucial information which at first he withholds.

Once these convergences are completed, however, the book falters. The capture, trial, conviction, and execution are anticlimactic, foregone conclusions. Therefore, we must deal with two aspects of *In Cold Blood:* the use of arrangement as novelistic—how effective, how not; and the question of authorial withdrawal in terms of analysis of latent, subjective elements. Capote's choice of arrangement was made from many he could have used. In purely journalistic terms, he could have related what occurred as an unfolding story. That would have meant, roughly, a chronological sequencing. Or else, he could have modified chronology and given us the conviction and execution first. In *Looking for Mr. Goodbar,* Judith Rossner's novel based on the brutal killing of a young teacher, we learn of the murder and the killer on the first page; the novel is located elsewhere, away from suspense, in the area of "why" rather than "how." Capote has eschewed "why," to the extent that he has insisted on the nonfictional aspects of his material. In addition, there were several other possible chronologies. Capote's choice was to use convergence; but that method's brilliance is diluted by what happens when the convergence has had its inevitable run. We can say that arrangement, alone, is insufficient for the materials.

The second point, the question of authorial withdrawal, must be connected to the first; for by negating analysis in favor of factual presentation, Capote has set back the novel, not advanced it. He has tried to destroy voice or voices, and yet he has despoiled his own work; he is not neutral. I do not, however, believe with many critics that he mocked the Clutters and their normalcy while showing sympathy for Perry Smith and his perversities. The Clutters come through touchingly, especially Nancy, but also the father and even the mentally ill mother. Their generosity and basic decency emerge, despite rigidity in other areas. If they represent the backbone of America rather than the values of New York's Upper East Side, Capote gives them their due. He may not like them, but he respects the way they have ordered their lives, and he does like Nancy, whose death is especially poignant. And he also likes Perry Smith, the muscle man with stunted legs and tiny feet, who pops aspirins for killer headaches, a man without education who aspires to knowledge, and is yet a raging killer.

Capote despoils his work when he retreats from the very areas which would, outside of arrangements, make his book novelistic. Although the Clutters needed little fictional treatment—they seemed to be what they were—Mrs. Clutter's mental illness amidst all this order and stability would appear to indicate that other factors were operating in the family life or in the marriage. We see relatively little of her, but she *is* there, and we wonder how such discordant elements came to pass. She is, in a sense, some form of sacrifice, so that the rest of the family can survive on its terms. Shunted off to an upstairs room, which she keeps to when people visit, Bonnie Clutter is a mystery, like Rochester's Bertha, someone who haunts what is otherwise a normal household, the "madwoman in the attic."

Analogously, Capote fails to deal with elements that went into Hickock and Smith. Hickock's childhood and upbringing were not abnormal, and yet he turned into a vicious criminal, not only a potential murderer but a rapist and pursuer of young girls. He married two sixteen-year-olds, but his tastes ran to girls half that age. He is really the accumulated deposits of a civilization's debris, and yet he remains a mystery, as Gary Gilmore would prove to be to Mailer. Perry Smith, whom Capote favors, is presented with greater detail, and he is potentially a character of considerable novelistic qualities. Yet the very areas which provide the dimension of fiction are neglected. They are difficult, and probably one reason Capote withdrew was that he recognized he was out of his depth.

The designation "nonfiction novel" was a way of avoiding an essential fact: the kind of crime committed meant an application to the novel at such a profound level that the author was moving into territory occupied by Dostoyevsky, Conrad, Balzac, Stendhal, Musil; territory marked off as psychopathological and, therefore, requiring the finest novelistic skills to make sense of motivation and character traits. The book as Capote wrote it is a considerable achievement, and when he went wrong it was at a high level.

But he was pretentious in labeling his book a "nonfiction novel," a false trail which his supporters followed. The book is nonfiction, with authorial intrusions, part of the so-called new journalism, which allows the writer to intrude into his material. But it is not "novelistic"; that is something else, and Capote cannot have it all, having recognized he could not do it all.

The Clutter case would be the first of several hideous killings, those mass murders of the 1960s which accompanied the political assassinations. The Manson murders were, of course, the most sensational of this type. And such murders, like the assassinations, provided a great number of books, not because the killings were considered anomalous or atypical but because they seemed to define us. They were acts of will which were not far from those acts of self which intruded into every aspect of the decade's life. The killings and assassinations carried such power because they conferred on the seemingly atypical act what was acceptable in the uses of will, choice, self. Perhaps for the first time, as Capote was quick to perceive, a society was ready to define itself in terms of its murders, or its ability to murder.

Long before Capote, Norman Mailer had recognized murder as a way of capturing the sense of a society, in his own life and in his fiction and nonfiction. His fine novel *Why Are We in Vietnam?* cannot be disentangled from his *The Armies of the Night* (1968), for they appeared in successive years, possibly Mailer's most fruitful period thus far. It was in the novel that he brought together the several strands of his career: the desire for murder, the self-hype, the society capable of any act, the Texan as "White Negro," the Huck Finn aspect of his American fantasies, the dreams that result in death and destruction, the vivifying powers of will and self, which in turn can be dangerously destructive (as we will see in Gary Gilmore). What Mailer began in the novel he carried over in the two parts of *The Armies of the Night,* subtitled "History as a Novel / The Novel as History." More appropriate would have been: "History as Autobiography / Autobiography as History."

Although Mailer calls the first part "History as a Novel: The Steps of the Pentagon," it is closer to a segment of autobiography. Mailer turns the peace movement into a solipsistic perception: it exists because Norman Mailer was *there.* None of this interferes with his observation of the march on Washington and the attempt to "seize" the Pentagon; but it does indicate that Mailer has assimilated or ingested the schizophrenia of America as his own, and by describing himself—the two, three, perhaps infinite Mailers—he hoped to define America.

To compare his effort with Tom Wicker's in *A Time to Die* is instructive in the way we perceive history and then reproduce it as either fiction, nonfiction, or autobiography. Wicker places himself at Attica as "Wicker" so that he can play off against his own observations events there during the siege. As a successful white journalist, Wicker needs himself in order to establish an angle of perception; he is interested not only in historical events, but in how those events appear to someone who should ordinarily be sharply antagonistic to the inmates and their acts. Accordingly, Wicker has a two-way tension: the inmates versus the guards and state police (the actual historical event) and the inmates versus Wicker's own background and conditioning (the personalized, "new journalistic" aspect).

Mailer offers a similar fictionalized scheme, *except* that he draws a distinction between history as Mailer "makes" it and history as it seems to him that it was actually created; thus, the two parts of *The Armies of the Night*. The reason Mailer works it this way is that he wants to develop the schizoid nature of the American experience, *which he shares*. Wicker's aim is quite different: to find some common denominator in that experience. If he can identify with the aspirations of the inmates, some of whom have been hideous criminals, then there is established, for that time and place, a common ground between white middle class and (mainly) black/Hispanic underclass. It is not that Wicker can believe in a resolution of elements; but he senses that perception of the "other" is itself a good.

Mailer observes separate and distinct Americas, what he would note, also, in his companion volume to *The Armies of the Night*, the much weaker *Miami and the Siege of Chicago* (1968). Although Mailer shows considerable courage, the later book is often perfunctory. He is tired of activities, tired of tumult, tired of being forced to reexamine his own political and social ideas so intensely, tired of the pressure cooker. In *Armies*, however, he is fresh, innovative, often inspired. And yet his theme is American schizophrenia. He perceives that the Vietnam War, that obscene event in the American experience, "provided him new energy—even as it provided new energy to the American soldiers who were fighting it." This is a great discovery in the self: that the presence of the war brought vitality, that the hated thing was the source of revitalization. He could, in a sense, live off it, first with a novel, now with journalism.

This brings him to his full observation: "He had come to decide that the center of America might be insane. The country had been living with a controlled, even fiercely controlled, schizophrenia which had been deepening with the years. Perhaps the point had now been passed." In *Miami and the Siege of Chicago,* as he observes the Hippies and Yippies moving through Chicago during the Democratic convention that nominated Hubert Humphrey, he repeats that until the appearance of these groups, perhaps no one quite recognized "the depth of that schizophrenia on which society is built. We call it hypocrisy, but it is schizophrenia." This is also Mailer's subject in the Pentagon march, embodied in the several Mailers—clown, actor, novelist, speaker, the man fearful of being clubbed, the antagonist of Robert Lowell (himself several parts: great poet, Boston Brahmin, depressive). Mailer speaks of the American as caught between his machines and his intense desire for a personal existence; between messages passed along by technology and his need for his own "imperfect impressions still afforded by him by his distorted senses." Such words are an updating of the debates between Hearn and Cummings in *The Naked and the Dead,* or the inchoate discussions of *Barbary Shore.* They are of a piece with his "schizoid America" in *Why Are We in Vietnam?*

Mailer's ground plan for *The Armies of the Night,* consequently, was nothing less than Whitman's cry of "I am America" or "America is Me"—"I celebrate myself, and sing myself," as the song of America. What occurs historically on the march on the Pentagon is of less interest to Mailer than his need to graft himself onto an America which slips from his grasp. If he can, like Whitman, or like Ginsberg (in "Howl") and William Carlos Williams (in the "Paterson" poems), remake America into himself, make it the reservoir of his perceptions, then he can define and redefine himself to reflect what America is. In this act, Mailer identifies with that tradition in American literature we associate with Emerson, Thoreau, Whitman. He uses historical events as they used themselves as historical counters.

The process is novelistic because it forces the writer to enter a no-man's-land of behavior, one neither cowardly nor courageous, but the result of several irresolvable ingredients. Mailer at his best becomes a complex person, as complex as the issues. One reason the "Miami" section of the later book is weak is that the Republicans meeting for convention cannot offer much complexity. Mailer can only react in a singular way, as a Jew to a WASP culture; and in so doing, he reduces himself and that culture. In the "Pentagon" section of *Armies,* Mailer refused simplistic descriptions. He also refused to simplify himself.

He speaks of his modern quotidian half as being servant "to a wild man in himself"; a position he can maintain as long as Robert Lowell is present. The novelist Mailer needed a foil for the "wild man," and Lowell, who reveals his seething in his wild lines of poetry, is the perfect sounding board: Mailer becomes alternately clown, saint, straight man, jokester, Merry Prankster, finally a man who respects, admires, feels awe. Lowell's presence allows Mailer innumerable acting roles, all focused on the Jew sucking up to the WASP, which Mailer perceives as the way of America as well. The triumph of this section lies not only in the sensitive way in which Lowell appears, but the way Mailer, without simplifying either, lines up a Jewish America against a WASP America. If the latter rules by a rounded shoulder, a shuffling walk, a look of elegant weariness, the Jew is energy, words, foulness, vitality, elements concentrated as if in a clown: thus Mailer.

Beyond is the Pentagon, that WASP-like structure of the imagination and of reality, the "Nazi monument" to every sensitive person. To penetrate its inside is, for the soldiers who make up the armies of the night, tantamount to penetrating America itself, piercing virginity and forcing experience upon it. The aim of the "real Americans," marshals with their look of violence and hatred, government officials with their officious language, is to prevent penetration: to keep the Pentagon intact and untouchable, a mythical and mysterious place which can transmit its schizophrenic signals without fear of reprisal. The aim of government, then, is to preserve for itself a schizoid stance that remains unquestioned.

The schizophrenic dimension increases: not only Mailer versus the Pentagon; not only Mailer dissolving into several selves; not only the Pentagon sending out its contradictory signals; but through it all, a British film crew making a film of Mailer, capturing on reel his decisions. The crew had no plan except to pursue its subject, and it follows him to prison, waits for him outside, is his shadow. Everything Mailer does is at once a free act, based on dissolving selves, and something "caught in history" by the camera. Thus, in addition to all the other factors, Mailer is an actor playing himself and himself playing an actor. The device, which he could have exploited more intensely in a novel, is worthy of exploration; it is, in fact, more inventive than Mailer's usual novelistic

ploys, where his lack of strategical inventiveness weakens his work.

Dissolving selves, film crew, Pentagon people, guards hoping for a bloodbath all enable Mailer to blur the distinction between consciousness and solipsism. In French existentialism, which lurks behind many Mailer attitudes, consciousness (that awareness of being which is so essential for choice) is distinct from solipsism, that megalomaniacal position in which the world is one's construction because only oneself exists. It was essential, however, for being to be separate from solipsism so that choice freed rather than enslaved one to the world. In Mailer, the distinction is blurred. The self is so overwhelming—its essentiality is the strategical reason Mailer divided *Armies* into Novel and History—that in the first, and better, part of the book we sense the Pentagon march would cease to exist if Mailer no longer perceived it. This insight, which is the stuff of megalomania, is also the stuff of creativity. Without the perception of Marcel, in Proust's novel, the world ceases.

The problem with the book as an ultimate fiction or nonfiction can be located in a Lowell remark, early on. " 'You know, Norman,' said Lowell in his fondest voice, 'Elizabeth and I really think you're the finest journalist in America.' " Mailer picks up on all the nuances of this, some of the comment not so subtle. He responds: " '. . . there are days when I think of myself as being the best writer in America.' " By using "writer," not novelist, Mailer plays a cat-and-mouse game. He holds back. Perhaps he decided to divide the Pentagon book into Novel and History as a response to Lowell. His life was, in many ways, intertwined with the lives of some of the other celebrities on the march: Lowell's wife, Elizabeth Hardwick, had reviewed (badly) *An American Dream* for *Partisan Review,* and Dwight Macdonald had in hand *Why Are We in Vietnam?* for review in *The New Yorker.* Mailer's presence on the march, his shaky alliance with Lowell, his stance on Macdonald all played in and out of themes in his career. Lowell's remark about Mailer's being such a fine journalist touched a significant chord; and Mailer could not respond about being a novelist, even though he was then planning novels.

Yet the Lowell remark rankled, and Mailer tries to locate himself in the novelistic realm. He comments frequently on the fictional component of what he is doing: that is, writing a journalistic account and yet escaping the "stigma" of journalism, reaching toward novelistic practices even when a novel will not come. At the beginning of Part IV, when Mailer has been taken, voluntarily, and he knows jail is just ahead, along with a crack on the head, he self-consciously pauses, speaks of the pause as a "necessity which was a Victorian practice." The "momentary delay in the proceedings," like a Trollope or Thackeray intrusion, is a form of self-mockery, but it brings Mailer back into fiction at the same time it places him as actor in his own drama: the pause is to inform us that the film crew headed by Dick Fontaine is making a documentary on Mailer. Once again, the consciousness of Mailer becomes indistinguishable from his solipsistic self: Mailer as perceived, Mailer as maker of the world, which Mailer can then perceive, ad infinitum, Nietzschean in his egomania.

Much later in the book, in the section devoted to the historical event that was the Pentagon march, Mailer picks up on the novel-history, fiction-journalist split. He speaks of the superiority of the novel: history is interior, and the novel "must replace history at precisely that point where experience is sufficiently emotional, spiritual, psychical, moral, existential, or supernatural to expose the fact that the historian in pursuing the experience would be obliged to quit the clearly demarcated limits of historic inquiry." Mailer indicates that while he will now be keeping closer to documentation, he will be entering "that world of strange lights and intuitive speculation which is the novel"; as earlier he had entered the "interior world" of history while maintaining a novelistic pose.

Mailer keeps us so tuned to his methods because he is defensive about journalism, smarting from Lowell's remark, and aware the literary world now perceived him this way. Yet Mailer's remarks are simplistic commentary for a man who wants to be considered our Tolstoy and Balzac. His sense of the novel is still naturalistic, without the sophistication that would be commensurate with his creative vision. The problems from his early fiction remain: too little novelistic strategy to communicate what he wants to be a thickly textured novelistic experience, too little creativity for creative work.

In *Miami and the Siege of Chicago,* Mailer has forsaken methodology and settled for journalism, although heightened and given the perceptions he is capable of. Yet even here, in a more straightforward format, he tends to bury events, in a way completely alien to Wicker in *A Time to Die,* where the great tragedy of Attica remains planted in our consciousness. With all Mailer's shrewdness and verbal pyrotechnics, we rarely *see* an event in either book, and

except for Lowell in *Armies,* rarely experience people in depth. Macdonald, for example, is a cartoon figure. Even Mailer's careful effort to create Chicago as the archetypal slaughterhouse—first the stockyards and then the parks where Hippies and Yippies are "massacred" by Daley's gestapo—even in that long-drawn-out metaphor, we do not perceive reality, only metaphor.

For instance, Mailer roves back and forth between the typical antagonisms in American history, pastoral and urban, nature and technology. For him, pastoral is associated with Neanderthal men, those who believe in God and America, but have, under their squared-off exteriors, a nasty, narrow, violent sense of experience. He overstates their belief in America, as he also overstates their ease in being Americans. Small-town America is not at all the way Mailer presents it, but full of genetic errors, alcoholism, madness, suicide. Inbreeding has done its work, even among the middle classes; and among the economically lower classes, small-town whites are as disadvantageously positioned as urban blacks. Small-town racism, which Mailer takes for granted, is often a class matter, the result of economic and social pressures, directed at all threatening differences. There is great cultural complexity here, but Mailer reduces it; and his easy generalizations—guards versus Hippies or Yippies, town versus city—undermine his novelistic stance.

THE TAPE-RECORDED NONFICTION NOVEL

In the following four selections of "new journalism" or "nonfiction novel," we have the use of taped comments which are then rearranged; or, in the instance of *Hiroshima,* the equivalent of tapings in Hersey's reporting. Oscar Lewis, in *The Children of Sánchez* and then in *La Vida* five years later, commented that he was working along the lines of something new, a new mode of "social realism," as he called it. In the next decade, Theodore Rosengarten did for Nate Shaw, an eighty-four-year-old black man, what Lewis had attempted for the Sánchez family, taping what would come to thousands of pages and then editing them into a functional narrative.

Such methods create certain problems, and the results are often different from what their authors or editors claim for themselves. Rosengarten is quite modest about what he attempted; but Lewis, and Hersey more indirectly, were concerned with breaking new ground, establishing a different genre or sub-genre.

The tape recorder, used in taking down the life stories [of the four children of Jesús Sánchez, a Mexico City worker] in this book [*The Children of Sánchez,* 1961], has made possible the beginning of a new kind of literature of social realism. With the aid of the tape recorder, unskilled, uneducated, and even illiterate persons can talk about themselves and relate their observations and experiences in an uninhibited, spontaneous, and natural manner. The stories of Manuel, Roberto, Consuelo, and Marta have a simplicity, sincerity, and directness which is characteristic of the spoken word, of oral literature in contrast to written literature.

What Oscar Lewis claims is only partially true. For except for a few anthropologists who can understand city Spanish and who will listen to the original tapes, the information, ideas, expression, individual styles, and anthropological evidence in this book will be derived from reading, not listening. Although Lewis sees the tape recorder as a way of creating an "oral literature," that orality is transmitted through the written word. Once we hear his characters by way of written, not spoken, words, we have somewhat different expectations; when an oral tradition becomes the written tradition, separate generic conditions obtain.

By means of this "new technique," as Lewis calls it, he hoped to enable each member of the family to tell "his own life story in his own words" and by this approach "give us a cumulative, multifaceted, panoramic view of each individual, of the family as a whole, and of many aspects of lower-class Mexican life." The scope was Tolstoyan: the individual, the family, the social class, the country itself. What Tolstoy attempted in his major novels is now delegated not to the novelist but to the anthropologist; and the mark of the book is how close Lewis came to writing a great novel without writing a novel. As he indicates, he arranged and selected the material from the tapes, eliminating his questions so as to create a flow, a controlled stream of consciousness. He organized the materials "into coherent life stories." He adds: "If one agrees with Henry James that life is all inclusion and confusion while art is all discrimination and selection, then these life histories have something of both art and life."

The evocation of James is important, for while James would have been horrified at this use, yet what Lewis says is partially valid. If the tapes do demonstrate a voice, literary or otherwise, and those tapes are then rearranged, selected, prepared to give a coherent life story, how does this differ from fiction—in fact, from very great fiction? We must ask this, since anthropology here becomes embedded in a modern literary method. For these "voices," the four children, and Sánchez himself at beginning and end, are not unlike Joycean or Woolfian voices, coming to us from great interiors, the heart of a Mexican *vecindad* or *barrio.* Words emanate from people who must create themselves not by way of anything Lewis may say, but by way of what they say. Their stream and interior monologues "construct" them; they are made a whole stream.

As we examine *The Children of Sánchez,* we must recognize that we are not only in a nonfictional form which purports to enter into fictional areas; we are in the heart of modernism and its methods. The author, Lewis, is hidden, disguised, out of sight, remaining an objective voice himself. Yet he manipulates, as does any author, and his manipulations are the shaping force. He has eliminated the context, altered the original language, foreshortened the responses, rearranged the prepared the materials of the text, put them in an order suitable for reading, not hearing, and transmitted them in a form for which they were not prepared. Even the Sánchezes' street Spanish has no English equivalent: the problems of translation are intensified here by the fact that the speakers use local idioms, local slang, the argot not only of Mexico City but of their particular *vecindad.*

The fictional progression of the book, which comes chiefly in the increasing revelations of character, is in turn blocked by the repetitive nature of the revelations. What is of interest for the anthropologist, the repetition and overlapping, is of lesser interest for the literary reader. After some time—halfway through this long book—the characters' revelations are not revelatory; and there is no pacing or rhythm to compensate for the lack of new information. Everything becomes supportive detail for what has already been established; whatever derives from succeeding "rounds" is restatement, rearrangement of point of view, revelation of powers of expression, especially with Consuelo, who is the most expressive. Everyone ages, but without changing or gaining greater understanding of themselves.

The tapes, accordingly, are both revelatory and entrapping. For the fictional dimension, the method is original and binding. Once Lewis decided to present the tapes as this family's "autobiography," he could not go beyond them, except for superficial cutting and editing. The tapes record history, but they are also bars to fictional or literary treatment. The directions the lives take on the tapes are fixed. The tapes are traps, also, in the sense that Lewis cannot intervene to complicate the narrative line; he cannot loop around to show future development. He is caught within the direction of the speaker, who is not acquainted with the other tapes. Interactions that do occur take place only in the mind of the speaker, not as part of the complications developed by the authorial hand. In this respect, every line of development is singular. Furthermore, for both anthropological and literary readers, the "meaning" of what is narrated has no dimension beyond the narration itself. The observations of Lewis, which must have been intense and varied, are lacking.

Thus, methodologically, there appears to be as much missing as included. Each Sánchez child distorts, and there is no working out of either the distortions or the self-knowledge implicit in the distortions. We cannot distinguish self-knowledge, in fact, from illusions. In fiction, we are often confronted by illusions supported by partial self-awareness, and we must judge what is valid, what is not. Here, we cannot tell. At the beginning of her first narrative, Marta tells us her "childhood was the happiest any girl would have." But the development of her narrative displays little to support this. She says she felt free—"Nothing tied me down, absolutely nothing"—and yet her sense of freedom is a delusion, since each step she takes further enmeshes her in the trap of the *vecindad,* and, as well, in the trap of her family life. Where does self-knowledge enter, since the tapes preclude comment on her sense of herself?

Consuelo, on the other hand, begins her first narrative by saying she "had nothing but bitterness all through . . . childhood and a feeling of being alone." Yet her tapes reveal little that is different from Marta's, except for their perception of what their lives were. Similarly, the details of Roberto's and Manuel's lives suggest that only their perceptions of themselves differ, and that these perceptions after a while become homogenized. Because we find no interference, one life for us begins to run into another; and the supporting cast of friends, relatives, neighbors, acquaintances becomes indistinguishable from the main cast.

Yet even as they come to this realization—this sense of "Oh, God! our lives have come to nothing" —we wonder as readers (not as listeners to the full tapes) how much of this derives from their precise thoughts and words, how much from Oscar Lewis. In editing, what did he compress to bring together these great moments? He realized, we assume, that these long narratives, making up a book of about one-quarter of a million words, needed some dramatic climax. If so, then he must have felt the need to reshape raw experience; perhaps not to put words into mouths, but to bring them to this stage. He hides his questions, and yet their wording is essential for the response. If he led them into this awareness of themselves, then the idea of self-revelation is as much his as theirs, as in a courtroom procedure a lawyer can elicit responses not consciously held.

In a more traditional use of fictional materials, a central consciousness serves as a director of events, a sorter and placer; also, he or she may be a person who develops. Conrad's Marlow, for example, not only observes but experiences. In *The Children of Sánchez,* we have a central intelligence who, because of the method, can never appear. Thus, whenever the book reaches out toward fiction, the method brings it back toward history or anthropology. The book fits into the pattern we have discovered for nearly all nonfictional novels: they succeed best when they use fictional methods—narrative intrusion, subjective reporting, creation of atmosphere, scenic effects—but do not pretend to fiction. As long as we do not ask large questions that take us into fictional areas, as long as we stay with the singular narratives of the Sánchez family, we have a genre which justifies itself. But if we respond to the larger questions suggested by the method, we find shortcomings of sensibility, revelation, arrangement. It is not that these latter elements are missing, but that they loom larger in our expectations than can be met by the format. To the extent that Lewis arranges and edits the materials so as to raise our fictional expectations, he is bound to disappoint us, the way Mailer has in some of even his most famous reporting. But to the extent that he retreats from fictional methods and remains within a reportorial function, with the tapes themselves, then his characters' stories are intense and moving. Put another way, the four children may be searching for an author, but they succeed in their stories to the degree that they do not find one.

The most telling point, however, is the lack of ethical or moral dimensions. Except for brief moments of revelation, the characters do not judge themselves, nor is there any external element (except the law in Robert's case) which judges them. The frame of ethical or moral judgment usually provided by an authorial presence—by way of contrast, counterpoint, context, analogy—is missing. The result is that the narratives float free of a context or society; even the rest of the *vecindades* do not intrude as moral entities, but serve only as extensions of the characters themselves. A narrative which exists in itself can be a statement of sorts, even a moral statement; but once again, that can be obtained only with a suitable preparation. We do not possess that sense here. Ultimately, the lack of moral dimension undermines the narratives as literary elements, and forces them back into anthropological structures, where no judgments are necessary. The structure *is,* no more.

In *La Vida* (1966), a more elaborate book than any of the other Lewis studies, the author plays a dual role: Joyce's author sitting like God above his work paring his fingernails, and also a self-conscious, self-reflexive presence. Before the tape recordings of the members of a particular family were begun—the total of such tapes to be the "history" of the Ríos family in San Juan and New York—Lewis established his procedures. "The methods used in this study are a combination of the traditional techniques used in sociology, anthropology, and psychology, and include [besides two "lower-class Mexicans"] questionnaires, interviews, participant-observation, biographies, a limited number of intensive whole-family case studies, and the application of selected psychological tests, such as the Thematic Apperception, Rorschach and the Sentence Completion."

Lewis himself conducted many of the personal interviews, helped administer the "basic schedules" of household inventory, employment records, migration information. An additional five hundred questions were posed to the family, including friendship patterns, views on labor and religion, knowledge of history. Furthermore, Lewis was involved in family activities well beyond the questioning level: in wakes, hospital visits, releases from jail, emergencies. Only when he was virtually part of the family did the tapes begin.

The tapes convey the tones and attitudes of the members of the Ríos family, the mother and her children, plus some of their mates and their children. Lewis maintains that the tapes capture the "full flavor of the speech of the people, the slang, the nuances, the hesitations, the laughter, the tears. Autobiographies based on tape transcriptions present living documents of a type that are difficult to match by any other method." The tapes are, of course, in Spanish; but the transcriptions altered the Spanish of the original.

While the English is rough and often obscene, it is grammatically correct, spelled uniformly, punctuated—something quite different from the actual flavor of the Ríos speech patterns.

In addition to the questionnaires and the interviews that led to the taped histories, there was the desire to gain a multiple point of view: "the much broader canvas of the family portrait, the intensification of the technique whereby individuals and incidents are seen from multiple points of view, and the combination of multiple biographies with observed typical days." Thus, the biographies provide a subjective view of the individual, whereas the "typical days" are more objective. "The two types of data supplement each other and set up a counterpoint which makes for a more balanced picture. . . . And because the days include a description not only of the people but also of the setting, of the domestic routines and material possessions, the reader gets a more integrated view of their lives." We have, therefore, two basic kinds of information feeding into us as readers: the oral taped histories of the character in question, his or her responses to questions, a stream of material obviously controlled by the interviewer at some stage, but nevertheless a stream; and the second, the objectively located "day" in which the character is observed. Behind this basic pattern lie all the questionnaires and schedules, more for the anthropologist and sociologist than for the general literary reader.

As "manipulator," Lewis has his hands on a great many controls, all of which help him to create the materials of the book. Like a novelist, he has data to work with, related to characters, setting, social levels, housing, friends and relatives of any character in question. Yet the method ties him to a linear presentation of characters and their milieu. While Lewis can manipulate almost infinite information in any way he wishes, as long as he holds to certain patterns, his imagination is haltered by the sequentiality of the presentation: one character at a time, other characters in the distance or on the margins. He cannot break from one to the other, unless the taped history introduces that character.

Lewis's elaborate methods approximate a sophisticated form of naturalism. The "typical days" are settings or locales that assert a deterministic fix on the characters; and the increase in data as we acquire it only demonstrates how little choice characters have, even as they roam frenetically from one relationship to another. There are multiple attachments of every kind, couplings and children, foster children, adults moving back and forth. Sexually, these have been the most liberated people in the Western world; and yet with all this movement, they are caught, in the subculture of poverty. It defines them, and they accept it as belonging to them. Whenever they have the opportunity to move from it, by virtue of a better income, they forsake the chance, and return to the poverty cycle, which is familiar. They seek constant change and yet fear real change. Because his characters cannot "select" another life—they are caught by La Vida —Lewis is himself mired in naturalism, though he seems to have potentially infinite power. Their lives, like his method in dealing with their lives, keep him within limitations that stop short of fictional possibilities.

THE NOVEL AS NONFICTION: HERSEY AND THEROUX

In *Hiroshima* (1946, entire August 31 issue of *The New Yorker*), John Hersey attempted to convey the effects of the atom bomb dropped on that city on August 6, 1945, through retelling the event by way of six lives. His six are not quite representative—two are doctors, one a German Jesuit—but they are ordinary enough to satisfy his needs. To scale the devastation down to human terms, Hersey conceived of not describing the overall damage primarily, but observing what occurred to these six on that day as they went about their ordinary business. They were all far enough removed from the blast's epicenter to survive the immediate explosion itself, although nearly all suffered from some injury or illness as the result. The plan of *Hiroshima* was to see how the blast wrecked their lives, that tight interrelationship of families, children and parents, jobs, routine activities which make up a culture.

What makes the idea of devastation manageable in human terms—and what turns this narrative into novelistic terms—is the withholding of scientific matters until near the end; individuals are primary. Accordingly, Hersey has two "sides" to his presentation: first, he brings the disaster down to six individuals; then he uses them to observe the bomb's effects and enlarges their vision to encompass the whole. There is a double action, from large down to small, followed by small back to large. With a "neutral" prose, the author outside as in traditional journalism, Hersey avoids the note of panic or hysteria, all in keeping with the Japanese reaction. The Japanese, Hersey demonstrates repeatedly, accepted the disaster almost as part of a natural event, complaining little and, even

when suffering dreadfully, not crying out.

Remarkable about the bomb is how closely it recalls Creation and Armageddon. Fire and water are the twin agents: the blast itself, in which destruction is created on a greater scale than anything except the Dresden firebombing; followed by strange fires which seem like unusual forms of punishment and redress. That is succeeded, in turn, by weird behavior of water patterns—rivers overflowing, streams filling, floods in some areas responding to primitive and inexplicable natural causes. Hospitals and houses built on beautiful sites slide into the river; or else streams rise and claim horrendously injured people, too weak to move. ". . . the Ono Army Hospital, where a team of experts from Kyoto Imperial University was studying the delayed affliction of the patients, suddenly slid down a beautiful, pine-dark mountain side into the Inland Sea and drowned most of the investigators and their mysteriously diseased patients alike." Fire and water, in tandem, continue their work long after the blast.

But the main arena is the lives of the six as they try to handle what has occurred. Miss Sasaki, a clerk, is injured and lies helpless and unattended. The Reverend Tanimoto becomes a demon of energy, as does Father Kleinsorge, both forgetting themselves and attempting to help others. The two doctors lose their hospitals, Dr. Fujii's slipping into the water, Dr. Sasaki's badly hit. Mrs. Nakamura, a housewife, is concerned for herself and her three children, whom she rescues. For her, as for Miss Sasaki, there is only the hope of individual survival. For the others, there is the need to help, to forget themselves in the disaster.

If momentarily we compare this short work with another "disaster" piece, Tom Wicker's *A Time to Die,* about the siege and storming of Attica Prison, we see how different nonfictional techniques may be. Hersey keeps himself out, for the most part, whereas Wicker becomes, as observer and negotiator, part of the scene. Wicker's plan was to make events at Attica credible by sifting them through *his* eyes, personalizing the siege and turning a sociopolitical event into one with deeply individual experiences. To accomplish this, he delves into the personalities of the prisoners as well as those of the observers; we have novelistic characters, although without the depth we expect of fictional creations. Hersey's plan, an inchoate form of new journalism, was different. As an observer subsequent to the event, he is objectively outside; and he does not give us any real sense of the six. He conveys what is necessary, absolutely minimally, as if in some Didion novel where information seems so valuable one handles it like diamonds.

Hersey gives us lives, but does not let the lives overwhelm the disaster; they serve as a conduit for the experience. We recall that in 1945–46, the atom bomb was as mysterious to Americans as to Japanese; most Americans welcomed the dropping of the bomb as a means to an end, the end of the war and the way by which the American military presence could be diminished. The possibility of an invasion of the Japanese mainland was removed by the bomb, and for this, as well as for purposes of revenge, the bomb was welcomed. For those who desired revenge—a good part of the population, for whom Pearl Harbor meant far more than Hitler's racial policies—the death of perhaps 80,000 to 100,000 Japanese in the atomic blast was almost meaningless. Wartime propaganda presenting the Japanese as racially inferior, plus reports of repeated Japanese atrocities and the Japanese treatment of Americans in the Philippines, made the widespread deaths at Hiroshima and then at Nagasaki either an indifferent or an accepted matter. On a smaller scale, Wicker was dealing with hated inmates at Attica, desperate criminals, no better than scum, who in the eyes of most deserved their fate.

Hersey, however, had a national and international event to bring home: not just a prisoner complaint that turned into a massacre, but an event of the greatest historical importance. He felt, this novelist, that no work of fiction could serve; although only a few years later he would publish *The Wall* (1950), which was an attempt to capture in the German extinction of the Warsaw ghetto something not very different from the bomb. In that, also, Hersey is as much reporter as fictionist.

Why did nonfiction serve more effectively, especially for the atom bombing of Hiroshima? There was, first, the knowledge that the event was greater than any imagination, as the blast itself outdid all previous blasts. Second, there was the need for immediate communication; Americans had to comprehend what the bomb was. Third, the historical dimension became immediately apparent, and Hersey had an event of such significance for mankind he couldn't take the chance of fictional treatment, with its exaggerations, distortions, and other literary needs. Nonfiction was transparent. Fourth, his own sensibility, which, despite his previous fiction and fiction yet to come, accommodated reporting more than acts of imagination. *The Wall,* his most ambitious effort, would indicate that Hersey could not get away from reportorial work, for even that novel comes to us as reportage, observational, part of a historical archive.

Fifth, there was, through nonfiction, the opportunity to demonstrate sympathy for the Japanese, cruel and lacking in compassion though they had been during the war. The Japanese character possessed something heroic, as well as something very worth keeping—the ability to withstand terrible suffering without complaint, the mutuality of aid in situations of need. Sixth, there was his urgency to say something quickly. His choice of six people through whom he could sift the events of August 6 meant a brief nonfiction study, whereas a fictional treatment by way of the six could prove as long as *The Wall.*

A question we must ask about *The Wall* is how a novel based on such intrinsically compelling material as life in the Warsaw ghetto under Nazi rule could become so inert. Essentially, Hersey was writing an equivalent of the war novel such as *The Naked and the Dead, The Gallery, The Young Lions,* even *The Caine Mutiny.* Instead of squads, patrols, and companies, Hersey has various Jewish groups, each with its own chain of command, its officers and men. The Judenrat, or Jewish Council, is the most prominent of these; but the groups extend to Socialists, Communists, labor units, and most of all, families, in the extended sense. One "family" has as central figures Dolek Berson and his wife, and it includes Rachel Apt and her sister, Halinka, Rutka, Mazur, and the various young men they attract. Marginal to the group is Noach Levinson, the keeper of the archive, the historical record of what the Nazis, with the collaborative aid of Poles, Lithuanians, Latvians, and Ukrainians, did to the Warsaw Jews.

Hersey chose to tell this story as "history," a form he achieved by placing all activity within the journal kept by Noach Levinson. The tactic entombs the material; it is as though Mailer had told the story of his patrol by way of a document found on a dead body, or James Jones had narrated the events in his company by way of some historian's journal discovered in a library. By turning dramatic events into history, Hersey achieved a certain nobility—what *The New York Times* applauded in its review—but at the expense of novelistic elements. Yet at the same time, Hersey is quick to remark that the work is a fiction, that the archive is a "hoax," that the characters possess imaginary names, faces, and traits. This insistence on the fictional quality of the work brings with it quite a different set of coordinates from those a purely historical accounting would obtain. In a novel whose subject matter is purely the question of humanity, of the very survival of human values in an uncivil-ized setting, there are, curiously, almost no instances of human life in its processes. Hersey's Jews are forbearing, noble, intent on their religious values, proud of their Jewishness—all excellent qualities, *if* dramatically countered by doubts, fears, deficiencies.

Since the archive forces Noach to approach his material from his vantage point as a witness, he avoids speculation, dramatization, adversary feelings. The historical process has in reality dried up the human element. A potentially interesting character is Pan Apt, who decides to leave his family and "pass" for a Gentile beyond the wall. Yet we get little more than his decision, none of the countering values warring in a man who feels self-preservation is more important than racial or family identification. Pan Apt chooses, and in a brief time he is outside, beyond our view and beyond Levinson's analysis. Levinson has an overview that is not the same as a novelist's, for he cannot invent; he must record. As historian of the Warsaw uprising, he must stick to sources, but sources do not contain human values.

Toward the end of the novel, the family moves in with a Polish woman, a person of considerable interest, since she seems trapped by internal conflicts she cannot control. She harbors Jews, but does not appear to like or even sympathize with them. "Berson came to the conclusion that Pani Szilepska gave sanctuary to Jews not out of conviction, not out of real understanding and altruism, but as a self-indulgence." Here is a potentially dramatic and compelling figure, whose conflicts could extend well beyond her to the very people she is harboring. Yet Hersey skips over the internal elements, having shown a flash of what his material is capable of revealing. The role of historian overwhelms the novelist's function. The episode ends, and we never see her again; more significantly, we never have the conflicts suggested in her extended outward to others. These are, after all, civilians, Jews whose past lives have not included force, men and women whose interests have been in the arts, in books and crafts. When their survival is at stake, we expect less than heroism.

The consequence is a gray inanimate mass, without the vitality we associate with a "war novel" or its equivalent. Hersey's book reminds us of Cozzens's *Guard of Honor,* a stratified view of the war that strangles the very emotional life which would have made the novel compelling. In a story of only twenty pages, "This Way for the Gas, Ladies and Gentlemen," the Polish writer Tadeusz Borowski says more about the Polish Jewish experience than *The Wall* in its seven hundred pages. First of all, Borowski is devastatingly ironic, beginning with the title; irony gives him a point of vantage missing in Levinson, who is dogged without being sufficiently intense. Second, Borowski's irony underscores the view that one man's death is another's life; one measures not in terms of numbers, but of individuals. "Suddenly I see the [extermination] camp as a haven of peace. It is true, others may be dying, but one is somehow still alive, one has enough food, enough strength to work." Through his ironic tone, he demonstrates he can tolerate an SS man's shooting a little girl who has fallen down, limbs that come loose from sockets, corpses whose hands close around the living, a one-legged child who will be burned alive. These become casual incidents; one adapts to them in order to survive. The inner toll is, of course, enormous—Borowski later committed suicide, by gas!—but control of the monstrous material by way of irony works far more effectively than Hersey's sober manner.

Part of the problem is that Hersey has little insight into Jewish life, despite his assimilation of materials, which he uses well. The awareness of Jewishness is lacking, as the sense of black life is missing from Updike's presentation in *Rabbit Redux* or Malamud's *The Tenants.* We find intelligent observation without real insight, willed writing. Hersey's Jews are not self-mocking, they are too much the standard-bearers of civilization, they are insufficiently divided in their sense of themselves, their faith is taken for granted, they reveal too little. When Hersey's Jews laugh, it is at formal jokes. Jews in reality are always laughing at themselves and at others. Their tone is mockery, and what saves it from indulgence is the way in which it can be directed against themselves, their family, their children, their friends. Hersey is fearful of undermining them, and yet the novelistic sense of something as momentous as the destruction of Polish Jewry depends on the very human elements the historical view has sieved out.

Like much fiction of the 1960s and early 1970s, *The Great Railway Bazaar* (1975) indulges a narcissistic fantasy; it is a nonfictional version of those circular fictional narratives—Mailer, Barth, Bellow come to mind—which pamper the self and cosset the ego. Paul Theroux has made a journey from England to Japan by train, without any goal but the journey itself. The chief motif is aimlessness; one travels, in Theroux's terms, simply for the sensations traveling conveys. "Anything is possible on a train," he says; and he takes his experience from what occurs to him in chance meetings and from what he has to give of himself in those encounters. At the center is not the journey to something, but the self under difficult circumstances attempting to achieve its balance.

Theroux is like Bellow's Herzog journeying into the past for its own sake: indulging sensations. Small triumphs make up the adventure and, therefore, do not threaten. Theroux always has sufficient money to lay in supplies, buy a local meal, pay the baksheesh necessary to obtain clean accommodations. The adventurousness is admirable, but the sensibility is clearly capitalistic, middle class, racially condescending. The book makes a great read if one suspends judgment; if not, the enterprise turns sour.

Theroux has adapted Mailer's "American Dream" into a footloose existence. The journey, with no pressures, removes him from wife and children, suspends him in time and space, regains for him bachelorhood, withdraws responsibilities, and reinforces an Eden—of food, drink, and rest. While hippies, dropouts, and other disaffected Americans and Europeans join the masses in third class, or in slightly better conditions in second, Theroux pursues his journey in first, often trying to hold a compartment for himself. There is, of course, nothing wrong with taking one's comforts—and first class on several lines is minimal comfort. Nevertheless, the stress upon baksheesh or even ordinary tipping becomes as significant in Theroux's routine as what he observes and experiences. The subjectivity of the journey distracts from what, late in the book, he very finely describes as the nature of travel:

> Train travel animated my imagination and usually gave me the solitude to order and write my thoughts [he kept a diary or journal]. I travelled easily in two directions, along the level rails while Asia flashed changes at the window, and at the interior rim of a private world of memory and language. I cannot imagine a luckier combination.

Train travel, in this observation, fits almost precisely into young Marcel's description of tea and madeleine in Proust's novel: the two levels of experience, including the level related to memory and language. Yet in Theroux's instance, we see little of memory. His narrative thrusts forward in the direction of the train; and his opportunities to become more novelistic, through memory and language, are dissipated in descriptions of creature comforts. Observations, which might associate present hurtling along on level rails with memories, are perfunctory, lacking social or political resonance. He sees hundreds of Indians squatting to excrete along the rail

line and quotes from something a man in Delhi "had called 'The Turd World.'" The pitch for a quick laugh negates what could have been a disturbing scene. Humans in the roles of animals deserve better. Similarly, in Madras, he leads a taxi driver—who has, he says, "the look of the feral child in the psychology textbooks"—on a merry chase looking for an English whore, whom Theroux does not want anyway. He imagines someone like Conrad's Lena, in *Victory,* but the brothel owner shows him only small Karala girls. Theroux rejects them and says he came only for a drink, making everyone angry and putting the taxi driver into a bad situation—a long ride and no business. The scene has overtones of racial condescension; what is life and death for these degraded people is sport for the affluent American.

Theroux's view of "danger" reveals that his sense of the novel is Conradian, but without the internal moral pressure Conrad imposed on his major characters and without their dangerous loss of ethical center. Theroux's defense of his own kind of journey is connected, we can speculate, to his waffling on what a novel is, the American novel in particular. When he arrives at Sapporo, Japan, to lecture—and lectures are the financial underpinning of this costly journey —he reviews what he has said about the novel. He recalls that in Istanbul, he had spoken of the American novel as having a tradition which was "special and local." In India, he says, he contradicted this, and by the time he came to Japan, he had "come full circle," asserting "there was no real tradition in American writing that was not also European." In this view—held for how long?—he felt the American novel derived from the Western cultural tradition, so that even writers as American as Faulkner or Twain were influenced by the British novel as much as by American fiction. Not unusually, the Japanese were upset by this, and began to cite Leslie Fiedler, at which point Theroux interrupts his narrative.

His shifting of attitudes, finally, accommodates his own needs, rather than any patterning of people, events, scenes. His chief attitude is as bemused witness. The farther he travels from London, the more he perceives cultural oddities. Oddities they are, but they should be more significant for what they are than as sources of amusement for Theroux. He homogenizes experiences and loses their structure by refusing to perceive them as unique expressions. When, for example, he returns to Singapore, a locale he knows well from three years of residence, he has little but criticism, although he has kind feelings for it. Much of his criticism is well taken, since Singapore is run as a dictatorship, only more efficiently than most because of its small scale. One has no quarrel with Theroux's point here; what is lacking, however, is a sense of the cultural forces in Singapore—its location, heritage, small scale, encirclement by huge countries and major powers—which have helped to shape it.

One of the drawbacks of the journey book, apart from Theroux's handling of it, is that it becomes like the picaresque novel: numerous episodes and people, but no time for settling in. On a trip, characters do not recur; once met, they, like oneself, pass on. In the picaresque, this, too, is a problem; for the novelist must constantly invent, not analyze. His work depends on the discovery of the new, while what has already been presented lies unexamined. In the journey book, the episodic nature disallows all but one's wonder at it all. The alternative for Theroux was some coherent pattern in his own mind, something to serve as a measure. Yet his views are to him as much a source of amusement as what he sees. His reorganization of his lectures on American literature, saying this to Istanbul, that to India, something else to Japan, assumes his audience knows little; but more important, that history, tradition, the culture itself can be manipulated to mean anything. That lack of intellectual stringency depletes the book's energy, makes it more a description of creature comforts than of a vast experience. Theroux wearies as he goes along, but as much from his inability to put together what he has observed as from the four months of arduous travel under some poor conditions.

The nonfictional novel, as we have observed, works best when it least pretends to a fictional presence. The mode, whether labeled "new journalism" or something else, is a graft, a mutant, an anomaly; but it remains nonfiction, a form of inventive, ego-centered reportage. It was a response to a self-oriented decade, to an age of indulgence, and it has reached its finest moments in those who discarded theory and observed sharply: Wolfe, Kingston, Wicker, Haley (in his version of Malcolm X's *Autobiography*); Mailer, Chambers, Capote, Lewis, and Hersey in part. Confusion in the use of "nonfiction novel" or "new journalism" intensifies when the mode is compared to fiction itself. The latter remains distanced from these efforts, even the finest of them, in a different dimension, on another level of imagination; and all efforts to blur distinctions only indicate that the nonfiction novel may borrow and imitate while remaining, nevertheless, nonfiction. Tom Wolfe's joyful accusation that the novel is tottering, like the Roman Empire in its day, and awaiting a new conqueror in the form of the new journalism, is a casual, self-serving observation, belied by the excellence of Wolfe's own work. When we dissect the "nonfiction novel," we should stress it as novel nonfiction, shifting the noun to adjective, the adjective to noun. In its own world, the novel lives!

Chapter Thirteen

||||||||||||||||||||||||||||||||||||||||||||||||||||||||||||||||

WHO WE ARE AND
WHERE WE ARE GOING

I pose you your question:
shall you uncover honey
where maggots are?
I hunt among stones

CHARLES OLSON,
"The Kingfishers"

At the precise center of the nineteenth century, Herman Melville, a great prophet as well as a great novelist, spoke of America's destiny as a nation. He had not as yet entered his embittered period, when irony was his sole defense against the delusions and destructive illusions he observed overtaking the American people. He wrote here, in *White-Jacket,* in terms that add a theological and hortatory dimension to what de Tocqueville had said in more moderate terms earlier.

> The Future is endowed with such a life, that it lives to us even in anticipation . . . the Future is the Bible of the Free. . . . in many things we Americans are driven to a rejection of the maxims of the Past, seeing that, ere long, the van of the nations must, of right, belong to ourselves. . . . And we Americans are the peculiar, chosen people—the Israel of our time; we bear the ark of the liberties of the world. . . . God has predestined, mankind expects, great things from our race; and great things we feel in our souls. . . . Long enough have we been sceptics with regard to ourselves, and doubted whether, indeed, the political Messiah had come. But he has come in *us.*

Perhaps, in 1850, he did not foresee that the American writer would have to become a trickster, a developer of magical potions, a deployer of strategies, in order to deal creatively not with a national destiny but with empty space which, somehow, could not be filled. It would prove to be internal as well as external empty space. Melville's vision of the future was to prove very complicated, since the mere fact of our having ingested the messiah did not create miracles. He did see that America was an entity of historical and visionary qualities, a reality as well as a symbolic presence. Yet history, our symbolic role, that ingested messiah who failed, those vast, unfilled spaces, our predetermined relationship to nature, that Calvinist heritage, that insidious growth of delusions about ourselves and our increasing disconnectedness from others—all such developments, plus a classic sense of his own failure, drove Melville into bitterness and irony; into taking on roles of confidence man and trickster. Right after this statement, he embarked on *Moby-Dick,* in which he questioned, through Ahab, his crew, and his quest, that very sense of national destiny he had expressed the previous year.

The trickster role which Melville himself came to play later is so significant because for the American novelist every serious work becomes a balancing act of irresolvable elements. In our examination of turn-of-the-decade fiction, we saw a growing awareness of history, the past, memory; and yet everything else pulls the novelist from that. Melville's "national destiny" is, of course, no longer possible; but historical awareness, as we see in Barth's *Letters,* is, and even some of our most experimental writers, such as Pynchon, roam deep in the past, whether the mail system or the Nazi era, for their coordinates.

Yet as we observe some historical awareness emerging, the dominant mode of American fiction must be rejection. The very foundation of American culture and its literature rests on that withdrawal from certain forms of history and our thrusting ourselves into different roles and poses. The Confidence Man, not Uncle Sam, as the archetypal American remains too powerful a pull. Or else that descendant of Cooper (Fenimore, not Gary), in Henry Nash Smith's words: "a benevolent hunter without a fixed place of abode, advanced in age, celibate, and of unequalled prowess in trailing, markmanship, and Indian fighting." The celibacy would have to go, although the myth of the Garden would help to keep "perfect sex" alive as an ideal.

No matter what eventualities occur in the future of our literature, certain ideas which define us must remain steadfast. We may move from Northeast to Southwest, we may suffer a loss of influence and power in the world, the energy crisis may intensify, as may racial tensions, we may fight meaningless wars, and we may deceive ourselves in multitudinous ways; but certain constants come through in our fiction. That uneasiness with history is one such constant, as something alien to the American temperament, the isolationism that derives from Garden worship. The American novel must depend on co-opting alternative modes and styles, which is one reason why our future novel must depend on some strong relationship to American forms of modernism and postmodernism.*

---

*One detects in several critics' use of "postmodernism" a desire to have done with it all. That is, the term is used as a kind of terminal case: now that postmodernism is with us, we can say farewell to modernism and be finished with it. The "post" aspect suggests, for them, that we can enter a new phase of reason, perhaps strong narrative again. Such feelings derive not only from staff reviewers, who, understandably, would like to read narratives, but from entrenched critics who pay lip service to the great modernist works of the century. Their critical hero would appear to be Van Wyck Brooks, who, after a career as a "radical," settled into old age attacking everything new or avant-garde; somehow setting himself up as protector of the Republic against a subversive literature. There is, of course, a strong political basis to these attacks on postmodernism. Many such readers have trouble accepting modernity itself, the very

Melville's national purpose led to national emergence, American power, and this, in turn, led not to homogeneity, but to an incorporation of disparate elements whereby the emergence could occur. Whatever happens in American history, life, and culture must occur haphazardly, given our assumptions; and the literature that truly reflects this can be little different. Assimilation as a gigantic devouring mouth or digestive system is our key metaphor: America as devourer, whether of energy, goods, or ideas. Emptiness must be filled, whether with success or with failure. The superficiality of so much American postwar fiction, despite adroit technical means and striking verbal gifts, results from the absorption of ideas before they have unfolded; and, therefore, we find marginal, incomplete assimilation. One reason we do not have large, striking political novels is that our writers turn politics to satire before they see it as structure, modalities, a culture in itself. A great political novel like Conrad's *The Secret Agent* would be impossible here, because Conrad had so absorbed the political atmosphere of the last third of the Victorian age he could toy with it; it lay at his pen tip. American novelists have no such means. History, when noted, may serve as parallel, metaphor, even satire; but it cannot be used simply for itself. It is part of the battle, not the resolution. Conrad's satire moves beyond history, whereas the American writer is still trying to escape it. One can foresee no resolution of this dilemma.

Because fixed values are so difficult for the American novelist to deal with, it is imperative for him (her) to discover strategies to finesse what is undigestible. I feel this can come only from a cultural balancing act, in which history is recognized, but, more, in which techniques can, somehow, find equivalents for American life. Critics of American culture are always seeking means of assimilating us to older ideas, making the American experience far more homogeneous than it is. Van Wyck Brooks found himself in this position in an earlier time, Lionel Trilling in our own. But Trilling recognized the dialectical nature of American life and did not attempt to simplify it, although in the later 1960s he was appalled at the direction American culture was taking. But those drastic turns in the culture were not anomalous; they *were* American culture, whatever one's personal feelings about them.

Richard Chase—whose early death deprived us of

---

era, no less its works. They are the true victims of the pastoral tradition.

perhaps our most perceptive postwar critic of American fiction—wrote that the "past convinces him [the avant-garde critic] that discontinuity and contradiction have always been of the essence of American culture. The present convinces him that among critics only the most powerful and resilient of 'suspended' minds are capable of keeping alive the avant-garde spirit, or any spirit, or of embodying cultural contradictions of any sort without collapsing under the great strain into a formless middle way of feeling and thought."

The critical atmosphere in which the more adventurous fictionalists have had to fend has been dispiriting. Staff reviewers, for the most part, repeat aesthetic lessons they absorbed, apparently, in high school, with little sign of growth or openness. Free-lance and more established critics, several of whom write books in addition to reviews, seem inclined to seek in literature some ideal by which to measure man, or to provide a viable social and political basis for continuing American life. They are, of course, antagonistic to experimentation, simply to the idea of it, although many of them have applauded and continue to applaud the classics of modernism. If, however, those "classics" appeared freshly, they would be condemned. One can only imagine the reception for *Ulysses,* no less *Finnegans Wake,* or "The Waste Land," or the first volume of Proust. The reception would divide into those who urged forthright dismissal and those who, fearful of being caught out, would counsel wait and see. Several of them now use postmodernism as a term of somewhat malevolent force.

The academic critics have been more receptive to experimentation, to the avant-garde, and surely to modernism and postmodernism. The very establishment and assimilation of modernism has depended on the academy. But most academic discussion now, which I feel is essential to provide both scholarly and critical bases, is of little use to our novelists, even those who stick close to the academy. That is, apart from the sense of support they may receive generally, the nature of the discussion has taken a turn so completely from culture into strategies (of structuralism, deconstruction, linguistic balancing acts), or into the primacy of criticism, that the novelist must await some synthesis before he can find useful directions.

All this is another way of saying that American culture remains pulled apart, which is as it should be. The novelist should have to struggle against contradictions, as Hawthorne and Melville did. The ordering and shaping of adversary roles, rebelliousness, and marginality is a condition of writing serious fiction. Such novelists would recreate the contradictions and adversary nature of our earlier writers in the nineteenth century, establishing a line of continuity that our culture also represents. Those who cry that we are in a cultural trough are often the very ones who wish to see us there, so that they can write off the novel as lacking a social or political center, which was not what American novels were about in the first place. Mary McCarthy's *Ideas and the Novel* (1981), The Northcliffe Lectures, was respectfully received in many quarters because it retrieved the "novel of ideas" and blamed all the "art writers" beginning with James for having sidetracked us. She and those who support her (a virtual army) are fighting the old battles of modernism. We are back in the 1920s and 1930s. Only now, instead of strictly political pressures being laid on the novel, we note the pressure of ideas, history, society. She is echoing John Gardner, who was already an echo.

The novelist who succumbs to this—and much of it is based on novelists' or critics' special pleading for their own work—will not only lose wit (so essential for viewing American culture) but will be persuaded of others' delusions. For the experimental novel, that adjunct to modernism, the onset of what some choose to call postmodernism, is hardly dead or even dying. The 1950s saw *The Recognitions,* Hawkes, and Burroughs; the 1960s, *V.* and *The Crying of Lot 49, Ada* and *Pale Fire, A Smuggler's Bible,* the stories of Barthelme; the 1970s, *Gravity's Rainbow, JR, The Dead Father, Chimera* and *Letters, Lookout Cartridge, Hind's Kidnap;* the deployment of modernist techniques in more traditional writers like Styron, Roth, and Malamud. This is a sampling, but it suggests the impulse is not moribund, nor does end-of-the-decade fiction indicate an end, even if the work overall is not quite equal to that listed above. Every time the novel lessens in its hold on the culture, there is a rush to declare its demise. And that declaration is made gleefully, as if the novel in its potential chaos represents a threat to the very orderliness of American life.

If it does represent a threat, then it is indeed alive, if not always in practice, then as an idea of what its potentiality is. It should be a threat at its most serious and best; and wit and irony, as we have observed, are its weapons. Our novels may be "cities of words," that place elsewhere, but they are also deep comic structures, where wit is embedded in image, metaphor, trope: that is, as part of thought.

A blueprint for the future novel is, of course, impossible to draft. Nor should we try. An anatomy of our past fiction will suggest that the novel will co-opt, perhaps too rapidly, whatever occurs; that some few novelists will get ahead of the larger culture and foresee what is yet to come, as part of that vision of America Melville perceived. The lower levels of culture will remain to weigh heavily on novelists, and many will succumb to praise, as many have. There are areas in the visual arts and nonarts which may profoundly affect the atmosphere in which novels are conceived and written. In the 1960s, the arrival of the art film in abundance and in quality—the films of Godard, Bergman, Truffaut, Antonioni, Fellini, De Sica, Malle, Kubrick—served as a cultural distraction. Movies became "films" and inevitably there was a cultural competition with the written word, although the precise relationship between the two media is difficult to pinpoint. Nevertheless, the written word was, in part, displaced. At the same time movies were becoming film, the impact of television was clear; but most television was at such a low level of performance that the serious novelist was not much affected by its advent. The situation in the 1980s is somewhat different. The serious film has receded; many of the directors above have fallen on hard times, and the excitement of seeing their new films has, by and large, passed. Some, like Kubrick, Godard, and Truffaut, are struggling, if their new work is any indication.

But something is happening with television that may prove significant. It is not a question of improvement of quality, but of a whole new array of devices which will make television and its electronic products a cultural entity in their own right. All the gadgets coming on the market, the advent of cable in multiple forms, the introduction of films on videotape into the home, the possibility of opera and concerts, even Broadway productions, being televised directly to subscribers, are signs of a cultural revolution. How this will affect the atmosphere in which the novelist writes cannot be predicted, but it must affect something as culturally sensitive as the novel; as much as the conglomerates in publishing, large advances, worship of celebrities began to change the literary atmosphere of the seventies.

I am not predicting that these developments need injure the serious novel. We could, in fact, argue that by driving the novel into a corner, such developments might make fiction seem more important, as it is in countries which practice censorship. But whatever specifically occurs, conditions will change for the writer seeking to hold himself intact. Words and sounds will come in profusion from other sources. The sole prediction is that onslaughts on his or her creative integrity—for those who still possess it—will be far greater; that fewer will be able to withstand not only the rewards but the atmosphere itself; that attacks on serious culture will be more intense than ever; that pressures from less penetrating forms of culture and their advocates in the press and television media will be more insistent.

This much is self-evident. What is less obvious is that the autotelic nature of current fiction—that is, its self-containment, its nonreferential quality, its establishment of internal values—is a healthy response. This autotelic quality is the very artifact which has come under so much criticism for its elite qualities, its distancing of itself from reality (however defined), its disregard for readability, narrative, recognizable characters. That self-contained artifact is not the emblem of the novel's demise, but a signal that the novelist has discovered strategies for preempting what has always belonged to art, and as such is being threatened.

For what the artist could always count on was a regard for the art object as separated from the culture that gave it form and support. Art signified something, and it still does in totalitarian countries, where the presence of serious art means the presence of danger. In postwar America, the art object means less, since it has been bagged with television and film, forms of entertainment in which larger distinctions are lacking. In such company, whatever the quality of the film or television program, the novel must seek different shapes, or else lose definition. Autotelic fiction—and "fiction," for some, has replaced novel—is both a defensive maneuver against annihilation and a positive step toward redefinition. It will, like most such maneuvers, become outmoded in time, very possibly before the 1980s have passed.

For a country that has based itself so powerfully on illusions—illusions which inevitably have become delusions, especially in the politics of the postwar era—there is a terrible fear of losing control of reality. A good part of the attack on experimentation and the rejection of what smacks of modernism goes deep into the American psyche; so that experimentation is observed not only as elite (although by elitists), but as disconnected from the realities of land, place, area of renewal. Experimentation touches American isolationism, since it seems an import, not native; and, therefore, somehow un-American, the lot of the foreign adventurer. Yet these arguments or feelings are delusions, for experimentation, whether good, bad, or indifferent, need not be antirealistic. It need not take us away from the matter of America.

I would argue the opposite: that the matter of America can only make sense in this lengthening postwar era by way of techniques of dislocation, jarring, upsetting of expectations in narrative, character, scene, value systems. Our best experimentalists have demonstrated this, as such writers and artists did in the first decades of the century. At an earlier time, we believed that the open frontier provided the free land which allowed for regeneration and rebirth; that in the movement toward free land which bordered the frontier wilderness, we discovered our finest self. "Our village life," Thoreau wrote, "would stagnate if it were not for the unexplored forests and meadows which surround it. We need the tonic of the wilderness." The growth of technology and broader social values eroded that belief; so that at present we believe in an illusory sense of it, not the reality. Yet in our fictional values, we continue to feel that our finest self is still found in works of realism, easily mirrored selves; when in reality, like the free land on the frontier, it is now all illusion. Realism by itself does not reflect us; it shields us from reality. As Albert Guerard has said, we need not seek the alternatives of certain French writers, which is "no story, no entertainment, no other reality than consciousness and language." There are other ways.

Such ways are in a continued absorption of what the early modern masters had to offer, lessons which the American novelist (except for Dos Passos and Faulkner) came to well after World War II. Strange as it may seem, American writers still have not fully absorbed the lessons of modernism, which had been exhausted in Europe in a previous generation. Irving Howe may have said a decade ago that the great battles for modernism have been won; but the winning was in the minds of the Eastern Seaboard intelligentsia, not in the writers themselves, certainly not in the media critics or the reading public. The writer is caught in a peculiar bind, for even as a sophisticated critic tells him it is all over, the media critics and the public let him know that experimentation is not marketable. At the same time, he is still learning his lessons from Kafka, Proust, Joyce, and the rest, lessons which involve strategies, language, broad ranges of technical matters. To seek homogeneity in such a stew is to forget what America is. The serious novelist must, as always, negotiate a difficult path.

In his "Custom-House" introduction to *The Scarlet Letter,* Hawthorne tried to discover the wellsprings of his imagination, which he finally unearthed in ordinary objects. "Thus, therefore, the floor of our familiar room has become a neutral territory, somewhere between the real world and fairy-land, where the Actual and the Imaginary may meet, and each imbue itself with the nature of the other. Ghosts may enter here, without affrighting us. . . . if a man, sitting all alone, cannot dream strange things, and make them look like truth, he need never try to write romances." Methods change, romances become fables, allegories, funhouses, and labyrinths; but the rest remains. American fictions must become America's fictions.

NOTES

FOREWORD

p. xi: staging, even clothes: One could cite the historical panoramas of Robert Wilson.

p. xi: useful as critical tools: Some are not. *Harvard Guide to Contemporary American Writing* (1979) tries fixed categories, with separate sections, for example, for women writers and black writers. What happens, however, when some of the women are black, some of the blacks women? Or what occurs when Jewish authors are fitted into one category, realists in another, when several Jewish writers are realists? And how is experimental fiction to be isolated from all other categories?—which is to say that experimental fiction is left entirely to those not Jewish, black, female. Further, the chapter on "Intellectual Backgrounds" is separated from literary criticism, poetry, and the novel, as if those areas of creativity functioned without intellectual background.

The result is confusion, no matter the effectiveness of individual essays. A writer like William Gaddis, who deserves lengthy treatment however one feels about him, gains two paragraphs in "Experimental Fiction." Heller's *Something Happened,* an intense, conventionally styled novel, also appears as an "Experimental Fiction," dismissed in a paragraph for something called "heavy joylessness" and "male narcissism." What is experimental about that?

Most novels once mentioned receive their paragraph or two, whether the book is a major achievement or simply a pimple on the face of fiction. But far more deleterious is the imprimatur of Harvard given to those meaningless distinctions of black, Jewish, female, and so on. Is Ralph Ellison as black a novelist as Mailer is a Jewish one? If Ellison is categorized this way, how do we account for the many themes in his book not distinctly "black"? Similarly, how do we explain the ideas in Mailer that are not the province of Jews but of all writers, such as wife-murder? Are Jews wife-murderers, to the exclusion of Slavs, blacks, Anglo-Saxons? Is Salinger hiding behind his Jewishness in *The Catcher in the Rye?* Does even writing about Jews make one a "Jewish writer"? or about blacks a "black writer"? Criticism must distinguish, whereas this guide bunches. Inapplicably, it provides theories of taxonomy and nosology to literature.

p. xii*n*: "the Nobel Prize": *Literary Disruptions* (Urbana: University of Illinois Press, 1975), p. 61.

p. xiv: "tangled web of fate": "On the psychology of the Trickster-Figure," *The Archetypes and the Collective Unconscious,* Princeton Bollingen Series, Vol. IX, No. 1 (Princeton, N.J.: Princeton University Press, 1959), p. 271. Jung also foreshadowed Pynchon's "ghosts" when he said that "the trickster obviously represents a vanishing level of consciousness which increasingly lacks the power to take express and assert itself' (p. 265). "images of the Uncertainty": *Gravity's Rainbow* (New York: Viking, 1973), p. 303.

A Polemical Introduction: WHO WE ARE!

p. 2n: "being well known": *Time to Murder and Create: The Contemporary Novel in Crisis* (New York: McKay, 1966), p. 67. Van Wyck Brooks, as early as 1918, caught the same phenomenon: "Of how many of our modern writers can it be said that their work reveals a continuous growth, or indeed any growth, that they hold their ground tenaciously and preserve their sap from one decade to another? . . . the American writer, having struck out with his new note, becomes—how often!—progressively less and less himself. The blighted career, the arrested career, the diverted career are, with us, the rule. The chronic state of our literature is that of a youthful promise which is never redeemed." *America's Coming of Age,* with *Letters and Leadership* (New York: Anchor, 1968), p. 164.

p. 2: "The Novel Dead or Alive": *The Griffin* (Reader's Subscription), February 1955, p. 5. "The End of the Novel": *Waiting for the End* (New York: Stein & Day, 1964).

p. 3: "charge of 'imitation' ": *The Novel of Manners in America* (1972; Norton, 1974), p. 265.

p. 3: "has been overlooked": *Curious Death* (Baton Rouge: University of Louisiana Press, 1967), pp. 9–10.

p. 3: "the received version": *The Death of the Novel* (New York: Dial, 1969), p. 41.

p. 4: eliminate plot and character: "John Hawkes: An Interview," *Wisconsin Studies in Contemporary Literature* (Summer 1964), p. 146.

p. 4n: "been swallowed up": p. 162.

p. 5: "harmless and sanguine self": (New York: New Directions, 1964), p. 1.

p. 7: associated with language: An example from the general culture: John Kennedy's assassination became fixed, for many of us, by the way in which we first heard about it, on radio or television, in the printed word, or from another person. It became embedded in our aural-visual history even as it occurred, and it derives from the language in which it was expressed; we fixed it in memory as continuous with our experience because of language. In a completely different language, the event would have registered differently. When Malcolm X heard of the death, he said it was the "chicken coming home to roost." The point he expressed was considered radical and malicious, but what concerns us here is how American it is, a typically home spun American usage, as much a white man's expression as a black's. The remark was used later to castigate Malcolm X for cruelty, but he was suggesting that the assassination was politics as usual, reacting to it as an American, not as a black.

p. 9: mind cannot be encouraged: In *Culture on a Moving Frontier* (Bloomington: Indiana University Press, 1955), Louis B. Wright shows that while many early settlers remained devoted to aspects of English culture even while living under duress, the conditions for the development of indigenous tales were poor.

p. 9: rewards can be very high indeed: Not just now, but in the nineteenth century also. George Eliot struck tremendous deals with her publishers and extracted every cent she could from Blackwood in complex arrangements.

p. 11: fits that function: Lionel Trilling was cautionary, not supportive, in this area. ". . . it seems to me that the characteristic element of modern literature, or at least of the most highly developed modern literature, is the bitter line of hostility to civilization which runs through it." "On the Teaching of Modern Literature," *Beyond Culture: Essays in Literature and Learning* (New York: Viking, 1965).

Chapter One: THEMES AND COUNTERTHEMES

p. 12: "hump the boss' daughter": *Why Are We in Vietnam?* (1967; New York: Berkley Medallion, 1968), p. 221.

p. 13: "whawng! and whoong!": Ibid., p. 144.

p. 14: "bowl around this pond": Ibid., p. 215.

p. 14: "Brooks Range electrified mind": Ibid., p. 220.

p. 14: In his *Journal:* February 1857.

p. 15: "act of subversion": *The Paranoid Style in American Politics and Other Essays* (New York: Vintage, 1967), p. 23

p. 15: "socialist and communist schemer": Ibid., p. 23. In 1980, they helped elect Reagan President, although for some he was too liberal.

p. 17: "child as well as a man": "Song of Myself," l. 330ff.

p. 17: "universe perpetually flow": Ibid., ll. 405–6.

p. 17: "appearance as its picture": "Nature," *The Complete Essays* (New York: Modern Library, 1940), p. 15.

p. 17: "rare and sublimer beauty still": *Cape Cod* (New York: Crowell, 1961), p. 14. Following quotation from same page.

p. 19: updated in the postwar novel: Anyone writing on the subject of Puritan and Indian is indebted to Richard Slotkin's *Regeneration Through Violence: The Mythology of the American Frontier, 1600–1860* (Middletown, Conn.: Wesleyan University Press, 1973). See also Richard H. Pells, *Radical Visions and American Dreams* (New York: Harper & Row, 1973), especially Chap. 8.

p. 21: "each person works for himself": *Letters from an American Farmer,* third letter: "What Is an American?" There are twelve letters.

p. 21: "learn nothing rightly": *Essays,* p. 124.

p. 22: Puritans with the Indians: Although D. H. Lawrence's *Studies in Classic American Literature* are more intuitive and prophetic than empirical, and are *not* to be taken as gospel, his analysis of Cooper's novels is compelling. Even here, however, while his view of white-Indian relationships in early America is accurate, his conclusion is wide of the mark. He writes: "The desire to extirpate the Indian. And the contradictory desire to glorify him. Both are rampant still, to-day [1916]. . . . The minority of whites intellectualizes the Red Man and lauds him to the skies. But this minority of whites is mostly a highbrow minority with a big grouch against its own whiteness. So there you are."

Now the conclusion: "But you have here the myth of the essential white America. All the other stuff, the love, the democracy . . . is a sort of by—lay. The essential American soul is hard, isolate, stoic, and a killer. It has never yet melted." (New York: Anchor, 1951), pp. 51, 73.

p. 22: Skinner Galt is unearned: *The End of My Life* (1947).

p. 23: In his excellent book: *The Crisis of the Negro Intellectual* (New York: Morrow, 1967).

p. 24: "Faulkner, Wolfe and Fitzgerald": From *Genius and Lust: A Journey Through the Major Writings of Henry Miller* (New York, Grove, 1976), p. 5.

p. 24: transcended this time or that place: Although in his essay "On the Teaching of Modern Literature" Lionel Trilling is wary of the hostility to civilization modern literature demonstrates, he is, perhaps, even more wary of its removal from history.

p. 25: "tolerate this age": *Lancelot* (New York: Avon, 1978), p. 170.

p. 26: reliance on language alone: Perhaps echoing Emerson's fine phrase "language is fossil poetry."

p. 27: "far deeper thinker than most": Robert Coles in his study demonstrates how Percy has pondered theological, philosophical, and historical issues. Coles writes: "Percy, in his philosophical writings [collected in *The Message in the Bottle* (New York: Farrar, Straus & Giroux, 1975)], tries hard to affirm Dostoevski's position [that Christ was ultimate truth] without appearing to be quite so careless of the word 'prove'—that is, without ignoring the Western tradition of scientific rationalism. In those writings, he involved the more humble and self-critical elements of that tradition—for instance, the open-minded 'pragmatism' of the American philosopher Charles S. Peirce—in order to indicate how imprecise any 'proof' is. Percy also showed how the assertiveness of all too many natural scientists (one cannot even begin to discuss in the same breath the dogmatism of social scientists) is derived from an illusion—the illusion of certainty, of knowledge that is sure. And he tried to indicate that the 'existentialist' viewpoint—so variously advocated by Christians and non-Christians alike, from Kierkegaard to Heidegger, from Dostoevski himself to Camus and Sartre—need not be opposed to the empirical or rational position." *The New Yorker,* October 9, 1978, pp. 84–8. Some of this is excessive, to be sure, but Percy does do battle with ideas without reducing them.

Chapter Two: AMERICAN SPACE AND SPATIALITY

p. 31: spatial frontiers were closed: In Emerson's insistence on the superiority of soul to matter, space was dominant. "Nothing is as fleeting as form," he said. This is, Matthiessen reminds us, a meeting ground of philosophy, art, and religion. ". . . it is the doctrine of a revolutionary movement, of a period in religion that insisted that the living spirit had rendered forms hollow and unnecessary, of a period in social evolution that thought it imperative to throw over conventions in order that the inner man might be free." *American Renaissance,* p. 25.

p. 31n: a still emerging Eden: See Paul Ginestier, *The Poet and the Machine* (Chapel Hill: University of North Carolina Press, 1961), p. 80 and passim.

p. 32: "Nearly every American novelist": See Helen Weinberg's *The New Novel in America: The Kafkan Mode in Contemporary Fiction* (Ithaca, N.Y.: Cornell University Press, 1970). Weinberg sees Kafka's K. in *The Castle* as a spiritual activist hero and then traces this idea in several (Jewish) postwar novelists. She fails to examine, however, how the Kafka protagonist also works against the grain of the American experience; so that one could argue as strongly against her thesis as for it.

p. 32: *"a writer, and a Jew":* The full title of the essay, from Kafka's "The Hunger Artist," is " 'I Always Wanted You to Admire My Fasting': or, Looking at Kafka," in *Reading Myself and Others* (New York: Farrar, Straus & Giroux, 1975).

p. 34: "man is an analogous figure": *Encounter* XXI: 25.

p. 34: "emptiness within himself": Ibid.

p. 34: fervent hatred of the self: See "Puritanism and the Self," Chapter 1 of Sacvan Bercovitch's *The Puritan Origins of the American Self* (New Haven: Yale University Press, 1975). We have already noted the dualism of soul and self in Emerson and Melville. Thoreau, of course, argued the opposite; for him, in R. W. B. Lewis's words, "Everything associated with the past should be burned away." *The American Adam: Innocence, Tragedy, and Tradition in the Nineteenth Century* (Chicago: University of Chicago Press, 1955), p. 21.

p. 35: "within their proper bounds!": *The Blithedale Romance* (New York: Dell, 1969), p. 154; lines above from p. 166.

p. 35: "multiple layers of the self": *Failure and Success,* p. 9. By the time I became aware of her brilliant study (it was published in 1978), I had already formulated many of my own ideas, which, I was gratified to see, were reinforced by her own strategies.

p. 37: "rattling of chains, always was": *Studies in Classic American Literature* (New York: Anchor, 1951), p. 17.

p. 37: "and conscience tinned": from "Key West."

p. 38: "every sort of extension agent": *A New Life* (1961; New York: Dell, 1963), p. 41.

p. 40: "in search of a real refuge": *Poetics of Space,* p. 81. That "hut dream" is the source of William Gass's irony in *In the Heart of the Heart of the Country.*

p. 41: "transcends geometrical space": Ibid., p. 47.

Chapter Three: THE PERSISTENCE OF PASTORAL

p. 42n: "unadaptable to Eastern life": *Portable Fitzgerald* (New York: Viking, 1945), p. 163.

p. 43: "repetition of the cosmogony": Ibid., p. 82.

p. 43: "ascend to heaven": Ibid., p. 26.

p. 44: paradise into Paradise: See Emma Rothschild, *Paradise Lost: The Decline of the Auto-Industrial Age* (1973; New York: Vintage, 1974), p. 169.

p. 44: "deluge of light": *Journals,* V: 76.

p. 45: confessional poetry is self-oriented: An interesting study would be one that tries to connect confessional poetry, with its self-reflexive focus, to later developments in the autotelic novel, a fiction always curving back to its own terms.

p. 45: "the unforgettable scenery": *Speak, Memory,* rev. ed. (New York, Putnam, 1966), p. 229.

p. 45: "garden of the literary covenant": *The Dispossessed Garden: Pastoral and History in Southern Literature* (Athens, Ga.: University of Georgia Press, 1975), p. 39. I am indebted to many aspects of this fine study.

p. 46: distinguished for John Adams: Letter to John Adams, October 28, 1813. Jefferson's views on slavery are found in *Notes on the State of Virginia,* 1782, the result of an official inquiry which Jefferson received in 1781.

p. 47: "holy emblem" to Emerson: *Journals,* V: 177.

p. 48: "articulated foundation": *The Uncommitted* (New York: Delta, 1965), p. 77.

p. 48: "distance from others": Ibid., p. 25.

p. 48: "as a physiographical region": *Frontier: American Literature and the American West* (Princeton: Princeton University Press, 1965), p. 9.

p. 48: contrast with civilization: Edwin Fussell is illuminating here: "A further threshold was crossed when American writers learned to double their basic metaphor, especially the frontier-as-space, by involving it with social, psychological, philosophical, or other situations analogously reconciling opposites through interpenetration and transcendence." Op. cit., p. 17.

p. 49n: "shiftless half-breeds": *Custer Died for Your Sins: An Indian Manifesto* (New York: Avon, 1970), p. 12. The story he tells occurs on p. 11. Also see Roy Harvey Pearce, *The Savages of America: A Study of the Indian and the Idea of Civilization* (Baltimore: Johns Hopkins, 1953).

p. 49: man's own imperfections: See Lewis, *The American Adam,* Chap. 6.

p. 49: a small factory town: One that "manufactured table silver and a few other small industries." *The Wapshot Chronicle* (1957; New York: Bantam, 1958), p. 19.

p. 50: "then this was gone": Ibid., p. 58.

p. 50: "flesh and blood": Ibid., p. 19.

p. 50: "the glow of love": Ibid., p. 264.

p. 50: "kingdoms of Riverside Drive": Ibid., pp. 267–8.

p. 50: "head and the groin": *The Wapshot Scandal* (1963; New York: Perennial, 1973), p. 141.

p. 51: "be nothing at all": Ibid., p. 244.

p. 51: "refused to crack": *The Field of Vision* (New York: Signet, 1957), p. 61.

p. 52: "beside the point": Ibid., pp. 37–8.

p. 52: "the bullring that afternoon?": Ibid., p. 172.

p. 53: "is a native son": *Ceremony in Lone Tree* (New York: Signet, 1962), p. 118.

p. 53n: "Geography of the Sentence": *The World Within the Word* (1978; Boston: Nonpareil, 1979).

p. 54: "anything plausible may": "The Concept of Character in Fiction," *Fiction and the Figures of Life* (1971; New York: Vintage, 1972), p. 36.

p. 54: "signposts, handles, keys": Op. cit., p. 47.

p. 54: "heart of the country": *In the Heart of the Heart of the Country* (1968; New York: Perennial, 1969), p. 180.

p. 54: "trembling has overcome them": Ibid., p. 181.

p. 54: "loud cantankerous dog": Ibid., pp. 181–2.

p. 54: "heart of the country": Ibid., p. 191.

p. 54: "It does not exist": Ibid., p. 194.

p. 54: "within it's dead": Ibid., p. 195.

p. 55: *Wisconsin Death Trip:* In *The World Within the Word,* Gass includes a brief essay called "Wisconsin Death Trip."

p. 55: "a fit of insanity": Both quotations from *Wisconsin Death Trip* (New York: Pantheon, 1973), unpaged.

p. 55: "arc of their pursuit": *Omensetter's Luck* (New York: Plume, 1972), p. 60.

p. 55n: "forms of daily talk": *Fiction and the Figures of Life,* p. 32.

p. 55: "a kind of abandon": *Omensetter,* p. 126. Following quotation from same page.

p. 56: "interest like a shade": Ibid., p. 166.

p. 56: "old leaves, I guess": Ibid., p. 21.

p. 56: "country-headed thing to say": *Fiction and the Figures of Life,* p. 27.

p. 57: "musicked deep with feeling": Ibid., p. 33.

p. 58: "made it part of him": *At Play in the Fields of the Lord* (New York: Random House, 1965), p. 202.

p. 58: "intimation of his fate": Ibid., p. 398.

p. 58: "the eye of Heaven": Ibid., p. 399.

p. 59: "sewer under the floor": *One Flew Over the Cuckoo's Nest* (New York: Signet, 1963), p. 30.

p. 62: "useful misconstruction 'mutual love'": *On Moral Fiction* (New York: Basic, 1978), p. 46.

p. 63: "like an Amish woman's": *Nickel Mountain* (New York: Ballantine, 1975), pp. 224–5.

p. 63: "idea of magical change": Ibid., p. 298.

p. 64: "blasphemy and high treason": *October Light* (1976; New York: Ballantine, 1978), pp. 1–2.

p. 64: "ancient Sumerian or Indian": Ibid., p. 223.

p. 65: product of Henry Waugh's imagination: The Universal Baseball Association parallels in some ways the American Professional Baseball Association, a computer-designed game. Participants served as team managers and worked with cards which gave hitting, fielding, and pitching stats for players in both leagues, dating to the 1950s. The idea was to outguess the actual managers of those games and to win more games than they had. One was pitted not against chance, as in Coover, but against the actual outcome. This game had more factuality than Coover's Association, for the participant team manager could adjust, juggle, and redo actual lineups to gain more strength than the original manager had.

p. 65: "need the game": *The Universal Baseball Association, J. Henry Waugh, Prop.* (New York: Random House, 1968), p. 121.

p. 65n: "woodwinds and violins": *The Summer Game* (New York: Viking, 1972), p. 4.

p. 66: "still in the right": Ibid., p. 160.

p. 67: "expulsion from Port Ruppert": *The Great American Novel* (New York: Holt, Rinehart & Winston, 1973), p. 366.

p. 68: "pitch with my nose": *The Southpaw* (1953; New York: Bard, 1977), p. 193.

p. 68: "finish in a sprint?": Ibid., p. 139.

p. 70: "a unicorn has been born": In *The Fantasy Worlds of Peter S. Beagle* (New York: Ballantine, 1979), p. 38.

p. 71: "Andrew Carnegie of Trout!": *Trout Fishing in America* (New York: Delacorte, 1967), p. 3.

p. 71: "Seen to be Appreciated": Ibid., p. 104.

p. 71: "in dealing with us": Ibid., p. 39.

p. 72: "without any sign": *The Optimist's Daughter* (*The New Yorker*, 1969; New York: Random House, 1972), pp. 197–8.

p. 72: "her how to feel": Ibid., p. 201.

p. 72: "She was coming": Ibid., pp. 201–2.

p. 73: "patterns restored by dreams": Ibid., pp. 207–8.

p. 73: "her age was nine": *Delta Wedding* (New York: Harvest, 1979), p. 3.

Chapter Four: THE WAR AND THE NOVEL —BEFORE AND AFTER

p. 75n: "part of us at all": *The Radical Novel in the United States, 1900–1954* (Cambridge, Mass.: Harvard University Press, 1956), p. 1.

p. 76: one percent in all: My statistics derive from John Kenneth Galbraith, *The Great Crash* (Boston: Houghton Mifflin, 1972).

p. 79: "Towards Proletarian Art": This article appeared in the February 1921 issue of *The Liberator.*

p. 79: Walter Rideout comments: *Radical Novel,* p. 232.

p. 80n: "he is alienated from": *Partisan Review* XIX (May–June 1952), p. 299.

p. 81n: Hemingway, Cummings, and others: Daniel Aaron, *Writers on the Left* (New York: Harcourt, Brace, 1961).

p. 81 "seldom bother you": *On the Line* (New York: Dell Laurel, 1978), pp. 72–3.

p. 82: "making of automobiles": Ibid., p. 84.

p. 83: "revolutions in Russia and Germany": *The Managerial Revolution* (Bloomington: Indiana University (Press, 1966), p. 254.

p. 83: "evened the score": *Native Son* (New York: Signet, 1950), p. 162.

p. 84: "or catch tarpon": *Dangling Man* (New York: Vanguard, 1944), p. 10.

p. 85: "or outdo in daring": Ibid., p. 9.

p. 86: nurses or emasculators: See Victoria Sullivan's "The Battles of the Sexes in Three Bellow Novels," in *Saul Bellow,* ed. Earl Rovit (Englewood Cliffs, N.J.: Prentice-Hall, 1975).

p. 86: "Tuesday from Saturday": *Dangling Man,* p. 81.

p. 86: "six-sided box": Ibid., p. 92.

p. 86: "disease would spring": Ibid., p. 68.

p. 86: "this part or that": Ibid., p. 137.

p. 87: Harvard undergraduate years: *The Cannibal* was begun in Albert Guerard's writing course at Harvard.

p. 88: "blinking the pink-lidded eyes": *The Cannibal* (New York: New Directions, 1949), p. 153. In his 1979 fiction, *The Passion Artist,* Hawkes recreates the madhouse riot as a prison riot.

p. 88: "recompense or absolution": Ibid., pp. 189–90.

p. 88: "sun was frozen and clear": Ibid., p. 194.

p. 89: does not or could not: *Across the River and Into the Trees* (1950) was an embarrassing failure, displaying a loss not only of vision but of language.

p. 89: by *Time* and *Life* magazines: That rewriting by editors of all reportorial files not only homogenized the style; it reduced all distinctions to Luce's editorial policies.

p. 90: nostalgia for Truman: In *The Culture of Narcissism* (New York: Norton, 1979), Christopher Lasch demonstrates how a society that vaunts nostalgia trivializes all issues, past and present.

p. 91: nature of things: Lasch's *The Culture of Narcissism* would give credibility to this specious argument.

p. 91: decade of tremendous excitement: See Edmund Wilson's *Patriotic Gore* (New York: Oxford University Press, 1962) for a contemporary view of the era.

p. 93: "it was waiting": *A Walk in the Sun* (Philadelphia: Blakiston, 1944), p. 187.

p. 93: "a marvellous thing": Ibid., p. 45.

p. 94: not at all ignored: For example, Mario Puzo called his novel of the German occupation *The Dark Arena* (1955), and his Americans and Germans square off literally in a capitalistic arena.

p. 95: space with imminent death: Combat has its analogies with the animal kingdom; they share spatial considerations. Wild animals have a combat zone, in which they attack; and a retreat zone, in which they withdraw. Although such distances may differ from species to species, the question of space is significant. In one's dealing with a wild animal, as with an enemy in a battle zone, the issue becomes the difference between "flight distance" (withdrawal in the face of superior force) and "critical distance" (the battle zone itself, where confrontation becomes unavoidable). John Keegan, in *The Face of Battle,* attributes this distinction between spatial elements to the zoologist Hediger. What the animal kingdom lacks is that third spatial zone, which I call the "good wound."

p. 98: with Croftness intact: Richard Poirier, in his brief Modern Masters study of Mailer, attempts to "thicken" the intellectual quality of Mailer's work, but his effort, I feel, owes more to Poirier's own considerable qualities as a critic than to Mailer. Too many critics who write on Mailer's work are desperate to discover a literary hero.

p. 99: destruction, doom, and death: The Galleria, whose mirrors and mirror images reflect illusions, fantasies, and myths intrinsic not only to soldiers but to all America, has several postwar analogues. Walker Percy uses telescopes, Hawkes a second skin, Pynchon the Tristero System and V. herself, Gaddis forgeries and counterfeit, Nabokov Zembla and Antiterra.

p. 100: "much less than myself": *The Gallery* (1947; New York: Bantam, 1960), p. 291.

p. 101: "island of Sicily": Ibid., p. 80.

p. 101: "Except us, the dead": Ibid., p. 92.

p. 101: "admit of cowardice": Ibid.

p. 103: what has happened to her: *From Here to Eternity* (1951; New York: Signet, 1953), pp. 593, 594, 794, for example.

p. 103: "against his kind": Ibid., p. 630.

p. 104: "feel anything about it": Ibid., p. 594.

p. 105: "Old Re-enlistment Blues": Ibid., pp. 819–20.

p. 105: "role of the hero": "Notes on the Decline of Naturalism," *Image and Idea* (New York: New Directions, 1957); reprinted in Marcus Klein, ed., *The American Novel Since World War II* (New York: Fawcett, 1969), p. 31.

p. 106: "Regrets card": *The Thin Red Line* (1962; New York: Signet, 1964), p. 190.

p. 106: "shuttle forward": Ibid., p. 52.

p. 107: "fingers against the tabletop": Ibid., p. 83.

p. 108: long and unfinished novel: After Jones's death, Willie Morris completed the final three and a half chapters in the form of a summary.

p. 108: Maxwell Perkins at Scribner's: Before beginning the first part of the trilogy, *From Here to Eternity*, Jones submitted to Scribner's, in 1945, a manuscript called *They Shall Inherit the Laughter*, whose matter was derivative of Thomas Wolfe. A. Scott Berg in *Max Perkins: Editor of Genius* (New York: Dutton, 1978) describes the relationship between Jones and Perkins, Scribner's famous editor, especially pp. 433–7.

p. 108: "a superior quality": *Whistle* (1978; New York: Delacorte, 1978), p. 297.

p. 109: "things have happened already": *By Love Possessed* (1957; New York: Harvest, 1957), p. 118.

p. 109: "doing them justice": *Guard of Honor* (1948; New York: Harvest, n.d.), p. 234.

p. 109: "in terms or facts": Quoted by Matthew Bruccoli, ed., *Just Representations: A James Gould Cozzens Reader* (New York: Harcourt, 1978), p. 390.

p. 110: "to them reserved": *Guard of Honor*, p. 166.

p. 111: "fat behind with my mother": *The Caine Mutiny* (1951; New York: Doubleday, 1954), p. 496.

p. 113: "squeezed into a few days": *The Wolf That Fed Us* (New York: Doubleday, 1949), p. 152.

p. 114: "They are the same": *Dog Soldiers* (1974; New York: Ballantine, 1975), p. 316.

p. 116: "Instead they were arrested": *Going After Cacciato* (New York: Delacorte, 1978), p. 228.

p. 116: "aware of his body": Ibid., p. 58.

p. 117: "had got a shirt": *A Flag for Sunrise* (New York: Knopf, 1981), p. 376.

p. 117: "own land here": Ibid., p. 401.

p. 117: " 'Hast thou a flag for me?' ": Ibid., p. 380.

p. 117: " 'handmaid of the Lord' ": Ibid., p. 416.

p. 119: "heat and the glare": *The Victim* (1947; New York: Vanguard), p. 51.

p. 120: "never see the flame": Ibid., p. 258.

p. 121: "where we were": *A Fable* (New York: Random House, 1954), p. 295.

p. 121: "you were competent for": Ibid., p. 328.

p. 121: "salute this time": Ibid., p. 13.

p. 121: "its own success": Ibid., pp. 71–2.

p. 121n: "never look back": *The Faulkner-Cowley File* (New York: Viking, 1966), p. 128.

p. 122: "a pheasant drive": Ibid., p. 305.

p. 122: "other two Marys": Ibid., p. 105.

p. 122: "the Resurrection": *Selected Letters of William Faulkner*, ed. Joseph Blotner (New York: Vintage, 1978), p. 179.

p. 122: "midst of war again": Ibid., p. 180.

p. 122: "overwriting, dullness, etc.": Ibid., p. 251.

p. 123: "short-sighted society": *The Mortgaged Heart*, ed. Margarita G. Smith (New York: Bantam, 1972), p. 141.

p. 123: "he was suspended": *The Heart Is a Lonely Hunter* (1940; New York: Penguin, 1946), pp. 303–4.

p. 123: as much Lawrentian: Lawrence's short story "The Prussian Officer" seems to have been an active influence on the shaping, not the content, of the novel.

p. 124: "old El dreams": *The Man with the Golden Arm* (1949; New York: Pocket Books, 1951), p. 130.

p. 125: "became the Tates": *A Rage to Live* (New York: Bantam, 1950), p. 132.

p. 127: "unconfidence and fear": *The End of My Life* (New York: Bantam, 1949), p. 27.

p. 127: "felt very domestic": Ibid., p. 134. Preceding quotation from p. 46.

p. 128: "make it funny": Ibid., p. 277.

p. 128: "no ethics, no standards": Ibid., p. 119. Following quotations from same page.

p. 128: "sake of running": Ibid., p. 43.

p. 128: "ever would do": Ibid., p. 218.

p. 128: "a private affair": Ibid., p. 276.

Chapter Five: GROWING UP IN AMERICA: THE 1940S AND THEREAFTER

p. 130: "long, long time": *Growing Up Absurd* (New York: Vintage, 1962), pp. 240–1.

p. 131: "new psychological quests": "Protean Man," *Partisan Review* XXXV (Winter 1968), p. 17.

p. 131: key figures Eisenhower, Nixon: The novelists were up against Nixon's referring to the State Department as "The Dean Acheson College for Cowardly Containment of Communism," in 1953. Did American politics start here?

p. 132: "than I do Moscow": Richard Hofstadter, *The Paranoid Style in American Politics* (New York: Knopf, 1965), p. 98.

p. 133: "the rest cringing away": *Call It Sleep* (1934; New York: Avon, 1964), p. 27.

p. 133: *"The hammer!"* Ibid., p. 83.

p. 134: "and it was light!" Isaiah 6: 6–7.

p. 134: "bulged and / billowed": *Call It Sleep,* p. 426.

p. 134: "a rock shears water": Ibid., p. 35.

p. 134: "call it sleep": Ibid., p. 441. Following quotations from same page.

p. 135: "a mind inside": *The Mountain Lion* (1947; New York: Farrar, Straus & Giroux, 1972), p. 177. Plath's *The Bell Jar* seems deeply indebted to several images of death in the Stafford novel.

p. 135: "socket of rocks": Ibid., p. 158.

p. 135: "dirty words you know": Ibid.

p. 136: "her golden hide": Ibid., p. 220.

p. 136: "fruit in her forehead": Ibid., p. 229.

p. 137: pastoral image reemerges, energized: Herbert Gold's *Therefore Be Bold* (1960) is a minor emanation from *Rye*. Although Gold fixes adolescently on his protagonist's need to "make out," he does catch the nature of the dispossessed garden in which a young person grows up. There is an idyllic overnight in which the boys take to the woods. They make their fire with a *Plain Dealer* that asserts Roosevelt is bankrupting the nation (this on the eve of the war), capitalism will be sucked in and destroyed by foreign machinations. The boys are transformed by whiskey—stolen from their parents and poured into milk bottles!—which stirs their souls, even when a storm closes in and threatens their idyll. "We had each drained off into milk bottles a sample of alcohol from our parents' closets in order to ease the way toward immortal truth and beauty." Like Holden, Gold's Dan Berman reaches for an already compromised purity.

p. 138: "along with the heartbeat": *Franny and Zooey* (1961; New York: Bantam, 1964), p. 113.

p. 139: *"Seymour's Fat Lady":* Ibid., p. 201

p. 139: "Christ Himself, buddy": Ibid., p. 202.

p. 140: "sacred human conscience": Ibid., p. 105.

p. 140: "the all-knowing": Ibid., p. 143.

p. 140: "electrocuted the Rosenbergs": *The Bell Jar* (1963; New York: Harper & Row, 1971), p. 1.

p. 142: "make it look so": *The Adventures of Augie March* (New York: Viking, 1953), p. 117.

p. 142: "first to knock, first admitted": Ibid., p. 1.

p. 142: "have a fate": *The Griffin,* September 1953.

p. 143: *Paris Review* interview: Reprinted in *Writers at Work,* ed. George Plimpton (New York: Viking, 1968), pp. 175–96.

p. 143: "easy and banal": Ibid., pp. 189–90.

p. 143: "excitement of discovery": Ibid., p. 182.

p. 145: "existence is worth-ful": Ibid., p. 192.

p. 145: "shameful and impotent privacy": *Encounter* XXI: 25.

p. 145: "force in James Baldwin": *Soul on Ice* (New York: Delta, 1968), p. 103.

p. 146: "writer on world events": *Amistad 1,* ed. John A. Williams and Charles F. Harris (New York: Vintage, 1970), p. 50. Following quotation from same page.

p. 146n: "bow to a *black man":* Ibid., p. 109.

p. 147: "a holy man, neither": *Go Tell It on the Mountain* (1953; New York: Signet, 1954), p. 114.

p. 148: "Washington—now Portnoy": *Portnoy's Complaint* (New York: Random House, 1969), p. 235. Parts were published separately, beginning in 1967.

p. 148: "perhaps to begin. Yes?": Ibid., p. 274.

p. 149: "and will never have": *Cosmicomics* (New York: Harbrace Paperbound Library, 1976), p. 29.

p. 149: "close to contempt": Ibid., p. 185.

p. 149: "with three letters!": Ibid., p. 184.

p. 149: "Not stupid at all": Ibid., p. 194.

p. 150: "the human world": *The Painted Bird* (1965; New York: Pocket Books, 1966), p. 42.

p. 150: "bouquet of wildflowers": Ibid., p. 44.

p. 151: "a fierce attack": Ibid.

p. 151: "of encouragement, any weakness": Ibid., p. 135. Following two quotations from same page.

p. 151n: "taken place in the mind": *Notes of the Author on The Painted Bird* (New York: Scientia-Factum, 1967), p. 13.

p. 152: "a vicious circle": *Painted Bird,* p. 137.

p. 152: "new powers for me": Ibid., p. 138.

p. 152: "his own existence": *Blind Date* (1977; New York: Bantam, 1978), p. 97.

p. 152: "abandoned dance": *Painted Bird,* p. 140. Preceding quotations from same page.

p. 152: "ghosts and ghouls": Ibid., p. 28.

p. 152: "warmed it during the day": Ibid., p. 20.

p. 153: "fact of being alive": Ibid., p. 198.

p. 153: "Jews on the fourth": Ibid.

p. 154: "for ordinary people": Ibid., p. 101.

p. 154: "Gavrila and Mitka": Ibid., p. 205.

p. 154: "wished to protect him": Ibid. Following quotation from same page.

p. 154: "paralyzed his muscles": Ibid., p. 207. Following quotation from same page.

p. 155: "belonged to him": *Ada, or Ardor: A Family Chronicle* (New York: McGraw-Hill, 1969), p. 542.

p. 155: "in me, adds Ada": Ibid., p. 297.

p. 155n: "in Osberg's novel": Ibid., p. 83. See, for example, pp. 507 and 613, for other self-referential material.

p. 155: "glowworm of strange truth": Ibid., p. 79.

p. 156: themselves given Latinized form: Andrew Field draws our attention to the fact that the fictional treatment has a real basis: "The catherine's wheel of languages in *Ada* is the way the Nabokovs, not just Vladimir, really do speak —in the households of Nabokov's father and grandfather it was French at the table, English in the nursery, and Russian elsewhere." *His Life in Part* (New York: Penguin Books, 1978), p. 59.

p. 156: "coolness of its continuum": *Ada,* p. 571.

p. 156: "some aspect of Space": Ibid., p. 574.

p. 156: "itself is incomputable": Ibid., p. 576.

p. 156: "of Technology Fiction": Ibid., p. 578.

p. 156: references to Tolstoy: Alfred Appel, Jr., in *"Ada* Described," has an excellent paralleling of the Nabokov novel with *Anna Karenina,* some elements of *War and Peace,* and Tolstoy generally. See *Nabokov: Criticism, Reminiscences, Translations, and Tributes,* ed. Appel and Newman (Evanston, Ill.: Northwestern University Press, 1970), p. 168ff.

p. 157: "followed by another": *Ada,* p. 585.

p. 157: "part of the nowness": Ibid., p. 586.

p. 157: "utopia, progressive politics": Ibid., p. 596.

p. 158: some critics have felt: See Appel, op. cit., p. 174.

p. 158: "metaphors picturing transition": *Ada,* p. 579.

p. 159*n*: "nymphet of ten": Ibid., p. 415.

p. 159: "fixed on the screen": "In Dreams Begin Responsibilities," *In Dreams Begin Responsibilities and Other Stories,* ed. James Atlas (New York: New Directions, 1978), p. 1.

p. 160: "upward and forward": Ibid., p. 5.

p. 160: "hope alive in me": *Black Boy* (1945; New York: Signet, 1951), p. 186.

p. 161: an Italian, Nick Romano: For example, pp. 368ff., 426, 450. *Knock on Any Door* (1947; New York: Signet, 1950).

p. 162: "judgment day. In innocence": *The Fortunate Pilgrim* (1964; New York: Lancer, 1969), p. 286.

p. 162: *Children at the Gate* (1964): Published posthumously.

p. 163: "ghost stories": *Children at the Gate* (1964; New York: Popular Library, 1964), p. 116.

p. 163: passage leading up to: *Other Voices, Other Rooms* (1949; New York: Signet, 1949), p. 45.

p. 165: "whims and visions": *Color of Darkness* (1957; New York: Bantam, 1970), p. 125.

p. 165: "were flesh or not": Ibid., p. 138.

p. 166: "hardly feel I exist": *Malcolm* (1959; New York: Avon, n.d.), p. 49.

p. 166: "shone like gold": Ibid., p. 5.

p. 166: "of her mansion": *Color of Darkness,* p. 117.

p. 167: antagonism to women: This is the subject of a good short study by Mary Allen, *The Necessary Blankness: Women in Major American Fiction of the Sixties* (Urbana: University of Illinois Press, 1976). She is particularly shrewd in discussing those novelists, like Updike, who ostensibly like women and yet who perceive them in traditionally derogatory terms. In *Rabbit Redux,* for example, Updike has created a new woman in Jill: "In creating a new type of woman and brutally disposing of her Updike seems unaware of what he does, not only in terms of artistic distortion but as a revelation of his determination to preserve a bovine image of woman" (p. 127).

p. 167: "clutching at a straw": *Malcolm,* p. 130.

p. 167: "Vernon retorted": Ibid., p. 121.

p. 167: "feathers, Mrs. B.!": Ibid., p. 106.

p. 168: "times without fail": *Cat's Cradle* (1963; New York: Delta, 1963.), p. 13.

p. 169: *"The Books of Bokonon":* Ibid., p. 216.

p. 169: chances of more light: For example, *The Sirens of Titan* (1959) begins: "Everyone now knows how to find the meaning of life within himself" (p. 7).

p. 171: "blue turban in the Hague": *The Centaur* (1962; New York: Fawcett, 1964), p. 63.

p. 171: "infinitesmal feathers": Ibid., p. 191.

p. 171: "is all about them": Ibid., p. 196.

p. 172: "is dead, *mein kind": Birds of America* (New York: Harcourt Brace Jovanovich, 1971), p. 340.

p. 173: "magic and poetry": *Even Cowgirls Get the Blues* (Boston: Houghton Mifflin, 1976), p. 379.

p. 173: "most effective of all": *The Teachings of Don Juan: A Yaqui Way of Knowledge* (New York: Ballantine, 1969), p. 183.

p. 173: "simpler, rustic lifestyles": *Even Cowgirls,* p. 268. Echoes of Lawrence's study of American literature are apparent, especially his remarks on early Melville.

Chapter Six: THE COUNTERFEIT DECADE

p. 177: "urgently be confronted": Yergin, op. cit., p. 196.

p. 178*n*: "we all fear: totalitarianism": February 1950, p. 105.

p. 178*n*: In the later symposium: May–June 1952.

p. 178: "himself as an artist": "The American Action Painters," *The Tradition of the New* (1959; New York: McGraw-Hill paperback, 1965), p. 31.

p. 179: *Commentary* would applaud: As Christopher Lasch phrased it, in *The Agony of the American Left* (New York: Knopf, 1969): "The freedom of American intellectuals as a professional class blinds them to their un-freedom. It leads them to confuse the political interests of intellectuals as an official minority with the progress of intellect. Their freedom from overt political control (particularly from 'vigilantes') blinds them to the way in which the 'knowledge industry' has been incorporated into the state and the military-industrial complex" (p. 98).

p. 180: "see what I mean?": *The Recognitions* (1955; New York: Meridian, 1962), pp. 450–1.

p. 181: "genuine article must endure": Ibid., p. 230.

p. 182: "artist you forge": Ibid., p. 250.

p. 182: "where mine goes": Ibid. Following quotation from same page.

p. 183: almost five hundred pages later: On p. 487.

p. 184: "national recognition": Ibid.

p. 184: "only hands but eyes": Ibid., p. 494.

p. 185: "descriptions of reality": *City of Words,* p. 27.

p. 186: "though seldom played": *The Recognitions,* p. 250.

p. 186: monumentally conceived *JR: JR* won the National Book Award for the best novel of 1975 and then sank into oblivion.

p. 186: "the light of day!": Libretto for Solti *Ring,* p. 26.

p. 187: "we saw it. Lifeless.": *JR* (New York: Knopf, 1975), p. 3.

p. 187: "me to find it?": Ibid., p. 133.

p. 188: "use it to play the": Ibid., p. 464.

p. 189: "bellies and learned the": Ibid., pp. 472–3.

p. 190: "into the atmosphere period": Ibid., p. 527.

p. 191: "next conflicting phase": *Invisible Man* (New York: Signet, n.d.), p. 498.

p. 191: "more overt action": Ibid., p. 16.

p. 191: "conform to a pattern": Ibid., p. 499.

p. 191: "into its depths": Ibid., p. 12.

p. 191: "passion to perception": *Paris Review* interview, op. cit., 2nd series, p. 328.

p. 192: "death and destruction": *Invisible Man*, pp. 19–20.

p. 192: "stay down there": *Paris Review*, p. 330.

p. 192n: "come to him yet": *Invisible Man*, p. 42.

p. 193: "American Negro writer": *Paris Review* interview, p. 320.

p. 194: explained to John Hersey: In the *Paris Review* interview.

p. 194: "late afternoon Harlem": *Invisible Man*, p. 218.

p. 195: "you're white, you're right": Ibid., p. 190.

p. 195: "effects of the knife": Ibid., p. 206. Following quotation from same page.

p. 195: "trustees and such": Ibid., p. 217.

p. 196: "ace in the hole?": Ibid., p. 381. Following quotation from same page.

p. 196: "corn before the harvest": Ibid., p. 502.

p. 197: "center leak out": *Ralph Ellison*, p. 6.

p. 197: "that air-conditioned AIR": *American Review*, February 1973, p. 264.

p. 197: one's private vision: See "The World and The Jug," *Shadow and Act* (1964; New York: Signet, 1966), pp. 119, 123, 130.

p. 197n: "constantly observed object": *The System of Dante's Hell* (New York: Grove, 1963, 1965). This phrase was added for the 1965 edition, in the Finale.

p. 199: "if put to it": *Go* (1952; New York: Appel, 1977), p. 35.

p. 199: "streets themselves": Ibid., p. 36.

p. 199: "argument over coffee": Ibid., p. 35.

p. 199: "sense of defeat": Ibid., p. 207.

p. 200: "in the book": *Go*, p. xi.

p. 201: "way to Los Angeles": *On the Road* (1957; New York: Signet, 1958), p. 5.

p. 201: "I was unrecognizably caked": Ibid., p. 202. Following quotation from same page.

p. 202: "shooting out from it": Ibid., p. 212.

p. 202: "bulk and bursting ecstasies": Ibid., p. 212.

p. 204: "long way from shadows": *Flee the Angry Strangers* (1952; New York: Charter, 1962), p. 364.

p. 205: "end of every fork": *Naked Lunch* (1959; New York: Black Cat, 1966), p. xxxvii.

p. 205: "long newspaper spoon": Ibid., p. xliv.

p. 207: "a cop says": Ibid., p. 15.

p. 207: "does it come from?": Ibid., pp. 12–13.

p. 207: "his enemy direct": Ibid., p. 21.

p. 208: "open in *Silence*": Ibid., p. 224.

p. 208: "rancid ectoplasm": Ibid., p. 230.

p. 208: "psychic process": Ibid., p. 221.

p. 208: "instead of in words": *The Job*, p. 133.

p. 208: "function of words": Ibid., p. 28.

p. 209: "TRAK to unknown sanctions": *The Soft Machine* (1961; New York: Black Cat, 1967), p. 47.

p. 209: Phi Beta Kappa address: Reprinted in *Harper's*, May 1961, pp. 47–9.

p. 209: "years and centuries": *Soft Machine*, p. 164.

p. 209: from the contemporary sensibility: A critic as finely tuned to the nuances of the contemporary sensibility as Lionel Trilling could not confront Kafka enthusiastically in a full essay or in any extended evaluation. In *Beyond Culture*, Trilling does not begin to grapple with the cultural implications of Kafka's anarchy and/or nihilism. See "On the Teaching of Modern Literature."

p. 209: "flickered like old film": *Soft Machine*, p. 71.

p. 210: "clean fall out": Ibid., p. 72.

p. 210: "spitting blood laugh": Ibid., p. 177.

p. 210: "Base Headquarters": *The Ticket That Exploded* (1962; New York: Grove, 1967), pp. 5–6.

p. 211: "cool blue wind": Ibid., p. 128.

p. 211: "that is to nova": Ibid., pp. 54–5.

p. 211: "contains a random factor": Ibid., p. 166.

p. 211: "by what we hear": Ibid., p. 205.

p. 211: "into the street": Ibid., p. 210.

p. 212: "air into thin air": Ibid., p. 217.

p. 212: "unborn feet forever": *Nova Express* (1964; New York: Black Cat, 1965), p. 11.

p. 212: "lines of the earth": Ibid., p. 20.

p. 212: "entire heat syndrome": Ibid., p. 40.

p. 212: "same planet": Ibid., p. 52. Following quotation from same page.

p. 213: "exploded in smoke": Ibid., p. 129.

p. 213: "window people and sky": Ibid., p. 154.

p. 213: "long time ago": Ibid., p. 155.

p. 213: "a Mexican city": *The Wild Boys* (1971; New York: Black Cat, 1973), p. 3.

p. 213: "started in 1969": Ibid., p. 143.

p. 213: "the Blue desert": Ibid., p. 147.

p. 213: "carrying nerve gas": *Exterminator!* (New York: Viking, 1974), p. 85.

p. 213: "destruction of wild life": Ibid., p. 86.

p. 213: "his unpopular thesis": Ibid., p. 40.

p. 213: "more you need": Ibid., p. 166.

p. 213: "your own body": Ibid., p. 168.

p. 215: "under the talons": *The Owl*, in *Lunar Landscapes* (New York: New Directions, n.d.), p. 139.

p. 215: "narrow driving streets": Ibid., p. 141.

p. 216: "marrow and gut given": Ibid., p. 147.

p. 216: "despite webbed feet": Ibid., p. 156.

p. 216: "intimate unnatural pattern": Ibid., p. 192.

p. 216: "to his collar-bone": Ibid., p. 239. *The Goose on the Grave*, like *The Owl*, goes back, in its conception and writing, to the later war years, when Hawkes was not yet twenty.

p. 216: "over-anxious oar blade": Ibid., p. 262.

p. 217: "into the darkness": Ibid., p. 56.

p. 217: "with the little": Ibid., p. 57.

p. 217: "water level of the dam": *The Beetle Leg* (New York: New Directions, 1951), p. 17. Following quotation from same page.

p. 218: "keep up with it": Ibid., pp. 67–8.

p. 218: "fruitful of emergencies": Ibid., p. 121.

p. 218: "its wire legs": Ibid., p. 123. Following quotation from same page.

p. 220: "numbers on the slate": Ibid., p. 92.

p. 220: "rubbers beside him": Ibid., pp. 94–5.

p. 220: "to be accounted for": Ibid., p. 49.

p. 220: "on Rock by Plebeian": Ibid.

p. 221: "quite out of time": *Second Skin* (New York: New Directions, 1964), p. 46.

p. 222: "dead dry locusts": Ibid., p. 25.

p. 222: "sleep, sleep, sleep?": Ibid., p. 161.

p. 223: "Two months old. Human.": Ibid., p. 202.

p. 223: "but about love": Called "The Last Lover," *The Griffin,* August 1958.

p. 224: and mirror reflections: Nabokov's Russian novel *Despair* (written in 1932, published in Russian in 1934; in English in 1937) turns on reflections and mirror images. As Hermann says, " 'I was still on admirable terms with mirrors.' " (New York: Capricorn, 1966, p. 74.) Hermann resembles Humbert slightly, to the degree that Nabokov in his foreword to the Putnam edition felt the need to reject any close similarity. "Hermann and Humbert are alike only in the sense that two dragons painted by the same artist at different periods of his life resemble each other" (p. 9).

p. 224n: alluded to in "The Magician": See Andrew Field, *Nabokov: His Life in Art* (Boston: Little, Brown, 1967), pp. 328–9; also *The Annotated Lolita,* ed. Alfred Appel, Jr. (New York: McGraw-Hill, 1970), p. xxxvii.

p. 225: Field quotes: Op. cit., p. 324.

p. 225: "Chateaubriandesque trees, etc.": *Lolita* (1955, 1958; New York: Crest, 1959), p. 133.

p. 227: "huge engorged heart": Ibid., p. 63.

p. 228: "it transcend its time": *Pale Fire* (1962; New York: Lancer, 1963), p. 209.

p. 228: elements of a mirroring process: Kinbote writes: "My commentary to this poem, now in the hands of my readers, represents an attempt to sort out those echoes and wavelets of fire, and pale phosphorescent hints, and all the many subliminal debts to me. . . . In other words, everything will be done to cut off my person completely from my dear friend's fate." (*Pale Fire,* p. 210.)

p. 229: "discovering Peking man": *The Habit of Being,* ed. Sally Fitzgerald (New York: Farrar, Straus & Giroux, 1979), p. 366.

p. 229: "passive diminishment": Ibid., p. 53.

p. 230: "what was called it": *Wise Blood,* in *Three* by Flannery O'Connor (New York: Signet, n.d.), p. 63.

p. 231: "matters of life and death": Ibid., p. 8.

p. 232: Cain and Ishmael: "He felt it building from the blood of Abel to his own, rising and engulfing him." *The Violent Bear It Away,* in *Three,* p. 447.

p. 233: "dull green of the tree": "The Displaced Person," in *A Good Man Is Hard to Find* (1954). In *The Complete Stories* (New York: Farrar, Straus & Giroux, 1972), p. 200.

p. 235: "implacable, to descend": *Complete Stories,* p. 382.

p. 235: "better things in it": *The Habit of Being,* (November 28, 1961), p. 356.

p. 236: "to do with Styron's": Ibid., p. 461.

p. 238: "could possibly handle": *Set This House on Fire* (1960; New York: Signet, 1961), p. 60. Lines like that may have convinced Tony Tanner to leave Styron out of his *City of Words,* which covers 1950–70, the very period of Styron's body of work.

p. 238: "full freedom": Ibid., p. 148.

p. 239: "There was nothing": Ibid., p. 465.

p. 239: "murder, suicide and rape": *Cannibals and Christians* (New York: Dial, 1966), p. 110.

p. 240: "trumpet of your defiance": *Deer Park* (1955; New York: Signet, 1957), p. 318.

p. 240: "in the sexual humanities": "The Time of Her Life," in *The Short Fiction of Norman Mailer* (New York: Dell, 1967), p. 234.

p. 241: "voice of my novel": *Advertisements for Myself* (New York: Putnam, 1959), p. 235.

p. 241: "chaos may be ordered": "The Man Who Studied Yoga," in *Short Fiction,* p. 285.

p. 244: "prayers for the dead": *The Magic Barrel* (1950–58, 1958; New York: Vintage, 1960), p. 214.

p. 245: "did you a favor": *Pictures of Fidelman* (1969; New York: Pocket Books, 1975), p. 41.

p. 245: "loved men and women": Ibid., p. 192.

p. 246: "a creation of God": *Player Piano* (1952; New York: Avon, 1967), p. 286.

p. 247: "light years away": *The Sirens of Titan* (New York: Dell, 1959; original publication in paperback), p. 297.

p. 248: "the other two": *The Outsider* (1953; New York: Signet, 1954), p. 247.

p. 248: "played no role in it": Ibid., p. 127. Following quotation from same page.

p. 249: "bold and delicate book": *The New Yorker,* August 24, 1957.

p. 250: "other contemporary writer": *Harper's,* September 1957.

p. 250: "of Joan's possible?": *By Love Possessed* (New York: Harcourt, Brace, 1957), p. 176.

p. 250: "in supporting mysteries": Ibid., p. 569.

p. 251: "trespassed its margins": *The Poorhouse Fair* (1958: New York: Fawcett, 1964), p. 114.

p. 251n: "observations of people": *Time to Murder and Create* (New York: McKay, 1966), p. 166.

p. 251: "fault in the sky": Ibid., p. 55.

Chapter Seven: THE POLITICAL NOVEL: 1950S AND AFTER

p. 256: *"strike, strike!": Henderson the Rain King* (New York: Viking, 1959), p. 12.

p. 256: "world of their own": Ibid., p. 76.

p. 256: "want to live": Ibid., p. 77.

p. 257: "hand became incandescent": Ibid., p. 227.

p. 257: "gray Arctic silence": Ibid., p. 341.

p. 259: "doomed peoples": *The Dean's December* (New York: Harper & Row, 1982), p. 192.

p. 259: "a good many subscribers": Ibid., p. 193.

p. 259: "no coherence—none": Ibid., p. 266.

p. 260: "Day of Disaster": *The Coup* (New York: Knopf, 1978), p. 72.

p. 260: "posters of Mao": Ibid., p. 117.

p. 262: "it had ten horns": Daniel 7:7–8.

p. 263: "cannot have planned for": *The Book of Daniel* (1971; New York: Signet, 1972), p. 84.

p. 263: "how obscure we were": Ibid., p. 106. Following quotations from same page.

p. 263: "has been arrested": Ibid., p. 117.

p. 263: "amplifies its voices": Ibid., p. 136.

p. 264: "of affliction, a priest": Ibid., p. 186.

p. 264: "Cowardly Communist Containment": *The Public Burning* (New York: Viking, 1977), pp. 142–3.

p. 266: "Mormon Tabernacle Choir": Ibid., p. 510.

p. 266: "size of the principals": Ibid., p. 540.

p. 266: "up my ass": Ibid., p. 560.

p. 266: "I confessed": Ibid., p. 563.

p. 269: "some statistical median": *The Groves of Academe* (1952; New York: Signet, 1963), p. 51.

p. 270: "political realm": *Cannibals and Missionaries* (New York: Harcourt Brace Jovanovich, 1979), p. 226.

p. 270: "into pure gold": Ibid., p. 227.

p. 270: "a real place": Ibid., p. 81.

p. 270: "than being Swiss": Ibid., p. 80.

p. 271: "starting at the verbal end": *Our Gang,* subtitled "Starring Tricky and His Friends" (New York: Random House, 1971), from Orwell's "Politics and the English Language."

p. 273: "pissed them away": *The Fixer* (New York: Farrar, Straus & Giroux, 1966), p. 333.

p. 273: "will of the people": Ibid., p. 334.

p. 273: "see yourself destroyed": Ibid., p. 335.

p. 274: "going right through": *A Different Drummer* (New York: Anchor, 1969), p. 26.

Chapter Eight: THE 1960S: THE (WO)MAN WHO CRIED I AM

p. 276: "country any more": *Going Away* (Boston: Houghton Mifflin, 1961), p. 244.

p. 277: "Cabot or Stevenson": Ibid., p. 242.

p. 278: "no other tradition": Ibid., p. 444.

p. 278: "Help. Help": Ibid., p. 513.

p. 278: "vitality is its keynote": I am quoting the blurbs on the book jacket.

p. 279: "beneath her skirt": *The Magic Christian* (1960; New York: Bantam, 1964), p. 50.

p. 279: "twice in succession": Ibid., pp. 50–1.

p. 279: *"believe you me!"* Ibid., p. 83ff.

p. 279: "in four directions": Ibid., p. 85.

p. 280: "cut from his face": *Goodbye, Columbus* (1959; New York: Meridian, 1960), p. 28.

p. 281: "I'm a pancreas": Ibid., p. 51.

p. 282: "grace or election": *The Lonely Crowd* (New Haven: Yale University Press, 1950), p. 128.

p. 284: "Pass ALL or Fail ALL": *Giles Goat-Boy* (1966; New York: Fawcett, 1967), p. 571.

p. 284*n*: "later Gilesians, perhaps": Ibid., p. 765.

p. 285*n*: Barth writes: *Lost in the Funhouse* (New York: Bantam, 1969), p. ix.

p. 285: "over tremendous spaces": *Giles,* p. 87ff.

p. 285: "less severe neuroses": Ibid., p. 89.

p. 286: "be a human student": Ibid., p. 109.

p. 287: "prepare you to confront": *Giles,* pp. 445–6.

p. 288*n*: "original New Syllabus": Interview with John Enck, in *Wisconsin Studies in Contemporary Literature* VIII (1965): 8.

p. 288: "ultimately indistinguishable": *Giles,* p. 65.

p. 288: "cut other things": *Giles,* p. 333.

p. 289: Lord Raglan's *The Hero:* David Morrell, in *John Barth: An Introduction* (University Park: Pennsylvania State University Press, 1976), demonstrates how twenty-two of Raglan's points, from the hero's ambiguous birth to his own projection of his death, are reproduced in *Giles.* See pp. 61–4.

p. 289*n*: "knew to be accurate": *Giles,* p. 479.

p. 290: "elected my name": Ibid., p. 693.

p. 290: "remained to do": Ibid., p. 753.

p. 290: *"New Syllabus":* Ibid., p. 763.

p. 290: "blind, dishonored": Ibid., p. 764.

p. 291: "the Grand Tutor's own": Ibid., p. 766.

p. 292: "always be challenged": *The Man Who Cried I Am* (1967; New York: Signet, 1968), p. 280.

p. 293: "have been to themselves": *Amistad 2* (New York: Vintage, 1971), p. 5.

p. 293: "possess and understand it": Ibid., p. 9.

p. 293: "heritage of Negro writers": Ibid., p. 12.

p. 293: "assimilate these influences": Ibid., pp. 12–13.

p. 294: "writer and his environment": Ibid., p. 18.

p. 294: "ideas of their day": Ibid., p. 19.

p. 295: "of the other guy": *Man Who Cried,* p. 59.

p. 295: "born seeing precisely": Ibid., p. 53. Following quotations from same page.

p. 296: "nearest stretch of sky": *Sula* (1973; New York: Bantam, 1975), p. 142.

p. 297: "his bubbly laughter": Ibid., p. 52.

p. 297: "bottom of heaven": Ibid., p. 5.

p. 297: "for a woman": Ibid., p. 104.

p. 297: "she became dangerous": Ibid., p. 105.

p. 297: "one constant empty eye": Ibid., p. 105.

p. 297: "as being a man": Ibid., p. 123.

p. 298: "A secondhand lonely": Ibid., p. 123.

p. 298: "circles of sorrow": Ibid., p. 149.

p. 299: "her mother's body": *them* (1969; New York: Fawcett, n.d.), p. 182.

p. 299: "cycles to go through": Ibid., p. 194.

p. 299: Oates has chosen to introduce: In the Author's Note.

p. 300: "out of school": *them,* p. 314.

p. 300: "No shape": Ibid., p. 320.

p. 301n: "Clyde, Clyde!": *An American Tragedy* (New York: Dell, 1959), p. 526.

p. 304: "people who do": *V.* (1963; New York: Bantam, 1964), p. 356.

p. 305: "Mediterranean beyond": Ibid., p. 428.

p. 305: "he'd ever encountered": Ibid., pp. 265–6.

p. 306: "spies of Florence": Ibid., p. 181.

p. 306: "side of real-time": Ibid., p. 41.

p. 306: "rickety and transient": Ibid., p. 128.

p. 306: make something of himself: Ibid., p. 134.

p. 307: "country of his guts": Ibid., p. 287.

p. 307: in *Kenyon Review:* Reprinted in *12 from the Sixties,* ed. Richard Kostelanetz. (New York: Dell, 1967), pp. 22–35.

p. 308: "always continually increases": Ibid., p. 27.

p. 308: "new and elusive light": Ibid., p. 28.

p. 308: "absence of all motion": Ibid., p. 35.

p. 308: "Low-Lands": In *Epoch* magazine, 1960; reprinted by Aloes Books (London), 1978.

p. 308: "perspective of things": "Low-Lands," Aloes ed., n.p.

p. 308: "flame behind the altar": "Mortality and Mercy in Vienna," *Epoch,* Spring 1959; reprinted by Aloes Books, n.p.

p. 310: "far more universal": *Catch-22* (New York: Simon & Schuster, 1961), p. 8.

p. 311: *The Organization Man:* An interesting statistic: by the end of the 1940s, nearly 20 percent of American college students were majoring in business; and by the mid-1950s, business was the largest undergraduate major.

p. 315: "within it feel it": *The Moviegoer* (1961; New York: Popular Library, 1962), p. 20.

p. 316: "than Banquo's ghost": Ibid., p. 114.

p. 316: "dead, dead, dead": Ibid., p. 209.

p. 316: "will not fall": Ibid.

p. 316: "hardly up to it": Ibid., p. 184.

p. 317: "distinguished from edification": Ibid., p. 218.

p. 317: "ten-thousandth millimeter": *The Last Gentleman* (1966; New York: Noonday, 1976), p. 29.

p. 317: "leave it to luck": Ibid., p. 64. Following quotation from same page.

p. 318: "like an honest man?": Ibid., p. 379.

p. 318n: *"has been waiting for": The Message in the Bottle* (New York: Noonday, 1975), p. 146.

p. 319: "about his business": *The Last Gentleman,* p. 353.

p. 319: "pertain to salvation": Ibid., p. 354.

p. 319: *"imperative of understanding": Journals,* August 1, 1835.

p. 319: "with a heathen Englishman": *Love in the Ruins* (New York: Farrar, Straus & Giroux, 1971), p. 11.

p. 320: "apoplexy of conservatives": Ibid., p. 20.

p. 320: "happened at last?": Ibid., p. 3. Following quotation from same page.

p. 320n: "of the *ens soi*": "The Man on the Train," *Partisan Review,* Fall 1956, p. 484. Reprinted in *Message in the Bottle,* p. 90.

p. 321: "self from itself": *Love in the Ruins,* p. 5.

p. 321: "flashing holy fire": Ibid., p. 368.

p. 321: "soul from body": Ibid., p. 383. Following quotation from same page.

p. 321: "time in the world": Ibid., p. 383.

p. 322: "salesmen, imbeciles": *Cabot Wright Begins* (New York: Farrar, Straus & Giroux, 1964), p. 170.

p. 323: "dirty *hard* book": Ibid., p. 201.

p. 323: "nobody is to home": Ibid., p. 212.

p. 323: "Grover Kennedy Johnson": Ibid., p. 207.

p. 323: "women are in": These quotations, respectively, from pp. 120, 138, 164.

p. 324: "house of busted dreams": *Eustace Chisolm and the Works* (1967; New York: Bantam, 1968), p. 134.

p. 324: "committing adultery": Ibid., p. 15.

p. 324: "small separate armies": Ibid., p. 3.

p. 325: "mountain-high sea": *In a Shallow Grave* (1975; New York: Arbor House, 1977), p. 124.

p. 325: "thread with this world": Ibid., p. 118.

p. 326: "like Superman": *The Human Season* (1960; New York: Berkley Medallion, 1964), p. 134.

p. 326: "no bearded Torturer": Ibid., p. 143. Two following quotations from same page.

p. 327: "saw their ugliness": *The Pawnbroker* (New York: Harcourt, Brace, 1961), pp. 256–7.

p. 327: "aggregate of pains": Ibid., p. 257.

p. 328: "colors of the outside": *The Tenants of Moonbloom* (New York: Harcourt, Brace, 1963), p. 32.

p. 329: "I doubt my existence": Ibid., p. 59.

p. 330: "husband and wife": *Seize the Day* (1956; New York: Viking Compass, 1961), p. 98. Following quotation from same page.

p. 331: "daughter of my people!": Jeremiah 9:1.

p. 332: as one critic: Richard Poirier, in *Partisan Review,* Spring 1965.

p. 332: Bellow has spoken: In *Paris Review* interview, op. cit.

p. 333n: "is without genius": *Commentary* XLI (March 1966): 39.

p. 333: "considered having an affair": *Herzog* (1964; New York: Viking Compass, 1967), p. 19.

p. 333n: "what really counts": *Modern Occasions,* op. cit., p. 177.

p. 334: "their employment by us": *Herzog,* p. 272.

p. 335: "theology of suffering": Ibid., p. 317.

p. 335: "order within oneself": *Mr. Sammler's Planet* (1970; New York: Fawcett, 1971), p. 208.

p. 336: "male love affairs": Ibid., p. 101.

p. 336: "their own persons": Ibid., p. 37.

p. 337: nor can *Sammler:* In "Culture Now," written for Rahv's *Modern Occasions,* Bellow sensed he was on weak ground with Sammler's advocacy of Wellsian rationality: "It should not be assumed that I recommend common sense for the artist. Surrounded by lunatics, he must make rational judgments, but he is not bound by these in his art. The operations of common sense are only preliminary. Once a writer has understood the state of fantasy prevailing, once he has understood what an art-polluted environment this is, his imagination is free again to receive new impulses." Yet Bellow has, so far, quelled these "new impulses" in his fiction.

p. 340n: "how much I love you": *Tell Me How Long the Train's Been Gone* (New York: Dial, 1968), p. 272.

p. 341: "Christ crucified?": *William Styron's Nat Turner: Ten Black Writers Respond* (Boston: Beacon, 1968), p. 104.

p. 341: "with golden curls": *The Confessions of Nat Turner* (New York: Random House, 1967), p. 193.

p. 341: "all my lust": Ibid., p. 183.

p. 341: "spurts of desecration": Ibid., p. 367.

p. 342: *"I want her":* Ibid., p. 413.

p. 344: "make each joke work": *The Vonnegut Statement* (New York: Delta, 1973), p. 258.

p. 344: "like an alligator": Ibid., pp. 243–4.

p. 346: "common-sense cruelty": *God Bless You, Mr. Rosewater* (1965; New York: Delta, n.d.), p. 210.

p. 346: "named Montana Wildhack": *Slaughterhouse-Five* (New York: Delacorte, 1969), p. 22.

p. 346: "cry at his funeral": Ibid., p. 23.

p. 347: "people on the ground": Ibid., p. 144.

p. 347: "live at peace?": Ibid., p. 100.

p. 348: "hands elates him": *Rabbit, Run* (1960; New York: Fawcett, 1963), p. 9.

p. 348: "leaves his hands": Ibid., p. 24.

p. 348: "mild bodies of women": Ibid., p. 165. Updike reaches for theological, philosophical, even mythical dimensions which his characters cannot sustain. Recognizing the need for "meaning," he manufactures it. That is perhaps why women become refuge for his men: sexuality without further meaning. Marriage is a form of pastoral, adultery a species of Eden.

p. 349: "in her mouth *was":* Ibid., p. 123.

p. 349n: "fussy old nance": *Cannibals and Christians,* p. 121.

p. 350: "their thing, unself-consciously": *Rabbit Redux* (New York: Knopf, 1971), p. 159. Mary Allen, in *The Necessary Blankness* (p. 127), feels that Updike kills off Jill because he cannot handle her fictionally; she upsets his "bovine vision" of women.

p. 350: "Benighted States of Amurri-ka": *Rabbit Redux,* p. 231.

p. 353: *"furtively* hedonist": *Couples* (1968; New York: Fawcett, 1969), p. 113.

p. 353n: "out of ourselves": *Pigeon Feathers* (1962; New York: Fawcett, 1963), p. 157.

p. 353: "venerable universities": *Bech: A Book* (New York: Knopf, 1970), p. 62.

p. 354: "far from home": Ibid., p. 121.

p. 354: "titillating as pornography": Ibid., p. 129. Following quotation from same page.

p. 356: "things that really counted": *The Group* (1963; New York: Signet, 1964), p. 3.

p. 357: "larger hook I'm on": *Letting Go* (1962; New York: Bantam, 1963), p. 628.

p. 358: "Taylor's pubic bush": *Reading Myself and Others* (New York: Noonday, 1975), p. 36.

p. 358: "you really are!": *Zuckerman Unbound* (New York: Farrar, Straus & Giroux, 1981), p. 217.

p. 360: "Where am I?"—*The Crying of Lot 49* (1966; New York: Bantam, 1967), p. 114.

p. 360: "being an actor": Ibid., p. 20.

p. 361: "into the system": Ibid., p. 62.

p. 361: "with the gift": Ibid., p. 63.

p. 361: "tryst with Trystero": Ibid., p. 52.

p. 361: "will be its emblem": Ibid., p. 85.

p. 361: "in charge of faces": Ibid., p. 102.

p. 362: "to the Inverarity estate": Ibid., p. 127.

p. 362: "government delivery system": Ibid., p. 128.

p. 363: "Lamont Cranston voice": Ibid., pp. 2–3. "The Shadow knows."

p. 363: "screw up your signal": "Entropy," in *12 from the Sixties,* p. 29.

p. 365: "A CROSS OF GOLD": *A Hall of Mirrors* (1967; New York: Fawcett, 1968), p. 302.

p. 365: "It was very familiar": Ibid., p. 337.

p. 365: "bust up the bar": Ibid., p. 352.

p. 365: "as an invert": Ibid., p. 266.

p. 365: "crap-colored blue": Ibid., p. 267.

p. 366: "as it should be": *The Origin of the Brunists* (1966; New York: Ballantine, 1967), p. 25.

p. 368: "please or amuse us": *Saw* (New York: Knopf, 1972), n.p.

p. 368: "seeping to the surface": Ibid., p. 24.

p. 368: "that's where it's at": Ibid., p. 7.

p. 368: "communicate by coughing": Ibid., p. 103.

p. 369: "This book is an autobiography": Ibid., p. 126.

p. 369: "happened to anyone else": Ibid., p. 129.

p. 369: "forbidding in the moonlight": *The Free-Lance Pallbearers* (1967; New York: Avon, 1977), p. 92.

p. 369: "scholars in the movement": Ibid., p. 74.

p. 369: "psychological disturbances": Ibid., pp. 7–8.

p. 370: "then, Loop said": *Yellow Back Radio Broke Down* (1969; New York: Bard, 1977), pp. 122–3.

p. 370: "(NICK!) O.K.?": Ibid., p. 123.

p. 370n: "is a tip": *Blueschild Baby* (1970; New York: Dell, 1972), p. 93.

p. 370: "once he takes office": *Mumbo Jumbo* (1972; New York: Bard, 1978), p. 18.

p. 371: "the stateroom table": *A Smuggler's Bible* (New York: Bard, 1966), p. 1.

p. 371n: "designed to fracture": *Tri-Quarterly,* Fall 1975, p. 205.

p. 371n: "what bruder didn't say": *Smuggler's Bible,* p. 118.

p. 372: "HOLY BIBLE": Ibid., p. 298.

p. 372: "small objects of value": Ibid., p. 299.

p. 372: "faked amnesia": Ibid., p. 304.

p. 372: "right here after death": Ibid., p. 398.

p. 373: "last process of dying": Ibid., p. 235. Following quotation from same page.

p. 374: both God and devil: Drawing on a single mention of Robinson Crusoe in the text, Tony Tanner sees a dialectic between Crusoe and Sindbad the Sailor, who is mentioned more than once. Crusoe settles down on his island, although he journeys on it—thus he is both bourgeois and adventurer; whereas Sinbad is purely the adventurer. Tanner sees McElroy as holding these two elements in balance, "the emblematic extremes." (*Tri-Quarterly,* Spring 1976, pp. 223–4.)

p. 374: "Ellen": *Smuggler's Bible,* pp. 362–3.

p. 374: "two mad equations": Ibid., p. 394.

p. 375: "pier by the hospital": *Hind's Kidnap: A Pastoral on Familiar Airs* (New York: Harper & Row, 1969), p. 1.

p. 376: "reconstitution of place": *Proustian Space* (Baltimore: Johns Hopkins University Press, 1977), p. 66. French publication was in 1963.

p. 376n: Ortega y Gasset argued: See his essay "The Dehumanization of Art," in *The Dehumanization of Art and Other Essays.*

p. 377: "tractors and billboards": *Hind's Kidnap,* p. 239.

p. 377n: "real estate prices": *Lookout Cartridge* (New York: Knopf, 1974), p. 3.

p. 377n: "Other Concrete Abstracts": *Tri-Quarterly,* op. cit.

p. 378: "Near Nut Shells": *Hind's Kidnap,* pp. 205–6.

p. 379: "a stationary trust?": *Lookout Cartridge,* p. 289.

p. 379: "between which it lies": Ibid., p. 284.

p. 379n: "round in circles": Ibid., p. 339.

p. 380: "bulk of it": Ibid., pp. 4–5.

p. 380: "that of my pusher?": Ibid., pp. 263–4.

p. 380: "film of rain": Ibid., p. 460.

p. 380: "two by two": Ibid., p. 46.

p. 381n: "forth and back now?": Ibid., pp. 511–12.

p. 381: "all pulsing fields": Ibid., p. 447.

p. 382: "he never survived": Ibid., p. 282.

p. 383: "undreamt lookout dream": Ibid., p. 268.

p. 383: "not to think of": *Plus* (New York: Knopf, 1977), p. 147.

p. 383: "that inheres in relations": See Tanner, *Tri-Quarterly,* op. cit., p. 241.

Chapter Nine: THE POSSIBILITIES OF MINIMALISM

p. 385: "those I did want": *The Dead Father* (1975; New York: Pocket Books, 1976), p. 26.

p. 385: "vacant yellows": Ibid., p. 27.

p. 385: "handsome in its own way": Ibid., pp. 17–18.

p. 386: "should not be murdered": Ibid., p. 61.

p. 386: "made a speech": Ibid., p. 66.

p. 386: "a poor idea": Ibid., p. 141.

p. 386: "achieve very much": Ibid., p. 147.

p. 387: "dead fathers taken together": Ibid., p. 178.

p. 387: "passed it by": Ibid.

p. 387: "an attenuated form": Ibid., p. 179. Following quotation from same page.

p. 388: "in this house?": *Snow White* (1967; New York: Bantam, 1968), p. 59. Following quotations from same page.

p. 388: "I always hear": Ibid., p. 8.

p. 388: "packed with grace": Ibid., p. 77.

p. 388: "erected conventional ones": Ibid., p. 76.

p. 389: "in National Parks": Ibid., p. 62.

p. 390: "but still fluid": *Snow White,* p. 96.

p. 390: "of Snow White/etc.": Ibid., p. 181.

p. 390: "Heigh-Ho": Ibid.

p. 390: "in the dark": Ibid., p. 165.

p. 391: "is itself absurd": *Come Back, Dr. Caligari* (1964; New York: Anchor, 1965), p. 137.

p. 391: "room for irony": Ibid., p. 19.

p. 391: "smashed arms and legs": Ibid., p. 72.

p. 392: "a terrible predicament?": Ibid., p. 79.

p. 392: "too close to him": *Unspeakable Practices, Unnatural Acts* (New York: Farrar, Straus & Giroux, 1968), p. 40.

p. 392: "Latin America, for example": Ibid., p. 44.

p. 392: "whole of existence": Ibid., pp. 45–6.

p. 392: "came in clouds": Ibid., p. 3.

p. 393: "big, damaged ships": *City Life* (1970; New York: Bantam, 1971), p. 156.

p. 393: "army at all": Ibid., pp. 91–2.

p. 393: "ironic subject": Ibid., p. 95.

p. 394: "absolute bloody liar": Ibid., p. 17.

p. 394: "on tomb sculpture": *Sadness* (1972; New York: Bantam, 1974), p. 58.

p. 394: "part of the story line?": Ibid., p. 73. Joseph McElroy, in *Hind's Kidnap,* wrote an entire book about this phenomenon, in which accidentals become the pattern.

p. 394: "also in 'panting' ": Ibid., p. 75.

p. 394: "splashes, and roars": Ibid., p. 77.

p. 394: "by I. F. Stone": Ibid., p. 78.

p. 395: "or in dreams": Ibid., p. 80.

p. 395: "Ed clasps hands together": *Guilty Pleasures* (New York: Farrar, Straus & Giroux, 1974), p. 101.

p. 395: "by his own self": *Amateurs* (1976; New York: Pocket Books, 1977), p. 168.

p. 395: "all that peeling": Ibid., p. 172.

p. 395: "pure planarchy": Ibid., p. 173.

p. 395n: In a mail interview: Printed in *The New Fiction: Interviews with Innovative American Writers,* ed. Joe David Bellamy (Urbana: University of Illinois Press, 1974), p. 53.

p. 395: "make 'A Film' ": Ibid., p. 49.

p. 396: "rearrest of sixty persons?": *Great Days* (New York: Farrar, Straus & Giroux, 1979), pp. 98–9.

p. 396: "bodyguard is at fault?": Ibid., p. 99.

p. 397: "conflict and failure": *The White Album* (New York: Simon & Schuster, 1979), pp. 14–15.

p. 397: "narrow and cracked determinism": Ibid., p. 113.

p. 397: "their old life": Ibid., p. 118.

p. 398: "after a dance": *Run River* (1963; New York: Pocket Books, 1978), p. 18.

p. 399: "the hard way": *Play It As It Lays* (1970; New York: Bantam, 1971), p. 199.

p. 400: "Sidney Howard": Ibid., p. 97.

p. 401: "I think you will": *A Book of Common Prayer* (New York: Simon & Schuster, 1977), p. 201.

p. 401: "practices genocide": Ibid., p. 163.

p. 401: "be her witness": Ibid., p. 2.

p. 402n: "back to compress": *Head Over Heels* (1976; New York: Fawcett, 1978), p. 136.

p. 401: "into those of form": *Against Interpretation* (1966; New York: Delta, n.d.), p. 12. "Against Interpretation" appeared originally in 1964.

p. 402: "since those days!": *The Benefactor* (1963; London: Panther, 1966), p. 9.

p. 403: "were not mine": *The Benefactor,* p. 62.

p. 403: "model of my salvation": Ibid., p. 116.

p. 403: "pursuit of wisdom": Ibid., p. 113.

p. 404: "rhythm of aging": *Death Kit* (New York: Farrar, Straus & Giroux, 1967), p. 90.

p. 405: "house of death": Ibid., p. 303.

p. 405: "inventory of the world": Ibid., p. 312.

p. 405: "reminder of the self": *Steps* (New York: Random House, 1968), p. 24.

p. 405: "smoked day and night": Ibid., p. 38.

p. 406n: "metamorphosis of others": *The Art of the Self: Essays à Propos Steps,* p. 17.

p. 406: "of them as possible": *Steps,* p. 124.

p. 406: "been struck off": *Steps,* p. 127.

p. 407: "leaves brushing my feet": Ibid., p. 145.

p. 407: "only to be killed": Ibid., p. 64.

p. 407: "mortgages, and loans": Ibid., p. 133. Following quotation from same page.

p. 408: "a living body": Ibid., p. 134.

p. 408: "in love with me": Ibid., p. 129.

p. 408: "this impulse, this moment": Ibid., p. 131.

p. 408: "of a half dollar": *Nog* (New York: Random House, 1969), p. 3.

p. 409: "walls press in": Ibid., p. 106.

p. 409: "to go on": *Flats* (New York: Dutton, 1970), p. 79.

p. 409: "directing the bearer": Ibid., p. 16.

p. 410: "strangles my concentration": Ibid., p. 7.

p. 410: "pointing to myself": Ibid., p. 22.

p. 410: "in front of him": Ibid., p. 64.

p. 410: "to pull back": Ibid., p. 93.

p. 410: "shape to embrace": Ibid., p. 143.

p. 410: "Mobile crawl on": Ibid., p. 158.

p. 411: "he never arrived": Ibid., p. 159.

p. 411: "an antique shop": *Quake* (New York: Dutton, 1972), pp. 88–9.

p. 412: "Oooooooooh": Ibid., p. 158.

p. 413: "the Three Encirclements": *The Adventures of Mao on the Long March* (New York: Citadel, 1971), p. 73.

p. 413: "over the unnecessary": Ibid., p. 115.

p. 413: "giving up a little!": *Panama* (1978; New York: Penguin, 1979), p. 11.

p. 413: "close to the bone": Ibid., pp. 8–9.

p. 414: "shoring them up": *Speedboat* (1976; New York: Popular Library, 1978), pp. 104–5.

p. 414: "too hard on yourself": Ibid., p. 105.

p. 415: "the suicides": Ibid., p. 158.

p. 415: "I am leading today": *Sleepless Nights* (1979; New York: Vintage, 1980), p. 3.

p. 415: "it was a nightmare": Ibid., p. 51.

p. 415: "town gardener": Ibid., pp. 91–2.

p. 416: "silently in the night": Ibid., p. 138.

Chapter Ten: THE FEMALE EXPERIENCE

p. 417: "her artistic autonomy": *Feminist Literary Criticism: Explorations in Theory* (Lexington: University of Kentucky Press, 1975), pp. 13–14.

p. 417: "practical and political realms": *On Lies, Secrets, and Silence* (New York: Norton, 1979), p. 78.

p. 418: *Ms.* magazine interview: July 1972.

p. 418: "one becomes one": *Ms.,* July 1977, p. 16.

p. 418: "as freely as to Man": *Woman in the Nineteenth Century* (New York: Norton, 1971), p. 37.

p. 419: "feminine mystique": *The Feminine Mystique* (1963; New York: Norton, 1974), p. 69.

p. 419: "crisis in women?": Ibid., p. 71.

p. 419: "unlike her own": *A Room of One's Own* (New York: Harbinger paperback, 1963), p. 79.

p. 419: "soft in her hands": Ibid., p. 80.

p. 419: "say it in new ways": *Feminist Literary Criticism,* p. 17. Following quotation from same page.

p. 421: "abundance particularly gross": *Necessary Blankness,* p. 137.

p. 422: "always be a boy": *Meridian* (New York: Pocket Books, 1978), p. 70.

p. 424: "fulfillment of a curse!": *Memoirs of an Ex-Prom Queen* (New York: Bantam, 1973), p. 285.

p. 424: "where they work at all": *Necessary Blankness,* p. 183.

p. 426: "coals in the dark": *Small Changes* (New York: Fawcett Crest, 1973), p. 538.

p. 426: "this account will end": *The Women's Room* (New York: Summit, 1977), p. 458.

p. 426: "wombless Norman Mailer": Ibid., p. 212.

p. 428: "Joe Bob's triumphs": *Kinflicks* (New York: Knopf, 1975), p. 32.

p. 428: "subduing the chaos": Ibid., p. 429.

p. 429: "in it and will die": Ibid., p. 479.

p. 430: "high-strung narcissism": *Maiden* (New York: Pocket Books, 1973), p. 13.

p. 430: "test her disdain": Ibid., p. 14.

p. 430: "with anybody, Champ": Ibid., p. 108.

p. 430: "Very high camp": Ibid., p. 109.

p. 430: "made of flat rocks": Ibid., p. 185.

p. 430: "cold, wet tiles": Ibid., p. 191.

p. 431: with Bert Parks: With his Thoreauvian name, Parks MC's Miss America contests!

p. 433: "2x (reg; or)": *Such Good Friends* (1970; New York: Dell, 1971), p. 86.

p. 434: "to the former group": *Sula* (1970; New York: Pocket Books, 1972), p. 71.

p. 435: "But *she* will": Ibid., p. 143.

p. 435: "had learned to use": *Song of Solomon* (1977; New York: Signet, 1978), p. 280.

p. 436: "confronted with reality": Ibid., p. 179.

p. 437: "fundamentally funny fix": *Willie Master's Lonesome Wife* (New York: Knopf, 1971), unpaged. *Wife* appeared originally in *Tri-Quarterly,* 1968.

p. 437: "when I lie down": Ibid.

p. 437: "life pulses": *Hermaphrodeity* (1972; New York: Bard, 1974), p. 501. Parts appeared as early as 1968.

p. 439: "role they lusted after": *Sick Friends* (New York: Dutton, 1969), p. 76.

p. 439n: "art could adopt": *Styles of Radical Will,* p. 14.

p. 439: "predict or imagine": *Of Lies, Secrets, and Silence,* p. 158.

p. 440: "self, art, and society": *The Madwoman in the Attic* (New Haven: Yale University Press, 1979), p. xi.

p. 440n: "individual happiness": *The Second Sex* (London: Penguin, 1972), p. 278.

p. 440: "naturally superior to him": *Ms.,* July 1977, p. 16.

p. 441: "our cultural achievements": *The Prisoner of Sex* (Boston: Little, Brown, 1971), p. 194.

p. 441: "great causes, great wars": Ibid., p. 125.

p. 441: "on a delicate base": Ibid., p. 154.

p. 441n: "actual physical work": Quoted by Michele Wallace, *Black Macho and the Myth of the Superwoman* (1979; New York: Warner, 1980), pp. 96–7.

p. 442: "heart of gold": *The American Eve in Fact and Fiction, 1775–1914* (Urbana: University of Illinois Press, 1974), p. 265.

Chapter Eleven: THE 1970S: WHERE WE ARE

p. 444: "cliff across the lake": Frost, "The Most of It."

p. 445: "they're apart so much": *Gravity's Rainbow* (New York: Viking, 1973), pp. 176–7.

p. 446: veritably, a culture: For a witty tracking of some of these ideas, see "King Kong: A Meditation" by Kenneth Barnard, in *New American Review* 14 (1972): 182–98. Its sections are called: "Tarzan and Kong"; "How Big Is Kong's Penis?"; "The Mind and Heart of Fay Wray"; "Kong as Toad."

p. 447: for Pynchon is dismemberment: One could argue that it is *the* mode in postmodern fiction.

p. 447: "it's all theatre": *Gravity's Rainbow,* p. 3.

p. 447: "in ancient brandy": Ibid., p. 10. The bananas also represent the South, as against the North, a region of death, frozen, the "white visitation."

p. 447: "not be his own": Ibid., p. 13. Following quotation from same page.

p. 448: "not made clear": Ibid., p. 34.

p. 448: "days in advance": Ibid., p. 49.

p. 448: "wild plum sauce": Ibid., p. 65. In a dissenting view of Pynchon (*Commentary,* September 1973), David Thorburn cites this episode as a way of undermining Pynchon's achievement. He says that the episode is an "elaborately detailed appropriation" of the third and fourth chapters of *The Autobiography of Malcolm X,* in which Malcolm Little recounts his experiences as a shoeshine boy in the Roseland Ballroom's men's room, in Boston. From this, Thorburn extrapolates his own idea that "it is the facts of Malcolm's life, not Slothrop's, that explain the passage," and further, that this fantasy of "racial uprising and homosexual rape belongs not to Slothrop but to his tendentious creator" (p. 70). The facts and reasoning do not quite connect, for the episode is not an elaborate appropriation of Malcolm X's experiences; nor is the issue whether Pynchon or Slothrop desires homosexual rape at the hands of a gang of blacks led by Malcolm X. The point of the episode is the testing of Slothrop under the needle, the need to penetrate his fantasies, and to discover what such fantasies reveal as a way of using Slothrop's unique gift of prediction. The larger context is to employ such fantasies and revelations as a military weapon. Malcolm X, his presence and his autobiography, is what we call a conceit, that yoking together of dissimilars for a witty effect. Understandably, *Commentary* would disapprove of Pynchon and his works.

p. 448: "famous Infant Tyrone": *Gravity's Rainbow,* p. 84ff.

p. 449: "education in America": Ibid., p. 85.

p. 449: "it is feared, incurable": Ibid., p. 96.

p. 449: an unfathomable cosmos: Suggested by the 000000 rocket, with Blicero's boy lover Gottfried as passenger. This rocket will enter the white death and become the ultimate whitener, fulfilling Blicero's real name, Major Weissmann ("white man"), by passing into the "Other Kingdom."

p. 450: "closely as lovers?" Ibid., p. 209. Following three quotations from same page.

p. 451: "polyethers, polysulfanes": Ibid., p. 249.

p. 451: "aromatic rings": Ibid., p. 250.

p. 451: "found out in the world": Ibid., p. 285. Following quotation from same page.

p. 452: "nature of molecules": Ibid., p. 344.

p. 452: "parts of a tapestry": Ibid., p. 355.

p. 452: "single-moving as pawns": Ibid., p. 344.

p. 452: "mythical half-brother Enzian": Ibid., p. 338. Following quotation from same page.

p. 452: the long episode: Ibid., p. 408.

p. 452: "of everything else": Ibid., p. 411.

p. 453: "advanced kind of forgery": Ibid., p. 464.

p. 453: "without causing addiction": Ibid., p. 348.

p. 453: early Chaplin, etc.: See p. 503, for example.

p. 453: "without the other": Ibid., p. 348.

p. 453: "Germans began in 1904": Ibid., p. 317.

p. 454: "history fully lived": Ibid., p. 318.

p. 454: "twirls among them all": Ibid., p. 566.

p. 454: *waiting to rise*: Ibid., p. 470.

p. 454: "the kid knows it": Ibid., p. 674.

p. 455: "Raketen-Stadi": Ibid., p. 674.

p. 455: "CADENZA-A-A-A-A!": Ibid., p. 685.

p. 455: "endless ratchet": Ibid., p. 681.

p. 455: "enemies of the Reich": Ibid.

p. 455: "All right": Ibid., p. 663. Pynchon, of course, does not achieve order; in fact, he leaves many elements hanging, themes begun and discontinued, lines of argument whose ends hang free.

p. 455: "legally burned out": Ibid., p. 653.

p. 455: "dreams of men": Ibid.

p. 456: "perpetually in struggle": Ibid., p. 727.

p. 456: "on bulb efficiency": Ibid., p. 654. Following quotation from same page.

p. 456: "if not transformation?": *Duino Elegies,* 9, translated by J. B. Leishman and Stephen Spender (New York: Norton, 1939), p. 77. Following quotation from the fifth Duino, p. 47.

p. 457: black humorist or fabulist: Robert Scholes's insightful attempt to group Barth with Nabokov, Durrell, and Murdoch, among others, does fudge differences in order to create a semblance of a movement. "Fabulation, then [he writes in *The Fabulators*], means a return to a more verbal kind of fiction. It also means a return to a more fictional kind. By this I mean a less realistic and more artistic kind of narrative: more shapely, more evocative; more concerned with ideas and ideals, less concerned with things." (New York: Oxford University Press, 1967, p. 12.) Such groupings are valuable, but Barth, whose *Giles* becomes Scholes's linchpin at the end of the study, really cannot be fitted into any group that includes Hawkes, Durrell, or Murdoch. Verbally, they all are daring, but Barth's concern with fictional strategies goes well beyond their efforts. Compare Durrell's four-layer novel in the *Quartet:* what remains is a good deal of plain, romantic, conventional storytelling.

p. 457: "climax and dénouement": *Letters* (New York: Putnam, 1979), p. 49.

p. 458: to use documents: Ibid., p. 52ff.

p. 458: "less than a revolution": Ibid., p. 33.

p. 459: "cuckolding their killer": *Chimera* (1972; New York: Fawcett, 1973), p. 29.

p. 459: "patriarchy hasn't changed": Ibid., p. 45.

p. 459: "exists does exist": *Notebooks, 1914–1916* (New York: Harper Torchbook, 1969), p. 86e.

p. 459: "the *only* language?": Ibid., p. 52e.

p. 460: "story of her stories": *Chimera,* p. 63.

p. 460: "is the treasure": Ibid., p. 64.

p. 461: "unveiled it to myself": Ibid., p. 141.

p. 461: "everything in view": Ibid.

p. 461: "clear and objective": Ibid., p. 149.

p. 461: "my present transfiguration": Ibid., p. 111.

p. 461: "presumed to be endless": Ibid., p. 111.

p. 462: "be together forever": Ibid., p. 115.

p. 461: "they forever represent": Ibid., pp. 145–6.

p. 461: "collapses, dies": Ibid., p. 205.

p. 463: "seek their sense": Ibid., p. 203.

p. 464: "to Congress in 1811": *Letters,* p. 47.

p. 464: "wandered, dozed, dreamed": Ibid., p. 49.

p. 465: "manures the future": Ibid., pp. 80–1.

p. 465: "the action itself": *Notebooks,* p. 87e.

p. 465: "upon the glass": Quoted by William H. Gass, "The Concept of Character in Fiction," *Fiction and the Figures of Life,* p. 48. My reading of the passage differs from his.

p. 467: "no person at all": *The Sot-Weed Factor* (1960; New York: Grosset, 1964), p. 56.

p. 467: "thought a turncoat!": Ibid., p. 135.

p. 468: "fired his original desire": Ibid., p. 281.

p. 468: "winds of Chaos!": Ibid., p. 364.

p. 468: "more than you have": Ibid., p. 515.

p. 469: "his own fundament": Ibid., p. 728.

p. 470: "of us must sculpt": Ibid., p. 793.

p. 471: "cash, existential *Angst*": *Letters,* p. 217.

p. 472: "lest he mishandle them": Ibid., p. 211.

p. 472n: "I sink for it": *Lost in the Funhouse* (New York: Bantam, 1969), p. 3.

p. 473: "things out for himself": *The Floating Opera* (1956; New York: Bantam, 1972), p. 163. The Bantam edition restores the revisions and the original ending as Barth intended it.

p. 473: "has intrinsic value": Ibid., p. 165.

p. 473: "differences in kind": Ibid., p. 166.

p. 474: two contrasting voices: Reminiscent of Bellow's *Dangling Man* and, beyond that, the archetypal *Rameau's Nephew* of Diderot.

p. 474: "for remaining alive": *Floating Opera,* p. 169.

p. 474: "the floor joist": Ibid., p. 215.

p. 475: "upon subtle reflection": Ibid., p. 147.

p. 475: "to be sitting there": Ibid., p. 7.

p. 475: "cracked, smoking": Ibid., p. 239.

p. 475n: "such a perfect day": The Avon edition (New York, 1965) repeated the Appleton changes; see p. 266.

p. 476: "just as efficiently": *The End of the Road* (1958; New York: Avon, 1960), p. 34.

p. 476: tighter with anguish: We recall the twin busts in Jaggers's office in *Great Expectations,* busts which take on qualities of the Medusa.

p. 476: "did you fuck Rennie?": Ibid., p. 113.

p. 477: "against the facts": Ibid., p. 127.

p. 477: "abstract and unsuggestive": Ibid., p. 132.

p. 478: "beloved Fielding": *Letters,* p. 298.

p. 478: "I was not European": Ibid., p. 305.

p. 478: "revolutionary letters": Ibid., p. 331.

p. 478: "of Lily Dale": Ibid., p. 330. Following quotation from same page.

p. 479: "oral tradition": Ibid., p. 438.

p. 479: "whether disc or tape": *Lost in the Funhouse,* p. ix.

p. 479: "there is of him": Ibid., p. 127.

p. 479: "for their livening": Ibid., p. 97. Following two quotations from same page.

p. 480: "effacing herself absolutely": Ibid., p. 99.

p. 480: "generation go under": Ibid., p. 4.

p. 480: "of night and sea": Ibid., pp. 8–9.

p. 480: *"transcension of categories":* Ibid., p. 10.

p. 480: "destroyed their love": Ibid., p. 94.

p. 481: "experiment is unsuccessful": Quoted by David Morrell in his very useful *John Barth: An Introduction,* p. 96. The quotation derives from an address Barth gave before a Library of Congress audience on May 1, 1967.

p. 481: "especially relevant": *Lost in the Funhouse,* p. 74.

p. 481: "without anything happening": Ibid., p. 74.

p. 481: "supposed to be used": Ibid., p. 80.

p. 481: "Mercury's caduceus": Ibid.

p. 481: "favorite dessert": Ibid., p. 90.

p. 481: "of a pipe organ": Ibid., p. 93.

p. 482: "funhouses are designed": Ibid., p. 94.

p. 482: "Yours Truly": Ibid., p. 53. Following quotation from same page.

p. 482n: Morrell in his study: Op. cit., pp. 90–91n.

p. 482: "name he also shares!": *Letters,* p. 407.

p. 483: "extraterrestrial scripture": Ibid., p. 531.

p. 483: "science of fiction": Ibid., See also p. 534.

p. 484: "Louisiana Project": Ibid., p. 621.

p. 484: "fit either hypothesis": Ibid., p. 627.

p. 484: "acceptable to him": Ibid. But of course, he cannot be certain; and by indirection, Lafitte now becomes an agent in the episode.

p. 484: "his initial triumph": Ibid., p. 629.

p. 485: "correspondence as ours": Ibid., p. 651.

p. 485: "of your story": Ibid., p. 652.

p. 486: "a political revolution": Ibid., p. 720.

p. 488: "can be created": "Surfiction—A Position," *Partisan Review* 3 (1973): 428.

p. 488: "from the unconscious": Ibid., p. 429.

p. 488: "creation of the fiction": Ibid., p. 431. Following quotation from same page.

p. 489: except Bellow: *The Dean's December* was published in 1982.

p. 492: "bristling with night static": *Humboldt's Gift* (New York: Viking, 1975), p. 25.

p. 493: affirm or reaffirm himself: A different application of the idea can be found in Sacvan Bercovitch's *The Puritan Origins of the American Self,* p. 20.

p. 494: "mother made for me": *Something Happened* (New York: Knopf, 1974), p. 362.

p. 494: "one nation of ours": Ibid., p. 305.

p. 494: "and midgets. Carcasses": Ibid., pp. 400–1.

p. 494: "who cares about them?": Ibid., p. 210.

p. 495: "to extradite myself!": *My Life as a Man* (New York: Holt, Rinehart & Winston, 1974), p. 85.

p. 496: "crying—and bleeding": Ibid., p. 212.

p. 497: his primary defense: Ibid., p. 275.

p. 497: "issues of the story": *Reading Myself and Others,* p. 67.

p. 498: "vibrant and desirable life": *The Professor of Desire* (New York: Farrar, Straus & Giroux, 1977), p. 156.

p. 498: "deepest source of satisfaction": Ibid., p. 171.

p. 498: "well-being of the spirit": Ibid., p. 172.

p. 499: "was a veteran": *Breakfast of Champions* (New York: Delacorte, 1973), p. 106.

p. 499: "engorged with blood": Ibid., p. 148.

p. 499n: "self-indulgent things": *The New Fiction: Interviews with Innovative American Writers,* p. 205.

p. 500: "I know, I said": Ibid., p. 197.

p. 500: "during my writing career": *Breakfast,* p. 301.

p. 500: "feels like to me": *Slapstick* (New York: Delacorte, 1976), p. 1.

p. 501: "between one and twenty": Ibid., p. 162.

p. 503: "flowers of all kinds": *Being There* (New York: Harcourt Brace Jovanovich, 1970), p. 66.

p. 504: "used to have resonance": *The Devil Tree* (1973; New York: Bantam, 1974), p. 210.

p. 504: "out of the past": *Cockpit* (1975; New York: Bantam, 1976), p. 143.

p. 504: "make it undefinable": Ibid., p. 144.

p. 508: "down the stairs": *The Tenants* (1971; New York: Pocket Books, 1972), p. 211. Following quotations from same page.

p. 508: "with wet footprints": Ibid., p. 12.

p. 508: "in a sense love him": Ibid., p. 177.

p. 509n: "desire 'containing agony' ": *The New Fiction,* p. 105.

p. 509: "in chest expansion": *The Blood Oranges* (New York: New Directions, 1971), p. 16.

p. 501: "reach out to another man": Ibid., p. 149.

p. 510: "Who could tell?": Ibid., p. 196.

p. 510: "in a vast wood": Ibid., p. 209.

p. 510: "nude and alone": Ibid., p. 210.

p. 510: "signs of sex": Ibid., p. 203.

p. 511: "my global belly": Ibid., p. 5.

p. 512: "cluster of golden figures": *Death, Sleep & the Traveler* (New York: New Directions, 1974), pp. 104–5.

p. 512: "making her moist": Ibid., p. 4.

p. 513: "ordinary man's imagination": Ibid., p. 153.

p. 513: "seed of the poet": *Travesty* (New York: New Directions, 1976), p. 76.

p. 514: "way to a dungeon": Ibid., p. 75.

p. 514: "river of Scorpio": Ibid., p. 99.

p. 514: "innate design": Ibid., p. 59.

p. 514: "across an entire field": Ibid., p. 58.

p. 515: "lend that book to you": *Ragtime* (1975; London: Pan, 1976), p. 174.

p. 515: "their ultimate test": Ibid., p. 175.

p. 516: "and Joseph Heller": *Up, A Novel* (New York: Dial, 1968), p. 38.

p. 516: "revelation in print": Ibid., p. 223.

p. 517: "before the Wasichus came": *Out* (Chicago: Swallow, 1973), p. 136.

p. 517: "walk right outa here": Ibid., pp. 81–2. For whom is such a passage written?

p. 517n: sees this, also: In his section on Sukenick in *Literary Disruptions.*

p. 518: "connected with the Cathedral": *98.6* (New York: Fiction Collective, 1975), p. 35.

p. 518: "absence of wholes": Ibid., p. 167.

p. 518: "what it is": Ibid., p. 89.

p. 519: "acting through nature": Ibid., p. 123.

p. 519: "pregnant with prophecy": *Long Talking Bad Conditions Blues* (New York: Fiction Collective, 1979), p. 73.

p. 520: such a scene: *Picture Palace* (1978; New York: Ballantine, 1979), p. 160ff.

p. 520: "to be believed": Ibid., p. 344.

p. 521: "ways between them": In a letter from the author.

p. 523: "what I feel for you": *The Executioner's Song* (Boston: Little, Brown, 1979), p. 359.

p. 524: "accept them as such": Ibid., p. 305.

p. 524: "the consciousness stuff": Ibid., p. 526.

p. 524: "if Gary found out": Ibid., p. 745.

p. 524: "Call it possessed": Ibid., p. 746.

p. 526: "could not move": *The Passion Artist* (New York: Harper & Row, 1979), p. 69.

p. 527: "in different circumstances": Ibid., p. 77.

p. 527: "a block of stone": Ibid., p. 72.

p. 527: "malformed newborn animal": Ibid., p. 133.

p. 527: "frozen in place": Ibid., p. 145.

p. 528: "destined to become": *Virginie: Her Two Lives* (New York: Harper & Row, 1982), p. 9.

p. 529: "never be repaid": *Jailbird* (New York: Delacorte, 1979), p. 51.

p. 529: "the gas chambers": Ibid., p. 17.

p. 532: "stature and consequence": *Passion Play* (New York: St. Martin's Press, 1979), p. 31.

p. 532: "his way again": Ibid., p. 74.

p. 532: "quivers of desire": Ibid., p. 224.

p. 532: "only he could see": Ibid., p. 271.

p. 533: "on 45-inch Jap TV": *The Second Coming* (New York: Farrar, Straus & Giroux, 1980), p. 19.

p. 533: "the living death": Ibid., p. 271.

p. 533: "into a slaughterhouse": Ibid., p. 271.

p. 534: "one for you": Ibid., p. 148.

p. 534: "whole dark world": Ibid., pp. 148–9.

p. 536n: "any defining sense, *character*": Robert Boyers, "Weightless Characters," *Salmagundi* 49 (Summer 1980): 131.

p. 537: "lust for power": *Sophie's Choice* (New York: Random House, 1979), p. 190.

p. 538: "one will you keep?": Ibid., p. 483.

p. 538: "my little girl!": Ibid., p. 484.

p. 538: "classical Southern culture": Ibid., p. 48.

p. 539: "whole benighted system?": Ibid., p. 206.

p. 541: "her native Charleston": *The Ghost Writer* (New York: Farrar, Straus & Giroux, 1979), pp. 96–7.

p. 541: "how I will live": Ibid., p. 5.

p. 542: "she suffered": Ibid., p. 170.

p. 542: "the murdered Jews": Ibid., p. 150.

p. 542: "power of her book": Ibid., p. 144.

p. 542: "doors—everything": Ibid., p. 170.

p. 543: "dug to protect": Ibid., p. 58.

p. 544: "flying at each other": *Dubin's Lives* (New York: Farrar, Straus & Giroux, 1979), p. 162.

p. 547: "Jedediah cried aloud": *Bellefleur* (New York: Dutton, 1980), p. 558.

p. 548: "taking in centuries": Ibid., p. 114.

p. 548: "fast, and squeezing": Ibid., p. 135.

p. 549: "filthy London pub": *Just Above My Head* (New York: Dial, 1979), pp. 5–6.

p. 550: "with my pain": Ibid., p. 329.

p. 550n: "have it no more!": Ibid., p. 363.

p. 551: "laughs at you": Ibid., p. 293.

p. 552: "receives its color": *In the Future Perfect* (New York: New Directions, 1979), p. 1.

p. 552: "coloring book": Ibid., p. 6.

p. 552: "former concentration camp": Ibid., p. 9.

p. 552n: "being explored": p. 96.

p. 552: "pose a great problem": Ibid., p. 17.

p. 553: "in his brain": *How German Is It* (New York: New Directions, 1980), p. 13.

p. 553: "survival of Germany": Ibid., p. 81.

p. 553n: "strive for revolution": Ibid., p. 158.

p. 553: "attain a total harmony": Ibid., pp. 130–1.

p. 554: "What is existence?": Ibid., p. 167. Following quotation from same page.

p. 554: "exactitude and abstractions": Ibid., pp. 169–70.

p. 555: "end all dreams?": Ibid., p. 252.

p. 555: "to give this voice": *Mulligan Stew* (New York: Grove, 1979), p. 7.

p. 555n: Myles na gCopaleen: Ibid., p. 31.

p. 556: "playing trained *bears!*": Ibid., p. 152.

p. 556: "absurdist murder mystery": Ibid., p. 28.

p. 556: "high Boots, and MORE!!": Ibid., p. 109.

p. 557: "she becomes me": *Loon Lake* (New York: Random House, 1980), p. 13.

p. 557: "out of sight": Ibid., p. 41.

p. 558: "echoing off the hills": Ibid., p. 76.

p. 558: "admit we remembered": Ibid., p. 151.

p. 558: "disynchrous lives": Ibid., p. 254.

Chapter Twelve: THE NONFICTION NOVEL

p. 561n: "any political events": *The New Journalism, with an Anthology,* ed. by Tom Wolfe and E. W. Johnson (New York: Harper & Row, 1973), p. 29.

p. 562: "the reasoning individual": Mas'ud Zararzadeh, *The Mythopoeic Reality* (Urbana: University of Illinois Press, 1976), p. 28.

p. 562: "private world view": Ibid., p. 3. Following quotation from same page.

p. 562: "technetronic culture": Ibid., p. 4.

p. 564: "in case of a girl": *The Woman Warrior* (New York: Knopf, 1976), p. 86.

p. 565: "encouraging her": Ibid., p. 82.

p. 565: "than White Ghosts": Ibid., pp. 96–7.

p. 565: "with their dimes": Ibid., p. 97.

p. 565: "worked in China": Ibid., p. 98.

p. 566: "can make a living": Ibid., p. 201.

p. 567: "social aggressiveness": *American Hunger,* p. 45.

p. 567n: "Chief of State": *The Autobiography of Malcolm X* (1965; New York: Grove, 1966), p. 301.

p. 568: "part of human beings": Ibid., p. 371.

p. 568: "against Elijah Muhammad": Ibid., p. 414.

p. 569: "to grow up,' I thought": *Witness* (1952; New York: Gateway Editions, n.d.), p. 149.

p. 570: "lost its soul": Ibid. Up to this point, the narrative could be that of a naturalistic novel, a Dreiserian tragedy.

p. 571: "added up to Communism": Ibid., p. 473.

p. 571: the messianic role: David Halberstam in *The Powers That Be* (New York: Knopf, 1979) gives an excellent explanation of how Chambers fitted into Luce's plans at *Time.*

p. 571: "Communist International": *Witness,* p. 497.

p. 571: "department of the news": Ibid., p. 502.

p. 571: "Capitol it threatened": Ibid., p. 543.

p. 572: "could not do otherwise": Ibid., pp. 694–5.

p. 572: "fit their facts": *Advertisements for Myself,* p. 341.

p. 572: "rebels and the regulators": Ibid., p. 357.

p. 572: "overwhelmingly against me": *Witness,* p. 707.

p. 572: "continue to exist": Ibid., p. 715.

p. 572: "a living witness": Ibid., p. 747.

p. 574: "dusky rusky forests": *The Electric Kool-Aid Acid Test* (New York: Farrar, Straus & Giroux, 1968), p. 144. Parts had appeared by 1967.

p. 574: "subjective reality of it": Ibid., p. 433.

p. 574n: "to give a party?": *Radical Chic* (New York: Farrar, Straus & Giroux, 1970), p. 29.

p. 575: "sounds, touch—lightning—": *Acid Test,* p. 9.

p. 576: "the human predicament": *A Time to Die* (New York: Quadrangle, 1975), p. 90.

p. 577: "a getaway driver?": Ibid., p. 155.

p. 580: "who were fighting it": *The Armies of the Night* (New York: New American Library, 1968), p. 211. Following quotation from same page.

p. 580: "it is schizophrenia": Ibid., p. 140.

p. 580: "by his distorted senses": Ibid., p. 174.

p. 581: "finest journalist in America": Ibid., p. 32.

p. 581: "best writer in America": Ibid., p. 33.

p. 582: "a Victorian practice": Ibid., p. 152.

p. 582: "of historic inquiry": Ibid., p. 284.

p. 583: "contrast to written literature": *The Children of Sánchez* (New York: Vintage, 1963), p. xii.

p. 583: "lower-class Mexican life": Ibid., p. xi.

p. 583: "both art and life": Ibid., p. xxi.

p. 584: "any girl would have": Ibid., p. 133.

p. 584: "feeling of being alone": Ibid., p. 88.

p. 585: "Sentence Completion": *La Vida* (New York: Random House, 1966), p. xix.

p. 585: "any other method": Ibid., p. xxii.

p. 585: "observed typical days": Ibid., p. xxv. Following quotation from same page.

p. 586: "diseased patients alike": *Hiroshima* (New York: Knopf, 1946), p. 94.

p. 588: "a self-indulgence": *The Wall* (1950; New York: Pocket Books, 1953), p. 544.

p. 588: "strength to work": *This Way for the Gas, Ladies and Gentlemen* (New York: Viking, 1967), p. 28.

p. 589: "a luckier combination": *The Great Railway Bazaar* (1975; New York: Ballantine, 1976), p. 166.

p. 589: "psychology textbooks": Ibid., p. 140.

p. 589: "not also European": Ibid., p. 285.

Chapter Thirteen: WHO WE ARE AND WHERE WE ARE GOING:

p. 591: "he has come in *us*": In *The American Jeremiad* (Madison: University of Wisconsin Press, 1978), Sacvan Bercovitch cites this passage as an epitome of American life. See p. 177ff.

p. 592: "and Indian fighting": *Virgin Land* (New York: Vintage, n.d.), p. 102.

p. 593: "feeling and thought": "The Idea of the Avant-Garde," *Partisan Review* XXIV (Summer 1957): 375.

p. 593: already an echo: Wearing blinders is not restricted to critics of the novel, nor to novelists, of course. In 1957, *The New Poets of England and America,* an influential anthology edited by Donald Hall, Robert Pack, and Louis Simpson, omitted the new with a vengeance: the Beats, the Black Mountain poets, the New York poets, among others. By 1957, what was "new" for them was already established.

p. 595: "tonic of the wilderness": *Walden* (New York: Mentor, 1957), p. 211.

p. 595: "consciousness and language": "Notes on the Rhetoric of Anti-Realist Fiction," *Tri-Quarterly* 30 (Spring 1974): 49. The critical battles continue to rage, even over what constitutes modernism and postmodernism. Gerald Graff, in "The Myth of the Postmodernist Breakthrough," argues that postmodernism is not something new, but an outgrowth or "a logical culmination of the premises of these earlier movements." (*Tri-Quarterly* 26 (Winter 1973): 385.) In the same issue, Philip Stevick argues the opposite point: "What recent fiction tells us on every page is that it is of another age than the modernist masters" (p. 338). Yet the terms Stevick uses to describe the new apply to Kafka, who is part of the old. Cf. the following: "It is partly the result of the revival of interest in pre-novelistic forms, the fabulistic, proto-realistic works that echo through much of new fiction, allowing a kind of power to grow out of the invention itself rather than depending upon the solidity with which the figures of the fiction are placed" (p. 361).

INDEX

women *(cont.)*
  careers of, 35, 421, 424–425, 428
  as comforters, 36, 85–86, 240, 292, 320, 333–334, 366, 422, 443, 490, 492, 494, 498–499
  death and, 35, 421, 424–425, 428, 496
  depersonalization of, 70–71, 199–200, 252–253, 291, 323, 352, 403, 418, 421–422, 436–437, 504–505, 509, 511, 555
  "Earth Mother" stereotype and, 60, 172, 352, 440–441, 509–511
  eating and, 224, 299, 398, 421, 424, 533
  in experimental fiction, 368, 388–390, 459
  imprisonment of, 224–225, 388–390, 421, 425
  "Lily/Rose" stereotypes of, 60–61, 127
  as male castrators, 60, 86, 166–167, 304, 322, 442–443, 496, 526, 528
  narcissism of, 280–281, 397, 399–400, 431–433, 437
  physical appearance of, 173–174, 237–238, 299, 423, 434–436, 509, 539
  sex and liberation of, 103, 296–299, 302, 423, 429–433, 435, 438
  spatial escape of, 39–40, 244, 296–300, 388, 398–399, 420–421, 424–425, 443
  violence against, 237–238, 298–299, 301–302, 423, 425, 497, 517
  virginity and, 320, 429–430, 528, 532
Women and Men (McElroy), 521
Women in Love (Lawrence), 544
"Women's Movement, The" (Didion), 397

Women's Room, The (French), 423–427
women writers, xiii, 6, 8, 102, 130, 148, 167, 283, 292, 397, 417–443
  aesthetics of, 79–80, 417–420, 439–443
  black, 296, 422, 434–436
  ethnic, 129, 564–566, 590
  experimental, 396–405, 414–416, 429–431
  naturalistic techniques used by, 298–299, 301, 420, 422–423, 425, 433
  separatism advocated by, 40, 80, 424–425
  spatiality and, 26, 36, 39–40, 420–422, 424–425
  unique perceptions of, 300, 418, 427
Wonderland (Oates), 420–421
Wood, Robert A., 16
Woolf, Virginia, xiii, 8, 11, 52, 155, 418n, 419, 443–444, 458, 583
Wordsworth, William, 179, 256, 286
"Work of Art in the Age of Mechanical Reproduction" (Benjamin), 181n
World According to Garp, The (Irving), xiin, 168, 174–175
"World and the Jug, The" (Ellison), 146
World More Attractive, A (Howe), 146n
World War I, 89, 94, 121–123, 155, 216
World War II, 7, 87–88, 90, 128, 209, 220, 346–347, 356, 587
  American idealism and, 22–23, 35, 46–47
  modern novel and, 28, 99, 379
  Pacific vs. European theater in, 96–97
  see also Holocaust; war novel

World Within the Word, The (Gass), 54
Wouk, Herman, 39, 79, 111–112
"Wreck of the *Deutschland,* The" (Hopkins), 215
Wright, Richard, 75–77, 80, 83–84, 131, 145–146, 160, 161, 247–249, 274, 291–295, 340n, 343n, 566–567
  Communist phase of, 47n, 83, 293–294
  in ideological disputes, 79, 83–84, 145n–146n, 293–295, 567
  modern mode used by, 247–249
  naturalism in, 83–84, 160, 293
  underground experience in, xiii, 83, 196–197, 317
  "war novel" by, 83–84, 129
"Writer as Moralist, The" (Bellow), 334n
Wroth, Lawrence, 467
Wurlitzer, Rudolph, 283, 358, 384, 389, 408–412

Yeats, William Butler, 23, 24, 47n, 57, 66, 75, 88, 99, 149–150, 158, 244n, 335, 444, 508, 518, 527, 534
Yellow Back Radio Broke Down (Reed), 370
Young, Stark, 14n
Young Lions, The (Shaw), 22, 39, 94, 112, 267, 587

Zavarzadeh, Mas'ud, 562n, 563
Zen and the Art of Motorcycle Maintenance (Pirsig), 174
Zola, Emile, 106
Zuckerman Unbound (Roth), 356, 358, 495n, 540n